the sources of Swiss Anabaptism

CLASSICS OF THE RADICAL REFORMATION

Cornelius J. Dyck, Editor
Institute of Mennonite Studies

In cooperation with John S. Oyer, Goshen College, Goshen, Indiana; John H. Yoder, Notre Dame University, South Bend, Indiana; and Jarold K. Zeman, Acadia Divinity College, Wolfville, Nova Scotia.

Classics of the Radical Reformation is an English language series of Anabaptist and Free Church documents translated and annotated under the direction of the Institute of Mennonite Studies (the research agency of Associated Mennonite Biblical Seminaries, 3003 Benham Avenue, Elkhart, Indiana 46514) and published by Mennonite Publishing House (Herald Press, Scottdale, Pennsylvania 15683).

1. The Legacy of Michael Sattler.
   Translated and edited by John H. Yoder, 1973.
2. The Writings of Pilgram Marpeck.
   Translated and edited by William Klassen and Walter Klaassen, 1978.
3. Anabaptism in Outline: Selected Primary Sources.
   Edited by Walter Klaassen, 1981.
4. The Sources of Swiss Anabaptism: The Grebel Letters and Related Documents.
   Edited by Leland Harder, 1985.

the sources of Swiss Anabaptism

the Grebel Letters and Related Documents

Edited by
Leland Harder

1985

herald press scottdale, pa.
kitchener, ont.

Library of Congress Cataloging in Publication Data
Main entry under title:

The Sources of Swiss anabaptism.

(Classics of the radical Reformation ; 4)
Bibliography: p.
Includes indexes.
1. Grebel, Konrad, 1498?-1526. 2. Anabaptists
—Switzerland—Correspondence. 3. Anabaptists—
Switzerland—History—Sources. 4. Switzerland—
Church history—Sources. I. Grebel, Konrad,
1498?-1526. II. Harder, Leland, 1926-
III. Series.
BX4946.G7A4 1985   284'.3'09494   85-5520
ISBN 0-8361-1251-2

*Photos by Jan Gleysteen, from the Anabaptist Heritage
Collection, Scottdale, Pennsylvania.*

THE SOURCES OF SWISS ANABAPTISM
Copyright © 1985 by Herald Press, Scottdale, Pa. 15683
  Published simultaneously in Canada by Herald Press,
  Kitchener, Ont. N2G 4M5. All rights reserved.
Library of Congress Catalog Card Number: 85-5520
International Standard Book Number: 0-8361-1251-2
Printed in the United States of America
Book designed by Jan Gleysteen

90 89 88 87 86 85 10 9 8 7 6 5 4 3 2 1

To the memory of the three predecessors
in this Grebel "life and letters" project

Harold S. Bender
Edward Yoder
Ernst Correll

and to Elizabeth Horsch Bender
who in the eighth decade of her life
translated most of the German documents in this collection.

Contents

General Editor's Preface

For many years a committee of German and North American historians known as the *Täuferaktenkommission* (TAK) has published source materials of the sixteenth-century Anabaptist movement under the title *Quellen zur Geschichte der Täufer* (QGT). More recently a similar organization has begun work in the Netherlands with Dutch source materials. It is known as the *Commissie tot de uitgave van Documenta Anabaptistica Neerlandica* (CUDAN). These developments have, obviously, been deeply rewarding to scholars and others as the multitude of articles and books using these documents amply verifies.

There are, however, still relatively few sixteenth-century Anabaptist materials available in the English language, though their number is increasing. It is to meet this need that the *Classics of the Radical Reformation* (CRR) series was begun some years ago with the aim of making available in the English language a scholarly and critical edition of the primary works of major Anabaptist and free church writers of the late fifteenth, sixteenth, and early seventeenth centuries. The first volume in this series, *The Legacy of Michael Sattler* by John H. Yoder, appeared in 1973. *The Writings of Pilgram Marpeck* by William Klassen and Walter Klaassen, appeared in 1978, and *Anabaptism in Outline: Selected Primary Sources* by Walter Klaassen, in 1981. Other volumes are in process.

In preparing these translations it has not been considered essential to the purposes of the series to include every known document of the writers under translation and, unless some contribution can be made to a fuller understanding of the text, it has not been considered essential to pursue at length critical textual issues. Those scholars interested in the details will, in any case, turn to the original language text. Where a choice had to be made between clarity and awkward literalism, the translators were encouraged to favor readability but without compromising the text.

15

Most of the volumes in the CRR include the writings of one author only. The central focus in the present volume is the correspondence of Conrad Grebel, but the scope has been enlarged to include also the documents most relevant to the unfolding of the Swiss Brethren story written by others, as the editor explains in his preface. The original intention of the editors was to include this volume in the *Studies in Anabaptist and Mennonite History* (SAMH) series of the Mennonite Historical Society, as well as in the CRR series, in view of the fifty-year interest of the Mennonite Historical Society in the project, but marketing and other considerations led to its inclusion in CRR only. The long history of the development of the project is explained fully in the editor's preface.

It is a pleasure to express appreciation to editor Leland Harder for his "labor of love" of many years, as well as to Leonard Gross, J. C. Wenger, and John H. Yoder, who served the editor and the Institute of Mennonite Studies as consultants, and to the Editorial Council of CRR as listed across from the title page. The North American Committee for the Documentation of Free Church Origins (NACDFCO), of which Professor George H. Williams, Harvard Divinity School, serves as chairman and Walter Klaassen as secretary, was helpful with its encouragement and counsel during the initial stages of the launching of the CRR series. Finally, without the commitment to the work of the church on the part of Mennonite Publishing House (Herald Press) and its willingness to include the series in its responsibility to society and the church, this venture could not have been undertaken.

Cornelius J. Dyck, Editor, CRR
Institute of Mennonite Studies
Elkhart, Indiana

Eðitor's Preface

Plans for the publication of this book began over fifty years ago, before the present editor was born. My own interest in the project was sparked as a graduate student twenty years ago, and half a decade has already elapsed since the role of editor was assigned to me. Over this span of time there have been six proposals in sequence for the completion of this project.

A. Proposals for Publishing the Grebel Letters

1. *The Original Proposal.* The initial plan was formally approved at the first regular meeting of the Mennonite Historical Society (MHS), November 7, 1924, and publicized in the *Goshen College Review Supplement* for January 1926. The biography and writings of Conrad Grebel were to have been one volume with three authors: Harold Bender, Ernst Correll, and Edward Yoder. The book "was planned to be modest in size and popular in character." Although it was to have been published in June 1925 as a quadricentennial volume celebrating the beginning of the Anabaptist movement, the discovery of new sources and the need to gain better command of the material led the authors to postpone publication. Subsequently, Yoder resumed teaching duties at Hesston College following completion of his doctoral studies, and Correll left Goshen College, making the three-way collaboration more difficult.

2. *The Yoder-Correll Proposal.* The next proposal was a two-page memorandum dated 1938 following the completion of Bender's doctoral dissertation on Grebel at the University of Heidelberg. It was sent from Scottdale, Pennsylvania, where Yoder was now on the staff of the Mennonite Publishing House; and it emerged from "an extended discussion of the present status of the Grebeliana Studies" between Yoder and Correll, who was now Professor of Economic History at the American University

in Washington, D.C. The chief elements in the Yoder-Correll plan were (1) the publication of the Grebel letters in the original languages, (2) the publication of additional documents in the original languages not written by Grebel but related to the content of his letters, (3) an English translation of all the included letters and documents, (4) an extensive annotating of the letters and documents with philological, critical, biographical, and historical notes, and (5) the securing of a subsidy from some learned society or foundation for the financial underwriting of the project.

3. *The Bender-Hershberger Proposal.* On behalf of the directors of the MHS, Bender and Guy F. Hershberger replied jointly to the Yoder-Correll proposal, reporting their intention to reactivate the original plan as approved in 1924. That plan had not called for reprinting the letters and writings in the original languages because they were already accessible in transcribed and published form with only several exceptions. Nor had the plan called for a comprehensive or erudite annotating of the documents, but rather (as was indicated in the *Mennonite Quarterly Review* when the Grebel-to-Myconius letters were published) the making of notes "as brief as seemed consistent with an intelligent understanding of the letters by the general reader," plus some "references added for the convenience of those interested in the sources." This counterproposal was greatly concerned about keeping the cost manageable in a time of severe economic depression. It was estimated that $900 would still be needed to publish the biography and writings in a single volume much more condensed than the Yoder-Correll plan would have required.

4. *The Separate Publication of the Biography.* In 1950 the Bender biography of Conrad Grebel was published by Herald Press at Scottdale as Volume 6 in the "Studies in Anabaptist and Mennonite History" (SAMH) series of the MHS. The preface acknowledged the prior translation and research contributions of Yoder and Correll and explained why their further participation in the project had ceased and why the biography was published without the letters. Yoder had died in March 1945 and "the difficulty of financing the publication and other factors compelled the postponement of full publication and also led to the decision to publish in two volumes what was originally intended as one." Bender added, "Dr. Correll ... continues to look with me toward the completion of our original program of collaboration: a full presentation of all *Grebeliana* extant, with critical commentary and English translations of essential sections."

5. *The Present Editor's Proposal.* The untimely death of H. S. Bender on September 21, 1962, and the retirement of Correll from research and teaching labors caused another indefinite postponement of the completion

of the project. The interest of the present writer in picking up the fallen baton began in the autumn of 1957 when Bender loaned me the Yoder translations for use in a graduate course at Northwestern University. Then in the autumn of 1972, following a sabbatical year during which I resumed this interest which had been dormant for yet another fifteen years, I received an informal mandate from the editors of the SAMH series to bring this project to completion as soon as possible. There was some question as to whether this essentially historical assignment should be entrusted to a sociologist, but it was recalled that Bender had once taught sociology at Goshen College and that Correll had been an economist. In November of that year, John H. Yoder, then serving as Associate Director of the Institute of Mennonite Studies (IMS) at the Associated Mennonite Biblical Seminaries (AMBS), secured approval for the idea of making this volume a joint project between the IMS and its "Classics of the Radical Reformation" (CRR) series and the MHS and its SAMH series. An advisory committee consisting of John H. Yoder, J. C. Wenger, Leonard Gross, and Cornelius J. Dyck was appointed and there was periodic review of manuscript contents and drafts.

6. *The Advisory Committee Enlargement.* In December 1977, the Advisory Committee took serious note of the way the manuscript had grown substantially larger than originally envisioned. However, instead of deleting any of the supplementary materials, the committee was of one mind that it would take little more time and effort to make the manuscript an even more comprehensive documentary of the beginnings of Swiss Anabaptism to 1527. The editor and two committee members—Yoder and Gross—were asked to search for any other documents which should still be included to tell a more complete story. Yoder subsequently recommended a number of items with particular reference to the pre-history of Zurich Anabaptism and the events leading up to the December 1523 "turning point in the Zwinglian Reformation," to use his phrase. Moreover, he wrote to Heinold Fast, Emden, Germany, eliciting several more recommendations. Gross suggested that the chronological coverage be extended to include an excerpt from the Bern Disputation of 1538 and recommended the composition of a "Cast of Characters" to round out the dramatic format for the book.

Finally after another half-decade of what Grebel would have called *vigiliae* (lamplight labors) or *lucubratio* (moonlighting), the book is nearing completion at this moment of writing. Its main purpose is still to publish a competent and readable English translation of the seventy-one Grebel letters together with other letters and documents that bear directly upon the themes and events in the Grebel letters, with sufficient notes to make the material understandable to the general reader, including interested church members as well as students of Anabaptist history and theology. The documents accompanying the letters number approximately 100 in all. They relate to the Grebel letters in the following ways: (1) extant documents from his pen besides the letters (1B, 5B, 26A, 47D); (2) nonextant documents from his pen preserved only in a refracted form by others (71F, Epi.C); (3) statements by Grebel reported in minutes, court records, etc. (47C, 57C, 71K, 71M); (4) letters written to Grebel (Prologue, 1A, 54A, 67D, 67E); (5) documents that do not mention Grebel personally but are indirectly related to his involvement in the event or subject matter contained there, 7A, 9A, 19A, 25A, 47A, etc.); and (6) documents that mention Grebel's direct involvement in an event or conversation (all the rest). In place of publishing the texts in their original languages, I have put the key Latin or German phrases into the notes, indicating problems of variance in interpretation and translation. Moreover, transcriptions of the original texts of the letters and documents are otherwise available in published form, with the following exceptions: Prologue, 1A, 3A, 5B, 7A, 39A, 57E, and 67E. A number of documents in the present collection have common published sources as follows: the Wyss *Chronicle* (47B, 71R), (2) Bullinger's *Reformationsgeschichte* (68B, 68L, 71L, Epi.A), (3) Kessler's *Sabbata* (65A, 68F, 68H, 69A, 69E, 70A, 71E, 71J, 71R), and (4) Zwingli's *In Catabaptistarum Strophas Elenchus* (59A, 66A, 68F, 68L, 70D, 71J, 71N, Epi.B, and Epi.C).

B. Translations of the Letters and Documents

1. *Prior Translations.* To the editor's knowledge, the only piece of *Grebeliana* to have been translated prior to the present half-century-old project are the letters to Thomas Müntzer (63 and 64). There were five previous German editions between 1860 and 1962, and English translations were published by Walter Rauschenbusch (1905), George H. Williams (1957), and J. C. Wenger (1970). Perhaps additional research would identify other pieces that have been translated, especially from Latin into German. A small number of supplemental documents appeared in English translation, and these will be identified in Point 11, below, and in connection with each of these documents as it appears in the present collection.

2. *Edward Yoder Translations.* Yoder began his first-draft English translation of Grebel's Latin letters during his year of graduate studies at the University of Iowa, 1924-25. In a letter to Bender dated April 14, 1925, it is clear that Bender had contracted with him for such a translation and had provided photographs of the transcriptions from the *Vadianische Briefsammlung* (VB, 7 vols., 1888-1913) and the transcriptions from *Zwin-*

glis Briefwechsel (ZW, Vols. VII-X, 1916-29). The nine letters to Myconius had never been transcribed or published. Photographs of the originals had been sent to Correll by Hans Nabholtz, then director of the Zurich Staatsarchiv, where they were located. They were transcribed by Yoder, who wrote that "the orthography of the autographs is reproduced almost without change." Yoder's first-draft translation was continued the following year at the University of Pennsylvania, where he completed his doctoral studies in Latin; and the last two letters were sent to Bender on April 7, 1926. Yoder also translated a number of supplemental letters and documents from the Latin, which Bender and Correll used in their research.

3. *Bender-Correll Revisions*. Correll and Bender went over Yoder's draft, scribbling insertions and revisions. They based their insertions sometimes on an alternate rendering of the Latin but mostly on a preference for a different word order or selection. Thus, their revision constituted a rough second draft of Yoder's translation. Most of the revisions were in Correll's handwriting, indicating that he was doing much of the Grebel research at this stage. He went to Europe during the summer of 1926, spending full time in German and Swiss libraries. A 23-page handwritten report of findings which he sent to Bender from Zurich is preserved in the HSB files in the Mennonite Archives at Goshen, where a copy of this second-stage translation is also preserved, with only six letters missing.

4. *Edward Yoder Revision*. In 1929, Yoder, then serving as Professor of Greek and Latin at Hesston College in Kansas, completed what he considered to be "practically a final version, so far as I am concerned." Regarding his original draft he wrote, "I find that my first efforts four years ago were rather crude in spots, mostly due, I think, to my lack of background and perspective, but also partly to my immaturity in Latin. . . . I am making quite a few changes. I do not think there will be any great number of textual problems left over this time, with the help I have already had from Doctor Correll." Correll was teaching at the American University by this time, and it is evident that they were collaborating in the project somewhat independent of Bender. It is also evident that Yoder incorporated many of the Correll revision notes as he worked over his earlier translation. This draft also included first translations of the three Grebel-to-Vadian letters written in German, probably made by Correll and edited by Yoder. This draft also included Grebel's poem from Zwingli's *Archeteles* (47D). The original typewritten copy of this draft was bound and accessioned into the MHS, where it has been frequently used by students. The carbon copy retained by Yoder was graciously given to me by his widow, Estie Miller Yoder, in response to the request of my colleague, J. C. Wenger.

5. *The Alan Beck Translations.* In January 1972 I contracted with Alan Beck, then Honors Latin Scholar at Trinity College, Dublin, Ireland, to make a fresh translation of Grebel's Latin letters, plus the Burgauer-to-Grebel letter (32A) and the Vadian-to-Grebel acknowledgment letter (1A). Working from the various published transcriptions identified above, he completed his draft with notes by July of that year, without prior reference to any of Yoder's translations.

6. *The David Sudermann Translations.* In the summer of 1972, I contracted with David Sudermann, then doctoral student in Medieval German at the University of Chicago, to make a fresh translation of the three Grebel-to-Vadian letters written in German (Nos. 66, 67, and 68), plus the Vadian-to-Grebel letter (67C), the three Jacob Grebel letters (9A, 23A, and 57A), and several German postscripts to earlier Latin letters.

7. *The John H. Yoder Translations.* At my request, John H. Yoder made independent translations of the same three Grebel-to-Vadian letters, using the more recent and accurate text from the Muralt and Schmidt source volume (Quellen 1). Yoder also translated the Hegenwald-to-Grebel letter (69D), using an unpublished, handwritten transcription made for Bender by the head librarian of the Stadtbibliothek (Vadiana) of St. Gallen, Switzerland—Theodor Schiess. Moreover, the translations of the Hubmaier speeches at the Second Zurich Disputation (57C) and the Veit Suter commentary on that disputation (57E) were made by Yoder.

8. *The Letters to Müntzer.* The four prior English translations listed above, plus a new and independent translation made by Elizabeth Horsch Bender, were collated and a newly edited version produced.

9. *The Elizabeth Horsch Bender Translations.* Apart from the combined work of the three originators of the project, the largest contribution to its completion has been made by Elizabeth Bender. For the past half decade (not to mention her earlier collaboration with the original trio), she has worked closely with the present editor, chiefly in making new translations of more than forty supplemental German documents taken from the Wyss *Chronicle,* the Egli *Aktensammlung,* the Kessler *Sabbata,* the Muralt-Schmidt and Fast source volumes (Quellen 1 and 2), and *Huldreich Zwinglis Sämtliche Werke* (ZW, Vols. I-X), including the major parts of three anti-Anabaptist treatises by Zwingli heretofore unavailable in English (67C, 69C, and 70C).

10. *Other Translations from the Latin and Dutch.* The first and last documents in the collection, both written by Vadian, were translated by two scholars, respectively, at the Catholic University of America, Washington, D.C.: John Hickey-Williams, PhD Cand in Greek Patristics, and Robert Eno, SS, STD (Institut Catholique de Paris), Associate Professor

of Church History in the University's School of Religious Studies. Mr. Hickey-Williams previously served on the editorial staff for the publication of English translations of early Christian texts (*The Fathers of the Church*, published by the CUA Press) and was an Andrew Mellon Foundation Fellow in Early Christian Humanism. The 11-page document which he translated was the dedication letter found at the front of Vadian's published text of a book on meteors by the fifteenth-century Italian humanist, poet, and statesman, Giovanni Pontanus. The essay was Vadian's philosophy of education, addressed to his 18-year-old student from Zurich. The existence of this document was unknown to any of the scholars previously associated with the Grebel research, and Mr. Hickey-Williams worked with a photocopy of an original edition which I acquired from the Stadtbibliothek of Zurich. Despite Vadian's difficult style and penchant for the more abstract medieval Latin vocabulary, Mr. Hickey-Williams and Fr. Eno produced accurate readable translations that provide important termini for this source volume—the first dated six months prior to the first extant letter by Grebel, and the last dated fourteen years after Grebel's death.

The translation of 57A, which is Zwingli's defense of his booklet on the mass canon which he addressed to the Grebel group, was made by Daniel Sheerin, Associate Professor of Classical and Medieval Latin, The University of North Carolina at Chapel Hill.

The translation of 68F(3), known as the "Klettgau letter," chronicling the first Zurich baptismal service, was made from the Dutch by C. J. Dyck, Professor of Historical Theology at AMBS, Elkhart.

11. *The Reprinting of Existing Translations.* Some of the documents included in the collection come from previously published translations— 25A, 47D, 47F, 57F, 59A, 66A, 67B, 68C, 68E, 68F(1), 68L(2), 68L(3), 69D, 71J(3), 71M(1), and Epi.C—revised and incorporated with the permission of copyright owners.

12. *Editing and Completing the Translations.* The editor's role has been largely to fulfill the second half of the original publication plan as revised by Bender when, instead of a single volume, he projected a companion volume to his Grebel biography of 1950. As already indicated, the present edition of the Grebel letters is based on two or more translations of each. An attempt was made to solve all problems of variant translations and to report such differences in the notes when significant. In addition to the supplemental documents listed above, about a dozen were translated by the editor himself—3A, 5B, 19A, 39A, 47E, 47G, 67A, 68B, 68L(1), 71F, 71N, 71P, and Epi.A(1). The producing of the notes was a formidable task, made easier by the prior work of many scholars, especially the editors

of the source volumes from which the translators worked—ZW, Quellen 1, and Quellen 2. The editor's dependence on the copious notes of Fritz Blanke in ZW, VI, No. 108, will be apparent in the annotations for Epi.B. A number of students at AMBS assisted in the translation of notes from the German, especially Peter Letkemann, Franz Wiebe, Heide Koop, and Mary Klassen. Two members of the St. Louis Mennonite Fellowship assisted in a similar way—Rosemarie Matsuda and Cornelius Buhler.

With the aid of these and other sources, a diligent attempt was made to identify every name, place, and event mentioned in the letters and documents. Names or subjects occurring more than once were cross-referenced, using a comprehensive index of the letters and documents prepared by a summer high school assistant, Rita Hartman. The cross-referencing is done by document, page, and line, as follows: 63/260/12 = Document 63, page 260, line 12. After the page proofs arrived, Sue Ramseyer prepared the revised index and Bret Kincaid converted all of the cross references. Because Bret used a conversion table to correlate the new page proofs with the manuscript pages, thus avoiding the tedious task of rechecking every cross reference, the new line numbers will sometimes be off by a line or two. For all of these suffering servants of a shared scholarship, the editor is deeply grateful.

Leland Harder, Director
Great Plains Seminary Education Program
North Newton, Kansas
January 21, 1985
(the 460th birthday of Swiss Anabaptism)

Introduction

The subject matter of the Conrad Grebel letters is distinctly different from that of the other volumes in the MHS or IMS series. Although some of the letters have historical content adjunct to that of the first eighteen "Studies in Anabaptist and Mennonite History," and some even have doctrinal materials not unlike those of the first two "Classics of the Radical Reformation" source volumes, none of them is basically in the category either of historical documentation or doctrinal interpretation. Of all the extant letters, the two to Müntzer come closest to the aim of doctrinal explication, and Grebel's post-conversion letters begin to chronicle an emerging radical Reformation movement; yet, they are all basically personal letters reflecting an inward pilgrimage of struggle and faith and not the chronicling of a movement or the defense of its doctrines.

Grebel's nonextant *Taufbüchlein* (which Zwingli called the *libellus confutatio,* book of counterarguments), found in refracted form in Epi.C, might have qualified as theological argument; but the fact is that Grebel more than once admitted that his gift was in another area. He looked to Hätzer and Hubmaier to do the doctrinal explaining and considered his own work to be more in the arena of proclaiming the message and establishing the church of true believers. Therefore, the rationale for this volume is somewhat different from the others in the two series.

Except for its overly polemical and personal implications, the title *Confessions of an Anabaptist Ringleader* might have been used for this book. The term "Anabaptist ringleader" comes from the Latin *catabaptistarum coryphaeus,* which Zwingli applied to Grebel (see Epi.A/463/2) with a polemical meaning that Grebel might not have totally rejected. The term "confessions" is an apt description of the content of Grebel's letters to Vadian, his father confessor. He often used terms like these to describe his relationship to his former teacher: "You counsel me so well and like a

25

father that I do not know whether my own father has acted as well the part of a counselor in my affairs" (5/72/30-32). Spanning seven of the last eight years of Grebel's life, these letters have the characteristic of free-associative expression. Toward the end of one long letter in which he was aware that his thought had been given free rein, he wrote, "All this I have blabbed out so that from the top of the head to the bottom of the feet, inside and outside the skin, you can observe my whole posture, attitude, affection" (6/80/33-35). Because they are so confessional in content, these letters are an extraordinary repository of subjective data for the behavioral analysis of the true believer, and we are indebted to Vadian and a dozen generations of St. Gallen archivists for the fact that they are still available nearly half a millennium later. A volume of documents portraying how one bright young Swiss patriot became a fervent, influential leader of the Anabaptist movement is long overdue in the rediscovery of Reformation roots. It might well have been the first volume in the series, for it is the beginning point in the portrayal of the tragic drama of the left wing of the Reformation.

Indeed, the basic format for this book is the drama with five acts, prologue, and epilogue. The cast of characters includes a total of 107 names. The main characters are Conrad Grebel, the Anabaptist ringleader, and Huldrych Zwingli, the vicar at the Grossmünster in Zurich. Joachim von Watt, MA, MD, better known as Vadian, is the trusted correspondent of both men before and after their alienation from each other; and through him much of the tense dialogue is filtered. The script is supplied by the 170 letters and documents. There is much monologue in this drama, although it fits the soliloquy of ancient and medieval theater. The actions of the characters are suggested to the imagination of the reader through the words they speak, expressing love and hate, consent and dissent, humor and heartache.

Involved in all of the actions is the extended family of Grebel:

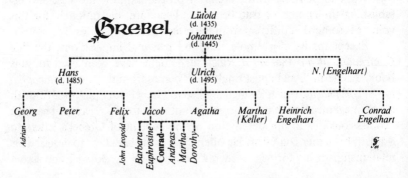

They were residents of Zurich since the late fourteenth century, when Lütold Grebel, the great-great grandfather of Conrad, left his native Kaiserstuhl, a village on the Rhine, to become a citizen of Zurich in 1386. They belonged to the landed nobility by virtue of possession of a family estate at Kloten near Zurich, giving Jacob Grebel, father of Conrad, the title of Junker. Family revenue came also from an iron business begun by Ulrich Grebel and carried on by his son, Jacob, with some help from his grandson, Conrad (see 23/119/26). They belonged to the patrician guild, "zur Meise," with various members of each generation serving as guildmaster, usually with membership in Zurich's Great Council, Lütold from 1420-30, Johannes from 1428-44, Jacob from 1494-1526, etc. The family history included governorships (Jacob in Grüningen, Felix in Rheinthal, and Conrad Engelhart in Hyburg), membership in Zurich's Small Council (Jacob from 1512-26), and appointment to various missions on behalf of Zurich, such as legate to the diet of the Swiss League, deputy to peace negotiations, etc. Felix Grebel carried an official message to the pope, and Jacob was sent on more than thirty missions from 1521-26 (see Schelbert, p. 37).

The family tradition also included service in the church, with Peter Grebel, a canon in the Grossmünster, Aunt Agatha and sister Euphrosine, nuns in the Oetenbach Convent, and Heinrich Engelhart, the pastor at the Fraumünster. More significant for the dramatic events depicted by the letters and documents, members of the Grebel family displayed the whole spectrum of attitudes toward the Zwinglian Reformation. Peter Grebel was an adherent of the old faith who believed that Zwingli's reforms were radical and heretical. Heinrich Engelhart was an intimate colleague of Zwingli, willing to sacrifice his own office in the canonry so that Zwingli could replace him and thereby be relieved of his obligations to the diocesan bishop in Constance. Conrad Grebel was a Zwinglian disciple who also came to the conclusion that the Zurich strategy of reform was diabolical, not for being too radical but for not being radical enough to follow through on the very biblical principles that Zwingli had first proclaimed. Jacob Grebel was a moderate who supported Zwingli and tried to remain conciliatory toward the adherents of the old faith. The conflict was deadly. On the conservative end of the spectrum, Peter was finally forced to resign his benefice and move to the Roman Catholic bailiwick of Baden. At the radical pole, Conrad was finally imprisoned for life and died as an escaped fugitive. Caught in the middle, Jacob was beheaded for treason.

The Prologue takes us to the University of Vienna, where Vadian, a professor of classical literature, composes a vision for young Conrad's education. Act 1 features Conrad as the brilliant, promising student who writes the first of seventy-one letters, addressed to none other than Huldrych Zwingli, then the people's priest in Einsiedeln, thirty miles southeast of Zurich. Grebel confides in Zwingli, patron of Swiss university students, that he respects Vadian very much but that he longs to go to Paris to study under Glarean, who is still the greatest of Swiss teachers. The letter is supplemented by a memo from Vadian, published in the Vienna edition of his best known work, *Commentary on Pomponius Mela*, reiterating what he had already said in the Prologue that Grebel was a student of extraordinary potential for scholarship and leadership, if only he would apply himself to the liberal arts with a sprinkle of theology and a dash of rhetoric. In Vienna, Grebel applies himself to the art of sword-fighting; and following a brawl in which he nearly loses his hand, he is called home by his angry father. From Zurich he writes letters to Vadian and Zwingli anticipating (with Myconius, schoolmaster at the Grossmünster) the return of Vadian and a great celebration when he visits Zurich. The celebration takes the form of an expedition to the top of Mt. Pilatus by Vadian, Grebel, Myconius, and Zimmermann, recounted by Vadian in the Basel edition of the *Pomponius Mela*.

As Act 1 comes to an end, Grebel moves to Paris to study with Glarean, but not before expressing his hope that Vadian meanwhile might meet and marry his sister Martha. And Myconius takes up permanent residence in his hometown of Luzern, where he will receive nine of Grebel's letters and from where he will serve as mediator between Conrad and his alienated parents. Then at a later crucial point in the drama, Zwingli will call Myconius back to Zurich to assist in the work of the Reformation.

Act 2 features Conrad, the prodigal, living in Glarean's dormitory at the University of Paris, but getting distracted by too many quarrels, too much drinking, too much spending on "belly, books, and clothes," too many visits to prostitutes, and too much display of temper when certain bandits attack. It appears that he and several of his friends fight back, and several Frenchmen are killed. When the repercussions are almost more than he can bear, Grebel blames his father for getting him into this mess by misusing his influence in high government to secure questionable foreign stipends and failing to teach his sons to live within their means "on what has been earned." Apart from their paranoid overtones, these indictments prove to be incredibly prophetic when read in the context of the father's trial and execution eight years later (see Epi.A). But in Act 2, the father comes on stage only to announce the marriage of his daughter Martha to Vadian; and the facts that the match was his idea in the first place and that the father will not allow him to come home for the celebration throw Conrad into utter despair.

In Act 3, Conrad returns home to Zurich with a consequent, although temporary, uplift in mood. He is elated to be back, grateful to Myconius for reconciling his angry parents, ecstatic at Vadian's long-awaited letter which he "fondles the way children do with a rattle." When the reality of his parents' foibles returns into focus, he demonstrates his sharp wit by writing amusing descriptions of his mother's erratic behavior in one 24-hour period and his father's penchants for wine and pretty girls. He begins again to write poetry and tries to interest Vadian in reading the *Iliad* together in the original Greek. His father appears on stage again to make payment on Martha's dowry, and Myconius sends along a guilder owed by a friend. But then Conrad returns to his "rather more sullen" temperament, triggered by the deaths of Zwingli's brother Andrew and his own sister Euphrosine, a nun with malice toward none. His spirits are revived somewhat by the announcement that he has gotten himself a sweetheart, "my desire," as he calls her. This infatuation does not help his relationship with his parents because the girl appears to be resident in the local convent without dowry or character references. Through this and other dimensions of his struggles, Conrad is the seeker, searching for the door that opens to ultimate freedom, knowing there must be such a door, but not yet finding it. So, like Ulrich von Hutten, the knight, he "gambles and casts the dice" and runs off to Basel with Barbara, his "ganze welt," his "holokosme." They take an apartment and Conrad goes to work for Cratander, the famous book publisher, with special assignment to proofread the Basel edition of Vadian's *Pomponius Mela*.

Act 4 is the turning point in Conrad's life following the deepest agony of his soul. He is back in Zurich and takes advantage of a week's absence of his father on state business to marry Barbara. This is a mixed blessing because of the relentless opposition of his parents, his own awful sense of guilt and emptiness, and a weird premonition that his "Barbarity" will eventually betray him—another self-fulfilling prophecy. Nine months elapse before he writes again; and when he does, he is playing a new role as Zwingli's advocate and helper. And so he writes to Vadian, "Would that by the grace of God all would pray for me that I accept this ministry in earnest and triumph in it." The seven supplemental documents between letters 47 and 48 fill some of the gaps of information. He has become the vanguard for Zwingli's Reformation offensive, and apparently not without the reformer's blessing. His is a radicalizer role that is acceptable and functional at this stage of Zwingli's movement but that is destined eventually to alienate him from his leader after the movement has gained control of the social order and there is the troublesome resort to compromise in order to conserve the gains that have been won. As Act 4 comes to a close with the

29

momentous Second Zurich Disputation in October 1523, the mystery character is no longer Grebel but Zwingli, whose vacillation between the radicalism of his address to the Bishop of Constance (47D) and the conservatism of his " 'Introduction' to the Disputation Findings" (58A) becomes the new enigma in the unfolding drama.

Act 5 portrays the estrangement in the Zwinglian Reformation when the radicalizers are rejected by their leader and form their own Anabaptist church without his approval. The turning point occurs in December 1523 when Zwingli forsakes his promise to celebrate the new evangelical communion on Christmas Day and when Grebel comes to the realization that "the cause of the gospel is in a very bad way here." The climax of the drama occurs in January 1525 when Grebel performs the first rebaptisms, signaling the founding of the new church. During the year 1524, Grebel keeps Vadian informed of developments; and his brother-in-law responds with a certain appreciation for the struggle in Zurich because he is having his own not dissimilar confrontations with Benedict Burgauer, the conservative vicar of the church in St. Gallen. Vadian wants to know more about Grebel's correspondence with the reformers of Wittenberg—Luther, Carlstadt, and Hegenwald.

The year ends with Zwingli's first published tract against the radical proponents of believers' baptism and an exchange of letters between Grebel and Vadian in which are heard especially poignant expressions revealing an emerging disagreement between the two brothers-in-law, who had long been closer than blood brothers. "Would that we were brothers-in-the-truth-of-Christ" writes Grebel. To which Vadian replies, "My wish concerning you would be and always has been that you conduct yourself with humble propriety toward Zwingli and Leo and not be so demanding and contentious, with awareness that they are the ones who are engaged in furthering the Word of truth and are not able abruptly to throw out everything that has come into misuse through so many years." But Grebel observes that "Zwingli is writing about rebels or rebellion," prophesying that "this may well hit us. Look out! It will bring something. I do not think that persecution will fail to come." Once more Grebel's prophecy comes to pass. Four weeks later the Zurich City Council issues its first anti-Anabaptist mandate, and those members of Grebel's circle who are not native to Zurich (Reublin, Brötli, Hätzer, and Castelberger) are banished from the country.

In a touching letter to Castelberger as the latter closes out his bookstore in Zurich in preparation for his exile, Grebel asks him to sell his own precious books, for he too is leaving Zurich. Then as the St. Gallen chronicler, Kessler, tells the story of Grebel's missionary work north to Schaffhausen and east to St. Gallen, where he baptized several hundred persons in the River Sitter on Palm Sunday, we can almost picture the executioners, preparing the stake and arranging the firewood as three of his brothers in the faith become the first martyrs of the movement.

Another scene spotlights the coincidence of letters to Vadian written the end of May only two days apart, one from Zwingli (accompanying shipment of multiple copies of his second anti-Anabaptist treatise) and the other from Grebel (the last personal letter he wrote to anyone, so far as is known). As Zwingli puts it, "You see me fighting hard and bitterly with these enemies of the gospel." And Grebel pleads, "Turn away from the bloody faction of Zwingli, flee from your own to the divine wisdom so that you become a fool to the world but wise to the Lord. Become as a child or you cannot enter into the kingdom of God."

Zwingli's next letter to Vadian, dated the following October, reports the arrest and imprisonment of Grebel and Blaurock; and the drama moves swiftly into the events of their trial (including another public disputation on baptism) and their sentencing to life imprisonment on a diet of bread, mush, and water, including the announcement that henceforth unrepentant Anabaptists who are citizens of Zurich will be executed by drowning, and may God have mercy on their souls.

The next scene, following six months of imprisonment, is the mysterious escape of the Anabaptists on March 21, 1526. The two men who tell the story to the Zurich court are fellow prisoners too sick and weak to succeed in their getaway. The third witness is not an Anabaptist but testifies to having met Grebel on his flight in the direction of Glattfelden. Act 5 ends with the St. Gallen chronicler telling about the death of Grebel in Maienfeld in the Oberland and the execution of Mantz in Zurich soon after.

The Epilogue features an incredible series of documents that put the whole drama of Grebel's Anabaptist activities into variegated perspectives, like the successive shakings of a kaleidoscope—the weird trial and execution of Conrad's aged father (which one historian calls "Zwingli's liquidation of Jacob Grebel") and the eerie conversation between Zwingli and Grebel's "ghost in hell," the single-mindedness of Zwingli's irreversible compulsion to destroy the Anabaptist movement, the witness of the next two Anabaptist martyrs in Zurich, the survival power of the movement in other Swiss cantons, and Vadian's final reflections on the whole drama fourteen years after Grebel's death. Although neither Zwingli nor Vadian can change his mind about the illegitimacy of the Anabaptist dissent, neither can he get the dissenters out of his mind. "It seems funny to strive with ghosts," writes Zwingli. "With the greatest obstinacy, he began to

31

examine thoughts once fixed and firm," writes Vadian. The Anabaptist ringleader is gone, but the dialogue continues in a kind of mysterious universal perspective.

And now 4½ centuries later, the dialogue resumes in our Sunday schools, college and seminary classrooms, and ecumenical convocations. Neither Zwingli nor Grebel had a corner on the truth; but by the grace of their same Lord, each had a corner of the truth. Neither was totally in error; but under the influence of the prince of darkness, whom both acknowledged as a satanic power in men's lives, both contributed in different ways to the tearing asunder of Christ's church. Perhaps in the presence of the prince of light, their unresolved differences were ultimately seen in true perspective; but our piecemeal search for the truth proceeds meanwhile, "for now we see in a mirror dimly, but then face to face."

These letters and documents are not published for scholars only but for all seekers and believers who have the will to read this drama, not as disinterested spectators but as persons who are themselves actors in the universal tragicomedy of the human predicament and God's gracious sending of his Son that we might know the truth and live by it forevermore.

Illustrations

ZOLLIKON: THE THOMANN FARM

The Grebel house on the Neumarkt in Zurich. "The decision to hold this convention had been made in Grebel's house" (47A/151f/7-8). Shown is the second of three houses acquired by Senator Jacob Grebel: the "Thurm auf dem Bach."

IN·DIESEM·HAUSE·WOHNTE
1508-1514 UND 1520-1525
KONRAD GREBEL
DER·ZUSAMMEN·MIT·FELIX MANZ
DAS·TAUFERTUM·BEGRÜNDETE

Commemorative inscription *on the Grebel house in Zurich*

The town of Gruningen and the Grebel castle

The Grebel castle in Grüningen. "*Conrad Grebel together with George, that man of fickle mind, has been arrested at Grüningen and thrown into prison*" *(711/436a/ 16-18). Ironically, Grebel was imprisoned in the same castle in which he had lived until age 13, while his father served as chief magistrate in this bailiwick.*

Zurich: the Grossmünster. *"The last news from here is this: Huldrych Zwingli has been appointed rector of Zurich" (6/40/15-16). It was in January of 1519 that Zwingli began his ministry in the Zurich cathedral by preaching directly from the Bible instead of following the traditional lectionary.*

Huldrych Zwingli. *"I am bishop and priest in this town of Zurich, and to me is the care of soul's entrusted . . . and not the monks" (47B/154/17-18). With the Bible in one hand and the sword in the other, Zwingli masterminded the Protestant reformation in German Switzerland with a new church-state synthesis.*

The guildhouse "Zur Meise," Zurich. *"And after voting among themselves, they decided by a majority of one hand that if the weather was nice, they would have the meal at the Lindenhof, although Hottinger wanted it at the Meisen" (47A/152/2-5). Zur Meise was the ironworks guild in which Grebel's father and grandfather were guildmasters.*

Joachim von Watt (Vadian). *"I am studying under Vadian, a man singularly worthy of every honor, by whom (and this I must confess) I am esteemed as a brother" (1/8a/13-16). Known in his home town of St. Gallen as Joachim von Watt, Vadian was Grebel's university teacher in Vienna (1515-18), brother-in-law (1519), and chief correspondent (1517-25).*

Mount Pilatus, as seen from mount Rigi. "*In Switzerland, near the ancient and celebrated town of Luzern, there is a very high mountain . . . which is known in the vernacular as 'the Fractured One'*" *(3A/20a/1-4). The mountain was climbed by Vadian, Grebel, Myconious, and Xylotectus in August, 1519.*

Zwingli's "Apologeti" and Grebel's poem. "*It is called 'Archeteles' because it is masculine and is going to put an end to all controversy between those gentlemen and myself*' (47D/158/3-5). *Zwingli's first major Reformation writing, by which he hoped to establish his authority once and for all, was climaxed by Grebel's poem,* "*In fury let them burst, the bishops all.*"

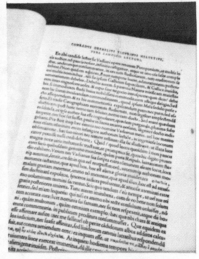

The Pomponius Mela. "*There is a* **Pomponius** *in the press, beautifully and well printed*" (35/23a/11-12). *The Basel edition carried Vadian's account of the expedition to Mt. Pilatus.*

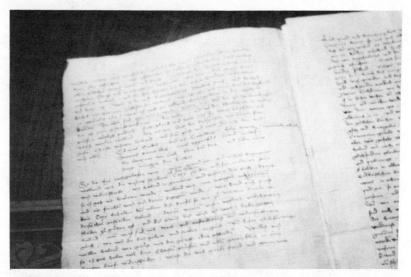

Grebel's letter to Müntzer. "*I am writing for the first time to Thomas Müntzer, whose second booklet on phony faith I recently obtained and read*" (62/257a/13-15). *This programmatic letter to the leader of the Peasants' War in Germany bore incisive witness to the way of peace and nonresistance which became the identifying mark of the Grebel-Sattler interpretation of Anabaptism.*

The first Zurich Disputation. "*Vicar [Faber]: 'Today I spoke as a vicar, but now as a John.' Zwingli: 'Yes, indeed, Had you long before today taken off your vicar's hat . . . I could have spoken with you as with a John'*" (51A/179/14-19). *The January 1523 disputation established the Reformation principle of* **sola scriptura** *in Zurich, to test all questions of faith and life by the final authority of the Scriptures.*

The Neustadtgasse in Zurich. *"Beyond this, they nevertheless proceeded at night to hold meetings on Neustadt, intending to set up a separate church"* (71K/442/8-9). *The time was late January and the place was most likely the home of Felix Mantz on the Neustadtgasse.*

41

Zollikon: the Rudy Thomann house. *"Your letter of safe conduct may be sent to Rudy Thomann's house in Zollikon. We will readily discern whether we have a safe conduct to you and back again to our refuge"* (71/421a/14-16). *The house of Rudy Thomann, who had joined the Anabaptists on Jan. 25, 1525, is still preserved at Gstadstrasse 23-25.*

Schaffhausen. *"We then went on to Schaffhausen, where we found our dear brother, Conrad Grebel, and where we were with the two doctors [Meyer and Hofmeister] and ate supper with them"* (68J/338/6-8). *Schaffhausen was a city and canton in northern Switzerland where Anabaptist refugees like Grebel and Brötli came in hope of winning the church leaders to their cause.*

Vadian and Martha *"You have married my sister, the most illustrious of suitors has come among us, and there has happened to me in this Platonic year nothing but this one happy event"* (10/51a/18-21). *Vadian and Martha Grebel were married at Wädenswil on Aug. 19, 1519.*

43

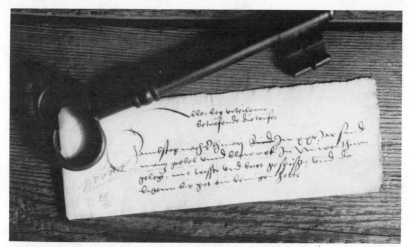

Notice of imprisonment. "On Saturday following [St.] Othmar's [Day] in the year [15]25, Mantz, Grebel, and Blaurock were placed into the New Tower to be fed on bread and water and there lie until God considers it enough." This is the translation of the jailer's note of Nov. 18, 1525, the original of which is owned by the Mennonite Historical Library, Goshen, Indiana.

The Sitter River. "On Sunday (it was Palm Sunday), they took him [Grebel] out to the Sitter [River] with them and received baptism from him" (69A/351/26-27). The Sitter flows toward the Rhine two miles west of St. Gallen.

Waldshut on the Rhine. "*He [Grebel] went to Waldshut to the Doctor Balthasar Fridberger [Hubmaier], the local minister, who although not unlettered allowed himself to be submerged in Anabaptism ... and by his cleverness succeeded so well that all Waldshut was baptized by him*" (69A/349A/25—350/6). *A town on the Rhine 25 miles northwest of Zurich, Waldshut was the seat of an Anabaptist congregation from April to December, 1525.*

Maienfeld. "*Not long after this, Conrad Grebel went to Maienfeld in the Oberland and fell victim to the plague and died*" (71R/464a/21-22). *Although not known for certain, the place of death may have been the home of his sister, Barbara, who lived here.*

Zurich: the Schipfge on the Limmat. "*On Saturday, January 5, 1527, the Large and Small Councils of Zurich condemned Felix Mantz to death ... and he was drowned that same afternoon at 3 o'clock*" (Epi.B/481c/1-4). *He was taken to the* **Schipfge** *by the executioner, bound hands and feet, and held under water until he expired.*

Cast of Characters

In Alphabetical Order
(For character profiles with references to the
letters and documents, see pp. 527ff.)

1. Aberli, Heinrich
2. Ab-Iberg, Fridli
3. Ammann, John Jacob
   Andreas on the Crutches (see
   Castelberger)
   Balthasar (see Hubmaier)
4. Binder, Jörg
5. Blaurock, Jörg
   Bodenstein (see Carlstadt)
6. Bolt, Eberli
7. Bosshart, Marx
8. Brennwald, Heinrich
9. Brennwald, Karl
10. Brötli, Hans
11. Burgauer, Benedict
12. Carlstadt, Andreas
13. Castelberger, Andreas
14. Charles V, Emperor
    Clivanus (see Collin)
15. Coct, Anemund de
16. Collin, Rudolph
17. Cratander, Andreas
    De Coct (see Coct)
    De Falconibus (see Falconibus)
    Dominik (see Zili)
    Eberli, Bolt (see Bolt, Eberli)
    Enderli (see Castelberger)
18. Engelhart, Conrad
19. Engelhart, Heinrich
20. Erasmus, Desiderius
21. Escher, Hans Conrad
22. Falconibus, William de
23. Falk, Jacob
    Felix (see Mantz)
24. Ferdinand I, Archduke
25. Filonardi, Ennius
26. Francis I, King
27. Giger, Gabriel
28. Glarean, Heinrich
29. Grebel, Adrian
30. Grebel, Agatha
31. Grebel, Andreas
32. Grebel, Barbara (1)
33. Grebel, Barbara (2)
34. Grebel, Conrad
35. Grebel, Dorothy
36. Grebel, Euphrosine
37. Grebel, Felix
38. Grebel, Jacob
39. Grebel, John Leopold
40. Grebel, Martha
41. Grebel, Peter
42. Grossmann, Caspar
43. Hätzer, Ludwig
44. Hedinger, Jörg
45. Hochrütiner, Lorenz
46. Hofmeister, Sebastian
47. Hohenlandenberg, Hugo von
48. Hottinger, Claus
49. Hottinger, Hans
50. Hottinger, Jacob
51. Hottinger, Margaret
52. Hottinger, Rudolf
53. Hotz, Hans

54. Hubmaier, Balthasar
55. Hujuff, Hans
    Huldrych (see Zwingli)
56. Hutten, Ulrich von
    Hypolitus (see Bolt)
57. Joner, Wolfgang
    Jörg of the House of Jacob (see
    Blaurock)
58. Jud, Leo
    Juflius (see Wetter)
    Kern (see Krüsi)
59. Kessler, Johann
60. Krüsi, Hans
    Kürsiner (see Roggenacher)
61. Lambert, Franz
    Landenberg (see Hohenlanden-
    berg)
62. Lehman, Felix
63. Leo X, Pope
    Lincki (see Lingg)
64. Lingg, Marty
    Lorenz (see Hochrütiner)
    Loriti (see Glarean)
65. Luther, Martin
66. Mantz, Anna
67. Mantz, Felix
68. Maximilian I, Emperor
    Megander (see Grossmann)
69. Müntzer, Thomas
70. Myconius, Oswald
    Nagel (see Krüsi)
71. Ockenfuss, Hans
    Oggenfuss (see Ockenfuss)
    Pannicellus (see Brötli)
    Pfister (see Pur)
72. Puccius, Antonio
73. Pur, Bartlime
74. Reimann, Heine
75. Reublin, Wilhelm
76. Ritter, Erasmus
77. Roggenacher, Anthony
78. Röist, Diethelm
79. Röist, Mark
80. Sattler, Michael
81. Schappeler, Christoph
82. Schinner, Matthew
83. Schmid, Conrad
84. Schumacher, Fridli
    Schorant (see Uliman)
    Sertorius (see Schappeler)
    Simon (see Stumpf)
85. Stumpf, Simon
86. Trinkler, Ulrich
87. Tschudi, Peter
88. Tschudi, Valentin
89. Uliman, Wolfgang
90. Ulrich, Duke of Württemberg
91. Ursinus, Caspar
92. Utinger, Heinrich
93. Vadian, Joachim
    Velius (see Ursinus)
    Verulanus (see Filonardi)
94. Walder, Heinrich
95. Wanner, Johann
    Watt, von (see Vadian)
    Weniger (see Lingg)
96. Westerburg, Gerhard
97. Wetter, Sebastian Wolfgang
98. Widerker, Anna
    Wilhelm (see Reublin)
99. Wirz, Hans
100. Wirz, Heinrich
101. Wüst, Michael
102. Wyss, Bernhard
103. Xylotectus, John
104. Zili, Dominik
    Zimmermann (see Xylotectus)
105. Zwick, Johann
106. Zwingli, Huldrych

PROLOGUE
1517

Prologue A
Vadian's Vision for Grebel's Education
Vienna, February 28, 1517

It is fitting to begin and end our source volume on the rise of the Anabaptist movement under the leadership of Conrad Grebel with two letters from the pen of Vadian, his university teacher, "father-confessor," and brother-in-law. Both make reference to Grebel as unusually talented. But the first is full of hope for his future, while the other is saturated with disappointment with his past. Early in their relationship Vadian wrote not only one but two public letters to his bright and promising student—the first one dedicating to Grebel his literary work on Pontanus (see fn. 40, below) and the second a tribute to him at the end of his 1518 edition of Pomponius Mela *(see 1A/ Intro.).*

The title page for the former work, translated from the Latin, appeared as follows: "Jovianus Giovanni Pontanus, inspired poet, and his work on meteors to his son L. Francisco. Together with an epistle by Vadian in which is beautifully explained how polished literature and the noble arts are joined together." Vadian's book was published in Vienna, presumably in Lucas Alantsee's printshop, sometime after February 28, 1517, when the letter to Grebel was written. Apparently only one copy remains, to be found in the Zurich Zentralbibliothek. It had originally belonged to Adrian Wirth, one of

> *"My dear Conrad, you should take this to heart. . . . You should develop a method by which you undertake a steadfast pursuit of knowledge and a gentle pursuit of words, because it is a matter of great importance to learn both the ideas and the art of communicating them."*
>
> —Vadian to Grebel, February 28, 1517.

49

the reformer-priests of Stammheim who were executed by confederate reactionaries in the Ittinger affair in 1524 (see 65/fn. 24).

The work has never been transcribed or reprinted and more research is needed concerning it. The translation presented here was made for the editor from a photocopy of the original by Mr. John Hickey-Williams of the Catholic University of America. To save space, only 62 percent of the letter is included, but sufficient to reveal Vadian's vision for the proper education of Conrad Grebel—model student.

A letter of Joachim Vadian[1] of Switzerland,[2] Poet Laureate of the Emperor, to his student, Conrad Grebel of Zurich, Switzerland, a noble young man of exceptional talent.

Today, dearest Conrad,[3] many people who are not in fact unlearned, think that their time and best efforts are spent well and to greatest advantage when their perpetual desire, to speak in jest, is that they may acquire for themselves by anxious recitation prolonged all the way to their gray hair the rich exuberance of the Greek and Latin languages. Whereupon to me, their opinion may be no more commendable than the madness of those who attribute nothing at all to the luster of language or the properties and elegance of vocabulary.

There is error, it seems to me, in both directions, for we cannot attain a knowledge of things without careful attention to vocabulary. Nor can even the most polished vocabulary devoid of any connection to a knowledge of many things have much benefit by itself. Hence those who are devoted to matters worthy of inquiry are freer of blame. They are pronouncing something for the sake of the advancement and excellence of the human mind, so that they seem to be keen on knowing, which is itself very natural to the human person. . . .

On the other hand, those who exhaust a stream of words and who, while neglecting the reality expressed, embrace the artificial ornamentation of words and do not feast on the whole hare are not only unlearned and uneducated but they are also ignorant of who they are. For they do not stretch their minds as much as they should in accordance with reason's dictates and the prescription of the human situation. . . . Such minds receive the pity of Apuleius[4] in his *de mundo*,[5] written for his son Faustinus: "They extol the heights of Nysa[6] and the hinterlands of Cirrha,[7] the sanctuaries of Olympus[8] and the steeps of Ossa,[9] and other isolated details of this sort. For they are seized by an insatiable admiration for objects of such mediocre value and insignificance. That these things exist (he says) is not so wonderful to them since they no longer wonder about the existence of anything greater, nor do they stretch to a reality worthy of more exacting observation. On the other hand, if they had been able to observe the earth and the whole universe at once, they would realize that the tiny details and single parts of the world merit less praise than the totality of which they are a part."[10] End of comment.

As I was saying, we should commend the person who acquires a rich vocabulary for himself with equal devotion to the noble arts[11] and to the most eloquent writers,[12] and especially the reestablished ones (unless, of course, a subject demands greater effort). To be sure, they tend to approach those disciplines that are concerned in any way with present places, times, races, or nations, without much capacity for work; for they are learned, it is believed, without difficulty through a process of analogy with daily events that occur. With respect to the eminent arts, however, while there are many and their individual purposes are almost distinct, none are considered by learned men to be more outstanding than those that encompass nature and divine truth from which the entire power of nature emanates.

The most outstanding among these is called theology.[13] It was eagerly attempted by the Greeks, Chaldeans, and Egyptians, and even more directly by the Hebrews. It has been done anew by us, however, since Jesus, the Lord of life and truth, appeared. But would that this faith were as pure today as it used to be! Would that it had not become entangled and confused by so many Aristotelian traditions over the past four hundred years more or less![14] For if I am not mistaken, the trouble over scholastic investigations and the alliance of Aristotle and our faith has become more intense since the rise of the orders of the mendicant friars (as they are called).[15] Inasmuch as many ardently praise this development, however, I will not object to it, especially since it appeared at the famous University of Paris![16]

On second thought,[17] you could say that the branch of learning that concerns itself with God and matters divine is no more noble than astronomy, for with a degree of certitude greater than the human mind seems capable of acquiring, it deals with the power, distance, and movements of the larger bodies of the heavens devoid of natural corruption.

The next place is occupied by those sciences which carefully examine the sources, causes, characteristics and activity of things consisting of a variable (although in this context I should say elemental)[18] nature. Then follow those co-sciences which study the location of places, the distance between them, and the currents of the weather and all those things which nature generally displays at random, one time or another, not by their single appearance but by the alternation of elements that are in them. Our scholars have resolved to call these sciences metaphysics,[19] just as the Greeks called them physics.[20]

With no temerity whatever,[21] I add here that distinguished profession, medicine, which is the most noble of all those arts whose benefit is bestowed on mortal man. This is true in my judgment because it is the dutiful servant of the mysterious and marvelous works of nature and has been linked in every way by an intimate connection with that very nature.

Although the branches of learning which pertain to the laws[22] and virtues of people and to the principles of equity and justice are manifold and have a rightful place, I do not overlook them (unless my judgment deceives me) when I include here only those which are suitable for all men and requisite for the administration of public government. Is there anyone who lives his private life well who does not discern between virtue and vice? Is there anyone who conducts his life with others well who does not have a norm for what is right and just? It is to be admitted, therefore, that these disciplines are indeed important and practical but with respect to their practice and method are less distinguished than those previously mentioned because the latter somehow seize and inflame the mind that has already advanced a little farther and is beginning to examine more deeply.[23]

The former disciplines usually nourish the mind with the sweet knowledge of nature's great mysteries[24] or with a certain divine ambrosia.[25] Moreover, just as the horses are led out of the starting gate onto the racetrack during the games, these disciplines lead out the native quickness of our minds incarcerated in the prison of weak bodies for a brief time (for indeed life is not long for us). [They ride them] through the earth, through the sea, through the sky, and through the heavens as well as the invulnerable structure of the celestial universe glittering with perpetual fires to an awesome respect for the total work of such a great Creator and to an understanding of its particular parts. For the human mind is capable of such understanding in proportion to the relationship between one's ability and one's endeavors and to the extent that we shall attain the goal as if for the awarding of an Olympic crown.[26] I am convinced, therefore, that there is in the universe a certain sustenance for the peaceful soul which no copious speech, no smooth diction, nor poetry, no matter how subtle the metaphor, can equal or excel.

This is not what I would say concerning God and divine truth, for which the mind is of less importance.[27] Indeed those in our religion who have purged the powers of their mind know better. With them contemplation can be so efficacious toward God that the mind, intent on God, elevates the body along with it, as stated in the thirteenth[28] book of *Platonic Theology* by Marsilio Ficino.[29] Speech, therefore, usually consists of those things which, having been humanly learned by studying nature, clarify and create a ready approach to divine things. In *Phaedo,*[30] Plato recalls these divine things when he states that the minds of philosophers acquire the wings by which one can fly to divine reality. . . .

But to return to our original point of digression. It seems to me that a bright person of honest judgment can bestow nothing on his language without a knowledge of the world. On the other hand, he can never bestow as much grandeur on his knowledge of the world when it is expressed in lowly speech and improper words as is usually produced by the pleasing facility of speech that flows aptly, fittingly. . . . But this fact is certainly not appreciated by those who prefer to be considered eloquent rather than learned, and thus neglect the rigorous disciplines. They are like starving poets, growing thin for lack of substance because they have been intent on their pleasure alone. Their total effort is directed at perambulating about the garden prepared for their delight; but it is devoid of any fruitbearing land. For such as these the ultimate aim of their study is to know the accomplishments of Philip in Macedonia and Greece, Artaxerxes in Egypt, Alexander in Asia, and Caesar in Gaul.[31] O such beautiful little minds, such delicate and little souls!

Codrus[32] writes (although not everyone ascribes the statement to him)[33] that Aristotle used to say that those who pursue other disciplines but scorn philosophy are like the suitors of Penelope during Ulysses' absence.[34] Since they could not have the lady, they used to flirt with the maidservants. Those who do not know how to link words with substantive knowledge are of the same lot, since they cultivate language but have nothing to say. . . .

My dear Conrad, you should take this to heart. Otherwise you might seem to some to be pursuing another course, either by a sloth that is blameworthy or an intellect that is weak. Because it is a matter of great importance to learn both the ideas and the art of communicating them, you should develop a method such that you undertake a steadfast pursuit of knowledge and a gentle pursuit of words. For in this way you will achieve your goal, as though on one course but with two chariots. Consequently the poetic words of Horace[35] should be recalled: "To discern is the source and font of writing well. The socratic pages can set forth your matter, and when the matter is in hand the words will not be loath to follow." . . .

Although the preceding days of winter have been spent in translating for a government stipend[36] the fifteenth book of the *Bibliotheca* of Diodorus Siculus[37] where he narrates the accomplishments of Philip of Macedon, and although Alexander the Great, who has been picturesquely narrated by Dionysius[38] in the sixteenth[39] book, remains to be done (for I must devote myself to its translation next February), I am making provision for an author who is very eloquent but also very learned whom I shall translate for the benefit of you and those like you so that no one will say poets are barren. . . .

Many others whom I have considered do not hit the mark as well as Pontanus.[40] He is certainly the most learned of all the poets of our day whom I have read on this side of the controversy. In the work entitled *Liber Meteororum,* he has explained with an unusual felicity befitting talent correct usage and substantive ideas which usually do not seem capable of such eloquent expression. Moreover, he exhibits outstanding learning which should be read by those fond of polished expression. I have explained my opinions on his talent in the twenty-ninth chapter of my *Poetica.*[41] You will receive from this outstanding writer what your own talent longs for. Indeed, you will receive something very useful both from his knowledge of the excellence of nature and from the well constructed elegance of the poem. And gradually you will ascend on the right path through those things which are more evident and more familiar to those which can only be acquired gradually. This, as Aristotle taught, is the ascent of understanding.

I know that from writers on the elements,[42] you have already learned the natural causes of various effects which inspire wonder for many people; namely, the source of dew and of hail, the source of the rivers and springs that flow continually from the mountains, the nature of thunder, and the nature of the meteors that burn at night as well as the diverse images they project, what hurls the comets in the heaven, the source of the winds and the rainbow, the reason why stars fall (as the uninformed think), and other things of this type which are very pleasant to know, no matter who the teacher might be. But they cannot be learned more beautifully from any other than from Pontanus. You ask why? Because he has enveloped all things in smooth rhythms; because he frequently mentions the places of Italy and other lands that have long inspired admiration for themselves; because he has a marvelous ability to weave narrative and physical science into a knowledge of reality from which education in narration can be understood to be neither empty nor frivolous, contrary to the statements of the ignorant. To the utmost of my ability I will do my best in the explanation of all these matters, to the end that by bringing forth garlands which achieve this purpose from the works of Aristotle, Pliny, Albert the Great, Seneca, and others, I will not in setting forth Pontanus be derelict in my duty to all my students, but above all, to you.

Vienna, Austria, February 28, 1517.

Original Publication: Vadian's *Joannis Joviani Pontani, poetae divini, ad L. Franciscum Filium, Meteororum Liber,* copy found in Zentralbibliothek Zurich, G. II. 147b.
Transcription: None.

54

ACT 1, 1517-1518:
THE STUDENT

1
Grebel to Zwingli
Vienna, September 8, 1517

Twenty miles southeast of Zurich—a six-hour journey by horseback—was the village of Einsiedeln, then as well as now a famous place of pilgrimage for Roman Catholics. Pilgrims come to the shrine of the Virgin Mary in the Abbey Church of St. Mary's to be touched by the mother of miracles. The people's priest here in 1517 was a 33-year-old leader, Huldrych Zwingli, who was destined to be called to the Grossmünster in Zurich a year later and to become the Protestant Reformer of German-speaking Switzerland.

Zwingli was a brilliant humanist scholar to whom many young Swiss university students looked as their role model; and he himself cultivated this relationship by writing personal letters of encouragement to them. One such letter that he wrote in the early autumn of 1517 was addressed to Conrad and Leopold Grebel, students at the University of Vienna. That letter has been lost; but the reply of the Grebel cousins, written by Conrad, has been preserved in the Staatsarchiv of Zurich. A translation follows herewith.

> *"I am studying under Vadian, a man singularly worthy of every honor, by whom (and this I must confess) I am loved as a brother. . . . I would still prefer to be enrolled among the French students of Glarean, my friend and yours, having come to the conclusion that he is the foremost teacher."*
> —Grebel to Zwingli, September 8, 1517.

Inasmuch as we little expected your letter,[1] most honored Zwingli,[2] a man indeed of such authority and renowned learning among the Swiss, it is with immense nostalgia (I speak for my friend and myself)[3] that we receive it, and we rejoice or rather in all sincerity we triumph in it no less than if you had sent us some magnificent gems, or a cornucopia,[4] or the hen's milk.[5]

Let others receive from friends the gifts of wealthy kings, if only you, Zwingli, continue to send to your Conrad these paper treasures of yours (which, like all your work, is so blessed by the Muses).[6] It will not matter to me in the slightest[7] if you charge me with presumption or stupidity, for I will continue to write to you in the hope of receiving your replies. We shall gain from them, aside from the choice Zwinglian elegance and polished style, the sure evidence of a new friendship, a keener and sharper spur for the study of the literary arts.[8]

I presume you want to hear about my career and other news. I am studying under Vadian, a man singularly worthy of every honor, by whom, and this I must confess,[9] I am esteemed as a brother, while he himself is loved, cherished, and revered by me as if he were a most devoted father.

In what are known as the seven liberal arts,[10] I have never won nor do I expect to win any laurels,[11] but this is how my temperament inclines me.[12] If today I am not settled down in the literary arts, I shall be wholly settled down in the future. Having been supported throughout this period of two years by a grant from the Emperor Maximilian,[13] I have cherished the aforementioned study of literature in Vienna,[14] just as I will continue to cherish it.[15] And though I might be enjoying some advantages here more than there, I would still prefer to be enrolled among the French students of Glarean,[16] my friend and yours, having come to the conclusion that he is the preeminent teacher[17]—I pay him the highest honor that is due and give him the garland appropriate to his fame—for he faithfully fulfills all the responsibilities of a learned, good, and true teacher. I felt the lack of these in Vadian, and I hope you will not mind my saying it—not that he was negligent, nor that he was lacking in ability, but that as a candidate in medicine he naturally is caught, so to speak, within the lattices of Orcus.[18] Engrossed in many projects, he is writing a commentary on *Pomponius Mela*,[19] with prolific annotations, to be published in Vienna.[20]

Nothing very newsworthy has happened here, unless it is news that the Aldine Press[21] has published this year in Venice the commentary on ancient texts of Ludwig Celius Rhodiginus,[22] who is still alive. We have purchased from the book dealers nearly thirty copies of the barbarous *Soliloquies* of Jacob Wimpheling,[23] that infamous hornet. So that less harm is done to the honor of the Swiss,[24] we bought them all. Master Joachim Vadian has a copy as do others. But there are still some left; so if you want a copy of Wimpheling, the "scourge of Switzerland,"[25] please let me know. I have also an edition of J. Baptista Egnatius' panegyrics on the defeat of the Swiss by the French king, and another of his on the lives of the emperors.[26] I am uncertain whether Pliny's histories[27] with the excellent index by the learned Camers[28] is being published here or in Basel. This man is working also to bring out the choice sayings of the poets and an index of proverbs. George Collimitius[29] and his friend Vadian are going to produce some commentary on the second book of Pliny's *Natural History,* which will be impressive even to the Italians.[30]

We have expected the emperor[31] for some time, but he has not come. Some have predicted that the plague would rage here, but to date they have been vain prophets. However, I do hear frequently of people here suffering and dying of other diseases. I willingly await the plague (provided it does not kill me) so that I may depart from here and go to Glarean.[32]

But enough of that. For not scorning to write to us who are unhonored, not learned, and in short worthless men of the lowest rank, we give you undying thanks, and we will make recompense to the best of our ability. Lastly, the friendship which you say you have initiated with humble, but in my opinion highly learned, eloquence, we will observe most avowedly and keep most solemnly. I should not fail to add that I have assumed the task of writing because John Leopold[33] was unable to write, prevented by his study of logic and expecting soon to take his final examination as a baccalaureate. He wishes, however, to greet you, as do Ulrich your agent[34] and Conrad Moser,[35] who delivered your letter. Although loved in other places, you will be especially loved when you write often, and I will not delay in writing back.

Farewell and love those who revere you as you deserve. Once again farewell, illustrious glory of Switzerland.

Vienna in Austria from our school in the year of salvation, the 17th beyond a millennium and a half, September 8.[36]

Your Grebels, John Leopold and Conrad.

To the man who is master of the noble arts and most vigilant guardian of souls at Einsiedeln in Switzerland, a most revered friend.

Original: Staatsarchiv Zurich, EII.339, p. 9.
Transcription: ZW, VII, No. 27.

1A
Vadian to Grebel
Vienna, May 1, 1518

Like Letter A, above, this was a public letter that Vadian addressed to Conrad Grebel as part of a published literary work. Vadian's edition of the Pomponius Mela (see 1/fn.19) was dedicated to Rudolph Agricola, professor of rhetoric and poetry from 1515 to 1518 at the University of Vienna, where Vadian also studied and taught; but at the end of the first edition (Vienna, 1518) there was the following printed tribute by Vadian to his student from Zurich.

Vadian of Switzerland to Conrad Grebel of Zurich, Switzerland, a young man of brightest talent,[1] greetings.

I hope, Conrad,[2] that I might have attained that for which I have labored thus far. For if to those somewhat more learned[3] I will seem to have wasted these past months and jeopardized my fame or name by hasty work,[4] I will not care one way or the other if in your[5] judgment I have not failed you in your studies. I am speaking of you and Rudolph Clivanus[6] and George Binder[7] from Zurich and the other young men of Switzerland[8] who have come to Vienna for the purpose of taking up noble literature,[9] for the interest I take in them is generated not only by a common love for our native land but also by their proven talents which augur well.[10] For in the future, unless my imagination deceives me, I seem to see many who are destined to bring certain special honors[11] of learning to themselves and their native land, if only they do not abandon the studies they have begun.[12] Indeed, whatever benefit my burning of midnight oil[13] will bring to others, it should be credited also to your account.[14]

With regard to the work[15] which I have accomplished, I might dare to claim that it has been restored to its rightful place among scholars, for the geography of the earth[16] and the knowledge of places should have no more proper place than among those authors who professedly teach these matters.[17] They make a great mistake here who without discrimination pick up some author,[18] cram whole margins full of commentary,[19] and trample over all the names as they are incurred on the way at random[20] like some undigested stew,[21] so that if in some poet the name of Zona[22] or of the star Bootes[23] or of some sea appears, they foolishly at once spin around long webs like spiders, scarcely ever arriving at the meaning of the matter in hand, which by heaven[24] would not happen if those who profess to teach would teach each thing in its own place and time as it should be done. Therefore in matters that pertain to geography we should inquire from geographers, and those things that are cosmographical from cosmographers, and likewise other things from their respective sources, all learned in their own context and elsewhere only referred to. So if I have described most things in a little too much detail,[25] it has been done for your sake and not out of context. For where more properly would one make lengthy mention of the Antipodes,[26] of the Antoeci,[27] and the Perioeci,[28] of the Nile, of the ebb and flow of the sea, of eclipses,[29] and of the climates of places, than in the book of an author-geographer? Even one who does introduce things may draw them together only so far; and unless you explain to eager beginners a little more faithfully,[30] you abandon them to shipwreck in the midst of Charybdis.[31]

Truly, most beloved Conrad, since I have admonished you for some time to be equipped for this noble task, I would wish especially that you would accommodate yourself to us[32] in this matter in keeping with your talents. Nor do I doubt that the rest of my pupils, among whom is Andreas Eck,[33] a most attentive disciple,[34] will accomplish a good work under my tutelage in their noble learning, if only they follow that which we commemorate in our catechesis.[35] Farewell. Vienna, May 1, 1518.

Original Publication: Vadian's *Pomponius Mela,* Vienna edition, 1518 (see end of volume).
  Copy in Mennonite Historical Library, Goshen, Indiana.
Transcription: VB, I, Anhang, Nachtrag No. 19.

1B
Grebel Addresses Mela
Vienna, May 1518

By way of introduction to his text of Pomponius Mela's De Situ Orbis,[1] *his commentary on it, and his tribute to Conrad Grebel (see 1A, above), Vadian included a number of poems by some of his students mentioned in 1A/ fn.8: John Winwiler, George Binder, Rudolph Clivanus, Christopher Crassus, and Conrad Grebel. The following is Grebel's poem addressing Mela.*

CONRAD GREBEL, HELVETIAN[2] OF ZURICH,
ADDRESSES MELA

Although, Mela, geographers now place
You too among their peers in foremost space,
    You shall possess a vast and valiant fame
Since he wished you a favored classic name.
A naked chief you were, you must assent,
With unkempt splendor, torso badly rent.[3]
    Uncouth you were at first, not wont to hear

59

Our greeting,[4] nor much known by those from near.
Now rich and prim and keen to face all men
So none can wound your nourished form again.
Then unrefined, now elegant, made sound
From defect, raised aloft to starry mound.
Antipodes[5] you know, the shades[6] unscanned
Till your blest polishing of Hermes' land.[7]
And now all knots are loosed with Phoebe's care,[8]
E'en those that some new bard had still to bare.
So shout to all the world and make a show,
Let no one now cry out, "Mela, ho! ho!"
Proclaim aloud the festive triumph due,
Earth has no one more learned now than you.
Yet do not stride too much, Mela, look out
For Nemesis[9] who 'venges too much flout.
With thanks hide not your source of such a gift;
Tell, what rash god was it gave you this lift?
Or was it Vadian of great Swiss fame
Who fully measured up to Phoebus' name?[10]
Of course, 'twas he who gave what now you see
And by his love for home gave it to me,
To prove Swiss victors strong for god of war[11]
Are no less victors now in teaching lore.

Original Publication: Same as 1A, above.
Transcription: *The Goshen College Record Review Supplement*, Vol. 27, No. 8 (May-June 1926), p. 50.

2
Grebel to Vadian
Zurich, July 23, 1518

About the middle of June 1518, Vadian and several of his students—Christopher Schürpf of St. Gallen and Conrad Grebel of Zurich—left Vienna to return to their homes. Although Vadian had planned this move for some time, their departure may have been somewhat sudden, for he and Grebel left their books behind (see 5/72/19-21), Grebel had made no arrangements for the final payment of his university stipend (see 5/73/30-34), and Vadian had to return to Vienna the following November to close out his affairs. Bender (p. 27) attributes the suddenness of their departure to the plague which was spreading in Vienna at the time (but see the Introduction to Letter 3, below). Vadian must have discussed with Grebel the possibility of his coming to

Zurich, for one of the first things Grebel did upon his arrival was to work out the arrangements for the entertainment of his teacher. In the following letter, he confirms the invitation after some unexplained delay in Vadian's coming. The latter must have left St. Gallen soon after receiving this letter, for he arrived in Zurich on August 4.

Conrad Grebel sends many greetings to Vadian, his most beloved teacher.[1]

It is your duty, eminent sir, to come swiftly to Zurich to those who have awaited you now for a long time with greatest longing. Mine it was in truth, when you did not come, to beg of you to whom I owe such gratitude to fly here at once when the letter of Ofnerius[2] has been delivered to you. This I would certainly have done, had you not promised that you would be with us so soon and had I not hoped that Master Jacob Walther[2] and John Ofnerius would persuade you, since you stayed away, not to stay away longer, because, I say, so many men even now through my untiring praise of you long for [you] to be here. Among them are my father[3] and I, who bore it ill since we hoped daily that you would be here and because you postponed your coming for so long a time. To make up for whatever had been neglected in not writing, we would not refrain from sending a messenger[4] of our own, for the reason, first, that father very much wanted to move up the day of your arrival, since he will not regard you as a friend unless you come to his house[5] to be the guest of your student, just as I was at your house for not a few days as the guest of my teacher, who by Almighty God[6] is the most beloved to me of all men by far. We did so also because I was not able to be here long. I would have gone off to the baths[7] and to my sister[8] who has been waiting there for some time if you by your delay (your annoying delay, I would add) had not deterred me. But if I have spoken frankly, forgive me, for such is your kind nature. Finally, know that the messenger has been sent because you are reported by our cardinal's musician[9] to have said that you will not come here before I have invited you by letter. I invite you therefore and beg you again and again by our love so happily mutual that you inform my father and me by letter on what day you will arrive. For if you do not come to my father's house, you will be doing a most ungracious, indeed most grievous something, not only to my parents but also to your Conrad.

And now to repeat what I have said: I order you to come to us and to my house in four days[10] and to choose no other in which to live for that time. What I was able to do for your interests I did so willingly that if the thing you desire were in my power, I would long since have done it. What I have accomplished I shall relate to you when you are here.

I have a marriageable sister.[11] If you are not pleased when you see her and if you do not marry her when you have seen her and been pleased, you will not be able to say that it was I who deterred you. I am your friend, and I wish also to be your best man. I am joking.

Give my regards to your parents, to whom I owe much, to Othilia and Katherine[12] and my Helen and Anna, the maids, to Andreas Eck,[13] my brother, who I hope will come with you. Farewell.

Zurich, on the day of Apollinaris.

Conrad Grebel, most obedient servant of your humanity.

To a man in every way most learned and upright, Joachim Vadian, poet and orator laureate and most illustrious doctor of health-giving medicine, most revered master.

Original: Stadtbibliothek (Vadiana) St. Gallen; VB. II.114.
Transcription: VB, II, Anghang, Nachtrag No. 2.

2A
Myconius[1] to Vadian
Zurich, July 23, 1518

With the following letter, we introduce another important character in the drama—Oswald Myconius—Grebel's former teacher, Zwingli's sponsor in the call to the Zurich pastorate, and the frequent correspondent of both men. Nine of Grebel's 71 extant letters were written to Myconius. The letters of Zwingli to Myconius dated July 24, 1520, and August 26, 1522 (see 19A and 47E) are important documents in the collection. Moreover, the following paragraph is the first of five excerpts from the letters of Myconius to Vadian included. Its date is identical to that of Conrad's letter (No. 2, above), and the two letters were probably dispatched together. The excerpt constitutes about one fourth of the total content of the letter.

We are all wondering at once, my dear Vadian, what cause could delay you so long from your coming which you promised and which we are longingly awaiting. Whenever the parents of those whose teacher you were at Vienna meet each other, likewise when our Conrad and I meet, the first talk is about the coming of Vadian....

Original: Stadtbibliothek (Vadiana) St. Gallen, VB. I. 123
Transcription: VB, II, No. 128.

3
Grebel to Zwingli
Zurich, July 31, 1518

The forwarding of Vadian's gift of a copy of the newly published Pomponius Mela *was Grebel's main reason for writing the following letter to Zwingli, although it is evident that he wanted also to try to explain why he had terminated his Vienna studies. Grebel alleges that "father ordered me to return," but this seems to be a partial explanation at best. Bender (pp. 27-8) speculates on additional motives. In any case, another reason for writing to Zwingli at this time was to invite him to come to Zurich upon Vadian's arrival, which was actually only four days after Grebel wrote this letter. Zwingli was still at Einsiedeln, only "six hours' journey to Zurich" as he once put it.*

G[reetings].

Once upon a time when I was far removed from you among the Austrians with Vadian my teacher (a most famous man, to put it briefly), you predicted a quite indissoluble friendship between us.[1] At last, now that I am at Zurich among my own people, I renew that friendship by a more appropriate theme.[2] For I came with the aforesaid man, the light of all Switzerland, traveling from Austria as far as St. Gallen,[3] and by his orders (why need I say "request" by a teacher so great and learned, to whom I owe so much) I am sending you with care along with a little letter the *Pomponius Mela*[4] with his excellent commentary as you will judge for yourself. I have seen to it especially because it seemed that no mean glory would come to me if (by my own diligence) the work of so great a man should be forwarded to so great a man. This provides a unique opportunity for me to send my little letter, such as it is, so that you may note that I especially esteem the learned and exemplary cultivators of friendship—I mean men like you.

My illustrious Vadian, not [just] a teacher, not [just] a man in every way most learned, but a most avowed friend (above all), has promised to come to us.[5] I wish therefore that you would also come.[6] Then indeed I shall be renewed for awhile by the sight of three men—Myconius,[7] Zwingli, and Vadian; and for the while, as God loves me, I shall not care about nor marvel at kings resplendent with lavish pomp like gods. If you could steal away from your tasks, I should not wish for anyone else from the whole of Switzerland to come to Zurich but Zwingli. But if it will not be possible for you to do this, see at least that your letters fly to me. When I see them I shall receive them with such joy and kiss them with so many kisses that eventually the Zwinglian letters (full of learning as usual) will always want to be sent to Grebel. I have chattered on like this so that you will at least write, or that you will come, which I would prefer.

You ask why I have come.[8] I was wounded,[9] but in truth had already recovered. A friend, who was not a friend, reported this to my father before my return, and he lied saying that I was worse than I was. Worried because of this, father ordered me to return from Vienna at once, going along with Vadian. So I returned, but not before the family of Vadian had graciously entertained me at St. Gallen.

You ask to know what I shall do here. I am waiting for my teacher, so that together with my father and everyone in Zurich I may welcome him with as much honor as possible in his own native land as previously in Vienna he treated me so kindly. He will stay at my father's house (when he comes) as I can testify by his own words, for he wrote to me as follows: "If father Jacob on his oath will promise moderation, I shall be his guest." And that he should be our guest I have entreated him by a letter sent to him by its own messenger, and I think I have succeeded in my entreaty. Would you call me at all unlucky[10] into whose home the most learned, most humane, and most upright man among the Swiss will enter (I speak without affront)?

But I have tarried longer than necessary on these matters. If you are coming, come as quickly as possible; if you are going to write, write no more slowly. By doing either you will gratify me deeply, but by the former most of all. I am willing that my slight letter be slighted by you, if only my very well-wishing attitude toward you should please you a little.

Farewell and best wishes.

From Zurich, on the day before the first of August in the year of salvation, 1518.

Conrad Grebel, your poor friend who respects you much.

To Huldrych Zwingli of Toggenburg,[11] pastor[12] at St. Mary's in Einsiedeln, a most learned man and my special friend.

Original: Staatsarchiv Zurich, E.II.339.p.14
Transcription: ZW, VII, No. 39.

3A
The Ascent of Mt. Pilatus[1]
Near Luzern, August 1518[2]

Sometime after Vadian's arrival in Zurich, Myconius and John Zimmerman, the pastor in Luzern, took Vadian and Grebel on a mountain-climbing expedition to the summit of Mt. Pilatus to visit the legendary lake that is mysteriously situated there. A permit for the ascent was secured from the au-

thorities in Luzern and the climb commenced in August 1518. The editors of several versions of the following account by Vadian (see fn. 1, below) claim that this was the first time that Pilatus was scaled for scientific purposes. Indeed, the humanist scientist tells us himself that his purpose was to test the legend that the lake at the summit had properties of magic and that the waters boiled up a storm of demonic destruction whenever anything was maliciously cast into it by a human hand. But the humanist part of him got the better of the scientific part, and the experiment had to be scuttled.

In Switzerland, near the ancient and celebrated town of Luzern, there is a very high mountain, which because of its fractured roughness and precipitous steeps is still known in the vernacular as the Fractured One,[3] a strange crude vestige of the name Fracmont.[4] Below the summit lies a lake with the most revealing and quite majestic name, Pilatus,[5] really more a swamp than a lake. It was claimed that anything deliberately thrown into the lake arouses the greatest tempest and floods the whole region. But if it happens accidentally, it does not provoke the lake in the least, just as though it could clearly perceive by human sensation that no one was to blame for the chance happening. Taking it as settled fact, the townspeople relate that some persons, swept away by disturbing the peace of the lake, subsequently subjected their neighbors to calamity on their account.

Last year in the month of August, when I had come to Luzern for the purpose of visiting the lake, I was welcomed very courteously by the pastor at Luzern, John Xylotectus,[6] a very learned man endowed with the noblest character, and on the next day was conducted up the mountain itself, having as my companions Oswald Myconius,[7] a man of learning and perfect integrity, and Conrad Grebel of Zurich, a noble young man of exceptional ability, brother to my Grebelia.[8] And indeed at daybreak we left the town and rode on horseback almost halfway up the mountain by a track that was difficult and not very well traveled. Later on when our horses could go no farther, we let them loose in a nearby pasture, hired a shepherd to guide us, and wound our way on foot up the remaining height by a very narrow path, climbing first one side and then the other of huge cliffs, a journey that would not have been possible for everyone.

Eventually we arrived perspiring at the edge of the swamp. The mountain itself, which is otherwise generally steep, is a pasture at this location. A vast boundless valley has been formed in the shape of a circular depression, in the midst of which, set off by itself as if in meditation, is the lake, attired with sparse reeds, enclosed with prickly woods, and confined on all sides by a deep silence that inspired quite a sense of awesome reverence. Nothing flows into or out of the lake. The water has a blackish hue like the Phlegethon;[9] but like a marsh, it has less flow, its lethargy not

65

readily aroused by the wind, for it is firmly protected from the south and west winds by the back of the highest mountain, while from the east and north the depth of the location and density of the forest provides this shield. Noteworthy also is the fact that neither from the snow of the winter nor the heat of the summer is there any change in the level of the water, constantly straining (as they say) to maintain an uninterrupted course for itself within its own environs.

I should have mentioned that during our ascent, the shepherd guide tried to bind us to a sacred oath that at the sight of the lake we would not try anything improper or throw anything in. He wanted to convince us by saying repeatedly that we were playing a deadly game endangering his life, and by admonishing us to propriety and silence as though he were escorting us to a holy spot. Consequently, I was almost anxious enough to concede some credulity to the old local legend that Pilate in his judicial robes could be glimpsed in the depths of the water and that whoever beholds this apparition would not live out the year, even though this type of legend should surely be consigned to fairyland.

So it is with man's superstitions, that the places that have eerie phenomena of nature he associates with the deceptive details of a legend. And meanwhile, it is the nature of man in his ignorance that he unreluctantly believes what he hears when, on one hand, religious credulity entices him to a certain degree, and on the other hand, there is also to a certain degree the desire for some new experience. In conclusion, I would have to say that I can neither lend validity to this myth about the memorable lake nor make claims about its falsity because it was impossible for me to test it without causing great panic; and so the myth of the lake's mysterious attributes will continue to be told by the local inhabitants of the region. Moreover, the numerous wonders of nature that many perceive in experience and attest with authority to be extraordinary should serve as warning to us not to proclaim too hastily that what is alleged to be the guardian spirit of a place is nothing more than a natural phenomenon.

Truly, the height of the mountain can be gauged from the fact that we started up toward the lake at daybreak, climbed to the top of the mountain, soon turned back without delay or empty talk, descended to our horses, and landed in town in the dusk following sundown. We spent about two hours resting and taking nourishment halfway down the mountain.

Original Publication: Vadian, *Pomponius Mela.* Basel edition, 1522, p. 34.
Transcription: Bernard Studer, *Geschichte der Physischen Geographie der Schweiz bis 1815* (Bern, 1863), p. 64, and P. X. Weber, *Der Pilatus und seine Geschichte* (Luzern 1913), pp. 249-51.

3B
Myconius to Vadian
Zurich, September 15, 1518

Following his return from Luzern, Grebel proceeded with his previously announced plan to visit his sister Barbara and her husband near Baden and to "take the cure" in the public baths while he was there. Some of the excerpts in our collection are included primarily for the purpose of providing a larger context for some of the minor, personal events in Grebel's life. In the following excerpt, for instance, Myconius tells us what the great Erasmus of Rotterdam was doing in Basel while Grebel was trying to find healing in Baden for the sores on his back. See Letter 4, below, for more information concerning Grebel's chronic illness.

Erasmus has written a *Praise to Marriage* and *The Art of Healing*.[1] If I had found it here, I would have sent it to you. I hope, however, to have it very soon. And then you will have it yourself. Be sure to inform me in the shortest time possible about all your affairs. Grebel has not yet returned from Baden.[2] Farewell.

Zurich, from my table on September 15, 1518.

Original: Stadtbibliothek (Vadiana) St. Gallen, VB(?).
Transcription: VB, II, No. 133.

4
Grebel to Vadian
Zurich, September 26, 1518

In the following letter, Grebel reports his decision to go to Paris to study under Glarean. It sounds as though this was new information, at least in part, which is further evidence that this was not a malicious strategy on Jacob's part to secure the French pension on top of the one previously received from the emperor (see Intro. to Letter 3, above), but was a calculated choice from several alternatives under consideration. The letter also reveals Vadian's serious interest in Martha Grebel, and it seems that negotiations for her hand in marriage had already begun. Four days after writing, escorted by Jacob's servant, Conrad and his two friends left for Paris on horseback.

Greetings, most eminent man.

Please do not ascribe to negligence that I have not written to you for so long, for on the 19th of September I returned from my sister[1] and from Baden,[2] where I was taking the baths. And when I had barely reached home, the sore in the middle of my back had gotten so bad that I could do nothing, least of all write.[3] And even if I had been able, there was no messenger at hand to carry the letter. So a personal messenger has been sent with this letter, in which I give you my everlasting thanks which I will continue to give as long as I live for all your goodness and love for me, for your faithful teaching, and for doing all you could for Conrad (and I call you not just my most learned teacher but above all my most beloved).[4]

I send good health and best wishes to you, your household, and your bride-to-be, whoever she is. By my father's wish and my own, I am taking myself off to Paris[5] to study literature and especially to do so under Glarean;[6] and I shall set out from my dear homeland next Thursday.[7] I shall be accompanied by two students from Zurich[8] [who are going] on a grant from the king by decree of the Zurich City Council, about all of which the messenger can give you more details.[9]

I shall now speak of the matters that remain. When you left me in Elligoew,[10] you requested that I should inform you as soon as possible what my father had meanwhile decided about his daughter[11] and with what dowry he would give her to you.[12] In keeping with my promises and in fulfillment of my duty, I have asked Father what he intends. He responded in this manner, naturally so after observing the bridegroom: Such a man as you by parentage, birth, education, influence, and reputation, perhaps did not really desire my sister or you would have broached the matter with my seniors in age and authority. However this may be, if you wish to act in earnest (for he thinks you were in jest), since he is yours, he wishes his daughter to be yours also, if you take her without a greater dowry to wed a wealthier maid (so I heard from him).[13] And if father and you do not come to an agreement sometime on this matter, he wishes to be in accord with you as much as possible in other matters, to esteem you no less than ever before, and to be wholly yours and entirely at your service. As for me, there is no reason for you to doubt that I love and respect Vadian, the excellence of whose name I shall continue to extol as long as I have strength and life.

To change the subject,[14] I beg and beseech you, when you return to Vienna,[15] to have my things, I mean my books,[16] sent here along with yours; or if the merchants of Ravensburg[17] will bring them, see that all is well packed so that they can be conveyed more easily and conveniently. I have nothing more to add to this. Everyone sends greetings. Please give mine to all your family, as many as there are. Good-bye.

From Zurich, September 26, 1518 years from the birth of Christ.

Conrad Grebel of Zurich to Vadian, were he not so great a man, altogether a brother, but since he is so great a man, a most devoted servant.

Please give my regards to my teacher Master Wolfgang of Bohemia,[18] and his pupils and yours who are at Vienna, when you get there.

Original: Stadtbibliothek (Vadiana) St. Gallen, VB. I. 133
Transcription: VB, II, No. 135

4A
Myconius to Vadian
Zurich, October 15, 1518

Vadian was working on his Concerning Poetry and the Theory of Verse *as early as February 1517 (see Pro.A./fn.41), and it was evidently off the press in Vienna in the autumn of 1518. He sent a copy to Grebel with the suggestion that he present it to Myconius (see 5/73/11-12), but Grebel took it to Paris on the assumption that Vadian had said he could keep it and that Myconius himself had concurred.*

I have glanced casually at your *Poetica*.[1] I do not say what I think, lest you accuse me of flattery or at least say that I am carried away by the blindness of love. Grebel has carried it away with him.[2] Therefore I beg you, be sure to send another as soon as you possibly can, so that I may have what I have long wished for....

Original: Stadtbibliothek (Vadiana) St. Gallen, VB?
Transcription: VB, II, Anhang, Nachtrag No. 39.

4B
Zurgilgen to Vadian
Paris, October 26, 1518

John Jacob Zurgilgen, Latinized to A'Liliis, came from Luzern. He was Vadian's student in Vienna from 1511 to 1515 and then went to the University of Basel, where he and Grebel may have met (see Bender, 1950, p. 10). From 1517 to 1519 he studied in Paris, where he was associated with Grebel as friend and fellow student following the latter's arrival. In a letter dated October 21, he introduced himself to Zwingli as a good friend of the reformer's brother James, who had just died. It is known that Vadian's decision to give up his influential teaching position in Vienna for a small-town career in St. Gallen disconcerted some of his former students, but Zurgilgen wanted to give Vadian support for that decision.

Grebel of Zurich, your friend, has informed me regarding your whole situation and circumstances and has told me that you have returned to Vienna, which I do not hear with my usually happy mind, fearing and suspecting that your former conduct and habits among the scholarly and cultured should delight and allure you more than the crude and common folk. Therefore I would wish you to take thought for your prudence, lest you disappoint the hope and expectation of those who are most interested and concerned for you and you acquire the name of hater of your native city.

Grebel likewise brought the annotations to your *Mela*,[1] which we received with joy, with applause, and with a certain favorable omen. Indeed, the more pleasantly and agreeably, the more they were longed for, because previously the report was noised about that you intended to check and overwhelm the stench and the blind flatteries of some people[2]. . . .

When that messenger from Zurich who brought Grebel here[3] said he could not conveniently take this along, and I was also rather certain that you would spend the coming winter abroad, I put it off until January 1, intending to have a letter-bearer of my own who does nothing else. . . . [4]

Original: Stadtbibliothek (Vadiana) St. Gallen, VB?
Transcription: VB, II, Anhang, Nachtrag No. 40.

5
Grebel to Vadian
Paris, October 26, 1518

It took twenty days for the four horsemen—Grebel, Frey, Holtzhalben, and Hedinger—to ride from Zurich to Paris. They went by way of Freiburg and arrived on October 20. Paris was a city of a quarter million people and the residence of the king of France. Its university had been the world's most renowned but was on the decline because of the reactionary stance of the faculty toward the new Humanism. But it was still a respected center of scholarship and learning. Grebel presented his letters of recommendation to Glarean and received his assignments in Glarean's bursa. In the following letter he tells about this, but only after he lauds his former mentor, who he still hopes will marry his sister.

Greetings, my Vadian, whom I ought to have addressed as "most learned," since I knew you as a man so learned as to be second to none among the Swiss, as "most faithful teacher," since you taught me so faithfully, and as "most upright," since you are no less upright than learned. But since you wrote so like a brother to me on my departure, I am not able to address you by any other salutation. And would that I (with the goodwill of the Muses[1] and all the poetic deities and even of Almighty God)[2] might be brought to that elevation of learning that I might be able to be your fellow philosopher (which you say you desire very much), that is, to live with you like a brother and to be allowed to call you brother. Truthfully, however (since I cannot reply at once to all the parts of your letter),[3] I shall reply: I do not expect, what you do not doubt, that I or all my grandsons will ever equal you in learning.[4] When you say that I will, you are moved by your most constant love and you are nobly playing the part of a teacher, solicitous that your pupil should outstrip you by a far distance, whom you have left and will leave a million miles behind.[6]

You asserted that often I have been advised by you concerning eloquence and the fluency of ready speech[7] (I repeat your very words). Indeed, most loving teacher, I have so fully forgotten what you advised that I do not even blush to beg you to rehearse what you said more than once before and to write to me in a copious letter what I, a poor little creature of the most deplorable talents, should do in order to scrape together from somewhere or other the fluency of ready speech and eloquence. You would prefer, dearest of all teachers, that I should become first in my native land rather than that I should be second to the first and less than another. Again and again you love me, that is, you compel even a monosyllable to be your little slave.[8] I could wish, therefore, that I might one day deserve to be numbered among famous men, not to acquire for myself a reputation that would endure for a time or one brief day, but so that I might be able to live with Vadian more unreservedly, yet not more unreservedly but more intimately, I who can scarcely live more intimately, to be like him in some small way, yet not like him unless formed in the likeness of the same Muse. But what is this you say? That I should have the principles of the illustrious arts on the basis of which all eloquence rests. If you love me (but you love me most dearly), please expound once more in a long Iliad[9] what the illustrious arts are.

I gave your regards to Glarean,[10] the best of men, and I promised from you whatever you can do. The matter which I disclosed to you on the journey you thought should be so concealed, although it is wholly honorable, that you immediately cut out and tore up the little verses in which I expressed the matter a little more candidly than in my letter.[11] You will assuredly play the part of Harpocrates[12] and of some Angerona[13] and the mute Pythagorean[14]—in other words, the part of a teacher (I have barely expressed it).[15]

You command me to write to you frequently. I shall write to you most frequently, more often than you instructed. You commended me to Bude[16] and Glarean, not because you considered it to be necessary but rather that I might know that your love for me is most constant. And the task will be slight, indeed no task at all, to persuade me that Vadian's love for me is most constant. I have certainly come to know that your love for me is that; indeed, not once have I known it to be more constant than the most constant and more ardent than what is ardent. Do not, I ask of you, relate to me my own dream, as they say.

In advising me also to have concern for the body, lest I be seriously endangered should I be attacked by a slight fever,[17] you show yourself the physician; and I trust that those whom you (no quack doctor)[18] treat may recover if they are ill and may become ill if they are well.

You rejoiced that my sister was still in an unmarried state.[19] I should also have rejoiced, but I would have been elated if such a man as you had wished to mention the idea of becoming my sister's husband. Certainly you could have done so if you had wanted. You are held by an alternative noose, but not that of love (that is your word). I pray that you might be held and happily, but not for long, so that indeed you may wed a pretty, wealthy, upright, and frugal bride, solemnize the wedding with the nuptial song,[20] and that from your wife, whoever will be your wife, you may rear children worthy of you, who will bear your likeness, if not in everything, at least in some ways, or who in short may complement you perfectly. You say that you refresh yourself and your spirit in the thought that you will be one of the Grebels, even if you will not be a son-in-law or brother-in-law to a Grebel, and you wish to be a friend of the family of Grebel, as though it were of great name.[21] The role of a friend you will act and do act, since the intervention of the abominable fates[22] prevent your acting the part of a son-in-law or brother-in-law.

I owe my soul to you, to whom I already owed everything, for promising to send to Switzerland along with your own my store of books left at Vienna;[23] and by thus loading me with huge favors you display to me, as you say, brotherly (better still, fatherly) affection. Moreover, sweetest teacher, have you not exhorted me well, do you not still teach me most faithfully, when you admonish me so to apply myself to virtue and study while I am absent from my native city, so that when I return to my dear parents I should not lack good character and learning, lest someone hurl at me that saying of Homer's, "Shameful 'tis to have tarried long and returned empty"?[24] By Jove[25] I will strive, and diligence will never be lacking in me, if only talent and the Muses,[26] whose gates they say proverbially stand open, do not fail this poor miserable creature.[27] You counsel me so well and like a father that I do not know whether my father has acted so well the part of a counselor in my affairs.

First you are making for Krakow, then indeed your beloved Vienna, more illustrious than Paris, if you look for learned men. May the gods, I pray, protect your household and your wife-to-be in the meantime, and also may they not begrudge you a happy return to your native land unharmed and unchanged. You will visit Krakow[28] and Vienna, the latter the city or metropolis of Austria, the former of Sarmatia;[29] and you will visit the former because of your brothers and relations,[30] the latter you will revisit because of learned men and your valuable books and library. Meanwhile your Conrad will nowhere and never be absent from you. While you promise this, will you also greet my friends in Vienna; there is nothing that you will not promise and surely nothing that you will not do.

You promised to send a little gift to [my] sisters; no doubt you sent it and gave it, as none outside my family have been so honored and showered with many kindnesses. And so you act that I am quite in doubt whom, next to Almighty God and my most devoted parents, I should love and respect more than you; no one certainly.

The mutilated copy of your *Poetica*,[31] which is worthy of the warmest praise, you sent when I was still waiting for that golden letter of yours in Zurich on the condition that when I had read it (rather glanced over it, since I was soon to depart) I should give it as a gift to Myconius,[32] a man quite learned and upright and the bright light of his native Luzern, or that I should keep it myself. I have kept it and did so with the consent of Myconius himself, so that after reaching Paris I might present it along with illustrious *Pomponius Mela*[33] to Glarean and Bude as a great testimonial of your learning.[34]

Your letter,[35] which I would not exchange for the wealth of Croesus,[36] has been answered. You will hear now of my affairs. I am living with Glarean, and I both eat with him and attend his lectures; and in the senate, which he has set up by Roman custom, I am a second Scipio and Leopold Grebel is a third Cato; that is, he has been made the censor.[37] It is wonderful to tell how he welcomed me when I arrived with joy in his face and speech, and how he loves and respects you, whom he used to hate and despise and how he defends you and gives you the palm for your learning. This defense is actually being fought also by Leopold, so that with a change of climate, I believe his mind has been changed too.[38]

Now learn what I wish you to do for me, since there has been enough of this joking. When you return to Vienna, let Clivanus[39] know my circumstances, and say that they are respectable enough and that he should show you the letter I sent to him. Further, if any money has been given for me by the emperor's paymaster, you may hand it over to Clivanus to apply to his own use.[40] I shall lend it to him, if he wishes; and if he ever comes to me sometime, I shall not ask for it back. And if you are going to write to me, give this letter of mine to Clivanus to copy, for I surely want him to have what I wrote in reply to your letter. This indeed is the original[41] sent to you.

Receive herewith the letters of Glarean, glory of Switzerland, and Bude of France, who hold you in highest esteem. I have enclosed for Clivanus the dialogue concerning the great Pope Julius II, written they think by Erasmus.[42] There is nothing new at Paris besides this, so you get the letters and the dialogue is my gift to be delivered.

If Jörg Hedinger[43] comes to you, do not be reluctant to lay your medical hands on him; he comes wishing to be healed with your help. Write to me as often as possible, and let me know what you advise, but not in a short letter. Give my greetings to your parents, your fellow citizens who honor me as the shadow following the body, which is you, and especially the priests,[44] your sisters and brothers, and Andreas Eck,[45] my brother.

At Paris,[46] from my study, October 26, 1518 years from the Virgin Birth.

Conrad Grebel of Zurich in Switzerland, disciple of Vadian.

> To Joachim Vadian, a man in every way humane, learned, and upright, a poet crowned by the emperor, and orator and physician extraordinary, to his most beloved teacher and incomparable friend. [Outside address] to a man most learned and upright, a physician and poet laureate, Joachim Vadian, by far my dearest teacher.

Original: Stadtbibliothek (Vadiana) St. Gallen, VB. I. 135
Transcription: VB, II, No. 136

5A
Myconius to Vadian
Zurich, November 12, 1518

As the following excerpt of a letter indicates, one of the roles that Grebel tried to play in Paris, as he had done in Vienna and Zurich, was to serve as a contact between respected scholars of separated residence—Vadian in St. Gallen, Zwingli in Einsiedeln, Myconius in Luzern, and Glarean in Paris.

Glarean[1] has written as follows. He too is very highly pleased because he is mentioned so often and so respectfully in your *Poetica*[2] and in other products of your night labors[3] which our friend Conrad has presented to him. As much as lies in me, I pray God that the friendship begun by your letter may remain forever. Permit me meanwhile to lie at your feet. Farewell most happily and gratify a friend.

Zurich, November 12, in the year 1518.

Original: Stadtbibliothek (Vadiana) St. Gallen, VB.I.136
Transcription: VB, II, No.138

5B
Grebel's Poem "To Joachim Vadian"
Paris, 1518

After their return from Vienna, Vadian sent Grebel a copy of his newly published book, De Poetica et Carminis Ratione *(Concerning Poetry and the Theory of Verse; see Pro.A/fn.41, above). Vadian had inscribed this copy with an original composition, a Latin elegy on Phoebus. He had asked Grebel to give the book to Myconius, but added that he could keep it if he wanted it very much (see 5/73/8-14; 4A/69/9-11). Grebel kept it and wrote the following on the inside front cover: "Impressus Vienna DDDXVIII, Dono datus a I.VVVV, Tiguri, XVIII, Illigatus Lutecie, XVIIII, Scriptum ante hoc DDDXX (Printed in Vienna in 1518, presented as a gift in Zurich in 1518, carried to Paris in 1519, written before the present 1520). Then followed a poem also in Grebel's handwriting entitled* Ad Joachimum Vadianum *(To Joachim Vadian). The poem had not been inscribed until his return to Zurich in 1520, but had been composed sometime before that, perhaps soon after his arrival in Paris. It is written in typical humanist style.*

To Joachim Vadian[1]
To willing sire of gods[2] Euryn'me[3] bore
Three Charites[4] like snowy bright candor.
More fruitful far than gods are you, Joachim,[5]
Six hundred three times four you spawn supreme.
Moreover
To high-born Thunderer[6] with fertile fame
Mnem'syne[7] bore nine nymphs, Castalian[8] name.
But you, Vadian, played with your Cam'nae[9] gang
And nine times three times nine is what you sprang.
Moreover
Pierus[10] implants a multiple of three
To reproduce one less than ten, you see.
The ancient sire upsets his Ardalides[11]
And though the test[12] of who are real decides
A thousand stars no one can number still.
A seer[13] says, Vadian, you will fulfill.
Moreover
Βίβλια ταύτα, ἴδων ταυτοῦ Θαύματ᾽ ᾽ιδέαϑαι
Μνημοσύνη, φεῦ, ἔχω μύρια τέκνα ᾽έΦη;
[One look at such a sight, this book will cry
"Now see, Mnem'syne, a thousand sons have I!"[14]]
Conr. Grebel
Here Inscribed   Zurich

Original: Zentralbibliothek Zurich, Gal.Tz.295 (inscribed inside front cover)
Transcription: None

THE PRODIGAL

6
Grebel to Vadian
Paris, January 29, 1519

On January 1, barely six weeks after his arrival in Paris, Grebel left Glarean's boarding school following quarrels with his teacher. His expectations of a close relationship like that which he enjoyed with Vadian in Vienna and Myconius in Zurich were shattered. In the following letter to Vadian, he details the series of events that led to his departure with two other students— conflicts over housing conditions and a drinking party in which Grebel offended Glarean's sense of propriety. (For the larger context of this letter, see Cast of Characters No. 28.)

Grebel's refractory behavior was only one piece of a totally unhappy situation for Glarean in Paris. Having received no mandate to lecture publicly and having been greatly disappointed by the low quality of the public lectures of others, he had earlier written to Erasmus, "So now I stay at home, making a little music to my pupils and abandoned to idleness. I enjoy myself with my beloved Horace and laugh with Democritus at the folly of the world" (Erasmus, 3, p. 55).

Greetings, dearest teacher.

I sent you a letter longer than the long Iliad[1] and perhaps much wordier than your most learned ears deserved. It was wordier, however,

> *"It was only on the ninth of January that I received father's letter written on the fourteenth of September. He commanded me to leave the sinful companions who had twice cast me into the danger of losing my money and my life, lest I be cast into that snare a third time and he be forced to cast off his son and there be no helping hand from him to draw me out."*
> —Grebel to Vadian, January 14, 1520

because I wanted to disclose how I feel toward you, that I am most devoted to you, and all the details of my situation. But now that all my affairs have been turned upside down, I cannot unravel the tangled web of my situation with many but only with myriads of foolish words. Please wind the thread[2] of my complaints or nonsense[3] cool-headedly as you always do, for this reason, that you are the one among all my teachers whom I revere and trust with most fervent love and tireless esteem because of your great kindness to me, and then because of the previous distinctions of learning and fortune that are yours, and finally because of my assurance that I have been and am so specially loved by you that I have never been thoroughly annoying to you by my wordiness, whether it was unspoken or spoken.[4] And why should I not dare or be duty-bound to pour out[5] to him all the ponderings of my mind since next to my most dutiful parents,[6] whom I should venerate not just by divine law but also by natural instinct, I do embrace him utterly,[7] and so embrace him that it is beyond the power of my words to express. Now I shall pour out.[8]

Induced by the commendation of father and Myconius,[9] and by my own prayers, Glarean[10] was persuaded to accept me among his pupils and table companions. There was a place vacant in a room of the house in which he was living and I was put in there. Three students shared it with me,[11] which was perhaps to the detriment of my studies. The winter froze my limbs which are impatient with the cold, and there was no fireplace by which I could ward off the cold by kindling a fire after the French custom.[12] I went to Glarean for his permission to change my compartment in the same house. He did not forbid me nor allow me but reproached me for being soft and opposed my plan. Meanwhile, though he often promised to move into more spacious quarters, he did nothing about it nor did he intend to do anything until some of his students had given serious offense to his landlord (by only a trivial misdemeanor). He was disturbed and ordered Glarean to get out of the house. So he paid the landlord and moved, and I moved with him. I chose a room that had a fireplace[13] and a study. It was granted to me but not without some grumbling. Along with my friends, I installed a stove[14] in the study. Not burning well because of the dampness, the stove smoked and infuriated those nearby. They threatened to smash the stove and menaced us with many insults and threats. Though I did not want to leave unless I was on good terms with Glarean, it seemed that there was no other way out except for me to change lodgings immediately and leave Glarean along with some of his students before we came to blows, considering the usual rows between us; for if this had happened, it would have given rise to even greater bad feeling and hot anger from him. Moreover, since other things excited me to anger, I swore that though it would be at my own expense, I would say a final farewell to Glarean's house as soon as possible. Subsequently (for he was not present), I related all that had happened to us, and I explained my plan to him and added that along with some others I had found and taken a house in which steam heating[15] had been installed; and so I was going there. What his arguments were and how he fought against it and what were my counter-arguments and what others said, I cannot easily relate. Since I would not reverse my decision and could not because of my oath,[16] I implemented what I had planned. Because I had begged to be admitted and he had been persuaded by the commendation of Father and Myconius as I mentioned and had brought me in, he got enraged and threatened to write the whole affair to Father and to you. But I was not intimidated by this, and on the first of January I said good-bye to my teacher and his students and left.

Before this happened, Glarean had a violent row with me, and the cause of the row was as follows. Leopold Grebel,[17] my relative, had invited some royal cavalrymen to a meal. They came and, as soldiers do, they drank prodigiously, drinking to my health and others. I was the only one disposed to keep up with them, and so the soldiers became merrier and I became drunker. Silently, surely, that sweet poison wine, with no warning of intoxication, took hold of me. Then, as the saying is, when the wine settles down, the words float up. Apparently, I swore in jest by the wounds of God in the presence of Glarean and behaved like a bacchanalian.[18] I was taken away on the orders of Glarean. Thrown down on the bed (and this let me say with all due respect for your refinement) I disgorged the wine I had intemperately imbibed. When he heard about it through informers, he was furious,[19] and (when I greeted him) he spoke few words to me and replied brusquely in a low voice. He appeared unwilling to deem me worthy of pardon, but when one of his students committed the same sin he got far kinder treatment, and he did not correct me as a teacher should. When I discerned that this was the case, I did not ask for his pardon, but I intended to ask for it, had he admonished me as was his duty. But he let the matter ride for the first few days and then finally delivered a rebuke in friendly words. I performed my part,[20] and with what words I could, I asked him to pardon one who would henceforth live as soberly as possible and I begged him to overlook my first offense. I thought he would pardon, but I knew he would be slow to love me; and I observed by sure signs that I was repulsive to him because of what I had done. Even sightless I could have seen him cherish the grudge. I suffered great torture because of this and because I was obliged to live with persons to whom I was repulsive; and when the matter I have related developed, I lived with Glarean no longer, as I said, but elsewhere at the house of an honorable citizen, lest anyone should think I am inclined to play the Greek[21] or carouse with someone.

And what of it, if there I did not pursue the frigid labor of literature? For I am attending the lectures of Beraldus,[22] who is a learned man and is lecturing on the *Oratorical Institutes* of Quintilian[23] together with [the manual of] Valla.[24] Glarean has banned me from his lectures, but he cannot ban me from his public lectures if he gives any as royal poet, which he has not yet done. The stipend which he is said to have on account of the Swiss students will either be increased, as he hopes, or he or Beraldus will take up the chair of poetry, which is doubtful.[25] I do not know how long I will stay in Paris. I have in mind some time surely to visit Bologna and Italy.[26] It is more the lack of companions than of money or will that prevents my proceeding to Italy.[27]

Now for something that concerns you. Budé[28] disagrees with you concerning that place in Pliny[29] where I recall you showing me that you thought the negative ought to be altered. Glarean does not admit that the Swiss today are Germans. Like all learned men he is keenly interested in Greek, and in inventing new words, particularly for family names and place names that do not derive from the Latin. If Vadian is attacked[30] by those who cast reproach on his name, be sure that Leopold[31] and I would fight a valiant fight on your behalf. Those who know you personally and by your writings readily award you the palm for comprehensiveness of learning and for your integrity.

And now back to me. You advised me in your last letter[32] to take the greatest care of my body. I would if I could or knew how, since my feet are in no better condition than they were when I was still in Vienna.[33] The cause, I think, is that they were abused by too much winter cold and of course they give me pain, and deservedly so, because I have often consorted with prostitutes.[34] It was not easy for me to confess that, but the face of a letter does not blush. So now you also know it but will not let it appear that you do.[35] You are my teacher when something needs to be disclosed, and a Harpocrates[36] when it comes to keeping silent. Please be my doctor too, since you are a doctor. For unless you bring me aid in my exile and give me advice as to how I might find a remedy to combat the ailment, I despair of my feet getting well. Do what you will.

Kobler's son-in-law[37] came to Paris and had a meal with me, and he said that you were in Vienna and had not yet taken a wife. So I was premature in sending my best wishes and congratulations (thinking you had already married). Let me say what I feel, but I fear that you may think that I speak insincerely[38] and that what is on my lips[39] does not come from the bottom of my heart.[40] You are a man who stands above all others, easily the first among all the Swiss for integrity, humanity, and learning combined, rich in the gifts of fortune, graced with the most splendid and previous titles (which you alone of all deserve), blessed at home with most honorable and rich parents,[41] and they in turn blessed with such a son as you. In short, you are the oracle of all our native land. You will wonder what is the point of this. I have a sister[42] (as if you did not know) of a marriageable age; and she has parents who are perhaps not as rich as honorable.[43] But let me not eulogize them nor reproach them with the charge of poverty. She is innocent as you will find, desirous of you[44] because of what you are, chaste because she has been so taught. Her parents will betroth her to you and choose you as a son-in-law above all others because you stand out above all others, and I could not but be blessed in you as my brother-in-law, nor my sister but be blessed in you as her husband. Because you are not bound by the bond of matrimony, the opportunity still exists of taking my sister as your wife, and especially as you rejoiced that she was still uncommitted,[45] that is according to your letter. She is there especially if you want her, but hardly if you require in your future bride, whoever she may be (which I doubt) sensational beauty and a huge dowry with the daughter from a father, whoever he may be, famed far and wide for having you as his son-in-law. We shall blame the malign fates[46] if my sister is not that girl who will be carried off to Thalassio.[47] How tactless you are, you undoubtedly are saying, how childishly you write, how emptily you yelp, with what senseless prattle you cry![48] But love prompts all of this, my love for you, which makes me revere you more than you believe or can express, you who have been so very generous to me for so long, my teacher most loving to me whom I yet adore and will adore in return for your love, for the very longest the fates allow, and the more so the more you will be related to me, but the less so the less you will be related to me. For I, so to speak, your alumnus (I chatter,[49] but in truth) have laid such foundations of love and reverence toward you (mutually vying for the palm) that neither fortune's malevolence nor time's decomposition can destroy. All this I have blabbed out so that from the top of the head to the bottom of the feet, inside and outside the skin, you can observe my whole posture, attitude, affection, and veneration of you, and not less the goodwill of all my family toward Vadian, a man most distinguished everywhere.[50]

While I was engaged in writing this letter to you, or better still, while I was thus entertained, it was reported that the emperor[51] had left this life and his empire, and that a certain notable Francis[52] with a great conscripted army is going to besiege the Swiss cities which revolted from the empire. Our native land, so often stigmatized for that one retreat,[53] does have valiant men to defend the republic, but she also has men who are cowardly, who alas are intent on their private affairs. I will have nothing to fear from the former but much from the latter; but yet not, for when it comes to his own safety everyone will be mindful and become a defender.[54] The king of France (as some vainly say) promises himself the Roman Empire of Germany and the title of emperor, see how well both go together.[55]

That was the last news from here, and also this: Ulrich Zwingli[56] has been appointed rector[57] of Zurich, and Valentin Tschudi,[58] who is taking to father my letter to you from France, has been appointed to Glarus.

Whatever you do with my things I left at Vienna, you will do well. Please give my regards to Master Wolfgang,[59] your fellow in philosophy, my patron truly, to whom for his kindnesses I will always owe the same, for his love, love in return, and for his learning, the bond of adoration, and to your brother,[60] who is like you and has been bound to me in friendship, to John of Hinwil,[61] my old friend, to Clivanus,[62] who has all the merits of a very close friend, to Binder,[63] who though he wills it not is yet dear to me, to Andreas[64] if he is with you, who is bound to me by love and mutual services, and finally to all those who would not reject my good wishes.

Unless you who are able to order me in everything order me to write more briefly in the future, I will discourse with you at greater length than before, like the swallow,[65] when once admitted to dialogue with you by letter, endlessly and more noisily than the Dodonean breeze,[66] as often as I have the chance. But whatever you order or do not order, I shall never reckon my wordiness to be unseasonable (though some could call it all unseasonable) because my love is not unseasonable. Nor is my love obtrusive, for no nonobtrusive love is obtrusive, unless it be in this very fact that I chatter. Let that not be, you have ordered. I pray you by the Lord God Almighty[67] to reply to my previous letter, and to this one too as soon as you can. I will be pleased to have your letter giving me your impression of Pontanus.[68]

Good-bye, most learned and dearest teacher. I shall say both "vive" and "vale"[69] as long as I unceasingly love and esteem and extol you. From Ile de la Cite,[70] Paris. 29 January in the year of salvation 1519.

Conrad Grebel, footstool of the feet of your humaneness.[71]

> To the most upright man, to the most famous poet, to the best doctor, Joachim Vadian of Switzerland, his most revered teacher.

Original: Stadtbibliothek (Vadiana) St. Gallen, VB.I.138
Transcription, VB, II, No. 140

7
Grebel to Myconius
Paris, January 30, 1519

In the following letter to Myconius, who was still resident in Zurich (see Cast of Characters No. 70), Grebel gives a milder judgment of Glarean than in his letter to Vadian above, perhaps because he is aware that Glarean will write his own interpretation of the conflict to Myconius (see 6/78/11-12 and 7A, below). The letter expresses Grebel's awareness of the serious nature of his break with Glarean but spares Myconius the sordid details that he sent to Vadian. These differences in the content of Letters 6 and 7 may account for the fact that Myconius apparently replied with words of advice and counsel while Vadian shunned his former student for months.

Greetings my Oswald:

When Valentin Tschudi was preparing to leave to visit his father's home,[1] I debated, while writing to a number of persons, whether a letter should also be sent to you, not that my letters are usually polished and for that reason pleasing, nor that I imagine your welfare depends upon them, but because you seemed to wish this when on my departure you made me promise to write to you as often as possible.

I fear you may have changed your mind about this and you changed it because of Glarean,[2] a man I say placed beyond the hazardous judgment of myself and my fellows,[3] my teacher most beloved.[4] Since I may have offended him as deeply as anyone ever did when I left him, I quite realize that you cannot ignore this and that perhaps you will be no less vexed than he whom I forsook, since you commended me to him and are so bound to him in affection that no one can offend Glarean lightly without also making you less friendly.[5] So when I pondered this and feared that I had estranged two men at one stroke, I scarcely dared to send my poor letter[6] to you.

Then further I am not proficient in letter writing[7] nor so favorably gifted that I can do without long hesitation and blushing what many young men accomplish readily and learnedly, fearing always to give you something to laugh over. But when I called to mind your love for me and mine for you and the respect and bond that linked me to you before my departure and safeguarded against your receiving these uncouth lines more chilling than the song of Ialemus[8] (as the saying is) with the scorn and disgust they deserve, love and the bond of friendship made me bold, and so bold that I was not ashamed to send to you this doleful dirge. Receive then this letter and welcome it with both hands and arms outstretched,[9] admire it, laud it with praises, declare it to be Ciceronian,[10] and intoxicate yourself with joy over it, saying that from my dear Conrad is this passably learned and charming little letter.

Now hurrying on to other things perhaps you wonder where I am living. And with whom. I am staying at the house of a printer,[11] a very upright citizen, and with me is John Henry Eleutherius of Zurich,[12] who left Glarean before me. And also a certain Probapolitanus[13] and a fourth person, a servant. I have not space to report on my studies. I am sending you the work of the clever Pontanus on the flight of the Swiss,[14] clearly an epic, not because it deserves your attention but so that you may see that a blind man has written blindly.

Please give my regards and those of J. Henry Eleutherius to your wife and family. All best wishes.

Your friend Conrad.

Ile de la Cite, Paris. January 30 from the birth of the Virgin 1519.

[P.S.] I rejoice that my friend Ulrich Zwingli has been appointed pastor in my native city.[15] I rejoice that my city has found such a one. Please reply if you love me.

Original: Staatsarchiv Zurich, EI.1.no.28
Transcription: MQR, II, pp. 231-32.

7A
Glarean[1] to Myconius
Paris, June 7, 1519

Grebel suffered two calamities in Paris (see 10/90/7). The first was his break with Glarean on January 1, described in Letters 6 and 7 to Vadian and Myconius; and the second was his involvement in the slaying of two Frenchmen on May 1, first mentioned in the following letter by Glarean and alluded to by Grebel himself in Letter 8, below. Bender interprets the episode as follows: "Glarean's students had been involved in several brawls before, but this was the most serious of all, so serious that although Glarean referred to the affair several times in letters to Myconius, Zwingli, and Peter Falk, he endeavored to keep the details as secret as possible. Among the other students involved were apparently Peter Tschudi and a certain Zophius of Glarus who had participated in a similar serious brawl the year before.... A plausible explanation of the affair is that a group of Glarean's students had been attacked by bandits and that in self-defense they killed two of the bandits in the battle. Grebel mentions the bandits twice later [see 10/89/14-15 and 13/97/33-34 after 9/86/24], when he speaks expressly of 'our war with the bandits....' All the available evidence indicates that Conrad Grebel and his fellow students who were involved in the affair were not guilty of an intentional crime, although the incident placed the whole group of Swiss students, and even the pension of Glarean itself, in serious danger" (1950, pp. 40-41).

Good heavens, sweetest Myconius, what a long 'ἐπιχείρημα [treatise] you compose on our love. But this may readily be ascribed to love itself, and deserves to be pardoned.

In regard to my return to Switzerland I promise nothing as yet. For everything is in turmoil. My stipend has been turned over to Faustus.[2] Indeed, I am not driven to reading in public unless I am pleased to do so. Our students killed two Frenchmen on the first day of May, relying on I know not whose influence.[3] The affair is extremely perilous indeed to all the others.

Also here with his *Weidlicheitate*[4] [grandiosity] was he whom I do not wish to name.[5] He, moreover, about whom you also[6] seriously inquired in a recent letter to Ammann[7] who left my hospitality,[8] about whom I say but one thing: I treated the fellow in the kindest manner. I overwhelmed him, as it were, with many favors. He not only did not thank me for it, but even inflicted loss and well nigh disgrace upon me. But he now has what he sought for, although to my sorrow. If the father resembles the son at all, which I for my part do not believe, I would expect the same things from him. But do keep still, lest in trying to perform the duty of a friend, which will surely do no good, you would make enemies for yourself. I shall look out for myself when the time comes, and meanwhile truth itself will fight on my behalf. Nor indeed am I of such hopeless fortune that this one fellow should overthrow me, although even the most worthless can do one harm. My favors bestowed on the son not even the son himself can have denied. Let the father deny them if he wishes. I for my part will not rank it as of great moment. . . .

It is strange why for almost four months now I have received no letters, except one or two, not even now from Zwingli, to whom I do not write now myself, I who formerly together with our friend Ammann used to write long letters every fortnight.[9] Farewell, dear Myconius.
In the year of Christ, 1519, the 7th of June.

Original: Staatsarchiv Zurich, EII.336, fol.4
Transcription: None

8

Grebel to Myconius
Paris, June 9, 1519

The "wretched plight" to which Grebel refers in the following letter is his embroilment in the killing of two Frenchmen reported by Glarean in the previous letter (7A/84/7-9). The affair placed Grebel and his partners in a dangerous position that could have meant their execution, and it is no wonder that it greatly clouded the remainder of his stay in France. He is purposely vague in speaking about his circumstances; consequently a number of allusions are obscure. The fact that the letter was sent to Myconius without salutation, signature, or address adds to the mystery, and its "regards to you all" (86/4) may indicate an assumption that Myconius would share the letter with Grebel's parents (see 9/87/27-28 and 12/95/37). Grebel almost always signed his name to his letters, except when he wanted to conceal his identity from prying eyes that might chance to read them in transit (see Letter 69, below). Ammann left for Zurich before Grebel could write the letter, and another five weeks elapsed before another carrier was available (see 9/87/25-26). So Letters 8 and 9 were sent together, and Grebel adds the request that Letter 9 be read by no one else (9/87/28), implying that Letter 8 could be shared.

If I[1] have not written to you for some time, believe me that it was not due to my fault, but to others. Believe me, I say, that when I do not write, it is that I cannot. Perhaps John Jacob[2] has revealed to you the wretched plight into which I have fallen.[3] He was not able to alert me sooner that he was going to leave, since I was staying in another town beyond the Seine for the sake of peace, nor had he foreseen that his departure would be so hurried, nor was I in a position to engage in letter writing when he did announce it because I was about to attend the court[4] with some other students, endeavoring to obtain some support. I have not the time to tell you about this affair and about my present situation. If you have not heard, I would prefer that you learn of it from my father.

I wonder much why I have received no letters from Clivanus,[5] since I wrote to him almost ten times after I left Vienna. It was understood that he should let me know about my books, whether they were burned or not or brought to my home.[6] I do not want anyone else but you to have the books which were brought by Clivanus and are now in your keeping. What I desire to have done with them I will specify in my next letter or when by chance I should return myself.

I have nothing to report about [editions of] Valerius[7] and Juvenal,[8] for the book dealers are in the university, which is in another quarter of the city. I have done all I could. I have arranged for her who delivers the letter to you to buy the books you want and take them along.[9] I do not know how this will turn out. If she does not get the job done, I shall send them myself. Whatever you do I accept in the spirit you do it. I am exceedingly distressed that you did not receive the reward which you earned from the Council of Zurich.[10] My unsettled state, enormous misfortunes, affliction of mind, and insoluble business so press on me that I know not where to turn, what to do, what to fear or hope for, what men or gods to entreat. So there is reason for you to disregard my worthless, illiterate letters,[11] muddled and wild[12] quite like my present state.

My regards to you all. Please give my greetings to John Jacob,[13] if he has not yet set off from Zurich. Farewell.

The day before Pentecost, from Paris, the sewer of thieves[14] and filth, a most hapless place for me.

[P.S.] If I do not reply to your bishop,[15] forgive me and beg him to ascribe it to the pressure of my business and not to despair of me. Indeed, I will write a letter different from his and will act far more uprightly.

Original: Zentralbibliothek Zurich, Ms.F82, fol.476 (Thesaurus Hottingerianus t. 47)
Transcription: MQR, II, pp. 232-33.

9
Grebel to Myconius
Paris, July 18, 1519

During the eight-month period of silence in the correspondence with Vadian, Grebel wrote Letters 7, 8, and 9 to Myconius, probably because the latter was responsive to his misfortunes listed in the following letter: the bandits, the plague, and his chronic bad health. Apparently, Letters 8 and 9 were dispatched together by the same messenger.

Hello most beloved, yea most eminent Myconius.[1]

My affection for you is so great and so devoted, I swear, that I long to speak to you as often as possible, by letter when there is no other way. I am quite delighted that a messenger has appeared to bear my lamentations[2] to you; and occasionally one is compelled, as the saying is, to seize the cicada by the wing.[3] So it has come to pass that I could not keep silent on this occasion, though Fortune stands over me like a malevolent stepmother and has all but strangled me in her noose.[4]

Those bandits[5] about whom we have often talked should be condemned for making the state a wilderness. In truth they are so besieging our shrines that sometimes it is not possible to practice our religion in safety; that is, to visit churches on holy days, to transact the most essential business; and with impunity they lie in ambush on each and every one, already distressed by affliction. This is utterly intolerable and equally abominable to me. Moreover, another thing is infinitely more unbearable, which shows no mercy to anyone of any class and which has recently tried to reduce the human population—the plague.[6] It began to rage among us, and if you knew what various schemes I have devised to avoid it, you would have called me a Proteus.[7] Of them all I shall adopt one, and it is this. They say that the plague can be avoided if one flees the place where it runs rampant. And so I have decided to do just that. Following the course of the Seine, I shall retreat ten miles from the city. I shall have companions who are trying to get out of the path of the same danger.[8]

On top of this I am taxed with uncertain health,[9] to the extent that I would prefer to be stricken with a definite disease than with a plague not definite. These ills are small and I should have borne them somehow with strength of mind if it had not seemed to me that the words of Vergil's Dido, "nowhere is trust safe," were truer than truth itself.[10] Time and time again these ills would have been as nothing if I could have been able sufficiently to lament and bemoan my Lemnian woes[11] without provoking a laugh of scorn for some deed or other. I would not tarry longer on these matters. There is something else that I should wish for you now to know.

I have this one desire only, that I should be able to spend what is left of my life's span in the understanding of literature. I do not know where I can more easily pursue this plan than in Italy,[12] and how better than in the company of John Jacob,[13] provided he does not spurn me.[14] I would like for you to try to sound out my parents on my plan, but most of all John Jacob, whom if I do not love, let none love me, neither men nor gods. If he becomes my companion, no Eurymnus[15] is going to cause a breach between us, and all the way to Italy he will be ever a "loyal Achates"[16] and I to him.

I have sent a longer letter along with this so that you could see that it was the courier's fault and not mine that they have not reached you sooner. If you wish to read all the letters, they are both addressed to you. I should prefer that others not read this letter. I say things to you that I do not to another. The books which you requested I assume you have and are already using. If you want anything else, give me the nod, make use of me, and it will be done swifter than you can write. As the gods love me I am your friend, and would that their love made me more worthy. My regards to your wife and family. Best wishes and good-bye.

Paris. July 18, the year of salvation 1519.

[P.S.] Jodocus Mauroticheus sends his best regards to you, but he prefers to be called Melanticheus.[17]

Original: Staatsarchiv Zurich, EI.1, No.27.
Transcription: MQR, II, pp. 233-34.

9A
Jacob Grebel[1] to Vadian and Hans Wirz[2]
Zurich, August 26, 1519

One of the reasons why Vadian failed to write to Conrad during most of the year 1519 was his preoccupation with the courtship of his sister Martha, which culminated in their marriage on August 19 in the chapel of the Wirz family castle in Wädenswil. Here, on the estate of Hans Wirz, stepbrother to Jacob Grebel, they lived for a number of months to escape the plague in St. Gallen. The following letter is the first of only three (9A, 23A, 57B) from the pen of Jacob, all written in German, that have survived. Inasmuch as his public duties as a senator in Zurich usually took priority over his domestic affairs (see Schelbert, p. 39), it is all the more interesting to read these letters, dealing mostly with private family matters.

My greeting and wish for everything good.

Dear doctor and brother:

We are highly pleased to hear that you are in good health and hope soon with God's help to have a happy reunion.

Master Jörg[3] is writing you[4] concerning the books. I have given the letter you wrote to St. Gallen to the messenger and entreated him earnestly to make haste in delivering it, but there is no word yet. One cannot help wondering and worrying whether you are somewhat annoyed. If it is important to you, let me know. I will do the very best I can.

Dear brother, I thank you always for your kindness, both on behalf of my folks who are with you and also in our behalf. I desire to be of service always.

Concerning the parish fair so soon at hand, our wish is that you will attend it with us. May the Lord God permit us to experience this one and many more in happiness. May you be commended herewith constantly to the Lord God.

Given on Friday before Verena, in the year [15]19

Jacob Grebel

To the learned doctor Joachim von Watt, now at Wädenswil, and to my dear brother and governor of the same.

Original: Stadtbibliothek (Vadiana) St. Gallen, VB.I.163
Transcription, VB, II, No. 166

10
Grebel to Vadian
Melun, October 6, 1519

After a silence of more than eight months, the correspondence between Grebel and Vadian resumes following the arrival of several letters from Wädenswil. Grebel's reply is written from Melun (see 9/fn.8), capital of the region Seine et Marne, twenty miles up the River Seine from Paris. For about six months, this was the refuge of Grebel and five fellow students while the plague was raging in Paris. Glarean had taken his pupils still farther from Paris to Marnay s. Seine, where he continued to teach them Greek.

S[alutation].

I cannot express in words how delighted I was to see and read your letters,[1] most illustrious man and most caring of my sister, full of your usual humanity. For how could I easily tell with what great joy I was affected, since I am poor in talents[2] and a fit plaything of the most cruel Fortune.[3] I could, perhaps, if any man could feel happiness amid unalloyed tears and gain a respite from wretched turmoil, if the dread of bandits, if the horror of the fierce plague would give him leave to smooth the wrinkles from his brow.

Truthfully, before I could learn from letters I had not yet opened, which the messenger had not yet delivered, that my way home to celebrate the wedding—you know which[4]—was blocked, I seemed to myself to be mad with happiness to hear that you had married my sister. But then when I discovered father's mind from the fact that no money for the journey was sent, it is beyond words to describe how depressed in spirit I was and how many tears I poured forth. And to make it more credible to you, may the gods doom me to wail in everlasting misery if I did not grieve most bitterly, for the reason I have said, if I did not most bitterly groan and weep. However the anger of a father and the hatred of fortune torment me to death in their usual way, you have married my sister, the most illustrious of suitors has come among us, and there has happened to me in this Platonic year[5] nothing but this one happy event: a marriage will be celebrated and the joy of both your family and mine will be great. That it will always be prosperous, auspicious, and fortunate for you and your wife and for all of us, I do entreat and implore the Almighty Lord Jesus Christ[6] with all manner of prayers. I should have been present to address and salute that divine man, soon to be my brother-in-law, and as bridesman to escort the bridegroom,[7] to venerate him, to embrace him, and finally to adore him with all my attention. As one suddenly turned prophet, I ought to have called you to the wedding chamber with the nuptial song which has been used so many times before, if like the cento[8] that sort of song could be composed from unbroken tears. Father should have aided me with money so that it could have been done. I should have been there, father should have provided the way. But what instead? My sinister guardian angel,[9] treachery, misfortune, and all the sea of evils tossed me and all but drowned me in the waves.

You grieved that I have been overwhelmed a second time by misfortune. You did this, I know not how to express it, but let me say, like a father. You rendered me more obligated, but again I cannot get the right word, if only this mind, your alter ego[10] (but am I not shameless and do your immortal Muses[11] permit this), be bound and in no other way but most tightly alone to you, if it please you and is the will of the gods. You invited me to the wedding; but I could do no less, I could do no more, than sweetly cry, both when I reread your letter, and as I reply with this weeping letter of mine. You tell me that your father-in-law is festively merry with you and that my father is still implacable toward me, but in this you have told me my own dreams and you agreed precisely with the divining seer.[12] You advise me to take care that none of my misfortunes could appear to have happened by my own fault. I have taken care and have complied. No offense has been committed by my own fault, for no offense has been committed. I am a suppliant, I curse myself, but if I sin again, let him forgive, let him pardon, let him be appeased and reconciled, and let him forget the things which so far have rained upon my head.

Why do you urge me to come to terms with Glarean?[13] His passions are the stronger, and not even friendship itself could have brought me back into his favor. I say this to you alone, because that man will not give up a grudge he has once assumed,[14] with the assistance of some unknown Nessus, unless on his death pyre.[15] You will say, I suppose, that I am not getting away from my nature.[16] So be it, I will not get away from it. However, time itself and the future will prove how true I was to my nature, even short of my nature, you know what I mean. Not long ago I sent you a letter[17] which poured out a great tragedy between him and me—so it seemed then—which now you might rather call a more unturbulent comedy if you knew what uproar and wondrous wrangling finally happened between us. The gods gave each his own mind, his own will. Not to say more—for should I say more?—he accused me of taking illegal foreign money[18] and with all his might he damned the son of your father-in-law, who had enough misery already to arouse pity from enemies. Justice will weary that advocate to death. I will add nothing to this, but if you want the whole case set forth from the brow of the accuser to the feet of the condemned, write back.

90

Write back what that matter is that you would have related had you not been occupied, and whether father has decreed to keep me in perpetual exile in Gyrara of France.[19] Meanwhile, until that is done, I shall indeed think of nothing that has to do with the life of the bridegroom. I shall be cheerless, I shall dread everything, I mean everything: the plague which rages also here at Melun up to fifteen miles from Paris. Either death will free me from distressing cares, or father, if he summons me and sends money to one who is a suppliant and penitent. If I do not see my native land again, honor me with an epitaph; for I hope that he whose wedding I could not attend will attend my funeral rites. Forgive me if I speak of epitaphs instead of epithalamia.[20] I am not sober, willingly or otherwise, I am drunk from the sorrow and wretchedness of my condition, and I could not but bewail to you. I am alone and miserable, but it is not an omen, even if no owl, or little light appears.[21]

I would like to know before you become ours in every respect whether you will become a permanent citizen of Zurich. I was going to come speaking one language, if the gods had willed; but now nearly dead I send you bilingual and even trilingual letters and the corpse of Calliope.[22] I shall terminate this incessant chattering and joking like a shade.[23]

Valentin Tschudi, rector of Glarus, asked me to convey his regards to you. I believe you know this gifted young man.[24] Peter Tschudi sends his regards from Paris,[25] and also Leopold.[26] Glarean, if you do not know, intends to take his students ten miles out of Paris to avoid the plague, but in another direction. I could not write all these events more briefly, nor my sufferings more joyfully. Forgive, I beg you, and waste a little hour from your nuptials. Please give my good wishes to your wife, to Zwingli, and Oswald Myconius, men learned and humane in every way, whose servant I am, and to whoever speaks of me. Good-bye and good wishes to you all, and may everything prosper as happily as it has miserably for me, and may your marriage be successful as you wish.

Melun, 6 October in the year 1519.

Conrad Grebel, most unfortunate son of your father-in-law, and yours as you wish, etc.
  To Joachim Vadian, poet, orator, and distinguished doctor, devout and dutiful son-in-law to his father.

Original: Stadtbibliothek (Vadiana) St. Gallen, VB?
Transcription: VB, II, No. 170

11
Grebel to Vadian
Paris, January 1, 1520

As a new year arrives, Grebel's melancholy frame of mind abates somewhat as he writes the following brief letter to Vadian, just to let him know that he is "alive and well and still your friend."

So have fortune, my spirits, and messengers combined that you receive from me a shorter letter than before; but what more do you want than to let you know that I am alive and well and still your friend? I have heard that you are not in good favor among the people of your hometown because you withdrew from there to the district of my uncle the Ammann,[1] leaving behind so many cut down by the plague.[2] They will speak well of you in the future when with your immortal work[3] you present the aliens[4] of your homeland with a much different sort of life and free them at last from another plague. But enough of that.

Please do not let my father neglect me, his son, especially at this time. I commend to you this messenger[5] who was formerly your pupil. John Leopold Grebel[6] is wonderfully delighted to have you as a kinsman. Valentin Tschudi and his kinsman Peter Tschudi[7] send you their best wishes, and Peter has high regard for you and scarcely holds back from writing letters to you, and he would not hold back his hand, as he said himself, if you were known as well personally as you are by name.[8]

Think well of Grebel, your friend, who could not have served you any more diligently at this time. Good-bye, most revered sir, live happily throughout the new year and more.

1 January, in the year of salvation 1520.

Conrad, who is always your most obedient servant.

[P.S.] I could not seal the letter. Please excuse me for this, both you and father; confession should atone somewhat, as will he who bears this letter. But still if I have done wrong in this, in the Euripus[9] of my fortunes it will be made good by me at another time unless I have launched my barque to be buffeted by endless waves.

Greet my parents from me, my uncle's family,[10] my sister or rather your wife.

To Joachim Vadian, most worthy for humane learning and uprightness, for his kinship but mostly for himself.

Notes, 622-3
Original: Stadtbibliothek (Vadiana) St. Gallen, VB. I. 175
Transcription: VB, II, No. 176

12
Grebel to Myconius
Paris, January 14, 1520

*On January 9, 1520, Grebel received three letters from Switzerland—
one from his father, one from Vadian, and one from Myconius. The message
that he read in the first two was that he had largely lost the confidence of his
parents and his new brother-in-law. While painting a sober picture of the
mood in the Grebel household in Zurich, Myconius remained the faithful
intercessor. With this kind of encouragement, Grebel sat down five days later
to write long replies to his two former teachers. Following is his letter to
Myconius, which expresses deep gratitude for the counsel of his friend and the
hope that he could still be worthy of his teaching, as once he was.*

G[reetings].

I received all the letters which the tradeswoman[1] brought to me; they
all came through, thanks to a little tip.[2] From them all I have learned
exactly what you want. You ask what I have decided about the books that
I sent you first from Austria and then from France.[3] I directed you to keep
them and do so now, so that it was correct of you to write that you are using them just as if they were your own. Whatever is to be done about this
from now on, I have made my reply; so let me know shortly. I could only
wish what you wish, and until you tell me what you want I await your
requests or advice.

Up to this point I could easily see the beginning and ending of my letter to you. I am in no doubt what I should turn to next, but I hesitate, all
but strangled in the noose of Fortune, a noose I say which threatens me,
and it is so menacing that she has all but flung it around my neck.[4] You tell
me of enormous tragedies and how the cudgels will rain upon my
miserable head.[5] Father (so you have heard from mother) grieves, rages,
fears: that I have lent money to swindlers and squandered it, that I have
wasted time I can never recover, that I never moved to William's,[6] all due
to my cruel stepmother Fortune,[7] and you do not know whether he feels
more in sorrow or in anger, or neither. He fears that a greater disaster may
attack me while I am still unimpaired. He has ordered me back because the
plague is approaching, because he is annoyed, because he spends sleepless
nights in fear that I have gone beyond the bounds of virtue. He is not pacified by your entreaties nor those of Vadian. I urge him not to worry, and
not to do what you mentioned in your letter, and I wish I could so
persuade him. Swindlers have devoured the least part of my money, barely
a twelfth; the greatest part has been eroded by the passing of time and has
been emptied into the abyss of Fortune (where I should like to throw quite

a few things). I did not move to William's;[8] but he did not order me to do so, nor could I, and anyway it would not have pleased him. You would agree if you had read father's letter and if you had known my circumstances in Paris. So it is not easy to see how I was disobedient to father in this matter. Let there be no fear of a greater disaster, especially since I have stolen nothing, I have not engaged in piracy, I have done nothing Italian,[9] nor lastly have I committed anything that has the slightest scent of dishonesty. I do not see how France sets snares for me, only perhaps that they are again the evil schemes of Fortune, whom I have been forced to bear this long as my tormentor. But if it is not from that source that he fears disaster awaits me, from what source, I pray then, does he fear danger, and what and why is he so greatly afraid? Let him call me away (but how the Furies[10] do meanwhile drive and drag me)[11] provided he will not call me away from Scylla to Charybdis[12] and from one plague to another. When he has called for me, he will not be able to frighten me with his wrath or with the plague and to exclude me from home or let the winter pass before my money is sent. Let him sleep as sound as Endymion[13] if he wishes, for my deeds do not prevent that. If anyone strives to the contrary, I cannot prevent him since I have no alternative—I nearly said something else.[14] If no prayers can reconcile him, if by the entreaties of brother-in-law, friend, child, he is a Toronaean harbor,[15] if the family on first approach should react with inhospitable anger, what shall I do? I shall play the part of a man who scoffs first at Fortune but then soon yields to her dire duties and fearful furies at the bidding of calamity. I shall suffer and behave like a typical character in tragedy.

Such is what disturbs my so wearied soul, and you foresaw this before and you decided to give me advance warning, lest I should slip heedlessly into a worse danger. You are the same Myconius. Thanks I owe to you, but I cannot repay. Be assured of the fact, however, that I am everlastingly grateful to you. Use and abuse this poor fellow just as need requires. I am yours, overwhelmed by your goodness.

I have babbled[16] quite enough about father and yourself, enough to rouse nausea and bile in another. On your counsel, it is mother's wish that I should better remain here, if possible, until father's anger subsides, and you Myrmidons cease to perish by whole companies.[17] But I should stop cracking jokes.[18] You say that it is the clear wish of my parents and yourself that I should do what I believe best, but in such a way that my intentions are known to you, that this is my mother's wish. Yet how can I discern what is best, when the opportunity of better things never looms near enough to me to grasp it by the hair? But whatever the flow of Fortune back and forth like the Euripus,[19] it will assuredly buffet and mock me with the obscene finger[20] as I here await the plague with the return of spring and in the fear of other assailants; and in terror, above all, of what the Dread Sisters will weave secretly until then.[21] I may be exiled from my father's home by the same plague and by the wrath of my sire if a Fortune which is not moved to tears by even these evils deals me the final blow. Would you not say that I am holding the wolf by the ears,[22] standing between the victim and the knife?[23] So I pass no decree, and until my consul gives me orders and my people carry it out, I will enact nothing[24] but will yield to be dragged at the heels of Fortune[25] and father.

Would that I had never met the Phrygian whom I should have known to be a Phrygian and not only a Zurichian.[26] The fellow perished when summoned by no one; he went to the abode of the dead laden with my money.[27] If it cannot be paid out of a stipend here or from what remains at his mother's home, I shall remit to his soul what he owes.[28] Meanwhile I must use all means to scrape together what I can for my own need. In whatever final state that man is, after the end of all troubles, I hope he finds God more merciful than his deeds deserve.

Now that you have moved to Luzern, may everything turn out according to your wishes;[29] and I pray that you and your family may escape the plague. I long to share your company; would that I could stay worthy of your teaching as once I was somewhat. My regards to John Xylotectus,[30] a man highly learned and compassionate, and to your wife as many times she could never greet me, I will not say a thousand times, and to the other members of your household. Good-bye my solace in hardship. Paris, from our workshop of torment, would it were a workshop of literature,[31] January 14, 1520.

[P.S.] I gave you instructions in a previous letter to compose an epitaph for one soon to die.[32] If you have done it, please change the inscription (to keep it current) and let this be the elegy: Unless perchance from dumb departed ghosts[33] or from Pythagoreans[34] he has learned to speak by speaking naught, I absolutely loathe Clivanus' silence. I have written six hundred times and have received nothing in return. It seems to be his style not to send a reply. Then I will importune him no longer with repeated requests for his sheets of paper. But if at last he takes the warning and writes, he will get back from me a whole Iliad, and if that does not sate his excessive greed for reading, I will add to that the wanderings of Ulysses.[35]

I nearly forgot this: forward this letter to Zurich or wherever father is staying. If you let me know who advises father so prudently or what they are up to, you will do me a most welcome favor.

Original: Zentralbibliothek Zurich, Ms.F80 fol.604 (Thesaurus Hottingerianus t.45)
Transcription: MQR, II, pp. 234-36

13
Grebel to Vadian
Paris, January 14, 1520

The following letter is certainly one of the best written, most honest and poignant of all the letters that Grebel wrote to Vadian. Like his Christmas letter of 1522 (No. 50), it is an unfeigned heartfelt confession of his innermost soul to his "physician" (96/33). With funds depleted, he was compelled to return to Glarean's bursa for a place to dwell but without obligation to participate in its rituals. With diminishing pretense, he examines his situation and gains new insight about himself and his father. He is sick of his French pension and feels that in the eyes of his compatriots he and his father are traitors. He indicts his father, not for illegal behavior in the technical sense (although he can only hope that he "has not accepted forbidden gifts" (97/41), but for pushing him to accept the French stipend. Conrad admits that it was he, not his father, who received the royal grant; but he has an uncanny premonition that a future day of reckoning is coming (see Epi.A, below) "if one day the republic rises to the heights of fame and glory" (98/26-27). His concern is not only for his own and his father's culpability, but for the immorality of spending the king's money extracted from the poor by oppressive taxation. In short, this letter, according to H. S. Bender, "bears evidence of an ethical awakening and witnesses to a certain nobility of sentiment which here appears for the first time in Grebel's extant correspondence. He begins to think seriously about death in view of the state of his health and the plague, and suddenly a remarkable sentence appears in his letter to Vadian: 'I do not ask for death, but I would not fear death if it comes to me, for I am prepared to meet Christ'" (HSB, p. 44). The prodigal son has not yet turned toward home, but he is near the end of his journey into a far country and his squandering of money in loose living (Lk. 15:11ff.).

Greetings, my Vadian.

I sent you a hurried letter[1] because I was not forewarned of the departure of Henry Lingk[2] of Schaffhausen. I will be able to learn whether you got it when at last you reply to my third letter since your marriage.[3] My last letter, brief because of the hurry of the messenger,[4] promised a longer one. It remains to be seen whether I will give satisfaction with this.

Smitten by the wounds of miserable fortune, I shall reveal myself to you fully, physician. I returned to Paris, from which the winter had driven the plague. I am living at the house of Glarean,[5] not bound to him in any way, and I move in respectable company. It was not in vain that I returned here, for you will know from this that I am staying in a safer place than before. All that money I had when I left home[6] I have spent for belly, books, and clothes. I returned it to fortune and idleness,[7] or if you prefer, it returned itself to the fickle giver of the Tolosian gold.[8] So I wrote to father to ask him to help me by sending more money as I had lost my purse and was thrown into straitened circumstances. He did what I hoped: he entrusted twenty scutatos[9] to a royal courier[10] to deliver them to me. But poor me, I received the letter but not the money. Mark an unfortunate creature born under stepmother Juno[11] in the fourth quarter of the moon. For he lost the money by means of which I was supposed to return home at Father's order. It was only on the ninth of January that I received father's letter written on the fourteenth of September.[12] He commanded me to leave the sinful companions who had twice cast me into the danger of losing my money and my life, lest I be cast into that snare a third time and he be forced to cast off his son and there be no helping hand from him to draw me out. In Vienna they were honest and upright young men who led me into those turmoils from which I barely emerged without having my whole right arm cut off;[13] and they were likewise honest who led me a second time to the dangerous point of nearly costing my head.[14] Some time you will know in what way. So what he attributed to bad company, which was not, and to me, who was not wholly to blame for these misfortunes, I could wish that, knowing my fates,[15] he would sometime learn to excuse my guilt on the basis of extenuating circumstances. I relate these things to you from father's letters.

Now hear what Myconius says, your friend and mine.[16] He says that father grieves because he fears I have committed something beyond the bounds of honesty, and that he spends sleepless nights in misery since he worries so. Had he known better what I had done, he would surely have been less of a Tieresias[17] to my motes, leaving that well-known beam.[18] I talk like this to you, Joachim, because you alone have been a Vadian,[19] a man learned in everything, a Harpocrates,[20] a brother-in-law. You began to discover the beam when you were ready to go to Luzern on horseback.[21] He heard that I am in bad repute because of the fight between ourselves and the bandits.[22] The truth is I am in no repute, never mind a bad one; and whenever mention of it is made, I have no need to blush or beat my breast with a thousand pangs of conscience. My mind is free, and I fear no reproaches. But he does not know what I suffer on his account because I was handed over to the support first of the emperor[23] and afterwards of the king of France.[24] If he had only taught me to live on little and on what had been earned, as a father should[25] (and I still hope that he who has sworn by the sacred stone of Jupiter[26] has not accepted forbidden gifts), and if he had not wished me to spread my wings further than the nest (although he with beam affixed[27] decides no less than this for his second son,[28] that my brother in the nest should spread his wings to the vultures), I would not fear that whenever the fathers of the fatherland inveigh against traitors, they mean to include my father among them, for they scarcely let me think otherwise, and that because the son receives a royal pension they believe his father too is growing rich.[29] Then as such talk is bandied about, I would not be blushing red or growing pale, the gilded knights or others would not be saying that my father always supports the interests of the king of France,[30] I would not be mortified, I would not believe that everyone is aware of the matter as many surely are, that time and perhaps this very day will disclose all[31] even though father tries to hide it like the ill-omened Harpocrates,[32] so ignorant despite such wide experience in the world. Then too I would not have to think of repaying, the vulture of worry would not eat my heart out,[33] I would not be a slave to money, if all things had not obeyed it according to the proverb;[34] I would not have sold my liberty for gold nor my good reputation for worthless metal, and most of all I would not believe that I had sold my name which is more precious than gems or the gifts of kings, I would not owe my soul itself because of that wrongdoing to I know not whom, I would not be exposed to every kind of misery, had I not looted that Delphic gold[35] from Tolosa,[36] which, if I dare to say this and no more, torments me with worry as nothing else does, I presume because it [the French money] is not less sacred to God than the Tolosan I mentioned. The king sucks up the wealth of the people and the wolf snatches the food from their mouth so that I can adorn myself splendidly and dine sumptuously; and if one day the republic rises to the heights of fame and honor, I do not know what reaction it will bring about. I should not have forfeited the liberty of Switzerland by my deeds, to be made the slave of so many masters so many times. But to speak freely what I feel, father hardly acted prudently, for he was the cause of my receiving this royal stipend again. It seems to me that I was more prudent in accepting it reluctantly than he was in forwarding it promptly.[37] You might say that I am raising a great storm over a small matter and belittle these arguments on the grounds that either everyone always loots from everywhere and everyone, or that custom has practically established the principle of looting as a law. If this were the case, believe me I would not conform to it and no one nor even eloquence could wrest this concern from me. I have pursued riches, I have been a pauper. I spent much, fortune took back much. I squeezed into the cupboard a lean weasel; having become a little fat with the pleasure of the gods, I shall not again be able to escape from my prison, nor will I be able to disgorge again what I ate. You have heard both sides of the case;[38] consider whom the fatal judgment ought to send to damnation.

But now let us pass on from this and let me report the advice Myconius gave to me. He says that father in his wrath does not want to yield that much to your entreaties or to his, either, that if I should return from France, he would still be extremely angry, or that if I came to Zurich in spite of this, he did not think that I could enter father's house. Assuming then that father will be so inhospitable, I do not know whether or not I should leave France for somewhere else, especially if someone provided more than a pittance of money. But if he should summon me, why should I not come? There are those who would persuade him that he should not let me continue living here for the reason that the plague could rage no worse than my father, nor he less than it; they are in fear, whoever they are, that my situation and fortune conspire to make miserable me perish miserably. Without doubt their aims and prayers will not fail them; for either my father will summon me, or if not, I shall be here to be harvested by the sickle of the plague when it returns with warmer weather at the beginning of the spring, and what I would not avoid there, I shall have conversely endured here, suffering the same thing.

I cannot easily predict therefore when you should expect me. What would happen if I never returned to Switzerland, what if I would die, what would become of me if I did, I care not in the least; I fear death no more than the name, and if I should come to Christ prepared,[39] since so many things have happened to me beyond those I mentioned, I could have no reason to pray for a longer life from the gods. Meanwhile, perhaps, you think that there is no true cause for my complaints. You see me, I think, wearing a very fine shoe with the mark of the crescent;[40] but where the soft shoe pinches me, there you do not look. If you have subdued my subduing father[41] and swayed him from anger to mercy, which I have always been able to rouse in an enemy and which I deserve more,[42] you will take from my mind a great anxiety. If you accomplish less than you wish, I must bear all fortune and the Dread Furies.[43] I shall pass from the peril of death into another, no less than from exile into exile. My one solace shall be this, that you have promised the gift of hospitality, so that when I am shut out when I should not have been, you will take me in. Laugh at all these things, as you will do, or find grave fault in my letter; I could not have been true to my promises and have jested about matters other than were in my mind. There is nothing else I would wish you to know except that I am yours and no one else's, and take care of this letter, as of the others. Please give my regards to your parents, if you have returned to them from the district of my uncle[44] and if they are with you, and to your sisters and your wife, and cease not to give me a father's care, and tell me in your next letter what is said about me, or what you hear about me as Myconius does. Good-bye, dearest of men, best wishes, and love me as always.

Paris, January 14, 1520.

Conrad Grebel, your servant.

[P.S.] My friend Leopold[45], not like the fellow of Vienna, and Peter Tschudi,[46] both ask me to send their respects to you.

> To the man incomparably learned and humane, doctor, poet and orator, Joachim Vadian, his brother-in-law very very highly esteemed. To Zurich

Original: Stadtbibliothek (Vadiana) St. Gallen, VB.I.180
Transcription: VB, II, No. 179.

14
Grebel to Myconius
Paris, March 7, 1520

The prodigal continued to feel lost and depressed during his remaining months in Paris. Depleted of funds, hounded by the cheap advice of "friends who are no friends" (101/16), threatened by the return of the spring plague, he writes to the only loyal friend he knows—Oswald Myconius, now of Luzern.

I bid you well, the most needed of all my friends. It is impossible to describe with what great profit, not to mention pleasure, I read your letter,[1] how at the beginning I cried out, and now I am plainly miserable. You showed the care my father ought to have shown; you showed what should have been my mother's concern and Vadian's. The day they come to the aid of their son or brother-in-law, even in a vision or dream,[2] let all the gods and goddesses turn against me and remain implacable by any sacred expiatory rites (as a good part of mankind does of late). Unless indeed you would say they do appear thus, that they laugh at me and my messages and then in the end desert me in such disasters when I especially need to be helped and rescued from the sea of troubles in which I have been tossed for so long.

They have not written, I suppose, in order not to neglect their own responsibilities, for this they could not do, yet they did not reply to my letters when they had the spare time to write up volumes.[3] They gave me no promise of hope, and the message they finally sent only added many tears to my other worries. I see no way to lay hold of any money, should I need it, and they make bold to reply by messenger only that whenever there is

100

need I know well where to borrow money. How I may have hurt my parents' name or Vadian's feelings has me completely in the dark. However, as often as I fall on my knees and beg them and importune them, and gain nothing but rebuff, I could easily have restored the good will of hardhearted enemies with my prayers.[4] If they persist, they will propel me on a bad way.

I do not yet see what I should do within the constant bounds of virtue to get out of this. If only fate would allow my shattered barque to be thrown out of this Scylla into a Charybdis,[5] or by the favor of the gods to escape both and be cast upon the shore. If this is not possible, and by the Almighty God it is not possible, I hand myself over to Fortune to be tormented by the gods until their fury puts an end to my life.

With the coming of March, the plague has opportunely begun again the slaughter it had left over from the autumn before. I pray not to avert death; I pray only to avert an untimely one. I pray for the end of troubles, as I am near the end. Friends who are no friends pray the same for me. They urge me to pray together with many others as occasion presents and they admonish me with their eyes not to try to prolong life irrationally by prayer. So each moment of time is a waste for me. If I return alive to you, I shall have lived the life of Nestor,[6] and I shall be born again in another body as the Pythagoreans say.[7]

Now I turn to another matter, if I can possible drag myself to any matter more real to me. You expressed thanks for the books I sent.[8] I did not expect this nor did I send them for that reason, but for you to know that I wanted to give you pleasure, for such your merits deserve, as often as I have the chance to return your favors. You must make full use of my services, great or small as they may be, as often as you like, since you will never exhaust them.

You longed so much for the promised edition of Asconius Pedianus[9] that I would by all means have sent it to my friend if it had been published and if I could have scraped the money together to buy it, though I am so poor and scarcely have enough to live. Now you know why it has not been sent. I do not see how it might be sent before its availability abroad unless you send what must be paid for it. A depleted or rather exhausted purse makes one stingy, and time impoverishes and disasters drive one mad. Please advise and tell me what to do and watch for. There are books of outstanding quality from the Aldine Press on sale here for very little and in both classical languages.[10] Two books are bound together here at a cheaper price and better at that and more beautiful than anywhere outside France. I do not know what your choice would be among them all. If you know from anyone how they might reach you, send the money and I will attend to it as ordered with all necessary care. If you have been reading Greek, as you usually do, I think you would like Homer, since you delight in the poets. An edition beautifully bound in gilt is on sale for less than two scutati.[11]

About Conrad[12] I have what you write. We are friends, just as if we were not separated by mind and location. More about this later.

You urge me to return. In my present shipwrecked condition I have as little power to do that as to stay here. Danger stalks in hiding in either case[13]. I have decided this much at least: to accompany some friends who are going to Melun to flee the plague, not necessarily for the same reason, but to take advantage of their support.[14] If fate follows me there, I shall put all the blame on father, who was responsible for my being unable to escape, because he failed to show a parent's feeling toward a son in trouble and to recall me.

My regards to your family, that is, your wife and son and the students. Good-bye.

Paris, March 7, 1520.

Yours, Conrad Grebel.

To Oswald Myconius, a most learned and cultured patron of all literature, my most esteemed friend.

Original: Staatsarchiv Zurich, EI.1, No. 32
Transcription: MQR, II, pp. 236-8

15
Grebel to Myconius
Paris, April 13, 1520

As another five weeks slip by, "the clouds become darker, and Grebel's melancholy was intensified. By the middle of April, he felt himself nearer to shipwreck than to the harbor, a sick and weary young man who knew not what the morrow might bring. As a last desperate expedient, he sent a letter to his father with Glarean, who was just then undertaking a journey to Switzerland" (HSB, p. 45). Grebel tells about it in the following short letter to Myconius.

Greetings my glory and ally Oswald.

When Glarean departed from here[1] and I had just written a letter[2] to my parents, great misfortune befell me, which further prevents me from writing to you at greater length.[3] However, by divine aid or the care of physicians this will soon leave me and return whence it came. Do not be worried at all about it, if you love me. But you will be worried, and I do not wish that any concern of mine should be kept from you. And since you never cease to write to me so warmly and regularly, and since my parents and Vadian, on whom I should depend, certainly do not give a care about me, I write to you by choice even though I am not in best condition for composing letters because of my ill health. I am yours if you permit it, and you are mine even if you do not.

I have not procured your copy of Asconius Pe.[4] yet because of the printers and my poverty, and it is not my fault that your wish has not been fulfilled. Please send my regards to J. Xylotectus,[5] to all your family a thousand times, and to my Conrad.[6] Best wishes and good-bye.

Conrad Grebel, your friend, your most loving of all your friends.
Paris, 13 April, 1520

[P.S.] Please reply to my previous letter which that remarkable old woman[7] surely delivered, for of course you will reply to this one.

I am tossed and thrown from Scylla to Charybdis,[8] and I fear that I may be nearer shipwreck than the harbor. I call upon the aid of the gods. I am torn between hope and fear until I come out free from these troubles or go under the waves.

Original: Zentralbibliothek Zurich, Ms.F80, fol.603
Transcription: MQR, II, p. 238

16
Grebel to Vadian
Paris, April 13, 1520

Having written to his father and to Myconius, Grebel decides to write to Vadian also, even though he has not heard from the newly married couple since the days following their wedding the previous August (see 10/89/9). He knows they have returned to St. Gallen, and he knows that Glarean wants to go there to talk with Vadian. He knows that if he does, they will talk about him, and he wants Vadian to keep in mind that he will be "dealing with a mind that is not rational" (104/20).

Greetings, my brother-in-law.

If you are well, great; if your family is well, I rejoice. I am not very well and especially at this time of writing.[1] But I write, not because you would feel the lack of my letters. I write that by my frequent urging you might be drawn in this direction and that you might not neglect me by writing nothing in reply. But you do neglect me; and with such leisure, with so many means, with so many messengers at hand, you do not send letters, not even a letter,[2] to someone who loved you so ardently, who was so miserable. You have offended my character. I should have been acknowledged, not dismissed. You are occupied the whole day in associating with your friends. An hour could have been allotted to me who surrendered to you my time and my whole being. Other things prevented you from being able to speak to me, and you have a weighty and just cause for silence. Now the blame will not be yours but that of my fates,[3] who make me restless and still miserable. I have long roused your sharp anger because I attacked you so freely,[4] but as one equal to another. Believe that it was done by one who loves you; for if I did not love you, I would not care so much for you or your sheets of paper. But in summary and in short: I should wish that you would overlook my rudeness or do nothing that I need to criticize, if I criticize.

Now about Glarean.[5] He said that he would visit your city because of you. I asked you in the last letter, and I ask you in this, to receive him with all hospitality, and not to expect a man who cannot be other than himself, that is, who cannot disguise his feelings, who gives long expression of his opinion, and who prolongs an argument. If you choose to doubt it, try it out; then you will discover that you are dealing with a mind that is not rational. I wish to be able to be yours for a long time, if you let me. I hope your family is well. Good-bye and best wishes.

Conrad Grebel, your pupil and brother-in-law, who is your servant.

To the lord doctor Joachim Vadian, teacher and most revered brother-in-law.

Original: Stadtbibliothek (Vadiana) St. Gallen, VB.I.185
Transcription: VB, II, No. 185

16A
Tschudi[1] to Vadian
Paris, June 20, 1520

Peter Tschudi, brother of Swiss historian, Aegidius Tschudi, was a close friend of Grebel throughout the Paris episodes, and Grebel mentions him in five of his letters. In 11/92/17-19, Grebel writes that "Peter has a high respect for you and scarcely holds back from writing letters to you; and he would not hold back his hand, as he himself said, if you were known as well personally as you are by name." The following letter is valuable not only for the light it sheds on Grebel's peer relationships but also for dating Grebel's departure from Paris (see 17/fn.1), which was probably the occasion for writing the letter. There is evidence not only that Grebel took the letter with him to Zurich but that he did not get around to forwarding it to St. Gallen until

September 11, when he wrote to Vadian, "Read the letter of Peter Tschudi and smile, if for no other reason than that he speaks and thinks about you most sincerely (23/121/2-3).

I would not want you, my very learned Vadian, to ascribe either to impudence or to my rashness the fact that I as an unknown man of the meanest fortune, without ever having personally met you, have not blushed to write to you, but in part to my love for you, which cannot be other than absolutely sincere, and in part indeed to your brother-in-law, Conrad Grebel, a youth of the most brilliant talent, who furnished such incentives for writing that it would have been surely an act of the greatest impudence not to comply with the man's so insistent entreaties. The more I tried to beg off from this duty, the more zealously he kept insisting; and he never stopped urging me until he had wrested this letter from me, such as it is. He did this of course as one who mentioned beforehand a certain wonderful mildness of your character and a comprehensive erudition in literature, tempered by a very affable courteousness that very politely overlooks the blunders of those who are uncultured, the result of which was that my pen itself almost demanded to scribble a letter to you and already impelled of its own accord chose for itself this task of writing before it could be entirely turned from its purpose. . . . [2]

Original: Stadtbibliothek (Vadiana) St. Gallen, VB. I. 197
Transcription: VB, II, No. 199

THE SEEKER

17
Grebel to Myconius
Zurich, July 6, 1520

Soon after Tschudi wrote his letter to Vadian (16A, above), Grebel left Paris for home, taking the letter with him. Two days out of Paris, he met Glarean on his way back, traveling with several students, one of whom was carrying Myconius's letter to Grebel. It was a positive letter regarding Grebel's homecoming and served to alleviate some of his fears of his father's wrath. Grebel's arrival in Zurich on about July 4 was no occasion for roasting a fatted calf. The father was apparently away on state business, but Myconius had planned a way to effect his reconciliation with Conrad in due course.

Meanwhile, Grebel "has returned to the paternal roof in Zurich, weary of life, and filled with uncertainty and anxiety about the future. In the autumn of 1514, he had left that roof full of youth and enthusiasm, riding out into the world equipped with everything that the heart could desire—money, social prestige, talent, the future bright and large before him; but after six years of university study in Basel, Vienna, and Paris, he returned to his home

> *"Note this: I have said a final farewell to roaming about. . . . In my private study, if it please the gods, I shall read something from Lucian and I shall taste the wit and elegance of the Greek epigrams. But this will probably be my last exercise in the literature of both languages. I have been most unsuccessful in devoting diligent attention to my studious inclinations, troubled by intolerable calamities. . . . I have loved them, and I love them now, you know how."*
> *—Grebel to Vadian, November 2, 1521.*

frustrated and in conflict, a relative failure. In this mood he struggled for two [more] years before finding the way out" (HSB, p. 53).

In our drama, these two years comprise Act 3, appropriately entitled "The Seeker." The act opens with a note of thanks to his faithful intercessor.

Greetings, my Oswald.

Your letter was luckily delivered to me on the road two days out of Paris[1] by my friend Publicola[2] (for some students who had previously met with Glarean met us).[3] I was delighted with the letter when I opened it and read it, as much as anyone possibly can be and as you would scarcely believe, or perhaps as you do believe if you know me inwardly. You do know, at least, that I am always extremely eager for you and your letters. You are assured of this and therefore you write to me often, and often by these wonderful pleasures you call me out of my sad and afflicted self and lighten my brow. You endeavor to do what Vadian endeavors to neglect. Although I try to be magnanimous and disregard and discount such petty things, I would not wish you ever to fall silent like him. But let me confess in all sincerity that I have never expected this of you, nor would I ever.

Now as to Glarean, he said after greeting me that he was not yet fully recovered from an injury he incurred after a fall from his horse,[4] and he wished to rest for two days and recover his strength before proceeding to Paris, though he could have reached his destination in two days even with tired horses.

I have had the copy of Asconius bought in your name and bound very elegantly, and the cost is half a gold piece.[5]

As for me, what action father will take I must divine from you rather than from him.[6] Whatever it is, you will know too. You do not know how indebted I am to you for writing to me often. I beg you never to cease writing, and I for my part will never be remiss. But let me correspond more cheerfully in our old laudable way.

Please send my sincere regards to Xylotectus, a most cultured and learned man,[7] your wife, son, and my friend Conrad.[8] Good-bye my dear Oswald and best wishes.

July 6, 1520. Zurich.

Conrad Grebel, your brother, if you will.

> If one whom I revere with love that's true
> Revoke his prior sway, let death ensue.
> Three ties bind you to me, a steadfast friend:
> A kindness that obliges without end,
> A candor unrestrained, and oft a line
> Brings cheer for gloom, a thousand joys assign.

Not even gifts of scholarship are sure
To join our trust and make it to endure.
But this awes me: Apollo[9] often girds
One at the point of doom with gracious words.

[P.S.] Please forgive the meter if it limps, but the verses came so quickly that I fear the feet[10] might have tripped over the rather inelegant rough stones.

Original: Staatsarchiv Zurich, EI.1, No.34
Transcription: MQR, II, pp. 238-39

18
Grebel to Vadian
Zurich, July 13, 1520

On his return to Zurich, Grebel had little to do. It took two months to get his books from Paris. He had few close friends. His parents were "appeased" but not above "tears" or "scorn." The vacuum in his life is indicated by the fact that he wrote five letters to Myconius and Vadian in the three weeks after his arrival. He still had not heard from Vadian or Martha after nearly ten months of silence (see 16/Intro., above). If he could have waited four more days, he would have had letters from both of them (see 19/110/11); but because he could not count on that (see fn. 3, below), he wrote the following letter. The death of their sister Euphrosine would have been sufficient reason to write; but that entry comes later in the letter, following another lengthy reproach for the intolerable silence.

Greetings, most eminent man.

When I left here you admonished me in a letter that I should compensate for my absence, which would be an age for you, by writing. I did this so diligently that no one ever departed from me to you without a letter; and I outdid myself in this most of all because you promised me always to write. When you demonstrated what this meant, that your letters to Conrad appeared no more than those which are never seen or which hide in Cimmerian darkness,[1] I began to wonder to myself what sin I had committed against you to turn you from a tuneful poet into a mute brother-in-law.[2] That comment in your one and only letter[3] excused you indeed when you wrote that you feared that your letters were not being delivered. By Mercury,[4] you are a cautious man, wishing not to entrust your words recklessly to sheets of paper nor to just any female hawker,[5] but you will deliver them only through the throat.[6]

Then finally you invented other reasons: it was because messengers were seldom there when you were about to write that you were never able to write; but the truth is you were never willing when a million chanced to be at hand. But why do I reprove a brother-in-law? Again I turned it over in my mind. Paper must be got from another continent, from Africa; the reed of the Nile is not coming into Europe; ink must be sought from the cuttlefish.[7] So the brother-in-law is not able (if he wishes, I say) to reply to so many and so wordy letters, and the immature youth does better to send a reply to another of his own age.[8] See what righteous reasons I have for your silence, and I have suppressed still more (lest I deafen one who already recoils from my words); and you ask whether, if you could labor with the pen for three months—three ages surely—you should not then have to suffer the hardship and misery of composing letters. You will love me for this favor, that I am an instant far-seeking Calchas,[9] who often foresaw the ruin of cities.

But I fear that you may cease to be my Harpocrates[10] or that Angerona Soliniana,[11] whom I recall you read to us an age ago, will now be your role. I gravely fear, I say, for you have not yet put off [the role of] Vadian,[12] that is, of a man in all hours renowned for his courtesy, nor have I, I speak seriously, for I am still immersed in dangerous seas in which, like the stone of Sisyphus,[13] I am tossed now from Scylla to Charybdis[14] and back and forth again. I came to my own home, which is not my own, to friends not my friends, to my appeased parents,[15] both of whom received me in a human way,[16] the one with a father's scorn, the other with a mother's tears. I imitated the two of them in turn. As did the parents, so did the son.

When I returned, sister Euprosine, our vestal virgin, whom I loved not a little, had cast off her mortality.[17] I grieved as much as ever I grieved, and I offered up prayers that she should receive the rewards of her pure life.

I shall send the Asconius[18] soon, when it comes. When I was on horseback on the journey two days out of Paris, I met Glarean, and he informed me that he was still suffering from the fall from his horse.[19] I know you will wonder whether I laughed. Do not wonder. I laughed as much as Philistion[20] ever did. I await the coming of you and of sister. Give my regards to your parents and to all yours in the name of us all.
Zurich, from my parents' house, 3 Ides,[21] 1520.

Conrad, your most devoted brother-in-law.
[P.S.] I have left enough of the paper clean if perhaps you wish to write back. I am jesting by our Graces[22] and do not take it badly. But snatch it now, and may the gods snatch me away if I could have added any more.

To the lord Joachim Vadian, doctor, orator, and poet, thrice famous and learned, most revered by his brother-in-law.

Original: Stadtbibliothek (Vadiana) St. Gallen, VB.I.179
Transcription: VB, II, No. 230

19
Grebel to Vadian
Zurich, July 17, 1520

After a silence of ten months, Grebel finally received two letters from St. Gallen, one from Vadian and one from Martha. The former was only the second letter from Vadian since Grebel left Zurich nearly twenty-two months earlier. No wonder Grebel was pleased to receive it, having written seven to Vadian during that time, not counting the present one, No. 19. But he was also irked by Vadian's charge of ingratitude and dual personality, and he tried hard to respond to these reproaches in a lighter than usual mood, playing with Greek figures of speech and beginning here for the first time to use some of the Greek phrases that he was learning.

G[reeting].

I received your two letters[1] (which you entrusted to dependable messengers) as I cherish, love, and admire you always. First, in the former you rebuked me at the end of the letter; then in the latter, you even invited me to come, and you so besought me that you seemed to suffer from my absence and to be able no longer to do without Conrad. If this is so—and I have no doubt that it is—I shall come as quickly as possible. However, I should wish very much to await the Asconius[2] and something else that I would not want father to see and that will be delivered from Basel[3] to me here, so that I may come to you with my Iliad[4] as my companion and your gift of the Pedianus.[5]

Meanwhile, since you depict me everywhere to be a double person,[6] namely, judge and plaintiff in my own trial and everything but Jupiter Fulminator,[7] I am amazed that, making a fly out of an elephant,[8] you do not impute σκιομαχίαν [shadowboxing][9] to your Jupiter Grebel. But to fight with shadows was too lowly for the majesty of the Homeric Thunderer,[10] who can guide all the gods at once by the slightest will, who can call them forth and if he wills suspend them by a chain from the heavens as claimed. So I rather wish that you had said αἰγεριομαχίαν [goat boxing],[11] if like you I may invent a term; why, I ask, was it not so disgraceful to Jupiter that Homer often delighted to call him αἰγίοχον [the aegis-bearer][12], so magnificent a title for Jupiter, which surely means that he was suckled by a goat, or that this saying was not undignified: quarreling over goat's fleece.[13]

What is this, that you say I do not acknowledge your many kindnesses to me? Take care lest you at the same time accuse and condemn a man in whom no sin has so small a place, indeed no place at all, than does that pestilent but nonetheless widespread sin of ingratitude. I acknowledge whatever you have done and I give you the greatest thanks I possibly can, and I admit that I owe you more than any other man;[14] but since I wrote so rashly, disturbed by the paucity of your letters, you inferred immediately that I was not acknowledging your kindnesses. As to whether or not I took them for granted, whether or not I feel indebted for them, what I intended when I blabbed[15] everything out, which you perhaps did not read with an impartial mind, whether I would have become an enemy to Vadian, and finally about the accusations that were written and innumerable other things—when I come as a guest to your house, I will prattle[16] about them more fully, more safely, more confidently (although I did speak too confidently the last time and without due respect for your great learning and your age). But prattle I shall, since you promise to spend whole days in deep reflection with me, since thus you invite and await me as you neither could nor would more eagerly await an exiled brother.

And your parents invite and call him too, and your Grebelia,[17] your little heart as you say, and also the priests.[18] So to come to them I shall devour the road, but on what day I have not yet decided; and I would come more freely if I knew that you would moderate your splendid entertainment and your excessive courtesy. And would that I would find at your home when I come the simplicity you promised in your letter, without need for apology, rather than sumptuous banquets at which studied speeches, like in some public assembly, have to be made to prove that one is grateful.[19] Please tell me not to fear these things and please ask me not to wish to spurn frugality and I will not visit you in fear of lavish kindness without frugality.

To my sister,[20] who longs for me, I will not unwillingly give my tender thanks in person when I come. The reason that sister received no letter from me in return—and this is my excuse—is as follows: I had to write pages to the merchant at Basel[21] to persuade him by entreaties to cause my things to follow their owner without delay; and I also had to send a letter of respect to Zilianus,[22] who gave you a French sword for a gift; the whole of another day was wasted in finding messengers and other business, and so I was unable to fulfill my duties as a brother and writer to her. She will forgive me, I trust, when you tell her the cause; and you will no less grant me pardon for speaking too freely, forwardly, and shamelessly to you. The heart of a good man can turn again and be changed, as the famous teacher of Achilles said,[23] nor was I so disturbed in France that there was no hope of an end to our war, if war there was, as you expected and as you say you feared. I will add nothing more to all the many things that I have said.

I send my prayers to all your family, indeed mine, and my family here sends their prayers too. Farewell with your family until I hasten to come under the most favorable auspices.

From Zurich. July 17, 1520.

Conrad, truly yours.

> Strange thing: ere now you thought me Ζεύ*ς ἀστεροποίτης*
> [Lightning Zeus],[24]
> Who hurls his borrowed bolts from Gallic sky.
> Now vexed, you grant but *σχιονμαΧίαν* [shadowfight] to Zeus
> But poet[25] grows from elephant a fly.[26]

To the lord doctor Joachim Vadian, poet and most eloquent orator, most revered of all kinsmen.

Original: Stadtbibliothek (Vadiana) St. Gallen, VB.I.202
Transcription: VB, II, No. 202

19A
Zwingli to Myconius
Zurich, July 24, 1520

Myconius was schoolmaster in his hometown of Luzern from 1518 to 1522, but it was a period of intense conflict for him because of his Reformation activity in a conservative Roman Catholic stronghold. At the same time, Zwingli's preaching in Zurich was rapidly gaining opponents as well as adherents, the former coming chiefly from several canons in the local ecclesiastical hierarchy and from the monks of the three monasteries in Zurich—Dominican, Franciscan, and Augustinian. These conservative clerics were determined foes of change in what they believed to be divinely ordained and essential church ceremonies. They had considerable power in the canton and diocese; and the safety of Zwingli, as of Myconius in Luzern, was not at all assured. In a letter to Myconius dated the last day of the previous year, Zwingli had written, "As to that base herd of antichrists accusing me first of imprudence and then of impudence, you ought to hear that calmly, for now I begin to be not the only heretic, though they meanwhile are boldly, not to say lyingly, asserting it. . . . As to their assertion that my doctrine (it is Christ's and not mine) is of the devil, that is alright. For in this assertion I recognize the doctrine of Christ and myself as its true herald. Likewise the Pharisees declared that Christ had a devil, and that they were in the right" (Jackson, 1900, p. 146). The following letter is included in our collection for three reasons: (1) It is the first of fourteen writings of Zwingli included, and it is a good representation of his first two years in Zurich. (2) The letter reveals the Nachfolge (discipleship) motif of his earlier writings which Anabaptism was later to develop at greater length—the righteousness of God in Christ as revelation of what man should be and the place of suffering in a faithful witness to that revelation. (3) The letter helps to set the stage for the development of the Reformation in Switzerland at the moment of Grebel's return to his home country in relation to such influential leaders as Myconius, Zwingli, and Luther. Note that Grebel writes to Myconius on the very next day (see No. 20, below), and note Zwingli's reference to a Bible study group "with some beginners" that may well have included Grebel (see 115/13; 47E/186/ 26).

Your spirit is troubled, dearest Myconius, by the uncertainty of our time.[1] Indeed, everything is in such up-and-down ferment,[2] everything is so confused, that no one is able to recognize the original shape of things. Yes, confusion is so general that nothing can advance to the fore but that the exact opposite also appears from the other side.... The mighty hope for a renaissance of Christ and the gospel has also awakened, for many good and learned men have begun to steer with oars and sails[3] (as the saying goes) toward the goal of bringing the seed to fruition. But this hope is weakened when one sees the weeds sown among the seeds by the enemy while people are sleeping or not on their guard.[4] And since the weeds have already taken deep root, it is to be feared that they have by this time entwined themselves so intimately with the roots of the wheat that the wheat cannot be purged of them ἀκινδύνως [without danger]. What can be done to remedy this, you ask? Listen to Christ: "Let them grow together quietly, until the harvest time, etc."[5] Thus, my very prudent Myconius, the gold must pass through the fire and the silver must be purified of its dross. Christ said to the disciples, "In the world you have suppression,"[6] and at another time, "And you will be hated by all men for my name's sake,"[7] and "The hour is coming when whoever kills you will think he is serving God."[8] ... Yes, as I teach Christians, we shall never lack those who persecute Christ in us, even though they proceed most arrogantly in the very name of Christ. For only he is a Christian who has the mark by which Christ wants his own to be recognized, when he said, "By this, as by a sign, will all men know that you are my disciples, if you do what I have commanded you."[9] ... Man's life on earth is a warfare. Armed with Paul's weapons, he must fight in battle array[10] who wants to acquire the reputation of having felled this world which has raised itself on high like a Goliath, to overthrow it with three very clear pebbles....[11] Did not Christ speak of many kinds of seeds, of which only a fraction fall on good soil?[12] Did he not affirm that he had come to cast a fire upon the earth and concerning which he wished that it would flare up brightly?[13] How could we more correctly interpret it than by understanding this fire to be steadfastness in trials, a steadfastness that makes us hate even our parents[14] when they try to lead us back into unfaithfulness or receive our brother who is delivering us to death?[15] Is this not the fire that proves the character of

113

each man's work, whether he goes into the battle for the honor of this world or of Christ?.... All these things are said to us so that I may encourage running,[16] as it is said, and so that pressing on,[17] I might enlist many soldiers for Christ, who one day are to fight courageously for him, to give them more and more courage so that the more cruelly persecution strikes, so much the less will they take to their heels. For I also want to tell you this openly: I believe that as the church was brought forth in blood, so it can be renewed through blood and in no other way. Continue therefore to preach only Christ to your charges; yes, precisely the greater the ignorance you see growing in his church, the more people you must arm properly, so that, like Hercules,[18] they will little by little clean the stables after so many bulls without letting themselves be stopped or lose courage even though whole swarms of insect pests buzz around them. And of course, they cannot expect any reward in this world and must not have been offended if they displease men very much, so long as they whisper to themselves, "If I were still pleasing men, I would not be a servant of Christ."[19] Or as a summary of everything, I teach that "blessed are those who are persecuted for righteousness' sake, etc."[20] Never will the world agree with Christ and that reward that was promised by Christ with persecution....

For Luther's life I fear very little, for his soul not at all, even if the ban-bolt of that Jupiter be launched against him,[21] not because I belittle excommunication but because I believe that such condemnation strikes the body more than the soul, if it is unjustly inflicted. But whether men are dealing justly or unjustly with Luther is not mine to decide. Nevertheless, you already know my views. One of these days I am going to the papal legate William[22]; and as soon as the conversation on this subject opens as it has before, I will urge him to warn the pope not to issue an excommunication, because I think it would be greatly to his own advantage [not to do so]. For if it is issued, I predict that the Germans will despise the ban and pope alike. But be of good cheer, for our time will never lack those who teach Christ faithfully, and who are willing to give up their lives for him, even though their names are very badly reported among men after this life, since that is already beginning, namely, that he has been called a heretic, a corrupter, a good-for-nothing. Of course, among the kind of men saying this, it is truthful men who are counted as corrupters. As far as I am concerned, I look for all evil from all men, I mean ecclesiastics and laymen. I beseech Christ for this one thing only, that he will enable me to endure all things courageously, and that he will break or form me, his potter's vessel,[23] as it pleases him. If I be excommunicated,[24] I shall think of the learned and saintly Hilary,[25] who was banished from France to Africa, and of Lucius,[26] who though expelled from his seat at Rome was returned again with great honor. Not that I compare myself with them, but I would take this comfort with them, that inasmuch as they were better than I, they suffered the greater ignominy though they were innocent. And yet if it be permitted to glory, I would rejoice to suffer insult for the name of Christ. But let whoever thinks that he stands take heed lest he fall![27] I have read scarcely anything of Luther's lately, but what I have seen of his writings so far does not seem to me to stray from evangelical teaching.[28] You know, if you recall, that what I have always said in terms of the highest commendation of him is that he establishes his position with authoritative witnesses, etc....

I am determined to take up Hebrew again in the next few days, for if Christ is willing, I would like to read the Psalms with some beginners next December and the next [Lenten] fast.... Farewell in Christ.

Original: Not extant, but see Epistolae 1536, fol.173bff., Opera 1581, Tom.I, 412f.
Transcription: ZW, VII, No. 151

20
Grebel to Myconius
Zurich, July 25, 1520

The contrast between Letters 19A and 20, both written to Myconius, is evident: Grebel is still preoccupied with his readjustment to life at home and seems unaware of the evangelical concerns that Zwingli was discussing so poignantly. Thanks to Myconius, Grebel's reconciliation with his parents has been completed and he can talk of accompanying his father on state business to Luzern to visit the two friends with whom he made the expedition to Mt. Pilatus two years before.

G[reeting].

I received your letter with great delight, not just because of your pleasure in my homecoming, but especially because of your long and newly evident friendship. Your reconciling my angry father to me so nobly has long since convinced me that your love for me is far above the common sort; and by constant intervention on my behalf, you may have appeased him again.[1] But most of all you gave encouragement to a man of no refinement[2] and in no way like yourself in the splendor of your learning. And so you could not bear witness to your love unless you were disposed of your own accord to make it evident. As often as you do this, you seem to reveal my own dreams[3] and to count my fingers and nails.[4] You see that it is not difficult for you to show me your feeling toward me, and it is easy to obtain what you desire from one already convinced.

I in turn need not recount at length my loyalty to you. Let me tell you only this much for your information: after my parents, to whom is due the highest degree of love, I can hardly number one or two that I respect more deeply than you and to whom I would wish to be more bound and committed, nor, I say, is there anyone for whom I would strive with more zeal and loyalty to do a favor as often as ability and energy permit. More of this later.

The Swiss Diet soon to be held in your city nearly summoned me,[5] and if father had been sent with the delegation I undoubtedly would have accompanied him to Luzern, and the only thing I would have sought and admired there would have been my friend Oswald and his family, and my friend John Xylotectus,[6] men so learned, so cultured, and what means much to me, so affectionate toward me that even if father should never go there, I shall go on a visit sometime myself. Perhaps it will be when Fortune[7] successfully brings me back from Vadian. Meanwhile, as I wait for some of my books, I cannot leave, and I can hardly tolerate the unwanted delay. I hope you do the same, while you are waiting for the arrival of your much-desired Asconius[8]; but it will grow feathers yet and fly to you. I jest.

I will tell Vadian the matter you entrusted to me. If Clivanus's[9] copy of Livy[10] is here or at his place, I will send it. Hold on to my copy of Juvenal[11] until yours is bound. Now let me be careful to add no nonsense that might offend you. There are stories about some townsmen of yours who did not act wisely in dealing with the Duke of Württemberg,[12] a Phalaris[13] and a curse to Switzerland. And there are some mischievous rumors here about the plague. However, Conrad will select more cheerful subjects as this sort of thing should not be entrusted to a letter. If I can help it, I do not want to write sorrowful epistles.[14] Farewell.

My regards to all yours, your family, John M. Xylotectus,[15] and others. Best wishes to you, Oswald, of all my friends.
Zurich. On St. James Day [July 25] 1520.

Your Conrad.

Original: Staatsarchiv Zurich, EI, 340, fol.10
Transcription: MQR, II, pp. 239-40

21
Grebel to Vadian
Zurich, July 29, 1520

According to the following letter, Vadian has invited Conrad to St. Gallen "three times to date," but Grebel cannot leave until his books arrive from Paris, which did not actually happen until the middle of September. The delay frustrates other members of the Grebel family, who are eager to have him visit Martha and Vadian; but what they cannot know is that the shipment from Paris contains some secret items which "father must not see."

G[reeting].

I would [not][1] want you to think that the smoke of his homeland is more welcome to the wandering Ulysses[2] than yours and that I strain to come at a later time to you who long as much to see me. There are not that many of my old friends who could hold me back with their company for even one day, and thus tear me away from Vadian. Nor has any Thais of Zurich,[3] to clear myself of guilt on this, put a spell on me after my arrival, or with Circean brews[4] turned me into another being, one who refuses so often to visit those who give invitations. But the whole reason why I am not with you is that I am awaiting my books,[5] among which are other things which my father must not see. If they come in a week, or if they do not, I will then be unable to feign an excuse for not taking to the road, since I had not thought to feign any, and at no turtle's pace, but flying there as quickly as possible.

My parents have ordered me to assure you that this is the reason. It is the wish of everyone that I visit you, and especially of those who might have wished me to depart, the books not awaited.[6] If I might have wished for them especially much, then in fact I have so wished,[7] but I fear that in my absence father would see some bird flying over which I do not wish for fathers to see.[8] After having been invited by you three times to date, I am writing this in reply. Give my regards to my sister, to all your family, who are also mine. Farewell, most beloved of teachers and most revered of relatives. Ours send their greetings to you and all.

Zurich, 29 July, in the year 1520.

Yours, Conrad Grebel.
To the lord doctor, Joachim Vadian, poet and laureate orator, most revered of all men.

Original: Stadtbibliothek (Vadiana) St. Gallen, VB.I.205
Transcription: VB, II, No. 205

22
Grebel to Vadian
Zurich, August 3, 1520

This letter is the fourth by Grebel to Vadian within a three-week period, concerned mainly with plans for his visit to St. Gallen. What is special about it, apart from the visit of sister Barbara and her daughters to escape the plague, was his reference to having read the Philirenus *of Myconius and a letter of Erasmus regarding the "Luther affair," both in manuscript form. Apparently, Myconius asked Grebel to evaluate them with a view to their possible publication.*

Greetings, my glory, dearest of men.

Fortunately, since to date I have not been able to get away at all because my books have not yet arrived, my sister[1] and her two daughters visited us, fleeing the plague[2] but leaving her husband behind, though only upon his insistence.[3] Now that I have received her as a brother, I shall be able to stay with you longer than if she had come in my absence, for then I should have felt obliged to return in haste to fulfill my duty toward her.

You meanwhile are tormented with desire for me along with many other things, as your letter indicates. I could wish very much to be or to become worthy of such expectation, to be humane[4] in your presence and of character[5] acceptable to you. If I shall not so appear, it will be the task of you all so to receive the uncorrupted loyalty of my mind toward you, that you cannot believe that there is anymore refinement to be gotten from me, even from that man, as he was, in separation from the companionship that is peculiar to you, who wants very much to be equal to all occasions so that it is not possible for him to approach even a finger's width closer.[6] However it may be, you are not unaware what sort of man I am; and still you invited me so persistently that, were you my enemy, I would not want to stay away. I have written for the third time to the merchant at Basel[7]; and I hope finally to obtain what is delaying me. In the meanwhile, I shall console my sister, who weeps much over the fate of her sister.[8]

For your expression of concern for my welfare, lest upon my return to my native climate I might be taken from the midst of men, I thank you very much. I beg you, however, not to be concerned about this matter, for there is no certain report as yet that the plague is making its rounds among us.

This Mars[9] has now begun to rage in Paris, as I learned from the letters of Glarean[10] and others which were given to me. But I shall relate all these things when I see you. With nothing else to do, I have read the *Phili-*

renus, Myconius' dialogue "on not going to war," which by reason of its truth deserves to become a classic.[11] I saw the epistle of Erasmus which had much to do with the Luther affair.[12] Both items are to be printed and to be out to the public, and Myconius wanted them back almost before he had sent them, so there is no chance to send them on for your judgment. Well, you can do without them. Take it for the best.

The servant girl knows when I wrote this letter and how long I anticipated her departure.[13] My parents and two sisters[14] wish you and your whole family good health, nor would I wish less. I have nothing further to write. So good-bye, my stay and strength, and may you all live happily. Zurich. 3 August 1520.

Your Conrad.

To the lord doctor Joachim Vadian, poet and orator laureate, his dearest kinsman.

Original: Stadtbibliothek (Vadiana) St. Gallen
Transcription: VB, II, No. 207

23
Grebel to Vadian
Zurich, September 11, 1520

The books that Grebel awaited for two months have finally arrived from Paris, but he still is not free to go to St. Gallen. He is temporarily tied up in his father's iron shop or foundry, since Jacob is away on missions of state, and Beatus, the new manager, is just learning the business. Meanwhile, in the following letter, under the inspiration of his new knowledge of Greek, Grebel becomes Vadian's teacher for two paragraphs and delights in the momentary reversal of roles. He finally remembers to forward the letter from Tschudi (16A, above), which he brought along from Paris.

G[reeting].

You think you have waited a year; indeed, I have hurried a whole lifetime to come to you. And the books have been delivered so that I am less detained.[1] But then the business of our iron shop was pressing; and since father was away on a mission and Beatus is not yet experienced in the work, I was forced to stay with it.[2] Now, after father has returned, I do not see what should delay my departure, unless the coming market[3] should occasion something, and I, poor wretch, should be compelled to tarry longer. Nor has fear of the plague frightened me, as you feared, since I heard by chance that it was raging among you.

Then what you say, that if I did not want to visit you though urged by so many letters, I should come for the sake of my sister.[4] May the gods utterly destroy me if I do not long to see you, to greet you from my heart, to venerate you, and when welcomed by your hospitality to love you. But what will you do with a creature who is dragged at a father's feet,[5] not to mention my lack of initiative in this matter? May the gods above, I hope, and a propitious Mercury,[6] grant the fulfillment of my heart's most ardent desire, that is, that by your kindness I shall be released from this prison of my native city and sent there, where I hope there dwells the Lethe of my cares[7] and there flows the perpetual ocean of joys,[8] where there waits for me, I say, a man whom I venerate in place of Apollo, the Muses, and all the Graces,[9] my star, my life. I lie not; if I flatter, may I die.

In the meanwhile, in my absence, enjoy this Asconius,[10] and also the *Paraphrases*.[11] The former I send to you as a wedding gift, the latter is from Zwingli.[12] The volume of *Antibarbarians*[13] is for you also, plus my Greek-Latin Aesop with its supplements,[14] if you are going to read Greek. I wish that you would not be without the works of Lucian[15] and Homer and would obtain from somewhere a copy of the *Iliad* at least, for this reason, that if you intend to become familiar with the oracles of this prince of the Greek poets,[16] you would be able to read this work with the help of my collection of notes, written especially for this purpose. I can hardly get along without them when I am especially engaged in my study, such as it is (when business permits).

If, like the pig to Minerva,[17] I am able to advise you at all, do not scorn my rashness; not that you could learn anything from me, whose descendants and forebears you have taught and do teach, but that there be someone to furnish you with the opportunity of stopping up the mouths of the slanderers, who, if it pleases the gods, taunt you with nothing other than the malevolence of the fates and of places, because you have not pursued the knowledge of Greek literature. You will gratify me as well as yourself, and what they took so many years to grasp, you will gain in a far shorter time. You will believe it, moreover, after you have barely saluted those Attic venerables[18] from the threshold. I will bring with me the *Dialogues* of Hutten,[19] each Homer, and if it pleases your fancy, the fables of Aesop and two books of the *Odyssey* for you to keep.

Regarding the two hundred guilders, father did not reply when I wrote to inquire; therefore it happens that I also can remit nothing; but I shall see to it, provided it does not seem unwise to him, that I bring it along.[20]

They say that our neighbors engaged in battle with the Rotweilers[21] and came off the better and inflicted heavy losses on them. I do not yet believe it, since I have often been misled by uncertain rumor. Our legate

120

Puccius[22] has returned so that he might reconcile the Swiss and the French.

Read the letter of Peter Tschudi[23] and smile, if for no other reason than that he speaks and thinks about you most sincerely. All mine send their prayers to you. Until I come, extend my prayers to your family.
Zurich. On the day of Saints Felix and Regula, 1520.

Conrad Grebel, ever yours.

To the lord Joachim Vadian, doctor of medicine, poet and laureate orator, most revered kinsman.

Original: Stadtbibliothek (Vadiana) St. Gallen, VB.I.190
Transcription: VB, VII (Ergänzungsband), No. 10

23A
Jacob Grebel to Vadian
Zurich, October 17, 1520

At last about the middle of October, Conrad went to St. Gallen for the long-anticipated reunion with Vadian and Martha. He could have been the carrier of the following letters 23A and 23B, except that Jacob preferred to send the large payment on Martha's dowry by special messenger, and Myconius arrived in Zurich after Conrad's departure. Jacob's letter deals primarily with the installment on Martha's marriage contract but also reports the securing of a two-year papal stipend for Conrad to study at the University of Pisa. The reader will tremble at the prospect of another financial arrangement so soon after the crisis of the French connection so poignantly exposed in Letter No. 13; but one of Conrad's purposes for the visit to Vadian, apart from the renewing of their relationship, was to seek his counsel on his future plans with particular reference to the advantages and disadvantages of going to Italy and the wisdom of accepting the papal grant. The excerpt from the letter of Myconius is interesting primarily as further attestation of his affection for Conrad.

First, my cordial greeting and wish for everything good.
Dear doctor:

Know that by divine grace we are all in good health and spirits. We always hope to hear the same and everything good from you.

I send you herewith these two letters. Will you please place your seal on the one and return it to me.[1] I am also sending you 120 crowns,[2] made up of 165 guilders in coin, 16 batzen to the gulden, and in addition, 35 guilders in solid plapharten and other coinage, making altogether 200 guilders,[3] 16 batzen to the gulden. Please do not be offended by this first payment—though I am quite ashamed of it, for it was my intention to give you the sum provided for in the marriage agreement.[4] But according to your wish and my ability, I will always be at your disposal. To the same extent that she desires to keep these bonds intact, mother wishes to do the best thing and settle this account next year together with the others. It would be my advice that you indicate your reaction, at your discretion, to my fellow administrator, even though he says nothing against me. But it seems to me, it would be honorable for you. And complain about him to his honest wife, God bless her.

Again dear doctor, Conrad has probably told you[5] that I have been with him to see the legate.[6] To this end he was in Baden on the next day. Together with others, I dined with him, and after the meal he drew me aside and told me that he wanted to show him a favor like the others who are at Pisa.[7] For that reason it is my friendly request and desire that you advise him and me what is to be done. For insofar as it would be agreeable to you and him, if he were to begin another two years of study with papal support, it would certainly be of value to him. Whatever then is in my power, I as a father will do at all times. I am sending Conrad a horse so that he may go down there and thank you cordially for all your good will which you have given him. We want very much to greet and extend our best wishes to your father and mother, as our dear brother and sister, as well as to the rest of you.

Recent news here is of large volume and depressing. May the Lord God see fit to frustrate the undertaking of the cities Luzern and Solothurn in conjunction with the duke of Württemberg[8] and other good-for-nothing people. And in Baden some time before Friday after St. Gallen Day. If it is not turned back there, much affliction and toil and bloodshed is to be feared. Question the bleacher who is bringing the horse; he can report all the developments to you. I did not wish to acquire the captaincy,[9] because the responsibility was too great, and one has that then plus other matters to attend to. Even so, I have no special regrets about that, other than in regard to you, that we might have hoped to have more to do with each other. May the Lord God help to bring us together successfully in another way and reveal to us what is good for our body and soul.

Given on Wednesday after St. Gallen's Day in the year [15]20.

Always your very willing Jacob Grebel.

The schoolmaster[10] sends you a letter and one gulden in gold that he collected for you from someone in Luzern.

> To the learned master, Doctor Joachim von Watt, city doctor in St. Gallen, my dear son-in-law.

Original: Stadtbibliothek (Vadiana) St. Gallen, VB.I.223
Transcription: VB, II, No. 221

23B
Myconius to Vadian
Zurich, before October 17, 1520

Greeting. I have performed the duty, dearest and most learned Vadian, of collecting the guilder, which I am now sending over to you.[1] I received it long before now, but never had anyone to whom I could safely entrust it. Restored to health after a very long and severe illness, I have come to Zurich, not the least reason being to visit[2] our Conrad and entrust the money to him, that he might dispatch it to you. In truth, because he was gone,[3] I gave it to his father, who will see to it[4].... I shall write to Conrad.

Original: Stadtbibliothek (Vadiana) St. Gallen, VB.I.231
Transcription: VB, II, No. 229

24
Grebel to Vadian
Zurich, November 7, 1520

Grebel returned to Zurich after a brief visit to St. Gallen. Vadian must have encouraged him to take the papal grant and go to Pisa, for in the following letter Grebel writes that he is preparing for the journey with the medicines that Vadian prescribed. It sounds as though Vadian sent the medicines by messenger along with a letter of further advice and counsel following Grebel's return to Zurich. The advice, having to do with more positive thinking, was timely, for Grebel was quite depressed by his indecision and aimlessness. Along with Vadian's counsel came a special request of some kind, perhaps to write a poem or epigram or introduction for the new edition of the Pomponius Mela *that was being prepared for publication (see 26A, below). Whatever it was, Grebel promised to do it promptly and with "the zeal of a Zwingli."*

Greetings, dearest of men.

When I saw and read your letter and fondled it the way children do with a rattle, you would scarcely believe with what joy it brought back to my mind the magnificent long-lasting benevolence of the Vadian household.[1] It brought this to mind because to be with you and your family is to be in the presence of the Graces,[2] humanity, and benevolence, whenever the gods wished to revive me by such occasions. Believe me.

I am grateful to you that you have so often given me joy, though you have seldom judged me so by the expression on my face, but rather

123

morose. Great God above, how uncouth is my sin;[3] mine it is, but the blame is not mine—alas, alas! But I fear that you may say that I am lamenting again, since you alone are inclined to call me happy before death,[4] against the examples of history, but you do not yet make me such. You say this because you know not where the heel of fortune treads on me, because you know not, let me say it in Greek, how τοξεύω ἀσκοπα [aimless I shoot].[5] What if it were known what a Silenus[6] I am revealed inside? Would you blame me for complaining? I would blame, you say. Well, the reply is: you would blame Niobe for her laments over the death of her children![7] You wonder why I have not opened up; I would have wondered myself, had not shame restrained me; and so near it came to not restraining me on the last night you were here, when I exclaimed:

Ah me! what grief and groaning, naught of mirth,
No joys in my whole breast are finding berth.[8]

O me, whose miserable misery (pity me!) falls nothing short of most miserably miserable,[9] and you say nothing is lacking for happiness. I'll be damned if I have countered you rashly.

Concerning that which you asked me to do, I will do it diligently, promptly, and not reluctantly, but with the zeal of a Zwingli.[10] You command me to send my Attic epigrams of my Mars,[11] that is my Boeotian[12] ones, since they came not from the city but from the country, not from an altar high but from a pigsty.[13] Send them I shall. Assign, signify, command, and enjoin, that I might be able to comply; let me die, if I do not act diligently; try me, I beg you. I shall write you an Iliad of a letter[14] in return for a letter, which will be the last of those to be written in Zurich.[15] I shall write, if it seems good then, my choriambic ode to Puccius,[16] such as it is that you request, such as the poet is. Now you have enough.

I am preparing myself for the journey with the medicines you prescribed.[17] Mureria asks for her letter back.[18] If you love me, if my sister loves me, send it. Expect words from a wordy one, and whatever else you expect. I hope your family is safe, secure, and happy, also my master Benedict Burgauer,[19] the pastor, heartily so, with Master Sebastian Wolfgang Juflius[20] and his family, and Master Bartholomew,[21] separated from Luther,[22] Master Lazarus.[23] Regards to my SISTER,[24] far more beloved than others by the blessing of the most high God. Farewell my joy, best wishes. Zurich, November 7, 1520.

Conrad Grebel, who cares not for himself, when he can be yours.

Please send my regards to the brethren to whom I owe a mutual debt of gratitude, and also to my pastor.[25]

Mother asks you to compound and send the medicine.

Mich wunderet, ob man üch und miner schwöster ansech, dass ir worden

124

sind tsu . . . schel(?). I wonder if by looking at you and my sister, one could tell that you have become too . . . scowling(?)[26]

> To Master Joachim Vadian, a doctor learned in every way, and most loving to his relatives, and to his father.

Original: Stadtbibliothek (Vadiana) St. Gallen, VB.I.223
Transcription: VB, II, No. 223

25
Grebel to Vadian
Zurich, Between November 19 and December 8, 1520

The first of the two following letters was undated and must have been written after November 19, the date of the death of Zwingli's brother referred to in 25/126/3-4 and 25A/128/10-12, and before December 8, when Letter No. 26 was written, telling about the return from the memorial visit to Einsiedeln anticipated in 25/126/34-35. Grebel's main reason for writing was to send the poems he promised in Letter No. 24, but he added two items of news, one humorous and one sad: (1) their respective brothers were on the way somewhere between Zurich and St. Gallen, riding their horses as if they were asses, and (2) Zwingli's brother had died of the plague. The letter as a whole is rather positive, although the note of uncertainty about the move to Italy is still apparent, partly because it involves the terrible risk of another foreign stipend. The epigrams were probably enclosed separately, for the poem appended to the letter was hardly more than a spoof of his "friend who was not a friend" (18/109/20)—George Binder.

Greetings.

Here are two letters for you and two epigrams[1] by your Grebel. Treat them as you will.[2] If there is something I have written poorly or rashly, as I doubt not, delete, replace, as seems best; and if many erasures will still not correct it, let one erasure blot it out altogether with my fullest approval, especially the poems, for I am uncertain what they are, what is their quality, since they have not yet been examined by Zwingli.[3] I ask, however, that my epigram of the previous edition be not printed again.[4]

The man from your wrynecked flock who flays the πρόβατα χρυσόμαλλα [golden-fleeced sheep][5] that is sheep with golden wool, truly the head man,[6] and the one with a big head, my blood relative,[7] are riding to you on horses, if indeed they are not actually riding on asses.[8] Welcome such men reverently, scrupulously, dutifully, ye Gallenite men.[9] Welcome, I say, these Gaulenites who come, since they come as triple Gauls, which is almost like your name, but very unlike your character. They are triple Gauls, lest I keep you in suspense, in faction, morbidity, and arrogance. I know not that they have received the golden eggs as yet. So much for this; now another matter.

Zwingli's brother has died, a young man of great hope.[10] May the gods bless the deceased; and you console the pastor as it should be done. The plague snatched him away alone, and no others, unless I have not heard what no one would be silent about, if it happened that more had died. I am hurrying to Einsiedeln to fulfill a vow to the Blessed Virgin.[11] Then soon, when I return, I shall visit Italy, either Bologna or Pisa. I shall visit them if the Almighty God visits me with his consent.[12] A horse is at hand to bear me and support me.[13] There will be no king, but a greater than a king, a pontiff.[14] O pupil, o patron, o jokes now, but then alas serious things seriously! Read the Dialogue of this youth,[15] so old; for I, lord, who am hardly a pope, have read it. If you love me, you read it too; let the other bosom friends read it too, they who hear the truth, which I so willingly hear, which I will not hear again. For if the fates[16] do not begrudge, I shall bear myself so that no one can say: a rich man is a rogue, or the son of a rich man.[17]

If it should happen that the Swiss should go mad and draft an army,[18] see to it that you become a general among your people, or at least a commander, and when you march into Italy, come as Jupiter Phileus,[19] a powerful divinity with me. I will be the host, as befits such a little man to such a great man. Only do come; you will test it, and you will prove it. You are annoyed, for I write such empty things, things that touch neither heaven nor earth. In truth, I willingly trifle,[20] lest willingly I should have whined.[21] But here I am whining. I did not want to unburden myself. I was no worse off before than now. This I fear, while I am in the mood for whining, that I should be perpetually invalid, that I should be perpetually miserable; for when I quit whining, what will you have to suffer?[22] I think, then, that you would suffer more undeservedly because I would not be able to whine. But when will I not be able to? When to my deaf ear, not by letter, you say farewell, not once, but thrice.[23]

By all the gods, do send the letter to Mureria.[24] Give my regards to your parents, your brothers and sisters, the whole family, Master Benedict the pastor,[25] Master Sebastian,[26] SISTER[27] and in short all your guests. Farewell, o life of mine.

If Binder[28] stopped to see me once a year,
    And if 'twere love impelled him to draw near,
You too "Ave" or Χαῖρε [Hail][29] from him had heard.
    He does not come, and business e'er deterred.
Comes not; to pour forth words for him is work
    Who far surpasses womankind in talk.

126

Never "Good health,"[30] 'tis base to say. The crow
    knows when to say the same to ask for more.
Meanwhile till he bears health[31] to you with zeal,
    If you be well,[32] yourself you cannot heal.

Furthermore

"Good-bye[33] Vadian," he said to you, to me,
    No "Hi," if I be sound and sane, whole be.

Furthermore

Quote Binder, "You I love"; if true, I die.
    He loves to death; I say I'll die; I lie.

Furthermore

If there is time and human law permits
    Divine law too and grim decrees of Fates[34]
That Binder could approach an old time pal,
    For me it's great I'd say and quite enough, it's well,
Still cautious I reflect: refused had he
    My hospitality, not his I'd be.

Furthermore

Binder owes us his soul, the name he bought,
    His right to bear and play the Lyrus pipe,[35]
A hybrid slave and master all at once
    To teach man arms he can, the joyless dunce.
He does not know; for him Vadian, let's pray.
    For what? forever arms[36] to teach alway.

Furthermore

That Binder rarely shares our place of rest
    You think is like a very wary guest.
Or that much business holds him back. This vice
    We swear from evil name may well arise.

Furthermore

Wish you to know my thoughts, how my mind guides,
    About this Binder what my heart decides?
Unless forthwith or ne'er restores what's mine,
    Or does repay,[37] there'll be no second time.

The verses of one written extemporaneously cannot be good whose poems written maturely are bad. As the man, so the speech. The speech of truth is simple, and should not be studied.

            To the lord Joachim Vadian, poet, orator, physician
        thrice famous, a kinsman especially dear.

Original: Stadtbibliothek (Vadiana) St. Gallen, VB.XI.99
Transcription: VB, III, Anhang, Nachtrag No. 69

Greeting,

I am doubtful whether the evils which befall me (if they are evils), ought to be communicated to you, who are a man of most sympathetic disposition. For I fear that if I do not warn you beforehand, you will fall into unrestrained grief, so regardful are you of me. And yet I beseech that you will endure my misfortunes with a calm mind, even as I myself endure them. Because now I endure with equanimity what formerly threw me into spasms of grief and mourning more than feminine, when I was suddenly and unexpectedly overwhelmed with sorrow. Still I recovered, so that now once more I stand firm. Thanks be to God! And so do you take it calmly when I tell you of the death of my brother Andrew, a youth of great promise and excellent parts, whom the plague slew on St. Elizabeth day [November 19], envious (I think) of our blood and renown. Had he lived a year longer, he would have come to you [at Luzern[to be instructed by you and your son in Greek. But so far am I from remonstrating with God that I am ready to offer myself. Enough of this.

I am awaiting your letter and those manifold songs recommended by Zimmerman, for which our people here are looking daily. Farewell, and love me in my bereavement as you are accustomed to do. Except for my loss, the plague grows no worse, for I do not know that within a month or so more than four or five have died. I send my good wishes for your wife and children, Zimmerman, the Provisor, and all.

Zurich, November 25, 1520.

I am not at home, driven out rather by the persuasions of my friends, than by my own fears of death; and I shall soon return. So you will not wonder that this letter is not sealed in my usual fashion. Francis Zinck greets you.

Original: Zurich Staatsarchiv E.II, 338, p. 1336.
Transcription: ZW, VII, No. 164
Translation: Taken from Jackson, 1900, pp. 64-65

26
Grebel to Vadian
Zurich, December 8, 1520

Grebel writes the third letter in sequence since receiving Vadian's last a month earlier, but he now tries hard not to reflect any resentment of this fact, as he had done so bitterly in Letter No. 18, above. But he is not entirely suc-

cessful in this resolve insofar as he imagines Vadian taunting him with the sign of the obscene middle finger. On November 7 he wrote, "I am preparing myself for the journey," and now a month later he still writes, "I am now at last preparing for the journey." The fact is that he never prepared for the journey; but it took him another half year to make a clear-cut decision not to go to Pisa.

Greetings, my Vadian.

I have sent you a number of letters by now. I do not know, of course, whether you have received them since I have not received yours. But it is enough if you are all well[1] and if what I sent with the letter, namely, the *Dialogues*[2] and that Zwinglian revision of the Greek expressions[3] have not been lost. About my own there is no loss if they have perished miserably, for this is deserved. When verbiage[4] is lost it cannot be burdensome; but when it is received and it jabbers, your ears are offended. They are offended, I know. But what will you do with a love that wants to appear so dutiful that it assembles a medley of uncouth words and causes the reader to waste valuable hours? Do not pardon me, pardon a love so loyal,[5] so fervent, yet so fair. Or rather pardon an absence which has no other way to console itself than through the benefit[6] of writing; and in this way, you who are a long distance away might imagine yourself to be present (though in my mind you are never, ever absent) when you send your worthy sheets to us. In this way also I reckon to restore the old friendship with you when through those mute messengers of the mind I blab out freely, charmingly, profusely, whatever casually enters my mind, whatever is on the tip of my tongue,[7] whatever demands to be spewed out. And I observe that that old silence of yours might be able to dissolve many friendships unless it is not able to produce inactivity in me. I also observe many other factors that bring blame upon me for this immoderate chattering.[8] It will be your task to bear it with equanimity: for I should not want you to feel compelled to write back when prevented by the flood of your affairs; and as a strong man is provoked to a fight by insults from a weakling, but hardly in the end either responds or scorns and taunts with his finger,[9] so with you, though I, the essence of ignorance and always impudently full of talk, strive to wrest letters out of a learnedly learned man who returns not a word, unless you have much leisure, when and if it pleases you. You ask why I diagnose it thus?[10] Because I shall reckon it sufficient for me if you love me without testimonial.[11] I will put the above most briefly. Reply when you wish and when you can. I have verily decided to caw like a crow until I am hoarse (unless someday I am radically changed).[12] So henceforth, as I have warned you, I will add no defenses for my much talking, unless you urge me.

When Beatus[13] and I entered the castle of Wädenswil[14] on our return from Einsiedeln,[15] we were received very courteously and treated magnificently, and also given much honor. But above all, the brief visit with Margaret,[16] a girl born under not unfavorable Graces[17] and beauty, delighted me more than anything else or any other girl, especially since she mentioned your presence and reported what you had been through with them to escape the plague, and what she had been through for you and because of you. When ready to depart, I presented her with no small memento and one of silver at that; and she with a little handkerchief and letter sent to Zurich renewed my affection for her.[18] How I wish, my dear Vadian, to do all we can for this blood relative by a pleasing and fitting marriage, and I would that it might be among you rather than among others.

I am now at last preparing for the journey, to make my way to Pisa.[19] I would have preferred to go to Saxony for certain sweet reasons;[20] I do not understand what prevents this. So I shall set out. The best of health to you, and no less to your equally dear wife, Martha, yours and mine; do love me in return and do not neglect me. Pray for a favorable journey, and a safe departure and an equally safe return. I pray that you may have your heart's desire. Good-bye, dearest friend, again and again, and a third time, good-bye, which is final, and rejoice together, if you can, with these loving tears I am about to shed. If you feel impelled, do reply.
Zurich. 8th of December, 1520.

Conrad Grebel, your friend from the inmost sanctuary of his heart.

Tell sister, please, I bid her well, the same to all your friends, to the pastor and fellow worker,[21] Master Sebastian,[22] to all my friends. I hope that sister is not upset that she has not had a letter. Before I leave here, perhaps she will get one, when I get the chance to fulfill the love that prompts me. Even though I speak not, I so love her from the heart that I could not more. She will take this well, unless I am mistaken.

Mother is waiting for the medicine,[23] and please tell her how much it costs. All my friends, who are no less yours, send you all their best wishes.

Εἴποτε, τί πράξω, ἀδαήμων ἐμέ γε μεταλλᾶς·
ἄσκοπα τοξεύω, κρόμμυα πάντα φάγω.
Χαῖρε σὺ καὶ μὲ ἔα τείρεσθ᾽ οὐκ ὄλβιον ὄντα,
ἡ κακά μοι κλώθει μοῖρ᾽ ὀλοωτάτη.

[Ask you what evil, now that I do:
     Aimless I shoot; onions[24] I chew.
Greetings, and leave me joyless to grieve,
     My awful lot Moera[25] to weave.]

Original: Stadtbibliothek (Vadiana) St. Gallen, VB.I.224
Transcription: VB, II, No. 224

26A
Grebel's Address "To the True Fair Reader"
Zurich, December 24, 1520

Grebel's address to the vere candido lectori *was the Introduction to the second edition of Vadian's* Pomponius Mela, *to be published in Cratander's printshop in Basel in January 1522. As it turned out, Grebel spent two months working on the project in Basel in the autumn of 1521.*

CONRAD GREBEL OF ZURICH, HELVETIA, TO THE TRUE FAIR READER [Introduction to the Basel edition of Vadian's *Pomponius Mela,* 1522]

Behold, fair reader, Pomponius[1] reborn through the labor of Vadian so that he may now present himself before the faces of students and learned alike, now that he is enlarged at many points, neater in not a few places, more accurate in countless passages, and to catch it all in a phrase, more perfect in all respects.

Surely to the previous edition, unless you were bristling with malice,[2] you owed your admiration. To this one, unless you are the epitome of Gallic contemptuousness and spite, you will owe your veneration for many reasons. Owe it you will if you want to gain with a minimum of effort an intimate knowledge of the marvelous majesty of Mother Nature. Owe it you will (I had better add) if you prefer to gain the most out of this most noble study. But this is not the place to impress such benefit upon you, which I think is only to be attained by an understanding perusal of Mela[3] and a searching consideration of this commentary. I not only believe this, I also proclaim it.

Geography he now teaches, foremost of golden studies and one not to be carelessly embraced. Since his day no one teaches it so happily and no one so learnedly. But certain points had need of restoration so that the [original] author himself could recognize them as his own. Some things had to be removed. Most points were in need of an interpreter who is trustworthy, and more importantly an interpreter thoroughly versed in obscure lore and especially erudite.

And so my friend Vadian and yours too because of this contribution performed all these tasks for our sake. By the untiring search of sources and the skilled investigation of passages, he has deliberately and independently restored a number of them. He has so elucidated others that one is compelled to believe they could not have survived without this light put upon them. What of those passages which had been assailed by not a few men of prestige whom he with the finger[4] provoked to make the severest criticisms with fabrications of their own rather than with studied arguments worthy of the community of lettered men? He has dealt with all of these in a courageous way. As a matter of truth Vadian has not placed his writings outside the common lot, but has thought and felt and believed that that is where they ought to be placed. In this common lottery are tossed the literary monuments of even the most widely accepted of ancient authors and monuments which gain scant favor or none at all among some persons, to wit, φιλαυτοὺς [egoists] who are jealous of another's glory. But among other persons, those namely who are cultivated to the highest excellence of learning and are unbiased judges, these monuments are approved and dedicated to the supreme deity of books for a venerable eternity.

Do you know what I am aiming at? Just this, that for the sake of your own benefit you will imitate the latter class. And you will be imitating them precisely when you not only think well of this man but speak well of him also. For unless he had sincerely desired to consult for your own best interests (although admittedly he has also had an eye to his own reputation, and that too, good heavens, by the example of many men, perhaps all men), he would not with such scrupulous care have improved for issuance to the public these annotations which are certain to be authoritative and valuable to you. These annotations are such, I for my part make bold to assert (and my judgment is not misled by the expert and favorable opinion of illustrious men, nor does kinship influence me; but an answer must be made to the doggish snarls of the envious, or at least they must be confronted). They are of the sort, I declare, that Μωμήσεται τις μᾶλλον 'ἢ μνμήσεται [sic], καὶ ὧν κλέος οὔποτε οιχήοεται [someone will sooner find fault than imitate them, but their glory will not pass away.] The present age, one might add, has this characteristic, that unmerited spite plagues the living. Someone feels bad that he is unexpectedly surpassed, while another is jealous of a foreigner. Verily, "an απροσώώην [unknown] posterity will judge them on merit."

I have dwelt on this matter at this length so that you might withdraw from the company of such persons and resist the practice (I might have said malpractice) of the surliness of this generation against a man from whom so great a contribution flows down upon you. If you will do this (and you may already be doing it diligently), I am eager to assure you that at some future time there will go out to your hands works not inferior to this that will not be disappointing to your nocturnal vigils. Moreover, whenever it is possible by means of extra hours snatched away from medicine or an increased leisure somehow to be found, he will produce such works and perfect and publish them, productions that will bring in their train perpetual laudations of his name. You will take my advice in

good part if you take note not of who it is who gives it but of what it is and how justly it is given. Farewell, fair reader. And to you, Envy, a long fare-well. Get thin, κρόμμυα ὀσφραίνου, κλαίε, οἴμόξε [sniff onions,[5] wail and go hang].
From Zurich. December 24 in the year 1520.

Original Publication: Vadian's *Pomponius Mela*, Basel edition, 1522
Transcription: None

27
Grebel to Vadian
Zurich, January 4, 1521

Vadian's father, Leonhard von Watt, a wealthy linen merchant and member of the Large Council of St. Gallen, died on December 28, 1520. Following is Grebel's letter of sympathy. It has been called the dolere *letter (see Rupp, p. 371) because Grebel used this Latin verb seventy-three times. The style is reminiscent of Ulrich von Hutten's poem "Nobody" in which the Latin pronoun* nemo *was used over and over again; and it seems likely that Grebel was using a literary pattern like it in contemporary humanist litera-ture. Whether or not this is true, the letter was defective both as an expression of sympathy to a grieving friend and as an imaginative piece of writing.*

Greetings, dearest of men.

I heard first that your father[1] had fallen seriously ill, and then from reliable messengers that he had passed away. It grieves[2] us all, and me especially, for I knew well the Christian integrity of the man. May the gods grant that all may be well for him there, as he wished well to all here. I do not know what I should add to this, for I lack reason and eloquence and wisdom. I will add this:

I am deeply grieved by the death of your father, and if I grieve not may the gods will that I grieve forever. I grieve for the sake of your mother, the most upright of all matrons;[3] and I grieve for the sake of your brothers and sisters.[4] What do you wish? Simple sincerity, Conrad's expression of sincerity from the depths. It grieves me; and I wish you to make known to all yours that it grieves us all. If you love me, make it known; if I lie, let everyone lie to me henceforth. It grieves me with a grief, greater than this alone, that its expression is not permissible or agreeable or possible. It grieves me that I am not there and yet I am there. It grieves me that I am at Pisa, it grieves me that I am at Zurich.[5] It grieves me with the grief of Vergil's Dido.[6] It grieves me, but if I should tell why I grieve, I would not be very convincing; I would not be convincing, because we all

133

play the part of Aeneas, that is, to whoever is allowed to speak with the words of Dido, if they should want to speak them, that nowhere is one secure.[7] It grieves me, but so do the Fates[8] decree that it should grieve you, that it should grieve us together, that it should grieve me, yea me by reason of the death of your father, and by reason of this (you want me to say it) that I am at Pisa and yet I eat the beans of Zurich, and in Zurich the beans are threshed out over my head.[9]

So this grieves me, that it grieves you. It grieves me, even if it does not grieve you. It grieves me because I am simultaneously in two cities, the one in Switzerland, the other in Italy, and yet I hang on in this city of Switzerland. It grieves me that I am neither in mind nor body at Pisa. It grieves me that I should want to be there. It grieves me because I am believed to be there, and yet I am not believed. It grieves me that I should grieve in body and mind. It grieves me therefore, if you do not know; it grieves me if you do know; it grieves me, if you wish it; it grieves me if you do not; and still it grieves me.

If you are well, if your family is well, it grieves me not that you are well, that they are well; but what grieves me, this indeed grieves me.[10] May the gods protect you as surely as I grieve; that is, may they most certainly protect you. They may not protect you, that you may grieve. They may protect you, that you may rejoice. If this happens not, I grieve. If something is not done by a certain person with respect to a miserable little Conrad Grebel (it is not done yet), it will grieve me not a little. It grieves me that although I do not want to be esteemed, I am not loved. It grieves me that if I should want to be esteemed, I would not be honored. It grieves me that I pursue neither the thing I want nor the thing I do not want, I who shall accomplish what I have accomplished. It grieves me that I cannot say what I shall accomplish in the future. It grieves me, therefore, that I am not a prophet. It grieves me, and not without just cause does it grieve me. It grieves me; but what grieves me is what concerns you; but it grieves me, that nothing is of concern to you, about whom everything is of concern to me. It grieves me, alas, alas, alas, alas! By all the exclamations of grief it grieves me. It grieves me that I can scarcely conceal why it grieves me.

It grieves me that my affairs, fortunes, and friends take on the same color.[11] It grieves me that the goose is rather long.[12] It grieves me that the product of the Nile is so dear in your city, which lacks nothing else.[13] Something far dearer[14] than all these things grieves me. What is dearer than this, you ask? It is a word of one syllable, which, if you form a false diminutive, becomes that by which human beings are begotten,[15] or it becomes the rod of the keeper of gardens.[16] It grieves me, not that the word of one syllable is so dear, but because that is so dear which the word of one syllable contains. It grieves me, if nothing else grieves me, it grieves me I say (if you have not yet heard me) that I will hear that you grieve because you have heard that I grieve.

I long to be well; but let me not be well, unless the death of your father grieves me, unless it grieves everybody. Let me not be well, if it grieves me not that you write such grievous things to my father, if it grieves me not that you write to my father that you believe me to be in Pisa when I am in Zurich. It grieves me, farewell. It grieves me, live well.[17] It grieves me; but do not take it seriously; and so good-bye with all best wishes. Live most happily.

Zurich, fourth moon of Hercules,[18] in Latin the fourth day of January, in the year in which to read my words is to disregard them (I quote from Cato[19]), that is, the year of 1521.

Conrad Grebel, your friend.

Yours at the altars, a Swiss of Zurich.[20]

To Vadian, physician and poet laureate,
a man by far most learned and revered,
the closest kinsman of all kinsmen.

Original: Stadtbibliothek (Vadiana) St. Gallen, VB.II.3
Transcription: VB, II, No. 232

28
Grebel to Vadian
Zurich, February 1, 1521

The months passed by in aimless existence without goal or plan. Grebel could do little without his father's consent, and yet Jacob had no plan for him apart from his attendance at the University of Pisa with papal grant. In this vacuous situation, Conrad continued to suffer his "most perverse disease," which had plagued him since his Vienna days; and in the following letter, he speaks candidly and mysteriously about the nature of his illness. It is a perverse malum, *translatable both as "disease" and "punishment." It is of long duration and chronic nature, known to Vadian by previous disclosure, perhaps curable if the cause could be controlled. As in Letter No. 13, Grebel speaks explicitly about his father's bad reputation as a statesman for being tempted by foreign bribes. Moreover, Conrad has a new interest in going to Basel, to which he alludes here for the first time but does not begin to clarify until Letters 34 (145/4-6) and 35 (147/13). In short, he is absolutely wretched, but not too wretched to write about it in rather fascinating, expressive terms.*

135

Greetings, dearest Vadian.

By the favor of your letter, I gather that this secret, most perverse disease which has afflicted me so long has finally been made apparent, mostly perhaps by my own disclosure.[1] As the matter stands, you would think that there was scarcely any hope of curing the disease, not because it was not curable, but because there was another problem.[2] I would prefer to unfold this wound to you personally and not to entrust it rashly to a letter. Although a letter does not blush,[3] I might indeed blush red all over and would that I had long since been nothing but red, or that this might somehow be less intolerable (to put it that way). Then beyond this there is one cause, one thing I have learned of man while I live, one thing I know, that like the proverb, I ἄσκοπα τοξεύειν [shoot aimlessly].[4] Why I specifically say, τοξεύειν [shoot], I would have explained to you personally had it been permitted by father, whom I implored but did not convince.[5] Now I do not expect your counsel nor your consolation, since all my affairs do not lie open to you and it may not be appropriate to pour out much more than this in a letter.

While I am stuck here, fit for nothing, disgracefully wasting my time under the pretense of literary study which I have not pretended since your departure, while, I say, I am stuck here fixed to these walls, fixed to others also, the desire to go to Basel[6] and live there has grown on me. There are reasons it has grown on me, which this sheet, if it could encompass them all, should not or would not want to encompass. I wish I could tell you personally how it happened that the aversion for Italy came over me, how I came to know it. How bad is the reputation of father and son because of my stipend,[7] my uncles[8] impress upon me daily. So it happens that I could not feel much joy in accepting this papal wealth. You do not believe me that I would feel no joy: I will document it. Scampius[9] reported what a certain French spokesman had said,[10] that if father was willing to support the king's party,[11] the richest wealth (that is, Tolosan gold)[12] could be carried off in carts by each of us. But if he continues to be the emperor's man, not even a lead coin would be brought back from France to the advantage, or disadvantage if you prefer, of either of us. This he said, adding further that we should tell him and the spokesman what our attitude would be. Then I indicated my unwillingness for father to hold or accept any royal gift, if he is forced by this to serve France and fetter his loyalty by betraying the republic and the liberty of Switzerland. What need to say more? It is very sweet, I grant, to accept; be this as it may, for me it is most bitter, and I do not want it.

In this manner, therefore, I shall reply to Scampius,[13] as I did to my father. How I wish now that I were some magician, so that by incantations

136

and the power of herbs I could meet with you. You would hear the history of my life, no less pitiful than wonderful, and far longer than the *History* of Livy, and even the entire [*History* of] Livy.[14] But since this cannot happen, that I might nevertheless, as it were, fly forth to you, let me add a few words. Unless I make my way to Basel,[15] anticipating, knowing, living, and seeing, I perish and perish by a miserable fate. Indeed, what burns me will burn me up and hurl all but utter destruction on my head. If I am prevented by the harshness of father from coming to you, I have decided to count every disloyalty as an act of loyalty and then to endeavor to do something beyond my hopes and also those of my parents, which is yet not dishonorable, but which would provoke the sorrow if not the anger of all the family and clan of Grebel.[16] Alas for me in my misery, whom neither consultations nor any good fulfillments favor, or if they favor at all, they do it so that it would be better to have lacked them than to have been in a position to expound all this, if one could begin afresh. In such plenteousness so penniless, the more unfortunate the more inarticulate I am,[17] that when contemplating τὴν τῶν ἐμῶν κακῶν ἀπειρεσίην θάλασσαν [the boundless sea of my troubles],[18] I seem not to have brought it upon myself. Therefore, I wish good health to your household, and fare not as Grebel does.

Zurich. From my Labyrinth,[19] February 1, 1521.

    Conrad Grebel, your friend.

    To the lord doctor Joachim Vadian,
    a most learned man, a most beloved kinsman.

Original: Stadtbibliothek (Vadiana) St. Gallen, VB.II.8
Transcription: VB, II, No. 239

29
Grebel to Vadian
Zurich, February 19, 1521

Two letters from Vadian arrived at the Grebel household—one for Conrad and one for Jacob. Although their content is unknown, it is possible to surmise that it had something to do with an accusation made by Zwingli at Jacob's trial in 1527: "He sent his son Conrad and his son-in-law—I do not know what dealings had previously taken place—to William de Falconibus, who gave each of them 50 guilders" (Epi.A/465/15-18). Whether the reference to "son-in-law" meant Vadian or Hans Conrad Escher, the second husband of Conrad's youngest sister, Dorothy (see Epi.A/fn.47), is difficult to know for certain. Vadian was a good friend of William de Falconibus, the papal paymaster in Switzerland (see Cast of Characters No. 22); and accord-

ing to Grebel, Vadian was "beset by money" (70/379/9-10). Escher, on his part, was arrested with Jacob on the same charge of illegal acceptance of foreign pensions. Whatever the case may be, it is evident in the following reply from Conrad that Vadian was implicated in something that would require a cover-up if it "does not turn out successfully."

Greetings, my glory.

I gave your letter to father; he has decided nothing as yet. What it will be I do not know, nor has it been permitted [to know]. But unless I am mistaken, I will learn presently how his opinion stands.[1] However it may proceed, the gods have granted that my affairs should turn out well and better than usual. Do not be concerned if something does not turn out successfully, for I will always clear you, so that no blame can be attached to you. Trust me, I shall prove it.[2]

A legate from the [papal] side[3] conscripted an army again from the Swiss. On Thursday next he will learn from the spokesmen at Zurich what his holiness can hope for. My brother[4] returned home together with Effinger.[5] They were among forty courtiers dismissed by Ferdinand.[6]

You would scarcely believe how conscious I am of the debt of hospitality that I acknowledge I owe you.[7] I would wish sometime to be indebted for your [medical?] counsel also. I am presently grateful nonetheless, since it does not depend on you,[8] that it may happen, what both should wish to happen, if the medicines are not helpful, etc.

Sister has given birth to a daughter.[9] She named her Cleophe. Would that I were loved as deservedly as I am loved unquestionably, and not just by one, and furiously.[10] More on this later. Best of health to your wife and you all; everyone here wishes the same. Concerning Janus the superintendent I reply nothing now.[11] You shall hear soon in the following letter; for I shall not set out so soon for Switzerland, nor for Basel[12] before first trying quite often to murder you with my chattering. Good-bye and best wishes; farewell, as you deserve.

Zurich, February 19, 1521.

Conrad Grebel, your friend.

Unless I wish the pastor together with Jufli[13] and the others to be well, may it never be well with me.

Binder and Leopold[14] send best wishes to you.

To Joachim Vadian, poet and orator laureate and physician, in all respects illustrious, kinsman most revered.

Original: Stadtbibliothek (Vadiana) St. Gallen, VB?
Transcription: VB, II, No. 242

30
Grebel to Vadian
Zurich, March 19, 1521

It seems strange to read Grebel's apology for not writing to Vadian in a month's time. Apparently his dependency needs are being better met somehow within his own environment. In his search for direction, he writes of two decisions that he is in the process of making—one negative and one positive. He will not go to Italy, and he all but closed that door when "the soldiers marched away, [but] I stayed." He will probably go to Basel, and will have more to report about that in his next letter.

To the lord master[1] Joachim Vadian, C. Grebel sends greetings.

I beg you not to be suspicious because I have not written to you when so many opportunities conveniently presented themselves. I shall repair whatever was neglected. Meanwhile, please forgive my silence, unless you prefer to forgive my talkativeness.[2]

When the legate[3] was about to depart with the army he had enlisted, I approached him and he promised my travel expenses and he again promised the stipend, but it must be paid at Pisa.[4] He set out for Uri,[5] expecting me to follow him there and from there to accompany him into Italy. The soldiers marched away. I stayed.

After Easter, unless I am mistaken, I shall go to Basel.[6] I have little time to write more now. I shall unravel all at great length by the next courier. Please give my best wishes to your family, and also those of my family. Good-bye and best wishes.

From Zurich, March 19, 1521 years from the birth of Christ, February 16.[7]

Regarding the matter under consideration[8]—you know which—it is not appropriate to write at this time. Unless I wish the health of sister and the pastor,[9] let me perish miserably. I shall send a little book along with this letter.

Milords of Zurich[10] are greatly displeased that the pastor of St. Gall[11] did not also attend the last Diet. They beg him by the sacred sword not to neglect doing them the honor of going with them to the French Diet at Luzern.[12] If I did not have to make my first confession soon and if I did not have so much to do, I would give him. . . . I have to write it, the lazy rascal![13]

To the most learned and humane man Joachim Vadian,
very dear and most revered kinsman.

Original: Stadtbibliothek (Vadiana) St. Gallen, VB.II.20
Transcription, VB, II, No. 250

31
Grebel to Vadian
Zurich, April 8, 1521

Vadian's letters are more frequent now, partly because Grebel is helping him to deliver the copy of his revision of Pomponius Mela *to Cratander's printery in Basel. Apparently Vadian and Martha are thinking of coming to Zurich for a visit; and although Grebel knows that he will probably not go to Italy, he gives the impression that he is about to depart in order to get them to come before he begins a long absence.*

Greetings, my sole defense.

Your previous letter to Cratander[1] I gave to the delegates of Basel leaving Zurich.[2] I will also give the later one. I do not know nor can I discern whether I myself will set out for Basel.[3] There arrived today the duke of Mecklenburg and the lord of Siebenbürgen[4] and also the bishop of Constance.[5]

My parents, if you believe me at all, are anxiously awaiting you with my sister,[6] that you fly here without delay. Nor do they just await you, they invite you earnestly, and so earnestly that unless you are here as soon as possible, they will hardly bear it. The reason why they wish this, especially in such an assemblage of various men,[7] I would not rashly judge to be other than their love for you. I beseech you by Almighty God,[8] if ever you come to me, a poor creature who is very fond of you, if you come to my family that is yours, do hasten to be present now. If you have never given way to earnest entreaties, do it now, my life, I implore lest you frustrate my so loving, so fervent hope of your coming. If I have ever been laden with favors from Vadian, I demand now indeed to be crushed by the presence of him and his wife.[9] Will you harden your heart and neglect these prayers? "Neglect them I will," you say; but then you will have me as a most insolent foe not only of yourself but of the whole name of Vadian. You will not neglect them, and I will be to the family of Vadian not just a kinsman, not most devoted, not most dedicated, but whatever unknown to me far and wide surpasses all these mentioned terms. Now it is not right for you to claim the doctor Apollo[10] or domestic affairs or anything else as an excuse to your father and mother-in-law, Conrad, and your other friends. You have devoted the whole year to these things; now bestow a brief time on us.

Do bestow it; for if I am to visit Italy[11] at all, such being my fortune or moral pettiness (I was minded to say perverseness)[12] and the habits of a life polluted by wickedness (to a certain extent): who will say when we shall enjoy each other's company again? Do you ask why I give this warning? If

I must go, I will go in such a way that it will be long before I see Zurich again, and then driven only by the most urgent reasons. Come if you want me to live. My father, had he not been engaged to entertain the leaders, wanted to invite you personally, so do not think that perhaps I am fabricating something. Farewell, and come with my sister if you wish me to fare well. Farewell. Give my regards to everyone.

Zurich. April 8, 1521.[13]

Conrad Grebel, most bound to your very soul.

Dear Sister:[14]

My brotherly greeting, first of all. I implore you kindly and earnestly to come here at the invitation of father and mother and to ask the doctor to permit it. I long from the bottom of my heart to see you, so also do father and mother. If you come, I shall always serve you eagerly, wherever I may be well able and apt. Therefore, do not delay and come as soon as possible and do not find some reason to stay at home. Nothing more, except that God keep you refreshed and well always. Given at Zurich on the eighth day of April in the year 1521.

Conrad Grebel, your devoted brother.

I beg you sincerely by God's will: come and bring brother-in-law Benedict[15] with you. Not for me alone but for our father and mother.

> To the Lord Master Joachim Vadian the Swiss, everywhere most eminent, a most beloved kinsman.

Original: Stadtbibliothek (Vadiana) St. Gallen, VB?
Transcription: VB, II, No. 254

32
Grebel to Vadian
Zurich, April 25, 1521

The plea of the previous letter for Vadian and Martha to come to Zurich becomes an imperative when their mother becomes very ill with pneumonia. The serious nature of her illness is indicated in the following letter by the facts that she breathes with difficulty and has already been given the last rites of the church.

Greetings, my Vadian.

Mother began to feel most severe pains in her lungs from very early today and is still suffering.[1] Her health is in jeopardy, and unless some Aesculapius[2] changes things for the better, Almighty God that is,[3] we despair. Her confession for her sins was heard at two o'clock[4] by Master Jacob,[5] and since then she breathes with difficulty. She seeks help first from God her Savior, and then she implored your help. She all but insists that you come, that you fly here as quickly as possible. If you come, you will relieve her great fear and you will revive her beyond measure with the hope of your presence and counsel (as much as is possible in this crisis[6]), and you will bind me to you most devotedly, if this also has any relevance to the matter.

Neither father, because of his business, nor I, because of my inflamed feet,[7] was able to attend to your request,[8] though at other times we would have readily performed anything in your behalf and for your sake. And behold mother down with such a distressing illness! Was it right then for the husband and son to go away? We are justifying ourselves to you, when necessity and your humanity do not require as much. Come if you can, persuaded by the prayers of my parents and of all of us.[9] Good-bye and good wishes, you who are the sole haven for me in this ocean of my troubles. Farewell again and again.

Zurich, April 25, St. Mark's Day, 1521.

Conrad Grebel, your friend, devoted to you from the soul.

I hope all your family are well.

To the lord Joachim Vadian, a man in every way most learned, the noblest and most famous kinsman honored above all.

Original: Stadtbibliothek (Vadiana) St. Gallen, VB.II.28
Transcription: VB, II, No. 260

32A
Burgauer to Vadian[1]
St. Gallen, April 28, 1521

We gather from the following letter from Vadian's pastor that upon arrival of the grave news of their mother's illness, Vadian and Martha set out for Zurich at once. The letter is also revealing of the sparring relationship between Grebel and Burgauer, who were former classmates in Vienna.

The company of our priests and sacrificers[2] hopes that you will soon return together with Conrad, my most affectionate brother, whom please greet for me ten thousand times, a million times; but please tell him that I am annoyed by his silence toward me in sending letters. And I sincerely wish that your father-in-law,[3] a man most honorable and respected by me, may fare well together with his wife and entire family.

From St. Gallen, April 28, 1521, most hurriedly.

Benedict Burgauer, Luther's most real lament concerning perversity.

The curate sends greetings to your wife, Martha, and makes no inquiry about you. And Master Adam[4] sends you his dogmas. Raise your ears upright again and be not afraid anymore. And Master Ulrich[5] invites you to stab the bear for its old wine to see if it flows, together with Conrad and the mush.[6] He knows well what I mean.

Original: Stadtbibliothek (Vadiana) St. Gallen, VB.II.293
Transcription: VB, II, Anhang, Nachtrag No. 74

33
Grebel to Vadian
Zurich, May 28, 1521

Vadian is back in St. Gallen, having left Martha in Zurich for an extended stay, perhaps to help in the care of her convalescing mother. Meanwhile, Grebel suffers the symptoms of his disease and tries to express his misery in an acceptable literary form, using the Greek he is learning.

G[reeting].

I shall see that your wife is escorted all the way to your house on the Sabbath Day.[1] In the meantime be patient and restrain Venus[2] during this time until your Grebelia comes. My parents beg and beseech you not to take badly nor interpret uncharitably that she cannot come sooner. Regarding your business, I will report to you in person.[3]

I have nothing new to add, not for many other reasons than that my old miseries[4] affect me so that to the matters at hand I have no more ears and judgment and memory last of all (νὴ τὸν τεσσάρωτα τὸν ᾿Απόλλωνα και νοῦν καὶ τὴν μνημοσύνην) [by the Apollo of four ears, mind and memory][5] than a tree trunk or rock cliff. I could therefore have exclaimed most τραγικωτάτως [tragically], or rather I should have if you had left any surplus from your more than τραγικωτάτη [most tragic] exclamation. But since you hardly exclaimed seriously or at least with dignity, should I not with raised voice shout aloud something scarcely other than τραγικώτερον [more tragic] for you and for me (by the faith above, o heaven, o earth!)?[6] I do shout aloud, I say, even if Homer's Achilles says οὐ γάρ τις πρῆξις πέλεταικρυεροῖο γόοιο [no good springs from chilling lament].[7] But how I now prove—all ye gods and goddesses!—how demented I am and with what a helpful memory (if I may say so) because I, though very plainly miserable, exclaim how you, you marvelous ποιητής [poet], I say, make me out to be nearly good luck itself. I will let up therefore with you, and I will begin now with myself to shout and to sing.

My whole family is well, only mother not being altogether well;[8] and they send their regards to you and your family. Farewell my glory and defense, and live most happily, as is due to your merits.

Zurich, the day before the feast of Corpus Christi, 1521.
Conrad Grebel, your friend.

> Martha, your mate, sends love to you
> And hopes that you are well,
> As well as one whom best health blest.
> O man fore'er esteemed
> And safe as safe can be at best,
> You could not but be well
> Since he whose wife commands be well
> Cannot be sick! χαῖρε [Farewell].
> To lord Joachim Vadian.

Original: Stadtbibliothek (Vadiana) St. Gallen, VB.II.33
Transcription: VB, II, No. 262

34
Grebel to Vadian
Zurich, between May 28 and July 14, 1521[1]

Grebel's antidote for misery was a love affair in which he hoped to find a measure of fulfillment even though he knew it would "provoke the sorrow if not the anger of all the family and clan of Grebel" as he had written five months before (28/137/11-12). Just when the affair began is not certain, but the following letter makes it fairly explicit and hints that the girl is either a nun or resident in the local nunnery where his Aunt Agatha serves as their counselor. It is a lighthearted letter in which he pokes fun at the eccentricities of his father and mother, but it is also a heavyhearted letter in which he threatens to "gamble and cast the dice" like Hutten, the renegade knight.

Greetings my Vadian.

The one who brought sister's letter to mother refused to carry the tunic with the linen garment which had been purchased, and this is the reason you have not received the tunic and indeed the garment. My parents promise their most ready service and they insist that if you need their help, you should use it. How then could that which the refusal of your courier prevented be ascribed to their negligence?

The news about father is this: for eight days he has been confined at home with kidney trouble. He has a stone, and by the doctor's opinion and his own it is large. He will break it up by pills (unless I am mistaken) and by baths. I hope indeed that he will be better soon both for his greatest advantage and mine especially (unless something comes between the cup and the lip).[2] Do you ask how so? Because then he will recover and will be relieved of the stone. Behold the benefit! With his health restored, father will allow me to go to Basel; and I can go with my life, that is, as you used to say here, with my passion,[3] who is most miserably in love with me and will follow ἀμεταστπεπτι [irreversibly] (irreversibly and *alsz hinder sich sen* [without looking back], that is her word).[4] Ah for the ocean of enjoyments and blessed happiness from out of the silliest and maddest, I nearly said something else by inserting a few letters.[5] There you have it, you know what I want. Hutten seized his freedom and cast the dice.[6] I am imprisoned and having been seized by love I shall gamble and cast the dice.

I accept what you advised about taking P.,[7] and I shall carry it out myself. What you did not counsel about her (unless I lie more than the Cretans)[8] I shall take care in the same way to carry out daringly, joyfully, energetically, and as early as possible. That I will be even more daring in this, here is the proof. I was complaining mightily (as I usually do) that my life would be a tragedy to the end. Grebelia[9] thought about it and urged that I not conceal it from the nuns;[10] and appealing finally through the ashes of our deceased sister, the nun, and once her pupil,[11] she persuaded and besought me to disclose this tragic Silenus,[12] not of Alcibiades[13] but of Grebel, promising that she would not divulge what I said to any mortal, as though it were the mysteries of Ceres.[14] So I disclosed it and with her consent I will make the trial of whether Fortune[15] is always against me.

About mother, she is well, she governs the house, she sleeps, arises, scolds, breakfasts, quarrels, lunches, wrangles, dines, and ceases not to be a nuisance. She bustles about, cooks, recooks, prepares, collects, heaps up, toils, is exhausted, and then does it all over again.

About me, what do you want, that I should caw?[16] Not at all; enough and more have you been stuffed full with these things. But I cannot pass over this: from a letter that arrived in Switzerland it was learned that the Frenchman[17] who led his forces against the emperor[18] and the Spaniards has lost eight thousand Capetian troops after the armies on both sides joined in battle and fought hand to hand.[19] If I review history, may the gods favor Charles, curse the Frenchman, who does and will (deserve) this and not only by my judgment but also by his merits (for as they say): the French spring an attack.[20]

With this farewell to you and sister, and my best regards and those of my family to everyone of yours, and believe me to be yours so much that I could not be more so. Good-bye and best wishes.
Zurich.
    Conrad Grebel.

Since he[21] could not burden his horse, I shall see to it that those things are brought by other means, unless you find someone who is coming here, who may forestall my arrangements.

I wish that you would greet
That witty parish priest,[22]
Deserving not, the first
Sinner[23], nor have we time
To give to greeting him.
But lest perhaps (he warned
As sister I returned)
He ban me with the bolt[24]
So fired by the pope
That he need say no more.
    About the Swiss[25]
Who until now no yoke has ruled
Tyrannicide the Swiss subdued
Why free (you ask) they ceased to be?
Because the king of France is used
To dole more gold than what is just.
    To the lord Joachim Vadian, poet, orator,
    doctor, thrice learned, thrice famous, thrice dear,
    and most revered of kinsmen.

Original: Stadtbibliothek (Vadiana) St. Gallen, VB.XI.101
Transcription: VB, III, Anhang, Nachtrag No. 78

35
Grebel to Vadian
Zurich, July 14, 1521

A year has passed since his return to Zurich, and Grebel's plans are still in limbo. He hardly wants to mention the anticipated departure for Basel; and his sister Barbara, who is coming to St. Gallen, will tell them more about his love affair, for she is the intermediary between himself and his parents. Until the fog has cleared, he "will scorn to utter a peep."

C.G.V.S.[1]

Greetings, my dearest Vadian.

Our parents are quite well. Zwingli is at Urdorf for hot bath treatments.[2] There is nothing new with us, I think, unless you have not heard of the tower in the castle of Milan, which was shattered by a thunderbolt and

146

killed nearly two hundred people in the ruins.[3] Then also this: the pope[4] has joined his army at Bologna with that from Spain under Emperor Charles, and because of this Ennius Verulanus, the first legate,[5] has come with utmost speed to demand that troops be led againat the French, who had invaded two towns there.

Regarding my departure for Basel, so often delayed, I cannot say a word. When finally I set out from home, then I shall say and shout: Grebel has broken through, has burst out, has escaped.[6] Vulcanus[7] sends you this Didymus[8] and says that there is a *Pomponius*[9] in the press, beautifully and well printed. Erasmus will go to Basel with all possible haste,[10] as soon as he learns what the emperor will do or which way he will move (for so he wrote to Froben).[11]

Regarding my traveling companion to Basel, I mean my passion,[12] you can inquire if you please from Barbara.[13] Since she knows the whole matter and is the go-between, why should she not most easily expound everything? Otherwise, let there be no Corycean[14] present, who could betray me! If she is not willing, you will learn from me at length, as soon as I have pulled up from this Tomitan shore[15] the anchor which has been so long fixed in Zurich. Before then I shall scorn to utter a peep about my hope of going.

All my family send their regards to yours and your parents. Ammann[16] sends his warmest regards. (And I, Master Georg Binder,[17] wish health to Vadian with all my heart[18] and to the venerable Master Dominicus,[19] schoolmaster by God's grace, and people's pastor at St. Lawrence's).[20] I hope that sister,[21] pastor Juflius,[22] and that drunken assembly of brothers,[23] your sisters,[24] the maid, etc., are all well.

The day after St. Margaret's, from Zurich, 1521.

Excuse the paper. It came unlooked for.

Original: Stadtbibliothek (Vadiana) St. Gállen, VB.II.35
Transcription: VB, II, No. 264

36
Grebel to Vadian
Zurich, July 22, 1521

Vadian thought that Grebel's plan to go to Basel to set up housekeeping was great; and in a letter that must have crossed enroute with Letter 35, above, he expressed surprise that Grebel was still in Zurich and wondered why Jacob was so opposed to the plan. In the following two letters (36 and

37), Grebel explains that the girl he loves has already moved to Basel at his expense, and that his father has simply refused to let him go. He hates to flee against his will, but he will not wait much longer before he goes "like Irus" and frees himself from the "Furies."

Greetings, my dearest Vadian.

Let me be damned if I did not receive your letter with the fullest joy. You are concerned to know why I am so slow to leave and you anxiously ask that I write the whole cause. It is as follows: One of my parents[1] detains me, whether the watching gods will this or my own evil genius. If I could relate without tears what has been said between us and how we argued over my departure, if I could do it skillfully and eloquently, either I would be made of stone or I would surely be a Cicero.[2] She on whom my whole welfare depends left for Basel at my expense; and unless I follow her immediately, I will perish miserably.[3] We love ardently, indeed we perish together. To be separated is hard, miserable, and calamitous. To be forever at home, even if love had no hold on me, is a cross and a punishment; and for two months now I have thought of choosing a Tomi[4] if the hesitation of my father continues to hold me. A horse will be ready if I flee against the will of my father. The papal money will help,[5] and divine aid will not be lacking. Take it that I will be going like Irus.[6] Fortune could not treat me more brutally. Surely, however, accused under those conditions I will be happier in that hope, as the human mind usually is. Freed from the Erinyes,[7] I shall stand nearer to Almighty God, since I will not pursue an empty Venus[8] and I will magnanimously disregard wealth. I shall endure painful events far more easily, I shall hang ambition,[9] and live.

But now I am variously troubled not only for whole days, even at night I am tortured and get so little rest that I scarcely know whether my dejection will turn into insanity before I give up the ghost,[10] or I will be laid to rest before I have understood human affairs with my wits dulled by many many evils.[11] Parental, family animosity, anger, delay, lovesickness, and the frequent ailment that attacks the joints of my hands and feet at the same time, then also that tragic woe of mine[12] and six hundred others, all so grimly predominate that I cannot discern anymore, even if the Pythian Apollo[13] were to tell me, what I am to do or how I should act or how I should regard myself.

But I will deal with these matters later, for I have been awake nearly all night and sleep jades my eyes. Innumerable are the things I might recount if sleep, cares, and their multitude permitted. In the next letter I will pour forth thousands[14] of words; for now spare me and also forgive me because I am more brief and more miserable. My family are all well and they pray well for you. Good-bye, from Zurich, on the day of Mary Magdalene.[15]

It was not possible for the M[aster] William[16] to write, because he was busy; (but) he was very greatly delighted by your letter. He commends himself to you,[17] he will reply when he returns and time permits,[18] and he asked me in the meantime to add his respects to my trifles.

C.G.T.H.[19]

Min gantze welt [my whole world], in Greek my ὀλόκοσμος [holokosmos][20] consumes me. Ach liden! [Oh suffering].

To Joachim Vadian, a man in every way most learned and incredibly dear.

Original Stadtbibliothek (Vadiana) St. Gallen, VB.XII.272
Transcription: VB, III, Anhang, Nachtrag No. 79

37
Grebel to Vadian
Zurich, August 4, 1521

Greetings my Vadian.

You ask the reasons for father's hesitation. I make up none of them, for I believe they are none other than the Dread Fates[1] of my life. I cling so to Zurich that I would not believe the fates could tear me away, even if they very much wanted to. This I have decided within myself about this matter: Let my parent detain me, let other things detain me; I prefer to be an exile voluntarily than a citizen of Zurich. But now because of the enormous weariness of reciting the same, if I dare to utter a word more, may the gods and all the goddesses exact the most terrible punishment from me. Why not put off the rest for another time? For certain things so torture my heart, they have the effect that what I would have encompassed in many bundles of words, I do not even touch with a very few.[2] If I know you, you will disregard my [state of] passion.[3] When the delegates[4] return from here to you, you will hear by word of mouth the singular account of everything behind my sheets of paper. Farewell. Everyone here sends prayers to you all.

Zurich. August 4, 1521.

Enclosed herewith finally is the letter from William.[5] It was not possible to send it sooner by messengers.[4]

Original: Stadtbibliothek (Vadiana) St. Gallen, VB.XI.2
Transcription: VB, III, Anhang, Nachtrag No. 80

149

38
Grebel to Vadian
Basel, August 21, 1521

Grebel's arrival in Basel the middle of August was the end result of a plan first reported six and one-half months earlier in Letter 28 (see 28/fn.6) and reiterated in 29/138/28, 30/139/18, 31/140/10, 34/145/3-4, 35/147/6, 9-10, 13, and 36/148/12-13. The opposition of his father to the plan was not overcome; and the trip had to be made in secret as anticipated in 36/148/18-19, financed by money from the papal treasury without the father's knowledge. Once in Basel, Grebel took lodging with Cratander, the printer of Vadian's second edition of Pomponius Mela.

Greetings, my defense and glory, my Vadian.

I have arrived at Basel. I have fulfilled the longing of my heart. My passion[1] is with me. All is well with us, except for the occasional storm of love between us. Brief is every conflict, such as it is, and there is immediate peace. She says she is mine; I am hers and could not be more so. The house in which we sleep together I have not yet rented; but I shall rent it immediately. When this is done, if she keeps true to me,[2] I do not see what could be added to all our joys; but let us await the outcome of the matter. For once the poor heart of Grebel is in ecstasy; therefore, if you love me, rejoice.

I am staying with Cratander,[3] who is kind and learned. He boards both Master Ursinus[4] and me. I have not yet arranged the terms. Ursinus promises to become a Swiss, if you arrange for his pension from France to be given to him, for you can now do so.

If you want maps to be added to the *Pomponius,*[5] let Master Cratander know by letter, for he promised to see to it with the help of Alantsee.[6] I am not yet my own master; may the gods graciously help me. For reason of enormous affairs, let this suffice. I shall write to you *ad nauseam,* when I shall have extricated myself from these cares, from this mass of business. My greetings to sister and you all; I except only Benedict Burgauer,[7] pastor of fools, of souls[8] I meant to say; the mistake was by a slip of the pen. Good-bye and best wishes.

Conrad Grebel, your friend from the heart.

1521, on the day before St. Bartholomew's. Master Velius[9] asks that you reply.

I beg you not to be (pro) French.[10] By my opinion, whoever from Switzerland plays that role is surely out of his mind. We should look at the aim of Charles.[11]

To Joachim Vadian, a man in every way most famous and most dear.

Original: Stadtbibliothek (Vadiana) St. Gallen, VB.II.42
Transcription: VB, II, No. 275

39

Grebel to Vadian
Basel, September 2(?), 1521[1]

Grebel lived in Basel for two months, boarding at the home of Andreas Cratander, the famous book printer, together with Kaspar Ursinus Velius, the famous poet. Cratander was delighted by the "learned vigorous conversations" carried on by the three of them, and Ursinus was delighted to have Grebel's help in the preparation of a volume of poetry for publication. Grebel was delighted to have his "mistress and passion" housed in a separate apartment where they could sleep together and begin to take more meals together for the sake of frugality.

Greetings, O bulwark and sweet glory of mine.[2]

I received your letter too late for it to be shown to Cratander.[3] He had left for Frankfurt[4] two days before your merchants[5] arrived.

About myself: Ursinus [6] and I are still boarding with Cratander. I do not know what we will pay; but if I can make a guess, we will settle with him for twenty-four gold pieces (for we live luxuriously). Then for twenty guilders I shall hardly support my mistress and passion,[7] about whom I have so often raved to you and about whom I have not rashly decided whether she will be a blessing to me or a disaster. We have acquired furniture for not a few guilders. William[8] gave a hundred francs, and father forty. Now note at what expense, at what price, for both to have to live separately, and consider how the money given and provided by the one and the other cannot be adequate. You say that I should ask father to help when the need arises; but he in the meantime will learn all about the stipend,[9] he will pay out nothing and in addition will rage against a love, and finally he will commit those things that will exceed our belief and expectation, although there is the hope that he will bear it all more easily when I have reviewed the history of my laments and my so bitter, or rather unending suffering (though hardly could I persuade him and he be placated and with a cheerful face). Indeed after hearing this, he declared that he would not be difficult in the future if I were to maintain a harlot for the pleasure of enticing and enhancing Venus.[10] However my sire will interpret the matter, whatever he will do, I have brought the greater evil with me;[11] for indeed, I maintain a woman, the greatest evil of three,[12] and may you hand down counsel for the better for me, from your tripod.[13] Now that Cratander has left, I will live[14] with my mistress at her house, because in this way (unless my calculation, not precisely thought out, misleads me) we will have enough money. Here is what I think will reach the ears of my parents forthwith. They will say: He stays under the same roof with a harlot,[15] he stays day and night, he lives with her, he is not to be torn from her because he is dying of love, he neglects the company of learned men since he neglects his studies, he dissipates himself and disgraces himself in love for a harlot, he will consummate it and brand ignominy on the Grebel family, he is enfeebling himself by idleness; let us be angry, let us not help him either by money or deeds, let us not heed a son who is not a son, who when living like this is unworthy of any kindness, even from an enemy. So will they speak, I think. But I shall not deserve it; so I shall bear it cheerfully, believe me, if any of this happens. I would justify my deeds to you with reasons, if it were not that the messenger departs sooner than I would wish and that I am deterred by the trustworthiness of a frail letter, so to speak. Would that you knew, Vadian my soul,[16] how hard it is to keep from unraveling to you the whole web of my life and Venus.[17] But at another time when it is more convenient and safer I will gratify your ears and my own desire.

Ursinus[18] awaits a reply from you. There is one favor which I would wish you would do for me, and when you have done it, you will make this creature completely your slave. It is this: I want to have a red silk cloak which they call damask;[19] and I wish that you would get somewhere from someone enough silk for making this and send it here without my parents' knowing. I will pay you in the coming year, unless all good fortune turns stepmother[20] toward poor miserable me. If without trouble to yourself, if you are willing, you can oblige poor Grebel[21] in this matter. If you cannot, if it does not seem that you ought to do it, then do not wish you could and let it not seem good that you ought to do so. For I should not want Vadian to be burdened on my account or to undergo any hardships, by whom just to be loved ought to be enough and more for me, such a poor[22] little creature (if I discern correctly).

I send best wishes to sister[23] from the heart and to you all. For the pastor,[24] I cannot pray worse than for myself. Farewell thrice, well and happily.

From Basel, September 2,[25] 1521.

Conrad Grebel, your friend.

The first night when one bed joined me to my mistress prompted this to me:

O sky, sea, earth,[26] palace of Pluto,[27]
She who just now called me lord
More than attentive with those special eyes,
Soon a slave, a naught, this empress
Makes, to sell for an empty nut,

Spurned, ridiculed, ruined,
Nothing is more Carthaginian[28] than girls
O sky, sea, earth, palace of Pluto.
>   To the lord doctor Joachim Vadian, a man in every way
>   most eminent and most dear to his kinsman.
>   and most dear to his kinsman.

Original: Stadtbibliothek (Vadiana) St. Gallen, VB.II.59
Transcription: VB, II, No. 290

39A
Cratander[1] to Capito
Basel, September 20, 1521

M[aster] Ursinus Velius,[2] the very well-known poet and great Greek scholar, and Conrad Grebel, an exceptionally talented youth whose sister married Joachim Vadian, are boarding at my house where this kind of learned vigorous conversation from my printshop will be frequent and enlightening. . . .

Original: Basel Kirchenarchiv Mscr.Ki.Ar.25, [a] No.48
Transcription: None

39B
Ursinus[1] to Vadian
Basel, October 1, 1521

. . . I beg you, if there is at your house any of the rest of my poems,[2] have them returned to me by right of retrieval. Many have thus slipped away and most have perished. For you have put it to the proof, how careless an observer of these things I have been. I have assigned this task to Grebel, a young man remarkable in all respects and wonderfully dutiful toward all, who will also talk with you about other matters which I refrain from writing. To your wife, a very respectable woman and, insofar as it is possible to guess from the talent of her brother, an agreeable young lady, you will give greeting even from a stranger. . . .

Original: Stadtbibliothek (Vadiana) St. Gallen, VB.II.48
Transcription: VB, II, No. 279

40
Grebel to Vadian
Zurich, End of October, 1521

Soon after Cratander returned from the Frankfurt Book Fair, Grebel returned to Zurich, allegedly to take the therapeutic baths at the insistence of his parents. As we discern from Letters 40 and 41, written only a day or two apart, his health must have been precarious at this time. He has to report to Vadian on the progress of the printing of the Pomponius, *but his need for medical counsel is uppermost in his mind. It is interesting that the subject of his love affair, to which he returns in Letter 41, is not even mentioned in Letter 40. Apparently Barbara accompanied him back to Zurich, where she was living alone somewhere with Conrad's financial support. A fourth subject of these letters (after health, the printing project, and his mistress) concerns his private study of the classical literature, which "I have loved and I do love, you know how!" Harold Bender speculated on what the two months in Basel might have meant to Grebel with reference (1) to contacts with humanists like Erasmus and Beatus Rhenanus and (2) to contacts with persons who later became Anabaptists like Reublin and Hugwald. But Bender is undoubtedly right when he concludes that "Grebel returned to Zurich much the same man as he had been when he left, very little changed by his two months in Basel. He had in no way been able to help himself by the Basel expedition, for the secret love affair had still to be kept secret, and the conflict with the parents had only been increased. What would ultimately become of his love affair was totally uncertain. Marriage apparently seemed out of the question, but he was firmly resolved never to give up his Holokosme" (HSB, p. 64).*

Greetings my Vadian.

I returned to Zurich,[1] summoned by my parents to take the baths. I will do it by your advice. If you love me, reply to us here in return. You know Grebel, his state of health;[2] you have thoroughly examined him internally, I believe. Therefore, I ask you to prescribe how I should take the baths. Your experience in medical matters is such that you understand, your knowledge of me is so precise that you are able, your friendship and kinship, to which add urgency,[3] is such that you ought to, indeed you should hasten to give me advice.

I have not seen your last letter to me which you gave to I know not whom. For when I had already arrived and it was not known to him that I had arrived, he proceeded on to Basel. This I learned from Valentin Tschudi,[4] who gave hospitality to the man while en route through Zurich.

Before my departure I gave your last letter to Cratander[5] upon his return and also the annotations. You would not believe with what elegant format, with what diligence the Catechesis[6] has already begun to be printed but laid aside because you were unable to make haste.[7] Nevertheless, the shop of Cratander will push toward publication by Christmas of the entire *Pomponius,*[8] recently produced by you. So the foreman of his shop has promised.

I will send you the bound edition of Tertullian[9] which was purchased for you, as soon as it is delivered here. Please give my greetings to sister and all yours (never do I wish ill to the pastor, the παντολάβω [grasper] I was tempted to say).[10] All the Grebels send their prayers, good-bye and best wishes.

Conrad Grebel, your friend.

I think they made me citizen of Zurich once again,
A candidate for balderdash from every sort of clan,
It may be grave or queer.[11]
As soon as opportunity presents itself to me
And many messengers are not in such a rush to flee
Prepare your ears to bear.[12]
To the lord Vadian.

Original: Stadtbibliothek (Vadiana) St. Gallen, VB.XI.98
Transcription: VB, II, Anhang, Nachtrag No. 83

41
Grebel to Vadian
Zurich, November 2, 1521

Greetings my Vadian, my glory.

I gave a letter[1] for you to the dealer Enderli.[2] I asked your advice about taking the baths. If you received it, please reply. Reply, even though in winter it might not be good to plunge into hot baths as I said, unless in a room,[3] as mother thinks.

Regarding my affairs (for I would not want any of them to be unknown to you, because you always help me with your advice; and when my mind is downcast with adversities and fortunes, you restore it to hope by your consolation) note this: I have said a final farewell to roaming about.[4] I prefer to be in my native land, whether well or rather miserable. In my private study, if it will please the gods, I shall read something from Lucian[5] and I shall taste the wit and elegance of the Greek epigrams.[6] This will probably be my last exercise in the literature of both languages. I have been most unsuccessful[7] in devoting diligent attention to my studious inclinations, troubled by intolerable calamities; and this is the reason that I am always immediately torn from the unlucky course of studies, so often

155

thwarted. I have loved (them) and I do love (them), you know how![8]

I have found a girl[9] of moderate beauty who loves me (if this can be believed of a woman). She charms me, to her I will cling, I will support her alone as long as she will be content with me, will be true to me, will love me in return. About wedding a wife[10] I think as little as if I belonged to[11] more a wife than a wife. My Barbarity[12] may, I imagine, deceive me someday. She will be the last one to deceive me.[13] For as I did the Muses,[14] I will cast from me to the furthest limits of men, I will repudiate and proscribe the whole race of women and the pleasure of Venus.[15]

Not a month do I live under such propitious powers but that I am distressed by some extraordinary misfortune. When I was about to leave Basel, I lost a silver cup which I had bought for gold, on the journey a leather vest, and then today a very elegant cap which was worth a scutatus. I bear all of this with such equanimity, however, that I am surprised at myself, and I would even scorn them, if only the attitudes of the people and citizens[16] at home were more just to me than is usually the case. So it will be that after a broken trust shall have been added to all these evils, I will extend the infamous finger[17] not just to the Muses and Venus,[18] but to all the snares of this deceiving world altogether at the same time, telling them all to go hang.

Greetings to sister and to you all. Farewell.

From Zurich, November 2, 1521.

To the lord doctor Vadian, a man in every way most famous.

Original: Stadtbibliothek (Vadiana) St. Gallen, VB.II.52
Transcription: VB, II, No. 285

42
Grebel to Myconius
Zurich, November 4, 1521

Fifteen months elapsed since Grebel last wrote to Myconius, and what follows was to be his last letter to the man who provided the most help during the times of stress and strain in Paris and effected the reconciliation to his parents in Zurich. One of the reasons this was to be the last of the nine extant letters to his friend in Luzern is that Myconius moved back to Zurich and the two were henceforth in personal contact, first as colleagues in Zwingli's Reformation and then as opponents in the anti-Anabaptist backlash. What is most revealing in the following letter is that after sixteen months of vacuous existence devoid of serious study, Grebel has joined a group that is reading

Plato with Zwingli. It is the first sign of a coming turning point for Conrad, which will become explicit in the 47-series of documents dated the following summer.

Greetings dear Oswald.

I hope and earnestly pray that you are well. I do not deny that for a long time I have been dumber than a fish.[1] The god of love tore out my tongue, that triple-sized fellow, and for some months he has assaulted and subdued me, certainly not in the likeness of a boy,[2] for he assailed me with such strength, as a veritable Hercules,[3] or whoever was greater and stronger than he. This one cannot be captured by the eyes and seen, since he hit me with a sure aim while Apollo watched,[4] he wounded me with the darts of his fury, and he attacked me with his torch and set me aflame. This Cupid is not winged, because he has stayed with me for such a long time.[5]

All this I have composed for filling up this sheet of paper. For what young man so devoted to the Muses[6] could yield to love? It is not true that I can love and study diligently. I lapse again into silence, but I ask you to converse with me again by exchange of letters and to wink at this wavering, for I will never again be accused of such behavior. You will have a more convenient opportunity than ever before, because I will not be going away again (unless father exiles me from my homeland), having been admonished so often by the disastrous outcome of unsuccessful sojourns that I shudder at the very mention of going away.[7]

All is well with Zwingli and your friends.[8] Zwingli, Tschudi, Ammann, and I are reading Plato.[9] When I am alone, however, if there is leisure to reflect on something at any time during a whole month, I interpret some Greek epigram[10] and turn it into verse (I nearly said curse).[11] Aside from these occasional and brief compositions, I am doing nothing. This accounts, my dear Oswald, for the fact that I know so little and am more ignorant than a Boeotian pig,[12] or if you prefer, than a monk. Moreover, it is for that reason also that I chatter[13] on to you in such an ungracefully uncouth and barbarian way, but such is the polite good nature and good-natured politeness of your amiable way[14] that you do not bear your friend's barbarity unfavorably. And you do not so bear it because you prefer inelegant words spoken from the heart to the charming embellished utterances from the mouth. In either case, I shall write and write again, and I shall write again and again, and I shall write you to death, so beware if you want to live.

Please beg Clivanus[15] for me not to take badly the fact that I have not replied, and tell him (if he is in Luzern) that it will require a longer delay than a certain person can give now. For this very evening, my father informed me of his departure early tomorrow morning. His unexplained haste accounts for my not sending another letter.

All the best wishes, my brother, if I can call you that. My regards to Master Xylotectus,[16] Tibianus,[17] and my other friends.
Zurich, November 4, 1521.

Conrad Grebel, yours sincerely.[18]

Original: Staatsarchiv Zurich, EI.1, No. 35
Transcription: MQR, II, pp. 240-41

43

Grebel to Vadian
Zurich, December 18, 1521

The first of five letters written within a seven-week period, followed by a nine-month moratorium on all letter-writing, opens with more nugarum *(trifles), but goes on to report the death of his younger brother, entreating "through Almighty God" that Vadian come to help erase the loss of Andreas. (The news that Vadian's younger brother, Melchior, had also died the end of November had not yet reached the Grebels in Zurich.) Conrad's letter is reminiscent of No. 18, in which he had written about the death of his older sister, Euphrosine, "I grieved as much as ever I grieved, and I offered up prayers that she should receive the rewards of her pure life" (18/109/25-27). Life was precarious indeed; and his appeal to* deus optimus *(Almighty God), still refracted through his humanist orientation, was made especially in those recurrent times of plague, illness, and death. But his faith was not yet the vital part of his life that it was soon to become.*

Greetings, my Vadian.

For not replying to your letter, forgive me, and that you have not yet gotten the Tertullian,[1] forgive me, O my glory. I do not deny that I may have been more negligent than was right, but this may have been because of love and that may have been at a time when a convenient bearer[2] was at hand. If you pardon me, I promise you in all sincerity that to my utmost ability (if you order it), I will never neglect, I will never be still, I will always perform, I will always converse.

Master de Falconibus[3] has informed you about the money of that soldier. I know not with what supply of trifles[4] I threatened you. If I really did threaten you, it has escaped my memory. You enjoy this in place of that; enjoy it, indeed. But if anyone could ever enjoy such lamentations, you might almost put them after those of Ialemas.[5] Truly, if you knew the style of my life so inactive, so averse to studies, you would expect this that is to be received instead of that which you did not receive, nor will you expect this long before you receive it forthwith.

I am unlearning what literature I had mastered (if I actually did master it) and I am unlearning more and more every day.[6] Love unteaches me. Consequently I will not be able not to trifle[7] with you! My parents hardly endure your absence, especially after the death of my brother Andreas,[8] the loss of whom you could erase with your presence, but in such a way that they would still not go beyond the bounds of dutiful affection. Come therefore, entreated through Almighty God. Father left on horseback right after reading your letter. He will reply when he returns. Erasmus is in Basel.[9] My life lives beautifully.[10] You also live beautifully, sweetest souls,[11] and best wishes ever.

Zurich. December 18, 1521.

Conrad Grebel, your friend.

Greetings to the pastor,[12] and my other friends.

To the lord doctor Joachim Vadian, a man in every way most learned, dearest kinsman.

Original: Stadtbibliothek (Vadiana) St. Gallen, VB.II.63
Transcription: VB, II, No. 293

44
Grebel to Vadian
Zurich, December 29, 1521

News that Vadian's brother, Melchior, had also died reached Zurich after Grebel's previous letter was sent. Hence, the following letter is mostly an attempt to offer comfort to Vadian, whose sense of loss was extraordinarily acute. The attempt might be judged harshly in the light of a modern theory of the grief process unless it is read in the context of an age in which the life expectancy was less than half what it is today. The letter is reminiscent of Grebel's "grief letter," No. 17, following the death of Vadian's father.

Greetings, my glory, my Vadian.

Such is my candor and my love for you and for Melchior,[1] while he lived, that since he of whom we expected many wonderful things has passed away, and you in this calamity all but languish away and lose your mind, I could not keep from grieving much. But what will you do? Weep at night? Weep in the day? No, by your own philosophy[2] you will not weep, but you will bear it because it cannot be mended. He was born to die at some time. He died accordingly, do you then grieve that he was born? Beware lest you begrudge a brother's birth. He died still an innocent youth; so there is reason the less to grieve, the less to weep, and the less for losing your mind. He has gone where the human race must go. He has gone whence none returns, whence we will not return. Why then do we not weep for ourselves, to whom will befall what he has already experienced, more happily now than later? What you have lost was not given to you forever; therefore, you have lost it. You will let go your possessions, you will let go yourself, and you will not grieve. Why therefore does your brother so disturb you and drive you out of your mind? You should be more moderately affected than other people, man, as one, if I might say, whose end has not yet been reached. You say that you are especially affected by your own family? I say not so, because the thing we lose is not yours or mine; therefore, do not be affected. It was the will of Almighty God who knows better than you what is right for a brother. Act like a Christian, that is, with serenity, to bear ἀνδριφόντην τὸν θεὸν [the god who slays men].[3]

My parents send their good wishes to the family of Vadian, distressed by your misfortunes, and they entreat you to hasten to come to us. Father will reply to you about the money when he returns from the convention.[4] Come to us, come to us, dearest to my soul. I am sending herewith the copy of Tertullian,[5] the best I could find and the soonest possible. Regard favorably this delayed effort. I shall send a longer letter with the legates.[6] Good-bye and keep safe for my sake.

Zurich, Sunday, the third last day of December 1521.

    Conrad, your friend.

      To the lord Joachim Vadian, the best man,
      the most learned and most dear.

Original: Stadtbibliothek (Vadiana) St. Gallen, VB.II.64
Transcription: VB, II, No. 295

45
Grebel to Vadian
Zurich, January 12, 1522

Vadian's copy of a work by Tertullian was delivered to Grebel in Zurich and forwarded by him to St. Gallen (see 40/155/5 and 44/160/22-23). Apparently Grebel had been slow in forwarding it (see 43/158/23-24 and then it was misplaced en route. It will finally arrive by the end of the month (see 46/162/9). The paragraph is a sprightly description of its "wanderings," plus other lighthearted news of Grebel's blissful life with his Holokosme and not-so-blissful life with his youngest sister, Dorothy.

Greetings, my Vadian.

That you have not received the Tertullian,[1] I invoke curses on the spirits of literature that have deprived you of the book you have awaited for so long. But perhaps it will be returned not panting from its wandering, strolling about under the gaze of the learned and exhibiting itself as to how new it is. It will be broken in by the journey and will be with you at last.

The news that circulates here circulates in such a way that I am not able to be informed. For after I feed the horses and sometimes greet my friends, I spend the rest of the time, whatever there is, with my Lysidice,[2] my Holokosme,[3] and there I flourish more blissfully than a Persian monarch,[4] although occasionally some annoying Nemeses[5] of our joys remind us forcibly of misery and upset us.

I have a barrel[6] full of books belonging to Johann Hasler[7] of Appenzell. I paid twenty-two ursigeri of scutati. Please see to it that those who return from him will reimburse me and carry the barrel to his place. I have no use for it, and I would have seen to it that it should be delayed here no longer, but it somehow always slipped my mind whenever I wrote to you.

Zwingli[8] has gone to Basel to visit Erasmus[9] during these days. I wish you would have gone with him from Zurich. Then we would have enjoyed your company.

The sister who was ill was Barbara,[10] not she whom you suspected, that little beast Dorothy,[11] who is more deserving of punishments, that special but not for long delight of her parents, that Maltese puppy,[12] and alas! that white mouse, the essence of paleness, the essence of greediness, the unbearable tyrant of our house, and the plunderer of her dear brother Andreas's clothes,[13] which are mine by the right of sex. I regret that this cross of mine was ever born, I regret it for a thousand reasons which with innumerable others you will hear from me personally when you are here. My regards to all your family. Good-bye and best wishes, my glory.
Zurich, January 12, 1522.

Conrad Grebel, your friend.

To your pastor, I almost said grasper[14] by an error of memory, do not give my greetings or regards, but tell him to attend the meetings and to be present at all the other gatherings.

To Joachim Vadian, a man most famous in every way and dearest kinsman.

Original: Stadtbibliothek (Vadiana) St. Gallen, VB.II.70
Transcription: VB, II, No. 301

161

46
Grebel to Vadian
Zurich, January 30, 1522

With relief we read that Vadian has at last received the tardy volume mentioned in four previous letters (40/155/5, 43/158/23, 44/160/22-23, and 45/161/4). The next two paragraphs refer to the imminent appearance from the press of Vadian's second edition of the Pomponius Mela, *which Grebel turns into a metaphor for his wish that Vadian would appear in person. The reason Grebel cannot appear in person is that he cannot be torn from his "darling."*

G[reetings].

I was full of joy at your enticing letter, not because I rejoice so much but because you received the Tertullian which for so long you desired, awaited, received with such joy; and having received, you will enjoy it. Take heed, my Vadian, lest I make you a Tertullian.

You will seem new to me, you who have not been seen for a whole age.[1] You will seem to be coming from the press and printshop. Though you have been formed slowly, you promise soon now to appear.

Then you disappoint by your absence, and later you put in your appearance by dispatching letters from home.[2] The cause that delayed you on the road or rather in your homeland has come to an end.[3] Therefore, you seem to have been intercepted, since you did not tiptoe[4] toward us as people who needed you so much. For why should I speak for myself alone? Anyway, you did not come on tiptoe, though you titillated us once with pleasing promises, because we looked for you with unpleasing ones, because we could not receive you. Therefore come to me, my Vadian, O come, because we long for you, we expect your promised arrival, how we welcome you, and would that we may welcome you soon. We welcome you that we may enjoy you. You came to Zurich three or four times in a brief while, and (now) you are not able to come briefly, and you will have robbed yourself from us for so long. Therefore, come as you can, that is, come late; and late you surely will come, even if you fly here as soon as possible. You would not believe by Almighty God how my parents command you, beseech you, desire you to come, and the rest of us, and especially Margaret from Wädenswil.[5] Do you see that you must come? I will not be torn from my darling,[6] from my life, from my Holokosme,[7] because I hope that you will come here first with my sister,[8] because we all with one voice ask you, and we all with one mind desire that it be done. Farewell, my Vadian, my best wishes to your parent, sister, brothers, and the pastor[9] along with the others, etc.

Zurich, January 30, 1522.

Ask concerning Bernhard your Councillor,[10] what he may have heard from my father. He urged me to write this, to speak for him,[11] but αὐτόματον [of my own accord].

Original: Stadtbibliothek (Vadiana) St. Gallen, VB.II.71
Transcription: VB, II, No. 302

46A
Falconibus[1] to Vadian
Zurich, February 1, 1522

The notorious William de Falconibus, purchaser of the favor of Swiss statesmen with the pope's money, recent bestower of 50 crowns each to Vadian and to Conrad (Epi.A/465/15-18), the person Zwingli believed could talk the pope out of placing the ban on Luther (19A/114/26-29), writes to Vadian in a vein most calculated to assure his favor—his high reputation in the world of scholarship in general and his intimate connections with the late great Angelus Cospus in particular.

I was lately reading, by the kindness of your friend Conrad Grebel, those two books of Diodorus[2] in which are told the deeds of Philip and of Alexander, published by Angelus Cospus of Bologna,[3] with whom I was once intimately acquainted at Florence and with whom I had almost common lodgings at Vienna, when we had recently been conferred our Latin rights and privileges. I have been delighted beyond measure by a text so learned and so crammed full of the manifold diversity of unstable Fortune; and all the more, because at the end of [the excerpt from] the book of Johann Monachus,[4] where indeed he had already given a taste as it were from the life of Alexander and other emperors, he [Cospus] promised that he would speedily give food, to say it thus, to all the scholars. If these were completed before his death, or might have been received for publication, although Grebel does not know this, I desire to know it from you especially, since you, I hear, have not only been in touch with the Greek and Latin labors of the same Angelus, but really have taken the lead like a second Aristarchus.[5]

Original: Stadtbibliothek (Vadiana) St. Gallen, VB.II.72
Transcription: VB, II, No. 303

163

ACT 4, 1522-1523:
THE ADVOCATE

47
Grebel to Vadian
Zurich, February 6, 1522

After living together for five months, Conrad and Barbara formalized their marriage, as the following letter indicates. Grebel did not "just now marry Barbara" in the modern sense of (1) a legal license, (2) a legal contract, (3) a religious ceremony, (4) a public exchange of vows, (5) a festivity, and (6) a first legitimate coitus. In some cultures like Zurich in 1522, these do not all happen or happen at once. In Zurich, the first item did not exist. The legitimacy of item 6 was not determined by whether or not one waited until the night of the wedding. The gradual way in which such alliances often happened made possible the kind of disagreement experienced between Conrad and his parents. That he was in their opinion "living with a harlot under one roof" (39/152/1-2) was more of a judgment on the fact that they failed to accept her as a daughter-in-law than on the morality of their living together.

What happened on February 6 was probably the drawing up of a formal document entitling Barbara and her children to inherit. That Conrad "confessed this" to Heinrich Engelhart, head priest at the Fraumünster, implies less of a religious ceremony than the fact that Engelhart, like Wirz, was a relative of Conrad's father; and both were thus in a position to intercede with Jacob on his return to Zurich. His Uncle Hans and cousins Dorothy and Margaret may have come to Zurich for other reasons, or perhaps they came

> *"Greet Conrad Grebel, who I hear has developed into an exceptional advocate of the gospel, a fact by Hercules that gives me no small joy, for indeed such eminently gifted and learned men who have returned to allegiance there can really advance themselves and all mankind."*—
> Macrinus to Zwingli, Oct. 15, 1522.

*primarily to give Conrad and Barbara the support they needed to go ahead
with their desire to formalize their marriage. Still, it was not the happy occasion for Conrad that it might have been with the approval of his parents.*

G[reetings].

Father has been away for a week. I have just now wedded Barbara,[1]
mine I hope. I confessed it first to our friend Hans Wirz,[2] and then to
Master Doctor Engelhart,[3] and to certain others who promised their
intercession when father returns. Mother sheds tears constantly. She is
intemperate toward me, no doubt the most unfortunate of all men. If
father continues to treat me in the same way and she to behave as she does,
you will have seen the last of Conrad in these parts. O my Vadian! If you
knew with what difficulty I tarry among my acquaintances, how I am exposed to all tribulations, how nowhere is there trust[4] when I put it to the
test. I had decided to choose exile had not the gray hair of my father called
me back from that intention.

Therefore in these circumstances my two prayers are these: that my
parents will consider me extremely unworthy, [and] that they will cease to
be parents and banish me to wherever they may want. I will not be happy
under any other conditions if these things do not come to pass. Come, my
solace, my Vadian, to aid your Conrad by your solace, lest I punish myself
either by exile or by emasculation.[5] Come, that you may for a little time
free my eyes from constant tears, my heart from incessant calamities. Face
to face, countless things.

Four copies of *Pomponius*[6] have been sent from Andreas
Cratander,[7] I guess. I do not know to whom I should give them. I like
them very much; and you will be delighted, I believe, when you receive
them. Why do you not transport them yourself, most beloved of all
messengers, however many there are. Come with my sister.[8] Dorothy and
Margaret Wirz[9] are here. There is no one here who does not await you,
especially my family. We will go to Erasmus.[10] Good-bye and best wishes.
February 6, 1522.

Conrad Grebel.

Unless you come, you are an enemy of Vadian.[11]

To the lord doctor Joachim Vadian, a man in every way most famous, dearest kinsman.

Original: Stadtbibliothek (Vadiana) St. Gallen, VB.II.75
Transcription: VB, II, No. 305

165

47A
Investigation of Plans for a Badenschenke
End of May 1522

The term Badenschenke *refers to a public gathering at a home or local inn to celebrate the return of one or a number of persons from the curative baths at Baden, twelve miles northwest of Zurich. For the camaraderie and folkways that attended this celebration, see Egli, 1910, p. 65, fn. 2. We are dealing here with the first of four episodes in Grebel's life during the nine months between February and November when no letters of his are extant. The other episodes are a preaching disturbance in a monastery (47B), an uproar in the City Council chambers (47C), and the Zwingli-Grebel reply to the bishop's admonition (47D). All of these episodes conform to a pattern that one can see quite clearly in the provocative violation of the Lenten fast on Ash Wednesday, March 5, which provides important background data for their proper interpretation.*

A. Background: The Ash Wednesday Fast Violation. *Historians refer to this event as "the beginning of the actual Reformation in Zurich" (Hillerbrand, 1964, p. 127). The event took place in the home of Christopher Froschauer, Zurich's renowned printer, who ate meat with his workers, alleging that a heavy work load compelled them to take nourishing food. The fact is, however, that Zwingli and some of his closest colleagues in the Reformation—Leo Jud, Heinrich Utinger, and Jörg Binder—were there, together with some of the more radical advocates of the Reformation—Hans Ockenfuss, Claus Hottinger, Heinrich Aberli, and Bartlime Pur (see Potter, 1976, p. 75, fn. 1). The event was more symbolic and less for the purpose of nourishment than Froschauer's court testimony indicated. He had produced two fried sausages, cut them up, and passed them around—hardly enough to nourish anyone. Almost everyone, including Jud, but not Zwingli, ate a piece.*

Although Zwingli abstained, he preached a sermon in the Grossmünster less than three weeks later in which he made it clear that he concurred with those who had violated the fast and that he assumed responsibility for their conduct (see Garside, p. 38). Considering the content of this sermon, it seems incredible that historians like Walton (pp. 59-60) would argue that Zwingli was taken by surprise, that the violators caused him only trouble, and that they not only constituted the nucleus of the radical group that later started Anabaptism which Zwingli opposed with all his might but were even now "proto-Anabaptists." Since Grebel was apparently not a participant in the fast violation, the relevant documents of that episode are not included in the present collection; but they are readily accessible in English translation (see Hillerbrand, 1964, pp. 127-31, and Potter, 1978, pp. 17-18). One of the four documents included by Hillerbrand comes from the pen of Heinrich Bullinger, who wrote that it was because of Zwingli's teaching "concerning freedom and choice of food" that some of his parishioners began to eat meat "during Lent and on Fridays." The offenders were tried before the City Council, reprimanded, and released.

It is more germane to a proper interpretation of the event to examine Zwingli's role as proto-typical than that of the offenders. From a behavioral perspective, Zwingli's attitude at this stage of his Reformation must be characterized as essentially *"radical"* in the sociological meaning of that term, i.e., favorable to fundamental change in the existing structures of one's social system. This need not imply that he was responsible for all of the actions of his most eager advocates. No doubt, some aspects of the fast violations caused some problems for him as the administrator of the Reformation in Zurich who had to steer a precarious course between tradition and change, and who had to supervise the actions of his own supporters on both the *"right"* and *"left"* of a middle course of planned change. On one hand, he moved cautiously and no faster than the system could move with him. But on the other hand, he prepared the way for change and then allowed things to come to a crisis. With a political ethic that has been described as *"Christian Realpolitik"* (Stayer, 1972, Ch. 3), he knew very well that there is no social change without provocation and innovation. Hence, there can be no doubt that Zwingli accepted the fast violations of March 1522 as functional for his Reformation. Moreover, as long as the innovators were a strategic part of the Reformation, even though they elicited occasional reprimand from the authorities or from Zwingli himself, they had little reason to act unilaterally as Walton asserts.

In retrospect, the historian can discern that in view of Zwingli's commitment to the concept of the state church, a schism sooner or later was likely. But as the documents in the present collection and our commentary will reveal, that break did not occur before December 1523; and until then, the more radical advocates worked more or less in harmony and in good graces with their leader. As our documents will show, Zwingli was essentially at this stage a change-agent himself, and they were his avant-garde. As Goeters (p. 252) put it, *"One may assume a partnership of conviction among Zwingli's radical disciples. To be sure, there are no definite indications as yet that cohesive groups were forming, especially in connection with the two [Zurich] pastors. Zwingli, deriving reliable support from the Large Council of Zurich, is always the dominating figure and the one who always knows how favorably to take advantage of incidents in relation to church politics. One can say, moreover, that if these actions did not result in harm to the activists, that was only because Zwingli always threw himself into the breach in the decisive hour."*

B. The Badenschenke in May. Like the other *"Grebel episodes"* to be documented in the present series, the idea of a Badenschenke came as an aftermath of the tumult over the question of fasting. Following the trials, the council passed a compromise measure to the effect that while Zwingli's teaching *"on freedom and choice of food"* was biblically sound, yet for the sake of peace the fasting ordinance should be followed until officially abolished. When the diocesan bishop of Constance heard about the uproar in Zurich, he and his advisers felt that the time had come to put a stop to the radical changes in that canton. Zwingli was already too powerful a figure to attack directly, so the bishop sent a delegation of three officials (see 47D/fn.4) to bring pressures on the rank-and-file clergy and councillors in Zurich not to depart from the old Roman Catholic order. The three delegates arrived in Zurich on April 7, 1522.

Although Zwingli was present at their meeting with the clergy, he was barred from their meeting with the Small Council (Senate). He would also have been excluded from their meeting with the Large Council, consisting of 200 members, had not some of his supporters within the council moved successfully to admit all three people's priests to the hearing. Until Zwingli finally got to speak in refutation of the delegate's complaints (see 47D, below), it appeared that they were making some headway in their goal to suppress him. But after he spoke, the council reaffirmed by vote its prior compromise ruling but added a request for the bishop of Constance to assemble the clergy and return with more agreement as to what should be done in his diocese.

In response to this proposal, the bishop sent letters to the clergy of the Grossmünster Cathedral chapter and to the Zurich Council, dated May 22 and 24, urging these bodies to suppress the heresy being preached and practiced in their city (see Kidd, p. 399, for an English translation of the bishop's letter to the council). According to Farner, 1943-60, III, p. 280, the two letters were sent to coincide with the meeting of the Confederate Diet at Luzern being held at this very time. An earlier letter from Pope Hadrian VI to the Confederates calling on them to do their duty and remain true to the church in this time of testing was to have been considered at the meeting in Luzern.

This was the first time that the threat of Zwingli's reform was the main agenda of the Confederate Diet, and it was crucial to Zwingli's cause that the delegates from Zurich, including Jacob Grebel, should be reinforced in their defense of Zwingli and of Zurich. In this decisive moment of history, the idea arose in Zurich for a large-scale public demonstration of support of Zwingli and the Reformation, taking the form of a Badenschenke to which up to 500 persons would be invited, including council members, clergy, laity, and of course Zwingli himself. Plans for the Badenschenke were made in Jacob Grebel's house. We know, however, that from May 9 to 27, he was out of town attending the Diet meetings in Luzern (see Schelbert, p. 37, fn. 30); and this according to Farner and Egli was the very time when the meeting in the Grebel house must have taken place.

From the following document there can be little doubt that it was Claus Hottinger and Heinrich Aberli who were promoting the idea, and it was Conrad Grebel who hosted the planning session. Bender (1950, p. 85) knew of this meeting; but because Conrad's name does not appear as such among the list of participants, he dismissed it as insignificant, although in a footnote (p.

250, fn. 49) he admitted that *"Grebel could have taken part in this dinner, of course, even though his name does not appear, particularly since the plans were discussed at Jacob Grebel's house."* Walton *(p. 64)* claims that *"there is no evidence that he [Zwingli] supported the scheme or even knew of it"* and that the Badenschenke if permitted to take place would have been a disaster for Zwingli's cause. Yet he knows that two of the same men who ate meat on Ash Wednesday in Zwingli's presence were now planning the Badenschenke. At the very least, an historian should be curious about the fact that Claus Hottinger and others involved in the preparations had been at Baden at the same time as Zwingli.

We know that Zwingli had a certain respect for this institution of the Badenschenke, for in August 1523 he sponsored one himself in honor of his prospective stepson, Gerold Meyer, on which occasion he presented his Lehrbüchlein *in dedication to him (ZW, II, 526-51; tr. Reichenbach, 1899).* One of the folkways of a Badenschenke was that all those visiting Baden from the same hometown would have a festive reunion in a local inn sometime after their return. The Baden group from Zurich included at least one councillor, Ulrich Trinkler, who was a loyal Zwinglian and good friend of the Hottingers (see fn. 14, below), and the document certainly suggests that he was privy to the plan for the celebration. The evidence is thin, to be sure; but in opposition to Walton's one-sided interpretation, we have already examined the likelihood of Zwingli's consenting role in the fast violations; and it would not have been out of character at this time for him to have condoned, if not abetted, the concept of a Badenschenke in May 1522. In his reply in August to the bishop's admonition *(see 47D, below),* he could claim, somewhat incredibly, that *"at Zurich, as far as the teachings of Christ are concerned, everything is as quiet as anywhere in the world, even the laymen in general are so well versed in the Gospel that they will not listen to any other teachings" (Jackson, 1912, p. 200).*

The support of the laity which Zwingli claimed and desperately needed to defend himself against suppression was considerably less apparent in May than in August; and the concept of a public display of mass participation in his movement might very well have been entertained by him and his friends at Baden. This is the hypothesis, alternative to Walton's, that will be explored in the present sequence of documents; i.e., that he may have encouraged, if not actually instigated, all of these acts of confrontation in the sequence.

Hearings concerning a "Schenke" of the evangelicals at the Lindenhof.[1] I. *Proceedings.* 1. Hänsli Freitag in the Clus, Engelhart Bleuler, Hans Wüst,[2] Heine and Ulrich Nötzli[3] testify that Claus Hottinger,[4] the salt retailer, and his brother Jacob,[5] had issued invitations to a "Schenke" at the (Linden)hof. Each invited person was to bring some good friends and let the hosts know how many so that they could arrange the purchases for the meal on the basis of the number of participants. The decision to hold this convention had been made in Grebel's house.[6] Two or three hundred people would take part. The banquet was to be festive and in good company. Some of Milords[7] would also be present. Jacob Hottinger told one of the witnesses "that some letters had come from Constance which they wanted to hear and discuss whether they had to comply with them or whether they should do anything other than what their people's priest is preaching."[8] .... 2. Proceedings, what [Claus] Hottinger and Aberli have schemed. a. Marx Schulthess said that he knew nothing special except that he had heard on the streets and from H[err] Caspar Göldli[9] that there was to be a Schenke in the Hof, and each would pay 9 d[enari][10] or angster. b. Heine Notz of Höngg said that on Saturday Hottinger had come to him before the Rordorfer Cottage and said, "Listen, Notz, you are coming at just the right time. I want to invite you also to come to the Hof on Saturday. Good fellows are meeting there to have a social meal. About four or five hundred of us are meeting. Then we are going to do some further business." And he asked him to tell this to his friends at Höngg; but he, the witness, refused to get involved in this affair. Meanwhile Ulrich Nötzli came and took him, the witness, aside and said he would invite their friends. And thereupon Heine Nötzli invited and listed about ten men at Höngg. Hottinger also said that the men from Zollikon, Hottingen, and the four parishes[11] and others thereabouts would also come to the Schenke. c. Niclaus Buri[12] of Höngg testified that he had heard nothing about Hottinger; but when he came home from Watt on Saturday, Heine Weber and Uoli Studer said that there was going to be a wedding or feast in the Hof in the city on Sunday morning, and 400-500 men were going to meet there. And in the morning when he, the witness, was about to go to church, Heine Wirtli approached him and asked if he did not know about the meal at the Hof; but then Milords canceled the meal. But Rüdiger Zurfel came to the two (testimony continues) and said that the five wounds of God must put to shame all those who canceled it, for I wanted to go to it also. And after the forenoon respite, one of his friends, Rüedi Stöubli, came to him and said, "Let's see what will come of this affair." Heine Nötzli came to us yesterday in the home of Rudolph Winkel, to the threshing floor, and had noted down the names of Cläwin Wiss and one other and said they must eat with them tomorrow at the Hof in Zurich; and when the meal was over, they would continue to discuss the affair. d. Similarly, Heini Wirtli of Höngg.

II. *Answers of Hottinger and Aberli.* 1. Claus Hottinger[13] gives his answer in the matter of the Schenke at the (Linden)hof as follows: a. Master Ulrich Trinkler,[14] he himself, and others recently had gone to the baths at Baden for several days; and when they returned home, several good friends came to him and told him that some who gladly heard the people's priest at the Grossmünster and the holy gospel and adhered to them were planning to invite him[15] and his companions who had been to Baden to eat and drink together in good brotherly love. Then as they were taking a drink in Jacob Grebel's house outside the city, called the Oberhof,[16] they talked about the proposed meal and drink, and he testified that they had asked him in particular where it should be held and who should be invited. And after voting among themselves, they decided by a majority of one hand that if the weather was nice and good they would have the meal at the (Linden)hof, although he, this Hottinger, would have preferred it to be at the "Meisen,"[17] and if there was not enough room, they could also use the "Schneggen." And it was surely not his or others' intention to create a disturbance, unrest, or unpleasantness thereby. They had intended rather to invite all who would like to be with them and would like to toast Master Ulrich and others, and especially those who liked to hear the people's priest and the holy gospel. They were told that there might be 500 people at the (Linden)hof. It was nothing more than that, and he knew well that there were about 34 men from the district who would come along with him. b. Further, he is reported to have said that it would not remain at that. After it took place, he believed that the evangelical doctrine and the Word of God would continue always to be effective and to increase among Christians and that those who now perhaps do not adhere to the gospel would be converted. Finally he went to Hänsi Binder and M[aster] Trüben's son.[18] He did not know to which of them he said that several matters regarding him were being discussed in the council that day. He received the answer that it was quite possible that he was being prosecuted. But he did not know which of them had said it. 2. Heinrich Aberli[19] gave the same answer about the supper as Claus Hottinger. [He said] it was probably true that the last time Milord Burgermeister talked to him and Hottinger before the councillors and representatives, and [they] had left, Hottinger said, "Several years ago they had also wanted to prohibit outsiders from assembling for Schenken and such." To this he had replied, "Yes, they had chopped off its head." But he did not say why its head was chopped off or what the reason was. He could well admit that the one who said this about him [was correct], that he could also say that he had given that answer. He also said that he had done so because at that time it was accepted and perhaps mostly because many an honorable man might remember its meaning so much the longer.

Original: Stadtbibliothek Zurich, Simml. Samml. 1522
Transcription: Aktensammlung, No. 246

The Wyss[1] Chronicle of Preaching Disturbances[2]
Zurich, July 1522

The journal entry of Bernhard Wyss for July 7, 1522, provides important information concerning the second episode in Grebel's Reformation activities during the nine months when no letters of his are available. It reports a summons to him and three others to appear before the Zurich Council on the charge of entering the pulpits of the monks to speak against them. The event is also reported by Bullinger, I, p. 77, who dated it June 7.

A. Background. *One of the strongholds of opposition to Zwingli's evangelical preaching was the monastic orders in Zurich—Dominican, Franciscan, and Augustinian; and the monks used their pulpits to denounce the Reformation program. Before this, in support of Zwingli, the Zurich Council ordered that all preachers in the canton, including the monks, should preach only what they could prove from the Bible, a principle that was formally confirmed in the Zurich Disputation of January 1523. When they discovered that their support among the civil authorities was getting weaker, the monks became increasingly antagonistic, seeking additional support from the papal authorities outside the canton.*

In a reply to the formal admonition from the bishop of Constance, Zwingli wrote that "while hitherto reckless mendicant friars had spouted forth in the pulpit whatever came into their heads, the Council has forbidden them to preach anything which they had not drawn from the fountainhead of the two Testaments of Holy Writ" (Jackson, 1912, p. 200). Zwingli was referring to the sequence of events from July 7 to 21, chronicled by Wyss in our present excerpts. The Wyss entries suggest that it was not unambiguous utterances of the monks to which Grebel and his three friends took offense. The focus of the preaching was the adoration of Mary and the saints. Zwingli had preached against the cult of the saints more than once, and by 1522 his attack on the doctrine was coming to a climax. According to Wyss in the entry just prior to the present one, Zwingli "rejected Mary and all the saints who are in heaven as well as their intercession and prayers addressed to them; in many writings he explained that one must pray only to God and to no other creature. But if one wanted to honor one of the saints, then one should imitate their good works. That above all would please them since they desire no honor but only that God be honored. It was for this reason that all the martyrs had suffered death, and in their suffering they called out only to God. No saint in his need would ever have called upon anyone else." And Wyss added the comment, "The entire city was informed of this" (Wyss, Chronicle, pp. 11-12, quoted in Garside, pp. 95-96).

Thus, the action of the four named persons in the Wyss entry was not unrelated to other current events in Zwingli's Reformation, even though its precipitate nature by unauthorized laymen received a mild rebuke in the Small Council. Further evidence that the four were pushing hard in the direction of Zwingli's own goals is found in the facts that this episode preceded by less than a month the decision of the Zurich Council to authorize the secular clergy of its three parishes to preach in the nunneries where previously only the Dominican monks had preached, and that finally on December 3, 1524, the council took action to close the three monasteries altogether.

B. The Pulpit Disturbance. *The details of the action requiring rebuke are not given. Bender thought that "it is hardly possible that the four accused had been speaking against the monks from their pulpits, for they were laymen (HSB, pp. 84-85). It now seems less unlikely that the four were doing exactly what the Wyss entry reports that they were doing—what Bender himself subsequently called an "active demonstration." As in the previous episode, Walton interprets the pulpit disturbance as an organized activity of an emerging radical faction already gathered around Grebel's leadership (pp. 62, 64-65). Walton apparently did not use the Wyss document, but based his critique upon Egli's* Aktensammlung *No. 269 (see 47C) and O. Farner, III, p. 264.*

Heinhold Fast presents the alternative interpretation in his paper, "Reformation durch Provokation: Predigtstörungen in den ersten Jahren der Reformation in der Schweiz" in Goertz, pp. 79-110. It was not only the monks, as Walton indicates (p. 64), but also the four pulpit stormers who brought the issue before the council and thereby forced it to take some action. As we shall note in 47C, below, the council was split in its decision in a tumultuous hearing; and although the four were admonished to refrain from such activity in the future, they had the support of a number of councillors. This was only the first of a long series of pulpit disturbances on the part of those who later became Anabaptists; and Fast raises the question whether such episodes occurred with or against Zwingli's will. Were they in any sense functional for Zwingli's Reformation, or did they only aggravate the situation?

Fast replies by pointing out that pulpit disturbances were not the tactic of the radicals only but also of Zwingli himself. In the same month in which the four agitators were called to account for their behavior, Zwingli interrupted the sermon of Franz Lambert, a Franciscan monk, who was preaching on the intercession of the saints in the Fraumünster. As he was talking about the intercession of Mary, Zwingli interrupted him openly and called out to him, "Brother, you are mistaken." Because of the dissention caused by this, a public debate was held in the Chapter House of the Grossmünster on July 17 between Zwingli and Lambert, at the conclusion of which Lambert declared himself as Zwingli's convert. In a letter to Rhenanus dated July 30, Zwingli wrote that Lambert "was not able to convince me with the assistance of a single passage of Scripture that the saints do pray for us, as he had with a great deal of assurance boasted he would do" (Jackson, 1900, pp. 170-71). Fast places these episodes in the context of the whole sequence of Reformation activity (abolition of the Lenten fasts, the marriage of priests, the destruction of icons, etc.) in which in each case an avant-garde of Zwinglian partisans led the way.

If we are to speak of fundamental differences of attitude at this stage, they are not between Zwingli and the four pulpit stormers but between Zwingli and the old faith adherents within the City Council and the governing chapter of the Grossmünster. Each issue had to come to a climax for the progress of the Reformation. The ecclesiastical reactionaries had a firm support in the Small Council while Zwingli's main support was in the Large Council, observable already in the dispute over the fast violations four months earlier. Following the intervention of the diocesan bishop in April, the matter was to be referred to a synod of clergy in the diocese, and therefore not to the bishop or pope himself. Far from constituting "the first crisis within the ranks of those of Zwingli's disciples who were dissatisfied with the slow pace of the rebirth of Christ and the Gospel in the city" (Walton, p. 59), it was a functional interdependence of men with a common goal, even though they proceeded in various ways and with different temperaments and roles.

The pulpit disturbances of July can best be interpreted in the same way. In place of fasting, the issue now being debated is that of monasticism and the worship of saints. While the monks were appealing to the council to suppress Zwingli's Reformation, the two most conservative canons in the Grossmünster Chapter—Conrad Hofmann and Johann Widmer—were writing memoranda of similar complaint to the other canons. The progress of the Reformation required concerted response to these attacks, and it was in Zwingli's interest that the matter be clarified in the Small Council and some principles for planned change be adopted. Fast believes that the pulpit disturbances by Grebel and his friends were a first step in this direction since they forced the council to deal with the problem. Fast admits that the four were too awkward to bring it to a neat conclusion and that Grebel may have been more aggressive than was good for the cause (see 47C). He agrees with Walton that it was possible for Zwingli's Reformation to be harmed by such provocations. But it could also be furthered by them, and Fast believes that Walton misinterpreted the action of the Small Council in its hearing of the case.

After Grebel's action forced the council to weigh the strength of the two sides in the dispute, and in effect to sidestep the issue at hand in giving its mild reprimand, Zwingli took the next step with his interruption of the sermon of Franz Lambert and the subsequent public debate on the issue. Thus, the Grebel/Aberli/Ockenfuss/Hottinger episode was merely a forerunner of the Zwingli-Lambert confrontation. Then on July 21, as Wyss reported in his Chronicle, the issue was brought before the council once more; and following additional discussion, Mayor Röist admonished all concerned to work together in peace and to take further questions of this kind to the provost and chapter in Zurich.

Zwingli considered this action too conciliatory to the monks who were opposing him, and he employed an even stronger weapon in his fight for his *cause—that of his office—when he said, "It is I who am bishop and priest in this town of Zurich...." By this outburst, Zwingli gained the additional response of the mayor's declaration that henceforth the monks should preach only the holy gospel, Saint Paul, the prophets, and the holy Scriptures.*

To summarize, the council's action of July 7 in the Grebel case attempted unsuccessfully to prohibit further sermon disturbances and agitation against the monks. Zwingli not only broke this command himself when he interrupted Lambert's sermon, but threatened to do so again when he appeared before the council on the 21st. Indeed, two weeks later the council took action to permit Zwingli and the other priests in Zurich to preach in the nunneries, where previously only the Dominican monks were allowed to preach; and shortly after that, Zwingli preached two sermons in the Oetenbach Convent, one on the supreme authority of the Bible and the other on the doctrine of Mary the mother of Jesus. Thus, the pulpit provocation of the Grebel group, followed by the tactics of shrewd and effective handling on Zwingli's part, brought his Reformation a little closer to fulfillment.

On Monday, July 7, 1522, under Lord Burgomaster Mark Röist,[3] Milord summoned Conrad Grebel, Claus Hottinger,[4] Heinrich Aberli,[5] and Bartlime Pur,[6] and forbade them henceforth to speak against the monks from the pulpits or to speak or dispute about such matters.[7] Then a great commotion ensued in the room.[8]

Later, on Saturday, July 12, a tall erect Barefoot Friar[9] and Observantist[10] came, Franz Lambert[11] by name, riding on a donkey. He came from Avignon, where for 15 years he had been reading from the Holy Scriptures. He did not know a word of German, but knew Latin well. He was given permission to preach four sermons in the Fraumünster, seated in an armchair in the choir before the high altar. And in the fourth sermon he referred also to the intercession of Mary and the saints; and because of a challenge by several canons and chaplains of the Grossmünster, he requested a debate with Master Ulrich Zwingli, for before and during the last sermon he [Zwingli] had interrupted him publicly and said, "Brother, you are in error there."[12]

Thus on Wednesday, July 17, toward ten o'clock, in the barroom of the canons, they began to debate until after lunch around two o'clock. Master Ulrich brought along the Old and New Testaments in Greek and Latin and got the monk to the point of raising both hands, thanking God, and saying that he would in all his needs call only to God and abandon all coronas[13] and rosaries[14] and follow God. The next morning he rode to Basel to see Erasmus of Rotterdam also, and from Basel to Wittenberg to Dr. Martin Luther, who was an Augustinian monk. There he discarded his robes and married a wife.

Then in 1522 on the eve of Mary Magdalene's Day [July 21], a Monday, Milords of Zurich summoned the master readers[15] of the three orders in the provostship and also all the canons, the Lord Doctor Engelhart,[16] people's priest at the Fraumünster, and Röschli,[17] people's priest at St. Peter's, also Conrad Schmid,[18] commander at Küssnacht, a learned man with a loud voice. Then from the Council Mark Röist,[19] burgomaster, Master Hans Ochsner[20] and Master Heinrich Walder,[21] two of the three leading guildmasters, and Caspar Frey,[22] city clerk of Zurich. Then at the opening of the affair, Master Ulrich began to speak from notes and confronted each Master Reader with his unauthorized preaching and all they had preached that was contrary or added to true Scripture.[23] This they denied, some while he was speaking. Therefore, after much argument and refutation—not necessary to report—the monks and Master Zwingli and all who had been listening were sent out [of the room]. When they reassembled, Burgomaster Röist said that they should be cordial to each other, and if something became of issue on the part of any, they should bring it before the provost and the Zurich Chapter. Master Ulrich Zwingli refused to accept that. They were hostile to him for the most part because he had forcefully attacked them in his preaching; and among the very elegant words that he spoke were these: "I am bishop and priest in this town of Zurich, and to me is the care of souls entrusted. I have taken this oath, and not the monks. They should pay attention to me, and not I to them; and however boldly they preach what is untrue, I will counter it even if I have to stand in their own pulpit and contradict it. For we have no use for your[24] begging friars, nor are you so regarded by God that we should have use for you."[25] Engelhart and Conrad Schmid also spoke in turn—the commander of Küssnacht on Master Ulrich's side—not necessary to record. And so they conceded that Master Ulrich Zwingli was right, and Burgomaster Röist said, "Yes, you gentlemen of the orders, this is the judgment of Milords, that you should henceforth preach the holy gospel, Saint Paul, and the Prophets which are the Holy Scriptures, and leave Scotus[26] and Thomas[27] alone." But some [of the councilmen] from the Large and Small Councils ate and drank regularly morning and evening in the monasteries. It is of concern that they [the monks] banded together and schemed against Master Ulrich, and that therefore in their preaching they overstepped the set limits and disregarded the advice of the above-named Lord Burgomaster, which as you will hear resulted badly for them and put them out of the monasteries, for the Word of God must have preeminence.

Original: Stadtbibliothek Zurich, Msc. B.66
Transcription: *Die Chronik des Bernhard Wyss 1519-1530,* ed. Georg Finsler (Basel, 1901), pp. 13-20

Uproar in the Council Chambers
Zurich, July 7, 1522

The following record from the Zurich Verbotbuch *(book of prohibitions) concerns testimony taken in September 1522, which referred to the episode of March 5 in which printers' helpers broke the Lenten fast at Froschauer's house (see 47A, Intro.) and to the episode of July 7 in which Grebel and three friends commandeered the pulpits of the monks (see 47B). Although the entire document is included because of its contextual unity, our interest is primarily in the latter event. It is supplemental to document 47B in its disclosure of a division of attitudes in the Small Council not only concerning the matter at hand but also concerning Zwingli's preaching "in a cow's ass."*

Miscellaneous examinations related to noctural noise and especially to menial printer's apprentices.[1] Witnesses are Trini Bernhart and her brother-in-law; Jacob Meier, baker; Steffa Bader; Marti Hantler, printer's apprentice from Bernang; Eustachius from Bayer-Oettingen; Jacob Messmer from the Rhine Valley; Hans Fider from Augsburg; Ulrich Stolz, shoemaker; Pauli Wegler; Hans Fiez from Herrliberg, laborer in the book printshop. Dates appearing were: Our Lady's Eve, our Lord's Day, "After Kermess," the latter in regard to Elsi Flammer's account of the supper at the house of Stoffel,[2] the book printer. Of interest is a report by Trini Bernhart:[3] Further, the said Marti once said that if the matter became serious, Milord Burgomaster Schmid[4] would have to be the first.

Her brother-in-law[5] also told how Jacob Grebel's son,[6] Aberli on the Rennweg,[7] Bartlime Pfister,[8] and [Claus] Hottinger[9] had appeared before Milords, and that on that occasion there was a loud banging[10] in the room and M[aster] Schliniger[11] said he thought the devil was sitting in the council chambers. Jacob Grebel's son Conrad said to M[aster] Schliniger: "The devil is not only sitting in the chambers but also among Milords, for someone is sitting among Milords who said the gospel might as well be preached in a cow's ass.[12] And if Milords do not allow the gospel to go forth, they will be destroyed." He said further that the fellows mentioned above had silenced Milords, and that they let them leave because they did not want to discuss the matter with them any further.

Original: Stadtbibliothek Zurich, A.Nachg.
Transcription: Aktensammlung, No. 269

The Zwingli-Grebel Reply to the Bishop's Admonition
Zurich, August 22-23, 1522[1]

The pamphlet which is excerpted here was Zwingli's Apologeticus
Archeteles adpellatus, *printed by Froschauer in August 1522. The full title in
English is "Defense Called Archeteles, in Which Answer is Made to an
Admonition That the Most Reverent Lord Bishop of Constance (Being
Persuaded Thereto by the Behavior of Certain Wantonly Factious Persons)
Sent to the Council of the Grossmünster at Zurich Called the Chapter." The
translation used here with minor changes was made by Henry Preble and
published in Jackson, 1912, pp. 197-292.*

The events leading to the publication of this pamphlet were the following: On Ash Wednesday, March 5, Froschauer, the printer, and some of his
workmen and friends violated the fasting regulation by eating meat on the
allegation that they needed solid nourishment for their heavy load of work.
On the third Sunday in Lent, March 23, Zwingli preached a sermon defending his parishioners for their breach of the Lenten fast. That week the Zurich
Council debated the matter and adopted a compromise resolution that the
New Testament provides no basis for prohibiting meat during Lent, but that
the fasting ordinance should be obeyed for the sake of the public peace until it
has been properly repealed.

When the bishop of Constance heard about the controversy in the wake
of other disturbing rumors concerning these wayward Swiss churches in his
diocese, he sent a commission of three men (a suffragan bishop, a cathedral
preacher, and a papal theologian) to investigate. Arriving on April 7, the commission assembled the clergy and presented the episcopal command to abide
by the established doctrines and ceremonies of the church. The commission
then presented the same command to the Small Council in the absence of the
clergy, after which the matter was referred to the Large Council for final
resolution with the stipulation that the pastors of the three Zurich churches
should not be present. However when the Large Council convened, its first action was to invite their pastors to participate in the debate.

As a result of Zwingli's strong defense, the council reaffirmed its former
compromise measure but added a request to the bishop to call a diocesan conference on the issues at hand. Instead of responding to that request, the bishop
on May 24 sent a formal admonition to the Zurich Cathedral Chapter and
the City Council to suppress heresy and obey the doctrines and rites of the
church.

A month later, on July 2, after the bishop persuaded the Diet of the
Swiss League in annual meeting in Baden on July 1 to adopt a mandate
against the preaching of Reformation doctrines, a number of the evangelical
preachers sent a formal petitition "to the Most Reverend Lord Hugo, bishop
of Constance, that he will not suffer himself to be persuaded to make any
proclamation to the injury of the gospel, nor longer endure the scandal of

harlotry, but allow the priests to marry wives, or at least to wink at their mar-riages." The last signature on the list of eleven was Huldrych Zwingli's. The issues were growing in number—abolition of compulsory fasting, compulsory celibacy for priests, the authority of bishops versus the authority of the Bible; and on August 22 Zwingli issued his most comprehensive defense entitled Archeteles, *because he hoped it would be "the beginning and the end" of the struggle with the bishop.*

At the end of the pamphlet appeared Conrad Grebel's poem "in gratitude for the gospel restored." The relation of this poem to the rest of Zwingli's treatise has been a puzzle to historians. Bender wrote that Zwingli's high regard for Grebel is indicated "by the fact that Zwingli permitted him to add a short poem as an appendix to his booklet Archeteles" *(HSB, p. 81). It is doubtful whether the words "permitted" and "appendix" are accurate in-dications of Zwingli's intent. It is not likely that he would have concluded this most crucial writing with Grebel's poem unless he felt that it added an im-portant element to his own response to the bishop's admonition, perhaps an indication of the grass-roots participation in the Reformation in Zurich which was a main point in his argument. Certainly, Potter's comment that the publication of the poem "marked almost the end of Grebel's friendship" (1976, p. 86, fn. 1) is totally without reason or substantiation.*

Goeter's conclusions are less incredible but also not fully convincing: "In August 1522 he [Grebel] comes into the literary limelight with a concluding poem for Zwingli's Apologeticus Archeteles. *With its attack on the bishops as rending wolves, Grebel outdoes Zwingli's tactically wise intention to put the responsibility solely on the advisers to the bishop of Constance for the [sending of] the episcopal emissaries to the chapter of the Grossmünster and the magistrates of Zurich on May 24, 1522, and to appeal to the bishop himself against such insinuators. Grebel,* on the other hand, *enthusiastically celebrates his teacher as the light-bearer and sharply points out the* contradiction *between episcopal power and the gospel. In the poem one can see what Zwingli* omitted *doing, i.e., a direct attack on the bishop's mandate to Zurich of August 22, 1522" (p. 244, type change added).*

The following excerpts from the Apologeticus Archeteles *will enable the reader to judge for himself whether or not Zwingli was less confrontative to the bishop than Grebel and whether or not Grebel's poem was so much more confrontative as to alienate himself from the very leader in whose sup-port he was writing. So far Zwingli had published very little: the April tract "concerning choice and liberty of food," a petition to the Confederates assembled at Schwyz to prohibit the recruitment of Swiss mercenaries, and the two petitions to the bishop of Constance and the Confederate states, respectively, that the preaching of the gospel not be suppressed and that priests be allowed to marry. His friends had long been urging him to go to press with his Reformation doctrines. Some sermons on faith and saint worship which he began to prepare for the press were never published.*

179

The first major piece of Reformation writing that Zwingli issued was his Archeteles, "the beginning and the end," because he hoped that by this writing he could establish his authority once and for all, if not to win over his bishop, at least to gain his freedom to proceed with the reform of the church. In this tract, which is a battle document rather than a doctrinal exposition, the appearance of Grebel's poem was surely part of a strategy rather than a gesture of courtesy as Bender suggests or a serious contradiction or tactical mistake as Potter and Goeters suggest. It literally assigned the "last word" to Grebel's witness on behalf of a "gospel restored."

To the Most Reverend Father and Lord in Christ, Hugo von Hohenlandenberg,[2] bishop of Constance, greeting from Huldrych Zwingli, preacher of the church of Zurich at the Grossmünster.

That I again trouble your highness with a letter, most noble bishop, overwhelmed as you are by such a mass of duties, I do not think will be laid up against me, for I know that I am speaking to one whose highest pleasure it is that the name of Christ be spread abroad as widely as possible; and his business, as it is not of men, so it can in no wise be undone by men. But now that for about six years[3] I have labored to the best of my ability with the talent entrusted to my keeping, that when the Lord comes and demands his gain, I might not slothfully bring forward with fear and shame the one idle talent wrapped in a napkin, lo! I am denounced before your highness as a destroyer of the Lord's fold, not its guardian or shepherd. And this thing, as was fitting, caused you to send to us at Zurich that unnecessarily magnificent delegation of three scholars;[4] and I rendered such account to them before the council of my teaching, which is not mine but God's, that every one might have been content with it, if only he had weighed the case in accordance with his judgment and not his feelings. And when I thought the matter had been settled in entire peacefulness, as has been the constant and only object of my effort, certain impatient fellows began to gnash their teeth, not so much because they had found anything wrong as because they had not conquered and slain their adversary and leveled everything with the ground; and they began to look for an opportunity to make a disturbance, until, having thought out a scheme for harassing me secretly and underhandedly, they made you the patron of their design. . . . For by their continual outcries and insinuations they finally dragged you into sending to the council of our canons, which we call the chapter, a document of admonition[5] that is as far removed from any learning as from any moderation. . . . This admonition is so full of violence and threats, so pregnant with them that it might bring forth if necessary, nay, has already brought forth, this pamphlet which you see dedicated to your highness. It is called "Archeteles," on this account, because it is masculine and is going to put an end, I hope, to all controversy between those gentlemen and myself, so that after this first engagement, with a continuous document at least, they will themselves make an end of strife and contention, and it may truly be the beginning and the end of the entire quarrel. . . .

Therefore, most kindly bishop, if you see them handled here a little freely, there is no reason to wonder; for they have deserved it by their recklessness and ignorance. And the same is demanded by the office that I fill. I must contradict and refute them, and like faithful Abraham, who when he heard that Lot had been captured by the enemy even slew kings to set him free,[6] I must rescue the sacred writings so wickedly tortured. . . . The opportunity to admonish or discuss shall be theirs at all times, so long as they grant that the sacred writings are a sacred anchor . . . and so long as they come squarely to try conclusions with me. . . . And seeking for a touchstone, I find none other than the stone of offense and the rock of scandal,[7] upon which are broken all who, after the manner of the Pharisees, make the Word of God of none effect through their tradition. Having therefore put these things together in this way, I began to try every doctrine by this touchstone, and if I saw that the stone reflected the same color or rather that the doctrine could bear the brilliance of the stone, I accepted it; if not, I rejected it. And finally it came to pass that at the very beginning of the test I began to discover whether there were anything added to the real doctrine or inserted into it, and then I could not be driven by any force or any threats to put in the human things, however they puffed themselves out and tried to appear fine, the same trust as in the divine. No, if any set of men taught their own notions that were not consistent, or rather were quite inconsistent, with the divine, I flung this saying of the apostle at them, "We ought to obey God rather than men."[8] . . . To this treasure, namely, the certainty of God's Word, must our hearts be guided. . . . For we ought to take the Holy Scriptures as our guide and master; if anyone uses them aright he should be unharmed, even though our little doctors be every so much displeased. Otherwise calamity will fall upon us sometime, for the knowledge of the sacred writings is today upon the lips not only of the ecclesiastics but of almost the entire community. . . .

What harm, pray, is going to happen to us if the whole rubbish-heap of ceremonials be cleared away, since God declares that he is worshiped in vain by these things? The sayings of the Lord are pure sayings, silver tried by fire and cleansed from earth, aye seven times cleansed. Are we, therefore, to mix dross with the silver again? Are we to change to dross those who have become the true metal of Israel?. . .

They do rightly who call us to the freedom of the gospel, for by that alone are we saved. Hear Christ in the last chapter of Mark: "Preach the Gospel to every creature. He that believeth" (after the gospel has been preached, to wit) "and is baptized shall be saved."[9] The truth has made us free; therefore we are truly free; the Son has made us free.[10] How shall a slave reduce us again to slavery?. . . .

Hence it is clear that all this brew of ceremonials is of no concern to those who have already come back to wisdom, but only to those who still stumble about in the darkness of human devices, disregarding Christ and his teaching. . . .

The common people, endowed with the harmlessness of the dove, will yield to the gospel alone, and the less vitiated with the dregs of human traditions, the more capable they are of receiving the heavenly teachings, to which they flee for refuge in confidence as to a sacred anchor. . . . They are the real spiritual, for they depend wholly upon the spirit—that is, the mind of God. . . .

I admit, as far as I am concerned, that I have often said that a fair proportion of the bishops of our time are not real but counterfeit bishops, and I do not think I ought to be blamed for it either, since Isaiah calls them "dumb dogs,"[11] and Christ calls them "thieves and robbers."[12] I am speaking of those who have not entered into the sheepfold by the door.[13] For you will find few who fill the office of bishop to the best of their ability, and do not rather conduct themselves as rulers and satraps and kings. I would that all who have spoken unrestrainedly in these days had spoken truly rather than passionately. It is the duty of all and especially of the heads of the church to see whether their ill repute is deserved or undeserved. For Paul teaches that an elder convicted of sin is to be rebuked publicly[14]. . . .

Offenses have been multiplying for about a thousand years, especially at the hands of those who do not care a snap for the little ones of Christ, whom he wished not to have made of little account when he said, "Take heed that ye despise not one of these little ones"[15] who believe in me. But these men, disregarding the words of God, teach the little ones their own sayings and turn to themselves the hope of those (I mean the little ones) whose only hope ought to be in Christ, stamping the grace of God as obsolete while marking with approval their own penances. They mercilessly frighten and drive to despair the feeble voice of conscience, selling that which ought to be freely given away[16] and requiring chastity,[17] which Christ left free, while they abuse their power of the keys[18] as they call it, and teach at the same time that all their fulminations must be accepted whether rightly or wrongly hurled forth. They defend their own luxury when compared with the gospel simplicity . . . and think it right to regulate even the clearly divine ordinances according to their own sweet will. The day would fail me if I tried to count up all their offenses, though these you regard not as offenses, but if a winedresser or a shepherd or a husbandman eats meat in Lent, as the sacred city of Rome ventures to do without harm, you call that an offense. . . .

For three years ago now (to give you an account of the preaching I have done at Zurich),[19] I preached the entire Gospel according to Matthew, and at that time I had not even heard the name of those persons to whose faction you accuse me of belonging. I added the Acts of the Apostles to the gospel immediately, that the church of Zurich might see in what way and with what sponsors the gospel was carried forth and spread abroad. Presently came the first epistle of Paul to Timothy, which seemed to be admirably adapted to my excellent flock. For there are contained in it certain canons, as it were, of the character worthy of a Christian. Here, inasmuch as certain smatterers showed perverted opinions of the faith, I postponed the second epistle to Timothy until I should have expounded that to the Galatians. Then I added the other. But the before-mentioned smatterers now went to such a pitch of mad impiety that they well-nigh made the name of Paul a disgrace, throwing out these pious ejaculations, which, of course, do not offend anybody: "Who was Paul, pray? Was he not a man? He was an apostle, to be sure, but a sort of outside one only, not one of the twelve. He never talked with Christ. He did not put together any portion of the faith. I believe as much in Thomas[20] or Scotus[21] or whom you will as in Paul." So I also expounded both the epistles of Peter, the standard-bearer of the apostles, that they might see clearly whether both men spoke under the inspiration of the same Spirit, and when I had finished these, I began the epistle to the Hebrews, that they might recognize more plainly the goodness and glory of Christ. From this they will learn that Christ is the great high priest, and they have in fact nearly learned it already. Nor is there any ground for your accusing me in regard to certain writings. For before these came into my hands I had begun the business, nay had promised to do so about a year before. They will learn also that Christ having been made a sacrifice once for all has accomplished their salvation forever.[22] This is the seed I have sown. Matthew, Luke, Paul, and Peter have watered it, and God has given it splendid increase, but this I will not trumpet forth, lest I seem to be canvassing my own glory and not Christ's. Go now and say that this plant (to come back to your point) is not of the Father in heaven. I have not, I say, used any false nostrums or tricks or exhortations, but in simple words and terms native to the Swiss, I have drawn them to the recognition of their trouble, having learned this from Christ himself, who began his own preaching with it. I have never drawn anyone away from harmony with his bishop, if he was a bishop and not a thief or robber such as Christ characterized in John 10:12....

Why, pray, do you cling so tenaciously to ceremonials? You yourself say they are to be kept only for a time.[23] To what time do you postpone their abolition? Do you think we ought to pay no attention to the divine goodness now calling us away from these ceremonials?... If ceremonials are to be kept for a time, they are to be done away with sometime. What hinders their being abolished now, especially as the world is looking for this and all the good and learned are moving in this direction? But you will say, wait till the time when undoubtedly certain τυφλεπίσκοποι [blind bishops] will suffer them to be done away with. Do you think that those whose life is a drunken spree, whose god is their belly,[24] whose mules and drinking cups, as well as their ceilings, are loaded with gold, are ever going to return to right feeling so far as to allow a thing to be done away with when that will lighten their plates and coffers?... But that Christianity which I advocate is adapted to all cities, obeys the laws and the magistrates of the nation, pays taxes to whom taxes are due, tribute to whom tribute is due, fees to whom fees are due. Under it no one calls any possession his own, all things are held to be in common; everyone is eager to outdo his neighbor in kindnesses, to exercise all gentleness, to share his neighbor's burden, and relieve his need. For he regards all men as brothers, abhors blasphemy, embraces piety, and helps it to grow among all....

If nothing is to be altered or changed, why has the communion been altered that used to be given under both forms,[25] according to the institution of Christ and the usage of the apostles? Or, rather, why has it been mutilated? Why has the function of bishop been changed into that of prince? Why is marriage forbidden [to the clergy]? Why are hundreds of other things altered? Christ and the apostles and the general opinion are all opposed thereto. Are you mightier than God, that you have ventured to forbid what Christ left free? Or wiser than God, that you complete what God inadvertently left unfinished? Or so stupid, that you think you are going to persuade consciences free in Christ not to regard as lawful what they know is lawful by the divine law, even though you shout till you are hoarse?...

The Scriptures can be compared to each other not only by those whose concern you say it is but also by those who trust in God and in his Word and who are pining with longing for him.... You see, therefore, that one may prophesy, though in a certain order, that all may learn the truth of the Scriptures, and all may be comforted by the Word of God,

184

which alone can give repose unto human longing. I want to leave you here for reflection from time to time the shameless statement of a certain smatterer who ventured to proclaim in a public assembly that it was unlawful for laymen to know or to read the gospel, but only for those to whom that function had been entrusted; namely, for our little priests and masters. Would that some Apollo[26] would give him an ass's ears because he does not remember or does not know that Christ said, "What I tell you in darkness, that speak ye in light: and what ye hear in the ear, that preach ye upon the housetops."[27] ... Country bumpkins! Do you not see that the spirit of God is everywhere like unto itself and ever the same? The more unskilled a man is in human devices and at the same time devoted to the divine, the more clearly that spirit informs him, as is shown by the apostles and by the foolish things of this world which God has chosen. And as it is a spirit of unity and harmony and peace, not of strife and dissension, it will inspire even the most ignorant if they are pious, in such manner that they will understand the Scriptures in the plainest way according to God's purpose.... Therefore, to come to an end at last, it is not the function of one or two to expound passages of Scripture, but of all who believe in Christ....

And as to the matter itself, so far am I from yielding to you that unless you leave me and mine—that is, the sheep of Christ—in peace and quiet, I shall proceed to deal with you far more roughly, without fear of your words or your frowns. You must deal with me by means of the Holy Scriptures bestowed upon us by God (and do not forget that point), and they must not be twisted.... May the Most High God cause all the hearts of all nations to be so illuminated by the divine ray that they become one in one faith and forever possess him who is one, Amen. Farewell.
Zurich, August 23, 1522.

In fury let them burst,[28] the bishops all,
So called in name, but grasping wolves[29] in fact,
For now again the gospel truth and light
Shines bright throughout the world like once of old.
And then intrepid tri-tongued Lucifers[30]
Were sent to us,[31] but God is now our Lord.
Indeed (I speak the truth as prophets spoke)
Their way of sovereignty and tyranny,[32]
Their keys,[33] their codes,[34] their lists[35] of simony,[36]
The slaying[37] of their brother's moral sense,[38]
Their grim array[39] of holy merchandise,
Their bulls, anathemas,[40] and δεισιδαιμονίαν [fear-based faith][41]—

185

All these are vanquished by the gospel Word
That leads, will lead, to everlasting life.[42]
So called in name, but grasping wolves in fact,
The bishops all, in fury let them burst.

Conrad Grebel,
in gratitude for the gospel restored

Original Publication: Zwingli's *Apologeticus Archeteles,* published 8/22-23/1522
Transcription: ZW, I, No. 13
Translation (except poem, above): Taken from Jackson, 1912, pp. 197-292

47E
Zwingli to Myconius
Zurich, August 26, 1522

*For promoting Zwingli's Reformation in Luzern, Myconius had gotten
into trouble with the magisterial authorities and feared serious recrimina-
tions. Luzern headed the Catholic cantons that remained zealously loyal to
Rome and took severe measures to suppress all Reformation activities. On
July 19 Zwingli had sent Myconius copies of his petition to the bishop (see
47D/Intro.) to circulate for signatures in Luzern, and Myconius dutifully
complied. Their good friend Zylotectus, the people's priest in Luzern, had
withheld his name because of the attending peril.*

*In his reply to Zwingli of July 28, Myconius reported that "all to a man
are insane, not against you particularly, but against the gospel. The rage of
war fills everybody." In letters dated August 4, 19, and 21, Myconius
reported the increasing hostility and his plans to move back to Zurich.*

Dearest Myconius.

Even though all Luzern forsakes you, please do not let it overthrow
you. For in what other way could you learn to fulfill what Christ commanded with his word "Pray for those who persecute and revile you"?[1]
Every time our troop[2] is together, we always speak of you with the greatest
sympathy and we offer our first resolve that we will in no way forsake you,
neither with our counsel nor with our funds. Therefore, be undaunted: to
this also God sets an end.[3] In Zurich you will be of service to us in many
ways. You will also be able to serve yourself, for after St. Gallen's Day,
Ceporin[4] will begin to read in Hebrew and Greek—a fine opportunity
which until now because of your incessant work you have not been able to
pursue. You will be with your friends Utinger,[5] Engelhart,[6] and Rey,[7] the
congenial older men; with Erasmus,[8] Zwingli, and Grossmann,[9] who are
by no means to be despised; and with Grebel, Ammann,[10] and Binder,[11]
who are the most sincere and learned younger men. Appearing finally will

be Leo,[12] who always roars with strength and thirsts for righteousness, who is smaller than Teucer[13] but mightier than Ajax.[14] Appearing again and again will be the dearest Administrator of Hermits, who is the father of all who honor God as Father,[15] together with our Franz,[16] who is the most charming and loving I have ever seen. These people I have listed, that you may take comfort when you must emigrate, and meanwhile we will be looking around that you might find employment when something opens up. Courage is everyone's native soil because here we have no lasting city, but we seek the one to come.[17]

Further, I send my *Archeteles*,[18] which has just now finally come from the printer, yet with many defects. It was written in a storm, as you will see, so take it for the best!

Original: Staatsarchiv Zurich, E.II.338.p.1342
Transcription: ZW, VII, No. 230

47F
Erasmus to Zwingli
Basel, September 8, 1522

Zwingli sent a copy of his Archeteles *(47D, above) to Erasmus, who wrote the rather characteristic reply here excerpted. Zwingli's relationship with Erasmus had been cordial since 1515 when, as the pastor at Glarus, he first went to Basel to see him. In a subsequent exchange of letters, Erasmus called Zwingli "a friend beloved as a brother." Zwingli had invited Erasmus to settle in Zurich on the latter's return from Louvain in November 1521, but the latter preferred Basel, in part perhaps because he had already begun to distrust the course of the Reformation in Wittenburg and Zurich.*

Zwingli went to Basel in January 1522 to see Erasmus personally (see 45/161/20), but we discern in the following letter that Erasmus was wary of Zwingli and read the Archeteles *as a rather arrogant expression of independence that did more harm than good. A final alienation between them occurred in August of 1523 after a serious conflict over Ulrich von Hutten, the German knight (see Cast of Characters, No. 56). Finally in a letter to Philip Melanchthon dated Sept. 6, 1524, Erasmus wrote, "As for Zwingli, his conduct is utterly seditious!" (Hillerbrand, 1970, p. 175).*

G[reetings] most learned Zwingli.

I have read some pages of your *Apologeticus*.[1] I beseech you for the sake of the glory of the gospel, which I know you would favor and which we all who bear the name of Christ ought to favor, if you should issue anything hereafter, treat so serious a matter seriously,[2] and bear in mind evangelical modesty and patience. Consult your learned friends before you issue anything. I fear that the *Apologeticus* will cause you great peril and will injure the gospel. Even in the few pages that I have read there are many things I wanted to warn you about. I do not doubt that your prudence will take this in good part, for I have written late at night with a mind that is most solicitous for you.

Farewell.

September 8, 1522.

Yours, Erasmus.

Very upright Master Ulrich Zwingli, pastor at Zurich.[3]

Original: Staatsarchiv Zurich, E.II.339.p.87
Transcription: ZW, VII, No. 236
Translation: Taken from Jackson, 1900, pp. 172-73

47G
Macrinus[1] to Zwingli
Solothurn, October 15, 1522

The following excerpt from the letter of Macrinus to Zwingli contains two phrases that aptly describe Grebel's character in Act 4 of our drama. One is studia converterint *(converted to devotion, changed to allegiance, returned to applied learning). This is the source for the term that Bender used in the title of Chapter VI of his biography, "Zwingli's Convert."*

*In the introduction to Letter No. 50, below, we will have reason to reinterpret the meaning of this term in relation to what really happened to Grebel in 1522 and 1523—not a conversion in the technical 20th-century evangelical sense, but a zealous commitment to Zwingli's Reformation goals in Switzerland. In this sense the other phrase of Macrinus is more descriptive of Grebel's role at this phase of the drama—*euangelii patronum *(patron of the Reformation, advocate of the gospel).*

Greet ... Conrad Grebel,[2] who I hear has developed into an exceptional advocate of the gospel, a fact by Hercules[3] that gives me no small joy, for indeed such eminently gifted and learned young men who have returned to allegiance[4] there can really advance themselves and all mankind. Moreover, greet all the other true Christians, of whom there are more among you by far, thanks to your work, than are to be known anywhere else in Switzerland.

Original: Stadtbibliothek Zurich, Msc. F.46.p.205/208
Transcription: ZW, VII, No. 241

188

48
Grebel to Vadian
Zurich, November 21, 1522

Nearly ten months have elapsed since Conrad's last extant letter to Vadian, the longest period of silence in his eight-year correspondence. His silence surely indicates that his dependency needs were being met by others than Vadian during this interim. Documents 47A, 47B, 47C, and 47D have given some information on his activities between February and November. In one respect, it is the most important period of his life, in which he makes a definite shift from seeker to advocate in the cause of Zwingli's Reformation.

The intervening documents record several of the events accompanying that shift: his summons to appear in court in July for preaching against the monks, his poem in August "in gratitude for the gospel restored," appended to Zwingli's Archeteles, *and Zwingli's letter to Myconius of August 26, calling Grebel one of "the most learned and dedicated younger men."*

The present letter also clearly indicates that a shift is taking place. Grebel expresses a personal interest in the Reformation writings of Zwingli, Luther, and Melanchthon. He champions the cause of Christoph Schappeler, known as Sertorius, an evangelical pastor at Memmingen north of St. Gallen whose Reformation preaching was being suppressed by two reactionary monks. He hopes to be able to counter such enemies of the gospel by "the inspired Scriptures of God," and he asks Vadian to pray for him that he can "accept this ministry in earnest and triumph in it."

Greetings again and again, my Vadian.

You have heard that Zwingli is producing a book on the mass.[1] It is unknown to me who can be touched by his hand from the vicinity of my home. Therefore, however much you await it you will not get it through me, nor even through Zwingli I think, as one who would never conceive of treating that kind of a subject. Enough of this nonsense.

Seriously, I ask you whether you have received the Angli produced by Luther,[2] which I would have given you as a gift if only you had paid the bookseller in advance; for neither does he give them to me gratis nor likewise do you feed me and my family. Enough of this seriousness also, so I will put an end to it.

How about a subject of neither kind?[3] For the transportation of Hasler's books I paid fourteen batzen.[4] I wish either that the same sum be paid to me, without the smallest reduction, or that the barrel be returned. Now you know what I desire. Do what you are to do, that is, do it as a friend, do not neglect it. For it was performed by me by scraping together that little money from the Zellani.[5] Burdened by debt, I flee; condemned by the tyranny of poverty, I go into exile. Nor will those affluent words of yours assist me at all, delusive prophet, by which you prophesied that I would be nothing else than a Midas.[6]

Fie on the abbot[7] together with Wendelin![8] Lips and lettuce,[9] as they say, both of them twice—that is, in life and also in ordination—the offspring of the devil[10] and the veriest offspring indeed, whom I as readily as you I note, would want to treat as they deserve, to show to the world and the whole earth the penalties which these are destined to suffer for their heresies and monstrous crimes, for their unforgivable blasphemies against the Holy Spirit, if I could wish as much, if I could do as much in the ϑεοπνεύστοις τοῖς γράμμασι [inspired Scriptures of God].[11] Meanwhile, let the will of the Lord be done, as long as I cannot and you wish not nor dare to at καιρὸν [this time][12] and as long as Zwingli, though he wished and dared, is prevented by the stress of his occupations.[13] But why does Sertorius[14] not write against that sorcerer Elymas,[15] the enemy of all truth, the sodomist? O my Vadian! If you knew me, how I burn with zeal to pursue this kind of wolves,[16] how in truth the rest of my life would not be dear to me, unless I could worthily pronounce anathema on them from the gods above and below, lest you think it be from mortals only. And would that by the grace of God all would pray for me, that I accept this ministry in earnest and triumph in it.[17] I add nothing more, since no wagons of words could represent this mind of mine, which is to be discerned after the test has been made.[18]

There is nothing new with us. Perhaps you desire the New Testament given by labor of Melanchthon[19] from the state of Germany (and from a very Greece), explained by notes inserted above. Since it will be brought to us first during these days, snap but your little finger and you will have it, and let me know as always how many copies you want.

As for the rest: good wishes especially to the bishop[20] together with the whole church, of which Christ is the head through the gospel of grace; and the same to your sisters[21] for their welfare together with the family of Vadian; and finally I order that she who is less yours, younger by birth, may return as quickly as possible to her parents, who bear her absence unwillingly and reluctantly.[22] Farewell, but hey! who wrote to me those blasphemies of Cimicis,[23] namely of Wentelin,[24] the pseudo-Christ? Again farewell, my Vadian, very much an evangelist.

From Zurich, November 21, 1522.

Conrad Grebel, your friend.

To the lord Joachim Vadian, a man eminently learned in every sort of literature, dearest to his kinsman.

Original: Stadtbibliothek (Vadiana) St. Gallen, VB.II.109
Transcription: VB, II, No. 326

Grebel to Vadian
Zurich, December 1, 1522

Again, in the second of his five letters written in the last five weeks of the year, Grebel's chief concerns are events of the emerging Reformation—the request of some nuns for release from their vows in response to Zwingli's preaching, the case of Sertorius's application for the Winterthur pastorate, and the arrest of the pastor of Fislisbach for his Reformation preaching. It is a succinct, lively letter, signed "most evangelically."

Greetings, dearest Vadian.

The matter of the nuns[1] has been handled with great tumult. They must not leave until Pentecost, but they have been permitted to choose priests to whom they prefer to make confession and give ears when they preach and with whom they may attend when they sacrifice, that is, when they crucify Christ anew. Those who are of the Dominican order[2] may have their own monks from this sect of perdition.[3]

Take care that my little sister[4] is greaved and shod and girded[5] for her journey. My parents will send horses for her transportation, and they also invite you to accompany her. If you do this (I know for sure), you will do something that will make us very grateful. Indeed, come with your Sertorius,[6] whose case if I have not supported I will certainly support. If there is anything I can do in the investigation of heretical violence,[7] speaking σοφιστιχῶς [sophistically],[8] you will seem to see Hercules.[9] Thus we travail like the mountain, miserable and unlearned as we are in truth; and from the ridiculous, ridiculous mice are born.[10]

Let this right hand of mine drop off, O Jupiter,[11] if I with all my business have been able to write to the bishop.[12] However, I hope that he is well, beyond reproach, the husband of one wife.[13] For what use would one have for a husband of two or more? I jest. Give my regards to Jufli[14] again and again together with all your family and the Christians[15] (wo sy wir die selben Christen [if we be Christians ourselves]). Farewell most evangelically.

From Zurich, December 1.

The bishop of Fislisbach[16] is in the hands of the thief and robber, the false bishop of Constance.[17]

To the doctor Vadian, a man in every way learned . . . his.

Original: Stadtbibliothek (Vadiana) St. Gallen, VB.XII.275
Transcription: VB, III, Anhang, Nachtrag No. 87

49A
Zwingli to Vadian
Zurich, December 8, 1522

Simon Mäglin of St. Gallen, since 1517 priest in Winterthur fifteen miles northeast of Zurich had been in trouble from the start. Earlier in 1522, the Zurich Council had appointed Jacob Grebel and Heinrich Walder to go to Winterthur to investigate some offense in which he had been involved. The charges were subsequently taken to the episcopal court at Constance, and the diocesan bishop ordered Mäglin's arrest, whereupon he resigned, or as Conrad Grebel put it, "returned his letter of investiture" (51/194/19).

Meanwhile, Vadian solicited the help of Zwingli and the Grebels to fill the vacancy with Christopher Schappeler, also of St. Gallen, who was serving as preacher at Memmingen. Known as Sertorius (see 48/fn.14 and 49/fn.6), he is the licentiate referred to in the following letter, in which Zwingli describes how he and the Grebels are working together to secure Schappeler's appointment. On the outcome of their efforts, see 51/fns. 3-10.

Greetings!

Now I must simply forego everything else and direct my words solely to the single matter that must be facilitated, disregarding all else. Simon,[1] who was preacher in Winterthur until recently, has been dismissed from his position.[2] I learned this just today and am writing this on December 8. Your father-in-law advises that the Schappeler[3] people immediately send a deputation to us in Zurich in such a way, if it seems right, that on traveling through they can meet the Winterthur Council and then secure from us the recommendation for the licentiate[4] to present to the Winterthur Council. Hurry but σπεῖδε βραδέως [hurry slowly].[5] To be sure, those who are dispatched to request the recommendation must hurry. Meanwhile, somewhat more slowly of course, but still with deliberate speed, I will allow the licentiate to be called; whereby the mentioned delegation will secure the place by making the attempt en route. I order speed, therefore, lest another gets the recommendation of our council. Meanwhile, the Grebels and I will not let up on diligence. Otherwise, the work proceeds nicely, even if somewhat slower than you wished. He[6] has never worked out anything by lamplight and you are not unaware how difficult are any first attempts. But custom[7] will cause no annoyance, for by Hercules he satisfies us in those things which we observe. I cannot write more for the messenger must leave.

Farewell.

Zurich, etc. 1522.

Greetings to Burgauer,[8] Schürpf,[9] and all the good to you.

Huldr. Zwingli

Original: Stadtbibliothek (Vadiana) St. Gallen, Litt.misc.II.115
Transcription: VB, II, No. 327; ZW, VIII, No. 255

50
Grebel to Vadian
Zurich, December 25, 1522(?)[1]

H. S. Bender began his chapter on "Zwingli's Convert" with the comment that "the year 1522 marked an epoch for Conrad Grebel which was to lead to a transformation of his entire life" adding that "it may well be called a conversion" (HSB, pp. 76-77). Indeed, we noted some of the signs of change in Grebel's Letters 48 and 49—a new awareness of the inspiration of the Scriptures, a new self-identity as a co-worker in the Reformation of the church, and a new concern for intercessory prayer on behalf of others and of others for himself.

But his was not a "conversion" in the 20th-century revivalist sense of specific time and place. The confessions he makes in Letters 50 and 51, below, simultaneously touch the lowest and highest points of his new self-consciousness to date—the awareness that "what troubles me" is (as he once put it) "deservedly so because I have often consorted with prostitutes" (6/79/29-30) and the awareness that each one must "put on Christ and become a new creature born again by the divine Spirit" (195/13-14). Like a miserable thrush, he has defecated on himself and cannot remove the stain (193/38); but then as one who knows that Vadian will "understand me better than this stammering expresses" (195/20) he prays directly to the Lord, "O Christ . . . send one like Vadian, who by your truth may teach me true endurance" (195/17-19).

Thus, these two letters combine the themes of repentance and submission in a remarkable way. Grebel had just read Zwingli's two published sermons on the Word of God and on Mariolotry; and at the very time in his life when he would throw his energies into the work of this Reformation which is just beginning, he finds those energies depleted because of his dissolute past life. He is simultaneously sick at heart and hopeful in spirit. Indeed, these are the psychological ingredients of evangelical "conversion" in any age!

Greetings most humane man.

Unless your letter, which is not at hand, proves me wrong, you already have the booklets that Zwingli, a most incorrupt man, has published.[2] He published two, and these two you have. Had he published a third, since you ask out of friendship, a third you would also have received.

Father is troubled by the λυσιμελὴς ἡ ποδαγρα [limb-troubling gout]; it troubles him, moreover, because it is the daughter of λυσιμελοῦς βάκχου καὶ λυσιμελοῦς Αφροδίτης [limb-loosing Bacchus and limb-loosing Aphrodite].[3] There is neither time nor space for what troubles me, which I am prevented from reciting for some other reasons also. I shall deal with it more at length another time. I have been foolish, to my own harm perhaps, because I, miserable thrush, have shit on myself.[4] I cannot improve unless you prescribe for me a rule whereby I can return and be wise, unless you not only pray for wisdom, but also reveal it to me, how it should be sought and from whom. Stupid, by Jove, and hard have I been. Once you forgive and teach me, I will be tractable and receptive of wisdom.

Farewell, most humane man, with my most human and dearest sister.[5]

Zurich, from my purgatory,[6] on the Lord's day after the heretical day, which was instituted or certainly confirmed by the heretic Thomas.[7]

Conrad Grebel, who unless he is wholly yours, may he be damned.

To your pastor,[8] to whom I owe my soul, relate my words of salvation and good news.[9] Unless I wish that you are all well, let me not live.

> To Vadian, a most human man, and also most learned, to the Homer of poetry[10] and the Hippocrates of medicine,[11] revered above all.

Original: Stadtbibliothek (Vadiana) St. Gallen, VB.XI.100
Transcriptions: VB, VII (Ergänzungsband), No. 12; M-S, No. 20

51
Grebel to Vadian
Zurich, December 29, 1522

Greetings, my Vadian.

First of all, if you can, send the money paid by the peasant of Appenzell.[1] If it has not been paid, collect it or do not let the barrel be given.[2]

Regarding the affair of Sertorius:[3] Simon Mäglin[4] has resigned his position at Winterthur. He has sent back the letter of investiture, and access to Winterthur has been forbidden.[5] A certain person spoke at a public meeting here in the hope of gaining this preaching position.[6] So I learned from Zwingli, who is the informant about this letter and the bearer of the news Zwingli heard from Schellenberg, the senator of Winterthur.[7] Since you commanded me to send news about this matter when there was occasion, have I not done so? There remains the need that there be legates at hand more vigilant and loyal than Captain Ambrosius,[8] whom I shall blame if Sertorius does not win out. It will be your duty to direct your influence to him.[9] We are already diligently fulfilling our responsibility.[10]

My parents express their thanks that you have entertained their daughter so well and so long; and they are thinking about bringing her back.[11] They wish that you would arrange to send her back with the legates, if possible; if it is not possible with them, that brother Benedict[12] might bring her. They wish above everything else that this be done. This courier[13] will follow on foot with the little sister, without legates or without Benedict as escort, but at the expense of father, whose will it is, not mine, for I am relaying his message that these things be done. He goes as his courier. So why should I pay anything? If I have as much as an obol,[14] may Plutus,[15] the mightiest god of this world, damn me, and may he be more sharp-sighted in punishing me as a liar than Lynceus.[16]

My Vadian, when I wrote my last letter to you,[17] I lost command of myself more than ever before because of the bad state of my mind. Would that you were here as soon as possible; and by whatever time it might be appointed, how could you not arrive most eagerly welcomed by me?

Mother is quite ungodly[18] toward me, toward my spouse she is even more rabid. I fear for her salvation, unless she puts on Christ and becomes a new creature born again by the divine Spirit.[19] And the time begins to appear when many—would that it not include her also—eat the body of Christ unworthily and to condemnation if they have not in brotherly fashion forgiven the sins of others.[20] O Christ, send to her, send to me, the ministry of Vadian, send one like Vadian, who by your truth may teach her to unlearn such ungodliness and who may teach me true endurance.

Please try to understand me better than this stammering expresses. If there is anything else, I shall write to you by Leopold;[21] for now I am in haste, lest the messenger not wait for me and leave. Give my prayers and good wishes to your dear ones. Zwingli instructs me to send his regards but he cannot write as he is occupied with capitular business,[22] as they call it. Zurich, third to last day of December, 1522.

Conrad Grebel.

My parents and I wish you a prosperous year.

Der Enderly ist gester von Nürenberg Kommen; spricht, der Luther hab von der mess und wider die bapstpaffen ein heftig büchly by XIII bogen geschriben. Hab er umm kein ½ (??) g(ulden) dahinnen wellen lassen, aber nit mögen zwegen bringen. [Enderli[23] arrived yesterday from Nuremberg. He reports that Luther has written an angry little book of 13 pages concerning the mass and against the papal priests.[24] He did not want to let it go for a half guilder, but he could not manage it.]

To doctor Joachim von Watt.

14 bazen heuschend vom Appenzeller [14 Batzen requested from the Appenzeller].[25]

Original: Stadtbibliothek (Vadiana) St. Gallen, VB.II.113
Transcription: VB, II, No. 332

51A
The First Zurich Disputation
January 29, 1523

The introduction of the Protestant Reformation in Switzerland is often dated from the First Public Disputation held in Zurich on January 29, 1523. As in the case of Lutheranism in Germany, the founding of the Reformed Church in Switzerland was accomplished under sponsorship by the state. Zwingli sought the support and alliance of the Zurich burgomaster and City Council for his reform proposals, appealing to them for permission to hold a public disputation at which they would sit as judges and award the victory to the side presenting the best arguments. The method of the disputation was borrowed from the medieval university and included such procedures as the publication of theses for debate, the appointment of impartial chairmen, free and open participation, especially by known opponents of the theses, and the writing of accurate minutes of the discussion for possible later publication.

As Jackson wrote, Zwingli "looked forward with great confidence to such a public debate, for which he had prepared the way by his preaching and writing and talking ever since he came to Zurich in December 1518. The City Council took up the idea and were perhaps flattered by the position they would take in this debate. They issued the invitation to the people of the canton and city of Zurich and to the bishops of Constance and of the adjoining dioceses. Zwingli prepared and had printed 67 articles as a program for the debate, and looked forward with great eagerness to the time set, which was the 29th of January 1523.

"On that eventful day six hundred persons—priests and laymen of the canton of Zurich, along with a few delegates from the bishop of Constance and some others—met in the Town Hall and held the debate, which is preserved for us by Erhart Hegenwald, a schoolmaster in Zurich, who informs us that he wrote it from memory immediately after hearing it. His account was edited by Zwingli and published in Zurich. John Faber (or Fabri), vicar general of the diocese of Constance, one of the ablest disuptants of the Roman Church side, bore the brunt of the attack upon that church. Zwingli was the principal speaker on the other side.

"Fabri also published his account of the debate: 'Ein warlich underrichtung wie es zie Zürich bey de Zwinglin uff den einen und zwentzigsten tag des monats Januarii rest verschine ergangen sey' (Leipzig? 1523). In it, naturally, he appeared to greater advantage than in Zwingli's account, but it seems to have given offense to an enthusiastic portion of the audience, and some of these young men thought they had a good opportunity to bring out a satire in the interests of the new faith, and so they concocted a book which they called 'The Vulture Plucked.' . . . This was a gross attack upon Fabri, and he was very indignant and appealed to the city authorities of Zurich to bring the offenders to book, but the city authorities regarded the whole affair

as a kind of joke and took no action in the matter. The three accounts of this important debate supplemented one another. . . .

"The result of the debate was the enthusiastic approval of Zwingli's teachings, and an order from the authorities not only to continue their presentation, but enjoining such teaching upon all the priests of the canton. Thus this debate, which is known as the First Disputation, is of great historical interest as marking the official beginning of the Reformation in German Switzerland" (Jackson, 1901, pp. 40-41).

It should be added for the sake of accuracy that the bishop's representative, Johannes Faber, had never really acknowledged the authority of the disputation to deal with questions of doctrine; and thus, as in the case of the later disputations on the question of baptism, Zwingli's "victory" was less of a decisive defeat of his opponents on specific issues than of a public assent to the authority of the Scriptures and a governmental mandate to preach the gospel on the basis of biblical authority. Included in the present collection is the edict that was issued by the City Council, followed by several brief excerpts from the debate itself. For an English translation of the entire disputation, see Jackson, 1901, pp. 40-117. What follows is a revised text based upon the version in Jackson.

After this the burgomaster of Zurich permitted everyone who did not belong to the council to go to his lodging to eat, until further notice, for it was now approaching noon. But the burgomaster ordered the councillors to remain, perhaps to consult further concerning this.[1] Thus they arose, and many of the visitors[2] went to their lodging. This much was done in the forenoon.

After everyone[3] had eaten, they were told to appear again in the city hall to hear the decision made by the wise Council of Zurich. After everyone had gathered, the following was publicly read before the assembly:

Whereas you now, in the name of the Lord and upon the request of the burgomaster, [Small] Council, and Great Council of the city of Zurich, and for the reasons indicated in the letters sent to you, have obediently appeared, etc., and whereas also a year has elapsed since the honorable delegation of our gracious lord of Constance[4] appeared here[5] in the city of Zurich before the burgomaster, Small and Great Council, on account of such matters as you have heard today, and when these matters having been discussed in various fashions it was reported that our gracious lord of Constance was going to call together the scholars in his diocese along with the preachers of the adjoining dioceses and prelacies to advise, assist, and confer with them, so that a unanimous decision might be reached and everyone would know how to conduct himself; but since to date nothing

197

much has been done in the matter by our gracious lord of Constance, perhaps for noteworthy reasons, and since the dissension among the clergy and laity continually increases, therefore once more the burgomaster, [Small] Council, and Great Council of the city of Zurich, in the name of God, for the sake of peace and Christian unity, have fixed this date and procured the honorable delegation of our gracious lord of Constance (for which they give their gracious, exalted, and diligent thanks) and have also for this purpose by means of their open letters, as stated above, written, called, and sent for all the people's priests,[6] preachers, and curates,[7] collectively and singly, out of all their regions into their city, so that those who accuse and call each other heretic might cross-examine each other.

And whereas Master Huldrych Zwingli, canon and preacher in the Grossmünster in the city of Zurich, has hitherto been much slandered and accused on account of his teachings, yet no one has arisen against him in response to his declaring and explaining his articles[8] or attempted to refute him by means of the Scriptures, and whereas he has several times also challenged those who have accused him of being a heretic to step forward, and no one has proved any sort of heresy in his teaching, therefore the aforesaid burgomaster, council, and Great Council of this city of Zurich, in order to quell disturbance and dissension, have upon due deliberation and consultation decided, resolved, and it is their earnest opinion that Master Huldrych Zwingli should continue and keep on as before to proclaim the holy gospel and the pure holy Scripture with the Holy Spirit according to his ability, as long and as often[9] as he will until something better is made known to him.

Moreover, all their people's priests, curates, and preachers in their[10] city and regions and districts shall undertake and preach nothing but what can be proved by the holy gospel and the pure divine Scriptures. Furthermore, they shall henceforth in no wise slander, calling each other heretic or other insulting word.

Whoever then appears contrary and does not sufficiently comply with this, the same shall be restrained to such an extent that they must see and learn that they have done wrong.

Done on Thursday after Carolus,[11] in the city of Zurich, the 29th day of January, in the year 1523.

HULDRYCH ZWINGLI

Thereupon arose Master Huldrych Zwingli and said: God be praised and thanked who wants his holy Word to reign in heaven and on earth.[12] And to you, Milords of Zurich, the eternal God will doubtless lend strength and might in other affairs also, so that you may uphold the truth of God, the holy gospel, and foster preaching[13] in your regions. Do not doubt that Almighty God will repay it and reward you in other matters. Amen!

Whether this decree that was read pleased the vicar of Constance or not, I really do not know, for he spoke as follows:

[VICAR][14]

Dear lords! Much has been spoken today against the praiseworthy traditions, usage, and ordinance of the holy popes and fathers, whose ordinances and decrees have until now been held in all Christendom to be true, just, and irreproachable. To protect and maintain this, I have offered myself [to speak] before the universities. But now when for the first time today I have looked and glanced through the articles of Master Huldrych (for I have not read them before),[15] it truly seems to me that these are wholly and entirely against the ceremonies,[16] that is, attacking and combating the praiseworthy majesty and glory of the churches, done and ordained for the praise and honor of God, to the disadvantage of the divine teaching of Christ. This I shall prove.

MASTER HULDRYCH

Lord vicar, do that. We would very much like to hear that.

VICAR

It is written, Luke 9[:50]: *Qui non est adversum vos,* etc., "He that is not against us is for us."[17] Now these praiseworthy services or splendor of the churches (like fasting, confession, having festival days, singing, reading, consecrating, reading mass, and other similar things) have always been decreed and ordered by the holy fathers, not against God, but only for the praise and honor of God Almighty, and it seems very strange and unjust to me to despise and reject them as though wrong.

MASTER HULDRYCH

When my lord vicar speaks and quotes from the gospel, "He that is not against us is for us," I say that is true. "Now the customs and ordinances of the church are ordered and decreed by men, not against God," etc. Lord Vicar, prove that, for Christ always despises human ordinance and decree, as we have in Matthew 15[:1-9]. When the Jews and Pharisees blamed and reprimanded the Lord because his disciples did not obey the teaching and tradition of the elders, Christ said to them: "Why do ye also transgress the commandment of God by way of your teaching and tradition?" etc. ... God the Lord cares more for obedience to his words—although you apply the word "obedience" to human obedience—than for all our sacrifices and self-made ecclesiastical practices, as we have it in all the divine writings of the prophets, apostles, and saints. The greatest and proper honor to offer to God is to uphold his Word, living according to his will, not according to our own notions and good intentions.

199

VICAR

Christ said, according to John 16[:12]: "I have yet many things to say unto you, but ye cannot bear them now. Howbeit when he, the Spirit of truth, is come he will guide you into all truth." Much has been inaugurated by the holy fathers inspired by the Holy Ghost, and especially the fasts and the Saturday[18] by the twelve apostles, which also is not described in the gospel, in which doubtless the Holy Ghost taught and instructed them.

ZWINGLI

Lord vicar, prove from the Scriptures that the twelve apostles inaugurated Saturday and fasts. Christ said in the passage above that the Spirit of God will teach them all truth, undoubtedly not human pomp. For according to John 14[:26] he said, "The Holy Ghost, whom the Father will send in my name, he will teach you (meaning the twelve apostles) all things and bring to your remembrance (advise and recall) all the things that I have said to you."[19] Undoubtedly as though he said, "Not what you think fit, but what the Holy Ghost teaches you in my name in accordance with the truth, not with human thoughts." Therefore, the holy apostles never taught, inaugurated, ordered, or decreed otherwise than as Christ had told them in the gospel. For Christ said to them, "You are my friends if you do what I have decreed and commanded [John 15:14]." The dear disciples did this diligently and did not teach anything other than as the true Master had sent them to teach and instruct, which is proved by the epistles of St. Paul and St. Peter. Hence your arguments can avail nothing. . . .

VICAR

Master Huldrych, you said in your articles that the mass is no sacrifice.[20] Now I shall prove that for 1400 years *missa* has been considered a sacrifice and called an offering. For *missa* is a Hebrew word[21] known by us as sacrifice, and the apostles also were known as *missam sacrificium.*

ZWINGLI

Lord vicar! prove that!

VICAR

Today I spoke as a vicar. Now I speak as a John.

ZWINGLI

Yes, indeed! Had you long before today taken off your vicar's hat, it would have suited you well at times today. Then one could have spoken with you as with a John.[22] I say that you should prove from the Scriptures that the mass is a sacrifice, for as St. Paul says (Heb. 9:12, 25, 26), Christ was sacrificed no more than once, not by other blood, but "by his own blood he entered once into the holy place," etc., nor yet that he should offer himself often, as the high priests in the Old Testament had to do for the sin of the people, for then Christ must have suffered often. Likewise, St.

Paul writes (Heb. 10:12), "But after he had offered one sacrifice forever, this man sat down on the right hand of God." Likewise (Heb. 10:14), "For by one offering he hath forever perfected them that are sanctified." Likewise (Heb. 7:11-28), by so much does this sacrifice surpass the sacrifices in the Old Testament performed by the high priest, by so much more powerful is this declared to be that it was sufficient once for the sins of all people. Who is so unreasonable as not to note that Christ must never be sacrificed in the mass as a sacrifice for us when he hears that the Holy Spirit speaks from the Scriptures, "For not more than *semel*[23]—once—by one offering entered he into the holy place; otherwise he must die often"? [Heb. 9:25-26]. Now matters have come to such a state that the papists have made out of the mass a sacrifice for the living and the dead, contrary to the clear Scriptures of God; they wish to protect this also, so that they may defend their reputation as scholars or their avarice. We also know well that *missa* does not come from Hebrew[24] or Greek; but you present nothing from the Scriptures.

VICAR

I will do that and prove it before the universities, where learned judges sit. And choose a place, be it Paris, Cologne, or Freiburg, whichever you please. Then I shall overthrow the articles presented by you and prove them to be wrong.

MASTER HULDRYCH

I am ready, wherever you wish, as also today I offered to give answer at Constance if a safe conduct (as to you here) is promised to me and respected. But I want no judge, except the Scriptures, as they have been said and spoken by the Spirit of God; no human being, whoever he be. Before you overthrow one article, the earth must be overthrown, for they are the Word of God.

VICAR

This is a strange affair! When only two are quarreling about a field or about a meadow, they are sent before a judge. They likewise accept him, and you refuse to allow these matters to come before a judge. How would it be if I should propose that you take Milords of Zurich as judges? Would you not accept them and allow them to judge?[25]

MASTER HULDRYCH ZWINGLI

In worldly affairs and in quarrels, I know well that one should go before the judges with the disputes, and I also would choose to have Milords of Zurich as judges, since they stand for reasonableness. But in those matters which pertain to divine wisdom and truth, I will accept no one as judge and witness except the Scriptures, the Spirit of God speaking from the Scriptures. . . . [26] The holy Scriptures are everywhere in agreement with themselves, the Spirit of God flows so abundantly, walks in them so joyfully, that every diligent reader, insofar as he approaches with humble heart, will decide by means of the Scriptures, taught by the Spirit of God, until he attains the truth. For Christ, whenever he argued with the learned Jews and Pharisees, referred to the Scriptures, saying, "Search the Scriptures" [Jn. 5:39]. Also, "What is written in the law?" etc. [Lk. 10:26]. Therefore I say the matter needs no human judge. But that at various times such matters generally have been brought before human judges and universities is the reason that the priests no longer desired to study, and paid greater attention to wantonness, at times to chess, than to reading the Bible. Hence it came about that those were considered as scholars and chosen as judges who had acquired for themselves only a certificate or reputation of wisdom, which they had previously purchased, who knew nothing concerning the right Spirit of God or the Scriptures. But now through the grace of God, the divine gospel and Scriptures have been born and brought to light by means of print (especially at Basel),[27] so that they are in Latin and German, wherefrom every pious Christian who can read or knows Latin can easily inform himself and learn the will of God. It has come to the point, God be praised, that now a priest who is diligent may learn and know as much in two or three years concerning the Scriptures as formerly many in ten or fifteen years. Therefore I want to have admonished all the priests who have benefices under Milords of Zurich or in their regions that each one be studious and strive to read the holy Scriptures, and especially those who are preachers and caretakers of the soul, let each one buy a New Testament in Latin, or in German, if he does not understand the Latin or is unable to interpret it. For I also am not ashamed to read German at times, on account of easier presentation. Let one begin to read first the Gospel of St. Matthew, especially the 5th, 6th, and 7th chapters. After that let him read the other Gospels, so that he may know what they write and say. After that he should take the Acts. After this the epistles of Paul, but first the one to the Galatians. Then the epistle of St. Peter and other sacred texts; thus he can readily form within himself a right Christian life, and become more skillful to teach this better to others also. After that let him work in the Old Testament, in the prophets and other books of the Bible, which, I understand, are soon to appear in print in Latin and German.[28] Let them buy such books and never mind the sophistical and other empty writings or the decree and work of the papists, but tell and preach to the people the holy Gospel written by the four evangelists and apostles. Then the people will become more willing and skillful in leading a peaceful Christian life. For matters have reached such a state that even the laymen and women know more of the Scriptures than some priests and clergymen.

Original Publication: *Handlung der Versammlung in der Stadt Zurich auf den 29. Januar 1523,* published 3/3/1523
Transcription: ZW, I, No. 18; Schuler-Schulthess, pp. 114-68

51B
Castelberger's Home Bible Study Fellowship[1]
Zurich, 1523[2]

"Matters have reached such a state that even the laymen and women know more of the Scriptures than some priests and clergymen." Zwingli's exclamation at the end of our last document presupposes the kind of informal Bible school led by Andreas Castelberger in various homes in Zurich in 1523. Although Conrad Grebel is not specifically mentioned in the following document, it is an important addition to our collection for a number of reasons:

(1) The close relationship between Grebel and Castelberger to be revealed in Grebel's letter to this intimate associate (see No. 69, below) presupposes their mutual participation in such a Bible study fellowship as this. Such lay Bible study groups began in 1522 and gathered around "readers" like Castelberger who were able to translate and exposit certain parts of the Bible to a small group gathered in someone's house.

(2) The strong attitude that Grebel expressed in his letters of June 17 and July 15, 1523, against the system of ecclesiastical tithes (see 52/207/32-33, 208/8-9, 53/220/21-29) presupposes a source context like that of the Castelberger circle, as revealed in the following document.

(3) The Anabaptist ethic of peace and nonresistance to which Grebel gave expression in his letter to Müntzer (63/290(10ff.) presupposes a similar contextual source. In 22/119/1, dated August 3, 1520, Grebel exclaims to Vadian about Myconius's unpublished dialogue "on not going to war," and it may have been Castelberger who returned this manuscript to Myconius through Zwingli in Zurich from the Froben printshop in Basel.

(4) Three of the names mentioned in the present document (Castelberger, Aberli, and Pur) were cosigners of Grebel's letter to Müntzer, and a fourth (Hochrütiner) was "my brother in God and Christ" who "has heard the word of God with us" (58/256/13-14). This is very likely a reference to the Castelberger Bible study group.

(5) The courtroom context for this document fits the edginess of reactionary councillors already revealed in Documents 47A, 47B, and 47C, which did involve Grebel. This indicates that certain authority figures within the power structure of Zurich were not entirely well disposed to such activities as home Bible study fellowships because of the way they gave to the oppressed groups a means of expression against such social problems as unjust taxation

203

and warfare by paid mercenaries. Such groups could certainly generate dissent and a serious challenge to the existing establishment.

(6) The document confirms the interpretation given to the 47A-47G series that to the end of 1523, the teaching of ethically sensitive laymen was not already undermining Zwingli's program as Walton and others have argued, but was in harmony with it "to a tittle" at this time, as Hans of Wyl testified. It was probably Zwingli's own sodalitium literarium Tigurinense *(Zurich Literary Association), which Grebel attended in 1521 (see 42/157/ 24-25) and which also began with a study of Paul's letter to the Romans, that provided the model for Castelberger's* sodalitium.

Goeters (p. 255) summarizes the group as follows: "Castelberger combined the exposition of the text with strong attacks against self-righteousness, spiritual pride, usury, and flavored this with concrete practical examples. Great emphasis was placed on the repudiation of war and mercenary service. Moreover, humanistic (i.e., secular) and evangelical (i.e., sacred) teachings were sharply differentiated. Because of the suspicions of loyal Catholic fellow citizens, the group became known to the Council and the object of its investigation, probably in the early summer of 1523. Since it was discerned to be unobjectionable, it was permitted to continue. The group ... should be considered the cradle of the Anabaptist movement in Zurich."

Proceedings concerning what Andreas on the Crutches[3] preached.

Heine Aberli,[4] baker, testified: Now that by the grace of God evangelical doctrine is being preached here in the city and elsewhere, he—this witness—likewise [Lorenz] Hochrütiner[5] of St. Gallen, Wolf [Ininger],[6] cabinetmaker, and Bartlime [Pur],[7] the baker, had at first with good friendly intentions planned together and reached a decision to meet and perhaps to choose and obtain someone who could open up to them the evangelical Christian teaching and the epistles of Paul and instruct [them]. Then they had gone into the home of this witness and begged Andreas on the Crutches that he undertake to do this with them as stated above, and teach them as well and as faithfully as he knew and was able. But when they had met in his house for some time several good fellows contacted them on the street and asked if they could not also go with them and listen to the teaching that they were conducting among themselves. Then, when he and the others gave them permission insofar as it was done with good intentions, and their room was too small for them and not large enough, they had moved the teaching into the house of H[err] Wolfgang,[8] the chaplain, at his suggestion, meeting there several days. And now during these days there were so many of them that they needed still more space, and they went into the home of Hans of Wyl[9] on his suggestion, and there Andreas on the Crutches gave them some good teaching; namely, reading, expositing, and explaining Paul's epistle to the Romans. And although the spirit, mind, and intention of this witness and of his other companions were always good and Christian—for this he called on God as witness—nevertheless because of the addition of several persons, among them some who did not come to learn but to attack Andreas in his admonition and teaching, some evil arose. For instance, when said Andreas in these days crossed over the bridge, Rudolph Ziegler came to him and said to him, "Lord People's Priest! When are you going to preach?" and the like. Andreas replied that he does not preach, that the pope had preached to him (Ziegler) and filled his purse. Then Rudolph Ziegler said that he would throw him off the bridge. Then Andreas said, "Throw your mother asshole off [the bridge]." Andreas himself told him that this is what happened. Right afterward, on the same day after the ninth hour, when Andreas began to teach down in the house of Hans of Wyl—not in a barn or cellar as has been said—and explained and exposited Paul's epistle to the Romans, several young fellows, like Rudolph and Heinrich Ziegler, M[aster] Grimm's son, Hänsi Wissgerber and others came to them, [and] they had mocked and laughed at them.

Then he, the oft-mentioned Andreas, had told them that M[aster] Huldrych [Zwingli] had previously said, "If a married woman calls another woman a whore and this married woman boasts of her piety and claims to be better and more righteous than the whore, then if the one accused of being a whore confesses herself to be a sinner before God, she is as good as the married woman." And again, he had read to them and said, "He who does not have need, be he clergy or laity, but engages in usury[10] with benefices and other things, or lays up more goods than he needs in order better and richer therewith to raise and feed his bastard children, and on the other hand a man with poor children steals because of his poverty to support himself and his children, then the one who steals because of poverty is as good and righteous in God's sight as those who have laid up so much usury and property beyond their need"—all with the explanation as above. He, Andreas, also said he does not mean that the usurer should be taken to the gallows like the one who steals out of poverty; but in God's sight and as taught in evangelical doctrine, the poor thief is as good as the other man.

Lorenz Hochrütiner[11] said the same things as Heine Aberli concerning the beginning when he and the others came together. And so much more. When they asked Andreas to open evangelical doctrine to them according to his best insight and understanding, Andreas asked them at the beginning to call upon God the Almighty for grace and for a good, peaceable Christian mind, and openly said to them a number of times that if they were ever about to argue with anyone and perhaps boast of their evangel-

205

ical doctrine and look down on the other because of it, he would rather simply not tell them anything or give them any instruction.

Likewise, Andreas said much about warring,[12] how the divine teaching is so strongly against it and how it is a sin, and expressed this opinion: "Anyone who could make do with his own paternal inheritance and goes to war, receives money and wages to kill good people and takes their possessions when they have done him no wrong—that warrior is a murderer in the eyes of God the Almighty and according to evangelical doctrine and no better than one who murders or steals because of his poverty, although that is not in accord with human laws here in the world, and is not so harmful."

He, this witness, and the others had not begun their undertaking for the purpose of gluttony, drunkenness or useless waste, but for the most part to avoid going into public drinking places; for at present people are so unpleasant to one another, and one says this and the other that, and people become so hostile to one another that they decided that their undertaking was better in the sight of God. People may have said that there was wine and drunken living; but there was not. Only when Andreas had finished his teaching and a few wanted to drink a glass of wine was it allowed.

Hans of Wyl[13] said: As Heine Aberli and Lorenz Hochrütiner have said about Andreas's teaching, so it was. And he was pleased with the affair, for Andreas's teaching agreed with M[aster] Huldrych's to a tittle.

Ulrich Trinkler[14] testified the same thing as Aberli about wives and stealing. About murder he could not say, for he had not heard it.

M[aster] Hans Scherer testified that he knew nothing about the beginning of the school and the other matters. He had merely heard that Andreas on the Crutches had said that a man who had income and money and would therewith drive a poor man from his house, fields, meadows, and whatever he owns, was worse than a thief and a murderer in God's sight, and that he had said that if anyone thought he was incorrect and not speaking the truth, let him come to him and he would test it with him from the Scriptures.

Original: Aktensammlung, No. 623
Transcription: Muralt-Schmid, Nachtrag, No. 397

52
Grebel to Vadian
Zurich, June 17, 1523

Since Grebel's last letter, nearly six months have passed, during which the First Doctrinal Disputation mandated the authority of the Scriptures for the Reformation in Zurich and Andreas Castelberger started his home Bible study meetings.

The depression of spirit that Grebel expressed in his Christmas letter (No. 50) has passed and he can open the following letter with the words "All is well." Then he turns immediately to matters concerning the progress of the Reformation—the closing of the convents and the petition of six villages in the domain of Zurich for the abolition of the tithe assessments (see 52A, below).

He closes with an expression of concern that his former friend and schoolmaster, Benedict Burgauer, the pastor in St. Gallen, is resisting Reformation changes by adhering to such questionable Roman Catholic doctrines as purgatory. Grebel predicts that Burgauer will either "vomit up this doctrine of abomination" or step aside so that a more Reformation-minded preacher can take his place.

G[reetings].

All is well. The nuns have been given the opportunity to leave the convent if they wish, now or later.[1] Four men of senatorial rank selected for this purpose will distribute to those who are leaving what of substance and possessions they brought into the order when they were initiated.[2] In fact, it was the counsel of the senate regarding their collective wealth and earnings that the convent should make a declaration, so that nothing could possibly be taken away from those who remain or turned over to the monks for their use.[3] It was a capital punishment to the "preaching monks" (as they are called) to see the nuns snatched from their wolflike jaws. Leo acts as pastor, but why did I not say bishop?[4]

The [Council of] 200[5] also enacted the following: Those whose means are small or whose credit [faith?][6] is not yet adequate to think of leaving the convent are requested not to change their monastic garb, for with different apparel from that of the order they would be a stumbling block to the weak or (if we prefer) to the rebels.

Nothing has been decided yet about the matter of the tithes,[7] but it will be decided five days from now.[8] There is nothing else that you ought to know from me, except that I grieve that Benedict, your bishop, has departed to purgatory,[9] as they call it, or rather as they wickedly contrive and dogmatically defend. I always feared that political expediency might turn him in a direction other than what was either worthy of him or that I could consider good. May the author of the gospel accordingly overrule this departure for the better, unless perchance he may not have been dismissed, who in these circumstances practically shouts that he will reverse himself by vomiting up the doctrine of abomination.[10] But if this is the situation, I would not lose hope that another laborer will succeed to the harvest of St. Gallen,[11] and that this one at last will be sent from God. I shall give a letter for you to Benedict, your brother[12] (if only Christ does not forbid), in which I shall let you know how the abuses of the tithe turned out and everything else that happens along with it. I pray for a true peace for all among you who seek not their own but the things of God.[13] I wish for a successful delivery for your wife[14] and that you are all well.

Zurich. 17 June, 1523.

Conrad Grebel, yours from the soul.

J. Jacob Ammaan[15] sends his prayers to you.

To Joachim Vadian, affectionately his from the soul.

Original: Stadtibliothek (Vadiana) St. Gallen, VB.II.131
Transcriptions: VB, III, No. 348; M-S, No. 1

52A
Council Decree on the Tithe
Zurich, June 22, 1523

In 52/fn.7, above, we referred to the importance of the tithe question in the early history of the Zurich Reformation. Although this issue was only incidental to the Doctrinal Disputation in January, Zwingli had claimed more than once (and probably in various sermons) to be opposed to the tithing system by which the clergy were supported. As in the cases of other early Reformation issues, such as the Lenten fast and the worship of images, he spoke his mind but waited for his parishioners, and particularly the magistrates, to begin to act on the principles that he was preaching.

The first to act on the principle of the voluntary support of the clergy vis-à-vis the compulsory tithe was a parishioner of Simon Stumpf in Hongg, who arbitrarily reduced the tithe on produce owed to the abbot of Wettingen, the administrator of the parish, and to the canons of the Grossmünster, to whom the abbot was accountable. The parishioner had no doubt been spurred on by Stumpf, who had preached that "one does not owe the tithe." The council jailed the violator and issued a decree on September 22 renewing the terms of payment on the grain tithe with the added provision that legitimate complaints could be presented to the council during the ensuing year.

Then in December 1522 Wilhelm Reublin was called by the local parish of Wytikon to be its priest in place of the interim chaplain assigned out of Zurich. To forestall a reaction in Zurich, the parish obtained permission to do

208

this from the Grossmünster Chapter in exchange for a promise to continue to pay the tithes until a new arrangement was made, presumably within a reasonable period of time. But when a review had not happened by March 1523, the Wytikon parishioners became increasingly unhappy over their double financial liability. So they petitioned for relief, and the council took the following action on March 19:

"To the people from Wytikon, who have come into conflict with the provost and chapter of the Grossmünster to which they belong as members and owe the tithe, in the matter of the appointing of their own priest and on account of the tithe, permission is granted to keep the priest they have appointed until a final decision by the council at the end of the year; but they are obligated to pay the tithe in line with their agreement to pay it willingly, unless others no longer give it, in which case they would also want to be released" (Egli, Aktens., No. 351, p. 125).

It was not long before other rural communities like Wytikon were unwilling to continue to pay the tithe, and in June six villages respectfully petitioned the Zurich Council for relief. The decision of the council of June 22 reported in the following document was a firm negative reply. Grebel's attitude to this action will be found in 53/220/23-24, where he writes that the "senate fathers," who should more rightly be called the "decimating fathers," are acting "tyrannically and like the Turk in this matter of the tithes." For Zwingli's attitude on the subject, see the introduction to document 52B.

(Monday of Ten Thousand Knights). Burgomaster Schmid, Councillors and Representatives.

1. The delegates of the parishes of Zollikon, Riesbach, Fällanden, Hirslanden, Unterstrass, and Wytikon complain about the provost and chapter of the Grossmünster in Zurich because of the tithe.[1] "They have now been informed and instructed by the holy gospel that the tithe is nothing but an alms,[2] and that some of the canons used such assessments for useless and frivolous things, as was known. For that they had to pay money for every sacrament and other things that really burdened them, such as bellringing, baptisms, tombstones, and burials; and they were hopeful that Milords would truly consider their grievances as well as the abuses that are practiced with the tithe, and come to the aid of their poor subjects." The chapter appealed to its old rights and liberties, which had not been increased by any new assessments; and it hoped to be defended in this, even though they might well tolerate "whatever good Milords could do."

2. The council decides that the parishes should give the tithe as in the past, payable when this has been written and twice published, except in the case new increases have been made in the past twenty or thirty years. In

209

such cases, the council will decide later whatever is necessary. Concerning the alleged abuses, the council will have its [appointed] members consult with the canons to undertake suitable and appropriate steps. The petitioners are to go home and be quiet.

Transcription: Aktensammlung, No. 368

52B
Zwingli's Sermon on Divine and Human Justice
June 24, 1523

The attitude of Zwingli on the issue of the compulsory tithe must be gleaned from various statements he made on the subject as early as 1520 and as late as the first half of 1525; but the excerpt from the following sermon that he preached on June 22, 1523, and published in pamphlet form on July 30 is certainly pivotal. John H. Yoder provides an excellent historical-theological background for understanding the document excerpt in its larger context:

"Since the favorable outcome of the disputation of January 29, 1523, one of the major themes in Zwingli's redoubled preaching of social renewal was the immorality of the tithes and interest by which the maintenance of the monasteries and many a priest's living were largely assured. Thesis 67 of the articles (Schlussreden) *proposed by Zwingli for the disputation had expressed his willingness to discuss further concerning 'interests, tithes, unbaptized children, and confirmation,' issues concerning which he differed from tradition without desiring to bring them to the forefront of the debate. In the* Exposition *of the 67 articles published later in the spring he further indicated, without extensive argument, that the only reasons which kept him and other preachers from attacking the interest system head-on were their respect for order and their fear of jeopardizing church income.*

"Zwingli held the charging of any interest—and not only of excessive rates—to be immoral by virtue of express prohibitions in the Old and New Testaments but, even more, because of the very nature of the Law of Love:

" 'God wills to reveal Himself to all creatures and to do good to them, without recompense, is not selfish nor changeable. He thus demands that we be like Him, for He speaks, "You shall be perfect, as your heavenly Father is perfect" (Matt. 5). Would we come into His presence, we must be perfect, i.e., pure, clean, beautiful, unblemished, not thinking of ourselves as being our own, but knowing that we belong to God; and if to God, then also to the neighbor [ZW, II, 522, lines 12 ff.]. *God commands us to give our goods to those from whom we can hope nothing and who cannot recompense us (Luke 6). He himself does the same; for He nourishes not only men but also the birds of the air (Matt. 6) without any return'* [ZW, II, 480, lines 16ff.].

"Thus profoundly does Zwingli reason with ethics as a reflection of God's nature. This is no left-over Erasmian or mystical humanism, conceiving

of man as by nature a partaker of the divine essence; this is Gospel, the righteousness of God in Christ as revelation of what man should be. This, as much as late medieval mysticism, is the origin of the Nachfolge motif which Anabaptism was later to develop at greater length. . . .

"It need hardly be said on what fertile ground such teaching fell, even though it was only incidental to the theme of the disputation and the Exposition. Suffering under the inordinate burdens of civil and ecclesiastical tithes which were soon to call forth outright rebellion all over German Europe, the peasants were all too ready to pick up the hint of social readjustments which might be called for the rediscovery of the pure Gospel. Fed by zealous followers of Zwingli like Wilhelm Röubli and Andreas Castelberger, who preached on the housetops what Zwingli told them in secret, the unrest centered especially in the villages whose tithes were owed to the Chapter of Zwingli's own Grossmünster. Röubli was himself preaching at Wytikon, one of these villages. Proceeding in an orderly, respectful fashion, these villages sent delegates to Milords of the Zürich Council asking for relief [see 52A, above]. . . .

"To this overture, as to the others of its kind which continued to come to the Council during the next two years as the impact of Zwinglian preaching reached different parts of the countryside, the Council responded with a clear negative, by a decision of June 22, 1523 [see 52A, above]. Two days later Zwingli preached his sermon 'On Divine and Human Justice and How They See [i.e., agree] and Stand Together,' which was printed as a pamphlet a month later. This sermon is Zwingli's response to a serious disappointment. It is not a poised, maturely weighed platform for a reformed social ethic, though it has been taken as such, but rather a heroic effort to adjust to the facts of life. Thus far the Council had moved with Zwingli, step by step, in the direction of Reformation. Now, as was to be the case again in October and in December, it refused to take the next step. Should he give up his confidence in Milords of Zürich as agents of his Reformation? Or should he change his understanding of the Reformation which he wanted them to implement? This latter task is what he takes up in this sermon" (J. H. Yoder, MQR, 1961, pp. 79-82).

The text of the published sermon, as transcribed in ZW, II, pp. 458-525, requires 67 pages, of which less than 12 (18%) is excerpted here. The sermon has two parts—an expository section giving the structure of Zwingli's practical ethics, and a section in which the biblical principles are applied to such issues as the charging and paying of tithes and interest. In the first part, Zwingli identifies the two levels of righteousness—divine and human. The divine righteousness is what God is and demands. The correspondence between God's own nature and his claims upon men applies to every area of social ethics: he demands by word and deed that we be like him. From the Sermon on the Mount, Zwingli derives ten dimensions of the divine righteousness that must become the standard for Christian behavior: "unconditional forgiveness, no wrath, no demanding of one's rights, chastity even in thoughts, no oath but absolute veracity, unconditional giving, loving one's enemies, no coveting, no vain words, loving the other as oneself" (ibid., p. 82, fn. 14).

The second level of human justice relates to the fact that people do not conform to the divine standard. "In order to prevent our sins from completely destroying society, God has therefore set up a second ... level of 'righteousness,'" on the assumption "that the first level will not be kept" (ibid., p. 82). Each of the ten dimensions of God's righteousness is broken down into the two levels of justice. Yoder subdivides human justice into levels B (prohibition) and C (punishment); but these dual-human responses can be interpreted more simply as components of the same level B, as the following collapsing of Yoder's example indicates:

Level A: Thou shalt not covet. This is the criterion of divine righteousness, which if followed would require no further provision.

Level B: Thou shalt not steal. This commandment is needed because level A is not followed. Those who do not steal are not necessarily righteous by the highest divine standard because they might still covet. Those who steal are not only unrighteous but also must be punished, and it is the function of the state to prosecute them.

Yoder summarizes the historical-theological significance of this sermon in relation to the universal problems of social ethics: "The highest level of love, truthfulness, altruism, etc., is not relegated to the cloister or the 'heart,' while elsewhere a different, lower-level Will of God applies. The highest divine righteousness is what should always be preached and what men shall be judged by. It is the standard by which the true believer shall be inwardly guided. The lower level of 'human righteousness' is only the result of sin; no 'order of creation' fixes its norms, no divinely mandated prince defines its duties. God's highest Law is not, as it tended to be in Lutheranism, removed from the realm of social ethics to serve only as a proclamation of men's inadequacy. Zwingli claims for the ethic of divine justice (which for him is largely the Sermon on the Mount) a relevance which was to be denied by subsequent Protestant theology until the age of Liberalism, yet he does so without expecting society to live by this high standard.... The function by which a state is to be measured is the maintenance of a livable social order, not the establishment of any one pattern of authority. It may consent to compromises, but its standards are fixed by Revelation. If it be ungodly, Christians are to bear the suffering involved as a divine chastisement; they may expect God to punish such a ruler in his turn, but they do not plan a rebellion in order to be the instruments of that judgment. Nowhere does Zwingli's treatment contain the assumption that the Christians whom he is counseling are pious men of state. He looks at problems of state from the position of the subjects, not with a view to the implementation of his principles of social reform from the top. He discusses the obligation to pay tithes and interest, not the authorization for the state, church, or landowner to demand them.

"This is basically the view of the state which continued to be held by the

Anabaptists.... What he wrote here was acceptable to Grebel, Stumpf, and the others whom Egli calls 'radicals' " (ibid., pp. 82-84).

In the following excerpt from Zwingli's sermon, the reader will note how close the Reformer comes to holding rulers accountable for applying the level A standard of God's righteousness (213/30, 216/38ff., 217/29-32, 36-41, 218/8-10, 24-30); but the reader will also note another sense in which rulers have no jurisdiction at all over the divine level of righteousness, i.e., they cannot legitimately legislate in matters of faith (214/4ff.). Yoder calls this "an unconscious shift" in Zwingli's argument, a "serious ambiguity" in his ethics (ibid., p. 83). Whether or not this ambiguity was conscious and deliberate, and whether or not it was already being detected and criticized by Grebel and his friends at this early stage of their involvement in the Reformation remains an unresolved question (see 53/fn.5), inspite of Yoder's strong argument for the negative.

Tithes. I will not attempt to speak here concerning the tithes that accrue to the laity, when the ground is their own and they have leased it out for an eighth, a ninth, or a tenth, or in some instances even a fifth. Rather, concerning the tithes that belong to the clergy or were purchased by them ... I say that every man is obligated to pay them as long as the government generally orders it.[1] The government may also punish the violator if he should refuse to pay it, for it is the consensus of the authorities; and all of the purchases were made on the basis of this consensus in such a way that the properties, according to whether or not they are tithe-free, were subsequently sold cheaply or dearly. Hence anyone who personally would refuse to pay the tenth contrary to this common consensus would be going beyond what was stated in an upright honest purchase considered just and proper by the authorities. Therefore such a man would be resisting the government; and he who resists the government resists God, as shown before. But in a case where an entire government, that could defend such action, should permit that one need no longer give the tithe, such a government would also have to see that justice is done to those who hold the tithe, or else those who hold the properties would maintain that they had not purchased them. But as long as that does not happen, everyone should pay the tithe as the government commands; and none should forcibly undertake anything for himself, or he would fall under the judgment pronounced on thieves and robbers. But the authorities must see to it that the tithe is not misused and correct it wherever that happens. For in short: if it does not punish transgression, it is an untrue government.[2] Therefore nobody should allow himself to be misled. Let everyone also consider that where one constantly sees a thing misused, one finally finds a way to abolish the abuse; and then it might happen with violence and disorder rather than with mature reflection. This brief opinion I offer to prove by Scripture.

Let not some hothead say here: the fact that you turn this over to the government to take under its protection indicates that we would have to hold the mass to be a sacrifice, that we would have to run to the priests for absolution from our sins, that the gospel must be preached according to the pope's pleasure, and that we would have to observe other like matters until a government orders other practices. Answer: No, it is not necessary to ask the government for those things, for it is not ordained over God's Word and Christian freedom, but over temporal matters,[3] as has been sufficiently shown. On the other hand, although the government might say as the Jews did to Christ's apostles in Acts 5[:2]: "We have strictly forbidden you to teach this matter"; then the preachers of the Word of God should say: "Our Lord Jesus Christ has foretold that for his sake we should be brought before kings, princes, magistrates, and rulers,[4] but he told us not to be afraid even if they should take the body; for they cannot injure the soul.[5] We therefore stand here and say with the apostles: We must obey God more than man.[6] God commands us to preach his Word and not keep silent about it, but at the opportune time. Therefore, if you rulers want to be Christians, you must permit us to preach the clear Word of God and then let it have its effect; for you are not lords over the souls and consciences of men. If you cannot suffer this, you will be like the unbelieving Jews and heathen tyrants, etc. Thus we see clearly that the authority that the government has over our temporal possessions and bodies cannot extend to the soul. Since paying the tithe concerns our temporal goods, it is in the competence of the government to command proper usage and payment or to change the method, but only without injury to common human amity and justice. Again I let stand the question, by what law tithes are due. If a proper, legitimate government demands it, I will be glad to pursue it further and establish it out of Scripture.

Likewise, it is obligatory to pay interest according to God's command, "You should pay all men that which you owe them."[7] For as soon as private ownership becomes the custom, the government cannot force anyone to lend out his property without hope for its return or profit.[8] But nonetheless we owe this in the context of God's commandment.[9] That is why Christ, in Luke 16[:9], calls riches unjust or imperfect, referring no doubt to the soil and the fruits that grow on God's earth, Psalm 23[:1], which he permits us to use and enjoy without payment. But we make a personal possession of what belongs to God. He permits this in the sense that we are nevertheless his debtors and are therefore obligated to use temporal possessions only in accord with his word and command. This debt is never remitted. For that reason, anyone who does not use his temporal possessions according to God's will is unrighteous before God, even though his use of it is not in conflict with human righteousness. Hence Christ justly calls wealth unrighteous, partly because we make our own what belongs to God and secondly, that we use that over which he permits us to be stewards, in ways not in accord with God's will. Therefore, all interest is ungodly.[10]

First, because all riches are unrighteous. That is why Christ said that it is easier for a camel to be drawn through the eye of a needle than for a rich man to enter the kingdom of God.[11] But let no one despair, for God's mercy is greater than our transgression. Nevertheless we must absolutely admit that all riches belong to God and that we must constantly hold them ready for the will and service of God and possess them as if we did not possess them. Otherwise, I could not understand how a rich man can be a believer when his heart is on his material possessions. But in fact his heart is on them if he does not at all times hold them in readiness according to the Lord's will and use them thus. That is why he has more regard for his treasures than for God. And so, if he is not a believer in this manner, he cannot be saved.

Second, interest is not godly, because God requires of us to lend or to sell on credit without expecting anything in return, Luke 6[:25]. Now since people are not willing to offer to the needy what they have made their own property, without some benefit or recompense, that is the reason why poor human justice has allowed that the borrower is required to give the lender some of the fruits of his loan according to the amount of the loan and also according to the harvest. Therefore, if the property is worth 100 guilders and the borrower receives fifty on its value, he is obligated to pay the lender half of the proceeds. If he has borrowed 25 guilders on it, he owes one fourth of the income, etc. Therefore, lawyers must understand, if they want to defend the paying of interest, that it is a purchase of the crop.[12] And truly, interest would not be such a great burden according to human justice if it were applied in this manner, although it is nonetheless unjust in God's eyes, as we said before. But that one must pay as interest on a property or field or vineyard what you lawyers call a *usufruct* or use rent, whether God grants a harvest or not, that is really too much. I am surprised that those who were in session in the Council of Constance or Basel[13] were, even in human justice, so heedless as to permit such an inequitable thing that would be too much even for unbelieving princes to permit among their people. Why did they not heed Christ's words: You should lend without hoping for profit from it?[14] How did the false priests

215

dare to speak and act in this way when even the princes should have been frightened off if they had proposed such a thing for themselves? But that they were not satisfied with the tithe but allowed themselves interest in addition shows me clearly that they raised this injurious interest. See, where are the lying fellows now? Yes, the councils are gathered in the "Holy Spirit!"[15] Does the Holy Spirit speak contrary to God? Nevertheless, if the taking of interest is supported by popular agreement and confirmed with government letters and seals, everyone should pay the interest on the principal that he has intentionally accepted for his possession; otherwise, he would be disrupting human peace. I say this only of that interest which is set at 5 percent according to human justice[16] (but which could almost be called something else here; for those who set the rate of interest have regarded neither the Word of God nor the law of nature). He also sins against God who commands us to pay to every man what is due him.

But the government should seriously seek to prevent abuses in the taking of interest. And my advice would be—and here I am advising as a human being as Paul did to the Corinthians, 1 Corinthians 7[:12]—for if I am to teach God's Word, I say: You should lend and expect nothing in return.[17] But here, where I always see that we have no taste for the perfection of divine righteousness, I advise all who possess interest rights to have the value of the property assessed, and every year accept a part of its produce in proportion to the loan.[18] Otherwise I greatly fear that many people burden themselves even more, by charging interest, than it is proper to overlook on the basis of human weakness, namely, that in their deliberate malice they are rogues in God's sight. Therefore—here I speak God's Word—no one can be too careful about the way he intends to lead his life. God feeds the ravens and other birds that do not gather or heap up possessions,[19] he clothes the little flowers of the field.[20] Of how much greater worth are we in the eyes of the Lord?[21] Indeed, he will also feed us and our children. These great abuses all come from unbelief and lack of knowledge of God. May he enlighten all men that they may acknowledge him and love him above all things; then these shortcomings will fall away without worry. Amen.

But interest that is not charged according to the government's orders shall be paid only according to the percentage of the principal. Look at it this way: One finds greedy men who demand as much of a part of fifteen as of twenty.[22] Moreover, there are rulers who confirm such rates with documents and seals. Herein the rulers act against their own justice and abuse their authority. Therefore they owe it to the oppressed one, even if he has signed the document, to help him get out so that no more will be taken from him than their feeble justice has prescribed; for falsehood and deception should hit back at the deceiver.[23] And even though they do this, they are still not just, but are merely eliminating the worst mischief, and too much harm still remains. Therefore, anyone who is burdened with an unjust interest contract may submit a grievance [to the authorities].

That is the opinion which I teach in the dirty business of taking interest. Now, however, my enemies are spreading the rumor that I teach that no interest whatever should be paid to anyone. And yet I am constantly shouting: He who assumed [a contract of] interest would be a thief if he refused to give what he has promised insofar, that is, as the contract is made in orderly terms in accord with humanly determined regulations. Regrettably, I must speak about it often, that I may close the mouths of those who dare to defend all vices and promote all injustice. All my effort seeks only to keep the interest-takers from committing a threefold sin[24] in God's eyes. For he who has the care of people's salvation should prevent all harm to those souls; otherwise, those that perish will be required of him;[25] and if he is unable to prevent all damage, he ought nevertheless not cease to warn; perhaps he might prevent the worst.

Concerning usury, I say this: Where a government allows usury,[26] then anyone who takes a loan is obligated to pay the usurious interest. But no government should deal so dishonorably with its subjects as to tolerate Jews or other usurers who would charge compound interest.[27] When the government does not condone usury, but also does not prosecute it, one is under no obligation to pay. Indeed, the government ought to penalize both those who give and those who take usurious interest when it becomes aware of them, although the debtor is obligated to return the principal unless the government decides otherwise. One finds this rhetoric in the lawmakers—if my memory serves me—which I must make use of in this messy matter of usury; for it is so repulsive to God that he will in no way tolerate it. Yet government has been established so that in these matters it might as nearly as possible approximate divine righteousness. It is also under obligation to remove all such ungodly burdens, insofar as it can do so without causing greater harm. In brief, a person should in all matters not shatter human society for the sake of temporal possessions; but if some matter is of great importance that he does not want to abandon out of regard for the Word of God, he should first explain it to the proper authority and not let Christ's teaching be accused of causing a disunity. But the government shall with its own eyes see to it that all abuses that are so contrary to God be abolished; or else long indulgence which will concede nothing will ultimately be perverted into madness. How can an honorable government tolerate the license of such clergy? How can it watch while its poor folk are being devoured by usurers and loan sharks? Therefore, God

217

is once again lighting the light of his Word that the refuse can be washed out and cleared away.

Regarding the tithe, Paul says: Give taxes to whomever you owe them; pay revenue to whom revenue is due; give reverence and honor to whom it is due.[28] These words are clear; they also apply to everyone. Nor am I concerned about the freedom of the clergy, whether or not they are considered free of taxes or revenues, just so there is no harm to other people, which is, however, nearly impossible. Let every government act according to its best insights. But I wanted to point out that they are not free on the basis of divine law or command.

In sum: The divine Word should rule over all people and shall be prescribed, proclaimed, faithfully published, and explained; for we are duty-bound to follow it. Only the grace of God through our Lord Jesus Christ can remedy our weakness. For the more we recognize our guilt and helplessness, the better we comprehend the glory and omnipotence of God, and acquire more and more the love and security of his grace, which more than anything else makes us righteous and God-fearing. But if on the other hand there are people who out of ungodliness and unbelief do not hear the Word, nor live up to it, God has given us lower commandments, not that by living in accord with them we may be righteous, but that the security of human society may be preserved and protected, and that watchmen may be appointed to pay serious attention to it, so that even the last fragment of our poor human righteousness will not also be snatched away from us. These watchmen are the legitimate government, but it is no other than the one with the sword; i.e., the one we call the secular government, whose office consists in directing all things in accord with God's will, and where that is not possible, in accord with God's commands. It should therefore abolish all things that are based neither on the divine Word or command nor on human righteousness and declare them illegal and unjust even for human righteousness.

This interpretation will be briefly summarized once more and the divine and human justice delineated in sequence:

1. God is the highest, most perfect good.

2. [He] wills to reveal himself to all creatures and to do good to them without recompense.

3. [He] is not self-serving or subject to temptation.

Moreover he demands also that we be [like this], for he says, "You shall be perfect as your heavenly father is perfect," Matthew 5[:48]. If we want to come into his presence we must be

1. perfect, i.e., pure, clean, beautiful, flawless,

2. and not consider ourselves our own, but know that we are God's; and if we are God's, we are also the neighbor's;

3. be utterly unselfish, not tempted by avarice or greed for position or luxury.

We should also seek the kingdom of God and his righteousness before all things,[29] i.e., become righteous as he is righteous. But since that is impossible for us, he assures us of his grace through his Son whom he gave to die for us. That is the gospel.

Since we are not able to achieve the measure of righteousness that God requires of us but are nevertheless commanded to become perfect, it follows that we must learn without ceasing what God requires in order that we may with unflagging zeal constantly grow in all goodness and at the same time not become proud of our virtue; for we have still not fulfilled what God requires. For that reason God has made some lower laws by which we can live as friends with one another, as Christ also told the Jews, Matthew 19[:8], that because of the unruliness of the Jews, Moses allowed them to sever a marriage, although it was originally not to be so. Consider that reference well! We still remain obligated to live in accord with divine righteousness, but we cannot do so, for

1. we are by nature evil and in darkness, Genesis 8[:21];

2. we are not willing to belong to other people, but want all things to be ours;

3. we are selfish from Adam's first fall and greedy for carnal things.

In order, then, that the flaws may not get so great that we run quite wild and become worse than the mindless beasts, God has given us two things that are to direct and control us—his Word and the government that controls our temptations by means of punishment.

1. In God's Word one learns how righteous we are duty-bound to be; and in that we find salvation by grace. No one is master over it, for it is above all men. For no one who was born in sin is so righteous or innocent that he may reach the demand of the Word; nor is there anyone who is not in need of the grace that is assured therein.

2. In order that violence may not grow out of our selfishness, we have government that subdues the disorderly, so that no one out of temptation may take another's possessions from him.

3. Also in order that we may not become shameless like dogs, the same government should discipline us; for that purpose it has been established.

Original Publication: Zwingli's *Von gottlicher und menschlicher Gerechtikheit,* published 7/30/1523
Transcription: ZW, II, No. 21

53

Grebel to Vadian
Zurich, July 15, 1523[1]

Soon after the First Zurich Doctrinal Disputation in January, Zwingli began work on his "exposition" of the 67 theses he had drawn up for that occasion. On February 19 he wrote that he was working on it day and night, adding, "It will be a sort of farrago of the opinions which are under debate these days" (Jackson, 1900, 196). With this writing he established his position as Reformation leader in Switzerland. It contained his first public explanation of his relationship to Luther, admitting doctrinal agreement on many points but claiming total independence from him.

Froschauer's publication of the "exposition," better known by the German word Schlussreden, *was delayed until July 14, the day before Grebel wrote the following letter to Vadian. Grebel's role in its distribution in St. Gallen and Nuremberg is the main subject of Letters 53 and 54, although he also updates the handling of the issue of tithes in Zurich (including a first slight note of disillusionment with Zwingli's apparent tendency to vacillate on an issue like this) and on the most recent Reformation writings by Strauss, Hutten, and Luther to have arrived.*

Greetings, my Vadian.

What you have waited for so very much you now receive from Zwingli—the very Christian book by Zwingli; and you receive it as a gift.[2] This for the present was what I had to write to you, unless you also want a report about the tithes.[3] What shall I reply more frankly and truly and what more appropriately evangelical[4] than this single comment which I now put forth, in a word: "The people of our world of Zurich are doing everything tyrannically and like the Turk in this matter of the tithe"? I said the people of the world, the tyrants of our homeland whom they call the senate fathers, but they should more aptly call them the decimating fathers.[5] Perhaps you will not believe this, but I believe it and I see it with my eyes; and therefore, you can learn about it from Zwingli, who (be careful) may have divulged everything to you as readily as I, sad babbler.[6]

There has been brought to us the book or most evangelical Articles of Jacob Strauss,[7] in which affluence is painted in its true color. Then another of the same quality has now reached us entitled *Balaam's Ass*.[8] Likewise, Hutten's invective against Erasmus has arrived.[9] To all these was added the judgment of Luther on the same Erasmus, which however was published without Luther's consent and knowledge.[10] Would you like these to be sent in one package? "Certainly I wish so," you say. I shall send them therefore whenever you advise me by letter, lest perchance you already have them and I do you a service which is not welcome.

I hope my mother is well and whoever is dear to you and to Christ, and I pray that your wife will have a happy delivery and that she begets a Christian child.[11] Farewell, on the day of [St.] Margaret, 1523.[12]

Conrad Grebel, yours.

Give my regards to Benedict Burgauer[13] and ask him to write to me about how many quarto pages of Zwingli's manuscript he has received, and how many remain to be added.[14]

> To the master lord Joachim Vadian, a man in every way learned and humane, his from the soul, etc.

Original: Stadtbibliothek (Vadiana) St. Gallen, VB.II.136
Transcription: VB, III, No. 353; M-S, No. 2

54
Grebel to Vadian
Zurich, July 16, 1523[1]

Greetings again, dearest Vadian.

The courier, or if you prefer, the courieress,[2] of my letter of yesterday had scarcely left with the book of Zwingli[3] and you asked about it in your letter to father,[4] whether it had been printed or not. Zwingli's book has been printed, which fact of course by now you know for yourself by the book sent to you. Now it is for you, Vadian, to decide what should be done and to make known how many copies you want. Or if you want to send three hundred to Nuremberg[5] (for so I have gathered from I know not whom), he who is to carry Zwingli's writing there[6] will come and fly them (here) to us. I do not see another way other booksellers could be anticipated.

I write this at lunch,[7] since the courier is in a hurry to be off. Therefore you should not scorn a letter written in a most unlearned style but yet in a friendly spirit. Such things I am accustomed to write almost learnedly when I am sober. For the time being, farewell in Christ, until another opportunity presents itself to give you my trifles in greater detail. Zurich, on the day following the letter which you received from our maidservant and $\dot{\alpha}\rho\chi\iota\gamma\rho\alpha\mu\mu\alpha\tau\acute{\epsilon}\omega\varsigma$ [chief clerk],[8] 1523.

Mureria[9] sends her prayers to her sister, to you, and yours.

Conrad Grebel, yours.

The family of Grebel sends best wishes to those of the Vadian name. Leopold[10] joins in this wish.

221

WE COMMAND[11] that your pastor[12] be secure in Christ and a learned scribe of the kingdom of heaven, who labors to draw out of both Testaments the new with the old,[13] divine things with divine inspiration, that is, that he may be what he is by the will of God, not only in body but also strong in the meetings and in the ministry of the gospel.

Hey[14] Benedict![15] Why are you silent? Why do you care not a scrap for your Grebel? Be mindful of (your) food. You wrote back something about pottage.[16] We call it Musio, wo muss heist ess [which is mush].[17]

I ask that my εὐλόγητος [blessed] Burgauer read these words in place of my sending a letter to him.

Benedict Vadian,[18] as much my brother as yours, I love from the heart, and I wish him well.

Master lord Joachim Vadian, dearest kinsman.

To Saint Gallen.

Original: Stadbibliothek (Vadiana) St. Gallen, VB.II.165
Transcriptions: VB, III, No. 376; M-S, No. 3

54A
Burgauer[1] to Grebel
St. Gallen, July 21, 1523

The relationship between Burgauer and Grebel, once cordial (see 24/124/31-32, 25/126/33-34, 32A/142/27), then sparring (34/146/4, 38/150/28-29, 45/161/34, 49/191/24-25), turned sour in Grebel's letter to Vadian, No. 52, in which he lamented the report that Burgauer was upholding such traditional Roman Catholic doctrines as purgatory and rejoiced in the rumor that he had been dismissed from his office as pastor in St. Gallen (52/207/34ff.).

Then upon hearing that Burgauer had not in fact been dismissed, Grebel sent him a more direct challenge to live up to his divine ordination and high call "in the ministry of the gospel" and "to draw out of both Testaments, the new with the old, divine things with divine inspiration" (54/222/1ff.). He authorized Vadian to give the letter to Burgauer to read, which he must have done together with Letter 52, because the following reply by Burgauer is obviously a reaction to both letters.

G[reetings].

If the modesty of the spirit of Paul did not compel me, I would not present one iota to my Conrad, teaching to return good for evil.[2] For you persuade yourself that you should be somewhat angry with me because I have turned aside from the evangelical truth, and so another has been substituted for the harvest of the gospel.[3] I have dealt sternly and summarily with certain people[4] who have striven to pervert the liberty of the Spirit into

222

an occasion of the flesh, who preached against prayers for the dead, that the sacrament of the Eucharist should be abolished from the church, that infants who have no faith of their own should not be baptized,[5] nor should we be deceitfully engaged in effort or at work in the vineyard of the Lord but that the passion of Christ is so overflowing that the mortification of the body and the life similar to Christ's is unbelief. These I have cursed as pseudochrists, who establish a pernicious sect, spreading darkness over men of sound doctrine and the light of truth. You know how men pervert isolated texts of the Scriptures into a liberty of the flesh, and not for the edification of the adjacent text, for which reason I prefer that those who claim to be the noblest and the most evangelical should not divide the gospel thus for the sake of passion, money, and gain. This is the evil by reason of which I am proclaimed by those babbling good-for-nothing fools to have turned aside from the gospel. Indeed, they have abused the elders,[6] they reject everything, and destroy custom and indulge in drunkenness. Then day after day they know no better than to defame the clergy by constantly calling them robbers and thieves;[7] this is gospel among these Christians. You have in brief what has disturbed me, you who need first to be nourished by drinking milk. Then the Scripture will judge you as still carnal from strife and envy. When I censure these evils which they incite, I also reproach shamelessness.

For the rest, you have sent 34 quartos to me, the last quarto is the letter M.[8] I ask that you send them along with the carrier, and whatever the expense, I shall repay it honorably to your mother.[9] Give my greetings to your wife,[10] your father, and the evangelist Zwingli.

From Saint Gallen, in great haste, July 21, in the year [15]23.

Your brother, Benedict Burgauer.

To the most upright Conrad Grebel of Zurich, a most beloved brother in Christ.

Original: Stadtbibliothek (Vadiana) St. Gallen, VB.II.137
Transcription: VB, III, No. 355

55
Grebel to Vadian
Zurich, July 28, 1523

The interpretation we gave in the introduction to Letter No. 50 of the evident correlation between Grebel's "conversion" and his recurrent depression because of ill health finds further substantiation in the following letter, in which he concurrently refers to the "feebleness of my body" and requests that Vadian "pray to Christ that I might keep a firm faith in him." We find here a total submission to the mercy of God "whatever finally happens."

Greetings, my Vadian.

We gathered from the Geiserani[1] that you are all well; but we are uncertain whether you have received our letters since you have written nothing in reply, the letters, I mean, of father and Dorothy.[2]

We hope that Martha[3] will have a successful delivery and that we will be informed as soon as possible after she has successfully delivered and that we can soon welcome the returning mother. Father will return to Berne three days from now.[4] He will go moreover as head of an embassy in the name of our lords of Zurich. I am scarcely able to write about all this, my Vadian, because of the feebleness of my body, which I feel may occasion the prelude to my death.[5] Father, however, prevailed on me, being scarcely able, to write for him, for Agatha,[6] and Dorothy.[7] I want to know how the pastor feels about my last letter[8] to him and how he interprets what I wrote in part to you.[9] We one and all pray that you are safe and prosperous. Farewell in Christ, and this in a word to my three souls: you, mother, sister. Zurich, in the year 1523, July 28.

Conrad Grebel, yours.

Pray to Christ that I might keep a firm faith in him, and I will pray that the same may be given you. Of me know this: If I am helped by the gift of mercy and divine grace for which I have prayed, I shall bear all things with disdain, whatever finally happens.[10]

Would that you could see me in the place where I am writing this and with what hope of health![11] I would not dare to complain since you, who have never tasted what I do, think I have complained enough and more, and you say so too.

To Joachim Vadian, a man accomplished in all respects, and dearest kinsman.

Original: Stadtbibliothek (Vadiana) St. Gallen, VB.II.140
Transcriptions: VB, III, No. 356; M-S, No. 4

56

Grebel to Vadian
Zurich, August 11, 1523

Vadian's emerging role of reformer in St. Gallen is running into severe resistance on the part of the head pastor, Benedict Burgauer. The growing conflict will lead to disciplinary action against Burgauer in February 1525 (see 68M/fn.2); but in the following letter, eighteen months before that happened, we can discern how Vadian was increasingly conferring with Grebel about Reformation happenings, keeping him abreast of developments in St. Gallen, and evidently even asking for his help to counter "the wolf that comes in sheep's clothing." The brothers-in-law are bound together by another event: they have both become fathers at about the same time. The brevity and straightforwardness of Letter No. 57 requires no introduction.

Greetings my Vadian.

How pleased I am with your writing and how joyous, Cicero[1] himself could not adequately express for me. How angrily, indeed, and with what indignation I will pursue that man whom you depicted to me, the evil worker;[2] and not if Archilochus[3] himself would furnish his iambics to me could I assail him as he deserves. But what do I accomplish by these emotions? The God of peace and the gospel has so hardened the man that instead of the shepherd he acts the part of the wolf, who is covered with sheep's clothing and devours the houses of widows and their souls under the pretext of long prayers.[4] He is one who menaces and stores up double damnation for himself. So I rejoice in Juflius[5] for you the most. I always had a far more secure hope for him anyway. Since I was not deceived about this, I can even rejoice that I surmised so wisely and hoped so successfully. May our heavenly Father grant that we may have Juflius with us for a long time and that he should carry out his ministry (which he does) with Pauline liberty and grace until the last day. 'Αμὴν [Amen].

I rejoice that you have born to you a Δωροθέαν [Dorothea],[6] although I would have preferred a Θεοδόσιον [Theodosius] or Δωρόθεον [Dorotheos].[7] You may in turn congratulate me (if you like) on my יֵשׁוּעַ; Jeshua, Ιησοῦν [Jehoshuah, Jeshua Jesus], Joshua.[8] If you like, I say, because father, Leopold,[9] Δωροθέα τε [and Dorothy] do not.[10] You guess what reasons could be attributed. I rather think the world is the source of this boorishness or jealousy. But these things and many others I reserve for your arrival. Meanwhile, however, know that I have so little hope left in father that I would prefer to depend on absolute strangers than on him alone.[11] And would that I had depended upon God and may depend on him, but when will I learn through some fire that is kindled by his will to possess this soul of mine in patience,[12] which has been exposed and tossed by many storms! Because of my pupils,[13] I treat this in a few words to you. Have concern for my soul, which is so cold, yet so affectionate to you, and will that it be kept safe whatever it is finally.[14] Farewell in Christ.

Conrad Grebel, ὁ σός [yours].

To the master lord Joachim Vadian, a man in every way most famous and dearest of all.

Original: Stadtbibliothek (Vadiana) St. Gallen, VB.II.143
Transcriptions: VB, III, No. 359; M-S, No. 5

57
Grebel to Vadian
Zurich, September 6, 1523[1]

Greetings, my Vadian.

I send to you (1) *The Sponge of Erasmus,*[2] (2) Oecolampad's *On Not Having a Levy of the Poor,*[3] (3) Phillipus' *Annotations on John.*[4]

I have swallowed the purge. I have opened my bowels twenty times at once. Now it remains for me to wash. The last is to say good-bye. The appendix, may you all be well.

From the paternal abode, on the Sunday after the day of Verona, 1523.

Conrad Grebel.

To the lord Joachim Vadian, a man in every way most famous.

Original: Stadtbibliothek (Vadiana) St. Gallen, VB.II.100
Transcriptions: VB, II, No. 323; M-S, No. 6

57A
Zwingli's Defense of His Booklet on the Mass Canon
October 9, 1523

Zwingli's view of the Lord's Supper developed over a period of several years and did not immediately imply the abolition but only the reform of the Roman Catholic mass. His belief that the mass is not a repetitious sacrifice was first enunciated in the First Zurich Disputation of January 1523 (see Article 18 of the 67 Articles prepared for that occasion; namely, "that the mass is not a sacrifice but a commemoration of the sacrifice and the assurance of the redemption which Christ has procured," Meyer, p. 41).

His next elaboration of that point was published in his Schlussreden *of July. Then on August 29 he published his first proposals for the revision of the mass in* De canone missae epichiresis *(Essay on the Canon of the Mass).*

Despite its reiteration of the doctrine of the Eucharist as a commemoration, the cautious character of this initial proposal was shown by its retention of the clerical vestments, the Latin chants, and the liturgical prayers; and Zwingli was immediately confronted by his more thoroughgoing disciples with the charge that he was retaining the ceremonies of the Roman Catholic Church out of a "false forbearance" for the weak in faith. This criticism compelled him several weeks later to add to the Essay *an "Apology" in which he declared his willingness to discard the priestly vestments and Latin chants in response to the arguments of his followers; but he rejected their third criticism against prescribed prayers.*

The Apology *was published on October 9 with the title* De canone missae libelli apologia *(Defense of the Booklet on the Mass Canon). This document is included in the present collection because it shows Zwingli's reciprocal relationships with the Grebel group (see fn. 5, below) and prefigures Grebel's concerns about the form of the Lord's Supper at the Second Zurich Disputation later in the same month.*

Goeters summarizes the evidence for the conclusion that in this tract, Zwingli was speaking to Grebel and through him to "his circle of friends" (p. 260), namely: 1. Grebel's protest of a "false forbearance" (see 59/276/10, 63/286/17, 26, 288/36-37, 289/36, 292/14, 26, 293/18, 67/302/19, 21. 2. His protest of liturgical singing (see 63/286/35ff.). 3. His protest of the adding of liturgical prayers to the New Testament words of institution (see 63/ 287/22-25). 4. His protest of the use of priestly robes and vestments in the administering of the Lord's Supper (see 63/288/21-23). These were the four issues raised by the unidentified group of dissenters to whom Zwingli spoke in the following document.

A forbearance,[1] ill-advised, as some think, but not at all unconsidered,[2] as you, renowned sir,[3] will clearly understand, compels me so soon and almost in the very travail[4] to write this defense of the canon dedicated to you. For there are those[5] who fear that certain people,[6] much given to my reputation, will more stubbornly adhere to those elements which I, with a certain dutiful forbearance, have allowed to the weak.[7] They consider that unless these features be wholly eliminated, they will bring back the old admonition by way of a legal right of return.

They place among the foremost of these objectionable features the adornment of vestments;[8] but they present arguments for this very different from any I have ever acknowledged.[9] I have always been of the opinion that the use of these vestments is a symbol of the abuse which Christ bore, as the veil with which we cover the head is a likeness and indication of what Christ, veiled, endured in the house of Caiaphas,[10] as thus the rest of the vestments which my concern for brevity bids me pass over.

At this point, they declare, all shadows have passed away.[11] And thus, he who makes provision for them, what else is he doing than to make those born again in Christ to Judaize? If you maintain those vestments in which treacherous avarice has hitherto marketed the Eucharist, what are you doing but bringing the simple people of Christ to believe again that it is an offering? To this objection I reply, "Quite correct!" For I too would not want the return of that veiled Moses[12] after the joyous and uncovered face of Christ has appeared. And though I might make considerable excuse here about the distinction between things which are a shadow of the future[13] and those which are a memorial of the past, foregoing all this, I honestly believe that those vestments which we have used hitherto should be done away with altogether, provided that it may be done without discrimination.[14]

But if any peril threatens, then let the weak first be taken in hand and clearly taught what vestments have to do with the case and what the consequences will be if they are not abolished. For I myself (to speak the truth), when I was undertaking to write this about vestments, had been exceedingly wearied of permitting the use of vestments to the weak. But lest I grant nothing, I then permitted those vestments which I now, in my concern, consider ought to be done away with, as I realize that they open a window to vain rites. And I pray all the brethren in Christ that they give no account to my reputation,[15] but rather weigh everything according to the scale of the heavenly Word and that if anything be contrary to this, they reject it. For it is certainly necessary to erect in the church of God a structure[16] which may abide as the fire rushes in and scorn its assault; but there can be no such structure but that which is raised upon the foundation which is Christ,[17] who sustains the edifice of both prophets and apostles.[18]

Secondly, they fear that the permitted chants,[19] namely, the *Introit,* the *Gloria in excelsis Deo*[20] and the rest may, like some sort of obstacle, impede the birth of a pure Christianity, and eventually furnish prey for ceremony.[21] To this I say virtually the same thing as I said before in relation to the abolition of vestments, though in this case we need not rush so anxiously, provided that we proceed without interruption, if we sing only texts which come from sacred Scripture. But I would wish that the epistle and Gospel[22] be read immediately in the language which is commonly understood.[23] And if it can be done at the outset, let the exposition of the Word of God take the place of singing. If not, we must put up for awhile with these lovely nightingales who cannot keep from singing, so long as they sing only heavenly things, until we can overcome all things by the Word of God. But wherever it is possible without disorder to abandon the uproar of ritual songs at the start, offensive once even to the prophet, Amos 5[:23], let them be set aside.

Now whatever I have said in this connection has been said on account of the weak, as I have attested many times. For I am zealous for peace, but a Christian peace.[24] I serve the weak, but only those of whose eventual strength there is some hope. I yield to the importunity of some, but only until their imprudent impulses may be restrained. Indeed, I am not unaware that the words of Paul in Ephesians 5[:19] and Colossians 3[:16[concerning psalmody and singing in our hearts afford no help to those who defend their swan song[25] by them. For he says "in our hearts," not "our voices."[26] Psalmody and the praises of God are, then, to be managed in such a way that our minds may sing to God. Nor in this matter ought only Romans[27] or Greeks to speak (for Christ is neither Scythian nor Greek),[28] but all who have given their names to Christ. Therefore let this barbarous murmur depart from the churches, for not even those who commend themselves under its name understand it. Indeed, it is no source of shame to term barbarous a language which the people do not understand, since Paul calls a man thundering forth foreign words in a haughty way a barbarian,[29] only let all things pertain to edification, not to destruction or ruin.

Lastly, they so carp at the prayers[30] which I have placed before Christ's Eucharist[31] that they practically allege a charge of *lese majesty*[32] because I have been so bold as to introduce prayers there. They proffer as the basis for their judgment that Christ employed no prefatory prayers, and that whatever God himself has not taught by word or deed is sinful.[33] At this point I lodge my appeal with impartial judges. If I have sinned at all in this matter, I will amend; if not, it would be only fair that they who have passed judgment without hearing the case give up their claim and alter their opinion.

And so, first, I suggest that they consider carefully how often in my book *On the Canon of the Mass,* I have taken precaution that no one suppose that a rule has been prescribed for him. And when they have found these precautions occurring quite frequently, then let them acknowledge that their leaping to slander so suddenly is quite unfair, particularly since I have subdued any suspicion that I was giving precepts, on these two accounts especially: because I am in no position to give precepts (for what am I?) and because my entire effort in that book is to the end that every man realize that he is permitted to pray according to the inspiration of the heavenly Spirit. For I do not think that he will approach there[34] who has not beforehand carefully examined his mind; namely, how much faith is in it, how great a hope of finding sustenance, how great finally a desire there is of union with the Son of God, the Spouse of the soul. I reckon this meditation or, if you like, deliberation of the soul to be nothing other than a prayer. And though others pour this out in their hearts, I, lest I ever fail the weak, have done the same thing openly.

But these men say: There is need for greater faith rather than that we should hope to accomplish anything by prayer. I agree; nor, indeed, do I believe that it can be fished out of my words that I attribute anything in this sphere to human activity. Although I attempt to rouse that faith which you[35] demand with material drawn all the way from the beginning of creation, yet not all have equal faith, and these prayers, what are they but stimuli to faith? But if any run of their own accord, let them run all the more, I pray, and go before me along with the weak! Let their spurs gain them profit! I will not begrudge them this; but I, all the while, will urge the feeble toward that measure which these now possess.

Now I readily grant that whatever God has not taught by word or deed is a sin.[36] For as he alone is good,[37] so good cannot proceed from any but him. However, I ask what have I said in any of these four prayers which is contrary to the holy words? I should like one iota to be shown which has not been taken from the celestial treasury, though in other words, so that everything may be both more simple and more obvious. But they counter: Granted that you have said nothing alien to the Word of God, yet in this place nothing in addition to the Lord's Prayer should be said, and what you are attempting—namely, to stir up the faith of the weak[38]—that ought to be accomplished by the preaching of God's Word.

To these remarks I reply as follows: I desire to learn from you where God has taught that we should say no prayer but the Lord's Prayer. Was it not permitted to Moses, Isaiah, Manasseh, David, and others to pour forth extended prayers? Did not Paul pray that the hard knocks, the guardians of his humility, be taken away from him?[39] Christ also prayed that the cup of his passion might pass.[40] He gave an abundant opportunity of praying to all when he said: "Whatsoever you ask of my Father in my name, he will give to you."[41] Only let us ask those things which it is not inappropriate for him to grant. Indeed, the apostles too once prayed that he increase their faith,[42] and this request (I believe) is not contained in the Lord's Prayer. As far as preaching is concerned, again I agree with you. But what difference does it make whether you call prayer or preaching that which you bring forward for the particular purpose of rousing minds, so long as you mean the same thing? And, to throw something up to you, from where in Scripture will you prove that the sermon ought to go before the Eucharist? If you allege Christ's act, you will be forced to grant that the sermon ought to be delivered after the eating of the body and blood. For Christ delivered that long discourse which John recorded after the banquet of his body and blood.[43] However, lest I give anyone opportunity for

230

contention, I shall present briefly what one ought to think about this controversy.

Just as we were not bound by prescriptions or conditions,[44] so too we were not bound by those things that are attended by conditions. For on the other hand, from the conditions of a person there follows an order.[45] Inasmuch as we have been freed from every consideration of person through Christ, we have been freed from the order which follows the person. To be sure, we have not been so freed from order that we ought not to observe it in all our Eucharists; but the order is in our will as well as person, place, and time, though this is not the place to prove it with evidence.

It is, then, the integral right of any private person or church to pray with many words or few. For who will prevent your spending entire nights in meditation on Scripture before approaching the table? Or your stirring up the devotion of the entire church with the fewest words? Or that you edify the minds of all with a prepared text, so long as it tastes of nothing but the Word of God? For when Christ bade his disciples that upon first entering cities they seek suitable hosts,[46] he did not, because he mentioned this first, so bind them to this order that, should an opportunity for teaching earlier present itself, they could not seize it straightaway.

So too we now see that we have not been bound to this or that order by any command of Christ. Christ offered his body and blood after a meal.[47] Paul did away with the meal and ordered them to dine at home.[48] Christ offered this food in the upper room; Paul, to be sure, in the crowded temple of the church. Christ gave his teaching after the feast; we teach beforehand. Why then might it not be permitted to replace the meal with prayers, and this (as I have said) according to the discretion of any private person or church, so long as the Eucharist of Christ be always maintained entire? To this no violence must be done; for again, this is subject to no extrinsic rules. If custom requires, sermon and prayer, meal and fast may be omitted, but the sacred words cannot be omitted. But since no mind approaches such wondrous mysteries boldly, I thought that I would be doing something of value, hardly contemptible, if I encourage the timorous with a prayer fashioned after the rule of Christ, which prayer each is free to employ or ignore.

I see then no remaining reason why they complain that I have written these prayers. For if the latter are in accord with Christ, and these men merely dislike their order, let them omit them. If, on the contrary, they are alien to Christ, let them show this; and if there be any sin, let them rebuke it in writing. For they shall never deprive us of this, that it be not permitted to pray before every Eucharist at what length and with what words you

231

would wish, so long as they be not contrary to Christ, just as Paul allowed an abundant opportunity of praying in every place. Since then I cannot be convicted of sin in this matter, so far as my prayers go, I beseech all who are Christ's to take precaution that they do not allow themselves to be led astray by their skills into a spirit of contention and dissension,[49] for God has called us to peace.[50] And let them frequently consider that knowledge puffs up, but charity edifies,[51] and that even in being wise, moderation must be observed,[52] so that we be wise no more than is fitting, but rather according to sobriety.

Gladly and willingly have I, in my hectic way, produced this little explanation, particularly to make clear to all that I allow nothing to the hypocrisy of vestments, nor do I approve of the barbarous, that is, of the unknown in the churches, even in the case of Scripture—all this only so that no one may eventually complain that he has been misled by my forbearance.[53] I have, in addition, all the while restrained those who, as the saying goes, look for a knot on the bulrush,[54] incorrectly interpreting what cannot rightly be thus interpreted, especially since I fortified everything with the required exceptions. I beg that all good men ponder all these considerations, and that the latter bring about this alone, that Christ's glory and not mine be increased.

May Christ preserve his church.

And you too, Diebold[55], venerable brother in Christ, farewell.

From Zurich, the 9th day of October 1523.

Original Publication: Zwingli's *De canone missae libelli apologia*, published 10/9/1523
Transcription: ZW, II, No. 26

57B
Jacob Grebel to Vadian[1]
Zurich, October 12, 1523

The background of documents 57B and 57C is the same. On September 1, 1523, Leo Jud, pastor at St. Peter's, preached a passionate sermon in which he not only denounced the worship of ecclesiastical images, pictures, and statues, but publicly asserted, perhaps for the first time in Zurich, that they should be removed from the churches. The reactions of conservatives and radicals were immediate. The most serious of these were several acts of iconoclasm in Zurich and its environs. The first occurred in Jud's own church on September 9, when one of the assistant priests, Lorenz Meyer, and one or two other "mass helpers" tore down some paintings and statues of the saints. Meyer was subsequently imprisoned for a week on order of the City Council.

Then on September 13, a similar incident occurred in the Fraumünster, where a weaver, Lorenz Hochrütiner (see Cast of Characters, No. 45), and a carpenter, Wolfgang Ininger (see 51B/fn.6), after reading a pamphlet by Ludwig Hätzer against idols and images according to the Scriptures (see 57C/fn.3), destroyed the "eternal lights," i.e., the oil lamps which hung near the altar. For this the two laymen were imprisoned in the tower for three days.

The most serious event of all occurred on September 23 near the lower gate of the city in the village of Stadelhofen, where Hochrütiner, following his release from prison, Claus Hottinger (see Cast of Characters, No. 48), and Hans Ockenfuss (see Cast of Characters, No. 71) removed the great village crucifix. All three had participated in the Lenten fast-breaking in Froschauer's house, and Hottinger had been associated with Grebel in the Badenschenke and pulpit disturbances (see 47A, 47B, and 47C). Their alleged purpose in the Stadelhofen incident was to sell the materials of which the crucifix had been made and give the money to the poor. At their trial, Hottinger named three members of the Zurich Council who had encouraged him in this act of iconoclasm, Ockenfuss testified that "one hears daily that such crucifixes and all other images of God our Redeemer are forbidden," and Hochrütiner declared that "since other people had taken images of the saints and crucifixes from the churches and no one had stopped them, he thought that he would do no wrong" (Egli, Aktens., No. 421, quoted by Garside, 1966, p. 121). The three were immediately consigned to the tower to await trial.

On Tuesday, September 29, following similar acts of iconoclasm at Höngg, where Simon Stumpf (see Cast of Characters, No. 85) was pastor, and at Wipkingen, the Zurich authorities appointed an 11-man committee composed of four members of the Small Council (one of whom was Jacob Grebel), four from the Large Council, and the three city pastors (Zwingli, Jud, and Engelhart) to review the biblical teachings regarding the Christian's worship of images and to bring a recommendation. On October 12, the committee recommended to the council that a public disputation be held not only on the question of images but also on the issue of the mass.

In the following letter on that same day, Jacob Grebel reports these developments to Vadian and urges him to attend. It is possible that the committee asked him to write to Vadian to invite him to come as a representative from St. Gallen. Vadian did in fact attend and served as one of the presidents of the disputation (see 57C).

First, my cordial greeting and wish for everything good.
Dear doctor:

I am letting you know that by the grace of God the Lord we are all in good health and spirits. We always desire to hear the same and everything good from you.

Further, I am letting you know that Milords, Councillors, and Representatives[2] took counsel together just now, Monday after Dionysius, [to invite] again[3] their lay priests and scholars in the city and their province, also abbots, plus Milord [bishop] of Constance, one burgomaster and councillor from the city of Constance, Milord [bishop] of Chur, Milord [bishop] of Basel, the University of Basel, and also all parts of the league.[4] They have been cordially invited for the sake of God and the Christian faith to appear on the Sunday before Simon and Jude [October 25] and then to assemble at the *Rathaus* [City Hall] on Monday to hold a disputation, especially concerning the mass and images and idols in the church.[5] These two points will be written up and posted everywhere, so that everyone will know how to observe them. Who is coming or staying away, I do not know,[6] though Milords expect everything favorable, and it is taking place with the best of intentions, when and if with God's help it can be brought to pass. It is therefore my request and desire that you, together with your cousin Jörg,[7] brother-in-law Bartholomew,[8] and whomever else you wish, will want to come. Bring them with you to my home and under no circumstances anywhere else. I hope you will not stay away and that you will be willing to take the time. If I judge correctly, you will not regret it.

We have gotten a great deal of wine, everyone much more than he would ever have believed; and it is our good judgment that it is better than in many years. You will want to help us sample it, although against you up there we cannot compete.

Greetings to you, your mother, Martha, brother-in-law Bartholomew, and cousin Jörg, and also all those of yours whom you hold dear, from my Dorothea,[9] sister Agatha,[10] Aunt Keller,[11] cousin Hans Lübolt,[12] and that naughty girl Dorli.[13] So be greeted herewith, and may God protect you from harm always.

Given on Monday after Dionysius in the year [15]23.

Jacob Grebel

To the learned Master and Doctor Joachim von Watt, my dear son-in-law.

Original: Stadtbibliothek (Vadiana) St. Gallen, VB.II.152
Transcription: VB, III, No. 364

57C
The Second Zurich Disputation[1]
October 26-28, 1523

Despite the disappointing response from outside the canton of Zurich (see 57B/fn.6), over 800 priests and laymen filled the Council Hall (Rathaus) *on Monday morning, October 26, for the convening of the Second Doctrinal*

234

Disputation. (For a discussion of the procedures of the disputation as a Reformation tool, see introduction to 51A, above). Burgomaster Röist (see Cast of Characters, No. 79) opened the meeting and appointed Vadian and two other delegates to preside over the three days of debate. The city clerk then read the official invitation and Zwingli made some preliminary remarks (see Hillerbrand, 1964, p. 144), interpreting the purpose of the disputation to discern the Word of God on the matters in question but not to specify the practical implementation of such findings, which he declared to be the prerogative of the Zurich Council.

As the following minutes reveal, however, there was subsequently some serious divergence of opinion on this very question of the council's prerogative in matters affecting the church. It emerged in a dialogue between Zwingli and Simon Stumpf, representing some dissenters (see 242/21ff.). Some historians (see Bender, 1950, pp. 98ff.) have pegged the beginning of Anabaptism to this debate, although others (see J. H. Yoder, 1958) have reinterpreted the question of Anabaptist origins in a larger time frame. In any case, this Second Disputation was an effort to continue the momentum for reform gained in the First Disputation nine months earlier, as newer questions such as the use of images in worship and the validity of the Roman Catholic mass arose.

The excerpts that follow highlight the participation of persons who later became Anabaptists (Grebel, Hubmaier, and Stumpf) and the role of Zwingli, still trying to shepherd the whole range of pro-Reformation attitudes within his jurisdiction. Thus, we hear him acknowledging his indebtedness to the dissenters on issues such as the priestly vestments on which he had "changed and withdrawn my former opinion" while also attempting to temper their alleged over-scrupulousness about other aspects of the celebration of the Lord's Supper. On the other hand, we also hear him recognizing the support of conservatives like Commander Schmid while clearly rejecting his idea of unlimited forbearance for the immaturity of parishioners who still depended on images in their worship of God.

[Excerpt from the First Day Concerning Images][2]
[Ludwig Hätzer]:[3]

In order that no one may think that private images[4] are to be permitted,[5] it is necessary for me to give an account, and [he] said:

Lord Doctor![6] Secret images are also forbidden. For this we have a clear passage of Scripture, Deut. 27 [:14f.]: Moses ordered upon the commandment of God: "The Levites shall declare with loudness to all the people of Israel: 'Cursed is the man who makes a melted image, an abomination to the Lord God, and sets it up in a secret place.' And all the people shall say, 'Amen.'"

No one can contradict this, he says.

Then spoke

Conrad Grebel:

Since there should be no images among Christians, there should also be no secret ones; for that would be *dispensatio divini verbi* [dispensing with the Word of God].[7]

Then everyone was silent. Anyone who wished to oppose him was urged to do so. But nobody did. . . .[8]

Following this summons[9] arose

Master Conrad Schmid,[10]

Commander at Küssnacht on Lake Zurich

and commented as follows: . . . One should not tear out of the hand of the weak the staff on which he leans. One should give him another, or one will throw him to the ground. So if a weakling clings to a crutch that totters with him, one should leave it in his hand, and show him a stronger staff nearby, so that of his own free will he will then let the crutch fall and grasp the stronger staff. So for the timid weak, let the outward images stand to which they still cling, and instruct them first that there is no life, holiness, or grace in them, and then that there is for the weak a crutch to help us, and point them to a stronger staff nearby, Christ Jesus, the only comforter and helper everyone comes to in trouble. Thus they will find that they do not need the images or even the saints, and will willingly let them go and joyfully take hold of Christ. And if Christ were thus in the heart of men in true knowledge, then all images would fall away without offense. For it is never good to injure the conscience of one whom Christ has made well by his death. . . .

Thereupon arose Master Huldrych Zwingli to speak as follows:[11]

Zwingli:

As my dear brother Leo Jud has pointed out here before, images should not be made, should not be worshiped, should not even be honored. That I also declare. For the Word is clearer than day. That my lord and brother, the commander, here advises that one should first fully instruct the world with the Word of God and preach the same unceasingly pleases me very much, and I am entirely of the same opinion that this be done faithfully to all. I also hope for that. My brother Leo and I have faithfully done this to all and spared nothing to that end. Indeed, I for my part have therefore here in Zurich from the hour I first arrived taken in hand to preach the holy Gospel of Matthew without any the accretions of human performances.[12] I have also declared openly before provost and chapter that I was undertaking this.[13] Thereupon I made my well-known introduction, like Paul, that he also might become well known. Consequently I have preached the Acts of the holy apostles, the epistle of Paul to the Galatians, the two to Timothy, both epistles of Peter, the one to the

Hebrews, and now Luke.[14] I believe therefore that there has been no default among us, that now everyone is well informed in the things concerning the grace of God, [and] that from now on the offense should have no recognition nor merit.

Here called to him

The Commander

and said to this: Master Huldrych! That is not what I said, that I find fault with you.

Replied

Zwingli:

I also did not say that you found fault with me, but rather that you want to believe that it[15] is the staff or cane of the weak. God forbid! Had the useless priests and bishops earnestly preached the Word of God as they ran after useless things, it would never have come to this that the poor layman who is ignorant of Scripture has had to learn about Christ from the walls and from the pictures.[16] Henceforth, images are not to be tolerated, for everything that God has forbidden is not an indifferent matter.[17] The commandments of God do not oversee so trifling a thing as eating meat. No! for the eagle "does not fly after gnats," as the common Greek proverb puts it.[18] It is shown throughout the prophets and in the New Testament that images should not exist at all among Christians. . . . [19]

There are two kinds of offense. Some take offense not because they are ill or weak in faith but because they are quite godless. That is not *infirmitas* [infirmity]; indeed, that is a real true *malignitas* [malignity], for they do not believe at all. Some, however, are really weak in faith. It is well to be forbearing[20] with them.

But that there comes an end to the taking of offense it is well to note, for Paul had Timothy circumcised but would not let Titus be circumcised. Why? It was time for the taking of offense to cease and come to an end. If one should wait with the idols[21] until no one took offense anymore, as is your opinion, then the commandment of God to throw out and do away with the idols would never be fulfilled. Likewise, if the outer idols should not be expelled until the inner idols of temptation are eliminated, we would never come to the point of abolishing the images. . . . Therefore, the images are not to be tolerated among Christians, for they are a real true abomination in the eyes of God. . . . [22]

This is now the summation of the words that he spoke. With regard to them

The Commander

said that he was fully satisfied and that they pleased him well. . . . [23]

237

And as everyone was silent, Dr. Balthasar Fridberger [Hubmaier], pastor in Waldshut, arose and spoke as follows:

D[octor] Balthasar [Hubmaier][24]

The all-powerful eternal God commanded us through Moses: "If you come across the ox of your enemy or a wandering donkey, lead him back to him, that is to say, to his owner; and if you see the ass of someone who hates you lying under his burden, do not pass by but lift him up" [Ex. 23:4f.[. Christ spoke similarly [Lk. 14:5]: "Which of you, if his ass or ox would fall into a pit, would not pull him out at the same hour, even on the Sabbath Day?" So much more should it be taken seriously if a person is in error in matters that have to do with the salvation of his soul, or if he has fallen into a pit of error or abuse, that he should be helped.

Now it cannot be denied but is rather public and clearer than the sun that for several hundred years much error and abuse has been infiltrated into Christian practices and added to them by the devil, who never rests. This has also happened on these two subjects; namely, the images of saints and the abuses of the mass. This is why the worthy, prominent, honorable, and wise lords, mayor, Large and Small Council, called the two hundred of this praiseworthy old city of Zurich, my gracious lords, esteemed and held that it would be good and Christian to carry out a friendly brotherly conversation so that such tension and division that had arisen, in that some want to stand by the old and others by the new, might be alleviated without disturbance or disorder. All of which cannot take place more fittingly nor properly than through the proclamation of the clear Word of God as written in both[Testaments. For in all divisive questions and controversies, only Scripture canonized and sanctified by God himself should and must be the judge, no one else; or heaven and earth must fall [cf. Mt. 24:35]. If the merciful God himself has set the judge on the judgment throne as we read in Ezekiel 44[:24]: "When there is a controversy, men will stand in my judgment and will judge." Now the judgments of God can only be known out of the divine Word, as Scripture truly testifies to us. The Word of God judges, John 12[:47-49]; Deuteronomy 17[:8]; Exodus 18[:13-27] and 28[:30]. Therefore Christ points us to Scriptures: "You research the Scriptures. They give testimony of me, etc.," and pointed us to Moses and the prophets whom we should hear; for he does not want to have testimony from men John 5[:39, 46]. This usage was held by Christ himself and also by Paul and the other apostles. When they spoke against the devil or against evil men, they usually stuck Scripture under their nose as the judge of all controversial talk and thereby convinced them. For holy Scripture alone is the true light and lantern through which all human argument, darkness and resistance, can be recognized. This the prophet David knew perfectly well as he said to God, "Thy word is a lamp to my feet" [Ps. 119:105]. Christ also himself taught us the same thing: that we should take the lantern of his wholesome Word in our hand, so that when the bridegroom comes we can enter into the marriage feast with him [Mt. 25:1-13]. Thus also the error and the abuses of making images and the mass shall be demonstrated only through the plumb line of the bright clear Word of God, thereby being recognized and moderated, and what is built thereupon will remain finally and permanently; for the Word of God is imperishable.

Here there was no one that would speak against that. . . . [25]

[Excerpt from the Second Day Concerning the Mass][26]

The Commander

On this it may be noted that one does not offer up Christ. For he who sacrifices gives some gift. But we give nothing when we observe the mass; on the contrary, we receive forgiveness of sin, grace, and mercy, and eternal life.

For that very reason I wish that one would speak more reservedly of the mass, that no one may be made worse thereby, but that all men would be made better thereby. For to me it seems a hard argument to say that the mass comes from the devil and that the devil has created and invented the monks and orders. That is speaking coarsely.[27] There is many a monk who wears the robes and is nonetheless a Christian for it.

It seems to me, if they[28] would leave us in peace, and not speak of it so immoderately and wickedly, they would not do so much harm. We who live in rural areas must listen to more things than you in the city. But I am going to take in hand the one who said such things (he may not be present here in this room) and say this to him between him and me alone, as Christ has taught and instructed us.[29]

That is the summary of that.

After this address in support of the monks, Zwingli arose and said:

Master Huldrych Zwingli

I could have done without having the subject of the monks dragged in by my dear brother and lord, since it adds nothing to the topic. Inasmuch as I myself have often preached like that in public from the pulpit, I am forced to give an answer for it.[30] For everything that God has not taught and that comes from men is never good.[31] Therefore, that such hypocrisy is never commended or instituted by God is clear. It is on the contrary always rebuked as a matter that is not of God but of the devil. I have also taught that the origin of good is from God, the origin of evil from the living devil, for there are always two wells from which flow good and evil. Thus, such hypocrisy has emanated from no other than the flesh and selfishness that has always wanted to be something too, like Adam in the garden. That is always diametrically contrary to God and is thus always from the devil, for such sects[32] are a cause of downfall of an entire Christian class.

But that more in the countryside than in the city speak immoderately of the mass and of the monks than is proper displeases me and I have never praised it but always censured it. I also wish that all the priests would be zealous in preaching the one Christ. Thereby in the course of time, if the Word is preached steadfastly, all sects, gangs, and orders together with other abuses would be put away.

I know well and it grieves me that some preach about it more immoderately than is perhaps good. There are many of those who retain only the words of that kind from my sermons. There are likewise many of those who refuse to learn from the learned Martin Luther in his books anything but the acrimony of his words which he often uses out of flaming, ardent love. But no one wants to learn from him the devout, faithful heart that he has toward true divine truth. I have been no less acrimonious in the pulpit at times; but I have never incited anyone except in a personal matter.[33]

You also know how I have made many concessions to you in the matter of the intercession of the saints; that I have always said, "Bring your laments to whomever you wish, I will bring mine to God"; that my way is sure, yours is unsure. Until now, I have thoroughly refuted the intercession of the saints with holy Scripture. Thus I have taught opportunely and inopportunely, that is, with harshness and with kindness. For this I have an example in Paul.[34] I would indeed like and prefer from my heart that everyone would strive to build and not to destroy, and firmly proclaim the Word of God, and speak in accord with it in the name of God as the Spirit teaches him.

That is the summary of his words. The commander was well satisfied.

Upon this,

Doctor Joachim von Watt [Vadian]

arose and again urged that if anyone cared to speak further, he should do so. . . .[35]

Then Dr. Balthasar Fridberger [Hubmaier] arose, saying:

D[octor] Balthasar Fridberger [Hubmaier]

Lord Burgomaster and other dear brothers in Christ! Yesterday it became thoroughly clear from Scripture that there should be no images. I myself would [have wished] that no image had ever come into Christendom. For the text of Exodus 20[4-6] is bright and clear. It stands firm as a wall. By means of two distinct prohibitions, it expressly forbids not only worshiping the images but also making them. Still more clearly it is said in

240

Deuteronomy 5[6-10], where God speaks by means of three distinct prohibitions: "I the Lord your God who brought you out of the land of Egypt out of the house of servitude" [Deut. 5:6]. Secondly, "Thou shalt not make an image or any kind of form of all of the things that are up above in heaven or below on the earth or in the water under the earth" [Deut. 5:8]. Thirdly, "You shall not honor them nor serve them, for I am the Lord your God, a jealous God" [Deut. 5:9]. Thus we find also that God hates not only the adoration which takes place before the images but also the making of the image. Therefore he commands them to be burnt and those who make them, he curses, Deuteronomy 7[25] and 27[15]: "And all the people shall say, 'Amen!' "

Now some people in the room said, "Amen!"

Now I want to add a Mosaic argument, which completely casts down the images with its two horns. That is: either it is or it is not commanded to possess images. If they are commanded, show us the Scripture and there will be no more question. If they are not commanded, then they should not exist. For everything which God has not taught us either with words or deeds should not be and is in vain. For as God is alone good [Mt. 19:17], so everything that is good must come from God alone. He who says otherwise accuses God the Father, the Son Jesus Christ, and St. Paul, of lying. God the Father speaks [Deut. 12:32], "What I have commanded you, do only that, nothing more, nothing less." God the Son has said [Mt. 15:13], "Every planting that has not been planted by my heavenly Father will be torn out." Likewise Paul [Rom. 14:23], "What does not arise from faith contributes to eternal damnation." Just one more thing. One of the two must be true: images are useful or useless in the church. If they are useless, what do you want with them? If they are useful, then God was not telling the truth because he said in Isaiah 44[9] that they are not useful to anyone. It is also a blasphemy to tell the people that the images call us, move us, invite us, and draw us to contemplation. For it is Christ who calls the sinner. He alone moves him to good deeds. He invites him to the wedding feast. God the Father is the one who draws those who come to Christ.

But now that the pictures have come into the church (which is most lamentable for me, because of the manifold abuses which take place), we have to look carefully how to deal with them, so that no one will be scandalized and so that brotherly Christian peace may not be troubled. For there are many persons who mightily adhere to the images. Therefore the true holy Word of God against images and idols in Old and New Testament must be shown to the people earnestly and often with care and thoroughness. This will exercise its authority and power and with time will drive all the images out. For it is impossible that the Word of God should be preached and not bring works and fruits in that whereto it was sent to God [Is. 55:10[. Thus Paul did in Athens and other places, as we find in the Acts of the Apostles. When that happens, every Christian will find in himself and recognize that the images are not any use at all. Then a whole parish church will gather and decide unanimously without any disorder that the images are to be moved out and laid to sleep. Then the powerful Word of God will have borne its fruit, for the sake of which it went forth from God.

When this doctor had completed his remarks, Doctor Joachim von Watt [Vadian] asked Doctor Hans Zwick of Constance whether he also wanted to say something. . . . [36]

Then arose

Conrad Grebel

and expressed the opinion that the priests should be given instructions[37] while they were still together how henceforth to proceed with the mass; for it[38] would be futile if they did not begin to change the mass.[39] Much has been said about the mass, but there would be no one who would be willing to stop this great abomination to God. In addition, there were yet much greater abuses in the mass. These also should be discussed.

Said

Zwingli:

Milords will discern how the mass should henceforth be properly observed.[40]

Thereupon spoke

Simon Stumpf:[41]

Master Huldrych! You have no authority to place the decision in Milords' hands, for the decision is already made: the Spirit of God decides. If therefore Milords were to discern and decide anything that is contrary to God's decision, I will ask Christ for his Spirit and will teach and act against it.

Replied

Zwingli:

That is right. I shall also preach and act against it if they decide otherwise. I do not give the decision into their hands. They shall also certainly not decide about God's Word—not only they but the whole world should not. This convocation is not being held so that they might decide about that, but to ascertain and learn from the Scripture whether or not the mass is a sacrifice. Then they will counsel together as to the most appropriate way for this to be done without an uproar,[42] etc.

Since the matter had continued until nightfall and it was not feasible to do anything more, the lord burgomaster said that they should come to the *Rathaus* again at twelve in the afternoon—for it was a holiday[43]—to discuss these matters further. Everyone could now go to his lodgings. This was done.

So much for the second day.

Actions of the Third and Final Day[44]

As the burgomaster had ordered everyone to return to the *Rathaus* at twelve, it was diligently done. Now, when all were again seated in the proper order, the burgomaster began to speak as follows:

Burgomaster

Dear gracious lords, you presidents! You may now in God's name resume the discussion of the mass, For I well foresee that you will not say much about purgatory today.

Then spoke

Doctor Joachin von Watt of St. Gallen [Vadian]

and admonished those who had begun to speak yesterday about the abuses of the mass to take it up again now with greater skill and as briefly as possible.[45]

After this arose

The Burgomaster

and expressed this opinion:

Gracious, dear lords and good friends! You have heard in what spirit this matter was begun, as Milords have also expressed it in briefest form in their mandate that here again no one should offend by speaking except from the Old and New Testament alone.

Therefore, dear lords, I urge and beg you to stay within this mandate and not to introduce anything that is unrelated to this article of faith. Later on, if anyone wishes to talk about purgatory or other things, a special day can be set for it and Milords will always be glad to grant it to you and accede to your wishes. Nevertheless, several of you have previously tried to bring other matters into the discussion that do not concern this article. Let each one keep such things for their turn.

The summation thereof.

This opinion was also expressed by

Doctor Joachim von Watt [Vadian]

Let everyone who will, be he clerical or secular, speak against this article today, but only on the basis of the Scriptures of God. Therefore, those of you who believe there are still many abuses of the mass which must be discussed may now again bring them up and announce them.

Then arose

Conrad Grebel

and expressed this opinion:

Dear brethren in Christ our Savior! Although it has been discerned and adequately demonstrated from the holy Scriptures that the mass is not a sacrifice, there are still many abuses which the devil has also added to this about which it is necessary to speak; for your mandate, Milords, concerns all the abuses of the mass. I therefore for God's sake urge those who can speak better—for I am not eloquent and have a poor memory—to be so kind as to open the subject here.[46]

Then Doctor Balthasar [Hubmaier] Fridberger[47] arose to speak:

Doctor Balthasar [Hubmaier] Fridberger

Concerning numerous abuses in the mass—which I would rather call a testament of Christ or a memorial of his bitter death—this is without doubt the main point of the abuses that we interpret the mass as a sacrifice. In order to speak to that subject, which concerns me, and since I want to let myself be taught by all Christian believers according to God's will but only through Scripture, I have not been taught otherwise to date than that I must confess with my dear brothers in Christ, Huldrych Zwingli and Leo Jud, that the mass is not a sacrifice but a proclamation of the covenant of Christ, in which there is a remembrance of his bitter suffering and his self-sacrifice, who offered himself once for all on the cross, and never more will again be offered; and that this is done by an external visible sign and seal through which we are made completely certain of the forgiveness of our sins. And whoever celebrates the mass otherwise is sealing a letter that has not yet been written.

The testimonies that move me to say this are found in Matthew 16[26-28]; Luke 22[:29ff.]; Mark 14[:22-24]; 1 Corinthians 11[:23-26]; Hebrews 7[:15ff.] and 9[:11ff.]. Christ said, *Hoc facite* ["This do"].[48] He did not say, *Hoc offerte* ["This offer"].

It follows from this, first of all, that the mass is of no use as a sacrifice either to the dead or the living. For if I cannot believe for someone else, I cannot hold a mass for him. Since the mass is established by Christ as a sign unto faith whereby the faith of believers is confirmed.

Secondly, because the body and blood of Christ are signs and seals of the Word of Christ which is spoken in the mass, the priest must preach nothing in the mass other than the pure clear Word of God of which these are signs. Whoever celebrates the mass otherwise does not hold a true mass.

Thirdly, whoever does not preach the Word of God does not hold a [true] mass. This was acknowledged by Christ and by Paul who learned it from him (Matthew, Luke, etc., as above): "This do in remembrance of me. As often as you do this, you proclaim the Lord's death."[49] The follower must be true to this or Christ must yield.

Fourthly, as the mass should be read in Latin to the Latins, therefore also in French to the French, in German to the Germans; for without doubt Christ did not speak Calcuttish[50] with his disciples at the Last Supper but rather loud and clear. So also to celebrate mass is to read a letter of testament. It would be ridiculous to read a Latin letter to a German who cannot understand Latin. For to celebrate the mass quietly and not to preach is to silence the Lord. Paul wants us to speak intelligibly in the church and would much rather have five words spoken with understanding to the profit of the church than ten thousand which are not understood, so that the people must be instructed and say, "Amen!" 1 Corinthians 14[:19].[51]

Fifthly, he who holds a true mass should give food and drink not only to himself but also to others who hunger and thirst in spirit, and that in both forms.[52] Christ taught this to us by word and deed, saying, "Drink all of it!"[53] He who teaches or does otherwise pokes a hole in Christ's letter of testament,[54] which even an angel from heaven has no right to do, much less a human being on earth, according to Gal[atians], chapters 1 and 3.[55]

Dear pious Christians! These are my convictions, which I have been taught out of Scripture, especially concerning images[56] and the mass. Where they are not correct or Christian, I beg you all through Jesus Christ our only Savior, I beseech and admonish you through the last judgment to be willing to correct me in a brotherly and Christian way with Scripture. I may err, for I am a human being; but a heretic I cannot be. I am willing— and desire it from the heart—to be instructed. I want to accept that from everyone with great thanks, confess my errors and subject myself to you willingly in all obedience according to the Word of God, and also truly to follow you as followers of Christ.

I have spoken. Judge and instruct me. I will pray Christ to lend us his grace so to do.

He also said that he was never more happy the whole year than when he learned that there was going to be discussion here of the abuses of the mass, of which there are still many more, as Conrad Grebel had indicated. Thereupon arose and expressed this opinion:

Conrad Grebel has demanded of us that we discuss the abuses of the mass. I say therefore:

All that is planted and added without being instituted by Christ is a true abuse.[57] But since these things cannot be abolished all at once, it is necessary to preach God's Word against them firmly and courageously. For instance, it is a foolish, useless, even treacherous matter for true divine worship that worthless chanting is rattled off in temples everywhere,[58] which not only the common man cannot understand but even many of the priests. Now Paul says clearly that he would rather speak five words with which he edifies others than blabber ten thousand with only his tongue.[59] Now nothing should ever be done in the church except what can be understood by all. That is an abuse that could well be changed.

Concerning the time: The testament [Lord's Supper] should not be bound to a specific time; but any time one desires it, he may receive it.

Likewise concerning the vestments which the priest wears when he administers the mass: Although at first, when I wrote about the canon,[60] I yielded on this point for the sake of the weak in faith, supposing it was a symbol of Christ's suffering, as is further explained in that booklet,[61] I have now been informed differently by several[62] that these vestments are derived from the vestments of the priest in the Old Law, from which there was good reason to consider the mass a sacrifice; therefore I have changed and withdrawn my former opinion.[63]

Since, then, neither chanting nor vestments is of any use except to detract from right, true prayer, which is raising one's spirit to God, these things must be put away and abolished at the proper time so that no uproar[64] or other disunity will arise among Christians. For the devil fences us in and often tricks us with ridiculous things, as Doctor Hans Zwick[65] said yesterday. The people must first be taught with the Word of God that neither vestments nor chanting contributes to the mass. For if anyone were to officiate at a mass at present without the vestments, there would be a disturbance.

Therefore, faithful, elect, dear brethren in Christ Jesus, I urge you for God's sake to take the Word of God in hand and present and preach it to your parishioners with the utmost clarity that they may learn from it what the mass is, and also that one may well have a mass without the vestments. If the people are thus built up, these things can be abolished without tumult.

This Zwingli said at greater length.

Thereupon spoke

Conrad Grebel:

There are other abuses besides these; for instance, he would like to know whether the bread should be leavened or unleavened; for it seemed to him that Christ used [ordinary] leavened bread, and the holy apostles likewise.

Answered

Zwingli:

He did not want to debate what kind of bread it was. That was not very important. Each parish should come to an agreement on what bread to use, leavened or unleavened.

Thought

Grebel:

It really should be considered, for the text says *"panis,"*[66] and it should not be "round" [wafers].[67]

Said

Zwingli

as before: But as to the shape it would not be right to insist that it always be round. He could easily tolerate the use of ordinary bread. Doing so would not be sinning.

Said

Grebel:

Then everything would be left to the parish.

Answered

Zwingli:

Yes, everything that is not clearly specified in the plain Word of God is left to the parish so long as nothing that is essential is changed. As to using leavened or unleavened bread that is left solely to the practice of the parish, for it is of little importance.[68]

Spoke

Grebel:

It is also an abomination to God that water is poured into the blood of Christ without any basis or reference to holy Scripture.[69] But God, the Almighty, has strictly commanded what all Christians should steadfastly and firmly observe—that we add nothing to it nor subtract anything from it.[70]

Said

Zwingli:

Conrad! You are right. No water should be added.[71]

Said

Grebel:

This is also an abuse: the priest's inserting [the bread] on the lay member's tongue, as though we had no hands and it were not as fitting for us to touch the body of Christ as for the priests.[72]

Said

Zwingli:

That is unimportant. We have no clear and plain Scripture concerning it. For that purpose they had deacons, i.e., servants, who distributed it.

Grebel insisted vehemently that each one take it himself.

Someone in the room said: But if we were all lame, we would have to have someone to hand us the sacrament and push it in.

Zwingli

says as before: We cannot tell from the Word of God whether Christ put his body [i.e., the bread] into his disciples' hands or not. For even though it says *accipite,* that is "take," that is not necessarily understood to mean that they took it in their hands. For it is also written: *Accepit acetum Christus in cruce,* that is, "Christ received the vinegar on the cross."[73] Now Christ could not possibly have received it in his hands, for they were nailed fast. It can therefore be left to each parish to decide how they want to practice it.

Conrad Grebel drew out further that for him they were trying to bind God's Spirit to time by insisting that the sacrament be taken in the forenoon and before eating, whereas Christ practiced and instituted it in the evening meal.

It was also deplored that the officiating priests had the Spirit only on those days when contracts of payment were due on their benefices. From this it can easily be inferred that they conducted the mass solely for the benefice and solely for the sake of the money.

Zwingli

replied: The sacrament is by no means bound to time. That was evident, for today mass was held at eight and tomorrow at ten. But if he wanted to insist so anxiously on practicing it in the same form and time as Christ did, then we would be bound to time and would have to be wearing clothes like those that Christ wore and would have to wash one another's feet beforehand.[74] Therefore it was left open to each parish to decide this matter for itself. But the sacrament should be given to everybody in both forms,[75] as Christ did.

Concerning the priests who conducted mass only on those special and certain days, he would surely be grieved if anyone would be so fond of temporal goods that he would sell God for them. "I hope," said Zwingli, "that you, Milords, will depose such mass-slaves and let them die off in

248

peace." The reason: It would be safer and better to give each one some other benefice so that he would not have to conduct a mass than that he would have to conduct a mass. This [way of] sacrificing and selling God is surely an abomination.

Conrad Grebel

remarked: No priest should serve himself.

Replied

Zwingli:

Everyone could serve himself the food and drink according to the leading of the Holy Spirit; for Christ, from whom we receive it, offers it to us himself.

This is in sum the dispute that arose here.

Since Conrad Grebel was now satisfied,[76] arose

Conrad Schmid

Commander at Küssnacht on Lake Zurich, and spoke very earnestly.... [77]

Following this all three doctors, the presidents, arose and Doctor Joachim [Vadian] spoke as follows:[78]

Doctor Joachim [Vadian]

Lord burgomaster, noble, austere, pious, dear, honorable, wise, and gracious lords of the Large and Small Councils of this praiseworthy city of Zurich! Whereas your honorable wisdom appointed and designated us— although insignificant—as presidents and moderators at the opening of this manifestly excellent and Christian convention, my fellow doctors and presidents have directed me to thank you in the highest degree for the honors, also the courteous and gracious goodwill. For that reason I together with them sought to merit and earn the same from your honorable wisdom. We would also like to petition our gracious lords to regard it as sufficient from us that we have not neglected to do our best according to our ability. In addition, now that you, my gracious lords, have singly and collectively, for two-and-one-half days, zealously and earnestly conducted, heard, discerned, and understood the disputation on the two main propositions, viz., on images or idols and on the institution of the mass and its abuses, how and to what degree these things were attacked with arguments and presumed Scripture by the learned M[aster] Huldrych Zwingli and M[aster] Leo Jud, your protectors and preachers, also how they were defended and maintained: it seems to us and indeed we have no doubt that the Holy Scripture, the divine Word, will remain firm and undefeated as to its content. But that it should be fitting or proper for us to speak or make any judgment in this matter, that is not warranted. Nor do we have any mandates from you or anyone else to do so. And we acknowledge that we could not do so without being suspected of committing a malicious and presumptuous deed.

Therefore, gracious lords, we commit the debate we have just now heard to your honorable wisdom to judge and to weigh, with great hope that God, the Almighty, will put into your minds and suggest to you as the magistrates, committed and inclined to defend the truth, ways and means by which the Word of God, which is and wants to be its own judge, may be applied and preached, and in addition, the abuses that have crept in for so long[79] a time because God had withheld his wrath may be abrogated and abolished without injury to the simpleminded in your canton. . . .

Lord burgomaster and gracious lords! Milords, fellow brethren, and presidents have directed me to ask your honorable wisdom faithfully to pray for God's will, that you will mercifully keep in mind, in appropriate measure and form, the poor prisoners[80] who have lain so long in severe imprisonment, as was presented to your wisdom in our name last Monday evening.[81]

Then arose

The Abbot of Kappel[82]

and admonished the lords of Zurich to pursue the cause of the gospel fearlessly and preach it effectively as the commander has said; for many of the priests are too unlearned to be able or competent to preach the gospel. As far as lay in his own power, he would not hesitate but with joy offer up his own person; for preaching must be done if they want to be called true Christians.

Concerning the prisoners, he too desired that for God's sake they be released from imprisonment, which had now lasted a long time.

This the provost and the commander of Küssnacht also desired.

Here in the briefest possible form is contained the entire summary and content of this disputation or debate on images and the mass, as it was conducted and took its course before many people and before the session of the honorable Christian Council of the praiseworthy city of Zurich, although many other speeches by a number of people have not been written down. The reason is that they did not serve the cause.[83] I[84] therefore did not write them down.

Transpired at the time and day as stated above.

Herewith I commend myself to all true servants of Christ in their prayers with the desire for an unburdening of their consciences.

The year 1523.

Original Publication: *Die Akten der zweiten Disputation vom 26.-28. Oktober 1523,* published 12/8/1523
Transcription: ZW, II, No. 28

57D
The Council's Mandate after the Disputation
Zurich, End of October 1523[1]

Near the close of the disputation, Conrad Schmid had proposed that the abolition of images and the mass should be preceded by a preaching-teaching mission mandated by the Zurich Council. As the following document shows, the council followed this suggestion and planned to send several of the most learned clergymen to speak in churches, admonishing the local priests to make way for them when they arrived. The council also ordered the writing and publication of an "Introduction" to the disputation findings, so that the local priests could better know "how to take God's teaching in hand and present it to their parishioners."

Meanwhile, everybody was to hold his peace, pending the orderly implementation of those findings. "Thus far," writes John H. Yoder, "the Council seemed to be moving forward, carefully but surely, in a way which justified the confidence placed in it to deal, not with questions of principle, but with applications" (JHY, 1958, p. 136).

Whereas this past year our gracious lords, the burgomaster, councillors, and representatives,[2] etc., solely for God's praise and honor and also for the salvation of Christ-believing souls, held a convocation[3] of all their priests, pastors, people's priests, and preachers, on account of some who did not understand the divine Word, and now in these past days—to the disadvantage or humiliation of no one—the aforementioned priests, pastors, people's priests, preachers, and all their other prelates and learned men were called together again[4] from all their cities and districts, and there the divine truth concerning the two matters—images and the mass—was sought and discerned out of the clear Word of God:

Now, therefore, concerning images, it is the prohibition, will, and intention of our aforesaid lords that henceforth until further information is given from the Word of God in the near future[5] (if God wills), no one, neither clergy nor laity, shall carry out of or into the churches or alter any kind of image, unless one has put his own image into the church. In that case he may take possession of it again, but in such a way that no disorderliness results.[6] Moreover, if some images were made by fellow parishioners or out of church funds, no one shall in the meanwhile alter them without the knowledge and consent of the fellow parishioners.

Concerning the mass, pending further information and explanation soon to come,[7] it shall remain as it is now, and no one shall malign or bait another with any kind of malicious provocative words.[8] And whoever behaves improperly or disobediently in word or deed in this matter our lords will punish severely in accordance with the circumstances of the case. And in order that none through lack of information or ignorance may be offended, it is the will and intent of our lords that all their pastors and preachers shall without delay[9] begin to preach and proclaim the holy gospel clearly and truly according to the Spirit of God. And in order that this may be the better accomplished, they have appointed some true and learned men to draw up a brief introduction[10] for the sake of the uninformed to instruct those who do not know how to take God's teaching in hand and present it to their parishioners.[11] This document will shortly[12] be issued in print telling how each should proceed, for this writing is not drawn from human reason but from the example and words of God (which cannot lead anyone astray). Also, in order that no one (as has already unfortunately been done by several) may evade or have an excuse, these our lords will send out several learned priests to proclaim the Word of God everywhere in their district.[13] Therefore, when these priests come into the parishes in this matter, the local people's priests wherever possible shall give place to them to make this proclamation and shall in no way interfere. And in order that the Almighty God may in many instances send and reveal his divine mercy and the light of truth in these and all questions that are of concern to us according to his praise and the salvation of our souls, etc., all the pastors shall in all their sermons admonish the people with the greatest zeal to call upon God earnestly and pray that this may be granted to us through the only begotten Son Jesus Christ in accordance with his will.

Original: ?
Transcription: Aktensammlung, No. 436

57E
The Report of Veit Suter
October 31, 1523

Veit Suter, an imperial observer in Zurich from Austria, wrote the following entry into his varied reports of Zurich affairs. It concerned the council's mandate after the disputation (see 57D, above) and contains two important pieces of information: (1) that the action of the council prohibiting any policy changes concerning images and the mass was motivated by fear of attack from the Roman Catholic cantons, and (2) that Zwingli had said very clearly at the disputation that the Zurich authorities had no right to pass judgment in these matters.

According to John H. Yoder (MQR, 1958, p. 134), "this letter confirms that really radical action was contemplated in the course of the disputation

252

and denies that there was any difference between Zwingli and Grebel with respect to the rejection of compromise. At the same time it indicates the real reason for the Council's hesitancy, which was nothing more theological than Zurich's fear of a war against all the rest of Switzerland. . . . This was the ground of the Council's reticence."

If Suter's interpretation is correct, how are we to understand Hätzer's minutes of the October Disputation, in which Zwingli is portrayed as submitting to the will of the Council? Bergsten (p. 85) hypothesizes that Hätzer, completing the writing of the minutes some weeks later after Zwingli began to compromise, was expressing his disappointment by reading the compromise back into the minutes, thus "exaggerating the differences of opinion between Zwingli and Grebel." Yoder (op. cit., p. 134), following Vasella, hypothesizes that it was Zwingli who edited Hätzer's minutes to fit later events, as evidenced by Hätzer's own comment that the text was seen by the authorities before printing (ZW, II, 673-4, 803). There is a third possibility that may be nearer to the truth, i.e., the Freudian mechanism of ambivalence—bipolarity of attitude. Zwingli may very well have been expressing the contradictory points of view that Hätzer's minutes accurately reflect. A Freudian interpretation does not negate Yoder's thesis of a December "turning point," although it mitigates some of the apparent contradiction between the interpretations of Yoder and Walton.

And on the 27th of this month [it was] further accepted that the mass is only a memorial and not a sacrifice.[1] But burgomaster, Small and Large Councils of Zurich, did not want to consent to this for the time being, but ruled imperatively to allow the figures of Christ and the saints to remain in the churches, also to respect and to hold the mass as heretofore,[2] for it is a common and open rumor that if they accept one of these articles as a precedent, the other confederates would attack them. Zwingli, contrary to this, spoke publicly before all those attending the said convocation that those of Zurich shall not sit in judgment over this,[3] but allow the Holy Scripture to decide both articles.

Original: Tiroler Landesarchiv, 6010 Innsbruck: Aktenbestand Pestarchiv Akt. XVIII, No. 235
Transcription: None

Lorenz Hochrütiner, a citizen of Zurich since 1520 and one of the three iconoclasts imprisoned just prior to the Second Disputation, was subsequently sentenced to banishment from the canton. Born in St. Gallen and a weaver by trade, he had asked Zwingli and Grebel to write letters of recommendation to Vadian, preparing the way for his return to his homeland. A comparison of their letters (No. 57F and 58) reveals that both were quite willing to do so for reasons that were both alike, indicating that a basic similarity of attitude between the two intercessors still prevailed, and also sufficiently different to suggest that some parting of the ways was beginning to occur.

The fact that Zwingli was willing to write on Hochrütiner's behalf indicates that his break with Grebel was not yet final. Grebel calls Lorenz his "brother," and Zwingli lamented the severity of Lorenz's punishment and actually called him a "good man." Egli observed that Zwingli and Haller of Bern had a special liking for Hochrütiner's "witzige Art" (witty manner), and that this was one reason both Reformers gave him a measure of protection in their respective cities (ZW, VIII, p. 130, fn.15).

Zwingli's comment, on the other hand, that "the prisoners have been treated with the greatest justice," was contradicted by Grebel's assertion that his judges were not impartial. Without mentioning his name, Grebel clearly alludes to Zwingli as the primary proponent of the abolition of images in Zurich, who had willingly sought and used Hochrütiner's help, thus making Zwingli an accomplice of injustice. Zwingli, though, indicates that the punishment of Hochrütiner, who was too outspoken before the council and too much of a rebel for the good of the Reformation "in this tempestuous time," is not entirely unfounded. The beginning of the parting of the ways, while not yet final, is nevertheless clearly discernible.

Grace and peace from God and our lord Jesus Christ.

It is not, most learned Vadian,[1] because you lived among us recently[2] in gracious, tireless labor that I now minister to you. You know yourself from whom rewards may be sought for yourself and whose work you were surely faithfully doing by that. Accept those that are later to follow. The council selected four from its own ranks and four from the citizens (as they are called),[3] that they might consult with the abbot of Kappel,[4] the provost of Embrach,[5] the commander of Küssnacht,[6] and the doctors Engelhart,[7] Leo,[8] and Zwingli, so that a plan can be provided by which to move the work of Christ effectively forward. It was agreed that a brief introduction[9] to the council's order should be written by me, by means of which those bishops[10] who had hitherto either been ignorant of Christ, or had been turned away from him, should be induced to begin to preach him. This was read on November 9 and pleased the council and is now being printed. It was also resolved that the abbot of Kappel should preach Christ under the authority of the city across the Alps,[11] the commander of Küssnacht around the lake[12] and in the province of Grüningen,[13] and I in those provinces which look toward Schaffhausen and Thurgau,[14] so that the sheep of Christ might not by anyone's negligence be deprived of hearing the Word of salvation. They will shortly[15] determine what will be done about the images, as soon as the people have been instructed; and the same with regard to the mass. In the meantime we are to go on in our usual manner, except that it is permitted anyone to remove his private images, so long as no one is offended.[16]

The prisoners[17] have been treated with the greatest justice. You know yourself what that might be. But still in these circumstances it has not been done without reason, for it does not escape you what sort of men[18] we have to fear in this tempestuous time, not so much for the thing itself as for the glory of Christ. For there are those who reject the gospel of Christ unless you yield to their weakness for awhile. For the sake of these I think that Lorenz Hochrütiner[19] has been treated a little too firmly, not to say harshly, a good man by Hercules,[20] but punished very severely because he has been far too free with his mouth. Nor is there any hope of his being restored now, although I could hope that in a short time a favorable alternative will appear, when of course all of us will have been taught better.

Accordingly, he is compelled to leave here; and in such a desolate world he can find no place except your city where he can settle.[21] He has therefore begged me to recommend him to you, lest you should desert him in the presence of your council.[22] He would not have needed to be in any anxiety in your home. Because he is a Christian, I had no doubt that he would be very highly recommended to you. Nevertheless, as we do not fear that you will take it indignantly to have an added spur applied, so we know that he will get along better for some time as a result of your effort. For you are aware of these squalls, that one must escape them by hiding until they cease raging. When these matters have settled down again and the sea been calmed, then at length it will be permissible to set sail in safety.

In short, be the protector before God of an excellent and innocent man. And whatever favor you will have given to him, you will have given to Zwingli. For you know how I am distressed by the stumbling blocks of all and how I long for all in the bowels of Jesus Christ. . . . [23]

Original: Stadtbibliothek (Vadiana) St. Gallen, Litt. misc.II.156
Transcription: ZW, VII, No. 321
Translation: Taken from Jackson, 1900, pp. 205-7

58
Grebel to Vadian
Zurich, November 12, 1523

Greetings, my Vadian.

I am sending to you my brother Lorenz,[1] who has been banished. He wishes to remain in his native land,[2] or rather to hide until certain persons not only among you but also among us become more lenient. Since he will need your defense and assistance privately or publicly, before civilians or magistrates, see that you do not fail him, I ask you through Christ. For he is worthy of your defense against wicked accusers, to aid and indeed to support his cause among the councillors who are inclined[3] toward him, so that he may be able to live among you in safety without pretense even in exile. It is for God to know the times, when he will return or not, and it is for him to know men's hearts and to convert, to soften, or to harden against; for if they repent, he[4] will return; if they harden them, he will not return. He is worthy, I say, because he is my brother in God and Christ[5]— for he has heard with us the Word of God—and because he has committed nothing against divine law, nothing against the laws and decrees of the state, nothing against his neighbor.[6] Moreover, if he had impartial judges, he is worthy because what he has done he did out of faith, and not that kind that is rash. For he[7] who brought up the sculpted images[8] asked his help and used it, nor would he have used it if Hottinger[9] had not previously persuaded him to get to work to demolish the statues,[10] on the decision and order of the Two Hundred[11] and also of many influential members of the council[12] to assault and demolish them. And many citizens with impunity have done the same thing, taken out and carried away idols[13] from the church before Hottinger[14] had ever thought up his crime. When he imitated them, not thinking that he was offending the council at all, he did offend it and paid for it by his long and miserable imprisonment, as though he had been condemned for having perpetrated a great abomination. Or I ask whether, after being sent into exile as well, he is not worthy to be welcomed, pardoned, encouraged, and even helped in every way by everyone, especially you, since he is so exceptionally learned in letters and Christian concerns. He will be helped here, since he is guilty of nothing against Scriptures and divine predestination, unless God does not work all things in all,[15] unless he does not number the hairs of our head[16] and see and appoint the sparrows to fall to the ground,[17] unless he does not direct and also lead our feet in another way than we had determined,[18] unless at Zurich on the occasion of the second assembly[19] (at which you, lord,[20] were present in person,[21] I speak plainly) we did not hear the Word of God on images and the mass. I have only suggested why he is worthy. You collect other arguments which you can plead yourself why my brother is worthy of you. But why do I wear you out with so much chattering? Hear him yourself and do what befits a Christian man. For you will be able to defend him since you are a Christian and learned and of great influence among your people. Farewell in Christ. Give my greetings to sister,[22] to Bishop Burgauer,[23] and to the co-bishop,[24] to the teacher,[25] and to the brothers. Once again, farewell.

Zurich, November 12, 1523.

  Conrad Grebel, your friend.

    To Joachim Vadian, poet, orator, doctor, theologian,
      councillor, kinsman, both Christian and dear.

  To St. Gallen.

Original: Stadtbibliothek (Vadiana) St. Gallen, VB.II.157
Transcriptions: VB, III, No. 369; M-S, No. 7

58A
Zwingli's "Introduction" to the Disputation Findings
Zurich, November 17, 1523

On October 29, the last day of the Second Zurich Disputation, Conrad Schmid, the head of the Johannite Monastery at Küssnacht and cautious supporter of Zwingli's Reformation (see Cast of Characters No. 83), proposed that careful preparation should precede the actual removal of images from the churches and abolition of the mass. He suggested a special teaching mission to all the communities in the canton (see 57C/fn.77). John H. Yoder observes "how Schmid's advocacy of compromise has changed under Zwingli's influence while his concern for education remains. He had first said there should be only teaching and no abolition order; now he asks for an abolition order including preliminary teaching" (MQR, 1958, p. 135, fn. 24).

* The Zurich Council not only followed this suggestion of a teaching mission but also mandated the writing and distribution of a "brief introduction" to the disputation findings "to instruct those who do not know how to take God's teaching in hand ... [and] telling how each one should proceed" (see 57D/252/7-10). The assignment of the teaching mission was given to Zwingli, Schmid, and Joner (see 57F/255/2-5) and the assignment of writing the introduction to Zwingli alone (254/36-37). He devoted one week to the writing of this document, which was read to the council on November 9 and published on November 17. The preface to the document was a new council mandate for all "clergy and laity" to study this "Introduction," dealing with sin and salvation, law and order, images and the mass, interpreted on the basis*

of "divine evangelical Scriptures of both the Old and New Testaments," and repeating the request for all to test the validity of these doctrines and report any errors that can be proved by the authority of Scripture.

On the two main issues, Zwingli wrote conclusively concerning the disputation findings: images lead to idolatry and should be removed from the churches, private homes, public marketplace, and wherever else people "do them honor"; and the mass is not a sacrifice and therefore is an abuse that should be abolished. The wine of the Lord's Supper should not be withheld from the laity and charges should not be made for serving communion. But Zwingli was quick to add that these reforms should be done cautiously and without disturbing the peace of the community.

He had two factions in mind to whom he spoke at length in the document. The first was the conservative old-faith party who were fighting these changes, for whose sake a measure of forbearance was required, especially the elderly "mass priests" who should be allowed "to die as they were born." The other was the radical party, identified by their past demonstrations against the current system of tithes (see 52A/Intro.) and certain other threats of revolutionary behavior, such as putting the idolatrous priests to death on the basis of Deuteronomy 13:5. Zwingli was referring indirectly to persons like Reublin, Stumpf, and Grebel on the tithes issue (see 52A, 53, and 54) and Stumpf alone on the execution of priests (see 71K/437/7ff.

On one hand, it is erroneous to conclude, as Walton does (1967, fn. 11) that the break between Zwingli and these individuals had already occurred long before the end of 1523. To be sure, it can be seen in retrospect that certain of these adherents who broke with Zwingli in December 1523 were already the more radical advocates in 1522; but this does not mean that they had already rejected his Reformation leadership or that they had already formed into a cohesive counter-group. But on the other hand, Zwingli was trying to carry out the difficult task of steering the Reformation to a successful conclusion; and while he was still wanting to be shepherd-leader to the Schmids on his right and the Grebels on his left, he was also prepared by this time to remove extremist factions on both sides—the papists who were still determined to suppress the Reformation in Zurich and the rebels who were bent on moving ahead without concern for social unrest and the threat of peasant uprisings. "The government must see to it that the malevolence of both kinds of ungodly men does not result in injury to the honor of God."

E. F. K. Müller describes Zwingli's document as "the first Reformed Confession of Faith" (quoted in Goeters, p. 272, fn. 199), and Goeters adds "rightly so, even if only with preliminary intention." Goeters summarizes as follows: "The current practical problems [of application] were not its subject. At the end, however, Zwingli indicated his point of view. Everyone should be intent on abolishing the sacrifice of the Mass and attaining evangelical communion. However, no one should plot tumult on the way to such goals. The reformer has his radical opponents directly in mind in the article on doing away with the law in which he repeats his reasons from the summer of 1523 *against the nonpayment of interest and tithes out of Christian motivation"* (*ibid; see also 52B, above*).

The following excerpt contains the Council's Mandate, Zwingli's addresses to the radical opponents, which by now included Stumpf, if not Grebel and Reublin, and the key paragraphs on images and the mass.

A brief and Christian Introduction which the honorable council of the city of Zurich has distributed to the pastors and preachers resident in its towns, districts, and domains, that they may from now on proclaim and preach the evangelical truth to their subjects with unanimity.

Issued on November 17, 1523

Mandate

First of all, we, the burgomaster, [Small] Council, and Large Council, known as the Two Hundred of the city of Zurich, convey our greetings, favor, and all good wishes to one and all—clergy and laity, prelates, abbots, deans, people's priests, pastors, parish pastors, and the preachers of the divine Word, who reside in our towns, lands, and districts. And as you read in the last mandate[1] that we issued to you and learned from it that we promised to send you as soon as possible[2] a brief, printed introduction[3] drawn up by the learned men from the divine Scriptures, this document has been written. We have heard it read, and in our opinion it is firmly based on divine evangelical Scripture of both the Old and New Testaments. We therefore, according to our promise, will not keep it from you but have decided to have it distributed to you corporately and to each one individually.

It is our demand and intention that you comply with this latest mandate mentioned above and faithfully study this introduction that we have now sent to you, diligently look up all the evangelical Scripture references in their original form, in the hope that they will lead you and many others further into the knowledge of true divine Scripture. This we counsel you in all seriousness and for God's sake to do, as each one's office requires in God's order and Christ's command, so that the true knowledge and glory of God, Christian love, and unity, as well as true improvement in our practices, may be learned from the Word of God and continually increase. For it is our opinion that your teaching should in all respects be earnestly toward that end and in agreement with it. But if there should be someone among you who would be negligent or obstinate,[4] and act without a basis in the holy, divine, and evangelical Scriptures, we would express ourselves in such a way that they would see that they had acted in error and contrary to Christ's teaching. And as we, in a public proclamation, have already issued a friendly invitation and request to all of you—our gracious lords bishops of Constance, Chur, and Basel, also the university of Basel, and also the loyal confederates of the twelve towns as well as others—to a disputation[5] on the two articles of images and the mass, that they through their learned messengers might help us by presenting statements on those articles based on true, divine, and evangelical Scripture. And then if anyone on the basis of the Holy Scriptures can instruct us better or differently, we want to accept it with special thanks and joy. We herewith also ask each and every one again that if they find us in any respect to be contrary to God and to be in error or wrong about his Word of the holy Gospel, they should for the sake of the honor of God, truth, and Christian love, point it out to us from the true Word of God and the gospel. We will accept it and receive it with deep gratitude. . . .

Concerning Doing Away with the Law[6]

Many are they who speak very ineptly about doing away with the law. In consequence of this, the ignorant, or more exactly, the malicious mischief-makers[7] soon speak so indiscreetly[8] that it dishonors God. Therefore as indicated above, there results from this an abrogation of law. . . .

Now there are two ways by which we are released from the law. One is the way of ceremonies, i.e., of observances or church practices.[9] The other is by way of punishment for our misdeeds. And if we are completely committed to God, we no longer need the law. For then it is God himself who leads us; and as God has no need of any law, therefore, he in whom God dwells likewise needs no law, for God leads him. For where the Spirit of God is, there is liberty, 2 Corinthians 3[17]. And so he who is committed to God is also free of the laws that concern the inner man. He cheerfully and freely performs everything that is required of a Christian. One sees by their fruits who is free in that sense. If they are humble, it is the work of the indwelling Spirit of God; Christ was also humble. If they are concerned for the salvation of others, Christ was too; thus, the concern must come only from Christ. If they are patient, likewise; for Christ was patient too. If they are peaceable, it is also from God; Christ was peaceable too. If they are valiant for the glory of God, Christ was too. If they are cheerful in adversity for the glory of God, it is all from God, etc.

But here we find a great number of false Christians who claim to be founded in God and free, but have no humility within them, but are trying thereby to become great, affluent, or important. Where they ought to be concerned for others, they are concerned only for themselves; they can

260

endure nothing for God's sake, but they endure all things for their own benefit and name's sake. They are quarrelsome; their purpose is nothing but to quarrel, create dissension, and tear people apart, although the glory of God is severely damaged thereby. To defend their deeds, however wrong they may be, they are learned and brave; but in promoting the glory of God and kindly correcting the neighbor, they are useless, and although it is occasionally necessary to treat one of them roughly and because of a slight adverse action in which they lose some slight temporal benefit, they collapse, etc. But when it comes to judging others, pardoning nothing in the weak-minded, boasting of their knowledge, which they, however, do not have, bragging about how the priests should be put to death,[10] the monks burned, the nuns drowned, and how the things should be punished of which they suppose they are free—in short, quickly adopting outward things without taking counsel, yes, there they are good Christians. But in the end, if you do not discover that they are self-made Christians, you will know them well by their fruits. Thus God's teaching is disgraced by many and badly perverted for those who are good Christians with respect to the body and outward appearance, though in time the misuse of these things must also be abandoned. But they refuse to touch inward weaknesses, though it is to be hoped that insofar as they have begun to believe the Word they will in time conduct themselves right. . . .

Now those in these times who dare to exempt themselves from all obligation to pay interest and retail taxes or tithes (for these have become a legally correct practice; everyone more easily purchases the land that he tithes, though the abuses of the tithe must [certainly] be discontinued or everything will be ruined) and other honest debts, are all transgressing the commandment "Thou shalt not steal."[11] They are far more wicked thieves than others, because they use Christ as the defense of their thievery. If it should ever come to the point that among Christians one should not give a pious man what is owed him and in addition, not be obedient to the government, it would be better to live among the Turks than among such people. No greater blasphemy of God can be committed than to protect one's rascality with his name. But let every government be on its guard against fraudulence, usury, and deception in interest;[12] and since God has put the sword into its hand it should be careful not to fight for its own benefit but to punish the evildoer with it and protect the good; otherwise, God would soon and easily find ways to destroy its authority like that of the papacy. In regard to the papacy, these offenders are also in error; for certain individuals dare to slander, impoverish, and put them to death, all of which is unchristian. This matter should be treated in this way: correct them in their errors and put them aside[13] and let them die in peace as they were born,[14] insofar as legal obligation is concerned. . . . But if some are so obstinate that they refuse to yield to God's Word even though they cannot basically oppose it, with such no private citizen should deal but only the government. It will then take the appropriate action according to Matthew 18[17] and Deuteronomy 13[5].[15] In brief: As to the ruthless, who can do nothing but rob and steal [and] are such noxious people when they are so bold as to justify it with the name of Christ, we would rather have that many Turks in their stead.

Similarly noxious are the rich priests who want to push[16] everything through their insolence and power. In these matters the government must seriously see to it that the malevolence of both kinds of ungodly men does not result in injury to the honor of God. And so in short: every Christian should pay to everyone what he owes him, Romans 13[7]. That means a debt that is recognized as a debt by the government. At the same time, however, it should see to it that it forbids or alters the debts that are not just in God's sight. And even if the priesthood were limited to a minimum number, the property they now possess does not belong to you or anyone else but to the poor, according to regulation by a government or each parish. It is not good to keep writing about this now. Insofar as the preacher of God's Word has a clear, sound eye,[17] he will not act dangerously.

Anyone can probably discern that this brief introduction, prepared for the unlearned, was given for those instances where the preachers do not first earnestly ask God to give them grace, and then search the Scriptures zealously and walk in them by day and night, and finally have a spirit to build true Jerusalems. But if they strive to promote the glory of God and the benefit of souls as is their duty, and do not regard the temporal but the eternal, God will richly impart to them the Word of truth. He turns the shepherd Amos into a preaching prophet.[18] Therefore, they should be rich in the Word of God and present the gospel, which cannot be understood without the law, in such a way that both the good and the bad may know the road by which one comes to God. There are also many intractable people who must be sharply reprimanded. They boast of being free of the law, but nevertheless need much severer laws that they may be held to the right way and in general taught which works are most pleasing to God; namely, those that he teaches in Matthew 5—7 and John 13-17; also gently or severely forbid excessive gambling, drinking, clothing, cursing, warring, quarreling, and greed. These are such monsters that one has enough to do to oppose them, and one can preach neither fables nor sophistic arguments.[19]

So much on the introduction to divine doctrine.

262

Concerning Images

Concerning images, as it has been learned that images are prohibited by God, this should be taught by everyone in order that the simple and ignorant, now instructed and built up, will soon accept action regarding them. For this purpose the pamphlet[20] on the removal of images that was recently published will serve, for it has much scriptural information. . . .

This is sure, that God has forbidden all images and paintings simply because men should not begin to honor anything besides him or offer honor to any created thing except to him, as can be clearly discerned from Deuteronomy 4[1-20]. We can clearly see from this that such figures as ornaments, lions' heads, winged creatures, and the like, which can never be taken for God or Helper, are not prohibited,[21] for Solomon would not have allowed such trees and ornaments to be made for the temple or ordered God to be put on the candlestick if they would have created the danger of idolatry. But the images, the paintings, that we have in our temples—it is obvious that they have created the danger of idolatry. Therefore they should no longer be allowed to remain there—neither in your room, nor in the marketplaces, nor anywhere else where they would be reverenced in any way. Above all, they are not to be tolerated in the temples, for everything that we have in them is sacred to us. If someone should have one as a historical memorial[22] outside the temples without a suggestion of bestowing reverence upon it, it could be allowed. But when anyone begins to bow before it and bestow reverence, they are not to be tolerated anywhere on earth; for they would soon become an accessory to idolatry or even idolatry itself.

Concerning Mass

If one intends to speak of the mass, he must first explain, in order not to offend anyone, that it is no one's intention to discard or criticize the body and blood of Christ or to teach that it is naught, but that the mass has a different meaning than to partake of the body and blood of Christ. For it has always been taught that the laity and priests partake of a thing when they partake of the body and blood of Christ. That is true, for Christ established an ordinance and institution in this matter. Nevertheless, many centuries ago, erring priests made a sacrifice of it, which, however, it is not. For no layman considered it anything other than food for the soul; and that is what it is and that is what God established it for and nothing else, as will be clearly explained below. Here it is necessary to explain what was meant by calling it a sacrifice and what a sacrifice is. Briefly, in the Old Testament the word "sacrifice" means a gift that someone has offered to God. The priest then took and lifted it onto the altar and burned it or raised it or moved it back and forth, depending on the kind of offering it was. In that way in those times they cleansed their sins. But all of this was only a figure of the coming of Christ, the true Priest, and became not an animal or a slaughtered sacrifice for the sins of the whole world, but a pure, unblemished one. But that could not be found among all the people except in himself. He therefore offered himself up when he suffered on the cross for us and with his own death cleansed and paid for the sins of all the world unto eternity. The basis for this real meaning is found in the epistle to the Hebrews, especially in chapters 6—10. Now as Christ has but once suffered death on the cross, he was also but once sacrificed. His death is his sacrifice for us, and his sacrifice is his death; his sacrifice is the cleansing of our sin, and his death is also the cleansing of our sin. Hence, as he died unto sin but once, Romans 6[10], he has thus also suffered death but once, and has now been sacrificed but once. And therefore, since we find in Scripture that Christ's death has taken away our sin, and find also that his sacrifice has taken away our sin and his shedding of his blood has taken away our sin, as in Colossians 1[22], all of this has one meaning, namely, that Christ has redeemed us and paid for our sin by sacrificing himself and offering himself up for us in his death on the cross. As he died only once, so he has been sacrificed only once.

But when the priesthood claims that the priests are offering Christ up for other people, they have invented it out of themselves without a basis in the Word of God, out of which two serious blasphemies of God and two great errors have arisen.

The first blasphemy is that the great value and cost of the suffering of Christ is obscured thereby. Christ, who was God and man, is of such great value and so high and worthy that his death, offered up only once, is sufficiently rich and precious to pay for the sin of all the world unto eternity, for he is eternally God. . . . Now, if the priests claim to be making the sacrifice for sin, it amounts to saying that Christ with his one-time suffering did not completely finish it or that it is no longer valid. For as we believe that he, once offered up, has redeemed and paid for us, i.e., the believers, for eternity, it must ever be a blasphemy for him who practices it again just as if it had not been already completed.

The second blasphemy and abomination is that no one can sacrifice anything higher than himself, which sacrifice Paul teaches in Romans 12[1]: "I appeal to you therefore, brethren, by the mercies of God, to present your bodies as a living sacrifice, holy and acceptable to God, which is your spiritual worship." Note that this is the highest sacrifice that a human being can offer—himself. If he then undertakes to offer up God, he is blaspheming God, for he makes himself so big as if he were able to sacrifice God. But no one can offer up Christ except he himself. For as the sacrifice had to be pure, so the priest would also have to be pure. But as we have no priest in all the human race who is without sin except only Christ, no one can offer him up but Christ himself. Therefore, any man who claims to be one who makes the offering takes the honor from Christ and gives it to himself. That is an intolerable abomination.

The two errors are these: The first is that the erroneous interpretation of the sacrifice has strengthened and implanted all the vices; for all robbers, usurers, betrayers, shedders of blood, and adulterers have supposed that if they have a mass held for their transgression, they have cleared their case. And it cannot be otherwise than that they sinned afterward. We can see this clearly in their founding of benefices and ordering of masses, which they would not establish if it were not their last refuge. So fond they are of the good life!

The second error is that with the mass they have accumulated so much temporal wealth and accepted it in exchange for the false sacrifice. And even if it had been a [valid] sacrifice, it would still be an abomination to take money and payment of temporal goods for it. But that was still not enough; they also dealt arbitrarily and even took from the poor what belongs most of all to them; for most of the alms were used for them. . . .

First, they called what they were enjoying a mass, i.e., the equivalent of an offering or a vicarious offering,[23] which it cannot be, as explained above. For Christ established it only once and in one method, and did not call it an offering or mass, but a testament and remembrance. Therefore, that name was wrongly applied to the body and blood of Christ.

Later, they cut off one form—namely, the blood—which they did not give to the common people, but which Christ nevertheless established; it is a matter of concern if only for the reason that one is considered as an offering and the other is not—with many other ceremonies, garments, crucifixes, and alien ideas.

But in order that it may become clear to everyone how Christ instituted this food for the soul, one should himself look at Christ's words in Matthew 26 [26-29], Mark 14 [22-25], Luke 22 [19ff.], and explain them to the people. Then those words will become much clearer from Paul's words in 1 Corinthians 11 [23-26], which we want to apply to ourselves here: "For I received from the Lord what I also delivered to you, that the Lord Jesus on the night when he was betrayed took bread, and when he had given thanks, he broke it, and said, 'This is my body which is [broken] for you. Do this in remembrance of me.' In the same way also the cup, after supper, saying, 'This cup is the new covenant in my blood. Do this, as often as you drink it, in remembrance of me.' " These are the words of institution. Here we see, first, that Jesus says, "The body which is broken for you." That is, "Just as I am breaking the bread, so will I be tortured and put to death for you. Do this in remembrance of me." Note that he himself, when he instituted the Supper, calls it a remembrance. By this we know that Christ did not offer himself up after the Supper when he gave his disciples his flesh and blood, but only on the next day when he died on the cross. However, his flesh and blood is to be a memorial of this deed that he did, as is explained below. Now, after the words concerning the blood, he did the same with the cup following the Supper, saying, "This cup is the new covenant in my blood. Do this, as often as you drink it, in remembrance of me. For as often as you eat this bread and drink the cup, you proclaim the Lord's death until he comes." These are the words concerning the blood of Christ, in which we are to understand that the word "cup" is used for "drink." Then he calls the drink the new covenant; i.e., the new testament and bequest. For, as said above, with his shed blood he reconciled us again with his heavenly Father and made an everlasting covenant by which we come to God through him. And when we consider the nature of the covenant, a bequest is not carried out until the maker dies. Thus, Christ's testament was not carried out until his death on the cross. And as impossible as it is for a human being to make such a bequest as Christ made, it is equally impossible to make the sacrifice; but he can indeed remember what Christ did. And if he places his confidence in Christ's suffering and redemption, he becomes whole. Of this he left us a sure, visible symbol of his flesh and blood and commanded both the eating and the drinking to be as a remembrance. And here Paul clearly expresses how this memorial is to be observed: "For as often as you eat this bread and drink the cup, you shall proclaim the Lord's death until he comes." And so we learn that the proper observance of this sacrament should be like this: As often during the year as the parish decides, we should proclaim and preach the suffering and death of Christ, then tell what benefits and peace it has brought us, and feed the believers who desire it in the firm association of the observance with the body and blood of Christ. That in short and simply explained is the intention of Christ.

Now that we see that the mass as such was never instituted but yet was considered a sacrifice by human beings (for this sacrament is nothing other than eating and drinking[24] the body and blood of Christ), all men should do their utmost to have such misuse abolished, in which one person claims to be sacrificing himself for another; but it should be done with such moderation and prudence that uproars do not occur in the process. Appropriate ways will be found to abolish it. Therefore, the preaching priests should not censure the common mass-offering priests. They did not invent this error; hence, they should not be held responsible. Admonish everyone to let them die in peace as they were born; for most of them are old and can no longer be drawn into the task. And no Christian should destroy the work of God for the sake of what he eats, Romans 14[20]. Even if some should react improperly with resistance not based on God's Word, no one should take any specific action against them but leave it to the government. It will deal with them in the proper way. So in short: When the Almighty God reveals his Word, man must see that he complies with it. Otherwise, he will bring God's wrath upon himself.

Conclusion

And if you on your part carry out what we require of you as stated above, which is your obligation, we have the sure hope in God that he will make his Word bear fruit and increase his glory with our improvement and peaceful life. May God grant this to us through Jesus Christ, our Redeemer and Preserver. Amen!

November 17, 1523.

58B
The Turning Point in the Zwinglian Reformation
Zurich, Between December 10 and 19, 1523

The heading for this series of documents comes from the title of John H. Yoder's article in MQR (April 1958) drawn from his Basel dissertation, Die Gespräche zwischen Täufern und Reformatoren in der Schweiz 1523-1538. *Although the beginning of Grebel's doubts about Zwingli's resolve came earlier than Yoder claimed (see 53/fn.6), the overall evidence tends to confirm Yoder's hypothesis against that of Walton, chapter 11. The five following documents can be dated between December 10 and 19, and it was during those ten days that the final "breaking point" occurred between the Grebel circle and the Reformation leaders. To be sure, as Yoder acknowledges, there were numerous earlier indications of potential rift; but it was not until the end of 1523 that "the actors in the drama themselves became aware of the problem" (p. 129). All of our documents in the 47-58 series confirm Yoder's observations (pp. 129-36) that a functioning unity between Zwingli and Grebel survived until this time.*

Then as the first document in the present series indicates, a new agitation against the mass occurred in Zurich just prior to December 10, including the destruction of some liturgy books, the taunting of conservative priests, and a demonstration against torture and capital punishment at Zurich's place of execution. The council was called into emergency session and took action to reissue the mandate issued at the end of October (see 57D) for everyone to hold his peace pending the working out of practical regulations for the new worship in Zurich and to request an advisory memorandum from the three people's priests. The result was the second and third documents in the present series.

The mandate of December 13 was identical with that of the October mandate, except for three significant differences. One was the more current reference to "these crazy days," indicating a new mood of anxiety if not of panic. Another was the addition that the agitators would face severe punishment if they did not cease and desist. The third was the omission of all four promises in the earlier mandate for speedy and impending action on the new regulations (see 57D/fns. 5, 7, 9, and 12). "Apparently Zwingli and his friends had become aware of new reasons for fearing that the Council would procrastinate," for in the third document below "they expressed ... a kind of determination which surpasses anything they had said before" (Yoder, p. 136).

Article 5 of the Zwingli-Jud-Engelhart memorandum announces the intention to abolish the mass and introduce the new evangelical communion on Christmas Day, two weeks hence. As Yoder put it, "This document states a truly revolutionary platform which, if applied by its authors, could have changed the whole course of Protestant church history" (p. 137). But as the fourth document shows, the plan was scrapped for an alternative proposal, adopted by the larger commission of fourteen men (see 57F/fns. 3-8), including Zwingli and his two colleagues. Yoder believes that the three people's priests were overruled by the other eleven; but in any case, there is now no minority viewpoint presented concerning an evangelical communion on Christmas Day.

The alternative proposal is clearly a compromise plan, indicated by the adverb "however" at the beginning of the second paragraph, for which the first paragraph was preparing the way. As Yoder put it, "The second memorandum expresses the same ideals and goals as the first, but not the same determination; and at this critical point, that made all the difference in the world."

Then in the fifth document of December 19, the council rejected not only the first memorandum (III, below) but also the "alternative opinion" (IV) and ruled that no change at all be made in the liturgy of the mass pending more disputations in Zurich, consultations with the diocesan bishops in the Confederacy, and the outcome of such further process between then and the following Pentecost "to see how the dispute and course of events proceed." The one concession that the council made to the commission was that no priest should be forced to conduct mass against his conscience. Nothing was mentioned of the commission's recommendation that individual congregations be permitted by consensus to abolish the mass, and the recommendation that the mass be given in both kinds (bread and wine) was rejected.

I

[Dec. 10]. Thursday after St. Nicholas Day.[1] [In the presence of] Burgomaster Röist, councillors, and representatives. (1) Provost and chapter[2] at the Grossmünster complain before the council in the presence of the chaplains and assistants that the latter are no longer willing to conduct the mass. When H[err] Hans Widmer conducted the mass of the people's priest, someone said, "There is seen the butcher of God." Also several liturgy books[3] were taken from the church and some pages were torn out of the "Directory" and thrown before the door of the provost's house. Finally they took the iron collar to the fish market and cut down the gallows.[4] The canons request direction on what attitude to take to preserve the peace. (2) After the interrogation of the three people's priests, it was decided to have the ruling concerning images and the mass[5] announced again[6] in the three churches, with the addition that the transgressor shall be punished "summarily."[7] Furthermore, the abbot of Cappel, the commander at Küssnacht, the provost of Embrach, Master Ochsner, and others previously appointed by Milords and active in this matter shall consult about the article on the observance of the mass and give advice on the position to be taken in the future on these matters at the hands of the councillors and representatives. Relative to the remaining complaints, Master Thumysen[8] and Conrad Escher[9] shall conduct an investigation.

II

[Dec. 13]. *Mandate*.[10] "Whereas our lords, burgomaster, [Small] Council, and Great Council, etc., in these crazy days[11] issued an order in their city and likewise in all their domains and provinces regarding images and the mass, namely that concerning the images no one, neither clergy nor laity, shall carry out of or into the churches or alter any kind of image, unless one has put his own image into the church. In that case he may take possession of it again, but in such a way that no disorderliness results. Moreover, if some images were made by fellow parishioners or out of church funds, no one shall in the meantime alter them without the knowledge and consent of the fellow parishioners. Concerning the mass, it shall also remain as it is now until further notice. Our afore-mentioned gracious lords hereafter by special summary[12] command and authority let it remain unchanged and wish that no one will malign or bait another with any kind of malicious, provocative words; and whoever behaves improperly or disobediently in word or deed in this matter will be severely punished by Our Lords according to the circumstances of the case. Hereafter let everyone know how to conduct himself."

III

[Between Dec. 13 and 19]. *Advice and Opinions on the Mass, announced by the Doctor at the Fraumünster,*[13] *Master Huldrych Zwingli,*[14] *and Master Leo,*[15] *People's Priest at St. Peter's.*

First, it is not their opinion that nothing should or may be abbreviated or subtracted from the body and blood of Christ, but that it should be observed according to Christ's institution and not otherwise;[16] for speaking of the body and blood of Christ is not the same thing as speaking of the mass. And the name mass and its usage is nowhere found in the Word of God. But the use of the body and blood of Christ has a foundation and observance in the clear Word of God. Also, if the body and blood of Christ were identical with the mass, it would follow that everyone who partakes of the body and blood of Christ must also be observing mass; but that is not the case.

Second, if the mass is presented as if it were paying for other people by means of sacrifices, but it is plainly found that this is not so (for that would be a special insult to the suffering of Christ, just as if, having once been offered up he had not done satisfaction for the sins of the whole world), then every Christian must be stirred up to abolish, remove, and utterly destroy it if it is regarded without foundation in the divine Word, yea, as an insult to God, out of human arrogance.

Third, it is therefore their opinion to stay with the pure Word of God and then let God rule. For whenever one considers an opinion, insofar as it is contrary to the Word of God, it must be done away with. For every planting that is not planted by the heavenly Father must be uprooted.[17] And even though other regulations were to be considered, we would always again and again struggle with the Word of God insofar as they are against the Word of God, from which disturbances would arise daily.

Fourth, it is the sum total of opinion from the Word of God that one should present to the Christian people the body and blood of Christ with both wine and bread[18] as a memorial of Christ's suffering, proclaiming the Lord's death whenever we use this food and drink,[19] as the thought is clearly expressed in Matthew 26[26-29], Mark 14[22-25], [and] in the first epistle to the Corinthians, chapter 11[23-29].

Fifth, we intend to hold a public observance of this form on Christmas Day, entirely according to the institution and practice of Christ, for we can no longer withhold the correct practice from the world; and even if they do not permit us, we must offer both body and blood, bread and wine,[20] to those who desire, or otherwise stand [condemned] as lying by the Word of God.[21]

Sixth, it is also necessary, however, since the human soul is daily attacked by sin, that it be daily strengthened by the Word of God. It is therefore our request that we see to it among one another that at a suitable time every day we preach a quarter or half an hour on a portion and part of the Holy Scripture and then if anyone desires it, give him food and drink according to the content of the Word of God.[22]

Seventh, if anyone considers himself burdened with the great number of lethargic priests, he should consider that it is far better that we let them pass away to their homecoming in peace than that we force them to act contrary to God's order;[23] for it is better to have been lazy than to have acted falsely and wickedly. It is to be feared that if it were to become habitual to break the promises [made to them] for their living, in time one would also take the liberty of attacking other provisions, which could bring forth a clear disorder against God and Christian peace. But if no new priests would be engaged, the present number would disappear sooner than we suppose; for many of the canons and chaplains would be endowed with parishes.[24] There are also many other ways by which to reduce their number daily.

Accordingly, [even] if your love and wisdom would refuse to accept this proposed way, we know of no other way that would be so much in agreement with God's Word. We therefore beg your honorable wisdom that it would at the very least see to it that no priests would be forced to conduct mass;[25] for this sacrament is always only a human institution. Then no layman would let himself be forced to go so often to God's table. Likewise, no Christian, even if he is a priest, [should be] forced to do so, for we feel it necessary to conduct this and other sacraments in simple fashion in accordance with the content of God's Word.

It is therefore our earnest opinion for the sake of God's honor that your wisdom might faithfully and fearlessly hold to God's Word, for all those who have thus taken this position are not forsaken by God. You have a basis for your decision, namely, the clear Word of God; and those who oppose it have nothing but the word of men. And so, if God is on our side, who can be against us?[26] Let God have control among his people, and whatever he commands, obey it like obedient sons, and you will not err nor be defeated. Amen.

IV

[Between the Preceding Memorandum and Dec. 19]. *The Alternative Opinion* [on the Mass][27]

1. The preceding opinion presented by the three people's priests is without doubt the most correct and most conformed to the Word of God. Therefore nothing shall be undertaken in this matter that does not aim

toward the point at which, with time, we will come directly to the practice of the pure Word of God.

However, since the hearts and beliefs of people are divided at this time—for many are still as immature as we were in common a short time ago—it will be necessary to make some concessions to the immature until they can come to the age and strength for solid food.[28] On this it has seemed not inappropriate for us to announce an opinion that will not be disadvantageous to the mature nor advantageous or offensive to the immature, in the following form, in the hope that the Almighty God will look graciously upon our intent to build up and not to break down:

2. That the people's priests shall give to all who desire it this holy sacrament of the body and blood of Christ with [both] the bread and wine,[29] for the very mouth of God has given and instituted this conception; and therefore no one can deny it according to God's ordinance. And in whatever way the mass is observed now and in the future, no one shall be refused the practice of the sacrament according to Christ's institution. In that way the body and blood of Christ will always persist and will have to be practiced according to Christ's institution.

3. Although it is clear and plain through the Holy Scripture that the mass is not a sacrifice, and still there are so many immature and ignorant that the mass cannot be abruptly done away with without offending the simple, also in view of those who have until now practiced the mass knowing that the body and blood of Christ is nothing but food and drink for the believing soul, we have weighed the two weaknesses against each other: the one refuses to give up the mass, and the other cannot adhere to it. It is therefore our judgment that no one can be compelled to observe the mass, nor should those who do so not be humiliated with insulting words, but all should earnestly ask the Almighty God to lead all men to the light of truth so that we will without delay[30] come to the pure and plain practice of Christ.

4. In this, however, it is our earnest request and appeal to all the prelates and people's priests, also to all the priesthood, to adopt such a position regarding the observance of the mass that they do not give definite reason for disturbance and unrest, but earnestly see that the Word of God is firmly adhered to, even sometimes instead of the mass, and that for awhile yet the mass should not be abolished[31] except in case the parishioners are so well instructed that they would feel no offense and where there is only one or few priests. But where there are several, we hope that, as Paul says, "Love bears all things,"[32] they will out of love of Christian peace give no one cause for complaint or come short and will henceforth adapt themselves thereto out of good faith. And this will be

made easy with the only Word of God and all burdens lightened on both sides, that we hope that nothing but peace and unity will be planted among us.

5. But the manner of practicing the mass we leave to each pastor after he is well informed out of Scripture about the intercession of the saints and that the mass is not a sacrifice and knows what position he should take.

V

[Second Part to the Preceding Memorandum]. *Concerning the images, the opinion of all commission members*[33] *is unanimous,*[34] *to wit:*

1. It is our opinion that the panels[35] [that exhibit pictures] should be closed at once and not opened until further notice. For after all, they are closed during the fasts and the other images are covered. But the silver and gold or otherwise ornate images[36] shall no longer be carried out on festival or other days, but the greatest treasure of the Word of God should be carried in the hearts of men, and not the idols in the processions.

2. Moreover, we stand by the recently issued order that no one shall carry images into or out of the temples unless he has previously put them in, or unless a majority of the parish agrees to do this, and all of this without any insult, mockery, and malice or anything that could wantonly offend anyone.

3. Finally, since it has now been learned from the Word of God that the mass is not a sacrifice, and also that one should not have images, but some priests[37] in our city continually oppose this [conclusion] with seditious, erroneous, unfounded words, it is our final decision to speak to them in some way or other, with penalties or deprivation of benefices, etc., when they can produce nothing out of God's Word.

[Dec. 19]. *Conclusions by the Council.* Burgomaster Röist, councillors, and representatives. Since in recent days two different proposals[38] concerning images and the mass have been presented to our gracious lords, burgomaster, [Small] Council, and Large Council, etc., by those who were especially appointed for it, these our lords have formally and thoughtfully sat in session and have discerned and decided that concerning the mass, it should remain as it was at their last decision, with the proviso that no one shall be constrained or forced to conduct it, but that each may conduct it or not, and those who want to conduct the mass shall do it orderly, chastely, and in a way that complies best with the will and Word of God, so that those who do not conduct the mass and think their consciences are burdened by it should not censure the others by word or deed by calling them God-eaters or God-butchers or provoke, label, and taunt them with other improper insulting words, but on both sides live in a cordial, brotherly way and in good harmony with one another. And if anyone is opposed again to that which may be decided at the next convocation or disputation and thinks he can refute it with the appropriate divine Scripture, let him do it or let the matter be as it is. Milords will have it this way; and as to the giving of communion or the sacraments, if anyone wants to receive it, it should continue to be done according to our former practice.[39] And for further explanation of Milords' will and pleasure, all the priests in the city will be summoned before the councils and the burgomaster next Holy Innocents' Day [Dec. 28] to discuss with them further, as they will hear.[40] Moreover, it was decided to write to the bishop of Constance, the bishop of Chur, the bishop of Basel, the University of Basel, and our compatriots of all the cantons, enclosing the pamphlet issued by Milords, requesting that if they ever presume to refute it with the appropriate divine Scripture, that they should do so and write us their cordial reply in the matter. And when such answers have been received and it is seen how the dispute and course of events develop, the matter will again be taken in hand by Pentecost,[41] and a conclusion reached that will be pleasing to God and in line with his holy Word. And our lords named above will surely see to it that the honorable clergy in their city will live according to this insight of theirs and that for the sake of peace, quiet, and good harmony will also avoid greater offense, dissension, and unrest, in best acceptance and obedient demeanor.

Originals: (1)?, (2)?, (3) Staatsarchiv Zurich E.I.1.1, (4) E.I.3.1, (5)?
Transcriptions: Aktensammlung, Nos. 456, 458; ZW, II, No. 29: I,II; Aktensammlung No. 460.IV.2

ACT 5, 1523-1526:
THE RINGLEADER

59
Grebel to Vadian
Zurich, December 18, 1523

That there has been a decisive turning point in the Zwinglian Reforma-
tion is further evidenced by the following letter of Grebel's. The context for
this letter is clearly the December events documented in 58B, above, including
(1) the emergency session of the council following renewed public agitations
against the mass, (2) the reissuing of the end-of-October mandate for
everyone to keep the peace, (3) the first memorandum by Zwingli, Jud, and
Engelhart promising a new communion liturgy and service on Christmas Day,
(4) the alternative compromise memorandum by Zwingli on behalf of the 14-
man commission to retain the mass with certain revisions, and (5) the deci-
sions of the council to postpone even these revisions in favor of further disputa-
tions.

Grebel's letter expresses total disillusionment with the way the Reforma-
tion was being administered by Zwingli and the city magistrates and marks
the beginning of the final act in our drama.

Greetings, Vadian.

Since you request and even demand as my duty that I write to you,[1]
or rather reply, I have written as many things allow, [things] which seem to
obstruct for many reasons. Not by accident, the cause of the gospel is in a
very bad way here (if you can still believe a mistrusted one rather than a

"For this reason they, the Anabaptists, Conrad Grebel
first of all, baptized one another in a home at night as a
true testimony that they considered infant baptism to
be no baptism, but that theirs was the true baptism, and
likewise their assemblies (where the true baptism was)
were considered by them to be the holy Christian
Church."—Johannes Kessler, *Sabbata*

275

liar),[2] and it began[3] when you with senatorial foresight served as president when the consultation was held.[4] On that occasion (God sees and it is in his ears), the Word was overthrown, set back, and bound by its most learned heralds.

Now I shall report how in dealing with the matter of the mass both councillor bodies assigned this knot to be unknotted to eight councillors,[5] Zwingli the introducer,[6] the abbot of Cappel,[7] the provost of Embrach,[8] and I know not what other tonsured monsters.[9] They have disregarded the divine will on not celebrating the mass, and have prescribed a middle ground[10] with diabolical (I know) prudence.[11] This matter will be referred to both councils tomorrow,[12] and so there will be mass. The pastors will see to that, etc. Farewell. Judge, but not as heretofore.

'Αξίωμα [Axiom]

Whoever thinks, believes, or declares that Zwingli acts according to the duty of a shepherd[13] thinks, believes, and declares wickedly. When you ask for a defense of ἀξιώματος [this axiom], I shall reply and send it.

On Friday before the festival of Thomas, 1523.

> To the lord Joachim Vadian, most famous president of the Zurich Consultation, dearest kinsman.

Original: Stadtbibliothek (Vadiana) St. Gallen, VB.II.161
Transcriptions: VB, III, No. 374; M-S, No. 8

59A
The Grebel-Stumpf Alternative Plan
of a Separatist Church[1]
Zurich, before December 23, 1523[2]

The plan of reform described in the following document was presented to Zwingli by Grebel and Stumpf sometime before December 23, 1523, as an alternative to his own state church Reformation strategy. Since none of Grebel's letters refers to it, the chronology of Stumpf's life is the major resource for its dating. The Zurich Council dismissed him from his Höngg pastorate on November 3, with strict orders to move out of the parish. Following an appeal by members of his congregation, the action was reconfirmed on November 14. On November 19 he wrote to Zwingli from Wettingen, requesting reassignment within the jurisdiction of Zurich. He subsequently reappeared in Höngg and was placed under custodial arrest by the Zurich authorities.

Between then and his total banishment on December 23, Stumpf was resident in Zurich, presumably with sufficient freedom for the kind of conversation with Zwingli that the following document describes. So, the first op-

tion for its dating would be December 1523, perhaps as an alternative to the compromise memorandum, 58B/IV, above. The other option is to date it before Stumpf's departure from Höngg, perhaps as early as June, as Goeters does (pp. 273-74); but there is not the slightest support for Goeters' hypothesis in any of Grebel's Letters 52 to 58. The plan best fits the mood of Letter No. 59, marking Grebel's first clear reference to a schism between himself and Zwingli.

The following account of the plan is taken from Zwingli's infamous Latin tract, In catabaptistarum strophas elenchus (Refutation of the Tricks of the Anabaptists) published on July 31, 1527. Although it is an emotionally charged account written three and one-half years after the event, its underlying reliability is confirmed by several other less detailed accounts of the same event. Our comments on the background, nature, and organization of the Elenchus will be given in relation to Epilogue C, below. The present excerpt appears toward the beginning of Part I of a three-part writing, prefaced by a dedicatory letter addressed to "all the ministers of the gospel of Christ." It is only the first segment of a summary which Zwingli had written regarding the origin of the Anabaptist movement. Continuing segments of this summary dealing with events of later chronology will be found in the following documents:

1. 59A. The Grebel-Stumpf Alternative Plan, before 12/23/1524.
2. 66A. The Tuesday Disputations, 12/6/1524—12/13/1524.
3. 68F. The First Believers' Baptism in Switzerland, 1/21/1525.
4. 68L. The Second Public Disputation on Baptism, 3/20/1525.
5. 70D. Procession of Zollikon Prophets to Zurich, after 6/12/1525.
6. 71J. The Third Public Disputation on Baptism, 11/6-8/1525.
7. 71M. The Tenth Disputation with the Anabaptists, 3/5-7/1526.
8. Epi. B. The Banishment of Blaurock, 1/5/1527.
9. Epi. C. Zwingli's Dialogue with Grebel's Ghost, 7/31/1527.

It is a somewhat mysterious writing in which the original leaders of the Anabaptist movement are not named, and the one whose ghost is addressed is deceased. Moreover, the accuracy of the present account by Zwingli is suspect because of its extremely polemical nature. But as Stayer points out (pp. 98-99), "It has been used by historians favorable to Anabaptists as well as by others, because it is a firsthand report of discussions and arguments he had with Grebel and his following. Furthermore, parts of Zwingli's statements agree with the testimony of the Swiss Brethren themselves, and the whole series of reminiscences can be joined coherently with the rest of what we know about the split in the Zurich Reformation. This separation of Zwingli the witness from Zwingli the polemicist does not produce an unchallengeable historical record. But the record that emerges is better than none."

Zwingli wrote two earlier accounts of the origin of Anabaptism which were included in his Taufbüchlein of May 1525 (see 69C/363/34ff.) and in *his* Answer to Balthasar Hubmaier's Taufbüchlein *of November 1525 (ZW, IV, p. 591.23ff.), but again the names of the characters in the drama were withheld. It was in the "Täuferprozess" (the trial of Grebel et al.) of November 9, 1525 (see 71K/436/29ff.) that the originators of the alternative plan are identified: "First Simon of Höngg came to him and Master Leo and said argumentatively that they ought to establish a special people and church and have in it Christian people who lived completely without blame and also clung to the gospel, and who were not involved in interest or other usury. . . . Then Grebel also came to them and made an approach similar to Simon of Höngg's." The account in the* Elenchus *not only contains more information about this Grebel-Stumpf plan of reform but also dates that plan as part of the events connected with the career of Stumpf (see Cast of Characters No. 85) and the "turning point of the Zwinglian Reformation" (see 58A).*

You should know, most pious reader, how their sect[3] began.[4] When their leaders,[5] clearly fanatics, had already determined to drag the liberty we have in the gospel into carnal liberty, they approached us who administer the word at Zurich,[6] courteously at first to be sure, but consistently,[7] so that as far as could be seen from their appearance and action it was clear that they had in mind something inauspicious.

They approached us therefore in the following way: "It has not escaped our attention that there will always be those who will resist the gospel, even among those who boast in the name of Christ.[8] It is therefore never to be hoped that all souls will be so established in unity, as Christians should be permitted to live.[9] According to the Acts of the Apostles those who had believed separated from the others, and then as others came to believe, they joined those who were already a new church. That is just what we must do."

They begged us to make a declaration to this effect: Those who want to follow Christ should stand on our side. They promised also that our forces would be far superior to the army of unbelievers.[10] Next the church of the devoted itself was to appoint its own council from the devout prayerfully.[11] For it was evident that there were many undevoted both in the council and in this promiscuous church.[12]

To this we responded[13] in the following way: "It is indeed true that there would always be those who would live unrighteously and hold all innocence and even piety in contempt, even though they confess Christ. Yet when they declare and contend that they are Christians, and are such by their deeds which even the church can endure, they are on our side. For who is not against us is on our side."[14]

So Christ himself had taught in just such a beginning of things as we were experiencing. He had also commanded us to let the tares grow with the grain until the day of harvest,[15] but we boldly hoped that each day more would return to a sounder mind who did not have it at present. If this should not happen, still the most devoted should always live among the least devoted.

I feared that in that state of affairs a separation would cause some confusion.[16] The example of the apostles was not applicable here, for those from whom they withdrew did not confess Christ, but now ours did. Many of them would be unwilling to consent to any separation on our part, even those who embraced Christ more ardently than we ourselves. It is the continuous action of the Word alone that should be promulgated, with which all men should become acquainted, unless they want to forsake their own salvation. I did not doubt that without disorder the number of the believing would ever grow larger[17] by the unremitting administration of the Word, not by the disruption of the body into many parts. Although the council seemed to them to be of varying complexion, we were not of that mind because nothing humane seemed alien to them;[18] and far from opposing the Word they frankly favored it equally with that Jehosaphat who with his cohorts strengthened the priests and Levites by the law itself that they might the more freely preach the Word throughout Judea.[19] Yet one should make special note of the fact that there were ten virgins awaiting the bridegroom, but only five of them were wise and prudent, and five were slothful and foolish.[20] Replies along this line we would make to them when they pressed us. And when they saw that they would not be successful, they attacked in another way. [To be continued in 66A, below.]

Original Publication: Zwingli's *In catabaptistarum strophas elenchus,* published 7/31/1527
Transcription: ZW, No. 108, pp. 32-36
Translation: Taken from Jackson, 1901, pp. 132-33

60
Grebel to Vadian
Zurich, February 26, 1524

Following the council decisions of December 19, postponing the abolition of images and the mass, two mini-disputations were held for the purpose of planning the next steps. The one held in Zurich on December 28, and restricted to the canons of the cathedral, the city magistrates, and the city clergy, "played itself out by the end of the very first day" (Garside, p. 153) and resulted only in the call for another debate.

The other was held on January 19 and 20 and was restricted even more—to five of the most stubborn canons, led by Conrad Hofmann, six councillors, and the three people's priests. "These fourteen men, representing the 'old believers' and the 'right believers,' respectively, met in private ... to discuss the problem of images and the Mass yet again.... While Zwingli was waiting to hear from the Confederate and episcopal authorities beyond Zurich in regard to his Brief Christian Introduction, *the city was still awaiting the Council's closing action on the removal of the images" (Garside, 1966, pp. 153, 155).*

These were the "public affairs" that Grebel did not need to report to Vadian in the following letter, which deals rather with the sponsorship of an apprentice tailor from St. Gallen.

G[reetings], my most learned Vadian.

How our public affairs[1] are I think you know full well from Beda Miles[2] or Zwingli,[3] so you have no need for a babbling narrator of what is happening among us. There is something else that I want you to know and (that I want) to take up with you. Eppenberg[4] has come here, joined to you by some connection, so he says. He has asked for my help, or rather for that famous Ulyssean[5] diligence of Grebel, by which I should aid him in finding a master tailor.[6] Upon his request and that of my brother Lorenz,[7] I did what I could. I found someone who would teach the man if I would stand surety for him; and I will not refuse to provide the surety if you advise it by reply to the letter which he is bringing, since you are familiar with his fortunes. So it will be for you to advise me what should be done. My Christianity is too unadventurous that I would hesitate to promise this for a man and brother, and especially since my creditors do not release me. If I were not so weighed down by their money, I would hardly have kept from promising surety for the position of Eppenberg, and I would immediately have promised it. Whatever you command, it will be settled and I will carry it out and discharge it. I hope your wife is well with your Theodosia[8] and all your household. From Zurich on the Sabbath Day after the feast of St. Matthew, 1524.

Conrad Grebel, your servant.

To the lord Joachim Vadian, a man in every way most learned and most dear.

Original: Stadtbibliothek (Vadiana) St. Gallen, VB.II.174
Transcriptions: VB, III, No. 383; M-S, No. 9

61
Grebel to Vadian
Zurich, July 31, 1524

The content of the "question" to which Grebel refers in the first sentence of the following letter is unknown. Five months have elapsed since his last letter to Vadian, and there must have been some contact in the interim to which allusion is here made. Perhaps it had to do with his own teaching and writing activities in the radical wing of the Reformation in Zurich which he mentions in his next letter in connection with what he calls the "rock" to which he is clinging. Perhaps it had to do with the latest developments in Zwingli's Reformation at this time.

Following the mini-disputation in January (see 60/Intro., above), the city awaited the decree of its magistrates on the removal of images. On May 14 on the eve of Pentecost when the statue-carrying processions to the Lindenhof and to Einsiedeln usually took place, with its possibilities for renewed iconoclasm and demonstrations, the council issued for the third time (see 57D and 58B/II) its mandate for everybody to keep the peace: "And since Pentecost is now here, unrest may consequently occur right away and our lords wish very much to be foresighted in this matter. And thus they command anew concerning these two matters, that is to say, images and the Mass, that still no one, be he woman or man, young or old, religious or lay, shall take up anything or do anything; but rather to wait for our lords who will take action in this matter as they think necessary and good" (Garside, p. 155). Again, new outbreaks of iconoclasm mobilized the 14-man commission (see 57F/fns.3-8) which brought a set of five less-than-thoroughgoing recommendations by the end of May (Garside, pp. 156-58).

Finally on June 15, following the death of Marcus Röist, the conservative burgomaster, the council adopted the decisive resolution to remove all of the remaining images from the Zurich churches. The actual removal took place systemmatically between June 20 and July 2 (Garside, pp. 159-60), just four weeks before Grebel wrote this letter. Meanwhile, however, the mass remained essentially unchanged for another nine months.

G[reetings].

The question which I said I would put to you I now put off, Vadian; and this is the reason. Sister Dorothy[1] is becoming more and more ill every day, but still she is not in bed; or rather, she is in bed today. There is great hope of her getting well if you come with your wife, our sister. Your father-in-law and mother-in-law ask and beseech that this be done, so much that I do not see how you would refuse or postpone your presence. However, come you must as quickly as you possibly can without tarrying, for this is what the situation demands should be done. And we shall discuss audibly face to face (unless God prevents) what is difficult for me to write now, and might have been also at any other time. Nor would I have written anything today, however able, had not my parents asked me to write to you by this messenger for the sake of sister; and they asked that you should fly here with your wife and that I should urge you. Hear my parents and me also and come with your soul, Martha; and when you come, give yourself to Grebel for one brief hour. The whole house of Grebel in which is also John Jacob Ammann,[2] send their regards.

The last day of July. Zurich, in the year 1524. Farewell and best wishes.

> Conrad Grebel,
> on behalf of Jacob Grebel his father.

To the lord Joachim Vadian, physician of St. Gallen, senator and most famous theologian.

Original: Stadtbibliothek (Vadiana) St. Gallen, VB.II.200
Transcriptions: VB, III, No. 402; M-S, No. 10

62
Grebel to Vadian
Zurich, September 3, 1524

For the first time in his letters to date, Grebel reports his own Reformation activities to Vadian—contacting other radical Reformation leaders like Carlstadt and Müntzer, preparing curriculum for Bible study groups, and leading one such group himself.

As Bender explains, "The thirst for a greater knowledge of the gospel was so great, and there were so many who either could not read or could not readily interpret, that many of the common people gathered around 'readers' to whom they listened for exposition of the Scriptures. . . . It is to be assumed that leading men like Zwingli welcomed such popular groups for Bible study, for this was exactly what all of them, from Erasmus on down, had advocated, namely that the common man should drink at the fountain of life. There is reason, however, to believe that at times the religious leaders were not altogether well disposed to such activities, being fearful of possible complications among the people. In these groups expression could be given to the social needs and the economic desires of the common man . . . as well as to his conviction that he ought to have a share in determining the course of the Reformation. . . . The longer Zwingli . . . postponed a concrete program of reform, the greater grew the danger that the whole evangelical movement would suffer because of the development of parties or factions, each promoting its own program of reform" (HSB, pp. 90-91).

Grebel has waited long enough and he is full of things to say!

Greetings, dearest Vadian.

In your letter to father you indicated that you wanted me to come. Father[1] gave it to me to read; and when I had read it, he asked what I had in mind. Inasmuch as I had detected that it would be pleasing to you both, I replied on the spot that I had made up my mind to prepare for the journey, especially if I should have a companion, for I am very skilled at wandering off the right road on journeys. But then when I thought of one thing after another and weighed it up, I began to incline with all my being to the other opinion. It was this, that I should cling to my rock. I have reasons of great weight with me, but you will not hear them accurately explained until willy-nilly either I come to you or you to us. While I was pondering many things to myself, there came my companion Michael,[2] but father[3] was away. And so I stayed, and it appears that I should stay here.

You ask what it is I am doing. I am writing a reply to Andreas Carlstadt.[4] And I am writing for the first time to Thomas Müntzer[5] (whose second booklet on phony faith I recently obtained and read).[6] And perhaps I shall challenge Luther also,[7] impelled by confidence in the divine Word. Then I am reading the Greek Gospel of Matthew to some pupils, interpreting it by my own abilities, not prophesying.[8] Last of all, I shall list and assemble passages—judge these words without laughter and without that preconceived opinion of yours about the passages[9]—indeed on two general themes; and unless someone else does it first, I will thrust these upon the public.[10]

Look at the reason for all my audacity:[11] I have waited, and they have not spoken. They stood still and have not responded. I shall both respond on my part and declare the knowledge of God.[12] For I am full of things to say, and the spirit in my inner being[13] compels me. Behold my belly[14] is as new wine without a vent, which bursts new wineskins. I shall speak and I shall take a little breath. I shall open my lips and I shall respond. I shall not accept the person of man,[15] and I shall not equate God with men. For I do not know how long I shall tarry or if after a short while my Maker will raise me up, ἀκούετε ἐπίσκοποι! [hear ye shepherds!][16] And as Daniel prophesies,[17] there will be in the temple an abomination of desolation, and the desolation will persist until the consummation and end, for according to Ezekiel,[18] when they drink the purest water, they muddy the rest with their feet, and the sheep feed on that which has been trampled by their feet, and they drink what their feet have muddied. They lay out plans,[19] not by the Spirit of God. They take counsel and not from God, so that sin is added to sin, so that they descend into Egypt without consulting the mouth of the Lord, so that hope is put in the help and strength of Pharaoh, and confidence is placed in the shade of Egypt, so that the strength of Pharaoh becomes a confusion and the confidence in the shade of Egypt becomes a disgrace. Etc.

In addition, my wife detains me[20] (this I might more appropriately have left unsaid) almost as much as all other causes, also the danger of the journey and the evidence of my health[21] which I tested on a short journey. So whatever I can do by mutual letters, I would prefer to do for this time rather than to travel to you and to be torn away as it were from my flesh and rib, my concerns, studies, vigils, and undertakings. Take it for good that I do not yet know when I shall be with you. If there is anything I could do by any effort in order that you might come here to live also, I would not hesitate. If father would urge me, perhaps I would not be able to refuse.[22] Cease not to invite me, if for no other reason than that we may feast together, that I may be received by you with kindness, and that I be cherished and refreshed by conversations together. If there is anything that is more fitting, let it be ordered, etc. Give my regards to sister together with all yours. Farewell in Christ.

Zurich, September 3, 1524

Conrad Grebel, yours.

You would do me a favor if through Michael[23] you would send the 9½ batzen[24] in payment for your wife's will. I would have paid it myself if I had not been so very poorly off. Therefore, charge it not to my impudence but to my poverty that I remind you of the debt.

To a Christian and famous man, Joachim Vadian, very dear kinsman.

Original: Stadtbibliothek (Vadiana) St. Gallen, VB.II.203
Transcriptions: VB, III, No. 404; M-S, No. 13

63
Grebel to Müntzer[1]
Zurich, September 5, 1524

Letters 63 and 64 comprise what J. C. Wenger calls "the programmatic letters of Conrad Grebel" because they contain, more than any other document in this collection, the vision of a believers' church free of the state which he and his friends had developed before the autumn of 1524. These letters were first translated into English in 1905 by Walter Rauschenbusch, father of the "social gospel." This version was revised and republished by George H. Williams in 1957. Then in 1970, J. C. Wenger published his own translation. These are the first of Grebel's extant letters written in the German language. As far as is known, he had previously used German only in brief phrases and postscripts, such as in 51/195/28ff. Following the present two epistles, Letters 65, 66, and 67 were written in German.

Latin was used primarily by scholars and clergy and was not understood by the masses. Most of the day-to-day commercial and civil business was transacted in German, including all of the court records. Although Müntzer and Vadian were proficient Latinists, Grebel's resort to German reflects a new interest in using the vernacular for Reformation discourse (see 57C/245/ 8-18). His decision to write letters to Müntzer, Carlstadt, and Luther was announced to Vadian in Letter 62.

Müntzer was preacher at the Church of St. John's in Allstedt from Easter 1523 until the middle of August 1524. Grebel did not know that he had already fled to Mühlhausen. It is not known whether he received the letter; but the fact that the original is extant in the Vadian archives in St. Gallen may indicate that it was returned to Vadian undelivered, perhaps by the messenger himself, since Grebel expressly states in 63/294/15-16 that he had not kept a copy.

Another obvious possibility is that having informed Vadian about his intention to write to Müntzer, he decided to send Vadian a copy of his own, so that he could better know what Grebel's new approach to the Reformation was. Perhaps this is "the question which I said I would put to you" (61/281/ 31), namely: What do you think of this free church vision for the Reformation of the church?

Peace, grace, and mercy from God our Father and Jesus Christ our Lord be with us all, Amen.[2]

Dear Brother Thomas.

For the sake of God, please do not let it surprise you that we[3] address you without title and ask you as a brother henceforth to exchange ideas with us by correspondence, and that we, unsolicited and unknown to you, have dared to initiate such future dialogue. God's Son, Jesus Christ,[4] who offers himself as the only Master and Head to all who are to be saved and commands us to be brethren to all brethren and believers through the one common Word, has moved and impelled us to establish friendship and brotherhood[5] and to bring the following theses[6] to your attention. Also the fact that you have written two booklets on phony faith[7] has led us to write to you. Therefore, if you will accept it graciously for the sake of Christ our Savior, it may, if God wills, serve and work for the good. Amen.

Just as our forefathers had fallen away from the true God and knowledge of Jesus Christ and true faith in him, from the one true common divine Word and from the godly practices[8] of the Christian love and way, and lived without God's law and gospel in human, useless, unchristian practices[9] and ceremonies and supposed they would find salvation in them but fell far short of it, as the evangelical preachers have shown and are still

285

in part showing, so even today everyone wants to be saved by hypocritical faith,[10] without fruits of faith, without the baptism of trial and testing, without hope and love, without true Christian practices, and wants to remain in all the old ways of personal vices and common antichristian[11] ceremonial rites of baptism[12] and the Lord's Supper, dishonoring the divine Word, but honoring the papal word[13] and the antipapal preachers, which is not like or in accord with the divine Word. In respect of persons and all manner of seduction they are in more serious and harmful error than has ever been the case since the foundation of the world. We were also in the same aberration because we were only hearers and readers of the evangelical preachers who are responsible for all this error as our sins deserved. But after we took the Scripture in hand[14] and consulted it on all kinds of issues, we gained some insight and became aware of the great and harmful shortcomings of the shepherds[15] as well as our own in that we do not daily cry earnestly to God with constant sighs to be led out of the destruction of all godly living[16] and out of human abominations and enter into true faith and practices of God. In all this, a false forbearance[17] is what leads to the suppression of God's Word and its mixture with the human. Indeed, we say it brings harm to all and does disservice to all the things of God—no need for further analysis and detail.

While we were noting and lamenting these things, your writing against false faith and baptism[18] was brought out here to us and we are even better informed and strengthened and were wonderfully happy to have found someone who is of a common Christian mind with us and ventures to show the evangelical preachers their shortcomings—how in all the major issues they practice false forbearance and set their own opinions and even those of antichrist above God and against God, not as befits messengers of God to act and to preach. Therefore we ask and admonish you as a brother in the name, power, Word, Spirit, and salvation which comes to all Christians through Jesus Christ our Master and Savior, to seek earnestly to preach only God's Word unflinchingly, to establish and defend only divine practices, to esteem as good and right only what can be found in definite clear Scripture, and to reject, hate, and curse all the schemes, words, practices, and opinions of all men, even your own.

[No.1.][19] We understand and have read that you have translated the mass into German[20] and instituted new German chants.[21] This cannot be good when we find in the New Testament no teaching on chanting,[22] no example. Paul reproves the Corinthian learned more than he praises them for murmuring in their assemblies as if they were singing,[23] as the Jews and Italians pronounce their rituals in the form of songs.

Second, since chanting in Latin developed without divine teaching or apostolic example or practice and has not brought good or edified, it will much less edify in German and will create an outward appearing faith.

Third, since Paul quite distinctly forbids chanting in Ephesians 5[24] and Colossians 3[25] where he says and teaches that they should address and instruct one another with psalms and spiritual songs, and if anyone would sing, he should sing in his heart and give thanks.[26]

No. 4. Whatever we are not taught in definite statements and examples, we are to consider forbidden, as if it were written, "Do not do this, do not chant."[27]

No. 5. Christ commanded his messengers to preach only the Word[28] according to the Old as well as the New Testament. Paul also says that we should let the Word of Christ, not the chant, dwell in us.[29] Whoever chants poorly feels chagrin; whoever can do it well feels conceit.[30]

No. 6. We should neither add to nor take away from the Word what seems good to us.[31]

No. 7. If you want to abolish the mass, it cannot be done with German chanting, which is perhaps your idea or derived from Luther.

[No. 8.] It must be rooted out with the Word and command of Christ.

No. 9. For it was not planted by God.[32]

No. 10. Christ instituted and planted the Supper of fellowship.[33]

No. 11. Only the words found in Matthew 26, Mark 14, Luke 22, and 1 Corinthians 11 should be used, neither more nor less.

[No. 12] The minister from the congregation shall recite them from one of the Gospels or from Paul.

13. They are words of institution of the Supper of unity, not of consecration.

14. There shall be an ordinary [loaf of] bread, without idolatry or addition.[34]

15. For this causes a hypocritical worship and veneration of the bread and detracts from the inward.[35] There shall also be a common cup.

16. This would do away with the veneration and would bring about a proper knowledge and understanding of the Supper, because the bread is nothing but bread.[36] By faith it is the body of Christ and an incorporation with Christ and the brethren. For one must eat and drink in spirit and in love, as John indicates in chapter 6 and elsewhere,[37] and Paul in [1] Corinthians 10 and 11,[38] and is clearly observed in Acts 2.[39]

17. Although it is simply bread, if faith and brotherly love are already present, it shall be eaten with joy, for when it is thus practiced in the church it ought to show us that we are and want to be truly one loaf and body and true brethren to one another, etc.

18. But if there be one who does not intend to live in a brotherly way, he eats to his condemnation, for he eats like any other meal without discernment[40] and he brings shame upon love, the inward bond, as well as the bread, the outward bond.

19. For it also does not remind him of the body and blood of Christ, the covenant of the cross, so that he is willing to live and to suffer for the sake of Christ and the brethren, the Head and the members.

20. Nor should it be administered by you.[41] Thereby the mass, the individual meal, would disappear,[42] for the Supper is a sign of fellowship, not a mass and sacrament. Therefore no one shall eat it alone, whether on a deathbed or otherwise.[43] Nor shall the bread be locked away, etc., for any individual person, for no one shall take the bread of the fellowship for himself alone, unless he be in unity with himself, which no one is, etc.

21. According to all Scripture and history, it shall also not be practiced in temples, for it leads to false devotion.

22. It shall be observed often and much.[44]

23. It should not be practiced without applying the rule of Christ[45] in Matthew 18; otherwise it is not the Lord's Supper, for without the same [rule], everyone pursues externals. The internal, love, is neglected, if brethren and false brethren go there and eat.

24. If you ever intend to administer, we would wish it would be without priestly robes and the vestments of the mass,[46] without chanting, without addition.

25. Concerning the time, we know that Christ gave it to the apostles in the evening meal and that the Corinthians had also thus observed it. We do not stipulate any specific time, etc.[47]

With this, since you are much better informed about the Lord's Supper, and we have merely indicated our understanding, if we are incorrect, teach us better, and be willing yourself to drop chanting and the mass, and act only in accord with the Word, and proclaim and establish the practices of the apostles with the Word. If that cannot be done it would be better to leave everything in Latin, unchanged and uncompromised. If that which is right cannot be established, then still do not administer after your own or the antichristian priestly rites, and at least teach how it ought to be, as Christ does in John 6, teaching how one should eat and drink his flesh and blood.[48] Pay no attention to the apostasy or to the unchristian forbearance,[49] which the very learned foremost evangelical preachers established as an actual idol and planted throughout the world. It is far better that a few be correctly instructed through the Word of God and believe and live right in virtues and practices than that many believe deceitfully out of adulterated false doctrine. Although we admonish and implore you, we

288

do hope that you will do it of your own accord and are therefore admonishing you in deepest affection because you listened so kindly to our brother[50] and have confessed to him that you have been too lax, and because you and Carlstadt[51] are regarded among us as the purest proclaimers and preachers of the purest Word of God. And if you both properly impugn those who mix human word and practice with the divine, you should also logically break away from the priesthood, benefices,[52] and all kinds of new and ancient practices and from your own and ancient opinions and become completely pure. If your benefices, like ours,[53] are based on interest and tithes,[54] both of which are actual usury, and if you are not supported by one entire congregation, we hope you will withdraw from the benefices. You know well enough how a shepherd is to be supported.

We await much good from Jacob Strauss[55] and several others who are little regarded by the negligent theologians and doctors at Wittenberg.[56] We are likewise rejected by our learned shepherds. All men adhere to them because they preach a sinful sweet Christ[57] and they lack the power to discern as you show in your booklets, which have almost immeasurably instructed and strengthened us, the poor in spirit. And so we think alike in everything except that we learned with sorrow that you have set up tablets, for which we can find neither text nor example in the New Testament.[58] In the Old, it was of course to be written outwardly, but now in the New it is to be written on the fleshly tablets of the heart, as a comparison of the two Testaments shows, as we are taught by Paul in 2 Corinthians 3,[59] in Jeremiah 31,[60] in Hebrews 8,[61] and in Ezekiel 36.[62] Unless we are in error, which we do not think and believe, we hope you will again destroy the tablets. It developed out of your own opinions; it is a useless expenditure which would continue to increase and become entirely idolatrous and implant itself throughout the world as idols did. It would also create a suspicion that some outward object from which the unlearned could learn had to stand and be erected in place of the idols, whereas the outward Word alone should be used according to all example and commands of Scripture, as shown to us especially in 1 Corinthians 14 and Colossians 3.[63] This kind of learning from a single word[64] might in time become somewhat obstructing,[65] and even if it would never cause any harm I would never invent or establish any such innovation and thereby follow or imitate the negligent, misleading, falsely forbearing scholars, nor out of my own opinion invent, teach, or institute a single item.

March forward with the Word and create a Christian church with the help of Christ and his rule such as we find instituted in Matthew 18[66] and practiced in the epistles. Press on in earnest with common prayer and fasting,[67] in accord with faith and love without being commanded and compelled. Then God will help you and your lambs to all purity, and the chanting and the tablets will fall away. There is more than enough wisdom and counsel in the Scripture on how to teach, govern, direct, and make devout all classes and all men. Anyone who will not reform or believe and strives against the Word and acts of God and persists therein, after Christ and his Word and rule have been preached to him, and he has been admonished with the three witnesses before the church,[68] such a man we say on the basis of God's Word shall not be put to death[69] but regarded as a heathen and publican and left alone.

Moreover, the gospel and its adherents are not to be protected by the sword, nor [should] they [protect] themselves, which as we have heard through our brother is what you believe and maintain.[70] True believing Christians are sheep among wolves, sheep for the slaughter. They must be baptized in anguish and tribulation, persecution, suffering, and death, tried in fire, and must reach the fatherland of eternal rest not by slaying the physical but the spiritual. They use neither worldly sword nor war,[71] since killing has ceased with them entirely, unless indeed we are still under the old law, and even there (as far as we can know) war was only a plague after they had once conquered the Promised Land. No more of this.[72]

On the subject of baptism,[73] your writing pleases us well,[74] and we ask for further instruction from you. We are taught that without Christ's rule of binding and loosing,[75] even an adult should not be baptized. The Scriptures describe baptism for us, that it signifies the washing away of sins by faith and the blood of Christ (that the nature of the baptized and believing one is changing before and after),[76] that it signifies one has died and shall (die) to sin and walks in newness of life and Spirit and one will surely be saved if one through the inward baptism lives the faith according to this meaning, so that the water does not strengthen and increase faith and give a very great comfort and last resort on the deathbed, as the scholars at Wittenberg say.[77] Also that it does not save, as Augustine, Tertullian, Theophylact, and Cyprian taught,[78] thus dishonoring faith and the suffering of Christ for mature adults and dishonoring the suffering of Christ for unbaptized infants. On the basis of the following Scriptures—Genesis 8, Deuteronomy 1, 30—31; 1 Corinthians 14; Wisdom 12; also 1 Peter 2; Romans 1, 2, 7, 10; Matthew 18—19; Mark 9—10; Luke 18, etc.[79] we hold that all children who have not attained the knowledge to discern between good and evil and have not eaten of the tree of knowledge are surely saved through the suffering of Christ, the new Adam, who has restored the life that has been distorted, because they would have been subject to death and damnation only if Christ had not suffered, not afterward risen to the infirmity of our broken nature, unless it can be proved to us that Christ did not die for children.[80] But in answer to the charge that faith is required of all who are to be saved, we exclude children and on the basis of the above texts accept that they will be saved without faith and that they do not believe; and we conclude from the description of baptism and from Acts (according to which no child was baptized) and also from the above texts, which are the only ones which deal with the subject of children, and all other Scriptures which do not concern children, that infant baptism is a senseless, blasphemous abomination contrary to all Scripture and even contrary to the papacy, for we learn through Cyprian and Augustine that for many years after the time of the apostles, for six hundred years, believers and unbelievers were baptized together,[81] etc. Since you know this ten times better than we, and have published your protestation against infant baptism,[82] we hope that you will not act contrary to God's eternal Word, wisdom, and command, according to which only believers should be baptized and will not baptize children.[83] If you or Carlstadt[84] do not adequately write against infant baptism and all that pertains to it, how and why one is to baptize, etc., I (Conrad Grebel) will try my hand at it and will finish writing out[85] what I have begun against all (except for you) who have thus far written misleadingly and knowingly about baptism, and who have translated into German the senseless, blasphemous form of infant baptism, like Luther,[86] Leo,[87] Osiander,[88] and the Strasbourgers,[89] and some who have acted even more shamefully. Unless God averts it, I together with all of us are and shall be more certain of persecution by the scholars, etc., than by other people. We beg you not to use or adopt the old rites of the antichrist, such as sacrament, mass, signs, etc. Hold to the Word alone and administer[90] as all emissaries should, especially you and Carlstadt,[91] and you will be doing more than all the preachers of all nations.

Consider us your brethren and read this epistle as our expression of great joy and hope toward you through God. Admonish, comfort, and strengthen us as you are well able. Pray to the Lord God for us that he will come to the aid of our faith, for we are very ready to believe. And if God grants it to us to pray, we too will intercede for you and for all that we may all walk according to our calling and commitment. May God grant us this through Jesus Christ our Savior. Amen.

Greet all the brethren for us, the shepherds and the sheep, who accept the Word of faith and salvation with deep desire and hunger, etc. One thing more. We desire a reply from you; and if you publish anything, send it to us by this messenger or another. We would also like to know whether you and Carlstadt[92] are of one mind. We hope and believe you are. We commend to you this messenger, who has also carried letters from us to our dear brother Carlstadt. And if you should go to Carlstadt so that you would reply jointly, that would be a great joy to us. The messenger is to return to us. Whatever we have not adequately paid him will be reimbursed when he returns.

Whatever we have not correctly understood, inform and instruct us. At Zurich, on the fifth day of September in the year 1524.

Conrad Grebel, Andreas Castelberg(er),[93] Felix Mantz,[94] Hans Ockenfuss,[95] Bartlime Pur,[96] Heinrich Aberli,[97] and your other brethren[98] (God willing) in Christ. Until another communication, we who have written this to you wish for you and all of us and all your flock the true Word of God, true faith, love, and hope, with all peace and grace from God through Christ Jesus, Amen.

I, C. Grebel, was going to write to Luther[99] in the name of all of us and exhort him to desist from the forbearance[100] which he and his followers practice without scriptural authority and planted abroad in the world, but my affliction[101] and time did not permit. You do it according to your duty, etc.

To the true and faithful proclaimer of the gospel, Thomas Müntzer of Allstedt in the Hartz, our faithful and dear brother in Christ, etc.

Original: Stadtbibliothek (Vadiana) St. Gallen, VB.XI.97
Transcriptions: M-S, No. 14, pp. 13-19; J. C. Wenger, *Conrad Grebel's Programmatic Letters of 1524* (Scottdale, Pa., Herald Press, 1970)

64
Grebel to Müntzer
Zurich, sent with letter of September 5, 1524[1]

Dearly beloved brother Thomas.

After I had written in haste in the name of all of us[2] and assumed that the messenger would not wait until we also wrote to Luther, he had to delay and wait because of rain. And so I also wrote to Luther[3] in my name and that of the other brothers, mine and yours, and admonished him to desist from his false forbearance toward the weak,[4] which they are themselves. Andreas Castelberg(er) wrote to Carlstadt.[5] Meanwhile, there arrived here for Hans Hujuff of Halle,[6] our fellow citizen and brother who visited you recently, a letter and a shameful booklet by Luther,[7] which no one who claims to be *primitiae* [firstfruits][8] like the apostles ought to write. Paul teaches otherwise: *Porro servum domini,* etc. ["Next, the Lord's servant, etc."][9] I see that he wants to deliver you to the ax and hand you over to the prince,[10] to whom he has bound his gospel, just as Aaron had to have Moses as a god. As for your booklets and protestations, I find you guiltless. I do not gather from them that you utterly repudiate baptism, but that you condemn infant baptism and the misunderstanding of baptism. What water means in John 3 we want to examine further in your booklet[11] and in the Scripture.

Hujuff's brother writes that you have preached against the princes, that they should be combatted with the fist.[12] If that is true, or if you intend to defend war, the tablets, chanting, or other things for which you do not find a clear word (as you do not find for any of these aforementioned points), I admonish you by the salvation common to all of us that if you will desist from them and all opinions of your own now and henceforth, you will become completely pure, for you satisfy us on all other points better than anyone else in this German and other lands. If you fall into the hands of Luther and the duke,[13] drop the aforementioned articles and stand by the other like a hero and a soldier of God. Be strong. You have the Bible (which Luther rendered "bible bubel[14] babel"[15]) as defense against Luther's idolatrous forbearance,[16] which he and the learned shepherds around here have spread throughout the world against the deceitful lax faith, against their preaching in which they do not teach Christ as they ought. They have just opened up the gospel to all the world so that many can read it for themselves (or ought to read it), but not many do, for everyone depends on them. Around here there are not even twenty who believe the Word of God. They only believe humans—Zwingli,[17] Leo,[18] and others who are regarded elsewhere as learned. And if you should have to suffer for it, you know that it cannot be otherwise. Christ must suffer still more in his members, but he will strengthen them and keep them steadfast to the end. God grant you and us grace, for our shepherds are also fierce and enraged against us, reviling us from the public pulpit as rascals and *Satanas in angelos lucis conversos* [Satans turned into angels of light].[19] In time we too will see persecution come upon us through them.[20] Therefore pray to God for us. Once more we admonish you, because we love and respect you so sincerely for the clarity of your words, and we confidently venture to write to you: Do not act, teach, or establish anything according to human opinion, your own or borrowed, repeal what has been established,[21] and teach only the clear Word and rites of God, including the rule of Christ,[22] the unadulterated baptism and unadulterated Supper, which we touched upon in our first letter and upon which you are better informed than a hundred of us. If you and Carlstadt,[23] Jacob Strauss,[24] and Michael Stiefel[25] should not deliberately strive to be wholly pure (as I and my brethren hope you will do) it will be a sorry gospel indeed that has come into the world. But you are far purer than our clergy here or those at Wittenberg who daily fall from one perversion of Scripture into another and from one blindness into another that is worse. I believe and am sure that they want to become true papists and popes. No more now. God our captain with his Son Jesus Christ our Savior and his Spirit and Word be with you and us all.

Conrad Grebel, Andreas Castelberg(er),[26] Felix Mantz,[27] Heinrich Aberli,[28] John Pannicellus,[29] Hans Ockenfuss,[30] Hans Hujuff your countryman of Halle,[31] brethren to you, and seven new young Müntzers to Luther.[32]

In case you are allowed to continue to preach and nothing happens to you, we will send you a copy of our letter to Luther and his answer if he replies to us.[33] We have admonished him and our clergy here too. In this way, unless God prevents, we want to show them their shortcomings and not fear what may happen to us for it. We have kept no copy except for the letter we wrote to Martin, your adversary. Please accept favorably our unlearned, unpolished letter, and be sure that we have written out of genuine love, for we are one in Word and trial and adversaries, although you are more learned and stronger in spirit. Because of this common identity, we have spoken or rather written at length. Give our greetings to the Christians there, God willing, and write us a long letter in reply from all of you together. You will give us great joy and stir in us an even greater love for you.

This letter also is for Thomas Müntzer of Allstedt in the Hartz.

Original: Stadtbibliothek (Vadiana) St. Gallen, VB.II.204
Transcription: M-S, No. 14, pp. 19-21

65
Grebel to Vadian
Zurich, October 14, 1524

Grebel has known strain in his relationship to Vadian before, but the strain about which he writes in the following letter is of a new kind. It is not the result of the absconding of Eppenberg in violation of the arrangement worked out between Vadian and Grebel. It is not the result of Grebel's indebtedness to his creditors in an amount exceeding sixty guilders. It is not his having written to Müntzer or Carlstadt and playing host to Carlstadt's brother-in-law.

Rather, it is Grebel's antagonism to Vadian's friend and colleague,

Huldrych Zwingli, and his audacity to apply to the work of Zurich's great reformer the condemnation of Ezekiel, "Are you not satisfied with grazing on good herbage, that you must trample down the rest with your feet? Or with drinking clear water, that you must churn up the rest with your feet? My flock has to eat what you have trampled and drink what you have churned up" (Ezek. 34:18-19, NEB).

Greetings, most eminent man.

Eppenberg contracted with his master and disappeared.[1] A half year was completed. The fee is seven Rhenish guilders which he owes the master. He owes a half guilder to the tribunes, as they are called. You are the guarantor. Inform and prod his mother, I mean Conrad's, that Ochsner,[2] the master, should be paid as soon as possible, etc. For he expects satisfaction, that it should be soon.

Just as we said in our last letter to you that we[3] were going to write to the leaders at the University of Wittenberg, know that it has now been done;[4] and since we had written to Carlstadt not many days before, a letter from there returned recently.[5] Moreover, eight booklets,[6] more or less, were presented to us to read through the good offices of the messenger, who stayed with us in Zurich for six days and told and read how Carlstadt and Luther came in contact, how they argued, and before even a month and a half elapsed they repudiated each other, how Carlstadt accepted a guilder from Luther so that he should [dare to] write against him.[7] The name of the messenger is Gerhard Westerburg,[8] if by chance you have read his booklet on the *Sleep of Souls*.[9] When these booklets and their disputations are printed and reach us, soon I hope, I will see to it that you have a supply of them, unless you do not want it.

Having been offended, I suppose, by my last letter,[10] you have written nothing in reply. If you want to know my fortunes, if I may call them that, I do not complain at all, lest sometime I should be worse off. In the meanwhile, however, my peace is a judge of men,[11] for I am a most reliable index of what sort of men are stewards of good gifts to needy persons.[12] May the God of mercy and peace, and also of patience, grant to them a bounteous if not also a Christian hand, if not so much toward me as toward the most poverty-stricken, but also in regard to my creditors, to whom I am enslaved and bound by a debt of more than sixty guilders. If this does not happen, may Christ our Master teach me to rein in and possess my soul in patience, if he has not almost now already taught me, if it were not that my creditors are troublesome to me. If they received full payment from me, as God lives, I could not play the part of a Codrus,[13] I could not endure ἀπαξάπαντα [everything][14] with a sheep's heart. But even so, callousness will be reckoned a blessing of Christ. I have no one among the whole race of kinsmen and relatives who is sympathetic; but I am becoming accustomed to it day by day so that I bear it more serenely. The burden of sins within should not weigh on me alone by rights, but on all Christians, more than the storms of affliction that assail from without.

What I charged in the previous letter,[15] I do not avoid here. The most learned shepherds and they who seem to be pillars and leaders of the Word, as they are indeed, are they who drink the purest water and yet trample with their feet much water for the sheep to drink,[16] in not a few places which still adhere to the faith. You do not believe, I know, with what disturbed feelings I learn of this, and what's more that I care nothing for the chief leader of the Word, who maligns me as the purveyor of envy[17] [disguised] as an angel of light[18] and ὑποκρίσεως [hypocrisy] from Satan. What is happening here is happening also at Wittenberg, but the impartial reader will judge from the booklets of Carlstadt how Luther walks backward and how notorious a dawdler and vigorous a defender of his own stumbling.[19] Now that is more than enough of this.

What you owe to Chrysόφορψ [Christophorus][20] and how much to Andreas,[21] I will clarify in a short letter, unless you fly here with mother. Good-bye, and best wishes to your wife and you all.

Zurich, October 14, in the year of salvation 1524

Conrad οὐδείς, οὐκέτι Γρεβέλλιος[22]

[Conrad Nobody, no more Grebel]

The points which Bodenstein[23] treats you have learned, I believe, from him who brought you the letter of Zwingli. These rumors of war,[24] which terrified the wisest men of the laity and the most learned of the πρεσβυτέροις [elders], if they have not been quieted, will be quieted. A false prophet is Christ.[25]

Whatever sort they were, many have suffered a cause of offense.

To the lord Joachim Vadian, dearest and most eminent kinsman, and a Christian.

Original: Stadtbibliothek (Vadiana) St. Gallen, VB.II.209
Transcriptions: VB,III, No. 407; M-S, No. 15

65A
Anabaptist Beginnings in St. Gallen
St. Gallen, 1524[1]

*Document 65A is the first of nine chronological excerpts from Johann
Kessler's* Sabbata *included in this collection: (1) 65A. Anabaptist Beginnings
in St. Gallen, 1524. (2) 68F. The First Believer's Baptism in Switzerland, 1/
21/1525. (3) 68H. The Oldest Anabaptist Congregation: Zollikon. (4) 69A.
The Spread of Anabaptism in St. Gallen, 2/1525-5/1525. (5) 69E. The First
Swiss Anabaptist Martyr: Eberli Bolt, 5/29/1525. (6) 70A. The Reactions to
Anabaptism in St. Gallen, 5/1525-6/1525. (7) 71E. The Third Anabaptist
Martyr: Hans Krüsi, 7/27/1525. (8) 71J. The Third Public Disputation on
Baptism, 11/6-8/1525. (9) 71R. The Death of Grebel and Execution of
Mantz, 8/1526-1/1527.*

*Gordon Rupp describes Kessler as "one of the world's great storytellers,
and there is more life in a paragraph by him than in all the thousand pages of
the Vadianus MSS. He is an inspired gossip, a sanctified Pepys, with a gift
for making thumbnail sketches of people and events, and with the instincts
and imagination of a true historian. . . . There was no chronicler of the time
who could speak more charitably and truthfully about the Anabaptists" (pp.
368-70).*

*The first excerpt below tells the story of how the issue of baptism first
came up for discussion in St. Gallen, prior to the more intentional Zurich
Anabaptist mission to St. Gallen, chronicled in 69A, below.*

First I want to show clearly and with as few words as possible the
small vein from which thereafter such great Anabaptist gushes of water
poured forth among us (since I write especially for the chronicle of St.
Gallen).

Last year[2] when in my simplicity I read Paul's epistle to the Romans
to some Christian brethren who asked and called me to do this, no one in
St. Gallen knew anything about rebaptism. Nor had it broken out publicly
yet in Zurich, except that secretly (as described above) several asked if they
might bring it out.[3] Now it happened that as I was reading from chapter
six of the aforesaid epistle and speaking about the power of the Word,
baptism, and its significance, Lorenz Hochrütiner[4] was present, who was
expelled from Zurich for some transgression, a zealous disciple of the
aforesaid Conrad Grebel, the arch-Anabaptist.[5] He lifted up his voice and
ordered me to stop, saying, "I note from your words that you think infants
should be baptized."

I replied [that] I knew nothing to the contrary at present. It seemed
very odd and strange that there would be anyone who doubted it. I asked
why they should not be baptized.

He replied on the basis of the saying and command of Christ in Matthew 28:[6] He who believes and is baptized will be saved, etc. A child is an unreasoning being and it would be like dipping any other unreasoning animal, like a cat or a stick, into the water.

I answered [that] according to my understanding there is a striking difference between God's creatures that were created for man's need such as cattle, wood, and stone, and those who are ordained to the kingdom of God and eternal life, such as children, of whom, according to Jesus' promise, is the kingdom of heaven.[7]

And so a conversation began between us which I will omit as peripheral. In the end he hoped to produce a Scripture against and in opposition to me that would be hard for me to digest. Not long thereafter the oft-mentioned C. Grebel sent the brethren an eight-page letter[8] which I was to read to them, saying that all that I said about baptism was from the devil. He urged them earnestly to be on their guard against me. When the brethren gave me the letter and it was read, I admonished them against it. They should not be easily swayed by this letter, for I would refute it in my reply.

And thus a division occurred among the brethren, for those among whom the above Lorenz was living thought I had not adequately replied to the letter. Still the matter remained secret at that time and was delayed until the present year '25. [To be continued in 68F, below]

Original: ?
Transcriptions: Egli-Schock, pp. 143-44; Fast, pp. 602-3

66
Grebel to Vadian
Zurich, November 23, 1524[1]

The first paragraph of the following letter to Vadian was evidently written conjointly by Conrad and his father, and the rest was written by Conrad but largely on behalf of his father. Consequently, the letter contains no new information about Conrad's activities and very little about the Swiss Reformation except for the allusion to the very difficult Ittingen affair then being negotiated at the Diet at Einsiedeln (see 65/fn.20).

Jacob Grebel had been deeply involved in the prior negotiations in the July meetings of the Diet in Bern and Solothurn and in the August-September meetings in Baden. Schelbert writes that "his diplomatic experience and his conciliatory temperament seemed well fitted to calm the tense and conflict-laden atmosphere. But his efforts seem to have displeased Zwingli, who apparently made the Zurich deputy responsible for the negative outcome of the

Ittingen affair. He may have been informed in this sense by other members of the Zurich delegation" (Schelbert, p. 52).

My brother-in-lawly greetings, first of all.[2]

Dear Doctor.[3]

Be assured that your letter and booklet[4] have come to me and the matter is resolved. Hans Widerker[5] has been with the bailiff of Luzern. He said that he had sent letter and booklet to the innkeeper at the Crown in Winterthur.[6] The latter, however, pretended to know nothing of them and perhaps did not know. Then another innkeeper (I suppose at the Sun) tried to deliver the letter and booklet to the innkeeper at the Crown, but he refused to accept them. So they were sent here. And there has been no complaint about it otherwise, etc.[7]

The confederates at Luzern laid down certain propositions to Milords.[8] I suppose these have been written to you, etc. Besides, I myself have not been able to understand them very clearly from father.[9] And so it happens that I know nothing more about it to write. But in case you have not been informed and I learn more about it, including what is now being negotiated at Einsiedeln,[10] I will write to you. But please do not let father notice that I have written it to you. He holds it against you that the duke of Württemberg might be coming today and that we might be Württembergers (which does not please him and perhaps others also).[11] I do not know what it means and I wait to see what the wisdom of the world wills and will work out.

Mother wondered how you fared on the road, etc. Please write. Father was supposed to go with five council delegates and deputies to Einsiedeln on court day[12] and be a counselor, but the gout laid him low, so he asked me to write to you and send hearty greetings in the name of us all. Greet my sister[13] for me and brother-in-law Benedict[14] and Master Jufli[15] and whoever is dear to you.

More another time.

At Zurich, in haste, on Wednesday after Mary, 1524.

Conrad Grebel, your brother-in-law and
willing servant

To the lord Doctor Joachim von Watt, my dear master and brother-in-law.

At St. Gallen.

Original: Stadtbibliothek (Vadiana) St. Gallen, VB.II.199
Transcriptions: VB, III, No. 411; M-S, No. 17

66A
The Tuesday Disputations[1]
Zurich, December 6 and 13, 1524[2]

In Grebel's letter to Vadian of December 16, 1524 (No. 67) is found a reference to several interpersonal disputations with the three people's priests in Zurich on the question of baptism. According to Blanke (ZW, VI, p. 37, fns. 1-5), the Grebel reference is a trace of the Tuesday Disputations which occurred between the middle of November and the more public and official disputation of January 17, 1525 (see 68A and 68B).

Zwingli makes reference to these Tuesday Disputations not only in the following excerpt from his Elenchus *but also in five other places, as follows:*

(1) "Then they wanted a special disputation on baptism to be held. When we conducted two such disputations, they displayed such anger and hatred— for both times they were defeated—that all the educated men who were present could easily discern their spirit, and that it would not be advisable, but even dangerous, to hold further disputations with them" (from his Taufbüchlein, *ZW, IV, 207/12-18, translated below in 69C/364/4-9).*

(2) ". . . for all of us who preach in Zurich have examined the Scripture with them on the subject of baptism, twice in private and once before the Large Council" (also from his Taufbüchlein, *ZW, IV, p. 286.14; see 69C/ 372/35-37.*

(3) "Were these words not cited by Hätzer in the first two disputations?" (from the Elenchus, *ZW, VI, p. 70.3; see below Epi.C/497/9).*

(4) "We have met twice for debate with certain brothers on the subject of baptism, successfully indeed, insofar as the battle and its outcome are concerned" (Zwingli to Franz Lambert, December 16, 1524, ZW, VIII, p. 269.13; see below 67A/304/18-20).

(5) See fn. 4, below. The second of the above references tells us that the Tuesday discussions were "in private" in distinction to the disputation "before the Large Council," which undoubtedly refers to the convocation of January 17.

[Continued from 59A, above] Replies along this line we would make to them when they pressed us. And when they saw that they would not be successful, they attacked in another way. They suddenly, surprisingly, denounced infant baptism as the chief abomination,[3] proceeding from an evil demon and the Roman pontiff.[4] We met this attack at once. We promised an amicable conference,[5] scheduled for Tuesday of each week.[6] At the first meeting the battle was keen but without affront to us as we especially considered their accusations with calmness.[7] Let God be the witness and those who were present, from their side[8] as well as from ours.[9] The second was more severe.[10] Since they could do nothing with Scripture, some of them carried on the affair with open abuse.[11] When they saw

300

themselves beaten after a considerable conflict, and when we had exhorted them in friendly ways, we broke up in such a way that most of them promised that they would make no disturbance, although they could not promise to give up their opinions. [To be continued in 68F, below]

Original: Same as 59A
Transcription: ZW, VI, No. 108, pp. 36-37
Translation: Taken from Jackson, 1901, pp. 133-34

67
Grebel to Vadian
Zurich, December 15, 1524[1]

In the following letter, Grebel replies to Vadian's "letter and booklet" that had just arrived when he sent his last letter (see 66/299/5). The content of Vadian's booklet, discussed in 66/fn.4, was evidently a defense of infant baptism and included arguments that Vadian later incorporated in his treatise, Schrift wider die Täufer. *What Vadian's letter had requested that Grebel "could not do" was probably that he reconsider his position on baptism in the light of Vadian's new arguments, or at the very least, that he be more quiet and less of a "troublemaker" in his new opposition to infant baptism.*

With this letter, Grebel has severed his reliance on Vadian's approval; and from another base of support, which Vadian had called a "faction," he returns the challenge to Vadian to quit "dealing in divine matters with human wisdom," to begin to "stand by the truth," to take a stand against the practice of usury, to warn about the coming persecution of true believers, to reject the false forebearance of Luther and Zwingli in the delay of the reform of the ordinances of baptism and the Lord's Supper, and to repudiate the new Zwinglian preparations for war.

Dear Lord Doctor and Brother-in-law.

What you have asked of me I could not do.[2] Truth will not be bound to time.[3] Therefore, understand it in the best sense.[4] This is my wish, that it might be so.[5] Others who have understood divine truth concerning baptism do not want to have their children baptized.[6] They have been warned by Milords,[7] but have stood firm. Then they asked for a judgment[8] and pleaded and appealed to Scripture. Both councils[9] then decided that all who say that infant baptism is unchristian and do not want to baptize their children shall present their reasons before the three pastors[10] and the pastors theirs in return in the presence of four of the councillors.[11] Zwingli and the lords appointed thereto have disobeyed all of this instruction.[12] They summoned and abused the simplest one, yet nearest to God as God and

301

the world know how.[13] But with the help of God and his truth, he has put their wisdom to shame.[14] Moreover, both councils have decided anew that they should meet together as previously ordered.[15]

In addition to this, you ask for something new, which is at hand but not yet printed. The lion[16] is scratching with the renowned Kretz,[17] the sophist of Augsburg. Zwingli is writing on force.[18] Whether he will scratch with the same one, I do not know; it is possible.[19] He, Zwingli, is writing also about rebels and rebellion;[20] that may well hit us.[21] Look out, it will bring something.[22] May God prosper his truth and righteousness and put to shame all persons.[23] They are (that is, we all are) false; the best are hypocrites. Amen. May God grant us his mercy, that you might abhor dealing in divine matters with human wisdom, and us, that we with you might also stand by the truth, persevere and pray that God might strengthen the laborers sent into the great harvest.[24] So may peace, faith, and blessedness abide and be obtained.

One thing I must say. To place in personal usury and interest and the splendor of this world a passing, fading consolation and security,[25] or to be quiet about the usury of others,[26] or not to warn about the coming sword:[27] if this is to have believed and loved and forborne in a Christian way,[28] then the truth of God is the most untrue untruth. The same applies concerning the present warring,[29] forbearance,[30] baptism, and the Lord's Supper. I believe the Word of God simply by grace, not by artifice.[31] From the standpoint of artifice, you know it well, yes, a thousand times better.[32] For that reason I have spoken and still speak. For that reason may God give us his perfect mercy that we might obey, that you might submit to his Word without pretense and also obey accordingly. Otherwise, it is to be feared that the situation is not as good as we falsely console ourselves. The way is narrow.[33] Too many vestments make it hard to get in.[34]

Your letter[35] with the booklet which you sent to me gives us a nasty slap,[36] but God has his own seat of judgment, etc.[37] If I am a troublemaker, then I have sinned.[38] That you public persons are better is of necessity. In confessing the truth I know how it is with the pastors[39] and the others. Also concerning our so-called faction here, I rejoice that God is the judge. They are going to write about rebels.[40] They will be known by their fruits,[41] by their expelling and consigning people to the sword.[42] I do not think that persecution will fail to come. God be merciful. I hope to God that he will grant the medicine of patience. Amen, if it cannot be otherwise.

When the booklets are printed and I am still living and able, I will send them to you.[43] Pray to God for the furtherance of his will and all righteousness, mine above all. May God increase them through Jesus

Christ. Amen. Greet my sister[44] for me, and all the students and beginners in the divine Word and life,[45] that they (if they have the will) might also pray for us in these perilous times. God knows why they are perilous.

You have not written. I have not been angry about it and have answered. In a friendly spirit I have spoken to you in writing. Accept it graciously and simply.

Given at Zurich on Thursday after Mary, etc., in the year 1524.

> Conrad Grebel, your faithful brother-in-law.
> I would rather we be brothers-in-the-truth-of-Christ.

To the lord[46] Doctor Joachim von Watt, my dear lord and brother-in-law.

To St. Gallen.

Original: Stadtbibliothek (Vadiana) St. Gallen, VB.II.213
Transcriptions: VB, III, No. 412; Quellen 1, No. 18

67A
Zwingli to Lambert[1] and other Brethren[2] in Strasbourg
Zurich, December 16, 1524

The most detailed report available of the content of the Tuesday Disputations of December 6 and 13 (see 66A), mentioned only briefly in the foregoing letter by Grebel (No. 67), is found in the following letter written by Zwingli. The part included here is about half of the letter. The rest deals with other concerns of the Strasbourg brethren, who had written three letters posing four questions in all. The excerpt is Zwingli's answer to the fourth question, posed by Capito and Bucer, concerning "the only two ceremonies that Christ bequeathed to us—baptism and Eucharist."

Although Zwingli's comments are thus in reply to a question out of another context, they deal directly, as the excerpt reveals, with the two Tuesday meetings which had just transpired. It is thereby the first writing on the subject by Zwingli. It was not intended for publication, and Zwingli explicitly instructed the Strasbourg brethren to treat it confidentially and not to have it printed without his permission.

Grace and peace from the Lord. The reason I refrained from writing to you for so long, most beloved brethren, is the one with which one generally makes excuses: there was no courier at my disposal whom I could have completely trusted. But at the same time there was also so much work facing me that even if a courier had been available, he would have had to depart without my letter.... And so whether out of piety and humility you have submitted several points to me, or whether you are doing it with the intention of finally putting an end to my silence concerning your inquiries in three letters[3]—accept my answer here, but on the condition that you will warn me without hesitation wherever I may have carelessly erred against the plumb line of divine wisdom, i.e., against the faith. . . .

In the first letter[4] the question was whether it is allowable to force on unbelieving magistrates the works of the law and thus to teach hypocrisy?. . .

The second question was whether it is allowable to induce magistrates to remove pastors who do not preach the gospel or who falsify it when they preach. . . .

The third question, asked in later letters,[5] was whether a man who has married the wife of his deceased uncle may keep her without the church having to be scandalized thereby. . . .

Fourth,[6] you want to know my views on the only two ceremonies that Christ bequeathed to us—baptism and the Eucharist.[7] I shall speak frankly on both. First, on baptism.[8] We have met twice for debate with certain brethren on the subject of baptism, indeed successfully insofar as the battle and its outcome are concerned. We mutually obligated ourselves most conscientiously to discuss everything according to the norm of love. How well we may have succeeded in this will be known by those who preach and insist that infants should not be touched by baptismal water and who are therefore charged with contentiousness and stubbornness by many faithful Christians. Anyone who understands anything at all about using the Scriptures will readily see baptism to be an initiation[9] both for those who are already believers and for those who are just coming to faith. Concerning those who are already believers, there is henceforth no debate; they can, of course, be baptized. Concerning those who are just coming to faith, however, the controversy is very extensive.[10] There are some, as you know, who call it a terrible and abominable act, quite tangibly ungodly and most insolently shameful; and what especially gives them black bile[11] is when someone, particularly a Christian, baptizes an infant with water. If one presents to them the scriptural reasons, which I shall presently discuss, it makes no more impression on them than if one held beets or herbs[12] in front of their faces.

That baptism may have been instituted also for those who are still to come to faith is very clear in John 1[:26]. When John the Baptist answered the challenging question on whose authority he baptized, he said, "I baptize with water; but there stands one among you whom you know not; he it is who is coming after me, etc." And so John was baptizing in the name of one whom they did not know at all at that time. Here, it is evident that there is no opening for an escape, as if John might have spoken these words only to those people who had been sent out to him, that is, to the priests and Levites, who of course did not know Christ. For soon he added [John 1:30-31], "After me comes a man who was chosen before me; for he was before me. And I knew him not; but that he might be made manifest to Israel, I come baptizing with water." Here we see clearly that John baptized the people in order to reveal to all the one who was to come after him, not into the world, for he was already thirty years old, but that through him human sin would be recognized. He says that he is baptizing in order that Christ would be revealed to the people of Israel. In Acts 19[:4] Luke analyzes this as follows: John baptized people with the baptism of repentance, telling about him who was coming. He baptized therefore on Christ, who was still to come. And lest this may seem unintelligible in any way, I add the point that such was the baptism of John that whoever believed his words when he exclaimed that the ax was already struck at the root and when he claimed to be himself the voice in the desert, warning about the coming Christ [Mt. 3:3, 10] and when he declared himself to be of so little account that he would not be worthy to touch his shoe [Jn. 1:27] and when he promised that this very one was to be the Lamb who was going to atone for the sins of all [Jn. 1:29]— whoever, I say, believed his words were now among the penitent whom he therefore baptized already at that time as if with this sacrament he was pledging them and thus winning them to his coming Lord so that he could then save them. John thus baptized with the intent of giving his people over to the coming Christ. Baptism therefore preceded acquaintance with Jesus. Between the baptism of John and that of Christ I make no distinction; for even though in each of the two it was performed with different words, it was still the same sign or sacrament. Therefore, in my opinion, it must not be overlooked that all who were baptized after coming to know Jesus from the apostles could not after the end of life proceed to the Father before Christ had died and risen. Baptism was thus even for the apostles who had seen the Savior in the flesh the sign of the coming Savior; and if they had died before his own death, they could have been baptized six hundred times and believed ever so strongly in his redemption—they would still not have experienced salvation through Christ until he arose as the conqueror of death. Moreover, if the apostles were baptized at the beginning in order that they might gain temporarily, they were for two reasons baptized first upon the Christ who was to come later: first, because they did not really learn to know him until he arose from the dead, and second, because the resurrection had not yet become fact when they were baptized. And baptism is after all an image of the resurrection, for "we are buried with Christ in baptism, etc." [Rom. 6:4]. With all this I merely want to show that baptism was also given for those who would only later come to faith. They were then baptized for the very purpose that they should later come to know Jesus. But this is exactly what these people with their howling call the worst ungodliness.

So now I want to tell with which places in Scripture I support my view that infants must be baptized. For in such argumentation of ideas one must be able to come up with a sure reference in which our view is very clearly contained. Therefore, hear the brief passage in Romans 4[:11]: Circumcision was the sign of a faith that was already there. But it was always performed eight days after birth on infants who would only many years later come to faith. Baptism then took the place of circumcision.[13] It follows then that baptism, like circumcision, should be performed also on those who will not come to faith until later. Of course, secondary circumstances of place, person, time, and method must be taken into consideration. All of this is clear and plain, except the middle clause, that baptism is the Christian's circumcision. But this assertion is also as clearly stated when Paul in Colossians 2[:11] says, "In whom also you are circumcised with the circumcision made without hands, by putting off the body of the sins of the flesh by the circumcision of Christ, buried with him in baptism." In regard to the meaning of this passage, it is very clear what Paul meant to say here, namely, that he who becomes a Christian is a new creation [2 Cor. 15:17]. But I want to come back to what I was going to say. What, I ask, could have been said more clearly than this, that the circumcision of Christ has been performed on us when we are buried with him in baptism, etc. [Rom. 6:4]. Consequently, the circumcision of Christ is also administered to infants on the authority of God's Word, not the pope's, just like earlier the circumcision of Abraham.

Moreover, Christ commanded the disciples to let the little children come to him, for of such is the kingdom of heaven; and he blessed them [Mt. 19:14-15]. If anyone then says on that ground that infants should not be baptized in the name of the Father, the Son, and the Holy Ghost, he is after all forbidding them to come to Christ. Against this, our opponents marshal this argument into the field: to be sure, Jesus commanded that the children be brought to him, but we read nothing about his baptizing them. Therefore, they should not be baptized. Our reply to that is: Christ never baptized anyone, as is seen in John 4[:2], "Jesus himself baptized not, but his disciples" baptized in his name. Then it would follow that no one should be baptized; but everyone sees well enough how senseless that is. No, for the present, "of such is the kingdom" is still valid. When we hear further that Peter in the house of Cornelius saw that they had received the Holy Ghost and then said, "Can any man forbid water, that these should not be baptized, who have received the Holy Ghost as well as we?" [Acts 10:47], then surely we can also say, "Since they are also God's children, who can forbid baptizing them with water?" But then they flare up again and say that Christ said "of such," not "of these"; he was speaking there more of people who are like children than of the children themselves. But they fail to see that such an interpretation is contradicted by the following words: "And he took them up into his arms, put his hands upon them, and blessed them" [Mk. 10:16]. Whom? Those, I suppose, who were like children! That is the way of the quarrelsome: they must always say one thing more even if they no longer know what. Here Christ did two things —he took the children up in his arms as his own possession, honored them by the touch of his hand, and sincerely prayed for them; but at the same time, as was his custom, he moved from them to us to lift us out of the material and visible world into the heavenly. But those people must tell me one thing: What, after all, does this have to do with faith, without which, as they say, no one may be baptized? They will no doubt answer: This, because we have become certain of being God's children through faith, we live throughout our entire earthly life in complete guiltlessness after the example of Christ, in order that one day we may enter into his kingdom. And so living in humility and blamelessness means to live a Christian life? Certainly. But Christ teaches that we must learn both humility and blamelessness from children. From this it is evident, therefore that children are what we must still become. And so, if we who are God's have difficulty before we have become as innocent as children, it is surely clear that Christ was speaking of the children themselves and not simply in parables of such as are like children. He placed their life before us as an ideal. And if it is the image of God, how much more it is then the ideal of God. If it is the children of God who are meant here, who would then, as Peter said, want to say they should not be baptized with water?

Paul also says in 1 Corinthians 7[:14] that the children of a marriage in which one spouse is a believer are holy, and Paul generally calls those holy who are believers. If then the children of parents of whom only one was a believer are nonetheless counted among the holy—that is, believers—who will say that one must not baptize with water those persons who are already holy, and are already what we are still to become? Some, to be sure, understand that Paul here calls the children of Christians holy in order that the parents could stay with them, which would not have been the case if they had been unclean simply because they were born of unbelieving parents. To this view, if I may say so, I cannot assent; for Gentiles who had been converted from pagans into Christians did not have such Jewish pride; that was certainly true of the Corinthians. It would never have occurred to them to feel aversion toward unbelievers, for they had even eaten with them at the sacrificial meals until someone took offense [1 Cor. 8:1ff.]. But when it was said in a preceding verse, "The unbelieving wife is sanctified by the believing husband" [1 Cor. 7:14], that should not be misconstrued as to make "sanctified" mean "made pure and clean" in the sense of fleshly purity; we must think of it as meaning that an unbelieving wife can be brought to faith by a believing husband, as has often happened. Right afterward he says, "For what knowest thou, O wife, whether thou shalt save thy husband?" [1 Cor. 7:16]. Now, of course, one person cannot save another; he is therefore speaking of conversion to faith. But even if we were to admit that this, or perhaps that, is the meaning of this passage, surely the child of a Christian is in a different situation from one whose father is an unbeliever; it will, of course, be in the same situation if the father denies his faith. Thus, the child will always be better off if it is brought up in the faith. But at the beginning we said that those who were only about to become believers had already received water baptism, as, for example, the disciples who had been baptized by John—assuming that we agree that they were indeed baptized. Accordingly, children who are to be brought up in the faith can likewise be baptized.

I shall now briefly respond to the replies of the opposite side and open up that knot. The first is: Nowhere do we read that the apostles baptized children with water.[14] Consequently, in the absence of a specific Word and example, they should not be baptized. I answer: The Word is not lacking, but you do not grant its validity, namely, that baptism is our outward circumcision [Rom. 4:11]. I am saying two things with reference to outward circumcision: it is of no value as long as we are not inwardly circumcised; and in reverse, what I say of inward circumcision, that is for the time being only the outward circumcision, which points to the inward; the outward preceded the inward. Similar wording should be used with reference to baptism; even Paul speaks in those terms. Nor is there a lack of examples, as we saw above when I wrote about John, who baptized upon Christ when he was yet to come. In addition, Paul baptized the household of Stephanas (1 Corinthians 1[:16]) and also the jailer with his whole family [Acts 16[:33]; in both of these instances there were, more likely than not, some children. It is also probable that there were in those families some adults who had neither known nor had faith until that very day, but nevertheless all of them became followers of the Lord.

The second objection they make is this: When the apostles baptized, they first examined the applicants as to their faith.[15] I answer: Occasionally such examination did in fact take place, but sometimes it did not. You are simply whispering a lie into the minds of the simpleminded when you say that the apostles always required faith. No; following Christ's example they did not, for in some instances he asked those he was about to heal concerning their faith, in others he did not. In Matthew 9[:28] he asked two blind men who begged him to restore their sight if they believed he could do it, and when they said Yes, he said it would happen according to their faith, and their vision was immediately restored to them [Mt. 9:29]. Likewise in John 9[:1ff.] he gave sight to a man born blind who did not know him at all; for when Christ faced him later he asked, "Do you believe on the Son of God?" the previously blind man answered, "Who is he, Lord, that I might believe on him?" [Jn. 9:35ff.]. Here the sign came before faith. This can also be considered to have been the case when Jesus looked upon the faith of the men who let the paralytic down through the roof to be healed [Mt. 9:2].

Their third objection is this: "He who believes and is baptized shall be saved; but he who believes not shall be damned" [Mk. 16:16].[16] Faith must therefore be present first, or one might just as well baptize a raven. I answer: This verse cannot be applied to children, for just before these words, he said, "Preach the gospel to every creature" [Mk. 16:15], and then "he who believes"—that is, when he has heard the gospel. But since it can neither be preached to infants nor heard by them, it clearly follows that they were not meant in this admittedly very important passage, but only those who hear the preaching and then either believe it or evade it.

Fourth, they bring this argument into the battlefield: It would be a far more powerful and effective act if everyone openly confessed his faith before he is dipped into the water. I answer: It will be easier to learn to know faith if he has been baptized as an infant than if that is not the case. For the two principal vices innate in the family of men—namely, wantonness and insolence[17]—can be more easily restrained in a baptized child than in an unbaptized one. For if parents are shamelessly permissive[18] with a shamelessly wanton child, the nearest relatives will feel it their duty to warn the parents as well as the children, saying, "Are you raising your child[19] in such a way that all the brethren[20] will be offended and our God blasphemed?" And then if the rebuked child should perhaps grow bold and protest, "Who am I anyway? I will be a Christian whenever I like; what concern of yours is it?" then most certainly the situation can be more easily handled if the child has been baptized than if he has not. Infant baptism, like circumcision before it, is a sacrament by which we are, for the time being, obligated to learn the law of the Lord and to ennoble our lives, but by which the parents are at the same time obligated for the kind of training that clearly shows: you are the offspring of Christian parents and will, in accord with that status, lead a clean life, just as one could see in the circumcision of those who were Abraham's descendants whether it was of the flesh or of the spirit. But if those people believe that something is still missing—namely, that each openly confesses his faith on his own impulse, we say, that will be easily dealt with at the Lord's Supper if it is properly observed. For it is after all simply a solemn thanksgiving to God by those who by the death of Christ feel awakened to new life and rejoice in it; and yet it is at the same time the most intimate union of the body—that is, of believers in Christ; and if we observe in it that spirit, each one will surely examine himself inwardly as to whether he is right-minded toward Christ and toward his members. And if he is, then he should eat that bread in the common giving of thanks as a cement and sacrament or symbol of union, and shall drink of the cup, while being aware that it would be the worst wickedness to repudiate this obligation, this bond and this body.

In brief, concerning infant baptism, I need to give this one warning—we should not expect of baptism what only the grace of God can do—that is, we should not think that the soul is cleansed by the baptismal water (which we surely do not imagine), but solely by the teaching of the divine Spirit. So we read in 1 Peter 3[:21] that the Spirit reconciles us to God in the same way as the flood cleansed the whole world, not, to be sure, in washing the body, but by causing the conscience to examine itself and [for the person] to be quite clear within himself of his intent toward God. Thus, if man's salvation is dependent on the grace of God and if what Peter says here about the answer of a good conscience (still they are nonetheless assured of God's grace)—I say we then have no reason to argue so violently about the outward sign. Such quarrels result only in offense and injury. But the devil[21] is full of sly tricks; in strange ways he incites us to self-love and a greedy desire for honor and whispers to us that it is the highest honor to stand undefeated. May the merciful God deliver us from his devices! And if this baptism is really such a blasphemy, may he bring it about that we baptize no longer,[22] but otherwise may he instill the spirit of peace into the hearts of contentious people that these men may take what they have expended on this conflict until now and turn it to the cause of peace and quiet.

May Christ preserve his church.

Zurich, December 16, 1524.

> Yours from the heart,
> Huldrych Zwingli

Original: Staatsarchiv Zurich, E.I.3.1 (Zwingli-Schriften) No. 10
Transcription: ZW, VII, No. 355

67B
The Mantz Petition of Defense[1]
Zurich, between December 13 and 28, 1524[2]

For many decades scholars ascribed to Grebel the authorship of the following petition, the original of which had neither signature nor date. It was written in a German script that is not Grebel's; but a note at the end in still another handwriting—"Con. Greb. de Anabaptismo"—was the chief source for the confusion. In an article in Zwingliana *(IX, 1, pp. 139-49), Walter Schmid demonstrated conclusively on the basis of internal evidence that the petition belonged not to Grebel but to Felix Mantz. It is included in the present collection because it was prompted by the impasse of the Tuesday Disputations, as its content clearly implies.*

One can discern Mantz's attempt to achieve what the Tuesday Disputations had failed to achieve—a point-by-point refutation of Zwingli's train of thought. The latter, as we said in the introduction to the previous document, was reiterated by Zwingli in his letter to Lambert; and thus, by reference to these two documents, we can reconstruct the main arguments that were orally and only partially presented for and against infant baptism in the Tuesday Disputations.

The petition also correlates with comments in Grebel's Letter 67, above, particularly the comment, "They summoned and abused the simplest, yet nearest one to God, as God and the world know how; but with the help of God and his truth, he has put their wisdom to shame" (67/301/33ff.). In this comment, Grebel may have had Mantz and his "Protest and Defense" in mind (although an alternative hypothesis was given in 67/fn.13). The Anabaptists seldom had time for systemmatizing their theology, and the Mantz petition is a good example of the way their doctrines were articulated mainly in antithesis to the arguments of the Reformers.

Wise, considerate, gracious, dear lords and brethren:[3]

It is well known to your Honors that many strange opinions have appeared. First, some hold that newborn infants are to be baptized as they come from the womb and that this can be proved from the Holy Scriptures, others that infant baptism is wrong and false, and has arisen from and been invented by that antichrist, the pope and his adherents, which is true as we know and believe from Holy Writ. Among whom I too have been held and accused by some as a rioter and wretch,[4] which is however an unjust and ungracious charge that can never be raised and proved on the basis of the truth, for neither have I engaged in rioting nor in any way taught or encouraged anything that has led or might lead to rioting (which all those with whom I have ever been associated can testify of me). For this reason the charge is unjust. Since, however, I have been accused of being such a person, it becomes necessary for me to give to you, my gracious and dear lords, an account and reason for my faith, as follows.

I should have thought that all this would have been clear to you simply from the truth itself, for your shepherds[5] have often asserted that the Scriptures, to which we are not to add or subtract anything,[6] must be allowed to speak for themselves. Although this was the intention, it was never carried out and we have never been given opportunity to speak, nor has the Scripture been heard, for our speech is cut off in the throat as soon as they suppose that we are about to speak the truth. They interrupt and demand proof from the Scripture although they ought rather to furnish such proof and stand by the truth—God knows that they act thus![7] They know full well,[8] much better than one could ever demonstrate, that Christ did not teach infant baptism and that the apostles did not practice it, but that, in accord with the true meaning of baptism, only those should be baptized who reform, take on a new life, lay aside sins, are buried with Christ, and rise with him from baptism in newness of life, etc.

Further Y[our] H[onors], for God's sake and for the sake of the common name which we bear with each other, I wish to beseech you, having put down persons, to sort out earnestly, diligently, and amicably, the clear, authentic truth which has been opened to us through the Word, judging well what is presented there, not letting it offend you for a moment, for, although it is well to forgive others, it is no small matter to practice the only two ceremonies left to us by Christ[9] otherwise than as Christ commanded.

In the first place God in his eternal decree ordained for his only Son a forerunner who should prepare the way by pointing out to his people their sins, and calling upon them to forsake them and reform, for the ax lay at the root of the tree, and everyone who did not bring forth good fruit would be cut down and cast into the fire.[10] To those who wished to reform, he showed the Lamb of God that taketh away the sin of the world[11] and also baptized them that their sins might be forgiven in the coming suffering of Jesus Christ, and that they might henceforth with changed lives bring forth proper fruit. All this you will find in Matthew 3[v. 10], Mark 1[v. 9f.], Luke 3[v. 9], John 1:4.[12]

Just as John baptized only those who reformed, forsook evil works, and did good, as is clearly shown [in the Scripture], so also the apostles received from Christ at his ascension a commandment in these words: "To me is given all power in heaven and on earth, go ye therefore and teach all nations and baptize them,"[13] and in Mark: "He who believes and is baptized shall be saved,"[14] as was done by Peter, as we have it in the Acts of the Apostles,[15] in the 10th chapter, where, as he was sent for by Cornelius and asked him why he was sent there,[16] Peter began to declare to them

312

how Christ came, taught, healed the sick, was slain and rose again.

Then follows further: "Him God raised up the third day and gave him to be made manifest, not to all the people but unto witnesses who were chosen before of God, even to us, who ate and drank with him after he rose from the dead. And he charged us to preach unto the people, and to testify that this is he who is ordained of God to be the Judge of the living and the dead. To him bear all the prophets witness, that through his name every one who believes on him shall receive remission of sins. While Peter yet spoke these words, the Holy Spirit fell on all them who heard the word. And they of the circumcision who believed were amazed, as many as came with Peter, because on the Gentiles also was poured out the gift of the Holy Spirit, etc."[17] From which words one can clearly see how the apostles understood the command of Christ from Matthew, as related above, namely, that as they went forth they should teach all nations, that to Christ is given all power in heaven and in earth, and that forgiveness of sins in his name should be given to everyone who, believing on his name, should do righteous works from a changed heart. After the receiving of this teaching and the descent of the Holy Spirit, which was evidenced to those who had heard the word of Peter by the speaking in tongues,[18] they were thereafter poured over with water,[19] meaning that just as they were cleansed within by the coming of the Holy Spirit, so they also were poured over with water externally to signify for the inner cleansing and dying to sin.

And as evidence that this is the meaning of baptism, we read in the 22nd chapter of the Acts of the Apostles, where Paul tells what happened to him on the road to Damascus, and how Ananias came and spoke these words, "And he said, 'The Lord God has appointed you to know his will, and to see that it is right, and to hear a voice from his mouth. For you will be a witness for him to all men of what you have seen and heard. And now why do you tarry? Arise and be baptized, and wash away your sins, calling on the name of the Lord, and now what more do you lack than to be baptized and have your sins washed away after the name of the Lord has been called upon.' "[20] From these words we clearly see what baptism is and when it shall be practiced, namely, upon one who having been converted through God's Word and having changed his heart now henceforth desires to live in newness of life, as Paul clearly shows in the epistle to the Romans, the sixth [chapter], dead to the old life, circumcised in his heart, having died to sin with Christ, having been buried with him in baptism and arisen with him again in newness of life, etc.[21] To apply such things as have just been related to children is without any and against all Scriptures.

The entire New Testament Scripture is full of such passages and their

313

like, from which I have now clearly learned and know for sure that baptism is nothing else than a dying of the old man and a putting on of a new,[22] [that] Christ commanded to baptize those who had been taught, [that] the apostles baptized none except those who had been taught of Christ, and [that] nobody was baptized without external evidence and certain testimony or desire. And whoever says or teaches otherwise does something which he cannot prove with Scripture; for I should like to hear anyone who, out of true clear Scripture can prove to me that John, Christ, the apostles baptized children or taught that they should be baptized.

Then since this cannot be proved, no more talk is necessary to show that infant baptism is against God, a disgrace to Christ, and a treading-under-feet[23] of his only true eternal Word, and is also against the example of Christ, who was baptized at thirty years, [although] circumcised at eight days.[24] Now Christ has given us an example that as he has done so also ought we to do. For this reason I have entreated Y[our] H[onors] cordially and most urgently to receive my writing for the best, for truly to me honor, name, fame, do not matter, nor do I do this out of envy or hate as I am accused,[25] but only because it is the eternal truth of God which no one can overcome, nor may an angel from heaven[26] teach other than is expressed above. And the eternally true Word of God will sing in the heart of each one that this is the truth, whether he be against it or not.

I want to admonish Y[our] H[onors] also that you should remember the contention over the incident of the idols, which bound to the time was first right and then wrong, on account of which his life was lost.[27] [I] am sure that M[aster] Ul[rich Zwingli] has exactly this same understanding of baptism and that he understands it much better than we.[28] [I] do not know, however, for what reason he does not declare himself. [I] do, however, know for sure that if the only Word be allowed to speak for itself freely and simply, no one will be able to withstand it, and that God will bring to naught the devices of the ungodly. Just as it was possible with respect to other matters and abominations, so it will go all right in this case, if only freedom is given and the truth is treated as truth. If however it is said that it makes no difference as to how baptism is practiced, this cannot be proved from the Scripture. But what will be proved is that God wills that we keep his commandments and ceremonies, as he has commanded us. We have also many examples of how God severely punished the transgression of the external commandments, as for example the two sons of Aaron [who] were consumed,[29] and countless other examples to tell of which would be too lengthy here.

I wish to admonish Y[our] H[onors] also of this that civil and public law will be neither weakened nor improved by anything touching baptism.

314

For this reason I entreat you most earnestly that you do not stain your hands with innocent blood,[30] supposing that you do God a service should you kill or exile persons, lest wholly innocent blood be required of your hands.

Be Y[our] H[onors] also entreated of this: Since Master Ulrich thinks he can prove from Scripture, which I nevertheless do not believe, this same infant baptism which has been fabricated by popes,[31] and which is even contrary to the earliest popes and their constitution as is clearly to be seen from the histories, and has been instituted and contrived by men, so I wish to entreat Y[our] worthy H[onors] most earnestly that he[32] do this same in writing, as he has heretofore offered to do to all those with whom he has been dealing from time to time. Then I will listen well and reply to him. To speak is not pleasant for me, nor is it easy,[33] for he has already so often overwhelmed me with so much speaking[34] that I was not able to answer or could not find room to answer because of his long speeches. It would also avoid much wrangling and discord[35] that comes from discussing things about which he supposes me to be extremely opinionated.[36]

Therefore do I call upon you, my gracious, dear lords and brethren, as a citizen, and testify herewith that I am of this very view and understanding and not without special basis in the holy and divine Scriptures. Now should there be anyone, whoever he may be, who really believes from the divine Scriptures that young, newborn children should be baptized, let him give evidence of the same to you, my lords, written and in writing. I will give answer to each one. I cannot dispute very well, neither do I wish to do so,[37] but only wish to deal with the holy Scriptures and whether they plainly read concerning baptism that young, newborn children were baptized by the apostles according to the injunction of Christ. I believe, yea, I know, that no man on earth can prove that.

Original: Staatsarchiv Zurich, E.II.340, fol.8 & 9
Transcription: Muralt-Schmid, No. 16
Translation: Taken from Correll-Bender, 1

67C
Zwingli's Treatise on Rebels and Rebellion
Zurich, between December 7 and 28, 1524[1]

When Grebel wrote to Vadian that "he, Zwingli, is writing also about rebels or rebellion; that may well hit us" (67/302/7-9), he was referring to Zwingli's booklet, Welche Ursach gebind ze Ufruren *(Those Who Give Cause for Rebellion). For the selection of an English word for* Aufruhr, *rang-*

315

ing from a mild "disturbance" to a capital "sedition," see 67/fn.20.

Despite its vitriolic language, the tract can be read as an earnest attempt to preserve the unity that is being threatened by the opponents of infant baptism and other "rebels." In order to do that, Zwingli is willing to make certain concessions: the biblical case for infant baptism is admittedly weak; his differences with the dissenters are not on essential points but on incidentals; and unity is still possible if they can overcome their spiritual pride.

Those who give cause for rebellion. Who the true rebels are. And how Christian unity and peace may be achieved. By Huldrych Zwingli at Zurich, etc. Read to the end and do not evaluate it alone by how severe it is, but how true it is. . . .

The first party[2] are those who listen to the gospel only out of envy and hate for the papacy. God's Word falls on them like seed falling on a rock[3]. . . .

The second party of those who give offense toward the gospel and occasion for unbelievers to rebel are those who go so far as if it were permitted to sin. But Paul warns earnestly against this in Galatians 5: "Brethren! You have been called unto liberty; only use not that liberty for an occasion to the flesh, but by love serve one another."[4] . . .

The third party, who do most of all to bring hatred upon the gospel, are those who search it only to try to find ways to refuse to pay anyone that is his—whether interest, tithes, or other obligations. Against that, however, Paul's clear word in Romans 13 proclaims, "Give to all men what you owe them."[5] . . .

The fourth party who bring hatred upon the gospel are those who are more inflated with knowledge of the gospel than ignited with love. They exercise themselves more with quarreling than with gentle Christian living. They want to condemn and teach all men but do not teach themselves. They see in others what is lacking in their own Christian lives, but in themselves they see no fault. In their minds the way they act is the right way; where they tread, there is a violet or a rose. If Momus[6] could see them, he would probably also say, "Their eyes are misplaced." For if they are to see first their inward state, their eyes should be turned inward. But since they are turned outward, they do nothing but judge and condemn those who are before them and quarrel about external things. First they reject the state, then they want to keep the state; and yet no one in government is a Christian.[7] Now they want to have their own church,[8] later the government shall not use force to protect the preaching of the gospel. First the misleading priests should be put to death,[9] before long they should be permitted to preach freely. If one baptizes infants they cry out that there is no greater abomination, atrocity, or sin in Christendom than baptizing infants. And they daily bring forth more silly arguments than Africa produces strange beasts. But still they do not tame their tongues from slander, gossip, envy, wrath, strife, and hatred, but they say that whoever does as they do has a just spirit. They are too good to greet anyone they meet who displeases them. And if someone else who talks to everybody greets those who resist the gospel, they immediately attack from leather[10] with the words of John the Divine, "Do not greet such a one."[11] . . . Nor do they consider that Paul in 2 Timothy 2 defines serving God as avoiding verbal strife,[12] which is of no benefit but contributes to the misleading of those who hear. They argue in all the corners, streets, shops, wherever they can manage to do it. And if one opposes them in this and forbids it, they have fight-houses[13] of their own where they slyly meet in secret, sit in judgment and condemn everybody. And when they have finished that, they pour such bitterness upon one another that one could often bathe in the abundance of gall. Such a miserable, perverted, bitter mind is known among them as spirit, though it is nothing but a saturnine, melancholy carnality that inspires such envy, bitterness, and quarrelsomeness. It cannot abide where there is peace and longsuffering. It strives less determinedly to master itself than to control others. They are unable therefore to be happy with anyone at all, not even with themselves. If we teach that our despair is to be comforted and made happy with the sure mercy of God which has assured us that Christ Jesus died for our sins and has become our righteousness, they say: You preach grace too much. And they have no rest unless they can lead those who are now won for God back into doubt or complete despair, from which I fear they will fall into ruin. If we teach them openly from the pulpit, they run at once to the preacher and ask if he was referring to them. Consider whether or not this is the weakness of the flesh, pure carnal lack of strength that refuses to be touched. I dwell as much longer in eradicating their faults in the hope that they will be willing to learn that their spirit is nothing but carnality which, however, has the Scriptures in its hands and on its tongue. . . . I therefore admonish these brethren to face the devil directly and not accept any suggestion that anything is spiritual when it is pure carnality. He[14] can do it easily. He has thus suppressed the gospel and has even dared to suppress it again, for it seems to me that he is again pretending to give you justification by the works of the law, a religion of works, which is the source of all hypocrisy. However boldly you outwardly contend and accuse, if you would fight against the old Adam, your pious living, Christian walk, and ardent love would much more destroy what must be removed and build what must be built up than all the contention and slander, as Peter indeed teaches you.[15] Otherwise you are among those who also cause much injury to simple folk who say, "See, they are also learned, and speak against the government and the baptism of infants, etc.," whereas not one of them is learned. . . .

Why do you continually rage about purely external matters? Indeed, if your diligence is only that one live in a Christian manner, you must not infuse those who are not living in a Christian manner with disparagement and accusation, but with gentleness and unceasing love. In short, this is my request of you, that you work as hard on yourselves to kill the greatest monster and poison to Christian living—namely, spiritual pride. . . .

Before we change the subject, we must admonish the children of God not to stumble because of the contention to be seen at present even among some Christian scholars, but to hold themselves to what they have received. When you see two excellent scholars disputing with each other, hold to the one who has a clear Word of God which he understands correctly on the basis of the faith; thus you will not be following a man but God. For example, there is argument even among Christians as to whether there should be images or not. For this problem, look at Exodus 20,[16] and you will clearly find that we should not have them. Then people try to introduce much human, false argumentation on how the images teach us and stimulate us to worship and to courage. All of this takes place without a basis in the faith. Where there is true faith it knows well that it did not come from the idols and images on the walls but from the drawing of God's Spirit. It also knows that its God is invisible and cannot be represented by an image. Thereby he is to be distinguished from false gods to whom ornaments and delusive images have been erected. For these reasons and faith the apostles also expelled idols from the hearts and eyes of men. First Corinthians 12 and Thessalonians 1 and 1 John 5.[17]

Secondly, if you see the one cite a Word of God that is plain and clear in its one meaning, and the other cite another verse equally clear but in obvious contradiction to the first, then consider which ascribed more honor to God and which to man. For example, if you see two men arguing about the freedom of the will or about works, one of whom cites a verse that sets the will free and the other a verse that says that we can do nothing without God, and therefore all things take place by his order, wisdom, and foresight, then follow the one who gives God the honor and ascribes to him all deeds, glory, and honor. And do not be surprised that he[18] himself ascribes the reward to us and the choice to our will, for it is by his grace that he ascribes to us what is really his, just as he also ascribes to himself the sin that is really ours.

Thirdly, it often happens that in permanent outward matters no clear and plain word is found in the New Testament. Where tension arises in these things, according to Christ's teaching, we are set over Moses and the prophets, lest he rebuke us with the Sadducees, "You err because you do not understand the Scriptures,"[19] Matthew 22. We should therefore learn from the divine Word what is to be done to solve the difficulties in the existing circumstances, as we have proved from Scripture in *Choice of Food.*[20] For example, marriage is an eternal necessary usage. But as to the way it is to be entered into, we have no statement in the New Testament. So in Leviticus 18[21] we find a criterion, to wit, that it should be done with the consent of the father and mother (examples in many places). Yet we do not find that children acting against their express will and public objection are living in adultery. Another example to show my mind and rationale: when speaking of the baptism of infants, those who refuse to baptize them have no clear prohibition against baptizing infants. On the other hand, those who baptize them have no clear word commanding that they be baptized.[22] (I say this simply to grant this point to the obstinate so that the two spears will be of equal length, lest they bring up Matthew 15, "They worship me in vain, etc."[23] and "Every plant that my heavenly Father has not planted, etc."[24] and they counter with, "Go therefore and teach all nations, baptizing them in the name, etc.")[25] Much strife is generated out of this from both sides, even though the latter proof-texting is the clearer. (Since this is not the place to debate doctrine, I will let it pass.) Hence we must inquire of the Scriptures. Now, we do not find in the New Testament that infant baptism is either commanded or forbidden. For by raising the objection that the apostles did not baptize infants, and therefore they should not be baptized, they prove nothing; else I could also argue: the apostles baptized no one in Calcutta, hence nobody in Calcutta should be baptized.[26] We must therefore see whether there is anything in the Old Testament about it. We find nothing on baptism, but we do on the practice followed in the place of baptism, namely, circumcision.[27] That is a sign of preceding faith which Abraham had in his uncircumcised state, as Romans 4 says.[28] Further, this sign was given the infants on the eighth day,[29] when they doubtless knew nothing of faith; but circumcision is nevertheless a sign of preceding faith. That baptism was instituted in the place of circumcision is proved by the usage that each was a sign of faith. Paul also touches on the same point in Colossians 2: "In whom (Christ) you are circumcised with the circumcision made without hands in that you have put off the body of sin by the circumcision of Christ, that you are buried with him in baptism, etc."[30] I know, of course, what Paul is speaking of. I quote this passage simply to show that we know a verse that shows baptism as taking the place of circumcision. Accordingly, it follows from this that as circumcision was given to infants in the Old Testament and baptism has come to take the place of circumcision, the children of Christians should also be baptized. For, in brief, all who are to be brought up to grow together in one faith need a common symbol no less than Abraham's seed. Those who oppose the baptism of infants have accomplished one good thing, that we cannot attribute to this or to any other sacrament the remission of sins, but that each is a sign of God's elect, as Peter himself has said in [epistle] 1, chapter 3.[31] Besides, it is better to assume that the apostles baptized the infants of believers than not, as Paul says in 1 Corinthians 1: "I also baptized the household of Stephanas."[32] And in Acts 16: "When Lydia was baptized with her household, etc."[33] And soon after this: "He was baptized that very hour, he and all his household."[34] It is more likely than not that in such households there were children. I wanted to point this out briefly as an example because I have discovered that the contenders, who are so spiritual, do not mention to the simpleminded whom they lure away from infant baptism this interpretation of mine, so they can hear it from my mouth. Not that infant baptism is so important to me, but when I gauge the infirmity of all people, I find no abomination in this—as they scream, as though there had never been a greater sin than infant baptism—but rather a succession to God-fearing Abraham, who circumcised Isaac on the eighth day,[35] and I believe also to the apostles. And if I saw any dishonor to God or hindrance to Christian living resulting from it, I would not hesitate to change my mind. But since this is not the case, why does the opposing party contend the point as though it were the sum total of the faith? Our eyes also want to see, for otherwise Christ would not have instituted baptism and the blessed bread. It is therefore to be feared that if infant baptism were discontinued, we too would cry for circumcision like the Christians of Antioch and like it is still done by the Marranos in Spain.[36] The children of Christians are children of God, Matthew 18 and 1 Corinthians 7.[37] Who wants to advocate that they should not also bear the sign of the children of God, as Peter says in Acts 10?[38] The counter argument that it would be good for children to grow to a mature age before they are baptized so that they can confess their faith for themselves is more of a contention than a requirement; for although one teaches the children, the law begins to grow in them just as in anyone. And when they are matured in the faith the law has died in them and they to the flesh or to themselves. Then if they have already received the sign, it is happening to them as to the blind man in John 9.[39] He was also illuminated but did not yet know the Son of God. And the obligation that they want to see in baptism is becoming fulfilled in the sacrament of the body of Christ. There the person is to show himself with his faith and assume his obligation with other members of Christ. That is the test of which Paul speaks in

1 Corinthians 11.[40] So much for that. The world also wants its children to be marked with a sign. Therefore, now that I have begun to warn, I repeat: Let no believer permit himself to be weakened in faith—even when the learned quarrel violently among themselves about externals—but persist firmly in the faith that we are made children of God by the Son of God; and upon the faith which we have in the mercy of God our Father test all questions of dispute as to whether or not they are in agreement with the faith. Then we shall see at once who provokes wanton foolishness or who does not.

Original Publication: Zwingli's *Wer Ursache gebe zu Aufruhr,* published 12/28/1524
Transcription: ZW, III, No. 42, pp. 374-412

67D
Vadian to Grebel
St. Gallen, December 28, 1524

Apart from the two Dedikationepisteln *(#A and #1A, above), document No. 67D is the only personal letter from Vadian to Grebel to have been preserved. And as his chief biographer, Werner Näf, writes, "what extraordinary good fortune!" The best qualities that Näf, Staub, Ninck, and Rupp have observed in Vadian come out in this letter: his transcendence of demagoguery, his knack for seeing two sides of a quarrel, and his humility of mind in the face of the unfathomable truths of God. But this letter was written months before the followers of Grebel in his own city caused him to abandon his attitude of tolerance and to castigate the work of Grebel and his movement in the bitter language that we will find in the last document in our collection.*

However, at this stage just before the great year of truth testing commences, Vadian laments the emerging sense of alienation expressed by Grebel toward him, foresees a future time when their differences over baptism can be resolved, and asks Grebel to make some allowance for Vadian's "wretched understanding of the truth of these things." His closing declaration of openness to be counseled undoubtedly accounts not just for the admonitions with which Grebel responds in his final letter to Vadian (No. 70) but also for Grebel's expression of deep appreciation for "the kindnesses you have shown me" (70/378/25).

It is not known whether Vadian retained a copy of his letter to Grebel, or whether the original was somehow returned to him; but there is evidence that Grebel received it because certain parts of Letter 70 (379/37-380/18) reply to it. Since Letter 70 was not written until May 30, it is possible that he did not receive it until sometime after Letter 68 was written; or perhaps he read it when he visited Vadian for the last time during the pre-Easter season. At least there is nothing in the Grebel to Vadian letter of January 14 that replies to it; and one must assume that it had not yet been delivered.

My greeting with devotion as I am able.[1]
Dear brother-in-law Conrad.

I have received your last written letter.[2] It surprises me that you assume that I get much pleasure out of shaming you.[3] That is not my way at all. My wish concerning you would be and always has been that you conduct yourself with humble propriety[4] toward Zwingli and Leo[5] and not be so demanding or contentious, in the awareness that they are the ones who are engaged to promote the Word of truth and yet who are not totally able to throw out and abruptly[6] abolish everything that came into misuse through so many years. That is practically what the conflict over baptism is all about. With time it will undoubtedly be regulated according to the witness of the Word of truth, as will other things. For this cause I would always be especially glad to see peace between you and a healing understanding. But if you intend to proceed radically,[7] I cannot prevent you or others. Nevertheless, as a kinsman I want always to have admonished you to proceed with discretion and meekness as befits the gospel and not imagine that I am shaming you whenever I do not immediately subscribe to everything. And also, some allowance is to be made for me when I have a wretched understanding of the truth of these things and am ready to allow myself to be counseled. Therefore, take all these things for the best and be commended herewith to God.

Given at St. Gallen on the commemoration of the [Christ] child, in the 24th year.

Joachim von Watt, D[octor].

Send me whatever new comes from Zwingli or Leo. I will reimburse you. Further, let me know what you intend to do with the booklet[8] I sent you.

To the upright, learned Conrad Grebel, citizen of Zurich, my dear brother-in-law.

Original: Stadtbibliothek (Vadiana) St. Gallen, VB.II.219
Transcription: VB, III, No. 414

67E
Hegenwald to Grebel
Wittenberg, January 1, 1525

The fact that not too much is known about Erhart Hegenwald may be the result in part from his own aversion to recognition. As he writes in the following letter, "I do not want to make myself a name on earth nor do I want to ... be considered as one who is attempting to intervene in these matters unless it should be that God would definitely impel me thereto through convincing coercion" (329/40ff.). He was once a teacher in the Pfäffers

Monastery, canton of St. Gallen, and in the Schola Carolina in Zurich. Thus, he was the local schoolmaster at the time he attended the First Doctrinal Disputation in Zurich in January 1523 and served as its recorder and author of its minutes (see 51A, above).

In the present letter Hegenwald speaks protectively of Vadian and the preachers in St. Gallen, and it would seem that he knew them personally as he did Grebel. He also mentions correspondence with Oswald Myconius about baptism. Although his letter to Myconius is lost, a reference to it in Zwingli's Elenchus *suggests that it dealt in part with the meaning of Acts 8:12 as it applied to the question of infant baptism (see Epi. C/494/22-25, 33-34).*

It is known that Hegenwald was a student at the University of Wittenberg from 1524 to 1526 and was in personal touch with Luther as he reports at the end of the present letter. In a brief biography in the Allgemeine Deutsche Biographie, *it is reported that "Erhard Hegewaldt" earned the MD degree at Wittenberg and was serving as city physician in Frankfurt a.M. in 1540. Another brief note in* The Lutheran Encyclopedia *reports that "Erhardt Hegenwalt" was the author of the hymn, "Erbarm dich mein, O Herre Gott," published in the Erfurt* Enchiridion *(1524), translated by Coverdale in 1539 with the English title "O God, be merciful to me," and again by Jacobi in 1722 with the title "Show pity, Lord, O Lord, forgive."*

As lines 3-5 of the first page below reveal, there was more correspondence between Hegenwald and Grebel than this one extant letter. There had been a prior letter from Hegenwald to Grebel and at least one from Grebel to Hegenwald, to which the latter was now replying. And as 330/14-16 reveals, there was prior personal contact between the two in Zurich when Hegenwald had tried to prevent Grebel from writing against Vadian and the preachers of St. Gallen (331/3-4, 6-7). It is barely possible that the two met at the First Zurich Disputation; but given the content of the present letter, it is more likely that they met in Zurich sometime following Grebel's disillusionment with the Reformation program after October 1523. Since there is no evidence that Hegenwald attended the Second Disputation held that month, he must have come to Zurich in the latter months of 1523 or in 1524.

The following background is reflected in the present letter and in other information: After Hegenwald returned to Wittenberg from Zurich, Grebel wrote one or more letters "to the leaders at the University of Wittenberg" (65/295/14-15). One letter was addressed and dispatched to Martin Luther (62/283/16-17, 63/292/13, 24, 294/12, 67D/331/2-7). Since Hegenwald specifically stated that he had not read Grebel's letter to Luther (331/6), his first letter to Grebel was not in direct reply to that. Nor was his first letter a reply to one that Grebel had previously addressed specifically to him since he admitted that he took the initiative to answer Grebel "uninvited" (324/33, 325/4). Yet, we know that Hegenwald's first letter was a reply to a letter from Switzerland and one apparently written by Grebel (see 328/12ff.). Perhaps Grebel had sent two letters to Wittenberg, one of which was addressed to Luther, and the other to someone else, the latter somehow coming into Hegenwald's hands for reply. It is evident that like his letters to Müntzer, Grebel had written on behalf of a small group of "fellow brethren in Christ at Zurich" (331/12-13).

In his first letter Hegenwald had expressed appreciation for Grebel's "Christian conviction" but also mentioned a number of criticisms (308/1-2). Grebel replied by refuting those criticisms in thirteen points (324/36, 329/ 35), the last of which was on infant baptism. Grebel had requested a reply by return of the same messenger; and in his attempt to comply with that request, Hegenwald had written so much on the first point that he had barely enough time before the messenger's departure to write briefly on five of the six remaining points.

He writes enough, however, to identify the main content of the six points: (1) How one can know that the spirit of a Christian comes from God. (2) How one should understand the nature of the "call" to preach the Word of God. (3) How one should understand the nature of Christian freedom in outward things according to the Word of God. (4) How one should interpret the meaning and practice of the Lord's Supper. (5) How Hegenwald failed to base his proof on the Scriptures. And (6), Why infant baptism is "a senseless blasphemy" (329/36-37). Some of the content of Grebel's lost letter can also be inferred from several writings of Carlstadt which he may have been quoting or paraphrasing (see fn.56, below).

Before replying the second time, Hegenwald had asked Luther whether he also wanted to write something in reply to his own letter from Grebel (331/ 2-3), to which Luther had replied that he did not know what to write but that Hegenwald should give Grebel his greetings and say that he was not unfriendly toward him. There is evidence that Zwingli also knew about Hegenwald's letters to Grebel and considered them to have effectively destroyed Grebel's credibility (494/33-34). To the editor's knowledge, the present letter has never been transcribed or published or translated before.

Grace, peace from God the Father through the Son Jesus Christ be with us all, etc.

Dear brethren[1] and good friends.

Since in response to my writing (in which I perhaps uninvited[2] took it upon myself with good intentions and confidence toward you to reply) you have now again requested [response] by messenger and have divided your concern against me into articles[3] [to show] my error which I committed the other time against you, I intend now in turn to organize my response in this way[4] in order to be more successful this time. And since you want a reply from me (although I am overloaded right now with many necessary studies) I will let you know my understanding in the simplest way.

First,[5] you accuse me of having attacked and depreciated your spirit, life, and work as witnesses of the faith.[6] You write: How could I say that your Christian conviction pleases me and then soon afterward say that you should first give attention to the fear of God[7] and *pietatem.*[8] I answer: Dear friends and brothers. Previously I took the initiative to answer you uninvited. So I would not have anything to be angry about (even if I wanted to be), should you hold this against me. But I say: If I have attacked your life, work, spirit, or faith (as you say), I am not aware of it. Nor do I believe that I have done that as far as I know. If, however, that should have happened (unwittingly), it would be fitting for you to forgive me for the same in Christ. But I rather believe that it is this way: I urged you, first of all, long before you begin anything (either in writing or otherwise) that you should first of all give attention to the fear of God, to *pietatis,* and should determine "whether your spirit, etc."[9] I really believe that I did not do that against you, for the following reason: You know, dear brethren, how all of us need and lack nothing more than the fear of God and that knowledge of him which is called *pietatem.* For a man does his human thing, what pleases him well, what seems to him to be reasonable, right, and godly, which, however, may be quite against God's will, knowledge, fear, as it is written: There is a way which pleases man well and which he thinks is good; but the end of it leads to death.[10] We can also read this about Manassah[11] and other kings of Israel who burned their daughters[12] for the glory of God. Again the children or the people of Israel elected and desired a king, Saul, believing that they were doing right.[13] But then God revealed and showed through the prophets their ungodliness (1 Kings 9) which flesh is otherwise unable to recognize (as will be said below). They paid attention and saw their mistake and also had to pay for it surely and painfully.

Nor has it any weight that you answer me: We have the Word of God on our side but they did not have it who sacrificed their children, etc. I answer: That would please God, and I would want to grant you that. Am I wrong when I admonish you to observe and take account of the fear of God, of *pietatis,* and to test whether your own opinion is from God and the spirit is from God as John himself teaches,[14] *Proate spiritus, etc.* (Test the spirits, etc.)? Dear friends, I know well that the shameless hypocrisy, which I would call ungodliness, lies so secret and so deeply hidden in the heart of man that no man can recognize it in himself correctly, yea, no one but the true Spirit of God as it stands written: He will judge the world concerning righteousness and concerning judgment.[15] There the Lord certainly means not outward righteousness which we call hypocrisy.[16] For that a human being can also observe. He means that ungodliness which no one can see, not even the person himself, unless the Spirit of God reveals it to him, because it is he who knows the hearts.[17] For the way (or the actions)

325

of a man are pure (they even sparkle) before his eyes, Proverbs 16,[18] that is to say, he pleases himself well enough. We are all unfortunately too blind, so that we do not always see the will of God, to say nothing of the fear of him and other things. This I would demonstrate as follows: Our flesh (of which we cannot be rid as long as we live) can do nothing except that it seeks after honor, profit, pleasure, renown, self-justification, the esteem of men. It never takes account of the fact that it may be against God and may be itself ungodliness, unless the Spirit of God should reveal that. For this is formed a part of us so that even the great saints complain of it. How often did David complain of it, Psalm 118. He was able to observe it but the friends of Job could not recognize their ungodliness (Job 2, 3, 6, etc.), until finally God himself spoke his judgment. Even then they still wanted to be right and quoted many divine Scriptures. Why does this happen? For this reason: As soon as the fear of God slips away from us (and it is very slippery), we can no longer see the will of God, but only our own will, Proverbs 14, from which it follows, as the Ps[almist] says, that some make for themselves a name on earth,[19] from which it follows further that he [who] despises and forgets the judgment of God can no longer discern and reckon (if something perhaps displeases him): "Is that perhaps God's will? What will you do about it?" He believes only wickedness, that he might go right on, as it is said, "Hatred must go into the bag";[20] and just as Elihu scolded the pious Job and condemned his speech, he[21] did not feel (nor did Elihu) this ungodliness in his heart. All of which happens very frequently to many and to most of those who now write. I wanted to admonish you (not that you did not know it before) but rather remind you that you should not forget those things completely.

But I notice that perhaps you did not understand me, which often happens. Therefore I want to interpret the words for you better. For your spirit to be in line with the Spirit of God, I bid you (in agreement with Paul everywhere)[22] to have a consoled spirit, which creates the true knowledge of God in us, whereby you can carry out something that you begin, driven thereto by the public Word of God[23] and with a peaceful conscience. Such courage and peace or thirst the world cannot object to without condemning itself, Matthew 12,[24] and the devil himself cannot knock it down or trouble the consciences with it. On the other hand, I call it a false spirit when a man undertakes something, acts without a command of God, without true faith, without the fear of God, just as Saul started a war with the Gibeonites[25] and Josiah with the king from Egypt.[26] So I wanted to warn you that in case anything was lacking in this respect, you would pray to God for it. For I take for granted that something will still be lacking among you, and that like Paul[27] you would not claim to have apprehended everything. But you want me to show where it all stands written, every word one by one. Otherwise you want to claim that I am presenting my own ideas. But let me make fun of that.[28] You should not be angry. To walk without the appearance of ungodliness I do not think means shunning the outward evil life, for that can also be punished by secular justice, and it should be.[29] What I call "walking," as Scripture uses it, means to look to the will of God, to follow it, not to propose to ourselves our own desires, high and rare prestige, as hypocrisy or *impietas*[30] do, but rather stick to the Word, yet in such a way that the fear of God is not forgotten. And even if one should be partly right and convinced of being in the right, still to fear God, as Job said,[31] and not like Job's friends (who also thought there was nothing ungodly about them), not frivolously scold other people for unrighteousness, as the friends of Job also did, with real convincing Scripture,[32] and yet they were wrong.

What I call *pietatem*[33] is the knowledge of God which exists in Christ Jesus, whom the Father commands us to hear.[34] Him we recognize (or perhaps better), him we find in Scripture and recognize only at the cross. As Paul boasts, he knows nothing but Christ and him crucified.[35] Dear brethren, here we all very much fall short, and I on my part especially much. I cannot properly recognize Christ on the cross, although in itself I see in Scripture *verbus patris* [a Word of the Father], a Word, a power, the glory of God, etc. I can speak beautifully of it but I must not let myself think that I know anything, as Paul says, Corinthians 8.[36] For if a dispute should arise,[37] Paul could well say, *Nondum cognovit, quemadmodum oportuit eum cognoscere* [He has not yet known as he ought to know].[38] And why? For this reason: he must himself say (Paul would say) that he has not yet known the power of the glory of God in all its patience and longsuffering with joy, etc., Colossians 1.[39] Therefore, dear brethren, let us pray with Paul that with one another we may be filled with the knowledge of the will of God in all wisdom and spiritual understanding, so that we walk or behave so that we please God in all things, Colossians 1.[40]

Now you see with what kind of intention and why I wrote you, and not otherwise. I believe I have thereby answered your other points, where you make many words on the subject of the call.[41] All right, dear sirs! He who is or comes to be called, only God knows. I am afraid we might make ourselves something of a cloak with Scripture and someone might think too easily that he is called.[42] Let that be entrusted to God.

Nor do I have any power to prohibit you, whether you should write or preach. I have exhorted you in a friendly way, as written above. I have the impression that you want to turn it around for me and accuse me as if I were the one who were writing and preaching.[43] You say, for instance, that

327

those who are called should add nothing to the Word, to the practices and the wisdom of God, or take nothing away from it,[44] like Martin [Luther], you (there you perhaps mean me), etc., and naming me personally you say, "as you do with the idols,[45] etc." To that let me say: Not much debate is needed about the idols. I have not written you anything about them, unless some other companion might have tried to interpret to you my opinion. I have never circulated any writing, and if God wills, I shall never do so unless God convincingly[46] constrains me thereto. But now Martin is publishing a book on whether or not it is sin that a Christian has images.[47] From that you could be better informed than what I could babble to you at length about it. You also excuse yourselves much, as your letter does not admit, that you intend to write against Martin. The letter is still at hand in which it was said: If several from Switzerland, from Swabia, or maybe from among you in Saxony would write against the ungodly, etc., do not be angry, etc.[48] It was in response to that that I admonished you, because I know well what is your opinion[49] and in part I know well[50] that we are unfortunately all too impetuous and too bold, and if we all begin to write, there will be no end to the strife. Therefore I have admonished you.

Secondly,[51] you say that I am talking against the Scripture, [when I say] that one may use outward things as one wills.[52] I say, that might well be true. I could also easily say, from my limited understanding, that the great saints speak contrary to Scripture at points where I do not understand them and I am still stuck in the flesh. As for the particular argument that you hold against me, which says: If that is the case, then we will have to complain that Scripture is inadequate, etc. I answer: Christ said, *Verba mea spiritus et vita sunt* [My words are spirit and life].[53] But I can observe what you still lack. Therefore I beg you to read the book that Martin is now publishing concerning images, which he wrote to the Reformers in Strasbourg.[54] It is too much for me for this time. The messenger was already in a hurry and I had as many as ten letters to write, so I am less able to inform you adequately.

Next, what you believe about the Lord's Supper I can let stand.[55] Soon a book will be published against Carlstadt which will probably clear things up.[56] So be of your opinion, whoever will; what does it matter to me? But watch out (as Paul says) that you do not claim to know and understand too much.

Fourthly,[57] you say that I do not prove with Scripture that you draw the [meaning of the] Supper of Christ (as you call it)[58] by external appearances and should not attach it to persons.[59] I say: Dear sirs, to prove that would take much time and Scripture. I will for now say it briefly thus: John in his first epistle, chapter 4, says: Every spirit which confesses Jesus

Christ as having come in the flesh is from God.[60] Whoever tears Jesus Christ[61] apart is not of God. Here we would have to clarify what it means for Christ to come in the flesh and what it means to tear Christ apart. But that would take too long. However, say it this way: As soon as you want to hang and press Christ on a few outward things so that salvation must depend upon a work (apart from faith) and no other way (although Christ and the kingdom of heaven, of which he is the head, is a hidden mystery, as Paul says), you make of him a Moses.[62] For he said: The Son of man is lord of the Sabbath,[63] which yet God had especially commanded.[64] Why then not all Christians? But that argument would not be enough for you. You will refute me with: *Hoc est corpus meum* [This is my body], etc.[65] Therefore I beg of you, be quiet until Martin will have torn Carlstadt's argument apart for him and shown how the devil has broken in and taken for himself the scriptural text, *Hoc est corpus meum,* in order to fight against the Spirit.[66] When you see then what the Wittenbergers write about it, then you can believe or write whatever you wish. I just wish (as Job also says, chapter 13) that you would be quiet and hold still awhile and not think you are getting so clever.[67] Look at the text itself and lie if you are not assuming persons,[68] even though you are not aware of it. Enough of that, etc.

Fifthly, you say that I do not prove anything with Scripture. For God's sake, do you think I have nothing else to do than to write the whole Bible to you about it? But when you say it is impossible and against all Scripture when I said that it does not matter how one does it as long as everything is done in true faith, etc., and you object that he who believes will also freely believe the Word of Christ, my answer is: Why not? Why then do you not believe: *Caro non prodest quidquam* [The flesh does not reveal anything],[69] or: *Filius hominis dominus est sabathi* [The Son of man is lord of the Sabbath]?[70] *Suma sumarum* [To sum it all up]: The purpose is different than you perhaps think and than I can tell you. It probably has another foundation than we suppose.[71] So I beg you again as before, be patient and wait until you hear what the Wittenbergers will write against Carlstadt; and if then something dissatisfies you, do what you wish and feel like.

But since Conrad Grebel writes a conclusion to the thirteen [articles],[72] he addresses me: Dear Erhart, I say that infant baptism is a senseless blasphemy. I intend to prove, etc. So this is my reply: Dear Conrad, what you maintain is not my business. But as to what I maintain, I have written a few conclusions concerning baptism to Myconius. These you can very well read. But I did not write that for print. (If God wills) I do not want to make myself a name on earth nor do I want to hold that I should be considered as one who is attempting to intervene in these matters unless it should be that God would definitely impel me thereto through convincing coercion.[73] You can read the above [letter to Myconius] and thus you will discover and see my foundation. I wish that you would not count me together with Martin [Luther], whom I call Elijah, and with Zwingli, as you do when you repeatedly say: "Martin, you, and Zwingli." *Quis ego sum vermiculus miser–* [Who am I, poor little worm?] I have after all written nothing and want to write nothing (that I hope before God) which would become of public note. We shall well see (without our initiative) what will be determined, if God wills. Therefore I would wish that you would suppress your Adam[74] a little better and not write so stormily, as if you were doing it out of utter gall. I do not say this on my own behalf because I know your mind well, and I also know well that you mean it much better in your hearts than you are able to write it. I know well that once (when I was still with you in Zurich) you also wanted to write against the doctors and preachers at Saint Gallen. I entreated you about that. You listened to me that time and I do not think that you are sorry you did. I say this on behalf of the doctor, to whom you have all probably written sharply enough, etc.

Now look, for God's sake, what I am doing. Now that I have your letter before me and want to answer every point, I discover for the first time and take account of the fact that you are asking me not to write to you about infant baptism and other kinds of blasphemy (which I would of course lament) and you say I should explain my statement where I say that I would wish that you would behave in a seemly way and not proceed so aggressively but let things lie. Dear Conrad, if I had seen that the first time I read your letter and paid attention to it, I would really have written you nothing because I see that you in fact (perhaps just this time) were not speaking carefully. Have you not everywhere in your Paul[75] that we should benevolently admonish one another,[76] or graciously be patient with one another,[77] and bear with one's weaknesses for a time,[78] or fraternally admonish one another to patience,[79] etc.? But then perhaps you are of the kind who do not need any of this. Very well, let God dispose. Perhaps you do not consider me a brother in Christ.

Lastly, you ask whether you should write against my argument or not and attack my theses. Let me say: I am not aware of any theses which I wrote to you except perhaps to want to show you a little how it appears to me that others would speak. I did not write thus because I wanted to debate much, in which case I would have spoken differently. But whether you write or do not write, I have already said that as far as it depends on me I will not write anything, even if you publish a special book against me.

You will have enough to write about if you have such great concern.[80]

And with this I conclude: Martin suggested to me (when I asked him whether he also wanted to write something to you all) that I should give you his greetings so that you would not think that he is unfriendly to you. He said, however, that he would not know what to write you about such a letter as yours. What you had written I do not know. But perhaps you will find an answer in the book against Carlstadt which will soon be issued in a congregation.[81] With this, may the matter be left in the hands of God. Let him give us his grace and wisdom.

Given New Year's Day, 1525.

Erhart Hegenwald.

To Conrad Grebel and his other fellow brethren in Christ at Zurich.

Original: Stadtbibliothek (Vadiana) St. Gallen, Ms.31.222
Transcription: None

68
Grebel to Vadian
Zurich, January 14, 1525

The first words of the following letter are like the opening of Letter 52, "all is well." Although there is no evidence in the present letter that Grebel was responding to Vadian's admonitions of December 28, it reveals nonetheless a marked absence of argumentation. The letter is mostly a report of the most recent developments not only in the disputes over baptism but also in the wider Reformation issues, such as Zwingli's recent sermon on the nature of the body and blood of Christ in the mass, which he is still celebrating according to traditional Roman Catholic rite.

Grebel reports the birth of his third child, the first who will not be baptized as an infant. We find in 68C, below, that in just four days this child (and other unbaptized infants) will be the subject of the council ultimatum giving Grebel one week to have Rachel baptized, or he "with wife and child and possessions" will be forever banished from the land (68C/336/10-13).

My greeting first of all.

Dear lord doctor and brother-in-law.

We are all well. Caspar Trismegander,[1] the preacher at the hospital, defended infant baptism in the sermon to the preachers[2] last Thursday.

Jacob Hottinger[3] interrupted him, but he behaved moderately and nothing has been done to him by Milords. However, a disputation has been set for next Tuesday in the presence of both councils, to which all who are for and against infant baptism are to gather.[4] It will be announced tomorrow.

My wife gave birth Friday, a week ago yesterday. The child is a daughter named Rachel.[5] She has not yet been baptized and swamped in the Romish water bath.[6]

Some say that the doctor from Waldshut[7] will also be invited. But I do not believe it because he is against Zwingli on the matter of baptism and will write against him if he does not back away. Others will do the same.

Urban Rhegius, the merchant preacher at Augsburg, has written against Carlstadt on the Lord's bread.[8] Zwingli and the Zwinglians have 96 theses in defense of the antichristian water bath.[9] The clear light of day must be deceiving and blinding them. Until today Zwingli has been referring in public sermons to the bread and wine of the Lord as the very body and blood of Christ. No longer.[10]

I beg you to be willing to give my affair with Conrad Eppenberg your serious attention, and he also, etc.[11] I am desperately needy.

There are new booklets at hand.[12] One against infant baptism ($\tau\rho\iota\sigma\alpha\rho\chi\epsilon\tau\epsilon\lambda\acute{\epsilon}s$) [trisarcheteles],[13] one on fornication,[14] one on the new birth,[15] one against interest and tithes, an *Archeteles*,[16] one against the new idol of forbearance,[17] a daring one, one on force,[18] one on war.[19] Zwingli has underway a fine booklet [to be dedicated] to the king of France,[20] [and] one on the love of God and one's neighbor.[21] On Friday, yesterday, he preached a warlike sermon $K\alpha\rho\acute{o}\lambda\eta\nu$ [with all the trimmings],[22] and the crowd applauded!

Greet all my supporters, my sister,[23] and all your relatives.

Given at Zurich, on Saturday after the 20th day [after Christmas], in haste.

Conrad Grebel, your faithful brother-in-law.

Greet my dear brother-in-law Benedict for me.[24]

To the lord Doctor Joachim von Watt at St. Gallen, my dear lord and brother-in-law.

Original: Stadtbibliothek (Vadiana) St. Gallen, VB.XII.105
Transcriptions: VB, II, No. 420 + Ersatz in VII, p. 303; M-S, No. 23

332

68A
Notice of a Public Disputation on Baptism
Zurich, January 15, 1525[1]

The scheduling of a public disputation on baptism for January 17 was seen by Grebel as already something of a victory for his group. In his letter to Vadian of December 15, he had reported that when the two Tuesday Disputations of December 6 and 13 had failed to follow the ground rules laid down by the two councils, "both councils decided anew that they should meet together as previously ordered" (67/302/2-3). Nevertheless, as the following public notice clearly indicates, the Anabaptist position was presupposed to be erroneous even before the disputation convened; and its implied purpose was to secure the conformity of the dissenters or to authorize appropriate action against them.

Whereas some have expressed erroneous opinions[2] that young children should not be baptized until they come to their days [of accountability], our g[racious] lords, the burgomaster, [Small] Council and Large Council of the city of Zurich announce that all who intend to hold to such views, be they clergy or laity,[3] shall appear before them in the Town Hall[4] next Tuesday at the regular time of meeting[5] and shall state and prove from the pure holy Scriptures the reasons for their opinions, after which our lords will take whatever further action is appropriate.

Original: Staatsarchiv Zurich, A.42.1
Transcription: Muralt-Schmid, No. 22

68B
The First Public Disputation on Baptism
Zurich, January 17, 1525

Harold Bender was probably wrong in supposing that the public disputation on baptism was set up "in the style of those which had been held in 1523, to which they invited foreign guests" (HSB, p. 134) To be sure, there had been a report that Balthasar Hubmaier of Waldshut had been invited (68/332/8ff.), but he did not come and there is no evidence that other dignitaries were invited. Unlike the two disputations of 1523, no record of the proceedings is extant, although Heinrich Bullinger apparently kept some minutes. It is known that he attended as a young man of 20, and on page 16 of his Diarium, *he wrote that he kept minutes for an Anabaptist disputation, which was probably the January 17 debate because of his firsthand knowledge of the proceedings as recorded in his* Reformationsgeschichte, I, p. 238.

With the following excerpt from Bullinger's account, we begin a series of documents on the public disputations on baptism in Zurich. Bullinger provides brief reports on three of them (68B, 68L, and 71J) and a letter from the Zurich Council to the Grüningen magistrates also lists these same three public disputations (71J/435/35ff.). But there were more than three. Myconius writes that he was present "at nine friendly conferences and earnest disputations" with the Anabaptists (Jackson, 1912, p. 15). Zwingli speaks of ten conferences on baptism "public and private" (71M/444/17-18). Although he does not precisely identify these meetings, it is possible to specify six private and four public disputations, as follows:

SIX PRIVATE DISPUTATIONS

1. Spring of 1524
2. Aug. 11, 1524

In his Taufbüchlein *of May 1525, Zwingli refers to "two private discussions on baptism held last summer." See ZW, IV, p. 257, line 24, and Bromiley, p. 150, line 29. See 67/fns.6 and 7 for further details.*

3. Dec. 6, 1524
4. Dec. 13, 1524

The Tuesday Disputations. See 66A, also ZW, IV, 286.17=69C/372/35-37; ZW, VI, 37.1=66A/280/5-6; ZW, VI, 70.3=Epi.C/490/34.

5. Feb. 7, 1525
6. Mar. 16, 1525

The prison disputations with the Zollikon brethren. See Muralt and Schmidt, #37, p. 47 and #59, p. 67, also Blanke pp. 44 and 57.

FOUR PUBLIC DISPUTATIONS

1. Jan. 17, 1525
2. Mar. 20, 1525

See 68B, also ZW, IV, 286.17=69C/372/35-37.
See 68L, also ZW, IV, 230.26, 242.24, 252.26, 257.2, 24, 279.14, 19, 24; also Bromiley, 140.6, 149.7, 157.1, 160.1=69C/369/29. Also ZW, VI, 43.17-44.5.

3. Nov. 6, 1525
4. Mar. 5, 1526

See 71J, also ZW, VI, 44.5-44.11
See 71M, also ZW, VI, 44.12-45.7.

Although Myconius called them "friendly conferences," they can hardly be described as objective and impartial inquiries into the truth of the matter. Three were actually held in prison with Anabaptists held in custodial detention (Private 2, 5, 6) and three were held in public locations with Anabaptist principals who were brought from prison for the discussion, after which they were sentenced to further confinement (Public 2, 3, 4). The prejudiced nature of these conferences also characterizes the first public disputation of January 17, 1525, although it certainly had the positive effect of bringing out into the open the private arguments on both sides of the baptismal question. That Bullinger wrote from firsthand participation is clear from the comment in his Diarium, *"I who write this have a personal relationship to all this and was present there."*

So a conference or disputation was scheduled by the authorities for the 17th of January to be held at the *Rathaus* before the councillors and representatives[1] of Zurich and before the learned ones. Attending there in particular were the above-mentioned Mantz and Grebel, also Reublin,[2] arguing their case[3] that infants could not believe or understand what baptism is. Baptism should be given to believers to whom the gospel had previously been preached, who have understood it, and who thereupon requested baptism for themselves, and killing the old Adam, desired to live a new life. Because infants knew nothing of all this, baptism did not apply to them. For this they drew on Scripture from the Gospels and the Acts of the Apostles and pointed out that the apostles had not baptized infants but only adult discerning people. Therefore, it should still be done in that manner. And as long as baptism is not done in that manner, infant baptism is not valid and one should have himself baptized again.

Thereupon Zwingli replied methodically in all of the comprehensiveness of his arguments and answers that he later encompassed in the book that he had written to the people of St. Gallen, *Concerning Baptism, Rebaptism, and Infant Baptism.*[4] The Anabaptists from then on could do nothing with his arguments nor maintain their [own] opinion.[5] I who write this have a personal relationship to all this and was present there.

After the conclusion of the disputation, the Anabaptists were earnestly admonished by the authorities to forsake their opinion and to be peaceful, since they could not support their cause with God's Word. But this had no effect on them. Then they said that they must obey God more than men.[6] And the unrest and discord grew stronger and longer. They continued to thrive especially towards Zollikon.[7] There they planted their great confusion and formed their separate congregations with total defiance and outrageous adventurousness. [Bullinger's account of three public disputations to be continued in 68L, below]

From the Original Publication: Heinrich Bullinger's *Reformationsgeschichte,* I, pp. 258-59

68C
Council Mandate for Infant Baptism
Zurich, January 18, 1525

Whereas an error[1] has arisen in the matter on baptism, namely, that young children should not be baptized before and until they have come to their days [of accountability] and know what faith is, and some have consequently left their children unbaptized, our lords and burgomaster, the [Small] Council, and the Large Council called the Two Hundred of the city of Zurich, have permitted a disputation to be held on the matter on the basis of Holy Scripture, and have decided that notwithstanding this error, all children shall be baptized as soon as they are born. And all those who have hitherto left their children unbaptized shall have them baptized within the next eight days. And anyone who refuses to do this shall, with wife and child and possessions, leave our lords' city, jurisdiction, and domain, and never return, or await what happens to him. Everyone will know how to conduct himself accordingly.[2]

Effected Wednesday before Sebastian's Day, 1525.

Original: Staatsarchiv Zurich, EI.7.1 & A.42.1
Transcription: Muralt-Schmid, No. 25

68D
Zwingli to Vadian
Zurich, January 19, 1525

Zwingli's letter to Vadian, only 22 percent of which is included here, starts with a report of writings in press or recently published: (1) Jud's reply to Emser concerning the Lord's Supper, (2) the Latin translation of Zwingli's treatise of December on rebels and rebellion (67C, above) entitled "De seditiosis," (3) Zwingli's tract, "Concerning the Fatherhood of God, and (4) an important document issued by the Zurich Council entitled "Content of Some Interactions," directed to all the townships within the Commonwealth of Zurich and dealing with the state of affairs in the confederacy that were threatening the peace of Zurich. The Catholic cantons had become increasingly hostile, referring to Zwingli's Reformation as the "idolators' war against the Christian church" and talking about expelling Zurich from the confederacy. Rumors were rampant that Zwingli would be assassinated or arrested. The Ittinger affair (see 65/fn.24) had added fuel to the fire.

In the month preceding Zwingli's letter, a "secret council" had been appointed in Zurich to which Zwingli himself belonged, empowered to mobilize various strategies of defense and to deal with enemies from within the commonwealth, including suspected members of the Zurich Council. In the letter to Vadian, Zwingli identifies one of these for the first time, i.e., Jacob Grebel, Vadian's father-in-law. The sentence is intentionally vague but clearly negative. After reporting the council document appealing for unity within the Zurich Commonwealth, he added, "At the same time in other respects it [the City Council] sends either your father-in-law or his patron [Joachim Amgrüt]." To be associated in Zwingli's mind with Amgrüt (see ZW, VIII, p. 371), an adherent to the old faith whom Zwingli later called a Hurensohn (son of a bitch, see ZW, IV, pp. 730-31), did not augur well for Jacob in the coming political showdown.

By January 4, Zwingli had designed his famous strategy of war (Plan zu einem Feldzug) in the event of attack by the Roman Catholic cantons. In the wake of these developments, this was no time for the toleration of an Anabaptist dissent, not only within the Zurich bailiwick but in other allied cantons as well, like St. Gallen. It was too late for reconciliation efforts and the time had come for stronger procedures against the dissenters.

Best regards to all the brethren. Warn them above all not to incite tragedies regarding the nonbaptizing of infants. For yesterday, when we replied to their objection, we disputed so over baptism that those who were present with calm emotions declared that it must be that the world should hear this view of baptism. Certain it is that I so disputed as no one has seen until now. But the Lord will judge.[1] The council moreover issued this decree: Within eight days let all baptize their children, those who have not been wetted, or leave the city and the entire jurisdiction.[2] Conrad Grebel and a few others persist; they are of no account. Farewell and may the Lord preserve and protect you with your wife and children. . . .

Original: Stadtbibliothek (Vadiana) St. Gallen: Litt. misc. II.226
Transcriptions: VB, III, No. 421; ZW, VII, No. 360

68E
Council Decree Against Anabaptists
Zurich, January 21, 1525

As the following decree reveals, the Zurich authorities were in a harsh and intolerant mood in consequence of the disputation on baptism of the preceding week. They had come to a decisive moment in their encounters with the dissenters. Either they had to suppress the dissent or allow a degree of religious freedom that endangered and threatened to destroy the precarious gains of the Reformation. The latter required a serious modification of the ancient structure of the state church. Moreover, the increased hostility of the Catholic cantons had thrown the Commonwealth of Zurich into a crisis that augured poorly for the toleration of opponents from within. The authorities opted decisively for suppression, and Grebel's previous prophecies that

337

persecution would surely come (63/291/22-24, 67/302/35-36) were beginning to be fulfilled.

Resolution of the council, Saturday following St. Sebastian's[1] in the presence of Lord Röist,[2] Small and Large Councils.

Following the preceding resolution on baptism, etc.,[3] it is further decided that the mandate shall be executed, and henceforth the special schools[4] that deal with such matters shall be discontinued and Conrad Grebel and Mantz[5] shall be told henceforth to desist from their arguing and questioning[6] and be satisfied with Milords' judgments; for no more disputations will be permitted hereafter.[7] But if on account of belief some article becomes of concern to them, they may indicate it to the burgomaster or three headmasters,[8] who may, as appropriate, give them further information, etc. And in order that from now on we may have more peace on account of such people, it is further decided that these shall be banished from Milords' territory, namely, the priest from Wytikon,[9] the assistant from Zollikon,[10] Ludwig Hätzer,[11] and Andreas on the Crutches.[12] And they shall leave within eight days.

Original: Staatsarchiv Zurich, V.VI.248.fol.227b
Transcription: Muralt-Schmid, No. 26

68F
The First Believer's Baptism in Switzerland
Zurich, January 21, 1525

When it had become clear that the Zurich authorities had irreversibly opted for suppression of the dissenters of pedobaptist doctrine and practice, the latter were forced to a decision concerning their own next steps. The hour of decision came soon—probably on the evening of the same day that four of the brethren were banished (see 68E, above). According to the report that Zwingli had heard (see first document, below), fifteen brethren had come together, probably in the Zurich home of Felix Mantz (see 71K/fn.6); and the first service of believers' baptism in Switzerland took place, marking the birth of the Anabaptist church.

The second account of that event included here is that of Johann Kessler, chronicler of St. Gallen, who like Zwingli wrote from the state church perspective. The third is very likely a firsthand reminiscence of one of the original "fifteen brethren" contained in a letter sent from Switzerland to Cologne in the first half of 1530 in response to an inquiry about the facts of the origin of the movement. From Cologne the letter was taken to the Netherlands, where it was lost, but fortunately not before it was translated into the Dutch language and copied several times.

Three variants of the letter have survived, dated 1603, 1615, and 1620.[1] *The first and third identify their source as a booklet entitled* Beter Verlicht *(Better Enlightenment), in which the Dutch Anabaptists publicly denied the charge that they were descendants of the violent Münsterites. The second version, contained in the document entitled* Het beginsel der scheuringen *(The Beginning of Divisions), is shown by H. W. Meihuizen to be the closest to the original.*[2] *Its author states that his version comes from "an old document of the Anabaptists in Switzerland, sent many years ago to their brethren in Cologne." One gathers from his comment that he had the original before him. Moreover, his version contains germanisms absent in the other two. For instance, all three say* heeft het hem begeven *("and it came to pass"); but where the other two say* daarentusschen *and* daerna *("thereupon" and "after that"), this version writes* in dien *("at this time") in direct translation of the German* in dem.

Another factor which throws light upon the events of its transmission is its close relationship to the early account of the first baptism preserved in the Chronicle of the Hutterite Brethren.[3] *This is the account that has been used by nearly all historians to date,*[4] *because it was more widely known and available in contrast to the letter, which was known by few until Meihuizen wrote about it. The author of the Hutterite version is known to be Caspar Braitmichel, who was the first appointed Hutterite chronicler from about 1534 to 1542. This account is so parallel to the Swiss letter sent to Cologne that a direct dependence of one on the other (or both on another common source) is indicated. The definitive study of these relationships remains to be made.*

Meanwhile, we can assume that the letter is the earlier of the two accounts for at least three reasons. First, it is the shorter version[5] *and the accumulation of evidence indicates that when documents like this were reproduced, they were changed more often by the increase of their contents than by their decrease.*[6] *Occasionally, of course, the user will refine and abbreviate a borrowed work; but in our case there are two other reasons to conclude that the chronicle is later than the letter. The chronicle is obviously a historical rewriting in which certain facts are altered in relation to other information at hand. For instance, Uliman is declared to be the "eleventh" martyr of the movement, not the "seventh" as reported in the letter.*

Finally, its additions are transparently apologetic in nature, reflecting a later stage of church order and establishment of leadership. The letter lacks the concern for proper ordination of the one who baptized the others, so prominent in the chronicle; and it is the layman, Grebel, who does the baptizing, rather than the ordained priest, Blaurock. The chronicle adds an excursus describing how Blaurock came to be called by his name, and his prominence in Hutterite history is indicative of his actual presence in the Tirol after May 1529. The letter, on the other hand, refers to several leaders who were never present in Hutterite territory—Johann Brötli, "our servant in the region,"[7] and Michael Sattler. The reference to these men indicates that the letter came from Northeast Switzerland, where these men labored, perhaps from the district of Klettgau in the canton of Schaffhausen. Like Blaurock, Brötli was surely one of the fifteen participants in the Zurich baptismal service of January 21, after which he went to Hallau, where he had a large following before the Austrian suppression of Waldshut in December. The fact that the martyrdoms of Sattler and Brötli (1527 and 1528 respectively) were mentioned in the letter, but not that of Blaurock (September 1529) may indicate that the letter was written before the writer knew of the latter's death.

Meihuizen's conjectures about the transmission of the letter are as follows: "The Cologne Anabaptists who asked the Swiss for information about the beginning of the movement must have been the very first at that place. We cannot with certainty identify any Anabaptists in that Rhine town before 1530, but in May 1530, Melchior Hofmann must have traveled through Cologne on his way from Strasbourg to East Friesland. He who had already attempted to persuade the City Council of Strasbourg to place a church building at the disposal of the Anabaptists must have been looking for kindred spirits in Cologne. It is not unthinkable that he made contact with Dr. Gerhard Westerburg,[8] who had returned to the town of his birth and who had been in contact with the Mantz and Grebel group. He had left Switzerland before the first believers' baptism took place, but when Hofmann asked for more information about further developments in the group which Westerburg had visited, the latter gave him the address of someone who was present and most certainly had experienced what had taken place."[9]

[*Zwingli's Account, continued from 66A, above*] When they saw themselves beaten after a considerable conflict,[10] and when we had exhorted them in friendly ways, we broke up in such a way that most of them promised that they would make no disturbance, although they could not promise to give up their opinions. Within three, or at most four days,[11] it was announced that the ringleaders of the sect[12] had baptized[13] fifteen[14] brethren.[15] Then we began to perceive why they had determined to collect a new church and had opposed infant baptism so seriously. We warned the church[16] that it could not be maintained that this proceeded from good counsel, to say nothing of a good spirit, and for these reasons: They had attempted a division and partition of the church, and this was just as hypocritical as the superstition of the monks.[17] Secondly, though the churches had to preserve their liberty of judging concerning doctrine, they had set up rebaptism without any conference,[18] for during the whole battle about infant baptism they had said nothing about rebaptism.[19] Third, this rebaptism seemed like the watchword of seditious men.[20] [*To be continued in 68L, below*]

[Kessler's Account, continued from 65A, above] There were at first in Zurich some good-hearted evangelical men, citizens and foreigners, though always maligning and being obstinate and more inclined to meet together in a particular manner and form. By name they were especially Conrad Grebel, well taught in Latin and otherwise, for he had been a [university] student at Vienna in Austria and at Paris, Felix Mantz, Blaurock, and one who was called "strong George" because of his great faith,[21] and other companions and related brethren. These persons supposed that those who had become evangelical ought to separate themselves from and part from all things of the papacy and have an unspotted church without sin.[22] But the ministers of God's Word, especially Huldrych Zwingli, did not want to permit such schism and separation,[23] because they were increasing daily, claiming to enlarge and improve the Word of God. When their activity was forbidden, they met secretly in cliques in their homes.[24] But when they carried on this ganging and meeting so frequently with daily increase, the honorable authorities of Zurich saw cause to look after it. They were beginning to spread out and proclaim their cause and admonition; namely, that infant baptism is not of God but was initiated without scriptural basis and invented by the devil through the pope. They insisted so strongly on this article that all their teaching and proclaiming was nothing but pondering and rummaging[25] for why infants should not be baptized; but nobody knew where they were trying to come out with this. When they were about to be watched more closely, they asked to have a disputation[26] with the ministers of the Word in Zurich. The honorable Zurich government granted this graciously and helped to bring the disputation about. But when they were declared defeated, they became hard and tried to continue the debate and refused absolutely to be considered overcome. In this it became clear why they sought with such fervor and rigor to overthrow infant baptism: in order that if it was wiped out, it would be necessary if one wished to be Christian at all to be baptized again, one and all; thereby their plan to separate would be achieved and their assemblies would gain a great increase.[27] For this reason they, the aforementioned ἀρχικαταΒαπισαι [arch-Anabaptists], Conrad Grebel first of all, baptized one another in a home[28] at night as a true testimony that they considered infant baptism to be no baptism, but that theirs was the true baptism, and likewise their assemblies (where the true baptism was) they considered to be the holy Christian Church [*To be continued in 68H, below*]

[*The Klettgau/Cologne Letter*][29] Therefore, dear brethren,[30] since you have asked us[31] about the beginning of the brotherhood of the Swiss Brethren,[32] it was about the time when men wrote the year 1522[33] that

Huldrych Zwingli, Conrad Grebel, a nobleman, and Felix Mantz—all three very learned men, experienced in the German, Latin, Greek, and Hebrew languages,[34] came to discuss matters of faith, and discovered that infant baptism is unnecessary, also not known as a baptism.[35] Thereupon the two, Conrad and Felix, believed and confessed that one must, according to Christian order, be baptized according to the words of Christ: he who believes and is baptized shall be saved.[36] This led to disunity among the three, and Huldrych Zwingli did not wish this[37] and said it would create a disturbance.[38] But the two previously mentioned men held that one could not ignore God's command because of that.

Meanwhile it happened that a priest by the name of Jörg, of the house of Jacob, who was called Jörg Blaurock because he wore a blue coat,[39] also came with a particular zeal which he had toward God's will. He was held to be an ordinary and simple priest but with a godly zeal in matters of faith, who through the grace of God which was given him acted in an extraordinary manner.[40] He came to Zwingli and talked to him about the faith, but achieved nothing. Thereupon he was told that there were others who had more zeal than Zwingli. These he sought out and came to them, namely, to Conrad and Felix, and talked with them; and they became united in these things.[41]

And it happened that they were together.[42] After fear[43] lay greatly upon them,[44] they called upon God in heaven,[45] that he should show mercy to them.[46] Then Jörg arose and asked Conrad for God's sake to baptize him;[47] and this he did.[48] After that, he baptized the others also.[49] After this, more priests and other people were added[50] who soon sealed it with their blood. So also Felix Mantz, named above, who was the first; he was drowned at Zurich.[51] Wolfgang Uliman[52] was burned at Waldsee with ten others, including his brother,[53] who was his companion. He was the seventh.[54] After him a cleric named Hans Pretle [Johann Brötli],[55] who was also our servant in the land. And thus it spread through persecution, as with Michael Sattler[56] and many of his relatives. Thus also Melchior Vet,[57] who was Jörg Blaurock's companion, who was burned at Dracha.

Thus you have the facts about what happened at the beginning. Later many things happened, so that many ran disorderly.[58] But the sure foundation of truth remained. The Lord knows his own.[59] Let those who call upon the name of the Lord forsake unrighteousness. And so you have the account of the beginning concerning which you should have no doubt, for we have most surely experienced it.

Originals: Same as 59A; same as 65A; non-extant
Transcriptions: ZW, VI, No. 108, pp. 37-42; Kessler, pp. 141-42/Quellen 2, pp. 599-600; Carel van Ghendt, *Het beginsel der scheuringen* (see fn. 1, below)
Translation of Zwingli's Account: From Jackson, 1901, p. 134

68G
Reports of Illegal Anabaptist Activity
Zurich, January 30, 1525[1]

The movement that began with the baptismal service on the Saturday evening of January 21 spread quickly to the village of Zollikon south of Zurich. During the next week various meetings were held for witness, baptism, and communion—all in violation of the January 21 decree of the council. By the end of the week at least thirty-five persons had been baptized.

On Monday, January 30, Mantz and Blaurock and twenty-five others were arrested and imprisoned for what Blanke describes as a "conversion custody" (p. 44). A week later, on February 8, all but Mantz and Blaurock were released after payment of maintenance and a joint fine of 1,000 guilders. The following document is an excerpt from the testimony of several of the prisoners.

Further: Clewy Kienast[2] said that he was never present when such acts were performed. But since the last prohibition,[3] Conrad Grebel and Felix Mantz went into some houses every morning and evening. And others frequently gathered there from Balgrist and other communities. Beyond this he saw nothing more. . . .

Hans Ockenfuss[4] answered [that] he was present when they baptized one another, but last Sunday[5] he was going to take to Wilhelm [Reublin] of Wytikon[6] a coat he had made for him and when he got there Fridli Schumacher[7] was standing at the well at Hirslanden[8] and said to the priest's assistant:[9] "Well, Hans, you have taught me the truth, for which I thank you and ask for the sign." And so the assistant baptized him. About two weeks ago[10] he was at Zollikon in Jacob Hottinger's house.[11] Conrad Grebel and others were there talking about baptism and the Lord's Supper. Then Grebel cut a loaf of bread and distributed it among them. He ate of it too, to symbolize that they would henceforth live a Christian life.[12] He has not accepted baptism yet but intends to do so.

Original: Staatsarchiv El.7.1 & 7.2
Transcription: Muralt-Schmid, No. 29, p. 38 & No. 31, pp. 41-42

68H
The Oldest Anabaptist Congregation: Zollikon
St. Gallen, 1525

Zollikon, a suburban village south of Zurich, was the location of the first persistent Anabaptist gathering in Switzerland. It existed for seven months from the end of January to August 1525—"the only Anabaptist congregation ever established in or in the immediate vicinity of the city of Zurich" (ME,

343

IV, 1036). It was not "established" in the sense of a local counter-congregation because its members conceived of the existing village church as their own. In fact, not until 1527 do we find local groups of Anabaptists organized as separate congregations (see the "Congregational Order" document of the Schleitheim Confession in JHY, 1973, pp. 44-45).

The population of Zollikon numbered about 90 large and small farm owners at this time (see Blanke, 1955, pp. 41-42), half of whom joined the movement. They met in small groups in homes but continued to attend the proto-Protestant church in the village, where Blaurock on more than one occasion preempted the pulpit with the words, "Whose community is this? Is this God's community where the Word of God should be proclaimed? Then I am here as an ambassador from the Father to proclaim the Word of God" (Quellen 1, No. 109, p. 110.) They even performed some of their baptizing in the village church (ibid., Nos. 55, 104, 105). Blanke identified a total of 35 persons who were baptized in the days following the banishment of the movement from Zurich, including members of such small farm families as Breitliner, Bleuler, Hottinger, Kienast, Murer, Rutschmann, Thomann, Schad, Schumacher, and Umholtz.

Johann Brötli, the assistant priest in the local church for a time, was the first to baptize another Zollikon resident (see 68G/343/20-23) following his own baptism by Grebel in Zurich on January 21. Grebel himself led the first communion service here a day or two later (see 68G/343/25-27), although he did less preaching and baptizing here in those early days than Mantz and Blaurock because he moved on to Schaffhausen. The elder of the group was Jacob Hottinger, in whose house the communion service was held, whose identity as an Anabaptist persisted long after the collapse of the congregation.

Blanke's fascinating account verifies the authentic nature of the movement here, which came to an end only after repeated arrests and imprisonments finally broke the will of the members to continue (see Blanke, 1955, pp. 66ff.).

[*Continued from the Kessler Account in 68F, above*] When the Zurich government became aware of this, they absolutely refused to allow it in their city. Since they believed that the Anabaptists were defeated with the Holy Scripture, they issued the order: No one should be rebaptized or leave his children unbaptized on penalty of banishment from the city, canton, and domain.[1] Thereafter the clergy were to baptize all children, even against the wishes of their parents who had neglected to have them baptized.

Now when the founders of Anabaptism noticed that not much room was granted them in Zurich[2] for their activity, they turned to the countryside into the villages again and again. Always their teaching and preaching was about rebaptism against infant baptism. They asked nothing but: Why don't you get baptized? Why do you have your child baptized? This occurred mainly in a place not far from Zurich called Zollikon,[3] where they had their center. There water was prepared and if anyone desired baptism they poured a panful of water on his head in the name of the Father, Son, and Holy Spirit.

Now because Zollikon in general had itself baptized, and they assumed that they were the true Christian church, they also undertook, like the early Christians, to practice community of temporal goods[4] (as can be read in the Acts of the Apostles),[5] broke the locks off their doors, chests, and cellars, and ate food and drink in good fellowship without discrimination.[6] But as in the time of the apostles,[7] it did not last long. It would be praiseworthy and desirable wherever it might have a basis on account of false, lazy Christians. But since it cannot be, we must show our mercy to the poor in other ways and pity their poverty, as I mentioned above concerning the regulation for the poor.

But when they became aware of the activities at Zollikon, their honorable wisdom, the governors of the city of Zurich, were as unwilling to tolerate such separation in their canton as in their city, but issued their command and prohibition also throughout their domains.[8] But because the Zollikon people persisted, the burgomaster and council decreed that the baptizers and baptized be seized and imprisoned in the Wellenberg (which was done).[9]

Now when the arch-Anabaptists felt the force and knew that the government would not tolerate their activities, the second article [of faith][10] arose among them that they proclaimed that no secular ruler could be a Christian, and no Christian could be a ruler; for Christians use no force other than the ban or exclusion, of which Christ speaks in Matthew 18.[11] But the preachers and the ministers of God's Word thought it was a secret and covert attack to do away with government among Christians,[12] so that they—if they ignored the ban—could without resistance quietly carry out their intention. [*To be continued in 69A, below.*]

Original: Same as 65A
Transcriptions: Kessler, pp. 142-43; Fast, 600-2

68I
Prison Disputation with the Zollikon Anabaptists
Zurich, January 30–February 8, 1525

On Monday, January 30, 1525, twenty-five Anabaptist brethren of Zollikon were imprisoned in the old Augustinian monastery in Zurich. During their nine-day confinement, January 30 to February 8, they were cross-

examined by a delegation appointed by the City Council for the purpose of "reconverting the Anabaptists to the Zwinglian standpoint." Thus, Blanke describes it as a "conversion custody." The committee, composed of the three city preachers—Zwingli, Jud, and Megander—and the three council members who had supervised the arrests in Zollikon, were assigned to go to the monastery "to listen and discern what they adhere to and what position they take" (Quellen 1, No. 37, p. 47). In the course of this prison disputation, which is undoubtedly one of the so-called "private disputations" in Zwingli's list of ten (see 71M/444/18 and 66A/Intro.), something interesting happened, which is documented in the following two records of the investigation of the role of the prison guard, Hans Hottinger, an Anabaptist sympathizer and later adherent. Blanke describes the incident in the following paragraphs:

"The representatives of government and of theology came to these country people in prison to dispute with them. In the face of this superior force, the position of the prisoners was the more awkward, because they were separated from their spiritual leaders and were thrown entirely on their own resources.

"The theological discussion in the Augustinian monastery concerned the scriptural proof for rebaptism. Zwingli declared that nowhere in the Bible is there any mention of one and the same person being baptized twice. The men of Zollikon contradicted him by referring to Acts 19. Here in verses 1-7, it is recorded that Paul met some men in Ephesus who had been baptized by John the Baptist....

"These Ephesian disciples of John did in reality receive baptism twice, first from John the Baptist, then from Paul. Zwingli, however, would not admit this, the only possible interpretation. He maintained that these men were not baptized by John, but merely instructed by him....

"This tortured interpretation was not convincing. We are therefore not astonished to hear that the prisoners felt themselves very sure in their cause. We have information about the feeling among them from Hans Hottinger. He was a Zurich craftsman and served as night watchman on the side.... He was able to visit the prisoners without being seen, probably at night. Through him they sent a message to their relatives. And so after supper one evening in the first week in February, Hans Hottinger went to Zollikon. The families and friends of the arrested men were called together in the house of Hans Murer. There must have been a dozen men and few women present. To them Hans Hottinger related what he had heard and seen.... In answer to the question ... concerning how the dispute over baptism between their 'brothers in Christ' and Zwingli had developed, Hans Hottinger reported that Zwingli had thus far not been able to accomplish anything. 'On the contrary,' he added, 'your brothers have routed Zwingli!'

"That sounds very boastful and doubtless does not correspond to the facts. Still it deals with a statement for which a reason is given, and we must examine the reason. The reference states, freely translated ... 'It was possi-

ble for the brethren to convince Zwingli, for Zwingli declared to them that when Lent comes, he, too, will accept the godly life.'

"It is quite possible that Zwingli did say something similar. . . . At that time (February 1525) baptism and the Lord's Supper were still celebrated according to old Catholic usage in the city and its surrounding territory. It was the Anabaptists of Zollikon who no longer could endure this half measure and were the first to abolish the Roman rite. It is very probable that these questions came up for discussion in Zwingli's dispute in the Augustinian cloister. Zwingli may have declared that very soon, in Lent, he would carry through the reorganization of the ceremonies. . . . Perhaps he had also hoped in that way . . . to take the wind out of the sails of the Anabaptist cause. The Anabaptists must have gained the impression that Zwingli was yielding to them on these liturgical points and interpreted it as a victory achieved over the Reformer" (Blanke, 1961, pp. 44-47).

1. *Investigation of Hans Hottinger, the Guard, Feb. 18-25, 1525*

Information on what Hans Hottinger,[1] the guard, said at Zollikon about how Master Huldrych Zwingli is to be [declared] defeated.

Heine Murer[2] of Zollikon said that Hans Hottinger, the guard, came to him, the witness, and to others, and said he had come from those who are being kept in prison, and they are well. Further, he told him, the witness, and the others, that Master Huldrych Zwingli had demanded of them the Scripture for saying that it cannot be found in Scripture that anyone was baptized twice. Then they pointed out to him the Scripture for it.[3]

Heine Bleuler[4] said that Hans Hottinger had come to them only after the Supper, but he, the witness had joined them only after that conversation was finished and done with.

Rudy Murer said that Hans Hottinger came to his house, the witness's, and said to them: Dear brethren, I am to give you greetings from the other brethren, and they should be happy, for they [the prisoners] were also happy and in good spirits. Further he told them that Master Huldrych Zwingli had said that it could not be found in any Scripture that anyone should be baptized twice. And when they indicated to him the Scripture, he said: "Ha, that happened once."[5]

Claus Murer testified with exactly the same words as Rudy Murer. . . .

Hänsi Thomann testified that he has heard from Heine Schänik, how they had defeated Zwingli on several points.

Heine Schänik testified: When Hans Hottinger came to them again in the evening after the Supper, he gave them greetings from the others who are imprisoned in the Augustinian monastery and admonished them to remain cheerful and steadfast. When they asked what had taken place, he reported that Master Huldrych Zwingli had said that no one was baptized twice. And when they showed him the Scripture, Zwingli said that it had not happened more than once. They replied that they also had been baptized only once.

Uli Merger testified like the preceding witness, Heine Schänik, with this addition, that Hans Hottinger on the same night when he was with them in Zollikon, appointed another guard who kept watch with him, etc. Also that he, the witness, did not baptize his child until two weeks after his wife had given birth.

Felix Horner testified: When Hottinger came to Zollikon, he greeted them and admonished them to be steadfast. Further, he said that he understood that Hottinger had told how they had defeated Zwingli at the monastery.

Heine Horner testified: When Hottinger was with several others at Zollikon and they asked him what had happened at the monastery between their brethren in Christ and Zwingli, he told them what they had discussed with Zwingli and that they had convinced him with their arguments. And when Lent comes, Master Huldrych Zwingli would also accept this godly life.[6]

Jacob Kienast[7] testified that Hans Hottinger had told them that those at the monastery were in good spirits, and if God wills, Zwingli would not be able to defeat them with Scripture.

Information on when Hottinger, the guard, spoke to Zwingli.

Rudolf Asper testified: When they were all talking about Master Huldrych Zwingli and he, the witness, supposed that they were glad when Zwingli preached, Hottinger said, "I don't know why I should be glad. Today he preaches one thing, tomorrow he takes it back. Years ago he preached that infants should not be baptized,[8] and now he says they should be baptized. And when he says that God commanded that infants should be baptized, he is lying like a rascal, a villain, and a heretic." Then when they rebuked his fellow guard for such talk, he repeated his former words, an opinion that he wanted him also to have in his throat.

Hans Schärer testified that Hans Hottinger said he did not at all enjoy Zwingli's preaching and would probably see what he would preach one of these days when he was sitting in the branches,[9] and now he has preached about the children like a rascal and a heretic, for which he must die. The witness also said that Hans frequently left his post, sometimes leaving a substitute, sometimes not. . . .

2. *Examination of Hans Hottinger, the Guard, Feb. 25, 1525*

Hans Hottinger, the guard, gives his answer thus and confesses:

Recently when Milords put several people of Zollikon into the Augustinian monastery and elsewhere because of baptism, he went there to [visit] them, for he had some friends among them—Conrad Hottinger was his closest friend—to see how they were and how they were planning to defend themselves. Then they asked him to go to Zollikon to their wives and children to see how they were getting along and to tell them that they were in good condition and to bring them greetings. This he did, going to Zollikon after the evening meal. Then some of the women and also some men met in Murer's house. There he told them what he had been asked to say. Afterward they asked him how matters stood between themselves and Master Huldrych. He replied that they had had a discussion [with Zwingli], but he did not know what it was about, for he had no knowledge about it. Master Huldrych then said it had already happened once; and Master Huldrych had then expounded and pointed out to them that John the Baptist had baptized once and Paul also once.[10] Never had he [Hottinger] said that Master Huldrych had ever been defeated.

Concerning the guarding, he did not think that he had ever neglected his guard duty. When on occasion he was not able to serve because of business or because he was sick, he asked a Spital servant or one of his companions to serve as guard for him.

Later, when the guards were drinking at the Rathaus, he told his comrades that he had heard Andreas on the Crutches[11] say that when Master Huldrych tries to prove that infant baptism was instituted by God, he is lying like a rascal. Furthermore, this Andreas also said that he would prepare himself and get ready; and if Master Huldrych could prove that the baptism of infants was instituted by God, he would let himself be burned to ashes as a heretic. Felix Lehman[12] of Hirslanden, etc., was also present and did not think that he [Hottinger] had ever said that Master Huldrych was a rascal and refused to confess it.

Original: Staatsarchiv Zurich EI.7.1
Transcription: Quellen, Nos. 43, 46

68J
Brötli to the Brethren in Zollikon
Hallau, February 5 and 19, 1525

As one of the four Anabaptist leaders banished from Zurich on January 21 (see 68E/338/15), Hans (Johann) Brötli left the canton on or before January 29. As the following letter indicates, he admonished the infant Zollikon congregation before he left to remain faithful and to beware of apostasy.

Accompanied by Wilhelm Reublin and perhaps by another Zollikon brother by the name of Merger, he set out with his wife and child on his way to exile. He mentions various villages along the way—Spanweid, Cloten, Eglisau, and Hallau, where he remained with his family. From there he and Reublin went to Schaffhausen, where they met Grebel, who had gone there earlier in the week. The four of them called on the two leading clergymen of the canton, Sebastian Hofmeister and Sebastian Meyer, after which Brötli returned to his family in Hallau and Reublin and Merger went on to Waldshut to see Balthasar Hubmaier.

The dating of this letter is based on Brötli's own reference to having preached a sermon "last Sunday," February 5. Also, word had already come to him that his brothers in Zollikon had been imprisoned, which occurred on January 30.

1. *Letter written after February 5*

John,[1] a servant of Jesus Christ,[2] called to proclaim the gospel of Christ through the will of God the Father, to the devout Christians and the called of God in the Christian congregation at Zollikon, grace and peace from God the Father and our Lord Jesus Christ.

You know, dear brethren, how while I was with you[3] I proclaimed to you the Word of God faithfully, clearly, simply, and did not treat it like the untrustworthy innkeepers who pour water into the wine. You know too how I would have liked to live among you, to work with my hands and to be a burden to none. You know too how I was driven away from you for the sake of the truth according to the will of God. You know how faithfully I admonished you, when I was about to part from you, not to fall away from the grace in which you were called. God grant that you still abide in it. I still testify today by heaven and earth that I taught you the truth, and if you stand fast in that truth you are God's and he is yours and you are saved. But if you fall away you will be children of damnation and God is against you and you are miserable and without knowledge and will flee from every gnat that flies past. Oh, how ardent my heart is toward you since I have begun to write these things to you. Oh, how I would have liked to shout aloud. I pray God earnestly that you stand fast in the faith. Oh, how I would like to be with you, so that I could encourage you to stand fast.

I have heard that several brothers are in prison.[4] God grant that they may be joyful in God, as I also am. Oh, how fervent and happy I was when God bade me leave you. Yes, yes, I left you joyfully. Yes, yes, I did not weep when I went away from you, but sang. Oh, how joyful I will be if God directs me to you again. When I got as far as the Spanweid,[5] Christ came to us, yes Christ, in his people. A devout brother from Bern named Christen went with us as far as Cloten and the next day parted from us.

350

Yes, yes, I often slipped on the way but did not fall. Yes, yes, when we approached Eglisau, Wilhelm[6] and I had considered our lives lost. But I believe God averted it. We strayed from the right road and wandered, lost half of that day through brush and wilds, but God willed it thus. At night we came to some devout people. Finally we got to Hallau,[7] and there I left my wife and child. We went on to Schaffhausen.[8] There we found our dear brother Conrad Grebel.[9] We were with the two doctors[10] and ate supper with them. Yes, Dr. Sebastian was of one mind with us regarding baptism. May God grant that he will improve in all things.[11] We then went from Schaffhausen back to Hallau. The next day Wilhelm and Merger[12] went to Waldshut.[13] I stayed at Hallau. Wilhelm did not come back to me. I don't know where he went. Perhaps Merger knows. . . .

Johann Brötli, your servant in Christ now living in Hallau.
To the devout Fridli Schumacher[14] of Zollikon and others of his dear brothers in Christ at Zollikon.

2. *Letter written after February 19*[15]

Wilhelm[16] has since left me and come back to me again and now finally left me again, and I do not know where he is. He is distressed in Christ on your account, as am I, etc. Let this messenger be commended to you. He is a good Christian, a pious man, who was also ruined by the hail and had to beg for alms. If you give him something he will be helped. Be sure to send me a Bible, etc. Stand fast in the faith, let no one frighten you from it. Then God, who is strong, will strengthen you. Oh, how strong, I hear, my brother Felix Mantz is, and Jörg,[17] but especially Felix Mantz. God be praised! Conrad Grebel is distressed, but in Christ.[18] Wilhelm was with me recently. I admonish you by the Word and faith that you have once received: If you abide in it, send a pious brother to me, and if you do not supply the messenger with the things I mentioned to you, then write that to me and I will supply them, etc. Greet one another with a greeting of peace. God and his grace be with you!

Johannes Brötli wrote this with his own hand, etc. Your brother in Christ.
To Fridli Schumacher[19] and other devout Christians at Zollikon.

Originals: Staatsarchiv Zurich, EI.7.2
Transcriptions: Muralt-Schmid, No. 36, p. 45, & No. 44, p. 55

Sentences Against Two Anabaptists
Zurich, February 18, 1525

Three generations of Mergers figure in the following Anabaptist story— an unaccountable unbaptized infant girl, a grandfather who sanctioned the unlawful act of prohibiting his granddaughter's baptism, and the father of the child who devoted most of his time to the spread of the movement. Meanwhile, back in St. Gallen, Gabriel Giger's father may not have approved his son's running off to Zurich to be baptized by Grebel; but he will have him back home just as soon as the Zurich authorities get around to banishing him from their bailiwick.

Heine Merger[1] answers that he has not baptized anyone and has not been baptized, and was never present at such baptisms.

Heine Merger is to be released upon swearing an oath and payment of costs, but he shall pay five pounds penance as punishment for refusing to have his son's child baptized, etc.

Passed on Saturday following St. Valentine's Day, 1525, in the presence of lord Walder, Burgomaster Emeritus, Small and Large Councils.

Gabriel Giger[2] of St. Gallen answers: When the Spirit of God came upon him he hastened to Zurich to Felix Mantz's home and Conrad Grebel baptized him.[3]

It is decided that said Gabriel shall be released upon an oath and payment of costs. And he shall be told clearly before the Small and Large Councils that he must henceforth forsake such conduct and keep still in such matters, etc.

Original: Staatsarchiv Zurich, EI.7.1
Transcription: Muralt-Schmid, No. 41

68L
The Second Public Disputation on Baptism
Zurich, March 20-22, 1525

The Second Public Disputation in Zurich was even less impartial than the first (see 68B). It was more of a judicial trial than a doctrinal dialogue. Mantz had been held in detention since February (see Krajewski, ch. VIII) and Blaurock had been arrested several days earlier. They were brought from the Hexenturm to the hearing at the Rathaus, where for three days they and their associates came up against the three people's priests, the two schoolmasters, the abbot of Cappel, the commander from Küssnacht, and the prefect of Embrach, plus the burgomaster and five councillors (see Quellen 1, No. 62, p. 70). Grebel was doing missionary work in Schaffhausen during this time.

[*Continued from Bullinger's Account in 68B*] Again, therefore, on the 20th of March, a disputation was held with them and their adherents, of whom several had been arrested. They did no more with God's Word in this disputation than they had done in the first one. And the debate and dispute with them was very active. The honorable council thereafter talked very earnestly with them and admonished them to forsake their opinions because such pernicious division and segregation would be suffered no more.

Moreover, several were kept in detention and several were banished from the canton. All of this settled nothing more with them than that they continued with their cause and thrived further in the jurisdiction of Grüningen,[1] where they subsequently caused much dissension. [*To be continued in 71J*]

[*Continued from Zwingli's Account in 68F*] When the evil had somewhat subsided, so that the majority seemed likely to judge the matter impassively, joint meetings were appointed.[2] But as often as we met, either publicly or privately, the truth that we had on our side ever came off conqueror. They promised then that they would prove by blood[3] what they could not by Scripture. They did this with such great boldness and boasting that I do not doubt that they were a burden to themselves. They practiced rebaptism contrary to the will of the senate and people. The public servants and police were turned back, and some of them harshly treated.

Finally, a meeting was appointed[4] where each side should be heard to completeness; and when they were brought from the prison[5] to the court[6] or were taken back again, one would pity the city and another would make dire threats against it.[7] Here hypocrisy tried its full strength, but accomplished nothing. While some womanish breasts bewailed and turned to pity, yet the truth, publicly vindicated, came off best. For all were allowed to be present during the whole three days' fight. [*To be continued in 70D, below*]

[*From Zwingli's Taufbüchlein written in May 1525*] The Anabaptists claim that only those who know that they can live without sin ought to receive the sign of baptism.[8] In so doing they make God a liar and bring back the hypocrisy of legal righteousness. My proof of the first point is as follows: In 1 John 1[:8] it says, "If we say that we have no sin, we deceive ourselves, and the truth is not in us. . . . " But the Anabaptists do hold that they live without sin.[9] This is proved by what they and some others write and teach concerning the *perseverantia justorum,* or perseverance of saints. In this they are committed absolutely to the view that they can and do live without sin. How far that claim is borne out by their envy, lying, clamor, evil-speaking, and blasphemy I leave on one side. But the following anecdote will show that they do regard themselves as righteous. The Anabaptists were eventually granted a disputation[10] by the City Council. But after three days[11] of effort, all that one of them could say about baptism was this: "I would willingly justify my position from the Word of God but none will understand it except those who are without sin." What answer do you think should be given? That of silence? Not at all, for only the Lord Jesus Christ can say, "Which of you convinces me of sin?" (Jn. 8[:46]).

Therefore I spoke up and said, "Did you not make a mistake when you said that none will understand you except those who are without sin?"

He answered, "That is what I said, and that is the case."

I said, "But you yourself understand this question of infant baptism?"

He answered, "Yes."

Then I said, "Therefore you must be without sin. But as long as you are in the flesh, that is impossible, for all those who are in the flesh are sinful."

He replied, "I would to God that all men were as conscious of their sins as I am." But then he said that he did not mean that he too was a sinner. But all good Christians may judge for themselves whether this boasting is anything but empty words, or any less arrogant than that hitherto made by the monks and nuns[12]. . . .

One of the good results of the controversy has been to teach us that baptism cannot save or justify. Yet I cannot but think that in other respects the Anabaptists themselves set too great store by the baptism of water, and for that reason they err just as much on the one side as the papists do on the other. For though the whole world were arrayed against it, it is clear and indisputable that no external element or action can purify the soul. But in the disputation there were some who maintained openly that they had experienced a great release at the moment of baptism.

To this Myconius[13] answered, "Did you not come to baptism with considerable apprehension?"

One of them replied, "Yes—for they claim that no one should be baptized unless he knows that he can live without sin."

Then Myconius said, "The release which you experienced in baptism was simply a cessation of that apprehension which you yourself had created."

They affirmed, however, that God had done something quite new toward them—the very experience which at one time we had in penance. For there, too, we were in great fear and distress before we made our confession: but the moment we had made it we said, "God be praised, I feel a great joy and refreshing." But all that we really felt was a relaxation of the previous tension. Yet the penitent could easily claim that in penance or papal absolution he experienced within himself a great renewal the moment he made his confession. And it was simply the removal of his apprehension. This is proved by the fact that our lives did not undergo any great change in consequence. Now those who allow themselves to be rebaptized make much of a similar experience. Its true source is the fact that rebaptism has no foundation in the Word of God. Hence the conscience opposes it, and it is anxious and afraid. But as the deed is done we brace ourselves and accept the risk, and then we want everyone else to do as we have done in order to free ourselves from reproach.

"Oh," but they say, "formerly we were sinners, but now we are sinners no longer."

Answer: The monks used to talk like that,[14] and we answered, rightly, that in making a statement of that kind they were committing the greatest possible sin. And now the devil is leading us back to the same evil ways. We disclosed his stratagems and revealed the hypocrisy of the monks. And now he is trying a new trick—he is using the light itself to bring us back to darkness.[15]

Again they say, "We allowed ourselves to be rebaptized in order that our Anabaptist brethren might have power and authority to restrain us when we have the impulse to sin."[16]

Note well that this is nothing other than monkery, separatism, sectarianism, a new legalism. For we Christians do not act rightly under the compulsion of law, but by faith. But it is no longer by faith when a man acts rightly because he is compelled to do so by his brethren in baptism. Naturally there are certain offenses which have to be punished, but even there the punishment ought to be administered by the church and not by the Anabaptist sect.

But they say, "We are the church, and those who do not belong to our church are not Christians. The church was founded by us: before us there was no church."

Answer: Exactly! It is just as I have said from the very first. The root of the trouble is that the Anabaptists will not recognize any Christians except themselves or any church except their own. And that is always the way with sectarians who separate themselves on their own authority. It is what the papacy itself did, claiming to be the true church without either the approval or the consent of genuine churches. Study carefully the passage in Acts 20 [:29] which speaks of wolves drawing the people after them, and you will find there a picture of yourselves. No, you despoilers. You should accept as Christians even those who do not rebaptize, and you should rejoice that they too accept you as Christians.[17]

Original Publications: Bullinger's *Reformationsgeschichte,* I, 259; Zwingli's *Elenchus* (same as 59A); Zwingli's *Taufbüchlein* (same as 69C)
Transcriptions: ZW, VI, No. 108, pp. 43-44; ZW, IV, No. 56, pp.
Translations: (2) Taken from Jackson, 1901, p. 135
              (3) Taken from Bromiley, pp. 139, 140, 156-58, used by permission

68M
Zwingli to Vadian[1]
Zurich, March 31, 1525

After two months in the canton of Schaffhausen, Grebel returned to Zurich about March 20, 1525. Although back for only a few days before going to St. Gallen on March 25, he must have been active in underground activity on behalf of the movement, as the present excerpt from Zwingli's letter reveals. In order to get a feel for the larger context of Zwingli's reference to Grebel, about 70 percent of his letter is included.

Grace and peace from God. Your *Axioms,*[2] dearest Vadian, I have read with much rejoicing, most of all for this reason, that they show that Christianity has been properly explored by you.[3] They are reverent and scholarly, but the printing press was held up with those necessary things at the Frankfurt Book Fair.[4] I send you my *Commentary*[5] as a gift, which with almost unspeakable toilings I have at length given out completed. In this I have treated many things in an entirely different manner than has so far been observed by many. Weigh all things carefully, for I certainly do not want to do violence to the truth anywhere.

Grebel is among us,[6] everywhere drawing to his faction whomever he can, and so reproaching and slandering our ministry that, even if we were at all the sort that he declares, still it was least of all fitting for him to be so ungrateful to one who deserves better. Strengthen yourself, lest you be seduced by his opinion; for he has this peculiarity, that he is silent about those very things which we present, yelping his own. The next task, after the one I have now in hand against a certain Uranian,[7] will be on baptism,[8] which I will treat very differently from the way any ancient or modern writers have treated it, although it is not I who will treat it that way but the Word itself, which nevertheless must be interpreted differently than has been done so far. But now you will get a foretaste of it in this *Commentary* of mine. . . .

Original: Stadtbibliothek (Vadiana) St. Gallen, Litt. misc.II.231
Transcriptions: VB, III, No. 425; ZW, VII, No. 366

69
Grebel[1] to Castelberger[2]
Zurich, April 25, 1525[3]

During the early months of the spread of the movement, Grebel moved back and forth from his Zurich haven. He was at home barely a week between his missions to Schaffhausen and St. Gallen. Upon return to Zurich in the week between Palm Sunday and Easter, he considered it necessary to dispose of his books, pay off his debts, and prepare for an indefinite transitory underground existence. It was during these days that he wrote the following fascinating letter to his brother in the faith, Andreas Castelberger, who was under a deferred sentence of banishment and was himself closing out his Zurich bookstore and place of residence. The letter reveals some of the difficult conditions under which Grebel lived at this time, complicated by the fact that his feet were badly infected.

My brother, much peace be to you in Christ Jesus our brother and Lord.

I had written to you that I was going away. I was going along with Felix Mantz,[4] preparing to leave by night on Sunday. Then my wife (how Satan never rests) said she would betray Felix,[5] who on the previous night had left my house again and gone to his own to await me there. I disregarded the great[6] insolence of Eve and went out. She went out through another door to father's house,[7] where she stirred up no small tragedy[8] over my departure. In the meanwhile I come[9] to the gate nearest me, which was locked.[10] I go up to the neighboring one, with fear of being recognized. I wanted to be cautious. I knocked to have it opened. Then Lady Meis[11] calls to me from her house saying that no one was being let out through that gate (which was also true), as it was for me at the Neumarkt gate. On my return I pray the Lord to show me what would be the best thing to do. It occurred to me at once on the way back to my house that if I should later be banished or Felix betrayed by my wife, the possibility for the brothers from Zollikon to come secretly might be cut off through the placing of guards.[12] By then I barely hobbled along because the sores on my feet hindered me.[13] For the third time the closing of a gate held me back.[14] So I have returned and await something else from the Lord.

I have listed all my books in a catalog while I remain at home.[15] I think I am seen by everyone when I look out and admit the brothers. I do not go out, however, because this is my asylum against captivity by Zwingli,[16] who is himself going into captivity according to the Apocalypse.[17] Give your advice as to whether they can be sold together and whether this catalog should be sent to one of the abbots, the abbot of Cappel,[18] or to some scholar who could inspect it and either buy the whole lot at once, which I hardly expect, or at least some of them. On those whose price has not been marked I do not set a price, intending to throw them in free as an addition to those that are priced. On those that are priced, I will allow a slight reduction (but only if the buyer is prompt). You know me better and more profitably[19] than I can explain. If your state of health allows,[20] you will not fail, I know, for such is your love. If Jacob[21] is with you, let him circulate the catalog if you think best. Do not worry that I am here and that this can be detected from my handwriting.

Regarding Adrian Grebel,[22] you have not replied whether he has paid you, although I doubt not that the man has not yet made settlement. I wish, however, to be informed so that when I send him a letter I might be able freely and less rashly to coax him somehow to pay up at last.

If you have anything definite regarding Zwingli's writing against me[23] and my infallible[24] passages from Scripture,[25] reveal it to me in a few words if it is possible and safe for you to do so. I hear that there is a book in the press. May I speak frankly?[26] It must be a falsely shameless and a shamelessly false book. Against which if I do not write a reply to make fun of this present [city] state,[27] I will never reply again. I will be more silent and dumb than a dead fish.[28] The passages which they say Zwingli has are those which they testify I gave to a certain person in Schaffhausen.[29] If that is so, I gave them to Erasmus,[30] and he in ignorance or persuasion by the spirit and $\Psi\epsilon\upsilon\delta\alpha\delta\epsilon\lambda\varphi\iota\alpha$ [false brotherhood] of the deceased Anemund[31] sent them to Zwingli.

While these gospel purveyors who have come into their reign after the beast, while these kings with one consent hand over their power to the beast, while they fight against the Lamb that will defeat them in his own time,[32] may you in the meanwhile be strong in the peace and patience of the Lord. Reply if you are able, if the interregnum of your illness allows you to write letters.[33]

The grammars of Theodorus[34] and Urbanus,[35] the Metamorphoses,[36] and perhaps the annotations of Erasmus on the New Testament,[37] you have I think in your bookshop; also Lucretius[38] and Horace[39] with the commentaries.

I shall send them bound, or I shall allow them to be carried down if someone should wish to see them or a prospective buyer should come to my house. If the zealous grammarians expect a Greek school,[40] there is the hope that they will come at least for the Greek manuscripts.

Original: Staatsarchiv Zurich, EII.349.No. 312
Transcriptions: M-S, No. 63; MQR, I (July 1927), pp. 41-53

69A
The Spread of Anabaptism in St. Gallen
St. Gallen, 1525

The spread of Anabaptism from Zurich to St. Gallen was told in the pre-face to 65A. Under the leadership of Lorenz Hochrütiner and later of Wolfgang Uliman and Eberli Bolt, the movement grew rapidly. Grebel ar-rived about March 25 and worked with these men for about two weeks, baptizing a large procession of people on Palm Sunday, April 9, in the Sitter River. A local chronicler, Fridolin Sicher, wrote that "the sect of the Anabaptists had completely taken over, on Sunday rushing into the water called Sitter, just as if it were a procession" (Quellen 2, p. 588).

[*Continued from 68H, above*] So much for the origin of Anabaptism. Anyone who wants to know their basis and writings, there are several booklets which they printed for that purpose;[1] likewise in the books of Huldrych Zwingli[2] and others in which they are refuted. Now we want to show how it flowed out into other towns and cantons, and especially to us here in St. Gallen, where it ruled and dominated most, and in the highest degree.

I have previously at another place described how the Almighty and merciful God and Father so graciously visited our city of St. Gallen with his saving Word of his holy gospel, turned it away from false worship and caused it to long for the knowledge of true righteousness, so that we knew that no outward or elemental thing[3] serves as righteousness before God. We St. Galleners run like the Galatians, whom we resemble somewhat in name and gesture. God wanted (I believe) to test us and cause us to know whether we understood this knowledge correctly and whether our hearts were properly secured in the truth of the faith in Jesus. He also allowed such a schism to occur among us and a testing by the glistening element,[4] as the Galatians with circumcision, so us Galleners with baptism which takes the place of circumcision among Christians, Colossians 2.[5]

I have often had to wonder about this, since this innovation[6] to the gospel of Jesus Christ so closely resembles it in words and deeds; for as the former needed circumcision for justification, so these require rebap-tism. . . .

Meanwhile it happened that the noted Conrad Grebel (as is known) left the city and canton of Zurich that he might tap other areas for his Anabaptism and besiege the learned preachers chiefly in the Protestant towns and cantons and try to convince them of his Anabaptism and give his work more promotion and prestige. Thus he went to Waldshut to the Doctor Balthasar Fridberger [Hubmaier], the local minister.[7] And al-though he was not unlettered, he nevertheless allowed himself to be com-

359

pletely submerged in Anabaptism, to the extent that he undertook to defend and shelter Anabaptism with open writings and publication of books. But because he was eloquent and not unpleasant to listen to, he gained no small approval and by his cleverness he succeeded so well that all Waldshut was baptized by him.[8] For as they had previously learned Christ from him, it seemed strange and unreasonable to them to accept another baptism. They thought it was futile and unnecessary, for they knew that they were baptized. When he saw that they would not be lured, he played a trick; namely, he let a report go out about him that he was planning to go away (though he knew well that they would not let him go) because he discerned that the Word of God would bear little fruit among them since they refused to accept Christian baptism. And so, because they loved him and trusted him, rather than let him go and be called bad Christians they yielded, let themselves be baptized, threw the baptismal fonts out of the church, calling them bathtubs[9] and calling infant baptism a child's bath, etc.[10]

Further it happened that our citizen and one of the brethren of whom I have written elsewhere, Wolfgang Uliman,[11] how he had earlier been taught against infant baptism by Lorenz Hochrütiner,[12] met with Conrad Grebel on his way to Schaffhausen and was so thoroughly convinced by him in favor of rebaptism that he would not have merely a pan of water poured over him but entirely naked and bare was pushed under and immersed in the Rhine by Grebel.[13] When he got back home, he boasted of great mysteries and revelations[14] that came to him on the journey, on which the true grounds of justification and salvation depended. Many brethren were very eager and thirsty to hear about this, what it might be; for we thought—indeed, we knew—we had the gospel of Jesus Christ. On March 18 a great number of brethren assembled in the Weavers' Hall in the marketplace with the intention of calling the aforementioned Wolfgang Uliman and asking him to help Dominik Zili,[15] the schoolmaster, conduct the reading in the church, to see whether one could learn the basis of salvation. But he soon appeared, stepped into the middle of the room, and said with a loud voice: "The heavenly Father has revealed to me that I should not proclaim his Word in the church from the pulpit (at that time there were still images in the churches), for the truth is never spoken there and none can be spoken. But if you want me at some other place, be it at the marketplace, on the Bruol, etc., I am willing to reveal to you what my heavenly Father gives me." Many brethren were shocked at these words and an inquiry was held. Then one said: "Dear friend, you know how eagerly and earnestly you requested the government last year and received permission to have room in the church for reading. If we leave this again and make use of other unusual places, we will be regarded as irresponsible; therefore consider it well." After him another said that it seemed strange and unreasonable to him that Wolfgang spoke such seemly but yet indefinite words; for he had never heard nor read that the apostles compelled the people to hear the sermon according to their pleasure, but they were glad when they could be heard in quietness, whether in the temple, synagogues, before the devil and hell. Everywhere they drove out the devils, idols, and images; the devils and idols did not drive them out. But he, Uliman, persisted, and those who adhered to him abandoned our Bethel[16] or house of God for Bethaven,[17] or place of lies, ganged together in homes, hills, meadows, and considered us as heathen, but themselves as the Christian church. And that was the first split among the Protestants here at St. Gallen.

Eight days later[18] (may God always grant his protection) the oft-mentioned Conrad Grebel himself came, for which those who rejected infant baptism had great joy in the confidence that they would now bring forth to the light of day the project with which they had been pregnant now for a whole year. But they did not detain him long. On Sunday, it was Palm Sunday,[19] they took him out to the Sitter [River] with them and received baptism from him.[20]

After this his adherents among the citizens arranged to have him brought to the Weavers' Hall to open to the public his admonition about infant and adult baptism (which happened), to see if they might catch some into their gang. But this was his manner and custom: If anyone wanted to contradict him he answered, "If you wish to discuss with me, then come to me naked,"[21] meaning that there should be no interruption but credence granted to his reasons. They were not allowed to argue.[22] For this reason some listeners were turned off,[23] thinking that he ought to tolerate and reply to opposition good-naturedly.

But as soon as Conrad Grebel left that same week, several of the imprisoned men of Zollikon (mentioned above)[24] came in his stead in order that the game that had begun should not fall apart, but that God's testing might abundantly move believing hearts who were newborn through the gospel; and with them [came] the clamor among the Anabaptists that the doors of the prison in Zurich had opened by themselves,[25] as is read in the stories about Peter.[26] But before long it was discovered that they had been opened with the aid of a strong iron rod or lever. [*To be continued in 69E, below*]

Original: Same as 65A
Transcriptions: Kessler, pp. 143, 144-46; Fast, pp. 602, 603-4

69B
Charges Against an Unnamed Person [Grebel?]
St. Gallen, May 15, 1525

The following document is a succinct, curious minute of the Small Council of St. Gallen concerning some informal evidence brought against an unnamed person whom Fast guesses to be Grebel (Fast, 1973, p. 382). Some evidence for this conclusion is given in footnotes 2, 3, and 5, below. If, indeed, the accusations pointed toward Grebel, they were heard a month after his departure, for it is known that he left St. Gallen before Easter, April 16.

On the 15th day of May 1525, what the Small Council [heard]:
1. [He] slandered Our Lady with seven children.[1]
2. [He] stripped the people naked[2] and baptized [them].[3]
3. Woman and man in common as the Grubenheimers.[4]
4. If he had not eluded them, they would have seized him and chopped off his head.[5]

More information [requested].

Original: Stadtarchiv (Vadiana) St. Gallen, RP.110b
Transcription: Fast, No. 447

69C
Zwingli's Treatise on Baptism, Rebaptism, and Infant Baptism
Zurich, May 27, 1525

The writing of the following treatise On Baptism, Rebaptism, and Infant Baptism, *often designated by the short title,* Taufbüchlein, *was important to Zwingli for two reasons. First, the doctrine of baptism was important to him because of its connection with his themes of covenant and election. He had first announced his intention to write a separate treatise on baptism in his* Commentary on True and False Religion, *published in March 1525. Second, as Bullinger reported (see 68B/335/27-30), he had done much of the research on the subject in preparation for the January and March Disputations with the Anabaptists, and as he explained in his letter of March 31 to Vadian (see 68M/356/23-29), the publication of his conclusions was important as a further step of suppressing these allegedly heretical and seditious doctrines.*

As he began to work on the treatise, his first intention was to dedicate it to the May family of Bern; but when the conflict with the Anabaptists in St. Gallen reached a level of crisis in May (see 70A/380), he decided instead to dedicate the Taufbüchlein *to "the entire community of the city of St. Gallen." Vadian had already written a* Schrift wider die Täufer, *which was to be the subject of discussion before the council on June 5 and 6 (see 70B/384), and there is no evidence that he had asked Zwingli for help; but the latter felt especially responsible since the movement had spread directly from Zurich to St. Gallen through such leaders as Grebel and Hochrütiner, whose return to St. Gallen had been commended by Zwingli (see 57F/255/17-31). As soon as the book was off the press, Zwingli sent a shipment of multiple copies to Vadian by a courier who had delayed his departure until it was ready. For the fascinating account of its reception in St. Gallen, see 70A/383/22ff.*

The treatise was divided into four parts: (1) the letter of dedication, (2) the correct doctrine of baptism opposed to the views of the Anabaptists, (3) the false doctrine or rebaptism, and (4) the doctrine of infant baptism, including the reformed baptismal liturgy recently adopted in Zurich. Sections of part 2 were included in 68L, above, and a full English translation of this important section is found in Bromiley, pp. 129-75. Moreover, a translation of the new baptismal liturgy is found in Kidd, No. 192, pp. 423-24, and corrected by Bromiley, p. 122, fn. 16. Thus, only parts 1 and 3 are included here, which still leaves part 4 (except for the liturgy) unavailable in English.

To the honorable, wise lords, burgomaster,[1] councilmen, and the entire community of the city of St. Gallen, Huldrych Zwingli wishes grace and peace from God and our Lord Jesus Christ.

Honorable, gracious lords and dear brethren in God! I am deeply grieved by the storm[2] that has befallen the heyday of the expanding gospel among you. But I am not greatly surprised, for the enemy never acts otherwise. Wherever God has opened his Word, he has sowed tares among the seed.[3] In nearly all the epistles of Paul we find that some whose claim of believing was more hypocritical than real gave serious offense to the Word of God for the sake of external things. Likewise we see some in our times who, shortly before the beginning of Anabaptism cried to all the people: "External things are of no value. They cannot contribute to salvation. Let no one place his hope on them." And they were right to the extent that they spoke out of true love and with moderation. Yet now we see them shattering all Christian peace for the sake of an external sign and calling anyone who contradicts them a heretic and antichrist, even though their activity is nothing but heresy, that is, sectarianism[4] and partisanship. I mean [that] those who initiated the strife over baptism had previously urged us often to begin a new church,[5] that is, congregation or gathering, supposing that they would gather a church that was without sin. But when we saw the daily improvement and growth of the gospel, we refused to agree to a separation. Then they banded themselves together to such an extent that the council had to look into the matter. When things were made difficult for them, they brought up infant baptism. We were all surprised that they were so vehement about it; but at last we discerned that it

363

happened for the reason that if infant baptism were rejected, then it would be proper for them to rebaptize themselves and actually gather their church by means of rebaptism. When I say "we" I mean all of us who teach and watch at Zurich.[6] Then they wanted a special disputation on baptism to be held. When we conducted two such disputations,[7] they displayed such anger and hatred—for both times they were defeated—that all the educated men who were present could easily discern their spirit and that it would not be advisable, but even dangerous, to hold further disputations with them. Therefore we addressed them with such earnestness and admonition that they would consider the risk of quarreling with the learned and would strive for peace and innocence, that we parted from one another in such a spirit that we thought they would conduct themselves properly. Since they were unable to defeat us and the honorable council refused to allow secret meetings, they went out to the countryside and turned the minds of the believers to only the scandal of rebaptism. That was the topic of all their preaching. For even though they taught other Scriptures, their chief teaching was always that infants should not be baptized. I say this only as proof, so that everyone may be able to judge how rightly or reasonably they defamed us as heretics among the simple folk. That is enough to call it rebellion[8] and partisanship. They were refuted by doctrine and then initiated a church of their own, separated themselves and formed a party. On this I will not say a word. I will charge them with it before the honorable Council of Zurich and will prove the truth of what I say with irrefutable testimony. But let every devout Christian judge whether they have acted in a Christian way or not when they have everywhere in actual fact, without the consent of the established church, brought forth one of their own, for the simple reason that they were refuted by doctrine. If it should go on this way, that anyone could follow his own confused head and start whatever he wished without asking the church about it, there would be more deviates than Christians. Every church should act and decide on public matters, and not each individual or even one hundred separately, as we can judge from Matthew 18[:17] and 1 Corinthians 14[:29] and Philippians 3[:16]. Therefore, they are truly the people of whom John says in 1 John 2[:19]: "They went out from us, for they were not of us. For if they had been of us, they would have remained with us. But (this happened in order that) they could reveal that not all of them were of us." And even though they say, "The church of Christ has no sinners," they reveal their own hypocrisy[9] in that they consider themselves sinless, which is the greatest sin.[10] But if they consider themselves purer, why then do they separate themselves? I find that there are indeed many Christians who are not rebaptized and are nevertheless capable of bearing and suffering all things for God's sake. But look at the road they are taking! In the first place, they act like Alexander Pseudomantes.[11] He refused to perform his magic where there were Christians or Epicureans;[12] for they saw through his game.[13] Thus they say first, "Don't listen to Luther, Zwingli, and those who preach in Zurich. They are antichrists." Is that the case? I mean, they are afraid these named men can break up their thing. Second, they have about them the appearance of humility, with which the devil has always deceived the simpleminded [and] from which also all monkery arose. Of them Paul speaks in Colossians 2[:18f.], "Let no one deceive you, pretending to do so in humility and the spirit or adoration of angels, by becoming involved in that which he has not seen, vainly puffed up by the desire of his flesh, but not holding to the head, from which the entire body, nourished and bound together by the joints and ligaments, grows with an increase from God." Their pretended humility is clearly revealed to those who talk or debate with them, [who see] how hostile it is. But I do not want to be unfair to them[14] as they are to me and say things in derogation of me that have no basis in truth. I stoked the fire that closed the city and canton against them. But I have publicly in their presence pleaded before the council that they should not be allowed to go underground and I said privately to individual persons that it would be better to let them stay in the canton than to expel them;[15] we have always, after all, been the victors. I do not shudder at an enemy when I know beforehand that he will be defeated. That is the injury that I have inflicted upon them and had great pity for them in all their woes, and have so often begged them in a friendly way to desist from their wrong ways, all of which they cannot deny. Now let everyone judge which of the two acted in a more Christian way toward the other. I will not mention their dishonorable talk in which they indulge in their secret meetings contrary to all truth, with such hateful words that I wonder how it happened that the Holy Spirit spoke so hatefully in earlier times. What is now to be done with these confused people? If you plead with them kindly, it does no good. If you overcome them and expose their lies, they revile you and want to refute everything with slander. They subsequently act no less according to their own heads than before. They egg the simple-hearted on with the external, elemental thing—baptism—and some of them also with community [of goods], who try to say that everything should be held in common,[16] concerning which we have this to say briefly: As far as the possessor is concerned, one should always earnestly teach that he give to the needy as to a member of our body. But that the needy should conclude from this that they may take another's possessions, that is wrong. Now the disturbers try to teach this, several of whom go to that extent when they speak so arrogantly of community. Of this it is not appropriate to speak now. Nor should one let the untruth that might be to the disadvantage of a Christian people pass unanswered, as when they say among the simple people as in Deuteronomy 4[:2] and 12[:32]: "You shall neither add to my Word nor take away from it." Since God did not say that infants should be baptized, infants should never be baptized.[17] To this one can give them two answers which they cannot refute, but still they fight. Then comes defiance, so that he would rather lose his life than yield and reform.

The first one is: Does it say anywhere that infants should never be baptized? No. And so they are adding to the Word, not we. For those who say that they should not be baptized are the ones who raised the issue. They should also show where it is written that infants should not be baptized. Otherwise, they are adding to the Word. For we are not adding to it; we include the children in "people" and "men." But then when they counter with Matthew 28[:19f.], "teach and baptize them," the consequence will be that they do violence to the Word, for baptism was not instituted at that place.

The second answer is: It does no good to say in reference to things which should be forbidden, "Add nothing to my Word," but only to the things that should be considered sin; for they must show a prohibiting law. "For where there is no law, there is also no transgression," Romans 4[:15]. Now if infant baptism is not forbidden with a law, it is not sin. If their error were allowed to spread, when a matter has its basis in God's Word, but the arguers do not understand it so but say it has no basis and want to undertake whatever they wish on their own assertion and quickly run through all the lands and when they are proved wrong and defeated by the truth in one place cause disturbance in another, then I would have to admit that I do not know what Christ is.

Now I hear for a fact that some of them present some strange interpretations from the Old Testament to the simple people. I cannot understand how they dare to do this, for they never granted me the analogy to circumcision[18] for which I had a clear word, indeed, not analogy but in the Old Testament it was precisely what baptism is in the New. But that is unimportant. We shall not allow the Jewish fables to lead us astray, Titus 1[:14]. For we are well instructed that every firm believer desires no less than Abraham to dedicate his child to God [Gen. 17:23-7; 2:4] and makes it his highest concern; thus, the children with their godparents are saved by the parents so that if the parents should die, the children will not fall into faithless hands or teachers and be turned away from God. And nonetheless the salvation is God's alone, but it comes from the devoutness of the faith of the parents.

366

Therefore, devout, wise lords and brethren, as you have hitherto been widely noted for your worldly wisdom and in all kinds of negotiations,[19] see to it at this time when the devil is assailing us so, tempting with dissension on external matters where the sword cannot reach, yes, see to it in every way that the gospel does not divide you; for there are many Christians who are capable of enduring for temporal things as much as your merchants for their possessions. I will not mention the vagabonds who seek a hiding place with it among the simpleminded, but do not want to have a word said about it, but use God's Word as a pretext for all their faithlessness, which is not merely idle talk but a way of life.[20] Do not lose courage. The confounded Anabaptists will not win the day.[21] It is not of God, for a thousand years ago[22] it was also unable to gain the upper hand.

Accept my writing favorably.

Let us pray to God for one another. May he graciously keep you. Amen! Zurich, May 27, 1525.

Your Wisdom's willing Huldrych Zwingli.

Concerning Baptism

[For an English translation of this first part of the tract, see Bromiley, pp. 129-175]

Concerning Rebaptism

Thirteen hundred years ago, rebaptism brought much strife also and caused so much confusion[23] that the present rebaptism is child's play[24] by comparison. But it was nevertheless subdued.

The cause of our Anabaptist movement is not unlike the cause of the earlier one. As there were at that time many causing disturbances and divisions, just so at present every saturnine blockhead[25] begins a new sect. At that time the bishops assembled, that is, the priests and watchmen, and searched what basis in the divine Word the strange ideas might have; and when they found that these brash men defended their useless activity (for they proudly promoted very strange, foolish opinions which do not need to be related here) out of their own obstinancy, not with the truth of the divine Word, they warned them kindly. But those who subsequently still refused to abandon their false wisdom were avoided as sectarians, rebels, or segregationists. We call them heretics. On their account strife arose in the following way:

The unstained Christians who held to the Word of God supposed that those who were baptized by the rebels[26] should be baptized again by those who were not stained with heretical error. Here you will notice at once that they did not rightly understand baptism, and that they thought the cleansing given by baptism was sullied by the unclean minister. The others, who understood the matter better, thought that anyone who had been baptized properly in the name of the Father and Son and Holy Spirit should not be rebaptized because the error of the heretic who baptized him did not adhere to him; for baptism kept its nature and power, provided it was administered as God instituted it.

Now I shall here omit the error that was involved in their opinion as to the power of water baptism, for it has been sufficiently shown above that no external thing can cleanse the soul.[27] I shall confine myself to rebaptism. In like manner our Anabaptists have found a basis on which to prove that they can also baptize. They say: Either we have previously been baptized in the pope's baptism or we do not know whether we have been baptized at all; and therefore we have ourselves baptized again so that we know and are sure of it.

I shall first discuss the former objection. I must teach you who have made a big affair of rebaptism among the common people and plainly bring your lying intentions to the light of day. You have falsely said that infant baptism was first instituted by Pope Nicholas II.[28] That would be about six hundred years ago. But you surely know that you fabricated that, for you have both by word of mouth[29] and in writing[30] admitted what Augustine writes about infant baptism[31] in which he proves it to be valid. You are pretending now to be able to reverse that. How? Well, Augustine lived nearly eleven hundred years ago. How could he then have initiated infant baptism only six hundred years ago? You are not uninformed about Augustine's time and teaching. Thus, if you pretend to the common people that it began under Pope Nicholas, knowing well that it is so very old, it must follow that you have undertaken by the lying use of the pope's name to make infant baptism odious. You cannot deny that you have done this. And in the first disputation[32] you have expressly said that infant baptism is not only of the pope but also of the devil.

Here I must tell a good story by which one may discover what a truthful spirit the Anabaptists among us have, so that if they display it elsewhere as well, it can be the better recognized. In the last disputation,[33] when all of us asked over and over again how it came about that they ascribe infant baptism to the pope, which is of course not true, they were to admit that to us or indicate those from whom they learned such error, for the common people cannot know when it began. But they absolutely would not indicate their source, even though they themselves had so vehemently brought it up in the first disputation.[34] Then I quickly attacked and demanded simply to know from whence he got this error which I had so often pointed out to all of them, that infant baptism was by no means introduced by the pope, for it existed earlier and was not papal, nor had any pope even been named or given such authority.

But the one whom I was asking was by far the most arrogant of all and could not read anything but simple German. When he said that infant baptism was of the pope, I said, "No," and denied it as strongly as I could simply to push him to the point that one could discern who had sowed this error among them, for I knew well that he had not read the decree.[35] For those who were similarly taught and publicly had said in the first debate that infant baptism was of the pope, nevertheless did not want to be known as having promulgated that idea. Nor would those who had learned it from them admit that they had learned it from them. I therefore continued to push this audacious fellow and said, "I charge you with lying. You say untruthfully that the pope was the originator of infant baptism."

He said, "It is a fact. Infant baptism is of the pope. I read it myself."

I asked, "Where?"

He replied, "In the papal book."[36]

I said, "Can you read Latin?"

He answered, "No."

I said, "How can you say you read it in the papal book if you do not know Latin and it has not been translated into German?" He blushed with embarrassment. I continued, "You said recently that those who rebaptized you are not lying. Isn't that a lie? Here you say everything depends on truth, which is not true." Then he began to be angry again and to rant with great malice. God forgive us all our sins and direct us onto the way of truth!

To the second reply that they make saying they have themselves baptized because they do not know whether they have been baptized or not,[37] we gave them this instruction. We asked what their names were. And then when they gave their names, we asked them where they got those names. They said they did not know. Then we proved to them that they were dealing in denials and lies, for they knew very well that among Christians names are given at baptism. Then we also asked them if they did not have godparents. They said: Yes, but they still could not know whether they were baptized or not. Then we said, If they were going to continue in this line, they should tell whether they knew they were born of their mothers. They said, "Yes." We replied: As far as their personal knowledge was concerned they could not know whether they were born of their mothers any more than whether they had been baptized. But on the contrary, they could know just as well that they had been baptized by their names, by their godparents, by the daily baptizing of infants as that their mothers were actually their mothers. For in either case they would have to learn it from others. But among Christians it is just as general and certain that infants are baptized as that they are born of their mothers. Therefore their counter-argument was shown to be merely an illusion. We have to point out these fantasies so that all may realize that they cannot show any other basis for their rebaptizing or their own fantasies; for when they attempted to defend it by the verses in Acts 19[3,5], this weapon was immediately snatched from their hands when the meaning was presented as above.[38] Then they turned to these evasions: They were either baptized in the pope's baptism or they did not know whether they were baptized at all. All of which of course are nothing but fantasies on which one should not build so wickedly in such important matters as rebaptism. And even though it is an outward thing, one should not start anything new without a clear Word of God; for although it is a ceremony, it has nevertheless been given in the New Testament as a general sign of the people of God. It should therefore not be repeated.

But these arguments of Anabaptism are false, vain, and wicked. I shall now prove this so clearly and powerfully that no one can gainsay it. You Anabaptists want to defend yourselves so that you may rebaptize on the ground that in Acts 19[3, 5] those who had not been properly baptized before—for they were baptized into John's baptism—were baptized again. So you too have previously been baptized in the pope's baptism, and so you too want to be baptized again. Hear my answer: You were taught in the section above[39] that infant baptism does not come from the pope, and the same from your own mouths and writings[40] (although I shall add Augustine's words below).[41] Hence your argument that you were baptized in the pope's baptism has already been refuted. Now the example in Acts 19[3, 5] remains. Against that you have heard sufficient refutation,[42] that the words, "Into what baptism have you been baptized?" must be understood to mean the baptism of doctrine and does not refer at all to water baptism.[43] But even if it were the case that the people there were rebaptized—which cannot be, as will be more definitely proved later on— you would still have to admit that they acted erroneously, rather than that one should rebaptize. Very well; and I shall now speak in your manner, as you insist on the Word. What Christ has taught and done, that only are we to follow after, and not regard any other master teacher. This will now be proved with Deuteronomy 4[2] and 12[32] and Matthew 15[13], where Christ says, "Every plant that my heavenly Father has not planted will be uprooted." Note clearly here how I am saying it; for I mean that in the things for which we have a clear word and example of Christ, that he had taught and done a certain thing, there we shall in no way act otherwise. Here now your argument against infant baptism is not valid when you say:

We do not find that infants were baptized, hence they should not be baptized. For that does not follow from the force of this saying. Reason: We are speaking here of things that have a clear teaching and example in Christ Jesus, and not of those that have neither example nor teaching in him; for in John 13[15] he says, "I have given you an example that as I have done you should do also." Now if the first saying is certain, that as Christ has instituted baptism for us and has given us his own example, we should not observe it in any other way. Now Christ was baptized in the baptism of John, as well as the apostles, and he was not rebaptized nor were the apostles. It follows therefore that one should by no means be re-baptized. For then it would have to follow that those in Acts 19[3, 5], if they had been rebaptized, would have done wrong and their example should not be followed. You Anabaptists cannot make this syllogism apply. For if the baptism of John (we speak here only of water baptism, for that is the only dispute) had been so weak that it had to be repeated, Christ would not have given us a perfect example of baptism. Also, if one were to be rebaptized he would not have been right in not having himself and the disciples rebaptized. Hence you are hereby defeated by your own arguments.

Accordingly then, baptism should not be repeated for the reason that he who repeats it is doubtless trying to find something in it that he did not have before; and then immediately that would follow which has previously led us into all manner of blindness, namely, that we would seek comfort for the soul in external things. Now the Anabaptists cannot lie that they attribute nothing to baptism; for they let it be known that they have received great quickening of the spirit by it,[44] although that is only old-womanish and foolish chatter. But if they would continually claim it, many would be rebaptized not just once but a thousand times. For if water baptism renews, strengthens, and comforts the soul, no one would refrain from being baptized again as often as he was tempted; and then the manifold ablutions or baptism of the Old Testament would come again.

Third, baptism typifies Christ's death, for as we have already heard in Romans 6[4], we are in baptism led into Christ's death. Now Christ died only once and cannot die again. Just as those who claim that Christ sacrifices himself daily sin grievously because his one-time sacrifice on the cross is sufficient unto eternity to atone for the sin of the whole world, so likewise those sin grievously who kill him again with their rebaptism. They also revile his resurrection. He arose only once; so also we are to be pulled out of the water only once and from that time on sin no more, just as Christ will never die again. But faith should prevent that, and where [faith] has been in opposition to him, [faith] again reforms, and not external duties. They shall correct only in the notorious, unconfused vices, and not [by] each separate sect. For as soon as a sect announces itself to be a church, it is all over with Christian peace and unity, as Paul warns in Acts 20[28-31], as has been said before.[45] Therefore all Anabaptists ought to see to it that they amend their lives; for they have enough to do in being baptized once. According to [the obligations assumed in] baptism, one is to live irreproachably. That can be done as far as God grants without any rebaptism. Therefore rebaptism is instigated only by those who want to be noticed for external things no less than those who in past times hung up their ornaments and weapons[46] in their temples. I know well how arrogantly they will react to my modest writing. But no matter. I know well what leads to peace, reconciliation, and friendship. And so also every believer knows what the true fruits of faith are. Among these fruits they will not find the schism of Anabaptism. And even if they rage violently enough, it is of no consequence. They will not win,[47] for their activity is not out of God's Word. And even if they call me bad names as they are already planning, I will none the less present the truth to them if God wills, and not be silent until the whole world realizes their obstinacy. For God's sake live as Christians and reject Anabaptism, which is now used as a cover for sectarians. The honorable Zurich Council knows well how the letter sounds that was read to them,[48] how in it one man boasts of having been the founder of Anabaptism with two others.[49] But that is unimportant. I submit the judgment of their presumption regarding Anabaptism to the intelligence of all believers; for as soon as their spirit is discerned, they reject everything with this shield: "Why do you judge me?" They indeed do not want to be judged, but whether they judge or not will no doubt soon be seen by what they write.

I have no doubt that some of those who have been baptized will become dissatisfied with themselves, for they will probably see that they have not weighed Anabaptism well. Those I want to ask for the honor of God not to be ashamed of yielding to the truth. For if they should persist in their error, that would be a sure indication that they are trying to win their case by obstinacy. I would have gladly shown them that the meaning of baptism as it is [written] above and will soon be concerning infant baptism below has not been unknown to those who began rebaptism; for all of us who preach in Zurich have examined the Scripture with them on the subject of baptism, twice in private, and once before the Great Council.[50] But they always departed in defeat and betook themselves to the countryside and did not proclaim our understanding of baptism. This they cannot deny. If they have done likewise elsewhere and not proclaimed our understanding, I let everyone judge how good a spirit they have; for they readily say of any one they do not like, "He is ungodly; the devil speaks in him." They call that speaking the truth. And if you tell the truth about them, you have fallen from the truth, you are ungodly or the devil himself. I therefore speak according to the truth by which I will be judged on the judgment day, that I have seen nothing in the founders of Anabaptism but either—as physicians say—a saturnine,[51] melancholy stubbornness and madness, or an immoderate thirst for honor; and the latter they call a mighty spirit. This writing will be requited with disfavor! But I will let our whole church together with the honorable council judge. They have seen and heard their manner, conduct, and words. But we are all blind, as one of them [said][52]—a big, tall fool, yea, so rabid that he truly could not read the German Testament before the council. Yet he had been a priest for several years. After he was banished from the city and canton, he wrote to Myconius a letter so dishonorable, shameful, and lying, and also against our honorable council, that I have never heard a bun-peddler[53] defame anyone more arrogantly, so that we took counsel together not to worry the honorable council with this wicked maniac, but to suppress the letter.[54] In the letter there was a line with nothing but "blind, blind, blind, blind, blind, blind." Among them no one is a Christian unless he acts as they do. Now I know of course what Paul means in 1 Corinthians 7[7], "I wish that all men were as I." But that one out of the world who wished all men were as he they took for a fool. How much greater is the presumption when you refuse to have anyone numbered among the children of God unless he is a blockhead like you? Is one instantly pious when he has been rebaptized? Then we all want to be rebaptized. If rebaptism does not make him pious, why do they repeat it, especially since they have no Word of God for it? Must that not come from pretension or madness? Yes, they say—so that I will not forget their counter-arguments—[that] much has been added to baptism that does not belong to it, [that] therefore one should be baptized in a different way, [that] children are salted and oiled and spittled upon, etc.[55] Answer: It has already been abundantly shown[56] where these things have come from. We will therefore not say anything more about them. But if the key words have been used—"I baptize you in the name of the Father and Son and Holy Spirit"—I ask them whether or not that is the right formula. They will not be able to deny that it is the right baptism. For all theologians and papists have always said these were the right ceremonial words. So now let them tell me whether baptism performed with these words can be invalidated by prior although yet faulty prayers and accessories? If they say, "Yes," then the devil would be more powerful than God, if God's work can be destroyed by the devil's power. If they say, "No, the baptism of Christ is not destroyed thereby," we will have won our point that they were previously correctly baptized. Oh, devout Christians, what troubles we make for one another with such unfounded assertions. We are baptized and properly baptized; for any woman could baptize herself. The most important thing is that we are new creatures bearing the cross of Christ, daily dying and being dead, both at the same time; for the flesh too continues to bring forth its fruits. These must be continually subdued. But all of this takes place by the power of God, which by grace lives and works in us, not by rebaptism, which has not the least appearance in all of Christ's teaching that would resemble it. For what is shown in Acts 19[3, 5] is clearer than light, namely, that they had not previously received water baptism.[57] Let everyone consider not how learned he is or what he hopes to achieve arguing over Scriptures but that he is living altogether blamelessly and giving his brother no cause for stumbling.

So much for Anabaptism, which will later be still more strongly refuted in the discussion concerning child baptism. For they have as their strongest argument: Since infants should not be baptized, they have the right to rebaptize themselves. But if infant baptism is proved to be of God, good and just, this argument of theirs will be overthrown also.

Original Publication: Zwingli's *Von dem touff, vom widertouff unnd vom kindertouff*, published 5/27/1525
Transcription: ZW, IV, No. 56

69D
Zwingli to Vadian
Zurich, May 28, 1525

Zwingli's Taufbüchlein *(69C) was just off the press when he wrote the following letter to Vadian to accompany the copies he sent to St. Gallen. The fact that they were sent to Vadian and not to the burgomaster, Christian Studer, or to the head pastor, Benedict Burgauer, indicates that Vadian was the leader of the Reformation in St. Gallen. He was an influential member of the City Council and was himself to become burgomaster by the end of the year. Grebel knew "that the decision lay in Vadian's hands" (HSB, 145). So he also wrote to Vadian at this time (see Letter 70, below) with an appeal to remain neutral at least if he could not be won over to the Anabaptist cause. The battle for Vadian's allegiance was intense.*

Grace and peace from the Lord.

I have changed my plan of inscribing the book, for it seemed better upon reflection to dedicate it to you rather than to the May family of Bern.[1] Accordingly I will inscribe to them what I had intended to give to you.[2] I feel rather ashamed of the tediousness with which the book is full.[3]

Indeed, it necessarily had to be so. Those people[4] prepare so many lies, they use so many tricks[5] and subtleties, that unless we had exposed those things, unless we had earnestly withstood them, I know not what sort of confusion they would have caused at length. Unless we had published these trifles,[6] they would have persistently tried to yelp among the unlettered common people: "Thus we have done away with those things!" even as they are nonetheless going to do despite us, that is, despite the truth itself crying out against them.

You should remind your council in our name, if you can, that no more serious opposition will ever come to them for defending the purity of the gospel than that of Anabaptism.[7] They so turn themselves to everything unless very quickly they run up against the council and the church's preaching. Among us their commotion has been made tolerable but at the cost of such great efforts as no one would have imagined. You see me fighting hard and bitterly with these enemies of the gospel. All the previous battles[8] were child's play[9] compared with these. For here I am unwilling to attack unrestrainedly lest I incense the council against them,[10] although in the meanwhile they themselves think no better of us, even with articulate words, than of a parricide, mercenary, thief, murderer, impostor, poisoner, and whatever criminal and crime one can think of. Let the Philippics of Demosthenes[11] and Tullius[12] be silent when these beasts bellow forth their words. Truth always conquers. Those people had not studied baptism very carefully, and when we set forth those very things which you see here,[13] although perhaps we spoke more copiously[14] on some points now than before, they were astonished at all we said, although they could have previously gotten a sufficient taste in special meetings,[15] if prejudice had not taken possession of their judgment. But we accomplished nothing, although certain ones did desist, not that they changed their minds, but their nerve. Thereafter, they were really overcome, having already left for the country,[16] [where] their lips found similar lettuces.[17] You should explain therefore that resistance must be severe. You will find in the dedicatory epistle soon after the beginning[18] the reason why they must be so vigorously attacked. It is a sedition, a faction, a sect,[19] not baptism. For at the same time, they teach that a Christian man cannot perform the role of magistrate[20] and they snarl their scandalous and false teachings to everyone: We must obey God more than men.[21] Concerning all the best and most innocent men, they speak no differently than if you should hear the barkings of a three-throated Cerberus.[22] They have put off all human reason, but they have put on the reason of beasts and maintain that this is Christian. You see therefore what they might provide. . . .

When Erasmus of Rotterdam received my *Commentary*,[23] he exclaimed, as a friend of his reports: "My good Zwingli, what do you write that I have not first written?" I tell you this that you may see how far self-esteem can carry us. Would that Erasmus had treated my arguments with his pen! The world would then have been persuaded, so that I should not labor under such a burden of enmity. I always preferred to stay in the background, but the Lord did not wish it; and his will be done. Would that the name of Erasmus had been attached to my book! Then shamefaced-ness would not have held me in its bonds, nor the fear of vainglory. I thus speak before the Lord: After my writings have been read by all, I would wish that my name should fall into oblivion. Glarean[24] rages against me, and takes all measures not only against me but also against Oecolampad.[25] See how the thoughts of the heart are revealed when Mary, i.e., those who are Christ's mother, sister, and brother, are stricken with the sword of persecution.[26] Who would have thought that there was in the former so great a desire for glory, and in the latter so much malignity and venom! The most learned men everywhere congratulate the Swiss, and a Swiss chafes because of Zwingli!

Original: Stadtbibliothek (Vadiana) St. Gallen, Litt. misc. II.269
Transcriptions: VB, III, No. 429; ZW, VII, No. 371

69E
The First Two Swiss Anabaptist Martyrs:
Bolt Eberli and an Unnamed Priest
Lachen, May 29, 1525

Bolt (Hypolytus) Eberli of Lachen, Catholic canton of Schwyz, was burned at the stake in his hometown on May 29, 1525, the first martyr of the Swiss Anabaptists, along with an unnamed priest accomplice. The events leading to his joining the Anabaptists and his martyrdom are told by Johann Kessler in the following fascinating although one-sided report. Incidentally, following a miscue from Kessler, most scholars, including Heinold Fast (Quellen II, p. 728), have placed the family name first.

[*Continued from 69A, above*] Now there was at Lachen in that canton of Schwyz a pious, goodhearted man who had suffered much for the sake of the gospel, called Hypolitus, or commonly Bolt.[1] Several of the es-capees[2] came to him, namely Anthony Kürsiner[3] and a priest,[4] also one called Hottinger,[5] and told him that they understood that there were also some goodhearted brothers at St. Gallen. They were on their way to them. Bolt replied, "I greatly yearn to visit those of St. Gallen, for I have heard much about their faith. I might as well go with you now, especially since the Easter holidays are at hand."[6] Now this Bolt had not been rebaptized, but had on the contrary resisted it. But they insisted so strenuously that he finally allowed himself to be drenched with rebaptism here at St. Gallen. And because he was skilled in the Holy Scripture and had a gift of pleasing speech, they urged him to preach. He yielded willingly wherever they wished him to speak. When our Anabaptists heard that he would preach wherever he was asked, they feared that after the above-mentioned sermon by Wolfgang Uliman[7] they would be judged untruthful and contentious. So they suggested to him that he should not offer to preach everywhere, or he might perhaps have to go into a heathen temple. Then they took him out before the gate to the hill known now as Berlisberg, which faces the shooting range toward Gossau.[8] Almost the entire town gathered there to hear the peasant. The first part of his sermon was on the sacrament of the body and blood of Christ, as he learned it in Zurich from Huldrych Zwingli. At that time this explanation was unknown to the world, and our priest Benedict Burgauer[9] and other brethren were entirely of Martin Luther's opinion, and the other Anabaptists were of Carlstadt's opinion. For this reason the aforesaid Benedict came forward out of the crowd of people. He had himself gone out to listen, fearing that danger threatened the faith of his flock, and as an obligation of his office placed himself in open conflict with Hypolit and his following. But since now the assembly was beginning to get restless, it had to adjourn without completing its objective. After this Hypolit preached at the Butcher's Hall in the city on the Easter holidays and every day of the following weeks. Although he carefully based all articles of faith on the Holy Scripture with abundantly eloquent and Christian doctrine, nevertheless at the instigation and concoction of the kindred Anabaptists, he had to conduct all of his teaching and preaching against infant baptism and toward the propagation of adult baptism. And so with lofty words he proclaimed Anabaptism, speaking of great and striking powers received by the Anabaptists, e.g., how all desire and lust for sin was extinguished by it. For that reason he would let him who wished to receive the water ask for it. Hereupon many of the citizens and rural people consented, especially from Gotzhus and Appenzell. They came to the city daily and asked where the baptism house was and then left again as if they had been to the barber's. After a week Hypolit went away. As soon as he arrived at home in the canton of Schwyz, he was arrested and sentenced to death as a heretic together with the priest who was with him. Soon both approached the fire stakes with joyful bearing and died willingly and joyfully. [*To be continued in 70A, below*]

Original: Same as 65A
Transcriptions: Kessler, pp. 146-47; Fast, 606-7

70
Grebel to Vadian
Zurich, May 30, 1525

On the assumption that no letters were lost, four and one-half months elapsed since Grebel's last letter to Vadian. In that interim the Anabaptist movement had gone underground in Zurich and out to the surrounding cantons. We have read Kessler's firsthand account of how it came to Vadian's town of St. Gallen (69A). Grebel had come here about April 1 and baptized a large number of persons in the Sitter River on Palm Sunday, April 19.

Did he stay in Vadian's home during that time as he had done on every previous visit? If so, did he read for the first time Vadian's letter to him written before New Year's but perhaps never sent (see 67D/Intro.)? This would account for the facts (1) that Vadian's letter was retained in his own file and (2) that although Grebel had written on January 14, the present letter replies to certain comments in Vadian's letter of December 28 as if he had just read it.

In any case, the present letter, while expressing appreciation for all past kindnesses, also indicates a strained relationship. The salutation and opening sentence seem to anticipate that this was to be the last of his fifty-six extant letters to his former teacher, father-confessor, physician, brother-in-law, and colleague in the work of the Reformation—covering eight of his short span of years. Six days later, their alienation became total and permanent, as we will see in documents 70A and 70B. The following letter represents Grebel's last attempt to win his dearest friend to his side or at least to win him for the principle and practice of religious tolerance.

Best wishes to you and peace in the Lord, not in the world, so that it can be in the Lord.

I am very grateful to you for the kindness you have shown me,[1] and I wish and desire that you may be wonderfully rewarded by the Lord God, the God of good gifts. But then[2] when I ponder,[3] when there comes to my mind your wrestling[4] against those who are truly my Christian brothers,[5] I say freely and frankly and as a Christian: I could not wish for another to be requited more liberally than what has been generously done to me by you, so that exonerated, I might be able to say to you what must be said,[5] for though you know this yourself, you have not been moved to give a ready ear more to the doctrine of the Spirit than to the doctrine of the flesh.[6] Be it as it may[7] that you are burdening me; be it as it may that you know it yourself; yet you do not care.[8] Be it as it may that you know it, I say, still I declare: all or at least most of the blame is yours if anything is decreed against them by way of prison, monetary fine, exile, or death.

Beware, beware of innocent blood, for it is innocent. Whether you know it or do not know it, whether you wish it or do not wish it, it is innocent. Their suffering and the end of their lives and the great day of the Lord[9] will prove it. Unto your own ruin were you born to the end of accursed learning,[10] to the end of authority in the state,[11] unless you take heed and recover your senses. I call on heaven and earth as witnesses. Let me say this, I beg, which is true in truth through Christ our Lord and Savior. The Lord permitting, I shall even unto death bear witness to the truth,[12] in which they surely abide and you could (also). I know what is besetting you: money besets you, I think,[13] or your knowledge of the flesh,[14] or the unjust faction of Zwingli,[15] the enemy of the truth in this matter. Do not destroy yourself, I beg. If you deceive men here, you will not escape notice before the presence of the Lord God, the knower of hearts and the just judge.[16] Rather, turn away from the usury of money.[17]Trust God, humble yourself, be content with little, turn away from the bloody faction of Zwingli,[18] flee from your own to the divine wisdom so that you become a fool to the world but wise to the Lord.[19] Become as a child, or you cannot enter into the kingdom of God.[20] Why for your salvation do you not believe even Zwingli, who proclaimed in public according to clear Scripture—Psalms 14, Ezekiel 18—that money leads to damnation?[21] And Gregory, the ninth pope of that name, excluded from the Lord's Supper anyone who had exacted from a debtor anything more than the principal.[22]

If you do not want to stand with the brethren, at least do not resist them, so that you may be less blameworthy and an example of persecution is not given to other (city) states.[23] I declare to you assuredly and truthfully by my faith in Christ, by heaven and earth and whatever is in them, that it is only from my love for you that I have admonished you in this way. Therefore I entreat you through Christ, do not despise me as I speak, warn from Christ, and take careful heed, so that it will have been said to you for the recovery of your senses and not [only] for testimony.[24] If you yield, I shall lay down my life for you. If you do not yield, I shall lay it down for those of our brethren against all who would oppose this truth. For I shall give testimony to the truth with the plundering of my goods and even of my house, which is all that I have. I shall give testimony with imprisonments, exiles, death, and the writing of a booklet,[25] unless God should forbid. But if I do not write in reply, others will not sleep.

You approve the doctrine, Zwingli disapproves it. Why do you wait then, since you know it beforehand?[26] Do you wait so that you may have a pretext for rejecting the doctrine and even persecuting it? My Vadian! Why do you not give testimony as we do? Why do you act only by the power and arm of the flesh, appropriating the Scripture against us after your own inclination? Do you think that we are mad, or all from hell, or, worse yet, full of demons.[27] that we are prepared to testify even unto death, to that death moreover which Zwingli and the others prepare while they withhold the truth in falsehood?[28] If the doctrine is sound, as sound it is, as you admit with partial assent,[29] and you deprive them of election,[30] why do you not elect yourself or another, or why were you not elected, or why does the council not do it and baptize? Why does it not elect? Why do not the priests, *die wider die ler sträbend und nit erwelt sind* [who strive against the doctrine and are not elect]?[31]

See how you trip yourself up and betray by your own words that you have one thing in mind and your words sound another. For if these were not baptizing, not one of you to whom you assign this duty and who you say are the elect should baptize. So you betray yourself to desire that baptism might be held up to derision and contempt, the doctrines and precepts of baptism approved by you. For the doctrine and precepts of the Lord are given in order to be fulfilled and put into practice. Again I say, if you deceive the council,[32] who do not give attention to this, you will not deceive the Lord.

Pray for me to the Lord that his just will alone extend to us, and I in turn will pray fraternally and unceasingly. Endure with a Christian and patient spirit and take care. Farewell in the Lord Jesus Christ. Greet my sister[33] and family for me with expressions of thanks.

Zurich, the Tuesday before Pentecost, 1525.

To Joachim Vadian, my brother-in-law and brother in the Lord.

Original: Stadtbibliothek (Vadiana) St. Gallen, VB.II.238
Transcritpions: VB, III, No. 430; M-S, No. 70

70A
The Reactions to Anabaptism in St. Gallen
May and June, 1525

When the Anabaptist movement in St. Gallen grew rapidly over the Easter holidays of 1525, the local City Council under Vadian's leadership was reluctant to take the same suppressive steps that Zurich had taken; but when it was reported that over 800 persons had been baptized within several weeks, the council proceeded to act. The first step, taken on May 12, was to schedule a written exchange of views in a week, first by the Anabaptists in the form of a defense of their position and then by the local pastors Burgauer and Wetter in the form of a response.

From his secret hideaway, Grebel responded to the request of his brethren in St. Gallen to furnish a "writing" that they could use for their part of the exchange, which he did in the form of a letter addressed to the burgomaster and City Council. According to the following court record, the letter was subsequently taken to Zurich, supposedly to ascertain whether the Zurich authorities might want Grebel returned to stand trial for violation of the Zurich mandate against promulgation of Anabaptist doctrines and practice; and the letter is no longer extant.

The response of the St. Gallen clergy to the letter was written by Vadian himself in the form of a treatise which, although also lost, is known today as his Schrift wider die Täufer *(see Näf, II, p. 552). Näf observes that "it lay before them as if already prepared, finished after a few days, and it was soon known to the leaders of the Anabaptists, whereupon they proceeded to explain to the council that the treatise was too extensive and they found it too difficult to respond immediately." The council was considerate and agreed to allow two more weeks, until Pentecost. In all likelihood, the St. Gallen Anabaptists turned again to Grebel for assistance. On June 5, the two sides met in the Rathaus, where, instead of the free exchange earlier envisioned, a letter from Grebel was read, Vadian read from his treatise, and the formal response to it by the Anabaptists was postponed till the next day.*

(Continued from 69E, above) But in the jurisdiction of our city, they, the Anabaptists, set up their camps in the shooting lodges and in the fencing hut under the lindens in front of the Multerthor [gate].[1] There they preached long almost every evening. Their subject matter amounted to nothing more than opposition to infant baptism, how it was not instituted by Christ, never practiced by the apostles, but invented by the popes without foundation; for since only believers are to be baptized, infants can cry better than believe. One might perhaps baptize someone in infancy, (but) when he comes to his years of understanding he might wantonly prefer not to be baptized. Therefore one should wait until someone in adult years can submit to baptism and now to rebaptism by his own consent. They were greatly concerned that an evildoer after receiving baptism should not again want to become pagan. But because they were of the common people, not much practiced in the Scripture, they tried to reject this and defend the practice by always quoting at the beginning of the sermon the verse in Matthew 11[:25]: "I thank thee, Father, Lord of heaven and earth, that thou hast hidden these things from the wise and understanding and revealed them to babes." Besides, they protested that they only wanted to speak what the heavenly Father gave and revealed to them. By this lofty and striking designation, the listeners were captured, so that they held the ordained clergy to be scribes and therefore seducers. Some considered nothing to be true and from God but what was said by the Anabaptists, who boasted of heavenly voices and revelations. At the

same time their conduct and attitude seemed quite pious, holy, and blameless. They avoided costly clothing, despised costly food and drink, dressed in coarse material, covered their heads with broad felt hats, their walk and life very humble. They carried no gun or sword or dagger, except a broken-off bread knife. They said the former were wolves' clothing which the sheep should not wear.[2] They did not swear,[3] not even the obligatory civil oath to the government. And if one transgressed herein, he was banned by them, for there was daily excommunication among them. In speaking and arguing they were hard and sullen and so unyielding that they would rather have died. They insisted more powerfully on justification by works than the papists. Thereby those newly born through the gospel became quite confused in their conscience and were made depressed, for they had just recently learned that it is the grace of Jesus Christ, received by faith, that saves. In such trials and blows I always took for myself Paul's saying to the Galatians [3:2], "Did you receive the Spirit through the preaching of the law or through faith? etc."

Indeed, they claimed to keep their church so pure and unspotted that Felix Mantz, one of the arch-Anabaptists of Zurich, adduced and alleged that they were without sin;[4] for to the man who has received the faith and later falls back into sin, no further absolution after forgiveness for sin could be claimed. He thought he had the basis for this in Hebrews 6, without considering that such a conception contradicts the entire totality and intent of the epistle, which presents Christ to us as a priest who eternally represents us before the Father, yea, one who knows and understands and pities our weakness, etc.

Then, since our town of St. Gallen was divided into so many ideas and faiths, such as papists, Christians, and Anabaptists, and the Christian congregation known as St. Lawrence[5] daily lost members to the Anabaptists—they no longer wanted to attend the preaching services but to run after the Anabaptists around mountains, forests, and fields—our government sought to prevent this and ordered: If anyone wanted to preach or teach, which they would not forbid anyone to do (so that they would not be considered to be tyrannical or using force), he should do so, (but) in town in the churches in accord with the regulation of the community, so that the community does not become so split up and the common alms for the poor decline. If one preaches the Word of God, he has the right; if not, he can be brought before the four appointed judges and called to give account of his teaching and to forestall error.[6]

When they, the Anabaptists, were presented with this order, they became as angry as a dog from whom a bone is taken from his maw and absolutely rejected it. They would rather die than walk into our church. In the evening the oft-mentioned Wolfgang Uliman, preaching in the Shooting Lodge,[7] made a speech against the magistrates, calling them heathen who rebel against Christ (Psalm 2) (and) defaming them before the community with such heat that it was to be feared, unless God in his mercy prevented it, that an uproar would ensue.[8]

Thereupon, our lord Doctor Joachim Watt [Vadian] offered to explain to the honorable council from the Holy Scripture how the manner and practice of preaching of the Anabaptists was an improper misdemeanor against the custom and teaching of the apostles and undertaken by their own choice without any Christian calling; and he would base it on Scripture. Then they, the Anabaptists, offered to present their reply in writing.[9] And so the statements of both parties were presented in writing to the honorable Large Council and read on June 5.[10] The Anabaptists thought they had thoroughly refuted and overthrown the doctor's arguments, and refused to be convinced to the contrary. Therefore, persisting in their activity as before, they began to take the matter in hand with greater force. Soon 800 Anabaptists were counted!

Meanwhile, when Huldrych Zwingli heard that our town was so overgrown with Anabaptists, he wrote his book, Concerning Baptism, Infant- and Re-Baptism, as a comfort and instruction to the honorable council and community of St. Gallen, and had it published on May 27.[11] When the book reached the hands of Dominic Zili,[12] one of our preachers, he was excellently instructed by it and strengthened against the Anabaptists, and subsequently offered in one of his sermons to read Zwingli's entire book to the entire parish that evening. The Anabaptists were also to be present and reply to the arguments, whether they could refute them with the truth of the Holy Scripture.

In the evening the burgomaster, council, and parish assembled in the church of St. Lawrence. The teachers of the Anabaptists were also summoned and invited there. They stationed themselves in the back of the church on the balcony.[13] When Dominic began to raise the book to read from it, the oft-mentioned Wolfgang Uliman[14] among the opponents in the balcony lifted up his voice and cried out, "Oh, I am sorry that the poor people present here are to be misled by such a book. Stop reading and give us God's Word[15] instead of Zwingli's."

By these words they won over the assembly. The people regarded them as if the truth of God were with them, but they regarded Dominic as if he were giving the doctrine of men. It made no difference how often Dominic might say, "Dear brethren, these are not Zwingli's and not man's words, but founded on God's Word." But they insisted that he lay the book aside. In this tension the burgomaster began to speak, at that time it was Christian Studer: "Dominic, you are to read the book, and they are to reply to the arguments and Scriptures." Then another Anabaptist said: "We are waiting also for a writing by Brother Conrad Grebel. When we get it, we will give answer." Thereupon the burgomaster said, "Since you could speak so happily at the Shooting Lodge without Grebel, do it here too." They replied again, "We have a letter here from Conrad Grebel to the burgomaster and the council.[16] We want to read it, so listen carefully to what C. Grebel has to offer against Zwingli." The burgomaster said: "If you have kept letters from us, why do you not give them to us? You should hand them to us and not read them."[17]

After this, how many words were spoken back and forth! Finally the Anabaptists left the balcony and departed with these words: "If you have Zwingli's word, we want to have God's Word." Here the authorities in such a disunited parish, in order to avoid civil strife and division, could not lay an unrestrained hand on anyone, but first had to have one hundred men selected who would have the sworn duty to come to the defense and protection of the government if need should arise.[18] *(To be continued in 71E, below.)*

Original: Same as 65A
Transcriptions: Kessler, pp. 147-49; Fast, pp. 608-11

70B
Court Proceedings in St. Gallen
June 5 and 6, 1525

At a public hearing scheduled by the St. Gallen City Council for June 5, Grebel's letter to the burgomaster and council (see 70A/384/6-7) was read and Vadian read his Anti-Anabaptist treatise with the followers of Grebel present. On the next day the Anabaptists were permitted to read their formal response to Vadian's treatise, ideas for which were probably also sent by Grebel (see 70A/384/3).

A discussion ensued, resulting in certain actions against the Anabaptists. They were to cease all irregular meetings but were permitted to meet in the Church of St. Lawrence on Sundays at 5:00 or 8:00 o'clock. Within the next several days, the council approved heavy fines for all who were rebaptized and banishment for all who attended the irregular meetings apart from those approved in the St. Lawrence Church. Moreover, a special squad of 200 men was mobilized (see 70A/fn.18) to handle any exigency of mass revolt against these mandates.

The Great Council on Monday after Pentecost [June 5], 1525.
After listening to [a reading of] Conrad Grebel's letter,[1] Burgomaster Emeritus Jacob Krom[2] and Hans Rainsperg[3] were commissioned with the

mandate to present the letter before the council at Zurich and there to inquire what attitude Milords should take to it.[4]

Doctor von Watt [Vadian] read aloud his book[5] that he had prepared against the Anabaptists. Thereupon they asked to be allowed to let the writer[6] who had written his reply read it. It is the opinion of m[y] l[ords] that they should read it themselves tomorrow and meanwhile stop reading, baptizing, and breaking bread in the city and its domain and also everywhere outside,[7] or see what will happen to them because of it, namely, to them and their adherents. But they are permitted to proclaim God's Word in the churches at the proper times.[8]

Giger's sacrilege[9] that he committed in the balcony[10] at the Church of St. Lawrence shall be postponed until the conclusion of the [present] business.

Joachim Blatter[11] has allowed himself to be seen at Uli Mayer's.[12] This shall not be tolerated and a warning is issued.

On Tuesday after Pentecost[13] [June 6] the Anabaptists read aloud their writing[14] against Doctor von Watt and handed it in. Thereupon the Great Council decided:

1. To keep the books[15] and order them to stop disputing.[16]

2. To cease the table [of the Lord] and baptism inside and outside the city and never again within.

3. To confiscate Grebel's letter,[17] which is improper and deserving of corporal punishment; otherwise with best intentions toward him to forbid them once more to hold the table of the Lord or to baptize, by word or deed, in or near the city, or he will be arrested and banished from the city with wife and children.

But it was granted that on the days when there is reading or preaching at St. Lawrence's[18] they may read at five or at eight o'clock.

Original: Stadtarchiv (Vadiana) St. Gallen, R.P.112a & 112b
Transcription: Fast, Nos. 456 & 457

70C
Zwingli's Tract Concerning the Office of Preaching
Zurich, June 3, 1525

In spite of the suppressive measures taken in Zurich and St. Gallen, the Anabaptist "menace" would not go away. Zwingli had a premonition about this "hidden ulcer" when he wrote in his Taufbüchlein that although he "stoked the fire that closed the city and canton against them," he felt "that they should not be allowed to go underground." He could not have it both ways, and underground they went as they took the movement to the smaller villages around Zurich and St. Gallen, in the latter case "to Golddach in the east, Teufen in the south, Oberdorf and Gossau in the west, and Cappel and Fredorf in the north" (see 71E/423/8-10). Hans Krüsi baptized nearly the entire village of Tablat, and Kessler tells how the regular Protestant preachers were deposed by the Anabaptist (71E/423/10ff.).

When Zwingli heard about these feared developments around St. Gallen and in his home country of Toggenburg, he mounted his pen again and published another anti-Anabaptist tract "Concerning the Office of Preaching." The treatise reveals that there were other issues besides baptism that were being debated in the disputations, e.g., the doctrines of the church and its ministry. It attempts to refute the Anabaptist idea that all true believers are mandated to preach, especially when they commandeer the pulpits of the regular preachers.

The tract is a rich source of information about the early stage of development of the Anabaptist movement, which began as if transitory house fellowships and itinerant preachers were the only needed forms of the church and its ministry, i.e., without institutionalizing permanent local counter-congregations. As John H. Yoder writes, "It did this for a few months at least because the roving Anabaptist apostles conceived of the existing ('proto-Protestant') congregations as their own ('proto-Anabaptist') audience. Not until late 1526 or early 1527 (see the 'order' document in my Legacy of Sattler, *p. 44) do we find the local cell set up to run on its own, and only since Schleitheim has the local group its named 'shepherd' (who, however, does not baptize); that action, perhaps because it is a crime, is reserved for the itinerant" (MQR, 1970, p. 137).*

To the honorable and wise Regional Council and the entire community of the jurisdiction of Toggenburg,[1] and to his especially beloved lords and countrymen,[2] H. Zwingli sends prayers for grace and peace from God.

I thank God, the heavenly Father, that he has illumined you with the light of his Word and has led you so well into the knowledge of the truth that you stand so firm in his confession. . . .

Dear lords and brethren! The fact that you are engaged in moderate action to eliminate the worship of idols[3] and are pursuing the proper course to remove from the feeding trough the preachers who resist the gospel shows that you are growing in all godly knowledge and courage. But in this connection I admonish you to take heed that you do not let the devil smuggle in a flaw by which you might fall into an error[4] that would be more harmful to you than the former error. . . . But as I hear, this could soon be happening to you on the part of those who, without the consent of the parishes, come into them and begin to preach and to rebaptize on their own authority. The former [i.e., to preach] leads to a confusion of the truth and the latter [i.e., to rebaptize] leads to disorder. For rebaptism has been

386

initiated for no other reason than to make it possible to band together under false pretense and rebel against the government (when I speak of government I am by no means referring to the papacy; for the papacy is not to be a secular ruler, Matthew 20[25-27]). Both[5] are absolutely contrary to Christ. In the first place, no one should teach but the one who is sent. Secondly, rebaptism is absolutely contrary to God, for it is nowhere indicated or implied, neither in the Old Testament nor in the New. Circumcision is given only once—and it was the same sign to the ancients that baptism is for us.[6] Also, the New Testament does not know more than one baptism. Neither Christ nor the apostles ever repeated it or taught that it should be repeated. On this subject we published a special book[7] just before this one, longer and more tedious than I would have liked. But since these brazen people who set themselves up to be apostles and preachers would like to cause even greater disharmony, we also want to write about the office of preaching so that everyone may be on his guard against these obstinate, arrogant prattlers, and we will do this entirely by means of the clear Word of God. For if one is not on his guard against them, a new error turns up every day, as anyone can perceive. If it were appropriate for everyone in a Christian community to sow whatever he wished and if the church did not condemn him for it and repudiate his error, these people would come up with a new sophistry every day to show off their lofty wisdom and knowledge.[8] Today it is just as it was in the time of the apostles. At that time several men came down from Jerusalem to Antioch, Corinth, Philippi, Crete, [and] to the Galatians, and presumed to teach. But all their zeal was centered on external matters, principally circumcision; and because they were from Jerusalem and were Israelites, they were well respected and honored. To increase their credibility even more they claimed to have learned Christian doctrine from people who had heard it directly from Christ. It is probably true that some of them had seen Christ Jesus in the body. But their principal purpose in making this claim was to stir up opposition to Paul and to bring contempt upon him (for he strongly resisted their seductive errors—so strongly that at least in his epistles he overcame them with the truth). Thereby they caused division in the church. All this they did to make themselves important with the new doctrine and thus solicit their food. But when Paul became aware of their faithlessness, he exposed them to the light by many Scriptures, but especially Philippians 3[2]: "Look out for the dogs, look out for the evil-workers, look out for the mutilators" (this word Paul uses with precise intention). They were planting circumcision, but he called it mutilation, for they were dividing the newly believing people with their quarrel about circumcision, just as if one were now to call the Anabaptists "drowners,"[9] because by that means they are trying to cause great disunity among the believers and then also great harm and suppression to the gospel). . . .

Now let us compare our mutilators with those. First, they proceeded out of Zurich[10] and betook themselves to strangers[11] and duped them with surprise deceit to have themselves rebaptized. But let every pious Christian note how justly or truly they have done it. First, they have been publicly and privately defeated[12] and therefore they should not have presented their doctrine on baptism to other churches nor stained them thus with error. For if it should happen in general that one who is convicted of an untruth would nonetheless contaminate other churches, then there would be more dissension among Christians than among unbelievers. "For by one Spirit were we all baptized into one body, that we might have unity" (1 Cor. 12[v. 13]).

Secondly, in their preaching on baptism they have not disclosed to the simple minded the basis of infant baptism which they have seen indicated in Zurich. And then, as it is well enough known that we in Zurich practice infant baptism and forbid rebaptism—the government by word and deed, and we with the Word of God—they proceed without consideration and speak so disparagingly of the honorable council that it is too much. And they revile the clergy (especially me) so shamefully that all God-fearing people by right should be displeased with their inhuman defamation. It happens that they consider their name very important and accuse all who contradict them of ignorance and unbelief. They alone have the Spirit of God, for they denigrate all who refuse to be baptized or otherwise oppose them. But why do they denigrate them? It must be either because they are not baptized (and then it must follow that the more they disdain the unbaptized the loftier must be their opinion of themselves) or they look down on other Christians because they consider them unbelievers. If so, it follows that they have simply convinced themselves that no one besides themselves has the Spirit of God. Their perverse manner proclaims that they despise the intelligence and warning of so many learned, wise men, so many God-fearing, pious people, and have initiated rebaptism contrary to any basis in the divine Word and set themselves up as apostles. In every parish where the bishop[13] and lay members are indeed believers, they have begun rebaptizing without the consent or permission of the congregation. Are they not the mutilators, as Paul calls them? Could there possibly be greater enemies of the cross of Christ than they, although they protect themselves with a very humble manner? But who has ever begun sects or gangs without a pretense of humility? What is more humble in appearance than the Carthusians?[14] But they[15] had very little to say as to why they were involved in the Ittinger uprising[16] for which they were fined 12 thousand guilders.[17] Note that there is no field, meadow, vineyard, fish pond, field, forest, tribunal, jurisdiction, territory, etc., that has not been troubled by them. Then how many more of them must there first be? And this has developed so recently that many still remember when there were no Carthusians at Ittingen.[18] I mention all this as an example of the way that pretended humility develops into evil. Paul also warns to beware of them (Col. 2[v. 18]). For truly their God is their belly [cf. Phil. 3:19]. I know well what grief was caused by some of them. They begrudge the benefices in Zurich with the exception of the parishes. Nevertheless, some of them would have liked to edge their way into them so that they might lie on the necks of the poor[19] to be supported by them, and they taught (falsely, however) that no one could preach the gospel if he had a benefice.[20] They hoped that the priests would be expelled, and then the next step would be that they themselves would be put in as pastors. Publicly they said, I want no benefice. But if one were to be secretly given to them and pushed up their sleeve,[21] misappropriating the money like the Barefoot Friars,[22] who knows? Thus they would have served their belly no less than the men in Paul's time [cf. Phil. 3:19]. Several of them even came to me and asked me to recommend them for a benefice.[23] This they cannot truthfully deny. Therefore their fame is carnal, for to be rebaptized is nothing but an external thing, just as the former [Judaizers] boasted of their circumcision. These Anabaptists themselves sneak in just as those also tried to slip in. They begin the affair by speaking of God in lofty terms and they themselves present such a miserable appearance as if they had just escaped from a shipwreck. The simple people stand there amazed and frightened. But in the end it all comes to rebaptism, infant baptism, and that there should be no government, and that all things should be held in common, and that neither interest nor tithe should be paid, concerning both of which we have given Christian counsel elsewhere.[24] And in speaking thus they use this trick: in public they utter deep sighs and say: Woe, woe to him who takes in interest and tithes! but you should nonetheless pay it. But afterward they whisper into their ears: When you have paid interest for twenty years you do not owe your creditor anything more. Behold, pious, faithful lords and friends, what comes of this, namely, that they even those who have no interest in the gospel pretend to be more excellent than others and say they will carry through; but then when it comes to it, that no one owes anything to anyone on his debt. To that end the ministry of the Anabaptists and of the self-sent apostles leads. Although much material goods is misused indeed, especially by the clerics, these matters should be decided by the judge, that is, the government; and those who on their own authority either withhold or take from anyone that which belongs to him are robbers, not Christians. But where the government refused to act, God will certainly take care of it. Therefore it is necessary to have a government and for everyone to keep his promises and obligations. For if one were to begin by removing even a Christian government, it would be exactly as if the sheep were to be turned out into the wilderness without a shepherd.

For these reasons, beloved lords and brethren, I have been troubled that your simple pious people should not be thus led into error by these sacrilegious, seditious teachers; for you are at all times my concern as my lords and brethren. I also consider myself one of you forever. For you shall see that where only temporal or vain honor is considered, there no renewal can take place. But where the knowledge and fear of God are found and there is a striving to honor God, no one can defeat you or anyone else.

I therefore dedicate this booklet to you, so that you may be on your guard for run-about wandering babblers and rebels, who can get nowhere with their preaching except where the gospel has already been proclaimed. There they manage to tear down with externals what has already been built up.

May God keep you! May he complete that which he has begun in you. Written at Zurich.

Wherever I can serve you, command me. I shall ever be obedient to you.

Concerning the Office of Preaching

I shall not repeat my reason for writing this booklet. It has already been established that it is because some men are so malicious that without obtaining permission from the bishop[25] or the parish they run into others' parishes, ring the church bells, and preach whatever they wish, and rebaptize, thereby creating disorder and disturbance. And afterward they say that they are doing what is right, for they are sent by God. Herewith I intend to show that they are not sent by God and that they should not be permitted to do this in any parish unless by unanimous consent of the entire parish.

Although this booklet has the title *Concerning the Office of Preaching,* I will, if God wills, also be everywhere speaking of teaching as it was conducted at the time of the holy apostles.

For this purpose we want to consider first the words of Paul in Ephesians 4 [vv. 11-14], where he says, "And he (Christ) gave some to be apostles, some to be prophets, some to be evangelists, some to be pastors and teachers, that they administer the work (of God) for the perfecting of the saints and the edifying of the body of Christ until we all come unto the unity of the faith and the knowledge of the Son of God, therewith to become a perfect man in accord with the maturity and perfection of Christ, that we henceforth not be children tossed to and fro and thrown by every wind of doctrine by the cunning of men, by evil craftiness of deceitful error." These words of Paul mean that Christ has incorporated the offices named here (each of which we will discuss hereafter) into his body, that is, the church, so that he, his body, might become perfect and edified in the unity of the faith and in the knowledge of the Son of God, and become as perfect, strong, and well developed a body as Christ when he reached perfect physical manly strength according to human nature and age, and was slain in the fullness of his physical strength in order that we might not be tossed about by many kinds of bombastic doctrines that are invented in order that men should join them and be led astray.

Behold, all pious Christians! If these offices were instituted by God so that men may be on their guard against manifold doctrines, it cannot be the case that it is fitting for every man to proclaim himself a public preacher. For where there are so many heads and so many minds,[26] the rogue can easily hide.[27] No one undertakes anything so mistaken that he cannot give it the appearance of good. The pope defended his multitude of learned men with this: "Yes, they stand guard that no error arises." But nevertheless in our time they have openly taken up arms to suppress the truth. But shall everyone for that reason take the liberty of claiming to be a teacher or an evangelist? No! That will become clear in the following discussion.

Now first, we want to speak of the office of apostle, for all the offices have certain differences. An apostle means simply messenger. Therefore we Germans rightly say that there were twelve messengers. But still we are not permitted to say: Peter the messenger or James the messenger. The name [apostle] and the office were instituted by Christ. Luke 6[v. 13] says, "He called his disciples and chose from them twelve, whom he named apostles."

So much for the name. Their office is to preach the gospel, that is, to teach the world to know God and itself. Now, if a man knows himself, he must be displeased with himself. As a result, repentance and reform must follow to the degree that he knows God. But this is followed by real, new despair. When a man finds himself so sinful that he needs correction and then improves daily, he will still find such flaws, deficiencies, and imperfections that he despairs of reaching God. Then one reveals to him the salvation that God has graciously given us. That is the office of the apostle, and it is the highest of all the offices. . . . Hence all who preach the gospel have, because of preaching, no other office but apostleship. Thus the apostles surpass the prophets, evangelists, and teachers in this respect that they made the first beginning in the unknown, unbelieving world and spread the Word of God on long dangerous journeys, as we have seen in the case of St. Paul. And God allowed them no comfort or preparation for temporal aid or food and lodging; but for those who would be appointed later in their place, such things are pertinent, as will be discussed later. . . . Thus, there is no distinction among the servants of the Word between the apostles and the others, except that the apostles had to travel about without any preparation or equipment. That is why I have always said that those like archbishops and prelates who boast among Christians of being apostles ought to carry neither purse nor money.[28] They carry on so that even the devil could not do a more evil deed. They do not preach, but want to be called apostles. And they come with such a pile of goods that they surpass the tyrants of this world. They cannot possibly be apostles or messengers, for they not only fail to walk according to the Word but remain and dwell with their churches. Of such we will speak later.

Then in Paul's words follows the phrase [Eph. 4:11], "some to be prophets." This word "prophet" is not Hebrew but Greek and is derived from the word meaning "foretell" and actually means a foreteller, whom we call a predictor, who foretells a thing before it happens. That was the function of the prophet in the Old Testament, and is now the function of the evangelists, bishops, or pastors. They look out for human vices, either to prevent them or, where they have developed, uproot them, as God told Jeremiah [Jer 1:9-10]. . . . That is in short the prophet's principal function, to root out, break down, and destroy everything that has been set up against God and then to build and plant what God desires to have. At the time of the apostles there were, however, also some who were called prophets and who proclaimed the meaning of Scripture to whole churches. For at that time there were as yet no New Testament Scriptures, and the apostles taught by mouth. Then presently what the evangelists wrote some years later in their writings was already learned and understood and believed. Epistles were also written now and then to strengthen the faith that they had previously learned from preaching and had believed by divine leading. From this we learn that at the time of the apostles those too were called prophets who exposited the Old Testament Scriptures before the churches, as is well noted in 1 Corinthians 14[vv. 26-33]. . . . The meaning of these words of Paul is this: When you meet to hear the psalms or Scriptures, if there is one among you who is learned, who knows languages (especially if he speaks Hebrew), to whom God has given a special revelation, who can interpret and translate Hebrew words into Greek and the like, he shall take the matter in hand in order to edify with it. Those who can speak Hebrew . . . speak or read systematically in succession the passages of Scripture in which the prophets are speaking. Then one of them translates the same words into the ordinary language. And he who is not an interpreter or learned in languages should not speak before the exposition by the prophets, but be silent and speak only with himself and with God. Then when the Scripture has been read aloud in both languages, it is usually still not understood. Therefore the prophets now begin to explain the Scripture and to reveal the will of God. Here the prophets must always likewise have been learned in languages, for all the other gifts serve the purpose of reaching to the highest, that is, to the prophets, which means to exposit. 1 Cor. 14[vs. 26-33]. . . .

Now when the prophets have spoken one after another in an orderly way, and in the meantime God has revealed the meaning of the Scripture to someone sitting in the congregation, it would be proper [for him] to speak concerning the meaning of the Scripture, but with such order and discipline that if someone else begins to speak, the former one will be silent. Nor should still another begin to speak while the second is speaking, for it is fitting for them to speak in succession concerning the meaning of the Scripture while the congregation is assembled, yes, everyone in his own congregation and in succession in an orderly way, so that all may be comforted and taught the truth. Note that although it is proper for all the men in the church to speak about the Scripture, it is proper only following the prophets and when the prophet has not understood or brought out the meaning. Therefore those who pretend to be apostles or prophets do not, in expositing the Scripture, act according to the practice of the apostles. They do not stay in their own churches but run to other churches and speak there without the prophets. And whereas they use this passage by Paul to prove that they may also interrupt by speaking from Scripture, they refuse to be interrupted themselves. I could mention examples when the trained prophets were coming to their sermons in which they read from the New Testament; and when the prophets requested permission to speak on the subject, they got the answer: it ill behooves them to speak on it. And when they have explained the real meaning, the Anabaptists did not accept it even though the rest of the church accepted it. And so they do not come into the church because they want to learn but because they want to teach and be taught by no one, although they claim with words that they will accept teaching. Paul says further [1 Cor. 14:30-33]: The prophets gladly listen to one another peaceably, also to those seated if they bring truth to light. For the spirits of the prophets are subject to the prophets; that is, if they are the prophets of God, they will gladly listen to those who reveal the hidden meaning of Scripture. And all of this will take place peacefully; for God is not a God of disorder and dissention but a God of peace. Note how clear it becomes what kind of spirit the Anabaptists have, however humble their pose. Their spirits are not subject to the prophets, but they initiate the first dissension with them. For example, an honorable pious prophet gave to his church the true meaning of Paul's words in 1 Corinthians 3[vv. 13-15], which were thought until then to refer to purgatory, although he was not understood by an Anabaptist who attacked him. When the sermon was over, the Anabaptist accused him of lying. See how friendly the spirit of the prophet begins to speak! If they really have the God who has revealed his gospel to us in these times, they would have the God of peace and not a God of strife. But if they cause strife they certainly do not have the God of peace, who first of all so peacefully revealed the gospel through the prophets or evangelists. . . . Just like those who came to Antioch saying, "Unless you are circumcised you will not be saved" Acts 15[v. 5], thereby confusing the Christian people, likewise these people say, "Unless you are rebaptized you will not be saved," and thereby likewise confusing the people.

Thus we get two distinctions in the office of the prophets. One of them is this: As the prophets in the Old Testament warned against the evil and planted the good, so also the watchmen or pastors in the New Testament. Thus, the office of preaching, the office of pastor, and the office of the evangelist are all the same office.

The second function of the prophets is this: In the large congregations they reveal the meaning of the Scriptures, especially the Old Testament, when people meet to learn the Scriptures. This function has not yet been adopted everywhere. It will, however, if God wills, be established in Zurich in a few days,[29] for the preliminaries have been started already as it was previously promised in the reformation of the chapter of the Grossmünster.[30] And thus, to speak precisely, in this second conception of the office, there will be no prophets except those who can interpret languages.

Next Paul says concerning evangelists [Eph. 4:11]: "but some to be evangelists." This office of the evangelist is not distinct from the office of the prophet,[31] because the prophet is considered a watchman who uproots and plants. He is also no different from a bishop or pastor, as is clearly shown in 2 Timothy 4[v. 5], where Paul writes to Timothy, "Do the work of an evangelist, fulfill your ministry." Timothy was a bishop, and so it must follow that the evangelist and the bishop fill the same office. Paul's preceding words show that he considered the bishop identical with the evangelist, for he says in 2 Timothy 4[v. 2], "Preach the word, be urgent in season and out of season, convince, rebuke, and exhort, and teach." What is that other than the office of a bishop, a prophet, a pastor? This office is,

394

as to teaching, no different from the apostolic office; but the distinction is that the apostles were wanderers or travelers, whereas the bishop resided where he served as bishop or pastor. The apostles were not to have possessions, but for pastors it is proper to have their own possessions, as must be clear, although the envious, seditious sectarians teach otherwise among the simple people. Paul writes in Titus 1[vv. 5-9]: "That is why I left you in Crete, that you might amend the things that are still defective, and appoint priests or elders (here "priest" means bishop or pastor) in every town as I have directed you, one who is unimpeachable, has only one wife, has believing children, who is not charged with unchastity, excess, or insubordination. For a bishop (note that here he calls the man a bishop whom he first called a priest) must be blameless, as befits a steward of God, not self-willed, not quick-tempered, not a drunkard, not violent or slanderous, not insolent, greedy, covetous, but hospitable, a good man, sober, right-minded, just, devout, temperate, who is firm in the teaching of the faith, so that he may comfort and admonish with sound, saving doctrine, and confute and punish the gainsayers." From these words of Paul, which are known at last by all Christians, I want to point out just those things that serve our purpose.

First, there had probably been apostles in Crete who had preached the faith; but as yet there were no priests, bishops, watchmen, evangelists, pastors, or prophets. For he said [Titus 1:5], "That is why I left you in Crete, that you might amend the things that are still defective." Thus, the office of the apostle must have a wider sphere of work or be something else than that of the evangelist.

Second, where he says that the bishop's children should be believers and well brought up, we see that he is speaking of a housekeeping, resident, and respected man. Where are here the seditious who stir up the simple [by saying], "Your pastors should not have homes of their own. They should simply be lodged by others"? And then they raise the doubting question: "If he owns a house, can he ever speak the truth?" Again in 1 Timothy 3[:4], Paul also says regarding the office of bishop: "He must manage his own household well."

Then right after this [1 Tim. 3:5] he says: "If a man does not know how to manage his own household, how can he care for God's church?" Note how clearly the distinction between the apostles and bishops opens up, so that one may know the spirit of the god of sedition. I should like to indicate here that in making this choice, the very poor and destitute should be less chosen as bishops than the well-to-do, for the very destitute usually manage their households poorly. For where one governs well, one becomes well-to-do. But I will refrain from saying it, so that I do not give

395

anyone a reason to conceal his greed. Finally, we read here that a bishop is also considered competent if he can rule his household well. Hence he must have a home of his own. Indeed, he remarks that one who has a disorderly, quarrelsome, careless, destitute family is not suited to have the care of an entire congregation. What would you say now, you quarrelsome people, if Titus had immediately chosen a well-to-do, rich man to the office of bishop with the Cretans? Read the Scriptures more carefully and stop criticizing. The fact that Paul does not indicate rich or poor here, but nevertheless one who is a good householder should not be understood to mean that "housekeeping" implies the heaping up of wealth, for he says the bishop shall not desire base riches. From this the whole church has learned that sensual, bold, greedy persons, usurers or money-grabbers[32] should not be chosen as bishops. One sees clearly by the zeal with which he protects the bishops that they should be given support, that rich men were not always chosen for that office. "For it is hard," as Christ says in Luke 18[v. 24], "for rich men to get to heaven." Nevertheless, they must have chosen such as conducted their households with a certain degree of affluence. That state is not achieved by begging, for beggars have neither house nor household. On the contrary, Paul understood the householder to be a trustworthy man who could manage his household well, so that none would suffer, and was above reproach, obedient, and concerned about the right things. Where there is such a household and householder, care is always taken that there is sufficient to live on without having to be a burden to the neighbor by complaining or begging. It all comes down to this, that the bishops or evangelists are not anti-Christian or papal-oriented if they have their own houses and possessions, but are yet not greedy or inordinately fond of temporal possessions. However, when Paul then explains that the bishop should be hospitable, that is, that he is to accept the poor and lodge them, that is a clear indication that he must own a house if he is to receive people into his house; also that he must have some property if he is to feed the one who comes to him.

Here we want to repudiate the malicious slander that the critics put upon the evangelists when they say: He who has a benefice may no longer proclaim the truth; nor should he be considered a pastor. In Luke 10[v. 7] Christ says, "The workman is worthy of his hire," and he speaks openly about it with the apostles, that they would not be burdened in conscience because they would be eating in the homes of those to whom they were preaching. But if anyone raises the objection that here Christ was speaking only to the apostles, he should remember that Paul applied these words also to the evangelists, that is, the prophets, pastors, watchmen, bishops, and whatever other name they might have. . . .

Since we see here so clearly that those who teach us and walk before us with a good example ought to be supported by us, why do the seditious babblers come and say among the simple Christians: "He who has a benefice should not preach the gospel," also, "Having a benefice is from the papacy," when it is from God, unless you split the twofold gift, honor and benefice, and prove that they are not one and the same thing. What does it matter if you call the support of the ordained a wage (note how spiritual we are; Christ himself calls it a wage), a double gift, honor or benefice, if it is the support of the ordained teachers? Yes, they say, "No benefice should be established. He should live on what is voluntarily contributed."[33] Answer: The regulation of external matters lies in the hands of the Christian church, as Philippians 3[v. 16] says, that all things should serve for peace and unity, and as Paul did in the Lord's Supper or remembrance of Christ. There it was the custom to eat the entire evening meal together, as also Christ did. But when abuse began to arise, Paul abolished the evening meal, 1 Corinthians 11[v. 22]: "Do you not have homes in which you eat and drink?" And finally, 1 Corinthians 11[v. 34]: "If anyone is hungry, let him eat at home." Thus also with the benefices, we should consider that the benefices were instituted when begging became too difficult and too prevalent. Then when the benefices, that is, specified support, were instituted, it was because begging was to end. Still, the poor pastors had to resort to begging again, for the lords of the tithe took their products away from them and left them the stubble. I will cite an illustration. I have often been exhorted to give up the benefices, that then the honorable council would undoubtedly grant me at least one hundred guilders. That would be considerably more than before. God knows how much the confusing liars say I am getting. Besides, several citizens have made me large offers. My dear friend, tell me what I should have done? I saw clearly that if I had given up my benefices, I would have to beg. For I know very well what the pious monkish preachers and master-readers have taken in by their begging. Also much more than one hundred guilders a year has been promised me by private citizens, and Milords would have added one hundred more, and I could have accustomed myself to begging. How much more profitable would that have been than a benefice? But what would the consequence have been? My successors would have taken the same beggar's road as I, and all courage in preaching would have been perverted into flattery. Now since no one is too wise or too strong with respect to avarice, just as with the other lusts, and God tests us in many ways, I let my simple prebend be sufficient because I see that it is best by far to give a pastor a decent, definite annual salary. Then nobody needs to give him a secret supplement. For one who is used to begging acts in any case as if he had nothing and at the same time takes all he can get. But if he has a definite prebend, no one needs to pity him, for everyone knows that he has a suitable living, and begging is thereby completely abolished. Nor should the sectarian preachers laugh, as they jokingly can, about my stating this opinion; for I could easily relate to them how they, with the commission which they have bestowed upon themselves, have eaten and drunk away the possessions of the poor, while they had money in their pockets at the same time. I will gladly tell you what my practice has been whenever I have preached in rural areas, and of course I am not nearly as holy as they. I paid for what I consumed with my own money, and when people offered me money or other gifts, I did not accept them, although such offers have frequently been made. Enough said: "If your eye is sound, your whole body will be full of light," as Christ says in Matthew 6[v. 22] expressly on the danger of wealth. If you are a true servant of God, you will use the benefice to God's honor. If you are not God's servant—which will be readily revealed—you will set your heart on contemptible gain and begging. As soon as that happens you become savorless salt that is fit for nothing but to be thrown out. More courage can be expected from one who has a benefice if he strives for true doctrine than from one who must constantly fear that he will again be driven away. I have no respect for the babblers who come along and pretend that they have no interest in earthly possessions, for in fact they have an interest only in them. This is easily seen in their sneaking in[34] and their stratagems. I have unfortunately learned too late to see through them, and along with the common people I thought it was a *spirit,* but it was a *covet.*[35] But at the same time I also dislike the preachers to whom huge sums must be paid or they refuse to preach. I do not know if they deserve to be called preachers. I do not know many of this kind around here and therefore do not want to be overly concerned about them. For while it is rumored about us in Zurich what large benefices we have, the truth of the matter is this: In the past year of [15]24, I would have received not even sixty guilders if the provost and chapter had not contributed sixteen measures [of wine].[36] If the others have somewhat more, it is very little more. In truth, that is the three hundred guilders that my prevaricating enemies talk about, and the many benefices I am said to have! Nevertheless, I declare by the God who keeps and feeds me that I am content with that; and if I regret anything, it would be solely about the poor whom I cannot aid as amply as if I had more. And I would much prefer, if I could follow my natural instincts, to give up all the benefices on earth if only I did not have to preach. But the time and small talent that God has committed to me do not permit it. The contentious preachers compel me to speak at such lengths about my own affairs totally against my will. As to my wife, Anna Reinhart,[37] they spread the rumor everywhere of how rich she is. But she does not have a penny more of capital than four hundred guilders besides her clothing and jewelry. She has worn none of these things, neither silk nor rings, since she took me as her husband. She dresses like the wives of other ordinary laborers. The annuity[38] that her children, the Meyers,[39] give her she needs for personal expenses. She is nearly forty years[40] old and children come to her daily for sustenance,[41] for which reason I took her. And now they babble about her great wealth and costly dress. But everybody knows that is an injustice to her. But it is easy to tell lies at a distance. The one about whom the lie is disseminated does not always come their way. Her children have sufficient wealth. May God grant that they make the right use of it! But not a cent of all that capital comes to her except for her clothing and other small necessities and the annuity of thirty guilders. I gave my consent to have her wedding dowry included in this; and as her capital, I am not in the least interested in it. Paul also often defended himself against disseminated lies, for he felt that they resulted in noticeable disadvantage to the gospel. I too would prefer to forego this self-defense if the scandal-mongering were not injurious to the gospel of Christ. . . .

Why do you make the pious evangelists hated? For I am not talking about papal priests but of the upright, faithful servants of the gospel. If you have not been aware of the distinction between the apostles and the evangelists, you have flown out of your nest too soon[42] and your spirit has not yet put enough food into the feedbag; and your creating hatred for them is nothing but ignorant presumption. If, however, you have known the distinction but have concealed it, it is not without villainy, and it is not God that has sent you, but a goddess call Eris,[43] in German: Strife. Note, therefore, pious Christian, that when Christ speaks of the small or simple in Matthew 11[v. 25], he does not mean those who are ignorant, or I would be a highly learned doctor. He means the simple ones who are not the children of this age, whose eye of faith is single, who are not wise in order to be great in this world, but despise human greatness and can open their hearts before God. For he made the most learned his disciples: Nicodemus, Paul, Barnabas, Luke, Gamaliel, Ananias, Apollos, Agabus, Timothy, Titus, and many others. But all of them had to become small with their knowledge, deny themselves, become like little children, etc., and not depend on their knowledge nor do violence to the Word of God according to their own notions, nor elevate the intention of the flesh above the intention of the Spirit, nor be great in themselves, but must be humble, obedient instruments of God. And it is Christ's thought that the wise men of the world do not understand the nature of salvation, but the further

399

removed they are from human wisdom, the more clearly they recognize the will of God. However, it does not follow that everything any fool says is true and that he has been chosen an apostle by God. I would like to hear from you why you hold in such high esteem your learned men who agree with you concerning infant baptism and rebaptism.[44] For after all, they are all chancel preachers and paid with benefices. How then can they speak the truth?. . .

Secondly, in Acts 21[v. 9] it says: "Philip had four daughters who prophesied." From these words we can see even more clearly that this Philip had a household and raised his children to honorable living according to the order of the bishops, as was specified regarding the appointment of bishops. I hear that some of the apostles who have sent themselves are beginning to say in order to turn everything upside down: It would be better if the pastors were unmarried. But they are the very ones who used to cry out in favor of the marriage of the pastors. Does it not seem to you time to walk on our heads? Does it not dismay you that all people walk on their feet? You wise critics or Momuses,[45] that is, judges or faultfinders, when will you ever become aware that your struggles are nothing but a quarrelsome bilious bitterness, and not a Spirit? You repulsive highnesses! I do not doubt that it is more functional according to the gospel for a messenger or apostle to undertake journeys when he has no wife. But if he cannot control his passions he should also have a wife and take her about with him, as Peter and others did, as Paul relates in 1 Corinthians 9[v. 5]. But bishops should not be without wives in order to avoid the suspicion concerning which enough has been said; but the suspicion is so warranted and all flesh is to be so little trusted that, although one who now has well-raised children is undoubtedly advanced in age, the apostles want the bishops to have wives.

But I would like to hear from the learned, confused messengers what it was that these four daughters prophesied, since it is not appropriate for a woman to speak at a church meeting, 1 Corinthians 14[vv. 35-36]. It must therefore be noted that this word "prophesy" as used occasionally in the Scriptures means to hear a sermon or to listen to an exposition of the Scripture in church, as is definitely explained in 1 Corinthians 11[v. 5] where Paul says: "Any woman who prays or prophesies with her head unveiled dishonors her head." Here one sees clearly by the preceding and following words of Paul that he means nothing else but that when a woman prays in church, she shall be veiled; likewise, when she sits in church to hear God's Word she should also be covered. Occasionally the word "prophesy" is used in the Scripture to mean explaining the meaning of Scripture, as in 1 Corinthians 14[v. 31]: "You can all prophesy one by one." This means: If the prophets who spoke first about the meaning of the Scripture did not present the true meaning, but God has revealed the meaning to another of the listeners, it is appropriate for him also to prophesy, that is, to talk about the meaning of the Scripture under discussion. It has been indicated often enough above[46] what Scriptures were exposited before the church in those days, namely, the writings of the Old Testament, as is noted in 1 Corinthians 14[v. 26]: "Each one has the psalter," etc., for at that time the New Testament Scriptures were written in the hearts rather than in books. From all this we learn that these four daughters did not prophesy as did the prophets, nor as the common man in church, for women were not allowed to speak in church. Besides, we do not find that they foretold anything. So it must be that Luke is saying: Philip had four daughters who were instructed in the Holy Scriptures and according to them praised God in psalms and other hymns. Women were probably permitted to use those[47] at home. It has been an ancient custom among the Jews that the women also learned to understand the Scriptures and therewith praise God, chiefly with the psalms. And so it has been sufficiently proved that the seditious self-sent messengers do violence to the pious bishops and against God when they say of them that they should not have their own homes or specified food, and if they have them they do not speak the truth. . . .

Then Paul says further in Ephesians 4[v. 11]: "He gave some to be pastors and teachers." Concerning the pastors, everyone knows that he means those who watch. But the same function is almost everywhere also attached to the evangelists; for they are the true bishops and overseers, to whom Christ says in Matthew 24[v. 42], "Watch therefore, for you do not know on what day your Lord is coming." And in the person of Peter, John 21[vv. 15-17]: "Feed my sheep." In John 10[vv. 11-30] he speaks again and again of the office of the shepherd. Everyone knows that here he is referring to the office of bishop. Likewise 1 Peter, chapter 2[v. 25], puts the shepherd and bishop together and says: "You have now returned to the Shepherd and Guardian of your souls," meaning Jesus Christ our Lord. Enough has been said about that. It might, however, happen that in large churches or parishes, it might be too much for one alone to have charge of preaching and also of watching for any danger to the sheep. Then it might be committed to one to be on guard against increasing threats and open misdeeds and to another to proclaim the Word. In our church it is too much for one alone, yes even for two or three, to watch. And although all three of us[48] share the preaching, we have enough to do with just that.

By doctors and teachers, one should not understand those with red hats,[49] gold rings, silk raiment, or gilt linen shirt, but rather those who teach, who are also prophets in the other sense as explained above,[50] and teach the multitude and those who then equip others to teach by teaching languages, or for all who teach, apostles and evangelists. Thus we find that Paul calls himself a doctor or teacher of the Gentiles, 1 Timothy 2[v. 2], that is, an apostle to the Gentiles, as he says in Galatians 2[v. 2]. But here we can discern by the order that by doctors Paul means the learned who also taught, and that they taught those who would later teach, as we see in Acts 13[v. 1]: "Now in the church at Antioch there were prophets and teachers, Barnabas, Symeon who was called Niger, Lucius of Cyrene, Manaen, a member of the court of Herod the tetrarch, and Saul." In these words we note clearly that already at the time of the apostles there were many learned men in several large churches who were thoroughly instructed in the Scriptures and who continually taught others so that the Scriptures would not be subject to misinterpretation, as Paul shows in 1 Corinthians 14[v. 5]: "Now I want all of you to speak in tongues, but even more to prophesy." Here Paul wishes that the Christians knew all the languages,[51] but for the purpose of prophesying. Now he knows very well that not all men know the languages; but he indicates how useful it would be for Christians to know the languages in which the Scriptures are written by his wish that all men had this gift. But he wishes it for the purpose of using it for the benefit of prophesying, that is, the exposition of the Scriptures or sermon. Here the Anabaptists are making a great mistake by daring to derogate the knowledge of languages and saying: "One does not need a knowledge of languages. We understand the Scriptures as well as those who know many languages. It is a matter of the Spirit and not of skill."[52] But Paul does not without purpose wish that all might understand the Scripture. From this we can draw the conclusion: It is true and sure that the human heart will not be converted to God in any other way than by God who draws him to himself, however learned the man might be. Nevertheless, one must have a knowledge of the Scriptures because of those who do violence to it. For nothing is too much for their hypocrisy. It dares to present itself as if coming from the Spirit; but when one finds afterward that their speech does not conform to the Word of God, one knows what hypocrisy is. For serious violence has been done to the Word of God among the common people, for they do not understand. But then one must search for the meaning, whether or not what they say is true. Thereby the believer is well informed as to whether or not the true meaning has been hit. And this cannot be brought about as well in any other way than by a knowledge of the languages. For just as the Scriptures do not remain unknown to us when they are put into the German language, because all of us understand German so well, just so it is with the Hebrew

402

if we understand it like German, and so we can also penetrate the Old Testament. Likewise, if we know Greek as well as German, nothing in the New Testament can be hidden from us. Hence all commentaries and teachers are naught in comparison with a mastery of the languages, as we can see in Paul's words; for he does not say, "I wish all of you understood the rabbis and the commentaries well," but that "all of you were instructed in languages," which means principally Hebrew. But in these areas the common man cannot master them. Therefore it is necessary to have teachers at some places who do some instructing in the languages. And this is not a new proposal. We see that it was started in Antioch at the time of the apostles and has also been practiced in our country. May you and other lands therefore as the opportunity of events of God arises, let the unprofitable clergy die out and use a part of their income for the benefit of the poor churches. But the rest should be used to educate some scholars in languages for the benefit and aid of your country, for otherwise there will be great danger in reading, which is so common in our day, since one can easily see that more of those who read become simply learned and garrulous than pious and God-fearing. They then make their appearance with every outrage, which is clearly not based on the original language and meaning. They can also be overcome with the correct interpretation.

We are not all to be preachers, as Paul shows in 1 Corinthians 12[v. 29]: "Are all apostles? Are all prophets? Are all teachers?" etc., as if he were saying, No! It is therefore a great presumptuousness in the self-sent preachers that they bestow upon themselves all the offices and despise what they cannot lay claim to. I am going to give two examples by which everyone can see how in time they could mislead into serious bypaths if languages are neglected. I could give many, but to what purpose? Everyone who hears them will see that it is a great presumption. At Jerusalem there were thousands of believers, but there were no more than twelve apostles. Here all of them are apostles. I believe there are more apostles than believers! If one has attended a German school and has learned to spell, he appears in public and spells it out to the congregation. I am not repeating common gossip. I know the place where they have not been able to read the Scriptures. They stumbled over the words and one could see that they were just learning to read.

One of the examples is this: One Sunday at a certain place where there is a devout, competent evangelist or bishop, a weaver (I want to be forbearing and not mention any names; but they may recognize themselves) took over the pulpit by his own audacity; and when the pastor came, the weaver said, "I am going to preach." The pastor yielded to avoid confusion. Then the weaver began to read 1 Timothy chapter 4, which the upright people had frequently heard their rightful shepherd read with understanding. And they began to murmur at the weaver's presumption. Soon he came to the place [v. 2]: "whose consciences are seared." Then he said, "I cannot understand that." The pastor replied, "Then stop! I will explain it to you." When that happened, the upright people cried out, "Order him to come down!" Then the pastor replied, "If I should ask him to come down on my own authority, I would arouse suspicion. Therefore, you order him to come down from the pulpit." And so he finally came down. See here, all of you Christians, how the Spirit works. In the first place, he elevates himself without regard for the church as a whole. Secondly, he professes to be a godly spirit but cannot understand it even though he can read it. But then the godly spirit instructs even the unlettered concerning its meaning and interpretation. Thus it is obvious that it is not a divine commission but a spelled-out reading and a puffed-up ingeniousness.

The second example is this: When they teach rebaptism, they take up Matthew, chapter 3. There, among other things in the same chapter, is a summary of John's preaching in which he calls the Pharisees and Sadducees, "You generation of vipers," etc. [vv. 7-12]. Here some of them say before the simpleminded: "See how severely the godly John castigates the Pharisees for refusing to be baptized." Then the simple people are petrified with amazement and do not know where they stand. But that is not the meaning of Matthew's words. He wants to indicate in summary the severe warning of John to the Pharisees who he knew inwardly had not come for baptism with good intentions, and for that reason sharply scolded them, but with more words and teachings. For who could relate all the teaching continually performed by John? If we then have to expect such danger from those who know nothing but the mere letters [of the alphabet], it is more necessary than ever before to have some who are able to extract the actual meaning out of the letters. When there are so many peculiar opinions at the start, what would happen with the passage of time? Now that everyone sees that they so often fail in reading, but proclaim their idea to be spiritual, everyone can see what kind of spirit it is. It is the kind of spirit who refuses to hear what opposes him and wants to withdraw from all obedience and duty into the crowd of the rebaptized. I am speaking the truth. It is seen in the speeches and writings of some of them; but the true Judge, God, will reveal all things at the proper time.

No pious Christian has ever usurped all of these offices for himself at once, but only when he has been sent by God or chosen by the church or the apostles, which is also nothing other than a call or sending.... But the election [of preachers] took place in three ways: sometimes by the entire congregation, as shown above about Matthias; sometimes by the apostles and not by the whole church, as in Acts 8[v. 14] when Peter and John were sent to Samaria by the apostles; and thirdly, by a single apostle, as when Paul ordained and sent Titus to Crete. Here it is noted by nearly all Christians that election by the pope's own authority has been perverted into violence and tyranny, for either the high-ranking bishops, abbots, and feudal lords have made priests of their stable boys, cooks, and pimps[53] against the wishes of the congregation, or if the congregation made the choice, it did so without the advice of the devout, educated believers, choosing a bishop more on the basis of popularity than consideration of the gifts and qualifications stipulated by Paul. Therefore, as to the election, there is no more godly way than that the whole congregation, with the counsel of several devout, intelligent bishops or Christians, choose a pastor, as we see they chose Titus. Although Paul says [Titus. 1:5], "And you appoint," he [Titus] did not appoint them alone, as the tyrannical bishops want to interpret it. Reason: If the decision on the ban and on doctrine everywhere belongs to the church,[54] much more so is the choosing of a teacher not the duty of an outside haughty bishop or abbot, but of the church, which has the counsel of wise Christian prophets and evangelists. But it is also not simply the right of the sincere, naive congregation alone, as is clearly seen in Paul's teaching of the use of the Word, as well as in the preceding examples; for the teaching of Scripture is not committed to the naive congregation but to the prophets, interpreters, and those who are learned in languages, although the congregation is also given a voice in the matter.

Now we want to show in each kind of sending whether these self-sent apostles may be found to have been sent by God, and for the first consider the inward sending. Christ says [John 20:21]: "As my Father has sent me, so send I you." Now if Jesus created disturbances for the sake of temporal goods, then it is proper for them to create disturbances for the sake of interest and tithes. But since this can in no way be proved, it is obvious that they are not sent by God.

God's Word requires that we be obedient to the government whether it is a believing one or not. But they teach that no Christian can be a ruler,[55] even though the opposite is found in 1 Timothy 6[v. 2], 1 Peter 2[vv. 13-18], and Ephesians 6 [vv. 5-9]. By this it is clear that they are acting contrary to God and to Christian peace by their teaching and rebaptism. And even if they swore a thousand oaths denying it, it would still be obvious. As soon as the number of the rebaptized got large enough that they could hope to save themselves, they would set themselves against all government and emperor, that is, the authorities, and refuse to render what they owe it.

The third test by which one sees by the nature of their teaching that they are not sent of God is the truest and clearest to any simple person. Paul says in 1 Corinthians 14 [v. 33]: "God is not a God of confusion but of peace," as can be seen in any church of Christians. But since their baptizing and preaching results only in confusion, they by no means have the God of peace. That is also shown above. Then they say, "Christ said, 'I have not come to bring peace but a sword.' " Reply: The sword that Jesus mentions here is not to be among believers, but Christ means that the sword will be between believers and unbelievers. Now they continually cause dissension among believers for the sake of external things, just as in the time of the apostles, as explained above.

Now we come to the external matters by which we see whether they are sent by God or not. If they are sent by God, then God has revealed this to men either by a miraculous sign or by a clear choice which cannot be denied. But since they neither perform miracles nor are properly chosen by any church, they do not have the outward signs of the office of apostle or bishop. They are therefore definitely not sent by God. All of this has been made adequately clear in the Scriptures already discussed.

Now we want to look at the officers, whether they themselves live and act in accord with the criteria of their offices, which they have assumed for themselves. And again we find that they are not sent by God. If they are apostles, it is their responsibility to travel constantly among the unbelievers and convert them to faith, as it has been said above that the apostles and bishops have the same teaching office. But this is the distinction between them—the apostle travels among unbelievers, whereas the bishop resides among those entrusted to him. If they do not travel among the unbelieving but always impose themselves on believers and confuse what was previously in agreement and peaceful, then they are certainly not apostles.

Nor are they bishops; for they have not been chosen by any congregation of the church along with other excellent, well-informed, believing bishops to that office. Still less are they prophets and teachers. It follows obviously that they are nothing but disturbers.

They have two answers against this. One is: Now Paul says in 1 Corinthians 14[v. 31]: "You can all prophesy one by one," that is, speak on the meaning of the Scripture, and before the assembled congregation. Reply: Prophesying is not yet customary in any church, nor are we beginning it now. But even if one would like to speak there, it does not follow that he may elevate himself out of his own initiative to the office of apostle or bishop. Nor does it follow that he should begin to speak on his own initiative before the assembled church. He is permitted to speak only after the interpreters, language scholars, and prophets have spoken.[56] That is why Paul at that place earnestly admonishes that all things be done in order. For that reason no one should simply assume for himself the office of apostle or evangelist unless he has been called and designated inwardly and outwardly by God. One does not immediately become a bishop although he has spoken before the congregation explaining the Scripture, or Paul would not have needed to specify the many differences in the offices which he mentions not only here in Ephesians 4[v. 11] but also in 1 Corinthians 12[v. 28] and Romans 12[vv. 7-8].

The second objection is: John says in John 3[v. 34]: "He whom God has sent utters the words of God." Then anyone who speaks the Word of God has been sent by God. Reply: By this single verse all Christians can judge that they have not been born of the Spirit of God [cf. Jn. 3:6]. For in the first place these words refer specifically to Christ, but they apply them to themselves. Although it then also refers to those sent, it does not apply to those who are not sent. For it is not the same thing to talk about God and to be sent as an apostle or bishop. We will soon speak more about that. Second, the two ideas: "He whom God has sent utters the words of God." and "He who speaks the Word of God has been sent to the office of apostle or bishop" do not logically follow one from the other. In brief, we are not wantonly to set ourselves up as masters [cf. Mt. 23:8-10]; but every church must have a watchman or overseer in order that insurgent, malicious rams may be mastered, not by the power of the watchman but of the church. For if the office of watchman, that is, of the bishop or pastor, is so neglected and thrown to the dogs that anyone could set himself up as a bishop whenever he wished, serious division could ensue in a short time among those who now offer themselves for preaching. For just as they are now offering themselves and wanting to be considered teachers or apostles, in a few days another gang would come and want to venture to preach just as well as the present gang, and after them still another. This would give rise to serious dissension; for each would provide himself with a following. Yes, so many cranks and so many sects and disturbances would result. Nor am I speaking only of preaching openly in the church. I know, of course, that it is everyone's right to talk to anyone he likes about God and converse with him. But that it is everyone's right to start whatever he wishes in some corner without the consent and agreement of the church which is supposed to judge him and his project, or that it is everyone's right to set himself up as a teacher or pastor who can present himself on his own authority and say whatever he likes in a believing church (I do not call all those "believing" who claim to believe in Christ, but those who believe the gospel faithfully and let it be freely preached)—of those I say that it is not only presumptuous and wicked but actually anti-Christian; for from it no fewer errors would arise than if every citizen wanted to be mayor in his hometown.

Similarly, the objection based on 1 Peter 2[vv. 5, 9] is of no avail to them: "We are all priests."[57] For here I am not speaking of being consecrated or not, but of the office of the preacher. It is true that all of us are sufficiently sanctified for the priesthood that offers the sacrifices in the New Testament, for this consists simply in each offering up himself, Romans 12[1]. But we are not by any means all apostles and bishops, 1 Corinthians 12[v. 29]. And even if one is a bishop, he has no right to interfere in another's flock or bishopric at his own pleasure. In Romans 12[v. 20] Paul says, "I have eagerly preached the gospel of Christ, not where Christ is already named, lest I build on another man's foundation." So it is never appropriate to break into another's flock. I am always speaking only of the shepherds or evangelists who fulfill their office in a godly and proper manner that it may not occur to them to run into each other's churches without prior agreement and stir up animosity against one another. Hence, for the sake of God and Christian peace, I want to admonish all those who are full of restlessness to preach that they consider the words of James 3[v. 1], where he says: "Let not many of you become teachers, my brethren, for you know that we who teach shall be judged with greater strictness." See, the devout, holy apostle opposes this, [saying] that we should not count the office of teaching so lightly that we want to set ourselves up for it without preparation and equipment. But there are many of that kind who either out of desire for honor or out of hate or out of greed try to announce themselves simply as teachers, whereas it becomes publicly apparent that they accomplish nothing but dissension and hostility. O God, do they mean to imagine that nobody knows their spirit or acts, whereas every believing spiritual person knows and judges all things [cf. 1 Cor. 2:15]? We by no means want to keep anyone from preaching on account of his consecration or his person in the case that he is sent, that is, properly installed as a bishop or sent as an apostle. Then he will hasten to the unbelievers and not confuse the believers. But this matter of setting oneself up and creating confusion, introducing new outward things without the previous consent of the Christian congregation can never bring forth anything good, for it does not originate with God. The God of peace deals in a different way, is not so unmerciful, not so bitter, so dissentious as is often seen in their teaching. It is also seen that their products, that is, those who listen to their words, become quarrelsome people, greedy for temporal goods and vengeful, whereas they were previously calm, devout, and peaceful. Thereby one sees that it is a sensual desire, not an impulse of the Spirit. But the devil can come so secretly and in such luminous form [cf. 2

Cor. 11:14] that the plain people take him for a Spirit; but many of them are beginning to see that it is being pleased with oneself. May God remove from our eyes all the fog and deception that we may clearly know his will and also do it!

But I also want to admonish the workers for the gospel of Christ equally earnestly with the words of Paul in Colossians 4[v. 17]: "See that you fulfill the ministry which you have received in the Lord." God has appointed you as watchmen in the church and as shepherds. Watch and take care lest the wolves rend the sheep of Christ or that quarrels arise. Among believers there should be no quarrels, although among believers there is everlasting warfare between the believers and the unbelievers. Do not be distressed that the seditious Anabaptists and preachers accuse you and all that do not follow their way of being unbelievers; for each of you knows well that in God does one hope. Then if they call one of you who doubtless trusts in God an unbeliever, you see plainly that their spirit comes from the father of lies [cf. Jn. 8:44]. Do not be frightened by the doctors[58] who boast so loudly that they are on their side (we well know what they are capable of and what spirit they are); but consider that the community of the Anabaptists can never become more than a sect, and that presumptuous preaching brings forth only unrest, disorder, and dissension. For in any case the greater part of devout, quiet Christians will find no pleasure in the Anabaptist cause because they see at once that the Anabaptists are aiming at community of goods and the abolition of government. It can therefore never become more than a sect which God allows to exist until the elect are revealed and firmly established. See to it that your sheep are kept and walk free of adultery, drunkenness, pride, blasphemy, and all immoderation. Build the faith, the fear of God, and love for the neighbor. Teach that there is no greater service to God than to honor God free of guilt. Teach them not to lose eternal things with the temporal. For this you have a clear foundation in the Holy Scriptures. Do not grow negligent in your work [cf. Gal. 6:9] for these things; for we know well what effort it costs to spare them, as we have done.[59] And yet they talk of so much hardness. If they had been rewarded according to their bold, lying speech which they have practiced and are still practicing, there is no doubt that we would be rid of them. Fight therefore as good soldiers. Do not forsake your place and your office.

The Lord is coming soon. He is near, that he may not find us asleep. Therefore be brave and hopeful, and you will overcome without question. May God grant grace! Amen.

Original Publication: Zwingli's *Von dem Predigtamt*, published 6/30/1525
Transcription: ZW, IV, No.61

70D
Procession of Zollikon Prophets to Zurich
After June 12, 1525[1]

"In June, 1525, a peculiar procession wends its way toward Zurich—men, women, and children wearing willow twigs or ropes instead of belts. They are men and women from the farms of Zollikon. They proceed through the lanes and squares of Zurich, doubtless an astounding sight to the citizens of the town. Quite unheard-of is the message they bring."

So writes Fritz Blanke (p. 60), pointing out that in the context of 1525, unlike today, it was most unlikely for such an event to happen, given the way the rural communities were subject to the rule of the city. He asks where these people of Zollikon got the courage for this demonstration. First, they felt themselves to be messengers of God's revelation, calling for repentance just like the early Christians. Second, they felt that they were prophets of the coming age of the Lord. This eschatological theme is not prevalent in the public documentation of the movement but must have been a part of the private teaching given to new members. The prophets Daniel and Ezekiel and the Apocalypse of John are cited by Grebel in several of his letters (see 64/fn. 25) and in public testimony (see 70F/414/33-34).

Still, Grebel was probably away from Zurich at the time and was certainly not the immediate impetus for this procession. Blanke (p. 65) assigns this role to Hans Hottinger of Zollikon. "On Sunday of Pentecost, June 4, 1525, he disturbed the sermon of Pastor Billeter in the church of Zollikon by turning to the congregation and crying, 'Go out, go out and protect yourselves from the false prophet.' This outcry began with the explosion of an individual, but it was also surely the sign of a ferment. . . ."

[*Continued from Zwingli's Account in 68L*] Then when they learned this they came in great swarms into the city, unbelted and girded with rope or willow rods,[2] and prophesied, as they called it, in the marketplace and squares. They filled the air with their cries about "the old dragon,"[3] as they called me,[4] and "his heads," as they called the other ministers of the Word. They also commended their justice and innocence to all, doubtless after they were about to depart.[5] They boasted that already they hold all things in common, and threatened others with extremes unless they do the same. They went through the streets with portentous uproar, crying "Woe! Woe! Woe to Zurich!" Some imitated Jonah, and gave a truce of forty days to the city [cf. Jonah 3:4]. What need of more? I should be more foolish than they, were I even to name all of their audacity. But we who by the bounty of God stood firmly by the sound doctrine of Christ, although throughout the city one counseled one way and another the other, we believed that we should teach correctly the proof of the Spirit [cf. 1 Jn. 4:1]. Something was accomplished in this way, although they changed themselves into all shapes that they might not be caught. [*To be continued in 71J, below*]

Original: Same as 59A
Transcription: ZW, VI, No.108, p. 43
Translation: Taken from Jackson, 1901, pp. 134-35

70E
Grebel and Hottinger[1] in Waldshut
Zollikon, June 1525

Grebel returned to Zurich from St. Gallen a few days before Easter, April 16, with perhaps a short layover in Oberwinterthur (see 71B/fn.5). He probably remained mostly in Zurich from the middle of April until early June, when he traveled to Waldshut in response to an invitation from Hubmaier (for the chronology of the prior contacts between the two men, see Cast of Characters no. 54). Hubmaier had been baptized by Reublin on Easter Sunday and was entering the fray with all of his energies. He had read Zwingli's Taufbüchlein *and was writing his own response,* Vom Christlichen Tauf der Gläubigen *(Concerning the Christian Baptism of Believers), regarded as one of the best contemporary statements on the doctrine of believer's baptism. Perhaps Hubmaier needed information from Grebel concerning the context for the dispute in Zurich.*

Grebel asked his old friend, Jacob Hottinger, to go with him to Waldshut. Upon his return to Zollikon, Hottinger wrote the following letter to the Zurich Council. The letter was undated, but Egli (Aktens., No. 763, p. 360) claimed to have evidence that it was presented to the council on June 29, 1525. This would seem to indicate that the trip was made about the middle or early part of June.

Lord Burgomaster and gracious dear Lords. Recently now in the last days it happened by God's grace that my dear brethren and sisters were working together searching the Scriptures as Christ taught in John 5[:39]. From this, God willing, God's honor and praise will be increased and our lives improved. For this sole purpose we began and did this, and not to despise anyone but to draw all men, if God wills, to God, that we may live together in the will of God. Thereafter it happened that my brother, Conrad Grebel, asked me to go with him to Waldshut because the Doctor [Balthasar Hubmaier] wrote to him asking him to come to him. I consented; for Christ says [Mt. 5:41], "If any man compels you to go with him one mile, go with him two." I soon returned home.[2] On my way home I heard that Milords are seriously displeased with us. I am sorry, because I would like to be obedient to God and to Milords. Therefore, Lord Burgo-

411

master, I, Jacob Hottinger, ask you and my dear Lords not to hold it against us for God's sake.

Original: Staatsarchiv Zurich, EI.7.2
Muralt-Schmidt, No. 113

70F
Grebel's Mission
to the District of Grüningen
After June 29, 1525

Upon his return from Waldshut (see 70E, above), Grebel began his most fruitful missionary work in the upper area of Lake Zurich, first as a partner with Marx Bosshart in the area between Zurich, Hinwil, and Winterthur, and later in the district of Grüningen in association with Mantz and Blaurock following their return from Chur. Since most of this territory was under the jurisdiction of Zurich, their activities were clearly in violation of the mandate of January 21 (see 68E), and it was inevitable that conflict with the magistrates would ensue.

The following series of documents lead up to the imprisonment of Bosshart on July 8. The testimony of Jacob Schnider provides a connection between the earlier mission to St. Gallen and the new mission to the Zurich Oberland. The subsequent documents then deal mostly with the events of Sunday, July 2.

1. Events of June 29-30.

Jacob Schnider[1] of St. Gallen answers that he was for some time a priest, but has now put that aside, thinking that he would work and not say that he too was baptized at St. Gallen during the Easter holidays,[2] etc. And [he] applied himself to a trade. And about four weeks ago he came to Stadelhofen to the weaver Hans Paley,[3] who undertook to instruct him for the sake of God. But he forbade him to baptize or to preach. He consented to this. And he has been with him about four weeks now. On the following St. John's Day,[4] Heine Merger's son[5] came to him in Balgrist into his master's house and asked him to go with him, for he had something to discuss. However, he asked him to go along to his home and eat supper with him. When they had eaten supper, Merger read [the Bible] and asked him to read too. That he did not want to do. But he read the fifteenth chapter of John and the twenty-fourth chapter of Matthew word by word and did not add anything. He asked him to go with him to Zollikon the next day. He refused to do that. Instead he went to Felix Lehman's house at Hirslanden,[6] and there were several women there who asked him to read the gospel to them on that Sunday. He did this and read them the fourteenth chapter of the Gospel of John, and then went home with his master. Later, on the eve of St. Peter's,[7] he went back to Lehman's house, and his master's wife bade him take lunch and stay overnight. After supper watchman Hottinger[8] came and told them many things. After that he read the second chapter of John's epistle, and then they went to bed.

The next morning[9] Conrad Grebel also came and read to them. Then he[10] went home. And he requests Milords through the suffering of Christ to do their best for him, for it will be found that he has not baptized or preached except as stated. And he respectfully said that he would be obedient to them, and neither read nor baptize at such places. If, however, he should fail to do so, then Milords could deal with him according to their pleasure.

2. Events of Sunday, July 2.

Testimony in the affair between the officials and several priests in the Grüningen district. Sworn information received.[11]

Next Hans Kasper of Dürnten[12] testified that Lutenschlacher[13] came to him and asked him to go with him to Hinwil, for Grebel and Marx Bosshart[14] were there. And when they reached Hinwil they found Mr. Ulrich[15] in Mr. Hans's house[16] and asked him whether he would go with them to Bäretswil to hear what Grebel had to say. Then Mr. Ulrich said, "I do not feel quite right about it, but I will go with you." And when they got near Bäretswil, Mr. Ulrich said, "I know what Grebel will say. He will say he finds nowhere that infants should be baptized." He likewise cannot find that it should be done. And when they arrived at Bäretswil, there were Grebel and Mr. Benedict[17] at each other about baptism. But Grebel had Mr. Benedict cornered, so that he could not say anything against it. And when they departed from Bäretswil, Mr. Ulrich and also Grebel and Marx Bosshart went with them. And as they parted Marx Bosshart implored them to desist from their sins and from their gluttony and drunkenness. They arranged to meet at Dürnten in 14 days. And afterward Mr. Ulrich said, "I find nowhere in the Testament that infants should be baptized." But neither did he find that they should not be baptized. Hans Kasper said to Mr. Ulrich, "How do you like Grebel's preaching?" Then Mr. Ulrich said, "I like it well and it is God's truth."

Lutenschlager testified that when he and Hans Kasper and Mr. Ulrich went to Bäretswil, Grebel and Marx Bosshart were there too and were discussing with the pastor of Bäretswil about baptism and also about the bread; not necessary to report everything. However, when they went home, Grebel and Marx Bosshart and Mr. Ulrich accompanied them. When they were between Ringwil and Bäretswil, Grebel and Marx were

413

about to leave them. Then Mr. Ulrich bade them come to Dürnten in 13 or 14 days and preach there too. After they had parted, Lautenschlacher said to Mr. Ulrich: "Dear Mr. Ulrich, what do you think of Grebel's teaching about infant baptism?" And the moment Mr. Benedict opened his mouth, he said at once that Grebel was going to defeat him, and as they came closer to Hinwil near the Maagen mill, Mr. Ulrich said, "I regret nothing more than that I must baptize infants now, for I know that it should not be done. But if I discontinue it I am afraid I will lose my benefice."

Uli Bluntschli[18] testified that he and the shoemaker Golpacher[19] attended Grebel's preaching at Hinwil. Later, at home at Dürnten, he went to Mr. Ulrich and said to him, "Grebel spoke mightily about baptism. How do you like him?" Then Mr. Ulrich said, "I leave baptism as it is. I will not say that it is right or wrong." And he continued, if one wished to baptize as Christ instituted baptism, one should not baptize a person until he is mature, for he did not find it written anywhere that children should be baptized. Nor did he find that they should not be baptized. But for fear of offending our nearest fellowmen, infant baptism must be practiced. . . .

Hans von Tobel[20] said how sometime ago Grebel had been at Hinwil and spoke about baptism. Then he went to Mr. Ulrich and asked him how he liked Grebel's concern about baptism. Then he said, "Well, he will come to me soon and expound baptism." After that he went to Mr. Ulrich's house. Other people were there also and were talking about baptism. Then he said to Mr. Ulrich, "Beloved, if you regarded neither Milords nor anyone, would you baptize children, or not?" Then Mr. Ulrich said, "Then I would not baptize a child."

Hans Golpacher testified: When Grebel was at Hinwil, he [the witness] came to Mr. Ulrich and said, "If you had been at Bäretswil today, you would have had your head set straight."[21] Then he said, "How?" Then he replied, "Grebel debated with Mr. Hans about baptism and silenced him, so that he wept quietly." Then Mr. Ulrich said, "If I had been there I would not have debated with him on infant baptism," for he has no Scripture on it. Then he said, Grebel explained John's Revelation. Then Mr. Ulrich said, "There are not many who can expound it." Later when he went to Mr. Ulrich's house, his father was there too, who said, "Dear Mr. Ulrich, if you could baptize without fear, would you baptize infants or not?" Then Mr. Ulrich said, "I would not then baptize infants." Later, however, he went to Mr. Ulrich and asked him whether he was still angry with him for not wanting to baptize infants. Then he said, "Yes, I am still angry."

Next, Marx Hotz[22] testified that he and Hans Hotz[23] once came to Mr. Ulrich at the little door. Hans Hotz said, "If you had been with

Grebel at Hinwil, you would have heard him speak on baptism." Then Mr. Ulrich said, "I was with him at Bäretswil." Then Hans Hotz asked, "How did you like him?" Then he said, "Indeed, I have already told you about baptism. I told you too how Philip baptized the eunuch." Further Mr. Ulrich said in the pulpit, salvation does not depend on baptism, nor does damnation. We may practice baptism or not, as we wish. But because of offense, one ought to baptize [infants]. Then Jörg Hotz[24] came with his son's infant and said to Mr. Ulrich [that] if he had no Scripture that infants should be baptized, he should baptize him.[25] He heard no Scripture cited. But Mr. Ulrich said [that] even if infant baptism were not instituted by God, he would still baptize them because of causing offense. And he also finds that previously many souls were lost. He finds no Scripture commanding that infants be baptized. Also, he does not find that God has forbidden the baptism of infants.

3. Further Testimony Regarding July 2.

Ulrich Zancker of Kempten[26] testified: Wildyss of Kempten,[27] the shoemaker of Ettenhausen, had told him that Grebel and Bosshart[28] preached and read at Hinwil,[29] and Grebel had reported that Zwingli spoke and said that they should gladly let the peasants[30] fall before the city, they should be given weapons and shoot 300 or 400 to death. Then the others would think twice. Further, he had said that Zwingli had said that if Milords would take two or three or four of the most influential [leaders] who refuse to pay their tithes and cut off their heads, the others would think twice.[31]

4. The Zurich Council Summons of July 5.

Ulrich Ryhener[32] answers: When the Anabaptists were imprisoned here in the Augustinian monastery on Shrove Tuesday [Feb. 26], Marx Bosshart[33] was in the same cell with him. When they left the prison, Marx Bosshart said to him that he should go with them to Zollikon for the present and take some nourishment there with them. Thereupon he frequently went to Marx Bosshart's and ate and drank with him. Then when Marx Bosshart disappeared for several days, his people sent him to Bäretswil to tell Marx Bosshart that he should not run around with Grebel but stay here. He did so and looked for Marx Bosshart and gave him the message. Furthermore, he took Milords' proclamation of Wednesday[34] concerning the Anabaptists to Marx Bosshart at Winterthur so that he and Grebel would appear at the appointed time and prove that Huldrych Zwingli had lied,[35] which his people and bailiff Wüst[36] had requested.

Further, on Wednesday[37] about two o'clock, he went to Marx

Bosshart's home and he neither knew nor said anything about a warning. He stayed there overnight until morning. That could be proved.

While he was in bed, someone whom he did not know came in front of the house and called to Marx and told him to be on his guard, for the bailiff[38] was coming to arrest some, etc.

Originals: Staatsarchiv Zurich, EI.7.2, A.124.I, EI.7.1, EI.7.2
Transcriptions: Muralt-Schmid, Nos. 78, 174, 79, 81

71
Grebel and Bosshart to the Zurich Council
Winterthur[1] or Zollikon, July 6, 1525

On Wednesday, July 5, Grebel and Bosshart were summoned to Zurich for a hearing on the following Saturday on the charge of slander against Zwingli's book, Concerning Baptism, Rebaptism, and Infant Baptism *(see 69C). In reply to the summons, the two itinerant missionaries of the movement wrote the following petition to the Zurich Council for immunity against arrest upon appearance. When the council rejected the request, Grebel refused to appear; but Bosshart complied together with Hans Ockenfuss and Fridli Schumacher, all of whom were immediately imprisoned (see 71A). At a first hearing on July 11, Bosshart was accused of having said that "Zwingli has written plain lies" (71A/417/18).*

Lord Burgomaster, honorable, wise, gracious, dear Lords, Councillors and Representatives.

We, Conrad Grebel and Marx Bosshart,[2] have your Wisdoms' letter and summons[3] to all those who say that Master Huldrych Zwingli lies in his book on baptism,[4] and have read and understood it as of the date of this letter.

So this is our request and reply, also petition, that you, our gracious lords, give us a [letter of] free safe conduct[5] to your city and back again to our refuge, so that we may appear on Saturday[6] before the councillors and representatives. If we are not able to acquire the same from you, our gracious lords, which we hope will not happen and which we have not deserved, there are many good, sufficient, Christian reasons to stay away until God directs otherwise according to his good pleasure. It would be better to relate these reasons to you directly than to put them in writing here.

Your letter of safe conduct may be sent to Rudy Thomann's house in Zollikon,[7] etc. We will readily receive it and discern whether we will have a safe conduct to you and back again to our refuge, to which we shall be transported according to God's good pleasure.

No more for now. If we are able to serve you, our gracious lords, in all temporal, official matters, we are willing and ready; and we pray that you will not be offended by our simple letter and will grant what is necessary and do it not unwillingly. May God keep us all in his peace according to his will. On Thursday after St. Ulrich's Day, 1525,

Your obedient and willing citizens and servants,

Conrad Grebel and Marx Bosshart.

Original: Staatsarchiv Zurich, EI,7.1
Transcriptions: M-S, No. 80; Goshen College Record Review Supplement, Jan. 1926, pp. 31-2

71A
Imprisonment of Four Anabaptists
Zurich, July 11, 1525

The wisdom of Grebel's caution about obeying the summons to appear for a hearing without a letter of safe conduct was verified when Bosshart was immediately arrested and imprisoned upon appearance on July 8. His first hearing together with three accomplices occurred the following Tuesday July 11.

On Tuesday before St. Margaret's Day, in the presence of Lord Walder,[1] Burgomaster, Small and Large Councils.

When Marx Bosshart[2] and Felix Kienast[3] of Zollikon said that they wished to show that M[aster] Huldrych Zwingli has written plain lies in his booklet[4] in which he defends infant baptism, etc. Thereupon these two and all who wanted to present such talk were summoned again. And although the summons also went to Conrad Grebel, he refused to appear without safe-conduct.[5] Nevertheless, the other two together with Fridli Schumacher[6] and Ockenfuss,[7] the tailor, appeared. And after they had testified long and in many ways, they could not hold their ground and admitted that they did not know and could not tell it. Thereupon it was decided to imprison the four and on the following Saturday[8] to punish them further together with others like them because of such lying and because they baptized and preached, in order to get rid of such preachers, baptizers, and liars.

Original: Staatsarchiv Zurich, B.VI.249, fol.151b
Transcription: Muralt-Schmid, No. 83

417

71B
The Visit of Finsterbach and Friends
Zurich, July 1525

While in prison, Bosshart was visited by his brother-in-law, Arbogast Finsterbach, and two friends. Bosshart and Grebel were probably staying in Finsterbach's home in Winterthur when the summons to appear was issued in Zurich (see 70F/415/35-37). The three witnesses tended to deny their own involvement in the movement, but it would appear that their interest was greater than their testimony implied.

The answer of the three[1] from Oberwinterthur who were at Zollikon.

Arbogast Finsterbach of Oberwinterthur confesses that Marx Bosshart was his brother-in-law, to whom he and Gebhart Strasser of Oberwinterthur had gone during the Easter holidays.[2] At that time he was not at home, and so they went back home. Now recently he heard that Marx was in prison.[3] Then Hans Müller and Gebhart Strasser went with him to Zollikon to see how Marx was faring and whether he was imprisoned. And when they got there, he was in prison. Nonetheless, they went to the home of his brother-in-law[4] and spent the night there. And in the morning they heard that the Anabaptists were gathering in the village, and out of curiosity they went to them to see what their way was. They were there reading to one another and they watched them, but did not speak to them at all. And afterward they went home for breakfast and then back home to Winterthur. And so he said he and his companions had gone to Zollikon with no other intention than to go to his brother-in-law, Marx Bosshart. Before this,[5] Conrad Grebel had been at his home in Oberwinterthur, and he asked Grebel what one must do if he wished to be baptized. Grebel had answered, one must first desist from adultery, gambling, drunkenness, and usury.

Original: Staatsarchiv Zurich, EI.7.1
Transcription: Muralt-Schmid, No. 98

71C
The Bailiff's Report of Anabaptists in Grüningen
Grüningen, July 12, 1525

The district of Grüningen, of which the town of Hinwil was the capital, was a part of the canton of Zurich, where Anabaptism under Grebel's leadership developed into a strong movement of the people. This is where his father had served as bailiff for twelve years (1499-1512) and where Conrad had grown up. As Bender wrote, "The soil in Grüningen was well prepared for

the spread of the Anabaptist movement. For a long time there had been ten-
sion between the population and the city of Zurich. . . . As a result of the ten-
sion a strong radical opposition against the paying of tithes had developed in
the spring of 1525. Many of the local parish pastors supported the movement
and demanded a complete abolition of the tithes. . . . This was the situation
into which Grebel and his friends came with their message of a free church
composed of believers, in which 'divine right' and righteousness was to pre-
vail."

The bailiff now was Jörg Berger, a rather inept magistrate who
zealously schemed to maintain control of a popular movement that was more
than he could handle. The Zurich Council expected the Grüningen authorities
to enforce the new mandates against Anabaptism, and Berger wanted to do
this; but the twelve judges of the Grüningen district court were reluctant to
comply, not because they were protective of Anabaptism but because they
were jealous of their local authority vis-à-vis the centralized authority of
Zurich. The following letter is the first of a long series of 54 letters from
Berger to the Zurich Council written between July 12, 1525, and Feb. 13,
1529, concerning the power of the Anabaptist movement in the district of
Grüningen (see Muralt-Schmid, pp. 91-294).

Devout, firm, foresighted, honorable and wise, gracious Milords.

May your Grace at all times have my obedient, submissive service, ready especially to offer all honor. Gracious Milords ... I did not write you everything thoroughly concerning the priest of Hombrechtikon[1] as I knew it. This is how it was: After the sermon[2] when everyone had left and the deputy bailiff approached him, the priest dealt not without skill. And when the priest's wife ran to the bells and summoned the people, she could not raise the alarm. Then about twenty ran back to the church because of the bell. Then the priest asked them to lead him first to me. Then the peasants asked the [deputy] bailiff where he was taking him. He did not immediately reply, but they insisted on knowing. Then they asked him not to take him to Zurich. Then the priest begged them with kind words to keep quiet, for they did not understand the matter. Then after much parleying[3] the [deputy] bailiff took counsel with those who were helping him arrest the priest and decided to honor him by taking him first to Grüningen. The peasants favored this. And so they started out on the road to Grüningen. Then the peasants ran after them and asked for assurance that they were not taking him farther than Grüningen, and to give them a promise. But the deputy bailiff did not want to promise this. Then they took the priest. Then they kept the priest and gathered a group and sent their messenger to me: If I would keep him in Grüningen, they would release him to me. Then I told them what was necessary, which was quite mild: "I do not want him. You took him forcibly from Milords. I will

419

leave it thus and send word to Milords. Your deed was done on the lower border, which may be Stäfa territory."[4] It is my advice that you mete out justice to those who took him. They seized one who was yours to hear, who belongs to you. Previously it has been customary to take priests to Constance for their acts concerning the faith and the Word of God. You have also had the custom of calling before yourselves the priests who wanted to defend themselves.

Further in the case, gracious Milords, Conrad Grebel was at Hinwil on the Sunday before St. Ulrich's Day,[5] and Marx Bosshart[6] was with him. He preached there. Many people were present. Then he went to Bäretswil and spoke and read in a room there. The local priest was not allowed to debate with him, and it was said that he would preach at Gossau on Sunday, July 9.[7] That did not take place. I was waiting for it. And it seems to me that he took the liberty of staying away, and he must therefore be properly arrested. And he lets statements[8] go forth, as I heard from one who heard it from him, as is set forth in the enclosed note[9] that I got from him.[10] You gracious Milords may now be thinking what great disturbance, expenses, and work will result from this. Here it will be well to be prepared, and you probably are prepared for it. Begin the matter with the affair at Hombrechtikon and act as if you knew nothing about Conrad's action, and send me two carriers[11] on Tuesday. Then with God's help we will seize him and a sentence given by the Twelve[12] to set them straight. And if they refuse to obey at once, instruct your carriers to say to me, "Bailiff, if things do not go as would be reasonable, you know your duty to Milords. We admonish you on the orders of our Lords." And do not allow yourselves to be pressed. Let it be said, it is sharply spoken, so it must be true. If you do not take the affair in hand by force, it will not work out. If you now let Conrad's affair stand, he will find support. And if you begin with the Hombrechtikon affair, we will be able with the help of God to bring the case to a good conclusion and apply to it what is necessary, for the matter will come before our confederates in Bern[13] if you yield. I therefore ask Milords to send me a written reply and not to take it ill of me to have written at such length. It must be true. There are two or three other things I could write about but will leave them and, if God wills, do all with the help of the Almighty and not with force to make the disobedient obedient if you will help me. For some in our area, contrary to all mandates, have never set up a sheaf.[14]

I will omit tithing[15] for the present. We will create obedience. That is the most necessary thing now, and let me inform you as an unskilled fellow. And if I mislead you, punish me for it. I know my favor with you would be small. I will leave it to God. Things will improve with time.

Nothing more for this time, except that the Almighty God grant you peace and grace.

Written the day before St. Margaret's, 1525.

Always obedient to Your Graces,
Jörg Berger, Bailiff at Grüningen.

Original: Staatsarchiv Zurich, A.124.1
Transcription: Muralt-Schmid, No. 85

71D
Investigation of Grebel's Activities
Zurich, July 12, 1525

The following court testimony concerning Grebel's missionary activities was taken in the district of Grüningen and sent to Zurich by Bailiff Berger along with his letter of July 12 (see previous document, 71C).

The undersigned testified under oath:

Hans Müller of Kempten[1] testified that he and other companions were at Hinwil. There he heard that Conrad Grebel and Hans Hinwil[2] argued mightily with each other about baptism. Then Hans said, "Milords have issued a mandate; I will stick to it." Then Conrad Grebel said, "Are you a man? You should not regard Milords or anyone else and should do only what God has commanded and follow after what the mouth of God has spoken." And after all that, Conrad Grebel said, "It is a miserable affair that I do not receive any justice—not civil justice,[3] not heretical[4] justice, not divine justice."[5] Further Conrad said [that] even if they seized him and imprisoned him in the tower,[6] he would write if they would give him pens and ink. And if he could not overcome Zwingli, they should burn him and not Zwingli. For he had earlier debated with Zwingli before Milords about baptism,[7] and Zwingli was silent and said not a word in opposition;[8]

Jacob Falk of Gossau[9] testified that Conrad Grebel spoke at Hinwil and he had touched on heretical justice and on divine justice and on civil justice, but none followed or reached him.[10]

Further, Conrad said [that] if he were permitted to publish his writings,[11] he would dispute with Zwingli unto [death by] fire. And if Zwingli defeated him, they should burn Conrad Grebel, and if Conrad Grebel defeated him, they should not burn Zwingli.

Clauss Wolfensperg of Ettenhausen[12] testified that Conrad Grebel said he would like to debate with Zwingli. For it was Zwingli who got him into this matter and told him many things about which he does not now remain constant and from which he was now retreating.[13] Further, Conrad

421

talked to the pastor at Hinwil[14] about baptism. He should not baptize children until they reach understanding. Then Hans said, Milords have issued a statement on baptism, and he would be obedient to Milords. Then Conrad Grebel remarked that he ought to follow the right, and what the pastors now said was untrue.

Fridli Wolfensberg of Ettenhausen[15] testified that he had indeed heard Conrad Grebel say about baptism that children should not be baptized until they reached reason, and what the pastors now say is untrue.

Uli Lutz of Hinwil[16] testified that Conrad Grebel said he had appealed to Milords for heretical justice, also for civil justice and other kinds of justice, but he did not know what they were called. And he received and acquired none of them.[17]

Heini Eglof of Hinwil[18] testified that Conrad Grebel said he had appealed to Milords for heretical justice as well as civil justice and other justice, but he received none. Further Conrad said [that] he would ask nothing more than to be placed in the tower prison where he was,[19] and to be given pens and ink, and if he were refused a hearing he would be heard in his writings.[20]

Hansliss Uli of Ringwil[21] testified that Conrad Grebel said he had appealed for heretical justice and divine justice and civil justice, but received and acquired none of them.

Further Conrad said [that] if he were permitted to publish his writings in print he would debate with M[aster] Huldrych Zwingli unto the fire, and if M[aster] Huldrych won they could burn Conrad, but if Conrad won they should not burn Zwingli.

On the back: Investigation of Conrad Grebel,

Original: Staatsarchiv Zurich, EI,7.1
Transcription: Muralt-Schmid, No. 84

71E
The Third Swiss Anabaptist Martyr: Hans Krüsi
Luzern, July 27, 1525

It is not without historical significance that the Greek word for witness, martyr, carries over into English for one who voluntarily suffers death as the penalty for proclaiming the message. Document 69E, above, related that the first two Swiss Anabaptist martyrs were executed for their missionary work. This is even more evident in the case of Hans Krüsi, who was won to the movement by Grebel, "the first to witness to him," and whose story is told in the following three documents.

[*Kessler's Account, continued from 70A, above*] Thereafter our Anabaptists assumed the apostolic office as the first in the newly established church, believing that it was their obligation to follow Christ's command when he said, "Go ye into all the world, etc." [Mk. 16:15]. They ran beyond the city gate into the outlying villages, regions, and market towns to preach there, to Golddach in the east,[1] to Teufen in the south,[2] to Oberdorf and Gossau in the west,[3] and to Cappel and Freidorf in the north.[4] In what places and towns they worked first [mention should be made concerning], how they managed to stir up hatred for the Protestant preachers, so that they were deposed from the congregations and they [the Anabaptists] installed in their places; how in Teufen in the Appenzell district where Johann called Krüsi,[5] a bold teacher among the Anabaptists, accomplished so much with his loudness and arguments in the church that they deposed their aged, honorable, highly learned minister, Jacob Schurtanner,[6] who had faithfully instructed them and in the beginning broke the path for the gospel in Appenzell, not without great concern, trouble, and labor; to whom, for his zeal and honesty, Huldrych Zwingli dedicated and wrote his book called *The Shepherd*. Not long after he was deposed, he took to his bed and died a Christian death.[7] The aforesaid Krüsi, since he was a native of St. George and stayed and lived there, was seized in bed one night by the captain of the abbot of St. Gallen, Melchior Degan,[8] and other authorities and police. He was taken to Luzern, contrary to the custom and practice of the area,[9] and there sentenced and burned at the stake. [*To be continued in 71J, below*]

[*Krüsi's Confession Before Execution*] When Hans Nagel [alias Hans Krüsi][10] of Klingnau was put into my gracious lords' prison, he confirmed that in spite of the oath of banishment he took during his recent imprisonment,[11] he began to preach, read, and teach in the New and the Old Testaments.[12] He found that whoever believes and is baptized will be preserved; this he did at St. George.[13] There he also baptized so many that he did not know the number and the peasants conspired and called[14] him to read again—namely, Beda the turner[15] at St. George told him he should not fall away from the faith[16] and that his work was now easier for him than before,[17] also Hans Haffner, Marti of Teuffen, and Erler, also Zeidler of Tablat near St. George.[18] These four were subjects of the abbey.[19] And his companions had been Gulde the weaver,[20] Antoni Kürsiner[21] and Giger of St. Gallen,[22] and he had also been with the schoolmaster at St. Gallen[23] and also questioned him, for he had wanted to preach and at first he was proviser at Wil.[24] There his companions were Peter Keich, Ruggimann, Felix Gerwer,[25] and the schoolmaster at Klingnau.[26] And also Hans Nüsch in the Schnecken area[27] had been his companion who preached, and they both taught each other.

When he had finished reading and teaching, the people gave him and his wife[28] a gift and something to eat; Hensli Studer[29] of the town of St. Gallen gave him a guilder, and the Spichermanns[30] a solid pfennig, and several gave three batzen and some less so that he might learn the weaving craft.[31]

He spoke and preached that the relics and images and idols[32] should be removed from the altar and from the church and thrown out, which was done;[33] and Othmar Schwend[34] and his associates broke open the altar and took out the objects. This Othmar was also a subject of the abbey[35] and asked what was to be done with the bones of the rogues.[36]

When he was preaching to the congregation and the captain of [the abbey of] St. Gallen[37] came, he said they should pray to God for the captain that he might also come into their true faith. He also read and said the deaf and the ungodly would be judged,[38] and we owe God more than man;[39] and from the living Word of God no one should be obligated to pay tithes[40] and the like, and one should be subject to the Word of God and not allow oneself to be led away from the Word of God; and they should not be led away from one another and from this doctrine but all stick together.

When he was about to be seized, the whole congregation promised him to stand by him with body and goods and to protect him, namely, Straubenzell,[41] Rotmonten,[42] Bernhardszell,[43] and those from St. George and some thirty-one other villages.[44]

He bought the New Testament from a boy named Heini Locher,[45] near Wil, for eight batzen; and the Old Testament was loaned to him by Aberli Schlumpf[46] of St. Gallen.

He has confessed that he preached that the worthy mother of God and the dear saints can intercede for no one—only Christ Jesus [can intercede].

He preached that the mass is nothing and of no benefit, and he who believes in the mass believes in the devil and is of the devil, and one should pray in the privacy of his heart, and faith is in the heart: there one should have faith.[47] And when people offer sacrifice, he said, they are sacrificing to the field devil.

He said the sacrament is not flesh and blood, and one should not believe in it. This he preached and told the people, and anyone who believes in the sacrament, they are all heretics.

424

He said, as to the body, one should suffer injury there, but as to the soul, no one should let himself be led astray.[48] All things should be held in common, in the love of God and in faith.

Uliman[49] and Rugglisberger[50] were also his associates, and they had traveled together and instructed each other, and they converted many of the common people and attached them to themselves.

Young Grebel was the first to witness[51] to him and brought him a booklet, and [he, Krüsi] testified[52] that the booklet was handwritten and not printed.[53]

Upon this, his confession my gracious lords, C[ouncil] and One Hundred[54] sentenced him to death with fire and had him burned to powder and ashes as a heretic of the holy Christian faith and the ashes buried in the earth.

Original: Staatsarchiv Luzern, Ratsbuch No.XII, 137a-39a
Transcriptions: Kessler, p. 147; Fast, pp. 607-8; Fast, No. 354

71F
The Grebel/Krüsi Collection of Bible Passages[1]
Augsburg, 1525

In the summer of 1960 Heinold Fast was examining a book published in 1864 listing "recently discovered" letterpress materials printed as early as the sixteenth century. To his great surprise he saw the title of a German tract by "Hans Nagel of Klingnau" printed in 1525 and dealing with two main subjects: faith and baptism. He recognized immediately that this was the third Anabaptist martyr in Switzerland, more commonly known as Hans Krüsi. To his knowledge, moreover, there were only two other Anabaptist publications of 1525, both written by Balthasar Hubmaier. The century-old booklist cited Munich as the place of discovery of this document.

After several months of anxious search during which he almost gave up locating the tract, he finally had a copy in his hands. At first he was disappointed to observe that it was not a doctrinal or disputational writing but only a collection of Bible verses. On twelve pages there were 53 passages, 37 under the subtitle of faith and 16 under baptism. Only in thirteen instances was a word of commentary added by the author. The tract was illustrated by two woodcuts, one on the raising of Lazarus and the other on the raising of the widow's son at Nain.

But on further study and reflection, Fast came to the conclusion that the document was very significant. First, it reflects two theological doctrines very important to early Anabaptism: their biblicism and their priesthood of all believers. The conviction that the Bible was the supreme authority for discerning God's will led the brethren to read and study this book for themselves with whatever tools of interpretation were available to them. The more educated

425

leaders like Grebel, Mantz, Hubmaier, and Krüsi felt called to make the Bible accessible to the rank-and-file members who joined the movement. One way they did it was by the publication of what came to be called concordances—systematic collections of Bible quotations for use in Anabaptist study groups—a kind of sixteenth-century Sunday school curriculum.

Robert Friedmann wrote that "since the Anabaptists and Mennonites were (and are) biblicists, they showed a particular interest in such books, which to them are not only Bible indexes but to some extent real guides through the Bible for understanding and for arguing in disputations" (ME, I, p. 665). Christian Hege wrote that "for the [public] hearings by secular and clerical scholars, the Anabaptists found in the study of their concordances a help which enabled them to refute the objections of their counterparts. The unusual certainty of their biblical proof-texting astonished the theologians and often embarrassed them (ML, II, p. 542). In the history of Anabaptism there are a number of published concordances, but none earlier than the 1530s and 1540s when Schnabel's Anfrage *and Marpeck's* Testamentserläuterung *were published (1538 and 1544, respectively).*

Fast compared the Krüsi collection with these later concordances and found a remarkable similarity in arrangement, particularly on the subject of baptism, with the following typical order of sequence: the baptism of John, the command of baptism by Jesus, the practice of baptism in the Acts of the Apostles leading to the rebaptism in Ephesus, and the formal doctrine of believer's baptism in the epistles. One could hypothesize a direct dependence of the later collections on Krüsi's booklet, except for the further evidence that Krüsi was himself the recipient of still earlier collections.

Fast demonstrates a further similarity between the present document and the Grüningen Eingabe *(see Epi.E, below) and the Mantz* Protestation *and* Schutzschrift *(see 67B, above), both of which had connections with the ministry of Conrad Grebel, who was himself probably the first Anabaptist to construct a topical concordance of the Bible. In his letter of Sept. 3, 1524, Grebel reported to Vadian, "I will list and assemble passages ... of two general topics, and unless someone else does it first, I will thrust these upon the public" (62/283/19-23). That he actually completed this collection we learn from his later letter to Castelberger, in which he reports giving it to Erasmus Ritter of Schaffhausen, who sent it to Zwingli. Moreover, Grebel must have made a number of manuscript copies because as shown in the preceding document (71E/425/7-9), Krüsi confessed to his judges that "young Grebel ... brought him a booklet and [Krüsi] testified that the booklet was handwritten and not printed."*

It is surely more than a coincidence that the booklet printed under Krüsi's paternal name contained, as Grebel wrote to Vadian, two general topics or themes, of which baptism was one. The first theme of faith reminds us of Zwingli and Luther and their emphasis on salvation by faith alone; and the theme of baptism is the outgrowth of faith. As the title of the booklet states, "*Concerning the faith in God which alone saves . . . and concerning water which cannot save us,*" Fast hypothesizes that Grebel was indeed the first Anabaptist to construct a biblical concordance, and that Mantz, Krüsi, and the brethren in Grüningen, all used his collection. But since these are hypotheses, we present the document under both names: Grebel and Krüsi.

For the sake of conserving space, the verses themselves will not be translated, but merely listed by Scripture reference. Students who want to study the concordance in greater depth will have to use their own Bibles or the full German text in the Fast source volume, 1973, No. 355, pp. 265-73.

Concerning the faith of God which alone saves and is only given from heaven; [and] concerning the baptism of Christ. Concerning the water which cannot save us. Hans Nagel[2] [alias Krüsi] from Klingnau, a leather dresser,[3] 1525.

[1] Concerning the faith of God, which must come from heaven alone and through whom we are saved and thereafter baptized.

John 3:16-18a	Romans 14:23b
Genesis 6:13-14a, 8,[4] 22a	1 Corinthians 13:13
Genesis 4:4-5a[5]	Psalm 116:10
Genesis 15:1-2a, 4-6	Galatians 2:16[13]
Genesis 22:1-2[6]	Ephesians 4:4a, 5-6
Genesis 19:1a, 12-14a[7]	Philippians 1:21[14]
Exodus 3:1a, 3a, 5, 10[8]	1 Peter 2:6-8
Matthew 16:13b-14, 16[9]	Hebrews 6:1-6
John 1:47-50	Psalm 46:1
John 6:67-69	Luke 1:26-29, 31, 35a, 38a[15]
John 11:25-26b	Matthew 8:2-3
Romans 1:17b	Matthew 8:5b-8, 13a
Romans 5:1-2a	Matthew 9:1-2
Romans 8:9b	Matthew 9:27-29
1 Timothy 1:18-20[10]	Matthew 17:19-21[16]
John 20:26b-29[11]	Matthew 18:6
1 Peter 1:7[12]	Mark 5:25-26a, 27a, 28, 34a
Romans 10:13-15a, 16b, 17a	Digest of Mark 5:22-24, 35b
	Psalm 71:1

[2] The true and thorough Word of God concerning baptism.

Deuteronomy 1:39	1 Corinthians 10:2 (refers also to
Matthew 3:11, 13-15	Colossians 2:12, Romans 1f.,

Matthew 28:18-20
Mark 16:15-16
Luke 7:29-30
Matthew 20:20-23a
Luke 12:49-50
1Luke 3:21-23a
John 3:22[17]
Acts 2:38

Acts 22:16, (all concerning baptism)
Acts 8:35-37a
John 3:5
Acts 9:17b-19a
Acts 10:34, 44-48
Acts 16:17-34; 19:1b-4a, 5[18]

The peace of God be with us at all times.

Original Publication: Hans Nagel, *Von dem Glauben/Von dem Wasser,* printed in Augsburg, 1525
Transcription: Fast, No. 355

71G
Jud to Vadian
Zurich, August 8, 1525

As pastor of St. Peter's Church in Zurich and Zwingli's closest associate in the work of the Reformation, Leo Jud was undoubtedly writing to Vadian for Zwingli between the latter's two letters of May 28 (see 69D, above) and October 11 (71I, below). The letter reveals the further polarization of the Reformed Protestant and biblicist Anabaptist positions.

Grace and peace from God the Father through Christ. I think you people acted rightly, most learned man, when the boldness of the Anabaptists was checked by a decree of the council.[1] We are waging war daily with these most monstrous monsters, whether this happens because of our fault[2] or because of the fickleness of the magistrate, I'll not say his carelessness; nor yet do I believe it will ever be fought out to a successful finish, so terrible an evil is the quarrel, so stubborn is the hypocrisy, two plagues[3] which are simultaneously laying waste all charity (of which true Christianity consists) and are utterly annihilating it. It was a small matter and of no great difficulty to drive the antichrist[4] from his kingdom, to hurl back the clever eloquence of the Sophists,[5] and ἐπιστομίζειν [to stop the mouths][6] of the gainsayers; for as soon as the torch of the divine Word was brought to these gloomy places, the smoke had to disappear. But the fight is fiercer and the war far more difficult with these people who eclipse the darkness by the light itself[7] and obscure the Spirit of the divine Word by the very bright light of the Word itself. But their vices lie in ambush for their very good and noble points, and the foe sows on top of the good seed.[8] Herod tried to kill Christ growing into his prime;[9] and the apostles

428

did not lack false prophets[10] and false brethren who caused trouble for the young church. They complained of them in their epistles,[11] forearming us with great earnestness. Why does puffed-up knowledge wish something else for itself—to know more than it should and to cause the peril of false brethren? Why does worldly, sensual, devilish wisdom, strife, and envy wish it? May the blessed God give us the Spirit of unity and gentleness and of a steadfast mind at the same time, so that we may be enabled to endure these hardships. . . .

Original: Stadtbibliothek (Vadiana) St. Gallen, VB.II.239
Transcription: VB, III, No. 431

71H
The Arrest of Grebel and Blaurock
Grüningen, October 8, 1525

The following letter in the series by Bailiff Jörg Berger to the Zurich Council (see Introduction to 71C, above) narrates the arrest and imprisonment of Grebel and Blaurock. Sometime before this event, Blaurock and Mantz had returned from Chur and Appenzell to join Grebel in the flourishing Anabaptist mission to the district of Grüningen. In the rise of a powerful popular movement in his jurisdiction, Berger had to intervene to enforce the injunctions from Zurich. So on the weekend of Oct. 5-8, the bailiff, his deputy, and a servant rode their horses between Grüningen, Gossau, and Hinwil, trying rather desperately to keep the movement under control. Berger's report lacks a measure of coherence and reflects a certain fear and trepidation even as he tells about this "extraordinary day."

Devout, firm, farsighted, honorable and wise, gracious Milords.

May my obedient, submissive service be yours at all times, ready with all honor.

Gracious Milords:

As I told you, Lord Mayor and other Milords, about the Anabaptists on Thursday night[1] and also indicated how one whom I regard as one of them escaped from my brother-in-law Michael Setzstab and me at Balgrist. On Friday morning I returned home. On Sunday[2] when I came back from Gossau, Hans Brennwald,[3] priest[4] at Hinwil, was at my home and he said to me, "I am here and want to be your prisoner."[5] He refused to say anything more, for he told how the sergeant[6] at Hinwil was coming right away. When the two[7] then met, they began to tell how Jörg,[8] who calls himself "of the house of Jacob," who has a blue coat, a black hat, and a bald spot, came to Hinwil into the church and the pulpit and spoke there, where he said, "Whose place is this? If this is the place of God where the Word of God is proclaimed, I am a messenger from the Father to proclaim the Word of God." Then after the priest[9] came, he[10] stood there and preached. The priest at Hinwil remained silent and let him preach awhile until he got to baptism. There he interrupted him, since it seemed necessary to him to reply. Then a great murmuring arose in the church, so that he had to shout for order and then left, as reported earlier. Then the deputy bailiff[11] wanted to seize him. But the others said: "Were you ordered to do it?" And so there was so much commotion that he[12] gave him three more men and he came to me. And so I hastily rode up there with the assistant bailiff and a servant.

When I got to Hinwil they were in the church, more than I wrote, about 200 people. I spoke to them as seemed good to me, so much that the priest[13] called out for his rights and also wanted to go to Grüningen. So he stood beside me in the pulpit. What we talked about is not germane. He made all kinds of arguments, and it seemed to me he did not want to be seized. Then when we got outside the church, I called out to them to give answer to me in Grüningen, according to my sworn duty. They did not want to do this and replied that I could do it through my servant, which I did. And so I mounted my servant's horse, and the assistant bailiff and I took him[14] with us, my servant walking beside him. And such a crowd followed him, young and old, truly remarkable. Then the Anabaptists wanted to gather at Betzholz[15] to carry on their activities again. Then I gathered them together in a big group and asked them kindly not to baptize anymore and to desist. But they told me they would compel no one, but if someone asked for it they would baptize him and not desist from it until they could be corrected on the basis of the Holy Scriptures. When we came from Betzholz, to the field where the meeting was, Conrad Grebel and Mantz[16] arrived; and we thereupon immediately recognized both of them. One went with them. It was right at the Hof.[17] And I was amazed at them. And so the deputy bailiff and I stopped for a conference where there was no one else except as said, the deputy bailiff, my servant, and I. Otherwise, there were many people and Anabaptists around. We took counsel and I rode to nearby Ottikon[18] and gathered as many men as I could find and sent them back to the deputy bailiff; and my servant and I rode on with the one who is called Blaurock. And so they also arrested Conrad Grebel. Mantz escaped from them. We had an extraordinary day. I am giving you my best information now. I am sorry I cannot write what seems good to me.[19] They have clever managers who want to teach Milords, but I really did it with good intentions. You have never erred, thank God. Do not hold against me what I have told you. There would be more to do. Herewith may you be commended to God.

Sunday before St. Dionysius Day, 1525.

He says they call him Blaurock. He has been imprisoned three times.

Your Graces' always obedient Jörg Berger, Bailiff at Grüningen.

Original: Staatsarchiv Zurich, El.7.1
Transcription: Muralt-Schmid, No. 109

711
Zwingli to Vadian
Zurich, October 11, 1525

Bailiff Berger's Sunday report of the arrest of Grebel reached Zurich without delay, for Zwingli relayed the news to Vadian on the following Wednesday. His letter of October 11 expresses not only his hostility toward Grebel and Blaurock but also his defensive reactions to the publication of Hubmaier's booklet, Concerning the Christian Baptism of Believers, *Oecolampad's warning about the likelihood of a written attack from Wittenberg on Zwingli's views of the Lord's Supper, and the continuing role of Jacob Grebel in the political affairs of Zurich (leading to the episode documented in Epi. A, below).*

. . . . I am now writing a reply to the letter of Bugenhagen of Pomerania[1] which he issued against us too impudently. When we have completed this task, we will gird ourselves against Balthasar [Hubmaier] of Waldshut, who stupidly treats the baptism of infants and the ἀναβαπτισμόν[2] [anabaptism] of adults with much wresting and violence of the holy Scriptures.[3] They of Wittenberg charge our Sertorius[4] as though he had framed the terms of the articles of the seditious peasants,[5] as I have seen in a letter sent from there to Froschauer. But perhaps it will be of no advantage to tear their false notion from them. All unseasonable and raging opinions are now cured by the invective of Luther,[6] in which he has not only cut to pieces the twice unlucky men but has also thrown them to the most savage wild beasts. For Melanchton wrote against their articles in the German language,[7] doubtless bringing aid to Luther. Oecolampad in his last letter[8] advised me to have my pen ready, for there will be plenty of them who will write against us regarding the Lord's Supper.[9] I on my part have bidden him to stand fearlessly, although he has no need of an adviser.

Christian affairs with us are always in the same condition. Conrad Grebel together with Jörg, that man of fickle mind,[10] has been arrested at Grüningen and thrown into prison. Inclined toward evil signs by nature,[11] he has always sought some tragedy. Now he has found it. May Almighty

God grant that his Word may not be violated, for some fathers-in-law[12] are such that I would assign not only too little hope to them but even too little faith.

Farewell.

From Zurich, the 11th day of October, MDXXV.

H[uldrych] Z[wingli]

> To the most learned and most devout Doctor Joachim Vadian, our brother beyond all gratitude.

Notes, 1129-30
Original: Stadtbibliothek (Vadiana) St. Gallen, Litt.misc.II.243
Transcriptions: VB, III, No. 435, ZW, VII, No. 390

71J
The Third Public Disputation on Baptism
Zurich, November 6-8, 1525

Following the arrest of Grebel and Blaurock by Bailiff Berger on October 8, they were imprisoned in the Castle of Grüningen, where Grebel had grown up as a boy when his own father was the bailiff. Although Mantz had escaped arrest, he, too, was arrested and incarcerated three weeks later. The holding of a Third Public Disputation on baptism in Zurich was certainly not inspired by much hope on Zwingli's part for changing the minds of these three. It was due, rather, to two other factors.

First, the movement was spreading so fast that a repressive approach alone could not stem its advance. Some able new leaders were joining the movement who had not been part of the previous disputations. It is likely that Michael Sattler of Stauffen in the Breisgau, Ulrich Teck of Waldshut, and Martin Lingg of Schaffhausen were also arrested during these weeks because they were tried and sentenced along with the other three. Moreover, it was Hubmaier's published Taufbüchlein—a new and powerful defense of believer's baptism—that now provided the agenda for the disputation rather than the well-rehearsed doctrines of Grebel, Mantz, and Blaurock. This is evident by the fact that Zwingli's tract against Hubmaier was issued on the day before the disputation opened. Hubmaier had evidently asked for a disputation with Zwingli and was expected to attend the November meeting, but did not because of the threat of arrest, not by the Zurich authorities so much as by the agents of the emperor who were about to occupy Waldshut.

The other factor in the scheduling of yet another disputation was the formal request for it by Bailiff Berger and the Twelve Judges of Grüningen, who not only wanted to demonstrate a certain degree of independence from the arbitrary authority of a centralized government in Zurich but also wanted to try to control the popular movement by showing the Anabaptists from their district the greatest possible consideration. Thus the scheduling of a disputa-

tion was in direct response to the request for it from Grüningen, and the formal report of its outcome was sent to the Twelve Judges of Grüningen.

[*1. Continued from Bullinger's Account in 68L*] As mentioned above, the Anabaptists militantly laid hold of the city and canton of Zurich, but especially Gossau and of the jurisdiction of Grüningen. There Grebel, Mantz, and other previously named Anabaptists had thrived and won so many more followers that many whose spirits would not yet be stilled were becoming riotous and refractory[1] in this jurisdiction. Moreover, the Anabaptists protested that although indeed a disputation had been held, they had never fully been able to present their case. Zwingli would let no one come into the debate.[2] So the unrest and peril grew stronger and longer.

The honorable magistrates of the city of Zurich were prompted thereby to convene a conference that would be especially free and distinguished. Everyone was to be allowed to speak freely whatever they thought could be supported with Scripture. . . .

And on the day of the disputation, many Anabaptists were on hand from St. Gallen and other foreign districts. The doctor from Waldshut, who was also an Anabaptist, as mentioned above, was expected to come, but did not. Then Grebel and Mantz took the case in hand together with their comrades. Opposite them stood M[aster] Huldrych Zwingli, M[aster] Leo Jud, and M[aster] Caspar Grossman.[3] The theses for debate were to be these:

Children of Christians are no less children of God than their elders, as was true in the Old Testament. If they are already God's, who will keep them from water baptism[?]

Circumcision was to the ancients (who had this sign) what baptism is to us. Inasmuch as it is now given to infants, baptism should likewise be given to infants.

Rebaptism has no mandate or example or proof in God's Word. Therefore, those who are baptized again crucify Christ again, either by their own obstinacy or by inventing something new.

The lords presiding over this disputation were four [in number]: the lord of Cappel, Mr. Wolfgang Joner;[4] the commander of Küssnacht, M[aster] Conrad Schmid;[5] Mr. Sebastian Hofmeister, doctor from Schaffhausen;[6] and Mr. Joachim von Watt [Vadian], doctor and burgomaster from St. Gallen.[7]

The disputation began with prayer in the Rathaus before senators and representatives with open doors in the presence of the Twelve from Grüningen[8] and very many other clerical and secular people.

433

But as the place became too crowded, rails were installed in the sanctuary of the Grossmünster, in the nave, plus chairs and two tables, one for the presidents and preachers, and the other for the Anabaptists. The latter could speak as long and as much [as they wanted] without any cloture. The conference continued the whole day for three days in succession, November 6, 7, and 8.

What was debated there is too long to rehearse. The best arguments on both sides are listed in summary form in M[aster] Huldrych Zwingli's *Reply* which he has given to Doctor Balthasar [Hubmaier's] book.[9] The honorable council immediately sent a message to those in the jurisdiction of Grüningen[10] in which they also briefly summarized the proceedings of the disputation as soon thereafter as they could. I have also alluded to this disputation in Book 1, Chapter 5, of my writing against the Anabaptists.

At the conclusion of the conference, Grebel, Mantz, Blaurock, and other Anabaptist patriarchs were arraigned before the council[11] and admonished to forsake their opinions which had been publicly found to be erroneous. But because this had no effect on these quarrelsome heads, they were detained in the Tower. [*Continued in 71L, below*]

[*2. Continued from Kessler's Chronicle in 71E, above*] Moreover, Doctor Balthasar Hubmaier of Friedberg, quite submerged in the idea of Anabaptism (as stated above), offered and requested from the Zurich government to debate with Huldrych Zwingli. He [said he] would demonstrate from the Scripture that infant baptism was not ordained of God, but the baptism of adult believers was. Meanwhile he published his booklet, *Von dem [christlichen] Tauf,*[12] against Zwingli. But in order that such a booklet would not cause more division and sects in other places and the hearts of believers confused again, Huldrych Zwingli wrote his *Reply to Dr. Balthasar's Booklet*[13] to refute it.

But in order to settle this disharmony not only among the common people but also among the learned, the Zurich authorities ordered the suggested disputation to be held and announced widely that those who thought Huldrych Zwingli to be incorrect in his article on baptism should gather at Zurich on November 10,[14] and they would have Huldrych Zwingli there to give answer.

Thereupon the arch-Anabaptists and teachers, such as Conrad Grebel, Felix Mantz, Jörg of the house of Jacobs of Bonaduz, whom they called "strong Jörg,"[15] as well as some of their adherents, gathered. Everyone thought that Doctor Balthasar [Hubmaier] would be there. But he was prevented by His Imperial Majesty's agents, who were planning to occupy Waldshut.[16] The disputation was then held with the persons enumerated above.

A peasant of Zollikon, Christians Fessler,[17] an Anabaptist, was there. He wanted neither side to use books. He pushed through the crowd crying with a loud voice: "Gangway! Gangway!" Everyone got out of his way. No one knew what he wanted. Then he snatched up the books on both sides and put them on a pile, leaving none to anyone. On the first day they let him have his way.

Many pious, honorable people from other towns also made the journey. Their consciences were burdened and unsettled by the hypocritical good conduct of the Anabaptists and questioned whether, by hearing both parties, they would be sufficiently assured in heart and conscience by the truth; for example, Junker Conrad Mayer[18] from our town and guildmaster Mainrait Weniger.[19] They all said Zwingli had approached them with such fundamentals of Scripture that they were silenced, but they nonetheless persisted in their belief and did not know any answer to give, but that they had said they would testify with their blood that they were right and that Zwingli was a false prophet, to be compared with the beast of which John writes in Revelation 13,[20] and they would be innocent in their being condemned.

At the end the peasant from Zollikon arose and thought he would deprive Zwingli of his power and said, "Zwingli, I adjure you by the living God to tell the truth." Zwingli paid little heed to these words but overlooked them as the outpouring of an angry peasant's heart. Then the peasant adjured him the second time and the third time to tell him even one truth. When he would not desist, Zwingli replied, "Well, I will tell you one truth, that you are a rude, unskilled, seditious peasant."[21] Thereupon everyone departed. Anabaptism on that occasion was weakened and considered to be obstinacy. [*Continued in 71R, below*]

[*3. Continued from Zwingli's Account in 70D, above*] When finally their impudence though beaten also at that meeting, would not yield, an opportunity was again given them to fight. In the presence of the church[22] the contest raged for three whole days more,[23] with so great damage to them that there were few who did not see that the wretched people were struggling for the sake of fighting, and not to find the truth. [*To be continued in 71M, below*]

[*4. Zurich Council to the Grüningen Magistrates, Nov. 15, 1525*] Thereupon, although two disputations had [previously] been held[24] and it had always been proved that infant baptism is right and rebaptism was brought to naught, we consented, nevertheless, for more than good measure, to grant to your esteemed, honorable graces, and to your appointed associates from Grüningen, the Third Disputation and announced it to all those who wished to defend rebaptism. And so the Anabaptists Conrad Grebel, Felix Mantz, and Jörg of the House [of Jacob] called Blaurock and their followers and adherents disputed against Master Huldrych Zwingli, Master Leo Jud, and Master Caspar Grossmann,[25] and other learned men who defended infant baptism, for three successive days, morning and evening, in our city hall and in the Grossmünster[26] publicly in our presence and that of many men and women, and each one, learned or unlearned, spoke his ideas to the full without prevention or verification of his words (as you saw and heard)—took place on Monday, Tuesday, and Wednesday after All Saints Day in 1525. And so gradually and finally the strongest possible reasons were found on the basis of the Holy Scriptures of the Old and New Testaments (as found in the new booklet published yesterday by Zwingli against the doctor of Waldshut)[27] that Master Zwingli with his adherents freely defeated his opponents, repudiated rebaptism, and upheld infant baptism.

Originals: Bullinger's *Reformationsgeschichte,* I, pp. 294-96; Kessler's *Sabbata* (see 65A); Zwingli's *Elenchus* (see 59A); Staatsarchiv Zurich, F.II.a.185,p.126ff.
Transcriptions: Kessler, pp. 149-50 Fast, pp.611-3; ZW, VI, No. 108, pp. 44-45; Muralt-Schmid, No. 129, p. 132
Translation of para. from *Elenchus:* Taken from Jackson, 1901, p. 135

71K
The Trial of Grebel, Mantz, and Blaurock
Zurich, between November 9[1] and 18, 1525

Although the November Disputation was to be "especially free and distinguished," according to Bullinger, "with everyone to be allowed to speak freely whatever he thought could be supported with Scripture," the facts that most of the disputants from the Anabaptist side were prisoners of the state and that their trial on charges of sedition was continuous with the disputation placed incredible limitations on their alleged freedom of speech. The trial lasted intermittently for ten days, and on November 18 sentences varying from "penance" to perpetual imprisonment on a diet of bread and water were issued. The trial record is a fascinating account of the evidence brought against them by Zwingli and Hofmeister, who served as the state's chief witnesses.

1. Testimony Concerning the Accused.

Master Huldrych Zwingli testified: First Simon [Stumpf] of Höngg[2] came to him and Master Leo[3] and said argumentatively that they ought to establish a special people and church and have in it Christian people who lived completely without blame[4] and also clung to the gospel, and who

436

were not involved in interest or other usury.[5] They rejected this always kindly and cordially, etc.

Then Grebel also came to them and made an approach similar to Simon of Höngg. They also rejected his idea. Beyond this, they nevertheless proceeded at night to hold meetings on Neustadt[6] intending to set up a separate church.

Then Simon of Höngg talked to him awhile, that they could not do it unless they first put all the priests to death.[7] But he gave him a good answer. And when Simon heard that Zwingli had repeated this about him at several places, Simon denied having said it. Then at one time he took hold of M[aster] Leo and Mister Caspar[8] in the hospital and they charged Simon with having said this to him and now trying to go back on it and deny it and again made him responsible for the statement in the presence of these two.

After this, Simon came to him again in the transept of the Grossmünster and talked to him about interest and tithes and mentioned that he had frankly told the Twelve at Höngg[9] that they did not owe interest and tithes. And when he talked very severely to him, telling him that he had done wrong and that it causes him difficulty, Simon would have been glad to swallow his words. He said thereupon that he had said it privately to the Twelve and trusted them not to spread it, but that there was one among them who said it came from him and spread it abroad.

Thus Grebel and Simon talked to him more than once and always insisted that all things should be held in common.[10]

Further, Felix Mantz came to him once [11] in front of Hujuff's garden[12] and argued with him about the church, saying that no one could or should remain in the church except those who knew that they were without sin.[13] And when he asked Mantz whether he considered himself one of them, he gave him no real answer.

In a private conversation in Leo's home, Mantz said he expected him and his companions not to preach anything without their knowledge and without discussing it beforehand with them.[14]

Also a trustworthy man from Bern wrote that one called Martin[15] (who was here for a time among the Anabaptists) spoke in Bern and boasted that he thought the Anabaptists were right, that there should be no government.[16] He liked them very well both in their insistence on piety and also that all things should be in common.[17]

Further, he heard from Provost Brennwald[18] that Jörg Blaurock said in the Preacher's Monastery[19] to an Anabaptist from Zollikon that there were so many of them that they could overpower Milords if they moved at once in an attack.[20]

It was also well known how Conrad Grebel said at the disputation on Monday[21] that he thought the Messiah might be already present, but it is not known what or whom he meant thereby.

From all this he could come to no other conclusion than that it was their ultimate intention that they were daring to increase their numbers in order to do away with government. . . .

Doctor Sebastian [Hofmeister] of Schaffhausen[22] said and testified that Conrad Grebel had come to him at Schaffhausen together with Anemund, the French knight,[23] and talked much with him about infant baptism and tried to get him submitted to it also. But when he refused, Grebel began to say that the papacy could never be overcome more easily than with infant baptism. He also told him how the prisoners had so miraculously escaped[24] and he also had seen visions and revelations.[25] For this he reprimanded him and showed him clearly from the Scripture that he was in error and wrong. Later he came to him again and said that the pulpit preachers and those who had benefices could never proclaim the truth properly.

Conrad also accused Zwingli of adultery[26] and other things and said that Zwingli was set on his blood and if they had obeyed him, he and his comrades would have been killed. Thereby he tried again to denigrate Zwingli and persuade him to his cause and ideas.

Grebel had also told the French knight[27] all sorts of things against Zwingli, so that the knight was greatly displeased with Zwingli and went to Zwingli from Schaffhausen to find out if what he had heard was the truth or not. And when he returned to Schaffhausen, he heard that the knight was incensed against Conrad Grebel and had told him that he had not told the truth and that he was well satisfied with Zwingli. Then Grebel said he knew very well that if he went to Zwingli, he would inject his poison into him also.

Grebel had also said he knew very well that Leo and Caspar were also of their opinion, but they dared not own such a thing before M[aster] Huldrych.

Then Felix Mantz was also in Schaffhausen and talked to him about government, how there should be none.[28] Likewise, there should be no use of the sword,[29] but it could not be gotten rid of unless infant baptism was abandoned.

He also heard from them that all who are rebaptized live without sin[30] and that all who sit on courts and councils cannot be Christians.

He says further that he knew and remembered very well that they had attempted to establish their own church and assembly.[31]

Lord Provost Brennwald[32] testified that when he with others was at the Preachers' Monastery for alms, George Sitz,[33] at the Krummfuss, came to him, M[aster] Trinkler, M[aster] Stollen,[34] and other Milords, and related to them that Blaurock said to a peasant of Zollikon [that] when there were enough of them, they should prepare to make a resistance, if they would be suddenly overpowered by a company.[35]

Mister Jörg of the Krummfuss testified that when he and Anthony Walder[36] were assigned to [collecting] alms, a young fellow from Zollikon came along and asked them whether anyone was permitted to visit the prisoners. Then Mr. Anthony answered, "No, no one was admitted to them." The man from Zollikon then left but later returned; and when Mister Anthony saw him, he said to the witness, "Run, dear fellow, look, he will be able to think up a way to get to him." And he went there and when he reached the prison, the fellow was there. Then Blaurock asked him how it was out there and which party was the larger. He answered Blaurock, the other party was greater, meaning the party in opposition to them. Then Blaurock said, "When Milords attack you with arms, do not fear. Pay no attention to the use of force and be steadfast and brave." And Mister Anthony told him that the "young fellow" who was with him was a Hottinger. . . .

2. The Testimony of Conrad Grebel.

Conrad Grebel persists that infant baptism is of the devil and rebaptism is right and that Zwingli is teaching falsely and wrongly.

Next, he does not admit that he ever taught that one should have to give his property to anybody for nothing.[37]

Concerning the church he said that whoever is a coveter, usurer, gambler, or the like should never be [included] among Christians but be excluded by the ban, as taught in Scripture.

Further he said he had never expected Zwingli or others not to preach anything without first discussing it with one another;[38] but he had said in Leo's home that if one wanted to preach anything, he should take God's Word in hand and add no mediator or anything else to it.

Nor did he ever teach that one should not be obedient to the authorities. Also he could not recall ever discussing with the man from Bern[39] this matter about the authorities or having things in common.

Concerning Doctor Sebastian [Hofmeister], he had never said to him that government should be abolished.[40]

Concerning the escape from prison,[41] he said the same things as the other people.

Likewise, he never said that he had ever seen visions.[42] Jörg had told him of visions and revelations, but not he himself.

439

Likewise he never charged Zwingli with adultery[43] or any other vices to discredit him therewith. Also he did not doubt that Leo and Caspar as well as the others, if they would only speak the truth, knew very well that infants should not be baptized.

3. The Written Statement of Jörg Blaurock[44]

I am a door,[45] he who enters through me finds pasture but he who enters elsewhere is a thief and a murderer,[46] as it is written. I am a good shepherd.[47] A good shepherd gives his soul for his sheep. Thus I too offer my body and life and soul for my sheep, my body in the Tower, my life in the sword, or fire, or in the winepress have my blood pressed from my flesh like Christ on the cross. I am a beginner[48] of the baptism of Christ and the bread of the Lord together with my elect brethren in Christ,[49] Conrad Grebel and Felix Mantz. On this account the pope with his following is a thief and a murderer, Luther is a thief and a murderer with his following, and Zwingli and Leo Jud are thieves and murderers of Christ with their following until they acknowledge this. I have desired and still desire of my gracious Lords of Zurich to debate[50] with Huldrych Zwingli and Leo Jud, and am unable to get it. But I am waiting for the hour that my heavenly Father has ordained[51] for it.

When Jörg von Husen wrote the aforementioned document which has been read to Milords, the delegated spiritual and secular [authorities], M[aster] Huldrych Zwingli and M[aster] Leo talked and argued about three hours with said Jörg, called Blaurock. But after long arguing, Blaurock refuses to desist from his plan and says he will keep on baptizing. But finally he was brought to the point that he could no longer give a reasonable reply but departed as an obstinate erring man. And at the end he said: If the burgomaster and council and many at Zollikon and elsewhere believe and follow him and his adherents, he proclaimed that interest and tithes[52] should be paid. But if they do not adhere to him, there was no obligation to pay interest or tithes, etc. He also claimed that his heavenly Father had sent him to Zollikon[53] to look after his sheep there.

4. The Testimony of Margaret Hottinger

Margaret Hottinger[54] of Zollikon gives her answer.[55] She cannot say who brought her into this affair, for when Grebel and Mantz came to them in Zollikon and read to them there and spoke of these things, no one had yet accepted baptism until Blaurock came, who was the first to begin to baptize.[56] And so she also accepted baptism. She also said that she knows nothing at all of strikes[57] or pacts[58] or schisms.[59]

440

5. The Testimony of Jörg Blaurock

Jörg Blaurock's answer and opinion is, as it always has been, that Zwingli, Luther, the pope and their ilk, were like thieves and murderers,[60] for Christ says, anyone who enters by another door than through him is a thief and murderer. Thus, Zwingli teaches falsely, and infant baptism was invented by men, and what comes from man is also of the devil.[61] And so Zwingli teaches falsely and is a false prophet besides.

He also says it will never be found that he ever said that if there were enough of them to defend themselves, they would try to convince them with a small squadron.[62]

Likewise he said he had never given an oath to leave Milord's territory[63] and would rather die than forswear God's earth, for the earth is the Lord's.[64]

And as he had more than once said to M[aster] Wädischwiler[65] in the Tower, if they should order him and his brethren to leave, they will do so willingly and voluntarily. Of this he is now completely disavowed and agreed.[66]

6. The Testimony of Felix Mantz

Felix Mantz gives his answer that the Scriptures and their bases are so firm that they cannot be set aside or overcome, so therefore infant baptism is wrong and rebaptism right; and since Zwingli teaches it, he teaches wrongly and falsely.

And so nothing has impelled him to deny infant baptism and to oppose it but the clear and true Scriptures. And so also nothing else led him to rebaptism but that he knew well that he had not been baptized.[67]

And when they reminded him that they held their meetings at night,[68] he answered that while he was reading Hebrew in his home, several persons came to him and heard him there. After the reading everyone went home. Some good fellows had occasionally come to him, but they never held a meeting that could have been to anyone's disadvantage.

Further, it happened on a certain occasion that M[aster] Huldrych was standing before Hujuff's garden, talking with him about a Christian people.[69] He also joined them there and after a long conversation M[aster] Huldrych asked whether one could not be a Christian secretly and for himself. Then he [Mantz] answered M[aster] Huldrych: No, for Christian and brotherly love must be shown openly, each to the other, and it cannot be secret. He pointed out that Paul indicated when he wrote about it and said that fornication, lasciviousness, and adultery and other things should not be tolerated among Christians, and a Christian should report such things. Then M[aster] Huldrych answered him that he ought to do that

441

and expel from the church anyone who had such a vice. Thereupon he [Mantz] said it would not be fitting for him to do that, for he is not a bishop like M[aster] Huldrych.

Likewise he said he had not heard that M[aster] Escher[70] and M[aster] Kambli[71] ever said that he should avoid going to the meetings.

He also said that he had never demanded that M[aster] Huldrych or his comrades should not preach anything without first asking him about it or discussing it with him.[72]

Concerning government he said no Christian strikes with the sword, nor does he resist evil.[73]

7. The Judgment of the Council

Saturday after Ottmari [November 18] in the presence of Lord Walder, burgomaster, and Small and Large Councils.

Inasmuch as Conrad Grebel, Felix Mantz, and Jörg of the House of Jacob were imprisoned by Milords because of their rebaptism and improper conduct, etc., it is declared that all three are to be put together into the New Tower[74] and fed on bread, mush,[75] and water. No one is to visit them or depart from them except the prescribed attendants, as long as God pleases and it seems good to Milords, etc.

As to Margaret Hottinger, she is to be spoken to and asked whether or not she intends to persist in Anabaptism and the teaching of Grebel and Mantz.[76] And if she persists, she is to be imprisoned in the Wellenberg.[77] But if she desists, she shall do penance (if she has not already done so) before she leaves the prison.

Ulrich Teck[78] of Waldshut, who was previously seized at Grüningen, shall be released upon an oath and payment of costs, if he has it. In his oath he shall swear that he will leave Milord's territory and never have anything further to do with it. In case he should refuse to render the oath, he shall remain in prison.

Marty Lingg[79] of Schaffhausen and Michael Sattler[80] of Stauffen in the Breisgau shall be dismissed under oath never to return and payment of costs.

Originals: Staatsarchiv Zurich, El, 7.1 & B.VI, fol. 183b
Transcriptions: Quellen 1, Nos. 120, 121, 123, 124, 133

71L
Mandate of the Zurich Council to the
Grüningen Magistrates
Zurich, November 30, 1525

The request for the Third Public Disputation on baptism in Zurich had come from the magistrates of its Grüningen jurisdiction (see Intro. to 71J, above), and it was to those magistrates or "Twelve Judges" that the following mandate was addressed. Note that the form of the mandate presented here is a combination from two sources—Egli's Actensammlung *and Bullinger's* Reformationsgeschichte.

In spite of imprisonment, two disputations,[1] and the consequent promise to desist from rebaptism,[2] many Anabaptists have backslidden.[3] The council acceded to the renewed demand for a debate and set it for Monday, November 6.[4] In the debate held in the city hall and the Grossmünster between Conrad Grebel, Felix Mantz, Blaurock, Huldrych Zwingli, Leo Jud, and Caspar Grossmann,[5] infant baptism was shown to be biblical.[6] And because of this, it is our prohibition and serious judgment that henceforth everyone—men and women, boys and girls[7]abstain from all rebaptism, no longer practice it, but baptize the infants. For whoever acts to the contrary, whenever it occurs, shall be fined a silver mark.[8] And if anyone shows himself to be disobedient, we will deal further with him, and we will penalize[9] those who are disobedient in this regard in accord with their deserts, and we will not let up.[10] Everyone will know how to conduct himself. All by virtue of this open letter sealed with the city's seal and proclaimed on St. Andrew's Day, 1525.

Original: Bullinger, *Reformationsgeschichte,* I, p. 296; Aktensammlung, No. 873
Transcription: Muralt-Schmid, No. 139

71M
The Tenth Disputation with the Anabaptists:
Their Retrial and Sentencing
Zurich, March 5-7, 1526

Oswald Myconius wrote that he took part in "nine friendly conferences and earnest disputations" with the Anabaptists (De Zwinglii Vita et Obitu, trans. Jackson, 1912, p. 15). Zwingli, nevertheless, in the following excerpt from his Elenchus, *reports a tenth* collatio, *which was certainly less of a disputation than any of the previous nine listed in the Introduction to 68B, above, but was in fact nothing more than the* Täuferprocess *(Anabaptist retrial) itself, which began March 5, 1526.*

At least eighteen Anabaptists were individually interrogated by three appointed prosecutors: Guildmaster Heinrich Huber, Guildmaster Heinrich Trüb, and Hans Usteri. The defendants included four women and fourteen men, chief of whom were Grebel, Mantz, Blaurock, and Hubmaier (who was being held in solitary confinement). The brevity of their testimonies indicates that the spirit of true dialogue was gone and the proceedings were purely juridical. Mantz gave his testimony in writing, saying that he does not argue but only witnesses to his faith.

Two days later, sentences were pronounced on sixteen of the defendants plus two other women. They were to be returned to their places of confinement on a continued diet of bread and water until they do one of two things: recant or die. Moreover, a decree was issued which mandated for the first time in Zurich capital punishment by drowning for incorrigible Anabaptists.

[*Continued from Zwingli's Account in 71J*] By this battle,[1] their forces were so cut up that we began to have much more tranquility, especially in the city; but they wandered through the countryside by night[2] and infested all[3] to the best of their ability.[4] After the next conference,[5] which was actually the tenth after the others both public and private,[6] the senate decreed most explicitly that he who rebaptized another should be drowned.[7]

[*To be continued in Epi.B, below*].

[*The Retrial of the Anabaptists*]

Felix Mantz answers:[8] You will and you must learn that infant baptism is not right and not Christ's baptism. You have not permitted me to write[9] as I always hoped you would because you kept me in prison. I did not argue but witnessed to my faith. I shall confess it to the end in the power of him who will strengthen me with his truth. Concerning other things and charges of your law, I will answer as truly as is right.

Jörg Blaurock's answer is that he will stay by the baptism of Christ which he has accepted, and all those who baptize infants are murderers and thieves[10] against God. And if they want many answers, let them read the letter that he wrote to the preachers in the churches.[11] He will stay with that until death.

Conrad Grebel answers and persists in the belief that infant baptism is wrong and the baptism he accepted is right. He will stay by that and let God rule. He would otherwise be obedient to Milords in all other secular matters. He also hopes to show that Zwingli errs in these and other things, and also asks Milords to permit him to write,[12] like Zwingli. Then he can prove it. If he fails to do so, he is willing to suffer whatever God wills....

The answer of Uli Hottinger of Zollikon[13] is that it cannot be found that infants should be baptized; and because it cannot be found, one should not, in his opinion, baptize infants. He also will let Anabaptism stay the way it is.

Ernst von Glätz of Silesia[14] gives his answer thus: Last Thursday it was one week[15] since Karl Brennwald[16] baptized him in Widerkerin's house.[17] The furrier's wife[18] was also present and Widerkerin and another woman he does not know.[19] He holds infant baptism not right, for it would have been mentioned in the Scriptures; but one finds it nowhere in the Scriptures that infants should be baptized. He will stay with his baptism.

Doctor Balthasar [Hubmaier][20] gives his reply: He had answered Milords previously that he would put the [matter of] baptism to rest and be peaceable in word and deed and the like. He would abide by this selfsame answer and beg Milords that where he has otherwise provoked them and acted contrary to them, they would for God's sake forgive him for that, etc. The doctor's case was heard previously.[21] He asks them for permission to write on the four articles, namely, on government, interest, tithes, and community [of goods]. He would acquit himself to such a degree that they would be compelled to see that he had been treated unjustly.

Anthony Roggenacher of Schwyz[22] the furrier, answered thus: He considers baptism right for those who forsake sin and diligently follow Christ, for God gives him much grace. Otherwise it is of no avail if God allows one to be given baptism when he always proceeds to sin against him and will not stay with it.

Hans Hottinger of Zollikon,[23] the watchman, gives his answer thus: Had God his Father planted infant baptism, he also would like to be baptized therein. But let him stay as he is, for what God has not planted must be uprooted; and he wants to do all that Milords require as far as he is able.

Rudolf Hottinger[24] answered that he was not eager to baptize anyone nor to teach about it. He could also not find in his conscience that he had now done wrong with baptism. He also would leave infant baptism as it was and begs Milords for the sake of brotherly love to burden his conscience no further. When the verdict had been read to him, he had replied as he had stood before Milords and it was spoken to him that he would stay at home with his children and be peaceful. This he had done and had been obedient, and he begged Milords to do their best by him.

Hans Ockenfuss[25] gave his answer thus: Since no one can say that either the Old or New Testament asserts that infants should be baptized, he would stay on the side of the truth and seal the same with his blood just like his predecessor[26] Christ, but in all [other] things he would be obedient to Milords.

Karl Brennwald[27] answered that the furrier[28] had baptized him and that he had baptized M[aster] zur Eichs' servant[29] in Widerkerin's house;[30] and to the baptism he now had he would testify with his blood that it is right and leaves infant baptism as it was.

Agli Ockenfuss[31] answered that Fridli Ab-Iberg of Schwyz[32] had baptized M[aster] Stoltz's servant[33] in her house. She also would stay with her baptism and considers it right, for God had revealed it to her and he and his apostles had so practiced it. And if they erred, she would err with them; and if they had done right, then she would also do right.[34] . . .

Elizabeth Hottinger of Hirslanden[35] answered that what Christ had done and spoken was right. She would also stay with that to her death and considers the baptism that she had now accepted as good and right, for Christ had also practiced it so. . . . .

Margaret Hottinger[36] gave her answer that she would stay with her baptism, which she held as right and good, and whoever is baptized in it would be saved, but whoever would not believe in it and fight against it was a child of the devil.

Winbrat Fanwilerin of St. Gallen[37] answered that what God her heavenly Father had not planted must be uprooted[38] and burned with eternal fire. Inasmuch as no word can be found in the Scriptures that infants should be baptized, the same infant baptism was not right but the baptism that she received is right; for God had declared it and also commanded it to be observed. It was also a righteousness of God.[39]. . .

Fridli Ab-Iberg of Schwyz[40] answered that he was entreated by his friend from Schwyz[41] that he leave for awhile. This he had done and had come here and lived at the Salmon and the Rössli[42] and often gone to Ockenfuss,[43] who had been his tailor. On one occasion there came someone[44] who wanted him for God's sake to pour water on him. He refused at first, but he begged him so much that he poured water on him in the name of the Father, etc. Other than that, he has baptized no one.

Hans Heingarter of St. Gallen[45] gave his answer that he arrived here Wednesday evening, spent the night at the Linden [hof],[46] and sought to discover what his brethren were doing in prison. And on Thursday morning he asked for the furrier's[47] house, which was pointed out to him. And when he arrived there, the man from Schwyz[48] was there with Karl Brennwald.[49] He went into the city with them to the Salmon.[50] There he was arrested. He had never been here before. He also held Anabaptism to be right because it was of God and not infant baptism.

Anna Mantz[51] answers: Since the last imprisonment, no one has been with her but Heini Aberli.[52] Since Tuesday she has been with her people and brought them bread, stayed with them about an hour; and they talked about nothing other than the love of God. No other outsider visited her except some women. Conrad Grebel baptized her. She intends to stay by that, and she considers him just and good, leaves infant baptism alone as it was.

Anna Widerkerin,[53] M[aster] Bluntschli's[54] sister, gave her answer. M[aster] zur Eich's servant[55] together with her brother's servant came to her house with her knowledge and permission and were there a good while. Into the same [house] came Karl Brennwald,[56] accomplished in all matters. There M[aster] zur Eich's servant wanted the sign of baptism from Karl, and there Karl baptized him. Other than this she knew of no other endeavors.[57] She also will stay with her baptism, which she holds as right and good; for Christ and his apostles had commanded it so, and so it seemed good and right to her.

[Resentencing by the Council, March 7, 1526]

Wednesday after St. Fridolin's Day in the presence of Lord Walder,[58] senior burgomaster, and the Large and Small Councils.

The following Anabaptists are definitely known to be in Milords' prisons:[59] Felix Mantz, Jörg Blaurock of Chur, Conrad Grebel, Uli Hottinger of Zollikon,[60] Ernst of Glätz of Silesia,[61] Anthony Roggenacher of Schwyz,[62] Hans Hottinger,[63] Rudolf Hottinger,[64] Hans Ockenfuss,[65] Karl Brennwald,[66] Fridli Ab-Iberg of Schwyz,[67] Hans Heingarter of St. Gallen,[68] Agli Ockenfuss,[69] Elizabeth Hottinger of Hirslanden,[70] Margaret Hottinger of Zollikon,[71] Winbrat Fanwilerin of St. Gallen,[72] Anna Mantz,[73] and Widerkerin at the Green Shield.[74]

Concerning these Anabaptists, it is declared that upon their answers which each one gave[75] and their opinions persisted in, that they shall be put together into the New Tower;[76] and they shall be given nothing to eat but bread and water and bedded on straw. And the attendant who guards them shall under oath let no one come to them or go away from them. Thus let them die in the Tower unless anyone desists from his acts and error and intends to be obedient. That should then be brought to [the attention of] Milords' councillors and representatives. And then they shall be asked how further to punish them. No one shall have the authority to alter their confinement, behind the backs of said Milords, whether they are sick or well.

Similarly, the girls and women[77] shall be placed together and treated in every respect as stated above.[78]

It is further decided to issue an open mandate everywhere indicating the severe imprisonment of the Anabaptists. And [that] anyone who baptizes hereafter will be drowned without mercy and thus brought from life to death, etc.[79]

[The Mandate of the Council, March 7, 1526]

Inasmuch as Our Lords, burgomaster, [Small] Council, and Large Council, which are called the Two Hundred[80] of the city of Zurich, have for some time earnestly endeavored to turn the deceived, mistaken Anabaptists from their error, etc., but inasmuch as some of them, hardened against their oaths, vows, and pledges, have shown disobedience to the injury of public order and authority and the subversion of the common interest and true Christian conduct, some of them—men, women, and girls[81]were sentenced by Our Lords to severe punishment and imprisonment. And it is therefore the earnest command, order, and warning of the said Our Lords that no one in their city, country, and domain, whether man, woman, or girl, shall henceforth baptize another. Whoever henceforth baptizes another will be seized by Our Lords and, according to this present explicit decree, drowned without any mercy. Hereafter, everyone knows how to avoid this so that no one gives cause for his own death.[82]

This judgment shall be announced in the three parishes[83] on Sunday and in the districts of the land and announced by public written mandate. Put into force on Wednesday after Oculi Sunday, 1526.

[From the Chronicle of Hermann Miles][84]

During this [Lenten] fasting period[85] the Zurich authorities imprisoned Dr. Balthasar [Hubmaier] of Waldshut and Conrad Grebel and many other Anabaptists together in the Murder Tower,[86] condemned to eternal imprisonment; and each is to be given daily 2 d[enari][87] worth of bread and water; but anyone who is willing to recant his Anabaptism will be released; otherwise all are to die off. And the Two Hundred [Councillors] decided that anyone else who accepts baptism is to be drowned immediately without mercy.[88]

Originals: Staatsarchiv Zurich, EI.7.1; A.42.1; Vadiana Ms. 177, pp. 1-84
Transcriptions: ZW, VI, No. 108, p. 45; Quellen 1, Nos. 170, 170B, 170A, and 172; Miles, p. 309
Translation from the *Elenchus:* Taken from Jackson, 1901, pp. 135-36

In the following letter, another turning point is discernible in Zwingli's attitude toward his former disciples who had turned to Anabaptism. In his December, 1524, tract concerning "who gives cause for rebellion" (67C, above), he pleads with his radical associates to cease their chronic agitating and to cooperate with their pastors to whom the difficult office of preaching the evangelical faith had been assigned. He claimed that baptism, which had just become on issue, was not an important enough basis for controversy; and in all other doctrines essential to the Reformation, they were surely still in agreement.

Then in May of 1525 when he wrote his Taufbüchlein *(69C, above), Zwingli saw more clearly that the dissent went deeper than he had thought. "All of the previous fights," he wrote to Vadian, "were child's play compared with this" (69D/375/15-16). After two more tracts (70C and his reply to Hubmaier mentioned in 71I/431/17-18) and ten disputations on the same subject, the City Council finally approved the death penalty for incorrigible Anabaptists as Zwingli's own attitude toward them turned from forbearance (57A/227/27) to uninhibited anger.*

Grace and peace from the Lord.

This day, most honorable burgomaster, it has been decreed by the Council of Διακοσίων [Two Hundred][1] that the Anabaptist ringleaders[2] shall be cast back into the Tower[3] in which they previously lay [and] enticed by bread and water until they either die or surrender.[4] It was further decided that whoever is baptized hereafter will be submerged permanently.[5] This decision has already been proclaimed.[6] Thus patience has endured enough and finally erupted. Your father-in-law senator[7] implored mercy in vain. The incorrigibly impetuous audacity of these people first pains and then irks[8] me. I could wish that the newly reviving Christianity would not be inaugurated with a rumble[9] of this sort; but we are not God, who is pleased in this way[10] to provide against evils that are to come, as he once slew Ananias with a sudden and terrible death when he lied to Peter,[11] so that he might cut off from us all who dare to deceive, though we are by no means equally skilled at this. . . . [12]

Luther is vigorously feeding the conflict among the Swabians with letters.[13] But what will they accomplish if the truth is so obviously bent? Truth and principle stand with us.

Erasmus is writing a hurried book[14] against Luther's *Bondage of the Will*[15] (the title which the latter gave his book that he wrote against the διατριβὴν [diatribes] of Erasmus),[16] by which he may trim the victory for

449

the Lutherans somewhat. But these are foamy fights as far as the real issues are concerned. . . .

Original: Stadtbibliothek (Vadiana) St. Gallen, Litt. misc. II. 253
Transcriptions: VB, IV, No. 444; ZW, VIII, No. 459

71-O
The Prison Escape of the Anabaptists
Zurich, March 21, 1526

Fourteen days after the sentence of life incarceration was imposed on them, all of the male Anabaptist prisoners escaped from the New Tower through an unlocked window which they managed to pry open. With the aid of the same rope and capstan used to hoist them over the wall and down into the Tower, they pulled each other up and over the wall into the moat, which happened to be drained at the moment because the drawbridge was closed. It was a curious set of circumstances almost too propitious to be accidental.

In either case, by breaking the lock on the bridge, they reopened it and were free again. They fled in various directions by twos and threes. Wilhelm Exell and Fridli Ab-Iberg were too sick or weak to get very far and were recaptured within the city walls that same night. Two weeks later they stood trial once more, and following is the fascinating story they told the council.

Council Investigation of the Escape, Apr. 4, 1526

Wilhelm Exell [of Wallis][1] gives his answer: When Felix Bischoff[2] had given them their water for Wednesday evening[3] and they were drinking it and eating a little bread with it, Karl Brennwald[4] said he thought that the shutter would open; but [the idea it suggested] seemed objectionable to him as well as to Grebel, Blaurock, Mantz, and Ockenfuss.[5] They did not want to take advantage of it, but die in the Tower. Then they saw that there was a shutter lower down in the Tower, which they broke loose and with it pushed at the upper shutter. When they saw that it would give way, the servant of M[aster] zur Eich[6] climbed up the wall at the corner by means of the shutter and came out below the shutter and propped it up with books and blocks of wood,[7] so that it would be possible to get through. Then Felix Mantz also climbed up, and after him Anthony Kürsiner.[8] They let the rope down and pulled Karli Brennwald up. But neither he nor the others were minded as yet to go up. Then the four discussed the fact that everything was open up there and they could easily get up. Then he said he had seen Felix Bischoff[9] close the drawbridge and lock it. Then they said everything was open. He did not know how the four broke the lock on the bridge. And so they pulled him and the others up too, took down the rope with which they had pulled them up, and they all in succession let themselves down by the rope of the capstan. And when they were all down in the moat, the servant of M[aster] zur Eich,[10] being the last one, took down the rope by which they had been put into the Tower, knotted it under his arms, and lowered himself too. Then Ockenfuss[11] said he did not know what he would do, but thought he would go to the Horgerberg to work. But the others joked among themselves and said they would go to the red Indians across the sea.[12] One said he would go here, and another there. And so he went first to the gate. And after he knocked for a long time, Ockenfuss the gate watchman[13] came and let him in. Then came Ockenfuss the tailor,[14] and also Karli Brennwald. And while they were talking to Ockenfuss the guard, he did not at first recognize them, for he was surprised that they were there. And so Ockenfuss the tailor said to his brother that he was doing the best for his children and brought him the bag in which he had needles, shears, and thimble so that he could work. And he went to his master's house to turn in his sack. Then his master's wife was badly frightened upon seeing him. Then he did not linger long and as he was about to leave, his master got up and talked to him and told him to get away fast. And when he got back to the gate, Ockenfuss the guard said it was dark and the weather so bad, that nobody would get there. Then he asked if he would keep him overnight. Ockenfuss said yes. And so he went home with him. Then the police came and took them prisoner. He knew nothing further.

It was also true that the furrier from Schwyz[15] had said often that they had looked at the shutter and saw that it would open, but no one paid any attention. Then Heini Hottinger[16] said he begged them for God's sake to help him get out, for he could not survive in there. And it was their decision to avoid the grossest vices and to conduct themselves toward God in such a way that if he should call them, they would be able to give an account. And they had always agreed to stand by this decision and die. Mantz and the furrier[17] had each brought a flint and steel and some wax candles into the Tower in order to make a light when it was necessary. Karlin[18] also had a wire in readiness, by which he hoisted himself up while he was still down there. But he did not know what he did with it. He asked Milords to do their best for him and be merciful and let him stay at home in his country. He thought his baptism would not hurt anyone. He had never baptized nor taught and would not do so. And if they could show him that he was in error, he would gladly desist from it. At home nobody had warned him against going away but had always said that anyone who supposed he did not have enough grace and strength from God to stay at home, he might leave; but when he was away he should nonetheless avoid vices or the Christian church would not tolerate him.

451

Fridli Ab-Iberg of Schwyz[19] said the same as Wilhelm of Wallis about leaving. And when they helped one another slide down, he lost consciousness because of illness; and so he could not know what they discussed later. And when he came to, each was asking the other where he planned to go. They did not know where they wanted to go, but he said he wanted to go into the town, for he was not able to go anywhere else. And he would have liked to hire a boatman to take him at once to Horgen and then on the next day he would be at home. But he was so sick that he could not go anywhere, and so he begged Ockenfuss to give him food and drink. He did so. He gave him bread and cheese and something to drink with it. And then he was seized. He begged Milords to do their best for him. And if anyone could teach him a better way, he would gladly obey for he could neither read nor write.

Grebel, Mantz, and Blaurock had read and strengthened him and the others in the Tower. Then he had believed the Scripture; and if anyone could teach him something different with the divine Scriptures, he would accept instruction.

Sentence

For these two, it is decided to expel them under oath from Milords' jurisdiction and region. And if they come in again they shall that very hour be drowned without mercy.

Ratified on the Wednesday after Easter, in the presence of the Lord Mayor Walder, Councillors, and representatives, in the year 1526.

Original: Staatsarchiv Zurich, EI.7.1
Transcription: Muralt-Schmid, No. 178

71P
Zwingli to Michael Wüst
Zurich, April 10, 1526

This is the first reference in the collection of documents to the name of Michael Wüst, first cousin and former fellow student of Heinrich Bullinger (see Cast of Characters No. 101). Before he became an Anabaptist, Wüst had been the schoolmaster and pastor in Klingnau, home town of Hans Krüsi; and it is possible that he was the one mentioned in Krüsi's pre-execution testimony listing "the schoolmaster of Klingnau" (71E/424/1-2) among his Anabaptist companions.

It is likely, as the following letter implies, that Wüst met Grebel in Oberglatt, following the latter's escape from prison on March 21. Wüst was living here at the time; and it is known that this was the destination of at least one of Grebel's fellow prisoners, Carl Brennwald (see Cast of Characters No. 9). Moreover, with Brennwald in Oberglatt was Hans Küntzi, the wool-weaver, who reported meeting Grebel on his flight from Zurich (71Q/455/ 7ff.).

Zwingli attempts in his letter to free Wüst from the alleged captivity to the Anabaptists and its leaders like Grebel. Bullinger had similar concern, expressed in several letters. In one he reported that Michael had been misled by the Anabaptists, deserted the priesthood, and gone into wool-weaving (ZW, No. 467, fn. 1); and in the other he reported that he died among the Anabaptists in Oberglatt, presumably soon after Zwingli's letter was written (ibid.). Zwingli must have known that Grebel had been with Wüst in Ober-glatt, although as 71Q, below, indicates, Grebel didn't tarry there very long.

Grace and peace from the Lord.

My dear Michael:

This woman—I do not know for sure who she may be—came to me and ardently implored that I should snatch you away from the Anabaptists with a letter. At first, I firmly refused what she was asking, barely indicating how I had thoroughly discussed this matter with you not many days ago.[1] But finally, by the urgency of her petition, she wrested this letter from me in the midst of my busy occupations.[2] I suppose I am writing it more to satisfy the woman than to frighten you away from the hypocrisy of these people, for it is surely not adequate or appropriate for what they have been concocting. She asserted that you have not yet been rebaptized, but that it is to be feared that if you associate with these people much longer, you will be snatched over to their madness. Why, I ask, should I write to you at length? Are you a Christian? Then what dealings do you have with those who separate themselves from Christians?[3] But they say: We are the Christians and those men by whom you believe are not the Christians. Who, pray, disclosed that to you? Are you the ones who are to judge the hearts and reins?[4] If they steadfastly adhere to Christ with their heart, confess him with their mouth, and zealously follow him as much as God grants, why do they then judge the innocent brother? Indeed, how many myriads, do you suppose, are there in the church of Christ who in holiness of life, goodness of character, and temperance of speech tower above the most outstanding of the Anabaptists? But let us grant for the moment that the latter surpass them in holiness. What spirit tells them then, I ask, that when they may have advanced a trifle, they can pride themselves to be destined[5] above others? Or can they cite Christ as the teacher of this sort of arrogance? Or have the apostles presented the example for it? What examples of history have produced the idea that when they have made a separation from the church of the Christian masses, they might be a little better than the ordinary population? The orders of monks have done that, but were they any better because they thought so highly of themselves? I will pass over the blasphemous gossiping of the Anabaptists which surpasses every poisonous defamation, their foolish arrogance, their most pretentious stubbornness. What will they not do to be seen by men?[6] Moreover, a large number of them can easily do without luxuries, for they have landed in this port out of the lowest and most desperate dregs of the population in order that they might make a nobility out of their obscurity. If the opportunity would be present for them, Sardanapalus and Heliogabalus would be mere child's play compared with them. I know that [Conrad] Grebel, however much he perjures himself, has despaired of his parents for no other reason than the fact that they have not given him as much as his licentiousness was demanding. Such thirst for glory and ambition shakes the human mind unless it is actively firm against such gusts of wind. While all of them try to conceal it, the younger ones are less successful for they are usually detected. Therefore, open the eyes of your mind and see what befits a Christian man, not what these people do or say. This woman wants to bring you back to the city. I promise you my service and loyalty at any time.

Farewell.

April 10, 1526.

To Michael Wüst, his by no means casual friend.

Original: Staatsarchiv Zurich, EI.3.1, No. 18
Transcription: ZW, VIII, No. 467

71Q
The Flight of Grebel
Glattfelden, April 11, 1526

Although we have no direct evidence apart from the following court testimony, we can trace Grebel's flight on this and secondary evidence. We know that fellow prisoner Brennwald went first to Oberglatt, six miles north of Zurich, and then another five miles northeast to Embrach, where he worked for an indefinite time (see 71 M/fn.16). Mantz was also here awhile, for he is known to have taught and baptized a woman at this place (M-S,#200, p.216,fn.4). It is likely that Grebel accompanied Brennwald at least to Oberglatt, where he was apparently in contact with Michael Wüst (see 71-0, above) and met Hans Küntzi, who according to the following document was recently with "Grebel and others" and then accompanied Grebel as far as Glattfelden, ten miles north of Oberglatt. For his likely destination beyond Glattfelden, see 71R, below.

454

Hans Küntzi of Klingnau[1] gives his answer: He has never baptized nor been present when one baptized another, but he was baptized by Uli Teck of Waldshut.[2] He is willing to desist if he can be corrected with Holy Scripture. And when people came to him and wanted to talk about baptism, he always refused and did not let them say anything, for he supposed they did not understand it and knew nothing about it. Also, he knew absolutely nothing about any meetings; and when Grebel and others were with him recently, he accompanied them to Glattfelden. Then he asked Grebel where they were planning to go. Grebel replied [that] he did not want to tell. So he did not need to tell either, and begged Milords most kindly to do their best for him. He never wanted to create any disturbance for Milords in any way or manner.

Original: Staatsarchiv Zurich, EI.7.1
Transcription: Muralt-Schmid, No. 180

71R
The Death of Grebel
Maienfeld, August 1526

From Glattfelden to Maienfeld south of Liechtenstein is a long way around the Toggenburg. The report that Conrad Grebel died of the plague in this village comes from Kessler, who probably heard it from Vadian, who would certainly have been in the best position to know, for Conrad and Martha, Vadian's wife, had an older sister living in Maienfeld. Barbara Grebel married Beat Beli of Maienfeld (her second marriage), and it is quite possible (although not absolutely certain) that they had been married as early as summer of 1526. If so, it was probably at their home that Conrad died in the autumn of that year (probably August according to HSB, p. 162). It is known that he arrived at the time when the plague was raging in the canton of Appenzell. "Thus," wrote Bender, "Grebel escaped the martyr's death which was the lot of his brother-in-the-faith and co-worker Felix Mantz and which would certainly have been his portion if he [too] had come back to Zurich from Maienfeld."

[*From the Account of Kessler, continued from 71J, above*] There were also some among them who had earlier learned and heard from Protestant preachers[1] that the New Testament was a matter of the spirit and not of the letter, as Martin Luther also says in his foreword to his translation of the New Testament.[2] Because they now thought themselves more spiritual than anyone else on earth, they threw their Testaments into the stove, burned and tore them up, saying, "The letter is dead, the spirit gives life,"[3] and "God says through the prophet: 'I will write my law on their hearts.' "⁴ ... There were some among the first Anabaptists who were not stained with so many opinions but held only to those articles that they had learned from Conrad Grebel.⁵

See, my Christian reader, I am not surprised if it bothers you to read further about such fantasies.⁶ I must cease, for there is no end to the abomination. I do not believe, furthermore, that it would be possible to write or speak of it as it really took place. But God be praised, who allows none of his to perish; for many have been called out of these errors to an orderly life. The aforementioned Conrad Grebel and Felix Mantz, the arch-Anabaptists, were also deeply distressed by such coarse errors and fantasies; nor was it their intention when they began it. Therefore, they were soon compelled to preach and teach against such error in Appenzell and Gotzhus.⁷ But many would listen to them as little as to us; indeed, they regarded them as false prophets and scribes and lashed out at them. Not long after this, Conrad Grebel went to Maienfeld in the Oberland and fell victim to the plague and died.⁸ Felix Mantz returned to the Zurich area and was drowned at Zurich as a penalty for repeatedly breaking his oath of banishment.⁹ I understand that the aforenamed Doctor Balthasar Hubmaier went down to Moravia, where Anabaptism spread so rapidly that they have rebaptized some six thousand persons.¹⁰

May God protect from this sect all the Christian communities where the gospel is flourishing; for not without much effort and setback for the gospel from what is called not only Anabaptism but also a redrowning of the conscience have we experienced people who were made alive again from the errors of the papacy through the joyous gospel.

Original: Kessler's *Sabbata* (see 65A)
Transcriptions: Kessler, pp. 153, 164; Quellen 2, pp. 616-17

EPILOGUE
1526-1540

Epilogue A
The Trial and Execution of Jacob Grebel
Zurich, October 11-30, 1526

The execution of Jacob Grebel, a respected senator who had been sent on no less than thirty special missions on behalf of the Zurich Commonwealth, is one of the great enigmas of history. The most thorough review of the whole episode is that of Leo Schelbert (1969), who consulted thirteen historians who had studied the case, seven of whom had taken a pro-Zwingli position in varying degrees and six a critical attitude toward Zwingli in relation to the Grebel case.

Schelbert himself tried to avoid taking sides. Grebel, in his view, was both innocent and guilty, depending on how the issues are defined. Zwingli, on the other hand, "experienced the cruel alternative which is so common in that deadly game of rising ideologies. He either had to risk complete defeat of the truth as he saw it and to which his whole existence was committed, or he had to strike at the compromising ally with ultimate force. The choice was a tragic one because it was inevitable and imposed by the very search for the ultimate" (pp. 63-64). Apart from the question of whether or not such historical decisions affecting the life and death of people are ever inevitable, Schelbert's

"Take my own Conrad Grebel of Zurich, a man endowed with great gifts, born into an outstanding family. Yet, stirred up by the promptings of a few, he began to spread in Zurich the dogma that baptism must be repeated. With the greatest obstinacy, he began to examine things once fixed and firm so that he refused to listen even to me, whom he had once held in the highest esteem." —Vadian to Zwick, August 19, 1540

finding that the execution was "*Zwingli's liquidation of Jacob Grebel*" (p. 55) is convincing. Grebel, in his view, was neither an adherent of the old faith nor an Anabaptist sympathizer but "*stood for mercy and moderation at a most critical juncture of the emerging Zwinglian persuasion*" (p. 63). How and why, then, did Zwingli engineer Grebel's demise?

First of all, he was much on the defensive in view of the momentum gained by the partisans of Rome following the Baden Disputation of May and June. Johann Eck, foremost champion of the papacy against Luther at Leipzig (1519), was present at Baden to debate with Zwingli, who refused to attend because of alleged threats to his life. In spite of the fact that the Protestant position was represented by Oecolampad of Basel and Haller of Bern, the forty charges against Zwingli, including his alleged cowardice in failing to appear and his alleged responsibility for the radical innovations of the Anabaptists gave the official victory to the adherents of the old faith. The conference ended with a decree that Zwingli and his colleagues were to be cast out of the bosom and communion of the Roman Catholic Church. Representatives from the old faith cantons returned with a new sense of righteous authorization to prepare for the showdown with the ever probable military aid of Austria.

Secondly, as Schelbert (pp. 49f.) clearly points out, the legitimacy of Zwingli's leadership was questioned within his own city by not one but three groups, in each of which a member of the Grebel family played a major role. The first group, the defenders of the old faith, "*declared Zwingli's theological and institutional reforms erroneous, heretical, and diabolic; they were the natural allies of those cantons within the confederacy which came to the defense of the old creed.*" In this group was Peter Grebel, a canon at the Grossmünster and first cousin of Jacob (see Cast of Characters, No. 41), who "*was forced to resign his position in late August 1526 after the canonry had been transformed into an educational institution during 1525 under Zwinglian control.*" The second group comprised the followers of Conrad Grebel who "*denounced the reforms as unbiblical . . . and contradictory to the very ideals which Zwingli himself had proclaimed before.*" The third group, at the center of which Schelbert places Jacob Grebel, "*was the least organized and therefore more difficult to combat. In general it supported Zwingli's reforming zeal but remained committed to a conciliatory attitude toward the radical dissent as well as toward the old faith party; it advocated moderation and such compromise which would minimize disturbances resulting from the use of force.*" The elder Grebel's role in this group "*seems to have resulted less from actual choice . . . than from a series of events which increasingly alienated Zwingli from his trusted and influential ally and finally ended in deadly hostility.*"

In the firm belief that a crisis of no small proportions had been reached that required emergency political measures, Zwingli more and more assumed the role of "dictator" (see fns. 18 and 30, below). In the meantime, Zwingli's *alienation from Jacob Grebel, according to Schelbert, began in the late summer of 1524 over the so-called Ittingen affair (see fn. 78b, below). At this point, Zurich was still the only canton explicitly committed to the Reformation. The removal of the sacred images and statues from her churches at the end of June (see 61/Intro., above) had numerous repercussions in the confederacy, one of which was the vandalizing of the monastery at Ittingen by Zwingli supporters in retaliation for the arrest of the pastor at Stein am Rhein by confederate agents. A number of the leaders in the Ittingen episode were arrested and tried and three of them executed. Word got back to Zwingli that Jacob Grebel, one of Zurich's deputies to the Diet in Baden at this time, had whispered that one of the pro-Zwingli defendants had admitted his crime.*

That fall Zwingli drew up a comprehensive military strategy in the face of the increasing likelihood of a military attack by the old-faith cantons. A situation approaching martial law was declared and a "secret council" was set up "to act in secret manner whenever grave and great matters" came to their attention (Schelbert, fn. 136). "This secret council enabled the power elite to supervise, isolate, and remove suspected or inconvenient members from the councils [and] empowered Zwingli to dominate the government more and more, and to intimidate and liquidate his opponents. Although he was technically only an 'adviser,' the secret council became in reality the institutional expression of his 'prophetic-theocratic' dominance" (Schelbert, p. 53). Zwingli's suspicion of Grebel as a compromiser at both ends of the political spectrum continued to grow during the last year of Grebel's life (see 71I/fn.12 and 71N/fn.7), and by the summer of 1526, he decided to destroy all of "Catiline's conspirators" (see below, fn. 4) who in his opinion were trying to undermine his plan for a Christian commonwealth.

Grebel was the first of ten men placed on trial. He was clearly singled out as the test case and was the only one to be executed. The following documents and accompanying notes recount how Zwingli secretly built his case against him, first gathering incriminating information from oral testimony and from certain letters, probably those that Conrad had sent to Zwingli from Vienna and to Myconius from Paris many years before, then preaching a series of sermons about the money-grabbers and traitors to the fatherland, and finally systematically presenting his data to the various tribunals of "justice"—a Committee of Four Councilmen meeting on September 22, the secret council meeting on October 11, the report of the secret council to the Committee of Four on October 12, the public report to the Large Council on October 13, and the jury of eleven appointed to try and judge the defendants.

The extant record of the trial and the reactions of Bullinger and Vadian tell the rest of the story. Schelbert's specification of the seven counts of the indictment against Grebel and summary of the proceedings are as follows:

"1. Grebel had permitted his son Conrad to give up his citizenship and study in Vienna with the support of an imperial scholarship.

"2. Grebel had arranged for a large scholarship from the French king for the benefit of his son whom he had therefore recalled from Vienna; of the 900 crowns Jacob Grebel had personally collected 600 crowns.

"3. Grebel had arranged a papal stipend for his son in dealings with the papal representative Pucci and his aid, Wilhelm de Falconibus, from whom Conrad had actually received 50 guilders.

"4. Grebel had used some of the money for his own purpose and had refused to hand it over to his son's widow.

"5. According to a witness Grebel had received 4,000 crowns from somewhere.

"6. Grebel had secretly promoted the causes of the old faith in dealings with the papal party.

"7. Grebel had secretly held that Hans Wirth, bailiff of Stammheim and first martyr of the Zwinglian persuasian, was guilty of theft.

"Despite the application of torture, the aged nobleman rejected all the allegations as untrue. He admitted only that Conrad, after having given up his citizenship, had indeed received the imperial and French scholarships, of which money the father still owed a part. These stipends had been no secret. Conrad himself had informed Zwingli of his imperial grant in 1517, and Glarean and the Swiss circle in Paris, many of whom kept in contact with the Zürich Reformer, knew about the French money. That Conrad Grebel had received financial help from the papal envoy the father thought was not impossible; when Conrad had requested money his parent had sometimes given it and sometimes not. On an occasion when he refused to give any money, Jacob Grebel may have told his son, half in jest and half in annoyance, to go to the papal representative who might be willing to answer his request. Zwingli himself had been aware of Conrad's recurrent demands for money. On April 10, 1526 [see 71P/454/11-13], Zwingli had remarked of his former friend: 'I know that Grebel, however he may deny it, has turned from his parents for no other reason than because of their refusal to give him as much as his arrogance demands.'

"But all this counted for little in the emotionally charged atmosphere of these October days, after the principal accuser had been promised swift and radical action. Grebel was declared guilty, and the penalty was death, because he had violated the three mandates against pension-taking issued in 1513, 1518, and 1522. It was of no avail that Grebel calmly rejected the central charges which were based on hearsay alone: the acceptance of some mysterious 4,000 crowns, the alleged improper dealings with the papal party, and the secret approval of Bailiff Wirth's execution. His solemn appeal to the judges to grant him fair protection of the law was to no avail. The highest penalty of death was imposed despite the fact that his son's stipends dated back five to nine years, and that Zwingli himself had accepted an annual papal pension of 50 guilders for some years; despite the fact that the draft law of 1500, upon which the subsequent laws were based, included the provision

460

that acceptance of a scholarship was not to be construed as pension-taking. Jacob Grebel's tireless efforts to further peace within the confederacy, and his devoted service in the cause of the reforms that Zwingli advocated, seemed now meaningless. He was beheaded on October 30, 1526, at about two o'clock in the afternoon." (Schelbert, pp. 59-61.)

Schelbert characterizes the response in Zurich as one of "shock and unbelief," quoting Bullinger, who wrote that "there was great unrest in the town." Vadian's dismay is described in his own words in the last document in this sequence. He does not mention Zwingli by name but indicates his misgivings by vowing to sail on with shortened sails and by the fact that for the next nine months no letter was exchanged between them while during the nine months preceding Jacob's trial, they had written on the average of once a month. Vadian finally took the initiative to renew his correspondence with Zwingli; but exactly five years later when word came to St. Gallen that the Zurich reformer had died in battle at Cappel, taking twenty-four of the canton's preachers with him to their death, he broke into tears as he wrote into his diary, "with this punishment God has clearly indicated that servants of the Word should not conform themselves to war but to peace and its teaching."

[*Zwingli to Oecolampad and Capito, November 29, 1526*]

I really do not know, my dearest brethren,[1] what the father may have told his son Jodocus[2] by letter. But I do know this, that whatever he may finally have written does not need to be of very much concern to us. For in fact, the man is in the tow of his brother,[3] to whom he is passionately devoted. Just as we discern the faults of our own people last of all, so he supposes him to be a virtuous or at least an impartial man, whereas he may actually be the most perverted of Catiline's conspirators.[4] So now ἀφ' ἑστίας [from the hearth] the matter stands as follows. A session of the Diet had been held ἐν Θερμοπύλαις [at Baden][5] and an agreement reached that the Zurich Senate and people should be urged once more to permit at least one small mass.[6] When this was announced at Bern by him who had been appointed as legate,[7] a certain honest and loyal friend[8] of our city countered as follows: "Why do you take on useless trouble?[9] Do you not see that every day less and less progress can be made at Zurich?" And not innocently. It is being said, for instance, that not only there but everywhere and in general, "the mass is the mass celebrated." Then the legate said, "That decision would not have been made so rashly by us if there were not some[10] in Zurich who wrested it from us with entreaties, however subtle." This, I declare, the friend disclosed. Why, otherwise, would he have been indifferent to us? So, when everything was considered in perspective, it seemed appropriate for this boil of the pensioners, or rather the traitors and prevaricators, to be opened a little at a moment when everyone could clearly see that all the discussions at the Diet session could be corrupted by μισϑοδοσία [the payment of bribes]. Moreover, the μισϑόφορους [bribe-takers] let themselves be bribed in this way to resist the gospel and thus render assistance to the princes[11] against the interests of the fatherland. This much was certainly evident: Catiline's conspirators[12] kept running together, rejoicing whenever the church suffered any adversity, and all those who were under suspicion of foreign money stood most definitely against the gospel. Why mince words? It was evident that they acted in everything exactly as bribed men usually do. This kind cannot be unknown to you through your reading, since you once studied Sallust[13] and Cicero.[14] They are especially known to us, however, for we are experiencing living treason. Since this was the state of affairs and those people showed on every occasion by all their deeds and words that they were more to be feared than our enemies, I confess that I proceeded most rigorously against the vice of treason and the rascals themselves and striking with all the battering rams so that the confederates on our side could clearly see how the wall had collapsed. Although some acted horrified and angry because it was frightening, others still pretended with difficulty that it was just a circumstance. In some sermons I constructed the following parable, not thoughtlessly but deliberately: Goldfinches live on hempseed, but not unless it is ground.[15] Likewise with traitors to the country and bribe-takers: if they could be convicted by testimony (they resort to this or that anchor), who would be so foolish and careless about himself that he would admit eyewitnesses to such crimes? Therefore the traitor must be interrogated on the torture rack, for which in our country hemp ropes twisted and grated like the seed are applied. But no one can be stretched on the rack unless certain indicators are present from somewhere somehow. So I also alleged to know something of this affair. And I have not fabricated it without grounds. In fact, letters had been found[16] about which I was not supposed to know anything, although all the best-intentioned people were busily discussing them in secret; but from elsewhere I had untangled many things in a number of different ways and methods.[17] Therefore in the face of danger, a dictatorship is set up,[18] not of course after the Roman practice in which one man governed alone with supreme absolute power, but the jurisdiction for trial and sentencing is entrusted to eleven[19] of the most outstanding men. Evidence is sought and all kinds of things are found, both trivial and significant; but those who might once have reported things of which they were cognizant are now thinking of denial. That, of course, is typical of the rabble and that cowardly kind of man who turns yellow in the face of the judge's sword. Then [Jacob]

Grebel, a nobleman and of highest authority among us, the father of Conrad Grebel, who was the ringleader of the Anabaptists,[20] was beheaded because he might have accepted more than 1,500 florins from the emperor, the Frenchman, and the Roman pontiff, ostensibly for his son. Add to that (what I myself had not supposed at the time) that when the wife[21] of his son Conrad, who had died several months before,[22] had claimed the inheritance at the house of her father-in-law, which among us amounts to one third for wives, she was rebuffed by the father-in-law with the reply that the son had left no savings.[23] And shortly thereafter, 400 guilders[24] were still found which that man had withheld in his purse in the name of his son. After Grebel's execution, certain others escaped.[25] The gates were serrated to no avail, for the uncle of Jodocus[26] was carried out in an uninspected manure wagon.[27] Thus, they who betray the fatherland for the sake of their belly and manure have to find their safety in manure. They are now working for his restoration,[28] alleging innocence as a pretext that Grebel was too old to be cognizant of the affairs of men of that type, although he was imprudent in the partial respect that they had themselves become cognizant of his affairs. Also tortured was a certain man by the name of N. N.,[29] who was imperfectly grown. Right at the start, they tore out the left arm of this shameful and reckless man because it was shorter than his right arm. The Lord imposed this torture upon this perfect good-for-nothing. The dictatorship and inquisition are still in force.[30] During all of this, we have continually encouraged persistence so that the evil might be removed and have extensively cited examples in order that the inexperienced might be made knowledgable about this type of people. Καὶ ταῦτα μὲν ταῦτα
[Enough about this].

[Excerpts from the Trial of Jacob Grebel]
    [Proceedings of Thursday, October 11, 1526] For the concern of M[aster] Huldrych Z[wingli], present: B[urgomaster] Walder, M[ister] Röist, M[aster] Thumysen, Ochsner, Werdmüller, Jackli, Kamli, Sprüngli, Conrad Gull, Schneeberger, M[aster] Binder, etc.[31]
    [Zwingli] testified: He spoke on this matter at some length to the other men who were assigned to him.[32] He would therefore not weary Milords with a long speech. He said that he did not speak those words from the pulpit without deliberation,[33] especially because he saw that all those who are supplied with pensions are unitedly opposing the gospel and employing great tricks. He had also heard from several pious people of Zug and Schwyz that all the tricks came from this city. The young people were being pushed to the left by them and would grow up in this evil. For

that reason and because he did not want to have to answer before God's severe judgment if he kept silence and let this go on, he was moved to speak out, for he knew that pensions were being accepted in our city and other tricks are being carried on which were contrary to Milords' faith, mandates,[34] and plans. He would therefore never keep silence because Milords do not put a stop to such things and punish them appropriately, so that peace could be hoped for.

Further, some had been arrested but not punished who boasted afterward and rejoiced about it and said, "Wasn't I steadfast!" One got away just yesterday evening.[35] One tells the other about it. If those deserving punishment are warned and not punished, the evil practices will continue. Because Milords may learn of such things by other routes than through him and it may not therefore be his duty that all such things should come to them from him only, and because he might have some partisans and adherents, it seemed good to him to consider this an answer for the time being.

But if Milords wish him to reveal everything to them, he would first want to be convinced that they will pursue the matter in earnest, so that it can be seen that such evildoing will be stopped.[36] In that case he would open up so that it would be clear that he is so strenuously opposed to this evil, not out of thoughtlessness, but out of true love for Christian doctrine and the city of Zurich, but on one condition: that he may keep to himself anything that no one else knows. But if Milords also know it, he will faithfully and truly report it, for what he knows in common with others, he will present credible people and sufficient evidence, so that the actions, misdeeds, and malice of these people may be done away with; but he would not appear as an accuser but as one to be questioned. He therefore offered to appear before Milords whenever they want him to do so. . . .

Then the above-named appointed officials decided that the four Councillors previously assigned to this matter by the S[enators] and R[epresentatives] should examine Zwingli further and issue the announcement so that the reply reaches said officials by tomorrow, Friday, in order that the matter will reach the S[enators] and R[epresentatives] on Saturday. Said officials are to stay together in order to avoid suspicion, and none shall leave the group even if he has friends or relatives who are indicted or named in this matter. They agreed unanimously to abide by this.

[Proceedings of Friday] On Friday, October 12, M[aster] Huldrych testified before the four appointed officials—M[aster] Jacob Werdmüller, M[aster] Jäcklin, Schneeberger, and Conrad Gull[37]—first concerning the suspicions and testimonies that he alone knows of. . . . Concerning J[unker Jacob] Grebel, M[aster] Huldrych in a long story said among

464

other things that when the report was made, Old Tschudi[38] said among other things, "The old grubber had grubbed[39] until he accumulated 4,000 crowns.".... From all this M[aster] Huldrych in his own mind considers these designated persons to be completely damned and malicious. M[aster] Hyldrych related these things with such lengthy and credible information and circumstances that it was not possible to include everything in writing. Then M[aster] Huldrych reported the cases known not only to him but also to others, namely:

J[unker] Jacob Grebel's son [Conrad Grebel] told him: "My father accepted my pension and gives me as much as he likes and owes me about 335 crowns."[40] (Substantiated by an undated document.)[41] People who know about this are Heinrich Utinger,[42] Jörg Binder,[43] Enderli Kramer,[44] and Conrad's wife.[45] (In his deposition, Binder confirms Conrad Grebel's statement, but speaks of 800 g[uilders].)[46]

Further, he sent his son Conrad and his son-in-law[47]—he did not know what dealings had previously taken place—to William de Falconibus,[48] who gave each of them 50 g[uilders].[49] (Jörg Binder testified similarly)....

Jörg Hedinger[50] also knew and reported on Jacob Grebel's actions....

Further, when Stoffel Bodmer[51] was released from Milords' prison term, he said when some woman addressed him, "Yes, if I must be punished, then J[unker] Grebel must also be punished."...

Zwingli relates surprising things about the unusual proposals and actions that transpired and were done.

[Decisions of the council, Saturday, October 13] To be arrested: J[unker] Jacob Grebel to the bailiff's quarters,[52] Hans Escher[53] and Hans Löw[54] to the Wellenberg tower[55]....

[The Trial of Jacob Grebel, October 13-30][56]
Testimony of named witnesses.
M[aster] Jörg Binder,[57] schoolmaster at the Grossmünster, knows from his stay in Vienna about Conrad Grebel's journey to Paris, where he received 300 crowns.[58] Also, Conrad complained to him about his father, that he accepted 800 g[uilders] for him.[59] Conrad would have been satisfied with his as his paternal inheritance. The witness had personally seen and held in his hands the 50 crowns[60] that Conrad got from William de Falconibus.[61] With it Conrad went to school in Basel.

Myconius,[62] reader at the Fraumünster, was in a group in Enderli's house[63] at the time when the man from Kronburg[64] was here. After the rest had left when he got to talking with Conrad Grebel about payment of interest,[65] he said to him, "How can you do this and enjoy interest on it?" Conrad Grebel said, "Yes, for that my father is damned."

Andres Kramer[66] testifies he was Conrad Grebel's "good friend" until Anabaptism separated them. Grebel complained in his shop that his father was withholding the French pension from him and had little by little borrowed 55 g[uilders] from him, of which Conrad's sister, the nun at Oetenbach,[67] had repaid about 1,000 pounds.[68] The father Grebel, approached about this debt by Kramer, replied, "I don't think there is any need. Let the matter rest."

M[ister] Heinrich Utinger[69] testifies that he drew up a contract between father and son when Conrad incurred his father's displeasure by his marriage. Later, however, when he met Conrad in the Grossmünster, he complained that his father was giving him nothing. Then he, the witness, asked what his mother was doing. Conrad said, "Less than my father," and further: "If he would only give me what he has received from me!" Then he, the witness, said, "Be quiet! Disgracing your father!" But Conrad did not mention the amount.

Hans Landös,[70] shoemaker, testified that when Conrad Grebel was his neighbor, he at one time spoke and complained how poor he was, that his father was giving him nothing, and if an occasional poor man came to his door, he had nothing to give him. He pitied them, and if his father would only give what he owed him and had accepted for him! It amounted to about 1,000 crowns,[71] for which he wanted to sue his father as for his own property. The witness advised against this: "He ought not to bring shame on his father."

Hans Hab[72] testifies like the preceding witnesses. A new item: At one time Conrad Grebel feared a catastrophe because he had had money from three men—the pope, and Frenchman, and the Duke of Milan[73]. . . .

Jacob Grebel shall be asked: (1) From where he got the 4,000 crowns.[74] (2) What was his business with the cardinal's treasurer[75] behind the "Samlung"? (3) After drawing the French pension he sent his son Conrad to the cardinal's treasurer: "Go to the cardinal's treasurer; there you will get money."[76] Thereupon Conrad and his brother-in-law each got 50 g[uilders].[77] (4) How much of Conrad's pension did he still owe him? (5) What Jörg Hedinger[78] received. (6) How much pension money did Stoffel Bodmer[79] receive and accept? (7) Why his brother, the manager at Wädenswyl,[80] threatened him in Conrad Baumann's house.[81] (8) How he whispered to Hans Meyer[82] at Baden, "The bailiff committed theft."[83]

Notes from Grebel's Answers:[84] (1) He knew nothing about Hans Escher's remarks made at Aarburg, or he would have "reprimanded him."[85] (2) Nor does he know anything about his remarks made in Baumann's house;[86] for he pays no special attention to people's talk. (3) He had said nothing about the alleged theft by the bailiff of Stammheim.[87] Anyone who says he did is lying shamefully! For he never thought or knew of anything of the kind. Everyone should know also that wherever he could help him with body or property, that he was willing to do it. But anyone who says such things of him, let him be brought face to face with him.

Jacob Grebel's Answers.

On the journey with Conrad Engelhart[88] to the Diet at Luzern and then to the peace treaty with the king at Geneva,[89] Grebel denies having received money.[90]

Then, when he and Milord Wyss[91] were sent to the Diet at Freiburg,[92] Alexander, Stamp's cousin,[93] had frequently come to him and offered him money in his king's name and urged him to take it. He would never take it, neither demand nor accept it, but always rejected it. And when Alexander understood that he would never turn to him, he told Jacob that he should indeed take it. He would be his guarantor that he would receive what he asked for. And thus he answered Alexander and was very unhappy: what should he then ask for? Alexander said 3,000 crowns. They will be yours without fail if you want them. But he was unwilling to turn to him. Then Alexander said: "The lord has ordered me to ask you if you have sons, so he could give them something at least." Jacob answered: "I have two sons. One is a student in Vienna who might take or want it, and the other is at home; but I believe they will accept nothing."

After this they returned home and the lord rode to France. Then when he and Rubli[94] were sent to Bern on the same day and in Baden they were about to settle down for the night, Alexander sent a messenger and awakened him and said he had brought money that belonged to his son if he would accept it. Jacob said, No, he did not want it and they should leave him in peace. Meanwhile, the son came home from Vienna and accepted the money himself[95] and then rode away to Paris and asked his father: he had been promised an annual stipend of 300 crowns for three successive years, and would his father accept it in his name. He did this and gradually gave it to his son except for a certain amount, which he still owed his children, etc.[96] In short, he took or received nothing for himself,[97] and he expected that it will not turn out differently.

When Milords came to J[unker] Jacob again,[98] he admonished them on the basis of their oath to deal with him according to civil protection and law and protect and shelter him as is fitting and obligatory for a citizen to deal with another.[99] (Here a note: he had accepted 600 crowns for his son after the 300 were sent; the rest was brought to him by Helbing).[100]

467

As to the cardinal's treasurer,[101] he had eaten and drunk something with him at the "Samlung,"[102] but always in company with others. Then, even if he had wanted to make a deal with him, he did not know the language[103] and could not have understood what he was saying.

When his son and son-in-law went to the treasurer,[104] they were not sent by him.

Grebel knew nothing about the Hedinger affair.[105]

Concerning Stoffel Bodmer's case[106] he also knows nothing. What Bodmer said might have had reference to his son.

As far as he can remember, he did not write Conrad to come home from Vienna.[107]

He met with Puccius[108] to ask for a position for his son, but he was too late. Thereupon Puccius offered to give the son 30 g[uilders], and take him with him and find him a position in Bologna or elsewhere. He did nothing else with Puccius.

M[aster] Rubli[109] and Brennwald[110] had warned him and said that at Seefeld it was said, "All who go into Baumann's house[111] are pensioners; therefore, if he thought anything of himself, he would get out of the way. Those people are seeing to it that they also get into the soup."

He was asked again about having sent his son to de Falconibus.[112] He said he[113] sometimes gave his son money and sometimes not, for he was always too busy. He may have told him in response to the preceding charge, "Go, he will give you something after all."[114]

An offer of 32 g[uilders] at the papal expedition[115] as a "token" he rejected. He sold a horse to the clerk in the expedition, paid him on his return, and in addition gave him a gray damask doublet as a token, which he accepted.

He knows what he owes on his son's account, but he had forgotten it [his notes] in the Rathaus.[116] He has invested his son's money in his business, but hoped that such use would not be a disadvantage to him; for his son had given up his rights of citizenship before that and before he got the money.[117]

Jacob Grebel's Additional Answers.

When he and Rubli[118] got home from Bern and his son also came home, Alexander Stamp[119] brought (approximately) 400 g[uilders] in gold[120] into Grebel's house. On his journey to Paris from Freiburg, Conrad had commissioned his father to draw out the first payment for his son. Helbing brought him the second payment, 300 crowns, for the second year.[121] That money went to the son right after the peace treaty. He had paid his son all but the specified amount.

It is possible that his son received the money on his way to Paris, but he was not sure.

At Vienna his son received 7 g[uilders] every Quarterday,[122] a total of 28 g[uilders]. Jörg Binder probably knows about it, for he collected the stipend at the son's request until his return.[123]

Concerning the Pucci matter, he testifies as before[124] and really does not know in what year it occurred.

He also knows nothing, either, about M[aster] Erhart Wyss's case.[125]

Jörg Hedinger, Jacob Grebel's servant, is to be questioned on:[126] (1) What money Grebel received while he was in his service. (2) What business dealings he had with the Lord de Ambroise together with Eberhart von Ryschach, Thomas Wellenberg,[127] and Bernhart Blarer, that he wrote to the Rieux and other French emissaries about them. (3) What Wernhart Rat wrote about him to Eberhart von Ryschach and Thomas Wellenberg; for among other things he says in his letter that he aided the two captains against the "Grand Master," for which they should do their best for Jörg, or he would be completely forsaken. (4) About his statement to M[aster] Berger that he brought first 600 and later 300 crowns to J[unker] Jacob Grebel.

Jörg Hedinger's Answers (October 23 and 31).

He rode to Geneva with Jacob Grebel and Conrad Engelhart.[128] He did not know their transactions, except that each received 100 crowns[129] and the servants 4 or 5 crowns. The gentlemen received the servant's money and he himself got none.

Likewise he had gone to Freiburg with Jacob Grebel and M[ister] Wyss. When the latter was sent home, all kinds of things were discussed with Hedinger, urging him to press J[unker] Jacob to adapt himself in this matter. He told this to J[unker] Jacob, but received no reply at all. He did not know what J[unker] Jacob did at that time. When he returned home, he was asked if he wished to accompany the Grebel son to Paris, and agreed to do it. The son stayed two or three days in Freiburg en route. He heard from Felix Schmid[130] that Conrad Grebel was to receive a sum of money. His father had made financial arrangements that the son could study in Paris. When Jörg asked him, Conrad admitted getting about 90 crowns.[131]

After this Jacob Grebel sent him to Freiburg. Magistrate Falk gave him 300 crowns for Jacob[132] and then he got one g[uilder] as a tip.

Conclusions: "It is decided that Jörg Hedinger be kept in prison and meanwhile more should be learned from him. Decided on Tuesday, Oct. 23. He was released on Oct. 31 on an oath. He is to pay costs.

Milords, those appointed by the S[enators] and R[epresentatives] have come to the following judgments in the Jacob Grebel case.

1. First, they have considered the three mandates[133] gradually enacted by Milords about pensions and amended at times, the first of which is given in the thirteenth year of this century and begins, "We, the b[urgomaster], s[enators], etc."

2. In this connection Milords should consider that the Battle of Novara[134] took place in that year; also that in the autumn an expedition was made into Upper Burgundy and the French prisoners were brought here, who lay here as prisoners the fourteenth year and then escaped; and the promised peace was not kept. For which reason a march was made into the Piedmont,[135] where the Battle of Milan[136] was fought with unfortunate consequences.

3. In the same 15th year, Jacob Grebel gave up his son's citizenship, sent him to school in Vienna, where he received support from the emperor. It was also in this 15th year when the peasants massed before the city. The first mandate was still in effect.

4. Then in the 16th year, peace negotiations began which continued into the 17th year. In that year the treaty was signed in Freiburg.[137] Jacob Grebel was there and participated. And on that occasion, when he was accused of arranging for his son's money and pension, he was not entirely agreed; but after much persuasion Alexander Stamp[138] asked him if he had sons. He replied, "I have two sons; one is at home and cannot accept it; the other is a student in Vienna, who could perhaps take it if he wishes."[139] But he did not know if he would take it or not.

5. As to how this concerns him, this must be considered: When he returned home from Freiburg, he wrote to his son in Vienna.[140] Here must be noted what he achieved for his son in Freiburg. He confesses having written,[141] for the son came too and applied for the larger payment. Besides a reliable witness[142] to whom his son Conrad confirmed it in Vienna says his father sent for him; he had to go to France, where he would have 300 crowns annually.

6. In addition, he engaged his servant, Jörg Hedinger, to conduct him to Paris.[143] To this Jacob Grebel also agrees. That he then went to Freiburg and there found information and money, he also admits. And the servant says that there in Freiburg he received eighty or ninety pieces of gold.[144] He also lets this stand. So he went to Paris.

7. Then when the servant returned home, Jacob Grebel asked him whether he would go to Freiburg.[145] He did this and was supplied with documents, and he brought him 300 crowns from there. Jacob Grebel ac-

knowledges this, but says he does not remember who the messenger was that he sent for it; but Jörg Hedinger says clearly that he was the messenger.

8. Likewise Jacob Grebel also admits that he received 300 crowns from Helbing from Freiburg.[146] It must be well considered whether this happened in the seventeenth year; for the pensions apply from year to year. If so, it was still under the first mandate.[147]

9. Further, in the eighteenth year, the milder or middle mandate applies, under which Jacob Grebel without doubt drew the following pensions for his son, thereby taking provision or pension from the other gentleman.

10. Then in the twentieth year the pope's messenger, Antonius Puccius,[148] was here with William de Falconibus,[149] whom Jacob Grebel also approached to ask them to help his son to a new service; he now has the other service. This Jacob Grebel also admits[150] and that he promised to give him thirty guilders for a guarantee and do his best for him. Besides, when Conrad Grebel demanded money from his father, he sent him to William, who was to give him money.[151] Jacob Grebel admits this, but does not know the amount. But a credible witness says it was fifty crowns that Conrad showed the witness and that the witness held in his hand.[152] Therewith he secured funds for his son from the third gentleman.[153]

11. In the twenty-second year, the first mandate, made in the thirteenth year, again applies, but with the concession that the treasurer of the city or the messengers serving the city may accept gifts. Let every one consider how Jacob Grebel transgressed herein and became guilty.[154]

12. And although at the time when his son Conrad died Jacob Grebel excused himself and claimed to the forsaken widow and her appointed guardian as well as to Milords the executors of the city that he had no money that belonged to his son,[155] he has now confessed that he had received 1,600 crowns in his name which he, Jacob Grebel used for his own benefit and business;[156] and if that were subtracted which he paid for his son or still owes, it would amount to about 400 guilders[157] still owing to the son or his heirs.

13. When he was asked about the four thousand crowns concerning which an important citizen[158] is reported to have said, "The old grubber grubbed until he accumulated 4,000 crowns," he did not admit it. But he did say that such language was used against him by the manager Wirz of Unterwalden;[159] and when he heard about it he appeared before Milords and the entire community and accounted for himself. He had hoped that Milords and the community were well satisfied at that time. But this Bailiff

Wirz is not the one that was reported to Milords, but another.[160] He also insists that he, Jacob Grebel, has in no way incurred guilt in this matter and no honest man could charge him with that.

14. He was also asked whether he knew of Jörg Hedinger's doings and not-doings at home.[161] He answered, No, he knew nothing to say about that.

15. About Stoffel Bodmer,[162] he knows nothing. When he was told that Stoffel Bodmer had once said, "If I have to suffer, old Grebel has to suffer too,"[163] Jacob Grebel replied that Stoffel might have said that about his son.

16. And when he was asked whether he had made a deal on the occasion of the papal expedition, he said, No, the gentleman offered him thirty-two guilders as a token. He refused them and did not take them.[164]

17. He was also asked: When Hans Escher at Aarburg used improper language and said, "Milords and their canton were probably not in agreement," did he know anything about this?[165] He said, No, he could not recall hearing him; for if he had been there he would have reprimanded him for it.

18. When the poor people of Baden were sentenced,[166] Jacob Grebel is reported to have whispered to one that the bailiff had committed a theft.[167] He was asked whether he confessed saying such a thing or why he did it. He said, No, he was not guilty and had not done it, for he called God to witness that if he had been able to do it he would have come to his aid with life and possessions and would not have withheld it. No honest man should say such a thing about him.

[From Heinrich Bullinger's HISTORY OF THE REFORMATION, 1572]

On October 30, [1526], at 2:00 in the afternoon, J[unker] Jacob Grebel was executed by the sword at the Fishmart.[168] He was condemned by senators and representatives. Until the hour when he was to die, he had not expected this and proclaimed to the end that he did not deserve this. Thereupon there was much talk; and it was felt that had he not been executed in such haste, nothing would have happened afterward to his life.[169] For otherwise he had been an aged, honorable, wise, and very esteemed and respected man in the city of Zurich. Because he also was odious to many people, many thought that his very own son, Conrad Grebel, who was an Anabaptist[170] and had created much and extensive unrest (which was, however, offensive to him)[171] had not been the least cause of his father's late death. Others put the blame on others and others.

472

If you are asking about our state of being, it is all right; for I do not bear the wretched fate of my father-in-law, about whom you have undoubtedly heard, as bitterly as I would have borne it had I abandoned myself to the ocean of feelings and thoughts concerning that shameful affair. Now I am picking my way toward the shore by shortening the sails, not unaware of the shipwrecks into which even the most experienced seamen are thrust when once the seas of council politics begin to seethe up and break into tidal waves.

Originals: Zwingli's letter no longer extant. Trial records in Staatsarchiv Zurich. Bullinger's *Reformationsgeschichte,* I, pp. 373-74. Vadian's letter in Stadtbibliothek (Vadiana) St. Gallen, VB.II.282.
Transcriptions: ZW, VIII, No. 552; *Akten.,* No. 1050; VB, IV, No. 473

Epilogue B
The Banishment of Blaurock and Execution of Mantz,
Fourth Martyr of the Swiss Anabaptists
Zurich, January 5, 1527

Following their prison escape of March 21 (see 71-O), Mantz and Blaurock returned to the region of Grüningen to resume their preaching and baptizing mission (Quellen 1, p. 203). On December 13, they were recaptured by Bailiff Berger (ibid., pp. 212-13) and returned to the Wellenberg prison in Zurich for a quick retrial. Their sentences were pronounced and carried out on January 5, 1527.

Barely two months after the execution of Jacob Grebel, Conrad's dear friend and brother-in-the-faith, Felix Mantz, was condemned to death. He was bound and taken to the Fish Market, where he was put into a boat and taken off shore. His bound hands were stripped down over his knees and a stick placed between his knees and arms to prevent struggle. Then the executioner held him under the water until he expired (ibid., p. 226).

Blaurock fared better because he was not a citizen of Zurich and no evidence was presented that he had violated the mandate of March 7 (71M/448/13-15) "within their city, country, and domain." He was stripped to the waist; and with hands tied to the front, he was beaten down the street with rods from the Fish Market to the Niederdorf Gate, where he was to be formally banished by an oath administered to him (ibid., pp. 227-28). When he refused to swear the oath on the grounds of conscience, the magistrate ordered him returned to the Wellenberg. Upon this threat following injuries already incurred (see fn.8, below), he took the oath and departed, shaking the dust from his feet (see fn.12, below).

Schelbert (p. 62) concludes: "Zwingli had every reason for being gratified. His opponents were thoroughly intimidated; his authority and power were now established beyond dispute .... No Councillor would rise anymore and plead for mercy and tolerance for Zwingli's foes; no one would now risk such an audacious step. Zwingli was finally in firm and undisputed control."

[*From Zwingli's* Elenchus, *end of Part Two*][1] They rightly admonish us that our speech should always be "Yea, Yea!" and "Nay, Nay!"[2] Yet they do not seem to understand it clearly, or if they do understand it, they do not obey it. For though in many places they have said, "Yea," it has never been "Yea." When those ringleaders are banished against whom I write especially, and are asked for an oath, they will not take an oath but say that through the faith which they have in God they know they will never return; and yet when they are seen to have returned, they say, "The Father led me back through his will." I know very well that it is the father of lies[3] that brings them back. But they pretend to know it is the Father in heaven. The following is worth telling: When that Jörg [Blaurock] of the house of Jacob,[4] whom they all call a second Paul,[5] was cudgeled[6] with rods[7] before us even to the infernal gate[8] and was asked by the Council's officer[9] to take the oath [of banishment][10] and to lift his hands [as the oath was administered], he refused at first, as he had often done before and had persisted in doing.[11] Indeed, he had always acted as if he would rather die than take an oath. The officer of the council then ordered him to lift his hands and take the oath at once when put to the question, "or will you, guard," he said, "lead him back to prison." But now, persuaded by rods, this Jörg of the house of Jacob raised his hands to heaven and followed the magistrate in the reading of the oath.[12] So here, O Anabaptists, the question confronts you: Did that Paul of yours transgress the law, or not? The law forbids swearing. He has sworn, so the law has been transgressed. Hence, the knot is tied: You would be separated "from the world, from lies, from those who do not walk according to the resurrection of Christ but in dead works." How is it then that you have not excommunicated that apostate? Your "Yea" is not "Yea" with you, nor your "Nay" "Nay," but the contrary. Your "Nay" is "Yea," and your "Yea," "Nay." You follow neither Christ nor your regulations.

[*From the Wyss* Chronicle, *following 47B, above*][13] On Saturday, January 5, 1527, the Large and Small Councils of Zurich condemned to death Felix Mantz, the son of Hans Mantz, the canon.[14] And so he was drowned in the afternoon of the same day, about three o'clock, and [they]

474

beat his comrade, Jörg Blaurock, out of the city with rods on the very same day at about four. For Mantz had baptized persons in violation of the prohibition on penalty of death by drowning, and Blaurock had also returned to Milords' jurisdiction against their strict prohibition. And because with their preaching and rebaptism, many people agitated against the government, supposing that no Christian could be a ruler[15] and no one should be put to death,[16] as will probably be found in the large chronicles. Against this Mantz, also Blaurock and Conrad Grebel, who had died previously, and their many adherents, many of whom lived in Zollikon, Huldrych Zwingli had to dispute often and suffer on account of rebaptism and because they thought that infants should not be baptized but allowed to grow up until they believed and could themselves request baptism. But although he amply defeated them with the Old and New Testaments before about 600 men and in the Grossmünster before men and women,[17] they were still so hardheaded that no one could dissuade them, no matter how long they had to lie in the towers. And Milords had to endure great suffering, trouble, and work with them, for it was a very harmful sect and a rebellion against the government.

Original: Zwingli's *In catabaptistarum strophas elenchus,* published 7/31/1527; Wyss *Chronicle* in Stadtbibliothek Zurich, Msc. B.66
Transcription: ZW, No. 108, pp. 152-54; *Die Chronik des Bernhard Wyss 1519-1530,* ed. Georg Finsler (Basel, 1901), pp. 77-79
Translation (of *Elenchus*), adapted from Jackson, 1901, pp. 217-18

Epilogue C
Zwingli's Dialogue with Grebel's Ghost[1]
Zurich, July 31, 1527

The last of Zwingli's polemical tracts against the Anabaptists was entitled In Catabapistarum Strophas Elenchus *(Refutation of the Tricks of the Anabaptists) and published on the last day of July 1527. In the first of this series of tracts written two and one-half years earlier (see infra, 67C), Zwingli thought that the issue of baptism was not a serious threat to the unity of the church in Zurich; and in most things essential to the Reformation he and his radical disciples were surely still in agreement. Five months later when he wrote his* Taufbüchlein *(see 69C, above), Zwingli saw more clearly that the dissent went deeper than he had thought. "All of the previous fights were child's play compared with this" (ZW, VIII, p. 332). After two more treatises (70C and 71J/fn.13) and ten disputations, capital punishment for the crime of incorrigible rebaptism was deemed to be the only solution (see 71M and*

71N). The execution of Anabaptists was sanctioned in Zurich in March 1526 and first implemented in January 1527.

The Swiss historian, Ludwig Keller, concluded that "when Zwingli wrote the Elenchus [*in July 1527*], his battle against his Swiss opponents had come to an end" (*ZW, VI, p.57, fn.9*). The five Anabaptist leaders whom he specifically named in it had all been driven out of Zurich, Mantz had been drowned, Grebel had died of the plague, and there were no trained leaders left in Switzerland. Why, then, did Zwingli bother to write his longest and most impassioned "refutation of the tricks of the Anabaptists"? There are at least four reasons why he might have done so.

One reason was to give a justification of the extremity of the public policy against them in Zurich. At the beginning of the tract, he referred to the fact that many of his friends "who had not discovered the [*true*] character of these men think that what has been done to them is too monstrous" (*see below 413/481/20-22*). Following the execution of Mantz, for instance, Wolfgang Capito had written from Strasbourg raising various questions about the legitimacy of the public policy in Zurich (*Capito to Zwingli, Jan. 22, 1527, ZW, IX, 25-26*). Certainly after reading the Elenchus, if one is inclined to believe the charges that are alleged, one might tend to be more realistic about the threats posed by these fanatics and the measures of suppression taken against them.

A second reason for writing the Elenchus deserves deeper analysis by behavioral scientists. These actors were working out a life struggle within themselves that was not entirely coherent with the immediate events of their history. Zwingli sensed this himself when he wrote that "it seems funny to strive with ghosts" (*see below 488/10-11*). The chief Anabaptist ringleaders had been vanquished, but he could not get them out of his mind; and so the dialogue goes on in absentia in a kind of mysterious universal perspective. Whatever else this tract documents, it documents the inner workings of Zwingli's mind to do what he felt predestined to do.

A third reason which is more within the domain of historical research is that in spite of the excising of its leadership, the "hidden ulcer" within the corpus Christianum *had not gone away. As early as May of 1525, Zwingli had had a premonition of this malignant state of affairs when he admitted that "he stoked the fire that closed the city and canton against them," adding, "I have publicly ... pleaded before the council that they should not be allowed to go underground" (see above 69C/365/17-20). He could not have it both ways; and so now, in addition to striving with ghosts in hell, he was striving with ghosts in the underground movement of rural sanctuaries and forest hideaways. And to confound the problem, there was an unmistakable continuity between the two categories of ghosts.*

Grebel is gone, but his "booklet containing the refutation of our positions [*is*] passing through the hands of their brotherhood, who everywhere boast that they can so tear up Zwingli's positions that there will be nothing *left" (see below 481/ 4-7). Zwingli tried unsuccessfully to obtain the mysterious* libellum confutatio *until Oecolampad of Basel sent him a copy that he had luckily acquired from a nearby country preacher (Oecolampad to Zwingli, Apr. 24, 1527, ZW, IX, 100-1). Along with this booklet Oecolampad sent a second document, a* Decreta Catabaptistarum *(the Doctrines of the Anabaptists).*

Neither Oecolampad nor Zwingli had known anything about a meeting in Schleitheim earlier in the year, but now in April they were not only hearing about a corporate Anabaptist confession of faith but also reading it directly from handwritten copies that were being confiscated by clergy and magistrates. For on the very next day after Oecolampad wrote, Berchtold Haller of Bern also wrote to Zwingli that eight Anabaptists had come to his town from Basel and already had a following of twenty persons; and that in a search of the house where they were staying, a handwritten list of their doctrines or what Haller called their arma et fundamina *(arms and grounds) was taken from them, and Haller was now sending it to Zwingli with the request that he write a* scopas *(critique) of them so that they would better know how to refute doctrines like these in Bern (Haller to Zwingli, Apr. 25, 1527, ZW, IX, 103-4).*

So now in the span of a few days, Zwingli had received the Libellum Confutatio *and two copies of the Schleitheim articles, and a new battle had begun. Just at the point when the tumult had seemed to be under control, it was apparently only entering a new phase, described by John H. Yoder as "the coming-of-age of a distinct, visible fellowship taking long-range responsibility for its order and its faith" (JHY, 1973, p. 29).*

The fourth reason for writing the Elenchus, *which will be discussed in greater detail in the introduction to Epi.D, below, is Zwingli's plan for a new conjoint policy to control and suppress, once and for all, the Anabaptist menace.*

Zwingli's Refutation of the Tricks of the Anabaptists *contains a letter of dedication and three parts. The "First Part" was Zwingli's replies to twelve Anabaptist arguments contained in the unpublished, lost document which Zwingli calls the "Libellum Confutatio" (Refutation Booklet or Booklet of Counter Arguments). Before he begins to reply to its first argument, Zwingli digresses to review the history of the Anabaptist movement as he remembers it, beginning with an event we have dated in December of 1523 and ending with the tenth and last public disputation with the Anabaptists, dated March 5-7, 1526. The seven episodes included in this chronicle were excerpted separately and interspersed at their appropriate chronological places in the present collection (see 59A, 66A, 68F, 68L, 70D, 71J, and 71M).*

The "Second Part" is Zwingli's replies to the seven articles of the Anabaptist confession of faith adopted at Schleitheim; and this part of the document, not reproduced here, can be found in English translation in

477

Jackson, 1901, pp. 177-219.

The "Third Part" contains some additional replies to the "Libellum Confutatio" under the headings of Covenant, Election, and "That the Apostles Baptized Infants," plus an Appendix containing his replies to four miscellaneous Anabaptist doctrines—soul sleep, universal salvation, multiple ministry, and spiritualism (also not included here but found in Jackson, 1901, 251-7).

The question of the authorship of the "Libellum Confutatio" will be treated at greater length in several footnotes below (see fns. 33, 57, 97, 115, 116, 119, 143, 151, 179, and 187). Zwingli thought he knew who wrote it, but he could not be absolutely certain (488/8-13) because the author in his mind was "now a ghost . . . among the shades on the Phlegethon [in Hades]" (see 488/10, 496/9-10). Walther Köhler (1937, p. 12), H. S. Bender (1950, pp. 186ff.), Fritz Blanke (ZW, VI, p. 101, fn. 1), and S. M. Jackson, 1901, p. 155, name Conrad Grebel as the author. It is evident that Zwingli had in mind one of the original Anabaptist ringleaders who had died prior to his writing of the Elenchus *because he identifies by name the leaders who came after him (Hubmaier, Denk, Haetzer, Kautz), all of whom were still alive. The only two deceased leaders who might have written the booklet are Mantz and Grebel, both of whom requested permission at their last trial to write in defense of their position (see 71M/444/23-24, 36-37). Moreover, Zwingli surely indicated which one of these two he had in mind when he wrote, "I pass over, O Shade, what that Wittenbergian did to you when you were in the flesh" (494/33-34). This is without doubt a reference to Hegenwald's letter to Grebel dated January 1, 1525 (see infra, 67E).*

Perhaps the clinching evidence is the discovery of a sentence from the pen of Heinrich Bullinger identifying Grebel as the author of "the little writing . . . to which Zwingli replied in the Elenchus" *(see Walther Köhler, 1937, p. 12). In typical humanist style (see 7A/84/10ff., 47D/185/2ff., 49A/192/ 30ff., 57A/227/30ff., 58/256/18ff., 59A/278/15ff., 66A/300/29ff., 67/301/ 33ff., 67C/316/25ff., 69C/363/34ff., 70C/388/3ff., 71P/453/15ff., Epi.A/ 461/21ff.), Zwingli chose not to address Grebel by name but to refer to him anonymously as "the shade" (umbra: 488/10, 490/33, 494/33, 496/9-10), the "ghost" (larva: 488/11), and as "their [Anabaptist] head in hell" (apud inferos princep eorum: 487/28).*

Zurich, July 31, 1527

Huldrych Zwingli to all[2] the ministers of the gospel of Christ.[3]

Grace and peace from the Lord. It is an old saying, dear brethren, that success is the mother of evils;[4] and this is profoundly true. For after even so little was conceded to the passions[5] of certain ones through our idleness or blindness, they are now so unable to set limits on these[6] passions that they prefer to die and to destroy others than to give up what they have begun[7]. . . . The audacity of the Anabaptists[8] has been allowed

478

to proceed so far that they have conceived the hope of confounding all things. They are so untaught that by calling themselves by this name[9] they even hope to increase their reputation, so imprudent (while Christ would have the apostles prudent as serpents)[10] that by means of their imprudence they hope to realize by a lucky chance rather than to create by any skill the confusion for which they alone strive. This inauspicious race of men has so increased within a few years[11] that they now cause anxiety to certain cities.[12] And this in no other way than through unskilled and impious audacity. For while pious learning and discipline has no need for the ministry of hypocrisy (for through knowledge it is faithful to itself, and by the unaffected discipline of piety it commends itself to others), yet men of this kind are so thoroughly ignorant of that which they boast they alone know, so pretentious of that from which they are farther distant than the hall of Pluto from the palace of Jove,[13] that it is clear that they begin this web endowed with nothing but impious and untaught audacity. . . . Since there is so rich a harvest of these—not men (for why should one call them men who have nothing but the human form?)[14]—monstrous imposters[15] who reproduce offspring so prolifically day by day that the good seed which the heavenly Father so recently sowed in his field[16] must now be on its guard, I beg this, that we watch, act, and not let the enemy overthrow us as we sleep.[17] Let us judge soberly, lest we receive a wolf in sheep's clothing.[18] Let us labor, lest that evil that has arisen be attributed to our neglect. For there are, alas, not a few among us who are stricken and moved by every wind[19] and novelty, just like the untaught rabble which embraces a thing the more quickly the more unknown it is. The Anabaptists speak in round tones of "the truth, of God, the Word, light, spirit, holiness, falsehood, the flesh, impiety, desire, demon, hell," and all these kinds of things, not only beautifully but even grandly and finely, if only hypocrisy were more surely absent. If also you would investigate their life, at the first contact it seems innocent, divine,[20] democratic, popular, or rather nonworldly, for it is thought more noble than human even by those who think not illiberally of themselves. But when you have penetrated into the interior, you find such a pest as it is shameful even to mention. Does not the whole New Testament tend to this, that we should learn that Christ is our successful sacrifice and redemption? Out of what books do the Anabaptists draw their doctrine? When therefore they thoroughly deny the sum of the New Testament, do we not see them using Anabaptism, not to the glory of God or with the good of their consciences, but as a pretext for seditions, confusion, and tumult,[21] which things alone they hatch out? . . . For we frankly confess: "I have sinned, I will correct the error, I will flee through Christ to the mercy of God, from which I will not stray."[22] But they do not refer to Christ. They have put off all shame, and what will he correct who denies

479

that he has fallen?... You are more a beast than the wolf, lioness, or horse, which have some shame.[23] Against this class of men we must be on constant watch. All our forces and machines must be brought to bear, my brethren, and the more because they rage so in their hypocrisy and perfidy. For in this Empusa,[24] they excel Proteus,[25] the chameleon,[26] or Tarandus,[27] or whatever is inconsistent.... But all our material cannot and must not be sought elsewhere than from the armory of the Old and New Testaments. Do thou, Father of lights,[28] illumine their darkness, that they may see their error, and as thou wilt sometime do, eliminate this error from the church quickly, we pray! But you, whoever you are, who boast in the name or ministry of the most high God or of the gospel of his Son, consider what and whence these matters are which we allege. And laying passion aside, you will have granted the herb of truth.[29] Farewell!
Zurich, July 31, 1527.

Huldrych Zwingli's Refutation[30] of the Tricks[31] of the Anabaptists[32]

Thus far our preface. Now hear in what order we shall proceed! First, we shall reply to their misrepresentations,[33] in which they assert that they have confuted our fundamental arguments. Secondly, I will overthrow the basis of their superstition.[34] Then I will discuss the covenant and the election of God,[35] which abides firm and is above baptism and circumcision, or rather above faith and preaching. I will add an appendix in which, with the help of God, I will tear up certain errors recently wrought out by them.[36] But all with a light hand.[37] In the first two parts I will always put their words first, faithfully translated[38] from the German into Latin. After that, the reply. Here is how they begin:

The Anabaptists

"One of Zwingli's bases[39] for advocating the baptism of infants is the family of Stephanas.[40] For he says:[41] 'It is more likely than not that the apostles baptized the children of the faithful, for Paul says, 1 Cor. 1[:16]: "And I baptized also the household of Stephanas." A second is in Acts 16[:15]: "And when Lydia was baptized and her household." A third a little later [v.33]: "And he was baptized, he and his household immediately." In these families it is more likely than not that there were infants.' " So far they.

[Preface to the Reply]

Before I go to the regular reply, I would warn you of one thing, O Reader. This work is entitled *Refutation of the Tricks, etc.,* because this class of men so abounds and works in techniques[42] that I have never seen anything equally oily or changeable. Yet this is not surprising; for add to

480

their claims of holiness, which they are skilled in putting together, their readiness in contriving fictions and scattering them, now not only the simple but even the elect[43] are being led into peril, divine providence thus testing its own. The booklet of counterarguments[44] to ours they had for a long time been passing through the hands of their brotherhood, who everywhere boasted that they could so tear up Zwingli's positions that there would be nothing left.[45] I had meanwhile been looking and searching everywhere to see if I could get it, but could find it nowhere until Oecolampad,[46] a most upright man and also most vigilant, found one somewhere and sent it to me.[47] So the first trick was that secretly by the hands of the conspirators, who are as dim-sighted[48] in their ignorance as they are obtuse in their passion for propagating the sect,[49] they circulated their own writings, which through their seared consciences they knew could not endure the light.[50] They did not allow it to come into other hands. But the evildoer cometh not into the light lest his works be manifest.[51] But how could they submit[52] theirs[53] to the judgment of the church when they have seceded from the church?... Perhaps I obtrude these details[54] upon you to your great disgust, good reader; but it is not heat or bias that has prompted me, only a faithful watchfulness and solicitude for the churches. For many of the brethren who had not discovered the character of these men thought that what had been done to them[55] was too monstrous. But now that these people have begun to decimate their own sheepfolds, they are assailing us daily with letters and shouts, confessing that what they had heard[56] was more than true, that they who have not had experience with this evil may now be rendered the more watchful. I think that the world has never seen a similar kind of hypocrisy.... When it is seen whither their increase is tending and resistance is made, immediately he who is the instigator departs from their midst and leaves the miserable people to be mangled by the executioner[57].... Who does not discern by which master[58] these apostles are sent? Therefore establish your courage, good brethren! The hypocrisy of the Roman pope has been brought to light. Now we must war with hypocrisy itself[59].... "They have gone out from us for they were not of us."[60] ...

Now I return to their tricks and respond as follows:

The Reply

When you say that the family of Stephanas[61] is one of Zwingli's bases for insisting on infant baptism, you display singular maliciousness. For where, pray, have I ever postulated this, which you assert, as a foundation?[62]... My mention of the households of Stephanas, Lydia, and the keeper of the prison[63] came about in the following way: I was giving you many warnings not to argue unskillfully like this: "We do not read that the apostles baptized the infants of believers; therefore, they ought not to be baptized."[64] First, because of the absurdity, because we might just as well argue, "The apostles are nowhere said to have been baptized, therefore they were not baptized." And when you replied, "It is most likely they were baptized long before they baptized others," then I replied: "It was too true what Christ set forth that some see a mote in a brother's eye and are deceived about the beam in their own."[65] But when I had said that it was more likely than not that the apostles baptized believers' infants, what laughter καὶ χλευασμούς [and mockery] did not the faithless apostate Balthasar [Hubmaier] stir up against me? "These are the pillars," he said, "and they bring no other Scripture but futile conjecture. We demand clear Scripture."[66] See the crafty fellows! Under the same pretense they reply by conjectures and laugh at others who adduce conjecture simply as conjecture. Or rather, they falsely assert among themselves that we use conjecture as a foundation. After that I very properly adduced examples which showed that it was more probable than not that the apostles baptized infants—the families of Stephanas, Lydia, and of the warden of the prison. And these examples you will never be able to abolish, as I shall clearly show. You then continue to answer my examples in this way:

The Anabaptists

We reply, first:[67] Zwingli says in his book, "An act of the apostles can prove nothing,"[68] which is not true. Second: Concede it to be true! Then the obscure testimony which he alleges concerning the act of Paul, 1 Cor. 1[:16], and concerning Lydia [Acts 16:14f.], can therefore by his own admission prove nothing.[69]

The Reply

I recognize my own words and I will not permit them to be twisted by your violent appropriation of them other than as they were said. It was in this sense that I said that the acts of the apostles proved nothing: Everywhere we read that they baptized, but we cannot prove by that fact that they did not baptize those whom Scripture does not assert were baptized by them. For otherwise it would follow that the divine virgin mother was not baptized, for Scripture does not relate her baptism.[70] Therefore we want to say: A fact cannot prove a non-fact. We read that Christ was at Jerusalem, Capernaum, and Nazareth. It does not follow that he was not at Hebron because Scripture does not say so.... So our reasoning here is: It cannot be proved that believers' infants were not baptized by the apostles because this is not written, for there are many things done by both Christ and the apostles which were not committed to writing. . . . By this expression I would say then nothing other than this: "The acts of the apostles cannot prove anything" except that the apostles did not baptize infants, granting for the moment that they did not baptize them. But it does not follow that they are not to be baptized, or that a negative follows from an affirmative: because the apostles baptized adults and believers, therefore infants are not to be baptized. . . . To wit, infants may not be denied baptism simply because it is nowhere expressly said that the apostles baptized infants. Also there is the consideration that, as we shall show clearly, the fact that they baptized may not have been put down in writing. Moreover, if the acts of no one presuppose the truth, much less do acts not committed. So that even if it were down in plain words somewhere that "the apostles did not baptize infants," it would still not follow that they are not to be baptized. The inquiry would have to be made whether they simply omitted the performance or whether it was not right to baptize. This we prove by John 4[:2] where you read: "Although Jesus himself did not baptize." Here you have an example of fact and non-fact. Christ did not baptize. Must we therefore, according to you, not baptize? This would follow if you are to argue from a fact to a law. And you cannot say: "But it says in the same place that the apostles baptized." For we would reply at once: "Oh, if the apostles rightly baptized, even though Christ himself did not, we too rightly baptize infants, though the apostles did not." There is no difference in the cases, or rather our case is the stronger. We have Christ's not baptizing, yet also the legitimacy of baptizing. You have the apostles only, who did not baptize infants (supposing we concede that they did not). Yet, nonetheless, infants are to be baptized. For since baptism is legitimate although Christ did not baptize, so is baptism of infants although the apostles did not baptize them, unless it is forbidden by another necessity which prevents the baptism of infants. As to your reply in the second place[71] to the examples and facts which I adduced, as follows: "Concede it to be true" (i.e., that nothing can be proved by the deed of the apostles unless it is clear that they acted legitimately), "then the obscure testimony which he alleges concerning Paul's act can by his own admission prove nothing." In this you rally well; you turn the argument[72] on me beautifully. For if by acts one cannot prove legitimacy, but one must examine what is legitimate, then that Paul baptized infants in the families of Stephanas, Lydia, and the jailer cannot prove infant baptism. For I was not here intending by these examples to prove the baptism of infants as foundational but to show how rash and false was your argument when you said that the apostles never baptized them, for you have no testimony to this. And then to prove that it was more likely than not that they baptized them, I laid as the foundation the saying: "The children of believers are as much within the church and as much among the sons of God as are their parents."

The Anabaptists

Third: Just before this fundamental argument of Zwingli's, Paul says: "Some of the family of Chloe tell me that there are strifes and contentions among you, etc." [1 Cor. 1:11]. As infants here announced and could announce nothing (for they could know nothing), so the infants of Stephanas's family were not baptized, if indeed there were infants in that family. For Zwingli thrusts them into it, in spite of the testimony of Scripture.

The Reply

Who does not see that the church never had such impostors? They dare to reason as follows: "No infant of the family of Chloe could make announcements to Paul, therefore no infant of Stephanas's family was baptized." What is there here but imposture for those who are ignorant of argument? Who was ever so unskillfully malign or so malignantly unskillful[73] as to argue in this way? It can only be that they rely on the foolishness of men. As if I would argue: "No infant announced to Christ about the tower that fell, or about those whose blood Pilate mingled with the sacrifices;[74] therefore, Christ welcomed no infant."[75] Or: "It is written of a certain family that it announced certain tidings, so whoever could not announce could not be of that family." As if announcement or any other deed makes one a member of a family. What insanity is this?

The Anabaptists

Fourth: All the testimony that mentions families omits children.[76] This is self-evident.

The Reply

Therefore, when Christ was a boy, he was not of the house and family of David. Then why is the family of the foster parent Joseph so meticulously written down?[77] So when peace was given to the family of Zacchaeus,[78] if there were infants in it, were they excluded from that peace? In Exodus 1[:21], Moses asserts that the Lord had built a house for the children of Israel, i.e., given them family and posterity, when the midwives pretended that the Hebrew women had skill in helping on progeny.[79] So those children were not children, or the women bore adults and men; for infants, according to you, are not of the family. Exodus 12[:30]: "There was not a house in which there was not one dead." Therefore, no infant was dead. But why do I plead with the aid of testimony, as if there were need to tear away with the testimony of truth things said most foolishly? But what they add is elegant: "This is self-evident." As if any ass ever so yawned near a lyre[80] as to believe him who asserted that youngsters did not belong to the house or family.

The Anabaptists
Fifth: No one ought to baptize or do anything else according to the reason, opinion, and sentiment of man, but according to clear Scripture or fact, as the mass of testimony of divine Scripture verifies. Just as Zwingli himself often exclaimed[81] against the vicar general[82] and other enemies of God and will not accept anything which depends upon human judgment or the custom of the fathers. But now he hastens to do what the enemies of truth have done so far.

The Reply
I am always of the opinion you ascribe to me and have never held or will hold a different one while life lasts. But when you impute to me what the enemies of truth have done until now, you speak from that spirit which has been false from the beginning and has not been based on truth.[83] For what else have I ever done but verify by testimony of Scripture all that I have given out? Not by influence, although I have some modicum of that; nor with clamor or hypocrisy. This will appear to my readers in the progress of the discussion.

The Anabaptists
Paul teaches that whatever is not contained in the gospel or in the discourses of the apostles is anathema.[84]

The Reply
Where, pray, does Paul teach this? I suppose you refer to what he wrote in Galatians 1[:8]: "But though we or an angel from heaven preach to you otherwise than we preached, let him be anathema." I will expose your words here a little vigorously, for your ignorance and malice will both be manifest. Your ignorance, because you suppose that when Paul wrote this, the gospel records and apostolic letters were already in the hands of the apostles and authoritative. As if even then Paul attributed to his own letters (for they are not the least part of the books of the New Testament) that whatever was in them was sacred. Not that I would not want his let-

ters to be sacred, which they are, but that I would not want monstrous arrogance imputed to the apostles. As often as they, either Christ or the apostles, refer to Scripture, they mean not their own letters or the gospel records, which were either not yet written or were then in process of being written,[85] just as the times demanded; they mean the law or the prophets. You cannot escape by saying that you do not refer to the Gospels or the discourses of the apostolic writings, for you say: "Whatever is not contained." You use the word "contained." And this must refer to the documents. Here is stretched forth the finger of your malice and inconsistency. In this connection you have now at last come to the point that you can deny the whole Old Testament,[86] just as also at Worms[87] Denk[88] and Hätzer[89] and I know not which Kautz[90] deny in no obscure terms a full satisfaction through Christ,[91] which is nothing else than trampling upon the New Testament. At Grüningen[92] near us, they deny the whole Old Testament, as I have seen with my own eyes. For they have written to our Senate: "The Old Testament is antiquated and the testimony adduced from it is void, and so can prove nothing."[93] Here I look for your spirit,[94] I say, if you assert it to be a true one. For it takes away from us at the same time the Scriptures of the Old and the New Testaments, for at Grüningen you tread upon the Old Testament just as much as at Worms upon the New. If you contend it to be not true, what boldness is it to simulate the divine Spirit[95] with such persistency and wantonness? But in vain do I offer you this alternative, for you will never admit your spirit to be a lying one. I will prove it then by the very power of him who silences the kind of spirit in which you abound, so that it no longer dares to assert: "Thou art the Son of God."[96] For as falsely and faithlessly as you did, they say: "Thou art the Son of God." For as often as you confess Christ (by "you" I mean your leaders)[97] you make a confession worse than the demons. . . . Of this enough has been said above,[98] I think. For it is time to prove your spirit.[99] You openly teach that blessedness can come to none but by works of righteousness.[100] So Christ, whom the Father sent into the world to become a sacrifice for the despairing, is made void. . . . While infant baptism can be defended by the Old Testament, you reject the Old Testament. Since then you disparage part of the Old and part of the New, you only show that you are the very worst and most fickle of men, indeed ἀθέους [atheists]. For while you draw from the records that are written about Christ the matters that concern baptism, you make Christ himself of no account. So it is known to all that you do everything for contention's sake, however much you hypocritically simulate sanctity and simplicity. Further, since you reject the Old Testament for the reason that you cannot endure what is deduced from it with reference to infant baptism, you

486

clearly show that you make of no account him who is God both of the Old
Testament and the New. . . .

The Anabaptists[101]

In chapter 17, John gives a good reason through the mouth of Christ
as he says: "Not for these only [i.e., the apostles] do I pray, but for them
also who believe in me through their word."[102] The apostles have their
word from Christ, but Christ has his from the Father.

The Reply

Unite these words, reader, to those immediately preceding, that you
may see what trained perception[103] they have in citing Scripture and how
excellently they square with what they thus caw out[104] before an unskilled
people. What do they want with such an authority of Christ? Is it that he is
to be believed because what he has said and taught he has drawn from the
Father and his disciples from him? Then why do they not believe Christ,
who just said previously: "I sanctify myself for their sakes, that they also
might be sanctified through the truth,"[105] i.e., really and truly
sanctified?. . . These people then have not the purpose of proving that
faith is to be had in Christ's words and his apostles', for they have none
themselves. If they had, they would not assert justification by works.[106]

The Anabaptists

Sixth: By the same rule by which Zwingli thrusts infants into the
family, I thrust them out, but by Scripture. This Zwingli does without
Scripture, for infants cannot be counted among the baptized families.

The Reply

First, I ask by what rule do you think I thrust children into families?
By none? Do you not see then that men are born of men, that parents support and protect children? You see how these angelic[107] messengers of the
devil[108] have put off all human sense. Their head in hell[109] knows that a
demon is not born of a demon. So having become his slaves they suppose
that this has become obsolete among men, that man should beget men and
foster what he has begotton. Hear therefore what and why I would say: "It
is more likely than otherwise that the apostles baptized infants."[110] For in
the sacred Scriptures we have whole families baptized by them, in which it
is more than likely that there were children. So to you this does not seem
the more likely? Show the reason, and teach us how it is more likely that
there were no children in those households, of which we mentioned three.
"But by Scripture," he says, "I will throw them out." Who, pray, are you

that throw them out? "I throw them out," he says. He must be a man of great authority among you to promise that, yet he shows none, neither baton nor scourge. For however he promises, he furnishes no evidence by which he may demand that he be believed: αὐτὸς ἔφη [he himself said it],[111] no doubt! "Children," he says, "cannot be reckoned among the families baptized." Here is Scripture for you! That master of ours[112] thinks they cannot be reckoned in. Who will dare to contradict him? "Zwingli," he says, "thrusts children into the family without Scripture." You frenzied wild ass[113] (for I would not name the man who I judge[114] was baptized[115] among the shades[116] on the Phlegethon,[117] both because it seems funny to strive with ghosts[118] and because I am not certain, even though I am led by certain assured conjectures to conclude, who is the author of so learned a confutation!),[119] what then if on you I should load Scriptures[120] from which you might learn that children are to be reckoned in baptized families? In Acts 2[:44] we read: "And all who believed were together, and had all things common." Here I ask: Did the believers have their children with them or not? If they did, were they not in their families? If not, how is it we nowhere read that they were anxious because he who believed could not have his children with him? Was the spirit that impelled them so cruel as to dictate the abandonment of their children? Oh! You do not mean that they did not have them and nourish them, but that these were not reckoned with the Christian family![121] I ask them what you mean by family? You will doubtless say: "Those who had come to such an age that they knew what law is and what sin is, for he must repent who wishes to be baptized; but since infants cannot repent, they cannot be included in the family."[122] Thanks to God that you have learned to make so fine a rope of sand,[123] twisting out lie from lie. For having persisted in the statement that none is to be baptized but he who can repent, you will rightly assert that infants may not be baptized. But here a law was needed that would forbid and you have no law. You therefore are the law, and where the lion fails you, patch on the fox.[124] And why not? For you adopt whatever one of your brethren puts out, however rightly or wrongly. But we, who are accustomed to assert nothing not abundantly founded and supported by divine testimony, we know that Isaac, even when an infant, belonged to Abraham's family so completely that he compelled his father to send forth the maidservant and the child born to her.[125] Does not this seem so to you? But Paul joins Moses in saying: "The son of a maidservant shall not be heir with my son Isaac."[126] He was heir, and doubtless of the family. For even they who are not heirs, such as slaves and freedmen, are of the family. I do not mean to say here that by legal experts this son whom you ἀποκηρύττεσθε [disinherit] here is declared a member of the family. But I

488

lean in this way: In Exodus 12[:48] we read (we who go to the Old and the New Testaments as to two lights to prevent us from being deceived, while in the meantime you feed on your own spirit, as pearls do on their own juice, when nothing flows into or wets them from outside)[127] we read, I say: "And when a stranger shall sojourn with thee and keep the Passover of the Lord, let all his males first be circumcised, and then he shall rightly keep it."[128] Why is it said here: "All his males?" Does this pertain only to adults? Why then the precept to circumcise every male on the eighth day? Yet infants are not of the family. To me the opposite seems true, for they possess heirdom. But it is yours to prove by Scripture that they who received the sign of the church of God in accordance with the rite and religion of the parents belonged not to their parents' family. But that you will as soon do this as cut through an isthmus[129] I will show by other evidence. In Acts 21[:5], Luke writes: "And after some days we went on our way, all bringing with us wives and children, etc." Were the children here only adults? And if not adults, were they not of the family? What miracle is here, or what is the special attention, if the fathers of the family brought the apostle on his way with wives and youths or almost adults? This was the special attention, that fathers with their wives carried or dragged the children with them, as is customary during such eager times. Now they took with them not others, but their own sons. These were therefore in the family. There is no reason to remind you, good reader, that I am exposing some trick or guile. For what difficulty will there be in discovering this to be malice, in that they do not reckon the infants of believers with the father's family. For it cannot be foolishness,[130] they themselves are reckoned in the families of the Denks,[131] Hätzers,[132] and Kautzes[133] (amazing birds)[134] from their very claws![135]

The Anabaptists

Seventh: Granted that there were infants in these families. The truth still does not support the conclusion that those infants were baptized. But it follows with insult to truth and divine wisdom.

The Reply

Who can wonder enough at the confidence of the man? He admits that children were in those families but says they were not baptized. Yet in the first passage the words are: "But I baptized also the house of Stephanas."[136] In the second: "But when she was baptized and her house."[137] In the third: "And he was baptized and all his house."[138] How in the first passage could he [Paul] speak in general of having baptized the house of Stephanas, which he did not baptize if there were children in it whom he had not let in? The same must be said about the second passage. But in the last passage when he [Paul] asserts that the whole house was baptized, how is it that they do not see that in the beginning the same custom obtained as with Abraham and his descendants, who circumcised the whole group[139] of his servants, as well those taken in war as the home-born slaves and those bought, not to say the children, as appears from the passage just cited from Exodus?[140] There it is expressly commanded to circumcise every male of the family, and there is never any mention of believing or knowing God, which yet ought to be the special care of all. It follows, he says, with insult to the truth and wisdom of God. Though they know neither, they affirm insult to both. But what abuse is it to either God's truth or his wisdom that Hebrew infants were circumcised and included in the faithful families? But these words of theirs are high-sounding; this is their merchandise— bombast and words a foot and a half long.[141] To words of this sort, which they abuse with loud pretense, the unskilled mob erects its ears and then applauds.

The Anabaptists

Eighth. The last chapter of this epistle shows that the apostle would not have known nor baptized children. Zwingli dishonestly keeps this back. It works against his foundation of glass. Paul describes this family to the learned when he says: "You know the household of Stephanas, that it is the firstfruits of Achaia, and that they have appointed themselves to the ministry of the saints—that you submit yourselves to them and to every one who is helping and working with us."[142] Paedobaptism and paedobaptists do not understand a family of this sort. They do away with it, for it is contrary to them.

The Reply

As in many other places so here we easily detect the author of this frivolous confutation, although the greatest proof is the Swiss tongue, in which it is so written that it has no foreign or imported words.[143] Yet, as I have said,[144] since the man now undoubtedly burns in hell[145] as much as he froze here through his Anabaptist washings,[146] I have chosen to omit his name.[147] What impudence is this, O Shade,[148] that you assert that I wish to ignore these words of Paul? Were these words not cited by Hätzer[149] in the first two disputations?[150] Did I not reply[151] that they were synecdochic,[152] like 1 Corinthians 10[:1-2]: "All our fathers were under the cloud"? But there were also infants under the cloud, yet no individual mention is made of them. "All crossed the sea." Yet the infants could not have crossed. Therefore they crossed who did not, but were borne by those who did. So

490

in the family of Stephanas there were those who were the first believers of all Achaia.[153] There were also those who at the same time belonged to the church who in actuality, because of age, had not yet believed or taken part in the ministry of the saints. "All were baptized unto Moses." He speaks throughout of the fathers, the ancestors and forefathers, by which we understand that they who were then infants Paul now calls fathers, for out of these was the people of Israel. Therefore not only adults, but infants also, were baptized unto Moses. For if they who were infants at the crossing of the Red Sea were not baptized, the apostle did not speak correctly in saying, "All were baptized unto Moses," for they were, as I have just said, the fathers of their posterity. Now where do you turn? Not to bypass this: Infants are referred to by the apostles as then baptized. . . . You will find no crack by which you can escape. . . .

Now I return to the point[154] and assert that the children are spoken of by synecdoche[155] in "All crossed the sea." For to be accurate, crossing occurred only to those who were of an age and strength to cross, and that "all ate the same spiritual food" when those alone ate who were spiritual, yet nonetheless it is said of all that they ate. So also in this place, if Paul had used the word "all" and had said: "*All* of Stephanas's family have given themselves to the ministry of the saints," yet by the very force of synecdoche the infants also would be understood to be of the family, and [likewise] that they who then had believed had given themselves to the Lord. For this is the nature of synecdoche, that when as to any body that has different parts, and those parts are similar in some respects and different in others, anything is predicated of the whole body, it is understood of a part, and what is said of a part is understood of the whole. . . . So also I replied, though not in so many words, to that passage that Hätzer adduced from Paul,[156] by which he would exclude the children from the family of Stephanas. Yet that family appears to have been pretty large,[157] if we worthily weigh the generously ample words in which Paul treats of them. Children remain therefore till now in believers' families and are baptized, and when mention is made of those families, or they are written or spoken of, whatever is said or told pertains to that part to which it is applicable. . . .

The Anabaptists

Ninth: Paul, a man of truth, wished in this first chapter[158] to show that he had baptized but few at Corinth, but Zwingli and his witnesses make Paul a liar and say that he baptized many when they assert that he baptized infants in the house of Stephanas.

The Reply

Because we say that there were undoubtedly children in the families, does it follow? "Therefore they make a liar out of Paul who asserts that he baptized but few." As though, if infants were baptized, they who were baptized by him could not still be numbered as a few! What, pray, can you do with such a stupid kind of men? What kind of a church do you think that is which—I will not say believes, but—listens to a man asserting such things?[159]

The Anabaptists

Tenth: How the reality is, this text shows which says: "Let no one say he was baptized in my name"[160] and thereafter be puffed up on my account. If infants then should speak and be factious (as those Zwinglians would have it) they were rightly baptized.

The Reply

See how fine they are at syllogism! "Let no one say," he says. Infants cannot speak nor be factious, therefore they were not baptized. As if none could be factious but those who said they were of Apollos, Cephas, or Paul![161] And as if we had not just shown that by synecdoche[162] that is to be understood of any part which is suitable to it!

The Anabaptists

Eleventh: It is not true that Paul baptized Corinthian children.

The Reply

Speak gently, I beg of you![163]

The Anabaptists

Why? Because he baptized believers only or saw that they were baptized by others.

The Reply

Now you argue splendidly, for it follows at once: Believers only were baptized, therefore children could not have been baptized—provided you can establish that exclusion,[164] that believers only were baptized by the apostles.

The Anabaptists

As we shall establish it from Acts 18 and 19 to the confusion and disproof of the misleading paedobaptist contention.

The Reply
The mountains have gone into labor![165]

The Anabaptists
It is treated as follows in Acts 18[:8]: "When Paul was at Corinth, Crispus, the ruler of the synagogue, believed in the Lord with his whole house, and many Corinthians who were listening at the same time (I translate faithfully and literally, perverting nothing,[166] even when those fellows struggle and stammer in the German tongue)[167] believed and were baptized." Infants were not able to listen, therefore were not able to believe, much less to be baptized. But now the attentive faithful were baptized. And here the whole house was rendered faithful, from which infants are excluded, and they were so excluded because there were none there. Or if there were, they were not counted in it and accordingly not baptized, for the faithful families were baptized.

The Reply
Infants were not able to listen, but it does not follow that consequently they were not baptized. We have nowhere the prohibition not to baptize infants of believers unless they listen and believe. I require a forbidding prohibition. But you add beautifully: "And here the whole house was rendered faithful." I agree. Continuing: "from which infants are excluded." This I ask you to prove from sacred Scripture. I hear it said: "Infants are excluded," but nowhere by a divine oracle. Here the whole dispute hinges. There was a strife among the apostles whether the gospel should be preached also to the Gentiles or not.[168] This strife rested partly upon a false inference, partly upon probability. The fallacy was this: To us the Christ was promised, therefore not to the Gentiles. But who is so unskilled as not to see that it does not follow at all: The Messiah was promised to us Jews, therefore not to the Gentiles. For it may be that he was promised also to the Gentiles, and the Scriptures testify to this in various ways. So in the present passage: The writings of the apostles testify that they who listened and believed were baptized, but it does not follow at all that children were consequently not baptized by them. For it may be true at the same time that the apostles baptized believers and that the apostles baptized children. . . .

The Anabaptists
So also [Acts] chapter 16 [verse 31] has: "Believe in the Lord Jesus and you will be saved and your house." And that his house was saved with him follows on: "And they spoke the word of the Lord to him and to all

who were in his house."[169] Then further: "And he was baptized, he and all who were his, immediately."[170] He heard[171] the word of the Lord, and so he was baptized, and all who were in his house; they, too, heard and so were baptized. Whereby again infants are excluded, for they could not hear and believe, as follows on: "And he rejoiced with his whole house, because he had believed in God."[172]

The Reply

To pass over some things translated into the Swiss tongue without entire fidelity,[173] I briefly say: This whole knot may be cut by the one ax of synecdoche.[174] For if there were infants in that family, what is said about faith and doctrine we apply to those who could receive and believe; but what is said of baptism [we apply] to those who belonged to the family of the believing master, but who through age or weakness neither heard nor believed. For when God said, "Hear, O Israel, the Lord your God is one God,"[175] he spoke to all who were of Israel. But just because infants neither hear nor understand, he does not exclude them so that they are not of the congregation of the people of God or should not be circumcised with all who hear and believe.

The Anabaptists

Twelfth:[176] Philip preached to the whole city of Samaria,[177] where undoubtedly there were infants. Yet Luke speaks in these insuperable words: "And they were baptized, men and women."[178] "Men and women," says Luke. But if some scholastic would say, as a certain Wittenberg sophist[179] lately did, "Under the word 'women,' girls are also included; and under 'men,' boys," this is fiction. For preceding these words we find: "Philip preached, they believed." They, the men and women, I say, believed and were baptized. So here falls synecdoche, Zwingli's second foundation.[180] This synecdoche is a comprehensive mode of speech to the effect that where Scripture speaks of believers baptized, infants also are included among them, as he strives to prove by perverting the Scripture passages that do not contain this.

The Reply

I pass over, O Shade,[181] what that Wittenbergian did to you when you were in the flesh.[182] But this is sure, that this passage does not exclude infants, even though it does not mention them. For that does not exclude which does not explicitly mention; for to pass over is one thing, to exclude, another. That may be omitted which is in no way excluded. The excluded can never come into the account. Since then the omitted, as well as those expressly mentioned, are included by synecdoche (as has been sufficiently shown), we are still waiting for you to prove that exclusion of yours by which you assert infants are excluded. For we have proved that by comprehensiveness (i.e., synecdoche, except that the Latin word is not as appropriate as the Greek)[183] they are included. Insofar as you promise to show how I had asserted synecdoche only by twisting Scripture, again you are rich in promising but poor in delivering. For when you would tear away synecdoche, you establish it most firmly.

The Anabaptists

As for example in Acts 2[:44]: "All who believed were together and had all things common." Here Zwingli says, "If believers alone were there, whither had they removed the infants? If they had cast them off, they would have been fine believers to disown the children against the command of the Lord. So the children of believers were also numbered with believers and were baptized with them."[184] To which we reply: Zwingli speaks correctly when he says that they would not have been believers if they had cast off the children.[185] For how could it be that these who had all things in common did not have the children common nor educate them in common, according to the precept of the Lord? Infants then are not numbered or reckoned among the believers, but are included in this, that "the believers had all things common;"[186]

The Reply

You see, good reader, whither the lie turns itself.[187] They would rather number believers' children with their animals and baggage than with believers. For they will not include them with "all who believed were together" but with "and had all things common."[188] Among them, therefore, children are not like dear pledges,[189] are not our flesh and blood.[190] For what else will they deny when they deny that they are included among the believers and put them in what all have common? What tiger, pray, is so cruel? Surely to this pitch of insanity ought they to come who have put off not only the sense of piety, but also all human sensibilty.[191] Here I beseech you, pious heart, not to take offense at what I am about to say. For by right they[192] must be cited (not that we should yield so much to emotion, but that those despicable things must not be ignored by everyone which those people secretly perpetrate, like what Alexander Χαλκεύς [the coppersmith] did to Saint Paul)[193] so that we may the more easily protect ourselves from this pestilence. In describing their deeds I shall be candid and brief. They have their wives in common in such a manner as to desert their own marriage partners and take others; so also with the children, as to desert them

495

and leave them for others to support. These fine fellows! When lust persuades, they make common a brother's wife, even his virgin daughter. Though the very force of nature requires that they cherish their children by the sweat of the body, they make them common to others. . . . [194]

Now I return to the matter. Not without reason will they not reckon the children of believers who live within the church among the believers but put them among the things that are in common. . . . Those who are re-baptized unite with a church that denies, if they themselves commit it, that adultery and harlotry is a crime. For in relation to this, he who is now a shade once[195] said to me, when they were asserting that they were without sin: "They should shut out from the church at once anyone who committed any wrong." I at once reminded him of the man who had committed adultery at Wesen.[196] He replied: "Even though he committed adultery, he did not sin. They who are in our church cannot sin." Then I said, "So adultery is not sin among you?" "There is no adultery among us," he said. "I do not say whether it is sin or not, but that what you think is adultery is not. For since we have one and the same spirit, nothing can take place among us which is sin, for as we have one spirit so also we have one body."[197] They now preach this view openly. . . .

The Anabaptists

Otherwise Zwingli would be compelled to admit because of the following construction that infants sold their goods and distributed them, which is impossible and has nothing to do with them, for the property belonged to their believing parents. And from the construction it would follow that the infants who are reckoned among the believers and so baptized were obliged to celebrate the Lord's Supper because they were baptized. Similarly they must have prayer with the other believers, for the preceding and following construction is as follows: "And they continued steadfastly in the apostles' doctrine and fellowship, and in breaking of bread and prayer."[198] Who steadfastly continued? All who had been made believers. If then infants were made believers or were numbered among the believers, they also broke bread, which cannot be conceded by any reasonable truth; and by the same argument they were not baptized. For if they were baptized, they also broke bread, which Zwingli himself will not admit. Now see how synecdoche[199] hangs together!

The Reply

Why do you charge me viciously with a skill in arguing which I never assumed, but [which] is deceitfully attributed [to me] by those who cannot sustain the force of the truth on which I rely, since this whole paragraph is

496

only vicious reasoning? For when you oppose synecdoche, you make clear that you do not yet see what synecdoche is. For you do not yet understand that there is no synecdoche where the words are received in their simple and true sense. For where this is the case there is no figure [of speech]. That speech is figurative which does not bring us the sense which the first sight of the words' promise. Synecdoche is a figure, so where synecdoche is, there is another hidden meaning than what appears at first. Hence when you thus infer, "If infants were numbered among the believers, they also broke bread, prayed, sold their goods, and distributed to the needy," you take everything according to the letter. . . . "

The thing itself compels me willy-nilly, good reader, to cease to give the vain words of the Anabaptists and to draw to a close. So hereafter[200] I will proceed as follows: I will untie every knot, and whatever is said by them that has any force, I will quote with such fidelity as I have done thus far in rendering it literally into Latin. And for this reason in particular, that which they have thus far quoted against the synecdochic sense has been refuted in great part. What they are arguing[201] about the covenant[202] will be so treated and torn away when we come to the covenant.[203]

The arguments against the synecdoche in 1 Corinthians 10[:1-3]: "All our fathers were under the cloud, they all crossed the sea, all were baptized unto Moses, all ate the same spiritual food"—the arguments, I say, that they bark out against these synecdoches[204] are so foolish and faulty that they are not to be taken seriously. For they say they know that they ate, drank, crossed the sea, went to stool and urinated, but it must be proved by us by clear Scripture that infants were baptized. Then they insult us in this way: "See now how Zwingli stands with his synecdoche, which he affirms with his own peculiar cunning and sophistry, lest by acknowledging the truth he may suffer the persecution of the cross of Christ."[205] What can you do with these men? That I might expound synecdoche correctly I quoted these examples,[206] which they are so far from tearing apart that he who will may use them, not only as examples of synecdoche, but to show also that in the apostles' time believers' infants were baptized, as I have indicated above. They approach the matter with bitterness, since they can do nothing with the sharp energy of the Word of God. They charge cunning and sophistry,[207] of which I so express my abhorrence that all my writings can free me from the charge better than any oration prepared for this purpose. But I recognize and cherish the truth. And I should have to endure nothing if I should adopt your opinion, unless you are most dishonest, for you have promised oftener than I can say that all will turn out happily if I join you.[208] But you had to have recourse to trickeries and shouts when you undertook to overthrow synecdoche, for you saw this to be impossi-

497

ble. This remains, and will ever remain, synecdoche: "The fathers were all baptized, the fathers all ate the same spiritual food with us,"[209] as was shown in the foregoing sufficiently and will be treated again in what follows. Thus far I have replied to the first part of your refutation. To the rest[210] I will do the same in the course of the disputation. Now I proceed to the second part.

SECOND PART

This part is to overthrow the foundations[211] of your superstition; although you have never published them, yet hardly any of your people exist who have not a copy[212] of these well-founded laws, as you call them. . . . [213]

THIRD PART

In this part[214] I undertake to deal with two things—with the covenant or testament,[215] and with election, that it may stand firm. Here I shall also show with sure testimony and argument that it was the custom of the apostles to baptize the infants of believers.

[Covenant]

On the covenant, then, I speak after the following fashion. . . . Therefore[216] the same covenant which he entered into with Israel he has in these latter days entered into with us, that we may be one people with them, one church, and may have also one covenant. . . .

[The Anabaptists]:[217] See how that fellow would make Jews out of us, though we have always been told of two peoples, two churches, and two covenants. See Genesis 25[:23] and Galatians 4[:22-31].

[The Reply]: To which my answer is: Whenever there is held in Scripture that there are two distinct and diverse peoples, necessarily one of these is not the people of God. For both when the Jews were God's people and we who are Gentiles were not, and now when we who are Gentiles are God's people and the Jews were cut off, there is only one people of God, not two. When we read in Genesis 25[:23] that "two peoples shall be separated from thy womb," it is not to be understood as though both were and would be his people at the same time. But Jacob he loved and Esau he hated[218] before they struggled in her womb. Therefore in each case one and the same people is that which cherishes the one true and only God, from whatever parents it was born. And again, they are diverse who follow a diverse cultus, though one and the same birth pang produce them. When therefore he spoke of two peoples formerly, one was Jewish, the other Gentile. The Jew worshiped the high God, but the Gentile was impious.

498

Now when we speak of the church of the Gentiles, it is the same as that former one of the Jews, and the people of the Gentiles or the impious are now the people of Israel. For we are put in their place after they have been cut off, not in some place next to them. But two covenants are spoken of, not that they are two diverse covenants, for this would necessitate not only two diverse peoples, but also two gods. . . .

[The Anabaptists]: The ancients had access to God, not by Christ, but by observance of the law. . . . Therefore . . . there are two testaments, one that leads to servitude and the other that pertains to freedom of the spirit through Christ.[219]

[The Reply]: They think then that the old requires observance of the law for salvation, not Christ, not seeing that the law even when kept does not save. "For if righteousness is through the law, then Christ died for nothing"[220] (that is, in vain). In my opinion, the law would save, i.e., we would be saved, if we kept the law entirely and according to the will of God (for the law is spiritual); but this is possible to no flesh. Through the law, then, we learn only our condemnation, for by it we are included in sin and bound unto the penalty. From this it is easily inferred that they also who were under the law saw that by one salvation through Christ both they and the whole world are saved. This Christ himself teaches clearly when in John 8[:56] he addresses the hypocrites of the law: "Your father Abraham rejoiced to see my day; he saw it and was glad." Therefore, Abraham desired nothing so much as the coming of him who as promised he did not doubt would be to his great good. Still he had not yet come. When then the time was fulfilled[221] and Christ was in the world, Abraham already rejoiced. Therefore as they had one and the same Savior with us, they were one people with us, and we one people and one church with them, even though they came before us a long time into the vineyard. It is also clear what the bosom of Abraham[222] is, about which many have anxiously inquired. . . .

[The Anabaptists]: What difference is there [then] between the Old and New Testaments?

[The Reply]: Very much and very little, we reply. Very little if you regard those chief points which concern God and us. Very much if you regard what concerns us alone. The sum is here: God is our God; we are his people. In these there is the least, in fact, no difference. The chief thing is the same today as it ever was. For just as Abraham embraced Jesus his blessed seed, and through him was saved, so also today we are saved through him. But so far as human infirmity is concerned, many things came to them in a figure to instruct them and be a testimony to us. There are therefore the things which seem to distinguish the old Testament from the New, while in the thing itself or in what pertains to the chief thing, they differ not at all. First, Christ is now given, whom formerly they awaited with great desire. Simeon is a witness.[223] Second, they who then died in faith did not ascend into heaven, but [went] to the bosom of Abraham; now he who trusts in Christ comes not into judgment, but hath passed from death into life.[224] Third, shadows were offered,[225] as is shown in Hebrews.[226] Fourth, the light shines more clearly, so far as pertains to the illumination of the understanding, for ceremonies, while they of themselves made nothing more obscure, yet added much to the priests, and these were not so strong in inculcating religion and innocence as they would have been if avarice had not brought pressure to refrain from ceremonies. Fifth, the covenant[227] is now preached and expounded to all nations, while formerly one nation alone enjoyed it. Sixth, there had never before been set forth for men a model for living as has now been done by Christ. For the blood of Christ, mingled with the blood and slaughter of innocent [animals],[228] would have lacked the model. Now I state the conclusion: Since therefore there is one immutable God and one testament only, we who trust in Christ are under the same testament, consequently God is as much our God as he was Abraham's, and we are as much his people as was Israel. . . .

[The Anabaptists]:[229] Paul wrote in Galatians 3[:7]: "Know ye, therefore, that whoever are of faith are Abraham's children," and like passages from Scripture. . . .

[The Reply]: If they had correctly weighed the discussion that Paul pursues here, or the force of synecdoche, they would raise no such objections. Paul's question is, do we acquire salvation by the works of the law or does grace come in? And he decides that grace comes in by faith, and not from works. All of these things he says synecdochically, as are all such things throughout Scripture which pertain to this argument. Abraham was justified by faith.[230] Here is synecdoche. If this were not so it would follow that Hebrew infants were not of the people of God, which has been shown to be false, for they did not believe; and therefore according to the Anabaptists' faith, they were not sons of Abraham. Therefore they believed who were destined for this by God when age allowed it and they were of the people of God; those who were circumcised grew and advanced until they attained intelligence and belief, and meanwhile they were of the people of God. Not only believers then are of the church and people of God, but their children. And when the Anabaptists admit that sons of Abraham according to the flesh were within the people of God, but suppose that our own sons according to the flesh are not, they commit a great wrong. For how is the testament and covenant the same if our children are

500

not equally with those of the church and people of God? Is Christ less kind to us than to the Hebrews? God forbid!. . . .

[The Anabaptists]: Then males only must be baptized, and on the eighth day only.

[The Reply]: These [physical] elements have been abolished so that we are bound neither to any race nor time nor circumstance, but under this condition that in these matters we do not transgress piety. For among the ancients, females no less than males were under the covenant, even if they were not circumcised. It results then after all this that just as the Hebrews' children, because they with their parents were under the covenant, merited the sign of the covenant, so also Christians' infants, because they are counted within the church and people of Christ, ought in no way to be deprived of baptism, the sign of the covenant. And the arguments of the Anabaptists, which because of their ignorance of figures and phrases they think valid, are of no avail against us. Nor shall we on account of our ignorance compel the Holy Spirit to lay aside its own method of speaking. He has always spoken to the whole church some things which did not fit a great part. But that part was not on this account cast out of the church, out of the people, out of the covenant of God. And the fact that the sacraments, so far as pertains to externals is concerned, were not the same, does not oppose the truth; for as far as meaning is concerned, they were the same. For as circumcision was the signature of the covenant, so is baptism;[231] as the Passover was the commemoration of the passage, so is the Eucharist the grateful memorial of Christ's death.[232] By reason of which St. Paul in 1 Corinthians 5[:7-8], 10[:18] and Colossians 2[:11] attributes baptism to them and the Eucharist or spiritual feasting to Christ, but to us the Passover and circumcision, and so makes all equal on both sides. So far upon one and the same testament, church, and people of God.

On Election

I am now compelled to treat election[233] or else forego my promise,[234] but not as fully as the subject demands.[235] For this is beyond my power and purpose. But I shall show election to be sure, i.e., free and not at all bound, and above baptism and circumcision; nay, above faith and preaching. . . . I think these arguments,[236] brief as I promised, will be clear and sure. But for what purpose? That I may reply to the Anabaptists. For they argue against me in the tract in which they suppose they have refuted me:

[The Anabaptists]: How are the Hebrews' infants of the people, of the sons or church of God? We believe the elect are of the people of God, like Jacob, by no means those thrust out or repudiated. For, according to

Romans 9[:11-13], when they were yet in their parents' womb and had done neither good nor evil, God said: "Jacob have I loved and Esau have I hated." How then could Esau be of God's people? It is then false what Zwingli asserts, that the Hebrews' infants were of the people and church of God.

[The Reply]: To which I think I may now the more advantageously answer, inasmuch as I have said these few things about election and predestination, in about the following manner: It is sure that with God no one is of his people or of his sons except he whom he has elected, and it is also sure that every one is his whom he has elected. But in this way, O Anabaptist, all your foundation has fallen away. For not only believers (as you would understand "believers" in practice) are the sons of God, but those who are elect are sons even before they believe, just as you yourselves prove by the example of Jacob.... [237]

[The Anabaptists]: How then were we sure of Esau's election when the Lord says, "Esau have I hated?" [238]

[The Reply]: Because we follow the law throughout. But if the Lord does something out of the ordinary, the law is not thereby abrogated. For privileges do not make the law common. [239] Though indeed it is my opinion that all infants who are under the testament are doubtless of the elect by the laws of the testament....

[The Anabaptists]: Where then do you put the infant Esau? Under the testament? But he was rejected.

[The Reply]: I respond in two ways. First, all judgment of ours about others is uncertain so far as we are concerned, but certain as regards God and his law. For instance, when it is said to an apostle: I believe in Jesus Christ the Son of God, [240] the apostle considers him who says this of the elect because of the certitude of the word. But they sometimes deceive who thus confess, as did Simon Magus [241] and the false brethren who came in secretly to betray the liberty of the gospel. [242] But God himself is not deceived, nor does the law deceive, for God knows the hearts and reins, [243] i.e., the inmost parts; and the law, if all is just and right, does also not deceive, but is eternal. Therefore we ever judge according to the law, as has been said, and the law for the sake of one or many may not be considered the less universal. The other reason may not be acceptable to all, but to me it is sure. All of those infants who are within the elect who die are elect. And this is my reason, that when I find no unfaith in anyone, I have no reason to condemn him; contrariwise, since I have the indubitable word of promise, "They shall come and sit down with the God of Abraham, Isaac, and Jacob," [244] I shall be impious if I eject them from the company of the people of God.

[The Anabaptists]: What then of Esau if he had died as an infant? Would your judgment place him among the elect?

[The Reply]: Yes.

[The Anabaptists]: Then does election remain sure?

[The Reply]: It does. And rejection remains also. But listen. If Esau had died an infant, he would doubtless have been of the elect. For if he had died, then there would have been the seal of election, for the Lord would not have rejected him eternally. . . .

[The Anabaptists]: Then would that he had died an infant!

[The Reply]: He could not die whom divine Providence had created that he might live, and live wickedly. You see then, O man, that almost all your ignorance of Scripture arises from your ignorance of Providence. But I return to my subject. Manifest then from all that precedes are those two inferences. That those two sayings: Whoever believeth, etc., and Whoever believeth not, etc.,[245] are not a touchstone[246] by which we may measure the salvation of infants, and that we condemn impiously not only the true children of Christians, but those of Gentiles. They alone are subject to our judgment of whom we have the word according to which we can judge.

[The Anabaptists]: If by election we come to God, Christ is in vain.[247]

[The Reply]: This is election, that whomever the Lord has destined to eternal salvation before the world was created, he equally predestined before the world was created to be saved through his Son, as Paul teaches in Ephesians 1[:3-8]. . . . [248] So I regard the whole Anabaptist argument as now overturned, and it is demonstrated that election is above baptism, circumcision, faith, and preaching.

That the Apostles Baptized Infants

In the foregoing I said that when Christ and the apostles referred to Scriptures, they referred to none other than that of the law and the prophets.[249] For not yet were the Gospels written or the apostolic epistles collected. But in this I would not speak as if I would take aught away from the canonical New Testament, since the books of the Old Testament also were not written at one time, and yet the authority of the later books is not less; but I would show that Anabaptist writers are in error in this, that they suppose the apostles to have directed baptism in accordance with that writing that was not yet written. . . . I have undertaken to prove a hard thing then, the Anabaptists think, but it is easy if we give ear to the truth . . . [for] the arguments I draw from no source but Scripture itself, as follows:

[First],[250] everyone knows how sharp was the contest among believers about circumcision, which contest is described in Acts 15. Some contended that those must be circumcised who had already been initiated into Christ, others opposing. But when there had arisen a great strife, the delegates from Antioch, the apostles, and the whole church guided by the Holy Spirit decreed that circumcision and all the externals of the law, a few exceptions being made in concession to the weak, should be abrogated.[251] Here then I will ask the Anabaptists whether they believe the disciples were less solicitous about administering the baptismal rite than about circumcision? If they say that they were not solicitous, then the piety of the parents which has regard for the children as well as for themselves leads us to think otherwise ... especially since in the beginning their infants had been circumcised. It cannot be then that if the apostles were unwilling to baptize the children, there would not have arisen some disturbance. But nothing is said of this, so there was no disturbance. So because of believers' opinions, children were baptized; and for this reason there is no distinct mention of it. . . .

But the second argument is insuperable, gathered by comparison of Scripture. Circumcision was abrogated by decree of the church gathered in the Spirit.[252] Infants were with their parents within the church. If, then, according to the Anabaptists' opinion, those infants or little children were not baptized, yet were circumcised, it follows that by a decree of the church children of Christians were cast out of the church and were sent back to the circumcision. For who is circumcised becomes a debtor to the whole law. And there is no reason why we should plead here that account must be taken of the time. For the strife about circumcision believers arose at Antioch, not at Jerusalem, where either circumcision or baptism was bound to have flourished.[253]

The third argument also is from conjecture—that we should consider the race from which the first believers came. They were of a race that so clung to externals that the apostles believed even after the resurrection that Christ would rule corporeally. It is not therefore likely that they left their children unbaptized. I leave the rest to you, reader, for much can be educed from these bases.

The fourth I have touched on in the foregoing,[254] i.e., that Paul in 1 Corinthians 10 makes us and the Hebrews equal. "All," he said, "were baptized, all ate the same spiritual bread."[255] And since all their children were baptized in the sea and the cloud, they would not be equal if our children were not baptized, as has been said. . . .

[The Anabaptists]: If they ate the same spiritual bread, therefore our children will also celebrate the Eucharist.[256]

[Reply]: That has no weight, for by synecdoche, to each part its own property is attributed. But since we have a precept for the celebration of the Eucharist—"Let each man prove himself"[257]—children are not competent for this, while they are for baptism and circumcision. It is clear that with Paul infant baptism was in use, but not infant Eucharist. . . .

[Anabaptists]: From Colossians 2[:11] we infer that children cannot be circumcised with the circumcision not made with hands nor lay aside the body of sin, therefore baptism did not come in place of circumcision, since circumcision is external and corporeal, but this is internal and spiritual. . . .

[The Reply]: We learn here that Paul attributed our externals to the Hebrews, though they had the internals alone, and the externals not in the same form but differently. No one denies that they ate spiritual bread just as we, for they, like we, were saved through him who was to come. But they did not carry around the bread and wine in the supper, but used other externals in place of these, manna and water from the rock.[258] Do you see how by analogy he makes the externals equivalent? how when they were different, the internals were the same? So he attributes to them that internal baptism, so that they as well as we were cleansed through Christ. External baptism he expresses by the analogy of "the sea and the cloud."[259] But to us he attributes internal circumcision, for we are under the same covenant with them and are renewed by the same Spirit, and by it are circumcised. That is, he is speaking by synecdoche in accordance with the age of each class. But he found no other external than baptism, for what cause would there be for making a comparison analogically between baptism and circumcision, when without that he could have spoken of the spirit being renewed, unless he had wished in the same way to make equal the internals as well as the externals, as he did in 1 Corinthians 10[:1]? It must be therefore that Paul entertained this opinion, that our circumcision is baptism. This he would never have held unless he had seen at that time the children of Christians baptized as he had formerly seen them circumcised. . . .

So the Anabaptists do nothing at all different from the false apostles in former times, of whom Paul thus speaks: They order you to be circumcised for this only, that they may glory in your flesh.[260] So these men glory in mobs and their seditious, or rather heretical, church. For I assert truly that in our time no dogma, however unheard of, can so rightly be called heresy as that of this sect, for they have separated themselves from the church of believers. They have rebaptized, and have their own gatherings.

Original Publication: Same as 59A
Transcription: ZW, VI, No.108, pp. 21-103, 155-87
Translation: Taken from Jackson, 1901, pp. 123-77, 219-51

Epilogue D
Joint Decree for the Suppression of the Anabaptists
Zurich, September 9, 1527

In the introduction to Epi. C, above, four reasons were cited why Zwingli might have written the Elenchus, in spite of the fact that the "Anabaptist ringleaders"—Grebel, Mantz, and Blaurock—were out of his way by this time. The fourth and main reason was that the persistence of the underground movement which they had created prior to their demise and which had recently surfaced in the areas of Basel and Bern convinced Zwingli that the time had come for a conjoint policy among the Reformed cantons on how to eradicate this "hidden ulcer" in the Swiss Confederation.

Until the summer of 1525, Berchtold Haller, head pastor at Bern, had differed with Zwingli on the use of violence to suppress the movement. He felt that Anabaptism was a symptom of the spiritual deprivation of the masses and he could not easily bring himself to approve the death penalty for a deprived people. But now that Bern was about to adopt the Reformation officially, the competitive methods of the radicals loomed up as more threatening to the success of the new evangelical order. So on August 2, 1527, the Zurich magistrates at Zwingli's suggestion sent letters of invitation to Bern, Basel, Schaffhausen, Chur, Appenzell, and St. Gallen, to send delegates to a joint consultation to be convened on August 12 (see Fast, 1973, p. 1, fn.1). Chur declined the invitation, Appenzell did not attend, Basel and Schaffhausen sent observers only, and Bern and St. Gallen sent delegates with full authorization and power of attorney.

Zwingli published the Elenchus just two weeks before this consultation as a means of generating support for the new policy of suppression that he desired. Thus, the Elenchus was mainly intended as a political policy document. For the preparations made in Zurich for the consultation, see Muralt and Schmidt, No. 226.

The consultation lasted for three days, Aug. 12-14, at the end of which the delegates were given a report with the lengthy title, "What these legates of the councils of Zurich, Bern, and St. Gallen, have decided concerning the Anabaptists; namely, that a public printed notice should be issued by all of them in the form below, to be brought back to their lords and magistrates, the two legates of Basel and Schaffhausen having had no authority except to be listeners at the sessions to what was dealt with." After reporting to their constituent city councils, the consultation was reconvened on Sept. 9 to reconsider the text of the report in relation to its reception in the respective councils. Bern did not attend this session and the Basel representative did not arrive until evening. Basel and Schaffhausen agreed with the content, but dissented to its publication at this time "in order that the other confederates might not think that we, for ourselves and behind their backs, intend to make

506

a separation." St. Gallen and Zurich accepted the text and decided to proceed with its publication, except to delete the part about fines, in deference to Bern, which had sent a memorandum on Sept. 6 that the plan was agreeable except that they reserved a free hand concerning fines. However, on Sept. 14, Bern withdrew its consent to the printing on the grounds that it did not seem necessary at that time; but by this time the document had already been printed with the names of its three sponsors: Zurich, St. Gallen, and Bern.

Samuel Geiser (ME, I, p. 667) summarizes its contents as follows: "(1) Whoever is suspect of the vice of Anabaptism will be summoned before the authorities and faithfully and seriously warned to desist and the penalties will be explained to him. (2) In order that this suspicion may come to light, every citizen is bound by his oath of loyalty to inform the authorities of any one suspected of Anabaptism. (3) Whoever openly belongs to this sect, and refuses to be corrected and to desist, is subject to punishment by the authorities. (4) Foreign Anabaptists are to be expelled. A foreigner is defined as one who is born outside the jurisdiction of the cities and cantons entering upon this agreement. (5) Whoever is expelled, and in violation of his oath returns, shall be drowned without mercy. (6) Citizens who backslide and are again stained with Anabaptism shall pay a double fine. (7) Whoever persists in his error, becomes a preacher or leader of the sect, or, having sworn to amend his ways and to desist from his error, backslides, shall also be drowned. (8) Anabaptists should not be absent from communion; they shall observe it with the other people of their local church. (9) Since many innocent persons are enticed by the hypocritical doctrine of the Anabaptists, we reserve the right to modify the penalty according to circumstances. (10) If an Anabaptist flees from one of the regions bound by the agreement to another, he shall not be spared, but shall either be expelled or extradited. (11) If neighboring cantons or cities wish to join us in this agreement, they may do so at any time. (12) The messengers shall immediately announce this mandate to their home governmental authorities, who shall then determine the amount of the fines to be imposed.

"The baneful effect of this concordat was soon in evidence. The death penalty for Anabaptists provided in it was now also applied in Bern. It was the first mandate issued by Bern against the Anabaptists and initiated a systematic persecution that lasted for centuries."

Decree of the cities of Zurich, Bern,[1] and St. Gallen on account of the uprisings of the Anabaptists.

We, the burgomasters, magistrates, councils, and citizens of the cities of Zurich, Bern, and St. Gallen, wish grace and peace from God through Christ to each and everyone before whom this our document will come, who read it or hear it read, and we herewith give you to know:

When in times past, alongside the eternal and saving Word of God, a sect and separation[2] of some people known as the Anabaptists occurred,

507

which was so impudent as to base and maintain its undertaking also on the sacred, divine, and biblical Scriptures of both the Old and New Testaments,[3] but has frequently been discussed and debated[4] by men learned in the holy Scriptures and shown on the basis of Scripture and reported to us that Anabaptism cannot stand according to the Word of God but is repudiated and against and contrary to common Christian order, and the baptism of infants as hitherto practiced in common Christian usage is right and in agreement with the Word of God, we in our domains and cantons have applied all possible industry to abolish this error of rebaptism, and first kindly admonished our people to desist from it and to adapt themselves to the common Christian custom. But because we found some among them obstinate and hardened who refused to be deflected, and this sect and separation[5] within and outside our confederation grew noticeably in numbers and in strength, because we also have thoroughly experienced that it is the intention, plan, and pursuit of the same Anabaptists and their adherents to aim and conspire to say and to practice and even command among themselves that none of their people are to attend and listen to the preaching and teaching of the preachers who are called and chosen by a Christian community to preach and to teach; for they teach and preach falsely, erroneously, misleadingly; they also accuse and libel them in the highest degree.[6] Moreover, they teach and preach for themselves in secret places in homes, corners, forests, and fields,[7] also at the time when a Christian congregation should listen together at an open customary place to the Word of God by preachers chosen by the church, who proclaim and teach the Word of God according to correct Christian interpretation, and thus have set up a separated meeting, mob, and sect, all to the disadvantage, offense, and suppression of usual Christian meeting and congregating of Christian people.

Item: At several places in our country and cantons,[8] they have some who, under the pretense of the Word of God and Christian and proper love, although they were obligated by proper marital bonds of matrimony have taken other women to themselves in the manner and form of a spiritual marriage,[9] exchanged rings and symbols of marriage, out of which obvious, shameless, and offensive abomination of adultery has come and resulted. Also, in many other ways, under the pretense of good, they carry on and practice improper deeds with married women and girls.

Item: They also, without shame and the fear of God and of all honorable authority, are so bold as to boast that God, by his command and the Spirit revealed to them and made them an example to commit horrible abominations like murder, even of their natural brothers,[10] and other evils, which kind of deeds actually happened.

Item: In times past they have at several places in our towns and countryside, under the pretense of divine order and miracles, made themselves appear as if they were in a trance or dead, and had seen divine mysteries and revelations.[11]

Item: They presumed, by misuse of divine Scripture, to hold that the devil will be pardoned and saved.[12] Some of them also hold and believe that since Paul said to the Romans that no external things could harm those who are in Christ, it was fitting for that reason to act and live in any way their frivolous and ignorant spirit leads them, without discrimination or differentiation according to their mood and desire. They therefore do not conceal or feel ashamed in the presence of authority[13] to curse and perform other offensive vices, but boast that this is and will be without disadvantage and harmless before God.

Item: Although not all of them make use of the outward water-sign of Anabaptism, they were nonetheless signed and marked with other signs and brands, namely, that none should carry a sword,[14] nor pay his outstanding debts[15] according to law and justice. They hold and say also that no Christian, if he wants to be a Christian, should give or take interest or rent from others for any capital,[16] that all temporal goods are free and common,[17] and everyone may have complete possession of them, which they frequently applied at the beginning of their self-proclaimed brotherhood, and thereby moved poor simpleminded souls to join them. All of these things and many more, which we omit for the sake of brevity, they have done under the pretense of peace and brotherly love and loyalty in order thereby to gloss over and conceal their rascality and their wanton and seditious life.

Item: They hold and teach without any qualms, also presume to maintain with Holy Scripture, that no Christian may be a magistrate.[18] And although the government could not be preserved nor exist without the duty and bond of the oath, still they teach and hold without any exception or distinction that no Christian nor anyone else may swear an oath[19] (even to the government), all to the offense and displacement of Christian and orderly government, brotherly love, and general peace.

Since we then, as stated above, were taught that infant baptism, by the all-inclusive verse, "Go ye and teach all nations, baptizing them in the name of the Father, Son, and Holy Spirit," comprises all men and nations and no one is cut off or excluded from it, and the Anabaptists make a distinction between the baptism of adults and of children, making an exception of infants without having God's Word and without any Christian and well-founded reasons, even though the secular authorities want us to stay by the common law until proper reasons for exceptions are announced;

also because it is after all not proper to judge on examples of what has happened but on what should happen, as the Anabaptists say: The apostles baptized [adults who] believed and comprehended and not infants; hence one should not baptize them. This is deception and false and should not be followed. It was also clearly found thus among the Christian teachers who lived not long after the apostles' time that the practice of infant baptism at that time came to them from the time of the apostles.[20] Hence, infant baptism has been held to be Christian and praiseworthy in Christendom in general.

For these and other Christian and well-founded reasons, which were sufficiently indicated earlier in the disputations that were held, we, as a Christian and proper government, since we are burdened with such defiled and seditious people, are moved to join together and take counsel in this matter of how we can root out and destroy these unchristian, malicious, offensive, and rebellious weeds, and have accordingly unanimously decided as is hereinafter successively encompassed:

First, we have considered and ordered to be observed and carried through that if a man or woman,[21] wife or husband, young or old, is suspected and accused of this vice of Anabaptism, that he or she[22] shall at once be sent to the authorities and faithfully and earnestly admonished to desist from it, upon penalty and punishment if they persist therein.

And in order that such a suspicion and charge may become publicly known, each of our citizens, subjects, and tenants[23] shall be bound and obligated by Christian obedience and the oath he has rendered, that he will inform his authorities where he knows and learns of man or woman[24] charged or suspected of such Anabaptism.

Item: Those who are citizens or inhabitants[25] of the place who fall into this sect and separation[26] of Anabaptism and refuse to reform and desist from it completely and get involved in open actual deeds or offense shall according to the will and pleasure of the authorities be penalized and punished according to the occasion and circumstances of the persons and the affair.

If, however, one or more aliens from outside our towns and cantons come to that point, if they have been found to be contaminated with Anabaptism, they shall first immediately be admonished by the authorities and banished and treated as foreigners who were born outside our town and canton or else as those who have immigrated and agreed with us in such.

Item: Anyone who then has been banished and expelled by a town or district and contrary to his oath returns to the area, he or they[27] shall be drowned without mercy.[28]

510

Item: If one of the citizens and inhabitants[29] of our towns and districts is contaminated with Anabaptism elsewhere and this has become known, he or they shall be punished and fined with a heavier penalty than previously.

But if a man or woman[30] refuses to desist from such intention but boldly persists in it or if one of this sect and mob is an important leader such as teacher, preacher, baptizer, or is a refugee, vagabond, or mob leader or has previously been released from prison, having promised, vowed, and sworn to reform and desist from it, which is the same thing among them, he or they[31] shall also be drowned.[32]

Item: Since we have discovered a division or split in the Lord's Supper among the aforesaid Anabaptists also, it is our view, will, and opinion that they come to terms with the other regular churches in the areas where they live and not separate from other churches but partake of the Lord's Supper with them, or abstain from it altogether to the extent that it can well be done.

And since we have also been informed that many poor, innocent, and common persons, women and men, young and old, who cannot realize or know the hidden poison, have been misled and led[33] into this sect by the smooth talk used by the Anabaptists, all of us reserve the right to moderate, reduce, and alter the penalties listed and defined above, according to the nature and circumstances of the persons and affairs, also according to each one's guilt, as it seems proper and right to us on any given occasion.

Item: We have united and agreed among ourselves that if someone who is suspected and accused of this Anabaptism seeks refuge and help in one or the other of our towns, territories, and cantons,[34] to flee there and maintain himself there, we will expel him from town and country or have him or her returned to those from whom he fled if they demand it.

In addition we have reserved to ourselves [the right] that if any other towns, territories, and commonwealths[35] adjacent and neighboring to us would enter upon, unite, and agree with us and we with them in the matter of these Anabaptists and their evil, vicious, and seditious actions, we may at any time take [additional] action in order that their evil intentions may be more efficiently suppressed, while now and henceforth always keeping inviolate and secure our treaties that we have made with our dear confederates.[36] And thus we command each and every one of our chief and assistant bailiffs,[37] etc.

Ratified this 9th day of September, 1527.

Originals: Zentralbibliothek Zurich, Ms.19; Staatsarchiv Zurich, EI.7.1, No.105
Transcription: Fast, No.1, pp.1-6

Epilogue E
The Fifth and Sixth Swiss Anabaptist Martyrs:
Jacob Falk and Heini Reimann
Zurich, September 5, 1528

Conrad Grebel devoted four months—June to October 8, 1525—to intensive evangelism in the township of Grüningen, canton of Zurich. It was here that his father had served as governor for twelve years—1499 to 1512—and where Conrad lived to the age of thirteen. It was here, more than a decade later, that he enjoyed his greatest following as an Anabaptist leader. He worked alone in this province, for Mantz and Blaurock were preaching in Chur and Appenzell until their return in early October. Bender (p. 149) writes that "on the whole it may be said that the Zurich Anabaptist movement had its greatest success in Grüningen."

As Document 70F, above, shows, there was a smoldering tension here between the peasants and the Zurich authorities over the paying of the compulsory tithes and the right of the local communities to choose their own pastors. Some of the local pastors supported the peasants in their protest by preaching against the system of centralization. The Zurich Council, which had promised to examine the complaints, subsequently decided on the advice of the governor Jörg Berger not to yield any further to the demands either for the abolition of the tithe or for local autonomy; and this reversal must have created a new sense of injustice in the district and a ready climate for the growth of the Anabaptist movement.

After the arrest of Grebel and Blaurock on Oct. 8 (see 71H, above), the Grüningen governor petitioned the Zurich Council to sponsor a new, objective disputation with the Anabaptists to which twelve impartial representatives from the province could be sent. This disputation was held in Zurich November 6-8. In spite of the fact that Grebel, Mantz, and Blaurock were now in custody in Zurich, the Grüningen Anabaptists continued to promote the movement, raising such charges that Zwingli wanted to suppress the peasants by force of arms. They refused to recant their Anabaptist beliefs, in spite of the decree that they should do so (see 71L, above). The twelve representatives from the district sought unsuccessfully to mediate between the Zurich authorities and the Anabaptists, but only thirteen of the latter yielded to the authorities while ninety remained steadfast.

Among the leaders of the movement at this time were two farmers from Gossau—Jacob Falk and Heini Reimann. Falk had heard Grebel's preaching as early as July of 1525 (see 71D/421/23-25) and was a participant in the November disputation. Then they were incarcerated in the tower of the governor's castle at Grüningen, but somehow managed to escape on Dec. 30. They were rearrested the following May when they took part in a meeting in the Herrliberg Forest, which was broken up by Bailiff Berger. When they fearlessly confessed to Berger that they had baptized many and would

512

continue to do so, knowing that it was a crime punishable by death, the Zurich authorities pressed for the death sentence. This the Grüningen court refused to do, not because they dissented from the Zurich mandate of March 7 (see 71M/448/4ff.), but out of consideration for the popularity of the movement in Grüningen and the maintenance of local autonomy.

On the basis of an ancient privilege granted by Austria, the Grüningen magistrates appealed to the Confederate Diet (Landtag) *in Bern, where the case was litigated over a period of eighteen months, during which time the two defendants "remained obstinate." In June 1527, they were granted the right of a written defense, in the form of the following petition, known as the "Grüninger Eingabe," an important document in the history of the movement. Von Muralt summarizes its contents as follows: "The government mandates are contrary to the Word of God and the command of Christ. We must obey God more than man, and must baptize according to the will of Christ. Christ calls baptism 'a righteousness' and 'a counsel of God,' a baptism to be performed only after repentance and only for believers. It cannot be given to children. Christ gave believers no other disciplinary power than the ban, since believers walk in the will of the Spirit. The baptism which we practice is the baptism of Christ and it is infant baptism which is the rebaptism" (ME, II, 606). For Zwingli's reactions, see Epi.C/486/14-29.*

It is interesting to note that at the time the two prisoners were writing their defense, they were visited by a group of five former Zollikon Anabaptists—Jacob, Uli, and Heini Hottinger, Jacob Unholz, and Felix Kienast. The Zollikon men had come to encourage their two brothers in the faith to remain steadfast. Uli Hottinger later confessed to a court in Zurich that "he had given the imprisoned brothers his hand, had encouraged them, and said that they should be steadfast and brave and not recant" (Muralt and Schmid, No. 219).

Blanke, who narrated this episode, comments, "What astounds us in this exhortation is that it comes from the mouths of men who had themselves recanted, for all five visitors had denied their own faith and had not found strength for martyrdom" (Blanke, 1961, pp. 69-70). The incident is noteworthy, nevertheless, for the degree of union it indicates between the Anabaptists of neighboring provinces, and also perhaps for indicating "that the Anabaptists of Zollikon had returned to the state church only because of despondency and fear, and not from conviction."

Over a year later, the confederate court finally decided the case in favor of Zurich and ordered the prisoners to be transferred to Zurich for trial. They were now separated for the first time and lodged in different prisons for two weeks on the usual diet of bread, water, and "mus" (see 54/fn.17). In their trial (see Muralt and Schmid, Nos. 257, 266, 268, and 273) the defendants refused to disclose by name whom they had baptized and declared that they would continue to baptize, strengthened only by the Son of God, who would never desert them. They were sentenced to death and drowned at Zurich at 1:00 p.m. on the afternoon of September 5, 1528. Their fellow prisoners were released on a bond of recantation, but two of them—Heine Karpfis of Grüningen and Hans Herzog of Stadel—rejoined the movement and were likewise drowned on March 23, 1532.

Appeal of the Prisoners to the Grüningen Diet in Session June 4, 1527:

Grace and peace from God our Father and the Lord Jesus Christ be with all those who sincerely desire it.

Dear Magistrates and Officials!

You have known the charge that the Councillors have made against us, that we have acted contrary to their orders and mandates and have promised and kept none of them and have been defeated with the holy Scriptures, and that the baptism that we practice has no foundation in Scripture.

We in turn testify and confess that their orders and mandates are contrary to the Word of God and Christ's command. For that reason we are more obedient to God than to men.[1] We wanted earlier to testify orally that we have baptized according to the command and will of Christ. But you refused to listen. Then we were satisfied. Then you ordered us to write, but not out of the Gospel that is found in the New Testament. With that we are satisfied. Further, you declared we could freely write from our hearts, and we have done so. Now we confess to God and before you and testify that we have been brought here and stand here before you for the sake of the truth and for the sake of righteousness, as we shall show.

When Christ was about thirty years old,[2] he came to John and wanted to be baptized by him.[3] But John objected and said, "I would indeed have need to be baptized by you, and you come to me."[4] Then Christ said, "Let it happen thus; for it is our duty to fulfill all righteousness."[5] Then he consented. Then he was baptized in the Jordan. Here at this place Christ calls baptism an act of righteousness.

The publicans came to John, repented, and assented that God was right, and had themselves baptized. But the Pharisees despised God's counsel and did not submit to baptism.[6] Here Christ calls baptism an act of righteousness and a counsel of God which takes place after repentance. Thus, baptism does not pertain to little children, for they are not in need of repentance, nor do they know anything about righteousness and the counsel of God. Therefore he says, "He who has ears to hear, let him hear!"[7]

After Christ arose and was about to ascend to heaven, he said to his disciples, "Go forth and teach all peoples,[8] and whoever believes and is baptized will be saved, but whoever does not believe is damned."[9]

Here at this place Christ commands and demands that one teach first,

514

and then whoever believes shall be baptized. Who wants to act to the contrary? Nobody with the truth. If Christ had been speaking of children, the children would have had to be damned before they could believe. But that is not the case, for what he taught and commanded he said to those who could understand good and evil. He therefore says, "He who has ears to hear, let him hear."[10] And he says, "Let the little children come to me and do not prevent them, for of such is the kingdom of God."[11] Therefore the children are his, and if we do what he teaches us we are his also.

Now take note, simpleminded man, how the false prophets[12] and the wise and clever are misleading you, saying baptism is nothing, it is only an external symbol and is only water; it is of no consequence. But you have well understood that Christ said to John, "Let it take place, thus it behooves us to fulfill all righteousness."[13] And second, he calls it a counsel of God.[14] And third, God commanded us to do it. Now take note—all who talk so against God's righteousness and against God's counsel and against God's command; and all who talk so will have no share in the kingdom of God unless they repent and be converted from their lying and falsehood.

As he commanded his disciples, so they acted. Peter preached the gospel and said: "Repent and every one of you accept baptism in the name of Jesus Christ, and you will receive the gift of the Holy Spirit."[15] And those who gladly received his word were baptized, and on that day about three thousand souls were baptized.[16] Now notice: How can a child repent who has no need of it? Or how could a child gladly accept his word? You say, the present and the past are not the same. We now have the baptism that they had; for there is just one baptism. If infant baptism were right, the three thousand would also have had their children baptized. And Philip preached the Gospel to the eunuch, and they came to the water, and the eunuch said, "Here is water; what prevents my being baptized?" Then Philip said, "If you believe from your heart, it may take place." Then the eunuch said, "I believe from my heart." So they both stepped into the water, and he baptized him.[17]

Let all note that one must believe with his whole heart before he is baptized. But a child cannot believe with his heart, as everyone well understands. Who will then want to contend against the Word of God and his apostles? No Christian is against it, but liars are always against it.

Furthermore, when Paul came to Ephesus he found several men there and said to them, "Have you received the Holy Spirit since you believed?"[18] Then they said, "We have never heard whether there is a Holy Spirit or not."[19] Then Paul said, "In what name were you then baptized?"[20] They answered, "In the name of John the Baptist."[21] Then

515

Paul said, "John baptized to repentance and told the people to believe in the one who would come after him."[22] Then they accepted baptism in the name of Christ. There were about twelve men.[23] Now everyone understood that there is just one baptism. John baptized to repentance and told the people that they believed in him who came after him, who is Christ. Christ commanded to teach and to baptize whoever believed. His followers have thus practiced it through his grace and the wisdom of his Spirit which is given to us. So we too practice it. Understand that the twelve men had not been sufficiently taught the faith of Christ. Hence it was no baptism. Hence infant baptism is nothing but a false, devilish doctrine since it is in every respect contrary to the Word of God.

Then again Paul says, "There is one faith, one baptism, and one Father of us all,"[24] and again Paul says, "How should we want to live in sins to which we have died? Don't you know that all of us who are baptized in Christ are baptized into his death? So we are all buried unto death through baptism, so that just as Christ was raised through the glory of the Father, we should also walk in new life;[25] as you once gave up your members to the service of unrighteousness, so now give up your members to the service of righteousness, so that you may become holy."[26] Now let everyone notice that baptism is for believers, for those who have given themselves over to the Son of God and desist from evildoing. Then note that an infant has never given his members over to unrighteousness. How can it then walk in a new life?

And further, Christ gave the believers no compulsion beyond the use of the ban and said, "If your brother sins against you, rebuke him between yourself and him alone. If he listens to you, you have won your brother; if he does not listen to you, take two or three others along; if he does not listen to them, tell the church; if he does not listen to the church, consider him a heathen and publican. Truly the one you bind on earth shall also be bound in heaven, and the one you loose on earth shall also be loosed in heaven."[27]

Now this applies to the believers who have died to the will of the flesh and are now walking in the will of the Spirit.[28] These are the fruits of the Spirit: love, peace, friendliness, kindness, faithfulness, gentleness, meekness, patience, righteousness, and truth.[29] Those who walk therein are the community of Christ and the body of Christ[30] and the Christian church. Now we hope and are assured that we are in the true church. Now they want to force us out of the true church into a different church.

Note now how the false prophet Zwingli, when he finds nothing on infant baptism in the New Testament, goes backward into the Old Testament, which he should not do, and says: Because children are included in the promise to Abraham, who shall refuse them the water? Now notice, simpleminded man: God made a covenant with Abraham and said, "You shall be a father of many nations, and from your seed all the nations of the earth shall be blessed, and I will give you the land of Canaan. And this is the sign between me and you: you shall circumcize all male children on the eighth day."[31] Notice now: the covenant that God made with Abraham he made only with the Jews and not with the heathen. The Jews considered the heathen unclean. But thus we are also by race and nature descended from the heathen. If infants should be baptized because of the covenant, why do they baptize our children since we are of heathen descent and not of the covenant of Abraham? So he could say: The promise that God gave Abraham that in his seed all nations should be blessed is Christ. Now if Christ has led us to the promise, we should carefully see what Christ teaches us and act accordingly. Everyone note: Christ was promised to Abraham. That has already been fulfilled for us. God gave Abraham circumcision to circumcize the infants on the eighth day, but not the little girls. But the little girls were included in the covenant as well as the little boys. Now notice, simplehearted people, as Abraham was obedient to God, so we should also be obedient to Christ, who said one should first teach and then baptize him who believes; for when Christ was about to begin preaching, there came a voice from heaven saying, "This is my beloved Son, with whom I am satisfied and well pleased."[32] And a second time, when Peter, John, and James were on the mountain with him, he was transfigured before them and a voice came from heaven saying, "This is my beloved Son in whom I am well pleased; hear him."[33] Note here, everyone, that it is the will of God and his command that we listen to the Son and obey him.

Further, Christ says, the law and prophets had prophesied until John,[34] and from that time on the gospel had been proclaimed. Christ is the gospel, therefore the law prophesied until the coming of Christ, as Paul also says: Christ is the end of the law.[35] And again Paul says: When Christ came he abrogated the former to establish the latter.[36] Notice in these words that Christ fulfilled the first testament, which ended in him, and established another, a new one, in which we are from now on to be in a new life and no longer in the old, and should not seek any other way; for he says, "I am the way, the truth, and the life. No man comes to the Father except through me.[37] I am the door to the sheep, and whoever tries to climb in anywhere else is a thief and a murderer."[38] Now no doubt everyone understands that there is no other way, nor can anyone come to the Father except through Christ alone. And he who seeks another door is a thief and a murderer. Now look at those who do not stay with the Word of Christ and say that because children are in the promise, who can refuse them the water? Then we say we know they are in the promise, for Christ says, "Of such is the kingdom of God."[39] But infant baptism is not a planting from the Word of God, and it will therefore be uprooted, and they seek another way and another door; therefore they are thieves and murderers of Christ. Now, beloved, we write such things to you that you may convert from darkness to the simple truth and light of Christ and recognize the tree by its fruit,[40] as Christ teaches us. The fruits of darkness are these: pride, greed, usury, envy, hatred, anger, strife, division, sectarianism, murder, gluttony, drunkenness, gambling, adultery, fornication, and all lusts of the flesh.[41] Therefore John also says, "He who transgresses and does not remain in the teaching of Christ has no God; but he who remains in Christ has both the Father and the Son."[42]

Now everyone has no doubt understood that in the charge [against us], they call the baptism of Christ a rebaptism without foundation in the holy Scriptures. But now we hope that you have heard and understood the Word of Christ which we have cited and which is written in the books and that there would be much more evidence that the baptism which we practice is the baptism of Christ and that infant baptism is the rebaptism.[43] And now we request that you let us stay by the truth. But if that cannot be, we are prepared to suffer for the faith through the grace and power of God which is given to us.

The grace of Jesus Christ be with all those who earnestly desire his grace.

Sentence by the Zurich Council upon Jacob Falk and Heini Reimann, September 5, 1528:

Since Jacob Falk of Gossau and Heini Reimann, both from the Grüningen domain, who are standing here, are guilty and have admitted that they have transgressed against the mandate and command of our lords,[44] the mayor, the Large and Small Councils, and the city of Zurich, which mandate of our lords, in brief, directs that anyone in their city, lands, jurisdiction, and territories shall rebaptize no one, whether men, women, or girls; for anyone who baptizes another again shall be imprisoned and be drowned without mercy, etc. And each of them has confessed that he rebaptized three persons and that they instructed and taught them their misleading, erroneous gang, sect, and ideas.

Also both of them, Jacob Falk and Heini Reimann, have continued to persist in their practice and have given no contrary evidence but that anyone who comes to them and has been taught and sincerely desires to be baptized, they will baptize him.

518

Therefore, as is known to many, to our lords and other honest people, concerning the two, Falk and Reimann, and also their adherents, that their activity, in commission and omission, is nothing but notorious offense, revolt, and rebellion against Christian authority, a rending of the common Christian peace, brotherly love, and unity of the citizenry, and finally followed by every kind of evil of the above-named Jacob Falk and Heini Reimann and for their misdeeds and wicked disregard for and transgression of the high and weighty mandates issued by our lords, and furthermore because, if they had the opportunity, they would have continued their rebaptizing for which they are charged, they are sentenced as follows:

They shall both be committed to the executioner, who will bind their hands, take them in a boat to the low hut, set them on the hut, strip their bound hands over their knees, and push a pole between their arms and legs, and thus bound throw them into the water, and let them die and perish in the water, whereby they will have atoned to the law and right.[45]

If anyone, no matter who, objects to or criticizes their death with word or deed, doing so privately or publicly, he or they shall be charged and stand in the bonds in which Jacob Falk and Heini Reimann are now standing.

This sentence and seal are ratified before Junker Hans Effinger, a governor of the state, upon the demand of lord Heinrich Walder, mayor. The property of the condemned has fallen to the mercy of the city and is confiscated.

Enacted on Saturday, September 5, 1528, before councillors and representatives.

Originals: Staatsarchiv Zurich, EI.7.1 & BVI.251, fol.77
Transcriptions: Muralt-Schmid, Nos. 212, 273

Epilogue F
The Preachers' Disputation with the Anabaptists
Bern, March 11-17, 1538

In the history of the Anabaptists, like that of the early church, the blood of the martyrs was the seed of the church. Their persecution in the canton of Zurich was a causative factor in their spread to other cantons like Bern, where Anabaptists settled in the areas of Solothurn, Aarburg, Lenzburg, Zofingen, Napf, Aarwangen, and the Emmenthal. Prior to his death on the battlefield of Cappel in 1531, Zwingli had frequent correspondence with Berch-

told Haller, the Bern Reformer, concerning the need to suppress the movement.

In April 1527, eight Anabaptists came to Bern with a copy of their Schleitheim articles of faith, which Haller sent to Zwingli with the request for help on how to refute it. One of the eight was Jacob Hochrütiner, the son of Lorenz Hochrütiner, (see Cast of Characters No. 45). Haller generally followed Zwingli's advice on how to deal with these Anabaptists, except that he had been reluctant to use the death penalty against them, until the joint decree of Sept. 9, 1527, was ratified (see Epi. C, above).

The following January, eight Anabaptists including Jörg Blaurock came to Bern to attend the doctrinal disputation which officially introduced the Reformation in Bern. The eight were not admitted to the sessions but were placed in custodial confinement. Then on one of the last days of the disputation, they were taken to the city hall, where they were questioned by Zwingli, after which they were banished on the threat of drowning if they ever returned.

In spite of several executions in the canton, the movement continued to spread, with the result that the Reformed preachers of the canton held three important disputations with the Anabaptists in the attempt to get them to recant and return to the church. The first was a disputation between Hans Pfistermeyer, the Anabaptist leader, and five Bernese preachers—Haller, Caspar Megander [Grossmann] (see Cast of Characters No. 42), Sebastian Hofmeister (see Cast of Characters No. 46), Franz Kolb, and Jacob Otherus, in the course of which Pfistermeyer recanted. Encouraged by this success, the magistrates of Bern engineered the idea of a major disputation involving more of the Reformed preachers and other Anabaptist leaders, who were offered safe conduct to appear at a place of meeting in Zofingen, in the midst of Anabaptist strongholds. This disputation was held July 1-9, 1532, and was attended by twenty-three Anabaptists. The minutes were published by the magistrates in the hope of suppressing the movement, but it had the opposite effect. With further numerical growth, especially in the Emmenthal area, came increased persecution by the authorities, including more executions.

The Third Public Disputation was held in Bern in March 1538, this time at the request of the Anabaptists themselves. In order to get approval for the debate and safe conduct to the place of meeting in Bern, the latter had to make two advance concessions: that government had been appointed by God to punish deviants and that the Old and New Testaments are of equal authority in the testing of divine truth. The disputation convened on March 11 and lasted for six days. The main spokesman on the Anabaptist side was Hanz Hotz, a native of Grüningen who was won to the movement by Grebel (see below 521/30-31 and 522/9-12 and above 70F/414/41ff.), and nurtured by Mantz and Blaurock (see 70F/fn.23). Hotz was a fellow prisoner with Falk and Reimann (see Epi. D. above) and was released one month after their execution. He and Martin Weniger (alias Marty Lingg; see 71K/442/30) were spokesmen in the Zofingen Disputation of 1532 (see above); and follow-

ing Weniger's recantation in 1535, Hotz continued to defend the movement with a spirit of steadfastness.

Following the Bern Disputation of 1538, the magistrates decreed that the Anabaptists should be escorted to the border and warned of summary death by beheading if they ever returned. The record of the disputation covers 208 pages, of which only two are here excerpted. Although the record was never published, four manuscript versions are extant, which the editors of Quellen, IV, identify with the letters A, B, C, and D (see pp. xxxiii-xxxiv).

Peter Kuntz,[1] Preacher

Since you confess that you first heard the Word from us, it is evident that we were the first to have the true Christian church.[2]

Hans Hotz,[3] Anabaptist Brother

As said before, we do not deny that you of the preachers made a beginning and were the origin. But by God's providence it happened that the books[4] were put into German. To the extent that you contributed to it, God thank you, although much was pointed out to us by the books of Luther, Zwingli, and others, so that we soon understood regarding the mass and other papist ceremonies that they are of no benefit. Nevertheless, I saw great lack in that they do not lead to Christian living, repentance, or conduct, on which I for my part set my mind and directed my thought and spirit toward a Christian life. So I put it off a year or two and waited, while there was preaching everywhere. The priest said much about reform, sharing, loving one another, desisting from evil, and forming community. I always felt that there was a lack in that we did not follow or establish what we were taught and the Word of God can accomplish. There was no initiation of godly conduct, for not all were so minded. And although the mass and images were abolished, there was still no penitence or mercy, and everything remained in evil living, gluttony, drunkenness, envy, hatred, etc., that should not have been in all the people. Because of this I found a reason for inquiring further in this matter. Then God sent his messengers, Conrad Grebel and others,[5] with whom I conferred on the basis of the apostles as to how one should live and also with whom. I started and established a church as those who had yielded themselves in true repentance according to the teaching of Christ concerning hearts, who by abstaining from wrongdoing, prove that they are in Christ, buried in baptism,[6] and risen in newness of life. As John said in his first sermon, "Repent, etc.,"[7] so Christ's teaching was also, "Repent, for the kingdom of God is near."[8] Likewise the apostles' sermons "pricked them in their hearts."[9] Peter also said, "Repent."[10] That was always the intent of their preaching. When I then found those[11] who led me to the life of Christ, the apostles, John, etc.,

521

on which alone we must build, and like whom they acted, I took them to be true apostles and a Christian church, for a Christian church must be like that.

Peter Kuntz, Preacher
A long speech is not to the point. Therefore, prove your call or commission to the office of preaching with Scripture, for I must ask what church commissioned the first Anabaptist, [Conrad] Grebel?[12]

Hans Hotz, Anabaptist Brother
Grebel was the first to teach me,[13] and I realized and perceived that he believed and followed what he taught me. I also found that it was in accord with the testimony of Scripture. I therefore accepted him as one who was commissioned by God.[14]

Erasmus Ritter,[15] Preacher
We say likewise that we are commissioned by God and the Christian Church. But that is by no means sufficient, for although you boast of a devout life for yourselves, supposing that you thereby prove your commission to the office of preaching, this does not have the power to commission, nor does a devout life prove a sure commission. For in 2 Corinthians 11, Paul faithfully warns the Corinthians that just as the devil masquerades as an angel of light, so also the false prophets masquerade as apostles of Christ.[16] To the Galatians in [chapter] 1, he said if an angel from heaven were to preach another gospel than he, they should not believe him.[17] Now if Paul warned of the angels, and the devil is able to masquerade as an angel of light and to arrange the very devoutest life outwardly, no life, however holy it is, can prove the commission. Therefore also Conrad Grebel's life (even if he lived piously) cannot prove for him a commission from God or anything else.

Hans Hotz, Anabaptist Brother[18]
Do not you, the preachers, also acknowledge that the Christian church should be changed[19] and converted to live in accord with God's order?

Hereupon the presidents admonished them to desist from details and prove their call and commission to the office of preaching from the Scriptures.

Original: Four ms. versions extant: A, B, C, D (see Quellen, IV, Intro.)
Transcription: Quellen, IV, pp. 281-83

Epilogue G
Vadian's Critique of the Lives of Grebel
and Other Anabaptists
St. Gallen, August 19, 1540

The foregoing collection of Swiss Anabaptist documents began with a letter from Vadian to Grebel, "a noble young man of exceptional talent." It ends below with another letter from Vadian, written nearly twenty-three years later, still referring to Grebel as "a man endowed with great gifts," but then presenting a bitter criticism of the lives of Grebel and other Anabaptist leaders whose natures were allegedly "scrupulously peevish and peevishly scrupulous." Written fourteen years after Grebel's death, it must be read in the perspective of the equally peevish attitudes of the alt-burgomaster and now 56-year-old Reformer of St. Gallen.

The last excerpt from his pen in the collection was a letter dated Nov. 24, 1526, concerning "the wretched fate" of his father-in-law (Epi. A/473/ 3ff.). Vadian vowed then to "shorten the sails," mindful of "the shipwrecks into which even the most experienced seamen are thrust." Following the execution of the aged Jacob Grebel, a silence of nine months in the correspondence between Vadian and Zwingli was broken by Vadian, who took the lead in restoring their collaboration in the work of the Reformation, including the joint decree for the suppression of Anabaptism, which they drew up together in 1527.

Vadian never forgave Conrad for what he considered the betrayal of his brother-in-law's confidence and counsel, or what in the following letter he calls his violation of "the laws of friendship and blood." The historian must assess the degree to which his personal resentment for having been "reviled and insulted ... publicly and in private" affected Vadian's appraisal of the movement. This sixteenth-century scientist, who in that first letter to Grebel of 1517 called him to a stance of fierce objectivity, was unable in the years following his young student's departure to sort out the evidences of authenticity in the movement he spearheaded from its also manifest distortions.

Nowhere is this failure more evident than in Vadian's Small Chronicle of the Abbey of St. Gallen, *written in 1532, in which he has a lengthy indictment of the heresies of "the terrible raging and raving of the Anabaptists which originated with some unruly persons in the city of Zurich.... They despised all justice, all governmental authority, all laws serving the civil community, all proper actions of secular and spiritual authority. They alone were holy and blameless, like the Donatists of Africa during St. Augustine's time. No church but theirs was the body of Christ; no faith but theirs was the justification of Christ ... they alone were sinless.... And what was the least of these—they repeated the baptism that they had first received and were rebaptized in rivers and ponds and poured out the baptism of infants as evil and*

523

damnable. *Their neighbor's goods and property was their property; they made him share it communally, not knowing God's command, 'Thou shalt not covet thy neighbor's goods.' None of them accepted interest or returns for their money, or on the basis of Scripture wielded the temporary sword, that is, for the protection of the godly and innocent and the punishment and repudiation of the guilty, especially in cases of capital punishment or anything touching on evildoing, saying that the use of the sword is tyrannical and heathenish, full of revenge and unmerciful. Likewise, no one could take an oath for any reason if he wants to be a Christian, holding strictly to the words of Christ, 'Swear not at all,' not seeing that in order to promote Christian doctrine and to establish the truth, the apostle swore frequently and Christ himself swore. . . . No Christian could wage war or carry or use arms for his own welfare or his neighbor's; and for that reason they wanted the gates of the city to be lifted from their hinges and removed. . . . In short, they made everything depend on the will of God . . ." (Fast, 1973, pp. 698-99).*

After the ordinance in St. Gallen forbidding Anabaptism, which Vadian helped to write (see 70B, above), the council swore in 200 men to be on call around the clock to appear at the Rathaus on a moment's notice with arms and weapons to suppress any indication of an Anabaptist gathering. Uliman, the main Anabaptist leader, whom Grebel baptized in the Rhine (see 69A/350/17ff.) was thrown into prison and subsequently banished from the canton and beheaded in Waldsee in Swabia. Anabaptism was broken in St. Gallen, not according to the example of Jesus or the precept of love, but according to the power and authority of the state, acting in concert with the established church.

By temperament and character, Vadian was a moderate and inclined toward tolerance. Thus Kessler wrote that *"Vadian sought to refute the turbulent nature, the incredible delusion of the Anabaptists, neither by means of the esteem which he enjoyed, nor through harsh punishment, but rather courageously through reason and evidence from the Bible"* (quoted in Ninck, 1936, p. 119). Yet Vadian was willing to use all of the powers of his office to suppress the movement and largely succeeded in doing so within the confines of his canton.

It is not surprising, therefore, that in the following critique of such gifted leaders as Hätzer and Hubmaier and such a noble spirit as Denk, not to mention the organizational contributions of Grebel, the "ringleader of the Anabaptists," he has little good to say. He sees only their alleged heresy. The letter was written to Johannes Zwick, the Reformer in Constance (see Cast of Characters No. 105), who, having attended the Second Zurich Disputation, may have remembered the young man Grebel and the questions he posed about the content and method of the reformation of Christ's church.

I have come to know by experience natures both most scrupulously peevish and most peevishly scrupulous.[1] They charge onto the field of scriptural study, but nothing ever pleases them save what they themselves have brought before the public as choice, sublime, rare, admirable, and unspoiled from time past. They praise and defend thoughtlessly hard and unusual things so that they should not even give an appearance of giving heed to someone who reminds them of better things, still less that they should seem to bear with them in any way.

Take my own Conrad Grebel of Zurich, a man endowed with great gifts, born into an outstanding family. Yet, stirred up by the promptings of a few,[2] he began to spread in Zurich the dogma that baptism must be repeated. With the greatest obstinacy, he began to examine things once fixed and firm so that he refused to listen even to me, whom he had once held in the highest esteem. I warned him time and again with great earnestness; but shortly thereafter, violating the laws of friendship and blood, he reviled and insulted me both publicly and in private.[3]

Take Denk,[4] that most promising young man. He was so outstanding that he even overcame the handicap of age and seemed older than he was. But he made ill use of his gifts, so that with great force he came to defend Origen's opinion[5] about the eventual freeing and salvation of the damned by a subtle use of Scripture you would not believe. He praised the fullness of God's mercy as if he were addressing a rally, so that it appeared to give hope that the most wicked and reprobate of men could gain a salvation which might come to them some day, albeit after a long while.

You remember Hätzer,[6] a man of most affable nature (for so highly do I speak of our own men), an outstanding man in so many ways, endowed with languages and an admirably quick nature, concerning whom I acted more than once lest he perish for going beyond what it is fitting to know.

More than once I tried to divert Balthasar Hubmaier[7] from the madness of my friend Grebel. He was burned alive at Vienna, a most eloquent and educated man, but to no avail and (the Lord is my witness) to my great personal sorrow. Some wondrous and incredible new mania had corrupted all of these men. Whatever they said, whatever they taught, was froth and foam (equal to Persius)[8] and thickness of shell. Within, all was bombast, the tipoff of unstable teaching, and words a foot and a half long. If you had entrusted the reins of the church's government to such otherwise learned, adjustable, and well-educated men (I maintain silence about the notoriety of the family of certain ones),[9] good God! What a holocaust, what a downfall from the simple and sensible teaching of Christ, what an evil for the world would they not have stirred up? No pope, no Sophists, no hypocrites of solid piety could have done as much harm in centuries as they could have done in a few years. The mythical fire of

Phaethon[10] and his rash impudence would not have been as great as the real one they would have caused for all of us.

Original Publication: *D. Joachimi Vadiani ... ad D.Joan. Zuiccium ... epistola ...* (Zurich, 1540), pp. 19a-20a
Transcription: Fast, No. 579

Chαραcter Profiles

(With References to the Letters and Documents)

1. **Aberli, Heinrich,** a baker on the Renweg in Zurich, was one of Zwingli's early Reformation Stürmer (assault party), together with Grebel, Pur, Claus and Hans Hottinger, Ockenfuss, and Hochrütiner. He was involved in the first violation of the Lenten fast (March, 1522), the planning of the Badenschenke (May; see 47A/170/8ff., 171/28ff.), the preaching against the monks in their own pulpits (47B/175/18 and 47C/177/22-23), and the Bible discussions at Castelberger's house (51B/204/22ff.). Together with Pur and Ockenfuss, he was one of the signers of Grebel's letters to Müntzer (63/292/8 and 64/294/7-8). Blanke's comment that he was "one of the most faithful members of Grebel's circle" (1961, p. 49) requires interpretation. On October 4, 1524, one month after he signed Grebel's letter to Müntzer, a contingent of volunteer soldiers from Zurich arrived in Waldshut to assist Hubmaier and the cause of Protestantism in their "war for the gospel" against their Austrian overlords; and the secretary of the Zurich contingent, Rudolph Collin (see Cast of Characters, no. 16), wrote to Aberli "to send us about forty or fifty honest well-armed Christian fellows" (quoted in Stayer, pp. 104-5 and Bergsten, pp. 118, 152-53). It is not known whether or how Aberli responded or whether in fact, like Hubmaier and later Brötli, he assented to the use of the sword for the cause of the Reformation. But evidence like this led Stayer to question the conclusion that nonresistance was a definitely and clearly formulated principle among the Grebel circle. It was in Aberli's house that Blaurock went upon release from prison on February 24, 1525 (Quellen 1, pp. 59-60). Aberli was subsequently baptized by Blaurock in the house of Jacob Hottinger (*ibid.,* p. 62). On March 16, he was arrested with Hans Ockenfuss, Michael Sattler, and others, and thoroughly cross-examined by Zwingli and selected councilmen (*ibid.,* pp.61-74). He was released upon his promise "to desist from such rebaptism and neither to speak nor act against infant baptism." He soon defied this order and resumed preaching and baptizing. Among those he baptized on the way to Hallau was his wife (*ibid.,* p. 159). In December he harbored Hubmaier in his home when the latter fled from Waldshut (*ibid.,* p. 161). He then took Hubmaier to an inn called the Green Shield, kept by a widow named Bluntschli, who with her maid, Regula Gletzli, had been baptized by Aberli a week before. Aberli was again arrested and brought to trial. In his self-defense, "he asked Milords to do their best for him and release him from prison to go home to his household. He would desist from such rebaptism (as far

as God would grant him grace) and be obedient to Milords, for he saw well that he was not called to baptize but to bake bread" (*ibid.,* pp. 163-4). On the basis of this testimony, he was fined fifteen pounds for each of six persons he admitted to having baptized and released. This is the last record of him in Quellen 1, and it does not seem likely that he was henceforth an active member of the movement.

2. **Ab-Iberg, Fridli,** came from the Catholic canton of Schwyz, where Eberli Bolt, the first Anabaptist martyr, was burned at the stake on May 29, 1525 (see 69E). Anthony Roggenacher and Jacob Hottinger, Jr., were in touch with Bolt at the time (see 69E/376/30-31), and it is likely that Roggenacher and Ab-Iberg fled Schwyz together. After an imprisonment in Zurich (see 71M/446/26ff.) and their escape (71-0/452/1) Ab-Iberg was recaptured and expelled from the canton on threat of death upon return (452/19-22). He accompanied Jacob Hottinger to Basel for awhile, where they worked as cowhands at the Rotten estate (see Quellen 1, no.187). Apparently Ab-Iberg returned to the Zurich area, for at the end of November, the Zurich magistrates received the following letter from his relatives: "Noble, strict, steadfast, pious, wise, above all, kind lords and good friends. Our friendly, willing service and whatever we honor, cherish, and possess be at all times with special diligence at the disposal of y[our] h[onorable] w[isdom]. Gracious lords and good friends: In recent years, our relative, Fridli Ab-Iberg, got unfortunately involved with the Anabaptists, so that he had to retreat from his fatherland and went to your city and lived there for a time and (as we understand) things went well for him for awhile. However, he finally loaded so much suspicion upon himself on account of the Anabaptists over the prohibition of y[our] h[onorable] w[isdom] that after his trial he was forced to leave your city and jurisdiction and was denied credit, employment, and residence in your jurisdiction. And now for awhile, he has been in perilous circumstances; and we, his relatives (as those who are utterly, sorrowfully burdened because of his actions) are writing. Inasmuch as he has quit the Anabaptists and will in no wise pay attention to them, we want to be helpful to him with all our ability on behalf of our lords and magistrates so that in due time he might return again to his own. Although we are aware that such is not found to be acceptable to our lords, yet we hope (the Lord God willing) that in time it will be obtained. Our aforementioned cousin has reported concerning this that he will henceforth in no wise pay attention to the mentioned Anabaptists; and in order that he may have a home place at which to stay, until we can help him on behalf of our lords, we humbly and diligently entreat y[our] h[onorable] w[isdom] to open again to our mentioned cousin your city and land and graciously allow him to reside there, in view of the fact that he was led into such error by other people because of his naiveté. We believe that from now on he will yield to your wishes and prove obedient. In so doing he will honor and give proof to y[our] h[onorable] w[isdom], in consequence of which we will be disposed to respect you for mercy and Christian understanding. This we desire always with special diligence to be indebted to you with good will. Dated November 27, 1526, and requesting herewith to receive your favorable reply. Always acknowledging y[our] h[onorable] w[isdom], Caspar Ab-Iberg, Uli Jacob, Adrian Vischli, Jost Lindower, all of the Council of Schwyz—relatives of Fridli Ab-Iberg" (*Ibid.,* no. 194, pp. 211-2).

3. **Ammann, John Jacob,** student of Glarean in Paris (1517-19), informant between Glarean and Myconius about Grebel's behavior (7A/84/11, 28-29, 41ff.),

returned to his native Zurich after the spring semester of 1519, then attended the universities of Basel and Milan (1519-21), together with his friend Collin (see #16, below). Upon return to Zurich he was part of a close circle of friends including Zwingli, Grebel, and Binder (35/147/21-22, 47E/186/26). On June 26, 1524, he married Grebel's youngest sister, Dorothy; but she was only fifteen years of age and the marriage was annulled on June 15, 1525. In 1526 he and Collin were appointed successors to Ceporin as Greek and Hebrew teachers in the theological school founded by Zwingli the previous summer. In later years he occupied the office of schoolmaster. He died in 1573.

4. **Binder, Jörg,** came from a leading Zurich family and was a student of Vadian (1513-19) and a fellow student of Grebel (1515-18) in Vienna. In the summer of 1519 he succeeded Myconius as schoolmaster at the Grossmünster in Zurich. He became an ardent supporter of the Zwinglian Reformation (see 47E/186/26). Grebel refers to him in four letters (6, 25, 29, 35). His reference to Binder "who though he wills it not is yet dear to me" (6/81/19-20) is given more elaborate expression in a poem Grebel wrote about him (25/126/36ff.). Apparently Binder had not become as close a friend as Collin; and in November 1526, he gave incriminating testimony in the trial of Jacob Grebel (Epi.A/465/31ff.) reporting among other things that for a time he had received Conrad's stipend in Vienna after the latter left for Paris (but see 5/fn.40).

5. **Blaurock, Jörg,** also called Jörg Cajacob, Romanesque form of the family name "Jörg of the House of Jacob," came from Bonaduz, six miles west of Chur in the Grisons, where in 1511 his father, Lutzi Cajacob, was a spokesman for five neighboring villages concerning some peasant grievances. Jörg attended the University of Leipzig in 1513 and apparently received the usual preparation for the priesthood. From 1516 to 1518 he served as pastor in the village of Trins in his native Roman Catholic diocese of Chur. Little is known about him from that time until his appearance in Zurich in January 1525, except that in 1523 he renounced his clerical vow of celibacy and married a wife. He arrived in Zurich in time to participate in the first believer's baptism (68F/341/7-8 and 342/11ff.) and perhaps also the First Public Disputation on Baptism (68B/335). It was said that he got his name, Blaurock, because he was wearing a blue coat at the disputation. In any case, he was the first person to receive believer's baptism, having requested Grebel "for God's sake to baptize him" (342/23). From then until he was whipped out of Zurich on the day Mantz was executed (Epi.B/474/7ff.), his story is closely intertwined with theirs, except for the peculiar style of his leadership. In Hinwil, he was a pulpit stormer, usurping the pulpit on a Sunday morning in October 1525, saying, "Whose place is this? If this is God's place, where the Word of God is proclaimed, I am a messenger from the Father to proclaim the Word of God" (71H/430/1-3). He had tried this in Zollikon eight months earlier (see Quellen 1, p. 39), and Blanke concludes that "for a hotspur like Blaurock, the development of the Anabaptist movement in Zollikon was too slow. He wanted to attempt to convert the population, if possible, at one stroke through preaching in the church. The authority for it he drew from his highly intensified sense of mission. He felt himself to be a prophet with a direct calling to spread the Word of God and cleanse the temple of God. But the test of strength failed in Zollikon. Blaurock could not deliver his message to the people. On the contrary, through his forwardness he

planted the seed of the downfall of the Zollikon Anabaptist congregation. For, through the incident in the church, the state authorities saw themselves induced to step in. On Monday, January 30, 1525, the city police appeared in Zollikon and arrested Blaurock, Mantz, and all the farmers who had been baptized in the past eight days" (Blanke, pp. 31-32, based on Quellen 1, pp. 37-39). Blaurock employed this same impetuous style in the disputations on baptism (see 69C/373/10ff.). He and Grebel were arrested in Grüningen following the October pulpit-storming incident described above (71H/430/19ff.). His trial testimony in November was a bitter declaration that Zwingli, Jud, Luther, and the pope and their ilk were all thieves and robbers (71K/440/12-19, 441/2-7). The hearsay testimony of Heinrich Brennwald that Blaurock had threatened the use of force by Anabaptists against the state (71K/437/38-41, 139/2-6) was denied by Blaurock (71M/441/8-10). Nevertheless, on November 18, he was sentenced to life imprisonment with Grebel and Mantz (442/14ff.), retried and resentenced in March (71M/446/38ff.), and escaped with them later in the month (71-0/450). He and Mantz were recaptured the following October, retried, and sentenced on January 5, respectively, to banishment and death (Epilogue B). Blaurock left the canton for the last time but remained active in the missionary spread of the movement in Bern, the Grisons, Appenzell, and in the Tirol, following his final departure from Switzerland. In a remarkable ministry in the region south of Innsbruck, where he provided a link between the Swiss and Moravian wings of the movement, he teamed up with Hans Langegger, with whom he was burned at the stake on September 6, 1529.

6. **Bolt, Eberli,** known as Hypolytus (Eberli was probably his family name), first Swiss Anabaptist martyr, was burned at the stake in his home town of Lachen, canton of Schwyz on May 29, 1525 (69E/376/25ff.). Kessler identified him as a peasant farmer and called him "a pious goodhearted man" whom Kürsiner and Hottinger talked into accompanying them to St. Gallen (376/28), where he was baptized and pressed into preaching service on behalf of the movement because he could speak well (377/3-4). The masses came to hear him on a hillside called Berlisberg (377/10-11). He presented a Zwinglian interpretatation of the Lord's Supper and was interrupted by Burgauer, the pastor at St. Lawrence, who held to Luther's view of the Supper (377/14ff.). He then preached believer's baptism at the Butcher's Hall in St. Gallen, where many from the city and surrounding region came to be baptized (377/22ff.). When he returned to his home a few days later, he and a priest companion were arrested, tried, and burned at the stake (377/35-38).

7. **Bosshart, Marx,** native of Zollikon, loyal companion of Grebel, with whom he worked in the district of Grüningen in July 1525 (see 70F/413/17ff., 415/17ff., and 71C/420/9-10). Prior to that he lived with his father-in-law, Ruedi Thomann, a prosperous Zollikon farmer, in whose home in Gstadstrasse (now nos. 23-25) a group of Anabaptists met on the evening of January 25, 1525 (see Blanke, p.25). Wilhelm Reublin and Hans Brötli, two of the Anabaptists who were banished from Zurich following the disputation on January 17 (68E/338), were invited to the Thomann house for a farewell supper. In the course of the evening they were joined by Mantz, Blaurock, Jacob Hottinger, Hans Bruggbach, and Heinrich Thomann. After Bible study and discussion, Bruggbach and Hottinger asked for baptism, after which the group celebrated the Lord's Supper. Bosshart was deeply moved by these events and could not sleep that night. Early in the

morning he woke his father-in-law, Mantz, and Blaurock, to tell them about his distress. Blaurock reminded him that he had been a lax young man and that in accordance with Ephesians 4:22-24 he needed to repent and put off the old Adam and put on the new. Bosshart was eager to do this on the basis of which Blaurock baptized him. He immediately became an active leader in the movement in Zollikon and the area between Lake Zurich and Winterthur, suffering several imprisonments in February (70F/415/26ff.). In a court hearing in March concerning an Anabaptist meeting in the inn, Zum Salmon, he observed that "Milords of Zurich wink at Zwingli's faults and Zwingli at Milords' " (Quellen 1, p.381). In the summer of that year when the movement in the highlands was at its height, he traveled with Grebel preaching and baptizing (70F/415/31-33). On July 5, the two were summoned to Zurich on a charge of slander against Zwingli's booklet on baptism (69C/363 and 70F/415/34ff.). Grebel refused to go without a letter of safe conduct (71/416), but Bosshart appeared on July 11 (71A/417), only to be imprisoned again until August 2, when he was released upon payment of a bond of 100 pounds, a fine of one silver mark, and a promise to quit preaching and baptizing (Quellen 1, pp.95-96). Nothing further is known about him, except that while he was imprisoned, three men from Oberwinterthur, one of whom was his brother-in-law, in whose home Grebel had visited, came to Zurich to see him (71B/418).

8. **Brennwald, Heinrich** (c.1476-1551), provost of the canons at Embrach, a monastic town ten miles northeast of Zurich. He matriculated at the University of Basel in 1494. In 1523 he was on the council-appointed commission to design a plan to implement the findings of the Second Zurich Disputation (see 57F/254/33-34, 59/276/7-8) and in 1524 he was one of the first priests to marry. In 1525 he was chosen by the Zurich Council as head of the newly established charity organization, and it was in this role that he testified against Blaurock in the November 1525 trial of the Anabaptists (71K/438/41). In November of 1526, his brother, Felix Brennwald, stood trial with Jacob Grebel; and Heinrich wrote about the affair to his son, Jodocus, who in turn informed the Strasbourg Reformer, Capito (see Epi.A/461/21-24).

9. **Brennwald, Karl,** was converted to Anabaptism in January 1526 by Anthony Roggenacher, who described the incident to the Zurich court as follows: "On Sunday, January 28th, Karl Brennwald came to him in his house, sat down by him, and said that since he had learned so much about the Holy Scriptures and was now a child [of God], he entreated him with tears in his eyes and for God's sake to give him the water of baptism. At which he (this witness) was startled, for he had not known what his convictions were. He thought perhaps he had wanted to persecute or ridicule him. He begged him kindly to release him from the request, but Karl Brennwald as before with tears in his eyes and for God's sake declared that he baptize him and down on his knees" (Quellen 1, pp. 165-6). Shortly thereafter Brennwald was meeting with some Anabaptists in the village of Oberglat, six miles north of Zurich (Quellen 1, no.169). On February 19, he accompanied Hans and Junghans Künzi (see 71Q/fn.1) to Seeb near Bülach to the home of Hans Meiers, which became a regular Anabaptist meeting place (Quellen, nos. 169 and 291). On February 22, he was at another Anabaptist meeting place, the Widerkerin house in Zurich, where he baptized Ernst von Glätz from Silesia (71M/445/4-7). By March 5 he was imprisoned in the New Tower along with

Grebel and the others (71M/445/34-38, 447/3). On March 21 he called attention to an unlocked shutter which led to their prison escape (71-0/450/18-20). He fled to Embrach, just ten miles northeast of Zurich, where he labored for an indefinite period of time. The circle here included Michael Sattler, Muprat of Constance, Hans Ockenfuss, Conrad Winkler, Hans Künzi, and others (Quellen, no.249), no doubt including Michael Wüst, the cousin of Heinrich Bullinger (see 71P/453). Here he and Sattler ministered to the others (Quellen 1, no.246). He then went to Basel, where he helped to lead the movement through his preaching and teaching. In June 1527 he was meeting with Pfistermeyer and others in the house of Hans Altenbach, when they were arrested by the Basel authorities. As part of his testimony to the court, he read a list of articles of his faith; and the court asked Oecolampad, the Basel Reformer, to write a refutation of them. It was entitled *Unterrichtung von der Wiedertaufe, von der Obrigheit, und von dem Eyd auf Karlins N. Wiedertäufers Artikel* (see ME, I, p.241). The Roman Catholic archbishop Augustinus Marius gave testimony that was milder in tone concerning the Anabaptists than that of Oecolampad, concluding that "to us and our dear Mother Church, Dr. Husschin and his published articles are worse than those of Carlin and his followers" (*Aktensammlung*, II, 63/291/p. 586.28).

10. **Brötli, Hans,** assistant priest in Zollikon (see 68G/343/20-21) until he, Reublin, Hätzer, and Castelberger were banished from Zurich for their unrecanted Anabaptism (68E/338/16). A former Catholic priest from Quarten am Walensee in the Grisons, he had been living in Zollikon since 1523 without parish assignment, serving as a kind of assistant priest instructing the peasants in the gospel following Paul's example of not living on tithes and offerings but by the work of his hands. He and his wife and child lived in the home of the local shoemaker, Fridli Schumacher, whom Brötli baptized, marking the beginning of the Anabaptist congregation in Zollikon (see Blanke, pp. 21ff.). Following his banishment, Brötli went to Hallau in the canton of Schaffhausen, where he had further contact with Grebel (68J/350/19, 351/24-25) and from where in February 1525 he sent two letters back to his former congregation (see 68G). Despite warnings from Zurich to Schaffhausen, Reublin and Brötli converted and baptized nearly the entire community of Hallau, which protected their new leaders from the Schaffhausen authorities. They got some support also from Hubmaier's town of Waldshut, until the Anabaptists were driven from the region by Austrian forces. Brötli was burned at the stake in 1528.

11. **Burgauer, Benedict** (1494-1548), student of Vadian and classmate of Grebel in Vienna, priest in Marbach on the Rhein, north of St. Gallen, people's priest at St. Lawrence's in St. Gallen (1519-28). In his early years in St. Gallen, he retained a friendship with Grebel (24/124/31-32, 32A/142/27-28) and a sympathy for the Zwinglian Reformation; but in 1523 his retention of Roman Catholic doctrines of the mass, prayers for the dead, purgatory, confession, and absolution (see 54A) and his growing opposition to the reform movement in St. Gallen got him into increasing conflict with Vadian and Grebel (see 56/225/13-21). Following the official council mandate for the Reformation in St. Gallen in February 1524, he was put through an official disciplinary process led by Vadian; and he was asked to retract his "erroneous" position and to agree henceforth to preach according to the official Reformation mandate (see 68M/fn.2). In 1528, because of his stand in favor of Luther's view of the Lord's Supper (see 69E/377/14-16), he was forced to

resign his pastorate in St. Gallen, accepting a call to Schaffhausen, where he remained until 1536. Grebel's references to Burgauer in letters 24, 25, 34, 38, 45, 50, 52, 53, 54, and 58 chronicle the transition from friendship to enmity and the bitter comment, "I hope that another laborer will succeed to the harvest [field] of St. Gallen, and that this one at last will be sent from God" (52/208/5ff.).

12. **Carlstadt, Andreas** (1480-1541). Following theological studies at Erfurt (1499) and Cologne (1503), he went to Wittenberg (1505), where he became professor of theology at the university and joined Luther in the work of the Reformation. In his own verbal and written attacks on the abuses in the church, he tended to be more radical than Luther and thus closer in attitude and style to the Anabaptists concerning such issues as faith and works, the oath, baptism, communion, and the priesthood of believers. When Luther returned to Wittenberg from the Wartburg in 1522, Carlstadt retreated to his pastorate in Orlamünde until he was banished from the territory in September 1524, about the time that he and Grebel entered into correspondence (62/283/14). It is not clear who initiated the correspondence, but the Grebel group wrote at least three letters to him and received two in return (see 63/291/4ff., 64/292/27, and 65/295/16-17). They read his writings and considered him one of "the purest proclaimers and preachers of the purest Word of God" (63/289/4-5), hoping that he would take the lead in writing against infant baptism (63/291/15-16). In October, Carlstadt's brother-in-law, Gerhard Westerburg, came to Zurich to oversee the printing of eight of his newly written pamphlets (see 65/295/17ff.). With the help of the Grebel group, arrangements were made for their printing in Basel, where they were taken by Westerburg and Felix Mantz. When Carlstadt fled Saxony, he came to Zurich on his way to Basel and Strasbourg and apparently met with the Grebel group sometime near the end of October 1524. The evidence for this is a comment Zwingli made that "the Grebel group prevented Carlstadt from visiting him during his stay in Zurich" (Bender, p. 110; ZW, IV, p. 464). When Luther had read the pamphlets and observed how widespread was their potential distribution and influence, he wrote his two-volume refutation entitled "Against the Heavenly Prophets Concerning Images and Sacrament" (see 67E/329/12ff.). Upon Carlstadt's request Luther consented to his return to Wittenburg in 1525; but the old hostilities recurred and forced him to flee again in 1529, this time to East Friesland in the Netherlands. In 1531 he was back in Zurich, where upon the recommendations of Bucer in Strasbourg and Oecolampad in Basel, Zwingli got him employment as a proofreader in Froschauer's printshop. In Zurich, where he became a chaplain at the Hospital, and in Alstätten, where he had a temporary pastorate, he supported the Zwinglian Reformation. In 1534 he became a preacher at St. Peter's in Basel and subsequently professor at the university, where he remained until his death.

13. **Castelberger, Andreas,** also called Andreas on the Crutches, Limping Andreas, or simply The Cripple, was a bookseller by trade. He came from Chur in the unfederated canton of Graubünden, worked for Zwingli and others as a colporteur between Glarus, Einsiedeln, and Basel, and then opened a bookshop in Zurich, stocking it with purchases he made directly from printers in Basel, Ingolstadt, Nurenberg, Frankfurt, and elsewhere (see 51/195/2). As early as 1522 he conducted an informal school in several homes at which he taught the Bible, particularly the Letter of Paul to the Romans (see 51B/204/21ff.). On Ash

Wednesday of that year, together with Zwingli, Jud, Utinger, Aberli, Pur, Ockenfuss, and others, he participated in the violations of the Lenten fast at the house of the printer, Froschauer. He became known for his witness against usury (51B/205/25) and war (206/4). He joined Grebel in the formulation of Anabaptist doctrines to send to Carlstadt (64/292/27) and Müntzer (63/292/7, 64/294/7) and the founding of the Anabaptist church, for which he was banished from Zurich by mandate of Jan. 21, 1525 (68E/338/16). Because of ill health, his banishment was postponed one month by council mandate of Jan. 28; and on Feb. 22, he addressed a petition to the council for permission to continue to live in Zurich with his family, referring to the severe illness he had suffered all winter (see 69/fn.2). A two-month stay of sentence was granted at the end of which Grebel wrote a poignant letter to him, asking Castelberger to sell his books along with his own (see 69/357/31ff.). Castelberger returned to his homeland in Chur, where he continued to promote the cause of Anabaptism.

14. **Charles V** (1500-1558), heir of the house of Hapsburg; grandson of Maximilian I (see Cast of Characters No. 68); son of Philip I, king of Castile, who died at 28 years of age; king of Bergundy (1506); king of Spain (Charles I, 1516); elected Holy Roman Emperor on June 28, 1519, ruling over a dominion so large by virtue of his grandfather's marriage treaties that it was said "the sun never set on his empire." In 1521 in a family pact between himself and his brother Ferdinand (see Cast of Characters No. 24), he gave the latter the Austrian share of their inheritance in exchange for a promise to act as the emperor's regent in all German lands and to renounce his claims to the Spanish-Bergundian inheritance. The back-and-forth Italian wars between Charles and Francis I that began in 1521 and lasted for eight years finally ended with the French acceptance of imperial superiority. Conrad Grebel was decidedly a pro-Charles imperialist (see 34/145/29-36, 35/147/1-5, and 38/150/34-36) while his father, Jacob Grebel, vacillated because of the pension from Francis I, allegedly given for Conrad's aborted education in Paris (see 13/98/9-10, 28/136/29ff., and Epi. A/463/2-6, 466/26-28, etc.).

15. **Coct, Anemund de,** a young French nobleman who studied at the University of Wittenberg and won the friendship of Luther and Spalatin. On his return to France, he visited Zurich, where he spent two months from the end of November 1523 to the end of January 1524. He was back in Switzerland in December 1524, with particular interest in the issues of baptism and the Lord's Supper. By January 25, he was on his way to France when he wrote from Wehr to a friend in Montbeliard to send some money with a messenger to Zurich to repay a debt which he owed to Conrad Grebel. While in Zurich, he had adopted a boy named Nicholas; and in February 1525, Myconius wrote to him that Grebel would tell him more about the boy and his welfare. Apparently de Coct and Grebel had become friends with a common interest in the subject of baptism. Hofmeister later testified that Grebel and de Coct had come to him in Schaffhausen, probably in February 1525, "and talked much with him about infant baptism and tried to get him submitted to it [believer's baptism] also" (71K/438/7-10). Hofmeister further testified that de Coct returned to Zurich to discuss the matter with Zwingli and became angry because Grebel had not told him the whole truth about Zwingli's view, after which Grebel had said that "he knew very well that if he [de Coct] went to Zwingli, he would inject his poison into him also (438/22-29)." Shortly thereafter,

perhaps on his return from Zurich, de Coct became ill and died at Hofmeister's house on about March 20 (see Bender, 1950, pp. 141-42).

16. **Collin (Buehlman), Rudolph** (1499-1578), also known as Clivanus, came from humble origin in Luzern and in 1516 was enabled by rich friends to study in Basel under Glarean, in Vienna under Vadian (1517-19; see 1A/58/7), and in Milan (1520-21). He then taught for two years in Luzern, coming to Zurich in 1524, where he learned a rope-making trade and conducted a boarding house. He became a friend of Zwingli, whom he accompanied on various diplomatic missions. In October 1524, he accompanied a group of volunteers from Zurich in the military defense of Waldshut, where Hubmaier was the Reformation pastor (see Bergsten, pp. 118, 152-53). Hubmaier later described Collin as "his special friend" (*ibid.*, p. 153). In 1526 he and John Jacob Ammann (see Cast of Characters No. 3), who was with him in Milan, were appointed professors in Greek in the Zurich theological school, a position he held for many years. Grebel refers to him in six of his letters: 5/73/28ff., 6/81/18-19, 8/85/26ff., 12/95/31-32, 20/116/22, and 42/157/39

17. **Cratander (Hartman), Andreas,** native of Strasbourg, became one of the leading printers of Basel (1518-36). He was a student at Heidelberg (1502-05), printer's helper in Basel (1505-12) and in Strasbourg (1512-18), proofreader with Adam Petri in Basel (1516-18), and an independent printer thereafter. A scholar and friend of humanists, he ran a press that was known throughout Europe for its fine editions of the Latin classics and church fathers. He published the second edition of Vadian's *Pomponius Mela* in 1522 (see 31/fn.1, 40/155/1-4, 47/165/24-27). Grebel helped to prepare the copy for publication, living with him for several weeks during the process (38/150/19-25, 39A) and serving as messenger between him and Vadian (31/140/8-9, 39/151/10-11, and 40/154/36ff.).

18. **Engelhart, Conrad,** bailiff of Hyburg, was the brother of Heinrich (see Cast of Characters No. 19) and a first cousin of Jacob Grebel (see p. 28). He accompanied Jacob to the Swiss Confederate Diet at Luzern and to the peace negotiations with the French at Geneva in 1516, following the ill-fated Battle of Marignano (see Epi. A/467/9-11).

19. **Engelhart, Heinrich** (c.1471-1551), pastor at the Fraumünster in Zurich, was the brother of Conrad (see Cast of Characters No. 18) and a first cousin of Jacob Grebel (see p. 28). He entered the University of Heidelberg in 1487, earning the baccalaureate and doctorate. He became the people's priest at the Fraumünster in 1496. He was later appointed a canon of the Grossmünster chapter, a position he resigned on April 29, 1521, so that Zwingli, with whom he was intimately associated in the cause of the Reformation, could be appointed his successor. The significance of this sacrificial resignation was that Zwingli could then resign as people's priest, thereby severing his obligations to the bishop of Constance and be locally appointed a canon of the cathedral chapter, thereby obtaining Zurich citizenship, local financial support, and direct authorization to preach the evangelical Reformation doctrine. Engelhart, who through Zwingli's Reformation leadership, "was changed from a doctor of Roman law to a poor scholar of Christ" (HSB, p. 80), remained as the loyal pastor at the Fraumünster, where Conrad Grebel and

Barbara were officially married in his presence (see 47/165/5-7) and where Myconius came to serve as the reader and schoolmaster (see Epi.A/465/38).

20. **Erasmus, Desiderius** (1466-1536), greatest of the 16th-century Christian humanists; born in Rotterdam; ordained to the priesthood in an Augustinian monastery in the Netherlands (1492); released from monastic life by his bishop in favor of a career of scholarship and travels; attended the University of Paris (1495-99); sojourned for various lengths of time in England, where he was befriended by Sir Thomas More and John Colet, with whom he collaborated to harmonize the old faith with the new spirit of humanism by abandoning scholasticism in favor of the recovery of biblical studies, and in Holland, Belgium, France, Switzerland, and Italy, where he received a Doctor of Divinity degree at the University of Turin (1506-09). He became known throughout Europe as the author of such works as *The Adagio* (1500), a collection of Greek and Latin proverbs, *The Handbook for the Christian Soldier* (1502), which advocated a return to the ethical teachings of Jesus, peaceful living, and the use of reason vis-á-vis warfare and religious superstitution, *The Praise of Folly* (1509), which debunked societal fictions and ecclesiastical abuses like the worship of relics. Apropos to our source volume, Erasmus had two periods of sojourn in Basel (1514-16, 1521-29), during which he met Froben, the printer of most of his subsequent writings, was a father figure to young Swiss humanist scholars like Glarean and Myconius, and served as a role model for the emerging Swiss Reformer, Zwingli. As the Reformation began to look like a revolt, threatening to split the church, Erasmus began to oppose Luther (See 71N/449/36ff.) and Zwingli (see 47F). Nevertheless, his contributions to the Reformation were substantial—especially public exposure of the abuses in the church and his edition of the Greek New Testament (Basel, 1516), which was foundational for the Reformation principle of *sola Scriptura* and the various Bible translations of the Reformation. Moreover, the Anabaptist movement was surely influenced by his ideas concerning pacifism and the return to the ethical teachings of Jesus; but this influence was tenuous in two respects. First, his pacifism was based more on rational and humanitarian interpretation of Scripture while that of the Anabaptists on a radical biblicist hermeneutic. Second, his method of reform was a gradual enlightenment and consequent reorganization—largely the work of scholars and princes rather than the common people—while Anabaptism was essentially a movement of the masses. This variance is evident in a letter from Erasmus to Morillon (1534): "The Anabaptists have flooded the Low Countries just as frogs and locusts flooded Egypt, a mad generation, doomed to die. They slipped in under the appearance of piety, but the end will be public robbery. And what is like a miracle, although they teach absurdities ... the populace is attracted as if by a fateful mood or the impulse of an evil spirit in this sect" (Allen, III, 1186, trans. in ME, II, 240). Grebel referred to Erasmus in nine letters (5, 22, 35, 43, 45, 47, 53, 57, and 69), and his deference to the man was evident throughout. He had inside information directly from Froben that Erasmus was returning to Basel (35/147/9-12); and he invited Vadian to go with him to see Erasmus (47/165/29-30), although they never went.

21. **Escher, Hans Conrad,** of Luchs, the second husband of Grebel's youngest sister, Dorothy. The Eschers belonged to the party known as Constafel (Walton) or Constables (Potter), a quasi-political organization of landed aristocrats and

merchants who were generally committed to the old faith against Zwingli's reforms and were well represented in the Zurich Council. Hans Escher, however, was an early supporter of Zwingli and was present at the Ash Wednesday, 1522, meeting in Froschauer's house, when the Lenten fast ordinance was publicly disobeyed, thus launching Zwingli's Reformation (see 47A/Intro.). He was a member of the Small Council as early as June 1523 and was one of four senators appointed to oversee the close of the convents and the fair distribution of monies to the departing nuns (see 52/207/17ff.). His sister, the Lady Meis, gave direction to Grebel when he was attempting to escape from Zurich in April 1525 (69/357/22). Nevertheless, in spite of Zwingli's strong opposition, many of the Constafel families, including the Eschers, "depended upon the revenues from mercenary service to compensate for the inadequate rents which their lands in the countryside yielded them" (Walton, p. 52). Hans Conrad Escher was one of the ten defendants, including Jacob Grebel, who stood trial in October 1526 for illegal acceptance of foreign pensions. "He was accused of having had secret dealings with the papal envoy, Ennius, of having received forbidden money, of having made disparaging remarks about Zwingli, and of having taken part in a nighttime disturbance aimed at the latter. Escher was released on 300 guilders bail on October 31 and fully rehabilitated on October 19, 1527" (Schelbert, p. 57). Some interesting things came out in his trial that reveal the mind set of Escher and other members of the Constafel. One of the prosecution witnesses testified that "Jacob Grebel, the manager of Wädenswyl [Hans Wirz, Grebel's stepbrother], Burkhart, Hans Escher, and Felix Wyss were sitting together in Conrad Baumann's house; and when they were in their drinks they happened to talk about pensions and the gospel. Hans Escher spoke up and said among other things, 'Milords have prohibited pensions and soldiering, and that we should not accept them from princes and lords; but I am going to accept them and have accepted them.' Then Felix Wyss said, 'the more the better, and I accept them too and intend to accept them.' Hans Escher said, 'I am going to take them, even if they do tend to disgrace God's fifth wonder [Zwingli] in the council' " (*Aktensammlung,* No. 1050, p. 501.)

22. **Falconibus, William de,** chaplain and secretary to a succession of papal legates in Zurich from *ca.* 1516 to *ca.* 1522 (Cardinal Schinner, Cardinal Pucci, and Ennius Filonardi). One of his assignments was the disbursement of papal pensions in Switzerland, including one to Grebel and another to Grebel's "brother-in-law" (Vadian) or Hans Conrad Escher (see Epi.A/fns.47 and 48), allegedly arranged by Jacob Grebel (see 471/12-21). Falconibus corresponded with Vadian, with whom he was a fellow student in Vienna (see 37/149/30, 46A, VB, etc.). As an official of the court of Pope Leo X *(commissarius pontifici),* he tried to be helpful to Zwingli in the early stages of the Reformation (see 19A/114/26-29; Jackson, 1900, p. 148, fn. 1); but he was gradually alienated by Zwingli's increasing anti-papal stance. Grebel refers to Falconibus in Letters 36, 37, 39, and 43, including his admission to receiving a papal gift of 100 franks from him (39/151/17-19).

23. **Falk, Jacob,** a farmer from Gossau, was the second Anabaptist martyr in Zurich, the fourth in Switzerland, executed by drowning in the Limmat on Sept. 5, 1528 (see Epi.E/518/26ff.). He was introduced to Anabaptist doctrines in July 1525, through the preaching of Grebel in Hinwil (see 71D/421/23-29). In November, he attended the Third Public Disputation on Baptism in Zurich (Quellen 1, pp.

232-33). He was probably in custodial detention at the time, for we know that he and his companion, Heini Reimann, escaped from the Tower in Grüningen on Dec. 30, 1525, and fled to Appenzell (*ibid.*, pp. 157-58). They were among fifteen Anabaptists arrested by Bailiff Berger at a meeting in the Herrlisberg Forest between Rubikon and Wetikon in May, 1526 (*ibid.*, pp. 232-34) and were henceforth imprisoned until their execution twenty-seven months later, boldly testifying that they had been baptized, had baptized others, and intended to continue baptizing whomever requested it, knowing full well that in doing so they were disobeying the public mandate against Anabaptism. During this period, they were the subjects of a long process of legal maneuvering between the Grüningen district court and the Zurich court, which was finally decided by the Confederate Diet in Bern in favor of Zurich (*ibid.*, pp. 239-43). Prior to their execution at 1:00 p.m. on Sept. 5, 1528, Falk and Reimann wrote a remarkable defense of their Anabaptist beliefs to the Diet (see Epi.E/514/4ff.) Jacob's brother Hans, a tanner from Gossau, was also a zealous Anabaptist (Quellen 1, pp. 257, 259, 276).

24. **Ferdinand I** (1503-64), archduke of Austria, was given the Austrian share of the Hapsburg possessions following the death of his grandfather, the Emperor Maximilian I, in 1519. Select young men from Switzerland served as courtiers in his court at Innsbruck. Among them was Andreas Grebel, younger brother of Conrad (29/138/11-12). Ferdinand's older brother, Charles I, king of Spain, succeeded Maximilian as emperor (1519); and Ferdinand in due course, as eastern regent for the emperor, became king of Bohemia (1526) and Hungary (1527) in addition to his Austrian crown. Upon Charles' abdication in 1556, Ferdinand himself had a short reign as emperor (1556-1564).

25. **Filonardi (Verulanus), Ennius,** bishop of Veroli, Italy (1503), was eight times papal legate in Switzerland (1513-33), appearing on the scene in Grebel's chronology in February 1521 following Antonio Pucci (see Cast of Characters No. 72) and returning to Italy in spring with a contingent of newly recruited Swiss mercenaries for the new phase of the Italian Wars (see 29/138/9-12), only to return again in July for another recruitment (see 35/147/1-5). *Persona non grata* in Zurich, he headquartered in Constance, from where he tried to suppress the "Zwinglian heresy," claiming that he would have debated Zwingli at the Second Zurich Disputation in October 1523 if he would have gotten "safe escort." He was named a cardinal in 1536.

26. **Francis I** (1494-1547), king of France (1515-47). Resuming the Italian Wars against Swiss troops fighting for the empire, he won the Battle of Marignano (1515) in which he bribed half of the Swiss troops to defect (see 6/80/41ff.); and the rest, including the battalion of which Zwingli was chaplain, suffered heavy casualties (see Epi.A/470/11-13). Thereafter Swiss statesmen like Zwingli began to renounce further military ventures and foreign bribes at the same time that Jacob Grebel accepted a pension of 900 crowns from the French king, designated as a three-year scholarship for Conrad's education in Paris (see 13/97/37-39, Epi.A/470/29-32). In the imperial election following the death of Emperor Maximilian I, Francis lost to Charles of Spain, his lifelong rival (see 6/81/6-7). Charles was a strong-willed monarch who knew how to arouse religious zeal and imperial loyalty while Francis was an impetuous, guileful spendthrift for whom war was more a

means of self-gratification than an instrument of monarchic policy (see 34/145/30-36, 146/18-19). For this and other reasons, Grebel took a strong stance against Francis (38/150/34-36). In the new phase of the wars between Francis and Charles that commenced in 1521, the Frenchman was defeated and captured at Pavia on February 10, 1525, and after eleven months of imprisonment was forced to sign the Peace of Madrid, renouncing further territorial claims, having in his words "lost all save life and honor." His subsequent search for new alliances against Charles prompted a beleaguered Zwingli to court his friendship by dedicating his major theological writing to him—*Commentary on True and False Religion* (see 68/332/23-25).

27. **Giger, Gabriel,** native of St. Gallen, was living in Zollikon at the time of his baptism by Grebel in the Mantz house (see 68K/352/16-18). He was arrested twice (February and March, 1525), along with other Zollikon Anabaptists. On March 16, he testified that because infant baptism had been introduced by the pope, he had let himself be baptized by the godly baptism, that he had not baptized anyone else so far, but that he would do so if someone requested it, and that "he is not his own; what God commands he will do" (Quellen 1, pp. 62, 73). For this audacity he was banished from Zurich, together with Sattler and Blaurock and several others: "Concerning the foreigners, namely, Peter Forster, schoolmaster from Luzern, Gabriel Giger from St. Gallen, Valentin Gredig from Savoy, Hans Bichtler from Walmenschwil, Jörg from Chur called Blaurock, and the brother in the white coat [Michael Sattler], it is decided that they shall swear out of Milords' jurisdiction and territory immediately, upon their vow to live here no longer" (Quellen 1, p. 74). Sometime after his departure, Giger wrote back to the Zollikon congregation, "Peace and grace be with you from God the Father and our Lord Jesus Christ, who gave Himself for our sins, that He might redeem us from the present awful world.... Do not take it ill of us that we did not write for so long; for there is not a week when we do not have to appear before the wolves. But we want you to know, dear brethren, that God is working in a wonderful manner among the common people. I believe that there are many who have been baptized in Christian baptism in St. Gall, in the canton of Appenzell, and in the abbot's jurisdiction.... Pray to God for us that He may not withdraw His grace.... There are probably 500 persons baptized in the Christian faith in the city and canton" (Quellen 1, pp. 75, 80; ME, II, p. 518). Giger returned to St. Gallen, where he became active in the spread of the movement. In a confession of faith prior to execution, Hans Krüsi mentioned Giger among those who had been his closest companions (see 71E/423/38). Giger was arrested in St. Gallen early in June for having committed a "sacrilege" in the balcony of the church on the occasion when Zwingli's book on baptism was being read to the public (see 70A/fn.14 and 70B/385/11-14). On April 4, 1526, he appeared before the court in Siebnen and testified that he held to the new baptism and not to the old baptism, for his first baptism had been in the name of the devil, and that he said this about the sacrament because of his love for Christ (Quellen 2, p. 418). Only two more references to him are extant. One dated April 18, 1530, is another court appearance in which he was charged with disorderly behavior and failing to attend the regular preaching service (Quellen 2, p. 453). Finally, an entry in the Rütiner diary of Dec. 18, 1537, tells of his death: "Gabriel Giger died fighting because his house was set on fire. He died the next day. Kessler heard that 'he convinced himself that he died from fire for the

sake of Christ.' In relation to the notorious Anabaptist frenzy in the public meeting, he had said, 'Who of you sits in judgment over that?' Recalling the dissention between Bolt Eberli and Benedict Burgauer [see Cast of Characters No. 11] that occurred immediately afterward, he exclaimed, 'You Burgauerites!' " (Quellen 2, p. 582).

28. **Glarean (Heinrich Loriti,** 1488-1563), brilliant Swiss humanist, Poet Laureate of the Empire (1512), instructor of Greek and Latin classics, University of Cologne (1510-14), where he took his MA under Busch and Caesarius (1510); University of Basel (1514-17), where he became an intimate friend of Erasmus and where he was licensed to operate a *bursa* (educational fraternity) in which he tutored over thirty boarders, including Conrad Grebel (1514-15); University of Paris (1517-22), where he reestablished his *bursa* with some of the same Swiss students, including Grebel (1518, 1520). After five unhappy and unfulfilling years in Paris, Glarean returned to the University of Basel (1522-29), where for a time he gave some support to the Reformation program of his old friends: Myconius, with whom he had attended Latin school at Rottweil; Zwingli, whom he had known as the people's priest in his home town of Glarus; and Oecolampad, with whom he was associated in Basel; but sometime before 1525 (see 69D/376/10-11), he turned against his Reform-minded friends and moved with Erasmus to the Roman Catholic university of Freiburg, where he remained until his death (1529-63) and was one of its most celebrated professors. In the course of his teaching career, he published numerous editions of the ancient classics, such as Livy, Horace, Ovid, Sallust, Terence, Lucian, etc. He wrote important works in the fields of geography and music: *Helvetiae Descriptio* (Basel, 1515), *Liber de Geographia unus* (Basel, 1527), and *Dodekachordon* (Basel, 1547), a 20-year study of secular and sacred music and musicians. In 1510 he drew a map of the world in which he was among the first geographers to use the name "Terra America" for the continent which was claimed to have been discovered by Amerigo Vespucci in 1497. In his younger years as a scholar and teacher, Glarean was a colorful, unruly intellectual whose "academic gang," according to Rupp (p. 371) "brawled from university to university." In Basel on one occasion, "when the hall was full of sophisters assembled for a disputation on the value of the *Parva logicalia"* (Erasmus Letters, 3, p. 81), he expressed his disdain by riding into the hall on horseback. His academic style attracted certain students but alienated others like Grebel who for one reason or another came into conflict with him (see 6/77/17ff., 7/82/19ff., 7A/84/10ff., 10/90/24ff.). Another student, Valentin Tschudi, wrote to Zwingli that "whom he loves, he loves passionately; and whom he hates, he hates without bounds" (ZW, VII, 56). Following Glarean's rejection of the Reformation and expressions of hostility toward Zwingli, the Reformer wrote, "Who would have thought that there was ... so much malignity and venom in him?" (69D/376/10ff.)

29. **Grebel, Adrian,** second son of Felix Grebel, second cousin of Conrad (see p. 26 and 69/358/8).

30. **Grebel, Agatha,** sister of Jacob Grebel and aunt of Conrad (see p. 26), a nun at the Oetenbach convent of Augustinian nuns on the outskirts of Zurich across the Limmat River. Conrad refers to her affectionately as "Grebelia" (34/145/17ff.) in connection with her counsel regarding his love affair with Barbara

(see Cast of Characters No. 33). When her convent was closed in June 1523, as a phase of the Zurich Reformation, she was among those nuns who elected to leave the order and return to the community (52/207/17-18). Her continued affection for Conrad is indicated by her having willed certain valuables to his children (Bender, p. 5).

31. **Grebel, Andreas,** younger brother of Conrad (see p. 26), served as a courtier of King Ferdinand of Austria in Innsbruck (*ca.* 1518-21; see 29/138/16-17). He died at home on Sept. 3, 1521 (see 43/159/7-8).

32. **Grebel, Barbara** (1), oldest sister of Conrad (see p. 28), married Leonard Karli of Baden (1512-20), from whom she bore three daughters, the last one following Leonard's death of the plague (29/138/23). Resident with her parents in Zurich, she tried to be a mediator in the conflict involving Conrad's love affair (35/147/13-14). She married Beat Beli of Maienfeld near Chur, where Conrad died as a fugitive in the summer of 1526 (see 71R/456/14-16).

33. **Grebel, Barbara** (2), Conrad's sweetheart and mistress (1521, first mentioned in 34/145/4-7), whom he officially married on Feb. 6, 1522 (see 47/165/5). Her identity has never been established. That she was unacceptable to Conrad's parents, perhaps because of a lower social status (39/151/36-152/9) or because she may have been a novice in one of the local nunneries (34/145/17ff.) is mentioned repeatedly in Grebel's letters. In either case, Conrad's sister by the same name served as a go-between in the difficult parental relationship (35/147/14-16). For more information, see 47/fn.1.

34. **Grebel, Conrad** *(ca.* 1498-1526), son of Councillor Jacob Grebel, student of Vadian in Vienna (1515-18), brother-in-law of Vadian (1518), fervent advocate of Zwingli's Reformation program (1522-23; see 47A-47G), leader of the dissenting group of radicals following Zwingli's strategic compromise (1523-25; see 57Cff.), founder of the Swiss Brethren called Anabaptists (1525-26). He grew up in the castle at Grüningen, where his father served as bailiff (1499-1508). He attended the Latin school in Zurich (1508-14), the University of Basel (1514-15), the University of Vienna (1515-18), and the University of Paris (1518-20). He married a girl named Barbara (Feb. 6, 1522), to whom were born three children: Theophil (1522), Joshua (1523), and Rachel (1525). He performed the first adult baptisms in Zurich (January 1525; see 68F), marking the start of the Anabaptist movement, which he subsequently promoted in Schaffhausen (February-March), St. Gallen (April), and Grüningen (June-October). He was arrested in Grüningen (Oct. 8), imprisoned in Zurich (October 1525-March 1526), escaped from prison (March 1526), and labored for six more months as a fugitive before he succumbed to the plague in Maienfeld (August 1526).

35. **Grebel, Dorothy,** Conrad's youngest sister (see p. 26), the "delight of her parents, the essence of paleness, the essence of greediness, and the unbearable tyrant of our house" (45/161/24ff.). Conrad mentions her in letters 45, 55, 56, and 61, once in reference to a serious illness (61/281/32-34). Her first marriage on June 26, 1524, at the age of 15, to John Jacob Aamann (see Cast of Characters No. 3) was annulled by the Zurich Court a year later. She was subsequently married to

541

Junker Hans Conrad Escher, member of the Constafel (see Epi.A/fn.47) and a Zurich Councillor (see Cast of Characters No. 21). Escher was arrested with Jacob Grebel in October 1526 (see Epi.A/465/27-28) on the charges of illegal acceptance of foreign money, disturbance of the peace in a local tavern, and disparaging remarks about Zwingli (Epi.A/fn.47). He was released on bail and acquitted of the charges a year later.

36. **Grebel, Euphrosine,** Conrad's older sister (see p. 28), entered the Oetenbach nunnery, where her novitiate was supervised by her aunt, Agatha Grebel (34/145/18-20), and where she died in July 1520 (see 18/109/24-27).

37. **Grebel, Felix,** first cousin of Jacob Grebel (see p. 28), made a pilgrimage to the Holy Land, for which he was knighted (*ca.* 1500). He was elected to the Large Council in 1510 and subsequently appointed bailiff in Rheinthal, where he also served as army inspector and imperial officer. He traveled to Rome in April 1519, as the representative of Zurich to lay before Pope Leo X some complaints about the peddling of indulgences by the papal commissioner, Bernhard Samson. He had twelve children (by three wives), the oldest of whom was J. Leopold Grebel, with whom Conrad attended three universities. He surrendered his Zurich citizenship in 1527 and moved to Rapperswil.

38. **Grebel, Jacob** *(ca.* 1460-1526), father of Conrad, called "Junker Grebel" because of his inherited landed nobility status. He operated an iron business begun by his father, Ulrich, was a member of the "zur Meise" guild, was elected to the Large Council (1494), and served as bailiff of Grüningen (1499-1508), with authority to collect taxes, make arrests, hold trials in civil and criminal offenses, and make official appointments within the regional jurisdiction. He was elected to the Small Council, in which he served for fourteen years (1512-26). In this office he served as occasional captain of recruiters (see 23A/122/27) and as Zurich's deputy to Diet meetings of the Swiss League. Schelbert (p. 37) knows of more than thirty such missions on which he was sent between 1521 and 1526, not to mention the many internal religio-political committees on which he served during the early period of the Zwinglian Reformation; and he concludes that "the available evidence reveals Grebel as a man of moderation intent on bridging dissensions by honest compromise . . . one of the architects of the religious reconstruction of Zurich and a consistent, if moderate and conciliatory, ally of Huldrych Zwingli" (pp. 37, 39). According to Schelbert's analysis (pp. 55-64), Grebel's execution on Oct. 30, 1526, on the charge of illegal acceptance of foreign pensions (see Epi.A, below) was a case of expedient "liquidation" by Zwingli, notwithstanding a measure of truth in the allegations.

39. **Grebel, John Leopold** *(ca.* 1496-1543), son of Felix Grebel, who was a first cousin of Conrad's father, Jacob (see p. 28). Thus, Conrad and Leopold were second cousins. Both boys studied with Glarean in Basel during the Winter Semester, 1514-15, and then entered the University of Vienna together in the spring of 1515. They studied with Vadian until the summer of 1518, when Leopold went to the University of Paris to study with Glarean again. Conrad joined him there in the autumn of that year (see 5/73/20-21). Conrad mentions Leopold thirteen times in his letters (see Index), the last time on August 11, 1523 (56/225/30-31). In 1532

Leopold became the administrator of the Grossmünster Cathedral Chapter. He died *ca.* 1542.

40. Grebel, Martha, younger sister of Conrad. Through his mediation, she married Vadian on Aug. 19, 1519. For six months following their marriage, they resided with her Uncle Hans Wirz at Wädenswil, after which they took up their permanent residence in St. Gallen. Martha had only one child, Dorothea, born in August 1523 (see 56/225/27-29).

41. Grebel, Peter, first cousin of Jacob Grebel (see p. 28), was a canon at the Grossmünster since 1484. He was forced to resign this office in August 1526, after the canonry was transformed into a theological seminary. As one of the last defenders of the old faith, he was warned by the council to conform to the Zwinglian changes or forfeit his benefice. He could not do this and moved to Baden (1526), where he died *ca.* 1534.

42. Grossmann (Megander), Caspar (1495-1545), an early supporter of the Zwinglian Reformation, was chaplain of the main Zurich hospital, a rest home for sick and infirm citizens located between the Dominican Cloister and the Limmat River. Served by the chaplain and a large staff of clerics, the hospital chapel was attended also by area residents. When the Dominican monastery was closed on Dec. 3, 1524, and the buildings were turned into another hospital, Grossmann became the pastor of the Hospital Church, an outlying parish in Zurich. The numerous public and private disputations with the Anabaptists were conducted by three of Zurich's pastors—Zwingli of the Grossmünster, Jud of St. Peter's, and Grossmann (Megander) of the Hospital Church (see 66A/fn.9, 67/301/30-31 68E/338/11-12, 70C/401/38-39, 71J/433/21-22, 436/5, and 71L/443/11-12). In 1528 Grossmann became pastor of the Münster Church in Bern and in 1538 returned to the Grossmünster in Zurich as archdeacon. He died here in 1545.

43. Hätzer, Ludwig *(ca.* 1500-1529). A native of Thurgau, he attended the University of Basel (1517-20) and studied Latin, Greek, and Hebrew with a steadfast purpose to master the Scriptures. Although he never earned an academic degree, he was ordained and became chaplain in Wädenswil on the south shore of Lake Zurich. Before the Second Disputation he moved to Zurich in order to get more directly involved in the Reformation. He wrote a definitive booklet tracing the biblical injunctions against the use of images and statues in worship (see Garside, 109-15, for a summary of its contents). Entitled *The Judgment of God Our Consort, What Man Should Do with All the Idols and Images, Drawn from the Holy Scriptures,* the pamphlet precipitated some acts of iconoclasm (see 57B/Intro.) and was a major resource document during the debates of the first day of the disputation, for which he served as recording secretary (see 57C/235/32ff., 250/28ff.). In 1524 Hätzer became increasingly critical of Zwingli's delay in implementing the reforms approved in principle in the disputation; and in another pamphlet dated June 29, he became the first member of the Zurich radicals to write against infant baptism. After the Tuesday Disputations (see 66A) and the January 17, 1525, Public Disputation on Baptism (see 68B), he was one of four dissenters to be expelled from Zurich (see 68E/338/16). Unlike the other three, however, he was not present at the first believer's baptism (see 68F); and following several precarious efforts at reform in Constance and Basel, he returned to Zwingli's side and testified against the Anabaptists at the November 1525 Disputation (see 71J). Moving to Strasbourg in 1526 he engaged in various literary and disputational activities with Hans Denk; and upon their removal to Worms, the chief fruit of his labor, in collaboration with Denk, was the translation of the Old Testament prophets, published in April, 1527—the first translation of the prophets in the Reformation period. Hätzer was arrested in Constance in 1528, tried on a contrived charge of adultery, and beheaded at the age of 29. For Vadian's critique of his character, see Epi. G/525/23ff.

44. **Hedinger, Jörg,** the servant of Jacob Grebel (see 5/74/1-3), accompanied Conrad on his journey to Paris by way of Freiburg, where they collected the first installment on Conrad's French pension (see Epi.A/469/29-35). Hedinger was forced to testify under threat of torture at the trial of Jacob in October 1526 (see Epi.A/469/20ff.).

45. **Hochrütiner, Lorenz,** a weaver from St. Gallen, became a citizen of Zurich in 1520. Zwingli liked his "witty manner" and accepted him as a Reformation comrade until his zealousness exceeded the Reformer's point of tolerance. Before that, he was a fellow participant in the act of fast-breaking in Froschauer's house on Ash Wednesday, 1522 (see 47A/Intro.) and a regular member of Castelberg's home Bible study group (51B/204,24, 205/36ff.). His involvement in various attacks on images and statues within the jurisdiction of Zurich prior to the Second Zurich Disputation (57F/Intro. and fn.19) resulted in his sentence of banishment from Zurich. Zwingli (57F) and Grebel (58) both lamented the severity of the sentence, but Grebel blamed Zwingli for willingly using Hochrütiner's iconoclasm in his Reformation strategy without defending him in his trial (58/256/18ff.). Zwingli claimed that the sentence, although harsh, was justified because Hochrütiner was too outspoken and rebellious for the good of the Reformation "in this tempestuous time" (57F/255/15). With letters of recommendation from Zwingli and Grebel, he returned to St. Gallen, where he began to promote Anabaptist doctrines. In a Bible class led by Kessler, dealing with a passage in Romans 6 about baptism on the death of Jesus, he spoke against the practice of infant baptism (see 65A/297/8ff.) and won Wolfgang Uliman to his point of view (69A/360/17-19). They were supported in their views by an eight-page letter from Grebel (65A/298/12ff.). When Hochrütiner and Uliman had gained hundreds of adherents, the civil authorities under Vadian's leadership moved against them (70A and 70B). Hochrütiner fled to Basel, where he was arrested at an Anabaptist meeting in August 1525 and expelled from the city. He went to Bern, where his son Jacob was promoting Anabaptism (see Epi.E/Intro.) and where Haller, the head pastor, gave him a measure of acceptance. He returned to Basel, where the rest of his family had remained, and was banished anew on July 24, 1526. He then went to Strasbourg, where in 1528 he acquired citizenship.

46. **Hofmeister (Oeconomus), Sebastian** (1476-1533), a Franciscan monk with a doctor of divinity degree from the University of Paris (1523), was an early convert to Zwingli's doctrine (1520). After attempting unsuccessfully to introduce the Reformation in Luzern and Constance, he became pastor in his home town of Schaffhausen (1522). He participated in both of the Zurich disputations in 1523

and was one of the three chairmen of the second conclave (57C/fns. 23 and 81). Although he first questioned the validity of infant baptism (68D/fns.10 and 11) and warmly received Grebel and other Anabaptist visitors (68J/351/6-8), he later denied this in sworn testimony (71K/438/39ff.). When the papal forces won the upper hand in Schaffhausen in August 1525, Hofmeister was sent to the diocesan headquarters in Basel for examination together with a letter that he had fomented disturbances and preached against the mass and infant baptism. He then found refuge in Zurich, where he became the copastor with Engelhart at the Fraumünster. He was one of the chairmen at the Anabaptist disputation of November 1525 (71J/433/35-36). In 1531 and 1532 he was in Bern again for the disputations with Pfistermeyer and the Zofinger Anabaptists (see Epi.E/Intro).

47. **Hohenlandenberg, Hugo von** (1457-1532), bishop of Constance (1496-1529, 1531-32). Born into landed aristocracy near Winterthur northeast of Zurich, he became deacon at St. Bartholomew's at Friesach (1477), provost at St. Mary's at Erfurt (1484), canon at Constance, Basel, and Chur (1487-92), apostolic prothonotary at Constance (1492), and bishop in 1496, ruling over the largest diocese in Switzerland and Germany, including 1,800 parishes, 350 monasteries and convents, and 17,000 priests. By virtue of his temporal rule over a territory in the vicinity of Constance, he was also a prince of the German Empire. The influence of Constance waned during his office as the number of cities in his diocese that turned Protestant increased, including Constance itself in 1526, after which he and his cathedral chapter withdrew to Meersburg, opposite Constance on the northern side of the lake, where he had restored a castle. He was at first sympathetic to Zwingli's reform goals, having ordained him to the priesthood in 1506, but was provoked by Zwingli's apparent disregard for such sacred traditions as the Lenten fast. He decided to send an official delegation to Zurich with his letter of admonition; and this in turn prompted Zwingli to write his *Archeteles*—his "once-and-for-all defense," which was a direct response to the bishop (see 47D), also marking the beginning of the latter's increasing hostility to the Reformation. Three months later, he arrested Hans Urban Wyss, Zwinglian preacher at Fislisbach, subjecting him to seven months of examination by interrogation and torture (see 49/191/31-32). This episode hastened Zurich's declaration of independence from the jurisdiction of Constance in November 1522. He refused to accept Zurich's invitation to attend the First Doctrinal Disputation in January 1523, but sent his official theologian, Johannes Faber, as observor (see 51A). In none of these ways was he able to check the Zwinglian Reformation, which finally forced him to resign his office in 1529, although the untimely death of his interim coadjutor compelled him to resume the see for the last few months of his life.

48. **Hottinger, Claus,** native of Zollikon, where his brother Jacob became the elder of the first Anabaptist congregation (1525; see 68/fn.3). Claus moved with his sister Margaret to a house in the Rennweg in Zurich, where he made a living as a shoemaker and salt-retailer. A zealous follower of Zwingli, he was in the group that violated the Lenten fast at Christopher Froschauer's house (see 47A/Intro.) on Ash Wednesday, March 5, 1522, the act that marks the operational beginning of the Reformation in Zurich. Next, he was in the group (including Grebel) that planned a *Badenschenke* in May of that year to dramatize the strength of Zwingli's support in response to the bishop's first move to suppress the Reformation in

Zurich (47A/170/21ff.). In July, he, Grebel, Aberli, and Pur were summoned before the council for preaching against the monks in their own pulpits (47B/175/ 17-21 and 47C/177/22-25). More seriously he was one of the three participants in the destruction of the large crucifix in Stadelhofen in September 1523 (see 58/256/ 18ff.), for which he was banished from Zurich on Nov. 4 for a specified two years. He went to Baden, where he spoke publicly against saint worship and the mass. He was arrested, brought to trial in Luzern, and executed on March 9, 1524, despite the intercession of the Zurich Council. His radical actions notwithstanding, he was memorialized in Zurich as the first Protestant martyr (see Bullinger, I, 145-51; Nüesch and Bruppacher, 49-51). He had been closely identified with the subsequent founders of Anabaptism and would surely have joined the movement had he survived.

49. **Hottinger, Hans,** a Zurich craftsman, serving also as night watchman in the Augustinian jail. He was sympathetic to the Zollikon Anabaptists during their imprisonment there in February 1525 and was the contact between them and their families (68I/347/15ff.). Although Blanke (p. 73) doubts it, it seems likely that this is the same Hans Hottinger who led the procession of Zollikon "prophets" to Zurich in June (see 70D/410/24ff. and Quellen 1, No. 73, pp. 80-81) and who was imprisoned with Grebel in March 1526 (71M/445/26), having been associated with him also in Grüningen (70F/413/3-5). Indeed he was more than merely the contact person in the February prison interrogations; he was himself on trial, during which it was testified that he had informed the Zollikon families that Zwingli had been defeated by their brethren, that Zwingli had claimed that there is no instance of a rebaptism in the Bible (68I/347/21ff.), that they had produced the incident told in Acts 19, and that Zwingli had admitted that they were right and would accept the "godly life" for himself (348/19). Hottinger had also charged Zwingli with inconsistency, first preaching that infants should not be baptized, and then reversing himself and "lying like a rascal, villain, and heretic" (348/27-31). He was released on promise to reform, only to stand trial again in March with Mantz and Blaurock (see Quellen 1, Nos. 54 and 64, pp. 61-62, 73-74). On the way to Waldshut to visit Hubmaier, Hottinger was baptized by Aberli. At the end of the year, the two of them harbored the fugitive, Hubmaier, in their homes in Zurich (Quellen 1, p. 161). Then in March 1526, Hottinger was imprisoned in the New Tower with Grebel and Hubmaier (see above) and told the court that "he would stay as he is" (71M/445/28). Upon his escape from prison (71-0/450/15ff.) he may have fled to Moravia and joined the Anabaptists there (see ME, II, pp. 819-20).

50. **Hottinger, Jacob,** an elderly wine-grower in Zollikon, elder brother of Claus, Hans, and Margaret (see Cast of Characters Nos. 48, 49, and 51). Like them he was identified with the Radical Reformation as early as 1523 when he openly repudiated the doctrine of transubstantiation and demanded that the cup of the Lord's Supper be given to the laity as well as the bread. When he publicly challenged people to refrain from participating in the mass until that was done, he was imprisoned and fined. Although he was not a signatory to Grebel's letter to Müntzer (Sept., 1524), he probably participated in the Tuesday Disputations, where he may have been the one "nearest to God" whom, according to Grebel, Zwingli "summoned and abused" (67/301/33ff.). If this supposition is accurate, Hottinger may also be the one Zwingli had in mind in his story of the unlearned

Anabaptist whose ignorance he exposed (see 67/fn.13). Hottinger interrupted Megander's sermon on infant baptism in January 1525 (see 68/332/1-2). On January 22 or 23, Grebel officiated at a communion service in his home (68G/343/23-27). He was subsequently baptized by Mantz in the home of Ruedi Thomann, probably on the Wednesday evening of January 25—the beginning of the Anabaptist congregation in Zollikon (see Blanke, pp. 25-26). Among the persons he baptized in turn were his wife and Hans Ockenfuss (see Cast of Characters No. 71 and Quellen 1, pp. 59-60). On January 30 he was arrested with Mantz and Blaurock and twenty-five men from Zollikon for having been rebaptized in violation of the council's decree (*ibid.*, p. 47). The two leaders were put into the Wellenberg Tower and Hottinger and his townsmen in the old Augustinian monastery, where they were questioned for nine days by the three Zurich pastors—Zwingli, Jud, and Megander—and released on February 7 (*ibid.*, p. 47). Hottinger's house was one of five places of meeting in Zollikon (Blanke, p. 53) and it was here that Heinrich Aberli (Cast of Characters No. 1) was baptized by Blaurock (*ibid.*, p. 62). Hottinger was the elder and disciplinarian in the congregation, admonishing his brethren against falling back into sin after baptism and reccommending the use of the ban in such cases according to Matthew 18 (*ibid.*, pp. 66-67). In June Hottinger accompanied Grebel to Waldshut to see Hubmaier (70E/411/21ff.). Hubmaier later testified to this visit (Quellen 1, p. 194). In August during a second imprisonment, Hottinger received a written order from the Zurich authorities that "he, this Hottinger and others, should not gang together, but go to church and there hear the Word of God (*ibid.*, pp. 103-04)." This was a crucial moment in the congregation for it prompted the brethren to a clear decision "to give up baptizing, simply live the Christian life together, and be obedient to Milords" (*ibid.*, p. 107). A year later (August 1526), however, Hottinger was imprisoned a third time because he had reneged on his promise to obey Milords, and again he seemed to be able to assure them that he would reform and was released (*ibid.*, pp. 205-06). In June 1527, he visited the imprisoned and condemned Anabaptists, Jacob Falk and Heini Reimann (see Cast of Characters Nos. 23 and 74), to encourage them to remain faithful to the end (*ibid.*, p. 247). The next report of him is dated April 4, 1528, when he was imprisoned on a diet of bread and water for leading meetings and refusing to attend the established church; but again he was released upon payment of a fine of five pounds and the usual oath of obedience, followed by the court's admonition "that he keep his sons, his wife, and servants from Anabaptism" (*ibid.*, p. 276). Following this there are several reports of appearances of a Jacob Hottinger in St. Gallen, and the record is confusing. On January 29, 1529, a Jacob Hottinger and Jörg Angenler were arrested and expelled (Quellen 2, p. 437). In his *Sabbata* (see 69E/376/29-30), Kessler reported that upon release from prison in Zurich at the end of March 1525, a priest named Anthony Kürsiner and a certain Hottinger (whom Fast, 1973, p. 606, fn. 63, identifies as the Zollikon elder) brought Bolt Eberli, whom they baptized on the way, to St. Gallen just prior to Eberli's execution in Lachen on May 29. Fast (*ibid.*, pp. 569ff.) also identifies Hottinger as the adulterer described by Zwingli in the *Elenchus* see ZW, VI:1, p. 85, line 10ff.); but this is a supposition based on flimsy evidence. Moreover, it is possible that all of these St. Gallen references pertained to a younger Jacob Hottinger (the adulterer in Zwingli's story still had dependent children at home), distinguished from "Jacob Hottinger der alt" (Quellen 1, p. 66; Blanke, p. 53). In contrast to Zwingli's indictment, Blanke refers to the elder Jacob as "the fulcrum and core of the whole

Anabaptist movement" because "before his eyes stood in particular brilliance the picture of what the early Anabaptist movement had sought to achieve. A great new idea had made him a fighter and, in the end, a man who walked alone. It was the idea of personal religious freedom and the free church. This finds expression in the answer he gave his judges in August, 1525, in clumsy language, but unmistakably clear meaning: 'For it is not given to any government to dispose over God's Word with worldly means of force. Is not after all the Word of God free?' " (Blanke, pp. 70-71; Quellen 1, p. 103).

51. **Hottinger, Margaret,** of Zollikon, sister of Jacob, Hans, and Claus. She lived in Zurich with Claus until he was martyred in Luzern in March of 1524. Little is known about how she joined the Anabaptist movement, except that she heard the preaching of Grebel and Mantz and was baptized by Blaurock (71K/440/33-38). For this, the Zurich Council decided that "she is to be spoken to and asked whether or not she intends to persist in Anabaptism and the teaching of Grebel and Mantz" and to be given the ultimatum either of imprisonment in the Wellenberg if she persisted or to do penance and be released if she recants (71K/442/20-24). She held fast to her beliefs and was imprisoned (71M/446/7-10 and 447/5-6); but following the escape from the Tower of all the male prisoners (71-0/450), she was pressured into recanting in order to gain her own release (Quellen 1, p. 183). A fascinating profile of her role in the movement was written by Anabaptist critic Johann Kessler: "Suddenly, there arose wild and arrogant error through the women of the Anabaptists, particularly one young woman from Zollikon in the canton of Zurich named Margaret Hottinger, a sister to the aforementioned Hottingers, who lived a disciplined way of life, so that she was deeply loved and respected by the Anabaptists. She went so far as to claim that she was God. And many other Anabaptists believed this and defended her against her opponents, protecting and sustaining her with the words of Christ, 'Have you not read in the law, you are gods, etc.' [Jn. 10:34] and 'Whoever keeps my commandments abides in me and I in him, etc.' [Jn. 15:10]. Moreover, this Margaret forgave and absolved the sins of those praying, and would say nothing about it nor give further judgment, but abide by the words. Following that she undertook to speak of things that nobody could understand, as if she were so deeply raised up in God that nobody could comprehend her speech, and then began to say, 'Is it not written, cursed is he who is hung upon a cross?' [Gal. 3:13]. But still [she] would say nothing further to anyone. She lived an austere life and overcame many obstacles, so that many of her followers declared that whoever speaks the most or can do the unusual which nobody can comprehend or evaluate, those were held to be the most devout and most immersed in God" (Quellen 2, p. 618).

52. **Hottinger, Rudolf,** was baptized together with his father, Conrad Hottinger, by Johann Brötli in the house of Hans Murer on January 27, 1525 (Quellen 1, Nos. 29 & 31). When he was arrested with fourteen of his Zollikon brethren, he testified that "he had been baptized and had also baptized a young woman who had beseeched him with tearful eyes; and was a servant and slave of God and must listen and wait what God's Spirit would show, teach, and tell him" (*ibid.,* No. 33). The prisoners were released nine days later after intensive cross-examination by the three Zurich pastors in the fifth so-called "private disputation" with the Anabaptists (see 68B/Intro.). He served as one of the "readers" in the Zollikon Bi-

ble study groups (*ibid.*, Nos. 56-57) and was arrested again on March 16, together with eighteen others, including Michael Sattler (*ibid.*, Nos. 54-64); and after the sixth so-called "private disputation," he was released on March 25 with a warning that a further relapse would result in banishment (*ibid.*, No. 65). Rudolf and three others were the only ones who stood by their confession, the others promising "that they would desist from such rebaptism and neither speak nor act against infant baptism (*ibid.*, No. 64, see Blanke, p. 59). The following July, the Zollikon group responded to a request from the village of Wassberg to send several brothers to read to them from the Bible; and Rudolf was one of the three sent (*ibid.*, No. 76). They were arrested on the way; and when asked how they could explain their activity in view of the prohibition, Rudolf replied that the Zurich Councillors had nevertheless permitted the Zollikon brothers "to go to each [privately] to read and also to instruct each other and to teach the Word of God" adding that "we have done nothing else than this in Zollikon; and as the request came to our church from outside, our church went outside also only as readers, not as baptizing messengers" (*ibid.*, No. 76, see Blanke, p. 67). When he was imprisoned with Grebel, Mantz, and Blaurock, in March 1526, he was more submissive to the authorities than the others, begging them "to do their best by him" (71M/445/19-28). Several weeks later, he was among the six prisoners who recanted their Anabaptist beliefs and were released (*ibid.*, No. 173). Nothing more is known about any further participation in the movement.

53. **Hotz, Hans,** Grüningen carpenter who first heard of Anabaptism during Grebel's mission to that district in July 1525 (70F/414/40ff.). In court testimony three years later, following a long period of imprisonment, he stated that "Blaurock first instructed him and also strengthened him, likewise Felix Mantz. Thus, they all encouraged one another in the Lord" (Quellen 1, p. 284). He was referring to an imprisonment with these two in Zurich between Dec. 3, 1526, when they were arrested by the Grüningen bailiff (*ibid.*, No. 198, fn. 1), and Jan. 5, 1527, when Mantz was executed and Blaurock whipped out of town. Hotz was kept in prison for another year and six months, continuing to testify that "infant baptism was the rebaptism and was not right" (*ibid.*, p. 281). He was one of a number of Grüningen Anabaptists cross-examined on this occasion, after which they were isolated in various towers and monasteries on the usual diet of bread and water. Two weeks later their leaders Falk and Reimann were executed by drowning (see Epi.E/514), and the rest were returned to court for strong admonitions to return to their regular churches to hear the Word of God and to acknowledge that infant baptism is right. Still Hotz declared that "he considers the baptism with which he was baptized in his infancy as wrong and useless; but the other baptism that he received was right; and he does not think that he has done wrong. Nor did he want to go to church to hear words of idolatry (*ibid.*, p. 288). This comment earned Hotz another month of imprisonment. It is not known when he was released; but during the next decade he was an articulate Anabaptist spokesman at the Zofingen Disputation near Bern, July 1-9, 1532, and again in the Bern Disputaion of March 11-17, 1538 (see Epi.F/521/12ff.). Following the latter disputation, the Bern Council declared that the aliens should be escorted to the border, subject to death by beheading if they ever crossed it again, because they were "leading people astray" (ME, II, p. 821). It is not known what happened to him after that.

54. Hubmaier, Balthasar (c.1480-1528), "the only trained theologian and the most prolific author among the first leaders of the Swiss-South German Anabaptist movement" (J. H. Yoder, 1959, p. 5). A native of the town of Frieberg near Augsburg, he studied at the University of Freiburg under Johann Eck, the renowned papal spokesman against Luther and other Reformers. After earning his baccalaureate here and being ordained to the priesthood, he followed Eck to the University of Ingolstadt, where he was appointed rector and earned the ThD degree in 1515. Known for his gifts of preaching, he was appointed to the Cathedral Church in Regensburg as chaplain of its newly erected chapel to the Virgin Mary, where pilgrims came and miracles were claimed. Growing doubts over the validity of the miracles led him to move to Waldshut in South Germany north of Schaffhausen (1521), where he served as pastor (1522-25) and where he began to embrace the evangelical Reformation. On May 1, 1523, he was in Zurich, conferring with Zwingli on a number of subjects, including a biblical doctrine of baptism. At that time, Zwingli had declared himself open to the idea of believer's baptism as he admitted it was practiced in the apostolic church. Hubmaier's participation in the Second Zurich Disputation in October 1523 further revealed his deep appreciation for the new leadership of Zwingli and Jud, whom he called "my dear brothers in Christ" (57/244/20-22). He spoke twice on the subject of the unscriptural worship of images and once at the request of Grebel on the abuses of the mass with particular reference to the use of the unfamiliar Latin language and the withholding of the cup from the laity (57/244/13ff.). His subsequent Reformation preaching in Waldshut met with the disapproval of the Austrian government, which attempted to suppress him by threat of military force. On September 1, 1524, he fled to Schaffhausen, where he appeared to be less safe than in Waldshut. Upon return, he gave support to an emerging resistance movement, for which freedom fighters from Zurich were requested through an old friend of Grebel, Rudolph Collin, who conveyed the request to Heinrich Aberli, a signatory to Grebel's letter to Müntzer (see Cast of Characters Nos. 16 and 1). Because of Grebel's strong nonresistant stand against all warfare (63/290/10ff.), it is unlikely that he approved Hubmaier's resort to resistance by force. In December 1524, about the time Zwingli was attempting to refute the arguments of Grebel and his friends on believer's baptism in the series of Tuesday conversations (66A/300/29ff.), Hubmaier wrote to Zwingli, asking him "for God's sake" to answer the questions on baptism he had sent earlier (ZW, VIII, No. 353, p. 254). Grebel may have known about these connections, because he wrote to Vadian in January that Hubmaier "is against Zwingli on the matter of baptism and will write against him if he does not back away" (68/332/9-11). It is not known how Grebel had come to know this when Zwingli did not. Bender (1950, p. 134) hypothesizes that Hubmaier told him about it in person during a visit to Zurich in October. It seems more likely that Hubmaier had written directly to Grebel about it, as he had done on another occasion (70E/411/29). Vadian later recalled that it was Grebel who really led Hubmaier to join the Anabaptist movement (see Epi.G/525/28-29), and Kessler told of a visit by Grebel to Hubmaier in Waldshut (69A/359/32ff.) that was probably earlier than the one reported in 70E/411, perhaps as early as January 1525. On January 16, Hubmaier wrote to Oecolampad that he had decided against infant baptism on principle, although he would still baptize infants if their parents demanded it. On February 2, Hubmaier published his first treatise on baptism, entitled *Public Entreaty to All Believers,* written as the basis for a disputation on the subject in Waldshut, namely, the thesis that in the Great Commission of Jesus, the command to baptize follows the command to evangelize. At about the same time, he was visited by several Zurich Anabaptists, Reublin and Merger, who may have been accompanied by Grebel (see 68J/351/22-28). Hubmaier is finally baptized by Reublin in April and in June asks Grebel to come to Waldshut for another consultation (70E/411/21ff.). In July he published his major treatise, *On the Christian Baptism of Believers,* which J. H. Yoder describes as "a minor masterpiece standing in sharp contrast to the disorderly construction of Zwingli's writings" (1959, p. 9). Hubmaier had read Zwingli's *Taufbüchlein* (see 69C/363/17ff.) but avoided entering into argument with it. Four months later, Zwingli published his *Answer to Doctor Balthasar's Taufbüchlein* just in time for the Third Public Disputation on Baptism in Zurich (see 71J/434/7-10). Hubmaier was expected to attend but could not get safe passage; so Grebel and Mantz were the main defendants (see 71J/433/18-20). Two weeks later, Waldshut fell to the imperial troops of King Ferdinand, and Hubmaier was forced to flee to Switzerland, where he was harbored for a few days by Aberli and Hans Hottinger (see Cast of Characters Nos. 1 and 49) and then arrested and placed into custodial confinement, pending interrogation by Zwingli, Jud, Grossmann, and Myconius. For reasons which Yoder examines in detail (1959, pp. 13-17), Hubmaier wrote a recantation, which he then repudiated; but after being subjected to torture on the rack, he renewed his recantation (71M/445/11ff.) and was deported to the Austrian border. He then fled to Augsburg and Moravia, where he had a fruitful ministry before he was kidnapped in Nikolsburg and taken to Vienna to stand trial. He was condemned to death and burned at the stake on March 10, 1528.

55. **Hujuff, Hans,** a signatory to Grebel's second letter to Müntzer (64/294/8), was a goldsmith from Halle on the Saale (near Wittenberg), the son of the court goldsmith of Cardinal Albrecht of Mainz. His brother had brought a supply of tracts by Müntzer and Luther from Saxony to Zurich (see 64/292/27ff.) and gave Grebel up-to-date information about the status of the Reformation in Germany, with particular reference to Müntzer's attitude on a number of issues (63/286/35ff., 290/12, and 64/293/7ff.). He became an active member of the Zollikon Anabaptists and is often listed with Aberli and Ockenfuss (Quellen 1, p. 414). His garden was the scene of a conversation between Felix Mantz and Zwingli (71K/437/25). On December 23, 1525, he was held for questioning on the charge of Anabaptism and released. His testimony reports having "gone [returned] to church" (Quellen 1, pp. 149-50).

56. **Hutten, Ulrich von** (1488-1523), a knighted scion of a noble family in Franconia, brilliant poet and scholar, prolific writer, fearless critic of the papacy, ardent supporter of the Reformation, impassioned advocate of German nationalism against the despotic rule of the duke of Württenberg. Among his many friends were Vadian, Erasmus, Glarean, Oecolampad, and Zwingli. After six years of reluctant novitiate in a Benedictine monastery where he was placed by his father, he escaped in 1505 and spent eight years as a wandering scholar at various universities. He stayed at Frankfurt-on-the-Oder long enough to earn a BA, the fourth to do so at the new university there. He came to Vienna and stayed with Vadian, who described him as a "wandering Odysseus," roaming from place to place, reading poetry and living off the gifts of admirers. Vadian told of how he

pulled a soiled manuscript from his pocket, revealing a poem on some loose sheets
on which he had scribbled during his travels. It was an ode to Emperor Maximilian
which Vadian and his housemates judged worthy of publication. Vadian edited it
and had it published in 1512 under the title of *Huttens Exhortatio ad D*[ominus]
Maximilianum (Hutten's Exhortation to Emperor Maximilian; see Näf, I, 189-91
and Böcking, III, 124ff.). Vadian included the foregoing account in his letter of
dedication to a colleague (see Böcking, I, 21ff.). Hutten moved on to Italy, where
he studied at Bologna and earned his bread by fighting as a mercenary in several
imperial wars. He returned home in 1513 and was reconciled to his family by his
successful avenging for the murder of a cousin by the duke of Württemberg, who
wanted to marry the cousin's wife. Von Hutten began by a series of literary *Exposures of Duke Ulrich,* published between 1515 and 1519 (Böcking, V, pp. 1ff.).
When enough public opinion against the duke had been accumulated, von Hutten
joined the armies of the Swabian League that waged the successful campaign,
March to July, 1519, that drove the duke from his kingdom. Meanwhile, von Hutten had won the friendship of Erasmus through contacts at Mainz (1514), revisited
Italy (1515-17), was crowned Poet Laureate by Maximilian (1517), and served as a
counselor to the archbishop of Mainz (1517-18). When Charles V succeeded Maximilian as emperor (1519), Hutten decided to commit himself to work for a united
Germany, attacking the territorial princes in writing and embracing the Lutheran
Reformation. His motto became *jacere alea,* "to cast the dice," or *jacta est alea,*
"the die is cast" (see 34/145/11). With increasing threats to his life from loyal papists, he fled in 1520 to the castle of his friend, Franz von Sickingen, on the Swiss
border at the Rhine, and remained for two years until Sickingen, with whom he
had fought against the duke of Württenberg, launched the ill-conceived Knight's
Revolt in August 1522, in which Hutten took part. This debacle forced him to flee
to Switzerland. He came to Basel and lived with Glarean for two months. By this
time, however, Erasmus was wary of him and refused to see him. Out of a sense of
betrayal, Hutten published a fiery attack on Erasmus, entitled *Expostulation of
Erasmus* (see Böcking, II, pp. 180ff. and 53/fn.8), accusing him of lacking the
courage to come out openly for the Reformation while secretly agreeing with
Luther (53/220/32-33). This attack so embittered Erasmus that he retaliated with a
brutal polemic of his own (see 57/226/9). Hutten then fled to Zurich, where
Zwingli gave him refuge and in so doing sacrificed his own friendship with
Erasmus and Glarean (see 69D/375/41ff.). Hutten died here on August 31. There
are six references to Hutten in the letters of Grebel, and further research on his influence on Grebel would be rewarding. Grebel made mention of two of Hutten's
"Exposures of Duke Ulrich" (20/116/26-27 and 23/120/32-33), including one
called *Phalaris,* which was modeled after the polemical style of the second-century
Greek satirist, Lucian, whom Grebel also admired above all ancient writers.
Moreover, Grebel knew that the controversy between Hutten and Erasmus represented the "casting of the die" on the part of Hutten and Zwingli (see 53/220/32-
33), and Hutten's motto became his own with reference to his breaking out of the
bondage of family and home when he went to Basel with Barbara (34/145/10). His
existential identity with Hutten shows up again when Grebel laments the estrangement of the Grebel family (October 14, 1524) and signs a letter, "Conrad Nobody,
No More Grebel" (65/296/22), the very signature Hutten used at the end of his
most quoted and reprinted poem, "Nemo" (Nobody), written at the point of his
own severe alienation from a strong-willed father who tried unsuccessfully to make
a monk out of him. The parallels between Hutten and Grebel are remarkable: they

552

were both born into landed nobility, having strong-willed fathers, alienated from parents, sojourners in foreign lands, living dissolute lives, suffering from similar symptoms of ill-health, attracted by the new liberating humanism, achieving self-identity as poets rather than scholars, debunkers of society, disillusioned by the fence-straddling of humanist-oriented Reformers, fugitives from arrest and persecution, yet sharp and witty in their writings, and finally experiencing premature death as fugitives.

57. **Joner (Rüppli), Wolfgang,** abbot of the Cistercian monastery at Cappel, thirteen miles south of Zurich (1519-31). He was a close friend of Zwingli and early supporter of the Reformation. He attended the Second Zurich Disputation (see 57C/250/18ff.), was one of the three spokesmen for the dissemination of its findings through the territory (57D/252/14, 57F/254/14-15), and was a member of the committee appointed by the council to design a plan of implementation of the disputation findings (57F/254/5-9, 59/276/7-8). All three spokesmen (Zwingli, Joner, and Schmid) died in battle at Cappel (1531). When Grebel was placed under threat of banishment for his unrecanted Anabaptism, he attempted to sell his books to Joner, who was also serving as headmaster of the Abbey School (69/357/37). In November 1525, Joner was one of four chairmen of the Third Public Disputation with the Anabaptists (71J/433/34).

58. **Jud (Keller), Leo** (1482-1542). Born in Alsace, where his father was a Catholic priet, he studied in Schlettstadt with an interest in medicine. He entered the University of Basel (1499), where he studied theology under Thomas Wyttenbach (MA, 1506) and had Zwingli for a classmate. He was pastor in his native Alsace (1512-19), in Einsiedeln, where he succeeded Zwingli (1519-22), and at St. Peter's in Zurich (1523-42), where he was Zwingli's partner in the work of the Reformation (see 47E/186/27ff.). One of his most valued contributions was the translation of tracts written by Luther and Erasmus. In March 1523, the Zurich Council authorized him to act as priest to the Oetenbach Convent, where previously only the Dominican monks provided the preaching and pastoral ministries to the nuns (see 52/207/23-26). In the summer of 1523, he published a new baptismal liturgy, modeled after one by Luther using the German vernacular (63/fn.87), and promoted the idea of a German communion service in which the bread and wine would both be given to the laity (see 57C/244/21ff.). In September 1523, he was the first of Zurich's preachers to call for the removal of images and statues from the churches, which led to several acts of iconoclasm in Zurich (see 57B/Intro.) and to the convening of the Second Doctrinal Disputation (57/Intro. and 57/236/27ff.). In his role as Zwingli's colleague, he was intensely involved in the disputations with the Anabaptists, who he claimed "eclipse the darkness by the light itself" (71G/428/28-29). Conversations between himself and Simon Stumpf were reported by Zwingli in the trial of Grebel on Nov. 9, 1525 (71K/436/17ff.), and Grebel testified that Jud and Grossmann had been of similar persuasion in favor of adult baptism, "though they dared not own such a thing before M[aster] Ulrich" (71K/438/30-32). Notwithstanding such claims, the three Zurich pastors carried out their assignment by the Zurich Council to interrogate the Anabaptists on numerous occasions (see 67/301/30-31, 68E/338/11-12, 70C/401/38-39, 71J/433/21-22, 436/5, and 71L/443/11-12).

59. **Kessler, Johann** (1502-74), "one of the world's great story-tellers" (Rupp, p. 368), author of a chronicle of the history of St. Gallen (1519-39), from which nine chronological excerpts are included in the present collection of documents: (1) 65A/297, Anabaptist beginnings in St. Gallen; (2) 68F/338, the first believer's baptism in Switzerland; (3) 68H/343, the oldest Anabaptist congregation (Zollikon); (4) 69A/359, the spread of Anabaptism to St. Gallen; (5) 69E/376, the first Swiss Anabaptist martyr, Bolt Eberli; (6) 70A/380, the reactions to Anabaptism in St. Gallen; (7) 71E/442, the third Swiss Anabaptist martyr, Hans Krüsi; (8) 71J/435, the Third Public Disputation on Baptism; and (9) 71R/455, the death of Grebel and execution of Mantz. Kessler (Latinized to Chesselius or Ahenarius) was a reformer, teacher, preacher, and chronicler. He was born in St. Gallen of humble parentage, attended the University of Basel, and then transferred to the University of Wittenberg in 1522. On his way there he chanced to meet Luther in the Black Bear Inn in Jena, as he was returning from the Wartburg disguised as a knight. It was here that Luther met Carlstadt and gave him the dueler's challenge to write in dispute of his interpretation of baptism and the Lord's Supper (see 65/295/19ff.). In less than two years, Kessler was back in St. Gallen without a degree but "with his head and his notebooks stuffed with first-hand and exciting notions from the lectures of Luther, Melanchthon, and Karlstadt" (Rupp, p. 368). Supporting himself as a saddler, he began to teach the Bible in homes. So many people came for his "readings," that the magistrates put a temporary stop to them. But when other "readers" continued in his stead with less ability to set limits on overzealousness, the authorities officially mandated Kessler to resume his teaching at the Church of St. Lawrence, assisted by the parish schoolmaster, Dominik Zili (see Cast of Characters No. 104). Henceforth, he was a close colleague of Vadian in St. Gallen's Reformation; and not the least part of his contribution was the writing of its history covering the years 1519 to 1539, giving it the title *Sabbata* because he wrote only on Sunday. His treatment of the Anabaptists was critical but also charitable. He tells us, for instance, that for all their radicality, Grebel and Mantz, before they died, tried hard to temper and restrain the excesses of their followers (71R/456/9ff.). It is interesting, however, that Grebel mentions Zili, Burgauer, Jufli, and other clerics of St. Gallen but never Kessler in all of his letters to Vadian. In 1537, Kessler became the parish schoolmaster and assistant preacher at St. Margaret's; and in 1542, he became the head pastor at St. Lawrence's, serving there for over thirty years.

60. **Krüsi, Hans,** alias Hans Nagel and Hans Kern (see Fast, 1962, pp. 456-75, Stayer, p. 110, and ME, III, pp. 250-51) was the third Anabaptist martyr in Switzerland (see 71E/423/3ff.). He got the name Krüsi from his mother's family in St. George, a parish on the southeast outskirts of St. Gallen, where he grew up. The family owned many acres of feudal land and his maternal grandfather was the "Praefekt," which refers either to the office of chaplain of the St. George Parish or of magistrate in the village of Tablat. He got his second name from his father, Mathias Nagel, a schoolteacher in the town of Klingnau. He also became a teacher in the village of Wil, 30 km. west of St. Gallen. During the two weeks before Easter, 1525, he was taken to one of Grebel's preaching meetings along the Sitter River east of St. Gallen by Johann Ramseyer, the son of a city councillor, and Martin Baumgartner (see Quellen 2, p. 583). It was here that Grebel "was the first to witness to him," not only through his preaching but also through a handwritten

collection of Bible verses that Grebel gave him (71E/425/7-9), undoubtedly the same collection mentioned by Grebel in two letters to Vadian (62/283/19-20 and 69/358/13), copy of which was recently discovered by Fast (see 71F/425). Krüsi was soon in close association with the leaders of the movement in the canton of St. Gallen—Uliman, Rugglisberger, Beda Miles, Antoni Kürsiner, and Gabriel Giger. Because of this involvement, he lost his teaching position in Wil but was quickly pressed into service by his new friends as Bible "reader" and preacher in his home environs of St. George, supporting himself and his wife through the trade of weaving, which he learned with money and tools given him by several Anabaptist friends. He had conversations with his pastor, Dominik Zili, of the Church of St. Lawrence in St. Gallen, where he may also have had opportunity to serve as "reader," although not as an Anabaptist. When his Anabaptist leanings became clearly evident, he was in immediate conflict with the authorities, who were especially worried about an alleged connection between Anabaptism and the peasant uprisings in the Catholic bailiwick of the Abbey of St. Gallen, where Hans was doing much of his missionary preaching. The farmers here lived under the oppressive rule of the abbot and his police; and during the month of March 1525, they actually took the legal advocate of the monastery hostage for a time. When these demonstrations failed to provide relief for their frustrations, the new message of Anabaptism provided a means of expressing their feelings of deprivation. Krüsi denounced the whole tax system in his preaching, declaring that "from the living Word of God no one should be obligated to pay tithes and the like" (71E/424/19-20). At the Swiss Confederate meeting of the Diet at Frauenfeld at the end of May, the decision was made to suppress both the Anabaptists and the rebellious peasants in the bailiwick of the abbey. Upon his return from Frauenfeld, Captain Melchior Degen, the constable for the district, heard that Krüsi was preaching and baptizing in Tablat; and when he went there with several soldiers to arrest him, he was confronted by crowds of Krüsi supporters who shouted that they had no magistrate but God, and the very ground on which they stood belonged to God. Some threatened to expel him, and a few rocks were thrown. Others told him to stay and hear the Word of God. Krüsi told the crowds to pray for the captain that he also might accept their true faith. The close relationship between the issue of faith and that of social justice was indicated by the fact that persons from practically every hamlet in the district volunteered to defend Krüsi "with body and goods" in the event of his attempted arrest. On the same day that the City Council of St. Gallen outlawed Anabaptists, June 6 (see 70B/384), Krüsi was called to preach, baptize, and celebrate the Lord's Supper. When he preached against the worship of images and relics in the church, some parishioners demolished the altar and threw out the bones of the saints that had been entombed there. A few days after his election as preacher, Krüsi was arrested by the constable of St. Gallen for alleged remarks he had made against the *Obrigkeit,* the governmental authorities, that they wanted to bury the gospel nine fathoms deep, etc. Krüsi was released on June 16, on the condition that he would not divulge the conversation held with him during his imprisonment. Kessler had visited him in prison and temporarily won him over to the Reformed faith, allowing him to remain in the city if he would abstain from preaching and baptizing. At his later trial in Luzern, he confessed that a fellow prisoner in St. Gallen, Beda Miles, admonished him against deserting the Anabaptist movement and convinced him to resume his Anabaptist mission in the bailiwick of the abbey. Now Captain Degen moved against him with greater stealth, capturing him in his bed one night and secretly transporting him first to the Oberberg Castle west of St. Gallen, and then to Luzern to stand trial. Although this procedure was irregular, it was partially legitimized by the fact that Luzern was one of four cantons serving as protectorates for the Abbey of St. Gallen. While in the Castle of Oberberg, Krüsi called out of his window, "Where are you who promised to protect me?" When the authorities questioned him about this, he told them about the pact that the peasants had made with him. Apparently Krüsi's followers did post guards around the castle, hoping to free him when he was brought out; but after a few days' delay he was transported to Luzern on July 20 for trial; and seven days later he was sentenced to death and burned at the stake. Rütiner wrote in his diary that when the fire got high, Krüsi's ropes were burned through and he was able momentarily to move away from the stake; but the executioner drove him back with a hay fork.

61. **Lambert, Franz** (1486-1530), was born in Avignon in the southeast of France and there in 1501 at the age of 15 entered the monastery of the Franciscan Observants. He was a gifted speaker and became *praedicator generalis,* a kind of itinerant preacher, expositing passages from the Psalms, Job, Jeremiah, Romans, and Revelation, using the common French language. Taken up with Luther's writings, he tested their validity in various ways, taking advantage of a special commission to carry letters to the general of his order to travel to Switzerland in 1522, riding on the back of a donkey. He traveled from Avignon to Lyons to Geneva to Bern; and from there, on the recommendation of Haller (ZW, VII, No. 214), he went to Zurich to see Zwingli. Here in public debate Zwingli corrected an alleged "error" of his concerning the intercession of Mary and the Saints (see 47B). From Zurich he went to Basel to see Erasmus, using a Latin name John Serranus. Early in 1523 he was received by Luther in Wittenberg, where he stayed for a year. From 1524 to 1526, he lived in Strasbourg, where he was closely associated with the Reformers, Bucer and Capito. While there he exchanged letters with Zwingli on the subject of the relation of church and state with specific reference to the recall of pastors who do not preach the evangelical faith (see 67A). In 1526, upon Luther's recommendation, he was invited to Hesse by the Landgrave Philip; and here he launched his own Reformation program, set forth in 158 theses which he entitled *The Paradoxes* and defended before the Synod of Hamburg on Oct. 26, 1526, which won for him the epithet "Reformer of Hesse." In theology, he was probably more a Zwinglian than a Lutheran. In 1527 he became professor of theology at the newly founded University of Marburg, where he died of the plague in 1530.

62. **Lehman, Felix,** Anabaptist in Hirslanden, north of Zollikon, in whose home some of Grebel's area meetings were held in June 1525 (70F/412/31ff.). He had been baptized by Heine Merger "out of great desire and longing" (Quellen 1, No. 131, p. 134). He was a friend of Hans Hottinger and testified in his behalf to the Zurich court (68I/349/26-29).

63. **Leo X,** first known as Giovanni de Medici (1475-1521), was named pope (1513-1521) by virtue of gross predilections by his famous Renaissance family, e.g., having been loaded with benefices since childhood, named to the College of Cardinals at the age of 13, and elected to the papacy without ever having been ordained to the priesthood. His reign is noted more for his work on St. Peter's Cathedral and

sponsorship of Raphael than for his struggles to cope with the outbreaks of the Reformation. Although he excommunicated Luther (1520), he failed to grasp the significance of the Reform movements in Germany and Switzerland and seemed indifferent to Zwingli's earliest published satire on the political intrigues of his office—*The Labyrinth*—in which he characterized Leo as a one-eyed lion. Preoccupied with the aggrandizement of Rome, he signed the Concordat of Peace with Francis I following the latter's military victory over the Swiss at Marignano (1515-16), and then signed a secret offensive alliance with Charles V against France (1521). Through his legates in Zurich—Cardinal Schinner and Cardinal Puccius (see Cast of Characters Nos. 82 and 72)—he succeeded in renewing the Mercenary Treaty of 1510 to send Swiss troops into the Italian Wars to help him recover some of his lands (Lombardy, Milan, etc.). Thus, the offer of a papal stipend to Grebel (28/136/27-28, 36/148/19-20) on top of those already received from Venice and Paris plagued Grebel's conscience and provoked the inner struggle depicted in his letters. This struggle was not unlike that earlier experienced by Zwingli himself who accepted an annual pension from Pope Leo until he finally renounced it in 1520.

64. **Lingg, Marty,** alias Martin Weniger, was an articulate Anabaptist spokesman from Schaffhausen. He was banished from Zurich on Nov. 18, 1525, together with Michael Sattler (see 71K/442/30-32), and went to Lostorf, canton of Basel, to Solothurn, to Bern, where he was known to have baptized a certain Flückinger on Easter, 1531, and to Zofingen, where he was one of the Anabaptist spokesmen at the Zofingen Disputation July 1-9, 1532 (see Quellen 4). In October of that year, he returned to the canton of Zurich to preach at Andelfingen and Ossingen, after which he yielded to pressure and made a public recantation at Schaffhausen (see ME, III, pp. 350-1). J. C. Wenger (1961, pp. 33-35) reviews an important Anabaptist essay on Christian doctrine written by Lingg in 1535 and entitled *Vindication.*

65. **Luther, Martin** (1483-1546), leader of the Protestant Reformation in Germany, attended the University of Erfurt (BA, 1504; MA, 1505) and then entered the Augustinian monastery there and was ordained to the priesthood (1507). He taught at the University of Wittenberg (1508-21), where his continuing search for a merciful God found fulfillment in his lecture preparations on the epistle to the Romans, especially Rom. 1:17, which he found to be the truest meaning of the gospel—the disclosure of God's forgiving love in Christ apprehended through faith and repentance. He launched the Protestant Reformation in 1517, predating the Zwinglian Reformation in Switzerland by two or more years. After his papal excommunication (1521) and self-exile to the Wartburg, the castle of Frederick the Wise, who served as his protector (1521-22), Luther returned to Wittenberg (March 1522), where he wrote prolifically and administered the work of reform. Grebel refers to him in Letters 22, 48, 51, 53, 62, 63, and 65. Until his break with Zwingli in December 1523, Grebel is interested primarily in Luther's Reformation work and writings. As early as August 1520, he refers to "the Luther affair" (22/119/2-4) in a way that shows his awareness of events in Germany, especially as they relate to events in Switzerland, i.e., the beginning of correspondence between Luther and Erasmus. He knows almost immediately about the publication of four of Luther's writings: (1) *Refutation of King Henry of England* (July 1522; see 48/189/27); (2) *Bull Concerning the Lord's Supper* (1522; 51/195/28ff.);

(3) *Opinion Concerning Erasmus of Rotterdam* (June 1523; see 53/220/33-36); and (4) *Letter to the Princes of Saxony Concerning the Rebellious Spirit* (1524; see 64/ 292/29). In September 1524, Grebel writes a letter of admonition directly to Luther (62/283/16-17, 63/292/13-14, 23-25, and 294/12, 15-16) about such concerns as the retention of the liturgical chant (63/287/16-17), the "blasphemous form of infant baptism" (63/291/20-21), the "idolatrous forbearance" (64/293/17-18), and his "walking backward" and being a "notorious dawdler" (296/15-16). Luther received Grebel's letter (see 67E/331/2-7) and asked Hegenwald "to give you his greetings." Thus, Hegenwald's letter is in one sense a reply to Grebel on Luther's behalf.

66. **Mantz, Anna,** the mother of Felix Mantz. Although there are only two references to her in the Muralt and Schmid collection of documents (pp. 178, 179), she is undoubtedly the same female Mantz mentioned elsewhere in connection with the names of Aberli and Guldi, both of whom spent time in her home (*ibid.,* pp. 159, 118). Aberli was to be questioned in January 1526, under torture if necessary, to tell "what he did on Neustadt at [Frau] Mantz' [house]." From other evidence it can be inferred (1) that this was also the home of Felix Mantz (see Bender, 1950, pp. 107, 256) and (2) that the female Mantz in this reference is identical to the Anna Mantz mentioned specifically in the Anabaptist trial of March 1526, where she admitted that Aberli had been with her recently (see 71M/446/32-33) and testified further that she had been baptized by Grebel and intended "to stay by that, for she considers him just and good, and leaves infant baptism alone as it was (446/35-38). For this she was imprisoned in the Wellenberg (447/7), which is the last reference to her, except that according to the *Martyrs Mirror* (ME, III, p. 474) she was standing on the shore encouraging her son to be steadfast as he was being executed on Jan. 5, 1527.

67. **Mantz, Felix** (*ca.* 1498-1527) was with Grebel one of the founders of the Swiss Brethren called Anabaptists and a signatory to Grebel's letters to Müntzer (63/292/7, 64/294/7), formulating their doctrinal position. His participation in the pre-history of the movement, however, cannot be dated positively until 1524, sometime following the Second Zurich Disputation (see 59A/fns. 1 and 5). Like Grebel, he grew up in Zurich, the son of the well-known chief canon of the Grossmünster, Johannes Mantz; and he acquired a good education in Latin, Greek, and Hebrew. He lived with his mother, presumably Anna Mantz (see Cast of Characters No. 66), in the Neustadt (see 71K/fn.5). It was probably here that the first believer's baptism took place on Jan. 21, 1525 (68F/340/25ff.). Several weeks prior to that, he wrote the first systematic biblical defense of believer's baptism (67B/311/26ff.). Henceforth, he was one of the most zealous missionaries of the movement (see 68G/316/9, 68J/351/23-25, 71H/430/28ff., etc.), suffering repeated arrest (see Krajewsky for an analysis of his imprisonments). He became the first Anabaptist martyr in Zurich, executed by drowning in the Limmat on Jan. 5, 1527 (see Epi.B/474).

68. **Maximilian I** (1459-1519), royal heir of the Hapsburg dynasty, king of Austria (1486), Holy Roman Emperor (1493). His dynastic policy enlarged his possessions to include the Netherlands through his first marriage, Brittany through his second, and the Duchy of Milan through his third, although this last accession

involved him in the Italian Wars that drained his funds and military forces (see Epi.A/470/7-13). A patron of humanism, he granted liberal scholarships to Swiss students for study at the University of Vienna, his capital (see 1/56/23-25) and awarded the laureate's wreath for poetry to Vadian, Glarean, Ursinus, Hutten, and others. His marriage policy secured for his grandsons—Charles V and Ferdinand I (see Cast of Characters Nos. 14 and 24)—one of the largest successions in history: Austria, Spain, the Netherlands, Bohemia, and Hungary. He died on Jan. 12, 1519 (see 6/80/38-41).

69. **Müntzer, Thomas** (1489-1525), a leader in the Peasants' War in Germany (1525), was born at Stolberg in the Harz Mountains and received a fine education at the Universities of Leipzig and Frankfort, graduating in theology. He became a priest (1513); and after serving as provost of a monastery and pastor of a convent, he became a preacher at the Church of St. Mary's in Zwickau (1520), where he collaborated with the so-called Zwickau prophets in envisioning a spiritualist society in which the peasants would become priests and prelates. Driven out of town for disturbing the peace, he went to Prague in 1522, where he wrote his "Prague Manifesto" for his new spiritualist church. Expelled from here he moved to Allstedt (1523) and was a preacher at St. John's for a year and six months. In this town of hardly more than a few hundred population, he drew an attendance of over a thousand persons by his preaching. It was here that he published two pamphlets that Grebel obtained and eagerly read (see 62/283/16, 63/285/33-34, and 286/21-22). By the middle of August 1524, unknown to Grebel, his increasing opposition to Luther and open threats of armed revolution forced him to flee to Mühlhausen, where he became a preacher in association with Heinrich Pfeiffer, who held similar views. This move accounts for the fact that Grebel's letters to Müntzer (63/285/23ff. and 64/292/21ff.) were never delivered but returned to Vadian in St. Gallen. Müntzer had to flee again, spending the last two months of 1524 in various locations in South Germany and Switzerland. Not much is known about his contacts during this time, and Heinrich Bullinger supposed without known evidence that Grebel made contact with him at this time and received from him some of the inspiration that led to the founding of the Anabaptist movement in Zurich several weeks later. By February 1525, Müntzer was back in Mühlhausen, where he helped to lead an overthrow of the City Council and established a communalistic theocracy. He then helped to lead the Peasants' Revolt, which ended in the tragic massacre in Thuringia (May 1525). Müntzer was captured and beheaded on May 27.

70. **Myconius (Geisshüsler), Oswald** (1488-1552), a native of Luzern and fellow student of Glarean at Michael Rubell's Latin school at Rottweil in south Württemberg. He attended the University of Basel (1510-14), where Erasmus was *parens et praeceptor* (father and teacher) to numerous young humanist scholars including Glarean himself. It was Erasmus who gave him the name, Myconius, perhaps because of early baldness (cf. Erasmus' *Adagia,* 1007). After taking his BA (1914), he remained in Basel as schoolmaster at St. Theodor's and St. Peter's. While here, he helped to edit the first Basel edition of Erasmus' *The Praise of Folly* (1514), he remained in Basel as schoolmaster at St. Theodor's and St. Peter's. riage he moved to Zurich in the autumn of 1516 to become schoolmaster at the Grossmünster (1516-19). Here he did some public lecturing on the *Paraclesis* and

Methodus of Erasmus and some writing on the geography of Switzerland. He helped with the editing of Glarean's *De Situ Heluetiae,* published by Froben in Basel in March 1519, and was celebrated in Glarean's published poem, *Ad Osualdum Lucernanum Heluitium Elegia Glareani.* At the end of 1518, Myconius was successful in promoting Zwingli's call to Zurich as people's priest at the Grossmünster, and the two became intimate friends for life. He returned to his native Luzern as schoolmaster in the autumn of 1519 but had to resign in 1522 because of his sympathies for the Zwinglian Reformation in a predominantly Roman Catholic canton. At Zwingli's urging (47E), he returned to Zurich as reader and teacher at the Fraumünster (1522-31), following an interim residence in Einsiedeln. During these nine years he was intimately associated with Zwingli and wrote the earliest biography of the Reformer upon his death in 1531 (see Jackson, 1912, pp. 1ff.). Myconius then became pastor of St. Alban's in Basel (1531-32); and upon the death of Oecolampad a year later, he succeeded to the title of Antistes and the chair of theology at the University of Basel, which he filled with moderate distinction, writing the first Basel Confession (1534) and unsuccessfully attempting to effect an agreement between Luther and the Swiss Reformers. He died in 1552. Grebel wrote nine extant letters to him (1519-21), in one of which he alludes to him as a former teacher (12/95/20-21), which may have been in Basel during the winter semester of 1514-15. In August 1518, Grebel accompanied Myconius, Vadian, and Zimmerman on an expedition to the top of Mt. Pilatus (3A). In August 1520, Grebel read and praised Myconius' dialogue "On Not Going to War" (22/118/ 29). Myconius was a friend of the Grebel family (1516-24) and took a sympathetic interest in Conrad during his conflicts in Paris, helping to reconcile him to his angry father (1520; see 17/107/26-27, 38). Like Zwingli, however, he turned against the Grebels, and in 1526 gave incriminating testimony at Jacob's trial, leading to his execution (Epi.A/465/38ff.). It is likely that one of Conrad's letters to him from Paris was also admitted into evidence to seal the father's fate (Epi.A/462/30-33). Moreover, Myconius supported Zwingli in the suppression of the Anabaptists. In his biography of Zwingli, he wrote, "I was present at nine friendly conferences and disputations. . . . They foamed at the mouth with palpable blasphemies and abuse, and in a word whatever revelation of evils John makes, they piled upon Zwingli. This plague, the more the efforts to repress it, the more fiery it became. Therefore, the Senate was at length compelled to assail it with imprisonment, exile, and death, not as Anabaptists but as perjurers, disobedient, and seditious persons" (Jackson, 1912, p. 15).

71. **Ockenfuss, Hans,** a tailor in Stadelhofen near Zurich, was one of Zurich's early Reformation *Stürmer* (storm troopers), together with Aberli, Pur, Hochrütiner, and the Hottingers. In March 1522, he was present at the meal at Froschauer's house when the Lenten fast was deliberately violated (47A/Intro.). In September 1523, he was one of the three men who broke off the crucifix at Stadelhofen, for which they were imprisoned; and in spite of several pleas for their release during the Second Zurich Disputation (see 57C/250/11-16, 25ff.), two of them were banished (57F/255/12, 58/256/2ff.). Ockenfuss, who was released, testified during his trial that in the light of Zwingli's preaching, in which "one hears daily that such crucifixes and all their images of God our Redeemer are forbidden," he sincerely believed "that he had neither acted unlawfully nor done wrong" (Egli, *Akten.,* No. 421). Ockenfuss was one of the signatories to Grebel's letters to

Müntzer (63/292/7, 64/294/8), declaring Anabaptist doctrines; and he was present at the first baptism at Zollikon (68G/343/17ff.). He did not accept baptism at that time but said that he intended soon to do so. He was then baptized by Jacob Hottinger (Quellen 1, p. 65) and was subsequently often arrested for his preaching and baptizing. When Aberli was arrested for harboring Hubmaier in December 1525, Ockenfuss had tried to send a warning to Aberli that the authorities were coming (Quellen 1, No. 157, p. 160). Soon thereafter, Ockenfuss himself was arrested and sentenced to life in prison with Grebel, Mantz, and Blaurock (71M/445/29ff., 447/3). After their prison escape, he considered going to Horgerberg to work (71-O/451/4-6) but apparently continued to live in the vicinity of Zurich. His name is found in the Zurich court records for the last time in January 1528 (Quellen 1, p. 273), but it is not known what became of him.

72. **Puccius, Cardinal Antonio,** priest of the Apostolic Chamber in Rome, subdean of the Cathedral of Florence, bishop of Pistoria, elevated to the College of Cardinals, delegate with the power of legate to Switzerland (1517-1519, 1520-21), bishop of Prato (1519-31), and bishop of Vannes (1531-44). He was in contact with Vadian, whom he described as "a small but shrewd man" and whom he tried to win "for the pope and against his enemies." During his second term in Switzerland, Pucci recruited Swiss mercenary troops to help drive the French out of Milan (23/120/41ff., 29/138/9-10). In this connection he was the potential source for a papal pension for Senator Jacob Grebel, allegedly for Conrad's education in Italy (23A/122/8-12). Conrad had mixed feelings about the propriety of accepting this money, which he thought of expressing in a "Choriambic Ode to Pucci" (24/124/25-26). Although he decided against going to Italy, he accepted 100 franks, which he used to support himself and his girlfriend in Basel (39/151/17-19). Vadian may also have accepted 50 guilders (see Epi.A/fn.49, 29/fn.2, and 30/fn.8). The whole episode was introduced as evidence to condemn Jacob Grebel at his trial for treason in 1526 (Epi.A/471/12-21).

73. **Pur, Bartlime (Pfister),** a baker in Zurich, was one of the Zwinglian storm troopers, having participated in the intentional transgression of the fasting ordinance on Ash Wednesday, 1522, testifying in court that he, Zwingli, Jud, and others "were in the kitchen of the printer Froschauer's house; and the printer produced two fried sausages. They cut them up and each had a little bit. All ate them except Master Huldrych Zwingli, people's priest at the Grossmünster" (Egli, *Aktens.,* No. 233). Although he abstained, Zwingli defended the act in a sermon in which he declared that "if Christ by his death freed us from all sins and burdens, then we also are in baptism, that is, in belief, released from all Jewish or human ceremonies" (Garside, p. 38). Pur was also in the group of *Stürmer,* including Grebel, Aberli, and Claus Hottinger, who were summoned before the council for preaching against the monks in their own pulpits (47B/175/18 and 47C/177/23). He attended Castelberger's home Bible study group (51B/204/25-26) and was one of the signers of Grebel's letter to Müntzer (63/292/8). He may have died soon after, because there is no further trace of him in Anabaptist documents, although it is known that his wife was subsequently baptized by Ockenfuss (Quellen 1, No. 56, p. 65, No. 57, p. 66).

74. **Reimann, Heini,** farmer from the upper region of Zurich near Grüningen, convert to Anabaptism following Grebel's mission to Grüningen in July 1525, the third Anabaptist martyr in Zurich and the fifth in Switzerland, drowned in the Limmat on Sept. 5, 1528, together with Jacob Falk (see Cast of Characters No. 23) by mandate of the Zurich Council (Epi.E/518/26ff.). Their appeal to the Grüningen Diet prior to their execution is a vibrant declaration of their vows of obedience to "the Word of God and Christ's command" (Epi.E/514/13ff.).

75. **Reublin, Wilhelm** (c. 1482-1560), pastor at Wytikon, five miles southeast of Zurich, had been ordained to the priesthood while attending the University of Freiburg. He served the parish of Griessen between Waldshut and Schaffhausen (1509-10), earned an MA degree somewhere in Germany, and moved to Basel, where he was pastor at St. Alban's (1521-22) and where his Reformation preaching drew large crowds. Expelled from Basel for preaching against the mass, he returned to South Germany as pastor in Lauffenburg but could not remain there long because of Austrian oppression. He came to Zurich (autumn 1522), filled the pulpit at the Fraumünster, and received an appointment as assistant priest at Wytikon, where the peasant congregation, ahead of a mandate from Zurich, soon chose him as their head pastor. Following Zwingli's petition to the bishop for marriage privileges for priests (July 2, 1522), Reublin was the first priest to marry publicly (April 18, 1523). About that same time, his preaching against Zurich's system of tithes and taxes led to the petitions of Wytikon and five other peasant parishes (52A/209/25ff.), which Grebel supported (52/207/32ff.) and Zwingli supported with qualifications (52B/213/15ff.). He was also the first in the territories of Zurich to preach against infant baptism, following which a number of young parents decided not to present their babies for baptism on Easter Sunday, 1524. For this he was arrested on August 11 and kept in custodial confinement for counseling by the three Zurich pastors. The first two of Zwingli's list of ten private and public conferences on baptism (71M/444/18) were held with Reublin and his followers (68B/Intro). He was probably a participant in the Tuesday Disputations in December (see 66A/300/29ff.) and was certainly at the side of Grebel and Mantz (see 66B/335/16) at the First Public Disputation on Baptism on Jan. 17, 1525, for which he was banished from Zurich (68E/338/14-15), but not before he had a coat tailored by Ockenfuss in a process that produced new converts (see Blanke, 1955, pp. 21ff.; 68G/343/18-19). He accompanied Brötli to Schaffhausen (68J/351/1ff. and 351/17ff.), from where he went to Waldshut (351/10) to see Hubmaier, whom he baptized at Eastertime. He then moved on to Strasbourg, where he debated with Capito, and to Horb, where he worked briefly with Sattler. Following the latter's martyrdom, he went to Reutlingen and Ulm, where he met Hans Denk. Following a lengthy time of transient missionary endeavor, he went to Moravia in 1530, where he participated in the emergence of the Hutterian Brethren. Because of internal dissension, he eventually returned to Switzerland, where he was reestablished with the help of Zwingli's successor, Heinrich Bullinger.

76. **Ritter, Erasmus,** a preacher at the Münster in Schaffhausen, to whom Grebel gave his collection of Bible passages on faith and baptism (69/358/19-20, 71F/427/10ff.). In 1536 Ritter became associate pastor in Bern with Sebastian Meyer; and the two represented a strict Zwinglian viewpoint at the Bern Disputation with the Anabaptists in 1538 (Epi.F/522/13ff.).

77. **Roggenacher, Anthony,** also known as Anthony Kürsiner, a furrier from Schwyz, was baptized in Zollikon on Feb. 26, 1525, by Blaurock (Quellen 1, pp. 59-60). He was arrested on Mar. 16 with eighteen Zollikon brethren, all of whom were held for interrogation by Zwingli (*ibid.,* p. 73). They were released on Mar. 25 with the warning that continued Anabaptism would result in banishment (*ibid.,* p. 74). He and Jacob Hottinger then went to St. Gallen, accompanied by Bolt Eberli and an unnamed priest, who were soon to be martyred in Schwyz (69E/376/27-30). He was also a companion of Hans Krüsi, the third Swiss Anabaptist martyr (71E/423/38). Back in Zurich, he was arrested in January 1526 (*ibid.,* pp. 165-67) and sentenced to life imprisonment with Grebel, Mantz, and Blaurock (71M/445/11). After their escape on Mar. 21 (71-0/450/27), nothing more is known about him.

78. **Röist, Diethelm,** succeeded his father, Mark Röist, as burgomaster of Zurich (1524). As Schelbert writes, "he shared none of his father's hesitancy, however; he became one of the most devoted followers of Zwingli and put the full power of his office at the Reformer's disposal" (p. 51). Consequently, his name is found on numerous official mandates against the Anabaptists (see 68E/338/4, etc.), including the mandate of execution of Felix Mantz (Quellen 1, p. 226).

79. **Röist, Mark** (1454-1524), knighted at Morat for gallantry with the Swiss troops under Hans Waldmann, member of the Zurich Council for thirty years, he was elected burgomaster of Zurich in 1509 at the age of 55. At the age of 61, he led a battalion of Swiss troops against the French at Marignano, where Milan was lost to the attack of Francis I and where over 10,000 Swiss troops lost their lives (see 6/fn.53). Upon his return, after serving briefly as captain of the papal bodyguard in Rome (1518), he was favorable to bringing Zwingli to Zurich and was generally his ally in the work of the Reformation, serving as chairman and honorary chairman of the First and Second Zurich Disputations, although he stood for caution against precipitous change. Wyss wrote that for Röist, "the removal of the idols [decreed on June 15, 1524, shortly before his death] had been a very repulsive thing and a great trial" (Schelbert, p. 50).

80. **Sattler, Michael** (c.1490-1527), Anabaptist leader and martyr in South Germany, author of the Schleitheim Confession of Faith that helped to consolidate the movement in 1527, first appeared in Zurich in March 1525, and apparently joined the Anabaptists at this time (Quellen 1, p. 73). Stayer (p. 331) calls him "Grebel's disciple," although H. S. Bender hypothesized that Reublin was his main influence (ME, IV, p. 427). After his expulsion from Zurich following his participation in the Third Disputation on Baptism in November 1525 (71K/442/30-32), he returned to his home at Stauffen and was an active Anabaptist advocate in Breisgau, Württemberg, and Strasbourg, prior to his execution in Rottenburg on May 20, 1527.

81. **Schappeler (Sertorius), Christoph** (1472-1551), native of St. Gallen, was Latin teacher there (1503-13), pastor at St. Martin's in Memmingen between St. Gallen and Munich (1513-25), where he championed the cause of the Reformation. In November 1522, he wished to return to Switzerland and applied for the pastorate at Winterthur northeast of Zurich but was opposed by the abbot of St. Gallen and Wendelin Oswald, the old faith preacher at the abbey church (see 48/

190/3ff.). When Oswald influenced the bishop of Constance against Schappeler, Vadian asked Zwingli and the Grebels to help him get the position directly from the Winterthur authorities (49/191/17-18, 51/194/18ff.), but they were not successful in this. Schappeler was one of three presidents of the Second Zurich Disputation in October 1523 (57C/249/16-17), serving with Vadian and Hofmeister. In the events leading to the Peasants' War in South Germany in 1525, it was suspected that the twelve articles stating the peasants' demands were written with Schappeler's help, if not directly by him (see 71I/431/20-21); and for this he was expelled from Memmingen and widely held in suspicion for a long time. After a brief pastorate in Münster near Schaffhausen, he returned to St. Gallen in 1527, where he was installed as pastor of the defunct convent chapel of St. James.

82. **Schinner, Cardinal Matthew** (c.1470-1522), bishop of Sitten (or Sion), fifty miles south of Bern (1499). His influence in all the Swiss cantons made him an important diplomat of popes Julius II, Leo X, and Adrian VI in their military efforts to expel the French and unite the empire. As a reward for an alliance that he secured with the cantons in which Swiss troops marched against Milan (although unsuccessfully), the pope made him bishop of Novara and cardinal in 1511. In 1512 he was appointed commander of a Swiss army that finally succeeded in driving the French from Milan and establishing Maximilian Sforza as its duke (see Epi.A/fn.73); and again in 1513, when Louis XII of France recaptured Milan following the death of Pope Julius, Schinner successfully led Swiss troops against him in the Battle of Novara (see Epi.A/fn.134). In 1515 when the French began a new offense under Francis I, Schinner led the Swiss troops against them in the unfortunate battle of Marignano (Epi.A/fn.89), in which Zwingli served as chaplain of the Glarus contingent, most of whom were killed. This was the turning point in Zwingli's attitude toward the mercenary system of recruiting Swiss men for foreign wars, which he vehemently began to oppose (see 23A/fn.9). Driven from Sitten by the local leader of the French party, George Supersax, Schinner lived in Zurich from 1517 to 1519. Zwingli later wrote that during this time he often spoke to Schinner "in the clearest language that the papacy had a false foundation and supported the same from Scripture" (Jackson, 1900, p. 109). For his support of Charles V in the election for emperor, Schinner was named bishop of Catania in Sicily (1520) and again in 1521 led a Swiss army against Francis I for the retaking of Milan. Following this achievement, Pope Adrian named him administrator of the States of the Church with residence in Rome, where he died of the plague in 1522.

83. **Schmid, Conrad** (*ca.* 1476-1531), son of a wealthy farmer in Küssnacht near Zurich, studied at Basel (ThB, PhM), and became the pastor at Seengen in Canton Aargau. In March 1519, he became the commander of the Johannite Monastery at Küssnacht. He had great respect for Zwingli, which was reciprocated by numerous invitations from the Zurich Reformer to preach at the Grossmünster and elsewhere. The two often worked together at the services of angelic dedication in Einsiedeln, in the Second Zurich Disputation, where Schmid's views were more cautious than Zwingli's (see 57C/236/8ff., 239/12ff.), in the visitation of churches following the Disputation (see 57D/252/12ff., 57F/255/2-6), in the design of a plan of implementation of the disputation findings (57F/254/31-36), at the disputation with Canon Conrad Hofmann in January 1524, at the disputation with

the Anabaptists in November 1525 (see 71J/433/33-34), at the Bern Disputation of 1528, and finally at the Battle of Cappel where they died on the field together.

84. **Schumacher, Fridli,** a shoemaker, lived in Zollikon (present address: 114-115 Kirchhof, according to Nüesch and Bruppacker, p. 74). At the time of Reublin's imprisonment for preaching against infant baptism (August 1524), Schumacher testified that his six-week-old son had not yet been baptized (Quellen 1, p. 10). Schumacher was baptized by Hans Brötli on Jan. 22 (68G/343/19-23), and his wife was baptized by Blaurock several days later (Quellen 1, p. 58). It was in Schumacher's house that Brötli (see Cast of Characters No. 10) and his family were living at the time. Following his banishment from Zurich, Brötli wrote several letters "to the devout Fridli Schumacher of Zollikon and others of his dear brothers in Christ" to encourage them during their imprisonment in Zurich (68J/351/14-15, 351/33). Then on March 16, Schumacher and eighteen of his Zollikon brethren were imprisoned for a second time and held for nine days (Quellen 1, Nos. 54-64, pp. 61-74). This time, however, they were put in separate rooms and questioned one by one by Zwingli and several Councillors. Only four stood by their profession of faith, and Schumacher was not one of them. But on July 11, 1525, when he was imprisoned for a third time along with Ockenfuss and two others (71A/417/25), he stood firm, testifying that "he had been baptized, which was not against God; and he would stand by that" (Quellen 1, p. 98).

85. **Stumpf, Simon,** a monk from Franconia, studied with Beatus Rhenanus in Basel, through whom he met Zwingli. In response to his letter to Zwingli of July 2, 1519, recalling their meeting, the latter helped him secure the appointment as pastor at Höngg near Zurich, succeeding his uncle, Nicolaus Beier, over the objection of the abbot of Wettingen, who was also supposed to have a voice in the appointment. Stumpf was a ready supporter of Zwingli's Reformation, being one of the signatories of his petition to the bishop of Constance to permit evangelical preaching and the marriage of priests, and being a member of his *Sodalitium*—an inner circle of friends meeting regularly for the study of the classic Greek language and literature with particular interest in the Greek New Testament. Under the influence of his preaching about church reform, Stumpf's parishioners appeared frequently in the Zurich court records for various offenses, such as involvement in the planning of the *Badenschenke* (47A/Intro.), protest of the system of tithes (52A/Intro.), and various acts of iconoclasm (57B/Intro.). In the autumn of 1522 (see Goeters, pp. 248ff.), he is alleged to have preached a sermon declaring that "no one has to pay the tithe," which led one of his parishioners to refuse to pay a portion of his grain and fruit tithe owed to the abbot of Wettingen. The Zurich Council jailed the parishioner on Sept. 22 and issued its first mandate ordering all delinquent sums to be paid immediately but promising to review the whole system within a year. Stumpf secured his parishioner's release by finding a sponsor for his debts and proceeded to preach even more vehemently against the abbot and monks of the Wettingen cloister, calling them "good-for-nothing clerics before God and the world for their robbing and stealing from the poor" (71K/437/15ff.). On complaint by the abbot to the bishop of Constance, Stumpf was summoned for questioning, but refused to go, asking the Zurich Council for protection. As part of the process of establishing its own authority vis-á-vis the bishop, the council asked him to drop the clerical trial, promising to bring Stumpf to trial in Zurich instead. The

bishop consented on Nov. 23, and Stumpf was brought before the provost and chapter of the Grossmünster and representatives of the council, reprimanded, and ordered to apologize to the abbot and monks of Wettingen. This did not satisfy the abbot, who appealed the case to the Confederate Diet in Baden, where the case was returned to Constance with a warning to Zurich against further interference. Thus Stumpf became a test case in the authority struggle between Zurich and Constance, along with the case of Hans Urban Wyss of Fislisbach (see 49/fn.17). When the Baden Diet of Jan. 5, 1523, confirmed the decision of the previous Diet, ordering Stumpf's surrender to Constance, the Zurich delegates obtained a delay, pending the convening of the First Doctrinal Disputation to deal with the basic principles of church reform (see 51A). The bishop, on hearing of the decision of the Diet, removed Stumpf from his pastoral office, only to reverse his action upon receipt of another petition from the Zurich Council but with a threat to depose Stumpf forthwith if any further complaint about him was received from the abbot. Stumpf avoided further acts of dissent until the end of September, when following the sermon of Leo Jud against images in St. Peter's Church (see 57B/Intro.), he declared from his own pulpit that the Zurich iconoclasts had done no wrong and that the congregation in Höngg should proceed straightway to remove its own statues and pictures. This actually happened, and Höngg became the first parish church in the Zurich bailiwick emptied of its images, but not without internal conflict. This occurred just after the Second Zurich Disputation in which Stumpf was an active participant (see 57C/242/25ff.); and was thus in violation of the council mandate for everyone to hold his peace until further notice (57D/251/15ff.). So again, the commission charged with these matters (57F/fns.4-6) was asked to deal with Stumpf. Their recommendation of Nov. 3, that he be dismissed from his pastoral office and prohibited from residing in the Höngg parish, was approved by the council on Nov. 14. Stumpf then went to Weiningen in the Baden domain, where he found asylum with the chaplain, Jörg Stähelin, another Zwinglian. It was from here that Stumpf wrote the penitent letter to Zwingli dated Nov. 19 in which he cited the words of the prodigal son and indicated his interest in another appointment as a "minor day laborer" (ME, IV, p. 648; see also 68F/fn.34, 69/fn.40, and 70C/fn.23). His penitent mood, however, did not restrain him from visiting his former parish against the mandate of the council, which had him arrested and put on trial. Apparently during or before his trial, Stumpf said to Zwingli that according to Deut. 13:5, the way to deal with false prophets who seduce people to worship idols was to put them to death (see 67C/316/39, 71K/436/26ff.). When the commission asked Stumpf whether he had made such a statement, he denied it, thus calling Zwingli's veracity into question. Zwingli then forced Stumpf to admit that he had said it. It was likely also during the processing of Stumpf that he and Grebel presented their alternative Reformation plan to Zwingli (see 59A/278/14ff., 71K/436/29ff.). On Dec. 23, 1523, Stumpf was sentenced to permanent banishment from Zurich and all its territories. Through this sequence of events, he thus became an early victim of Zwingli's politics of compromise following the Second Disputation (see 58B/269/1ff.), along with Hochrütiner and Claus Hottinger. Upon return to Weiningen, Stumpf and Stähelin were placed under arrest by Bailiff Fleckenstein. On March 9, 1524, the Confederate Diet at Luzern ordered the bailiff to whip the jailed Stumpf out of the Swabian country with rods and to banish him from all Confederate Switzerland. On the run, somewhere in the vicinity of Basel, Stumpf wrote a bitter letter to Zwingli (with a copy to Nikolaus Beier), accusing

Zwingli of deserting a brother and failing to deal with him according to the rule of Christ in Mt. 18:15-18. He blamed his sentence of banishment on Zwingli, who could have restored him. Thereafter, Stumpf lived in Basel, where he apparently attended the church of which Zwingli's friend, Oecolampad, was pastor. In April 1527, he was arrested in Zurich and again banished on threat of death should he ever return. Little more is known about him, except that he may have fled to Ulm.

86. **Trinkler, Ulrich,** one of the few members of the Small Council who were wholeheartedly in support of the Zwinglian Reformation. Zwingli refers to him in intimate terms as early as May 4, 1520, in a letter to Vadian. He was also a close friend of Claus Hottinger, with whom he planned the *Badenschenke* (May 1522) to demonstrate support for Zwingli's leadership against the repressive moves of the bishop of Constance (see 47A/170/21ff.). On Sept. 19, 1523, in a meeting in his house, Trinkler showed Hottinger "some images that he had in his house under the staircase and said that he had a great deal of expense concerning them, and still had carried them from the church so that no one would do reverence to them" (Egli, *Aktens.,* No. 421, quoted by Garside, p. 122). He attended the Castelberger home Bible study group (51B/206/25) and was often appointed to committees of the Small and Large Councils to resolve various Reformation questions: what to do with the monasteries, regulations concerning relief of the poor, etc. In 1526 he became the official administrator of the Grossmünster alms fund, continuing to work closely with Zwingli.

87. **Tschudi, Peter** (*ca.* 1503-32), native of Glarus, brother of Aedigius Tschudi, Swiss historian, whom Erasmus characterized as "the Swiss Herodotus" and cousin of Valentin Tschudi (see Cast of Characters No. 88). He studied with Glarean in Basel (1514-17) and in Paris (1517-21). Glarean addressed two of his poems to him, which were published in his *De ratione syllabarum* and *Elegiae,* both published in November 1516. A close friend during the Paris episodes, Grebel mentions him in four letters (10, 11, 13, and 23). On urging by Grebel, he wrote to Vadian from Paris (see 16A), and Grebel carried the letter to Zurich, from where he dispatched it by courier (23/122/12-14). On leaving Paris (*ca.* 1521), he settled at Chur, where he was sympathetic to the Reformation.

88. **Tschudi, Valentin** (*ca.* 1500-1555), cousin of Peter Tschudi (see above), native of Glarus, where he was one of Zwingli's parishioners and pupils. Zwingli sent him to study with Vadian in Vienna in 1512-13; but after only a year there, he visited Pavia and then attended the universities of Basel and Paris (BA, 1518; MA, 1519). The university careers of Grebel and Tschudi intersected at Basel and again in Paris, where they were apparently jointly involved in the skirmish with bandits in which two were killed (see 7A/Intro.), and where Grebel and his cousin, John Leopold Grebel, and the two Tschudi cousins lived together in Melun for five months to escape the plague (see 10/91/21ff.). Grebel mentions him in six letters (6, 7, 10, 11, 40, and 42). Upon Zwingli's resignation as pastor at Glarus (Dec. 19, 1518, although he had actually left Glarus two years earlier), Tschudi was called to that position, which he did not actually take up until Oct. 12, 1522. Prior to that, he lived in Zurich for a time, where he was in a circle of students including Grebel, Ammann, Binder, and Stumpf, who were studying Greek and reading Plato (see

42/157/24-25). He became known in subsequent years for writing a chronicle of the historical events in Switzerland, 1524-33.

89. **Uliman, Wolfgang,** also known as Schorant, was an Anabaptist leader in St. Gallen. Son of Andres Uliman, the tailor's guildmaster and master of the Large Council, Wolfgang became an apprentice monk at St. Lucius' Monastery in Chur. Already in 1515, however, he was expressing Reformation ideas. Returning to St. Gallen before taking final vows, he attended Kessler's Bible studies in 1524. When Kessler stopped holding the meetings following opposition by the authorities (see 65A/Intro.), Uliman began his own "readings" at the Slaughterhouse and often preached outdoors near the Mangen Church. When these meetings became popular, the authorities decided not to interfere directly but to ask Kessler to resume his readings officially at the St. Lawrence Church, together with Zili, the parish schoolmaster. There was back-and-forth traffic between the two meetings and a joint discussion arose on the meaning of "baptism into the death of Jesus" (Rom. 8:4). Lorenz Hochrütiner, who had been banished from Zurich at the end of 1523 (see Cast of Characters No. 45) interrupted the Kessler meeting and questioned the validity of infant baptism (65A/297/31-32). It was after having taken a stand against infant baptism that Uliman was immersed by Grebel in the Rhine near Schaffhausen sometime in early March 1525 (69A/360/17ff.). Back in St. Gallen, at a meeting at the Weavers' Guildhouse on the 18th of the that month, Uliman was asked by the authorities to stop his unauthorized meetings and give support to the approved meetings at the church; but he refused on the grounds that God had revealed to him that the established church was not open to the truth and should be avoided (69A/260/32-36). Summoned before the council on April 25-26, he defended Anabaptism on the grounds that "infant baptism was a later institution of the church without Scriptural foundation, that adult baptism implied the obligation to die to vices, live to Christ, and be obedient, and that their rejection of infant baptism was based on Jesus' command to the disciples to teach, believe, and baptize" (Quellen 2, p. 379; ME, IV, p. 787). The council then asked Uliman "for the sake of brotherly love to wait with the deed" (*ibid.*), which sounds like the advice of Vadian (see 67D/322/9ff.). When Uliman refused, the council threatened banishment, which was finally mandated on July 17 (*ibid.,* p. 400); but the sentence was reversed on October 2 upon his oath of obedience (*ibid.,* p. 405). In 1528, he went to Basel as an Anabaptist missioner, but was quickly expelled. Later that year he led several groups of Anabaptists to Moravia and was arrested in Swabia on his second trip. Those who recanted were sent back. Uliman and ten others were executed, the men by beheading and the women by drowning (ME, IV, p. 788).

90. **Ulrich, Duke of Württemberg** (1498-1550), was the despotic ruler of a territory in Southwest Germany from Lake Constance north to Stuttgart, between Baden on the west and Bavaria on the east. Originally a countship, this kingdom of an unbroken succession of princes that began with Count Ulrich I (1241-65) grew steadily larger, and was declared a duchy in 1495 by Emperor Maximilian I, since it had already incorporated the ruins of the old duchies of Swabia and Franconia. Because of his acts of violence, including the murder of the cousin of Ulrich von Hutten (see Cast of Characters No. 56), Conrad Grebel called him "a curse to Switzerland" (20/116/26-27) and Jacob Grebel called him a "good-for-nothing" (23A/122/23). In 1519 the extravagance and cruelty of Duke Ulrich led to a suc-

cessful military campaign against him by armies of the Swabian League (March-July), joined by Hutten himself; and the Duke was driven from his duchy and put under the ban of the Empire. In the six months interregnum between the reigns of Maximilian and Charles, the Duke thought he saw an opportunity to regain his duchy by championing the election of Francis I to the imperial throne. When that did not work, and the new emperor renewed the ban against him, he tried other strategies for several years, finally fleeing to Basel, where he embraced the teaching of Oecolampad in the hope of gaining an ally. Then on Nov. 18, 1524, he moved to Zurich, where he listened to Zwingli preach and alleged that Zwingli taught him to pray (Potter, 1976, p. 381). Zwingli in turn was not adverse to the idea that if Ulrich converted to Protestantism and regained his kingdom, "the Catholic-Hapsburg ring which surrounded Zurich" (*ibid.*) would be broken. Ulrich appeared before the Zurich Council on Nov. 23 and was granted citizenship. The opposition of Jacob Grebel to Ulrich's mission in Zurich (66/299/19-23) may have been another factor in the subsequent "liquidation" by Zwingli (see Epi.A). However, it was not until 1534, three years after the death of Zwingli, that Ulrich regained his dukedom with the military aid of Philip of Hesse.

91. **Ursinus, Caspar Velius** (1493-1539). Born in Silesia, studied in Krakau and Vienna, where he was crowned Poet Laureate by the Emperor Maximilian (1517).He was a good friend of Vadian and some of his poetry was published in the latter's first (Vienna) edition of *Pomponius Mela* (see 1B/Intro.). He was a prodigy among humanists all over Europe. The plague in Vienna in 1521 brought him to Basel, where a complete edition of his poetry was published in 1522, with the editorial assistance of Grebel (see 39B/153/12-20). In fact, the two men lived together in the home of the printer, Cratander (see 39A/153/7-11).

92. **Utinger, Heinrich,** a canon in the Grossmünster, had been one of the leading advocates of Zwingli since the latter's candidacy as head pastor, when he helped to interpret charges that Zwingli had been guilty of the sexual abuse of a girl in his Einsiedeln parish. Utinger became the godfather of Zwingli's first child and remained his faithful friend and adviser (see 47E/186/13). He was present with Zwingli, Jud, Pur, Aberli, and others at Froschauer's house on Ash Wednesday, 1522, when meat was eaten in open, defiant breach of the Lenten fast (see 47A/Intro.). Yet, as commissioner of the Grossmünster Chapter, appointed by the diocesan bishop in 1502, he remained in a position of mediation with old faith leaders. Bullinger called him "a gruff old man through whom the bishop of Constance accomplished much" (ZW, VII, No. 48, fn. 1). Utinger befriended Conrad Grebel at the time when his marriage to Barbara incurred his father's wrath and served as mediator in that instance also by drawing up a contract between father and son, providing for the couple's financial support (Epi.A/466/10-17). Upon his death in 1536, Bullinger wrote to Myconius that he had known Utinger as a man *tante fide* (of great faith)" (ibid.).

93. **Vadian (von Watt), Joachim** (1484-1551), Grebel's university teacher (1515-18), brother-in-law (1519), and chief correspondent (1517-25). He became the town physician (1518), Reformer (1521), and burgomaster (1525) of St. Gallen. Set apart for an academic career by his father, a linen merchant of St. Gallen, he was resident at the University of Vienna for most of sixteen years (1502-18), first as

a student (BA in 1504, MA in 1508, MD in 1518), and then as a professor of classical literature. He edited numerous classical texts (Sallust, 1511; Cicero, 1512; Ovid, 1512; Dionysius, 1515; Plinius, 1515; Pontanus, 1517 (see Prologue A); etc. He authored other books, including *Conversation with Death* (1511), *Concerning Poetry,* 1518 (see 5/73/8, 5A/74/29, 5B), *Lectures on Pomponius Mela,* 1518 (see 1A, 1B, 26A), etc. He was appointed Poet Laureate of the empire (1514), university orator (1510, 1515, 1516), and rector (1516-17). He made scientific expeditions to an underground river called Timavus near Triest (1507), to Mt. Pilatus near Luzern (1518), and to the salt mines of Krakau (1518-19). He earned the doctor of medicine degree (1517) and returned to St. Gallen as town physician (1518). Grebel accompanied him back to Switzerland; and a year later (Aug. 18, 1519) Vadian married his sister, Martha. They had one child, Dorothy, born in 1523. He was elected *Ratsherr* (Councillor) to succeed his deceased father (1521), and became *Burgomaster* in 1525, later *Altburgomaster* (senior mayor) and *Reichsvogt* (imperial officer). He became the lead Reformer of the church in St. Gallen, collaborating with Zwingli in the Swiss Reformation. In this connection, he was a delegate to the First Doctrinal Disputation in Zurich (January 1523) and served as president of the Second Zurich Disputation (October 1523; see 57C). Some of his unpublished writings concerning the Reformation were *Arguments Against the Primacy of the Pope* (1521-22), *With Respect to the Whole of the New Testament* (1522), *Commentary on the Acts of the Apostles* (1523), and *Theses [Concerning Penitence and Forgiveness]* (1525; see 68M/356/9-13). He organized a Bible academy in St. Gallen for the continuing theological education of the clergy, in which he did much of the lecturing, supplemented by Kessler, Schappeler, and Hubmaier (see Cast of Characters Nos. 59, 81, 54). Following a mandate of the St. Gallen Council for preaching on the basis of the Scriptures alone (April 4, 1524), Vadian was appointed the chairman of a committee of four to enforce the mandate, with special reference to the reactionary resistance of the head pastor, Benedict Burgauer (see 52/208/5ff., 54A, and 68M/fn.2). Another of his unpublished writings, *Essay Against the Anabaptists* (1524-25) was instrumental in the suppression of Anabaptism in St. Gallen (see 70A and 70B) and the gradual severance of the intimate relationship between Vadian and Grebel (see 67, 70, and Epi.G), whose previous devotion to each other was chronicled in the fifty-five extant letters Grebel wrote to him (1519-25) and in the three from Vadian to Grebel, the first two of which were in the form of open addresses published in two of his literary works (1517, 1518; Pro.A and 1A). Although Vadian followed Zwingli in the suppression of Anabaptism, his confidence in the Zurich Reformer's integrity was impaired for nearly a year by the latter's execution of his father-in-law, Jacob Grebel. But he never quite forgave Conrad for his Anabaptist betrayal "of the laws of friendship and blood" (Epi.G/525/13ff.).

94. **Walder, Heinrich** (c.1468-1542), a director of the Tailors' Guild since 1489, was elected to the Zurich Council in 1505. He was a field commander in the military service of Pope Julius II (1510), a war Councillor in Mailand (1512), and captain of recruitment of mercenaries (23A/fn.9), accompanying them to the infamous Battle of Marignano (1515). He was appointed bailiff of Wollishofen (1520), guildmaster of the Tailors (1520), war Councillor for auxiliary troops for Pope Leo X (1521), chief judicial magistrate of Zurich (1522), and burgomaster (1524-42). His name is found on numerous mandates against the Anabaptists (71A/417/15, 71K/442/12, 71M/446/39-40, 71-0/452/22-23, etc.), including the mandate to exe-

cute Falk and Reimann (Epi.E/519/22).

95. **Wanner, Johann,** leading preacher in the Cathedral Church in Constance since 1521, even though he already displayed some support for Lutheran doctrines and this was the seat of the Roman Catholic diocese. He had been brought to Constance through the efforts of a small circle of enlightened officials. He had earned a ThD degree and impressed Erasmus as "a man of evangelical integrity" (ZW, VII, No. 209, fn. 1). When the Lenten fast violations in Zurich in 1522 disturbed the religious sensitivities of conservative Catholics throughout the diocese, Bishop Hugo von Hohenlandenberg sent Wanner to Zurich as part of a three-man delegation to admonish the council to remain loyal to the old faith. Although Wanner was certainly of a different attitude than the other two—the suffragan bishop Melchior Wattli and the papal theologian Nicholas Bredlin—all three were subjected to the righteous anger of Zwingli and Grebel. Zwingli ridiculed them as "that unnecessarily magnificent delegation" (47D/180/23-24) and Grebel called them "intrepid tri-tongued Lucifers" (185/34). Wanner increasingly sided with the Reformers and was a frequent correspondent with Vadian concerning the Reformation in Constance and St. Gallen. It was to Wanner that Vadian could express his reservations about the excess cruelty of Zwingli in the execution of his father-in-law, Jacob Grebel (Epi.A/473/18-25).

96. **Westerburg, Gerhard** (*ca.* 1498-1558), was married to Carlstadt's younger sister and was in Zurich in advance of his brother-in-law to promote the publication and distribution of the latter's writings (65/295/14ff.). He was about the age of Grebel, with an MA from Cologne and a doctorate in civil and ecclesiastical law from Bologna. Through the influence of Nikolaus Storch of Zwickau, he early identified with the left wing of the Reformation. Expelled from Saxony along with Carlstadt in the autumn of 1524, he came to Zurich with eight pamphlets on baptism and the Lord's Supper which Carlstadt had written at the challenge of Luther (65/296/9-11). Accompanied by Felix Mantz, Westerburg proceeded to Basel, where they were printed, except for the one on baptism, which was refused. The others were printed in editions of 1,000 copies, some of which Mantz brought back to Zurich for distribution as Westerburg returned to Germany to work with various peasants' movements in Frankfurt and Cologne. He became an Anabaptist leader in the latter city (1529-34) and was drawn into the "New Jerusalem" uprising in Münster. As opposition increased, however, he left the Anabaptists to join the Reformed Church, serving his last years as a preacher in East Friesland and northern Germany (ME, IV, pp. 930-31). Grebel may have abetted the distribution of Westerburg's pamphlet, *On the Sleep of the Soul;* and nearly three years later Zwingli appended an attack on this alleged Anabaptist doctrine at the end of his *Elenchus* (see Jackson, 1901, pp. 251ff.).

97. **Wetter, Sebastian Wolfgang,** called Jufli, was the assistant pastor of the Church of St. Lawrence in St. Gallen. An ardent supporter of Zwingli and Vadian in the work of church reform, he found it difficult to work with the head pastor, Benedict Burgauer (see Cast of Characters No. 11) and served on a disciplinary committee to investigate the latter's recalcitrance (see 68M/fn.2). Grebel greeted Wetter in Letters 24, 29, 49, 56, and 66, and expressed appreciation for his commitment (56/225/21-26).

98. **Widerker, Anna,** matron at the Green Shield Inn in Zurich, where Anabaptist meetings were held. She may have been the wife of Hans Widerker (see 66/299/6), although by March 1526 she was a widow (ZW, VIII, p. 703.20). She was the sister of Guildmaster Uli Bluntschli, who with his wife also lived at the Green Shield (Quellen 1, pp. 159, 179). She and her maid, Regeli Gletzli, and Frau Bluntschli "and her maids" were all baptized in early December 1525, by Heinrich Aberli, who led Bible studies in her house (*ibid.,* pp. 159-63). It was in their inn also that Aberli harbored Balthasar Hubmaier for several days prior to his arrest on Dec. 20 (*ibid.,* pp. 158-61) and that Karl Brennwald baptized Ernst of Glätz (71M/ 445/34-35, 447/13-18). On Jan. 13, she and Regeli were fined five pounds each for allowing themselves to be baptized (*ibid.,* p. 164).

99. **Wirz, Hans,** stepbrother of Jacob Grebel through a second marriage of Hans's father to Jacob's mother. He served as Ammann (governor) of the district of Wädenswil, twenty miles southwest of Zurich. It was here in the Wirz family castle that Vadian and Martha Grebel were married August 1519 (see 9A) and lived for about six months to escape the plague in St. Gallen (11/55/3-6). Conrad Grebel's close friendship with his Uncle Hans is attested by the fact that he secured his intervention to soften the wrath of his father at the time of his own marriage (see 47/165/6). Wirz and his daughters, Dorothy and Margaret, were probably witnesses to the marriage of Conrad and Barbara in the Fraumünster in the presence of Pastor Engelhart, another relative. Wirz often warned Conrad and his father about their involvements with foreign pensions (28/136/24-26); and Jacob was asked at his trial "why his brother, the manager at Wädenswil, threatened him in Conrad Baumann's house" (Epi.A/466/35-37).

100. **Wirz, Heinrich,** brother of Hans, stepbrother of Jacob Grebel, *Ammann* (governor) of the jurisdiction of the monastery at Einsiedeln, part of the family estate since 1383. Hans and Heinrich Wirz were concerned about Grebel's foreign pensions and spoke to Conrad about the serious consequences which the pensions entailed (28/136/25-26).

101. **Wüst, Michael,** first cousin and fellow student of Heinrich Bullinger, University of Cologne, *ca.* 1519. They both came from Bremgarten, ten miles west of Zurich. Jacob Wüst, the older brother of Michael, held a Cologne MA and was already a reputable scholar, having become schoolmaster in the monastery of Muri and then pastor at Lunkhofen near Bremgarten; but Jacob died prematurely in 1524. In a letter dated 1526, Bullinger wrote that since their youth, Michael had been his traveling companion to such places as Emerich in the Netherlands and to Cologne, that he had become the learned schoolmaster and subsequently the pastor in Klingnau in the canton of Aargau, but that he had been misled by the Anabaptists. Bullinger added that "he died among the Anabaptists in Oberglatt" (ZW, No. 467, p. 561, fn. 1 and *Zwingliana,* I, p. 447), which indicates that Michael must have died in the same year that he received a letter from Zwingli, attempting to extricate him from the alleged Anabaptist entanglement (71P/452/24ff.). It is not known exactly how or when Michael became an Anabaptist. As recently as December 1525, Bullinger had the impression that Michael was still holding to old faith views, from which he tried to dissuade him (Quellen 2, p. 263, fn. 19). If he was won to the movement through the preaching of Krüsi before the latter was

executed on July 27, 1525, it must have happened without Bullinger's awareness. It is certainly probable that Wüst met Grebel following the latter's escape from prison on Mar. 21 (see 454/11ff.), because Oberglatt, where Wüst was living at the time, was the first destination of Grebel's fellow prisoner, Karl Brennwald. Moreover, with Brennwald in Oberglatt was the wool-weaver, Hans Küntzi, who reported meeting Grebel on his flight from Zurich (71Q/455/6-10). There was a group of Anabaptists in Oberglatt; and in another letter dated May 2, 1526, Bullinger wrote that "our Michael unhappily deserted the priesthood and has gone into wool weaving" (ZW, No. 467, fn. 1).

102. **Wyss, Bernhard** (1463-1531), native of Ravensburg, Bavaria, near the Lake of Constance, emigrated to Baden, Switzerland, in 1497, working as a baker. He later settled in Zurich, where he served as a Confederate guard in the role of "chronicler," using the vernacular German. The result of this assignment was the authorship of one of the best chronicles of the history of Zurich during the first quarter of the 16th century, including the episodes of Grebel's summons before the council for preaching against the monks (47B/175/17-21), Zwingli's confrontation with Franz Lambert (47B/175/22ff.), the first public marriage of a Roman Catholic priest, William Reublin of Wytikon, the execution of Felix Mantz Epi.B./474/36ff.), and the execution of Jacob Grebel.

103. **Xylotectus (Zimmerman), John,** was a canon and the pastor at the Beromünster in Luzern, a humanist and close friend of Myconius. Like Zwingli he sponsored young men in their study under Glarean at Basel and Paris and under Vadian in Vienna (see *Zwingliana,* 2, pp. 58ff.). By the end of 1520, he was labeled in Luzern as one of the eight *Haupterneuerer* (chief innovators) of Switzerland. As one of the priests who married ahead of official sanction, he was harassed by church officials until he was forced to seek refuge in Einsiedeln, then in Basel, where he died in 1526. Grebel sent greetings to him in all but one of his letters to Myconius at Luzern.

104. **Zili, Dominik,** was the schoolmaster in St. Gallen since 1521 and a preacher at St. Lawrence's since 1524. He was quite receptive to the Reformation, and Grebel greets him in a letter to Vadian (35/147/23-24). Because he served as the authorized Bible reader in place of the unauthorized Wolfgang Uliman, he had several confrontations with the St. Gallen Anabaptists. First, they wanted to have Uliman appointed as co-reader (69A/360/29-30), but Uliman himself refused to consider such an appointment. Second, when Zili gave approval to Zwingli's anti-Anabaptist *Taufbüchlein* and decided to read it to his parish in place of the usual Bible expository sermon, Uliman interrupted him from the balcony, saying, "Stop reading and give us God's Word instead of Zwingli's" (70A/383/34-35). In spite of these differences, Zili was always accessible to the Anabaptists (see 71E/423/39) and "remained open and sympathetic to their position on the ban longer than any of the other Zwinglian Reformers. . . . Early in 1526, Zili was himself accused of preaching radical ideas and being the founder of Anabaptism in St. Gallen [but] he was cleared of the charges by the Small Council" (Erwin Schlabach, pp. 158, 191, based on Quellen 2, pp. 411ff.).

105. **Zwick, Johann** (1496-1542), Reformation leader in Constance, the seat of the diocese that embraced Zurich. Born and raised there, he studied law at Freiburg (1509) and at Bologna (1518-20), where he earned a doctorate in civil and ecclesiastical law. He then taught law at Basel (1520-22), where he was introduced to Zwinglian ideas of church reform. Ordained to the priesthood in 1518, he was the pastor at Riedlingen near Constance (1522-24) when he attended the Second Doctrinal Disputation in Zurich (57C/246/29). Zwingli was especially glad to have him represent Constance because the bishop had refused to attend; but Zwick got into increasing conflict with his church authorities and was excommunicated as a heretic in 1526. Before that, however, he had a two-year preaching appointment in Constance itself (1524-26), where he was much loved as a compassionate and gifted evangelist, counselor, administrator, and hymn writer. Hence, he was able to return as head pastor in 1527 when the Reformation was officially accepted there in May, and he served there until his death. It was to him that Vadian wrote a fascinating, although largely negative, critique of Grebel, Denk, Hätzer, and Hubmaier in 1540, many years after all four had died—two by martyrdom and two by the plague.

106. **Zwingli, Huldrych** (1484-1531), lead Reformer in Zurich (1518-31), father of Reformed Protestantism in Switzerland (1523). Born into a rugged family of Swiss patriots in the village of Wildhaus in the mountain region called the Toggenburg, he received his early theological and humanist education under the supervision of an uncle, the parish priest in Wesen. He attended a private Latin school in Bern (1498-1500), the University of Vienna (1500-02), and the University of Basel (BA, 1504; MA, 1506). Then on his uncle's reccommendation, he became pastor at Glarus (1506-16), where he accepted an annual papal pension and served as chaplain in several foreign wars. Identifying himself with the humanist-pacifism of Erasmus (1516), he began to speak against the mercenary service of Swiss soldiers in foreign wars. After a brief pastorate in Einsiedeln 1516-18), he won the appointment as people's priest in the Grossmünster in Zurich (1519-31), although technically on Nov. 9, 1522, he resigned as people's priest so that he could be reinstated by the City Council as head of the Grossmünster Chapter, thus bypassing the authority of the Roman Catholic diocesan bishop. As head of the church in Zurich, he formulated and led a humanist-biblical program for Christian renewal and reform, first by systematic preaching from the Bible, then by published writings, e.g., *Concerning Choice and Liberty Respecting Food* (April 1522), *Apologeticus Archeteles* (August, 1522), which included Grebel's Reformation poem (47D), *On Divine and Human Righteousness* (July, 1523; see 52B), *Essay on the Canon of the Mass* (August, 1523; see 57A), *A Brief Christian Introduction* (November 1523; 58A), etc., and third by convening two public disputations in January and October of 1523 (see 51A and 57C), through which the majority support of the City Council was won for the principle of the Reformation on the basis of scriptural authority. A turning point in the Zwinglian Reformation came in December, 1523, when Zwingli made a fundamental concession to the reluctance of the council to act in the face of conservative resistance and indefinitely postponed abolition of the mass and images in the church (see 57D, 57E, 58B) and when a small number of his more radical advocates, whose precipitous actions were previously functional for Zwingli's reform program (47A, 47B, 47C, 47D, 47G, 51B, 52A, 52B, and 57A) began to form a pre-Anabaptist party in Zurich (59A, 66A, 67B,

67C, etc.). In opposition to this group, which initiated rebaptism in a private meeting in Zurich (January 1525), Zwingli wrote numerous letters (67A, 68D, 68M, 69D, 71N, 71P, etc.), held numerous disputations (66A, 68B, 68I, 68L, 71J, 71M, etc.), and published numerous treatises (67C, 69C, 70C, Epi.C, etc.), giving increasing sanction to their arrest, imprisonment, banishment, and execution. At the price of compromise, he not only gained a pro-Reformation majority in the council but succeeded in setting up a small secret council within the Large Council, by which he was able to crush the last pro-Catholic resistance and to execute its alleged leader, Jacob Grebel, father of Conrad (October, 1526; see Epi.A). Having gained almost unlimited power in Zurich, he designed plans for a war to reconstruct the old Swiss confederacy with the help of an anti-Hapsburg alliance with France. In the so-called Second War of Cappel to achieve these ends, Zwingli died in battle (1531); and his grandiose plan collapsed.

Notes

Pro.A. Vadian's Vision for Grebel's Education, Vienna, 2/28/1517

1. See Cast of Characters No. 93.

2. *Helvetii,* lit. "Swiss," the inhabitants of medieval Switzerland, originally a Celtic people occupying what is now Western Switzerland and governed in the first century BC as a political district of the Roman Empire. The terms *Helvetii, Helvetia,* and *Helvetius* occur often in the present collection and are translated "the Swiss," "Switzerland," and "Swiss" (adj.) or "Helvetian" (in poetry), respectively.

3. Lat. *Cunrade amatissime,* found also in 1A/59/8-9. This salutation is to be distinguished from the more common *charissime* ("dearest," or "most gracious"), found often in Grebel's letters to Vadian. As in letter 1, below, the salutation appeared as part of the first sentence of the letter. At the time this dedication letter was written, Grebel was at the midpoint of his three-year study at the University of Vienna and had gained a prominent place among Vadian's students.

4. Lucius Apuleius of Madura in Africa flourished around AD 150. Educated at Carthage and Athens, he traveled extensively before returning home. His most important work was his novel *Metamorphoses,* a satire upon the debauchery of certain orders of priests and the hypocrisy of their pretense to supernatural powers. The book may have been part of Grebel's personal library (see 69/357/31ff. and 358/29)

5. *De mundo liber* (Book about the World) was Apuleius's translation of a Greek work by a pseudo-Aristotle.

6. Nysa was the legendary scene of the nurture of Dionysus (Bacchus), the youthful effeminate god of wine.

7. Cyrrha was an inland town southwest of Delphi, the inhabitants of which levied contributions upon pilgrims on their way to the Delphic oracle, in consequence of which the Amphictyons destroyed them in 595 BC. The territory, the rich Crissaean plain, was declared sacred to the Delphic god and was not to be cultivated.

8. Olympus was the highest mountain in Macedonia and therefore the mythical abode of the Greek gods, of which Zeus was chief.

9. Ossa was a mountain in Thessaly, connected to Olympus on the northwest by the vale of Tempe and celebrated by Homer in the legend of the war of the giants.

10. The quotation from Apuleius is almost verbatim, except for several minor adjustments that Vadian made to fit it into his own context.

11. Lat. *illustribus artibus,* "illustrious arts" (see 5/71/20-21), i.e., the seven liberal arts (see 1/fn. 10).

12. Vadian is making a distinction between the seven liberal arts and literature, which he puts in a separate category.

13. Carefully as Vadian expresses himself in humanistic language, his longing for an evangelical faith clearly emerges in this paragraph on the importance of theology, which was *not* one of the seven liberal arts (see 1/fn. 12).

576

14. The priority that Vadian gives to theology is underlined by this disregard of Aristotle, which is inconsistent with the general emphasis on philosophy in the rest of the letter. Nevertheless, Vadian wants to make a clear distinction between the pure faith of primitive Christianity and the intellectualized formulations of Scholastic Theology (see also fn. 27, below). Historically, Scholasticism was more than 400 years old, for it began with the teachings of the ecclesiastical schools founded by Charlemagne to reestablish Christian learning by integrating Catholic doctrine with Aristotelian logic.

15. From this comment, it is clear that Vadian had the thriteenth century in mind, which has been called the Golden Age of Scholasticism, in which the founding of the mendicant orders (especially the Franciscan and Dominican), the rise of the universities (especially Paris and Bologna), and the translation of hitherto unknown works of Aristotle were all part of the most productive period of the movement.

16. "At Paris, the eager study and enthusiastic acceptance or rejection of Aristotle's works both in the original and in the interpretations of the Arabian commentator, Averroes (1126-98), resulted in violent controversies and the formation of three outstanding schools of thought" (J. J. Fitzgerald, "Scholasticism," Ferm, p. 695).

17. Vadian returns to the liberal arts and sciences; and perhaps sensing his slight inconsistency in the previous paragraph (see fn. 14), he becomes somewhat inconsistent for the second time by stating that theology, which is the "most outstanding" among the higher disciplines, is "no more noble than astronomy." Nevertheless, the logic of the statement comes through in the last clause of the sentence.

18. An element was one of the four substances—earth, air, fire, and water—constituting the physical universe.

19. *Metaphysics* was the title of Aristotle's treatise on the basic kinds of things and properties that make up the cosmos or universe. The Greek philosophers divided metaphysics into two branches: ontology and cosmology.

20. Physics, from the Latin *physica,* meaning natural philosophy or science.

21. Vadian had begun his study of medicine in 1514; and because he was about to earn his doctorate in this discipline, he felt slightly self-conscious about the high claims he was about to make for this profession. He may have been aware that M. Terentius Varro (116-27 BC) in his *Discipline* had added medicine and architecture to the list as basic to all education.

22. Lat. *mores,* "customs" or "fashions" or "rules." In a post-Comte period in the development of the disciplines of sociology and political science, in which the term "mores" has specialized meaning, it is fascinating to read this early sixteenth-century view of what we now call the social sciences.

23. In the unfinished analysis of the relationship of Humanism and Anabaptism, this comment throws light on the ambivalence that many sixteenth-century humanists felt about the role of social radicals in society. Vadian wanted Grebel to "examine more deeply" but apparently not so deeply as to question the fundamental structures of the social order.

24. Again, Vadian is involved in a slight inconsistency, or perhaps the paradox of a *scientia* which can threaten the existing social order and yet, by definition, must remain open to "the sweet knowledge of nature's great mysteries."

25. *Ambrosia* carries the double meaning of the food of the gods and the food that gives one "a certain divine" knowledge, like the tree of the knowledge of good and evil in the Garden of Eden (Gen. 2:16-17).

26. The reference was to the garland with which winners were crowned at the Olympic games in ancient Greece, held every fourth summer in honor of Olympian Zeus. The games were first confined to running, but boxing, chariot racing, and other sports were later introduced.

27. By this claim that pure faith requires a certain detachment and unique commitment, Vadian amplifies on his earlier criticism of an overemphasis on reason and logic in Scholastic Theology (see fn. 14, above).

28. The text has *decimotertio,* but someone, perhaps the original owner of the book (see Intro., above), scratched out *tertio.*

29. Marsilio Ficino (1433-99) was a Renaissance scholar in the Florentine Academy who translated Plato and other ancient Greek philosophers into Latin in order to make Platonism the bridge to Christian faith for the educated.

30. The *Phadeo* of Plato contains the moving scene in which Socrates spends his last hour on earth speaking to questions of ultimate significance with the young men he is leaving behind—the meaning of life and death and the quest of the soul for an afterlife.

31. Vadian was himself involved in translating Books 15 and 16 from the Historical Library of Diodorus Siculus (see fn. 37), which included accounts of Philip II of Macedon (382-36 BC) and his son Alexander the Great (356-23), and in true polyhistoric spirit is commending a truly integrated and comprehensive approach to knowledge.

32. Codrus was a poet of the Flavian period (AD 66-96) who wrote an epic, *Theseid*.

33. It is not entirely clear whether the parenthetical phrase qualifies Codrus or Aristotle. Although the Latin word order pushes the balance of the argument towards Codrus, it is possible that Aristotle is the one to whom the statement was not ascribed by all.

34. Penelope, the wife of Ulysses. During his twenty-year absence, she was beleagured by importunate suitors whom she put off by declaring that before she could make up her mind she must finish a large robe which she was making for Laertes, her aged father-in-law.

35. Horace (65-8 BC) was Rome's greatest lyric poet, best known for his compressed, elegant expressions, such as the one here quoted by Vadian from the *Ars Poetica*, 343.

36. Upon the death of Angelus Cospus late in 1516, Vadian succeeded to his chair as Professor of Rhetoric. One of the unfinished tasks of Cospus which he inherited was to finalize the publication of Cospus's Latin translation of the Greek work of Diodorus (see next fn.) and to carry out Cospus's lectures on the work of the ancient Greek historian. (See 46A/ fns. 2 and 3.)

37. Diodorus Siculus, Greek historian in the first century BC and author of *Bibliotheca Historica*, consisting of 40 books, only some of which are still extant. It was divided into three parts, and the two books that Vadian was translating were from the second part, which covered Greco-Roman history from the destruction of Troy to the death of Alexander.

38. The reference is probably to Dionysius of Halicarnassus, also a Greek historian and contemporary of Diodorus (see fn. 37, above). His great work was entitled *Roman Antiquities,* and contained 20 books. It is unlikely that Vadian was referring to one of these books, since only the first eleven are extant and the rest remain only in fragments. What is more likely is that Vadian was working exclusively with the fifteenth and sixteenth books of Diodorus, and that the sixteenth quoted extensively from the work of Dionysius. It is known that Diodorus followed special authorities like Dionysius in certain sections.

39. The text has *decimo sexto,* but *sexto* has been crossed out, perhaps by the original owner of the book (see fn. 28, above).

40. Giovanni (Lat. Jovianus) Pontanus (1426-1503) was one of the most gifted poets of the Italian Renaissance. He came to Naples as a penniless scholar, following the murder of his father in a small-town civil strife in Cerreto and his own exile with his mother to Perugia, where he was educated. In Naples his rise to political power was phenomenal, first as tutor to the sons of Alphonso the Magnanimous, and then in turn as political adviser, military secretary, and finally chancellor. At that point he founded an important academy in Naples for the encouragement of the literary arts. His writings are divided into prose (history, dialogues, dissertations) and poetry (elegies, idylls). It was as a Latin poet that he exhibited his greatest talents, especially in his didactic and cosmological poems such as *Urania* and *Liber Meterorum,* written in hexameters about stars and meteors and other atmospheric phenomena such as lightning and rainbows. Pontanus's writings were published in Venice by the Aldine Press (see 1/fn. 21), which issued a three-volume *Pontani Opera* in 1513, 1518, and 1519 (republished in Basel in 1538).

41. This was a prepublication reference to Vadian's *De Poetica et Carminis Ratione* (Concerning Poetry and the Theory of Verse), Vienna, 1518. The thesis of this volume is similar to the main point of Vadian's letter to Grebel: the art of writing must be joined to the understanding of nature and the universe. The book of thirty-two chapters had been in

process since 1513 in the form of readings and lectures and was published at the request of his students. Among the many questions discussed in the book is the relation of poetry to faith, and an entire chapter citing the Church Fathers was devoted to the thesis that poetry correlates with the deepest revelation of Holy Scriptures. See 5b/Intro., below.

42. See fn. 18, above.

1. Grebel to Zwingli, Vienna, September 8, 1517

1. Although Zwingli's letter has been lost, Oscar Farner reconstructs its contents in an article in *Zwingliana*, 1913, No. 2, pp. 34ff. Conrad Moser was the carrier of Zwingli's letter (see 1/57/26-27).

2. Zwingli had come to Einsiedeln the previous October after ten years as pastor in Glarus. See Jackson, 1900, chs. II and III.

3. Although Conrad wrote the letter himself (see 57/23), he was writing also on behalf of his second cousin, John Leopold Grebel (see Cast of Characters No. 39).

4. The horn of the goat, Amalthaea, or horn of plenty, an emblem of abundance.

5. A proverbial term for something very precious and rare. See Petronius, *Lena,* 38:1, and Pliny, *Natural History,* pref. 23.

6. The nine goddesses of arts and sciences: Calliope (epic poetry), Clio (history), Erato (lyric poetry), Euterpe (flute), Melpomene (tragedy), Polyhymnia (mimic arts), Terpsichore (dancing), Thalia (comedy), and Urania (astronomy). Grebel refers to them in general ten times and once in particular to Calliope (10/91/18-19).

7. Grebel used a familiar phrase from Roman comedy, "It will matter not the slightest."

8. Lat. *mansuetiorum literarum,* which could also be translated "of refined literature" or "of polite letters."

9. Confession as to the priest, Zwingli.

10. Lat. *artibus liberalibus, quas sempem vocant.* The seven liberal arts in the late classical and medieval periods consisted of the *trivium* (grammar, rhetoric, logic) and the *quadrivium* (music, arithmetic, geometry, astronomy).

11. A crown of laurel was used to indicate academic honors. Two meanings are possible: he would not distinguish himself as a scholar or he would not pass the final qualification for the baccalaureate degree.

12. Lat. *sed hoc meo suadente genio,* "but so my genii persuade me" or "but thus my persuading genius." There is less feeling content in this expression than in Grebel's later references to *ingenio meo,* "my nature" (10/90/28-29) or *affectibus meis,* "my moods" (37/149/24-25). It is a matter-of-fact statement with a possible implicit meaning. Young humanists, particularly those with a poetic interest, sometimes debunked academic degrees as part of the apparatus of defunct scholasticism. By disclaiming any laurels, Grebel might be expressing an attitude of nonconformity to the old order.

13. Maximilian I, emperor from 1493 to 1519 (see Cast of Character No. 68). Insofar as these scholarships were part of the strategy of the emperor, the king of France, and the pope to secure the support of the Swiss, they were a corollary to the pensions granted leading Swiss citizens to promote mercenary service by the Swiss in foreign armies. Although Zwingli later vigorously opposed such pensions, he was himself the recipient of a pension from the pope and was certainly not opposed to academic scholarships at this time. See Epi.A/fn.73.

14. Vienna, one of the great cities of medieval times, about 500 miles east of Zurich, was the residence of the Hapsburgs, whose possessions at this time included not only Austria but a large share of Central Europe, as well as Burgundy and the Low Countries. They had furnished the emperors of the Holy Roman Empire for many generations. Vienna had become a center of the humanistic studies north of the Alps through its celebrated university founded in 1364, the first in the German-speaking world. From 1500 on, it was at its height and drew students from all lands. There were about 600 students in attendance at this time (see King, *Geschichte der Kaiserlichen Universaität zu Wien,* I, p. 226). A stream of Swiss students began in 1500, reaching its height in the years 1510 to 1520.

15. Lat. *incubui ... incubiturus,* "to sit on top of," "to incubate," "to brood over," "to cherish," "to nurture"—a metaphor from classical literature, used of a miser over his chest of money, etc.

16. Henry Loriti (see Cast of Characters No. 28).

17. Fritzsche (pp. 11-12) writes that Grebel's superlative about Glarean was shared by other students, such as Valentin Tschudi, who said, "I doubt whether there are ten like him in all Switzerland," and Rudolph Collin, who called him "the most faithful instructor of all."

18. Lat. *inter Orci cancros herente* is susceptible to two interpretations. It could mean "stuck within the lattices of Orcus" or "stuck between the claws of the crab." Orcus was the god of the infernal region, and a similar expression occurs in Latin literature in Apuleius's *Metamorphoses,* 6, 25, where it means "among the lattices [cancelli] of the lower world." Orcus may also refer to the Crab (cancri), the constellation. If this was Grebel's meaning, there may be a slight reference to the famous eulogy of Augustus by Virgil in the beginning of the "Georgics": the new constellation of Augustus is in the sky, and Scorpio (the Scorpion) withdraws his claws (G.I. 34). Whether Vadian is entangled in the claws or behind the lattices, the meaning is the same: he is preoccupied *(haeret).*

19. Pomponius Mela was a Latin geographer of the first century AD, living in Spain under the Emperor Claudius. He was author of an extant work, *De situ orbis libri III* (Concerning the Geography of the Earth in Three Books), in which he describes the coastline of the Mediterranean and the interiors of various countries, reporting legends and customs in a form reminiscent of Herodotus. Although it contains many errors, it was considered the most competent geographical compendium of classical times. It was the first distinctly geographical work after Pliny's *Historia Naturalis.* It had been lost through the Middle Ages, and Vadian's new edition with commentary was his own most important work as a scholar. Its full title was *Pomponii Melae libri de situ orbis tres, adiectis Ioachimi Vadiani in eosdem scholiis, Addita quoque in geographiam catechesi, et epistola Vadiani ad Agricolam.* The first edition was published by Lukas Alantsee and printed by Johannes Singrenius in Vienna, May 1518. A second edition was published by Andreas Cratander in Basel in January 1522 (see 40/154/38ff.) and a third in Paris in 1530.

20. Lat. *sub prelo Vienne et in literariis follibus,* "under the press in Vienna and in the literary bellows." A number of terms borrowed from the blacksmith shop were applied to the process of printing in early times.

21. The Aldine Press was founded by Aldus Manutius of Venice (1450-1515), one of the greatest printers of the humanistic period. The press was noted for its splendid editions of the classics, as well as for the introduction of the simple italic type. Upon his death in 1515, his father-in-law, Andrea Torresano of Asola, carried on the press during the minority of Aldus's sons.

22. Ludwig Celius Rhodiginus edited classics and published his *Antiquarum lectionem commentari* in Venice in 1516.

23. Jacob Wimpheling (1450-1526), of Schlettstatt in Alsace, was professor at Heidelberg, dean of the cathedral at Speyer, for a time retired to a monastery in Strasbourg. His book to which Grebel refers was published in 1510 under the title *Soliliquium pro pace Christianorum et pro Helvetiis ut resepraesciant,* a political pamphlet written to influence the Swiss to return to the Holy Roman Empire. Grebel favors continuation of Swiss independence and therefore mentions the pamphlet with distrust.

24. The first of a number of expressions of patriotism by Grebel, in which he was influenced by the Swiss patriotism of his teachers—Vadian and Glarean. Bender writes, "When such men were away from home in foreign lands they thought of themselves as exiled Swiss scholars temporarily living abroad, not at all as international cosmopolitans. One of their chief aims was the development of young Swiss scholars, even though they taught them far from home in Vienna and Paris, scholars who would prepare for a greater and more glorious future for the fatherland in the field of learning" (1950, p. 233). On Grebel's expressions of patriotism, see especially 26A and 6/80/41ff. See also Index listings for "fatherland," "Swiss," "Switzerland," and "native land." Almost all such expressions came before 1520,

after which he tempered his patriotism to a great degree as his mind set changed. In 41/156/ 15-16, he actually expressed some hostility to the "attitudes of the people and citizens at home."

25. Lat. *Helvetiomastigis,* borrowed from the terms *Ciceromastix,* which referred to the lampoom against Cicero by Largius Licinius, and *Homeromastix,* which referred to the spiteful criticism of the Homeric poems by the Greek grammarian Zolius. See 6/fn.30.

26. Joannis Baptista Egnatius, learned printer of Venice, published the books mentioned in 1516. Their full titles were (A) *Ad Franciscum huius nominis primum de eius in Italiam adventu: Deque clarissima ex Helvetiis panegyricus* and (B) *Joannis Baptistae Egnatij veneti de Caesaribus libri III a dictatore Caesare ad . . . Maximilianum Caesarem.*

27. C. Plinius Secundus, called Pliny the Elder, was born in Northern Italy in AD 23. His greatest work, in 38 books, was his *Natural History,* which is really an encyclopedia, the first of its kind by a Roman writer.

28. Johann Camers (1458-c.1546) was born in Camertino, Italy, with the name Giovanni Ricuzzi Vellini. He was a leading professor and classicist of Vienna, and published an index to Pliny's *Natural History* in 1518.

29. George Collimitius (1482-1535), Latinized from Tannstätter, came from Bavaria, earned an MA degree from the University of Ingolstadt, and then became professor of mathematics and astronomy at Vienna. Like his student Vadian after him, he became poet laureate, rector of the unversity, and a doctor of medicine, all with a continuing interest in the classics. As the following footnote indicates, he and Vadian were close friends as well as colleagues.

30. Vadian had earlier published two editions of Pliny in connection with his lectures at the university. One was Pliny's *Introduction to World History* (1513) and the other was the seventh book of Pliny's *Natural History* (1515). The former was dedicated to Collimitius in appreciation for the impetus to do this work, and the latter was dedicated to the Vienna Boys' Choir. In 1517 Collimitius had prepared *scholia* on the second book of Pliny's *Natural History* on the basis of a lecture manuscript by Vadian. The commentary to which Grebel referred was not actually published until 1531, when it was issued as a Pliny edition by the Basel printer Jacob Ziegler. The names of Collimitius and Vadian appear as coeditors, although the former did most of the work on it. Näf, I, p. 180, fn. 5, gives the title as follows: *Iac. Ziegleri . . . in C. Plinii de naturali historia librum II. commentarius . . . Item Georgii Collimitii et Joachimi Vadiani in eundem secundum Plinii scholia quaedam.* The signature underneath included the following: "Georgii Collimitii Viennensis gymnasii mathematici ordinarii in C. Plinium librum secundum dictata Joachimus Vadianus excoepit."

31. Maximilian I (see Cast of Characters No. 68 and fns. 13 and 14 above).

32. See fn. 16, above.

33. See fn. 1, above.

34. Lat. *Institore,* "one who sells for another." The agent is Ulrich Kramer of Zurich, related to Zwingli through marriage. Zwingli sent him to study with Vadian in June 1517. He subsequently became a monk, and later a strong supporter of the Reformation.

35. Conrad Moser of Zurich was a friend of the two Grebels, having studied with them in Basel and Vienna.

36. In writing the date in Latin, *sexto Nonas Septembris,* Grebel makes two mistakes, so that it is uncertain which date he means. In the Roman system of reckoning dates, three days of the month had special names, the Kalends, always on the first day of the month, the Nones, in some months on the fifth and in others on the seventh day, and the Ides, in some months on the thirteenth and in others on the fifteenth day. Any day between these special days was counted as so many before the next following special day, never as so many days after the one before. The days at both limits were counted customarily. In September the Nones fall upon the fifth day of the month, so there could be no sixth day before the Nones. There may be a mistake either in the word sixth or in the word Nones for Ides, which being on the thirteenth would refer to the eighth day of September. Or he might have meant a different month. In the month of October the Nones come on the seventh, so that the sixth day

before would be October 2. Of the two possible days, September 8 seems preferable.

1A. Vadian to Grebel, Vienna, May 1, 1518

1. Lat. *candidissimi ingenii,* "of the most shining talent." See Pro.A/50/11, above.

2. As in Pro.-A, above, the salutation appeared as part of the first sentence of the letter.

3. Vadian was still a junior professor at the university that included such learned colleagues as the poet-rhetorician to whom he dedicated the work, Rudolph Agricola; the poet-historian and university rector, Cuspinianus; the Latin specialist, Angelus Cospus; the Latinist-theologian, Johann Camers; and the mathematician-astronomer, Collimitius. The rivalry and competitiveness were notorious (see fn. 17, below).

4. Lat. *quod gloriae meae nominive male in praecipite opere consuluerim,* "because I might have consulted badly for my glory or name in precipitous work."

5. The plural form, *vestris,* is used, anticipating the next sentence.

6. Rudolph Clivanus or Collin, see Cast of Characters No. 16.

7. George Binder, see Cast of Characters No. 4.

8. Bender (1950, pp. 18-19 and pp. 230-31, fn. 41) lists twelve others who were in Vienna at this time: Johann Hinwiler, Christopher Crassus, Jacob Zwingli, Conrad Moser, John Leopold Grebel, Ulrich Kramer, Ulrich Lener, Melchior von Watt, John Jacob Zurgilgen, Benedict Burgauer, Johann Bünderlin, and Andreas Eck (Eggius). To this list should be added the name of Christopher Schürpf (see 2/Intro.). Bender writes that Vadian's students lived together in the Brücken Bursa, located across the street from the main building of the university. The procurator of this bursa would give Vadian a receipt for payment of the accounts of all his students whom he had guaranteed.

9. Lat. *bonas literas,* "polite letters" or "noble literature."

10. Lat. *et spei plena,* "and full of hope."

11. Lat. *ornamenta,* "ornaments."

12. Vadian might be pointing this admonition at Grebel, who in spite of his great talents lacked perseverance in his studies. "This is the way my temperament inclines me," he wrote to Zwingli (1/56/20-21).

13. Lat. *Lucubratio,* "lamp-work."

14. Lat. *id vobis ceu acceptum debeitur,* "it will be due to you as a credit." Again (see fn. 5, above) the pronoun is plural in reference to the assistance and participation of all his students in the work now published.

15. I.e., the *Pompcnius Mela.* See 1/fn.19.

16. Lat. *situs terrae,* "situation of the earth" or "structure of the earth."

17. Lat. *qui ex professo illa tradunt,* "who by profession transmit these things." The sense of the Latin here clearly implies the known conflict between the humanists and the scholastics in Vienna and a disdain for those scholastics who by abilities to which they lay false claim do a disservice to the ancient writers. Vadian is probably referring especially to his colleague, Johann Camers, who had also published an edition of the *Pomponius Mela,* in which he took a very literal approach with the kind of scholastic deference to the untouchable authority of the classics that Vadian and Zwingli rejected. Vadian's model of scholarship was to test the theories of the great writers of the past by the empirical observations of the present, as he had tried to do in his own edition of the ancient geographer.

18. Lat. *arrepto scriptore aliquo,* "having seized on something that has been written."

19. The books which scholars like Vadian wrote and edited and published were used by their pupils as texts; and as the professor lectured on them, they would write additional notes between the lines and in the margins of their textbooks. See Näf, I, p. 326.

20. Lat. *ut passim obvia vocabula facta sunt,* "as the words were composed in their path at random."

21. Lat. *ceu farraginem quandam indigestam.* Juvenal had used this culinary metaphor, *farrago,* to describe the variety and realism of his writings. Here it means a mess, hodgepodge, or concoction of what comes quickest to hand. It is interesting that Vadian uses this term in the title of one of his important unpublished theological writings of 1525 (see 68M/356/9 and

582

68M/fn.2).

22. Zona, the name for the classical five belts of the earth's surface with respect to latitude and temperature: south frigid, south temperate, torrid, north temperate, and north frigid.

23. Bootes, a constellation in the northern hemisphere containing the bright star Arcturus.

24. Lat. *a hercle,* "by Hercules," a mild exclamation. Hercules was a hero of classical mythology noted for great strength, e.g., achieving the twelve labors imposed on him by Hera. The term can also mean "by heaven," referring to a northern constellation.

25. Greater length than someone who would take an overly literal, exclusively deductive approach to the text (see fn. 17, above).

26. Antipodes, those in opposite parallels and meridians.

27. Antoeci, those under the same meridian but opposite parallels.

28. Perioeci, those in the same parallel but opposite meridians.

29. Lat. *umbris,* "shadows."

30. Lat. *tyro,* "young soldiers."

31. Charybdis, a whirlpool off the Sicilian coast personified in Homer's *Odyssey* as a female monster who twice a day swallowed down the waters of the sea and thrice threw them up again.

32. Lat. *morigerari nobis,* "humor us" or perhaps "cooperate with us." This is clearly another well-placed admonition at the point of Grebel's weakness (see fn. 12, above).

33. Andreas Eck, a student of Vadian from his home town of St. Gallen. He is affectionately mentioned in two of Grebel's letters (2/62/5-6 and 5/73/6-7). After his return in 1527 from seven years of military service in Spain, he inquired of Vadian twice in letters concerning the whereabouts of Grebel, though the latter had died more than a year before. See V.B., IV, 477 and 493.

34. Lat. *meus a pedibus,* "mine at the feet" or "my pupil, who sits at my feet."

35. *Catechesis,* "oral instruction," but in this case referring to a manual for oral instruction, viz., Vadian's commentary on the *Pomponius Mela.* The same word was used in the title of the book (see 1/fn. 19). See also 40/154/38 and 40/fn. 6.

1B. Grebel Addresses Mela, Vienna, May 1518

1. On the person of Pomponius Mela, see 1/fn.19, above.

2. See Pro.A/fn.2, above.

3. It is not clear whether Grebel's imagery in this couplet refers to the ancient geographer Pomponius Mela, or to his writing *De Situ Orbis,* which was lost through the centuries. The text is often corrupt, and editors like Vadian attempted to restore its pure Latinity.

4. Lat. *audire salutem limine,* "hear one's greeting from the doorstep," proverbial for "to greet in passing" or "to touch upon slightly" or "not go into deeply." See *Ad.* I.9.91.

5. Antipodes, see 1A/fn.26.

6. Lat. *umbra,* which can mean "eclipses." See 1A/fn.29.

7. The Lat. *Antipodas calles et quas non attigit umbras Hermoleos terrae lima beata tuae* is vague. If Hermoleos refers to the Greek god whose Latin name was Mercury, among his many duties was to oversee roads and to protect travelers. His gold sandals carried him across land and sea with the speed of the wind.

8. Lat. *Jamque patent omnes Phoebeo vindice nodi.* Was Grebel referring to Phoebus, surname of Apollo in his capacity as the sun god, or to his twin sister, Phoebe, an epithet of Artemis in her capacity as the goddess of the moon? If the latter, her help might have come at night when Vadian burned the midnight oil for his writing (see 1A/fn.13).

9. Nemesis, the Greek goddess of retributive justice. See 45/fn.5.

10. Lat. *An Vadianus erat phoebum qui complet utrinque Ille vir Helvetici maxima fama soli?* Concerning the Greek god Phoebus (Apollo), see fn. 8, above, and 17/fn.9.

11. Lat. *Ut probet Helvetiam victrici Marte potentem Victricem doctis non minus esse viris.* Mars was the god of war (see 22/fn.9).

2. *Grebel to Vadian, Zurich, July 23, 1518*

    1. Lat. *Conradus Grebelius Vadiano, preceptori suo charissimo, S.D.P.*, the proper way to begin a letter in classical Latin. The initials stand for *salutem dicit plurimum*. From this letter and the following one, it is evident that Grebel had returned to Zurich in the company of Vadian sometime before the beginning of July. The *Pomponius Mela* was published in Vienna in May, and since Grebel brought copies with him (3/63/18-20), they could not have left Vienna before that time.

    2. The identity of John Ofnerius and Jacob Walther is unknown. This is the only place they are mentioned in Grebel's letters.

    3. On Conrad's father, Jacob Grebel, see Cast of Characters No. 38.

    4. Lat. *nuncium*, "messenger." Two similar terms used later by Grebel are *tabellarius*, "courier," and *vector*, "bearer." *Gerulus* (carrier) was also used (see 54A/223/23). Epistolary intercourse was haphazard, being dependent upon personal messengers, special couriers, or traveling friends. Once his letter was carried by *oratores* (37/149/25-26), apparently official emissaries who were en route.

    5. For location of this house (near the Grossmünster), see Bender, 1950, p. 3.

    6. Lat. *deum optimum maximum*, here used to designate the Hebraic-Christian God, was used by the humanists of the fifteenth century who fostered a return to the Latin of the Ciceronian age. Since the chief of the gods among the Romans was known as *Jupiter optimus maximus*, who corresponded to the Greek Zeus, the God of the Christians was styled *deus optimus maximus*. Grebel often referred to the Christian God and the gods of Roman mythology in the same sentence (5/70/33-35, 14/100/10-12, 36/148/22-24, etc.). As used here, the reference to Almighty God was a form of oath.

    7. Reference to the thermal baths taken for physical therapy, usually at Baden, twelve miles northwest of Zurich.

    8. The reference is undoubtedly to Barbara, his oldest sister (see Cast of Characters No. 32), who was living in or near Baden at this time. In the next letter to Vadian (4/67/33-34), he writes, "I returned from my sister and from Baden, where I was taking the baths."

    9. The identity of the cardinal's musician is unknown. He was evidently acting as messenger between Vadian and Grebel. The cardinal was either Matthew Schinner (see Cast of Characters No. 82), the papal legate until 1517 and a resident of Zurich for two years thereafter, or Antonio Puccius (see Cast of Characters No. 72), the papal legate from 1517 until 1521 (see 23/fn.22).

    10. Perhaps the length of time it would have taken Vadian to travel from St. Gallen to Zurich if he left immediately.

    11. The sister mentioned here is Martha (see Cast of Characters No. 40), whom Vadian did indeed marry a year later, August 18, 1519. The whole story of Conrad's ultimately successful campaign to accomplish their marriage is told in Letters 4, 5, 6, and 10. Conrad had two older sisters—Barbara (see fn. 8, above) and Euphrosine, a nun in the convent of Oetenbach in Zurich. Two younger sisters (Martha and Dorothy) were still at home. Martha could not have been more than 18 at this time, fifteen years younger than Vadian. A younger brother, Andreas, was a courtier of King Ferdinand of Austria at this time.

    12. Othilia and Katherine von Watt were sisters of Vadian. Näf (II) believes that Helen and Anna, listed here, were also sisters; but he bases this entirely on this letter, and Grebel seems to refer to them as maids. It is known that Othilia married Bartholomew Steck, an educated merchant in St. Gallen, on August 8, 1519. See 57A/fn.7.

    13. Andreas Eck, see 1A/fn.33.

2A. Myconius to Vadian, Zurich, July 23, 1518.

    1. Oswald Geisshüsler, known as Myconius (see Cast of Characters No. 70).

3. Grebel to Zwingli, Zurich, July 31, 1518

    1. The reference is probably to Zwingli's letter to Grebel in Vienna mentioned in 1/56/1-2, which prompted the first letter in reply.

    2. Lat. *commodiori argumento*, which could also mean "more extensive proof" (AB),

but since a longer letter was apparently not the intent, Grebel probably meant "more suitable subject" (EY).

3. See 1/fn.1.

4. See 1/fn.19.

5. By "us," Grebel refers to others like Myconius who were also anticipating Vadian's visit. See 2A/62/36-38.

6. Vadian actually came to Zurich for the promised visit on August 4, and Zwingli could readily have come too.

7. Myconius, see 2A/fn.1.

8. This inquiry of Zwingli's and that mentioned at the beginning of the next paragraph may indicate a second letter from him in addition to the one to which Grebel's first letter replied, although the questions might also be rhetorical.

9. The wound was evidently incurred in a sword fight in which his arm was badly cut. As he later described it to Vadian, perhaps in exaggeration, "I barely emerged without having my whole arm cut off" (13/97/17-18).

10. Lat. *me infoelicum,* a phrase found in Plautus, Amph., 1,1,171.

11. The Toggenburg is a valley in the lower Alps in the Canton of St. Gallen. Zwingli was often addressed by his friends as "Doggius," i.e., the Toggenburger.

12. Lat. *parocho,* "a supplier of needs," "a host." The term was transferred to the role of a parish priest, vicar, rector. The most universal equivalent in the English-speaking world is "pastor," if by this term is meant the traditional professionalized church leadership function and not simply an informal shepherding function. *Parochus* was Grebel's most often used term for the traditional priestly role; and even when he used other Latin or German terms *dominus plebanus* (35/147/24-25), *pastor* (59/275/10-11), *Pfarrer* (30/139/28), *Hirt* (67/302/32), there is little indication that he meant anything other than the traditional role. Hence, the word "pastor" will be used for all of these terms. Exceptions would be Grebel's references to *evangelische Prediger* (63/288/37) and *Hirten* in the Reformation free church sense (56/225/7, 63/286/24, 63/289/11-12,15, 63/291/36, 64/293/18-19, and 65/296/6-7). In the latter cases, "shepherd" is used instead of "pastor." In several instances, e.g., "the most learned shepherds" (63/289/15, 64/293/18-19, 65/296/6-7), an ironical usage was intended.

3A. The Ascent of Mt. Pilatus, August 1518

1. Vadian's account as published in the second edition of the *Pomponius Mela,* p. 34 (see 1/fn.19, above) was transcribed by Studer (p. 64) and by Weber (pp. 249-51). A translation into German by Götzinger was published in Schlatter, pp. 263-64.

2. The date of the ascent is indefinite. The account, published in January 1522, was written before December 1520, when the manuscript of the *Pomponius Mela* was in the hands of Cratander, the printer. We know from the account itself (65/21) that the ascent took place a year before the writing. Since Grebel arrived in Paris in October 1518, it must have occurred between June and when he was at home in Zurich. The phrase in Grebel's letter from Paris "when you were ready to go to Luzern on horseback" (13/97/31-32), probably refers to the Pilatus expedition. In the earlier letter of Sept. 26, 1518, Grebel mentions his farewell from Vadian "in Elligoew" (4/68/11), which was probably the return from Luzern when Vadian left Grebel and went on to St. Gallen. Willy Brändly (2, pp. 425ff.) suggests August 1518.

3. Lat. *fractum,* "fractured," "broken," "rugged." In his translation Götzinger (see fn. 1, above) used the term *gebrochene,* "the broken one."

4. Vadian used the medieval Latin name for the mountain, *Fracmont* (derivative of *Mons Fractus),* meaning "fractured mountain."

5. There are two theories about the origin of the name, Pilatus. One is that it derives from *Mons Pileatus,* "the hatted mountain," for the cloud cap that often forms around the summit at midday. Another, which is more pertinent to Vadian's account, is that it derives from Pontius Pilate of New Testament infamy (Mt. 27:2, etc.). According to an apocryphal account of the death of Pilate, Tiberius Caesar, afflicted with a serious illness, sent word to Pilate to bring the famous Galilean healer at once. But when Pilate could not oblige because he

had already crucified him, Tiberius ordered the procurator himself to be crucified. To avoid so disgraceful a death, Pilate committed suicide. His body was weighted and thrown in the Tiber River, but the demons which inhabited the body caused the water to boil as if in a storm. The body was then removed and sent to France, where the phenomenon was repeated in what is now known as *Mont Pilate* near Vienna. Then the body was brought to Luzern and buried in the lake at the top of Mt. Pilatus.

    6. John Zimmermann, known as Xylotectus (see Cast of Characters No. 103).

    7. Myconius, see 2A/fn.1 and Cast of Characters No. 70.

    8. Lat. *Grebeliae meae fratre,* "brother to my wife" or "my brother-in-law." Although not married at the time of the ascent, Vadian had married Martha Grebel by the time he wrote the account.

    9. Lat. *phlegethotae,* "of the Phlegethon," which in Greek mythology was the river in Hades containing fire instead of water. See Epi.C/fn.117.

3B. *Myconius to Vadian, Zurich, September 15, 1518*

    1. In September 1518, John Froben, the Basel book printer, published two writings of Erasmus under one cover. The first was the *Encomium Matrimonii* (In Praise of Marriage) and the other was the *Encomium Artis Medicae* (In Praise of the Art of Medicine). In his *De Conscribendis Epistolis* (On the Writing of Letters), published by Froben in 1522, Erasmus reissued the former as an example of expressions of dissent and advocacy.

    2. Lat. *Thermis,* used simultaneously for the name of the town and for the public baths located there (see 4/fn.2). For Grebel's references to this trip, before and after the fact, see 2/61/25 and 4/67/34-38.

4. *Grebel to Vadian, Zurich, September 26, 1518*

    1. See 2/fn.8.

    2. Lat. *Thermis* (see 3B/fn.2). Situated on the lower Limmat, about twelve miles northwest of Zurich, Baden was known from Roman times for the medicinal quality of its mineral waters and was much frequented at this time. Grebel had gone there for a cure (see next fn.).

    3. For a thorough discussion of Grebel's chronic illness, its symptoms, and a modern diagnosis, see Bender, 1950, p. 233, fn. 80. In 1937 a Zurich physician diagnosed the trouble as chilblain. It may have been something more serious, such as venereal disease (see 6/79/25-36 and 28/136/1-10). In either case, it was something which started in Vienna, caused pain and itching to his limbs and back, and plagued him to the end of his life (see 69/357/29-30).

    4. It is interesting to note the consistency between the gratitude expressed here and that expressed in Grebel's last letter to Vadian written in May 1525, after their relationship was severely threatened by the Anabaptist conflict (see 70/378/23-29). He lived up to his promise to be grateful "as long as I live."

    5. Grebel's decision to go to Paris is here first disclosed, although his first letter to Zwingli from Vienna revealed such a desire.

    6. See 1/fn.16.

    7. Lat. *die Jovis,* "the day of Jupiter."

    8. Bender (1950, p. 235, fn. 20) found a record in the Staatsarchiv of Zurich that identified the two students as "Hans Frey und des Holtzhalben sun." In *Zwingliana,* VI, 4, p. 213, fn. 27, Hans Wirz had identified the two students as J. J. Amann and Urs Hab, but Bender preferred the former evidence. Hans Frey is the same person mentioned in Grebel's letter to Myconius from Paris under the name of John Henry Eleutherius (7/83/5), who together with a certain Probapolitanus left Glarean before Grebel (see 7/fn.12). It is known also from the record of Jacob Grebel's trial that his servant, Jörg Hedinger, went with them at least as far as Freiburg (Epi.A/464/29-31). Bender (1950, pp. 33, 39) identified Probapolitanus as Heinrich Lingk of Schaffhausen; but the source for this information is not given.

    9. The trial of Jacob Grebel disclosed details about the allowance with which Conrad was to study at Paris. According to testimony given there he and his father had received 300 crowns yearly for three years (Epi.A/467/40-41, 468/35ff.). Leo Schelbert (p. 32, fn. 64) dis-

entangled the details of the disbursement of the funds: "Conrad had actually received 500 crowns.... In 1526, at the time of the trial, Jacob technically still owed his son some 400 crowns."

10. Elligoew, probably Elgg in the canton of Zurich, about halfway between Zurich and St. Gallen. Grebel and Vadian must have been here in the interval between Letters 3 and 4. Perhaps Grebel accompanied him this far on his return from their joint expedition to Mt. Pilatus in the month before.

11. Martha, married to Vadian August 18, 1519 (see Cast of Characters No. 40).

12. On the details of the dowry, see 23A/121/29-34

13. In a letter to Vadian dated 1516, Ulrich Lener thought Vadian would be interested in a pretty young widow in Appenzell, eighteen years of age, worth 2,000 guilders. An impression that Grebel carried of Vadian as late as May 1525 was that he was "beset" by money (70/379/9-10).

14. Lat. *Haec ut missa faciam,* "so that I may dismiss these matters."

15. Concerning Vadian's short trip to Vienna in the winter of 1518, see the references given in VB, III, 180, notes.

16. Grebel spent a good part of his stipends on books (see 13/97/2-3), first in Vienna and then in Paris. He had left his books behind in Vienna, and they were finally brought by Rudolph Clivanus and kept by Myconius pending Grebel's return from Paris (8/85/29-30). In financial straits as an Anabaptist fugitive, he finally sold all his books (69/357/32).

17. The Ravensburg merchants belonged to the big companies in Ravensburg, Swabia, only a few miles from the Swiss border. For the history of the great Ravensburg merchant companies from 1380 to 1530, see Schulte.

18. Wolfgang Heiligmaier of Bohemia, one of Grebel's teachers at the University of Vienna, whom he mentioned also in 6/81/13. Not much is known about him, although see VB, III, index and p. 296, and Joseph Aschbach, II, p. 136.

4A. Myconius to Vadian, Zurich, October 15, 1518

1. *De Poetica et Carminis Ratione* (Concerning Poetry and the Theory of Verse), Vienna, 1518. See Pro.A/fn.41.

2. Compare with Grebel's comment in 5/73/8-16.

4B. Zurgilgen to Vadian, Paris, October 26, 1518

1. *Mela,* see 1/fn.19.

2. See 1A/fns. 3 and 17.

3. The messenger was Jörg Hedinger, Jacob Grebel's servant. See Cast of Characters No. 44.

4. The reference is unclear in view of the fact that this letter was dated Oct. 26. It is possible the letter was not actually dispatched until the first of January.

5. Grebel to Vadian, Paris, October 26, 1518

1. See 1/fn.6.

2. See 2/fn.6.

3. The letter of Vadian to Grebel referred to here is not extant. Grebel is replying in the order in which Vadian's letter was written. The greeting of Vadian apparently referred to Grebel as a brother.

4. The only child of Conrad's who survived to marry was Joshua, from whom all his posterity was derived. Joshua was married on June 21, 1549, and had three sons and four daughters. One of these seven children was named Conrad, and he became the city treasurer in Zurich in 1624. His grandson, also named Conrad, became burgomaster of Zurich in 1669. A direct descendant of the thirteenth generation from the original Conrad Grebel, Hans Rudolf von Grebel, became the head pastor of the Grossmünster in Zurich in the 20th century.

5. [Omitted]

6. Lat. *mille millies parasangis,* "a thousand thousand parasangs." The parasang, a Persian measure of length (about 2.8 to 4.2 miles), was a literary construction of Grebel's.

7. Lat. *promptae narrationis copiam*, "abundance of prompt narration." Grebel was quoting Vadian.

8. Lat. *servulus*, diminutive of *servus*.

9. "In a long Iliad" means, of course, "in a long letter." Grebel uses this phrase frequently.

10. See 1/fn.16 and Cast of Characters No. 28.

11. The antecedence to the sentence would seem to indicate that the matter referred to had something to do with Glarean.

12. Harpocrates was the Egyptian god of silence or secrecy, represented as a boy with his finger on his mouth. Also interpreted as a Greek philosopher who enjoyed silence respecting the nature of the gods. Grebel used this reference five times.

13. Angerona was the Greek goddess of suffering and silence.

14. A follower of Pythagoras who took an oath of silence on his teaching. Pythagoras was a celebrated philosopher of Samos about 550 BC. At Crotona, 300 of his adherents were formed into a select order in lower Italy for the purpose of cultivating his doctrines. All that was done and taught was kept a profound secret from all outsiders.

15. Lat. *vix dixerim*, "this hardly expresses it."

16. William Budaeus (or Budé), born 1467 at Paris, was a leading Greek scholar at the University of Paris, a most zealous defender of the new learning. Grebel either attended his lectures or had personal conversation with him about some criticism of Vadian's regarding Pliny (see 6/79/15-18). Grebel delivered a copy of Vadian's *Pomponius Mela* to him (5/73/13-16), and sent to Vadian Budé's letter of response (5/73/37-38).

17. See 4/fn.3.

18. Lat. *non proletarius medicus*, "not a common doctor" or "not a doctor of the common people." The emphasis is on quality of performance, "not a quack."

19. See 2/fn.11.

20. Lat. *Hymenaeus*, the Greek god of marriage after whom the nuptial song is named. The "Hymanaeus" was sung by young men and maidens to the sound of flutes during the festal procession of the bride from her parents' home to the bridegroom's.

21. Lat. *nominis Grebeliana, quasi magni nominis*, "of the name of Grebel, as if of a great name."

22. There were three goddesses of fate or destiny: Clotho, who spins the thread of life; Lachesis, who determines its length; and Atropos, who cuts it off. They were called the Dread Sisters (see 12/95/2-3).

23. See 4/fn.16.

24. Homer, *Iliad*, II, 298.

25. Lat. *per Jovem lapidem*, "by the stone of Jove." The Latin proverb was "per Jovem lapidem jurare," said of one who swore by Jupiter, the supreme god of the Romans, identified with the Greek Zeus, who held in one hand a knife with which he pierced the sacrificial sow, and in the other a stone. This was regarded as the most solemn oath one could take. Grebel referred to his father as having taken this solemn oath as a senator (13/97/41).

26. See 1/fn.6.

27. Lat. *homuncioni*, diminutive of *homo*, man.

28. Krakow (Eng. Cracow, Ger. Krakau), a city in Galicia (south Poland) on the Vistula River. It was another center of Humanism in the Holy Roman Empire and seat of a famous old university on the eastern border of German territory, some 200 miles northeast of Vienna. Vadian studied here for one year (1501-2) and returned for a visit in the winter of 1518-19, including a visit to the salt mines of Wieliczka.

29. Sarmatia, ancient region of Northeast Europe in what is now Poland and part of Russia between the Vistula and Volga rivers.

30. See fn. 28, above. Vadian's brother Melchior von Watt was here for a time, as well as other kinsmen and friends, including Rudolph Agricola, with whom Vadian collaborated in some writing. Vadian's correspondence contains many letters from Krakow.

31. The full title of Vadian's *Poetica* was *Joachimi Vadiani Helvetii, de Poetica & Carminis ratione, Liber ad Melchiorem Vadianum fratrem*. It was published in 1518. Vadian's aim

in this work, which started as a lecture in the winter semester of 1513-14, was to relate the science of words to the wider realms of natural knowledge. He sent a copy to Grebel with instructions to pass it on to Myconius. When Grebel took it to Paris with him, Myconius wrote Vadian to send him another copy (see 4A). Grebel showed his copy to Glarean, who was "very highly pleased because he is mentioned so often and so respectfully in your *Poetica* and in other products of your night labors" (5A/74/32-35).

32. See 3/fn.7.

33. Lat. *illustrato* could also mean "illustrated," as the edition was, with maps.

34. See 1/fns. 16 and 19; 5/fn.16.

35. The letter received upon his departure (see 70/21-22, 27, above).

36. Croesus was a prominent king of Lydia in Asia Minor of the sixth century BC, whose wealth became proverbial.

37. The organization of Glarean's pupils into a Roman senate was described by Glarean in a letter to Myconius from Paris dated Sept. 1, 1520 (Zurich Staatsarchiv E.II, 336, p. 10, quoted in ZW, VII, 333, fn. 8). Scipio probably refers to Scipio Africanus the younger, 185 to 129 BC, best known as a military hero of the Third Punic War, 149 to 146 BC. He was also the center of a literary circle in which were numbered the historian Polidius, the poets Terence and Lucilius, and Laulius. The two Catos are M. Procius Cato the Censor (234 to 149 BC) and his great-grandson Marcus Cato (93 to 48 BC). The former was a statesman and writer who embodied the rigor of the old Roman character and spent his life combating the incoming tide of Greek and Hellenistic influence which was breaking down Roman morals. He is most distinguished as a rigid judge of morals. The censor was a Roman magistrate whose duties included the censoring of conduct and especially the punishing of the moral and political crimes of officials and men of high rank.

38. Apparently, John Leopold Grebel (see Cast of Characters No. 39) had some conflict with Vadian in Vienna, but was now defending him. See also 13/100/6.

39. Clivanus, Latinized from Collin. See 1A/fn. 6 and Cast of Characters No. 16.

40. The stipend is that which Grebel had received from the Emperor Maximilian for his studies in Vienna (see 1/fn.14). Testimony at the trial of Jacob Grebel indicated that George Binder, not Clivanus, received the stipend until Conrad returned to Zurich from Paris (see Epi.A/469/4-5).

41. Lat. *archetypon,* for which "archetype" would be the literal translation.

42. Authorship of the *Dialogus de Julio Pontifice Maximo,* written in 1513, performed as a drama in Paris in 1514, and published in Paris in 1517, was first attributed to Erasmus. This reference by Grebel confirms that assumption, further documented by P. S. Allen (Ep.502/Intro.). The *Dialogue* was a severe criticism of Pope Julian's military policies. He reigned from 1503 to 1513 and was succeeded by Leo X (see Cast of Characters No. 63).

43. Jörg Hedinger was a servant of Jacob Grebel and accompanied Conrad on his journey to Paris by way of Freiburg. Details are given in the trial of Jacob where Hedinger was compelled to testify (see Epi.A/465/19-20 and 469/20ff.).

44. Lat. *presbyteros,* "elders."

45. See 2/fn.13.

46. Lat. *Lutetie,* "Ile de la Cité," the center of Paris. "Paris" will be used unless the distinction is made, as in 6/81/35 and 7/83/14.

5A. Myconius to Vadian, Zurich, November 12, 1518

1. Glarean, see 1/fn.16.

2. *Poetica,* see Pro.A/fn.33.

3. Lat. *lucubrationibus,* "by moonlighting, "by nighttime writing," "writing done by lamplight." See 1A/58/23-24 where Vadian used the term with reference to his work on the *Pomponius Mela.*

5B. Grebel's Poem "To Joachim Vadian," Paris, 1518

1. On Vadian, see Cast of Characters No. 93. On his *Theory of Poetry and Verse,* see Pro.A/fn.33.

2. Lat. *diva parenti.* Zeus, the chief of the Olympian gods, husband of Hera and many rival wives, was often called the father of gods.

3. Eurynome, the mother of the Graces by Zeus. The daughter of Oceanus, she had also been mated to Thetis and Ophion. Hence Grebel's reference to Omnivolo, which means "all-willing" or "all-craving."

4. The Charites, called Graces by the Romans, were the three daughters of Zeus and Eurynome. Their names were Euphrosyne (joy), Thalia (bloom), and Aglaia (brilliance). They were the goddesses of music, poetry, and the arts, personifying grace and beauty.

5. Gordon Rupp (p. 363) has described Vadian as a "polymath"—a scholar of encyclopedic learning. It is this aspect of Vadian's work about which Grebel is poeticizing.

6. Lat. *Tonanti,* "Thunderer," epithet of several gods, especially Zeus (Jupiter). See 19/fn.9.

7. Mnemosyne, the personification of memory, was the daughter of Uranus and became by Zeus, the mother of the Muses.

8. Lat. *Catalides nymphas.* Castalia, a celebrated fountain on Mt. Parnassus, was especially sacred to the Muses, who because of this were sometimes called Castalides. For the names of the nine Muses, see 1/fn.6.

9. The Camenae were Roman divinities corresponding to the Greek Muses. The name is connected with *carmen,* an oracle or prophecy. They were, accordingly, prophetic nymphs. Two were named Antevorta and Postvorta. A third was Carmenta, a healing divinity who had a temple at the foot of the Capitoline Hill. The most celebrated was Aegeria.

10. *Pierides,* a surname of the Muses, derives from Pierus, king of Macedonia, whose nine daughters by Euippe or Antiope were given the names of the nine Muses. See fn. 12, below.

11. *Ardalides,* another surname of the Muses, derives from Ardalus, who was said to have invented the flute and to have built a sanctuary of the Muses at Troezen.

12. Lat. *certant,* from the infinitive certare, "to settle by contest." Grebel's reference is to the contest which the Pierides, the nine daughters of Pierus (see fn. 10, above), had with the nine Muses (the Ardalides; see fn. 11, above). When the Pierides were conquered, the Muses changed them into birds.

13. Lat. *Vates,* prophet, seer, bard, poet.

14. The last couplet was written in Greek as follows:

Βίβλια ταῦτα, ᾿ιδων Γοικτχ̄ θαυματ ιδεαθαι

Μνημοουνη, φεύ ἐχω μύρια τέκνα ἐφη,

Grebel published a slight revision of this couplet in the postscript to his Introduction to the Basel edition of Vadian's *Pomponius Mela* (see 26A/132/41-133/1).

6. Grebel to Vadian, Paris, January 29, 1519

1. See 5/fn.9. Grebel probably is referring to Letter 5, above, which is one of his longest letters.

2. Grebel continues the weaving metaphor.

3. Lat. *nugor,* "I trifle." This is a dominant theme in Grebel's letters expressed with a variety of words: *nugari* (trifle), *garrire* (chatter), *blaterare* (babble), *effutire* (blab), *loquacitas* (talkativeness), *garrulitas* (chattering), *battalogia* (verbiage), *multiloquia* (much talk), *verbosus* (wordy). The theme is common also to Zwingli's letters and to a general humanist self-awareness.

4. Lat. *muta aut viva,* "mute or alive," "by letter or by speech."

5. Lat. *evomere,* "to vomit out," often used metaphorically in classical Latin.

6. Lat. *pietissimos parentes,* "most pious [or dutiful] parents." *Pietas* means "faithfulness or dutiful conduct" in relation to the gods, to God, to children, or to parents. This is different from Christian love, but Grebel may not be pointing to a distinction at this point or to any lack in his parents.

7. Lat. *efflictim exosculer,* "kiss lovingly and utterly [i.e., to death]."

8. Second use of *evomere,* see fn. 5, above.

9. See 3/fn.7.

10. See 1/fn.16, 5/fn.10, and Cast of Characters No. 28. Glarean was conducting a kind of boarding school known as a bursa or pension because of the financial support (pension) received from the king of France for this purpose. He came to Paris in May 1517, bringing with him some of his pupils who had lived in his bursa in Basel. The first location of his bursa in Paris was a house in Rue St. Jacques in that section of the city known as the "vicus divi Jacobi," where printers and scholars lived. Grebel lived here from October to December 1518.

11. Perhaps the same three persons mentioned in the following letters, 7/83/5-7.

12. Three types of heating are mentioned in this paragraph: *caminus* (fireplace), *fornax* (which seems to have been a portable wood-burning stove), and *vaporarium* (steam heating).

13. *Caminus* (see fn. 12, above).

14. *Fornax* (see fn. 12, above).

15. *Vaporarium* (see fn. 12, above).

16. Lit. "nor was it permitted by oath to move the impediment." The meaning is not clear.

17. See 1/fn.33.

18. Lat. *bacchanalia celebrasse,* "celebrant of the feast of Bacchanalia," a feast held every three years in ancient Rome in honor of Bacchus, god of wine, the wildest celebration in Rome. The orgies of this worship were prohibited by decree of the Roman Senate in 186 BC.

19. Erasmus wrote to Regius (3/7/1516) that Glarean "has a great aversion to the intemperance of these fashionable drinking parties" (Erasmus, III, 251).

20. Lat. *Ego partes meas agens ... orabam,* "playing my part, I asked ... " an expression borrowed from the theater. See 12/94/23.

21. Lat. *pergrecandi,* an expression from Roman comedy, stereotyping the Greeks for their revels.

22. Lat. *Beraldum ... interpretantem audio,* "I hear Beraldus interpreting." Nicholas Beraldus first taught law at the University of Orleans, where he was born in 1473. Weary of the formalism of his work, he turned to the study of Greek literature at the University of Paris, where he became an ardent humanist and friend of Budé (see 5/fn.16). Beraldus made an ambassadorial trip to England in the fall of 1518, from which he returned at the end of October. He then taught at the university until the middle of March 1519, after which he made another ambassadorial trip to Southern France in the service of Bishop Poncher. Hence, Grebel could have heard Beraldus only from the beginning of November 1518 until the middle of March 1519. For further evaluation of Beraldus, see Bender, 1950, p. 252, fn. 121.

23. M. Fabius Quintilianus was a celebrated rhetorician of the first century AD., the first teacher of rhetoric ever supported in Rome at the expense of the state. His most important work still extant, and the one to which Grebel referred, was *De Institutione Oratoria,* a treatise in twelve books tracing the education of an orator from the earliest years of childhood.

24. Laurentius Valla (*ca.* 1407-1457) was an Italian scholar of the early Renaissance period. He taught classics and wrote Latin in a style that was later used as a model. He wrote a much-used manual of Latin usage, *De Elegantia Latinae Linguae,* 1471, which did much to expel the barbarisms of medieval Latin from the speech and writings of the learned. The reference indicates that Grebel was following the typical major interest of the humanists, namely, eloquence.

25. Glarean was trying to secure a teaching appointment at the university in addition to operating his own bursa. Bender (1950, p. 32) writes: "When the professor of poetry at the University of Paris, Faustus Andrelinus, died on February 25, 1518, he worked hard to secure the appointment to this vacancy, but his efforts were fruitless, the chair remained vacant. He did, however, receive the pension of 180 francs which Andrelinus had enjoyed, without being obligated in any way to lecture publicly at the university."

26. Lat. *Bononiam* refers to Bologna, which was in Grebel's plan as the place for future study (see 9/87/18,22-23; 25/126/7-8, 27/134/10, 31/140/34).

27. Six months later, Grebel has hopes that John Jacob Ammann will take him along to Italy (see 9/87/18-23).

28. On Budé, see 5/fn.16. Since Grebel does not specifically mention attending Budé's lectures, as he did in connection with Beraldus, it may be assumed that the information he is passing on to Vadian came by hearsay or in personal conversation. Bender (1950, p. 48) writes, "Since Budé was not a professor at the University, this cannot refer to regular lectures by Budé but probably to some group discussion by humanist scholars in which Grebel was present."

29. On Vadian's prior work on Pliny the Elder, see 1/fns. 27 and 30.

30. *Mastiges,* a Greek word meaning whip or scourge, here applied to persons, i.e., the "rascals" who do the scourging. This sentence may refer to Budé's criticism of Vadian three sentences earlier.

31. See 1/fn.33.

32. Grebel probably refers to the letter from Vadian received just prior to his departure from Zurich (see 5/fns. 3 and 35). If this is true, he has received no letter from Vadian since his arrival in Paris. Vadian is probably preoccupied with his courtship of Conrad's sister Martha.

33. See 4/fn.3.

34. Lat. *quum me saepe pensili venere mulieribus miscuerim,* "I have often joined myself to women for hired sexual love." Grebel apparently thought that his ailment and his visits to prostitutes were somehow connected. There is a possibility that he had syphilis.

35. Lat. *tu quoque haec adeo scies, ut nescire videare,* "you also know these things to such an extent that you seem not to know."

36. See 5/fn.12.

37. Kobler was a merchant of St. Gallen whose relations to Vadian are reported by Kessler in "Vita Vadiana" (Kessler, p. 602). The identity of Kobler's son-in-law is unknown. Vadian's trip to Vienna mentioned here is referred to frequently in the Vadian correspondence (VB, III, 180, fn. 1). The trip took place in the winter of 1518-19.

38. Lat. *ex animo,* "from the mind [soul, heart]."

39. Lat. *quod in buccis iam est,* "what is already in the cheeks [mouth]."

40. Lat. *ex animi vel intimis medullis,* "from the inmost marrow of my soul."

41. The von Watt family was prominent in St. Gallen, long established in the linen trade. Gordon Rupp writes, "If Leonard, Joachim's father, could not afford to live in the most fashionable part of town, he was a respected citizen, a Councillor *(Ratsherr),* member of the Inner Council of the oligarchy which rules the little republic. Wealth on the scale of a Peutinger or Pirckheimer he never knew; yet Joachim grew to moderate affluence, seems always to have had all the books he needed, and escaped the economic pressures which drove many to a clerical career" (p. 359).

42. Martha (see 2/fn.11 and Cast of Characters No. 40).

43. This is an important comment in the assessment of the charge of greed in the trial of Jacob Grebel (see Epi. A/465/1-3, etc.). Hans Wirz writes that the income was not sufficient to meet special expenditures like dowries and tuition costs (*Zwingliana,* VI, 209-10). Contrary to Wirz, Bender (1950, p. 46) views Jacob Grebel as an acquisitive man. Schelbert (p. 40, fn. 50) writes that Grebel's characterization of his parents in this text as *non tam divites quam honestos* ("not so rich as honorable") seems valid.

44. Lat. *tui cupida,* has a sensuous connotation, "passionate for you."

45. Lat. *superesse,* "left over."

46. See 5/fn.22.

47. Thalassio was a Roman senator under Romulus. At the time of the rape of the Sabine women, when a maiden of surpassing beauty was carried off for Thalassio, the persons conducting her, in order to protect her against assaults from others, exclaimed "for Thalassio." Hence arose the wedding shout with which a Roman bride was conducted to the house of her bridegroom. See Livy I.9.

48. Lat. *battalogia obstrepis.* See fn. 3, above.

49. Lat. *garrio.* See fns. 48 and 3, above.

50. In psychoanalytic terms, Grebel's prattling could be called "free association." In truth, Vadian served in the role of confidential counselor to him.

51. See 1/fn.14 and Cast of Characters No. 68. Emperor Maximilian died at Wels, Upper Austria, on January 12, 1519, just seventeen days before Grebel wrote this letter.

52. Francis I, king of France from 1515 to 1547 (see Cast of Characters No. 26), aspired to become emperor of the Holy Roman Empire. He had won a brilliant victory over the Swiss troops at Marignano in Northern Italy in 1515, which brought him an alliance with the Swiss cantons in the treaties of Geneva and Freiburg of 1516. The reference to the rebel Swiss cities probably refers to the revolt of the Forest Cantons in AD 1313, which began the movement toward the independence of the Swiss city states, rather than to any very recent secession. In Grebel's time the confederation included thirteen city states.

53. Grebel refers to the last of the four Italian Wars in which the Swiss fought: Ravenna and Pavia (1512), Novara (1513), and Marignano (1515). In the first three battles, the Swiss soldiers tipped the balance. At Novara, for instance, 30 miles west of Milan, occurred one of the most remarkable battles of history, in which 7,000 Swiss overcame 21,000 French, well supplied with cavalry and artillery, while the Swiss had neither. In 1515, however, a number of Swiss mercenaries had become disenchanted with the pope and defected to the French side, with the result that on September 14 and 15, the imperial troops were badly beaten in the battle of Marignano, ten miles southeast of Milan, and the reputation of the Swiss as the "ever victorious" was badly tarnished. Potter writes that "over 10,000 Swiss lay dead on the field. It was not as obvious then as it was later that the Swiss Confederation had ceased to be a great military power because, manifestly, if the Swiss forces had remained intact that September, a French retreat or defeat would have been certain" (1976, pp. 38-39).

54. A revealing expression of Grebel's early patriotism. See 1/fn.24.

55. *Caesar* and *Imperium*, emperor and empire (Julius Caesar being the first to rule the ancient Roman Empire). As Grebel says, Francis confidently expected to win the imperial crown of the Holy Roman Empire at the election following Maximilian's death on January 12. He had once exclaimed, "I will spend three million crowns to become emperor," but the election went to Charles I of Spain on June 28.

56. Zwingli was elected by the Zurich City Council to be the people's priest of Zurich on December 11, 1518. He arrived on December 27 and took up his duties on January 1. See 57C/fn.12.

57. The Latin title used by Grebel to designate chief priest is *parochus* (see 3/fn.12).

58. Valentin Tschudi, see Cast of Characters No. 88.

59. See 4/fn.18.

60. Probably Vadian's brother, Melchior von Watt, who had studied with Grebel in Vienna and who died in Rome on November 24, 1521 (see 44/159/20), according to a letter from Kaspar Wirth to Vadian dated Nov. 26 (see VB, II, No. 289, p. 403).

61. Johannes Hinwiler of Zurich, a fellow student of Grebel's at Vienna. His name appears with those of Conrad and Leopold Grebel in the Zurich "Bürgerbuch" as "Hans von Hünwyl, Jörgen von Hünwyls Sohn," when the three renounced their citizenship on "Zinstags St. Ulrich Abend, 1515" preparatory to leaving for Vienna.

62. Clivanus, see Cast of Characters No. 16.

63. Binder, see Cast of Characters No. 4. Note, however, that Binder added a personal postscript to Grebel's Letter No. 35 (35/147/22ff.); and in his own letter to Vadian dated January 1522, he referred in a personal way to Conrad and his sister Dorothy.

64. Andreas Eck, close friend and fellow student at Vienna (see 2/fn.13).

65. Probably a proverb that remains untraced.

66. Dodona, the most ancient oracle in Greece, was founded by the Pelasgians in Epirus and dedicated to Zeus. The responses of the oracle were given from lofty oaks or beech trees, probably from a grove consisting of these trees. The will of the god was declared by the wind rustling through the trees. In order to render the sounds more distinct, bronze vessels were suspended in the branches of the trees, which when set in motion by the wind came in contact with each other.

67. Lat. *per deum optimum maximum,* see 2/fn.6.

68. The Latin is *Pontani praeliminarem ad me scriptam.* The use of "impression" for the second word, which is not Latin, is purely a guess. The word was undoubtedly the same as the reference in the next letter (see 7/83/7-8). Grebel had sent both Vadian and Myconius a copy of the book by Petrus Pontanus, *De Helvetiorum Fuga.*

69. Lat. *vive et vale,* used in exchanging greetings: "Live [long] and be well."

70. See 5/fn. 46.

71. A suppressed quotation from Psalms 99:5, 110:1, 132:7, etc., suggesting both an identity and contrast between the footstool of God's divinity and Vadian's humanity.

7. *Grebel to Myconius, Paris, January 30, 1519*

1. On Valentin Tschudi, see 6/fn.58 and Cast of Characters No. 88. He was a fellow student in Paris. For his visit to Switzerland, which included some business connected with his appointment as pastor at Glarus, where Zwingli had served, he left Paris about February 1 and returned the following April.

2. On Glarean, see 1/fn.15, 5/fn.10, 6/fn.10, and Cast of Characters No. 28.

3. Lat. *extra iudicii mei meique similium aleam positum,* "placed beyond the hazard of my judgment and my fellows." This is a suppressed quotation from Pliny's *Natural History,* Pref. 7. The expression is unique and Grebel undoubtedly knew its origin. The compliment to Glarean is doubled if Myconius recognizes its origin. See 6/fn.29.

4. This comment contrasts with the hostile expressions of the previous letter.

5. The Latin reflects Grebel's uncertainty, for in the manuscript three words in succession in the last clause were crossed out and corrected.

6. Lat. *litterulas,* a diminutive of litterae, "letters." This is a common colloqualism in Roman letters.

7. Another example of Grebel's self-depreciation (see 1/fns.11 and 12, 57C/244/11-12).

8. Ialemus was the son of Apollo and the Muse Calliope. He was mentioned by the Greek tragedians as the inventor of the dirge or lament. Later, in the comic poets, his name became a proverb for cold, frosty, frigid poetry. A similar proverb was quoted by Zenolius (IV, 39), a scholar of Hadrian's time, and an edition of his work was published in Florence in 1497. It would be part of the equipment of a rhetorician.

9. Lat. *utraque manu et obviis ulnis,* a Roman proverbial expression (see Eras., *Adag.,* II, 9, 54).

10. "Ciceronian" had reference to a correct and lofty Latin style in the classical vein of the Ciceronian Age of Latin Literature.

11. Lat. *Calchographum,* a name printers gave themselves.

12. John Henry Eleutherius (Hans Heinrich Frey) was one of the three Swiss students who traveled together from Zurich to Paris (see 4/fn.8). A letter he wrote from Paris to his brother Abrosius was published in *Zwingliana,* 2, 92ff.

13. Probapolitanus, according to Bender (1950, pp. 33, 39), is Heinrich Lingk of Schaffhausen, but the source for this information is not supplied.

14. See 6/fn.68.

15. See 6/fn.56.

7A. *Glarean to Myconius, Paris, June 7, 1519*

1. On Glarean, see 1/fn.16, 5/fn.10, 6/Intro., and Cast of Characters No. 28.

2. Faustus Andrelinus, professor of poetry at the University of Paris, died on February 23, 1518. Glarean had tried unsuccessfully to be appointed to this vacancy but did receive Faustus' pension of 180 francs without obligation to lecture publicly.

3. See 8/fn.3.

4. In the *Deutsches Wörterbuch,* the word *Weidheitin* connotes a swaggering bravado.

5. Glarean probably refers to Grebel (see 7/82/17-25). Although Glarean's anger is evident, his attitude toward Grebel improved to the point where Grebel could return to his bursa seven months later; and between 1520 and 1522, after Grebel had returned to Zurich, Glarean greeted him five times in letters to Zwingli (see Bender, 1950, p. 239, fn. 77).

6. Lat. *Praeterea et is de quo in nupera epistula ad Ammanum data perquerebaris* might be read in two ways. *Et* can mean "also [in addition to Grebel]," in which case Glarean was complaining about two persons, or it can mean "also [in addition to my complaint]," in which case both Glarean and Myconius were complaining about the same person, i.e., Grebel. In the context of the total paragraph, the latter seems more likely.

7. John Jacob Ammann, see Cast of Characters No. 3, 8/fn.2, and 35/fn.16.

8. See Grebel's description of this episode in 6/78/15ff.

9. The previously close relationship between Glarean and Zwingli also ended in rupture (see 69D/376/10ff. and 10/fn. 14).

8. *Grebel to Myconius, Paris, June 9, 1519*

1. On the question of authorship, since this letter contains no salutation or signature, see Edward Yoder, MQR, II, 256, fn. 8.

2. The John Jacob referred to was probably not John Jacob Zurgilgen of Luzern (see 4B/Intro.) but John Jacob Ammann of Zurich (see Cast of Characters No. 3), since Myconius was still resident in Zurich (see 2A/fn.1). They were both pupils of Glarean and left for Zurich together in May 1519. Grebel referred to Ammann eight times in his letters but never to Zurgilgen, except perhaps in 19/111/33.

3. See Intro., above.

4. Lat. *aula*, "royal court," "hall," "palace," "auditorium."

5. On Clivanus (Collin), see Cast of Characters No. 16, 1A/58/15-16, 5/73/28ff., and 6/81/18-19.

6. On Grebel's books, see 4/fn.16.

7. Grebel probably had been asked to procure copies of these classical Latin authors for Myconius. Valerius could refer to any one of eight classical writers: Valerius Aedituus, Valerius Antias, Valerius Cato, Valerius Flaccus, Valerius Licinianus, Valerius Maximum, Valerius Soranus, or Valerius Martialis. An edition of Valerius Flaccus, *Argonautica,* was published in Paris in 1519, and may be the work cited. He was an epic poet of the Flavian period, AD 69-96.

8. Juvenal (Decimus Junius Juvenalis), AD 60-135, was a great Roman satirist. Jodocus Badius Ascensius issued an edition of his *Satires* at Paris in 1519 (see 20/fn.11).

9. A female courier is mentioned also in 12/93/11, probably the same person.

10. Just what the merited reward would have been is not known, but it may have had something to do with Myconius' leaving Zurich and returning to Luzern a month or two later.

11. Lat. *litteras illitteras*, "letters not letters."

12. Lat. barbaras, (1) of Latin style, "unpolished," (2) of manners, "wild," "fierce." Grebel deliberately forces the language to express his unsettled state.

13. See fn. 2, above.

14. Lat. *latrones*, "mercenaries," "robbers," "brigands." Grebel was probably referring specifically to the bandits who provoked the fight in which the Frenchmen were killed (see 9/86/32, 10/89/14-15, and 13/93/33-34).

15. Lat. *provisori*, "provisor," in medieval Latin a synonym for *episcopas* or "bishop." The reference may be to Zwingli, now the head priest in Zurich. Whoever was meant must have written Grebel a scolding letter.

9. *Grebel to Myconius, Paris, July 18, 1519*

1. Lat. *charissime immo clarissime*, a play on sound.

2. Lat. *Naenia*, a mournful song or dirge, chanted at funerals, was personified at Rome and worshiped as a goddess. She had a chapel outside the walls of the city.

3. The classical origin for this proverb is Erasmus' *Adagia*, I.9.28. It meant to catch a fast-moving opportunity.

4. Fortune was worshiped in Roman religion as the goddess of destiny, sometimes benevolent (the goddess of good luck) and often malevolent. Her worship became popular in later times when she was worshiped at Rome under many different titles. The image of

Fortune as a malevolent stepmother comes from Erasmus' *Adagia,* II.2.95. Grebel uses the image of Fortune and her strangling noose also in 12/93/22. In Roman literature, the sage often tells a malevolent Fortune to go and hang herself. Grebel imagines that Fortune is telling him to go and be hanged—a clue to Grebel's present self-image.

    5. See 8/fn.14.

    6. Grebel defers the real subject of the sentence until the end. He is intending a comparison between the devastation of the brigands and the plague, and so personalizes the latter and uses the same metaphors. The constant threat of the plague is indicated by the many references to it in his letters. It was very severe at Paris this year, more than 30,000 are reported to have succumbed to it, and the mortality among the students seems to have been especially high. Seven years later Grebel also "fell victim to the plague and died" (71R/456/15-16).

    7. Proteus, mentioned in Homer's *Odyssey,* IV, 351, the Man of the Sea. He had the power of assuming many different shapes to escape all who wanted to hear his prophecies. Hence, the English adjective "protean."

    8. Grebel, in company with four or five other Swiss students, fled to Melun, a town above Paris along the Seine, and returned to the city on January 1. According to a letter from Valentin Tschudi to Zwingli, dated January 2, 1520, he, Petrus Ricardus, Conrad Grebel, and two others had retired to Melun and remained there for six months.

    9. Grebel suffered continually from some ailment about which he often consulted Vadian. See 4/fn.3.

    10. From Vergil's *Aeneid,* IV.343. Dido cries out to Aeneus, who has betrayed her.

    11. Lat. *Lemnia mala,* "woes of Lemnos." Philocteles was left stranded on Lemnos with a snake wound by the Greeks going to Troy and suffered there ten years. A play of Sophocles on this story is still extant. The simile is based on physical and mental pain, on loneliness and desertion.

    12. See 6/fn.26.

    13. See 8/fn.2. Ammann spent a year and a half at Milan, from autumn of this year until the spring of 1521

    14. Lat. *me . . . respuat,* "spit me out." A classical though strong metaphor.

    15. Eurymnus is any person who tries to separate friends by calumny. The Achaean Eurymnus attempted to separate Castor from Pollux and was killed by Polydeuces.

    16. Lat. *fidus Achates,* from Vergil's *Aeneid,* VI, 158. The loyal companion of Aeneas became proverbial. Grebel is also drawing a comparison with the epic journey of Aeneas and Achates to Italy.

    17. The identity of this person is unknown.

9A. Jacob Grebel to Vadian and Hans Wirz, Zurich, August 26, 1519

    1. On Jacob Grebel, see Cast of Characters No. 38.

    2. On Hans Wirz, see Cast of Characters No. 99. Just a week before, Vadian and Martha Grebel had been married in the Wirz family chapel in Wädenswil, where Hans served as governor; and the couple remained here until early 1520 to escape the plague in St. Gallen.

    3. On Jörg Binder, see Cast of Characters No. 4. He had recently succeeded Myconius as schoolmaster at the Grossmünster in Zurich.

    4. This paragraph is addressed to Vadian, and the following one to Wirz.

10. Grebel to Vadian, Melun, October 6, 1519

    1. Letters written, perhaps, by both Vadian and Martha (see 19/fn.1). This was apparently the first letter from Vadian since Grebel arrived in Paris a year earlier (see 6/fn.32), which would account for the lapse of eight months between Grebel's last two letters to Vadian (Nos. 6 and 10).

    2. For this repetitive theme of self-depreciation, see 7/fn.7.

    3. See 9/fn.4.

4. Vadian's wedding to Martha Grebel on August 18, 1519.

5. Platonic year, the end of the time span in which the constellations return to the same place—15,000 years. Grebel means either an extraordinary year or an endless year (of misery).

6. This is the first reference to Jesus Christ in Grebel's letters. His present conception is certainly different from his later view (see 63/285/29ff., 289/16, etc.).

7. Lat. *ducere sponsum paranymphus,* "to lead the bridegroom as the paranymph." In ancient Greece the *paranymphos* was a bridesman who accompanied the betrothed man to fetch the bride.

8. A "cento" is a poem made up of verses of another poem. Grebel may be referring to the *cento nuptialis* (Wedding Cento) of Ausonius, poem XIII. Or the song is composed of many parts, as his misery is composed of many tears.

9. Lat. *sinister meus genius.* The last word connotes one's personal spirit or guardian spirit. To think of the guardian angel as sinister expresses the irony that Grebel intended.

10. Lat. *tuus ego alter,* "your second self."

11. On the Muses, see 1/fn.6.

12. Grebel means himself, interpreting his own dreams.

13. On the conflict with Glarean, see 6/77/17ff. and 6/Intro.

14. Grebel's judgment of Glarean is confirmed by the extant comments of others, e.g., Valentin Tschudi and Zwingli (see Cast of Characters No. 28).

15. Nessus was a centaur who attempted to rape Deianira, the wife of Hercules, who heard her screaming and shot an arrow into his heart. The dying centaur called out to Deianira to take his blood with her, as it was a sure means of assuaging the anger of Hercules and preserving his love. Later, Deianira had reason to fear that Iole would supplant her in the affections of her husband, and gave Hercules a robe anointed with the blood of Nessus, which penetrated into all his limbs and caused him the most excruciating agony. He tore off the garment, but it stuck to his flesh, and with it he tore away whole pieces of his body. He then ascended Mt. Oeta, raised an altar, placed himself on it, and had it set on fire. When the pile was burning, a cloud came down from heaven and carried him to Olympus, where he was reconciled to his enemies and honored with immortality. Grebel identifies Glarean with Hercules, but not himself with Nessus, who will have to be some "unknown" intervener.

16. See 1/fn12.

17. Letter No. 6, dated January 29, 1519.

18. Lat. *latrocinii crimine accusavit,* "he accused me of the crime of mercenary service [in a foreign army]." Since Grebel had never served in a foreign war, Glarean was referring to his taking of the French and imperial pensions (see 13/97/37ff.).

19. Gyrara, a small barren island in the Aegean Sea, one of the Cyclades, used by the Romans as a place of exile for criminals.

20. *Epithalamia,* a Greek word meaning nuptial songs. The play on the sound of this word and *epitaphia* (epitaph) is retained.

21. The owl and darkness are traditionally bad omens. Grebel means that in spite of everything he still has hope.

22. Calliope, chief of the Muses, the goddess of epic poetry. Because there is no mention of her death in mythology, to have sent Vadian her corpse implies the demise of his literary skills. The meaning of *bilingues atque adeo trilingues,* "two-tongued and actually [or almost] three-tongued" refers to the fact that Grebel has used three languages in his letters—German, Latin, and Greek. (See ZW, VII, pp. 251, 379, notes.)

23. Lat. *umbra,* in ancient Rome, an uninvited guest whom an invited one brought with him to dinner, usually a professional jester or clown. The reference is interesting by comparison to Zwingli's later calling Grebel an *umbra* [shade] in hell (see Epi. C/488/10, 490/33, 494/33, 496/10).

24. See 6/fn.58.

25. Peter Tschudi, cousin to Valentin Tschudi (see Cast of Characters Nos. 87 and 88).

26. John Leopold Grebel, Conrad's cousin (see 1/fn.1 and Cast of Characters No. 39).

11. Grebel to Vadian, Paris, January 1, 1520

1. The uncle is Hans Wirz, Ammann (governor) of the district of Wädenswil, twenty miles southwest of Zurich (see Cast of Characters No. 99).

2. Gordon Rupp writes: "It was between his betrothal and his marriage, when he was away from home, that the plague struck St. Gallen with unparalleled ferocity, carrying off a third of the inhabitants, over 1,700 in a few months. All this while Vadianus, town physician, stayed away.... It is a fact that many contemporary physicians added 'non-attendance in time of plague' to their terms of contract" (p. 346). The Latin for the last phrase, *sub cultro pestis,* "under the knife of the plague," is a metaphor borrowed from Horace from the victim at the sacrifice *(Satires,* 1, 9, 74).

3. By *aeterno opere,* Grebel may have meant in part his *magnum opus,* the *Pomponius Mela,* but as the rest of the sentence makes clear, he also meant his future work as a physician. Rupp writes: "The best proof that he knew there had been a failure of nerve came later, in his own courage in later epidemics, in 1530 and 1541. In 1541 he organized a large-scale evacuation to Marbach, and packed off his wife and his daughter Dorothy. He himself stayed, and in one of his finest letters wrote: 'I am not scared ... I stick to the job ... though I can neither eat nor drink, and joy has withered.' " *(Ibid.,* p. 365.)

4. I.e., Vadian has much more right to be a citizen, because of his worth.

5. According to 13/96/28, the messenger was Henry Lingk of Schaffhausen.

6. Cousin and fellow student of Grebel's in Basel, Vienna, and Paris (see Cast of Characters No. 39).

7. On the two Tschudis, see Cast of Characters Nos. 87 and 88.

8. Peter Tschudi did finally write to Vadian from Paris on June 20, 1520, in a vein similar to this sentence (see 16A).

9. Europus, the channel between the island of Euboea and the mainland of Greece, full of strong and dangerous currents. See 12/fn.19.

10. See fn. 1, above.

12. Grebel to Myconius, Paris, January 14, 1520

1. Lat. *nugivendae,* "dealer in women's apparel." If this is the same person mentioned in 8/85/35 and 15/103/14-15, the messenger was a woman.

2. Lit. "the grace of a little payment conveyed them all."

3. See 4/fn.16.

4. The image of the noose of Fortune is better developed in this sentence than in 9/86/31-32, though in the first part it is seen as a tightening knot, in the second part as being near to being slipped over his head. As Grebel writes, he does not always think in terms of the whole sentence. Sometimes he thinks by single words, but here he is thinking in clauses. The origin of the "noose of Fortune" is Juvenal, *Satires,* X.53.

5. Lat. *quae in hoc miserum caput cuduntur fabas,* "on my miserable head the beans are beaten." See also 27/134/6-7. This is a phrase from Roman comedy and balances the "tragedy" of the first half of the sentence. The phrase is used by a slave in Roman comedy, foreseeing punishment from his master (Terence, *Eun.,* 381). It thus adds a lighter touch, and Grebel is trying to poke a little fun at the serious family crisis. Myconius has apparently written Grebel about his efforts to mediate the family conflict.

6. Lat. *Guilielum,* "William." Is this the name of a man (EY) or place (AB)? The same name, clearly that of a man, occurs in 36/149/4, 37/149/30, and 39/151/17-18. In either case, the exact identity is unknown. The name of William Budé (see 5/fn.16) has been suggested.

7. See 9/fn.4 and fn. 4, above.

8. See fn. 6, above.

9. Italy with its papal abuses was the equivalent of what the English regarded as the morality of the Irish, clearly a stereotype in both cases. The humanists from the north of the Alps held aloof from the supposed moral looseness of the Italian humanists, and the term "Italian" was proverbial for moral turpitude.

10. Furies, the avenging sisters who drove Orestes mad as punishment for the murder of his mother. They represent the guilt that maddens. See 13/fn.42.

598

11. "Drive and drag" retains the sound effect of the Latin *agant exagitentque*.

12. Scylla (the monster) and Charybdis (the whirlpool) first experienced by Homer's Odysseus. If one did not kill you, and other did.

13. Endymion, the shepherd boy who was loved and put into a perpetual sleep by the moon goddess, Selene, who visited and kissed him each night in his sleep.

14. A word play in the Latin. *Moror* means "I hinder" or "I am a fool" according as the first vowel is pronounced short or long.

15. Lat. *Toronoei portus est,* "he is of the harbor of Torone." This refers to the harbor near the town of Chalcidice in Macedonia called Kophos, meaning "deaf." It was separated from the sea by two narrow passages so that because of its seclusion, the noise of the waves was never heard. From this arose the Greek proverb "deafer than the Toronaean harbor."

16. Lat. *blateravi* (see 6/fn.3).

17. A neat metaphor. Achilles, the Greek hero at Troy, refused to lead his troops in battle when he felt slighted. Because of his pouting and anger, many of his followers from Aetolia (the Myrmidons) were killed. Father Jacob Grebel is Achilles, brooding in destructive anger. The Myrmidons are the members of his family and others who suffer under his influence.

18. Lat. *Vt et hic garrire abstineam,* "But I should refrain here from talking nonsense."

19. *Euripus,* see 11/fn.9, proverbial for its seven daily current changes (see Aeschylus, *Agammemnon,* 292).

20. This refers to the ancient Greek and Roman habit of making an unbecoming and scornful gesture with the middle finger. It is mentioned in *Persius* 2, 33. Juvenal (*Satire* X) uses it of the sage mocking Fortune (53). Grebel quotes from the same line in 9/87/17-18 but has inverted the original phrase so that it is now Fortune who is mocking.

21. The Dread Sisters are the Fates who weave the cloth of life (see 5/fn.22).

22. To have the wolf by the ears suggests the desperate predicament of one who cannot keep his hold for long but cannot let go with safety. From Roman comedy (Terence, *Thornio,* 3.2.21).

23. Also an expression from Roman comedy (Plautus, *Capt.* 3.4.84). To stand between the victim and the knife is to be in the path of certain death.

24. The sentence is based on constitutional metaphors taken from the ratifying of a new law by the people: *velitis, jubeatis,* "as you wish, so you order."

25. For this proverbial expression, see Erasmus, *Adag.,* II.1.18.

26. Phrygian, the inhabitants of Phrygia in Asia Minor, stereotyped as slothful and disreputable (also called Trojans).

27. A possible double meaning: (1) "He has run away with my money, and it should drag him down to hell" and (2) the Roman practice of putting a coin in the mouth of a corpse to pay the fare across the Styx. The identity of the person to whom Grebel refers is unknown.

28. Grebel will forgive whatever remains of the debt.

29. Myconius moved to Luzern in the fall of 1519 to take charge of a school there (see 2A/fn.1).

30. Xylotectus, see 3A/fn.6 and Cast of Characters No. 103.

31. Lat. *ex officina nostra tortoria, utinam litteratoria* is hard to translate. A. B. had "from my barbershop, would it were a bookshop." Apparently, he thought Grebel meant *tonsoria* for *tortoria.* E. Y. had "from my headquarters, would they were educational rather than inquisitional."

32. There must have been another letter from Grebel to Myconius between Nos. 9 and 12 which has not been preserved, in what otherwise would have been six months of silence.

33. Lat. *Manes,* "souls of the dead." In Roman religion the Manes were originally the deified souls of the departed, but later the term was used in general for inhabitants of the lower world or infernal regions.

34. It was said that a novice who learned the Pythagorean system of philosophy was required to keep absolute silence for two years and merely to listen to what was told him (Erasmus, *Adag.* IV.3.72). Grebel mentions them also because they believed in existence after death. This was a deathly joke, intended as a message to Clivanus (see 8/85/26) to write back.

Since Grebel has not heard from him, he pretends he is dead.

    35. *Iliad* is proverbial for a lengthy literary composition.

13. Grebel to Vadian, Paris, January 14, 1520

    1. Reference is to Letter No. 11, dated January 1, 1520.

    2. Henry Linggius (Lingk) was a student from Schaffhausen who had studied in Vienna in 1514 and, like Grebel, had received a stipend from the French king to study in Paris with Glarean. Bender (1950, pp. 33, 39) reports that he and Grebel had left Glarean on January 1, 1519, and moved into a house with Hans Frey of Zurich.

    3. I.e., Letters 10, 11, and 13, written since Vadian's marriage on August 18, 1519. To date since his arrival in Paris, Grebel has written five letters to Vadian (counting the present one, No. 13) but has received only one from Vadian (see 10/89/9).

    4. Lat. *nuncii culpa,* "fault of the messenger."

    5. Grebel's return to Glarean's house indicates a lessening of the conflict between the two, in contradiction to Grebel's previous comment that Glarean never yields a grudge (10/90/25).

    6. For the evidence concerning the amount of Grebel's stipend, see 4/fn.9.

    7. Lat. *dissidiis,* probably *desidia.*

    8. The reference is to the sacking of Toulouse (Tolosa) in southern France by Q. Servilius Caepio in 106 B.C. He plundered the gold of the temples and was severely punished for sacrilege at Rome on his return. The fickle giver of the gold of Toulouse is presumably Fortune, who reclaimed her gift so soon. There is a reference to the gold of Toulouse in Cicero, *De Natura Deorum,* III.30.74.

    9. A scutatos was a French coin with the insignia of France on the shield, hence the name *scutum,* meaning "shield."

    10. Lat. *celeri regio.* "Celeres" was the name of the mounted body guards for Roman kings, from which was derived the adjective, *celer,* meaning swift, speedy, quick, rapid, or the adverb *celere,* meaning swiftly, speedily, etc.

    11. In addition to her role as wife of Jupiter, queen of heaven and protector of the female sex, Juno was guardian of new-born children. By making her a stepmother, Grebel was giving her a diabolical influence over him from birth. It is possible that Grebel also had in mind her added role of guardian of the finances, presiding over the temple on the Capitoline hill, which contained the mint.

    12. This letter, like all the letters from Jacob Grebel to his son, has been lost. Three letters from Jacob to Vadian have, however, been preserved. (9A, 23A, and 57A). The content of the lost letter of September 14, 1520, is partly summarized in the present letter.

    13. This escapade in Vienna was referred to in 3/64/3 and 3/fn.9 as the occasion for Grebel's return to Zurich at his father's urgent request.

    14. This second escapade in Paris was referred to in 8/85/17 and 8/fn.3.

    15. For a note on the Fates, see 5/fn.22.

    16. The reference here is to a lost letter from Myconius to Grebel. Myconius was at this time serving as schoolmaster in Luzern, but the letter was probably written from Zurich before his move.

    17. Tieresias, the celebrated soothsayer from Thebes in Greece, was blind.

    18. Matt. 7:3-5; Luke 6:41-42.

    19. At times Grebel appears to play upon the name Vadian. Perhaps he is thinking of the verb *vadere,* "to move, progress, advance, make one's way, get along well" (see 18/109/15-16).

    20. On Harpocrates, see 5/fn.12.

    21. This probably refers to the first visit of Vadian on August 4, anticipated in 3/63/29. It was probably on this occasion that Grebel and Vadian went to Luzern together for their joint expedition to Mt. Pilatus (see 3A).

    22. See 9/86/32, 10/89/14-15.

    23. See 1/56/23-24.

    24. See 4/68/8-9

25. In contrast to his earlier reports of these stipends (1/56/23-24 and 4/68/8-9), Conrad here assumes a critical attitude and speaks of having been pushed into this if not betrayed by his father. Bender (1950, pp. 45-46) cites this reference as evidence that Jacob Grebel "failed dismally in his parental obligations." In a similar vein, Hans Wirz (*Zwingliana*, VI, 213, fn. 27) describes the letter as "a shocking document which grants us a glimpse into the secret abyss of Confederate politics." In defense of Jacob, Leo Schelbert sees the letter more as "a typical document of a youth in trouble who blames his father in order to win back the favor of a friend whom he suspects of siding with the former" (p. 44). There is probably some truth in all of these interpretations of what is certainly one of the significant tragedies of history, leading to Jacob's execution (see Epi.A).

26. See 5/fn.25. Senators like Jacob Grebel took their oath of office by *Jovem lapidem,* "the famous [sacred] stone of Jove [Jupiter]."

27. Refers to lines 29 and 32, above, on the biblical reference to motes and beams.

28. Andreas, younger brother of Conrad (see Cast of Characters No. 31). He was still at home, but was soon to go as a courtier in the service of Duke Ferdinand (see 29/138/16-17), apparently at the instigation of the father. He returned from this service in early 1521 and died later that year (43/159/7-8).

29. Bender (1950, p. 43) writes: "Apparently the students of Glarean's bursa frequently discussed foreign pensions in a very patriotic spirit and condemned vigorously as traitors to the fatherland all such Swiss who sold their native land for money."

30. See 6/fn.52. The reference is to the struggle between Francis I and Charles V, the Holy Roman Emperor. The political function of the pensions as bribes was common knowledge.

31. Here and in lines 26 and 27, below, Grebel fears retribution on traitors in an independent Switzerland. His fear was prophetic (see Epi.A).

32. On Harpocrates, see 5/fn.12.

33. A reference to the Greek myth of Prometheus, who was punished by Zeus for stealing fire from the gods and giving it to men. Zeus punished him by chaining him to a rock, where vultures daily ate at his liver as it grew anew at night.

34. Lat. *non servus essem pecunie, et si illi iuxta adagium omnia obedirent.* Grebel was quoting from Eccles. 10:19, which in the Latin Vulgate reads: *Pecuniae oboedient omnia* ("everything obeys money"). RSV: "Money answers everything."

35. Gold was left for security in the temples of Delphi, and to take it was a terrible sacrilege. See also fn. 8, above.

36. See fn. 8, above.

37. At his trial, Jacob Grebel admitted that from the total scholarship of 900 crowns, he had held 400 back which he still owed his son (Epi.A/471/32-33).

38. Lat. *Intellexisti utriusque causam,* "you have learned [understood] the case [cause] of each side [both sides]."

39. Grebel's second reference to Christ (see 10/89/32-33), which is more personal than the first but is still followed by an appeal to the "gods."

40. The traditional mark of a Roman senator, hence someone with great wealth.

41. Lat. *oppugnatum patrem expugnaveris.* Note that the predicate and participle have the same verb stem, *pugnare,* "to attack," "to storm," "to subdue."

42. Grebel feels that as a son, he is above being a common enemy of his father's.

43. Lat. *Dirae Furiaeque,* "Dread Deities and Furies" or "Erinyes and Furies" (EY). The Furies were the goddesses of vengeance—Allecto, Megaera, and Tisiphone. Symbolizing the pangs of conscience, they pursued criminals relentlessly and frequently drove them mad. See 12/fn.10.

44. See 11/fn.1.

45. See Cast of Characters No. 39.

46. See Cast of Characters No. 87.

14. Grebel to Myconius, Paris, March 7, 1520

1. None of Myconius's letters to Grebel have been preserved. Most of Grebel's nine letters to him were replies to letters received.

2. For the idea of someone's intervention through dreams, see Erasmus, *Adag.* I.3.62.

3. Lat. *excudere*, lit. "to hammer out."

4. Same thought as 13/99/30. See 13/fn.15.

5. He wants to get out of one danger, even if it is only to fall into another. See 12/fn.12.

6. Nestor, famous in Homer, lived to rule over three generations of men. He was king of Pylos and at an advanced age joined the Greeks in the campaign against Troy.

7. The Pythagoreans believed in the transmigration of souls and that the same soul is reborn in different people. See 5/fn.14, 12/fn.34.

8. See 12/93/13-14.

9. Quintus Asconius Pedianus (AD 3-88), a learned grammarian of Padua, devoted especially to the study of Cicero, Sallust, and Vergil. His commentary on five orations of Cicero is extant. A copy was discovered by Paggio in St. Gallen in 1917. The "editio princeps" is dated 1477 (Venice), but it is not known who published the Paris edition (1520) to which Grebel refers here and in 15/103/8 and 17/107/22-23.

10. The Aldine Press (see 1/fn.21) reprinted classic works by Greek writers such as Theocritus, Hesiod, Aristotle, Aristophanes, Sophocles, Herodotus, Thucydides, Xenophon, Euripides, Demosthenes, and Homer. They also published Erasmus' *Adagia,* and he visited them in 1508. In 1501 they began publishing pocket editions of the classics.

11. See 13/fn.9.

12. This has reference to some other Conrad, perhaps Conrad Moser (see 1/fn.35). See also 15/103/11 and 17/107/32-33.

13. Lat. *Utrunque latens periculum fovet,* "Danger, in hiding, cherishes both (in her arms)," a curious mixture of metaphors.

14. There is no record that this second retreat to Melun here contemplated was carried out. See 9/fn.8.

15. Grebel to Myconius, Paris, April 13, 1520

1. Glarean made a visit to Switzerland in the spring of 1520, leaving Paris in April and returning in June. See 16/fn.5.

2. Lat. *vix ... litteras exarassem,* an elegant use by Grebel of a colloquialism common to Cicero's letters.

3. The "great misfortune" is not clearly identified, although it may have been a serious recurrence of the symptoms of his chronic ailment (see 4/fn.2).

4. See 14/fn.9.

5. See 12/fn.30 and Cast of Characters No. 103.

6. See 14/fn.12.

7. See 12/fn.1.

8. See 12/fn.12 and 14/fn.5.

16. Grebel to Vadian, Paris, April 13, 1520

1. See letter to Myconius (15/103/5), written on the same date.

2. Lat. *non literas, sed ne literam quidem mittis* could also be translated "do not send a letter, not even a word."

3. Fates, see 5/fn.22.

4. Lat. *in te invehar,* "laid into you."

5. On Glarean, see Cast of Characters No. 28. On his visit to Switzerland, see 15/fn.1. Various references in other letters permit the tracing of his movement. In ZW, VII, No. 133, dated April 17, 1520, Nepos of Basel expects Glarean shortly. In ZW, VII, No. 135, dated April 29, Hedio of Basel reports that Glarean had been in his company. In ZW, VII, No. 136, dated May 4, Zwingli reports that Glarean had been in Zurich for four days, is about to leave for his home in Glarus, and wants to meet Vadian. After taking the cure at Pfäffers, he plans

to return to Paris. In ZW, VII, No. 142, dated June 10, Hedio tells of Glarean's visit to Basel on his way back to Paris, indicating that he has just come from Zwingli in Zurich. In ZW, VII, 145, dated June 19, Zwingli reveals the purpose of the journey. Glarean had been planning to return to Switzerland if he could secure a position. It took another year and a half to accomplish this, and Glarean did not return to Basel until February 1522. On July 7 Glarean is back in Paris, writing to Zwingli (ZW, VII, No. 147). The time of his return to Paris is important because it enables the fixing of the date of Grebel's return to Switzerland, since the two met a two days' journey from Paris (17/107/7-9 and 18/109/28-30).

16A. Tschudi to Vadian, Paris, June 20, 1520
   1. On Peter Tschudi, see 10/fn.25 and Cast of Characters No. 87.
   2. This excerpt represents about one fourth of the letter, which proceeds to celebrate the accomplishments of Swiss scholars like Vadian and Glarean with particular reference to the literary arts.

17. Grebel to Myconius, Zurich, July 6, 1520
   1. The date of Grebel's departure and arrival can be fixed within reasonable limits. It took about two weeks to make the journey by horseback (see 5/Intro.). We can infer from Tschudi's letter (16A) that Grebel was still in Paris on June 20, perhaps leaving the next morning, since he would have needed at least that much time to have arrived before July 6, when the present letter was written.
   2. The further identity of Publicola is unknown.
   3. I.e., the students chanced to meet Glarean on the way to Paris (see 16/fn.5) and then chanced once more to meet Grebel on his way to Zurich.
   4. Glarean speaks of this accident with his horse in a letter of July 7, 1520 (ZW, VII, No. 147). Grebel found the incident quite amusing (18/109/31-32), but did not dare to make fun of Glarean to his friend Myconius.
   5. See 14/fn.9 and 15/fn.4.
   6. Even though Myconius is living in Luzern and Grebel is now at home in Zurich, Myconius, because of some unspecified plan to effect the reconciliation of father and son, has easier access to the father now than Conrad in the matter of discerning the father's mood and thought. The sentence implies some contact between Myconius and Jacob Grebel, either in Luzern or in Zurich.
   7. See 12/fn.30.
   8. See 12/fn.12 and 15/fn.6.
   9. Apollo was one of the greatest and most versatile of Greek divinities, son of Zeus and Leto, twin brother of Artemis. One of his many functions was to be the patron of young men like Grebel.
   10. The Latin for metrical feet (*pes*) allows the same pun as the ancient Greek and modern English. The origin of the pun is Artistophanes' *Frogs*.

18. Grebel to Vadian, Zurich, July 13, 1520
   1. The mythical Cimmerian people described by Homer as dwelling in a remote realm, enveloped in constant mist and gloom.
   2. Lat. *sonoro poeta mutum sororium* is an obvious play on sound and words.
   3. Grebel was in Paris from October 20, 1518, to about June 25, 1520, wrote six letters to Vadian during that period, and received only one in return (see 5/fns. 3 and 35, 6/fn. 32, 10/fn.1, and 13/fn.3).
   4. Mercury was a Roman god corresponding to the Greek Hermes, the son of Zeus and Maia. He had many functions, but his chief characteristics were inventiveness and versatility, united with trickery and cunning.
   5. One of several anti-female stereotypes in Grebel's writing, although actually Zwingli was more prone to employ such references.
   6. Lat. *jugulum*, "throat," but referring to the larynx.

7. Earlier, paper was manufactured from the pit of the papyrus plant, which grew mostly along the Nile in Egypt; and much of the ink was made from the black juice of the cuttlefish.

8. Vadian was fourteen years older than Grebel.

9. Calchas, a celebrated prophet in Greece before the siege of Troy. He had received the knowledge of future events from Apollo. On their departure for the Trojan War, the Greeks chose him as their high priest and prophet, consulted and obeyed him in connection with all the important events of that ten-year war. He figures prominently in Homer's *Iliad*, 2.329.

10. See 5/fn.12. As in 5/71/28, 6/79/33, and 13/97/31, to be a Harpocrates was seen as making a positive contribution as a confidant.

11. Goddess of suffering and silence, a friend who can keep confidences (see 5/fn.13). Gaius Julius Solinus, a Roman writer of the third century AD, wrote about Angeron in his *Collectanea Rerum Memorabilium,* better known by its later title of *Polyhistor* (see 1,6). In 5/71/28, to be an Angerona was seen as having "the role of a teacher," but in the present connection, Vadian's Angerona-like avoidance is disapproved of as an alternative to his Harpocrates-like friendship. The conjunction *aut* corrects what precedes.

12. See 13/fn.19. E.Y. thought that *Vadianum* was a play on *vadere,* and thus carried the added meaning, "a man equal to all occasions."

13. The punishment of the wicked Sisyphus in hell was to have to roll a huge stone to the top of the hill, only to have it always roll down again.

14. See 12/fn.12.

15. Although this was true in part as the result of the mediation of Myconius, Grebel probably intends this to be taken ironically.

16. Also to be taken ironically.

17. Euphrosine Grebel, older sister of Conrad (see Cast of Characters No. 36). The metaphor is from taking off a garment. She apparently died just before Grebel returned at the beginning of July.

18. See 17/fn.4.

19. See 17/fn.4.

20. Philistio, a writer of mimic farces, flourished at Rome during the time of Emperor Augustus (27 BC to AD 14). He was an actor as well as writer of mimes and is said to have died of excessive laughter.

21. Since the month is not given, the date of the month cannot be computed, because the Ides vary. The editor of VB simply placed it at the end of 1520. Staub, p. 23, dates the letter July 15, 1520. The month is probably correct, but the day cannot be. Since the Ides of July fall on the 15th, the date must be July 13.

22. Lat. *Charites,* see 5B/fn.4.

19. Grebel to Vadian, Zurich, July 17, 1520

1. Letters received from Martha as well as Vadian—their first since the post-wedding residence in Wädenswil (see 10/89/9 and 19/111/29).

2. Q. Asconius Pedianus (AD 3-88), commentary on the orations of Cicero. See 14/fn.9.

3. Grebel's baggage from Paris came by way of Basel and had evidently not yet arrived (see 19/111/31-32).

4. See 5/fn.9.

5. See fn. 1, above.

6. Lat. *duplicem hominem.* "Two-faced" (AB) is too derogatory, and "double character" (EY) is too psychoanalytical.

7. Lat. *Jovem fulminatorem,* "Jupiter with his thunderbolts." See 5/fn.25. The thunderbolt was Jupiter's special weapon of revenge and punishment.

8. Lat. *ex elephanto muscam reddens.* The common Latin proverb was *elephantem ex musca facere,* "to make an elephant out of a fly," or as it would be said today, "making a

mountain out of a molehill." Grebel intended to reverse the meaning of the proverb as indicated by 19/112/9. Vadian was making a small Jupiter (Grebel) out of a big one.

9. The Greek word was possibly quoted from Plato, *Apol.* 18,d.

10. The Homeric Thunderer was Jupiter (see fn.7, above).

11. The Greek word was manufactured by Grebel. The image of two goats fighting with their heads replaces that of a person boxing his own shadow. Perhaps the two goats in conflict were Grebel and Vadian.

12. Aegis-bearer is the storm cloud of Zeus, imagined in Homer as a shaggy shield fringed with tassels of gold and displaying in its center the awe-inspiring Gorgon's head. When Zeus shakes the aegis, it thunders and lightens, and horror and perdition fall on those against whom it is lifted. As the Greek word also means goatskin, it was explained in later times as the skin of the goat Amalthea, which had suckled Zeus in his infancy.

13. Lat. *de lana caprina certare,* another ancient proverb meaning "to wrangle over a goat's fleece," i.e., to split hairs, to dispute over trifles. See Horace, *Ep.* 1.18.15.

14. See 4/fn.4.

15. Lat. *effutiverim,* see 6/fn.3.

16. Lat. *garriam,* see 6/fn.3.

17. Lat. *Grebelia* refers to a female Grebel, viz., Vadian's wife, Martha, Conrad's sister.

18. Lat. *sacrificuli,* the officiating priests performing a religious sacrifice.

19. This is marked with a question mark in the published transcription (VB), to indicate that the reading does not make sense. The translation is probably what Grebel was trying to say.

20. See fn. 17, above.

21. The transportation of goods at that time was mostly consigned to merchants, a rather primitive form of the modern independent transport business. See 4/68/30-32, where Grebel speaks of the possible service of the Ravensburg merchants in delivering his books from Vienna.

22. Zilianus probably refers to A'Liliis (John Jacob Zurgilgen), a friend and fellow student in Paris (see 48/Intro.).

23. The teacher of Achilles was Chiron, the most famous of the centaurs, fabled monsters, half horse and half man.

24. See fn. 10, above.

25. Lat. *vati,* "seer," "poet."

26. The epigram is a restatement of the concern earlier expressed in 19/110/21-33.

19A. Zwingli to Myconius, Zurich, July 24, 1520

1. Lat. *expectatio nostrorum temporum,* more freely meaning "the thought of what our time might be coming to."

2. Lat. *omnia sursum deorsumque moventur,* "all things are changing topsyturvy."

3. Lat. *remis et velis,* prov. "with might and main" or "with tooth and nail."

4. Zwingli has Mt. 13:24ff. in mind.

5. Mt. 13:30.

6. Jn. 16:33.

7. Mt. 10:22, Mk. 13:13.

8. Jn. 16:2.

9. A fusion of Jn. 13:35 and 14:21.

10. See Eph. 6:11ff.

11. Lat. *tribus limpidissimis lapidibus.* Actually, it was "five smooth stones" (1 Sam. 17:40).

12. Mt. 13:3ff., Lk. 12:49.

13. Lk. 12:49.

14. Lk. 14:26.

15. Mt. 10:21.

16. See 1 Cor. 9:24.

17. See Phil. 3:13-14.

18. On Hercules, see 27/fn.18. Zwingli often referred to this mythological figure.

19. Gal. 1:10.

20. Mt. 5:10.

21. The papal bull of excommunication against Luther was dated June 15, 1520, but Zwingli did not know this, as he was writing a month later. It apparently arrived in Switzerland before the end of July, for it is known that Zwingli's influence with the papal legate in Zurich delayed the official deliverance in Wittenberg as well as in Zurich until the end of September.

22. On William de Falconibus, see Cast of Characters No. 22. He was not himself the papal legate (see Cast of Characters No. 72), but his chaplain and secretary. Nevertheless, as a representative of the court of Pope Leo X, he was given the title of *commissarius pontifici* (a representative of the pope).

23. Lat. *figulinum suum*. See Rom. 9:20ff. Zwingli used this same figure of the potter's vessel in his prayer song, *Gebetslied in der Pest*, written the previous December during his severe illness with the plague: "Thy vessel am I, to make or break altogether." See ZW, I, No. 5, pp. 62-69, and Jackson, 1900, p. 133.

24. It is revealing to learn that even before he knew that Luther had been excommunicated, he anticipated this possibility in consequence of his own Reformation work.

25. Hilary (c.300-67), bishop of Poitiers 353-68. A champion of orthodoxy against Arianism, he was exiled by Constantine to Phrygia (not Africa as Zwingli supposed) in 356; and while there, he attempted to bring about a reconciliation between semi-Arians and Roman Catholics. He was restored to his see in 364.

26. Lucius I, bishop of Rome 253-54, was banished in 253 soon after his election but returned before long, for which Cyprian congratulated him.

27. 1 Cor. 10:12.

28. For a chronological listing of allusions to Luther in the Zwingli correspondence of 1519, see Jackson, 1900, pp. 139-43. For instance:

Dec. 28: Myconius to Zwingli: "There has come into my hands through a Dominican monk an epitome of the discussion of Luther with Eck [i.e., the Leipzig Disputation]. I should have sent this to you if I had been sure that you did not have it. This is written by Luther himself, so that I have as much confidence in its accuracy as if I had been present and heard it all."

Dec. 31: Zwingli to Myconius: "I have that epitome of Luther, have read it and approved of it, and hope that Eck in following that elusive little wind of glory will throw away his labor."

20. Grebel to Myconius, Zurich, July 25, 1520

1. Lat, *propitium reddideris*, "may have rendered him favorable." See 17/fn.6.

2. Lat. *inelegans:* inelegant and lacking polish, culture, learning, wit.

3. A proverb found in Plato and Suidas used when one person tells something to another which he already knows better than the one telling it.

4. Fingers and nails because of the Roman method of counting by using all the joints. See Erasmus, *Adadio*, II.9.68.

5. This was one of a number of Diets of the Swiss Confederacy that met at Luzern in 1520.

6. See 12/fn.30.

7. See 9/fn.4.

8. See 14/fn.9.

9. See Cast of Characters No. 16.

10. Titus Livius (Livy), ca.59 BC-AD 17, second only to Tacitus among Roman historians. Grebel's reference is to Livy's history of Rome, entitled *Ab urbe condita*. It came out in installments, and only books 1-10 and 21-45 are extant.

11. Juvenal was a Roman poet who lived about AD 60-135. He is the author of sixteen satires in which he attacked the sins and foibles of his society with sarcastic wit. One calls to

mind such familiar phrases as "sound mind in a sound body," "who'll watch the watchmen?" "bread and circuses," "nobody ever became wicked overnight."

12. On Duke Ulrich of Württemberg, see Cast of Characters No. 90. The duke had allies in Switzerland, especially in the cantons of Luzern and Solothurn (see 23A/122/7); and Grebel may have been implying some sympathy for him on the part of Vadian (see 66/299/19-22).

13. Phalaris has two meanings in this reference. First, it refers to the rule of Agrigentum in Sicily (570-66 BC), who attained a proverbial celebrity as a cruel and inhuman tyrant. Second, it refers to the title of a polemical dialogue against Duke Ulrich written by Ulrich von Hutten in 1517 (see Cast of Characters No. 56, 23/fn.19, and Böcking, IV, 1ff.). Holborn writes: "The dialogue was composed under the influence of Lucian, whom Hutten came to know through the Greek studies so enthusiastically prosecuted at Bologna. The Lucianic form of question and answer offered a congenial mode for the expression of his inner thought and feeling, and the mould of *pro* and *con* stamped his polemic and exhortation with greater verve" (p. 85). Grebel also had a liking for Lucian (see 23/120/15-17 and 41/155/28-29). For comments about Hutten's influence on Grebel, see cast of characters No. 56.

14. Lat. *tristes Epistulas.* Grebel is probably intending a reference to the *Tristia* and the *Epistulae ex Ponto,* sorrowful poems written by the Roman poet Ovid in exile.

15. See 20/116/13-14 and 12/fn.30.

21. Grebel to Vadian, Zurich, July 29, 1520

1. The translator believes that Grebel intended a negative which he omitted by mistake.

2. See 12/fn.35. Homer's *Odyssey,* 1.58.

3. *Thais* was the name of a celebrated Athenian courtesan who accompanied Alexander the Great on his expedition into Asia. She is best known from the story of her having induced the conqueror during a great festival to set fire to the palace of the Persian kings.

4. Reference to Circe, famous witch in Homer's *Odyssey* who put spells on the crew of Ulysses. When Ulysses landed on the shores of her island near Italy, some of his comrades after being feasted were given the enchanted potion that changed them into swine and deprived them of all desire to leave the island.

5. See 20/116/18.

6. Lat. *qui me non expectatis libris voluissent abire.* This is a difficult clause, made complicated by Grebel's attempt to be witty. The translation by AB, "who did not wish [voluerant] me to desert [abire] the expected books [expectatis libris]," puts the negative with *voluissent* rather than with *expectatis,* but turns the former from pluperfect subjunctive to perfect indicative verb tense, and makes the intransitive infinitive, "to depart," transitive, "to desert [the books]." The translation by EY, "who would have desired [voluissent] that I go [abeo], were I not waiting [expectabam] for the books" retains the pluperfect verb tense, *voluissent,* but turns the infinitive ("to go") into a first person present indicative verb ("I go") and the participle ("waiting") into an imperfect indicative verb ("were waiting"), making Grebel the subject of the verb ("were I waiting"). The rendering here given is the simplest, most literal translation of all three verbs: *expectatis* ("awaited"), *voluissent* ("might have wished"), and abire ("to depart").

7. Grebel is trying to say that he could leave without the books except for the fact that he does not want his father to see something that will be delivered with them.

8. A cryptic reference to some other things which his father must not see. *Supervolitantem avem,* "overflying bird," suggests their transportation to Zurich although certainly not by airplane.

22. Grebel to Vadian, Zurich, August 3, 1520

1. Conrad's oldest sister, Barbara (see 2/fn.8 and Cast of Characters No. 32). Her husband (see fn. 3, below) died during the present epidemic, and Barbara consequently remained in Zurich indefinitely. A third daughter was born to her the following February (see 29/138/18).

2. A continuation of the epidemic that swept Switzerland in the latter half of 1519 and was still raging in certain towns.

3. Barbara was married to Leonard Karli; and the family was living in or near Baden, twelve miles northwest of Zurich.

4. Lat. *humanus,* meaning "courteous," "kindly," "humane."

5. Lat. *moribus,* meaning "manners," "character," "habits."

6. Lat. *ut ne latum quidem unguem accedere fas sit,* a difficult phrase in a difficult sentence with convoluted grammar. EY thinks that Grebel was quoting some proverb.

7. Again Grebel refers to his baggage from Paris which has not yet arrived via Basel. See 19/fns. 3 and 21.

8. The first sister is Barbara (fn. 3, above) and the second was Euphrosine, who had died a month before (see 18/fn.17).

9. Mars, the Roman god of war, used here as the personification of the plague.

10. On Glarean, see Cast of Characters No. 28. Grebel's feelings about him have improved somewhat after the intense hostility of the Paris sojourn. It is of interest to note that Glarean's hostility also mellowed. He sent greetings to Grebel in five letters to Zwingli 1520-22 (See ZW, VII).

11. The dialogue *Philirenus* ("Lover of Peace," also called "Über den Krieg" and "Dass man nicht kriegen soll") was written by Myconius in Luzerne toward the end of 1519. It was first mentioned in a letter of Hedio to Zwingli, dated November 21, 1519 (ZW, VII, 225), and had been sent to Basel to be printed. Hedio and Capito were at first enthusiastic about it, and sent it to Zwingli to read. It was given to Froben to print, but never reached the press because Hedio and Capito changed their minds and objected to its publication because they feared that its bitter attacks on the monks and its quotations from Erasmus would stir up bitter feelings against the budding Reformation. Grebel had the manuscript in his hands and evidently still expected it to be published. He was obviously deeply moved by this pacifist pamphlet, which undoubtedly was one of the sources for his own later pacifism (see 63/290/10ff. and Stayer, Ch3). Many of the Swiss humanists were pacifists, especially since the disaster of Marignano (see 6/fn.53). Indeed the whole northern wing of Humanism under Erasmus' leadership was tinged with the pacifist spirit. A major theme in the works of Erasmus was the folly of war, as in his 1517 antiwar pamphlet, *Querela Pacis* ("The Complaint of Peace"). According to Beatus Rhenanus in the dedication of one of his pamphlets published toward the end of 1518, there was a considerable group of Swiss leaders who were "studying peace and condemning war as a pestiferous thing unworthy of a Christian." In a letter from Hedio to Myconius dated December 10, 1519, the *Philirenus* was described as an antiwar polemic in the Erasmian vein. But on April 17, 1520, the ms. was returned to Myconius from Basel through Zwingli and was never published.

12. Allen (IV, p.98) identifies the "epistle of Erasmus" as the one written to Archbishop Albert of Brandenburg on Oct. 19, 1519. It had been entrusted for delivery to Hutten, who had it printed for the sake of promoting Luther's cause. It was widely circulated, recopied, and reprinted because it contained Erasmus' first detailed reactions to Luther, surprisingly affirmative although with typical Erasmian cautions. Grebel may have gotten it from Zwingli, who on July 16, 1520, sent an "Erasmi epistolam" to Myconius (ZW, VII, No. 146). In the June 15, 1520, papal bull of condemnation, *Exsurge Domine,* Luther had been given two months in which to recant (see 19A/fn.21). The "Luther affair" to which Grebel refers was moving toward the climax of thè Diet of Worms, April, 1521.

13. The sentence implies a female messenger for Grebel's letter. For other instances of women serving as messengers, see 8/85/35 arìd 12/93/11.

14. The two sisters were Barbara (see fn. 3, above) and Dorothy (see Cast of Characters Nos. 32 and 35).

23. Grebel to Vadian, Zurich, September 11, 1520

1. In three previous letters Grebel referred to his books as the obstacle to his awaited visit to St. Gallen—19/113/13-14, 21/117/16, and 22/118/10.

2. Jacob Grebel inherited the iron business from his father. Since 1500, when trade

increasingly affected Zurich's economy, iron ore from Northeast Switzerland was exchanged for salt, grain, wine, and manufactured goods obtained via Basel (see Birnbaum, *Archives de Sociologie,* IV, 18). It is not known whether Grebel's iron shop dealt in raw materials or in manufactured products. In either case, it is evident that the business suffered from the frequent absences which Jacob Grebel's public service required. Apparently, Conrad and Beatus, the new manager of the shop, developed a friendship because they made an excursion to Wädenswil together toward the end of the year (26/130/1).

3. Lat. *nundinae,* the Latin term for the Roman market day, held on the last day of their eight-day week. On this day the country people rested from their work and came to Rome to buy and sell as well as to do other business. Market day in Zurich was not a regular but a special day scheduled in advance.

4. The reference is to Martha, Vadian's wife, Conrad's sister.

5. Lat. *qui hic pedibus paternis trahar,* possibly proverbial, expresses his father's dominance over him.

6. See 18/fn.4. One of this god's functions was commerce and merchandising.

7. Lethe was one of the rivers of Hades in Greek and Roman mythology. Upon drinking of its waters, souls coming from this life forgot everything of their earlier existence. Hence the name was proverbial for release and oblivion.

8. Lat. *Oceanum,* in Greek mythology the mighty river of the world which flows around the earth and back into itself.

9. On Apollo, Muses, and Graces, see 17/fn.9, 1/fn.6, and 18/fn.22.

10. See 14/fn.9. Vadian's copy of the Asconius had finally arrived from Paris via Basel, and Grebel was sending it with the letter.

11. The Latin *Paraphrases of the New Testament* by Erasmus, prepared after his first edition of the Greek New Testament, was published in 1516. Although the *Paraphrases* were not known to have been completed until a date later than this letter, they were issued in part. The first part appeared in 1517.

12. This is the first mention of Zwingli since 10/91/26-27. If Zwingli was the "bishop" mentioned in 8/86/8, Grebel may have been offended in Paris by a letter of admonition from the Zurich leader. If that was true, it is evident here that a new warm relationship is beginning to develop.

13. A writing by Erasmus, published in Basel in May 1520. The full title was *Antibarbarium D. Erasm. Rot. lib. unus, quem invenis quidem adhuc lusit, caeterum diu desideratum, demum repertum non invenis recognovit, et velut postliminio restituit.*

14. Aesop was the famous writer of fables, the first author to create an independent type of story about animals. The stories of his life are mostly legendary, but he was probably a Phrygian by birth and lived about 600 BC. The specific edition which Grebel sent to Vadian was the 1518 Frobenius edition printed in Basel. See *Bibliotheca Vadiani,* 1973. p. 94.

15. Lucianus (Lucian) was a Greek writer and second-century sophist who flourished in the reign of Marcus Aurelius. The most important of his writings were his *Dialogues of the Gods* and *Dialogues of the Dead,* treated in a great variety of style from seriousness to satire, apology to polemics. See also 20/fn.13 and 41/155/28-29).

16. On Homer, see 5/fn.9.

17. Lat. *sus Minervam,* "as a swine to Minerva," a common proverb among the Romans and Greeks, equivalent to "the fool teaches the philosopher." Minerva, the same as the Greek Athena, was the goddess of wisdom and the crafts. In contrast to her as the embodiment of the highest intellectual wisdom, the pig was considered a type of the profoundest stupidity.

18. Lat. *Atticas Veneres.* Attica, the most celebrated district of Greece, with Athens for its capital, was the threshold (doorway) to Greek literature.

19. On Ulrich von Hutten, see Cast of Characters No. 56. His revised collection of previously published Latin dialogues was printed by John Schöffer in Mainz in April 1520, with the title, *Dialogi.* His German *Dialogues* appeared one year later with the title *(Gesprächsbuch.*

20. Jacob Grebel had an installment of 200 guilders due on Martha's dowry. For the details of this payment made on October 17, see 23A/121/28-33. Apparently it did seem

"unwise" to Jacob, because he sent the money by separate messenger after Conrad had left (see 23A/Intro. and fn. 5, 23B/fn.3).

21. Rottweil was a free imperial city, the seat of an imperial court, the jurisdiction of which extended over Swabia, the Rhineland, and Alsace. The conflict referred to was between this Swabian League and the kingdom of Württemberg. The cantons Luzern and Solothurn had promised to help the Duke of Württemberg recover parts of his duchy taken by the Swabians, but the Swiss patriots were mostly against him. For the attitude of Jacob Grebel, see 23A/122/21-23.

22. On Cardinal Antonio Pucci, see Cast of Characters No. 72. After a brief absence as bishop of Prato, he returned to Zurich for another papal mission to renew mercenary treaties. Since the defeat of the Swiss by French troops at Marignano (1515), there was a strong anti-French attitude in Zurich and a growing opposition to all foreign treaties. Pope Leo X was still an ally of Francis I against the Hapsburg emperors in the Italian Wars, but reversed his position in the next phase of the struggle that began in 1521 (see 35/147/1-5, 23A/fn.6, and 24/fn.16).

23. On Peter Tschudi, see Cast of Characters No. 87. He had written a letter to Vadian from Paris dated June 20, 1520, which Grebel probably brought along with him (see 16A). This may be the letter he is only now getting around to forwarding, or Tschudi has written another for which Grebel is also serving as carrier.

23A. Jacob Grebel to Vadian, Zurich, October 17, 1520

1. Perhaps a receipt for the large payment on Martha's dowry.

2. For notes and bibliography on medieval Swiss coinage, see Schelbert, fn. 64, and Fast, 1973, p. 722. Fast's table of money values indicates one crown worth 21-24 batzen. Grebel was here evaluating it at 22 batzen. A guilder (florin) was equal to 15 batzen, but a goldguilder was equal to 16 "gute" batzen.

3. In 23/120/35-38, Conrad referred to the 200-guilder installment on Martha's dowry, expecting to deliver the money to Vadian himself.

4. This is one of several comments that led Schelbert (pp. 39-40, fn. 50) to the conclusion that "the family income seems not to have been sufficient to meet such special expenditures as dowries and tuition costs." Bender (1950, p. 46) views the elder Grebel as a man of greed, but Schelbert accepts as true Conrad's reference to Martha's dowry: "She has parents who are perhaps not so rich as honorable" (6/80/7-9 and 6/fn.43).

5. "Told you" in person, present perfect tense, i.e., Conrad had arrived in St. Gallen before this letter. See 23B/fn.3.

6. The legate Puccius (see Cast of Characters No. 72 and 23/fn.22) was the potential source for another educational stipend for Conrad. This incident was cited as evidence in the trial of Jacob Grebel (see Epi.A/468/12ff.).

7. This is the earliest written indication of Conrad's plan to study in Pisa (see 25/126/8-9, 26/130/13, 27/133/31, etc.).

8. On the duke of Württemberg, see 20/fn.12 and Cast of Characters No. 90.

9. Captains were uniformed recruiters of mercenaries in the employ of the pope or a sovereign like the king of France with whom the Swiss Confederates had a pact. Captains were often noblemen with political power and were highly paid by their sponsors. In a fiery sermon preached from the pulpit on Sunday, March 6, 1525, Zwingli condemned two kinds of nobility who brought injury to the country. One were "the *pensioners,* whom he called pear-roasters, because they sat at home behind the stove and still got at the treasures of all the lords." It was on the charge of taking illegal pensions that Jacob Grebel was tried and executed in October 1527 (see Epi.A). The second were "the *captains,* who walk around in such rich silks, silver, gold and precious stones, with rings and chains, so that it is a disgrace to the sun and moon, not to mention God and man. One is gold above and silver below; another is gold below and velvet or damask above, and the clothing so slit and cut open that it is a disgrace that one should allow them to strut around so publicly before people's eyes. . . . They are like butchers who drive cattle to Constance; they drive the cattle out, take the

money for them, and come home without the cattle; then they go out again, and do likewise repeatedly. Thus, also, the pensioners and captains do. They have always succeeded (except once) in coming home from the battles and the cannon—I do not know where they stationed themselves—and bring their money-belts full of money, and have driven away the children of honest people. And immediately they begin again and collect another herd. These they also drive out; and thus they become rich. . . . For the pensioners sit everywhere in the regiments, do not wish to give up the pensions, and therefore do not wish to forbid war. And the captains lead astray as many sheep as they wish, and still people take their hats off to them" (quoted in Jackson, pp. 137-38). Grebel does not specifically indicate that he had ever served as a recruiting captain, although neither does he deny the legitimacy of that role.

    10. Oswald Myconius, schoolmaster in Luzern, who was visiting in Zurich. See Cast of Characters No. 70 and 23B.

23B. Myconius to Vadian, Zurich, before October 17, 1520
    1. See 23A/122/35.
    2. Lat. *ut convenirem Conradum nostrum ac aureum mandarem,* "that I might visit our Conrad and entrust the money [to him]." *Convenire* means "to meet," "to call upon," "to visit."
    3. I.e., he had already left for St. Gallen.
    4. I.e., Jacob would send it with his letter (23A) by special messengers.

24. Grebel to Vadian, Zurich, November 7, 1520
    1. Conrad had been in St. Gallen during the middle of October (see 23A/122/16-17 and 23B/123/6-7). The visit had been promised in July and delayed until October.
    2. Lat. *Gratias,* a purer Latin form of Charites, refers to the Graces (see 18/fn.22).
    3. Lat. *quam hoc meum vitium inurbanum.* The adjective means "inurbane," "inelegant," "uncultivated," the fault of language or behavior or lifestyle.
    4. Lat. *felicem . . . ante obitum,* classical saying loosely translated as "call no man happy until he is dead" (see Ovid, *Metamorphoses,* 3,137).
    5. ·A phrase from Lucian, *Tox., 62.*
    6. Silenus, the tutor of Bacchus. He is described as an old man with a bald head, puck nose, fat and round like his wine-bag which he always carries with him, and usually intoxicated. The note of depravity is what Grebel applies to himself.
    7. Niobe, because of maternal pride for her progeny of twelve children, ungraciously compared herself to Leto, who had only two children. To punish this presumption, Leto's children, Apollo and Artemis, slew all of Niobe's children with their arrows. The figure of Niobe trying to protect her youngest daughter from the slayers is a famous subject in art and sculpture.
    8. The two lines of poetry were written as a couplet in the tradition of elegiac couplets.
    9. Lat. *O me, cui ad miseriam miseram misere miserrimo (miserere!) nihil desit.* There is a word play here because the Latin for "pity me" is *miserere.* The translation "misery (pity me!)" retains something of the sound effect.
    10. This reference to Zwingli is interesting not only because it reflects Zwingli's zeal but also because it indicates the high regard in which Grebel held him at this time.
    11. Lat. *Attica mea epigrammata mei Martis.* For the first and last terms in this phrase, see 23/fn.18 and 22/fn.9. The reference to these lost verses together with the known verses published in the two editions of the *Pomponius Mela* (see 1B) and those attached to Zwingli's *Archeteles* (see 47D) reveal the interest that Grebel had in classical poetry as a model for his own creative writing efforts.
    12. Boeotia is a district of Greece proper lying to the northwest of Attica, whose capital was Thebes. The allusion is explained in the following clauses, Boeotia standing in contrast with the literary center of Athens, the capital of Attica. See 24/fn.12.
    13. Another word play, *non ab aris, ab haris.*
    14. See 5/fn.9.

15. As will be seen in the next two letters (25/126/7-9 and 26/130/13), Grebel was planning to leave soon for study in Italy, at Bologna or Pisa, both seats of famous universities.

16. Choriambic ode was a poem with the verses having feet of four syllables, the first and last of which are long, the two in the middle short, that is, a dactyl plus an iambus. True choriambic rhythms are rarely found in Latin. On Puccius, see Cast of Characters No. 72. As the papal legate in Switzerland, he authorized papal grants such as the one for which Grebel was applying. Vadian may have advised Grebel to send him a sample of his poetry. The secretary to Puccius was William de Falconibus; and for further connections see 43/158/16.

17. See fn. 15, above.

18. Lat. *Chartas suas reposcit Mureria.* The identity of Mureria cannot be definitely established. She is mentioned again in 25/126/32 and 54/221/28. Correll suggested it might be the nickname of one of Grebel's sisters. Bender (1950, p. 221) concluded that Mureria "must have been a daughter of Jacob Murer." The families were connected through Conrad's mother, who was a sister to Jacob Murer's wife. Thus, Conrad and Mureria would have been first cousins. Another hypothesis is that she was Murer's wife, herself—Conrad's aunt. Evidence to support this surmise is found in 54/221/28 (see 54/fn.7). According to Grebel's reference, she must have sent a *chartas* (which could mean "sheets of paper," "writing," "letter," "poem," "book") to Martha, Vadian's wife, and either wanted it back or wanted a reply. See 25/fn.23.

19. The first of a number of references to Benedict Burgauer (see 32/142/27-28 and Cast of Characters No. 11).

20. On Juflius, see Cast of Characters No. 97 and 29/138/33, 49/191/26-27, 56/225/21-24. and 66/299/28-29.

21. This probably refers to Bartholomew Weirmann (Wyerman), who was one of several chaplains at the Church of St. Lawrence in St. Gallen. Little is known about him other than Grebel's comment about parting ways with Luther and Näf's comment that he was an "able young cleric" (II, p. 210).

22. It is not clear whether *Luthero a secretis* is to be translated "secretary to Luther" (AB and EY) or "separated from Luther." The latter would seem to be the more literal rendering, and "secretary" would be designated by the Latin *scriba* or *amanuensis.* The reference to "separated from Luther" could refer to his having studied at Wittenburg like Kessler, who then returned to St. Gallen to teach.

23. Master Lazarus, an unidentified priest in St. Gallen. While these clerics are unknown to us, it is obvious that Grebel was on friendly terms with them, probably having learned to know them on his recent visit there. He will send subsequent greetings to Burgauer, Jufli, and "all my friends" (26/130/25), that "drunken assembly of brothers" (35/147/25-26).

24. Written in capital letters.

25. Benedict Burgauer, see fn. 19, above.

26. The German adjective *schel* means "squint-eyed," "asquint," "jealous," "grudging," "scowling," "frowning." It may refer to Vadian's admonition to Grebel in 24/124/16.

25. Grebel to Vadian, Zurich, between November 19 and December 8, 1520

1. The "two letters" might refer to Letters 24 and 25 if they were sent together. The term "epigrams" hardly fits the appended poem, written in the form of elegiac couplets, the usual meter for light verse. Perhaps Grebel enclosed the epigrams separately, for in the preceding letter (24/124/19-23) he had promised to send them in response to Vadian's request for something of Grebel's to publish in the Basel edition of *Pomponius Mela* (but see fn. 4, below).

2. Lat. *tu boni consule,* "take it for good" or "regard it favorably," a favorite humanist phrase. The sense is, "make up your own mind but with some favor toward your friend."

3. Zwingli at this time was just moving into his Reformation agenda as pastor in Zurich after almost two years of preaching and is apparently on friendly terms with Grebel, as evidenced by this reference to his reviewing Grebel's writing.

4. This sounds like a request to omit from the second edition of the *Pomponius* to be

published in Basel in 1522 the brief poem by Grebel found in the first edition, published in Vienna in 1518. In fact, the poem did not appear in the later edition. Instead, Grebel wrote the Introduction (see 26A, below). Vadian has apparently asked him to compose something for the new edition, either a new poem in place of the old one, or the Introduction, or both (see 24/124/18).

5. "Flays the golden sheep" is an allusion to the mythological story of the Argonautic expedition in search for the golden fleece. The story of the Argonauts arose out of the accounts of commercial enterprises which the wealthy Minyans, who lived in the neighborhood of Iolcus, made to the coasts of the Euxine.

6. "Head man" *(capitaneus)* is linked with the next word, "big head" *(capitosus)*—a skillful play on words.

7. Grebel is writing about two persons on their way to Vadian's in St. Gallen, but not necessarily from Zurich. One of them is related to Vadian, and the other to Grebel. It is possible that the former was Benedict von Watt, Vadian's brother, and the other was Andreas Grebel, Conrad's brother. It is known that Benedict was temporarily living with his Uncle Hector in Krakow in 1519, working in the family business there. Conrad subsequently refers to Benedict four times: 31/141/20, 51/195/2-3, 52/208/7, and 66/299/28-29. Another brother, Melchior, wrote to Vadian from Rome on April 22, 1521, asking Vadian to write to Conrad [Grebel—?] on behalf of Benedict. In June 1523, Benedict was apparently visiting the Grebel family, for he was going to be the carrier of Conrad's letter to Vadian (52/208/6-8). Grebel's brother Andreas had been away in the service of Duke Ferdinand (see 29/138/16-17). Benedict and Andreas met in Krakow and may have been returning home together between the dates of Letters 25 and 29.

8. The Latin term *inequitant* ("on horses") is linked in assonance with *inasinant* ("on asses").

9. By "Gallenites," Grebel refers to the people of St. Gallen, pronounced like "Gauls" or "Gallians," the Latin term for "French," here referring more to French characteristics.

10. Zwingli's youngest brother, Andreas, a promising youth, died of the plague in Zurich, November 19, 1520 (see 25A/128/11).

11. Einsiedeln, a monastery about 20 miles southeast of Zurich, is today, as in the sixteenth century, the greatest mecca of Roman Catholic pilgrims in Switzerland and South Germany because of the divinely dedicated shrine and image of the Virgin Mary, where miracles of healing are believed to be wrought. The monastery had only two monks at this time. Grebel may have made the pilgrimage and vow in memory not just of Zwingli's brother but of his own sister, Euphrosine, the nun, who had died the previous June (see 18/fn.17).

12. Grebel's plan to study in Italy was mentioned as early as January 29, 1519 (see 6/fn.26). See also 23A, in which Jacob Grebel speaks of getting Conrad a papal grant for study in Pisa.

13. Lat. *qui ferat, qui nutriat,* "that will bear and feed me." Grebel may mean that by selling the horse upon arrival, he will have money for food.

14. A pun. *Rex* in Latin means king, but also patron. The pope at this time was Leo X, 1513-21 (see Cast of Characters No. 63). He was taking the place of the emperor and the king of France as Grebel's prospective source of financial support.

15. The word *dialogum* is used often by Grebel, here not as part of the title of some published literary work (as in 23/120/32-33), but as a metaphor for his current letter-writing about his personal struggles in self-identity and decision-making.

16. Fates, see 5/fn.22.

17. For the sequence of Grebel's developing concern about his acceptance of questionable if not illegal stipends through the influence-peddling of his father, see 13/97/37ff., 28/136/23ff., 29/138/7-13, and 39/151/17-23. Up to this point he had received stipends from the emperor and the French king (see 1/fn.14, 4/fn.9, and 13/97/37ff.). He will vow never again to receive funds from these sources (Letter 28), but he will in fact accept one more stipend from the pope, allegedly to study in Italy but which he will use to support himself in Basel (see 28/fn.7, 29/fns.1,2, and 39/fn.9). On the question of the legality of these stipends,

see Schelbert, 1969.

18. The pope was endeavoring to enlist an army of Swiss to assist in the war against the Turks and in support of Charles V. This was the part of the mission of the papal legate Pucci. The political purpose of the scholarly stipends is thus unwittingly disclosed.

19. Lat. *Jovem Philium.* Various surnames were attached to Zeus. One cult was that of Zeus Philios, Zeus, the god of friendship, for whom a temple was built at Megalopolis, according to Pausanias 8,31.

20. Lat. *nugor libenter.* See 6/fn.3.

21. Lat. *querulus,* the same self-identification he used in the previous letter, there translated "lamenting" (see 24/124/3).

22. Lat. *quid feres,"* "what will you bear?" or more meaningfully, "how will you bear it?"

23. In Roman burial rites, the last act was to shout the word "vale" three times over the remains as a last farewell to the deceased. Grebel means he will quit lamenting only when he is dead.

24. Mureria, who was perhaps an aunt to Conrad and Martha (see 24/fn.18), had sent a letter to St. Gallen that she wanted returned for some reason (see 24/124/29).

25. See 24/fn.19.

26. See 24/fn.20.

27. Spelled in capitals.

28. On Jörg Binder, see Cast of Characters No. 4. Binder had replaced Myconius as schoolmaster at the Grossmünster in 1519. Grebel refers to him in terms that indicate some tension in their relationship.

29. The Latin term, *Pelasgicum,* follows the Greek term "Hail." Instead of saying Gracecum for Greek, Grebel used a literary adjective "Pelasgian," suggesting ancient Greek. Except for the sake of the meter, the line would read, "You also would have from him a Hail or a Greek 'Hàil.' "

30. Lat. *Salve,* a greeting like "Good day," but originally meaning "be healthy" or "I wish you health."

31. Lat. *salutem,* "Good health to you."

32. Lat. *salvus,* "well." The poem is formed on the two meanings of *salveo*—to greet, to be healthy.

33. Lat. *Salve,* "Hello," sometimes "Good-bye."

34. Lat. *Parcee,* the same as Fates. See 5/fn.22.

35. Lat. *Lyri pipium.* The editor of VB commented that these words were unintelligible to him. Pipulus means "chirping," "piping," and the first term may refer to the lyre.

36. Written by Grebel, *A Rma virum.* The two capitalized letters may have referred to the letters of a familiar name. Apart from that, the two words are the first words of the *Aeneid,* the epic poem by Vergil: *arma virumque cano, Troiae qui primus ab oris.*

37. At the trial of Jacob Grebel, Binder gave incriminating testimony that he had received Conrad's Austrian stipend in Vienna after Conrad left for Paris. Grebel is probably referring to the fact that Binder had never repaid him.

26. Grebel to Vadian, Zurich, December 8, 1520

1. Grebel does not want to complain that he has not received a reply from Vadian, a significant shift in attitude from 18/108/2-109/11, although he cannot help himself later in the letter.

2. The *Dialogues* of Hutten were mentioned in 23/120/32-3, but the use of the singular here may refer to Ulrich Hugwald's *Dialogus studiorum suorum prooemium et militiae initium* (1520). Vadian's copy was inscribed, "Conradus Grebelius D.D. [Domino doctori] Vadiano suo ex Tiguro Anno 1520, mit Marginalien von Grebel" (see *Bibliotheca Vadiani,* No. 840, p. 280). On Hugwald's 1525 involvement in Anabaptist activity see *Mennonite Encyclopedia,* II, p. 836).

3. Lat. *Graecarum dictionum illa Zingliana lima.* Since there is no published work of Zwingli to which this phrase could refer, it probably means a scribbled critique by Zwingli of

614

Grebel's "Attic epigrams" which he had promised to send to Vadian (see 24/124/20-23).

4. Lat. *battalogia*, lit. "pounded words" or "repetitious words."

5. Lat. *pio*. See 6/fn.6.

6. Lat. *munere*, meaning "service," "duty," "favor."

7. Lat. *que in buccam veniunt*, "whatever comes into the cheeks."

8. Lat. *garrulitatis*. See 6/fn.3.

9. Lat. *provocatque digito*, same meaning as *infamis digiti* of 12/95/1 (see 12/fn.20).

10. Lat. *praescribam*. Grebel uses a medical term in speaking to a doctor.

11. Lat. *si me absque testimonio ames*, "if you love me without deposition [proof]."

12. Recurrence of premonition of some future conversion. See 14/101/19-21, 22/118/16-24, 24/124/2, etc.

13. Beatus, see 23/fn.2.

14. Wädenswil was a small territory in the canton of Zurich about 20 miles south of Zurich. Here Conrad's Uncle Hans Wirz was governor (see 11/fn.1 and Cast of Characters No. 99). Vadian had fled there from St. Gallen in August 1519. He and Martha remained there until January 1520. Reference is made here to this sojourn.

15. Einsiedeln, see 1/fn.2.

16. Margaret Wirz, daughter of Hans Wirz. Grebel appears to have been infatuated with her.

17. Graces, see 18/fn.22.

18. Lat. *in sui desiderium rursus concitavit*, "roused again my longing for her."

19. Pisa, the Italian university to which Grebel was ready to go with a papal stipend (see 25/fn.12).

20. Saxony, in Northern Germany, originally a duchy, but in the time of Grebel only the territory around Wittenberg and Lauenburg. It is not evident what Grebel's interest there was. Had he met a girl from there? Was this the Barbara, whom he eventually married? Correll hypothesized that he was thinking of the University of Wittenberg, where Luther and Melanchthon were teachers. In any case, Conrad's father did not want him to go there.

21. Benedict Burgauer, the parish priest in St. Gallen (see 24/fn.19 and Cast of Characters No. 11).

22. Sebastian Wolfgang Wetter, called Juflius (see 24/fn.20 and Cast of Characters No. 97).

23. See 24/93/20.

24. The literary significance of onions is not known, if indeed it had such meaning for Grebel. He may have been thinking merely of the pungent taste of onions as a metaphor for his poignant life struggle.

25. Moera, the Greek name for the Fates (see 25/fn.34 and 5/fn.3).

26A. Grebel's Address "To the True Fair Reader," Zurich, December 24, 1520

1. On Pomponius Mela, the Spanish geographer of the first century AD, see 1/fn.19.

2. Grebel's chief purpose in this introduction was to champion the side of humanists like Vadian against their scholastic rivals like John Camers, who had also published an edition of the *Pomponius Mela*. For other references to this conflict, see 1A/58/12-15, 27-35, 4B/70/3-4, and 1A/fn.17. In his own introduction to the Basel edition, Vadian made mention of the conflict with Camers, as follows: "Some passages from commentaries on *Pomponius* have been quoted and referred to, in the judgment and evaluation of which John Camers, theologian ... and very learned man, in his interpretations on Solinus, does not exactly agree with Joachim Vadian."

3. Mela, see fn. 2, above.

4. Lat. *quos hic digito provocaret*. For the meaning of this reference, see 12/fn.20 and 26/fn.9.

5. For the reference to onions, see 26/130/33 and 26/fn.24.

27. Grebel to Vadian, Zurich, January 4, 1521

1. On Leonhard von Watt, Vadian's father, see Näf, II, 83.

2. Lat. *doluit,* the first of over seventy forms of the verb dolere ("to grieve") used in this epistle.

3. Vadian's mother Magdalena Talmann continued to live in the family home on Schmiedgasse in St. Gallen until 1524. Vadian's brother Benedict lived there with her until 1529, and another brother, David, from 1530 to 1541.

4. Vadian had four brothers—Konrad, Melchior, Benedict, and David—and three sisters—Othilia, Katherine, and Elizabeth. Vadian was the oldest in the family.

5. He is in two places at once. Psychologically, he is already in Pisa; but physically, he is still in Zurich. See 26/fn.19.

6. Dido was the queen and reputed founder of Carthage on the north coast of Africa. The Trojan hero, Aeneas, whose journey from Troy to Italy is told in the early book of the *Aeneid,* landed at Carthage after being driven by a storm. He won the affections of the queen and promised to marry her. But in obedience to the gods to settle in Italy instead of Africa, Aeneas stealthily sailed away, and the heartbroken queen committed suicide. The story is told in Book III.

7. Lat. *nusquam tutam esse,* from the *Aeneid,* 4.373. The original quotation is *nusquam tuta fides,* "nowhere is there true faithfulness." In longer proverbial sense, "Our confidence is everywhere misplaced" or "We cannot trust a single person." Grebel used the original quotation once before in 9/87/9, and in this second usage he leaves out *fides* and the language is more elliptical. When he gets onto an obsessive idea, he is inclined to repeat what he has said before and to summarize his ideas, perhaps because he is writing continually to the same correspondent.

8. See 5/fn.22.

9. Lat. *fabae in caput meum cuduntur,* a phrase from Roman comedy, quoted previously in Letter 12 (see 12/fn.5). Grebel uses *fabae* (beans) twice in the sentence—a conceit.

10. The meaning of this sentence is not clear. The editor of VB had difficulty with the text.

11. Lat. *Dolet, quod succus quidem rebus, fortunis, amicis meis concolor.* "It grieves because the sap is the same color in my affairs, fortunes, and friends." *Succus* means "sap," "strength," "vitality," "vigor," "juice," "taste," "flavor," i.e., all his affairs are equally depressing. It is a mixing of metaphors, combining *succus* with *concolor.*

12. This may refer to 25/125/16-22 and Vadian's request for a poem from Grebel to publish in the new edition of *Pomponius Mela,* on which Vadian was hard at work. As the swan is associated with the good poet, the goose is with the bad. Grebel is referring to Vadian's preoccupation in a not complimentary way. He might mean "because your 'goose' poetry is taking up so much of your time, you cannot write to me."

13. The product of the Nile is paper (see 18/fn.7).

14. A play on the double meaning of "dear": costly and cherished. The same double meaning occurs in the Latin.

15. The one-syllable word that Grebel has in mind is *mens,* meaning mind, intellect, understanding, reason, passion, impulse. With a slight change, the word *mentula* is formed, meaning phallus or penis. For a similar word puzzle, see 34/145/8.

16. The reference here is to Priapus, the Greek god of fertility, whose symbol was the phallus. Priapus, the son of Dionysis and Aphrodite, was worshiped as the promoter of fertility, both in vegetation and in all animals connected with an agricultural life. His *columna* to which Grebel refers was his "waterpipe" or "waterspout" (penis) with which he watered the land.

17. Lat. *Dolet; vale. Dolet; vive.*

18. Hercules, son of Zeus and Alcmene, celebrated for strength and especially for achieving twelve great tasks or "labors" imposed on him as the result of the hatred of Hera. The reference here, however, is to a northern constellation between Corona Borealis and Lyra.

19. Grebel quotes from *Disticha Catonis* in which is found the clause, *legere enim et non intelligere, negligere est,* "to read and not understand is to slight." The name of M. Porcius

Cato (234-149 BC) is erroneously given as the author of this collection of moral maxims in four books, much used as a schoolbook in the Middle Ages. The style of the writing shows it to date from about the third century AD.

20. Lat. *tuus ad aras, Tigurinus Helvetius*. The reference to altars may represent the funeral services for Vadian's father. The place names indicate the custom of Latin scholars of the Renaissance period to use names from classical Latin authors: *Tigurus* for Zurich, *Helvetia* for Switzerland. In Caesar's *Gallic War*, I, 12, he speaks of the *Tigurinus pagus* as a canton or division of Helvetia.

28. Grebel to Vadian, Zurich, February 1, 1521

1. Perhaps the disclosure of 6/79/25ff. Concerning the chronic nature of Grebel's illness, see 4/fn.3.

2. If, indeed, he suffered from venereal disease, the other problem to which he likely refers is his hard-to-manage sexual drive (see 6/79/25-36 and 27/fns. 15 and 16).

3. This is the same phrase Grebel used in 6/79/30-31 when he confessed to consorting often with prostitutes.

4. See 24/fn.5. The matter he does not disclose may be also the reason he accuses himself of being Silenus in 24/124/7.

5. The Latin has a play on sound: *peroratum non exoratum,* "supplicated but not placated." What his father would not permit is identified on the next page, line 18, as "prevented by father's severity from coming to you."

6. This is the first in a series of references to an attraction in Basel, which will be progressively revealed as his love affair. See 28/136/4-5, 29/138/28, 30/139/18, 31/140/10-11, 34/145/3-4, 35/147/6, 9-10, 13, 36/148/12-13, and 38/150/10.

7. Several interpretations of this reference to "stipend" are possible. Although the present tense was used, it could refer to the accumulating stigma attached to his past stipends from the emperor and the king of France (see 1/fn.14 and 4/fn.9). Or it may refer to the papal pension for study in Pisa, mentioned by Jacob Grebel (23A/122/9-16) and by Conrad (30/139/13-17). Although the latter reference by Conrad indicated that the papal stipend had not yet been negotiated, the reference in 28/136/27 to "papal wealth" indicates that Grebel's chief concern here is a pending decision whether or not to accept a new stipend from the pope. In either case, the opposition to such stipends in Zurich is clearly revealed here. Zwingli had given up his papal pension in the previous year (1520). See 25/fn.17.

8. The uncles referred to here were stepbrothers of Jacob Grebel: Hans Wirz, manager at Wädenswil; Heinrich Wirz, manager of the monastery property at Einsiedeln (see Cast of Characters Nos. 99 and 100); and Jacob Wirz. Uncle Hans was particularly close to the Grebel family (see 11/fn.1). At Jacob Grebel's trial, one of the questions to be asked the defendant was "why his brother, the manager at Wädenswil, threatened him in Conrad Baumann's house" (Epi.A/466/35-37). Compare Jacob's answer (467/12ff.) with Conrad's following disclosure.

9. Scampius is probably Alexander Stamp, referred to in Epi.A/467/12-13, probably a representative of the king of France (see Epi.A/fn.93).

10. Lat. *Scampius ex ore Gallici cauiusdam oratoris retulit,* "Scampius brought back a report from the mouth of a certain French orator." The blushing (line 8), Silenus (24/124/7), and shooting arrows (line 11) may all be metaphors connected with the same cause of guilt. It is typical of Grebel's style and allusiveness for various reasons to use clusters of metaphors, which suggest and refer to each other, once the idea comes into his writing.

11. The party in Switzerland favoring alliance with and support of the king, Francis I of France, was called the Royalist Party; and those supporting the Holy Roman Emperor, Charles V, the Imperialist Party. Jacob Grebel, previously pro-French, seemed to be vacillating at this time, while Conrad remained sympathetic to the Imperialist Party (see 34/454/33-34 and 38/150/34). The friction between the two parties was serious and almost led to civil war, since most of the other cantons wanted to engage in active military support of the French while Zurich had taken an official anti-French position. Citizens of Zurich were for-

bidden to support the French cause in any way; and on September 5, 1523, a certain Konrad Hedinger, mentioned in Jacob Grebel's trial, was condemned to death for violating this regulation (see Egli, No. 407).

12. See 13/fn.8. Since Toulouse was a political center in Grebel's time, as well as in ancient history, it is possible that the bribe to which he referred actually came from here, and that it then awoke in Grebel its classical associations.

13. See fn. 9, above.

14. See 20/fn.10. As indicated in the earlier note, less than 40 out of 142 of Livy's volumes are still extant. By "the entire history of Livy" Grebel includes the lost books were they to be found. During the summer of 1924 much interest was aroused by the report—later proved false—that those lost books had been found in Italy.

15. See fn. 6, above.

16. Grebel probably refers here to the possibility of marriage with a girl who was not acceptable to his family.

17. Lat. *In tanta copia tam inops, in tantis malus tam mutus sum,* "In such abundance, so destitute; in such adversity, I am so speechless." The assonance of the Latin *(copia . . . inopia, malus . . . mutus)* has been retained.

18. "Sea of troubles" is a frequent phrase in Greek tragedy.

19. A labyrinth was a structure full of intricate passages and windings, so that when once entered it is almost impossible to find one's way out without the assistance of a guide. There were four famous labyrinths among the ancients—in Egypt, Crete, Lemnos, and Italy. The one in Crete figured prominently in Greek mythology.

29. Grebel to Vadian, Zurich, February 19, 1521

1. Lat. *non intelligo nec licuit.*

2. Apropos of the introduction, above, it appears that Grebel was taking the lead in whatever the negotiations were, and that he may have had less to lose if not more to gain than Vadian (see 30/139/23-24). But see also Epi.A/fn.47.

3. Lat. *Legatus a latere* is elliptical, but means "from the side of the emperor" or "from the side of the pope." The campaign for Milan between Charles V and Francis I began in the spring of 1521. Francis had succeeded in winning all of the Swiss cantons but Zurich to his side. The legate was Cardinal Antonio Pucci (see Cast of Characters No. 72, 23/fn.22, and 24/fn.16. Pucci left Zurich with the Swiss troops at the end of March according to his own letter referred to in ZW, VII, p. 446, fn. 10. Zwingli preached against this business of mercenaries, but was not heeded at first. The adverse treatment which the Zurich contingent received convinced Zurich that the pope was no holier a master than any other prince, and therefore in 1522 Zurich withdrew from the mercenary business and tried to dissuade the other cantons to do the same.

4. One of only four references to Andreas, Conrad's youngest brother, two by name. See Cast of Characters No. 31. Andreas died September 3, 1521.

5. Effinger was a prominent family name in Zurich and one associated with the Grebels (cf. Staub, p. 3, where it is reported that "Schultheiss Hans Effinger" was a witness in 1515 when the two Grebels surrendered their citizenship). A son of Hans Effinger, Beat Effinger, is probably the companion of Andreas here referred to. He was named as one of the officers in a military campaign proposed by Zwingli in 1524 (cf. ZW, III, No. 17, p. 555).

6. Ferdinand I, archduke of Austria (see Cast of Characters No. 24).

7. One of the numerous expressions of gratitude to Vadian for his friendship (see 4/fn.4).

8. "It" in this sentence seems to refer to the restoration of Grebel's health. He hopes for healing with or without Vadian's medical help.

9. Barbara Grebel Karli (see Cast of Characters No. 32) had fled to Zurich in August 1520 to escape the plague and had remained with her parents. It is assumed that her husband died of the plague before or after her arrival in Zurich (see 2/fn.8 and 22/118/2-3).

10. Lat. *vehementer,* "vehemently," "impetuously," "violently." Grebel refers first to his

sister Barbara and her love for him, but he refers increasingly to another Barbara (see Cast of Characters No. 33), a secret sweetheart with whom he later went to Basel and whom he married in February 1522. All of this will be revealed in later letters.

11. An unknown person, possibly a shop foreman in Jacob Grebel's iron business.

12. Lat. *nec in Helvetiam nec Basileam perveniam.* Either "Switzerland" was written by mistake for "Italy," or he meant "Helvetia" to refer to other Swiss cantons outside of Zurich. His plan to go to Basel was first mentioned in 28/136/21 (see 28/fn.6).

13. References to the pastor and assistant pastor of the Church of St. Lawrence in St. Gallen (see Cast of Characters Nos. 11 and 97).

14. Jörg Binder and Leopold Grebel (see Cast of Characters No. 4 and 39). Binder was now schoolmaster in Zurich.

30. Grebel to Vadian, Zurich, March 19, 1521

1. Lat. *domino,* repeated twice.

2. Lat. *multiloquio,* see 6/fn.3.

3. The papal legate referred to in the previous letter (29/138/9 and Cast of Characters No. 72).

4. Pisa refers to the Italian university where Grebel had planned to study with a papal pension. The details concerning it are found in Jacob Grebel's testimony in his trial in 1526 (see Epi.A/468/12-14). In the present letter Conrad indicates that Puccius left Zurich with the Swiss troops before March 19 (see 29/fn.3).

5. Canton Uri, on the route from Zurich to Italy, 35 miles south of Zurich.

6. See 28/fn.6.

7. The latter date is a calendar error of Grebel's, for this letter is clearly later than the one preceding it, dated February 18. In the Latin the two dates are *14 Kalendas Aprilis* and *14 Kalendas Martii.*

8. Although we cannot know what the "matter under consideration" was, it sounds as though it is connected with the matter referred to in 29/138/2-8.

9. Burgauer, see Cast of Characters No. 11.

10. This postscript was written in German. Milords of Zurich refers to the Zurich City Council.

11. Burgauer, see fn. 9, above.

12. The German word for Diet was *Tag,* (lit. "day"), sometimes called *Tagsatzung* or *Tagung,* referring to a session of the representatives of the confederated Swiss cantons. "The French Diet" or "Frenchman's Day" (EY) refers to a special session at which a pending new treaty with France was the main agenda. Luzern, some 30 miles southeast of Zurich, was the meeting place for the next Diet scheduled for April 9, at which the proposed alliance with France was accepted.

13. Ger. *flaschböswicht,* "bottle scamp."

31. Grebel to Vadian, Zurich, April 8, 1521

1. Andreas Cratander, Basel printer (see Cast of Characters No. 17). A letter from him to Vadian dated October 19, 1520 (VB, II, No. 222, p. 315) says that Alantsee, the Viennese publisher of Vadian's first edition of *Pomponius Mela* (see 1/fn.17), had commissioned Cratander to print the second edition. The manuscript had been secured in December 1520 (see VB, II, p. 323) and was now in press (see VB, II, p. 346), but because of lack of helpers and a large number of commissions, the work was progressing slowly. Grebel served as intermediary between Vadian and Cratander in some aspects of the work. A letter from Cratander to Vadian dated April 20, 1521 (VB, II, p. 356) was written in reply to the one of Vadian's mentioned here as being forwarded by Grebel. Because of inadequate carrier facilities, Vadian frequently sent other letters along with his to Grebel, asking the latter to forward them at the earliest opportunity. The *Pomponius Mela* appeared in January 1522 (47/165/24-25).

2. The reference is to the meeting of the Swiss Diet at Luzern on April 9 (see 30/fn.12). Evidently the Basel delegates stopped at Zurich on their way.

3. Grebel's planned move to Basel has been mentioned in every letter since No. 28. See 28/fn.6.

4. These two unidentified names probably refer to legates of Emperor Charles attending the Luzern meeting. Meckelburg (Mecklenburg) is an area in Northern Germany, and Siebenbürgen (Transylvania) is an area in Eastern Hungary.

5. Hugo von Hohenlandenberg (see Cast of Characters No. 47).

6. Martha Grebel, Vadian's wife.

7. Grebel refers to the three named in the previous paragraph whom his father was helping to entertain (see 141/3-4).

8. See 2/fn.6.

9. Grebel continues the metaphor of being laden so heavily as to be pressed down.

10. Among the other functions of the Greek god Apollo was that of healing and medicine. See 17/fn.9.

11. See 25/fn.12 and subsequent references to possible study in Italy. These references reveal a painful ambivalence about this plan, including some attraction and considerable repulsion. In 28/136/23-25, he spoke of an "aversion for Italy." The implication of 30/139/16-17 was that the plan had been given up and removal to Basel chosen instead. Now he speaks again of the possibility of visiting Italy, but in a cynical and threatening way.

12. Attempt was made to retain the play on the Latin words *parvitas* ("pettiness") and *pravitas* ("perverseness").

13. Lat. *VI Nonis Aprilis* ("6th day before the nones of April") was clearly a mistake as indicated by the date in the German postscript that follows. In April the nones fall on the fifth day.

14. The postscript is the only extant note of Grebel to his sister Martha. The original, in German, was written on the back of the sheet.

15. Benedict von Watt, Vadian's brother. There will be three subsequent references to Benedict in Conrad's letters: 51/194/32ff., 52/208/7, and 66/299/28. Also see the letter from Melchior von Watt to Vadian dated April 22, 1521 (VB, no. 258, p. 359), in which Melchior writes from Rome, asking his brother to write to Conrad on behalf of Benedict. In 52/208/7, it is apparent that Benedict was visiting in the Grebel home.

32. Grebel to Vadian, Zurich, April 25, 1521

1. The most apparent diagnosis would be pneumonia.

2. Aesculapius, the Greek god of the healing art, son of Apollo. In Homer he is not a divinity but simply the "blameless physician."

3. See 2/fn.6.

4. The eighth hour, assuming Grebel used the Roman reckoning of hours, would be about 2:00 p.m. The Roman hour was one twelfth of the time between sunrise and sunset and therefore varied from 45 to 75 minutes according to the season.

5. Master Jacob probably was one of the Zurich priests, but his identity is unknown. Grebel referred to an unidentified "Jacob" also in 69/358/5. In July 1529 Vadian counseled a Zurich priest called Jacobus on account of the plague (see VB, III, no. 50, note 8).

6. Lat. *in his fluctibus,* "in these billows."

7. Lat. *mihi ob pedes adustos,* "because of my burned feet." See 4/fn.3.

8. We are not informed as to the nature of this request, evidently transmitted by letter from Vadian.

9. That Vadian and Martha did come to Zurich at once in response to this urgent request is revealed by the letter of Burgauer to Vadian from St. Gallen dated a few days later (see 32A, below). Vadian had entrusted to him the overseeing of his affairs in his absence. Also Conrad's next letter, dated May 28 (No. 33), reveals that Martha was still in Zurich, but that Vadian had already returned to St. Gallen.

32A. Burgauer to Vadian, St. Gallen, April 28, 1521

1. On Burgauer, see Cast of Characters No. 11. Vadian and Martha were visiting her sick mother in Zurich at the time. Grebel and Burgauer sent frequent brief messages to each other by way of Vadian, many of which expressed sarcasm.

2. Lat. *Collegium nostorum sacerdotum et sacrificulorum.* In addition to the leading priest, Burgauer, there were six other priests at the Church of St. Lawrence at this time: Clemens Hör, Bartholomäus Weiermann, Othmar Lieb, Ulrich Girtanner, Jacob Riner, and Hans Vogler. See Näf, II, p. 210, fn. 265.

3. Jacob Grebel.

4. Adam Moser, a deacon at the St. Lawrence Church, who later became a cathedral priest and preacher. He held rigidly to the old faith beliefs, which he was forced to retract in December 1528, in a disputation with the reformed-minded preachers (see Näf, II, p. 652).

5. Ulrich Girtanner, who although 56 years old, was identified by Näf (II, p. 368) as associated with Riner and Vogler as the reformed-minded priests vis-a-vis Hör, Weiermann, and Lieb. As the story unfolds, Burgauer later shifted sides from the liberals to the conservatives, or perhaps more accurately, from a Zwinglian view of Reformation to a strict Lutheran view.

6. A private verbal sparring was taking place between Burgauer and Grebel, having to do with *dem Muss,* the mush fed to prisoners. Evidently Burgauer had told Grebel that he would end up eating prisoner's mush. Grebel continues this sparring correspondence in 54/222/7-8.

33. Grebel to Vadian, Zurich, May 28, 1521

1. I.e., Martha is about ready to return to St. Gallen with special escort.

2. Venus, the Roman goddess of love, corresponding to the Greek Aphrodite. Grebel makes four subsequent references to her (see Index).

3. See 32/fn.7.

4. See 32/fn.6 and 4/fn.3.

5. The three characteristics of Apollo mentioned refer to the three personal deficiencies listed by Grebel: ears, perception, and memory. As indicated in 17/fn.9, Apollo was quite versatile, functioning also as god of music and prophetic discernment, the epitome of what Grebel lacked at the moment.

6. Lat. *o coelum, o terra* ("O heaven, O earth"), used also in Grebel's poem at the end of Letter No. 39, below.

7. Quoted in Greek from Homer's *Iliad,* XXIV, 524.

8. Grebel's mother had been ill with pneumonia (see 32/fn.1).

34. Grebel to Vadian, Zurich, between May 28 and July 14, 1521

1. The editor of VB (III, p. 227) believes that this undated letter was written between the letters of May 28 and July 14 (Nos. 33 and 35). The mention in the postscript of the recent return of Vadian's wife, which according to 33/143/11-12 took place the Sunday after May 28 (i.e., June 3) provides the date *a quo.* A comparison of this letter with No. 35, dated July 14, both with reference to political allusions and the proposed trip to Basel, shows that it was written prior to July 14.

2. Lat. *inter os et offam,* "between lip and lump," reminiscent of the Roman proverb, "There is many a slip betwixt cup and lip."

3. Lat. *cum affectibus meis,* "with my affection" or "with my desire." The appropriateness of the rendering here given will become more apparent, especially in Letter No. 38. The phrase will be used several times by Grebel (35/147/13, 37/149/24-25, 38/150/10, 39/151/15), with two meanings. It will be used to designate the object of Grebel's love (as a sort of affectionate nickname as in the present reference) and to describe his own emotional state or condition (37/127/24-25). This is one of a number of nicknames Grebel will use to refer to his new sweetheart. And now, the reason for his going to Basel is finally disclosed (see 28/fn.6).

Up to this point he had spoken obscurely about it. The identity of his sweetheart has never been established. Several German writers had hypothesized that she was Agathe von Fynland from Alsace, but without documentation. Bender (1950, p. 225, fn. 17) shows that this was "pure invention." That her name was Barbara will be revealed in 47/165/5, and see Cast of Characters No. 33. In 41/146/7-8, he calls her *Barbaries mea* ("my Barbarity"), a play on her name. He will use other nicknames: "Holokosme" (whole world, 36/149/9), "my life" (43/159/12), "Lysidice" (45/161/11-12, see 45/fn.2), and "my darling" (46/162/31-32). In the next letter (35/147/14-16), Conrad reports that his sister Barbara was the go-between in his love affair and knows "the whole matter" and can "expound everything." It has been hypothesized on the basis of line 18, below, that she was a nun in the local convent (see 34/fns. 9 and 10).

4. The editor of VB indicates that the part within the parenthesis was written in the margin of the original letter. It is likely an allusion to Lot's wife (Gen. 19:26). Note the phrase written in German.

5. Although it is not certain what Grebel is alluding to, the change of a few letters in the adjective *stulta* ("silly") produces the verb *stupro* ("to ravish," "to rape"). For a similar word puzzle by Grebel, see 27/134/38-41 and 27/fns. 15 and 16.

6. On Ulrich von Hutten, see Cast of Characters No. 56. When he declared openly for the Reformation, he adopted the motto *jacta est alea*, "the die is cast." For other evidence of Grebel's identification with the life and thought of Hutten, see 65/fn.22.

7. The letter "P" seems to be an abbreviation for his mistress, Barbara, since the following lines refer to her.

8. See Paul's judgment of the Cretans as liars in Titus 1:12, quoting the Cretan poet Epimenides of Cnossos, a half-mythical sixth-century BC Greek, variously described as poet, prophet, religious reformer, sage, and the reputed author of a body of literature extant in the first century. Epimenides called the Cretans liars because they claimed to possess the tomb of Zeus, whereas his devotees believed that he was not dead but alive.

9. Bender (1950, p. 226, note 17) concluded that this female Grebel was Agatha, Jacob's sister and Conrad's aunt (see Cast of Characters No. 30). The editor of VB (III, p. 225) holds that this "Grebelia" was Barbara, Conrad's sister, on the basis of 35/147/13-16, where Conrad tells Vadian that he could learn everything from Barbara, who knew everything. Bender is probably correct since "Grebelia" was a nun, which Barbara was not, and since Barbara was no longer a "Grebelia," but a "Karli." Moreover, Barbara could hardly have been the teacher of the deceased Euphrosine (see 34/145/18-19).

10. This comment may well indicate that Conrad's sweetheart, Barbara, had been a nun, or at least living in the Oetenbach convent.

11. Lat. *alumnae eius*, "her alumna," or "her foster daughter." The deceased sister was Euphrosine Grebel, a nun at the Oetenbach convent (see 18/109/24-25).

12. Silenus was the name of the tutor and constant companion of the Greek wine god, Bacchus. Much Greek drama, especially tragedy, grew out of the worship of Bacchus (see 24/fn.6).

13. Alcibiades (*ca.* 450-05 BC) was a Greek general who lived a life of widely varied fortunes. On the death of his father in 447, he was raised by his relative, Pericles. His youth was disgraced by his amours and debaucheries; and Socrates, who saw his great abilities, vainly tried to win him to the paths of virtue. Recalled from battle to stand trial for sedition, he escaped to Thurii, and thence to Sparta, where he acted as the avowed enemy of his country. Meanwhile at Athens, sentence of death was passed upon him and his property confiscated. He died later at the hands of assassins.

14. Ceres, the Roman goddess of agriculture and crops. She was identified with the Greek, Demeter, having similar functions. The center of her worship was at Eleusis, near Athens, where the famous Eleusinian Mysteries were celebrated, including an elaborate secret ritual into which candidates were initiated.

15. Fortune, see 9/fn.4.

16. The cries of a crow were considered a favorable omen, e.g., a sign of rain.

17. Francis I, king of France (see Cast of Characters No. 26).

18. Charles I, king of Spain, also Charles V, Holy Roman emperor (see Cast of Characters No. 14).

19. On May 8, representations of the emperor and the pope had signed an offensive alliance against France, which Charles had authorized only as a defensive pact. In this they had been swayed by Pope Leo X to go to war against Francis I because the latter had thwarted a desired extension of the papal possessions, especially of northern Italian principalities such as Milan. The war lasting eight years (1521-29) was a success for the emperor, although his generals had had several severe setbacks during the first year. The specific engagement to which Grebel referred is obscure, although it might have been the unsuccessful French attempt to reconquer the little duchy of Navarra in the Pyrenees undertaken in May. The number of casualties is probably exaggerated, for the major battle over Milan did not occur until 1522, but see 147/1-5.

20. Lat. *Gallus insilit*. Grebel's anti-French bias (see 38/150/34) was probably related to his bad experience in France and his recent entanglements with the papal emissaries Puccio and de Falconibus (see 23A/121/31-32).

21. The messenger or letter carrier.

22. Lat. *parochus* (see 6/fn.57). The reference is to Burgauer (see Cast of Characters No. 11).

23. Lat. *improborum Alpha*, equivalent here to "chief reprobate."

24. Lat. *nos fulmina mittat*, "send us the thunderbolt [anathema]" (see 47D/185/40, 47C/fn.8).

25. The five-line poem refers to the victory of the French ambassador at the recent Diet at Luzern in winning the support of all the Swiss cantons but Zurich in the conflict of the French against the emperor. This was achieved by general bribes of money in return for the promised mercenaries. It was said that the illegal royal pensions increased by 50 percent. The treaty of aid was adopted on May 5 (see Egli, *Aktens.*, No. 169). Despite all the pressure, Zurich refused to join the other cantons in the alliance. The reference to this event fixes another *terminus a quo* for the letter (see fn. 1, above).

35. Grebel to Vadian, Zurich, July 14, 1521

1. Conrad Grebel salutes Vadian.

2. Udorf was a small village near Zurich, popular for its medicinal baths. Zwingli mentioned his stay here in a letter from Zurich dated August 31, 1521 (ZW, VII, p. 470).

3. The castle of Milan, known as the *Castel Sforzesco,* was built in 1450 by Francesco Sforza. The splendid entrance tower was built separately by Antonio Averulino (Filarete) in 1451-53. It was this tower that was shattered in 1521, not by a thunderbolt as heard by Grebel, but by a powder explosion. It has been rebuilt in its original fifteenth-century design and is today one of the most famous structures in Italy.

4. The pope, Leo X (see Cast of Characters No. 63), had made a secret alliance with the emperor against France on May 8, 1521 (see 34/fn.19). With the help of papal forces the emperor was able to drive the French out of Milan by the following year. The pope succeeded in winning the consent of Zurich, based on the Treaty of 1510, to send troops to aid him in recovering some of his lands from the French. For this purpose Bishop Filonardi (see fn. 5, below) was sent, against Zwingli's wishes. The desired additional contingent was sent in the autumn. The Swiss regained Parma and Piacenza, the "two towns" mentioned here. The sending of the contingent is referred to in Egli, No. 195, dated Sept. 26. From Zurich 2,700 men went and were joined by still larger contingents on the way.

5. Ennius Filonardi Verulanus, see Cast of Characters No. 25. The Latin *legatus prior* could mean "former legate" or "foremost legate." Since he had just been appointed, the latter interpretation was given.

6. Concerning the plan to go to Basel, see 28/fn.6 and subsequent indexed references. The Latin *perfregit, erupit, evasit* ("broken through, burst out, escaped") has its source in Cicero, *Cat.* II, 1, where it was said of Catiline's leaving the city, *Abiit, excessit, evasit, erupit.* See 36/148/12-13 and 36/fn.2.

7. Vulcanus, the god of fire and the god of mechanical skill, also called Mulciber (the hammer god), was Grebel's metaphor for Andreas Cratander, who was publishing the second edition of Vadian's *Pomponius Mela* (see 31/fn.1).

8. Didymus, a famous grammarian, was born at Alexandria in 63 BC and flourished in the time of Emperor Augustus. He is said to have published 3,500 volumes on grammatical and scholarly subjects. Whether Cratander had sent a volume on Didymus or the name was metaphorical for some other volume being forwarded is not known.

9. Vadian's second edition of the *Pomponius Mela* (see 1/fn.19) was published by Cratander in January 1522. The book was in process during the entire year 1521.

10. Erasmus (see Cast of Characters No. 20) had been in Louvain since 1517. As the storm about Luther began to rise, he was accused by the reactionaries of the university of favoring Luther's cause. After the Diet of Worms, the papal bull of May 6, putting Luther under the ban of the church, and the imperial edict of May 26, putting him under the ban of the empire, he began to fear for his own safety. Early in June, Emperor Charles and the papal legate Aleander came to the Netherlands and proceeded to carry out their mission to stamp out heresy. From this time on Erasmus planned to flee to Basel, his earlier residence. He arrived in Basel on November 15.

11. Johann Froben, the greatest printer of Basel, had been in the business since 1491 and had earned world renown. Since 1514, when Erasmus came to Basel, they had been close friends and he lived in Froben's house at least part of the time from 1514 to 1517. Froben had printed the first edition of his Greek New Testament in 1516. When Erasmus returned to Basel in November 1522, he lived in Froben's house for another ten months.

12. Lat. *puto illum ipsum affectum,* "I reckon affection itself." Compare with 34/145/4-5 and see 34/fn.3.

13. Barbara Grebel Karli (see Cast of Characters No. 33).

14. Corycus was a promonotory of Ionia in Asia Minor whose high and rugged coast once harbored a wild and daring population, notorious for piracy. By disguising themselves and infiltrating the harbors nearby, they obtained private information on the course and cargo of merchant vessels. The secrecy with which their intelligence was procured gave rise to the proverb, "This, then, the Corycean overheard."

15. Tomi was a town of Thrace on the west shore of the Black Sea, renowned as the place of Ovid's banishment. Zurich was to Grebel as Tomi was to Ovid.

16. John Jacob Ammann (see Cast of Characters No. 3) had studied the year before in Milan from where he sent greetings to Grebel and Binder in a letter to Zwingli (ZW, VII, No. 153, p. 349) dated Sept. 11, 1520.

17. This sentence was written by a different hand, obviously Jörg Binder (see Cast of Characters No. 4).

18. The translation omits the unintelligible phrase, *et non zoyce.* The name Zoilus was proverbial for censoriousness, after a severe critic in the time of Ptolemaeus Philadelphus, a censurer of Homer. If this was the reference, the translation might be "and no criticism." According to Grebel, Binder tended to remain aloof (see the poem at the end of Letter 25).

19. Dominicus Zili (see Cast of Characters No. 104) was schoolmaster in St. Gallen since 1521 and became a preacher at St. Lawrence's in 1524.

20. Lat. *dominum plebanum S. Laurencii,* "people's master at St. Lawrence's" (see 3/fn.12). The people's priest was Benedict Burgauer (see Cast of Characters No. 11).

21. Martha Grebel, Vadian's wife.

22. Wolfgang Wetter, assistant pastor at St. Lawrence's (see Cast of Characters No. 97).

23. See 24/fn.23.

24. See 2/fn.12.

36. Grebel to Vadian, Zurich, July 22, 1521

1. The parent is Grebel's father. The "leaving" refers to the intended move to Basel mentioned in every letter since No. 28 except Nos. 32 and 33. See 28/fn.6.

2. Cicero (106-43 BC) was the most celebrated orator of ancient Rome. More than fifty of his speeches are still extant.

3. The reference is to his mistress (see 34/fn.3).

4. Tomi, the place of Ovid's banishment (see 35/fn.15). Grebel is thinking of an exile from Zurich.

5. In 39/151/17-18, Grebel discloses that William de Falconibus, the secretary to the papal legate (see Cast of Characters No. 22) had given him 100 francs. This is probably unrelated to the arrangement by the papal legate mentioned in 30/139/13-16, but was a direct gift (cf. Epi.A/468/12-15). At his trial in 1526, Jacob Grebel was asked about having sent his son to de Falconibus; and he replied that when Conrad asked his father for money, he had sometimes given it and sometimes not. On one occasion when he had not, he may have told his son to go to de Falconibus. Perhaps "he will give you something after all" (Epi.A/468/20-23). That Conrad was aware of his father's opposition to accepting money from de Falconibus is evident from 39/151/22-23).

6. Irus, the well-known beggar of Ithaca. His real name was Arnaeus, but he was called Irus because he was the messenger of the suitors of Penelope. He was slain by Ulysses.

7. Erinyes, called Furies or avenging deities by the Romans, were originally only a personification of curses pronounced upon a criminal.

8. Venus, the Roman goddess of love (see 33/fn.2). No "empty Venus" refers to the presence of his sweetheart in Basel waiting for him.

9. Lat. *ambitioni laqueum mandaturus*, "order the noose for [my] ambition" or "I shall bid ambition to go and be hanged."

10. Lat. *ego animam hanc exhalem*, "I will breathe out this spirit."

11. Lat. *multis malis malis*, repeated twice for emphasis, either "many, many evils" or "many evil evils."

12. Tacked onto the preceding list of difficulties was *illud meum tragicum malum*, "that tragic evil of mine."

13. Pythius, the Pythian, was the surname given Apollo when he slew Python, the celebrated serpent, thus winning control of the town of Pytho, renamed Delphi, considered to be the "navel of the earth." In Delphi there was a temple of Apollo and an oracle to which the Greeks resorted to discern the will of the gods.

14. *Chiliades* is a Greek word written in Latin letters.

15. The year is missing but 1521 is correct considering the content of the preceding and following letters concerning the plans for going to Basel.

16. William de Falconibus, see Cast of Characters No. 22.

17. The editor of VB refers to some letters in the margin at this point which cannot be deciphered.

18. See 37/149/30, 37/fn.5, and the letter from de Falconibus to Vadian, July 31, 1521 (VB, II, No. 270).

19. C.G.T.H. stands for *Conrad Grebel Tigurinus Helvetius*, "a Swiss of Zurich" or "a Swiss Zuricher."

20. *Holokosmos*, Greek for "whole world," was one of Grebel's nicknames for his mistress (see 34/fn.3).

37. Grebel to Vadian, Zurich, August 4, 1521

1. Lat. *vitae meae Diras* (see 36/fn.7).

2. Lat. *Nam ita quaedam meum cor urunt, ut, quae multis verborum fasciculis comprehensurus fueram, ne paucissimis attingam, faciunt*. The sentence did not make full sense either to the editor of VB, who added the mark (!) after *faciunt*, or to the translators. AB writes: "Grebel has left the sentence unfinished, because the result clause ('that. . . .') has not been put in. It is a jumble in Latin, the last word *faciunt*, 'they do,' being very strange and not fitting at all. The sense of the sentence would seem to be, 'For so do certain things torture my heart, that, what I would have enclosed in many bundles of words, I do not touch with the fewest.' " EY connects *faciunt* to *quae* and translates as follows: "For certain things so

distress my heart that *what* I had compassed in many volumes of words *cause* me not to touch with a very few." The present rendering connects *faciunt* with *quaedam*, "certain things . . . have the effect that. . . . "

3. The Lat. *affectibus meis* is the same pair of words Grebel used in 34/145/4-5, as a nickname for his mistress. In the present context, however, it refers to his emotions.

4. Lat. *oratores.* Grebel usually employs the word "nuncio" to refer to conventional messengers or letter carriers (see line 17, below). In this instance, his letter was evidently being carried by "delegates" returning to St. Gallen by way of Zurich from some official meeting. See 2/fn.4.

5. See 36/fn.16 and Cast of Characters No. 22. The letter mentioned here is probably that written to Vadian from Zurich dated July 31, 1521 (see VB, II, No. 270). The absence of an address at the close of Grebel's letter can be explained as due to the enclosing of this letter with that of Falconibus, as the editor of VB suggests.

38. Grebel to Vadian, Basel, August 21, 1521

1. Lat. *affectus mei.* Cf. 34/145/4-5, 35/147/13, 37/149/24-25, and 34/fn.3.

2. The doubt expressed by this comment is reiterated in 39/151/16-18 and 41/156/6-7.

3. Andreas Cratander, Basel printer. See Cast of Characters No. 17.

4. Ursinus (Caspar Velius). See Cast of Characters No. 91.

5. Grebel's main task at Cratander's was to help prepare Vadian's second edition of *Pomponius Mela* for the press. See 1/fn.19 and 35/fn.9.

6. Lucas Alantsee and his brothers were famous printers and booksellers in Vienna, where almost all of the local humanists published their works. He had published the first edition of Vadian's *Pomponius Mela* in 1518 and commissioned Cratander to publish the second.

7. See 24/fn.19. Apparently their friendship is beginning to cool. The hostility increases as time moves on (see 52/207/35-36, 54/222/6,9, and 54A).

8. Lat. *pastorem nebulonum, animarum,* a play on words in assonance. The middle word means "loafers" or "good-for-nothings." See 52/fn.9.

9. See fn. 4, above. The reference is probably to an expected reply to Ursinus's letter to Vadian from Constance dated August 3 (see VB, II, No. 271).

10. This was written in the margin. Grebel's bias toward the Imperialist Party against the French is here again disclosed (see 34/145/33-34).

11. Lat. *Videamus Caroli finem.* The literal translation, "We should see the end of Charles," can hardly be the sense of Grebel's conclusion, but rather the opposite, "Let us consider the aim of Charles."

39. Grebel to Vadian, Basel, September 2, 1521

1. For the problem of dating this letter, see fn. 25, below.

2. Grebel's salutation is a quotation from Horace, *Odes,* I, 1, 2. A high compliment is intended as Vadian is compared to Horace's patron, Maecenas, a nobleman and famous patron of the arts.

3. On Cratander, see 31/fn.1, 38/fn.3, and Cast of Characters No. 17.

4. Cratander was attending the semiannual Frankfurt Fair, a gathering of buyers and sellers from all over Europe. It became famous in the thirteenth century, and was first mentioned in 1150. It was credited with bringing prosperity to this medieval town. Part of the fair, which brought scholars and printers together, was the display of newly published books, which is why Cratander was there.

5. Merchants from St. Gallen enroute to the Frankfurt Fair, who delivered Vadian's letters to Zurich.

6. Ursinus, see 38/fn.4 and Cast of Characters No. 91.

7. Lat. *non facile educavero heram meam et affectus illos,* "I will not easily here have provided for my mistress and passions" or ". . . for my mistress and her whims."

8. William de Falconibus, see 36/fns. 5 and 16, and Cast of Characters No. 22.

9. Stipend from the papal legate through his secretary, de Falconibus.

10. Venus is a metaphor for rousing and enlarging a sexual appetite (see 33/fn.2). Grebel believes his father would prefer to have him keep a whore than this particular girl.

11. Lat. *abduxi malum maximum mecum,* "I have abducted the greatest misfortune with me."

12. The three evils: his lack of funds, his father's hostility, and living with a mistress.

13. The priestess of Delphi, called Pythia, sits on her tripod handing down oracles to the worshipers. It was thought that in the center of the temple there was a chasm, over which stood her tripod whenever the oracle was to be consulted. The words which she uttered, containing the revelations of Apollo, were written down by the priests, who then communicated to the worshipers in hexameters. Note the verse at the end of Grebel's letter.

14. Lat. *victum,* translated "eat" (AB) or "board" (EY).

15. For an interpretation of what this meant, see 47/Intro.

16. Lat. *mi anime Vadiane.*

17. "My life and love."

18. Ursinus, see 39/fn.6 and Cast of Characters No. 91.

19. Lat. *damast,* derived from *Damascus,* the place of origin for this material.

20. For the image of fortune as stepmother, see 9/fn.4.

21. Lat. *Grebeliolus,* dimunutive form of Grebelius.

22. Again the dimunutive *homulus* for *homo* ("man").

23. Martha Grebel, Vadian's wife.

24. The pastor, Burgauer (see Cast of Characters No. 11).

25. The Latin reads *IIII Nonis Decembris.* As Bender (1950, p. 247, note 57) concludes, December is probably another of Grebel's errors with dates (see 1/fn.36, 31/fn.13, etc.). The content of the present letter indicates that it was written between Letters 38 and 40. Letter 41, dated Nov. 2, 1521, was clearly written from Zurich, as was Letter 40, which was undated but probably written the end of October (see 40/fn.1). Letter 39 was written from Basel, and the period of the Basel sojourn was probably limited to ten weeks at most, from the middle of August to the end of October. Grebel's error gave rise to the theory that he was in Basel twice, as stated by Neff in *Gedenkschrift zum 400-jährigen Jubiläum der Mennonitem oder Taufgesinnten,* p. 73. There is nothing in Grebel's later letters to indicate a return to Basel, but just the opposite. In Letter 42, he wrote that he was glad to be home and resolved never again to leave Zurich for foreign sojourns (42/157/22-23).

26. The Latin *O coelum, mare, terra,* is similar to that used in 33/143/26-28.

27. Lat. *Ditis aula,* refers to the palace of Pluto, the god of the lower world, called Dis by the Romans and Hades by the Greeks. Grebel calls on all the elements of the universe, including heaven, earth, and hell.

28. Carthage, one of the most celebrated cities of the ancient world, situated northeast of Tunis on the northern coast of Africa, was renowned for its perfidy and faithlessness.

39A. Cratander to Capito, Basel, September 20, 1521
1. On Cratander, see 31/fn.1, 38/fn.3, and Cast of Characters No. 17.
2. On Caspar Ursinus Velius, see 38/fn.4 and Cast of Characters No. 91.

39B. Ursinus to Vadian, Basel, October 1, 1521
1. On Ursinus, see 38/fn.4 and Cast of Characters No. 91.
2. A complete five-volume edition of the poems of Ursinus was published by Cratander in 1522 under the title *Posteritati reliquit Elegias, Epigrammata, Panegyricos, Epitomes chronicarum Mundi et opus quoddam de rebus Austriacis. Poematum libri V.*

40. Grebel to Vadian, Zurich, end of October, 1521
1. This undated letter is the one referred to by Grebel in 41/155/19, which he had given the merchant Enderli; and it must therefore be dated shortly before that, or near the end of October. Since he had just returned to Zurich, he must have remained in Basel most of October. The letter of Ursinus to Vadian dated Oct. 1, 1521 (see 39B) refers to Grebel as

627

though he were still in Basel.

2. On the nature of Grebel's chronic illness, see 4/fn.3.

3. Lat. *necessitatem*, "necessity," "need," and by transfer "intimate connection," "familiarity." Probably this should not be translated "urgency" but "familiarity" as a progression from "friendship" and "kinship."

4. Valentin Tschudi (see 6/fn.58 and Cast of Characters No. 88) had been in Paris until very recently. He remained in Zurich until October 1522, when he took up his duties as pastor in Glarus.

5. Cratander (see Cast of Characters No. 17), the printer at whose house Grebel had stayed in Basel. This is another source for dating Letters 39 and 40, since it is known from the letter he wrote to Capito from Frankfurt (see 39A) that he was still at the Frankfurt Fair on September 20, and the present reference indicates that Cratander had just returned from the fair. The things given to him included a letter from Vadian and additional notes for the edition of *Pomponius Mela* which had come during Cratander's absence.

6. The Lat. *Catechesis*, meaning "oral instruction" or "manual for oral instruction." The reference here is to Vadian's commentary on the *Pomponius Mela* (see 1A/59/15-16 and 1A/fn.35.

7. Vadian had added to his commentary a catechism for the study of geography. It is named on the title page of the 1522 edition: *addita quoque in geographiam Catechesi,* "also added a catechism in geography." Apparently Vadian was slow in delivering the copy for this part of the book.

8. The new second edition of the *Pomponius Mela,* Vadian's commentary on the old Latin geography (see 1/fn.19), actually came from the press in 1522, the date on the title page. In a letter from Lucas Alantsee to Vadian dated Feb. 2, 1522 (VB, III, p. 418), it is said that "the *Pomponius* has appeared." Grebel was still awaiting it on Jan. 30 (46/162/13-14) and first mentioned having received copies in his letter of Feb. 6, 1522 (47/165/24). Falconibus writes on Feb. 1 from Zurich that he has heard that the *Pomponius* has been reborn (VB, II, p. 417). Binder in an undated letter probably written in January 1522 (VB, III, p. 233) asks Vadian for a copy of the new edition.

9. Tertullian (Q. Septimus Florens Tertullianus, ca. 160-230) was one of the earliest of the Latin Christian Fathers whose writings are still extant. He was born at Carthage in Northern Africa of pagan parents, converted in mature manhood, widely read in law, literature, and philosophy. The most interesting of his numerous works is his *Apologeticus,* or defense of Christianity. It was Erasmus who turned the scholars of Vadian's time back to the early Church Fathers, and new editions of nearly all of them were pouring from the presses.

10. This satirical reference was to Benedict Burgauer, pastor at St. Lawrence's in St. Gallen (see 24/fn.19 and Cast of Characters No. 11). The Greek word *pantalabus* means "all-grabber," one who takes everything. The same word play is found in 45/161/34.

11. Lat. *Civitate Tiguri donatum me tandem credo, / Nugarum genus omne candidarum/ Seu sit ridiculumve seriumve.* In order to attend foreign universities, students like Grebel were compelled to surrender their citizenship, which he had done on July 4, 1515 (see Bender, 1950, p. 18), before going to Vienna. Now finally, more than six years later, he is resuming his citizenship, although Bender (p. 247, note 70) found no trace in the state archives of Zurich of the formal reinstatement.

12. Lat. *Quam primum mihi per tabellionum/Non sic properantium licebit/Copiam, auriculas para ferentes.* The reference here is to a common theme in Grebel's letters, his chattering (see 6/fn.3). This goes back to the term *nugarum* in the second line of the poem, the "balderdash" or "nonsense" that constitutes a predominant theme in human communication. Vadian will respond to this cynicism (see 43/158/30-31).

41. Grebel to Vadian, Zurich, November 2, 1521

1. Conrad's undated letter to Vadian, i.e., Letter 40, above. See 40/fn.1.

2. Enderli, another form of the name Andreas or Andrew, probably refers to Andreas Castelberger, the book dealer in Zurich (see Goeters, p. 244, 51B/fn.3, and Cast of

Characters No. 13). If so, this is Grebel's first reference to someone with whom he was later associated in the Anabaptist movement. It is probable also that this is the same person referred to by Myconius at Jacob Grebel's trial when he testified that he and Conrad were "in Enderli's house" (Epi.A/465/38ff.). It is less likely that these refer to Enderli Kramer, who also testified at the trial that "he was Conrad Grebel's 'good friend' until Anabaptism separated them" (Epi.A/466/3ff.). Kramer operated some kind of a shop in Zurich and was apparently on friendly terms with the Grebel family as indicated by other parts of his trial testimony. Grebel refers to Enderli again in 51/195/27, where the context supports the identity of Castelberger. See Epi.A/fn.42.

3. The word was written in German: *stuba.*

4. The vow is more explicit in Grebel's letter to Myconius which follows. See 42/157/21-23.

5. For Lucian, see 28/fn.17. He was one of Grebel's favorite authors.

6. Lucian and the Greek epigrams satirized and mocked the pagan religious superstitions of his time, and it is interesting that Grebel turned to them at this point in his life. The next sentence indicates that he was tiring of much of his past humanist studies.

7. Lat. *infelix,* which could be translated "unlucky," "unfortunate," "unsuccessful."

8. Lat. *Amavi amoque, scis quibus modis,* could mean either "I have loved (my studies)" (AB) or "I have loved (a woman)" (EY). The latter interpretation would mean a thought transition from humanist studies to romantic love. Although the next paragraph makes such a transition, the phrase, "For as I did the Muses" (see below), indicates a love-hate relationship to both literature and women, which supports the AB rendering here given. See also 42/157/16-17.

9. His mistress, Barbara, with whom he had spent two months in Basel (see 34/fn.3).

10. Lat. *de ducenda uxore.* See 47/fn.1 for an interpretation of what that meant.

11. Lat. *quam si usore magis usor essem,* "as if I were more a wife than a wife." This makes little sense. Either Grebel intended *esset* ("she were") or the rendering we have given.

12. Lat. *Barbaries mea,* a pun on "Barbara," his mistress whom he later married (see 47/164/2).

13. Lat. *Imponat olim, fingamus, Barbaries mea; inposuerit ultima.* "My Barbarian might put me on in the future, I suppose; the last one to put me on." Several times in his writing, Grebel expresses a premonition of things to come. In 13/98/12-13, concerning his father's acceptance of illegal pensions, Grebel predicted "that time and perhaps this very day will disclose all," a prophecy that certainly came true in the trial and execution of his father. Here, he predicts that Barbara will betray him someday; and in 69/357/15-28, dated May 1525, he reports how she proceeded to do just that after he became an Anabaptist.

14. Muses (see 1/fn.6), the inspiring goddesses of the arts and sciences.

15. Venus, see 33/fn.2.

16. Lat. *genii hominum domesticorum civiumque.*

17. Extending the middle finger, an obscene gesture that goes back to ancient Greek and Roman usage. See 12/fn.20.

18. The Muses and Venus are specific metaphors here for literature and romance.

42. Grebel to Myconius, Zurich, November 4, 1521

1. Grebel really did read Lucian as he said he was going to in 41/155/28-29, because this phrase is a proverb from Lucian, *Gallen* 1.

2. Cupid, god of love, usually represented as a naked winged boy with quiver and darts.

3. Not just a boy, but with strength equivalent to three times his size, or to the invincible Hercules (see 27/fn.18).

4. Apollo (see 17/fn.9), the patron of young men like Grebel.

5. Cupid hits and flies, but Conrad's love endures.

6. Muses (1/fn.6), used here as a metaphor for the literary arts.

7. Paris and Basel represent bad experiments in living abroad for Grebel, and he will

be content to remain at home for awhile. In fact, the next time he goes abroad, he does so as an Anabaptist missioner over three years later.

8. Myconius was instrumental in bringing Zwingli to Zurich as people's priest in 1518 (see 3/fn.7). They became close friends as they worked together in the Grossmünster, Myconius as schoolmaster. Less than a year later after Grebel wrote this letter, Zwingli brought Myconius back to Zurich (see 47E) to work with his friends in the Reformation movement.

9. Lat. *Platonisamus*, "we Platonize," a term coined by Grebel to express their study of Greek. Valentin Tschudi (see Cast of Characters No. 88) had just returned from Paris (see 40/fn.4) and John Jacob Ammann (see Cast of Characters No. 3) from Milan. Together with Grebel, they were studying Greek with Zwingli (see ZW, VII, No. 190, note 4).

10. See 41/155/29-30 and 41/fn.6.

11. The assonance of the Lat., *carmen . . . crimen*, has been retained, although "curse" is a free interpretation of *crimen*, which means "crime," "charge," "reproach."

12. Boeotian was an epithet for the stupid and uncultured among the ancient Greeks (see 24/fn.12). The people of Boeotia northwest of Attica were proverbially dull and backward, in contrast with the culture and refinement of Athens. The phrase "Boeotian pig" was used by Piner, *Olympian*, VI, 490.

13. Lat. *garriam* (see 6/fn.3).

14. Lat. *benignorum morum humana facilitas rursusque facilis humanitas.* An alternate rendering (AB) would be "human courtesy and courteous humanity of your benign nature."

15. Rudolph Collin, see Cast of Characters No. 16.

16. John Xylotectus, Cast of Characters No. 103.

17. Tibianus is otherwise unknown, perhaps the assistant pastor in Luzern.

18. Lat. *tuus ex animo*, "yours from the soul."

43. Grebel to Vadian, Zurich, December 18, 1521

1. Tertullian, see 40/fn.9.

2. Lat. *vector*. Grebel usually used *nuncio* to designate the letter carrier, and occasionally *tabellarius* (see 2/fn.4). Apparently in this instance he wanted to single out the "butcher" who delivered Vadian's last letter by calling him *vector*. His identity is unknown.

3. Falconibus (see Cast of Characters No. 22). The identity of the soldier is unknown.

4. Lat. *nugarum*. The reference is certainly to the poem at the end of Letter 40, in which Grebel facetiously threatened to send Vadian *nugas* ("trifles"). He used the same word in both places.

5. *Ialemi*, proverbial for depressive writing (see 7/fn.8).

6. Quotation from Horace, *Odes*, 2.2.20.

7. Lat. *non nugari tecum*. See fn. 4, above.

8. Andreas Grebel, see 13/fn.28 and Cast of Characters No. 31. This is the first reference in Conrad's letters to his brother's death. See also 29/138/16-17 and 45/161/27-28. There is no evidence of much intimacy between the two brothers.

9. Erasmus had fled from Louvain to Basel for safety, having just arrived a month before. See 35/fn.10.

10. The reference is to Barbara, his mistress (see 34/fn.3).

11. The reference is to Vadian and Martha.

12. The pastor at St. Gallen, Benedict Burgauer (see Cast of Characters No. 11).

44. Grebel to Vadian, Zurich, December 29, 1521

1. Melchior von Watt, Vadian's younger brother, who died in Rome on Nov. 24, 1521. Conrad and Melchoir had been fellow students in Vienna, although the latter arrived only shortly before Vadian and Conrad moved back to Switzerland (see 6/fn.60).

2. Lat. *sapientiam*, connoting Vadian's philosophical orientation, including his Christian and classical training.

3. The Greek quotation comes from Homer's *Iliad*, 2, 651, where it was applied to the god of war, Ares.

4. Jacob Grebel often represented Zurich at the Diet of the confederated Cantons. The Diet was meeting at Luzern on Jan. 1, 1522. The money referred to is probably another payment on Martha's dowry (see 23A).

5. See 40/fn.9, 43/158/23, 45/161/4, and 46/162/9.

6. Legates, probably St. Gallen's representatives to the Diet, who would return by way of Zurich.

45. Grebel to Vadian, Zurich, January 12, 1522

1. The work by Tertullian (see 40/fn.9 and 43/fn.1) may have been the *Apologeticus*.

2. The identity of this name in Greek mythology is unknown, but its derivation is self-evident. *Lysis* is the Greek word for "loosen" or "release from" as in "catalysis" or "catalyst" and *dice* is the Greek word for "justice" or "judicial decree" as in *dictum*. Grebel uses the word Lysidice ("release from decree") to refer to his mistress.

3. Holokosme (see 36/fn.20). This is the third time he has used this name for his mistress.

4. Kings of the Persian Empire were proverbial for extreme luxury and happiness in classical Greek literature. See Horace, *Satires,* III,9, 4:*Persarum vigeo rege beatior.*

5. Nemesis was the Greek goddess of retributive justice. As here, it is often used in the plural to refer to various acts of retribution that one experiences. This latter usage was a post-Homeric personification of the moral indignation felt at all derangements of the natural balance of things, whether by extraordinarily good fortune or by the arrogance usually attendant thereon. Nemesis, as the goddess of due proportion, hates every transgression of the bounds of moderation, and restores the proper and normal order of things. She does this by chastisement and punishment. Two of Grebel's nemeses were debts and family hostility.

6. Lat. *dolium,* "wine barrel" or "wine cask."

7. According to Egli (1910, p. 127, note 1), the name of Johann Hasler is not to be found outside the four references by Grebel (45/161/15, 48/189/32-33, 51/194/16, and 51/195/32). Appenzell was the capital of the canton of that name southeast of St. Gallen.

8. That Zwingli actually visited Erasmus at Basel is confirmed by letters from Glarean to Zwingli dated March 4, 1522 (ZW, VII, No. 499) and from Myconius to Zwingli undated except for the month of March (ZW, VII, No. 500). The latter states that Zwingli had written to Myconius about the visit with Erasmus. A letter from Zwingli to Rhenanus dated March 8, 1521, indicates that the visit had been planned as early as this date (ZW, VII, p. 439). Jackson (1900, p. 145, citing ZW, VII, 192, 195, 196) reports two visits to Erasmus, one in 1520 and one in 1521. In 1522 Zwingli invited Erasmus to settle in Zurich, but he declined (ZW, VII, p. 580). In 1523, Erasmus turned against Zwingli over the Hutten affair (see 23/fn.19, 34/fn.6, and Chapter IX in Jackson).

9. Erasmus had returned to Basel from Louvain on Nov. 15 (see 35/fn.10 and 43/fn.9).

10. Barbara Grebel Karli, Conrad's oldest sister, now living as a widow with her parents (see Cast of Characters No. 32).

11. This is the first mention of Dorothy Grebel, Conrad's youngest sister, who was about 13 years of age at this time (see Cast of Characters No. 35). From this reference we gather that she was the pet of the family and the object of some sibling rivalry (see also 57B/224/25-26 and 57B/fn.12).

12. Lat. *catella Meliteae.* The reference is to the island of Malta in the Mediterranean, from where lapdogs, much petted by Roman ladies, were obtained.

13. Conrad's brother Andreas (see Cast of Characters No. 31) had died some time before Christmas, 1521 (43/159/7-8 and 13/fn.28).

14. Grebel may have forgotten that he had used this same word play in 40/155/6, although he used Latin characters here. The slur, of course, is directed at Benedict Burgauer, pastor at St. Gallen (see Cast of Characters No. 11).

46. Grebel to Vadian, Zurich, January 30, 1522

1. The verb *video* is used in its dual passive (seem) and active (see) meanings.

2. Just as the appearance of the *Pomponius* is metaphorical for the wished-for appearance of Vadian himself, the appearance of a letter from Vadian is metaphorical for Vadian's hoped-for coming in person.

3. Lat. *decumbit*, "has fallen in battle."

4. Lat. *adrepis*, "creep toward," "steel up on," "glide gently toward."

5. Margaret of Wadenswil (see 26/fn.16), Grebel's cousin, daughter of Hans Wirz, magistrate of the county of Wädenswil twenty miles southwest of Zurich.

6. Lat. *a delitiis meis*, "from my delight."

7. Greek word for "whole world" (see 36/149/9-10 and 4/161/10).

8. Martha Grebel, Vadian's wife.

9. Benedict Burgauer (see Cast of Characters No. 11).

10. Lat. *De Bernhardino consulem vestrum sciscitare.* The verb is either the imperative form of the deponent *sciscitor* or the infinitive of *sciscito,* "to inquire," "to examine," "to interrogate," "to ask." *Consulem* could mean either "councillor" or "counsel." *Consulem vestrum* ("your Councillor" or "your counsel") could modify Bernhard or be the object of the imperative verb, "Ask." Hence, the sentence is susceptible to the following interpretations: "Ask your councillor about Bernhard," "Ask about Bernhard, your councillor," "To ask your counsel about Bernhard." The rendering here given is influenced by the possibility that the name refers to Bernhard Züner, a known member of the Small Council in St. Gallen, representing the Tailors' Guild.

11. The pronouns probably refer to Conrad's father, Jacob Grebel.

46A. Falconibus to Vadian, Zurich, February 1, 1522

1. On William de Falconibus, see 36/fns. 5 and 16, and Cast of Characters No. 22.

2. On Diodorus, see Pro.A/fn.37.

3. Angelus Cospus had come to Vienna from Bologna in part to escape the war troubles in Italy. At the University of Vienna he was Professor of Greek and Latin Literature until his death on Nov. 2, 1516. Vadian succeeded to his chair and inherited several of his predecessor's unfinished tasks. One was to finalize the publication of Cospus's Latin edition of the Greek writings of Diodorus Siculus (see fn. 2, above) and the other was to lecture on the same in the university (see Pro.A/fn.36).

4. The name means "John the Monk." The National Union Catalog of Imprints lists twelve different authors who were known by that name, none of whom fits the content of the writing to which allusion is here made.

5. Aristarchus of Samothrace, the celebrated grammarian and critic of antiquity, who flourished 156 BC. He worked to the advanced age of 72 to restore the texts of the Greek poets, especially Homer.

47. Grebel to Vadian, Zurich, February 6, 1522

1. Lat. *ego dudum duxi Barbaram.* This is the same verb, *ducere,* that was used in 41/156/5-6. It is a verb of many meanings, one of which is "to lead in marriage" or "to marry a wife." Bender (1950, p. 64) interprets the sentence as follows: "But suddenly the wedding occurred after all. On February 6, 1522, at a time when his father had left for an eight-day business trip, the ceremony was performed, probably by Heinrich Engelhart, parish priest at the Fraumünster Church. Dorothea and Margareta Wirz, daughters of Hans Wirz, were present at the ceremony." This interpretation is based on Letter No. 47 and reflects the sociological context of a twentieth-century wedding. The letter does not say that Engelhart performed a religious ceremony, or that the Wirz cousins were present at such a ceremony. Marriages in Zurich were still being regulated according to Roman Catholic canon law which specified that persons 19 years of age or over could marry without parental consent upon proper notice of intent given in church in the presence of at least two witnesses. The origin and identity of Barbara whom Grebel "just now wedded" is unknown. Concerning the origin of the tradi-

tion and the argument for its rejection that her real name was Agatha von Fynland, see Bender (1950, p. 225, fn. 17). Concerning the development of their relationship, see 34/fn.3 and subsequent references. Apparently she was living in Zurich when they met, and they were living together in Basel and in Zurich for some months before their marriage. He tried to keep the affair from his parents as long as possible and felt that it might be necessary for them to leave Zurich if they married. As indicated in 34/fn.3, this might have been due to the scandal which would have resulted from the violation of a nun's vows, an interpretation based on 34/145/17-18. Some time after Grebel's death in the summer of 1527, Barbara married Jacob Ziegler, a citizen of Zurich. Adverse testimony concerning Jacob Grebel's treatment of her was heard at the latter's trial in October 1526, and she herself may have been the source for that information. The marriage of Conrad and Barbara was not very happy, especially after Grebel became an Anabaptist; and in 1525 he feared that she would betray Felix Mantz to the authorities (see 69/357/15-28). In fact, the present reference to Barbara is the last one by name, and he only refers to her as "my spouse" or "my wife" four more times (51/195/12, 62/284/3, 68/332/15, and 69/357/15, 27-28).

2. Hans Wirz (see 11/fn.1) was Conrad's uncle, stepbrother to his father. See Cast of Characters No. 99.

3. Master Doctor Heinrich Engelhart, pastor at the Fraumünster, was a first cousin of Jacob Grebel (see p. 26 and Cast of Characters No. 19).

4. A quotation from Vergil's *Dido* which he had used before in a letter from Paris (see 9/fn.10).

5. Lat. *mentulae excisione,* "penis amputation." Not very polite, but neither is the sentiment.

6. The second edition of Vadian's *Pomponius Mela* (see 1/fn.19, 35/fn.9, and 40/fn.8) is finally off the press. It had been in process for most of 1521. Grebel helped with the editing (38/150/23-25) and wrote the introduction for it.

7. Cratander (see 31/fn.1 and Cast of Characters No. 17) was the printer.

8. Martha Grebel, Vadian's wife.

9. The Wirz girls were daughters of Hans Wirz (see fn.2, above) and cousins of Conrad (see 26/fn.16 and 46/fn.4).

10. Erasmus had been back in Basel since Nov. 15, 1521 (see 22/fn.12). The visit by Grebel and Vadian never took place, although in a letter from Erasmus to Zwingli dated Sept. 5, 1522 (ZW, VII, No. 235, p. 581), Erasmus mentioned that he had read the work by Vadian and visited him in person. The date of this visit was probably June 1518, soon after Vadian's return from Vienna (see VB, II, No. 127). In his *Pomponius Mela,* published in Vienna in May of that year, Vadian had made honorific mention of Erasmus, to which further praise was added in the Basel edition. Erasmus responded in 1526 with a complimentary literary reference to the *Mela* in his commentary of *Adagia,* 1353. Apart from these literary references, there was no contact between them following Vadian's brief visit in 1518.

11. Grebel meant to say either "Grebel," or, more likely, "untrue to Vadian's real nature."

47A. Investigation of Plans for a Badenschenke, end of May 1522

1. The Lindenhof was an inn or tavern in Zurich, located across the Limmat River from the Grossmünster. Its prominence is indicated by the fact that every year on Palm Sunday and Pentecost the relics of Saints Felix and Regula, the patron saints of the Grossmünster, were carried in state from the cathedral across the Limmat to the Lindenhof and back, attended by a great procession.

2. Hans Wüst was the son of the deputy bailiff, later governor of the village of Zollikon, whose wife became an Anabaptist in March 1525.

3. Apart from Claus Hottinger and Heine Aberli, scarcely any information is available on the men who testified at the hearing. Heine and Ulrich Nötzli came from Höngg and were members of the church where Simon Stumpf was pastor (see 57B/fn.13). Four months after the present episode, when Stumpf preached a sermon against images in the church, the two

Nötzli brothers defended some acts of iconoclasm in that church (see Garside, pp. 112-24).

4. Claus Hottinger, a local shoemaker and salt-retailer. See Cast of Characters No. 48.

5. On Jacob Hottinger, see 68/fn.3 and Cast of Characters No. 50.

6. Bender (1950, p. 3) states that Jacob Grebel owned two houses at this time. Bender was not aware of a third Grebel house called Oberhof (fn.16, below) located outside the city gates. Of the other two, one was *an der nüwen Gasse* and the other was *Thurm auf dem Bach* or *Bilgerithurm.* It can be assumed from 47/165/4-14, 55/224/13-21, 56/225/33-35, etc., that Conrad was living with his new wife in one of these houses, but it is not clear what the living arrangement was. In 69/357/16-17, 18-19, Conrad referred to "my house" and "father's house" as separate although adjacent. In any case, as indicated in fn. 1, above, Jacob Grebel was away at Luzern from May 9 to 27 at the time this meeting was held in his house "outside the city" (see Strickler, IV:1a, cited by Schelbert, p. 37).

7. Several members of the Zurich Council, such as Claus Setzstab, Thomas Sprüngli, Heinrich Trüben, and Ulrich Trinkler (see fn.14, below), were known to be sympathetic to these acts to promote the Reformation.

8. The people's priest was, of course, Zwingli himself.

9. Caspar Göldli, an old-faith adherent rejected the Zwinglian Reformation and left Zurich in 1523 in order to oppose it. As it turned out, he and his older brother, Jörg, the commander of Zurich's military forces in the Battle of Cappel (1531), fought on opposite sides (see Potter, 1976, p. 413).

10. Denar is equal to a Pfennig. One guilder equals 210 denari.

11. Ger. *vier Wachten,* the four suburban villages (congregations, parishes) were Riesbach, Fällanden, Hirslanden, and Unterstrasse (see 52A/209/25-26).

12. The Buri family belonged to the Höngg congregation where Simon Stumpf was pastor (see Garside, pp. 122-23).

13. Claus Hottinger, see fn. 4, above.

14. Ulrich Trinkler (see Cast of Characters No. 86) was one of the few members of the Small Council who were ardent supporters of the Zwinglian Reformation.

15. Although it is possible to infer that the witness is here referring to Hottinger and not to Zwingli, this is not self-evident from the text. The pronoun is more in apposition to Zwingli than to Hottinger, and the plan to invite Zwingli is precisely what the testimony is about.

16. On Grebel's two houses, see fn.6, above; but the derivation of the name *Oberhof* is unknown.

17. Ger. *zur Meisen.* "The Meisen" was either a public inn or the guild hall of the patrician guild known as *zur Meise.*

18. Heinrich Trüben was one of three councillors (including Thomas Sprüngli and Claus Setzstab) alleged to be radically pro-Reformation (see Garside, p. 121).

19. Heinrich Aberli, a baker on the Rennweg in Zurich. See Cast of Characters No. 1.

47B. The Wyss Chronicle of Preaching Disturbances, Zurich, July 1522

1. Bernhard Wyss, chronicler of Zurich history. See Cast of Characters No. 102.

2. See Introduction, above.

3. Mark Röist (see Cast of Characters No. 79), already 68 years of age, had served as burgomaster since 1505.

4. Claus Hottinger, see 47/fn.7 and Cast of Characters No. 48.

5. Heinrich Aberli, see 47A/fn.19 and Cast of Characters No. 1.

6. Bartlime Pur (Pfister) was also a baker in Zurich. See Cast of Characters No. 73.

7. Ger. *und verbot man inen, nüt me wider die münch an canzlen z'reden und söltind nüt me von disen dingen disputieren und reden.* Heinold Fast (1975, p. 81, fn. 3) interprets this passage as indicating that the four agitators interrupted a monk during his sermon.

8. Ger. *Do liess die stuben ein grossen schnall.* The word *Schnall* connotes a precipitous action and the noise and commotion caused by it. The courtroom commotion is further described in the following document, 47C.

9. A member of the mendicant order of Franciscans.

10. Those members of the Franciscan order who maintained the primitive rule of St. Francis against the mitigations of the Friars Conventual. The Franciscans began as mendicants living in absolute poverty without property; but as this custom was relaxed, there were recurrent moves within the order to return to "pure" poverty. After the Observants were made independent in 1517, friars wishing still stricter observance formed the Friars Capuchin in 1525.

11. On Franz Lambert, see Cast of Characters No. 61.

12. Zwingli had been preaching for some months on the subject of the intercession of the saints and had considered publishing his sermons but never did. As early as Jan. 28, Haller of Bern had written that he hoped he could soon read Zwingli's sermon on saint worship (ZW, VII, No. 196).

13. Corona, from the Latin word meaning "crown," refers to one of five mysteries of the rosary.

14. Rosary refers to a string of beads consisting of five "decades" (sets of ten), each of which is associated with a mystery of the Faith. These mysteries number fifteen, so that a full rosary consists of this number of decades and corresponding prayers.

15. Ger. *lässmeister.*

16. Engelhart, see 47/fn.3 and Cast of Characters No. 19.

17. Rudolph Röschli was a canon at the Fraumünster prior to becoming people's priest at St. Peter's in 1503. Soon after this episode he resigned his post because he was opposed to Zwingli's Reformation. Nevertheless, in 1526 he followed other Reformation priests who rejected celibacy.

18. Conrad Schmid, see 57C/fn.10 and Cast of Characters No. 83.

19. See fn. 3, above.

20. Hans Ochsner had been on the Council of Twelve of the Guild *zur Meise* since 1510. He became guildmaster in 1519, chief master in the same year, and alms master in 1520. In 1532 he was appointed governor of Andelfingen. He died in 1535.

21. Heinrich Walder, councillor since 1505. See Cast of Characters No. 94.

22. Caspar Frey was born in Baden, Canton Aargau. He became a citizen of Zurich in 1516 and city clerk in 1518, which office he held until April 1526.

23. This comment makes one wonder how Zwingli got all these notes about the "unauthorized preaching" of the monks and whether one of the by-products of the Grebel-Hottinger-Aberli-Pur mission to the monasteries was the gathering of intelligence.

24. From the context of the sentence, it is evident that Zwingli is addressing those members of the council whose spokesman was Burgomaster Röist who were giving support to the monks in the dispute.

25. In line with fn.24, Zwingli is addressing the council itself in what must be one of his rare references to doubts about the moral legitimacy of the magistracy.

26. The reference is to Johannes Duns Scotus, thirteenth-century Anglo-Irish scholastic philosopher and Franciscan priest, founder of Scotism, opposed to Thomism (i.e., the school of Thomas Aquinas).

27. The reference is to the thirteenth-century Roman Catholic theologian and Dominican priest, Thomas Aquinas (1225-74).

47C. Uproar in the Council Chambers, Zurich, July 7, 1522

1. Ger. *Schwäbische Buchdruckergesellen,* "Swabian bookprinter's apprentices."

2. Stoffel, commonly used for Christopher, refers to Christopher Froschauer, Zurich printer from Bavaria who because of his craft was given citizenship on Nov. 9, 1519, and subsequently published Swiss Reformation books and the famous Froschauer Bibles until his death in 1564, when his nephew, also Christopher Froschauer, took over the business.

3. The rest of the excerpt is the testimony of Trini Bernhart, who presents hearsay evidence from two sources: Marti Hantler and Trini's unnamed brother-in-law.

4. Felix Schmid, then age 68, was one of Zurich's elder burgomasters until his death on June 13, 1524. He was a moderate who stood for caution and gradual change. The implica-

tion of the comment is that if the Reformation is to progress, Burgomaster Schmid will have to yield.

5. Referring to the brother-in-law of Trini Bernhart.

6. Conrad Grebel.

7. Aberli, see 47A/fn.19 and Cast of Characters No. 1.

8. Bartlime Pur, see 47B/fn.6 and Cast of Characters No. 73.

9. Claus Hottinger, see 47A/fn.4 and Cast of Characters No. 48.

10. Ger. *die stuben fast geknellt.* The word *knallen* means "bang," as in a shot or explosion. Fast (1975, p. 82, fn. 9) thinks it may have referred to the banging of doors as disgruntled councillors departed.

11. Guildmaster Schliniger was one of the members of the Small Council. Walton (pp. 65-66) claims that while he "had no use for Grebel's programme, he gave strong support to Zwingli," but he cites no proof for this claim other than the comment that the guilds in general supported Zwingli. Heinold Fast (1975, p. 81) cites a source to indicate that Schliniger was totally negative to the Reformation.

12. Ger. *man sollte das Evangelium in einer kuofud predigen.* Another witness (Egli, *Aktensammlung,* p. 78) reported that the "someone" who made this comment was Councillor Peter Meyer, who like Schliniger was a vehement opponent of Zwingli (Fast, 1975. p. 81. fn. 8). The Egli reference reads as follows: "Just then M[aster] Peter Meier came and said, 'Were you speaking of the people's priest? For on that day he said nothing good, but preached everything out of envy and hatred. It would be better if he preached in a cow's ass. People should not take it from him and should put him away because here in Zurich we have enough rule and animosity. . . . As long as the people's priest has been preaching here in Zurich we have not had good fortune. Furthermore what he says is all lies, for he preaches all his sermons out of envy and animosity.' "

47D. The Zwingli-Grebel Reply to the Bishop's Admonition, Zurich, August 22-23, 1522

1. Zwingli signed the preface on August 22 and the treatise was issued on August 23.

2. On Hugo von Hohenlandenberg, see 31/fn.5 and Cast of Characters No. 47.

3. Zwingli was installed as people's priest in Zurich on January 1, 1519, so he is predating his Reformation preaching to his Einsiedeln pastorate.

4. The three members of the bishop's delegation were Melchior Wattli, the suffragan bishop, Johann Wanner, the cathedral preacher of Constance (see Cast of Characters No. 95), and Nicholas Bredlin, papal theologian. Zwingli believed that Wanner, who was favorable to Reformation doctrines, participated against his will.

5. The Document of Admonition, published as part of Zwingli's pamphlet, contained 69 articles. The *Archeteles* was a point-by-point refutation of these articles.

6. Gen. 1:14-16.

7. 1 Pet. 2:7.

8. Acts 5:29.

9. Mk. 16:15b-16a.

10. Jn. 8:32b, 36.

11. Is. 56:10.

12. Jn. 10:1.

13. *Ibid.*

14. 1 Tim. 5:20.

15. Mt. 18:10.

16. Zwingli was referring to the papal practice of selling indulgences to raise money for papal wars, probably with reference to the appearance in Switzerland of the papally commissioned seller of indulgences, the Franciscan monk Bernhard Samson. It should be said to Bishop Hugo's credit that he was much opposed to the traffic in indulgences and had encouraged Zwingli to preach against the practice. An indulgence was a remission of the temporal and purgatorial consequences of sin offered in exchange for a sum of money.

17. A reference to the vow of chastity or celibacy required of all priests and nuns, including those in secular (i.e., parish) ministries.

18. The power of the keys refers to the supremacy of jurisdiction of the Roman Catholic Church as vested in the pope, assumed to have been mandated by Christ in his analogy of the keys in Mt. 16:19. As the one who holds the keys to a house possesses complete authority over that house and its occupants, so also the pope, the head of the house of God in this world, is supposed to have the power of the keys over the church and its members.

19. Zwingli presented similar testimonies of the sequence of his preaching in Zurich at two other times. The first was in his sermon of March 23, 1522, entitled "Concerning Choice and Liberty of Food," which was subsequently expanded and published by Froschauer in Zurich on April 16 (ZW, I, pp. 133ff., and Jackson, 1912, pp. 110ff.). The other was in a speech during the Second Zurich Disputation (ZW, II, p. 708, and below 57C/236/34ff.).

20. See 47B/fn.27.

21. See 47B/fn.26.

22. This is an anticipation of Zwingli's ground for the coming reformation of the mass, that it is not a repetition of the sacrifice that Christ made once and for all on our behalf.

23. Reference to Article 45 in the Bishop's Document of Admonition, "Let the general good also invite us to retain the observance of the ceremonials of the church at least for the time being."

24. Reference to Phil. 3:19.

25. By "both forms," Zwingli means the bread and cup of wine, referring to the Roman Catholic practice of withholding the cup from the laity.

26. Apollo, see 17/fn.9.

27. Mt. 10:27.

28. Lat. *rumpant ilia episcopi universa,* "the bishops all together may burst their belly [vent their spleen]."

29. Earlier in the *Archeteles,* Zwingli had described these grasping wolves as priests in shepherd's cloth who "seize upon, scatter, and destroy everything, in order to fill up the vast maw of their lusts, not satisfied to stuff their belly with the milk and wool and flesh even of the sheep which they had seized, but breaking their bones also and leaving no bit of cruelty untried."

30. From a supposed linkage of Lk. 10:8 and Rev. 9:1-11 to Is. 14:12, commonly but incorrectly translated "Now art thou fallen from heaven, O Lucifer, son of the morning star," the name Lucifer came to be used synonymously with Satan as identified with the rebel archangel before his fall. By "three-tongued Lucifer" or "Lucifer with three tongues," Grebel referred to the three members of the Bishop's Delegation (see fn. 4, above).

31. *Intrepidis trilinguibusque missis Luciferis,* "intrepid, tri-tongued Lucifers having been sent." Since the preposition is not supplied, it could mean either "sent to us by them" or "sent away by us."

32. Earlier in the pamphlet, Zwingli had referred to the tyranny of church ordinances as "whatever the prelate will, he may."

33. On "keys," see fn. 18, above.

34. Lat. *canones,* "canons" of the Roman Catholic Church.

35. Lat. *librum,* "register" or "book" or "lists."

36. Lat. *librum Simonis.* Simony was the polemical term for the practice still common in Switzerland at this time of buying or selling ecclesiastical preferment. It derives from Simon Magus, Samaritan sorcerer described in Acts 8:9-24, who attempted to buy the gift of healing from the apostles for his own financial gain. Zwingli himself began his clerical career as parish priest in Glarus by purchasing his appointment out of his own pocket for the price of 100 guilders.

37. Lat. *parricidia,* the murder of a member of one's own family.

38. Lat. *conscientiarum,* corporate conscience.

39. Lat. *agmina,* masses or herds.

40. Lat. *fulmina,* thunderbolts, fig. for vehement denunciation or censure, used often to

refer to the ban of excommunication solemnly pronounced by ecclesiastical authority (see 19/110/23, 19/fn.7, and 34/146/11, 34/fn.24).

    41. Gr. δεισιδαιμονίαν, "superstition."

    42. Lat. *ducit perpetuoque victa ducet,* "it leads and shall lead to perpetual living [way of life]."

47E. Zwingli to Myconius, Zurich, August 26, 1522

    1. Mt. 5:44.

    2. Lat. *contubernium,* "soldiers' tent." It is significant as further evidence against Walton's thesis (see 47A/Intro.) that Zwingli here includes Grebel in his troop (see line 14, below).

    3. A suppressed quotation from Vergil's *Aeneid,* I, 199.

    4. Jacob Ceporin (Wiesendanger) provided private instruction in Greek and Hebrew from 1522 to 1525, when he was appointed the first professor in the new theological school in Zurich (see 69/fn.40).

    5. Heinrich Utinger (see Cast of Characters No. 92), a canon in the Grossmünster.

    6. Heinrich Engelhart (see Cast of Characters No. 19), pastor at the Fraumünster.

    7. Junker Rudolf Rey, trustee of the revenues for the Grossmünster Chapter. To this position was added in 1525 the role of overseer of the poor relief for the area of the Linden Guard and in 1526 the job of city engineer. He died with Zwingli at Cappel.

    8. Erasmus Fabritius (Schmid), *ca.* 1492-1546, close friend of Vadian and Zwingli, was pastor at Stein am Rhein and a canon of the Grossmünster. He received his education at Freiburg (MA, 1514) and Basel. It was through Johann Oechsli, the pastor of a nearby castle parish, that he first began to relate to Zwingli and his "hermit friends." Zwingli tried unsuccessfully to win him for the position of pastor in Baden in 1521. In July 1522, Fabriti was one of the signatories to the petition to the diocesan bishop for permisson to marry (see 47D/Intro.) and participated in the First Zurich Disputation in January 1523. In the summer of 1524 he got involved in the Ittinger affair (see Epi.A/fn.83) and was forced into temporary exile. Following the Cappel wars, he was with Utinger a pillar of the church in Zurich by virtue of which he was called to Württemberg in 1535 as Reformer in the district of Reichenweier in Alsace.

    9. Caspar Grossman (Megander), chaplain and later head preacher at the hospital. See 68/fn.1 and Cast of Characters No. 42.

    10. John Jacob Ammann, see 35/fn.16 and Cast of Characters No. 3.

    11. Jörg Binder, schoolmaster at the Grossmünster. See Cast of Characters No. 4.

    12. Leo Jud, pastor at St. Peter's in Zurich. See 52/fn.4 and Cast of Characters No. 58.

    13. Teucer, son of Telamon and Hesione and brother of Ajax, who, after his return from Troy, sailed to Cyprus, where he founded the town of Salamis.

    14. Ajax brother of Teucer of the previous fn., who committed suicide because he failed in the contest with Ulysses for the arms of Achilles.

    15. Theobald von Geroldseck, administrator of the monastery at Einsiedeln, which had an office in Zurich where he and Franz Zinck often stayed when here on business. Zwingli's close tie with him went back to April 1516 when he brought him to Einsiedeln as people's priest. He left Einsiedeln in 1527, lived henceforth in Zurich as an active supporter of the Reformation, and died with Zwingli at Cappel. Zwingli dedicated his "canon of the mass" to him in August 1523.

    16. Franz Zinck was papal chaplain at the Einsiedeln monastery and lived in the Pfaeffikon Castle. He was receptive to the new ideas of the Reformation and defended Zwingli's actions.

    17. Heb. 13:14.

    18. Archeteles, see 47D/Intro.

47F. Erasmus to Zwingli, Basel, September 8, 1522

    1. Referring to the *Apologeticus Archeteles,* published August 22-23, 1522 (see 47D).

2. Erasmus is asking Zwingli to do what he himself certainly did not do in his famous 1511 work, *The Praise of Folly:* "treat so serious a matter seriously." One might wonder, in fact, whether the writing of Erasmus was not Zwingli's model for the writing of the *Archeteles,* particularly those sections that debunk the monks and bishops.

3. The letter was written by Erasmus, but the address was in another handwriting.

47G. Macrinus to Zwingli, Solothurn, October 15, 1522

1. Melchior Macrinus, alias Dürr, came from Solothurn, the canton between Basel and Bern. He attended the University of Basel about 1516 as a student in Glarean's bursa, together with Rudolf Collin (see 1A/fn.6). In 1521 he became the schoolmaster in the monastery of St. Urban in the canton of Luzern, where Collin succeeded him in early 1522. At this time Macrinus was appointed *scriba curiae* (Senate scribe) in his hometown. Then he was appointed schoolmaster in the service of the canons of the cathedral of St. Ursus, and in this position he is mentioned as a zealous promoter of the Reformation. Following some adverse shifts in loyalties of various council members, Macrinus was removed in February 1523. He then moved to Basel, where he found work in Cratander's printshop and also attempted to lecture on Homer at the university, but did not find adequate subsistence in either activity. At the beginning of 1524 he was back in Solothurn, writing to Myconius that he had found an employer, probably a reappointment to his position as schoolmaster. Nothing more is known about him.

2. In two subsequent letters to Zwingli dated Jan. 25 and Mar. 6, 1523, Macrinus closed with similar greetings to "Grebel and the church of Christ."

3. Lat. *mehercle,* a commonly used interjection.

4. Lat. *ad . . . studia converterint,* "converted to studiousness," "returned to devotion [to a person or cause]."

48. Grebel to Vadian, Zurich, November 21, 1522

1. It was not until August 29, 1523, that Zwingli's booklet on the mass came out. It was entitled *De canone missae,* "On the Canon of the Mass." Egli, the editor of the published transcription (ZW, II, 552ff.), states that Zwingli had planned this important writing for many months, and it was finally written in just four days. It was an important step forward in his Reformation because it dealt with the radical matter of using the vernacular in the liturgy and the doctrine now associated with Zwingli's name that the mass is not a sacrifice but a memorial and its effect is not the infusion of grace but of dedication. Zwingli publicly announced in the First Zurich Disputation in January 1523 that he would issue such a booklet.

2. Lat. *Anglos Lutherigenas,* "the Angli born of Luther." The title of this tract was *Contra Henricum regem Angliae, Martinus Luther, Wittenbergae,* 1522 ("Refutation of King Henry of England by Martin Luther of Wittenberg"). It was Luther's reply to the attack by Henry VIII on Luther's "Babylonian Captivity" of 1520. Henry's tract was entitled *Assertatis VII Sacramentorum* ("Defense of the Seven Sacraments"). The reply by Luther was published in July 1522.

3. "Either kind" refers back to the two paragraph themes of "nonsense" and "seriousness."

4. The matter of Johann Hasler's book first came up in 45/161/15 (see 45/fn.7). On the value of "batzen," see Quellen 2, p. 722.

5. Short for Appenzeller, referring to Johann Hasler.

6. Midas, the son of Gordius and Cybele, became the wealthy king of Phrygia in Asia Minor in the fifth century BC. The name became proverbial for great wealth.

7. The abbot of the monastery in St. Gallen was at this time Franciscus Geissberg, elected in 1504. See *Die Chronik des Herman Miles,* p. 10, and following footnote.

8. Wendelin Oswald of Thurgau, a Dominican monk and the official priest of the abbot of St. Gallen in the abbey church, the Münster (1522-28). He upheld the most conservative old faith doctrines, opposing Vadian's efforts to spread the new doctrines. Vadian began to assume leadership in the Reformation in St. Gallen after he was elected to the City Council

in the summer of 1521. Soon he began to gather about him the clergy and friends whom he led in Bible study. His first work was to give an exposition of the Acts of the Apostles, intending thereby to show his hearers what primitive Christianity was and to inspire them to remodel the church along New Testament lines. As the seed began to bear fruit, the opposition began also to develop. It centered in Geissberg and Wendelin, and Vadian had apparently written to Grebel with particular reference to their suppression of the evangelical preaching of Christoph Schappeler, called Sertorius (see fn. 14, below).

9. Lips and lettuce refers to a saying of M. Crassus, who upon seeing an ass eating thistles said, *similem habent labra lactucam,* "they have lips like lettuce," or as we would say, "like to like."

10. Lat. *cacodaemonis,* "defiling demon" or "evil spirit."

11. Grebel was quoting from his Greek New Testament from 2 Tim. 3:16.

12. The Greek word is *kairos,* meaning a fixed time or season. Zwingli did not get around to writing to Wendelin Oswald until Feb. 23, 1524 (ZW, VIII, No. 326).

13. Zwingli was deeply preoccupied at this time by preparations for the First Doctrinal Disputation which was to take place in January 1523. Just ten days before, he had succeeded Heinrich Engelhart to the position of canon of the Grossmünster, thus giving him a new political authority for the Reformation (see 47/fn.3). Two days later, Sebastian Meyer wrote Zwingli from Bern that they had heard that he had been forbidden to preach by the Zurich Council, a deliberate misinterpretation of the reasons why Zwingli sacrificed his people's priesthood on Nov. 9 (see ZW, VII, p. 244).

14. Sertorius refers to Christoph Schappeler of St. Gallen, pastor at Memmingen (see Cast of Characters No. 81). His Reformation preaching was being suppressed by the abbot of St. Gallen (see fn.7, above) and the abbot's chief priest (see fn.8, above). Because of the severity of his opposition at Memmingen, he is about to apply unsuccessfully for the pastorate at Winterthur (see 49/191/17, 49A, 51/194/18, 27, and 711/431/20).

15. Elymas is metaphorical for Wendelin (see fn. 8, above). Elymas is the name of the sorcerer encountered by Paul in Cyprus (see Acts 13:4-13).

16. Lat. *huiusmodi luporum,* comb. of singular and plural tenses.

17. The Latin of this important sentence, expressing Grebel's sense of call to evangelical ministry, is *Atque utinam gratia dei omnes pro me orent et ministerium hoc triumphaturus serio accipiam.*

18. Again, the Latin of this significant sentence reads *Nihil addo, quia nulla plaustra etiam verborum cognoscendum animum hunc meum facto olim periculo depingere possent.* The last phrase could be rendered more freely, "which discerns only after putting it to the test." The thought is similar to Hans Denk's motto, "No one may truly know Christ except he follow him in life." Indeed, both statements are reminiscent of Jn. 8:31-32.

19. Philip Melanchthon (1497-1560), precocious graduate of the University of Heidelberg at the age of 14, professor of Greek at the University of Wittenberg since 1518, Luther's co-worker and colleague, a prolific writer on evangelical themes. The work referred to here may be one of his recently published N.T. book commentaries (see 57/226/10, 655/ note 4) or perhaps as suggested by Dale Schrag, librarian at the Univeristy of Wichita (in personal correspondence with the writer), the Luther-Melanchthon translation of the N.T. itself, which first appeared with written introductions to each book and without identification of translator(s). Grebel's wording suggests a document with these two components: the N.T. text and the introductions.

20. Lat. *episcopum.* The reference is to Burgauer, pastor in St. Gallen (see Cast of Characters No. 11). That Grebel meant the term as sarcasm is clear from 52/207/26-27, "Leo acts as pastor, but why did I not say 'bishop'?" See also 49/191/24, 52/207/35-36, and 58/257/6.

21. See 2/fn.12.

22. This undoubtedly refers to Dorothy, Conrad's youngest sister (see Cast of Characters No. 35), who must have been visiting her sister Martha in St. Gallen. She is "less yours" because she belongs more to her father and mother in Zurich.

23. *Cimicis,* "bedbug," used also as a term of reproach, applied especially to a malicious

640

critic. See Horace, *Satires,* 1.10.78.

24. *Wanzen,* the dialect form of which is *Wentelen,* is the German word for "bedbugs" (see previous footnote), suggesting the name of Wendelin Oswald (see fn. 8, above). Egli (1910, p. 123, note 1) suggests that Grebel was calling Oswald a bedbug, and EY so translated for *cimicis.*

49. Grebel to Vadian, Zurich, December 1, 1522

1. The nuns were mostly members of the Dominican order resident in the largest convent in existence since the thirteenth century, Oetenbach in Zurich. About sixty nuns representing some of the most powerful families of Zurich were living there. Grebel's aunt Agatha Grebel was among them and his own sister, Euphrosine, was a nun there until her death. Shortly before September 6, Zwingli succeeded in preaching a sermon to the nuns on the authority of the Bible, thus breaking the sacred tradition that only the Dominican "preaching" monks were authorized to preach to them. Zwingli's sermon "On the Plainness and Certainty of the Word of God" stirred considerable ferment among the nuns, some of whom requested immediate permission to leave the convent, pleading that its views were contrary to the plainness and certainty of the Word of God. This embarrassed Zwingli; and the council issued a decree, dated on the very day Grebel was writing, ordering that they remain until the following Pentecost and await the contemplated reform of the monastic order in Zurich. The decree also took the convents out of the exclusive confessional control of the Dominicans, permitted the nuns to choose their own confessors, and authorized the secular priests to officiate or preach in the local convents.

2. The Dominican Order of Preachers, an order of mendicant friars founded by St. Dominic early in the thirteenth century, was one of the great monastic orders of the day. Zurich had three monasteries, which belonged to the Dominican, Franciscan, and Augustinian orders. The Dominicans especially were a troublesome source of opposition to the Reformation.

3. Lat. *e secta perditionis,* a literal quotation from 2 Pet. 2:1 (Latin Vulgate).

4. Probably Dorothy Grebel, Conrad's youngest sister (see 48/fn.22).

5. Lat. *ocreata utque caligata et praecincta.* The three articles of apparel have to do with wearing shin guards, boots, and a girdle or robe.

6. Sertorius, see 48/fn.14. Vadian had asked Zwingli and the Grebels to help him get the pastorate at Winterthur. See 49A/Intro., below.

7. Lat. *haeretice gravitatis.* "Heretical gravity" (EY) and "heretical enormity" (AB) are alternative renderings.

8. "Speaking sophistically," after the nature of a sophism, a formal argument embodying a subtle fallacy, but not intended as a deception. The term is derived from the Sophists, members of a class of teachers of rhetoric, philosophy, and the art of successful living in ancient Greece, who became prominent in the middle of the fifth century BC for their adroit and specious reasoning.

9. Hercules the hero, who undertook all his labors. See 27/fn.18.

10. Lat. *Sic parturimus montes, scilicet miselli indoctuli, et nascuntur e ridiculis ridiculi mures.* Grebel is quoting a proverb from Horace (*Ars Poetica,* 139), *Parturiunt montes, nascetur ridiculus mus,* "The mountains go into labor and a ridiculous mouse is born."

11. Jupiter, the supreme Roman god (see 5/fn.25).

12. Here and in 48/190/27, Grebel refers to Burgauer, chief pastor in St. Gallen, as *episcopus,* the bishop (see 48/fn.20). Evidently he had asked Vadian to remind Grebel that he had not written to him.

13. Lat. *unius uxoris maritum,* indirect quotation from 1 Tim. 3:2. The Latin Vulgate reads *unius uxoris virum.*

14. Sebastian Wolfgang Wetter, assistant to Burgauer (see 24/fn.20 and Cast of Characters No. 97).

15. Grebel may be referring to the group to which Vadian was lecturing on the New Testament (see Egli, 1910, p. 121).

16. Grebel refers to the case of Hans Urban Wyss, pastor of Fislisbach, village in the canton of Aargau in the jurisdiction of Baden. He was charged with disrespect for the saints, secret marriage, and disobedience to the bishop's mandate relative to the maintenance of the old faith teachings. Although he was supported by his congregation, the bishop of Constance had him arrested and imprisoned. This is what Grebel knows so far. He was still in prison on Feb. 24, 1523, when Zwingli wrote to him, urging him to stand firm in the gospel. Subsequently, when Wyss was released, Zurich made him assistant pastor in Oberwinterthur (see Egli, 1910, p. 101). The case of Wyss was the first attempt of the bishop to suppress evangelical ideas and thus caused great turmoil in Zurich.

17. Hugo von Hohenlandenberg, bishop of Constance. See Cast of Characters No. 47.

49A. Zwingli to Vadian, Zurich, December 8, 1522
1. Simon Mäglin of St. Gallen (see Intro., above).
2. Mäglin had been placed under arrest by the bishop of Constance and released soon after he submitted his resignation (see Intro., above).
3. Christoph Schappeler, see 48/fn.6, 49/fn.6, and Cast of Characters No. 81.
4. Lat. *licentiato*, i.e., Schappeler, holder of this academic degree in the mastery of the Holy Scriptures.
5. An Erasmian proverb, *Festina lente*, "hurry deliberately," fig. "haste makes waste." See *Adagia*, II.I.1.
6. It is unclear who is meant by the pronoun, whether Jacob Grebel or Conrad Grebel or someone else.
7. Lat. *Morae*, "inclination," "will," "way," "style," "habit," "behavior." It is not clear whether the word refers back to the pronoun, "he," or to customs affecting "first attempts" in general.
8. Burgauer, pastor in St. Gallen (see Cast of Characters No. 11).
9. Christopher Schürpf had transferred from Vienna to St. Gallen with Vadian in 1518 and later became assistant to Jacob Schurtanner, the pastor in Teufen. He was the son of Johannes Schürpf, Vadian's old school teacher in St. Gallen.

50. Grebel to Vadian, Zurich, December 25, 1522
1. The correct dating of this letter is uncertain. On the problem of month and day, see fn. 7, below. Grebel did not give the year. The editor of VB gives 1524 as first preference and 1523 as second, without documentation. Either of these dates seems highly unlikely inasmuch as Grebel by then expressed himself in sharp disagreement with Zwingli in contrast to the present reference to "Zwingli, a most incorrupt man." Moreover, he was by the end of 1523 quite alienated from Burgauer in contrast to the present reference to "your pastor, to whom I owe my soul" (see fn. 8, below). Several items of internal evidence support the date of 1522: (1) In 51/195/8-9, Grebel confesses, "When I wrote my last letter to you, I lost command of myself more than ever before because of the bad state of my mind." The present letter (No. 50) fits that description very well, e.g., his reference to having "shit on myself," no doubt the lowest point in his self-deprecation of all his letters, reminiscent of Paul's self-deprecation in Rom. 7:21-24. (2) With the hypothesized date of December 25, 1522, the two booklets by Zwingli mentioned in 50/193/29-31 can readily be identified. The one, published Sept. 6, 1522, was entitled *Von Klarheit und Gewissheit des Wortes Gottes* ("On the Plainness and Certainty of the Word of God," ZW, I, No. 3, pp. 328ff.). The other, published Sept. 17, 1522, was entitled *Eine Predigt von der ewig reinen Magd Maria* ("A Sermon on the Eternal Virginity of the Maid Mary," ZW, I, No. 15, pp. 385ff.). (3) These two pamphlets were originally sermons which Zwingli preached in the Oetenbach Convent in Zurich with the consequence of precipitating the decision concerning the nuns to which Grebel referred in 49/191/8-13 (see 49/fn.1). Thus, Letter No. 50 would seem to stand in immediate connection with Letters 49 and 51.
2. See fn. 1, above, for the probable identity of these two booklets.
3. These Greek phrases are quoted from an epigram in the *Palatine Anthology* (11/414) by a writer named Hedylus. As the Palatine manuscript of the *Anthology* was not dis-

covered until 1606, these quotations must be from the extract made by Maximum Planudes in the fourteenth century in seven books which were in circulation during the early Renaissance. Gout was a common affliction among the ancients and was probably correctly ascribed to dissolute and intemperate living. Bacchus was the Greek god of wine and Aphrodite was the Greek goddess of love and beauty. Their "marriage" and "offspring" are purely inventions of Grebel's, but the implication is that his father is an imbiber and adulterer. The two phrases repeat the word "limb" three times, and there is a pun on its double meaning. For gout it is "troubling the limbs." For wine and love it has another meaning, "loosening the limbs." In Greek these are separate derivations, both spelled the same. It is a clever literary creation.

4. Lat. *Desipui, meo forsitan malo, quod et ipsemet mihi cacarim infelix turdus.* This is a slight adaptation of the Latin proverb, *malum sibi avem cacare* ("evil wishes to shit upon itself") which was used of those who heedlessly brought trouble upon themselves. A discussion of the proverb is found in Otto, *Die Sprichwörter und sprichwortlichen Redensarten der Römer,* p. 52. Birdlime was commonly made from the berries of the mistletoe, and the ancients had the curious notion that the seed of the mistletoe did not grow until it had passed through the body of a bird. Thus, by defecating, the bird was involved in its own ensnarement.

5. Martha Grebel, Vadian's wife.

6. Purgatory, in Roman Catholic teaching, is an intermediate state after death for the purging of one's sins, especially of venial type. For reaction to this doctrine in Zurich and St. Gallen, see 52/207/35-36.

7. St. Thomas' Day was December 21, yielding the date of December 25 for the writing of this letter. The references to *haereticam diem* ("the heretical day") and *a Thoma haeretico* ("by the heretic Thomas") are free formulations by Grebel, perhaps expressing a sense of identity with the ill-reputed Thomas the doubter, although certainly not a heretic.

8. Pastor Benedict Burgauer of St. Gallen, see Cast of Characters No. 11. The editors of Quellen 1 (No. 20, p. 32, note 5) identify the reference here as Wolfgang Jufli (see 24/fn.20), the assistant pastor. Their reasons are not given, but perhaps Grebel's growing disdain for Burgauer (see 37/fn.7) did not seem to fit the descriptive phrase in the present letter, "to whom I owe my soul." It can be noted, however, that in 49/191/23-25, Grebel's message to Burgauer via Vadian was not entirely negative, although it turns negative again in 52/207/35-52/208/4.

9. Lat. *meis verbis salutem et evangelium dicito.*

10. The Homer of poetry, see 5/fn.9 and 23/fn.16.

11. Hippocrates (460-377 BC), famous physician of Greek antiquity and founder of a school of the scientific art of healing.

51. Grebel to Vadian, Zurich, December 29, 1522

1. The matter of concern here first came up in 45/161/15. See 45/fn.7 and 51/195/6-7. The "peasant of Appenzell" was Johann Hasler, who owed Grebel money for shipping his books.

2. See 45/fn.6. The reference was to Hasler's barrel of books.

3. See 48/fn.14 and 49/fn.6.

4. Simon Mäglin had been pastor at Winterthur, a city about fifteen miles northeast of Zurich, since 1517, but had been in trouble almost constantly. He had given offense to the Zurich City Council in 1522 because of which two delegates including Jacob Grebel had been sent to the City Council of Winterthur with charges which finally were taken to the episcopal court at Constance. The bishop ordered the arrest of Mäglin, whereupon he resigned (or as Grebel put it, "gave back his letter of investiture") on Dec. 23 and was freed on promise to stay out of the territory—the canton of Zurich to which Winterthur belonged. In spite of Vadian's recommendation and Zwingli's help, Schappeler failed to receive the appointment.

5. "Access ... forbidden" means that the custom of *probe predigen,* "to preach a trial sermon," was bypassed. Heinrich Lüte was later appointed to the pastorate (1525).

6. Grebel does not identify this "certain person."

7. Bender (1950, pp. 82-83) believes that Zwingli asked Grebel to write to Vadian about the Schappeler matter, since Zwingli was too busy to do so. He cites this as one of a number of indications of close relations between Zwingli and Grebel at this time. There is, however, no certain evidence to support the former conclusion. See fn. 10, below, and 51/194/29-31.

8. Captain Ambrosius was evidently a legate representing St. Gallen in Zurich (see VB, II, 328).

9. Vadian had, on Zwingli's suggestion, sent a letter of recommendation for Schappeler to the City Council of Zurich, dated Dec. 13 (see VB, II, 455). Vadian was evidently quite willing to bring his influence to bear to win the preaching post for his friend.

10. Bender (1950, p. 83) believes that the pronoun "we" refers to Conrad, Jacob Grebel, and Zwingli. That may be true, but the conclusion does not necessarily follow from the text.

11. The reference is probably to Dorothy, Conrad's youngest sister. See 48/fn.22 and 49/fn.4.

12. Benedict von Watt, Vadian's brother (see 31/fn.15). Benedict apparently accompanied Dorothy, since he was visiting the Grebels when 52/208/7 was written.

13. Lat. *tabellio*, see 2/fn.4. The courier bearing Grebel's letter was to return to Zurich and was apparently instructed to escort Dorothy to her home if the legates and Benedict were unable to do so.

14. Obol, a small Greek coin, the sixth part of a drachma. It traditionally expressed poverty.

15. Plutus, Greek god of riches.

16. Lynceus, mythological hero of the ship *Argo*. According to legend this Argonaut was so sharp-sighted he could see through the earth and distinguish objects at vast distances.

17. The particular reference is undoubtedly to 50/193/36ff.

18. Lat. *impia*, which could mean either undutiful or ungodly. The latter correlates with *rabida* (rabied) in the next phrase.

19. The wording in this sentence undoubtedly comes from the letters of Paul, especially Rom. 13:14; 2 Cor. 5:17; Gal. 3:27; Eph. 4:24, and Col. 3:10. Apart from the superficial references in 10/89/32-33 and 13/99/23-24, this is Grebel's first personal reference to Jesus Christ, although he had referred to Christ as head of the church in 48/190/28. Henceforth, there will be mention of the lordship of Christ in almost every letter, especially in Letters 62 and 63.

20. See 1 Cor. 11:27-29.

21. John Leopold Grebel, Conrad's second cousin (see Cast of Characters No. 39).

22. Lat. *negociis ... capitularibus*, capitular business related to a local ecclesiastical jurisdiction or chapter, and probably related to the administration of funds through the system of tithes. The business occupying Zwingli's attention just then was the tithes due the ecclesiastical treasurer in Zurich from certain parishes in the canton. There was a growing resistance to the payment of these tithes, and Grebel will soon take an aggressive position on this question. See 52/207/33, 52/208/8, 53/220/21-27, 63/289/9-10, and 68/332/22.

23. Enderli, probably Andreas Castelberger, the local bookseller (see 41/fn.2 and Cast of Characters No. 13). Grebel's occasional use of German at this stage of his correspondence reflects a personal aside and exception to his preference for Latin as the language of scholars. Later (see letters 63-67) he will elect to use German to reflect a new interest in the vernacular for Reformation discourse.

24. The reference is to Luther's *Bulla cene domini: das ist die Bulla vom Abentfressen der allerheyligsten hern des Bapsts* published in Wittenberg in 1522 by Melchior Lotter, in Augsburg in 1522 by Melchior Ramminger, in Augsburg in 1522 by Jörg Nadler, in Strasbourg in 1523 by Ulrich Morhart, and again in Wittenberg in 1523 by Melchior Lotter.

25. See fn. 1, above. On the value of the batzen, see Quellen 2, p. 722.

51A. The First Zurich Disputation, January 29, 1523

1. Bullinger, I, I, p. 102, portrays the burgomaster as saying, at this point, "and the sword with which he from Fislisbach was murdered does not wish to appear to fight" (quoted

by Jackson, 1901, p. 92). With reference to the same comment, the *Gyrenrupffen* (p. 47) reports Heinrich Wolf as saying, "The spear with which the pastor of Fislisbach was stabbed, nobody could find, although the Lord Burgomaster Röist himself sought him."

2. Ger. *den frembden,* "the strangers."

3. Ger. *mengklich.* Since the convocation was mostly between a few of the leading clergy and the City Council, the people about whom it was said that they could leave and return after eating were the nonparticipants and outsiders and more marginal clergy.

4. Hugo von Hohenlandenberg, bishop of Constance (see 31/fn.5 and Cast of Characters No. 47).

5. This visit took place on April 7-9, 1522 (see ZW, I, No. 9, pp. 137-54).

6. Ger. *lütpriester.* The most literal rendering is used because there is no better equivalent in English. It does not mean secular clergy in Roman Catholic usage but refers to a particular kind of clerical post, usually one per parish, with concentration on instructional preaching rather than on sacraments. There were only three people's priests in Zurich.

7. Ger. *seelsorger,* one who has "the care of souls."

8. The 67 articles prepared by Zwingli for the disputation (see Meyer, pp. 34-57, for texts in the original Swiss German, contemporary Latin, and modern English).

9. The German, *so lang und viel bis er eins bessern/bericht werde,* is not in the ZW text but in that published by Schuler and Schulthess, I, p. 144. Five editions of the official proceedings written by Hegenwald were printed, but apparently with a few slight variations.

10. Ger. *ire lütpriester ... iro statt.* The possessive pronoun is not "your" as in the Jackson translation (1901, pp. 93-94) but "their," referring to the people's priests employed by the City Council.

11. "Thursday after Carolus" was omitted from the ZW text. See Schuler and Schulthess, I, p. 144, lines 36-37: *Actum donstag nach Caroli.*

12. Bullinger (I, p. 104) wrote that "Zwingli spoke with great joy after the aforesaid decision had been read" (quoted by Jackson, 1901, p. 94).

13. Ger. *die warheit gottes ... handthabend und zu predigen furdert,* not "advance and preach the truth of God" as in Jackson (1901, p. 94), which implies that the Councillors do the preaching, but rather to foster the preaching of the people's priests.

14. Johann Faber (1478-1541), known also by the Latin name of Heigerlin, was vicar general of the diocese of Constance. Educated at the universities of Tübingen and Freiburg, he was an able disputant for the Roman Catholic position against the Reformation. He was author of *Malleus in haeresim Lutheranam* (1524), from whence came the epithet "Hammer of the Heretics." He became vicar general of Constance in 1516 and bishop of Vienna in 1530.

15. Zwingli's articles had not circulated ahead of time as they were supposed to have done. Hence Faber did not secure his copy until his arrival in Zurich. Bullinger (I, p. 104) reports that "here for the first time the Vicar became angry, saying, 'My dear lords, today for the first time I read Master Ulrich's Articles, which before now I had had no time to examine' " (quoted by Jackson, 1901, p. 94). In his *Unterrichtung,* p. 7, Faber wrote, "Master Ulrich had published the 67 Articles only a day before this session and before anyone at Constance or any other city knew a word of it, and Master Ulrich also admitted that it may perchance have been issued too late." Again on p. 46, Faber addressed Zwingli with the words, "You know that it is true that before I or all the priests had come to Zurich, no one knew your word, whereon the dispute was based, and I tell you that I would have thought sooner of death than that there should be a debate at Zurich ... concerning the intercession of the saints. Hence you probably marked well that I said I thought I had come to Zurich but I see I am in Picardy [place of the Manichean heresy of the fifteenth century], and this saying I explained to be from the heretic Picard. Hence although I had not prepared nor thought about the matter, still I desired to argue concerning it, and show wherewith I had proved the imprisoned priest whom you wished to make a bishop to be in error, so that you also might fall into the Arian heresy which was suppressed 1200 years ago" (quoted by Jackson, 1901, pp. 94-95).

16. Germanized Latin, *die Ceremonias.* The word had become a technical term in

Reformation disputations, centering on the question of whether numerous Roman Catholic rituals (e.g., Lenten fasts) are a legitimate extension of the authority that Christ gave to his church.

17. Faber's mockers wrote that "not [more than] six words were quoted from the saying of Luke 9" *(Das Gyrenrupffen)*.

18. Ger. *der samstag,* which refers to the vigils before high mass on holidays, often a Saturday midnight mass.

19. In his *Unterrichtung* (p. 34), Faber wrote, "Also, I did not refer to the saying from Jn. 16, for I knew the verse did not belong here, just as I said little about fasting Saturdays." Heinrich Wolf claimed that he was the one who quoted Jn. 16, "and Zwingli answered him and showed how he had distorted the word of Christ" *(Gyrenrupffen,* p. 54, quoted by Jackson, 1901, p. 97).

20. See Article 18 (Meyer, p. 41).

21. The word "mass" is an English translation of the late Latin word *missa,* which derives from the Latin word *dimissio,* "dismissal." At first, *missa* was applied to the dismissal of the catechumens before the Eucharistic service, later to the dismissal of all communicant members at the end of the service. Eventually, *missa* became the technical and almost exclusive name for the Eucharist itself. This derivation of the word, however, had long been forgotten by the sixteenth century, hence the rise of the fanciful explanation by Faber and other Roman Catholic apologists that *missa* derived from the Hebrew *missah,* or "oblation." Even Luther had accepted this explanation, but Zwingli somehow had acquired more accurate information on the subject.

22. Hans Hab was quoted in *Gyrenrupffen* (p. 17ff.) as follows: "Faber attacked the articles severely, but could not prove that they were unchristian. It happened as follows after the noon meal when the resolution was read: Just like peasant boys, you began to be in earnest after the matter was closed, and even then you did not wish to challenge any Article to declare it unchristian by means of the Scriptures as you challenged them, but you raised the Articles in your own hand and said, 'Now I do not wish to speak as a vicar, but as a John, and I say, Master Ulrich, that your Articles are not like unto the truth, and are not based upon the Gospel and the writings of the apostles.' " Zwingli was then quoted as follows: "Lord Vicar, if you had taken off your hat long ago, one could have treated about something. But in answer to your speech, I spoke thus: 'You should prove your malicious speech with the deed, and would do well to attack but one Article so that we may not let this day pass by in vain, for so well are these Articles founded that heaven and earth must shatter sooner than one of these Articles.' Upon this you answered, as always before, this was not the place to debate, but you wished to debate in writing and have judges. Thereupon Zwingli answered that he was indifferent whether everything that was said was recorded, but he wanted no judge over the Word of God, for the Word of God would judge the people, and not the people the Word of God."

23. The Latin adverb was used here.

24. The ZW text (II, p. 557, line 7) has *Latin;* but that from Schuler and Schulthess (I, p. 148, line 32) has *Hebräischer.*

25. In the *Gyrenrupffen,* Hans Hab remarked, "Concerning the way you teased Zwingli, whether he would not take those of Zurich as judges, Zwingli replied, 'No.' "

26. The omission following "Scriptures" includes two comments by Faber, three by Zwingli, one by Lord Fritz von Anwyl, majordomo of Tübingen, and one by Martin Blantsch of Tübingen, concerning the authority of Scripture, the direct authority of the Holy Spirit, and the temporal authority of human judges.

27. In February 1516, Johann Froben of Basel published the Greek New Testament edited and annotated by Erasmus, and frequently collated with the Latin Vulgate. During the following two decades, about forty reprints appeared, including the four major editions of 1519, 1522, 1527, and 1535. In December 1522, Adam Petri of Basel published an edition of Luther's German New Testament. For other contemporary publication achievements in Basel and Zurich in the area of biblical scholarship, see ZW, II, p. 562, fn. 2.

28. From December 1522 to the end of 1525, there appeared from the presses of Adam Petri and Thomas Wolff alone twelve editions of the New Testament in the German language. In Zurich, similar editions appeared from the presses of Christopher Froschauer and Hans Hager in 1524.

51B. Castelberger's Home Bible Study Fellowship, Zurich, 1523
1. This kind of group was known to the authorities as informal "Bible schools" (68E/ 338/6) and as public "Bible readings" (65A/297/4-5), considered quite legitimate until they were expressly outlawed in Zurich in January 1525 and in St. Gallen in June of that year (70B/385/6).
2. The dating of this document as *ca.* January 20, 1525, by Egli *(Aktens.,* p. 276, and Muralt and Schmid *(Quellen* 1, p. 385, fn. 1) is clearly incorrect. Its latest possible date is the banishment from Zurich of one of the witnesses, Lorenz Hochrütiner (see Cast of Characters No. 45) on November 4, 1523, as Egli later observed (ZW, VIII, p. 342, fn. 8). Egli *(Aktens.,* No. 252, p. 85) places the first mention of Castelberger's "Schule" in May 1522. Although a date anywhere between those two for the present document would be possible, it fits best prior to June 1523 when the issue of the tithes came to a head. The Zurich Council had decided on June 22 to maintain the tithes against which Zwingli had been preaching for several months (see 52A, below). In his letter of July 15 (53/220/21ff.), Grebel lamented the Council's action in words that seem to indicate the beginning of some vacillation on Zwingli's part as well (see 53/fn.5).
3. Andreas Castelberger, Zurich bookseller. See Cast of Characters No. 13.
4. On Heine Aberli, see 47A/fn.19, 63/fn.97, and Cast of Characters No. 1.
5. On Lorenz Hochrütiner, see 57F/fn.19, 58/fn.1, and Cast of Characters No. 45.
6. Wolfgang Ininger, a carpenter in Zurich, was associated with Aberli *et al.* in several incidents: the breaking of the Lenten fast in March 1522 (see Egli, *Aktens.,* No. 233) and the destruction of the lamps in the altar of the Fraumünster in September 1523, for which he and Hochrütiner were imprisoned for three days (Egli, *Aktens.,* No. 415). The name of Castelberger was mentioned in the testimony of the latter incident (see 57B/Intro.).
7. See 47B/fn.6 and 63/fn.96.
8. Wolfgang Grüter, chaplain at the Grossmünster. He later participated in the Second Zurich Disputation, declaring the mass to be unbearable to his conscience and that in the future he himself would serve both bread and wine to communicants who desired it. Following this declaration, the burgomaster had told him to be silent (ZW, II, p. 768). Again in December 1523, Grüter and other chaplains requested exemption from continuing to serve mass (see 58B/269/4-5). See Goeters, p. 255, fn. 111, and p. 277.
9. Hans Wieland of Wyl was a shoemaker, named as an Anabaptist as late as 1532 (see Quellen 1, pp. 328, 365-67, and Goeters, p. 255, fn. 112).
10. Ger. *wuocher,* "usury." This word was often used as a synonym for taxes/rents *(zins)* and tithes *(zehenden),* rather than specifically for a percentage interest on loans. See 52/fn.7, 63/fn.54, and 70/fn.17.
11. See fn. 5, above.
12. Ger. *kriegen,* "to lay hold of," "to seize," "to take military action." It is likely that the antiwar teachings of Erasmus were the source for several types of pacifism in Switzerland, the Zwingli-Myconius type that took a strong stand against unpatriotic aspects of Swiss participation in foreign wars but affirmed the use of the sword for national defense, and the Castelberger-Grebel type that developed into a more absolutist nonresistant ethic. These distinctions had not yet emerged, however, at this stage of development. See Stayer, 1972, pp. 95-96.
13. See fn. 9, above.
14. Ulrich Trinkler, see 47A/fn.14 and Cast of Characters No. 86.

1. See 49/fn.1. Grebel refers to the decree of the Council dated June 17, 1523 (Egli, *Aktens.*, No. 366), in which the nuns were allowed by the city authorities to leave the convent under the conditions he describes in the next sentence.

2. The four men of senatorial rank were Thumysen, Binder, Konrad Escher, and Heinrich Werdmüller. The fair distribution of money and property was of special interest to the Grebel family. A comment in Egli, *Aktens.*, No. 367, dated June 21, 1523, indicates that a large sum was paid back to Jacob Grebel in favor of Conrad's Aunt Agatha.

3. The monks had previously exercised considerable control over the convents. On March 7, 1523, following new tensions, a city decree forbade the Dominican "preaching" monks from entering the Oetenbach convent (see *Aktens.*, No. 346). Because of their vested interests, they stood strongly opposed to these new regulations. Cf. Egli, 1910, p. 82, regarding the continued controversy over the dissolution of the convents.

4. This is the first reference in Grebel's letters to Leo Jud, pastor of St. Peter's Church in Zurich since Feb. 2, 1523 (see Cast of Characters No. 58). He was preaching to the nuns by February 1523, and it was his appearance there that caused the bitter reaction of the Preaching Monks.

5. The Large Council in distinction to the Small Council.

6. Lat. *fidei* could mean either "credit" (AB) or "faith" (EY). In view of the prior clause, Grebel may have intended "credit."

7. The matter of the tithes refers to a petition from the villages of Zollikon, Riesbach, Fällanden, Hirslanden, Unterstrass, and Wytikon, asking relief from tithes that were owed to the Chapter of the Grossmünster because its canons allegedly misappropriated these funds and failed to use them to provide evangelical preaching in their village churches. This was the first of a number of references by Grebel to the problem of *zins und zehenden,* "interest and tithes" (see 63/289/9-10, 68/332/22). It was Zwingli who began this criticism; and in fact, it may be said that it was the subject which first introduced the Reformation into Zurich. As early as 1520 he had declared that tithes were not of divine authorization and that their payment should be voluntary. Jackson (1900, p. 156) writes that "as tithes were an important part of the ecclesiastical revenue, he was striking a serious blow at the further maintenance of the cathedral. No wonder that his brother clergy were alarmed. They knew all too well that voluntary payments of tithes or of any other moneys were sure to be small." In Thesis 67 written for the First Doctrinal Disputation the previous January, Zwingli declared his intention to discuss further such issues as "interests, tithes, unbaptized children, and confirmation" (see Meyer, pp. 48-51). J. H. Yoder points out that this particular thesis implies that on these issues Zwingli "differed from tradition without desiring to bring them to the forefront of the debate [at that time]" (MQR, 1961, p. 79). Moreover, as noted in Document 51A, above, the problem of tithes and interest was at the center of the agenda of the Castelberger home Bible study fellowship, which undoubtedly also contributed to Grebel's thinking on the subject.

8. The decision mentioned by Grebel is dated June 22, 1523 (see 52A, below).

9. On Burgauer, see Cast of Characters No. 11. Early in 1523 he announced in the pulpit of St. Lawrence's in St. Gallen that he was returning to some of the teachings of the old faith, such as belief in purgatory and the practice of confession. He had to answer for this to the City Council, which made him revoke his error in the same pulpit on February 20. See Egli, 1910, p. 124, and Burgauer's letter to Grebel dated July 21 (54A), which is a defense of his growing conservative views. For the later development of his troubles in St. Gallen, see 68M/fn.2.

10. "Abomination" was a major theme in Jewish and Christian apocalyptic literature. See Ezek. 8-10; Dan. 9:27; Mk. 13:14; Mt. 24:15, etc. See also various references to "vomiting up" false notions (Job 20:15; Prov. 23:8, etc.). For Grebel's use of this term in

its apocalyptic meaning, see 62/283/33. His premonition was truly prophetic because in spite of the disciplinary action taken against Burgauer, he remained pastor in St. Gallen until 1528.

11. Lat. *messem Gallensem,* an indirect reference to Mt. 9:38. *Gallensem* is short for *Sangallensem,* or St. Gallen.

12. Benedict von Watt, brother of Vadian. See 51/fn.12.

13. Grebel appears to be quoting from Phil. 2:4 and 2:21.

14. See 53/221/4, 55/224/11-13, and 56/225/27.

15. John Jacob Ammann, schoolmaster in Zurich (see 8/fn.2, 35/fn.16, and Cast of Characters No. 3.

52A. Council Decree on the Tithe, June 22, 1523

1. The tithes from land owned by the church were the chief source of revenue for the chapter of the cathedral in Zurich, and it is no wonder that the provost was protective of this system. After Zwingli's attack on the system in February 1520, the provost had written him a letter in which he scolded him for furnishing arms to laymen to use against the clergy (ZW, VIII, No. 121).

2. This comment was in response to the argument of the provost that the tithes were "a divine right" (ZW, VIII, No. 121). By "alms," the petitioners were saying that the payment of tithes should be strictly voluntary.

52B. Zwingli's Sermon on Divine and Human Justice, June 24, 1523

1. Zwingli does not mean to imply by this that the tithe system exists according to divine justice, which he had repeatedly denied. He states the same legal obligation to pay interest (see 214/32ff.) but writes nevertheless that "all interest is ungodly" (215/4-5).

2. Ger. *Strafft sy die missthat nit, so ist sy ein unredliche oberkeit.* The first criterion by which the validity of a state is to be measured is the punishment of transgression, in this case the injustice in the tithe system, as well as the refusal to pay the tithe.

3. I.e., the state has no jurisdiction to command false worship against the Word, or false authority of priests against Christian liberty. Zwingli seems to be shifting his level of abstraction from a prior distinction between divine and human righteousness, both of which are explicit ethical possibilities of action, to a distinction between sacred matters that are not subject to external controls and temporal matters that are (see J. H. Yoder, MQR, 1961, p. 81). It remains to be seen (58B, below) whether or not the rejection of the mass as a sacrifice is a possibility in practice as well as in intention.

4. Mt. 10:17; Mk. 13:9; Lk. 21:12.

5. Mt. 10:28; Lk. 12:4.

6. Acts 5:29.

7. Rom. 13:7.

8. I.e., against the ethical injunction of Lk. 6:35.

9. Cf. Ex. 22:25.

10. Ungodly, i.e., on the level of divine righteousness. On the level of human righteousness, Zwingli is about to make a distinction between interest and usury, the latter exceeding a humanly tolerable rate of 5 percent. Nevertheless, he continues to hold to his basic principle that "all interest is ungodly." In the spring of 1525 he attempted to ban usurers from the Lord's Supper, but was thwarted in this by the City Council.

11. Mt. 19:24; Mk. 10:25; Lk. 18:25.

12. Ger. *früchtkouff,* i.e., a rent in proportion to the value of the crop rather than a straight land-use rent payable without regard to whether or not the land produces a harvest.

13. Council of Constance, 1414-18; Council of Basel, 1431-49.

14. Lk. 6:35.

15. Quotation marks are inserted to indicate Zwingli's satirical reference, but the exclamation mark is in the original.

16. See fn. 10, above.

17. See fns. 8 and 9, above.

18. I.e., the interest received should be proportionate to the yield, not to capital (see fn. 12, above). That would make it like the tithe. This principle of a rent in proportion to the value of the crop rather than a straight rent for land use is more basic than the 5 percent distinction between a fair rent and unjust usury.

19. Lk. 12:24a.

20. Lk. 12:27.

21. Lk. 12:24b.

22. One fifteenth is 6.7 percent; one twentieth is 5 percent. Thus the person renting 15 acres is paying 1.7 percent more rent per acre to the same landlord than the one renting 20 acres.

23. Ger. *denn untrüw und betrug sol den betriegen den schlahen*. If the government functions as it should to recompense good for good and evil for evil, the deceiver who gets an ignorant person to sign a usurious note should be made to pay the price of that offense.

24. I.e., charging interest, charging exorbitant interest, charging illegal interest.

25. Cf. Heb. 13:17 and Ezek. 3:18.

26. I.e., allows in excess of 5 percent interest.

27. Ger. *die den rütschhart gar oder teilhafft bruchend*. The noun *rütschhart* (*Rutscherzin*) refers to interest computed on the original principal plus the accrued interest, sometimes called "interest upon interest." The modern English term for this is compound interest.

28. Rom. 13:7.

29. Mt. 6:33.

53. Grebel to Vadian, Zurich, July 15, 1523.

1. The editors of VB. III, No. 353, dated this letter erroneously. They took "the Day of Margaret" (53/221/4) to be July 13, which was true for the archdiocese of Mainz but not for the archdiocese of Constance. The latter celebrated this saint's day on July 15.

2. The reference is to Zwingli's famous work, *Auslegen und Grunde der Schlussreden* (Exposition and Proof of the Summary Theses). See ZW, II, pp. 14-457.

3. See 52/fns 7 and 8. The decree of the council of June 22, 1523, read that "the parishes shall give the tithe as in the past, payable when this has been written and twice published (52A/209/39-40). Grebel reports this decree with anger and disillusionment.

4. *Quidque magis evangelio probabilius*, which could have either of two meanings: (1) "what more probable to the gospel" in the sense of the disobedience of persons in authority (see Mt. 18:23ff.) or (2) "what more appropriately gospel" in the sense of Grebel's giving an indictment on the basis of the gospel.

5. The Lat. *patres conscriptos*, which would ordinarily be translated "senators" or "council members," is here rendered "senate fathers" to highlight Grebel's play on words with *patres decimantes,* "tithing fathers," or as Yoder prefers "decimating fathers" (MQR, 1961, p. 81). Yoder interprets the word play as "a Latinization of a German pun between *Zunftherren* and *Zinsherren* or *Zehentherren."*

6. Lat. *quam miser ego nugator.* Far from the kind of self-applied putdown typical of earlier use (see 6/fn.3, 25/126/24-25, 36/149/7, 43/159/6), Grebel is here expressing his first note of reservation about Zwingli's apparent vacillation on the question of tithes. Goeters (p. 258) discerns in Grebel's "unhappy babbler" self-reference "a bitterness and ... disapproval of Zwingli's position ... by an 'archscribe' of a formerly revered Reformer. Henceforth, no good word about his teacher comes from his pen anymore." For several years Zwingli had questioned the justice of the tithe system by which

the churches and monasteries were financed. But now in his sermon on "Divine and Human Justice," while reaffirming that on the divine level of justice, tithes and interest were wrong, yet on the human level of justice he was asserting that "everyone should pay the tithe as the government commands" (52B/213/37-38). John H. Yoder is too one-sided in his interpretation of the sermon as a definite reaffirmation of Zwingli's earlier condemnation of the tithe system (MQR, 1961, pp. 79-88) and he is mistaken in his translation of Grebel's sentence, above, as entirely pro-Zwingli ("Zwingli can tell you about all this better than I" (MQR, 1958, p. 130).

7. Jacob Strauss was born in Basel in 1482 and entered the ranks of the Catholic theologians with the Doctor of Theology degree sometime after 1516 after having been a Dominican monk since 1500. He became a Lutheran preacher in Hall dear Innsbruck (1521), in Wertheim (1522), and in Einsenach (1523-25), where his prophetic preaching against usury in the cause of the peasants cost him his position. He died about 1533 following an apparent return to Catholicism. The book to which Grebel refers was titled *Haubtstück und artickel Christenlicher Leer wider den unchristlichen Wucher* ("Principle Articles of Christian Teaching against Unchristian Usury"), a sermon preached at Eisenach in 1523. Two editions were published at Erfurt, one in Strasbourg, and one in Augsburg, all in 1523 (see 63/fn.55). It contained 51 theses against the practice of usury.

8. The reference is to the booklet by Mathis Wurm of Geydertheim titled *Balaams Eselin*. The title comes from the Old Testament account in Numbers 22. The lengthy subtitle tells more about its contents: "Concerning the Ban, That It Dare Not Be Imposed in Payment of Money Debts and Similar Slight Matters, and That the Clergy Are Responsible to Obey the Worldly Authorities If They Desire to Be Christians" (see Bender, 1950, pp. 312-15).

9. On Ulrich von Hutten, see 23/fn.19 and Cast of Characters No. 56. The title of his "invective" was *Ulrichi ab Hutten cum Erasmo Roterodamo presbytero theologo expostulatio* ("Expostulation of Ulrich von Hutten with the Elder Theologian, Erasmus of Rotterdam," Augsburg, July 1523). A second expanded edition was printed in Strasbourg a month later under the title *Expostulatio cum Erasmo* ("Expostulation with Erasmus" see Böcking, II, 180ff.). For the details of the controversy between Erasmus and Hutten, see Jackson, 1900, Ch. IX, and Holborn, Ch. XII.

10. The pamphlet to which Grebel refers was titled *Iudicium D. Martini Lutheri de Erasmo Roterodamo* ("Dr. Martin Luther's Opinion Concerning Erasmus of Rotterdam"), printed in Strasbourg by Hans Schott in June 1523. It contained three items: a letter by Luther concerning Erasmus originally dated May 28, 1522, a tract by Melanchthon comparing some of the sayings of Erasmus and Luther, and a letter by Luther to Capito originally dated Jan. 17, 1522. The reserved attitudes of Luther and Erasmus toward each other were gradually turning into indirect attacks. There were rumors that a direct verbal confrontation was imminent, and the uncertainty of Erasmus's stand on the Reformation heightened that possibility. It was in this situation that Luther wrote the letter of May 28 from Wittenberg to an anonymous addressee, probably Kaspar Borner, professor in Leipzig, saying, "I shall not challenge Erasmus; if challenged myself once or twice, I shall not hurry to strike back. I think it unwise, however, for him to array the power of his eloquence against me, for I am afraid he will not find in Luther another Lefevre" (see LW, Vol. 49, p. 7). By publishing the letter together with the other material, the Reformers in Strasbourg tried to force Erasmus to declare himself on the validity of the Reformation.

11. Martha's pregnancy was first mentioned in 52/208/10-11 (see 52/fn.13). Conrad's mother was visiting her in St. Gallen, perhaps to assist with the delivery and care of the mother and infant (55/224/13).

12. See fn. 1, above.

13. On Burgauer, see 24/fn.19, 52/fn.9, and Cast of Characters No. 11.

14. Vadian evidently complied with Grebel's request, for Burgauer writes to Grebel under date of July 21, 1523, and answers this very question (see 54A/223/22-24). On the

identity of the Zwingli writing to which Grebel refers, see fn. 2, above. Zwingli's Schlussreden had sixty-three quarto pages (see 54A/fn.8).

54. Grebel to Vadian, Zurich, July 16, 1523

1. Grebel dates the letter 1523 but does not give the month or day. He does write, however, "on the day following the letter which you received from our maidservant" (see 54/221/27). The editors of VB dated the letter July 14, but for reasons given in 53/fn.1, it should be dated July 16.

2. Lat. *tabellarius . . . tabellaria.* The former is a masculine noun, but the courier was female. So Grebel repeats it with a feminine ending. The courieress was probably either Conrad's mother, or their maidservant, both of whom had departed for St. Gallen the day before to attend Martha at the birth of her baby (see 54/221/27 and 55/224/7).

3. The book to which reference is made here, in 53/221/7, and in 54A/223/22-23 was the *Auslegen und Gründe der Schlussreden* (see 53/fn.2). In the Introduction to his edition of the *Schlussreden,* Egli cites testimony about how anxiously all of Zwingli's friends anticipated the completion of this important commentary on the 67 articles Zwingli had written for the First Zurich Disputation with the Catholic authorities on Jan. 29, 1523 (ZW, II, 1ff.).

4. Vadian's letter to Jacob Grebel has not been preserved.

5. Grebel's reference to the copies of the book to be sent to Nuremberg by Vadian is interesting. Schuler and Schulthess, the editors of *Huldreich Zwinglis Werke,* I, p. 169, quote it without reference. So did Egli in his introduction (ZW, II, 3); but because he was quoting from Schuler and Schulthess, he was unable to cite the source for the information and thus lacking proof speaks of this fact as only a possibility. Here is the proof in Grebel's letter, which was probably also the reference of Schuler and Schulthess. Nuremberg at this time was the government seat of the Holy Roman Empire, where the ambassador of Prince Elector Frederick the Wise of Saxony, Luther's protector, was especially interested in the Zwinglian movement (see ZW, II', pp. 3 and 431).

6. It is uncertain in the context of the sentence whether "there" (Lat. *istuc)* refers to St. Gallen or to Nuremberg.

7. Lat. *prandio* could be either "late breakfast" (AB) or "lunch" (EY), although technically there was no "breakfast" in that culture in the modern sense.

8. The Greek noun may refer to the maidservant, or perhaps may be Grebel's momentary nickname for his mother, their "chief clerk" (see fn. 2, above).

9. On the identity of Mureria, see 24/fn.18.

10. John Leopold Grebel, Conrad's second cousin (see Cast of Characters No. 39).

11. Written in capitals.

12. The reference is probably to Burgauer (see Cast of Characters No. 11) rather than to Wetter (see Cast of Characters No. 97) because of the clear distinction in 58/257/6 between the "bishop" (Burgauer) and the "co-bishop" (Wetter).

13. Grebel may mean "the New Testament as well as the Old," but is more likely quoting from Mt. 13:52.

14. Lat. *Heus,* "Hello there," meant to arouse attention.

15. See fn. 12, above.

16. This part of Grebel's postscript was meant for Burgauer (see fn. 12, above), who was to "read these words in place of my sending a letter to him." It is not known whether or not he actually read them. His letter to Grebel dated July 21, 1523 (see 54A), is a reply not to the present postscript but to Grebel's comments about him in 52/207/35-52/208/5, which Vadian must have let him read. The present postscript must be characterized as "inside conversation," the exact meaning of which is largely unknown to us, but which refers back to 32A/142/30-31.

17. Lat. *nos vocamus Musio,* followed by a phrase in German, *wo mûss heist ess. Musio* refers to a pap or gruel fed to prisoners sentenced to a diet of "bread and water."

For the earlier correspondence concerning this, see 32A/142/30-31. See also 71K/442/17.

18. Benedict von Watt, brother of Vadian (see 51/fn.12).

54A. Burgauer to Grebel, St. Gallen, July 21, 1523
1. On Benedict Burgauer, see Cast of Characters No. 11. Although receptive to Reformation ideas at first, he turned reactionary to the point that his reaffirmations of purgatory and penance elicited official discipline in St. Gallen in 1523 and again in 1525 (see 68M/fn.2).
2. Rom. 12:21.
3. Burgauer is responding directly to Grebel's reproaches of June 17 (see 52/207/35-52/208/5).
4. Heinold Fast (1973, p. 330, fn. 4) comments that the errors alleged by Burgauer cannot be associated with any one person or group of persons, except that the reference to opposition to infant baptism suggests Hubmaier, who had preached in St. Gallen at the end of April and beginning of May, and who had indicated serious doubts about the baptism of children.
5. This is the first reference in the present selection of documents to the issue of infant baptism, but it has a pre-history. Goeters (p. 280) writes that "Grebel apparently censured it in a letter to the preacher Benedict Burgauer of St. Gall. This letter is not preserved. In November 1523, Lorenz Hochrütiner had been banned from Zurich [see 57F and 58] and listened in 1524 to Johannes Kessler's interpretation of the Letter to the Romans [see 65A]. When Romans 6 was exposited he objected that this should not be applied to infant baptism; indeed, in the ensuing conversation he had a complete argument against it ready and this led to the writing of a letter by Grebel to St. Gall which brings about a crisis in the Bible school there. Hochrütiner obviously kept continual contact with his friends in Zurich among whom the question of baptism became priority in 1524, and he also was stimulated and encouraged by them. But we should not overlook the possibility that already in Castelberg's interpretation of the Letter to the Romans in 1523, all of this was already being discussed." Indeed, Goeters might have added that Zwingli himself, who was the starting point for almost all of Grebel's emerging points of view, questioned the validity of infant baptism as early as 1521 and identified it as an issue for scriptural discernment in the First Doctrinal Disputation in January 1523 (see 67C/fn.22).
6. Johann Kessler also cited an instance of abuse of elders (see 71E/423/15-21).
7. A frequent use of John 10:1, 8 by Zwingli (47D/182/19) and the later Anabaptists (71K/440/7, 441/3, 71M/444/29-30).
8. Burgauer referred to the publication of installments of Zwingli's *Schlussreden* (see 53/fn.2 and 54/fn.3). In 53/221/6-8, Grebel had asked Vadian to ask Burgauer how many quarto pages of the book he still needed. Fast (1973, p. 331, fn. 5) reports that the *Schlussreden* were issued in 63 quarto pages. The letter M referred to the 35th, which began the commentary on the 22nd Article.
9. Grebel's mother was visiting her daughter in St. Gallen at this time, awaiting the birth of Martha's baby (see 55/224/13).
10. This is one of the few references to Grebel's wife, Barbara, by any other than Grebel himself.

55. Grebel to Vadian, Zurich, July 28, 1523
1. The identity of the *Geiseranos* is unknown.
2. Dorothy Grebel, Conrad's sister (see Cast of Characters No. 35).
3. Martha Grebel, Vadian's wife, who was still expecting the birth of a baby (see 52/fn.13 and 53/fn.11).
4. Jacob Grebel was representing his city at the Swiss Diet at Bern with a special mandate to help to interpret the Reformation work of Zwingli, whose safety and freedom to proceed needed to be secured by the Confederacy (see Strickler, IV, p. 314).

On August 2, 1523, Zwingli wrote to Niclaus von Wattenwyl, an influential pastor in Bern, that the Zurich deputies Grebel and Walder were trustworthy men and would transmit a letter which von Wattenwyl might safely send along with them back to Zurich (ZW, VII, 107).

5. Concerning Grebel's chronic ill health, see 4/fn.3 and 6/fn.34. His anticipation of death was premature by about three years.

6. Agatha Grebel, Conrad's aunt, who until recently had been a leading nun at the Oetenbach Convent (see 34/fn.9 and 52/fn.2).

7. See fn. 2, above.

8. Either Grebel had written in reply to Burgauer's letter to him of July 21, 1523 (see 54A) or he had changed his mind (see 54/222/9-10) and written a separate letter to him after July 16, to which Burgauer's letter of July 21 might have been a reply which had not yet reached Zurich as he was writing the present letter on July 28.

9. Grebel refers to the note he wrote to Burgauer at the end of Letter No. 54 to Vadian (see 54/222/1ff.).

10. These two sentences indicate a significant maturation of Grebel's faith in contrast to prior fears and doubts concerning his ill health.

11. See fn. 5, above.

56. Grebel to Vadian, Zurich, August 11, 1523

1. On Cicero, see 36/fn.2.

2. The identity of "the evil worker" (the term taken from Mt. 7:23; see fn. 4, below) cannot be known for certain, but the editors of VB are probably correct in supposing him to be Benedict Burgauer (see 24/fn.19 and 52/fn.9). The reference to "shepherd" in line 7 would fit Burgauer's pastoral role. Also the reference to Jufli in line 21 fits his role as assistant pastor. On the deteriorating relationship between Grebel and Burgauer, on one hand, and between Vadian and Burgauer, on the other, see 54A/Intro. and 68M/fn.2, respectively.

3. Archilochus, famous seventh-century BC Greek writer of satirical poetry who attacked even his friends without mercy.

4. Quoting from Mt. 7:15 and 23:14.

5. Sebastian Wolfgang Wetter, see Cast of Characters No. 97. The implication is that Jufli, the assistant pastor in St. Gallen, has succeeded Burgauer as head pastor. However Grebel may have been led to that conclusion, it was not true. Burgauer did not leave St. Lawrence's until 1528 (but see 68M/fn.2).

6. The birth of a child to Vadian and Martha, anticipated in 52/208/10-11, 53/221/3-4, and 55/224/11-12 is announced at last. Dorothea was their only child. She grew up and married Junker Lorenz Zollikofer on June 4, 1544. They had eight living children—four boys and four girls. For portraits of Dorothea and Lorenz, see Näf, II, opposite 524. Grebel refers to her once more (see 60/280/27-28).

7. Theodosius and Dorotheos, meaning the same as Dorothea, i.e., a gift from God, are names of boys, indicating that Grebel would have preferred a boy to be born. Näf (II, 169) comments in his typically negative vein concerning the Grebels that Conrad was more concerned that the child was not male than that Martha had had a long and difficult delivery.

8. Grebel announces the birth of his second son, Joshua. Like the inscription over the Savior's cross (Jn. 19:20), the name is written in Hebrew, Greek, and Latin. For data on the two sons, Theophil and Joshua, see Bender (1950, p. 506). Theophil apparently died in 1541 without children. Joshua lived until 1589, and from him all of the posterity of Conrad Grebel derives. A direct descendant, Dr. Hans von Grebel, is presently head pastor of the Grossmünster in Zurich.

9. John Leopold Grebel, Conrad's second cousin (see Cast of Characters No. 39).

10. Dorothy Grebel, Conrad's sister (see Cast of Characters No. 35).

11. This reference reveals that Conrad is still dependent upon the support and

counsel of his father, even though he claims to have little hope left in him. In 62/283/13, he gives as one of the reasons why he cannot go to St. Gallen that "father was away." In 62/284/11-12, he writes, nevertheless, that "if father would urge, perhaps I would not be able to refuse [to go to St. Gallen]."

    12. Quoting Lk. 21:19.

    13. This is the first of two references to "pupils" Grebel was tutoring. In 62/283/17-20, he writes: "I am reading the Greek Gospel of Matthew to some pupils, interpreting it by my own abilities, not prophesying."

    14. See 55/fn.5.

57. Grebel to Vadian, Zurich, September 6, 1523

    1. Staub (p. 41) dated this letter 1524, and the editors of VB (II, 445) dated it Sept. 7, 1522, but later corrected it to Sept. 6, 1523 (VB, III, p. 36; VII, p. 30).

    2. The title was *Spongia adversus aspergines Hutteni* ("Sponge to Wipe Off the Aspersions of Hutten"). It was written in reply to Hutten's attack on Erasmus, entitled "Expostulation with Erasmus" (see 53/fn.9), and dedicated to Zwingli, who had befriended Hutten in his last days. It was printed in Basel in early September 1523.

    3. The title was *De non habendo pauperum delectu epistola utilissima* (Basel, July 1523). Oecolampad, the Greek form of Johannes Heussgen (or Hauschein), was born in Württemberg in 1482. He studied at Heidelberg, Tübingen, and Stuttgart. He became a preacher in Basel in 1516 and in Augsburg in 1518. He returned to Basel in 1522 where he was professor of theology and preacher in the cathedral. He was a friend of Erasmus and a close associate of Zwingli in the Swiss Reformation. He died in Basel in 1531 and was succeeded by Grebel's former teacher and friend, Myconius (see Cast of Characters No. 70).

    4. Phillipus refers to Philip Melanchthon (see 48/fn.19). The work was titled *In Evangelium Joannis annotationes* ("Annotations on the Gospel of John"), published in Basel in May 1523.

57A. Zwingli's Defense of his Booklet on the Mass Canon, October 9, 1523

    1. Lat. *indulgentia*. Zwingli's concept of "forbearance," introduced in the *Archeteles* of August 1522 ["Hundreds of times I have said openly, 'I beseech you by Jesus Christ, by our common faith, not to make any changes rashly, but to show to all men by your endurance, if in no other way, that you are Christians, in that on account of the weak, you bear things that by Christ's law you do not need to bear' " (Jackson, 1912, p. 256)] became an issue of controversy, both with his more conservative associates (see 57C/236/8-237/39) and with his more radical disciples (see 59/fn.8, 63/fns. 17 and 100, and 67/fn.30). In the former instance, it subsequently led Zwingli to differentiate between *infirmitas* and *malignitas*, defending forbearance only in the case of *infirmitas*, i.e., the innocent weak. In the latter case, it subsequently led Grebel to castigate Zwingli for his *prudentia diabolica* ("diabolical prudence," 59/276/9-10) and his *falsch schonen* ("false sparing," 63/286/18). In the present tract, forbearance is used with reference to two categories of persons—the innocent weak, for whose sake Zwingli had at first retained chants and vestments, and his radical followers, at whose insistence he was now setting chants and vestments aside. Note 229/3-6, "I serve the weak, but only those of whose eventual strength there is some hope. I yield to the importunity of some, but only until their imprudent impulses may be restrained." See also 230/8-12 and 232/13-15. As pointed out in 63/fn.17, Zwingli's practice of forbearance survived longer in his attitude toward the innocent weak than toward the importunate radicals.

    2. Lat. *inconsulta*, used in these two phrases in both of its meanings: "not consulted" and "imprudent."

    3. Both the *Essay on the Mass Canon* of Aug. 29 and the *Apology of the Booklet on the Mass Canon* of Oct. 9 were dedicated *ad Theobaldum Geroldseggium Eremi Suiten-*

sium administratorem ("to Diebold von Geroldseck, administrator of the Hermits [Monks] of Einsiedeln"). See 47E/fn.15.

4. "In the very travail" of having given birth to the earlier *Essay.*

5. "Those" refer to the associates who have confronted him about his cautious retention of vestments, chants, and prayers in his earlier *Essay.* Who were they? We turn for clues, first, to the document itself in which he refers to them as "importune" with "imprudent impulses" (229/4). They "carp at the prayers" (229/19). They are more radical than Zwingli because "they run of their own accord" and "go before me" (230/8-10). They must take precaution lest they lead others astray "by their skills into a spirit of contention and dissension" (232/4-5). They "look for a knot on the bulrush, incorrectly interpreting what cannot rightly be thus interpreted" (232/15-17). Yet, in spite of these negative comments, Zwingli is in genuine doctrinal debate with them as brothers. "They present arguments very different from any I have ever recognized" (227/36-37). The essay turns to second person plural usage following 230/6; and on two out of the three issues under discussion, he yields to their better wisdom and clearer biblical authority. Our second source of clues to their identity is found in the proceedings of the Second Zurich Disputation, held just three weeks later. On the third day of the debate, Zwingli defines his new position on chants and vestments as "abuses of the mass" and refers to the earlier discussion with his disciples as follows: "Although at first, when I wrote about the canon, I yielded on this point [vestments] for the sake of the weak in faith, supposing it was a symbol of Christ's suffering, as is further explained in that booklet, I have now been informed differently by several . . . therefore I have changed and withdrawn my former opinion" (57C/246/18-24). In this context, the discussion takes place in direct dialogue with the person of Conrad Grebel, and it certainly implies that it was Grebel and his friends who caused Zwingli to change his mind.

6. According to Zwingli, these "certain people" are viewed by the Grebel group as "stubborn adherents" to the old church but by Zwingli himself as the innocent weak on whose behalf he has to show forbearance until they can be properly taught (see fn. 2, above).

7. Lat. *infirmis.* In this tract, the weak in Christ are viewed in distinctly Pauline terms as fns. 12, 24, 49-52, indicate. On the first day of the Zurich Disputation three weeks later, Zwingli will acknowledge the other category of weak—the *malignitas,* the willfully stubborn (see fn. 2, above). Thus, on one hand, he can identify himself with the *infirmi* as a restraint of the *fortes* (the strong ones who are confronting him); but on the other hand, he can accept the fact that the *fortes* are right to a certain degree.

8. Lat. *vestium ornatum.* See ZW, II, p. 600, lines 14ff. for Zwingli's prior acceptance of vestments.

9. The dissenters had argued that Roman Catholic vestments "are derived from the vestments of the priest in the old law, from which there was good reason to consider the mass a sacrifice" (57C/246/21-24).

10. See Jn. 18:14, 28 and ZW, II, p. 600, lines 15ff.

11. See Col. 2:17, Heb. 10:1, 2 Cor. 5:17.

12. See Ex. 3:6, 2 Cor. 4:13.

13. See Heb. 10:1.

14. Lat. *sine discrimine.* Zwingli had used the same word four lines earlier. Although this time he might have meant simply "crisis" or "risk," the repetition of *discrimine* could also imply, "Let's get rid of all vestments without attempting to distinguish one as appropriate and another as inappropriate."

15. This refers to the first paragraph, line 5.

16. Lat. *statutum.* Although Zwingli is writing an apology for his revision of the mass canon, the term "structure" here is not simply to be identified with the canon, even in its amended form, but to a "structure that will abide." Zwingli finally abolished the mass altogether in April 1525.

17. See 1 Cor. 3:10-15, especially v. 11.

18. See 1 Cor. 12:28.

19. Lat. *cantiones,* translated either "chants" or "songs," as also the Ger. word, *Gesang* (57C/fn.58). Compare ZW, II, p. 601, lines 19ff., where Zwingli had still permitted chanting and 57C/246/8ff., where he reports having totally rejected it.

20. One of several liturgical doxologies beginning in Latin with *gloria.*

21. See 51A/fn.16.

22. See ZW, II, p. 603, lines 10ff.

23. Although Zwingli has said on the occasion of the First Zurich Disputation the previous January that he "was not ashamed to read [the Bible in] German at times, on account of easier presentation," he had allowed Leo Jud and other pastors to be the first to make the transition to the vernacular.

24. See Eph. 4:3.

25. Lat. *cigneos cantus,* "swan song," a song formerly thought to be uttered by a dying swan (see Otto, p. 104).

26. A faulty interpretation of the two Pauline passages later also put forth by Grebel (see 63/287/3-6).

27. Lat. *Latinis,* "Latins," although its derivation from Latium refers to the district of Italy in which Rome was situated.

28. See Col. 3:11.

29. See Eph. 4:17ff.; 1 Cor. 14:11, 17, 26.

30. The reference is to the earlier *Essay,* ZW, II, p. 596, lines 8ff.

31. Lat. *Christi actionem.* Although the literal meaning is "Christ's act," the noun also carries the technical meaning of *gratiarum,* the "expression of thanks" or "eucharist."

32. Lat. *lese magestatis* is carried over into the English as a crime committed against a sovereign power.

33. Zwingli affirms this hermeneutical principle himself in 230/13-14. See also 57C/239/35 ("For everything that God has not taught and that comes from men is never good") and 57C/246/5-6 ("All that is planted and added without being instituted by Christ is a true abuse"). See also 51A/200/17ff.

34. I.e., approach the service of the mass.

35. The verb is plural, hence the pronoun refers not to Diebold von Geroldseck (see fn. 3, above) but to Zwingli's confronters (see fn. 5). The address to them shifts back and forth between the third person "they" and second person "you" in this and the following paragraph but then continues in the first person for several more paragraphs.

36. See fn. 33, above.

37. See Mt. 19:17; Mk. 10:18.

38. The Lat. *nempe fidem infirmorum excitare* occurs also in the *Essay* as Zwingli's statement of purpose for the prayers (see ZW, II, p. 596, 8ff.).

39. See 2 Cor. 11:24ff. and 12:7.

40. See Mt. 26:39-44.

41. Jn. 16:23.

42. Lk. 17:5.

43. Jn. 14:1ff.

44. Lat. *circumscriptionibus aut circumstantiis.* The first word refers to the "limitations" or "restrictions" of the prescribed prayers to which the radicals were objecting. The second refers to the "confrontations" or "conditions" of the radicals themselves, from which flow a new set of restrictions or prescriptions (see next fn.). Zwingli is claiming freedom from both.

45. Lat. *Sequitur autem persone circumstantiam ordo.* The spokesman for the radicals lays down the condition that only the Lord's Prayer should be used in the Eucharist and in so doing merely replaces one order of worship with another.

46. See Mt. 10:11-13 and Lk. 10:5-7.

47. Mt. 26:26-29 and 1 Cor. 11:25.

48. 1 Cor. 11:34.
49. See 1 Cor. 11:12ff.
50. 1 Cor. 7:15.
51. 1 Cor. 8:1.
52. Rom. 12:3.
53. See fn. 1, above.
' 54. *In scirpo nodum quaerere,* "You look for a knot on a bulrush" (see Erasmus, *Adag.,* II.IV.76.
55. Diebold, see fn. 3, above.

57B. Jacob Grebel to Vadian, Zurich, October 12, 1523
1. This is the third and last extant letter of Jacob Grebel, all written to Vadian (see 9A, 23A, and 57B).
2. Ger. *mine heren rätt und burger,* referring to the Small and Large Councils.
3. The year 1523 was a watershed in the Zwinglian Reformation, created by the two official disputations, the first in January and the second now in October. The major accomplishment of the first was the tacit approval by the Zurich magistrates of Zwingli's Reformation leadership plus a formal affirmation of the supreme authority of the Bible in decisions that still had to be made to implement his Reformation preaching. The agenda for the second, in the light of the first, was what exactly should now be done about two issues on which reform had been proclaimed—the worship of images and the sacrificial rite of the mass.
4. The Swiss cantons were divided into three dioceses: Basel, Chur, and Constance.
5. Of the two main issues on the agenda, the worship of images was the more pressing for resolution (see fn. 1, above). Although the three Stadelhofen iconoclasts were imprisoned, there was considerable sympathy for them, as it was felt that they had sincerely tried to do what their preachers had taught. The pressure this put on the council to act was considerable. The reform of the mass, although less urgent, was even more at the heart of the Reformation—the use of the vernacular, the restitution of both elements (wine and bread) for the laity, the meaning of Christ's presence, etc. Zwingli's *Canon of the Mass,* published Aug. 29, had taken a number of innovative positions on these questions, and required official sanction also so that it could be used in the liturgy.
6. The disputation was as notable for who did not come as for who did. In Jackson's words, "Constance declared (October 16) that he would be answerable to both his rulers (Pope and Emperor) if he took part in the proposed disputation; [he] urged the Council to give the idea up, and leave all such questions for answer at the coming General Council. Basel declared that he was too old and weak to make the journey; that only the whole Church should undertake such changes, and also they should avoid schism. Chur sent no reply at all. The cantons, except Schaffhausen and St. Gallen, declined to send deputations. Bern and Solothurn replied in friendly fashion, but said the matter should be discussed by the Confederacy as a whole; the abbot of St. Gallen politely declined to come; Lucerne reproached Zurich for her persistency in error; Upper Unterwalden was bitter and abusive" (1900, p. 203).
7. Jörg von Watt, cousin of Vadian, lived next door to him and worked closely with him not only as a fellow member of the Small Council but also in the work of the emerging Reformation in St. Gallen.
8. Bartholomew Steck, married to Vadian's sister Othilia, was an educated merchant in St. Gallen who took an interest in Reformation activities. He became a member of the Large Council in 1526.
9. Jacob's wife, Dorothea Fries.
10. Jacob's sister, Agatha Grebel (see Cast of Characters No. 30). It is possible that she was living in the Jacob Grebel house at this time (see 55/224/17-18).
11. Aunt Keller was Jacob's sister, Martha, who was married to a Keller.

12. Identity unknown.

13. Ger. *das böss meitlin Dorly.* The name refers to Jacob's youngest daughter, Dorothy, born about 1509 and according to Conrad "the pet of her parents and the tyrant of the house" (45/161/23-28).

57C. The Second Zurich Disputation, October 26-29, 1523

1. For good brief reviews of the disputation, see Garside, pp. 129-45, and Jackson, 1900, pp. 203-5.

2. From ZW, II, pp. 692ff. The agenda of the first day was the debate on the proposition: "The church images are forbidden by God and Holy Scripture, and therefore Christians should neither make, set up, nor reverence them, but they should be removed." For the second and third days' agenda, see fn. 26, below.

3. The name of Ludwig Hätzer does not appear in the text, but rather a mark of some kind that the transcribers have interpreted as the comments of the recording secretary himself (see ZW, II, p. 692, fn. 4). On Hätzer, see Cast of Characters No. 43.

4. Ger. *heimliche bild,* "household images."

5. Leo Jud (see Cast of Characters No. 58 and 52/fn.4) had just concluded a powerful condemnation of images, based on Hätzer's published exposition. Hätzer felt, however, that Jud did not make it sufficiently clear that "all images were forbidden everywhere, and not simply in places of public worship" (Garside, p. 132).

6. Hätzer is addressing Leo Jud, pastor at St. Peter's in Zurich (see fn. 4, above).

7. Grebel's comment, although simply an affirmation of Hätzer's thoroughgoing specification of the biblical prohibition of images, had a double significance. It spoke for those present who wanted to support the radical approach which Hätzer represented and yet it laid claim to a ground gained that was subsequently affirmed in the resolution of the first day (see next fn.). In his "Brief Christian Introduction" to the disputation findings published in November (58A, below), Zwingli reaffirmed this very point in words similar to those of Hätzer and Grebel: "They [the pictures and statues of the saints] should no longer be allowed to remain there—neither in your room, nor in the marketplaces, nor anywhere else where they would be reverenced" (58A/263/17-20).

8. Following a period of silence, Sebastian Hofmeister (see Cast of Characters No. 46), one of the three presidents of the disputation, asked if anyone wanted to respond. Heinrich Lüti, the assistant priest at the Grossmünster from 1520 until June 1523, and thereafter in Winterthur, took the floor to initiate a debate with Leo Jud (Garside, pp. 131-35).

9. When the Lüti-Jud dialogue (see previous fn.) was played out (see ZW, II, p. 699), Hofmeister summoned the group to some new topic.

10. From ZW, II, 699.15-18, 704.30-705.9. On Schmid, see Cast of Characters No. 83.

11. From ZW, II, pp. 707.21ff. Garside writes that Schmid's speech "represents the moderate point of view at its best" (p. 136). If that is true, then by contrast Zwingli's reply can only be described as progressive if not radical in the sociological sense of the expeditious reform of an existing abuse without further delay.

12. Zwingli began his career in Zurich on Jan. 1, 1519, by announcing that he would not follow the traditional pericopes and interpret them patristically, but that he would preach whole books of the Bible in sequence. He explained that the pericopes were an imported innovation from the time of Charlemagne, but that preaching from the Bible was a method that went back to St. Augustine and St. Chrysostom. In his first sermon on the next day, he began the continuous exposition of the Gospel of Matthew, inductively preaching on the life of Christ.

13. When he presented Zwingli before the canons of the Zurich Chapter for his induction, the provost mentioned the duties of the people's priest to maintain the revenues of the cathedral. Zwingli expressed thanks for electing him, requested their prayers, and then announced that he would begin the next day with a series of sermons on the Gospel

of Matthew, which he would preach according to the Bible itself and not according to the Church Fathers.

14. This was the third time that Zwingli recited his early preaching sequence. The first time was in his sermon of March 23, 1522, "Concerning Choice and Liberty of Food," following the Ash Wednesday fasting violations (see ZW, I, p. 133, lines 3ff., and Jackson, 1912, p. 110) and the second time was in his reply to the bishop's admonition titled *Apologeticus Archeteles,* published Aug. 22-23, 1522 (see 47D/183/7ff. from ZW, I, p. 284, lines 39ff., and see 47D/fn.19). This clearly identifies Zwingli's basic attitude in the Second Zurich Disputation, at least with respect to images, with his earlier more aggressive, confrontative stand of 1522-23, and casts further doubt on Walton's thesis about a serious alienation between him and the so-called "Grebel faction" as early as the 1522-23 phase of the Reformation (Walton, Ch. 11).

15. Namely, the images.

16. Ger. *ab der wand unnd ab den brieffen.* According to ZW, II, p. 708, fn. 6, the last word refers to *Blätter mit Abbildungen* ("sheets with illustrations"). Thus, perhaps "sheets" would be the more exact translation, parallel to "walls."

17. Ger. *ein mittelding.* The technical term *adiaphoron* would be preferable, if it were known more generally.

18. Ἀετος μυίας οὐ ϑηπεύει. See Stephanus, *Thesaurus linguae gracecae,* I, 775.

19. ZW, II, 709.1-27 omitted.

20. On the issue of forbearance, see 63/fn.17.

21. Ger. *den götzen,* the more polemic term for images and statues used in the debates (see 58/fn.12).

22. ZW, II, 710.9-22, 25-28 omitted.

23. Following comments by Ceprinus, Edlibach, Widmer, Fry, and Jud (ZW, II, 711.1-716.7), Hofmeister summarized the conclusion to which the assembly had come and asked whether there were any more grounds for objection to the doctrine presented by Zwingli and his colleagues. Then Hubmaier spoke (ZW, II, 716.16ff.).

24. On Hubmaier, see Cast of Characters No. 54. On the first two days of debate, he spoke twice in opposition to the worship of images (ZW, II, 716.17-719.6 and 760.33-762.22). Only the first of these three speeches is included here; but for his speech on the third day on the issue of the mass (786.11-788.9), see below, 228.27ff.

25. After another invitation from Hofmeister (ZW, II, 718.5-9), Edlibach argued that the meaning of Exodus 20 is not that images should not be made or painted but only that they should not be worshiped. He claimed that pictures move the believers to contemplation and good works (ZW, II, 718.11-21). A counter question by Franz Zingk asked how images would move people who were blind, perhaps meaning to argue the priority of the spoken Word (ZW, II, 718.23-27). The debate threatened to degenerate when Hubmaier spoke up again (ZW, II, 718.31-719.6), reading Deuteronomy 27:15, "Cursed is the person who makes a carved or molded image, which is an abomination before the Lord God, and secretly places this image anywhere." Ludwig Hätzer, the recorder, added the comment, "This text resolved this debate completely and all were satisfied."

26. The first day of disputation ended with a summation by Chairman Hofmeister, thanking God that the day had been productive and that it had been decisively discerned from the Scriptures that the use of images by Christians should not be tolerated. Before adjourning the session, he made an impassioned plea for the three imprisoned iconoclasts, declaring that they had only put into practice what Zwingli and Jud had preached about the images and what had now been adopted by this assembly. Burgomaster Röist responded by promising that the plea would be considered when the trial was held following the disputation. On the second and third days, the debate was directed to the proposition: "The mass is no sacrifice, and heretofore has been celebrated with many abuses of its original institution by Christ. As we resume the debate at a point early in the day (ZW, II, 738.35), Commander Conrad Schmid (see Cast of Characters No. 83)

begins another colloquy with Zwingli like that above.

27. See 57C/fn.7.

28. It is not clear whether "they" refers to the monks or to those who ascribed them to the devil.

29. Mt. 18:15ff.

30. Zwingli's "answer" has two parts: a defense of his own condemnation of the monks and a support for Schmid's admonition against those who employ libelous language in their condemnations. Zwingli admitted that he had himself said that the monks were of the devil. But then he went on to argue that others who said the same thing deserved to be censured.

31. See 57A/fn.33.

32. Ger. *sömlich secten*. This is the first of Zwingli's numerous references to the phenomenon of sectarianism. This reference, repeated in the following paragraph, anticipates the argument in Zwingli's tract, *Those Who Give Cause for Rebellion* (see 67B), that two main sources for social deviancy in Zurich were the reactionary monks and papists, on one hand, and the radical iconoclasts and Anabaptists, on the other. At this point, however, there is little evidence that a "Conrad Grebel sect" is the object of Zwingli's present criticism, as Walton (1967, p. 189) supposes.

33. Ger. *nebenthalb von min selbs wegen*, "except on my own account."

34. 2 Tim. 4:2.

35. After another period of discussion on the mass a point was reached where momentarily no one felt like responding. In this pause, Hubmaier returned to the agenda of the previous day. There are several clues in Hätzer's minutes as to the purpose and intent of this "displaced contribution": (1) His comment in the middle of Hubmaier's speech that "some people in the room said, 'Amen!' " suggests that Hubmaier was speaking for a particular group of disputants. That this was the Grebel group becomes evident in 244/4ff. (2) Hubmaier begins his speech with the observation that "yesterday it became thoroughly clear from Scripture that there should be no images." Thus, the only question remaining on that subject was what to do about the images still in use in the churches. Notwithstanding the ground rule that after truth had been discerned in principle, the magistrates would decide how to proceed in practice, Hubmaier (on behalf of the Grebel group) wanted to add a procedural suggestion. (3) This suggestion came at the end of Hubmaier's speech, to wit, that "a whole parish church will gather without disorder to decide by consensus that the images shall be moved out and laid to sleep." Thus, the final decision was being reclaimed for the congregation rather than the state.

36. Following remarks by Zwick, Walder, Utinger, and others on the jurisdiction of the council on procedures concerning images and the mass, Zwingli reminds the disputants that they were not supposed to give practical advice but to leave that to the council, adding that of course the magistrates should not decide anything that was not based on the Word of God, in which case he would have to preach against it. The recorder, Hätzer, inserted a comment into the minutes that Zwingli wanted to avoid the impression that the ordinances of the church were to be observed because they were mandated by the magistrates rather than by the Word of God. After further debate on the second day's proposition on the mass (see fn. 26, above), Burgomaster Röist said, "In the name of God! Since this point has been thoroughly discussed, Milords will be glad to grant it." Receiving no dissent, he started to adjourn the session when Conrad Grebel arose to speak (ZW, II, 783.36ff.).

37. Ger. *man sölte den priesteren ein bescheid geben.* The phrase is difficult to translate. With a literal rendering, "One should give the priests instruction," the subject of the sentence could be either the disputation itself or the City Council. Hillerbrand thinks that Grebel meant the disputation itself, "otherwise Zwingli's response that the City Council would take care of this and the ensuing disagreement between Zwingli and Stumpf about the priority of the Spirit of God or the City Council would have been beside the point" (MQR, 1965, p. 310). But that Grebel may very well have meant the City Council is indicated in 244/9-10, below, where he says, "Your mandate, Milords, concerns all the abuses of the mass." Grebel's protest here would appear to be not that Milords did not have the authority to take care of

the matter, but that they should do so forthwith without further procrastination.

38. Namely, the disputation.

39. Ger. *so man nit ein anders mit der mess anhub [anhob]*. As in other instances, Grebel here anticipates what actually occurred, the delay of the actual reform of the mass for another sixteen months after that decision had been made in principle in the present disputation. For the controversial events that led to this postponement, see the 58B series of documents.

40. Zwingli was not here claiming any new authority of the state over the church, but was merely reiterating the basic ground rule for the disputation, that while it had the right to discern the scriptural teaching about images and the mass, the practical application of such discernments were to be left to the authority of Milords. See Yoder, 1958, pp. 131-35.

41. Simon Stumpf, pastor at Höngg since 1520. See Cast of Characters No. 85.

42. Zwingli's use of the German word *uffrur* anticipates his pamphlet of 1524, *Those Who Give Cause for Rebellion* (see fn. 32, above, and 67C, below). On the meaning which this word came to have for him, see Yoder, 1969, pp. 120-21.

43. It had been agreed to convene at noon on the third day so that all present could hear Zwingli preach in the morning on the subject, "The Shepherd" (see ZW, III, 1-68).

44. From ZW, II, pp. 784.35ff.

45. Vadian may have been admonishing Grebel to exercise less anxiety and more candor in his comments on this third and final day of the disputation.

46. This comment may be both a response to Vadian's admonition (see previous fn.) and an indication of an unfulfilled minority position in the disputation on behalf of which Grebel was speaking. His deference to "those who can speak better" might even indicate an advance plan that Hubmaier would speak for them (see fn. 35, above, and 68/fn.7).

47. On Hubmaier, see fns. 24 and 35, above, and Cast of Characters No. 54.

48. 1 Cor. 11:24b.

49. 1 Cor. 11:24b, 26; Mt. 26:26-28; Mk. 14:22-24; Lk. 22:17-19.

50. Ger. *caliquutisch*. The language of Calcutta, here "gibberish" (see 67C/fn.25).

51. 1 Cor. 14:19.

52. Both kinds, see 47D/fn.25 and 57B/fn.5.

53. Mt. 26:27b.

54. Ger. *der sticht Christo ein loch in sinen testamentbrieff*.

55. Gal. 1:6ff. and 3:15.

56. See 238/3ff., above, for the first of two speeches Hubmaier made on images, one right after lunch of the first day (see ZW, II, 716-19) and the other on the morning of the second day (ZW, II, 760-62). For the content of his second statement see fn. 39, above, and Garside, 143-44. He had expressed support for the inconoclastic position, which Garside interprets as "the impact of such a disputation on a sensitive mind in a state of transition between the traditional form-life of the Church and a radically new faith." Upon his return to Waldshut, he composed eighteen theses on images for local debate; and Garside translates the seventh as follows: "Images are good for nothing; wherefore such expense should be no longer wasted on images of wood and stone, but bestowed upon the living, needy images of God." The pictures and statues were actually removed from his church a full month before that happened in Zurich.

57. See 57A/fns. 33 and 36 and 57C/fn.31.

58. Ger. *das nüt söllend gsang, so man allenthalben in den templen rüchlet*. Garside's translation, "that the song which one sings off-key in the churches should not exist" (p. 54) is hardly correct. The reference is not to inept singing but to habitual liturgical chanting in what might be called a priestly voice or monotone "*mit unsircherer Stimme singt*" as the editors of ZW, II, 788, fn. 9, put it. The modern German verb would be *röcheln*, to rattle in the throat, to gasp out words. For a thorough analysis of Zwingli's position on singing, see Garside, pp. 7-75. A clear distinction should be made between liturgical singing in the medieval church and congregational singing in the post-Reformation church. The *Gesang* that Zwingli was describing could be translated "liturgical singing" or "chanting" to signify the priestly *Gesang* in distinction to the congregational *Gesang* that Reformers like Carlstadt were promoting.

However, rather than moving in the direction of allowing the laity to sing in congregational worship, Zwingli preferred to discard the *Gesang* altogether. In his Articles 44, 45, and 46 (see Meyer, pp. 44-47) prepared for the First Zurich Disputation, Zwingli had argued: "Those who pray truly call on God in spirit and in truth, without all kinds of shouting before men. Hypocrites do their works so that they may be seen before men; also, they receive their reward in this life. From this follows that singing in church [*Tempelgesang*] or crying out without devotion and only for merit stems either from a desire for recognition before men or gain." For Zwingli's amplification of these articles in his *Schlussreden* of July 14, 1523, see Garside, pp. 47-52. For the way in which Grebel became a thoroughgoing Zwinglian on this subject, see 63/286/37-63/287/13 and 63/fn.23.

59. 1 Cor. 14:19.

60. Zwingli refers to his *Treatise on the Canon of the Mass,* published Aug. 29, 1523 (see ZW, II, 552-608).

61. See ZW, II, p. 600, lines 14ff.

62. After some specific criticism from some of his disciples, Zwingli published his second treatise entitled *Defense of the Booklet on the Canon of the Mass* (see 57A, above), dated Oct. 9, in which he responded to the three criticisms having to do with his retention of Latin singing, priestly vestment, and liturgical prayers. The first two he was now ready to eliminate, in reversal of his earlier treatise, but he held to the third. The identity of the several disciples who influenced him to change his mind is not given, but Yoder (MQR, XXXII, 1958, p. 130) and Goeters (p. 260) conclude that it was the Grebel group.

63. This is a most revealing argument to compare with Zwingli's later defense of infant baptism, citing circumcision in the Old Testament as the model for infant baptism—a logic that was the reverse of the present argument relating to priestly robes.

64. See fn. 13, above.

65. Johann Zwick, pastor at Riedlingen near Constance, the seat of the diocese that embraced Zurich. See Cast of Characters No. 105. In view of the bishop's refusal to attend the October 1523 disputation, Zwingli was especially pleased to have Zwick represent the church in Constance. See also Epi.G/Intro.

66. The Latin Vulgate version of the Bible used the term *panis* for the original Greek word for "bread" in Mt. 26:26, Mk. 14:22, Lk. 22:19, and 1 Cor. 11:23. Grebel was correct in his exegesis of the Latin text, which he may have compared with the Greek text. The synoptic Gospels specify that Jesus used ordinary leavened bread *(panis)* instead of unleavened bread or *matzoth.* This has been taken as evidence that the Lord's Supper was not a celebration of the Passover meal. Although the question remains unresolved, it would have been quite proper to discuss it at the disputation in relation to the sacrificial mass versus the representative Eucharist. In view of his insistence on *sola scriptura* in the Disputation, Zwingli's refusal to discuss Grebel's question indicates the beginning of a diverging hermeneutic.

67. Small, round, unleavened wafers were used in the mass.

68. The fact is, however, that in his Reformed communion liturgy adopted on April 13, 1525, entitled *Aktion oder Brauch des Nachtmahls,* Zwingli specified that unleavened bread be used.

69. In Roman Catholic and Eastern Orthodox churches, the priest mixes some water with the wine as part of the offertory of the mass. Ancient church fathers like Irenaeus and Cyprian interpreted this as a union of Christians with God, related to the mystical union of the human and divine in Jesus. To Ambrose this was a symbol of the blood and water that flowed from Christ's side while on the cross (Jn. 19:34). Grebel was correct in pointing out that the official Roman Catholic claim that "at the Last Supper, following a Greek custom then common in Palestine, Christ mixed some water with the wine" has no basis in Scripture.

70. Deut. 4:2; 12:32; Rev. 22:18-19.

71. The editor of ZW, II, p. 791, fn. 6, reports that Zwingli spoke to this matter in his *Treatise on the Canon of the Mass* (see fn.60, above).

72. For the history of this practice, see ZW, II, p. 791, fn. 2. The *Ordo Rom. VI* from the ninth century prescribes that even the subdeacons in the mass "receive the body of Christ

from the hand of the bishop." A more general regulation on this matter dates from the council of Rouen of AD 880.

73. In order make a point Zwingli was paraphrasing John 19:30 from the Vulgate: *Cum ergo accepissent Jesus acetum* ("When Jesus had received the wine").

74. It was apparently hardly conceivable to Zwingli that there would be Reformation groups that would practice foot washing as an ordinance of the church.

75. See fn. 52 above, and 47D/fn. 25.

76. J. H. Yoder accepts this assent as evidence that the "turning point in the Zwinglian Reformation" did not come in October, as some scholars have argued, but two months later (1958, p. 129).

77. Conrad Schmid (see Cast of Characters No. 83) proposed at this point (ZW, pp. 793ff.) that the abolition of images and the mass should be preceded by a teaching mission mandated by the Zurich Council. As 57D/252/12-16 reveals, the council followed this suggestion, in addition to ordering the writing and publishing of an "Introduction" to the disputation findings (see 58A). The summation comments by the three presidents are found in ZW, II, pp. 800ff.

78. Our excerpts of Vadian's comments are taken from 800.23-801.21, 802.13-18.

79. Compare with Vadian's letter to Grebel, 67D/322/8-10.

80. The three imprisoned iconoclasts—Hottinger, Ockenfuss, and Hochrütiner—had been much in the minds of the disputation participants, for it was their action at Stadelhofen that precipitated the conference. The failure of the Zurich authorities to release them without the penalty of banishment was a source of considerable disillusionment for Grebel and an important factor in what is soon to become the "turning point in the Zwinglian Reformation" (see 57D, 58, 58B, and 59).

81. At the end of the first day of the disputation, chairman Hofmeister had made the first plea on behalf of the prisoners (see fn. 26, above).

82. On Wolfgang Joner see 57F/fn.4 and Cast of Characters No. 57. His concluding comments are found in ZW, II, 802.20ff.

83. The recorder of the disputation apparently omitted comments that were not considered to be germane to the two main propositions being debated, either by the burgomaster or one of the three presidents, or by the recorder himself. In his concluding remarks, Burgomaster Röist also referred to "several of you [who] have introduced things here that would not have served the cause; those I ordered to be silent and desist." Another indication that Conrad Grebel was not as persona non grata as Walton (Ch. 11) supposes is the considerable space given to his comments in the official record.

84. The recorder of the disputation, Ludwig Hätzer (see fn. 3, above, and Cast of Characters No. 43).

57D. The Council's Mandate After the Disputation, Zurich, end of October, 1523

1. Although this document is undated, its temporal boundaries are fairly narrow. It looks back to the October 26-28 Disputation, and Zwingli's letter of Nov. 11 (57F) looks back to it (i.e., the council's mandate). Egli *(Aktens.,* No. 436) gave it a date (Oct. 27) during or following the second day of the disputation, perhaps because its mandate on images is a bit more explicit than its mandate on the mass; but this date cannot be correct because the mandate refers to the implementation of several specific suggestions made by Conrad Schmid at the end of the disputation on Oct. 28 (see 57C/fn.77). It seems most likely that the council issued this mandate soon after the adjournment of the disputation.

2. Ger. *unser gnädig BM., R. und der gross Rat, etc.* The initials refer to the burgomaster and *Ratsherren,* respectively, the latter meaning the members of the Small Council, usually called councillors (or senators) in distinction to the members of the *Grosser Rat* (Large Council), usually called representatives. Another familiar sixteenth-century Swiss designation of the two Councillor bodies was *Raedten und Bürgern.*

3. This convocation was the First Zurich Disputation held on Jan. 29, 1523 (see 51A).

Its doctrinal agenda centered in the 67 theses written for debate by Zwingli, and its principal conclusions were a commitment to the Bible as the central authority for faith and life and a mandate for Zwingli and his colleagues to continue to preach a Reformation doctrine based on the Scripture.

4. The second convocation was the Second Disputation just concluded, with its two principal doctrinal concerns: images and the mass.

5. This is the first of four promises in this brief document of a speedy implementation by the Zurich authorities of the disputation findings regarding the images and the mass. When by the middle of December it became evident that these promises would not be met, a rupture between the moderates and progressives became inevitable.

6. This was the only procedural decision reached by the council following the disputation: persons who had given paintings or statues to the churches could now retrieve them if they wanted to do so. This idea was first voiced following Leo Jud's iconoclastic sermon of Sept. 1, when a conservative Catholic by the name of Thomas Kleinbrötli complained that the only right the iconoclasts had was to remove their own images (Garside, p. 105).

7. The second promise of speedy implementation of disputation findings (see fn. 5, above).

8. See 57C/238/6-10 and 58B/269/33-35.

9. The third promise of speedy implementation (see fns. 5 and 7 above).

10. Although the plural reference is to a commission of 14 men assigned to the task of recommending ways to remove the images from the city churches and to implement an evangelical communion liturgy (see 57F/fns. 3-8), it was to Zwingli himself, a member of the commission, that the task of writing "a brief introduction" to the findings of the disputation was given (see 58A). He finished it before Nov. 9, when it was read before the council and approved for publication. It appeared from the Froschauer printery on Nov. 17, bearing the title *Eine kurze christliche Einleitung* (A Brief Christian Introduction). On the two main theses of the disputation (see 57/fns. 2 and 26), Zwingli summarized the conclusions reached. But it is also clear that he had pushed these Reformation ideas into the disputation in a way that was independent of the consensus reached there and that he anticipated the application of these new principles in the near future (Garside, pp. 147-51).

11. Ger. *iren undertanen,* "their subjects," in distinction to the word used for parishioners in the second paragraph above, *kilchgnossen,* "church members."

12. The fourth promise of a speedy procedure (see fns. 5, 7, and 9, above).

13. This was in response to Schmid's proposal (see 57C/fn.46). The three spokesmen were Zwingli, in villages toward Schaffhausen; Schmidt, in the Grüningen and Lake Zurich area; and Joner, in the territory of the Abbey of Cappel (see 57F/255/2-6).

57E. The Report of Veit Suter, October 31, 1523
1. See above, 57C/243/13-15.
2. See above, 57D/251-2.
3. See above, 57C/242/33-39, although Hätzer's additional assertion, "That they [the magistrates] will counsel together as to the most appropriate way for this to be done without an uproar," suggests less of a discrepancy between the consensus of the disputation and the subsequent decree of the council that Suter's report would indicate.

57F. Zwingli to Vadian, Zurich, November 11, 1523
1. Vadian is addressed in this letter in his dual role as the most influential political leader in St. Gallen, through whom an acceptance of Hochrütiner can be arranged (255/23ff.) and as the chief reformer in his canton, to whom all other local reform-minded clerics and laymen looked for ecclesiastical leadership as well.
2. Vadian served as one of the three presidents of the Second Disputation, Oct. 26-28 (see 57C, above).
3. Lat. *civium* for the Ger. *Bürgers,* referring actually to representatives of the trade

665

guilds of Zurich in the Large Council, although including in this case the *Ratherren* (councillors) on the special commission. The eight councillors and representatives, who had been elected on Sept. 29 to carry responsibility for "regulations concerning images and other things" (Egli, *Aktens.*, No. 424), were Jacob Grebel, Conrad Escher, Hans Usteri, Heinrich Werdmüller, and guildmasters Setzstab, Berger, Binder, and Wegman.

4. The abbot of Cappel, thirteen miles south of Zurich, was Wolfgang Joner, who had been at the Cisterian Monastery since November 1519 (see Cast of Characters No. 57). He and two men named in the following two footnotes were the three prelates of the province according to the still existing hierarchy of the Roman Catholic Church.

5. The provost of the canons at Embrach since 1517 was Heinrich Brennwald (see Cast of Characters No. 8).

6. The commander of Küssnacht was Conrad Schmid (see 57B/fn.11 and Cast of Characters No. 83).

7. Heinrich Engelhart, see 47/fn.3 and Cast of Characters No. 19.

8. Leo Jud, see 52/fn.4 and Cast of Characters No. 58.

9. On Zwingli's document, *A Brief Christian Introduction,* see 57D/fn.10 and 58A.

10. Lat. *episcopi,* a term Zwingli often used to refer not only to bishops in the Roman Catholic hierarchy and to people's priests or pastoral overseers in a local community.

11. Assuming that these preaching assignments were confined to the canton of Zurich, the editors of ZW, II, p. 130, fn. 10, identify this one as the Monastery of Cappel on the road to the town of Zug.

12. Lake Zurich, including such towns as Zollikon, Kussnächt, Meilen, Rapperswil, Horgen, and Wädenswil.

13. The district of Grüningen was located east of the eastern shore of Lake Zurich.

14. This was the "Weinland" country to the north of Zurich on the way to the canton of Schaffhausen. With one exception there is no extant information on Zwingli's preaching mission here (see ZW, II, p. 130, fn. 12).

15. Zwingli makes the same promise of speedy action on the recommendations of the disputation as the City Council (see 57D/fns. 5, 7, 9, and 12).

16. A reference to the one and only procedural decision made by the council so far (see 57D/fn.6).

17. The three prisoners following the Stadelhofen episode (57B/Intro.) were Claus Hottinger (see 47A/fn.4 and Cast of Characters No. 48), Lorenz Hochrütiner (see fn. 19, below, and Cast of Characters No. 45), and Hans Ockenfuss (see 63/fn.95 and Cast of Characters No. 71). The first was exiled for two years, the second for life, and the third was released.

18. As the next sentence indicates, Zwingli was not talking about the prisoners, whose acts of iconoclasm precipitated the second disputation, but about the devout Catholics who resisted any change in doctrine and practice, for whose sake consessions of time had to be made, especially those like Conrad Hofmann, Anshelm Graff, Rudolf Hoffman, Erhart Battmann, and Heinrich Nüscheler.

19. Lorenz Hochrütiner, a weaver from St. Gallen, living in Zurich since 1520 (see Cast of Characters No. 45 and Intro., above) was banished from the city just before this letter was written. The iconoclastic event that precipitated his banishment was an important juncture in the events leading to the coming "turning point" in the Zwinglian Reformation (see 58B, below). On Sept. 1, Leo Jud, pastor at St. Peter's, preached his impassioned sermon against the worship of images (see 57B). The first act of iconoclasm in Zurich occurred on Sept. 9 in consequence of that sermon. Then on Sept. 13, Hochrütiner and Ininger destroyed the "eternal lights" in the altar of the Fraumünster, for which they were imprisoned for three days. Then on Sept. 23, in response to a sermon against images by Simon Stumpf, pastor at Höngg near Zurich, Hochrütiner, Hottinger, and Ockenfuss dug up the large crucifix standing before the city gate at Stadelhofen. Adherents of the old order denounced the action as sacrilege and secured the arrest and imprisonment of the three offenders. Zwingli, as in the case of the earlier violators of the Lenten fast (see 47A/Intro), acknowledged the convictions behind the iconoclasm and visited the offenders in prison, whom he considered not as crimi-

nals but as overly zealous. When the case was tried in court shortly after the Second Zurich Disputation, the politics of the Reformation seemed to require stringent measures against the radicals. Although Hottinger was the main offender in the Stadelhofen incident, Hochrütiner was permanently banished from Zurich. With the letters of recommendation from Zwingli and Grebel, he returned to St. Gallen, where he soon began to promote Anabaptist doctrines.

20. "By Hercules," a mild oath by the name of the famous son of Zeus (see 27/fn.18).

21. Hochrütiner had previously been a citizen of St. Gallen and was thus returning to his hometown where other family members were still living.

22. Lat. *coram vestris*, lit. "in the presence of your [people]." The object of the preposition is understood, and Fast (Quellen 2, p. 331, fn.4) presumes that it was used as an equivalent of "before your council." Vadian had been a member of the Council since 1521.

23. Zwingli is quoting Phil. 1:8.

58. Grebel to Vadian, Zurich, November 12, 1523

1. On Hochrütiner, see 57F/fn.19 and Cast of Characters No. 45. Grebel refers to him as "brother" again in line 12, below (see fn. 5).

2. St. Gallen was his native land.

3. Lat. *illi pacatos,* "pacified to him" or "appeased toward him." "Senators" refers to the members of the Small Council.

4. The pronoun refers to Lorenz Hochrütiner, not to God.

5. It is significant that Grebel refers to him as his "brother" here and in line 2, above, while Zwingli only calls him a "good man," "a Christian," and an "excellent and innocent man" (57F/255/18-19, 27-28, 34). Goeters believes that in addressing him as a brother, "Grebel writes as the spokesman for a certain group. The person banished from the country becomes to Grebel one sent by them; and though separated in space, he remains a 'brother' of the close-knit group remaining in Zurich" (p. 273).

6. This was a frequent usage in Grebel's later court testimony (see 71D/421/17-18, 24-25, 422/11-12, 15-16, 21-22).

7. The pronoun refers to someone other than Hochrütiner, someone who carried fundamental responsibility for raising the issue of images and sought and used Hochrütiner's help. It might refer to Claus Hottinger, except that in the third phrase, a distinction is implied between the unidentified "he" and Hottinger. Goeters writes that "this can only refer to Zwingli, who in the eyes of Grebel has consequently become nothing but an accomplice of injustice" (p. 273). The present translation was made on this assumption that the pronoun refers to Zwingli, who had not actually "destroyed images himself," which is one possible translation of the verb *sustulit,* but had himself "raised" or "brought up" the question of images, which is another meaning of the verb. See also 65B/fn.27. At the Second Disputation he had brought all of his influence to bear to move in the direction of abolition, in principle first, and then in practice. It was the indefinite time gap between these two parts of the decision that prompted the radicals to take things into their own hands. In the letter of Nov. 11 to Vadian, quoted in fn. 1, above, Zwingli wrote that a committee "will shortly determine what will be done about the images, as soon as the people have been instructed; and the same with regard to the mass. In the meantime we are to go on in our wonted manner, except that it is permitted to any to remove his private images, as long as no one is injured."

8. Lat. *sculpta imagines.*

9. Claus Hottinger (see 47A/fn.4 and Cast of Characters No. 48), was one of the three participants in the destruction of the crucifix in Stadelhofen. For a thorough analysis of this episode, see Garside, pp. 119-22.

10. Lat. *statua.*

11. See 52/fn.5.

12. Lat. *tum patrum conscriptorum,* "also of the conscript fathers," or "of the members of the senate."

13. Lat. *templo idolis,* a more polemic designation for "images" and "statues," above.

14. See fn. 9, above.

15. 1 Cor. 12:6.
16. Mt. 10:30.
17. Mt. 10:29.
18. Prov. 16:9; Is. 42:16; Jn. 21:18.
19. The Second Disputation in Zurich held Oct. 26-29, 1523 (see 57C).
20. "Milord" refers to Vadian's role since 1521 as St. Gallen city councilman.
21. Vadian served as one of the presidents of the disputation.
22. Martha, Conrad's sister, Vadian's wife.
23. Benedict Burgauer, see Cast of Characters No. 11.
24. Wolfgang Wetter, see Cast of Characters No. 97.
25. Ernest Correll raised the question whether Grebel refers to Johannes Kessler as "the teacher"—the former student of Luther's who was influential in St. Gallen as a Bible teacher. If so, it would be the only reference in Grebel's letters to the St. Gallen chronicler of his own Anabaptist missionary activities. This identification, however, is impossible since Kessler did not return from Wittenberg until Dec. 9, 1523, nearly a month later. The "teacher" greeted by Grebel was probably Dominic Zili, schoolmaster in St. Gallen since 1521 (see Cast of Characters No. 104), who later assisted Kessler in the Bible study groups there (see 35/fn.19).

58A. Zwingli's "Introduction" to the Disputation Findings, Zurich, November 17, 1523
    1. See 57D, above.
    2. See 57D/fns. 5, 7, 9, and 12.
    3. See 57D/252/7-10.
    4. Ger. *sümmig oder widerwertig,* "careless or in opposition."
    5. See 57B and 57C, above.
    6. Ger. *Von abthŭn des gsatztes.* Zwingli is concerned in this article about both legitimate and illegitimate abrogation of laws.
    7. Ger *unverstendigen, oder eigenlicher: mŭtwilligen,* "uninformed, or more exactly rogues."
    8. Ger. *ungeschicklich [ungeschickt].*
    9. Ger. *ceremonien [Zeremonien].* See 51A/fn.16. "Zünselwercken oder kilchengespänsten" has a derogatory connotation difficult to translate into English.
    10. Ger. *ze tod schlahen.* The revolting claim that false prophets should be put to death is cited three times in the full text: ZW, II, pp. 650.24, 652.25, and 663.13. For evidence that Zwingli had Simon Stumpf in mind, see 71K/437/7-14. The charge was first mentioned without identification in Zwingli's October 1523 sermon, "The Shepherd" (ZW, III, p. 61), and repeated in his December 1524 tract on "Rebels and Rebellion" (see 67C/316/39) and in November 1525 court testimony (71K/see above). In the sermon, preached on the third day of the Second Disputation, he talked about how to deal with false shepherds and why the erroneous view of certain impetuous persons that they should be put to death in accordance with Deut. 13:5 and 18:20 was unbecoming to Christians. They should rather be disregarded and allowed to die in peace as they were born, for most of them are old and can no longer be recruited for the Reformation. Thomas Müntzer, in his July 1524 sermon, "Fürstenpredigt" [Sermon to the Princes], also quoted the Deut. 13:5 text in his allegation that priests, monks, and godless rulers should all be put to death; and it was the duty of Christian princes to do so! (See *Thomas Müntzer Schriften und Briefe* ed. Paul Kirn and Günther Franz, p. 259.
    11. Ex. 20:15.
    12. Ger. *falsch [Falschheit], wŭcher und varlicheit* [Gefährdung] *der zinsen.*
    13. Ger. *dieselben dennen tun [entfernen, beseitigen].*
    14. Ger. *wie sy har sind komen,* "as they came here."
    15. Zwingli condemned Stumpf for suggesting that unrepentant idolatrous priests be put to death on the basis of this verse, calling such an idea "unchristian" (see line 2, above); but he is citing the same passage in Deut. to legitimize government's authority to execute heretics.
    16. Ger. *hyndurch trucken.*

17. See Mt. 6:23.

18. Cf. Amos 1:1.

19. See 49/fn.8.

20. Written by Ludwig Hätzer (see 57C/fn.3 and Cast of Character No. 43).

21. Zwingli had just reaffirmed that "God has forbidden all images and paintings" (57C/fn.5), but now he makes an exception in reply to his conservative critics who cited 1 Kings 6:1, that Solomon "had cherubim, palms, and many kinds of paintings made for the temple" and that therefore "it is doubtless also fitting for us to have such paintings or pictures" (ZW, II, p. 658.)

22. Ger. *geschichteswyss,* "historical representations." Garside writes: "What Zwingli intended by the word *geschichteswyss* is not precisely clear from its immediate context, but its implications may in great part be explained by a significant passage from the later *Answer to Valentin Compar.* Within the Great Minster there stood an altar panel on which was painted a kneeling Charlemagne, together with a replica of the Minster. Outside the Great Minster there had been set in a niche high up on the so-called Charles tower a statue of Charlemagne seated on his throne. Of these works of art Zwingli wrote to Compar: 'We have had two great Charleses: the one in the Great Minster, which was venerated like other idols, and for that reason was taken out; the other in one of the church towers, which no one venerates, and that one was left standing, and has caused no annoyance at all' (ZW, IV, 95.18-21, 96.1). The painting, merely because it stood within the Minster, was potentially capable of a religious interpretation, whereas the statue outside was not. The former, moreover, represented Charlemagne in a religious role, as legendary founder of a church; the latter represented him in a secular role, as legendary founder of a city. Consequently, the altar painting belonged to that category of images which for Zwingli 'have clearly given birth to the danger of idolatry,' whereas the statue was a pertinent example of the purely secular representational art to which he had no objection. Yet almost as if reiterating his earlier statement in *A Brief Christian Introduction,* Zwingli pointedly warned that with regard even to the statue of Charlemagne on the tower 'as soon as anyone goes astray also with idolatry, then that, too, will be taken away' (ZW, IV, 96.1-2)."

23. Ger. *gesandtes opfer.*

24. Ger. *das neissen [geniessen].*

58B. The Turning Point in the Zwinglian Reformation, Zurich, between December 10 and 19, 1523

1. December 10.

2. Ger. *Propst und Capitel,* i.e., the ruling canons of the cathedral chapter and their provost or administrative head.

3. Ger. *Jahrzeitbücher,* the mass-annuals containing the daily readings and liturgies for the church year.

4. Ger. *Endlich habe man ihr Halseisen genommen und an den Fischmarkt getragen, dazu den Galgen umgehauen.* The details of this demonstration are not available, but it was patently a challenge to the existing practices of torture and capital punishment in Zurich, and thus a serious challenge to the authority of the state to use these methods of enforcement.

5. The reference is to the end-of-October mandate (see 57D).

6. This was done on Dec. 13 (see the next document).

7. Ger. *dass Uebertreter "gestrax" gestraft werden.* Actually, the earlier mandate contained the wording, "And whoever behaves improperly or disobediently in word or deed in this matter our lords will punish severely . . . " but the present mandate was strengthened in this respect by the word *gestrax* (see fn. 12, below). This means implementation without delay or the usual legal formalities. This kind of expedited disposition was justified only in special cases.

8. Guildmaster Rudolf Thumysen, a member of the Large Council, was a bell founder by trade, a close friend of Zwingli with whom he died at Cappel in 1531. He was often used as a council delegate on commissions concerning the abolition of the monasteries, etc.

9. Conrad Escher *vom Luchs* was a member of the *Constafel,* a political organization identified with the ancient families of Zurich's noble and merchant class. They were strongly represented in the Small Council and in general represented the more conservative element in the city in alliance with the canons of the cathedral. Sometime after June 15, 1525, when her first marriage to John Jacob Ammann was annulled, Dorothy Grebel, Conrad's youngest sister, was married to Escher. She was only 16 years of age, having been first married at the age of 15.

10. This mandate was essentially the same as the October mandate (see 57D), except for three significant shifts mentioned in fn. 1, above.

11. Ger. *diser verruckter tagen.*

12. Ger. *solichem gebott und ansehen gestrax.* See fn. 7, above, for the meaning of the word *gestrax,* here translated "summary," meaning "done without delay or formality."

13. Heinrich Engelhart, see 47/fn.3 and Cast of Characters No. 19.

13a. It is assumed that the memorandum was written by Zwingli himself, and indeed its language bears this out.

14. It is assumed that the memorandum was written by Zwingli himself, and indeed its language bears this out.

15. Leo Jud, see 52/fn.4 and Cast of Characters No. 58.

16. Apparently, some loyal papists in Zurich had argued that nothing should be added tion, but see 57C/246/5-6 where Zwingli used the same argument.

17. Mt. 15:13.

18. In the mass as practiced, the wafer was administered to the laity but not the cup of wine, which only the priest drank (see 57B/fn.5).

19. 1 Cor. 11:26.

20. Ger. *unnd ob man unns den glich nüt erloubti, müssent wir beide, lichnam unnd blůt, brott unnd win, den begerenden reichen,* which J. H. Yoder translates as "and even if it should not be permitted, we must offer both body and blood, bread and wine to those who so desire" (1958, p. 136). It is doubtful that Zwingli was saying, as Yoder thinks, that he would go ahead to celebrate the new evangelical communion in place of the mass on Christmas Day "whether the council so desires or not" (p. 136). Rather, he was saying that if the council objected to replacing the mass with the new communion by that time, he would at least insist on giving the cup to the laity along with the wafer *within the liturgy of the mass* (see Goeters, p. 278). This was precisely the extent of the gains he won when the council delegates to the commission did so object, as the fourth document, below—"The Alternative Opinion"—indicates: "That the people's priests shall give to all who desire it this holy sacrament of the mass . . . with the bread and wine." A difference in the degree of determination still exists between the two memoranda, but it is not as contrasting as Yoder indicated.

21. Ger. *oder aber lügenhafftig bei dem wortt gottes stan.* Walton translated this "or appear untrue to the Word of God" (p. 202). The preposition *bei* requires a more emphatic declaration.

22. Another indicator of the turning point in Zwingli's Reformation was the shift in frequency in the celebration of communion. The December memoranda provided for its daily celebration, but such frequency thereafter was "less important than maintaining the unity of the whole people through uniform religious observance" (Yoder, 1958, p. 139).

23. Still another indicator of Zwingli's turning point, more important than the criterion of frequency, was the principle of tolerance. The memoranda here and subsequently clearly specifies that no force is to be used to compel a uniformity of observance. If the progressive priests are not to be forced to say mass, the "lethargic priests" are not to be forced to quit saying it. Within months this gives way to the necessity of uniformity in a magisterial church, and "persecution becomes a theological necessity" (Yoder, 1958, p. 140).

24. The predicted shift from administrative to pastoral assignments for ordained clergy did occur for a number of canons in the Grossmünster Chapter.

25. On Zwingli's principle of tolerance at this time, see fn. 20, above.

26. Rom. 8:31.

27. Ger. *Die ander meinung.* In view of the contrasting content of the two memoranda,

670

as indicated by the opening words of this one, "The other opinion," or even "The second opinion" would not be contrasting enough. The "alternative opinion" was the compromise decision of the commission members listed in 269/14-15, above, and the three people's priests—Zwingli, Engelhart, and Jud.

28. Heb. 5:14; 1 Cor. 3:1ff.

29. See fns. 16 and 17, above.

30. This alternative memorandum had some of the same wording as the first, but expressed with very different assumptions. The phrase "without delay" is contradicted by the phrase "for awhile yet" in the very next sentence.

31. Zwingli's new policy of compromise is clearly in contrast to the determination of his first memorandum (see 58A/III).

32. 1 Cor. 13:7.

33. The three people's priests plus those named in 57F/254/31ff—fourteen persons in all.

34. The point of unanimity is made because the previous (alternative) opinion concerning the mass was not unanimous. In spite of the unanimity, it was the decision of the council (see below) to take no action about the images until Pentecost; and it was not until the end of June when the images were actually removed (see Garside, pp. 159-60).

35. These were panels of pictures near the altar, so constructed that they were hung by hinges and could be opened or closed by rotation.

36. This refers to the silver gilt busts of Saints Felix and Regula and similar reliquaries, carried in procession to the Lindenhof and back every Palm Sunday and Pentecost (see 47A/ fn.2 and Garside, p. 152).

37. For the identity of some of these reactionary priests, see 57F/fn.18.

38. The "two different proposals" could refer either to the two memoranda III and IV, above, concerning the mass, or to memoranda IV and V, which were the ones adopted by the council. The latter meaning is probably intended because "images" and "the mass" are expressly mentioned.

39. Not only was the traditional mass retained but even the request in the commission's "Alternative Opinion" that both elements (bread and wine) be given to the communicant was not approved.

40. A "Third Disputation" involving the canons of the Grossmünster, the members of the two city councils, and all the clergy of the city, was held on Monday, Dec. 28, for further discussion of the problem of images and the mass. The one-day session resulted only in the call for yet another disputation on Jan. 19-20 between the three people's priests and the adherents of the Old Church party.

41. The promise to resolve the problem by next Pentecost, five months after the Christmas Day communion service promised by Zwingli in Memorandum III, above, was not kept. The actual reform of the mass in Zurich was not completed until April 11, 1525, and it was this indefinite postponement which first became evident in December 1523 that was the "turning point in the Zwinglian Reformation."

59. Grebel to Vadian, Zurich, December 18, 1523

1. This is an interesting reversal in role of complainant for not having written (compare with 18/108/20-31), perhaps another sign of Grebel's changing self-identity.

2. The name-calling, so common in the subsequent conflicts of 1524 and 1525, began at this point when Grebel began to be labeled by loyal Zwinglians as suspect and the Grebel group in turn began to indict Zwingli as a liar. As Hans Hottinger later put it, "Today he preaches one thing and tomorrow he retracts it" (68I/348/26-28).

3. "His indignation at Zwingli's present compromise has led Grebel to see as well that its seeds were already present in October, namely, in the utterly unrealistic distinction between matters of principle and of application which had been accepted there" (J. H. Yoder, 1958, p. 138). On one hand, Zwingli kept reiterating his new understanding, so clearly enunciated in the *Einleitung* ("Introduction") published November 17 that the Lord's Supper is not a sacrifice to be repeated by a commemoration of a sacrifice given once and for all (see

58A). But on the other hand, while concluding that the old practice of the mass was an abuse that should be abolished, he continued to celebrate it, warning that its abolition should be done so cautiously that it would not prompt a disturbance. As early as August 29, in his *Treatise on the Canon of the Mass*, he had issued the outline of a new evangelical communion liturgy to replace the liturgy of the mass; yet he continued to sing the Latin mass. In his *Apology for the Tract on the Mass Canon*, he had to defend himself against the charge that he kept using the old liturgy out of deference to the weak (see 57A.201/1ff.). No doubt Grebel was temporarily reassured by his numerous statements to the contrary and by the repeated promises in the end-of-October Council Mandate for an expeditious implementation of the disputation resolutions; but by Dec. 18 he could see in retrospect that the gap between principle and practice had existed at least as early as October.

4. Vadian had served as one of the presidents at the disputation in October.

5. For the identity of these Councillors, see 57D/fn.3.

6. Lat. *Zinlio, commendatori*. Muralt and Schmid (Quellen, p. 8, fn. 3) are probably in error in concluding that the comma in the text indicates two persons and supposing that the *commendatori* refers to the Comtur of Küssnacht (see Cast of Characters No. 83) who was also on the commission. It is more likely that it refers to the special assignment given to Zwingli to "write a brief introduction to the council's order ... by means of which those bishops [ruling pastors] who had hitherto either been ignorant of Christ, or had been turned away from him, should be induced to begin to preach him" (see 57F/254/10-13 and 57F/fn.9).

7. The abbot of Cappel was Wolfgang Joner (see 57F/fn.4 and Cast of Characters No. 57).

8. The provost of Embrach was Heinrich Brennwald (see 57F/fn. 5 and Cast of Characters No. 8).

9. Lat. *monstris rasis*. The adjective refers to the Roman Catholic rite of admission to the clerical state by the clipping or shaving of the head. Also included on the commission were Conrad Schmid, the commander of the Monastery at Küssnacht, and the other two people's priests in Zurich—Leo Jud of St. Peter's and Heinrich Englehart of the Fraumünster.

10. The "middle ground" to which Grebel refers was the commission's compromise memorandum which Grebel had probably just seen (see 58B/IV, above).

11. Lat. *prudentia diabolica* is Grebel's first reference to a concept developed further in his later German letters (63/fn.17), where he calls it *falsch shonen* (false forbearance).

12. For the council's action on Dec. 19, see 58B/V, above. Grebel apparently had a premonition or some inside information a day in advance of the action that was taken.

13. On the morning of the third day of the October Dispuation, Zwingli had preached to the entire assembly on the subject, "The Shepherd" (ZW, III, pp. 1-68). It was an ardent appeal to the pastors present to give themselves to the cause of the Reformation as shepherds give up their lives for their sheep. As Yoder indicates (1958, p. 138, fn. 31), "Grebel's use of the term, 'shepherd,' is in all probability a direct play on the theme of Zwingli's October sermon."

59A. The Grebel-Stumpf Alternative Plan of a Separatist Church, Zurich, before December 23, 1523

1. The name of Felix Mantz is deliberately omitted, although the *Täuferprozess* of Nov. 9, 1525 (see 71K/437/25ff.), refers to him in a way that could be interpreted as participating in the Alternative Plan along with Grebel and Stumpf. However, Krajewsky (pp. 29-31, 37, 40-41) doubts that Mantz was present at the Second Zurich Disputation and believes that he became involved only after Stumpf had been banished from Zurich in late December 1523. If this is true, he would not have been party to the earliest version of the Stumpf-Grebel Alternative Plan.

2. The reference to Simon Stumpf of Höngg in 71K/436/29 (see Intro., above) establishes a *terminus ante* for the event that Zwingli describes in the present account, since it must have occurred prior to Dec. 23, 1523, when Stumpf was expelled from the canton of

Zurich (see Cast of Characters No. 85). There is no definite *terminus post* in the excerpt; but the alternative plan of reform would hardly have been presented prior to the Second Disputation in October, and the sequence of subsequent events makes it most likely that it was presented as part of the negotiations chronicled in 58B and particularly as an alternative to Zwingli's compromise memorandum.

3. Lat. *sectam.* Zwingli first used this term in the Second Disputation when he expressed the hope that through the preaching of the Word "all sects, rabble, and orders together with other abuses would be rejected" (57C/240/2-3). It was mostly after 1525, however, that he used the term; and the listing of usages found in ZW, VI, 23/fn.1, reveals that for Zwingli the essence of the sectarian is the arbitrariness with which he undertakes innovations in the church without consulting the whole congregation (see 69C/364/28ff.).

4. As indicated in the Intro., above, this is one of three accounts which Zwingli wrote of the origin of the Anabaptists. All three reports begin with a similar preface and follow a similar formula, e.g., "In the first place, that Anabaptism is a sect or gang is clearly seen because their origin has shown this" (ZW, IV, p. 590.3).

5. The identity of the leaders, as indicated in the Intro., above, is revealed in Zwingli's court testimony of November 9, 1525 (see 71K/436/29-437/25). In addition to Grebel and Stumpf, there is slight evidence that Felix Mantz was also involved in this earlier approach (71K/437/25ff.), but see fn. 1, above.

6. In the trial of Grebel *et al.* of November 1525, Zwingli testified that in addition to himself, the leaders also approached Leo Jud (71K/436/30, 437/3, 30).

7. Lat. *constanter,* "consistently." The clear implication is that the approaches were plural. This is confirmed in Zwingli's *Taufbüchlein:* "Those who initiated the strife of Anabaptism had previously often urged us to begin a new church" (69C/363/33-35) and also in Zwingli's court testimony, "Thus Grebel and Simon [Stumpf] talked to him more than once . . . " (71K/437/23-24).

8. This sentence seems to refer back to a sentence in the December memorandum concerning images, i.e., "some priests in our city continually oppose it [the Word of God] with seditious, erroneous, unfounded words . . . when they can produce nothing out of God's Word" (58B/274/12-17). For the identity of some of these "gospel-resisters," see 57F/fn.18.

9. This presupposition speaks directly to the situation of December 1523 when the disunity in Zurich over Reformation procedures had reached a crisis. The Grebel-Stumpf claim, according to Zwingli, is that the resistance of some to the mandates of Scripture should not be permitted to obstruct the obedience of others.

10. The claim of superiority which Zwingli heard in connection with the Grebel-Stumpf plan was probably a superiority in numbers, as indicated in the following paper, lines 7-8. Such a claim would find some confirmation in Roland Bainton's comment that "Anabaptism, if unimpeded by the sword of the magistrate, might have become the prevailing form of the church in Germany" (Hershberger, p. 320).

11. Lat. *Iam ecclesiam piorum suis, iisque piis, senatum suum lecturam esse votis.* That Zwingli seems to have interpreted the Grebel-Stumpf plan as a political strategy for the election of a new City Council made up only of committed Christians who would govern in a thoroughly Christian manner is confirmed by his other accounts: "First they reject the state; then they want to keep the state, and yet no one in government is a Christian" (67C/316/35-37) and "From all this he could come to no other conclusion than that it was their ultimate idea that they were daring to increase their numbers in order to do away with government" (71K/438/4-6). Fritz Blanke accepts these accounts as true to fact (pp. 11-13). There is nothing in the present text, however, to warrant Zwingli's claim or Blanke's conclusion regarding it. It is just as possible to interpret the Grebel-Stumpf plan as the first signs, however embryonic, of a new vision for the separation of church and state. When Grebel demanded at the Second Disputation that the assembly should give immediate directions to the pastors concerning the mass, Zwingli replied that the council would decide how the mass should henceforth be celebrated, whereupon Stumpf declared that he had no right to give the judgment into the hands of the council (57C/242/26-30). This comment clearly implies that participation by the secular authorities in the decisions of the church is to be rejected. Seen as a

follow-up of this view, the Grebel-Stumpf plan is that the faithful church should elect its own council to make its own decisions. The issue in question is whether or not it was their intention that this church-elected council should replace the secular council. Apparently Zwingli thought that it was; but at his trial in November 1523, Grebel claimed that it had never been his intention "that one should not be obedient to the authorities" (71K/439/32).

12. Lat. *Palam enim esse, quam multi sint et in senatu et in haec promiscua ecclesia impii.* In his other accounts, Zwingli claimed that the proto-Anabaptists demanded a church of sinless people (69C/363/36, 71K/436/28-32, 71K/437/26-28). His account from the *Elenchus* says nothing about sinlessness but talks rather of the demand for an *ecclesia piorum* (church of believers; see fn. 11, above). There are demands in the other accounts which are not mentioned in the present one: abolition of taxes, execution of the priests, community of goods, the duty of the people's priests to confer (71K/436/31-32, 437/8, 23-24, 30-32). In the present account, Zwingli restricts himself to the main demand for an *ecclesia piorum*. For his fuller refutation of this concept of the church, see Jackson, 1901, p. 241.7-11.

13. Lat. *respondebamus,* the imperfect tense implying repeated replies.

14. Mk. 9:40. It is uncertain in the text whether the quotation ends here or at the end of the next paragraph. The paragraph divisions in our translation are not in the original text.

15. Mt. 13:27ff. For an interesting analysis of "The Parable of the Tares as the Proof Text for Religious Liberty to the End of the Sixteenth Century," see the article by Roland Bainton in *Church History* (June 1932), pp. 77ff. It is interesting that Zwingli compares the tares to the unbelievers within the church from whom one should not separate rather than with heretics whom he was very ready not only to excommunicate but also to execute.

16. Zwingli's apprehension is also mentioned in the Klettgau/Cologne letter (68F/342/7-9).

17. This comment probably refers to the claim that Zwingli heard in the Grebel-Stumpf plan (see lines 14-15 of the previous page) that in time a church of believers would outnumber the magisterial church in Zurich. Here, Zwingli accepts the goal of a church of believers, but rejects the idea that the goal should be reached through separation rather than through a faithful proclamation of the Word in the magisterial church.

18. Lat. *etsi humanum ab eis nihil alienum.* This is a suppressed quotation from the *Hautontimoroumenos* of Terence, Roman comic playwright of the second century BC (I.1.25:*Homo sum; humani nil a me alienum puto.)* ("I am a man, and deem nothing that relates to man alien to my feelings.")

19. See 2 Chron. 17:7ff. It is characteristic for Zwingli to return to the Old Testament for a biblical basis to his doctrine of church and state.

20. Mt. 25:1ff.

60. Grebel to Vadian, Zurich, February 26, 1524

1. For the resolution that emerged from the meetings on January 19-20, see B. J. Kidd, No. 201, p. 442.

2. Beda Miles, a citizen of St. Gallen in whose house (or woodworking shop) a Bible study group of about twelve persons was assembled with Johannes Kessler as "reader." Kessler had returned in December from the University of Wittenberg, where he had studied with Luther. Beda Miles was a radical in Reformation activities, a strong opponent of Roman Catholic practices, and a participant in the first act of iconoclasm in St. Gallen in 1524. He was identified with the Anabaptist movement from 1525 to 1532. Several scholars have conjectured that he was a nephew of Hermann Miles, the chronicler, or perhaps his illegitimate son (see Fast, 1973, No. 405, fn. 6). The relationship between Grebel and Miles and between Miles and Vadian, alluded to here, is not clear. Fast describes the role of Miles in the context of this letter as a *Verbürgsmann,* one who answers or vouches for another.

3. Zwingli had written to Vadian two days earlier (see ZW, VII, No. 327) and it is possible that their letters were carried by the same messenger.

4. Conrad Eppenberg, mentioned in Kessler's *Sabbata* (pp. 360/22 and 370/45) was one of Vadian's friends. See 65/fn.1 and 68/fn.11.

5. Ulysses was famous for his energy and endurance. After the fall of Troy he wandered in far parts of the earth for ten years before returning home.

6. Lat.*artifice tondendorum pannorum,* "skilled in clipping rags."

7. Lorenz Hochrütiner, see 57F/fn.19 and Cast of Characters No. 45.

8. The daughter born to Vadian and Martha the previous August (see 56/fn.6).

61. Grebel to Vadian, Zurich, July 31, 1524

1. Dorothy, Conrad's sister, had been married just a month earlier (June 26) at the age of 15 to John Jacob Ammann (see line 16 and Cast of Characters No. 35). This marriage was annulled by the Zurich courts on June 15, 1525. See 45/fn.11.

2. On John Jacob Ammann, see 35/fn.16 and Cast of Characters No. 3.

62. Grebel to Vadian, Zurich, September 3, 1524

1. See fn. 22, below.

2. Michael was probably the traveling companion mentioned in line 6, who delivered the letter of Grebel when the latter decided not to go to St. Gallen. See also 62/284/20. Although Michael's identity cannot be definitely known, in April 1526 Zwingli expresses concern about Grebel's influence upon Michael Wüst, a cousin of Heinrich Bullinger (see 71P/454/11).

3. See fn. 22, below.

4. This is the first of a dozen references in later letters to Andreas Rudolf Bodenstein Carlstadt (see Cast of Characters No. 12). Grebel had evidently written previously to Carlstadt, whereas he was writing "for the first time" to Thomas Müntzer (see fn. 5, below); and Carlstadt had evidently sent a response, to which Grebel was now "writing a reply." Unfortunately, none of these letters has been preserved.

5. Unlike Grebel's letters to Carlstadt and Luther (see fn. 7, below), his letter to Müntzer plus a lengthy postscript (see Letters 63 and 64, below) are extant. On Thomas Müntzer, see Cast of Characters No. 69.

6. Grebel had procured and read two recent pamphlets by Müntzer (see 63/285/33-34): *Von dem getichten blawben auff nechst Protestation ausgeganzen Tome Münzers seelwarters zu Alsted,* 1524 (Hans Hillerbrand suggests the English title, "On Phony Faith"; see 63/fn.7) and *Protestation odder empiettung Tome Münzer von Stolberg am Hartz seelwarters zu Alstedt seine leren betreffende unnd tzum anfang von dem rechten Christen blawben unnd der tawffe,* 1524 ("Protestation or Declaration"). The reference here is to the former.

7. Martin Luther (see Cast of Characters No. 65) had returned from the Wartburg in March 1522 to resume the leadership of the Reformation in Wittenberg. High on his priority of goals was to reverse trends toward evangelical radicalism initiated by some of his colleagues and to prevent further religious and social acts of revolution by formulating and implementing a doctrine of submission to constituted secular authorities in the matter of religious innovations, including the concepts of gradual reform of beliefs and institutions and the unacceptability of radicalism in the work of the Reformation. He wrote a number of pamphlets along these lines that angered the more radical reformers, such as his *Warning Against Tumult and Revolt* (1922), *On the Civil Power* (1523), *Letter to the Princes of Saxony Concerning the Rebellious Spirit* (1524), and *Against the Murderous and Thieving Peasant Bands* (1525). Through these writings the peasants, who had previously believed that his appeal to the New Testament was an appeal to the social ethics of the Sermon on the Mount, now came to believe that the new Protestantism protested less against their socio-religious oppressors than against the oppressed. As Letter 63 will indicate, Grebel was less interested in Luther's social conservatism than in his theological conservatism. That he actually wrote to Luther is documented in 67E/331/2-6, and Hegenwald's letter to Grebel (67E) is in part a reply to Grebel's letter to Luther.

8. Grebel first mentioned his tutoring activity in 56/226/2-3 (see 56/fn.13). His reference to "interpreting" and "prophesying" implies a distinction between tutoring for hire and teaching the faith in Paul's charismatic terms (see Rom. 12:6; 1 Cor. 12:10; Eph. 4:11).

9. The editor of VB reports that the words between the dashes were written in the margin of the original.

10. As shown by Fast, 1962, 456-75, the passages which Grebel was assembling on the two themes of faith and baptism were published under the posthumous name of Hans Krüsi sometime after July 27, 1525, the date of the latter's execution (see 71E and 71F). According to Krüsi's final testimony, Grebel had given him a handwritten manuscript, probably a copy of the passages here referred to (see 69A/360/35-37). See also 69/358/12-14.

11. What follows is a verbatim quotation of Job 32:16-22 out of the Latin Vulgate with one exception noted in fn. 12.

12. Grebel substitutes *dei* (God) for *meam* (my) in quoting Job 32:17b.

13. Lat. *spiritus uteri,* "spirit in my belly [womb]."

14. Lat. *venter,* meaning stomach, belly, or womb.

15. Lat. *personam viri,* "mask of man," as in theater, or "humanity of man," as in theological vocabulary.

16. The Greek phrase was written in the margin of the letter and was perhaps a paraphrase of Jer. 25:34.

17. In what follows Grebel is quoting almost verbatim from the Latin Vulgate version of Dan. 9:27b. On the apocalyptic influence in this comment by Grebel, see 64/fn.25.

18. Grebel is quoting from the Latin Vulgate version of Ezek. 34:18b-19a, the first verse verbatim (except *bibant* for *biberetis)* and the second verse more loosely paraphrased. See also 65/296/8-10.

19. The rest of the paragraph is a paraphrase of Isa. 30:1-3 from the Latin Vulgate.

20. This is the first mention of Barbara, his wife, since 51/195/12. In fact, the last mention of her by name was 47/165/5, reporting his marriage. Even his report of the birth of their second child (56/225/28-30) makes no mention of her. The present reference indicates her growing hostility toward Conrad's activities. This will be more evident in 69/357/14-18.

21. Concerning Grebel's chronic ill health, see 4/fn.3, 6/fn.34, and 63/fn.101.

22. In spite of Grebel's loss of hope in his father (56/225/33-35), it is obvious in the present letter that he is still dependent on and to a certain degree subservient to his counsel and support.

23. See fn. 2, above.

24. On the value of *Batzen,* see 48/fn.4 and Quellen 2, p. 722.

63. Grebel to Müntzer, Zurich, September 5, 1524

1. For an analysis of the points of agreement and disagreement between Grebel and Müntzer as revealed in this letter, see Bender, 1950, pp. 171-83.

2. In this opening sentence, Grebel was quoting the introductory verses of Paul's letters to Timothy and Titus. See 1 Tim. 1:2b; 2 Tim. 1:2b; and Titus 1:4b.

3. Grebel employs the plural pronoun because he was speaking for a group of persons named in 292/8-9 and 294/7-8.

4. Concerning Grebel's previous references to the lordship of Jesus Christ, see 51/fn.19.

5. This ecumenical note contradicts the frequent charge of Zwingli that Grebel and the Swiss Brethren were separatists and schismatics (see 69C/363/33, 69D/375/33, etc.).

6. Ger. *Artikel,* translated "points" by Rauschenbusch and Williams, and "articles" by Wenger. Grebel uses the term in two ways: as a general term for faith "issues" (286/13,25 293/13-14) and as a specific term for listed or numbered programmatic "theses" (285/33, 293/15-16). The latter style of dialogue is reminiscent of the numbered theses of Luther and Zwingli.

7. For the full titles of these two Müntzer tracts, see 62/fn.6. The translation "phony faith" was suggested by Hans Hillerbrand in his volume, *A Fellowship of Discontent,* p. 10.

8. Ger. *götlichen brüchen,* translated "divine institutions" by Rauschenbusch and Williams and "divine rites" by Wenger. For the word *brüchen* Rauschenbusch used four renderings: institutions, customs, practices, and usages. There are at most two meanings that need to be distinguished. The word "rites" has been used when Grebel's reference was specifically to the ordinances (sacraments), i.e., baptism or the Lord's Supper (285/4-6, 288/34, 291/24-25, 293/36). Otherwise, the word "practices" was used (285/39-40, 286/3, 31-32, 34, 287/1, 288/40, and 289/5-6). In the latter cases, however, it is still probable that Grebel was thinking specifically of the mandated ordinances of the church.

9. Ger. *unchristlichen brüchen,* translated "unchristian customs" by Rauschenbusch and "unchristian rites" by Wenger. Compare this reference with 286/4, 26, 288/34, 36, and 295/24-25 in which several words with similar but distinct meanings are used. The words *unchristlichen* or *widerkristlich* are here rendered by the informal adjective "unchristian." The words *Endkristlichen* or *Endkristen,* usually capitalized in the original, are rendered "Antichristian" or "Antichrists." The latter indicates a more resolute attitude against not only Roman Catholic but also Lutheran and Zwinglian rites and practices. It was a denunciation of Luther and Zwingli for perpetuating traditions considered to be apostate.

10. Ger. *in glichsendem glouben,* which Rauschenbusch translated "by superficial faith" and Wenger translated "by a make-believe faith." See also 286/40 and compare the reference in 287/2 to *usserlichen schinenden glouben,* "outward appearing faith."

11. See fn. 9, above.

12. This is the first reference in Grebel's letters to the issue of baptism which later became the symbolic point of dissension between the Reformers and Anabaptists. See 63/290/20ff.

13. Ger. *in verachtung dess götlichen worts, in achtung dess bepstlichen,* one of the numerous wordplays in Grebel's letters, better preserved by "dishonoring . . . honoring" than by Wenger's "despising . . . following." Rauschenbusch had "in disrespect for the divine word and in respect for the word of the pope."

14. Grebel used this same figure of speech in later court testimony. See 71K/439/30.

15. The word "shepherds" is used for *hirten* instead of "pastors" because a free church functional usage is intended, rather than a tradition, vocational usage. In some subsequent references to "the learned shepherds" (63/289/15, 64/293/18-19, 65/296/6-7) an ironical meaning was intended.

16. Ger. *götlichen wäsens.* Grebel may have meant to say *gotlos* rather than *götlichen.* The text can be read either way.

17. Grebel's first reference to the concept of *falsch schonen* (see 57A/Intro.), translated "false caution" by Williams and by Wenger, was found in 59/276/9-10, where he used the Latin phrase *prudentia diabolica* ("diabolical prudence"). See 59/fn.8. He refers to this concept six more times in the letters to Müntzer (see 286/26, 288/37, 289/36-37, 292/14, 26, and 293/18-19) and twice in a later letter to Vadian (67/302/19, 21-22). The concept was used earlier by Müntzer in his "Sermon Before the Princes," the full title of which was "Exposition of the Second Chapter of Daniel the Prophet Preached at the Castle of Allstedt Before the Active and Amiable Dukes and Administrators of Saxony by Thomas Müntzer, Minister of the Word of God" (Allstedt, July 13, 1524), and it seems likely that Grebel was intentionally elaborating on Müntzer's concept. The concept is a relational term; hence, Williams' "false caution" is too general. It connotes more than the "unworthy diminishing of the demands for total obedience and discipleship" (Wenger, 1970, p. 12). It is also a rebuke of the gross inconsistency with which the Reformers "spared" the laity in the churches but not the radicals. See 57A/fn.2 and 67/fn.28.

18. *Protestation . . . von dem rechten Christenglawben unnd der tawffe,* 1524, "Protestation . . . Concerning the Right Christian Faith and Baptism." See 62/fn.6 and 63/fn.7.

19. The twenty-five theses appeared partly in written and partly in numeral form, and Nos. 1, 8, and 12 were not indicated. Theses 1-9 deal with liturgical singing or chanting, 10-25 with the Lord's Supper.

20. Grebel had evidently read Müntzer's three *Messordnungen* ("Liturgies of the

Mass"), reprinted in Sehling, pp. 472-507 with the titles: (1) *Deutsch Kirchenampt,* Allstedt, 1523; (2) *Deutsch Evangelische Messe,* Allstedt, 1524; and (3) *Ordnung und Verechnunge des teutschen Amptes zu Alstadt,* Eylenburg, 1524. It is evident that these publications made less impression on Grebel than the two previously mentioned tracts on false faith.

21. Ger. *nüwe tütsche gsang.* This is the first of twelve references to the *Gesang* or *Singen* which Rauschenbusch translated "hymns" and "singing," with particular reference to the liturgical mass. These words could also be validly translated "chants" and "chanting," as does Williams (1957, p. 76, line 6), especially if what Grebel was criticizing was the priestly *Gesang* rather than the congregational *Gesang.* In his translation, Wenger inserts "liturgical" in brackets before "singing" (see p. 23, 1. 116). For a helpful discussion of this matter, see Garside, pp. 58-60. He points out that Müntzer had accepted Carlstadt's challenge to prepare a choral liturgy to be sung in the vernacular by his congregation at Allstedt. But because of the low state of congregational singing in Zurich at this time, which Garside also describes (pp. 17-22), it is not likely that Grebel was protesting specifically against congregational singing, but against the retention of liturgical music of any kind, including the Gregorian chants and the choral polyphony performed by monks and nuns and professional choirs. In the diocese in which Zurich was located, it had long been "forbidden for laymen to sing in public congregations as it is forbidden to them to preach and to expound Scripture" (p. 21); and rather than move in the direction of congregational singing in the vernacular, Grebel preferred to discard the ecclesiastical *Gesang* altogether on the assumption of a total incompatibility between the traditional singing practices and the new evangelical consciousness. In most of his arguments against liturgical singing, he was simply reiterating Zwingli's theses 44, 45, and 46 of Jan. 19, 1523 (see Meyer, pp. 44-47), his subsequent exposition of them in the *Schlussreden* of July 14, 1523 (see ZW, II, 18-19), his *Defense of the Booklet on the Mass Canon* (57A/228/27ff.), and comments he made at the Second Disputation (57C/246/8-14, 25-27).

22. Ger. *singen.* Except by gross error in biblical interpretation, Grebel could not have meant "singing" in view of such New Testament references as Mk. 14:26; Acts 16:25; Rom. 15:9; 1 Cor. 14:13; Eph. 5:19; Col. 3:16; Jas. 5:13; Heb. 2:12; and Rev. 5:9. Grebel himself refers to three of these passages in the following arguments.

23. Grebel was referring to 1 Cor. 14:9, 16, a passage Zwingli also quoted on the same subject (see 57C/246/10).

24. Eph. 5:19. Bender (1950, p. 176), assuming that Grebel was arguing that Paul forbade singing, concluded that Grebel "felt it necessary to find scriptural proofs for a position which cannot be supported from Scripture." If, on the other hand, it was chanting, not singing, that Grebel was arguing against, his argument is quite valid: Paul's admonition to sing "to the Lord with all your heart" is indeed a corrective to liturgical chanting.

25. Col. 3:16.

26. In his exposition of thesis 45 (ZW, II, p. 18), Zwingli also referred to Col. 3:16, and said, "Here Paul does not teach us mumbling and murmuring in the churches, but shows us the true song that is pleasing to God, that we sing the praise and glory of God not with our voices, like the Jewish singers, but with our hearts" (tr. Garside, p. 59).

27. This hermeneutical principle came from Zwingli (57A/230/13-14, 57C/239/35-36, 246/5-6), who later rejected it (Epi.C/485/28ff.). The fact is that he had earlier invoked this same principle against liturgical singing in his exposition of Thesis No. 45 (see fns. 21 and 26, above).

28. Ger. *Christus heisst sine botten allein dass wort uss predigen.* Wenger placed *allein* with *botten* ("only command") and Rauschenbusch placed *allein* with *predigen* ("simply proclaim"). It is more accurate and literal to render it "preach only the Word."

29. See fn.25, above, regarding Col. 3:16.

30. In the latter phrase Grebel was echoing Zwingli's Thesis No. 46, "From this follows that singing in church or crying out without devotion and only for merit stems either from a search for praise before men or gain" (Meyer, p. 47), and Zwingli's exposition of this thesis, "Those who are unmusical will be distracted by their awkward attempts simply to follow the

678

notes, whereas those who are musically talented, regardless of how much or how little, will be overwhelmed, because they are by virtue of their competence the more susceptible to music's power" ZW, II, 18-19, tr. Garside, p. 49).

31. This hermeneutical principle came from Zwingli (see 57A/fn.33), who based it on Deut. 12:32.

32. "Rooted out . . . planted by" *(gerütted . . . gepflantzet)* is a reference to Mt. 15:13.

33. This point seems self-evident but takes on meaning in the context of the times. In opposition to Luther, who retained the name and certain ritual elements of the mass, such as the elevation of the host, Grebel is supporting Carlstadt's insistence on using the name "Lord's Supper."

34. Grebel had expressed this same point in the Second Disputation (57C/247/3ff.), a point Zwingli had not thought very important.

35. This point is reminiscent of Carlstadt's dissent from Luther's retention of the ritual elevation of the host.

36. By insisting that "the bread is nothing but bread," Grebel was rejecting both the transubstantiation doctrine of the Roman Catholics and the consubstantiation doctrine of the Lutherans in favor of a Zwinglian view of the spiritual presence of Christ in the Supper.

37. Jn. 6:52-63.

38. 1 Cor. 10:16-22; 11:20-29.

39. Acts 2:41-47.

40. The words "condemnation" and "discernment" were admonitions taken from 1 Cor. 11:29. Grebel obviously had an open Bible before him as he wrote.

41. As Williams points out (1957, p. 76, fn. 10), "The objection here appears to be against the perpetration of the priestly conception of administering the elements. To avoid any suggestion of a sacerdotal act, Müntzer, ordained to the old priesthood, should relinquish to a server from out of the congregation the distribution of the elements."

42. Ger. *darmit gieng die mess ab/dass einig essen.* Rauschenbusch translated this, "That was the beginning of the mass that only a few partook," and Wenger rendered it, "That is how the mass originated, namely, individual participation." The verb, *abgehen,* does not mean "to originate" or "to begin," but "to exit," "to end," "to terminate," "to discontinue," "to disappear." Moreover, *abgieng* is subjective rather than past tense.

43. Grebel rejected the practice of a Roman Catholic priest celebrating the mass in private.

44. On the significance of the frequency of the practice of communion in the Zwinglian Reformation, see John H. Yoder, MQR, 1958, pp. 139-40.

45. The "rule of Christ" was the term often used by the Anabaptists for the formula of church discipline outlined by Jesus as recorded in Mt. 18:15-18 (see 289/39, 290/22, and 293/36). As the last reference indicates, it had the character of a mandate or mark of the church among Anabaptists, cognate with baptism and the Lord's Supper. It represented the rule of love in the church in place of a political establishment of religion in the form of a state church.

46. The question of priestly robes and vestments was discussed in the Second Disputation (see 57C/246/17ff.). Zwingli said there that when he wrote his *Essay on the Canon of the Mass* (Aug. 29, 1523; see ZW, II, No. 23), he had retained the use of vestments in the mass "for the sake of the weak in faith," but that he had since been led by certain thoroughgoing followers (undoubtedly Grebel and friends; see 57A/Intro.) to change his mind (see 57A/228/5ff.). Now he believed that it was necessary to abolish chanting and robes, although only "at the proper time, so that no uproar or other disunity will arise among Christians." Neither chanting nor robes were actually abolished until April 12, 1525.

47. The question of the time of day for the celebration of the Lord's Supper also came up in the Second Disputation (see 57C/248/21ff.). On this matter Zwingli had agreed with Grebel, except that he felt he was also bound to time by insisting so strongly that the Supper be practiced in the evening as Jesus had done. The present statement would seem to indicate more flexibility on Grebel's part than Zwingli had supposed.

48. See fn. 37, above.

49. See fn. 17, above.

50. The brother referred to here is Hans Hujuff (see Cast of Characters No. 55), mentioned again in 63/290/12, 64/292/28, and as a signatory to the second letter to Müntzer, 64/294/8, where he signs himself as "your countryman of Halle." In the present reference and in 64/292/28, it is reported that Hujuff had recently visited Müntzer. Two scholars have accepted these references as proof that Hujuff had personal contact with Müntzer: Otto Schiff (p. 291) and Karl Simon (pp. 50-54). Bender (1950, p. 257, note 56) rejects the validity of Grebel's assertion that Müntzer "listened so kindly to our brother and . . . confessed to him that you have been too lax." Bender writes: "It seems scarcely possible that Müntzer would have accepted an 'admonition' from Hans Hujuff and confessed to him a shortcoming; Müntzer was not likely a man to confess shortcomings; furthermore, there is no evidence that Müntzer modified his program in the direction of the ideas of Hans Hujuff and his brethren in Zurich." George H. Williams (1957, p. 78, fn. 13) believes, on the other hand, that a personal contact between Hujuff and Müntzer is "more than plausible," and thus sides with Schiff and Simon.

51. Carlstadt, see 62/fn.4 and Cast of Characters No. 12.

52. A benefice was the common means of support for the clergy, deriving its income from the rents paid by peasants living on the land owned by the church.

53. I.e., in the Zurich parishes.

54. *Zins und Zehenden.* The twin terms referred to a number of feudal economic practices that tended to exploit the poor, and Bender (1950, p. 315) concludes that "Grebel joins *Zinsen* and *Zehnten* as one evil, meaning thereby the whole evil system of economic exploitation of the poor in his time, particularly in rural areas." The problem, however, had specific elements and the following references attempt to sort them out: Correll, pp. 28-29; Claus-Peter Clasen, pp. 196-99, 467/fn.104; Köhler (ZW, IV, pp. 25-29. *Zins,* sometimes called "small tithes," included *Erbzinse* (inheritance taxes), *Bodenzinse* (ground rents), *Lehenszinse* (feudal taxes), *Fruchtzinse* (taxes on produce, paid in kind), *Geldzinse* (taxes on produce, paid in coin), and *Kinskauf* (interest on capital loans). In his reference to *Zins,* Grebel was most concerned about the *Zinskauf* (see 67/302/16-18 and 70/379/13-22), and hence the English word "interest" rather than "taxes" or "rents." Another more polemical name for it was *Wucher* or *Wucherzinsen* (usury). *Zehenden* referred primarily to tithes exacted for the support of the church and its institutions (see 52/fn.7 and 53/fns. 5 and 6). Zwingli remained favorable to the demands of the peasants for relief of the "small tithes," but considered the ecclesiastical tithes as binding on practical, if not on Scripture, grounds.

55. On Jacob Strauss, see 53/fn.7. In 53/220/30-31 Grebel identified one booklet by Strauss which he had read, but it is likely that he read others, such as *Von dem innerlichen und äusserlichen Tauff* (May 1523), *Widder den Simonieschen Tauff unnd erkaufften Chrissum und oel, auch worynn die recht Christlich tauf begriffen sei* (1523), and *Das wucher zu nemen und geben unsern christlichen glauben und brüderliche lieb entgegen ist* (June 1524). Grebel may have been in error in thinking that Strauss was "little regarded" by Luther, who wrote in a letter of April 15, 1524, that he had "the best opinion" of Strauss. Bender (1950, pp. 312-15) concluded that Strauss remained a faithful Lutheran preacher all his life and was never alienated from either Luther or Melanchthon.

56. By the "Wittenberg doctors," Grebel refers primarily to Luther and Melanchthon, in distinction to "the learned shepherds" of Zurich—Zwingli and Jud.

57. Grebel probably got this phrase from Müntzer himself, who wrote, "He who does not have the bitter Christ will eat himself to death from honey" (quoted by Hillerbrand, 1967, p. 10). The phrase is also found in Hans Denk's *Selection IV.*

58. The reference is to two stone tablets inscribed with the Ten Commandments, which Müntzer had set up in his church shortly before Grebel wrote. The source for this information was probably Hans Hujuff, who had visited Müntzer recently (see 292/27-28). For Grebel, Müntzer's tablets were too reminiscent of the struggle in Zurich to abolish all images and idols in the church (see lines 25-29, below). Grebel was anticipating the universal accessi-

bility of the "outward Word alone" (line 31), i.e., the Scriptures, and he did not want anything to substitute for the supreme authority of the Bible.

59. 2 Cor. 3:3.

60. Jer. 31:33.

61. Heb. 8:10.

62. Ezek. 36:26-27.

63. 1 Cor. 14:36; Col. 3:16.

64. Ger. *den einigen wort,* i.e., the stone tablets set in the church in place of the Scriptures.

65. Ger. *möcht . . . hinderstellig werden,* which Rauschenbusch, admitting that "the connection is not clear," translated incorrectly as "might lag" and Wenger as "might become inferior." The translation by Williams, "might become insidious," is too strong. The adjectives "hindering," "impeding," or "obstructing" are more accurate.

66. Mt. 18:15-20. See fn.45, above.

67. Ger. *gebett und abbruch,* which Rauschenbusch translated incorrectly "prayer and decision" and Wenger "prayer and restraint."

68. Mt. 18:15-17. This refers to Grebel's references to the "rule of Christ" in 288/17 and 289/39.

69. Grebel may be thinking here of Paul's reference to "the destruction of the flesh," 1 Cor. 5:5, which was often used in his time to justify the execution of heretics. If so, he is comparing Paul's disciplinary procedure in the case of the Corinthian sinner with that outlined in Mt. 18, implying that "to deliver this man to Satan" means excommunication (Mt. 18:17), not execution.

70. Ger *alss wir durch unseren brucher* [sic] *vernommen hand dich also meinen und halten.* The "brother" providing the information was Hans Hujuff (see fn. 50, above). Wenger translated the sentence: "We learn from our brother that this is also what you believe and hold to," suggesting that Grebel learned from Hujuff (see fn. 50) that Müntzer agreed with his own nonresistant position. Williams drew a similar conclusion, adding, "of course, Grebel is deceived (1957, p. 80, fn. 23). Bender (1950, pp. 111, 179) did not think Grebel was deceived at all but knew clearly what Müntzer's militant position was and that they were in disagreement. Compare 293/5-8, in which Hujuff clearly reports that Müntzer "preached against the princes, that they should be combatted with the fist."

71. By "worldly sword" is meant the office of government, according to Rom. 13:4.

72. It is not completely clear whether Grebel meant "no more war" or "no more of this subject," probably the latter (see 65/296/17).

73. On Grebel's prior thinking on the subject of baptism, see 54A/fn.5.

74. In his tract, "Protest or Declaration," (see 62/fn.6), Müntzer had argued that the practice of infant baptism had its source in an inadequate understanding of the Christian faith. He wrote that "the entrance into Christianity has become an animal-like monkey-business." He challenged the "scribes" to prove by Scripture that Christ and the disciples baptized children and argued that "in the days of the apostles only adults were accepted, after a lengthy period of instruction" (tr. Hillerbrand, p. 10). Bender (1950, p. 116) was thus in error when he wrote that Müntzer "never advocated adult baptism and never mentioned it in his writings." Bender correctly pointed out, however, that Müntzer never actually put believers' baptism into practice and that as late as 1524 he composed a German liturgy for the baptism of infants entitled *Von der Taufe wie man die heldet* (see fn. 83).

75. See fn. 45, above.

76. *(Dem getoufften dass gmut enderenden und dem gloubenden vor und nach.)* The prior translations of Rauschenbusch and of Wenger disclose their difficulty with this parenthetical phrase: "(to him that is baptized, changes his mind and believes before and after it)," "to the one baptized that his inner self has been changed and that he believes, both before and afterward" [Wenger omitted the parentheses].

77. See fn. 56, above. Luther sought to combine the traditional Catholic doctrine that baptism was necessary to salvation with his belief in justification by faith alone. Thus he

denied the *ex opere operato* character of the sacrament, making it conditional upon the faith of the recipient (including infants who he claimed had a "sleeping faith" given by God), but he taught a strict baptismal regeneration.

78. Tertullian and Cyprian are Ante-Nicene Fathers whose contributions to a Catholic orthodoxy predated the Council of Nicea in AD 325. Augustine was converted in AD 386 and is thus Post-Nicene. It is uncertain to which of several churchmen by the name of Theophylact Grebel was referring—an eighth-century bishop of Antioch, an eighth-century archdeacon elected antipope by a small faction in AD 757, an eighth-century bishop of Tudertum or Todi, or an eleventh-century archbishop of Achris and well-known biblical commentator in Constantinople. Williams (1957, p. 80, fn. 25) believes that it was the eleventh-century Theophylact. Hubmaier also referred to an unknown Theophylact who he claimed wrote in AD 189 as a contemporary of the Apostolic Fathers (see Sachsse, p. 34), Among the four writers listed by Grebel, it is Augustine who is best known for the doctrine of baptism to which he refers. Tertullian had earlier asserted that true baptism was to be found only in the Catholic Church (De Baptismo, 15). Cyprian applied this doctrine to the controversial question of the validity of baptisms in heretical sects, asserting that such persons should be rebaptized. Augustine established the validity of baptism *ex opere operato* apart from the faith or worthiness of the minister, asserting that the chief effect of the sacrament, provided it was conferred in the name of the Trinity, was the removal of the stain of original sin which bars even the newborn child from the kingdom of heaven. Henceforth, the infusion of saving grace was generally recognized in Roman Catholic doctrine to be the result of baptism.

79. The verses dealing with the subject of children cited by Grebel were: Gen. 8:21; Deut. 1:39; 30:6; 31:13; 1 Cor. 14:20; Wisdom 12:19; 1 Pet. 2:2; Mt. 18:1-6, 10; 19:13-15; Mk. 9:33-37; 10:13-16; Lk. 18:15-17. The texts in Romans are uncertain.

80. Grebel's theology of children reflected Zwingli's teaching, "They are free from original guilt through Christ's gracious work." (Schuler-Schultess, IV, p. 125).

81. Grebel probably means that Cyprian, born in a pagan family, and Augustine, born in a Christian family, were both baptized on confession of faith. He might also have reference to the persistent although controversial practice of rebaptizing believers previously baptized in the "heretical sects" (see fn. 79, above).

82. Muntzer's *Protest and Declaration.* See 62/fn.6 and 63/fn.75.

83. Grebel apparently knew about the contradiction between Müntzer's declaration on believer's baptism and the liturgy he wrote for the baptism of infants (see fn. 74, above). In a conversation with Oecolampad of Basel late in the autumn of 1524, Müntzer mentioned his own practice of baptizing every two or three months those born in this interval (Herzog, I, p. 302).

84. See fn. 51, above, 62/fn.4, and Cast of Characters No. 12.

85. Grebel did publish a *Taufbüchlein,* which is not extant except for excerpts quoted verbatim by Zwingli in the *Elenchus* (see Epi.C, below).

86. The reference here is to Luther's *Das taufbüchlin verdeutscht,* published after Easter of 1523.

87. Leo Jud's baptismal liturgy was modeled after Luther's rite (see above), with the title *Ein kurze und gemeine Form fuer die schwach gleubigen kinder zu Thouffen* (Zurich, summer of 1523; see ZW, IV, 710-13).

88. Andreas Osiander's German liturgy of baptism was entitled *Ordnung wie man Tauffet, bissher im Latein gehalten, verteutscht* (Nürnberg, 1524).

89. The Strasbourg booklet was published with the title *Ordnung des Herrn Nachtmal; so man die mess nennet, sampt der Tauff und Insegnung der Ee, wie jetzt die diener des wort Gottes zu Strassburg, erneuert, und nach göttlicher geschrift gebessert haben uss ursach in nachgenender epistel gemeldet.*

90. Ger. *schalten wie allen gesanten.* The verb means to rule, direct, operate, officiate, control, manage, govern, function, administer. Wenger misread *schelten* for *schalten,* and translated it "rebuke as ambassadors should." Rauschenbusch omitted the verb altogether.

91. See fn. 84, above.

682

92. See previous fn.

93. Castelberger, see 51B and Cast of Characters No. 13.

94. Felix Mantz, see Cast of Characters No. 67.

95. Hans Ockenfuss. See Cast of Characters No. 71.

96. Bartlime Pur, see Cast of Characters No. 73.

97. Heinrich Aberli, see Cast of Characters No. 1.

98. In 64/294/7-10, Grebel mentions two others not named here, and then adds "and seven new young Müntzers to Luther."

99. That Grebel did in fact write to Luther, see 64/292/24, 65/294/32-65/294/1 and 67E/331/2-6.

100. See 63/fn.17.

101. On Grebel's "affliction," see 4/fn.3 and 6/fn.34. The chronic nature of his illness is evident in his later letters as well (see 62/284/5, 69/357/29-30, etc.).

64. Grebel to Müntzer, Zurich, sent with letter of September 5, 1524

1. The following letter has usually been treated as a postscript to Letter 63. That Grebel thought of it as a separate letter is indicated by 64/293/38, where he referred to Letter 63 as "our first letter."

2. Ger. *in unser aller namen geschriben,* which Rauschenbusch incorrectly translated "subscribed all our names."

3. See 63/fn.99.

4. On "forbearance," see 63/fn.17.

5. On Carlstadt and Castelberger, see Cast of Characters Nos. 12 and 13. The letter is not extant. It was evidently a third letter written to Carlstadt by the Zurich brethren following two written by Grebel (see 62/283/14 and Bender, 1950, p. 108).

6. On Hans Hujuff, see 63/fns. 50 and 72, and Cast of Characters No. 55. It was not Hujuff, as Wenger supposed (1970, p. 39), but a letter from Luther that "arrived here." Hujuff had returned to Zurich from his visit to Müntzer sooner than the interim between Grebel's two letters, if we conclude (what seems probable) that it was Hujuff who was the "brother" referred to in 63/289/2, "you listened so kindly to our brother."

7. The reference was to Luther's tract, *Ein Brief an die Fürsten zu Sachsen von dem aufrührischen Geist* ("Letter to the Princes of Saxony Concerning the Rebellious Spirit"), Wittenberg, 1524. See also 71I/fn.6.

8. Lat. *primitiae,* "firstfruits," although "preeminent leader" would be the general sense of the term.

9. The reference is probably to 2 Tim. 2:24.

10. The prince was Frederick III (1463-1525), called "the Wise," the ruling monarch in Saxony, Luther's protector. A member of the Ernestine branch of the ruling family in Saxony, he succeeded his father as one of the seven electors of the Holy Roman Empire in 1486. He founded the University of Wittenberg in 1502 and appointed Luther and Melanchthon to professorships. When Luther was placed under papal and imperial ban, the elector provided refuge for him in his castle, the Wartburg.

11. This is another reference to the *Protest . . . Concerning the Right Christian Faith and Baptism,* 1524. See 62/fn.6 and 63/fn.18.

12. Ger. *funst,* "fist," although "violence" (JCW) was the general sense of the term. Müntzer's sermon was preached in Allstedt on July 13, 1524, and later published with the title "Exposition of the Second Chapter of Daniel the Prophet Preached at the Castle of Allstedt Before the Active and Amiable Dukes and Administrators of Saxony by Thomas Müntzer, Minister of the Word of God." For notes and translation see Williams, 1957, pp. 47-70, especially 64, 68ff.

13. See fn. 10, above. Among his various titles—Landgrave of Thuringia, Margrave of Meissen—was also Duke of Saxony.

14. Ger. *bubel,* "to drum," hence "to utter raucously," "to proclaim flamboyantly," "to blare."

15. *Babel*, a reference to the Tower of Babel in Gen. 10:10 and 11:9; hence to a confusion of sounds and noises, to babbling. Grebel was quoting this alliterative phrase from Luther's tract, *The Letter to the Princes of Saxony Concerning the Rebellious Spirit* (see fn. 7, above). He did not know, apparently, that the phrase was originally Müntzer's own words, that the Bible as used by radicals had led to *bubel* (strife) and *babel* (confusion). See Williams, 1957, p. 84, fn. 42.

16. On "forbearance," see 63/fn.17.

17. See Cast of Characters No. 106.

18. See Cast of Characters No. 58.

19. See 2 Cor. 11:14

20. Compare with 63/290/13-17 and 67/302/7-9.

21. Grebel means specifically the German mass and chants (see 63/286/36), priestly robes (63/288/22), and stone tablets (63/289/19-20).

22. On the "rule of Christ," see 63/fn.45.

23. See Cast of Characters No. 12.

24. On Strauss, see 53/fn.7 and 63/fn.55.

25. This is the only reference to Stiefel in Grebel's letters and cannot be taken to indicate that he knew much about him, except perhaps for the booklet *Das Evangelium von dem verlornen Sohn* ("The Gospel of the Prodigal Son"), published in 1524. Michael Stiefel (1487-1567) began his career as an Augustinian friar and concluded it as a mathematics professor at the University of Jena. To the end of his life he was a staunch Lutheran preacher, first in the service of Hartmut von Kronberg (September 1522 to May 1523) and then of Count von Mansfeld. At the time that Grebel heard of him, he was deeply involved in apocalyptic studies of Daniel and Revelation, and had set the date for the end of the world—October 19, 1533. It is possible that the several eschatological references of Grebel (62/283/30-34, 69/357/34-36, 69/358/23-27, 70/378/17) are due to Stiefel's influence.

26. See Cast of Characters No. 13.

27. See Cast of Characters No. 67.

28. See Cast of Characters No. 1.

29. John Pannicellus, better known as Hans Brötli, assistant priest at Zollikon (see Cast of Characters No. 10.

30. See Cast of Characters No. 71.

31. See Cast of Characters No. 55.

32. "Young Müntzers to Luther" was a euphemism for dissenters. The seven persons were the signatories to the two letters: Grebel, Castelberger, Mantz, Aberli, Ockenfuss, Pur, and Brötli.

33. See fn. 3, above.

65. *Grebel to Vadian, Zurich, October 14, 1524*

1. On the Conrad Eppenberg affair, see 60/fn.4 and 68/fn.11. The details of the contract for apprenticeship for which Vadian stood surety were reported in Letter 60. The "master" refers to the master tailor to whom he was apprenticed.

2. The master tailor was Hans Ochsner, elected to the Large Council in 1510, guildmaster in 1519, deputy burgomaster in 1524, and district bailiff of Andelfingen in 1532. He died in 1535.

3. Grebel uses the plural pronoun as he did in the previous letter to Müntzer (63/fn.3) because he is speaking on behalf of a group of friends.

4. See 63/fn.99 and 64/fn.3. It is known that Grebel wrote to Erhard Hegenwald and Martin Luther, both of Wittenberg.

5. Grebel first mentioned writing to Carlstadt in 62/283/14 (see 62/fn.4). However, since the plural pronoun is used in the present reference, it is possible that the letter to Carlstadt referred to here was the one written by Castelberger in the name of the Grebel

group and referred to in 64/292/26-27. See Bender, 1950, p. 108.

6. See fn. 7, below.

7. Luther had arrived in Jena on August 21 on a mission to try to stem the rising tide of unrest associated with the preaching of Müntzer and Carlstadt. The next day he and Carlstadt had a personal confrontation in the Black Bear Inn in Jena. Carlstadt defended his new views on the Eucharist and insisted that he was not to be identified with Müntzer's violence. When he complained that his adversaries refused to hear his position, Luther challenged him to state it publicly in writing and tossed him a gold coin as a sign of the challenge—an old German custom to signal a duel and a commitment to fight each other in the open. Carlstadt accepted the invitation and within less than a month and a half produced eight tracts—five on the Lord's Supper, one on false forbearance of the laity, one on faith and unbelief, and one in opposition to infant baptism. He sent them to Switzerland with Westerburg to get them printed with the help of friends. It is not known how or whether Grebel was involved in the negotiations, but arrangements were made for the printing to be done in Basel, where they were taken by Westerburg and Mantz. For the titles of the eight pamphlets, see ZW, IV, p. 464, fn. 1, and Sider, 1974, p. 202, fn. 5. The tract on baptism was subsequently confiscated by the authorities. In his two-volume refutation of Carlstadt entitled "Against the Heavenly Prophets Concerning Images and Sacrament" (see 67E/fns. 47 and 66), Luther twice referred to the episode of the gold coin. In the first paragraph of Part I, Luther claimed that Carlstadt would never have come out into the open "unless I had lured him out with a guilder." And toward the end of the refutation he wrote, "I should like to give Dr. Carlstadt two guilders again if only once in all this discussion he would help, not me, but his own cause by doing one of two things: either by producing passages from Scripture, or by showing that a selected text demands an interpretation proving his cause to be right" (LW, Vol. 40, p. 185).

8. On Westerburg, see Cast of Characters No. 96. As Carlstadt's brother-in-law and colleague, he was in Zurich to promote the publication and distribution of his writings.

9. During Westerburg's visit (Oct. 8-14), Grebel apparently read his pamphlet entitled *De sopore animarum* ("Of the Sleep of Souls"). Although there is no further evidence of its influence in Grebel's writings, it is interesting in this regard to read Zwingli's attack on certain alleged Anabaptist teachings regarding "the sleep of the soul," with probable reference to Westerburg's pamphlet (see the Appendix of the *Elenchus*, Jackson, 1901, pp. 251ff.).

10. Grebel supposed that Vadian might have been offended by the increasing indications of radical attitudes and activities.

11. *Iudico ... pacis meae homines,* "I judge men (by) my peace."

12. Grebel is referring to his own state of poverty.

13. Codrus was an Athenian king who sacrificed his life for his city. The Delphic oracle had predicted that the Dorian army, which was besieging Athens, would be successful if they would not harm the king of Athens. Knowing this Codrus disguised himself, went to the Dorian camp, quarreled with some persons, and was slain. On learning that they had slain the king, the Dorians gave up the siege and retreated because of the oracle. Grebel sees a connection between the sacrifice of Codrus and his own enduring the pain of indebtedness, but the connection is not clear. Is he comparing his own endurance of the pain or indebtedness to the sacrifice of Codrus? Or is he refusing to sacrifice himself for the cause of his creditors? Both interpretations are possible, although the next sentence would seem to favor the latter.

14. Grebel may be quoting 2 Tim. 2:10. The Greek word is the same.

15. See 62/283/35-62/284/8.

16. See 62/fn.18. Grebel is quoting Ezek. 34:18-19.

17. Lat. *invidentiae tabernam,* "shop or factory or hovel of envy."

18. Compare with 64/293/29-30.

19. The controversy is best described by Luther himself in his reply to Carlstadt's insistence on a German liturgy of the Lord's Supper: "I would gladly have a German mass today. I am also occupied with it. But I would very much like it to have a true German

character. For to translate the Latin text and retain the Latin tone or notes has my sanction, though it doesn't sound polished or well done. Both the text and notes, accent, melody, and manner of rendering ought to grow out of the true mother tongue and its inflection, otherwise all of it becomes an imitation, in the manner of the apes. Now since the enthusiast spirit presses that it must be, and will again burden the conscience with law, works, and sins, I will take my time and hurry less in this direction than before, only to spite the sin-master and soul-murderer, who presses upon us works, as if they were commanded by God" (LW, Vol. 40, pp. 141-42).

20. The last three syllables of the name were written in Greek letters. The reference is probably to Christoph Klauser, a doctor in Zurich.

21. The reference is probably to Castelberger (see Cast of Characters No. 13).

22. It is highly probable that this self-identity—"Conrad Nobody"—was based on Ulrich von Hutten's most read and reprinted poem, *Nemo* (Nobody), transcribed by Böcking, III, 106ff. Hutten had also signed the 1518 edition of the poem, *Hutteni Nemo* (Hutten Nobody), having used the Greek/Latin signature, Ουτις ελεγν. *(Nemo dicebat* ["He Was Naming Nobody"] in the earlier 1513 edition). The title page also contains the word in both Greek and Latin lettering. Holborn describes the mood of the poet as follows: "All during his German and Italian travels we find a note of deep depression and bitter scepticism, which contrasts markedly with the self-confidence of his personal conduct. He felt himself to be as good as the next man, and better than most, but the riddle of existence still pressed upon him. Humanism filled him with hope for the progress of mankind; yet only gradually could the clouds of barbarism be dissipated. This observation and his own toilsome struggles overwhelmed him with recurring despondency as to destiny.... One recognizes the outward impressions which accompany the composition of the work: the chilly reception at home, the indignation of the family that he came back not as a doctor but as a 'nobody,' the contempt of the father for humanist 'humbug.' But it is not merely personal circumstances which come to expression, but also deeper concern for the future of the new learning. 'O mores, o studia! O ye leaders of this time! Why do we not dispel the clouds and turn to the truth?' " (Holborn, 52-53). The parallels between the lives of Hutten and Grebel, which the latter may have sensed when he mentioned or quoted him (see 20/fn.13, 23/fn.19, 34/fn.6, 53/fn.9) are considerable. They were both born into landed nobility, alienated from their parents, sojourners in foreign lands, living dissolute lives, suffering from similar ill health (syphilis?), attracted by the new liberating humanism, disillusioned by the fence-straddling of humanist-oriented Reformers (Erasmus and Zwingli, respectively), fugitives from arrest and persecution, yet sharp and witty in their writings. With reference to their past, they were both "nobody"; but in his negative self-identity Grebel went a step beyond Hutten, who was still "Hutten Nobody." Following the sense of abandonment by "the whole race of kinsmen and relatives" expressed in 65/296/1-3, Conrad could not even say "Grebel Nobody," because he was "no more Grebel." Hutten's source for the "nobody" theme was Homer's *Odyssey*. It was the Homeric Οὐτις [Lat., *nemo;* Eng. *nobody*] with which Ulysses mocked the Cyclops. For more on Hutten's poem, see D. F. Strauss, *Ulrich Von Hutten: His Life and Times,* tr. G. Sturge (London: Daldy, Isbister, & Co., 1874), p. 80.

23. I.e., Carlstadt. See Cast of Characters No. 12.

24. The "rumors of wars" (see Mk. 13:7) concerned the growing conflict in the Swiss Confederation between the Five Forest Cantons (Uri, Schwyz, Unterwalden, Luzern, and Zug), devoted to the Old Roman Catholic establishment, and the three cantons of Zurich, Bern, and Basel, devoted to the new Reformation order. The conflict frequently threatened outbreaks of violence from 1523 to 1531, when the Battle of Cappel occurred in which Zwingli died. In the summer and fall of 1524, a particular crisis arose, called the Ittinger affair (see Epi.A/fn.83). In the wake of the removal of the sacred images from the churches of Zurich, a group of iconoclasts from Stammheim had decided to imitate the example of Zurich; and when their leaders were captured by the confederate authorities, a mob retaliated on July 17, 1524, vandalizing and looting the monastery at Ittingen, twenty-five miles northeast of Zurich, near Franenfeld, completely destroying its tower. In subsequent meet-

ings of the Swiss Diet, representatives from the Forest Cantons threatened to expel Zurich from the confederacy, which would have perilously isolated her and exposed her to attack by Austria. As a direct response to this threat, Zwingli designed an elaborate defense strategy, including defense treaties with the cantons of Bern, Basel, and the Grisons, and an appeal to the king of France and the South German cities of Strasbourg and Constance (see "Plan zu einem Feldzug," ZW, III, pp. 539-83). Even the "rumor of war" which Grebel mentioned was part of Zwingli's strategy, for the latter hoped to consolidate the forces at home by propaganda concerning the impending confrontation between Zurich and the Forest Cantons.

25. Jesus had prophesied that "you will hear of wars and rumors of wars" (Mk. 13:7; Mt. 24:6), but Grebel believes that in the present situation in Zurich, the rumors of wars will subside.

65A. Anabaptist Beginnings in St. Gallen, 1525

1. The dating of the events that Kessler is describing is helped by several clues in the excerpt. First it is clear at the end that he is writing in "the present year '25." Second, at the beginning of the second paragraph, he writes that these events took place "last year," i.e., 1524. For more specific *terminus post* and *terminus ante*, see fns. 2 and 3, below.

2. We know that Kessler began his Bible study group in January 1524; hence, the events described in this excerpt could not have occurred before then.

3. The parenthetical phrase in this sentence refers to our excerpt 68F, which while chronologically later than the present excerpt actually came prior to it in the chronicle itself. From 68F, we learn that what "had not yet broken out publicly in Zurich" was either the debate over baptism in the Tuesday Disputations (66A) or the First Public Disputation on Baptism (68B), or more likely the First Believer's Baptism in Switzerland (68F). Thus, the *terminus ante* for the events described in the paragraph (as indicated above) is either December 1524 or January 21, 1525, at the latest.

4. Lorenz Hochrütiner, see 57F/fn.19 and Cast of Characters No. 45.

5. Ger. *Cunrat Grebels, des erzwidertoufers.*

6. The words are not from Mt. 28 but from Mk. 16:16.

7. Mk. 10:14, Mt. 19:14, Lk. 18:15.

8. Ger. *ainen vierboginen brief.* This letter by Grebel is not extant, unless it was a copy of Letter 63, which happens to be exactly eight pages in length. In any case, it is not likely that it would have been written before Letter 63 dated Sept. 25, 1524, in which he discusses baptism for the first time in his extant letters. In all, two letters and a treatise from Grebel to the St. Gallen Anabaptists are known lost (see 70A/384/3, 6-8).

66. Grebel to Vadian, Zurich, November 23, 1524

1. There has been some uncertainty about the proper dating of this letter. Grebel's dating was given in 66/299/30 as "Wednesday after Mary, 1524." Arbenz, the editor of VB (III, 94-95) interpreted this to be Dec. 11, 1524, on the assumption that the day of Mary was the Conceptio Mariae, December 8 (although in that case for that year the date would still have to be corrected to Dec. 14). But this does not accord with other internal evidence. Grebel referred in the letter to "what is now being negotiated at Einsiedeln." The reference was to the *Rechtstag* (Confederate Court) held in Einsiedeln on Nov. 23, 1524. Another clue is his remark, "The duke of Württemberg might be coming today." It is known that Duke Ulrich left for Zurich on Nov. 18, was heard by the Zurich Council on Nov. 23, and departed for Schaffhausen on Dec. 1 (Feyler, 1905, pp. 251-54). So the day of Mary must be understood, not as *Conceptio Mariae*, but as *Mariae Praesentatio*—Nov. 21—the Wednesday after which fell on Nov. 23.

2. Ger. *Min schwagerlichen grůtz zevor.* This is the first of three letters to Vadian that Grebel wrote entirely in the German language. Concerning his resort to German, see 63/ Intro. But in this case, there was another reason for writing in German: he was writing on behalf of his father, who probably dictated the first paragraph (see next fn.).

3. Although neither the editor of VB (III, 94-95, No. 411) nor the editors of Quellen (No. 17, pp. 28-29) were aware of it, it is evident that the first paragraph of this letter, beginning with the "Dear doctor" was written jointly by Conrad and his father, Jacob Grebel. The words "first of all" in Conrad's salutation anticipate Jacob's paragraph to come. Then comes Jacob's salutation, which is unlike any of Conrad's usual salutations but precisely like those of Jacob's previous letters (9A/88, 23A/121, and 57B/233). This conclusion is further confirmed by Conrad's statement in line 27, below: "he asked me to write to you."

4. The identification of the "booklet" which Vadian had sent is unknown. Vadian's chief biographer, Werner Näf, says nothing about a published or unpublished writing by Vadian in 1524 (Vol. 2, pp. 551-52). In his next letter, written three weeks later, Grebel writes, "Your letter with the booklet which you sent to me gives us a bad setback" (67/302/29). Two unpublished writings by Vadian would fit this description—*Farrago* and *Schrift wider die Täufer,* but these cannot be dated before March and May, 1525. The "booklet" is mentioned a third time in Vadian's letter to Grebel dated Dec. 28: "Let me know what you intend to do with the booklet I sent you" (67D/322/26). We know from the content of Vadian's letter (67/322/5-10) that he was critical of the Grebel group, accusing them of undermining the established authority of Zwingli and Jud in Zurich. The booklet may have been a first draft of materials that Vadian subsequently included in the *Farrago* and *Schrift wider die Täufer,* dealing with Reformation concerns in St. Gallen. This would correspond to Näf's comment that Vadian was able to produce the latter tract on very short notice after May 12, 1525: "We do not know how it happened that the treatise against the Anabaptists was not written by the two clergymen but by Vadian. It was submitted complete after a few days as if it had already been prepared" (Näf, II, 230-31). For further evidence that Grebel may have had one of Vadian's writings in manuscript rather than in published form, see 65/295/17, where Grebel refers to Carlstadt's unpublished manuscripts as "booklets." See further 67D/fn.8.

5. The identity of Hans Widerker is vague. He may be connected with "Widerkerin at the Green Shield" (71M/447/26-27), in which case he would be the innkeeper here (71M/fn.74). Hans Widerker is mentioned in Egli's *Actensammlung,* No. 238, p. 78, as a pro-Zwingli witness in the case of threats to Zwingli's life in April 1522. In the present reference, he seems to be a carrier or connecting link in the conveyance of Vadian's letter and booklet from St. Gallen to Zurich via Luzern. Perhaps delegates from St. Gallen to the Diet in Luzern carried it that far, and it sounds as though Widerker brought it to Zurich from there, delivering it to an acceptable depository—the inn in Winterthur. The other details of how it was finally delivered relate to the mystery that the Grebels are attempting to clear up.

6. Winterthur was situated sixteen miles northeast of Zurich.

7. The "etc." at the end of this and several subsequent sentences indicates that the matter could be discussed at greater length, but that the two Grebels had decided not to pursue it further. It marks the end of Jacob's collaboration in the letter, for the sentence two lines later ("I myself have not been able to understand them very clearly from father") indicates that Conrad is now doing the writing.

8. "Milords" was the standard title for members of the Small Council or Large in Zurich, i.e., all the magistrates of the city state. The items laid down at the Luzern meeting of Nov. 8, to which Milords were to respond, are summarized in Segesser, IV, I-i, 523ff.

9. Jacob Grebel was the Zurich deputy at more than thirty meetings of the Confederate Diet between 1520 and 1526, and was supposed to attend the current session in Einsiedeln (see 299/24-25).

10. The *Rechtstag* (confederate court) was meeting in Einsiedeln on Nov. 23, probably the very day Grebel was writing this letter. The agenda included the Ittinger affair (see 65/fn.24).

11. On Duke Ulrich of Württemberg, see Cast of Characters No. 90. He came to Zurich on Nov. 23 to address the council on the possibility of a Protestant alliance in exchange for Zurich's help in the recovery of his kingdom. Jacob Grebel's opposition to his coming and mission is apparent in this comment and may have been another factor in Zwingli's growing resentment of the senator (see Epi.A, below).

12. See fn. 10, above.

13. Martha Grebel, Vadian's wife.
14. Benedict von Watt, Vadian's brother (see 31/fn.15).
15. Wolfgang Wetter, preacher in St. Gallen (see Cast of Characters No. 97).

66A. The Tuesday Disputations, Zurich, December 6 and 13, 1524
  1. For further information as to who participated, see fns. 8 and 9, below.
  2. From the introduction, above, we note that the Tuesday Disputations must have occurred before Jan. 15; but the date can be established more definitely than that. The *terminus ante quem* for these disputations would be Dec. 16, the date of Zwingli's letter to Lambert (Intro., Reference No. 4). The *terminus post quem* is established by the fact that Ludwig Hätzer participated (Intro., Reference No. 3). Hätzer left Zurich on June 29, 1524, after completing the preface to his German translation of *Bugenhagens Paulusauslegung,* and went to Augsburg (ZW, VI, p. 39). He was still in Augsburg in September (ZW, VIII, p. 361.9). Sometime later he returned to Zurich and participated in the Tuesday meetings. The fact that they are mentioned both in Grebel's letter of Dec. 15 and Zwingli's of Dec. 16, just a day apart, suggests that these discussions had just taken place, i.e., between Dec. 1 and 15, probably on the Tuesdays of Dec. 6 and 13.
  3. Lat. *summam abominationen.* This is the Latin Vulgate translation of Βδέλϑγμα in Mt. 24:15, usually translated "abomination" or "sacrilege." In his letter to Müntzer (63/ 291/7-8) Grebel refers to infant baptism as a "senseless, blasphemous abomination."
  4. Again in his *Taufbüchlein* (ZW, IV, p. 279.13), Zwingli wrote, "And in the first disputation you have expressly said that infant baptism is not only of the pope, but also of the devil. . . . In the last disputation [Blanke thinks this refers to the March 20, 1525, Disputation; see ZW, VI, p. 44, fn.3], when all of us asked over and over again how it happened that they attribute infant baptism to the pope. . . . " Just prior to this excerpt, Zwingli wrote that the Anabaptists identified the introduction of infant baptism with Pope Nicholas II (AD 1058-61).
  5. According to Grebel's letter of Dec. 15 (67/301/27), it was the Anabaptists who asked for the disputations. This is confirmed in Zwingli's *Taufbüchlein* (69C/364/4-5): "Then they wanted a special disputation on baptism to be held."
  6. Probably the Tuesdays of Dec. 6 and 13 (see fn. 2, above). The reference seems to suggest that a series of Tuesday meetings was projected but goes on to imply that only two were held. In the first reference to these meetings in the *Taufbüchlein* (see 66A/Intro., above), Zwingli gives a reason why there were only two. The second meeting was so contentious that their continuation was considered to be too dangerous. In his letter of Dec. 15, however, Grebel seems to imply that only two meetings were intended from the start, one for presentations by the dissenters, and the other for rebuttals by the Zwinglians (67/301/28-32; 67/ fn.11).
  7. One detail that is missing in the present account is that the Bible was to have been the basis for the discussions in the Tuesday meetings (see Intro., Reference No. 2).
  8. The only participant on the side of adult baptism named by Zwingli is Ludwig Hätzer (see Intro., Reference No. 3). Documents 67 and 67B show, however, that Grebel and Mantz participated; and there were several others.
  9. The original first draft of Zwingli's *Elenchus* contains crossed-out sentences that provide additional information (ZW, p. 37, fn. 3). In connection with this phrase, Zwingli had scribbled the names of Caspar Megander, Leo Jud, and Oswald Myconius (see Cast of Characters Nos. 42, 58, and 70) as those who had fought with him in the two debates against the opponents of child baptism. This does not exactly correlate with Grebel's comment (67/ 301/30-31) that their meetings were with the "three pastors." It should be pointed out, however, that as pastor at the hospital of the now defunct Preachers' Monastery (see 68/fn.1), Megander's role was now cognate with that of the other people's priests. Therefore, the only participant on the side of Zwingli who does not fit Grebel's description is that of Myconius, who may have been standing in for Heinrich Engelhart of the Fraumünster. We know that Myconius was the teacher and reader there. Or perhaps Myconius was present in addition to Engelhart.

689

10. Traces of the severity of the encounter are found in Mantz's "Protest and Defense" (see 67B/311/36ff., etc.).

11. The handwritten first draft of the *Elenchus* (see fn. 9, above) adds information to this sentence. Apparently Caspar Megander (see Cast of Characters No. 42) was the special target of the Anabaptist attacks, "as they believed that he was the most responsive to them." Blanke points out that he was the only one of Zwingli's colleagues who grew up in Zurich with Grebel and Mantz, being slightly younger than they; and it is probable that there was some prior connection between the three of them from former times.

67. Grebel to Vadian, Zurich, December 15, 1524

1. In contrast to the previous letter (see 66/fn.1), Grebel's dating of the present letter—"on Thursday after Mary"—undoubtedly refers to the Thursday after *Conceptio Mariae*, or Dec. 15. The internal evidence for this conclusion is the reference to Zwingli's booklet, *Wer Ursach gebe zu Aufruhr*, which was written between Dec. 7 and 28, and was still in the writing process when Grebel wrote. The date assigned by the editor of VB (III, p. 95) must be corrected from Dec. 12 to Dec. 15.

2. What Vadian had requested that Grebel could not do is probably that he be more quiet and less aggressive with his new complaints about infant baptism (see fn. 6, below). This is confirmed in Vadian's letter of Dec. 28 (see 67D/322/5-10), and his earlier "request" was presumably in the same vein.

3. That "truth should not be bound to time" was a slogan in the Zwinglian Reformation. Both Zwingli and Grebel used it in the Second Disputation. It had various and sometimes contradictory meanings. One was that the Catholic tradition limiting the practice of the mass to the morning should be set aside. Another was the argument for slow and cautious change, even after the truth had been established. Still another was the criticism of delay in the implementation of reform while waiting for a better time. The third meaning seems to be implied here. Vadian had probably written what he then repeated in his Dec. 28 letter, "With time it will undoubtedly be regulated according to the witness of the Word of truth" (67D/322/10-12). Grebel rejects this argument which in other letters he calls a "false forbearance."

4. "It" refers to Grebel's rejection of Vadian's request.

5. Grebel's desire "that it might be" refers to his hope that Vadian would see his resistance in a good light.

6. In the next eight sentences Grebel reviews in sparse terms the developments of the past eight months concerning the issue of baptism. The issue first emerged in the villages of Wytikon and Zollikon in the spring of 1524 when Wilhelm Reublin and Hans Brötli (see Cast of Characters Nos. 75 and 10) began to preach against infant baptism in their respective churches, with the result that the parents in both places refused to have their newborn infants baptized.

7. The next event occurred on August 11 when the issue of baptism first came before the Zurich council. Reublin was imprisoned briefly for the purpose of interrogation by the three city pastors, and a first official mandate was issued against parents who refused to baptize their infants on threat of a fine of one silver mark. In his *Taufbüchlein* of May 27, 1525, Zwingli referred to "two private discussions held last summer" over the issue of infant baptism in which the dissenters "allowed themselves to be worsted" (ZW, IV, p. 257). He was probably referring to the spring and August encounters with Reublin and his supporters, rather than to the Tuesday Disputations (see 66A) as Fritz Blanke supposed (ZW, VI, p. 39). Egli concluded that Zwingli was here referring to two discussions which preceded the Tuesday Disputations *(Reformationsgeschichte,* pp. 289, 297).

8. Ger. *Do hand* [*sy*] *recht begert*, "Then [they] requested a judicial decision." Several items of information are given: (1) the request for a public discernment on the question of baptism came from the Anabaptists and not from Zwingli, and (2) the request was channeled first to the magistrates and not to Zwingli. Zwingli confirmed the first item in a comment in his *Taufbüchlein*, "Then they wanted a special disputation on baptism to be held . . . we conducted two such disputations" (ZW, IV, p. 207.12; see also 69C/364/4-5). Although Zwingli said nothing about the request having come first to the council, he alluded several times to the role of

the council in the decision-making process (364/14, 22-23).

9. In a plenary session of the Small and Large Councils of Zurich, a procedural decision was made to have several closed meetings involving the dissenters, the three city pastors, and four members of the Small Council. Blanke (ZW, VI, p. 39) is probably correct in concluding that Grebel here refers to the Tuesday Disputations (see 66A, above).

10. The three pastors would have been the people's priests at the Grossmünster, the Fraumünster, and St. Peter's—namely, Zwingli, Engelhart, and Jud. According to Zwingli, however, his side was represented by himself, Myconius, and Megander (see 66A/fn.9). An interpretation of this apparent discrepancy is that Megander, the pastor of the new Hospital Church, was ascribed a status cognate with that of the other people's priests, and that Myconius, the teacher at the Fraumünster, was standing in for Engelhart.

11. Ger. *den retten,* members of the Small Council. One can read this sentence as implying that two meetings were projected, the Tuesday Disputations, one for presentations by the dissenters and the second for rebuttals by the Zwinglians (see 66A/fn.6). Whether or not only two meetings had been projected from the start, Grebel implies at least that a two-stage procedure was to be followed. The action of the councils in effect set aside the earlier August mandate against Reublin *et al.,* pending a new clarification of the position of the dissenting parents and their pastors.

12. If, indeed, the ground rules for the discussions included an openness to the validity of the opponent's position, Zwingli's own description in the *Taufbüchlein* confirms Grebel's complaint. He admitted that his attitude in the discussions was that "it is for us to try the words of the novice, not for the novice to coerce us" (compare with 47B/176/20-22). He called the dissenters "blockheads," and added, "How dare you introduce innovations into the Church simply on your own authority and without consulting the Church?" (ZW, IV, p. 256).

13. Grebel was referring to one particular person among those who attended the Tuesday Disputations. Zwingli describes what may well be the same incident (ZW, IV, p. 279): "I must tell you a good story," he writes. He tells about two Anabaptists, one a learned leader, and the other an unlettered follower. The leader claimed "by word of mouth and in writing" that infant baptism was introduced by Pope Nicholas II. He had made this claim during the first Tuesday Disputation; but when confronted by Zwingli, he "did not want to be known as having promulgated that [false] idea." But during the second Tuesday Disputation, the unlettered follower, who was not only "the most arrogant of all" but "could not read anything but German" repeated the claim that infant baptism came from the pope. Then Zwingli "attacked quickly and demanded to know from whom he got this error." The story includes a verbatim account of what was said in the confrontation between them. Finally, when Zwingli had him cornered, the Anabaptist "blushed with embarrassment." Although the identity of neither is given, two names suggest themselves. The first is Felix Mantz (see Cast of Characters No. 67), whose description of his own participation in the disputation fits Zwingli's account of the learned leader. As Zwingli said, his verbal comments were put into writing in his "Petition of Defense to the Zurich Council" (see 67B, below), in which he reiterated the claim that the infant baptism "has been fabricated by popes" (67B/315/7). Moreover, Mantz's comment that "our speech is cut off in our throat as soon as they suppose that we are about to speak the truth" (67A/312/8-9) correlates with Zwingli's admitted attack in both Tuesday disputations. The "follower," however, refers to someone like the impetuous farmer-Anabaptist, Jacob Hottinger (see Cast of Characters No. 50). Whether Grebel had Mantz or Hottinger or someone else in mind, he implies in the present sentence that it was not a weakness to be "simple." It was the inquisitors who were showing weakness by their abuse. Blanke (1955, pp. 58-59) described Zwingli's strategy in a similar situation several months later: "Consider the fact that Zwingli and the Council members disputed with the simple farmers and craftsmen one by one in their cells. It required steel nerves to meet such a situation."

14. Ger. *hett geschendt.* Although the verb is present perfect indicative, the implication is that the shame was not immediately apparant, but that in retrospect or by some later act, the "simple one" put his accusers to shame. The subsequent writing by Mantz (see 67B) would fit this reference.

15. Finally, in the sequence of events, a report of the Tuesday Disputations was taken back to both councils, where the decision was made to meet again when the original ground rules would be better enforced. The reference seems to anticipate the public disputation of January 17, 1525, which was also on a Tuesday (see 68B, below).

16. The lion refers to Leo Jud, pastor at St. Peter's (see Cast of Characters No. 58).

17. Matthias Kretz or Gretz was a fellow student of Vadian's in Vienna before he became a preacher in Augsburg in 1519. The play on words cannot be fully preserved in translation, except by such unacceptable renderings as "the lion is scratching with a renowned scratch." Jud's tract was entitled "A Christian Counter-Attack Against Matthias Kretz's False Antichristian Mass, Together with a Letter of Ulrich Zwingli to All the Christian Brethren in Augsburg," and was printed by Johann Hager in Zurich in 1524.

18. Ger. *gwalt,* meaning "power," "authority," or "force." The sentence probably refers to the tract identified in fn. 20, below. Two writings by Zwingli are indicated in this and the following two sentences—the one on force, rebels, and rebellion; and the epistle to the Augsburg brethren against Kretz (see next fn.).

19. Grebel must have heard reference to the possibility that Zwingli was also planning to write against Kretz, which he did in the form of a letter published with Jud's tract. See fn. 17, above.

20. The reference is to Zwingli's tract, *Wer Ursach gebe zu Aufruhr* (Those Who Give Cause for Rebellion), which Zwingli began writing on Dec. 7 and finished on Dec. 28 (see 67C). The translation of *ufrureren oder ufrur* in the text and the term, *Aufruhr,* in the title has varied from EY's "disturbers or disturbance," which is a little too weak, to Bender's "seditionists or sedition," which is a little too strong (pp. 130-131). "Agitators or agitation" would be preferable, if it were not so cumbersome.

21. Grebel's premonition was accurate. The tract dealt with seven groups of agitators, the fourth of whom were the opponents of infant baptism (see 67C/Intro.).

22. The tract was printed in early January 1525, and on January 21 rebaptism was outlawed in Zurich. That edict, however, was not the consequence alone of Zwingli's tract, which was certainly more moderate in tone than Zwingli's later anti-Anabaptist writings. He did not at this time consider the Grebel group the most dangerous, nor their differences on the doctrinal issues of faith and baptism that important. See Blanke, pp. 18-19.

23. Ger. *alle personen* does not mean persons in the sense of individuals but the rule and status attributes that adhere to their office, including prestige and personal pride. Grebel uses the term pejoratively to include those, like Zwingli, who compromise their convictions in order to maintain their personhood, i.e., their position and power. He is saying that truth has no respect of persons and should prosper without asking who is for or against it.

24. Reference to Mt. 9:38 or Lk. 10:2. Grebel is already clear about the polarization into Reformation groups but he is hoping for God's mercy that this group tension might be managed constructively. He hopes that "they" and "you" (the Zwinglians and Vadian) would learn to think less of human wisdom; and for his own group he prays for perseverance and faithfulness in mission.

25. Grebel's concern about *wûcher und zinss* (usury and interest) was expressed in his letter to Müntzer, in which he referred to *zins und zehenden, bede warem wûcher* (interest and tithes, both of which are actual usury: see 63/289/9-10). By usury Grebel meant the receipt of unearned income in the general sense, whether by interest on capital one has loaned, by taxes on the selling and buying of produce, or by compulsory tithes to support the church. *Zinss* could refer to any of these forms of unearned income (see 63/fn.54). The tithes issue, not specifically identified here, was mentioned in 52/207/23, 52A, 52B, and 53/220/21, 23-24

26. What is new in the present reference is the more direct personal admonition to Vadian with reference to usury. The admonition becomes even more direct in 70/379/13-15. By "the usury of others," Grebel was distinguishing between receiving and giving interest on loans. Later Anabaptists continued to make this distinction, condemning the institutions of usury while continuing to pay interest on loans received from unbelievers. See Bender (1950, p. 276, note 80) and Clasen, p. 199. See also 71K/439/23-24, where Grebel is reported to have denied saying "that one should have to give his property to anybody for nothing."

27. The reference to the "coming sword" is striking because it has few parallels in this period. In this case it is probably not an apocalyptic reference as in 62/283/30-34, 69/357/34-36, or 69/358/23-27, but to the persecution of true believers which, according to Zwingli's own testimony in 1520 (see 19A, above) was inevitably going to be part of the price of true reformation.

28. On *geschonet* ("forborne") see 63/fn.17. In this reference, however, *geschonet* is regarded postively, while *schonen* is elsewhere (and only two lines later) negatively used. This criticism of Zwingli's faith, love, and forbearance (line 4) probably refers literally to Zwingli's self-interpretation; and as indicated in 63/fn.17, the concept had an ironical meaning for Grebel, referring to the inconsistency with which the Reformers "spared" the laity but did not "spare" the radicals.

29. Ger. *jetzigen kriegen* refers to the "rumors of war" mentioned in 65/296/25 caused by the current threat of attack by the Catholic cantons and Zwingli's "Battle Plan" (see 65/fn.24). Implicit in Grebel's challenge to Vadian to reject this kind of "warring" is his own new radical Christian pacifist faith ethic (see 63/290/10ff.).

30. On forbearance, see 57A/fn.1,63/fns.17 and 100.

31. By *künst,* translated, "artifice," Grebel refers to critical biblical exegesis, learned rhetorical analysis, and other academic ways of dealing with a text at arm's length without asking what it means for faith, commitment, and obedience. See next note.

32. Vadian's published writings to date were primarily in the areas of classical literature and medicine. He had, however, lectured on the Bible to clergy in St. Gallen, and in that connection had produced several impressive manuscripts of biblical interpretation, perhaps intended for publication. These included *Ex omni novo testamento* (According to the Whole New Testament, 1522) and *Collectanea in Acta Apostolurum* (Collected Notes on the Acts of the Apostles, 1523). Grebel had undoubtedly seen these writings and may have had them in mind when making the present comment, for Vadian was intrigued by the biblical humanism of Erasmus and the latter's Greek text of the New Testament with its critical apparatus. Concerning the manuscript on the *Acts of the Apostles,* Rupp writes that "Vadianus went about the business in a scholarly way, making good use of previous commentaries, notably of Jerome and Bede. There is also evident a humanist debt to Valla, to Budaeus and above all to Erasmus. It is perhaps a scholarly and academic rather than a theological commentary" (p. 367).

33. Mt. 7:14.

34. This reference to *vil mäntel* (many vestments) keeping one from getting through a narrow gate is a play on the word *fürmantel* two lines before, which was there translated "pretense," as in 1 Pet. 2:16.

35. Concerning the identity of this "booklet," see 66/fn.4 and 67D/fn.8.

36. Ger. *böse schlappen,* "an evil blow," "a wicked setback," "a bad loss." See 67D/321/12 for Vadian's response to this sentence.

37. Reference to Rom. 14:10.

38. Grebel is apparently refuting a charge leveled by Vadian that the Grebel group is leading to social unrest.

39. Ger. *der hirten,* see fn. 10, above.

40. See fn. 20, above.

41. Reference to Mt. 7:16.

42. In mid-December 1524, at a point when Zwingli is still overtly forbearing toward the emerging Anabaptist group, Grebel anticipates formal persecution by the state, to which he already believes Zwingli will resort.

43. Grebel refers to the booklets by Jud and Zwingli then in the press. See fns. 17 and 20, above.

44. Martha Grebel, Vadian's wife.

45. Grebel may have had reference to the small academy, which included the clergy, to whom Vadian often lectured on biblical and theological subjects. Or he may have had reference to the more informal Bible study group led by Johann Kessler, who returned to his hometown from Wittenberg just a year earlier. See 65A/297/25ff.

46. Ger. *hern (herren),* translated "lord" in the opening greeting and closing salutation, referred to Vadian's role as *Ratsheer* (Councillor) in St. Gallen.

67A. Zwingli to Lambert and other Brethren in Strasbourg, Zurich, December 16, 1524
1. On Franz Lambert of Avignon, see 47B/fn.11 and Cast of Characters No. 61.
2. "Other brethren" refers particularly to Wolfgang Capito (1478-1541) and Martin Bucer (1491-1551), Reformers of Strasbourg. Of all the early leaders of Reformed Protestantism, Capito was the most sympathetic to Anabaptism, having considerable personal doubt about the validity of infant baptism (ME, I, p. 512). Bucer was also conciliatory toward the Anabaptists, favoring conversation and public debates in preference to suppression (ME, I, p. 455).
3. The first letter, written by Lambert, has been lost. Probably written the end of October, it had posed the first two questions which Zwingli proceeded to answer (see below). The third question (also see below) was from Bucer in a second letter to Zwingli dated Oct. 31, 1524 (ZW, VII, No. 350). The question on baptism and the Lord's Supper was posed in the third letter to Zwingli, written in November by Capito and Bucer conjointly (ZW, VII, No. 351).
4. See fn. 3, above.
5. See fn. 3, above.
6. The fourth question to which Zwingli is replying was posed in a third letter from Strasbourg (see fn. 3, above).
7. The source for the Bucer-Capito question concerning baptism and the Lord's Supper was the recent appearance in Strasbourg of Andreas Carlstadt, distributing his new published pamphlets on these subjects (see 65/fn.6 and Cast of Characters No. 12).
8. The reference is almost certainly to the Tuesday disputations of Dec. 6 and 13 (66A/fn.1).
9. Lat. *Baptismum initationem.*
10. Lat. *multo maxima,* fig. "very long-winded."
11. Lat. *bilis atra.*
12. Lat. *betam aut malvam,* plants valued for their irresistibly savory and aromatic qualities.
13. See 67C/319/29 and 67C/fn.27.
14. This was one of Grebel's basic arguments. See Epi.C/489/29ff.
15. Mantz had asserted that "nobody was baptized without external evidence and certain testimony or desire" (see 67B/314/4-6).
16. Mantz had quoted this verse (67C/312/38-39).
17. Lat. *lascivia et audacia.*
18. Lat. *conniveant,* "to close the eyes to," "to wink at," "to overlook."
19. Lat. *filium,* "son" although the Lat. word for "daughter" is *filia.*
20. Lat. *fratrum.*
21. Lat. *cacademon,* a colloquial word for "devil," lit. "the evil spirit," "the bad omen."
22. Lat. *efficiat, ne tingamus, sin minus.* For evidence of Zwingli's vacillation on this issue of baptism, see 67C/fn.22.

67B. The Mantz Petition of Defense, Zurich, between December 13 and 28, 1524
1. The scholars who ascribed authorship of the petition to Grebel were Egli-Schock (p. 297), Fritz Blanke (ZW, VI, p. 39), and Harold Bender (1950, p. 129ff.). This mistaken assumption was corrected by Walter Schmid (pp. 139-49).
2. Our dating of this document between Dec. 13 and 28 is guided by the following considerations. If the assumptions that it stemmed from the Tuesday Disputations (see Intro., above) and that those disputations were held on Dec. 6 and 13 (see 66A/fn.2) are correct, it could not have been written before the second of those meetings, which Zwingli characterized as the "more severe" (66A/300/38). One *terminus ante quem* is Jan. 17, 1525, the date of the First Public Disputation on Baptism, on the grounds that the mandate of suppression that followed would certainly have been reflected in the Mantz petition had it been written after

that date. It is probable, moreover, that Mantz wrote this petition before the publication of Zwingli's first writing against the Anabaptists (67C), which was completed on Dec. 28, because he pleads with Zwingli to put his defense of infant baptism into writing, and it is evident that he made this challenge before he knew of any writing by Zwingli on this subject. Thus, the best dating of the petition would seem to be between Dec. 13 (the second Tuesday Disputation) and Dec. 28 (publication of Zwingli's tract on rebellion).

3. Ger. *Wisen, fursichtigen, gnedigen, lieben herren und brüder,* a remarkable salutation from one who is suspect.

4. Ger. *auffrurer und unman.* The latter term has the double meaning of eunuch (state of impuberty) and a contemptible, inhuman person, not conforming to the social requirements of human existence.

5. Ger. *euweren hirten,* the three chief pastors of Zurich: Zwingli, Jud, and Engelhart.

6. Mantz refers to the basic principle of *sola scriptura* that was established at the First Disputation of Jan. 29, 1523: "All your people's priests, curates, and preachers, in the city, canton, and dependencies, shall undertake and preach nothing but what can be proved by the Holy Gospel and the pure Holy Scriptures" (Egli, *Aktens.,* No. 327). This principle was often reiterated in the ensuing months in the phraseology that Mantz uses here.

7. Compare this complaint with that of Grebel (67/301/33ff.): "They summoned and abused the simplest, yet nearest one to God, as God and the world know how" (see fn. 1, above).

8. Mantz's claim that Zwingli also had questioned the biblical basis for infant baptism finds confirmation not only in the witness of others (see Bender, 1950, p. 126, 261/fn.106) but also in the admission of Zwingli himself (see 67C/320/34-36 and fn. 28, below).

9. Baptism and the Lord's Supper.

10. Mt. 3:10.

11. Jn. 1:29.

12. Mantz mistook Jn. 1:4 for Jn. 1:29.

13. Mt. 28:19.

14. Mk. 16:16.

15. Ger. *geschichten der botten,* an earlier form of *Apostelgeschichte.*

16. Ger. *wie er beschickt vom Cornelio, im furgehalten ward, worumb er dhaher beschickt wer.* The dual use of *beschickt* is a bit obscure, and it is difficult to discern whether the second use refers to the messenger who was sent or to Peter who was sent. Although our translation preserves this obscurity, the sense of Acts 10:21 confirms the former meaning.

17. Acts 10:40-45.

18. Acts 10:46. One wonders how Mantz interpreted the phenomenon of glossolalia. For Zwingli's understanding, see 70C/402/15ff. For the phenomenon among the Anabaptists, see ZW, VI, p. 151, fn. 2.

19. Acts 10:47-48. The reference is to baptism with water.

20. Prior to publication of this collection, the editor did not investigate the biblical text from which Mantz was working, whether from the Greek text that had been recently edited by Erasmus, from the Latin Vulgate, or from one of the earlier German translations. There are several variants in the present quotation when compared with the RSV: "The Lord God" for "The God of our fathers," "to see that it is right" for "to see the Righteous One," "calling on the name of the Lord" for "calling his name." Moreover, Mantz added the entire last phrase, "and now what more . . . called upon" from some unknown source, either by way of added explanation or from some additional material in the source from which he was quoting.

21. Rom. 6:2-4.

22. Eph. 4:22-24.

23. Grebel also used this figure of speech from Ezek. 34:18-19 (see 62/283/36 and 65/296/8-10).

24. Lk. 3:21, 2:21.

25. Compare with Grebel's similar comment in 65/296/11-13.

26. Gal. 1:8.

27. Mantz refers to Claus Hottinger's participation in the iconoclasm at Stadelhofen (see 57B/Intro. and 58/fn.9), on account of which he was banished from Zurich and later executed in Luzern (see 47A/fn.4 and Cast of Characters No. 48). Mantz here confirms Grebels' earlier judgment that "he who brought up the sculpted images asked his help and used it, nor would he have used it if Hottinger had not previously persuaded him to get to work to demolish the statues . . . " (see 58/256/18-20; 58/fn.7). The implication is that Zwingli is partly responsible for Hottinger's death. At the trial leading to his banishment, Hottinger himself had named three Councillors who had encouraged him in his act, and Ockenfuss testified that "one hears daily that such crucifixes and all other images of God our Redeemer are forbidden" (*Aktens.*, No. 421, quoted by Garside, p. 121).

28. See fn. 8, above.

29. Lev. 10:1-3.

30. See Grebel's similar warning to Vadian in 70/378/16-17.

31. See Zwingli's comment in 66A/300/32-33.

32. I.e., Zwingli.

33. Compare Grebel's comment, "I therefore . . . urge those who can speak better for I am not eloquent and have a poor memory . . . " (57C/244/27-28). See fn. 37, below.

34. See above, 67B/312/8-9.

35. Ger. *vil zangk und hader.*

36. Ger. *dingen er mich überauss beneigt sein vermeint.*

37. This is Mantz's second reference to his inability to debate in public. See fn. 33, above.

67C. Zwingli's Treatise on Rebels and Rebellion, Zurich, between December 7 and 28, 1524

1. The treatise can be dated sometime between Dec. 7, when Zwingli wrote the letter of dedication, and Dec. 28, when it came from the printers.

2. Zwingli discussed seven parties or groups of agitators: (1) the anti-Catholic evangelicals who were merely reacting to authority structures and figures, (2) the libertine evangelicals who confused freedom with license, (3) the nonpayers of taxes and tithes on the false grounds of conscience, (4) the opponents of infant baptism on the false grounds of spiritual pride, (5) the Catholic bishops, (6) the Catholic clerics, and (7) the Catholic princes. The first four types profess commitment to the Reformation but for the wrong reasons. The main thrust of Zwingli's attack was groups 5-7 who rejected the Reformation and so violated the gospel and rights of the masses that they constituted the first cause for rebellion. Our present interest, of course, is group No. 4.

3. Mt. 13:5.

4. Gal. 5:13.

5. Rom. 13:7.

6. Momus in Greek mythology was the personification of ridicule as a mocking and censorious god; hence, a carping critic. For instance, Momus criticized Hephaestus for making a man without providing a little door in his breast to enable one to look into his secret thoughts.

7. These were common charges against the Anabaptists some months later, as Zwingli's letter to Vadian of May 28, 1525 (69D/375/34-35) and his later court testimony (71K/437/35-36, 438/4-6) and Hofmeister's (71K/438/33-34, 38) reveal. For Grebel's reply see 71K/439/32, 36.

8. Zwingli and his associates made this charge against the Anabaptists more than once (see 71K/436/17-20, 438/39-40).

9. See 58a/fn.10.

10. On the expression "from leather," see Wander, II, pp. 1873ff., Nos. 59 and 71. It refers to drawing the sword from leather sheath or scabbard.

11. 1 Jn. 10.

12. 2 Tim. 2:23.

13. Ger. *kampphüser.*

14. He, meaning the devil of the preceding sentence.

15. 1 Pet. 1:13-25; 2:1-12; 3:3-29; 4:1-19.

16. Ex. 20:4.

17. 1 Cor. 12:2; 1 Thess. 1:9; and 1 Jn. 5:21.

18. God.

19. Mt. 22:29.

20. Zwingli referred to the booklet, "Concerning Choice and Liberty Respecting Food," published April 16, 1522 (see Jackson, 1912, pp. 70-112).

21. Lev. 18:6-18.

22. Although Zwingli's approach here appears conciliatory, it represents a definite shift away from an earlier doubt about infant baptism. As early as 1521 he had preached "that the little children who are not baptized will not be damned" (Bender, 1950, p. 126, note 101). The same doubt was expressed in the 18th Article for the First Disputation in 1523 (see Meyer, p. 41), but more particularly in his "Exposition" of that article published in July, in which he had written: "Although I know, as the Fathers show, that infants have been baptized occasionally from the earliest times, still it was not so universal a custom as it is now, but the common practice was as soon as they arrived at the age of reason to form them into classes for instruction in the Word of Salvation (hence they were called catechumens, i.e., persons under instruction). And after a firm faith had been implanted in their hearts and they had confessed the same with their mouth, then they were baptized. I could wish that this custom of giving instruction were revived today" (ZW, II, No. 20, tr. in Jackson, 1900, p. 243). Like his other articles on images, the mass, celibacy, etc., he had not yet proceeded to put this conviction into practice. Nevertheless, this earlier position was the source for the view of believer's baptism held by Grebel and his friends. As Grebel is reported to have said, "It was Zwingli who got him into this matter and told him many things about which he does not now remain constant and from which he was now retreating" (71D/421/31-33). This testimony finds further confirmation in Zwingli's own comment of May 1525: "For some time I myself was deceived by the error and I thought it better not to baptize children until they came to years of discretion. But I was not so dogmatically of this opinion as to take the course of many today, who although they are far too young and inexperienced in the matter argue and rashly assert that infant baptism derives from the papacy or the devil or something equally nonsensical" (ZW, IV, p. 228, tr. in Bromiley, p. 139). For further documentation see Bender, 1950, pp. 126-27, 260-61, and 68F/fn.35.

23. Mt. 15:9.

24. Mt. 15:13.

25. Mt. 28:19.

26. For another reference to Calcutta as the far-off foil, see 57C/245/10 and 57C/fn.20.

27. For the Old Testament basis for circumcision as the sign of the covenant people, see Gen. 17:10-14. It was in the Tuesday Disputations that Zwingli first used this argument of circumcision as the precedent for infant baptism and of baptism as the Christian's circumcision (67B/306/13).

28. Rom. 4:12.

29. Gen. 21:4; Lev. 12:3.

30. Col. 2:11.

31. 1 Pet. 3:21.

32. 1 Cor. 1:16. This particular proof-texting from 1 Cor. and Acts 16:15, 32, became a primary point of contention in Grebel's written confutation, which is extant only in the form found in Zwingli's *Elenchus* (see Epi.C, below, pp. 480ff.

33. Acts 16:15.

34. Acts 16:33.

35. Gen. 21:4.

36. The Marranos were Spanish Jews who adopted Christianity under the threat of expulsion while secretly adhering to Judaism. In that way they adapted to the social life of the Iberian Peninsula and gained considerable influence, part of which came through their syn-

cretistic doctrinal formulations and rites and through their interest in the Reformation.
37. Mt. 18:3-5; 1 Cor. 7:14.
38. Acts 10:47.
39. Jn. 9:36.
40. 1 Cor. 11:28.

67D. Vadian to Grebel, St. Gallen, December 28, 1524
1. Ger. *Minen grůss mit erbietung so ich vermag.* In his translation, "My greeting with offer to do what I can," Yoder misread *erbietung* ("offer") for *Ehrerbietung* ("respectfulness," "reverence," "deference," "dutifulness," "devotion."
2. Letter No. 67 dated Dec. 15. See next fn.
3. Ger. *das ich fil luschtz hab dich zu schmützen.* This is a response to 67/302/29 where Grebel accused Vadian of giving him "a nasty slap."
4. Ger. *khumlicher schiklikeyt.*
5. Leo Jud, see 52/fn.4.
6. Ger. *gachling ussstossen und abthůn,* "precipitously discard and dispose of."
7. Ger. *So du aber meinst, grundtlich ze faren,* "But if you mean to go radical." Bender (1950, p. 133) gives the following parphrase: "But if you intend to be thorough in the matter." The addition of "in the matter" suggests that the abuse of baptism was the sole concern here, but the context makes it clear that Vadian referred to Conrad's attitude toward reform in general. The fact that Vadian did not here use Zwingli's term, *aufrührerisch* (rebellious) suggests that Vadian did not put a totally negative connotation into his adjective, *gründlich* ("radical").
8. On the identity of this booklet, see 66/fn.4 and 67/fn.3. It is possible that the "booklet" to which Vadian refers is a manuscript draft of his lost tract, *Schrift wider die Taüfer* ("Writing Against the Anabaptists"), directed against the emergence of the movement in St. Gallen (see 65A/297-98, 70B/385/3, and Näf, II, pp. 230, 232) and indirectly against the proto-Anabaptist group in Zurich, which sparked the movement in St. Gallen.

67E. Hegenwald to Grebel, Wittenberg, January 1, 1525
1. Hegenwald was writing, not just to Grebel, but to the group he represented, his "fellow brethren in Christ at Zurich" (331/12-13).
2. Ger. *villicht unerfordert.* See 325/4, below.
3. Thirteen articles in all (see 329/35).
4. The phrase, "in this way," would seem at first to mean that his answer was going to be stated in specific articles, i.e., in a list of responses to the objections which were listed; but the rest of the letter does not really proceed like that, even though Hegenwald did assign numbers to six of his responses. Thus, "in this way" probably means simply "as follows."
5. The entire early portion of the text including point one (p. 324) to the beginning of point two (p. 328) has no paragraph divisions. The divisions begin when Hegenwald returns after all to answering point by point. The earlier divisions in the present edition were added on the basis of units of meaning.
6. In the disputations of that time, it was not unusual for the disputants to question each other's motives and basic integrity. Luther certainly did so in his refutation of Carlstadt to which Hegenwald referred in the letter (see fn. 47). To the extent to which Hegenwald had done so in his first letter to Grebel, the latter's reply raised an important ecumenical principle—their fundamental unity as believers—and question how one decides whether one's motives are truly Christian.
7. Ger. *furcht gottes.* Compare to the same usage but with quite different application in 68F/342/21.
8. The Latin *pietatis,* genitive case of *pietas,* means "dutifulness." It is applied, first, to dutifulness toward parents, children (see 6/fn.6), native country, etc. It is used, second, to indicate duty to God, usually as the norm for all other duty, Hegenwald used the term five times (325/2, 12, 15, 31, 327/15) and it is central to his main point. He defines it as "the fear of God" that produces the "consoled spirit" and "peaceful conscience" which constitute

Hegenwald's "test" of whether or not Grebel's opinion is from God. Hegenwald does not actually make that judgment but implies a serious question about it. The opposite of *pietas* is *impietas* (327/8)—hypocrisy, ungodliness, the "flesh" that can do nothing but seek after its own profit, pleasure, and recognition. A number of examples of *impietas* are cited: the friends of Job, who condemn by quoting many Scriptures; King Manassah, who thought he was returning to the early religion of the nation when he restored the old altars and sacrificed his son on one of them; the people of Israel, when they elected a king in the belief that they were doing God's will, etc. Hegenwald's definition of *pietas* in 327/15 emphasizes the otherness of Christ on the cross, whom no one can "properly know" or about whom no one can really "know something." Therefore, many claims like those of Grebel are *impietas* because they claim to know God's Word out of a contentious spirit and a blindness about their own true motivations.

9. *Etc.* means that Hegenwald is quoting his own or Grebel's sentence or a Bible verse in an abbreviated form (see 325/28, 32, 327/28, 328/3-4, 25, 329/25, 37).

10. Prov. 14:12.

11. 2 Kings 21:1ff. and 2 Chron. 33:1ff.

12. 2 Chron. 33:6. The reference is to the burning of sons, although *filios* in the Latin Vulgate may mean "children" of either sex. Perhaps Hegenwald was referring to the burning of Jephthah's daughter (Judg. 11:29-40).

13. 1 Sam. 8.

14. 1 Jn. 4:1.

15. Jn. 16:8; Ps. 96:13b; 98:9b.

16. Luther often referred to "the outward appearance of righteousness" as the ground of pride and works-righteousness that he so deplored in Carlstadt and other "heavenly prophets" (see fn. 47).

17. Lk. 16:15; 1 Sam. 16:7; Prov. 21:2; Acts 1:24.

18. Prov. 16:2.

19. Ps. 49:10-11.

20. An idiomatic expression of unknown derivation.

21. The pronoun was probably meant to refer back to Elihu, notwithstanding the next parenthetical phrase, *wie ouch Heliu* ("as also Elihu" or "nor did Elihu"), which Hegenwald probably meant to be *wie ouch Job.*

22. Rom. 8:16-17; Gal. 6:1; Eph. 1:17.

23. Ger. *durch das öffentlich wort gottes* (see fn. 32).

24. Mt. 12:24-27.

25. 2 Sam. 21:1-9. The circumstances of the massacre of some of the Gibeonites by Saul are known.

26. 2 Kings 23:29-30.

27. Phil. 3:13.

28. Hegenwald refers to the preceding sentence in which he exaggerated the insistence of Grebel and his friends on proof, yet without wanting to say that asking for proof is unimportant—likewise the sarcasm of his needing to say that they probably also have some shortcomings.

29. This sentence is a clue to Hegenwald's concept of *pietas.* He is trying to validate a test of Christian integrity and yet avoid any appearance of a works-righteousness of his own.

30. Lat. *impietas,* see fn. 8.

31. Job 4:6; 6:14; 15:4; 22:4; 28:28.

32. Ger. *mit offenglicher warhafftiger gschrifft.* If "convincing" is too strong a translation of *offenglicher,* "manifest," "evident," "plain" are alternatives.

33. See fn. 8.

34. Lk. 9:35.

35. 1 Cor. 2:2.

36. 1 Cor. 8:2.

37. Ger. *Den wo es zu ein treffen gieng.*

38. 1 Cor. 8:2b.

39. Col. 1:11.

40. Col. 1:9-10.

41. Ger. *der beruffung*. The word here does not mean individual job appointment but rather the moral grounds for acting like a preacher or teacher. It is the response to the question "Who called you?" or "Who gave you the right to preach?" The effect of Hegenwald's downgrading of the certainty of Christian vocation on the part of anyone, and therefore on the part of Grebel and his friends, is to leave such matters in the hands of the authorities on the grounds that it would take a special certainty to act against or without their appointment.

42. The subject of "the call" was prominent at that time in the arguments between Luther and Carlstadt, and it is possible that Grebel had echoed some of Carlstadt's points, to which Luther had replied, "I want to warn everyone truly and fraternally to beware of Dr. Karlstadt and his prophets . . . because they run about and teach, without a call. This God condemns through Jeremiah [23:21], who says, 'I did not send them, yet they ran. I did not speak to them, yet they prophesied' " (LW, Vol. 40, p. 222).

43. This disclaimer of a call to write on his own part is inconsistent with his earlier admission that he had written to Grebel "uninvited" (324/33, 325/4).

44. This phrase was characteristically Grebel's. See 63/287/14-15), who got it from Zwingli (see 57C/246/5-6), who got it from Deut. 12:32; but see 63/fn.27.

45. On idols, see 57B/fn.1.

46. Ger. *offenglich*. See fn. 28. Again (see fn. 35) the point is that there is a kind of clarity in divine leading which is unquestionable and irresistible, and without such clarity one should not go ahead.

47. The reference was to Vol. 1 of Luther's *Wider die himmlischen Propheten, von den Bildern und Sakrament* (Against the Heavenly Prophets Concerning Images and Sacrament), published in two parts. The first was finished by the end of December 1524, and the second a month later in January 1525. See fn. 66 below.

48. This allusion to another source of information is unclear, but it can be presumed to refer to an earlier letter from Grebel himself. See fn. 1, above.

49. "Opinion" implies not merely a position Grebel had taken privately but also the Grebel party.

50. "In part I know well" seems contradictory. The "in part" is one of the expressions of modesty which the author uses frequently, not claiming to know too much. But of the little he knows, he says, one piece of information is very solidly confirmed and that is the general impulsiveness of human nature, apparently illustrated especially in what happens when people publish.

51. This is where actual paragraph units begin in the text.

52. Luther had criticized Carlstadt because "he pounces on outward things with such violence, as though the whole strength of the Christian enterprise consisted in the destruction of images" (LW, Vol. 40, p. 67), and argued in favor of a Pauline freedom, "for just as I may with good conscience eat and drink that which has been offered to idols, and sit and dwell in an idol's temple, as St. Paul teaches, so I may also put up with idols and let them be, as things which neither make any difference nor hinder my conscience and faith" (LW, Vol. 40, p. 95).

53. John 6:63. Hegenwald does not really answer Grebel's accusation that he is assuming that Scripture is inadequate for certain purposes. To cite "my words are life and spirit" can itself be an argument against being too concerned about the details of biblical teaching, and Hegenwald can be read in that way. This means he really accepts Grebel's accusation that he does not give Scripture dominant authority in outward matters. It is, however, also a possible interpretation that here he is making a kind of confessional statement claiming that for him Scripture is authoritative whether he has been able to work out all its meaning or not. One of those approaches continues the argument, the other repeats his modesty. In either case, he is saying that he knows enough to see what is wrong with Grebel.

54. After Carlstadt was banished from Saxony on Sept. 18, 1524, he visited Strasbourg where he gained some support for his ideas. In November the Strasbourg Reformers wrote to

Luther for clarification of their differences with particular reference to the use of images and the mass. In his reply (LW, Vol. 40, pp. 65-71), Luther did not give them a detailed refutation but announced his intent to publish a lengthy refutation, which he did in the two-part work, "Against the Heavenly Prophets" (see fn. 47).

55. We can assume that the views on the Lord's Supper which Grebel wrote to Hegenwald were similar to those he wrote to Müntzer. See 63/287/21-288/26. See fn. 64, below.

56. The book to which Hegenwald referred was the same as fn. 47 above, directed largely against Carlstadt's doctrine of the Lord's Supper, in reply to the latter's *Wider die alten und neuen papistischen Messen* and *Dialogus oder ein Gesprächbüchlein von dem greulichen und abgöttischen Missbrauch des hochwurdigen Sakraments Jesu Christi* (both printed in Basel in October 1524; see 65/fn.7). It is evident that Hegenwald identified Grebel with Carlstadt, for four times (328/33, 329/12, 329/33, 331/7) he referred him to the booklet that Luther was writing against Carlstadt. He says specifically in the fourth citation that he will probably find in this writing Luther's answer to their own arguments relating to the Lord's Supper. Bender wrote: "This identification of the Grebel group as 'Carlstadtian' is noteworthy.... It is possible that the last letter by Grebel to Hegenwald reflected the influence of the Carlstadt pamphlets which were printed in Basel at the end of October 1524, and which were so diligently read and circulated by Grebel's friends. It is also probable that Grebel's letters to Hegenwald indicated a friendly attitude toward Carlstadt" (1950, p. 122).

57. The text did not have a paragraph separation for point four.

58. Although one cannot be certain why Hegenwald remarks on the fact that the letter he has received refers to the Lord's Supper as "the supper of Christ," it is possible to speculate on why the usage is different. Carlstadt had criticized Luther for retaining the terms "sacrament" and "mass" in reference to the Lord's Supper, the former because Christ and the apostles never used the word and he wanted a biblical word (see LW, Vol. 40, p. 149), and the latter because "mass" implies a sacrifice which all Protestants reject (*ibid.*, p. 119). The derivation of "mass" from the Latin *missa* was reminiscent of all unbiblical derivations and hence was repugnant to the radical Reformers.

59. Ger. *und wolt ye nit hängen an personen.* This is obviously a technical point that Hegenwald is making, referring to an alleged denial by Grebel of the objective grace of God imparted through the elements of the mass apart from the subjective faith and obedience of the recipients. In his letter to Müntzer, Grebel had written, "If there be one who does not intend to live in a brotherly way, he eats to his condemnation, for he eats like any other meal without discernment and he brings shame upon love, the inward bond, as well as the bread, the outward bond" (63/288/1-4). Hegenwald is hewing to Luther's view that the mass is not a rite by which persons give something to God (thus attaching it to persons), but a means of grace that Christ gives to the recipients. In his criticism of Grebel, Hegenwald is using the same wording that Luther applied against Carlstadt, i.e., "external appearances," signs of faith or works of love by which the Lord's Supper is supposed to be validated. "It is the same fiddle upon which he always fiddles, namely, that the *external appearance* is the main thing, according to which everything that the heart, mouth, pen, and hand confesses is to be regarded and judged. Therefore it does not help that we believe with the heart, confess with the mouth, testify with the pen, and demonstrate with deeds that we do not regard the sacrament as a sacrifice, though we still elevate it [the host]. The elevation is so important [to him] and by itself counts for so much, that it outweighs and condemns everything else. Is this not a vexatious spirit, who so juggles with *external appearance* against the truth in the spirit?" (LW, Vol. 40, p. 137, italics inserted). When Carlstadt denied that the unworthy can either dispense or receive the body and blood of Christ in the Lord's Supper, Luther also accused him of attaching the validity of the Lord's Supper to persons, i.e., to "spiritual participation" (*ibid.,* pp. 179-80).

60. 1 Jn. 4:2.

61. Ger. *Jhesum Christum afflöst,* "dissolves Jesus Christ." The phrase connotes a negation of incarnation. It is interesting that the argument that outward matters are unimportant

is based on the claim that Christ came in the flesh. Hegenwald is using the argument to say that if you make the doctrinal affirmation that the incarnation happened, that is all that is needed to be "of God." Therefore, the only criterion for faithfulness should be that kind of confession. Grebel, on the other hand, would have said that it is precisely because of God's entering into historical reality that historical reality in all its detail should be taken seriously and that Scripture should be respected wherever it speaks clearly.

62. I.e., "You make of him a lawgiver." Luther often referred to the polarity between Christ and Moses in his refutation of the "heavenly prophets," e.g., "These teachers of sin and Mosaic prophets are not to confuse us with Moses. We don't want to see or hear Moses. How do you like that, my dear rebels? We say further that all such Mosaic teachers deny the gospel, banish Christ, and annul the whole New Testament. I now speak as a Christian for Christians. For Moses is given to the Jewish people alone, and does not concern us Gentiles and Christians. We have our gospel and New Testament. If they can prove from them that images must be put away, we will gladly follow them. If they, however, through Moses would make us Jews, we will not endure it" (LW, Vol. 40, p. 92).

63. Mt. 12:8; Mk. 2:28; Lk. 6:5.

64. Ex. 20:8-11.

65. Mt. 26:26; Mk. 14:22; Lk. 22:19; 1 Cor. 11:24. Again, since Grebel's letter is missing, we have to look elsewhere for clues as to how Hegenwald understood that the Grebel circle used as an argument on their side the words of institution, "This is my body." Much of the debate between Carlstadt and Luther centered around these words. In his *Dialogus* (see fn. 56, above), Carlstadt denied that the body of Christ was corporeally in the bread, and to support this denial, he exegeted 1 Cor. 11:24: "This verse, 'This is my body which is given for you,' is complete in itself. At other points in the gospels it appears independently, though in different words, where Christ says nothing of the sacrament, for example in Mt. 16 [:5ff.]; Jn. 3 [:1ff.]; 6 [:25ff.] ..." (see LW, Vol. 40, p. 154, fn. 114). He argued that this verse is unrelated to the preceding action of blessing and distributing the bread. "This" refers to "my body" and not to the bread in the previous verse. In his letter to Müntzer, Grebel presented the same thesis but without the exegesis: "They are words of institution of the Supper of unity, not of consecration ... because the bread is nothing but bread; by faith it is the body of Christ and an incorporation with Christ and the brethren" (63/287/26-27, 33-35).

66. The second part of Luther's "Against the Heavenly Prophets" dealt mostly with Carlstadt's exegesis of 1 Cor. 11:24 (see previous fn.). See LW, Vol. 40, pp. 154ff. Luther concluded as follows: "I think I find evidence here that it is against his own conscience that Dr. Karlstadt denies that the blood and body of Christ is in the sacrament, and that in his heart he is hostile to God and wants to blaspheme and dishonor him, to the injury and vexation of his Word and sacrament. I believe, I say once more, that Dr. Karlstadt has surrendered himself and dared to become an avowed enemy of God, wanting to race rather than trot to hell" (*ibid.*, p. 217).

67. Job 13:5.

68. See fn. 59 above.

69. Mt. 16:17.

70. See fn. 63 above.

71. Ger. *es wil ein ander fundament haben, den wir wenen.* What Hegenwald means by this is not very clear. He could mean, on one hand, that "It is not really worth our carrying on this debate about the details of Reformation policy since the fundamental conflict at stake will not be decided on the level of debate about details." On the other hand, the coming Luther tract, which should clear up everything, was a masterpiece of detail, devoting eighty pages to a refutation of Carlstadt's exegesis of 1 Cor. 11:24.

72. Like the letter to Müntzer, Grebel wrote the bulk of the text in the first person plural on behalf of a Zurich group and then became personal under his own name in a later paragraph (see 63/291/17-18) and postscript (see 63/292/14).

73. Ger. *offentlichen zwang.* The adjective was used twice before (see fns. 32 and 46). Hegenwald has some specific conception of a particular divine leading which is what it would

take for him to get into publishing. He does not describe it but it seems clear that he would know if that compulsion came to him and that it has not yet done so.

74. Adam is, of course, the prototype of unregenerate fallen man (Rom. 5:14; 1 Cor. 15:22, 45).

75. "Your Paul" probably indicates that Grebel had appealed to the authority of Paul for much of what he was writing.

76. Rom. 15:14; Col. 3:16.

77. Eph. 4:2; Col. 3:13.

78. Rom. 15:1; Gal. 6:2.

79. 1 Thess. 5:14; 2 Thess. 3:15; 2 Tim. 2:24.

80. The line means that if they are that aggressive, they will have other targets for their criticism and need not pick on Hegenwald.

81. Although the German text for this sentence is perfectly clear, its meaning is unknown to translator or editor. At the time that Hegenwald wrote (Jan. 1, 1525), the first part of Luther's "Against the Heavenly Prophets" was in the press. Was its formal publication and commencement of distribution planned to take place in an announced congregational setting?

68. Grebel to Vadian, Zurich, January 14, 1525

1. This reference to Caspar Grossmann (see Cast of Characters No. 42) was apparently meant to be ironical, perhaps in the sense of "three-sided Megander" or "Number Three Megander" since he was the third of the three Zurich pastors (see 66A/fn.9 and 67/301/30-31). Grossmann had been recently appointed head preacher at the new Hospital Church in Zurich (see fn. 2, below).

2. Ger. *zun Predigeren* ("to the preachers") refers to the Dominican monks, whose monastery had recently been turned into another hospital and whose chapel had been made into the fourth parish church in Zurich (66A/fn.9).

3. Jacob Hottinger, see Cast of Characters No. 50.

4. The public disputation on baptism was held in Zurich on January 17, 1525. For the official notice see 68A/333. Grebel's implication that attendance at the disputation was mandatory for "all who are for and against infant baptism" is warranted by the wording of the mandate of the council, 68A/333/14-15.

5. The daughter Rachel must have died before her second birthday, for a record of the Orphans' Court following Conrad's death in 1526 mentioned all three children (Theophil, Joshua, and Rachel), but the subsequent records (1527, 1539, and 1541) mentioned only the first two (see Bender, 1950, p. 5).

6. Ger. *ist noch nit in dem Römschen wasserbad getoufft und gschwemmt.* The English "Romish" is used rather than "Roman" (*Römisch* or *Römer*).

7. On Hubmaier, see Cast of Characters No. 54. He had been pastor at Waldshut since 1521. News that he was planning to write a tract questioning infant baptism had apparently reached Grebel but not Zwingli. This is not surprising since Hubmaier had not indicated this publicly until January 16, 1525, when he wrote to Oecolampad that he had just written a booklet on baptism which the Basel Reformer would soon see in print. Oecolampad then wrote to Zwingli about it on January 18. It is interesting that Grebel had known about this earlier, and Bender (1950, p. 134) speculates that Hubmaier may have told him about it in person when he visited Zurich in October. It is more likely that Hubmaier had written to Grebel directly as he had on other occasions (see 70E/411/29). Vadian later wrote that it was Grebel who led Hubmaier to embrace Anabaptist doctrines (Epi.G/525/28-29).

8. Urban Rhegius (1489-1541) had attended the University of Freiburg and like Hubmaier had accompanied Johann Eck to Ingolstadt. After Emperor Maximilian crowned him poet laureate and imperial orator in 1517, he settled in Constance, where he learned to know Johann Faber, the bishop's vicar, upon whose recommendation he was assigned to Augsburg in 1520. Here he became a dedicated Lutheran preacher, theologian, and reformer, and from 1525 until his death he zealously persecuted the Anabaptists. The particular

pamphlet to which Grebel referred was entitled *Wider den neuen Irrsal Dr. Andreas Karlstadt des Sacraments halb Warnung . . . wom September 1524.*

9. Grebel's reference to 96 theses defending infant baptism probably represented the preparation on the part of Zwingli and the other Zurich pastors for the January 17 Disputation on baptism. Only Heinrich Bullinger recorded this disputation, having attended it as a young man in his early twenties. In his *Diarum,* he wrote that he recorded the proceedings of an Anabaptist disputation, undoubtedly referring to the January 17 meeting (see Bender, 1950, p. 263, note 2), but that record is not extant. In his *Reformationsgeschichte,* I, pp. 237-38, written in 1572, he recalls the January 17 Disputation and writes that "Zwingli responded with the reasoning and argumentation which he subsequently published in a pamphlet dedicated to the people of St. Gallen entitled *Von dem touff, vom widertouff unnd vom kindertouff* ["Concerning Baptism, Rebaptism, and Infant Baptism"]. The Anabaptists could neither refute his arguments nor maintain their own" (see Hillerbrand, 1964, p. 228). This recollection indicates that the "96 theses" to which Grebel referred were an early draft of the anti-Anabaptist tract which Zwingli published on May 27, 1525 (see 69C, below).

10. Grebel was referring to a turning point in Zwingli's program of reform with particular reference to the mass, in preparation for its abolition by the Zurich Council on April 12. The initial commitment to abolition came at the Second Zurich Disputation in October 1523, but strong resistance from other cantons and from within the Zurich church and council prevented its immediate implementation. For fourteen months the Roman Catholic mass continued to be celebrated, but in January 1525 a new vigorous attack upon it was made. This forced Zwingli's hand, and the sermon to which Grebel referred indicates a new pledge on his part to convince the City Council to decree a new evangelical communion service in place of the old mass. The first published summary of his new doctrine of the Lord's Supper appeared in his "Commentary on the True and False Religion," issued in March.

11. Concerning the Conrad Eppenberger affair, see 60/fn.3 and 65/fn.1.

12. The "new booklets at hand" are seven in number, but they cannot be easily identified since they are described by content rather than by author and title.

13. Apparently no scholar to date has been able to identify the author and title of the tract "against infant baptism," which Grebel describes with the Greek word *trisarcheteles,* loosely translated as "the first and last word on the subject three times over." Hubmaier's first tract on the subject did not appear before February 2. Carlstad's tract on infant baptism was rejected for printing in Basel the previous October (see 65/fn.6); and in any case he was more interested in the subject of the Lord's Supper than of baptism. Müntzer had criticized infant baptism in his *Protestation oder Empbietung* which Grebel had read the previous September (see 62/fn.6 and 63/fn.7); but like Carlstadt, Müntzer expressed only minor interest in the subject.

14. Ger. *einss von der hurery,* can be translated "one on sexual immorality."

15. Ger. *einss von der widergeburt,* can be translated "one on rebirth" or "one on regeneration."

16. Ger. *einss wider den zinss und zehenden, ein Archeteles.* Muralt and Schmid (Quellen 1, p. 34, fn. 6) interpret *ein Archeteles* as a separate publication, distinct from the tract against interest and tithes; and they identify it as Zwingli's *Apologeticus Archeteles,* published August 23, 1522. This is inaccurate speculation, and it is much more likely that *ein Archeteles* ("the beginning and the end" or "a work to end all argument") was Grebel's description of the otherwise unidentified tract against the compulsory collection of tithes and interest.

17. Ger. *einss wider den nüwen abgott dass schonen.* On the concept of the "new idol of forbearance," see 63/fn.17 and other listings in the Index. The tract to which Grebel referred may have been Müntzer's "Sermon Before the Princes," preached on July 13, 1524, and later published as a tract entitled *Ausgetrückte Emplössung des falschen Glaubens,* in which the concept of "false forbearance" is employed. See Williams, 1957, p. 63.

18. Ger. *einss von gwalt,* referring to a tract concerning the use of force or violence.

19. Ger. *krieg einss,* referring to some unknown tract on warfare.

20. There is no doubt that this refers to Zwingli's famous work, *De vera et false religione commentarius . . . das König Franz I. von Frankreich gewidmet ist und Ende Marx 1525 erschien* ("Commentary on the True and False Religion"; see ZW, III, No. 50, and Heller, pp. 43-337). In his introduction to the work, Zwingli said that he wrote it in three and one-half months for general circulation especially in France, thus redeeming his promise to French friends; and so he dedicated it to King Francis I.

21. Muralt and Schmidt (Quellen 1, p. 34, fn.8) report that a writing "on the love of God and one's neighbor," does not exist but may have been planned by Zwingli. It is more likely that the phrase was meant in apposition to the booklet dedicated to Francis, i.e., "The Commentary on the True and False Religion" (see fn. 20, above).

22. Zwingli regularly preached on Friday as well as on Sunday. The Greek *kai-holen* means literally "and all that," but it is more pertinently translated "and the whole bit" or "with all the trimmings." Considering the content of a letter that he wrote on Saturday, Jan. 14, to the magistrates of Rhaetia, the sermon defended himself and his fellow Zurichers against the charge of sedition by Emperor Charles and vowed to protect all whom professed the new doctrines of the Reformation from their enemies (see Jackson, 1900, pp. 266-67). For Zwingli's "battle plan" and war preparations, see 65/fn.24 and 67/fn.29.

23. Martha Grebel, Vadian's wife.

24. Benedict von Watt, Vadian's brother.

68A. Notice of a Public Disputation on Baptism, Zurich, January 15, 1525

1. The formal resolution *(Beschluss)* concerning the public disputation on baptism was approved on January 12, 1525 (Quellen, No. 21). Muralt and Schmid erroneously dated the formal proclamation *(Mandat)* on the same day (Quellen 1, p. 33, fn. 1), but according to Grebel it was made on Sunday, Jan. 15, probably in all the Zurich churches.

2. Since the opponents of infant baptism were already designated as the errant ones, the outcome was prejudiced before the debate began. For the outcome of the disputation held on Jan. 17, see documents 68C/336, 68D/337 and 68E/338.

3. Ger. *geistlich oder weltlich.*

4. Ger. *Rathaus.*

5. The "regular time of meeting" may refer not to a regular session of the council but to the "Tuesday Disputations" that were held consecutively in December (see 66A, above) with the same agenda of the present disputation: the question of baptism. The identification of this "first public disputation" as in fact the third of the "Tuesday disputations" would correlate with Grebel's comment of Dec. 15 that "both councils have decided anew that they should meet together [again] as previously ordered" (67/302/2-3) and with Zwingli's comment *ex post facto* that 'within three, or at most four, days [after the last, i.e., third, Tuesday Disputation], it was announced that the leaders of the sect had baptized fifteen brethren" (68F/340/29-31). The Tuesday Disputation to which Zwingli referred could not have been either of the two December meetings (if our dating in 66A, above, is correct), since Blanke dates the baptismal service on other evidence as Jan. 21 (see 68F/fn.11). But if Zwingli was here referring to a Tuesday Disputation subsequent to the December meetings, i.e., the Jan. 17 Disputation, then indeed the chronology works perfectly. Further evidence that this was Zwingli's intended meaning was his comment in the *Taufbüchlein* that they had met with the Anabaptists "twice in private and once before the Large Council" (69C/372/35-38).

68B. The First Public Disputation on Baptism, Zurich, January 17, 1525

1. Ger. *raedten und Burgern,* see 52/fn.5, 57B/fn.2, etc.

2. On Reublin, see Cast of Characters No. 75.

3. See 67/fn.6, 67A/304/18-20, and 67B.

4. See 69C, below. It is interesting to note that Zwingli was devoting major time at this early date to the refutation of the Anabaptist position.

5. Ger. *ir meynung erhallten.* It is not clear whether the possessive pronoun refers to "arguments" (i.e., "obtain their meaning") or to "the Anabaptists." The latter is used here.

6. See Acts 5:29.
7. See 68H, below.

68C. Council Mandate for Infant Baptism, Zurich, January 18, 1525
1. The Anabaptist position had been prejudged erroneous before the disputation was held (see 68A/fn.2).
2. Blanke (1961, p. 60) concludes correctly that "the result of the disputation on January 17 is in fact almost the annihilation of the Grebel group."

68D. Zwingli to Vadian, Zurich, January 19, 1525
1. A quotation from the Latin Vulgate of 1 Sam. 2:10.
2. A paraphrase of the mandate itself (see 68C, above).

68E. Council Decree Against Anabaptists, Zurich, January 21, 1525
1. I.e., the day after Jan. 20.
2. Diethelm Röist (see Cast of Characters No. 78) had been appointed burgomaster only a month before to succeed his father, Marx Röist, who had died the previous June.
3. See the mandate of the Zurich Council of Jan. 18 (68C/336).
4. Ger. *bsondern schulen.* There are two interpretations of the meaning of these "special schools": (1) Hillerbrand (1964, p. 230) believes that they refer to the Tuesday Disputations (66A), and he translated this phrase "the special gatherings arranged to deal with this matter." (2) Bender (1950, p. 136) interprets this as the meetings of the Castelberger-Grebel group for study of the Bible (see 51B, above). These meetings began as "Bible schools" that were allied with the Zwinglian Reformation with the approval of Zwingli himself (Bender, pp. 90, 199). It was these schools in general and the house meetings in particular which were now to be prohibited.
5. Felix Mantz, see Cast of Characters No. 67.
6. *Disputieren und fürnemen.* Bender (1950, p. 136) renders it "disputing and agitating."
7. The fact is, however, that two more public and several more private disputations were held in Zurich in 1525-26 (see 68B/fn.1).
8. Ger. *dryen obersten meistern.* They were Zwingli, Jud, and Grossmann.
9. The priest from Wytikon was Reublin (see Cast of Characters No. 75). He had been the first in the canton to preach against the baptism of infants, in response to which a number of parents refused to present their children for baptism on Easter 1524. He was arrested on Aug. 11 (see 67/fn.7) and imprisoned for a period of counseling by the three Zurich pastors. He, Grebel, and Mantz, were the three main dissenters at the January 17 disputation (see 68B/335/16), and it was for his disputing on this occasion especially that he was now being expelled.
10. The assistant preacher in Zollikon was Hans Brötli (see Cast of Characters No. 10).
11. On Ludwig Hätzer, see 57B/fn.3 and Cast of Characters No. 43.
12. On Andreas Castelberger, see Cast of Characters No. 13.

68F. The First Believer's Baptism in Switzerland, Zurich, January 21, 1525
1. The first version is found in the *Successio Anabaptistica* ("Succession of the Anabaptists"), the second as subsequently indicated in *Het beginsel der scheuringen,* and the third in P. J. Twisck's *Chronijk van den ondergangh der tyrannen* ("Chronicle of the Demise of the Tyrants"). The printed source for the excerpt included here (second version) is Carel van Ghendt, *Het beginsel en voortganck der geschillen, scheuringen en verdeeltheden onder degene die Doops-gezinden genoemd worden.* S. Cramer, ed., Bibliotheca Reformatoria Neerlandica, VII (Gravenhage, 1910), 24-25, 515-16.
2. H. E. Meihuizen, "De bronnen voor een geschiedenis van de eerste doperse doops-toediening," *Doopsgezinde Bijdragen,* nieuwe reeks 1 (1975), 54-61.
3. There have been three published editions of the Larger Chronicle to date: (1) Joseph V. Beck, *Die Geschichts-Bücher der Wiedertäufer in Oesterreich-Ungarn, etc., von 1526 bis*

1785 (Vienna, 1883, in Fontes Rerum Austriacarum XLIII). (2) Rudolf Wolkan, *Geschicht-Buch der Hutterischen Brüder* (Philadelphia: Carl Schurz Foundation, 1943). The third is a letter-perfect edition of the original text, and the account of the Zurich baptism is found on pp. 45-47.

4. E.g., Hillerbrand, 1964, pp. 230-31; Williams, 1957, pp. 41-46; Bender, 1950, p. 137.

5. The account in the Chronicle as translated in Williams, 1957, contains 1,143 words, compared to 499 words in the Klettgau letter. Even up to their last line in common, the Chronicle has more than twice as many words (882) as the letter (390).

6. See J. H. Yoder, 1973, p. 14.

7. In disagreement with Meihuizen's interpretation of the Klettgau letter (see fn. 2, above), Heinold Fast argues that this reference to "our servant in the land" is so idiomatically typical of the Hutterites of that time as to prove that the letter was no more than an excerpt from the Hutterite Chronicle, although evidently (because of its additional content) from an edition unknown to us. See Fast, "Wie doopte Konrad Grebel?" *Doopsgezinde Bijdragen,* nieuwe reeks 4 (1978), pp. 22-31.

8. See 65/fn.8.

9. *Meihuizen, op. cit.,* p. 60.

10. The "considerable conflict" of this sentence is in apposition to a series of Tuesday meetings referred to six sentences earlier (see 66A/300-01). That the series also included the third Tuesday meeting, which was the Public Disputation of Jan. 17 (68B, above) is indicated by Zwingli's later reference in the *Taufbüchlein,* "for all of us who preach in Zurich have examined the Scripture with them on the subject of baptism, twice in private and once before the Great Council" (ZW, IV, p. 286.14 and below 69C/372/35-38).

11. "Three or ... four days" after the "breakup" occurred on Jan. 17 (see fn. 10, above). For a detailed discussion of the problem of dating this historic baptismal service, see Blanke's comments in ZW, IV, p. 40, fn. 1.

12. Lat. *secte coryphei.* In his *Taufbüchlein,* Zwingli wrote that "the honorable Zurich Council knows well how the letter sounds that was read to them, how in it one man boasts of having been the founder of Anabaptism with two others" (ZW, IV, p. 285.23; see 69C/372/20ff.). The reference here is undoubtedly to Blaurock, Grebel, and Mantz (see 69C/fn.49).

13. The form used for these earliest baptisms was pouring or sprinkling out of a pitcher or basin (see Blanke, 1961, p. 22 and ZW, VI, p. 40, fn. 5). The practice of immersion came later (see 69A/360/21-23 and 69B/362/9. On Zwingli's charge of sectarianism, see 59A/fn.3, 69C/363/33, etc.

14. It is impossible to identify all fifteen persons. We know that Grebel performed the first baptism upon the head of Blaurock. At the first Anabaptist trial, Feb. 7, four persons are named among those who came from Zurich to Zollikon baptizing: Blaurock, Mantz, Brötli, and Rudolf Hottinger (see Cast of Characters Nos. 5, 67, 10, 52); and it is probable that all four were present on the night of Jan. 21. It is likely, moreover, that Reublin, Castelberger, and Giger were present (see Cast of Characters Nos. 75, 13, 27). Reublin and Castelberger were banished on the day of the baptism with Brötli and Hätzer (see 68E/338/14-16). We know that Hätzer did not accept baptism at this time because he disapproved of rebaptism; but we know from the cross-examination of Feb. 25 that "when the Spirit of God came upon him," Gabriel Giger "ran hastily to Felix Mantz's house; and there he was baptized by Conrad Grebel" (Quellen 1, No. 43, p. 52).

15. Zwingli here uses the name which the Anabaptists themselves used as a self-designation: "Brethren." Concerning the origin of the term "Swiss Brethren," see John Horsch, MQR, 1932, p. 243.

16. The church was the Grossmünster in Zurich, of which Zwingli was preacher. He undoubtedly would have used the sermon to convey his warnings. See Blanke, ZW, IV, p. 42, fn. 1.

17. For an elaboration of this point by Zwingli, see below, 68L/354/22-23, 355/15-18.

18. Zwingli's main reproach against the Anabaptists is not that they introduced rebaptism but that they bypassed the judgment of the church regarding rebaptism. What he understands by "churches" *(ecclesiis)* is the totality of all people in Zurich, i.e., the Zurich state

church. But in its stead in dealing with things of outward order, the City Council decided in the name of the people, for which the silent assent of the people was required (see Farner, 1930, pp. 102ff.). The Anabaptists did not recognize the judgment of the magistrates as the judgment of the church and could not therefore "submit to the jurisdiction of their church" (see Blanke ZW, IV, p. 31, fn. 4).

19. Lat. *catabaptismum,* "submersionism," although see Epi.A/fn.8 for the source of this Greek term and its meaning for Zwingli.

20. Somewhere in his discussions with the Anabaptists, Zwingli shifted from an accusation of doctrinal deviation that warrants a degree of forbearance to one of sedition against the state that warrants the use of force. In this reference, written in July 1527, Zwingli reads this shift back into the relationship in January 1525. This confirms Grebel's comment to Vadian on Dec. 15, 1524, "He, Zwingli, is writing also about rebels and rebellion; that may well hit us. Look out, it will bring something" (see 67/302/7-9). Certainly by May 1525, Zwingli was worrying more about the sedition of the Anabaptists than about their heresy (see 69C/364/19-21).

21. Kessler seems to have confused two of the names by which the same person was known: Blaurock, because he was wearing a "blue coat" at the Disputation of Jan. 17 (see 342/11-12, below), and "strong George," whom he knows as "George of the House of Jacob of Bonaduz" (71J/434/35-37). Blanke, however, cites sources to show that these names refer to the same person (ZW, VI, p. 153, fn. 3). Zwingli referred to another name used by the Anabaptists—"the second Paul" (see Epi.B/474/18 and Epi.B/fn.5). He was known in his home town of Bonaduz, 10 km. west of Chur, as Jörg Cajacob, which Blanke explains was the Rhein Valley, Romanesque form of the family name, meaning the same as "from the house of Jacob." For more on Blaurock, see Cast of Characters No. 5.

22. Kessler may be paraphrasing Zwingli's *Taufbüchlein:* "that they would gather a church that was without sin" (69C/363/33-36).

23. *Spaltung und absunderung.* Again, Kessler may be quoting from Zwingli's *Taufbüchlein,* 69C/364/20-21.

24. Ger. *rottenden sich sy in die hüser haimlich zûsamen.*

25. Ger. *nichts anderst was dann grublen und suchen.*

26. Although the Tuesday Disputations could be meant (see 66A), this is more likely a reference to the Public Disputation of Jan. 17 (68C, above).

27. Again, cf. the *Taufbüchlein,* 69C/363/41ff.

28. In whose home the baptismal service took place cannot be determined. Bender (1950, p. 264, note 3) says it was "the house of Felix Mantz in Zurich," and indeed the reasons behind this speculation are convincing. Additional evidence would be that Gabriel Giger of St. Gallen specifically testified that "when the Spirit of God came upon him he hastened to Zurich to Felix Mantz's home and there Conrad Grebel baptized him" (see fn. 14, above). This would settle the question if we could be sure that the occasion was the baptismal service of Jan. 21. Fritz Blanke first believed that the place was the "Obristen Haus" in Zollikon, but later changed his mind in favor of Zurich (see "Ort und Zeit der ersten Wiedertaufe," *Theologische Zeitschrift,* 1952, pp. 74-76, and Blanke, 1961, p. 20). Kessler's is the only one of the three 68F documents that says the baptism took place at night, but see 71K/437/5-6, where a street called Neustadt is given as their place of meeting, and 441/26ff., where the Brethren were reproached for meeting at night.

29. See Introduction to 68F, above.

30. The "brethren" in this context are members of an Anabaptist community in Cologne who had requested a letter from a certain Swiss brother describing how the Anabaptist movement arose in Zurich (see Introduction, above).

31. The pronoun refers to the Anabaptist congregation of which the writer was a member—probably located in the Klettgau district of the canton of Schaffhausen in Northeastern Switzerland (see Introduction).

32. See fn. 15, above.

33. Meihuizen concludes that our version mistakenly read 1522 for 1525. However, the

other two Dutch versions (see fn. 3, above) also have 1522, and the Hutterite version mentions no year at all. It is quite possible to read "1522" without misunderstanding. The Bible study groups here mentioned began in 1522 (see 51B, above) and the issue of baptism came up as early as January 1523, if not earlier (see fn. 35, below).

34. Mantz had expertise in Hebrew and Grebel in Greek, and the two might have become the teachers of these classical biblical languages in the new theological school established in Zurich in June 1525, except for their Anabaptist activity. Bullinger wrote, "Meanwhile, they began to look around for learned and practiced men in the languages. And since Mantz and Grebel, who would have been capable enough for the job, had cast themselves out and followed Anabaptism, H. Conrad Pellican of Basel was called to the Hebrew lectureship" (*Reformationsgeschichte,* I, p. 289). See also 62/282/31, 69/fn.39, and 70C/fn.23.

35. In the early years of 1521-23, Zwingli had indeed entertained the idea that infant baptism was questionable (see 67C/fn.22). As late as December 1524 he admitted that "we do not find in the New Testament that infant baptism is either commanded or forbidden" (67C/ 319/22-24).

36. Mk. 16:16.

37. Between "Ulrich Zwingli" and "did not wish this," the Hutterite Chronicle inserts, "who shuddered before Christ's cross, shame, and persecution."

38. This is probably a reference to Zwingli's tract of Dec. 1524, "He Who Gives Cause for Disturbance" (67C).

39. On Blaurock, see fn. 21, above. The Hutterite Chronicle adds the excursus, "because once when they were having a discussion of matters of belief in a meeting, this George of the House of Jacob also presented his view. Then someone asked who it was who had just spoken. Thereupon someone answered, 'The person in the blue coat spoke.' Thus thereafter he got the name of Blaurock."

40. Dutch *daer nae wonderlijck gehandelt.* The Hutterite Chronicle, which seeks to establish Blaurock's identity as the founder of the Swiss Brethren, has "he acted wonderfully and valiantly in the cause of truth" *(hat er wunderbarlich und mannlich gehanndlet im werck der warheit).*

41. The Chronicle adds, "and in the pure fear of God they recognized that a person must learn from the divine Word and proclamation a true faith which manifests itself in love, and receive the true Christian baptism on the basis of the recognized and confessed faith, in the union with God of a good conscience [this phrase from 1 Pet. 3:21], henceforth to serve God in a holy Christian life with all godliness, also to be steadfast to the end in tribulation."

42. Presumably at the home of Mantz on the night of Jan. 21, 1525.

43. Dutch *anghst,* "anguish."

44. The Chronicle adds "year, they were pressed in their hearts. Thereupon, they began to bow their knees to the Most High God in heaven. . . . "

45. The Chronicle has "and called upon him as the knower of hearts, implored him to enable them to do his divine will. . . . "

46. The Chronicle adds, "For flesh and blood and human forwardness did not impel them, since they well knew what they would have to bear and suffer on account of it."

47. The Chronicle adds "with the true Christian baptism upon his faith and knowledge. And when he knelt down with that request and desire, Conrad baptized him. . . . "

48. The Chronicle adds "since at that time there was no ordained minister to perform such work."

49. Dutch, *naemaels heeft hy die anderen oock gedoopt.* The Hutterite Chronicle, again seeking to establish Blaurock's preeminence, has "After that was done the others similarly desired George to baptize them, which he also did upon their request." The placement of the adverb "also" in the Dutch version tends to indicate that Grebel did all the baptizing. This is Meihuizen's interpretation (*op. cit.,* p. 54), with which the writer agrees, because the contexts of the two versions strongly indicate a disagreement in this regard for which the Chronicle required the excursus in defense of its claims for Blaurock.

50. The Chronicle adds, "for example, Balthasar Hubmaier of Friedberg, Ludwig

Hätzer, and still others, men well instructed in the German, Latin, Greek, and Hebrew languages, very well versed in Scripture, some preachers and other persons...."

51. The Chronicle adds "because of this true belief and true baptism, who thus witnessed steadfastly with his body and life to this truth."

52. On Uliman, see 69A/fn.11 and Cast of Characters No. 89.

53. The name of Uliman's brother is unknown. The place of execution is given in the Dutch version as Waltzen and in the German as Waltzra. Kessler identifies the place as Waldsee (see Fast, 1973, p. 636 and Clasen, MQR, 1973, p. 150), which was in Swabia and not in Switzerland, as the Chronicle has it.

54. The Chronicle claims "eleventh."

55. On Brötli, see Cast of Characters No. 10. Neither Brötli nor Sattler was mentioned in the Chronicle, one of the best clues as to the origin of this letter, since both men had worked in Northeast Switzerland.

56. On Sattler, see 71K/fn.80.

57. On Melchior Vet, see ME, IV, p. 819.

58. This whole paragraph is missing in the Chronicle, perhaps because it is local Swiss history and did not fit the purposes of Hutterite history. This reference to the "many [who] ran disorderly" is reminiscent of the cover letter to the Schleitheim Articles of 1527, which refer to "false brothers among us" and "It is manifest with what manifold cunning the devil has turned us aside" (see Yoder, 1973, p. 35).

59. See John 10:14.

68G. Reports of Illegal Anabaptist Activity, Zurich, January 30, 1525

1. For problems of dating, see Quellen 1, p. 37, fn. 1, and Bender, 1950, p. 264, note 3.

2. Two of the prisoners in whose home (now Rütistrasse 43) one of the baptismal services took place were Felix Kienast and his son Hans. Clewy Kienast was a kinsman who had not participated but provided testimony in the case. See 71A/fn.2.

3. The "last prohibition" was the council decree of January 21 (see 68E/338).

4. On Hans Ockenfuss, see 63/fn.95 and Cast of Characters No. 71.

5. This was Sunday, Jan. 22, the day following the Zurich baptismal service.

6. Wilhelm Reublin, see 68E/fn.9 and Cast of Characters No. 75.

7. On Fridli Schumacher, see Cast of Characters No. 84.

8. Blanke, p. 22, has a theory about the well of Hirslanden: "We may ask why the baptism did not take place in Schumacher's house, where Brötli and Schumacher both lived, but was performed out by the well of Hirslanden. Perhaps caution was the reason. It could be that Brötli, the leader of the baptistically inclined group in Zollikon, considered it advisable to administer outside of Zollikon the first baptism of an adherent from Zollikon."

9. On Hans Brötli, see Cast of Characters No. 10.

10. This reference to "two weeks ago" presents a problem for dating the document. If the testimony took place on January 30, the communion service was held prior to the Zurich baptism on January 21. Bender (1950, p. 264, note 3) does not believe that either baptism or communion services were held prior to the Zurich Council decree of January 21, and so prefers to date this document February 5. The alternate dates of January 30 or February 6 are given in Quellen 1, p. 37.

11. On Jacob Hottinger, see 68/fn.3 and Cast of Characters No. 50.

12. J. H. Yoder (1958, p. 140, fn. 35) writes that "it was probably the house meetings of the Anabaptists, who began celebrating the Lord's Supper in January 1525, more than Zwingli's teaching, which led the Zurich Council finally to accept the introduction of a Protestant communion service in April 1525."

68H. The Oldest Anabaptist Congregation: Zollikon, St. Gallen, 1525

1. See 68C and 68E, above.

2. Ger. *nit vil platz zu Zürich vergont ward.*

3. On the early history of Zollikon, see Nuesch-Bruppacher.

4. Compare with 69C/365/34-36, which suggests that Kessler was using Zwingli's *Taufbüchlein.* See also 71K/437/23-24.

5. Acts 2:45, 4:32ff.

6. Ger. *bruchtend spis und trank in gûter gemainschaft un underschaid.*

7. The radical community of goods of the early Christians was replaced by an organized *diakonia,* a daily "ministration" to the poor (Acts 6:1-2).

8. See Quellen 1, No. 35, p. 44.

9. See Quellen 1, Nos. 37 and 38, p. 47. Actually, only Mantz and Blaurock were put in the Wellenberg Tower. Its nine cells were too small to contain the twenty-five Zollikon prisoners, who were held in the old Augustinian monastery.

10. By "second article," Kessler is making a historical interpretation that the Anabaptist doctrines of community of goods (the first article) and nonparticipation in government (the second) were formulated after the separation took place. Certainly, the doctrine of nonparticipation in government was not formulated as specifically as Kessler here puts it until the Schleitheim Article No. 6 was written in 1527 (see Yoder, 1973, p. 40).

11. Mt. 18:15ff. The Anabaptist rejection of the use of force preceded their rejection of participation in government. Grebel clearly enunciated the former in Sept. 1524 (63/290/11ff.) but was still trying to reform government from within.

12. See 71K/437/35-36, 438/6, 34.

68I. Prison Disputation with the Zollikon Anabaptists, Zurich, January 30-February 8, 1525

1. On Hans Hottinger, see Cast of Characters No. 49.

2. Heine Murer was not one of the twenty-five imprisoned Anabaptists but was probably related to one of them—Grosshans Murer, in whose house, now Bahnhofstrasse 3, the meeting with Hottinger took place.

3. I.e., Acts 19:3-6, which the editor of Quellen 3, p. xxiv, calls the "trump card" of the Anabaptists, adding, "Zwingli appeared to be surprised by this argument at this moment" (see below 347/32-33).

4. Heine Bleuler, also probably a kinsman of one of the imprisoned men, Lienhard Bleuler.

5. I.e., water baptism could not have been applied more than once in this case on the assumption that this never happened in the New Testament (see 349/12-15, below).

6. For Blanke's interpretation of this testimony, see Intro., above.

7. Perhaps a kinsman to two of the imprisoned men—Felix Kienast and his son Hans Kienast.

8. See 67C/fn.22.

9. I.e., being burned at the stake for heresy.

10. Ger. *wie Johanes paptistans getoufft habe einest und Pauly noch einmal.* This wording of Zwingli's statement may not be precise. It was probably recorded by a court secretary who hardly had enough theological education to grasp the point Zwingli was trying to argue. Zwingli found himself in a twofold difficulty: he had to prove that Acts 19:1ff. could not be interpreted as rebaptism and he had to demonstrate that Paul in this incident did not reject the baptism of John, for as he had argued earlier concerning the institution of Christian baptism, John's and the apostles' baptism were identical (see 67A/304/38ff.).

11. Andreas Castelberger, see Cast of Characters No. 13.

12. Felix Lehman, see Cast of Characters No. 62.

68J. Brötli to the Brethren in Zollikon, Hallau, February 5 and 19, 1525

1. On Brötli, see Cast of Characters No. 10.

2. Brötli is obviously modeling his salutation after Rom. 1:1 and Phil. 1:1-2.

3. Brötli thinks of himself with considerable justification as the apostle of Christ who, having been baptized by Grebel on the night of Jan. 21 in Zurich, returned to Zollikon where he performed the first baptism at that place and thus founded the Zollikon congregation.

4. Twenty-five of the Zollikon brothers, plus Mantz and Blaurock, had been arrested

and imprisoned on Monday, Jan. 30, including Fridli Schumacher, to whom the letter was addressed. They were released on Feb. 8 (see Quellen 1, Nos. 29 and 38).

5. Spanweid refers to the location of a chapel, convalescent home, and public bath for therapy, in the community of Unterstrass.

6. On Reublin, see Cast of Characters No. 75. The two had been banished together.

7. Hallau, a village in the Klettgau district of the canton of Schaffhausen, not far from Waldshut, since 1525 a possession of the city of Schaffhausen. During the preceding year it had been subject to a variety of revolutionary ideas associated with Müntzer. Brötli preached here on Feb. 5 and probably founded an Anabaptist congregation at this place (see Stayer, pp. 109-10). Almost the entire village was baptized by him. The Schaffhausen authorities tried to arrest him but the peasant members of his congregation forcibly prevented it. See ME, II, p. 635.

8. Schaffhausen, city and canton in the north of Switzerland where refugees like Brötli came in the hope of winning the church leaders to their cause. Their efforts were not without some success because Brötli writes that the people's priest "was of one mind with us regarding baptism; may God grant that he will improve in all things." There was much concern about this in Zurich, for on Feb. 8 the Zurich Council wrote to the Schaffhausen authorities that "there had been error and dispute about infant baptism" and that the Zurich Disputation on the subject proved "that infant baptism is nothing wrong." On Feb. 11, the Schaffhausen Council issued a mandate "that young children shall be baptized." See ME, IV, pp. 439-40.

9. Following the Zurich baptismal service of January 21, Grebel devoted a few days to missionary work in Zollikon, after which he left for Schaffhausen in an attempt to win the leading priests to Anabaptism. According to Bender he spent the two months of February and March in this city (1950, pp. 138ff. and 69/358/18ff.).

10. The two doctors were Sebastian Hofmeister and Sebastian Meyer (See Cast of Characters No. 46 and ME, II, 785). Hofmeister was the head pastor in Schaffhausen and Meyer (1465-1545), like Hofmeister, was a Franciscan monk from Neuburg on the Rhine and an early Reformation promoter, one of the first to preach the new evangelical doctrine in Bern. Following his participation in the January Disputation in Zurich, he was expelled from Bern. He went to Basel, left the order, married, and went to Schaffhausen to become associate pastor with Hofmeister. After the Reformation was accomplished in Bern, he returned to succeed Berchtold Haller. Here he participated in the Anabaptist Disputation in March of 1538 (see Quellen 2, pp. 13-14), and ME, III, 665).

11. In his Der Uralten unnd gar neuen Leerern Urteil (see Quellen 2, pp. 13-14), as well as in his testimony before the Zurich court on April 11, 1525 (see Quellen 1, p. 195), Hubmaier reported that in Feb. 1525, Hofmeister had written to him, "For the sake of the truth we were not ashamed to testify openly before the council of Schaffhausen that our brother Zwingli strays from the track and does not proceed in accordance with the truth of the gospel if he wants the little children to be baptized. I have certainly not allowed myself to be compelled to baptize my children, and therefore you do what is exactly Christian when you reintroduce the true baptism of Christ that has been neglected so long."

12. In Quellen 1 the names of Heine, Jacob, and Uli Merger appear. Heine disclaims having been baptized, but was fined for not wanting to have his grandchild baptized (see 68K/352/11-13). His son Jacob had been baptized and as the more active adherent of the new movement (see 70F/412/23-24) would be more likely to have accompanied Brötli to Hallau. Or perhaps he was sent to Hallau to report the imprisonment of the Zollikon brethren, for no one by the name Merger was included among the twenty-five arrested. Merger may have been the carrier of Brötli's letter back to Zollikon.

13. Reublin went to Waldshut to visit Hubmaier, the local pastor since 1521. Hubmaier had already declared his assent to believer's baptism in his tract Oeffentliche Erbietung ("Public Commitment"), published on Feb. 2, and Reublin baptized Hubmaier sometime during this period. The town was located about twenty-five miles northwest of Zurich. The Anabaptist congregation flourished from April to December 5, when the town was captured by the Austrian forces.

712

14. Schumacher, see 68G/fn.7 and Cast of Characters No. 84.

15. On Brötli and the founding of the church in Hallau, see Cast of Characters No. 10 and fns. 1 and 7, above. The occasion for the writing of this letter was the report that had come that the Zollikon brethren had recanted in prison. The fact is that the twenty-five prisoners had been released on Feb. 8 on an oath of obedience. Mantz and Blaurock were still being held because they were obstinate (Blanke, p. 47). In the name of Reublin and Grebel, who were also distressed by the news, Brötli wrote to reprove the brethren for disowning their baptism and promising to curtail their witness.

16. Wilhelm Reublin, see 68E/fn.9, fn. 13, above, and Cast of Characters No. 75. He had returned from Waldshut, where he had gone to see Hubmaier (68J/351/10), and had departed again for Waldshut, where he remained for several months.

17. Jörg Blaurock, see 68F/fn.21 and Cast of Characters No. 5.

18. Grebel apparently moved between Schaffhausen, Waldshut, and Hallau during the two months he was in that region (see fn. 9, above). Brötli does not mean that he was generally distressed but that he was distressed about the reported apostasy in Zollikon.

19. On Fridli Schumacher, see 68G/fn.7 and Cast of Characters No. 84.

68K. *Sentences Against Two Anabaptists, Zurich, February 18, 1525*

1. Heine Merger, see 68J/fn.12.

2. On Gabriel Giger, see Cast of Characters No. 27.

3. In comparison to Blaurock and Brötli, who had baptized many in Zollikon, Grebel had baptized few, in part because he left almost immediately for Schaffhausen, and in part perhaps because his role was to make contact with and try to win the church leaders in Schaffhausen and Waldshut and to produce curriculum for the use of his brethren in their Bible study groups and disputations with their opponents (see 62/283/19-24, 69/358/12-22, 71F/427). His baptism of Giger, however, is significant for the connection that it provided with the spread of the movement to St. Gallen, as subsequent documents will show.

68L. *The Second Public Disputation on Baptism, Zurich, March 20-22, 1525*

1. Bullinger, writing almost fifty years after the event, erroneously read back into the spring of 1525 the spread of Anabaptism to Grüningen. Grebel was the first Anabaptist missioner to spend time there, and he did not arrive until July (see 70F). However, Mantz spent a few days there on his way to Chur after his escape from prison in April.

2. Blanke (ZW, VI, p. 44, fn. 1) believes that "joint meetings" here refers to "all the debates from the middle of December 1524 to mid-March 1525," and not specifically to the Disputation of March 20.

3. Zwingli, writing more than two years after the event, is compelled to interpret a stiffening sequence of penalties for Anabaptism (admonition, penance, fines, exile, and finally execution), which was sanctioned in March 1526 (see 71N/449).

4. According to Blanke (*ibid.*) this meeting refers to the Second Public Disputation, which lasted for three days (March 20-22) rather than for one day (March 20) as supposed by Krajewski (p. 93), on the basis of the Bullinger account, above. As the reports of the disputation from the *Taufbüchlein* following this excerpt reveal, the disputation was clearly of three days' duration.

5. This refers to Mantz and Blaurock, who were held in custody.

6. The Rathaus, where the trial was held.

7. Egli (1910, p. 328) believes that the threats came from Blaurock, the words of pity from Mantz.

8. For more on this charge, see 71K/437/25ff.

9. For Mantz's answer to this charge, see 71K/441/31ff.

10. This is the first of six references in the *Taufbüchlein* to the Public Disputation on March 20-22: ZW, IV, 230.26, 242.24, 252.26, 257.2, 279.19, and 327.17 (Bromiley 140.24, 149.29, 157.1, 160.1, and *infra* 368/33).

11. This substantiates Blanke's claim (ZW, VI, p. 44, fn. 3) that the disputation lasted

for three days and not for only one as in Bullinger and Krajewski (see fn. 4, above).

12. For other similar comparisons by Zwingli between living under monastic rule and living under the baptismal rule, see 68F/340/34-36 and 355/15-19.

13. On Myconius, see Cast of Characters No. 70.

14. See fn. 12, above.

15. Cf. 71G/428/28-29 and Epi.D/508/4-5.

16. Zwingli here bypassed the scriptural authority repeatedly cited by the Anabaptists for this teaching, i.e., the "rule of Christ," Mt. 18:15-18. See 63/288/17-18, 289/9-10, 290/21-22, 64/293/36.

17. Zwingli here states the basic principle of ecumenicity to which he himself did not continue to adhere. In the *Elenchus* (Epi.C/487/28, 491/23-25, etc.) he consigns Grebel and his kind to hell in justification for the use of force against them.

68M. Zwingli to Vadian, Zurich, March 31, 1525

1. This was the second of six letters Zwingli wrote to Vadian in 1525.

2. A number of important historical events in St. Gallen mentioned by Grebel in earlier letters (see 52/207/35ff. and 56/225/12ff.) preceded the sending of Vadian's "Axioms" to Zwingli. In February 1524, largely through Vadian's leadership, the Reformation had been accepted here as an official mandate of the City Council. But at the very time that this was happening, Benedict Burgauer, the people's priest, became defensive about the traditional doctrines of confession, absolution, and purgatory. The progressives called him a "stillstander" and wanted to replace him with the schoolmaster, Dominik Zili (see Cast of Characters No. 104). On June 17, 1524, when the dissatisfaction over his reactionary attitude had increased to the point of potential schism, the City Council appointed a committee of four to examine their pastor's position and had taken counsel with him accordingly. Members of the committee were Vadian, Wolfgang Wetter (see Cast of Characters No. 97), Dominik Zili, and Augustin Fechter, the town clerk. The discussion with Burgauer was oral at first; but when the opinions expressed did not seem to agree with the allegations, they asked for written statements from both sides. Burgauer wrote a position statement in Latin, and the committee wrote a 64-page counterstatement entitled *Responsio ad Parochum* ("Response to the Pastor"). The latter was dated July 27, 1524. The differences were still not resolved, and the council then set up a forum for Feb. 3, 1525, when Burgauer was supposed to answer orally some pointed questions about his views of purgatory and confession. The forum was continued on February 17, at which time Burgauer's defense in the German language was found to be in error. The burgomaster referred the matter back to the committee of four (replacing Wetter by Vadian's cousin, Councillor Jörg von Watt), which brought back a 10-page report on March 20 entitled *Antwurt der Vieren* ("Reply of the Four"). Finally, on that occasion, Burgauer admitted that he had been disproved and that he realized his mistake. Thereupon the council directed him to retract his former position from the pulpit of the St. Lawrence Church on the following Sunday and henceforth to preach according to the evangelical Reformation mandate. It was in the course of this investigation that Vadian wrote the pamphlet entitled *Farrago centum plus minus axiomatum, in quibus summatim, quod ad Christianam poenitentiam, contritionem, confessionem, absolutionem et satisfactionem attinet, comprehenditur, authoribus Georgio Vadiano, Dominico Zilio, Joachimo Vadiano, trimviris auscultandarum concionum apud St. Gallen, Anno MDXXV* ("A Medley of One Hundred Axioms More or Less Which in General Concern How They Comprehend Christian Penitence, Contrition, Confession, Absolution, and Justification, Authored by George Vadian, Dominik Zili, and Joachim Vadian, Three Men in Obedience to the Council of St. Gallen, 1525"). Vadian apparently sent the manuscript to Zwingli for printing in Zurich, but no print of it is extant if in fact it was ever printed. The manuscript sent to Zurich, however, has been preserved as has also an earlier rough draft in St. Gallen.

3. There were 101 articles or axioms in Vadian's *Farrago,* the first 42 of which were explicated in detail. Like Luther and Zwingli, Vadian used this occasion to affirm justification by faith against the works-righteousness and grace-dispensing of the Roman Catholic

Church, or what he calls "absolution." For a good summary of the content of the axioms, see Näf, II, pp. 217-20.

4. On the Frankfurt Book Fair, see 39/fn.3.

5. Zwingli referred to his *De vera et falsa religione commentarius* ("Commentary on the True and False Religion"), published in March 1525. It was dedicated, oddly, to Francis I, king of France, as a political maneuver to win France's support in case of war with the Catholic cantons. It was Zwingli's first attempt at a systematic theology and was the first formal publication of his anti-Catholic view of the Lord's Supper as not the repetition of the sacrifice of Christ but the faithful remembrance of Christ's once-for-all sacrifice, and of his anti-Lutheran view of the nature of the presence of Christ in the sacrament, not in bodily form (consubstantiation) but in the resurrected-ascended form of Christ's eternal existence.

6. According to Kessler's *Sabbata* (69A/361/14ff.), Grebel arrived in St. Gallen on March 25 and remained two weeks. Either Kessler was mistaken about the dating or Zwingli was unaware that Grebel had already left Zurich. For a thorough discussion of the problem, see ZW, VIII, p. 313, fn. 3, and Fast, 1973, No. 438, p. 373, fn. 3).

7. The reference is to Valentin Compar of Uri. The writing was entitled *Eine Antwort Valentin Compar gegeben,* and was published April 27, 1525.

8. Zwingli's writing on baptism was entitled *Von dem touff, vom widertouff unnd vom kindertouff,* and was published May 27, 1525 (see 69C).

69. Grebel to Castelberger, Zurich, April 25, 1525

1. Neither the writer nor recipient of this letter was named, but the evidence for the identification of Conrad Grebel and Andreas Castelberger as the persons is overwhelming. The handwriting is Grebel's (see 358/6-7), and the content confirms his authorship in many ways—the references to Felix Mantz, to "my wife," to "Father's house," to "the brothers from Zollikon," to "the sores on my feet" (cf. 6/79/26,36), to his books, to "Adrian Grebel," his second cousin, and to "my infallible passages from Scripture" (cf. 62/283/19-20). In fact, there is nothing in the letter that is out of character for Grebel (see Quellen 1, p. 70, fn. 2, and Correll-Bender-Yoder 2, p. 41).

2. The message of the letter fits all that we know of Andreas Castelberger (see Cast of Characters No. 13)—his residence in Zurich, his trade as a bookseller, his participation in the movement, his "state of health," and the evidence of a long background of relationship between the two men (see 51B/Intro.). Although on January 21 Castelberger had been banished from Zurich effective in eight days (68E/338/16), he was allowed to remain one month longer because of ill health (see Quellen 1, No. 28, p. 37). At the end of February he wrote a letter to the Zurich Council requesting permission to remain in Zurich indefinitely with his family because of illness and his bookselling business; and an additional two months' stay of expulsion was granted contingent upon continued ill health! (Quellen 1, No. 45, pp. 55-56). The letter was probably written at the end of that postponement; and in preparation for leaving Zurich, Castelberger may have been selling his own stock of books to which Grebel added his own. We know that Castelberger moved back to his home in Graubünden.

3. The letter was not dated but the time limits within which it had to be written are not difficult to establish. Correll-Bender-Yoder (2, p. 41) fix the limits of late March and early June, in the former case by Grebel's reference to the death of Anemund de Coct (see Cast of Characters No. 15), which occurred about March 20, and in the latter case by the reference to plans for the "Greek school," which was finally opened on June 5 (not 19 as stated by Correll-Bender-Yoder). Bender dates the letter "the latter part of May" (1950, pp. 146, 265/note 21). The only reason he dated it late May was the reference to Zwingli's forthcoming "writing against me"—undoubtedly the *Taufbüchlein* of May 27. But the *Taufbüchlein* had been in process since the completion of Zwingli's "Reply to Valentin Compar" on April 27 (ZW, IV, No. 53). Moreover, already in his letter to Vadian of March 31, he mentioned his plan to begin working on it (68M/356/24). Thus Grebel could have known about it much sooner

than the end of May. Closer definition of the *terminus post* and *ante* is possible by Grebel's reference to the imminent departure of Mantz, reported to be at his home at that moment. It is known that Mantz escaped from prison about April 15, and sometime later (probably within two weeks) he went to Schaffhausen and from there to Chur with Jörg Blaurock (see Krajewski, pp. 100-1). It is possible that Castelberger was in the Grisons also by then. Moreover, we know that Grebel was in St. Gallen until about Easter, April 16, when he returned to Zurich with a short stop in Oberwinterthur. This suggests that the letter could not have been written before April 16 nor later than May 1 and points to a date about April 25, which would have been the end of Castelberger's two months' stay of expulsion.

4. Felix Mantz, see 63/fn.94 and Cast of Characters No. 67. Apart from the fact that Mantz was signatory to the two letters to Müntzer (63/292/7 and 64/294/7), this is the only letter in which Grebel mentioned him by name. He lived at his mother's home in the Neustadt, a street near the Grossmünster (see 71K/fn.6).

5. Because of his reference to "Eve" in the next sentence, this may be an allusion to the second part of the temptation in the Garden of Eden recorded in Gen. 3:6. Compare this description of his wife with 41/156/6-8: "My Barbarity may, I imagine, deceive me someday" (see 47/fn.1).

6. Lat. *immensam,* "immense."

7. Grebel probably lived next door to his father, whose house was called *Thurm auf dem Bach* (see Bender, 1950, p. 3, and 47A/fn.6; but see also 47A/fn.16).

8. Lat. *tragoediam,* a favorite word of Grebel's for a crisis, borrowed from classical drama. In the present instance it also suggests that the fuss created by his wife was theatrical hysteria, not a reasonable response to the real facts.

9. Lat. *ego venio.* In his sense of immediacy, Grebel begins to shift back and forth between past and present.

10. Correll and Bender secured the help of Corrodi-Sulzer, specialist on sixteenth-century Zurich, to reconstruct Grebel's movements in his effort to flee. Given his residence next door to his father, he went to the nearest gate, the Neumarkt or Kronenthor. Finding this closed he went through a short alley called Untere Zäune, along the city wall to the Kirchgasse, which goes out of the city through the Lindenthor. The house of Lady Meis (see fn. 11, below) was on the corner of the Untere Zäune and the Kirchgasse, near the Lindenthor. Finding this gate closed, he returned to the Neumarkt gate, only to find it still closed. A picture of this gate taken from Murer's plan of the city in 1576 is found in Corrodi-Sulzer (1925).

11. Lady Meis was the sister of Hans Conrad Escher, the second husband of Grebel's youngest sister, Dorothy (see Cast of Characters No. 21).

12. Zollikon was a small village five miles southeast of Zurich (see 68H/Intro.).

13. Lat. *scabie pedum me* vexante, "the scabies [scabs, mange, itch] that troubled my feet." See 6/79/26 and 4/fn.3.

14. Having returned to the Neumarkt gate, Grebel's third attempt to get out through the city gates was thwarted and so he remained inside the city.

15. Grebel's letter was preserved, but not the catalog of his books which he enclosed.

16. The reference is to the growing power of Zwingli to secure mandates for the suppression of Anabaptism in Zurich rather than to any specific requests from him for Grebel's arrest.

17. The general sense of this comment is that in the future day of judgment, Zwingli will meet a like punishment. The biblical reference is to Rev. 13:10. See 67/fn.27.

18. The abbot of Cappel, Wolfgang Joner (see Cast of Characters No. 57).

19. Lat. *Rectius commodiusque me,* "more properly and profitably for me."

20. Concerning Castelberger's ill health, see fn. 2, above.

21. Bender (1950, p. 147) believed that this was Jacob Hottinger (see Cast of Characters No. 50).

22. Adrian Grebel was a second cousin of Conrad's (see Cast of Characters No. 29).

23. The pamphlet referred to was *Von dem touff, vom widertouff, unnd vom kindertouff,*

published on May 27 and dedicated to the people of St. Gallen to counteract the influence of Grebel and his followers there.

24. Lat. *infallibiles locos.* To avoid confusion with later Roman Catholic or modern fundamentalist usage, the adjectives "indubitable" or "unquestionable" might have been preferable.

25. Through the competent research and good fortune of the German scholar, Heinold Fast, who recently discovered an extant copy of what is undoubtedly this very collection of Bible passages in a later published form (see 71F, below), the following hypotheses are suggested: First, Grebel had written to Vadian on September 3, 1524, that he "was collecting and assembling passages . . . indeed two general kinds, and unless some other person anticipates me, I will thrust these upon the public" (62/283/19-23). Second, he had given handwritten copies of this collection to Anabaptist converts or leaders as an aid to their own individual and corporate Bible study. One of these was Erasmus Ritter (fn.30, below) and another was Hans Krüsi (also called Hans Kern and Hans Nagel), who later was reported to have testified, "Young Grebel was the first to witness to him and brought him a booklet . . . [which] was handwritten and not printed" (see 71E/425/5-6). Third, the collection was later published in Augsburg under the name of Hans Nagel. Among the convincing arguments given by Fast (1962, pp. 456-75) for Grebel's authorship is its conformity to Grebel's original description concerning "two general kinds" of passages, for all of the passages in the published edition are indeed arranged under two general categories: faith and baptism. For a transcription of the only extant copy known, see Quellen 2, No. 355, pp. 265-73.

26. Lat. *Vis dicam?* "May I speak forcefully?"

27. Lat. *civitatem hanc lusurus,* "mock this present community" or "make a fool of this state."

28. Lat. *Mortuo pisce taciturnior magisque mutus futurus.* Grebel was using an old Latin proverb, *Magis mutus quam piscis,* "Dumber [more silent] than a fish," but he added the adjective "dead."

29. Schaffhausen was a Swiss city and canton north of Zurich. Grebel came here at least twice—once for the two months of February and March and once in April—both times for visits to Hofmeister and Meyer (see 68J/fn.9).

30. This was probably Erasmus Ritter, preacher at the Münster in Schaffhausen (see Cast of Characters No. 76). It is less likely that he meant Erasmus Schmid (Fabriti), who had been canon at the Grossmünster in Zurich since 1521 but was temporarily expelled because of the Ittinger affair (see ZW, VII, No. 37, p. 84, fn. 1).

31. The young French nobleman, Anemund de Coct. See Cast of Characters No. 15.

32. Grebel is quoting the apocalyptic language of Rev. 17:13, 14, 17. See fn. 17, above.

33. Lat. *morbi interregno* probably means more than whether Castelberger was too ill to write but refers to whether writing would jeopardize his two months' stay of expulsion contingent upon continued ill health.

34. Theodorus Gaza (1398-1475) was a Greek scholar from Constantinople who came to Ferrara, Italy, in 1430 and published a well-known Greek grammar here in 1495. It was used by Budaeus in Paris and by Erasmus, who translated part of it into Latin.

35. The reference is undoubtedly to Urbano Bolzanio from Belluno, also called Urbanus Bellunensi (1443-1524), whose *Institutiones Graeco Grammatices* was published in 1498 in Venice by the Aldine Press. Grebel probably possessed the newest edition, *Urbani Grammaticae Institutiones, iam tanta adhuc iterum cura excussae* published in Basel in 1524 with a forward by Glarean, Grebel's former teacher.

36. This was either the *Metamorphoses* of Apuleius (see Pro.A/fn.3) or the *Metamorphoses* of Ovid, Roman poet who flourished at the beginning of the Christian era. Ovid's poem in fifteen books is a collection of all the mythological stories of transformations of things and beings into something else.

37. Erasmus' *Annotationes in novum Testamentum,* 1st ed., 1516; 2nd ed., 2 vols., 1518-19.

38. Lucretius (98-55 B.C.) was a poet philosopher at Rome. He is known for his poem

in six books, *On the Nature of Things,* which gives the best expression of Epicurean philosophy that we have from ancient literature. The poem was lost for about 1,000 years and rediscovered by Poggio in the fifteenth century.

39. Horace, see Pro.A/fn.35.

40. The "Greek school" for the study of biblical languages and theology was established by Zwingli in Zurich with Jacob Ceporin (Wiesendanger) as the teacher of Greek and Hebrew. The opening session was held June 5. Ceporin was succeeded by two of Grebel's former friends—John Jacob Ammann and Rudolf Collin (see Cast of Characters Nos. 3 and 16). One of the undocumented indictments against Mantz and Grebel is that they became Anabaptists in anger over not being appointed teachers of Hebrew and Greek in this new school. This allegation stems from Zwingli's statement that "several of them even came to me and asked me to recommend them for a benefice" (70C/389/18, but see also 70C/fn.23) and Bullinger's that "Mantz hoped to secure the Hebrew lectureship and Grebel the one in Greek, supposing that because they were children of citizens and came from good families they should be favored above everyone else. But Master Huldrych was not able at that time to accomplish what they desired but promised to promote them in the future.... But these fellows could not wait" (*Reformationsgeschichte,* I, p. 237; see also 68F/fn.29). For a thorough analysis of these allegations, see Bender, 1950, p. 251, fn. 12.

69A. The Spread of Anabaptism to St. Gallen, St. Gallen, 1525

1. Kessler was probably referring to writings by Hubmaier, i.e., *Vom Christlichen Tauf der Gläubigen* ("The Christian Baptism of Believers"), published about July 11, 1525, and regarded as the classic statement of the time on the Anabaptist doctrine of believer's baptism. Depending on when he was writing this entry, Kessler may also have had in mind Hubmaier's *Gespräch auf Meister Huldreich Zwingli's Taufbüchlein von dem Kindertauf* ("Dialogue on Master Huldrych Zwingli's Booklet on Baptism Concerning Infant Baptism"), written the end of November 1525 and published in July 1526, and perhaps Grebel's *Taufbüchlein,* which was apparently printed also about that time but is no longer extant.

2. Primarily three writings: *Von der Taufe, von der Wiedertaufe, und von der Kindertaufe,* published May 27, 1525 (see 69C), *Von dem Predigtamt,* published June 30, 1525, and *Antwort über Balthasar Hubmaiers Taufbüchlein,* published November 5, 1525.

3. Ger. *kain usserlich oder elementisch ding,* e.g., baptismal water. Kessler is quoting from Zwingli's *Taufbüchlein,* "hetzend die einvaltigen mit dem usserlichen, elementischen ding, dem tauf" ("egging the simple-hearted on with the external elemental thing—baptism"). See ZW, IV, pp. 210.27-211.1 and below 69C/365/33-35.

4. Ger. *bewernus in dem glissenden elementen.* The adjective can also mean "hypocritical." The latter noun refers to water baptism, which Kessler compared with circumcision. This was Zwingli's standard defense of infant baptism, first articulated in 67A/306/7ff.

5. Col. 2:11ff.

6. Ger. *dise infürung.*

7. On Hubmaier, see Cast of Characters No. 54. On Grebel's visit to Waldshut sometime before March 20, 1525, see Bergsten, p. 229, and below 70E/411/8-10. Grebel's visit preceded Hubmaier's baptism by Reublin on Easter Sunday, April 16.

8. See 68J/fn.13.

9. Ger. *badgelten,* "worth the equivalent of a bath," i.e., "bathtub."

10. Regarding these events see Bergsten, pp. 230-31. Grebel used similar words (see 68/332/6-7); and in view of his visit to Hubmaier prior to March 20, we can hypothesize a direct influence (see Epi.G/525/28-29).

11. On Wolfgang Uliman, alias Wolfgang Schorant, see ME, IV, 787-88, and Cast of Characters No. 89.

12. On Hochrütiner, see 65A/fn.5 and Cast of Characters No. 45.

13. Several scholars have taken this incident as normative. For instance, Vedder writes that "this is not merely a statement that Grebel immersed Uliman, which would be important, but also a testimony that, according to the writer's belief, such immersion was the

result of complete instruction in Anabaptism—in other words, that immersion was the usual practice of the well-instructed Anabaptists" (p. 143). Fast (1973, No. 447, p. 383, fn. 3) agrees that baptism by immersion had special meaning for Grebel and Uliman, not just because Kessler's account implies it but because of certain points of accusation in St. Gallen against an unnamed person whom Fast hypothesizes was Grebel. One of the accusations was that "the people stripped naked and baptized" (see 69B/362/9). Among the brethren in Zollikon, pouring was the method of baptism (see Blanke, 1961, p. 26); but both Fast and Vedder suppose that Grebel baptized by immersion in the Sitter River—"the only place near the city well adapted for immersion, and some two miles from the town. It would be silly to maintain that the people walked that distance to be sprinkled. This must be taken, therefore, as confirmation of the view that immersion was fast replacing affusion among the Swiss Anabaptists" (Vedder, p. 144).

14. Compare with 71K/438/12-14 and 439/40-440/1.

15. On Zili, see Cast of Characters No. 104.

16. Bethel, "house of God," was a well-known holy place in central Canaan. Two accounts are given of the origin of the name: (1) It was named on the spot by Jacob under the awe inspired by his vision recorded in Gen. 29:19. (2) It received its name on the occasion of a blessing bestowed by God upon Jacob after his return from Padan-aram, when his name was changed to Israel as recorded in Gen. 35:14-15.

17. Bethaven, meaning "house of iniquity" or "house of idolatry," was mentioned in Josh. 7:2; 18:12; 1 Sam. 13:5; 14:23; Hos. 4:15; 5:8; and 10:5.

18. "Eight days later" than the March 18 mentioned in 360/27, i.e., March 25.

19. Palm Sunday, April 9, 1525.

20. In his Chronicle, Fridolin Sicher wrote that the highway was filled with people as on a procession day (Quellen 2, p. 588). The Sitter River flows toward the Rhine past St. Gallen about two miles to the west.

21. See 69B/362/3 and 69B/fn.2.

22. This description of Grebel's missionary style is not verified by other evidence.

23. Ger. *abgewendt*.

24. See 68H/345/19-21.

25. This is one of several references to a prison escape prior to March 1526 (see 71K/438/12-13, 71-0/450ff.). Fast (1973, p. 373, fn. 3) concludes that "Kessler is very likely in error. The escape occurred only in 1526." On the other hand, Krajewski (pp. 99-102) accepts it as fact, at least of an escape by Mantz. See 71K/fn.24.

26. Acts 5:19.

69B. Charges Against an Unnamed Person [Grebel?], St. Gallen, May 15, 1525

1. It was alleged that the accused had claimed, no doubt on the basis of his knowledge of the Bible, that the mother of Jesus, whose perpetual virginity was already being taught in the Roman Catholic Church, had had seven children. The number derives from Mk. 6:3, where mention is made of four brothers and plural sisters of Jesus. Together with Jesus himself, that makes at least seven siblings.

2. Cf. 69A/361/25-26, where Kessler quoted Grebel as saying, "If you wish to discuss with me, then come to me naked."

3. Baptism by immersion is clearly implied. Cf. 69A/360/21-23: "He [Uliman] would not have merely a pan of water poured over him but entirely naked and bare was pushed under and immersed in the Rhine by Grebel." See 69A/fn.13.

4. The Grubenheimers are the Bohemian-Moravian Brethren. See Fast, 1973, p. 383, fn. 5, for the derivation of the name.

5. The charge here is that the unnamed Anabaptist himself made this claim. For Grebel's anticipation of martyrdom, see 70/378/21 and other similar comments listed in 70/fn.12, going back to 62/283/30-32. A fear of arrest would explain Grebel's rather quick departure from St. Gallen after a brief two-week mission. Cf. Kessler's comment, ". . . Conrad Grebel left that same week."

69C. Zwingli's Treatise on Baptism, Rebaptism, and Infant Baptism, Zurich, May 27, 1525

1. The burgomaster was Christian Studer. See 70A/384/1 and Näf, II, pp. 207ff. Vadian succeeded him on Dec. 28, 1525.

2. Zwingli refers to the rapid rise of Anabaptism in St. Gallen.

3. Mt. 13:25, frequently quoted by Zwingli.

4. On Zwingli's charge of sectarianism, see 59A/fn.3 and 68F/fn. 12.

5. See 59A/278/20ff.

6. Zwingli refers especially to the three people's priests and two schoolmasters, who were the principal spokesmen for the Reformed position at the Disputation of March 20-22 (see 68L, above).

7. It is possible that Zwingli was here referring to the two public disputations of January 17 and March 20-22; but we follow Blanke's conclusion (ZW, VI, p. 37, fn.5), based mostly on the internal evidence of this paragraph, that they refer rather to the two private "Tuesday Disputations" of December 6 and 13 (see 66A/Intro.). For instance, the reference to parting in a conciliatory spirit certainly fits the public disputations less than it does the Tuesday Disputations.

8. There is a definite shift here from the charge of sectarian heresy (primarily a doctrinal difference) to seditious rebellion (a political/legal indictment), which Zwingli now plans to bring before the magistrates.

9. Ger. *ir eigne glychsnery.*

10. Zwingli has 1 Jn. 1:8 in mind. See 68L/353/32-34.

11. Alexander of Abonoteichos, who lived in the second century AD, was a professional oracle to whom pilgrims came from all over the Roman Empire with their inquiries written ⟍ on sealed tablets, to which he then responded in metrical aphorisms or verdicts. It is said that around AD 166, when the number of these pilgrimages reached their peak, he distributed over 80,000 such oracles at a charge of one drachme and two obols. These oracles were extolled as remedies for all kinds of human need and deprivation. Apparently one group of people who tried to expose him as a defrauder and swindler were Christians. He in turn denounced them as unbelievers and attempted to incite mob action against them.

12. Followers of Epicurus (342-270 BC), a Greek philosopher who subscribed to a hedonistic ethic that among other elements held that the gods have no interest in human affairs and that we must consequently concentrate on present happiness and not fear the future.

13. Ger. *sahend im in's spil,* a proverbial expression in the same vein as "to look into another's cards."

14. Cf. 69D/375/16-20.

15. These two sentences are remarkable for their contradiction of each other, and it is difficult to believe that Zwingli was unaware of his dilemma.

16. See 71K/fn.10.

17. In the time between the two doctrinal disputations of 1523, Zwingli had himself affirmed this hermeneutical principle which he now repudiates. See 51A/200/17ff., 57A/230/13-14, and 57C/246/5-6.

18. See 67C/319/29 and 67C/fn. 27.

19. The city of St. Gallen was a flourishing commercial center by this time.

20. Ger. *ein läben.* Zwingli did not underestimate the intention of the Anabaptists to live their faith.

21. Zwingli here commits himself to their total suppression (see 312/15-16).

22. Zwingli refers to the third-century dispute in the churches of North Africa over the "Lapsi" (those baptized by heretics). Such baptism had been declared invalid by a group of North African bishops and such persons were rebaptized before they were received into the Catholic Church. The Roman Church, however, honored the Lapsi and received them by the laying on of hands provided that they had been baptized in the name of the Father, Son, and Holy Spirit. For an account of the conflict that ensued, leading to the convening of various synods and general councils, see ZW, IV, p. 214, fn.1.

23. See previous fn.

24. Cf. 69D/375/15-16.

25. Ger. *saturnischer lätzkopff*. Allegedly born under the influence of the planet Saturn, such persons were astrologically thought to have a sardonic view of life.

26. Ger. *von denen rotteren*, meaning the heretics or sectarians in this conflict. Zwingli's comparison of the Anabaptists with the third-century North African bishops under Cyprian's leadership (see fn. 22, above) is most interesting inasmuch as the latter were conservatives, not radicals, who wanted to keep the church pure from the stain of heresy.

27. In Part 2 concerning baptism (ZW, IV, p. 248.1ff; Bromiley, p. 153, lines 33ff.).

28. Nicholas II was pope, AD 1058-61.

29. See 66A/300/32-33 and 66A/fn.4.

30. The only known writing which Zwingli could have meant is the Mantz Petition of Defense, 67B/311/31-32, above.

31. Zwingli quotes the passage from Augustine later in Part 4, "Concerning Infant Baptism" (see fn. 41, below).

32. Blanke concluded that these references to "first disputation" and "last disputation" (lines 10-11) refer to the public disputations of January 17 and March 20-22 (ZW, VI, p. 279, fn. 3), but the editors of the text apply it to the Tuesday Disputations, although they believe that the second Tuesday Disputation was identical with the January 17 conference (ZW, IV, p. 279, fns. 14 and 22). The repetition of the reference to pope and devil (cf. 368/30-31 and 66A/300/32-33) would support the latter conclusion.

33. See fn. 32, above.

34. *Ibid.*

35. "Papal decrees [epistolae decretales] collected and inserted in medieval law books as well for the student of canon laws as for the faithful and clergy who are bound to observe them, but in particular for ecclesiastical superiors and judges who are to regulate their actions and judgments according to their tenor" (Ferm, p. 221).

36. I.e., in the *epistolae decretales* (see previous fn.).

37. This pretended uncertainty on the part of the Anabaptists as to whether or not they had been baptized as infants was one of the factors considered in the revision of the baptismal liturgy, which had just been published. See Kidd, No. 192, pp. 423-24.

38. Zwingli referred to his statement in Part 2, "Concerning Baptism," ZW, IV, p. 268.21ff. See Bromiley, p. 169.15ff.

39. See 360/26ff.

40. See fn. 30, above.

41. In Part 4, "Concerning Infant Baptism."

42. In Part 2 "Concerning Baptism," ZW, IV, p. 271.1ff.; Bromiley, p. 169.15ff.

43. Blanke (1961, p. 45) calls this "tortured interpretation."

44. Refers to Part 2. See 68L/354/30-31 from Bromiley, p. 157.1ff.

45. In Part 2, ZW, IV, p. 254.17ff., Bromiley, p. 158.11. See 68L/355/40.

46. Ger. *wappen*, i.e., shield and helmet with their jewels and ornaments. The word also refers to a coat of arms.

47. See fn. 21, above.

48. According to Blanke (ZW, VI, p. 40, fn. 2), Zwingli refers to the letter of February 18, 1525 (Quellen 1, No. 42A, pp. 49-50), in which one of the Anabaptists reported about himself that he had baptized several people. Blanke accepts the assumption of Egli and Finsler (ZW, IV, p. 285, fn. 26) that the author of the letter was Blaurock, but Muralt and Schmid (Quellen 1, p. 49, fn. 2) believe the author to be Mantz.

49. The three without doubt are Grebel, Mantz, and Blaurock. See Egli and Fensler, ZW, IV, p. 286, fn. 1.

50. All commentators (Egli and Finsler, ZW, IV, p. 286, fn. 15, and Blanke, ZW, VI, p. 37, fn. 5) agree that this refers to the two private Tuesday Disputations of December 6 and 13 (see 66A) and the first Public Disputation of January 17 (see 68B).

51. See fn. 25, above, and ZW, IV, p. 287, fn. 13.

52. This reference is clearly to Blaurock's notorious but nonextant letter to Myconius. See Quellen 1, No. 67, pp. 75-76.

53. Ger. *hüppenträger,* "itinerant sounder of his own horn" (see ZW, IV, p. 289, fn. 3).

54. This accounts for the fact that the letter is not extant.

55. Until that very month of May 1525, "infants were still baptized by Zwingli and the Reformed preachers according to Catholic usage with blowing, driving out the devil, crossing, moistening with saliva, and anointing with oil.... The baptismal liturgy by Leo Jud, which was introduced in Zurich in 1523, still contained all these Catholic features" (Blanke, 1961, pp. 22-23, 75).

56. In Part 2, "Concerning Baptism," ZW, IV, p. 247.8ff., Bromiley, p. 154.11ff.

57. See fn. 43, above.

69D. Zwingli to Vadian, Zurich, May 28, 1525

1. Lat. *Madiis Bernensibus.* The Mays of Bern were a Reformation-minded family to whom Zwingli had intended to dedicate his *Taufbüchlein* (see ZW, III, p. 524, fn. 2; IV, p. 458, fn. 2; and VIII, p. 327, fn. 2).

2. I.e., the *Subsidium sive coronis de eucharistia* ("Supplement to or Summary of the Eucharist"), published Aug. 17, 1525 (see ZW, IV, No. 63).

3. Part 3, "Concerning Rebaptism," is especially redundant.

4. Namely, the Anabaptists.

5. Lat. *strophis.* Zwingli used the accusative case of this word in the title of his last anti-Anabaptist tract of July 31, 1527 (see Epi.C/fn.31, below).

6. Lat. *nugas,* a familiar humanist term (see 6/fn.3).

7. Zwingli here uses the word *rebaptisantium* as a Latin equivalent of *widertouff* (see 69C/363/11). His later, more formal names were derived from the Greek words, ἀναβαπτισμός, Latinized *anabaptismus* ("Anabaptism"; see 71I/431/10) and καταβαπτισμός, *catabaptismus* ("Catabaptism"; see Epi.C/fn.8).

8. Lat. *pugne,* "fight," i.e., the struggle against the old papal church (see 71G/428/23-30).

9. Lat. *lusus,* "playing games," "dalliance."

10. See 69C/365/16.

11. Demosthenes was the most celebrated of the Greek orators (383-22 BC). During the fourteen years that he was prominent as an orator, he repeatedly delivered orations against the ambitious plans of Philip of Macedon to bring Greece under his sway. These speeches are known as the Philippics.

12. Cicero (see 36/fn.2 and 56/fn.1) delivered a series of fourteen fiery orations against Mark Antony in 44-43 BC. These are also called Philippics (see fn. 11, above), after those of Demosthenes against King Philip.

13. In the *Taufbüchlein.*

14. See fn. 3, above.

15. I.e., the six private and two public disputations to date (see 68B/Intro.).

16. I.e., to Zollikon, Hirslanden, Zumikon, Stadelhofen, Bäretswil, Hinwil, etc.

17. On this proverbial expression, see 48/189/20 and 48/fn.9.

18. See 69C/363/30ff.

19. See 69C/363/33 and 364/20-21.

20. This is the second reference in the collection to the Anabaptist doctrine of nonparticipation in government, which was not explicitly formulated until the Schleitheim Confession of 1527 (see 67C/316/36-37 67C/fn.7, and Yoder, 1973, pp. 39-41).

21. Acts 5:29.

22. Cerberus was the famous dog of Hades who was stationed at the entrance as a watchful keeper to prevent the living from entering the infernal regions and the dead from escaping. In the ancient poets he is mostly represented as having three heads.

23. "Commentary on True and False Religion," published in March 1525. This postscript is included here to portray the larger context of this letter and to indicate the overall defensive posture of Zwingli at this time.

24. On Glarean, see Cast of Characters No. 28.

722

25. See 57/fn.3.

26. Zwingli obviously failed to see the contradiction between his own receiving and inflicting "the sword of persecution."

69E. The First Two Swiss Anabaptist Martyrs: Bolt Eberli and an Unnamed Priest, Lachen, May 29, 1525

1. On Bolt Eberli, see Cast of Characters No. 6.

2. See 69A/361/34-37.

3. On Kürsiner, known also as Roggenacher, see Cast of Characters No. 77. He was arrested on March 16 along with eighteen other Anabaptists and held for questioning (see Quellen 1, Nos. 54, 59, and 60). Upon their release on March 25 (not escape, as Kessler thought), he went to St. Gallen, accompanied by Jacob Hottinger, Eberli Bolt, and an unnamed priest.

4. Fast (Quellen 2, No. 443, fns. 1 and 4) speculates that the unnamed priest was Jacob Schneider, but see 70F/fn.1.

5. Four Hottingers were involved with Kürsiner in the release from prison on March 25: Heine, Jacob, Jr., Hans, and Rutsch (see Quellen 1, Nos. 54-64).

6. Easter was on April 16, 1525.

7. On Uliman, see Cast of Characters No. 89. Regarding his sermon, see 69A/360.

8. Gossau was situated six miles west of St. Gallen. See 71E/fn.3.

9. On Burgauer, see Cast of Characters No. 11.

70. Grebel to Vadian, Zurich, May 30, 1525

1. The letter begins with a reference to their past intimate friendship and is reminiscent of several similar references in Grebel's earliest letters to Vadian (see 4/68/3, 19/110/32ff., and 29/138/13-17).

2. The conjunction that opens the second sentence indicates an immediate shift in mood and content, introducing the main concern of the rest of the letter—Vadian's growing opposition to the Anabaptists.

3. Lat. *cogito,* "reflect on" (EY) or "think to myself" (AB) are not strong enough renderings.

4. Lat. *lucta tua* translated "your combat" by EY and "your struggle" by AB.

5. The alternation of attitude is again striking, introducing the strong admonitions that are to follow.

6. The language of this clause reflects Jn. 6:63. It does not mean a technical doctrine of the spirit and the flesh, but rather "spiritual doctrine" versus "carnal doctrine."

7. Lat. *esto,* the imperative of the verb, "to be," lit., "let it be" (AB), fig., "granted" (EY).

8. Lat. *Esto me oneraris; esto ipse scias, non caves tamen.* Although it is barely possible for *oneraris* to have a positive meaning ("to lavish"), its predominant meaning is negative ("to burden," "to oppress"), and the positive rendering of both EY and AB has been replaced.

9. This is one of the biblical designations of the impending decisive intervention of God in the prophetic anticipation of the future kingdom. See 2 Pet. 3:10, 12, and 69/fn.19.

10. Lat. *literarum sacrarum. Literae* means "learning," "letters," "literature." *Sacrae* means "sacred," or in the negative sense, "accursed," "devoted to destruction."

11. From 1521 to the end of his life, Vadian's political offices and influence progressed from *Ratsherr* (City Councillor) to *Burgomaster* (mayor), to *Altburgomaster* (mayor emeritus) to *Reichsvogt* (imperial officer). Although he had not yet become burgomaster, he was already undoubtedly the most powerful leader in the city of St. Gallen.

12. This martyr-stance of Grebel was typical of the Anabaptist movement as a whole. For similar comments by Grebel, see 62/283/30-32, 63/290/13-17, 64/293/25-32, and 67/302/34-38. See also 71D/421/27-28 and 422/24.

13. This is not the first time Grebel admonished Vadian about the sin of exacting usury from the poor (see 67/302/16-18).

14. Lat. *sapientia tua carnis.* As in fn. 6, above, this refers not to "your philosophy of the flesh" but to "your fleshly [human] knowledge."

15. Lat. *parte Zinlii* is the same wording that Zwingli used against Grebel (see 68M/356/18 and 69D/375/33).

16. See fn. 9, above.

17. For the attitude of Grebel and the Anabaptists on the ethics of usury, see 63/fn.54 and 67/fn.25.

18. See fn. 15, above.

19. 1 Cor. 4:10.

20. Mt. 18:3; Mk. 10:15; Lk. 18:17.

21. This was a frequent theme in Zwingli's preaching and writing, which he summarized in the sixty-seven articles of January 19, 1523, as follows: "23. That Christ rejects the goods and glory of this world; from that follows, that those who amass riches for themselves in His name mock Him shamefully, so that they make Him a memorial of their greed and excess" (Meyer, p. 41). Zwingli stressed the demonic temptations of money whenever he preached against pensioners in Switzerland, and it is possible that Grebel was referring to his "Sermon Against Pensions and Pensioners" (ZW, III, No. 49, pp. 584-89). The Scripture references mentioned by Grebel were Psalm 15:5 (*censum ad damnationem promovere,* from the Vulgate, which omits Ps. 10) and Ezek. 18:5-18). The theme was stressed again in *Ratschlag betreffend Ausschliessung,* in which Zwingli condemned the *"unbillich gyt"* (unjust coveter). See fn. 22, below.

22. The pope to whom Grebel referred was not Gregory IX but Gregory X, who convened the second Council of Lyons (1274), which reaffirmed the canon of the third Lateran Council (1179) that "manifest usurers shall not be admitted to communion, nor, if they die in their sin, receive Christian burial," and added still another canon invalidating the wills of unrepentant usurers. The question of excluding usurers from the Lord's Supper was explicitly discussed by Zwingli in his "Advice Concerning Exclusion from the Lord's Supper for Adulterers, Usurers, etc." (ZW, IV, No. 52, pp. 25-34), published shortly before April 12, 1525. The tract dealt primarily with two questions—the right and wrong uses of the ban by the church and the legitimate and illegitimate charging of interest by Christians. As stated in fn. 21, above, Zwingli condemned the "unjust coveters," among whom, in strict adherence to canon law, he reckoned *Zinskauf* (the charging of interest), but he then went on to specify the legitimate uses of *Zinskauf* in the emerging capitalistic society, as he had done in his sermon on "Divine and Human Justice" (52B), warning that anyone who oversteps these bounds should be banned from communion.

23. The actions to suppress the Anabaptists in which Vadian participated in St. Gallen are described in documents 70A and 70B. His *Schrift wider die Täufer* ("Writing Against the Anabaptists") which he presented to the council on May 19 and read publicly on June 5 has been lost. On June 6 the council issued its mandate to forbid Anabaptist practices and deputized 200 men to be ready when called to move against the Anabaptists with armor and weapons. The local Anabaptist leader whom Grebel had baptized in the Rhine River, Wolfgang Uliman (see Cast of Characters No. 89), was imprisoned. Although the death penalty was threatened, it was not imposed as in Zurich. By principle and character, Vadian was more inclined toward moderation than his friend Zwingli. Kessler wrote that "Vadian sought to refute the turbulent nature, the incredible delusion of the Anabaptists, neither by means of the esteem which he enjoyed nor through harsh punishment, but rather courageously through reason and evidence from the Bible." No doubt the fact that his brother-in-law, whom he had loved more than any other former student, was one of the leaders of the outlawed movement was another important factor in his comparative leniency.

24. Grebel admits that his admonitions to Vadian have a more explicit purpose—the conversion of his brother-in-law—than the kind of nondirective testimony that merely defines one's position. Compare this with the court testimony of Felix Mantz (71M/444/22-27).

25. The booklet that Grebel wants to write is not the collection of Scripture passages referred to in 69/358/12-14 (see 71F), but the writing that he first describes in the letter to

Müntzer, "If you or Carlstadt do not adequately write against infant baptism and all that pertains to it, how and why one is to baptize, etc., I (Conrad Grebel) will try my hand at it and will finish writing out what I have begun against all (except you) who have thus far written misleadingly and knowingly about baptism" (63/291/15-20). See also 71M/444/37.

26. Like the booklet that Grebel wants to write against infant baptism, the doctrine to which he here refers is undoutedly the doctrine of believer's baptism. He is referring to the comment in Vadian's letter to Grebel, "This practically is what the conflict over baptism has to do. It will undoubtedly in time be brought, as will other things, into line with the witness of the Word of truth" (67D/322/10-13). Grebel read this as approval of believer's baptism in contrast to Zwingli's disapproval, and is asking why then Vadian would hesitate to act on that to which he claims to have assented (see 379/14-15).

27. These are the very terms that Zwingli used in his incredible conversation with Grebel's ghost in hell (see Epi.C, below). Vadian came to very negative conclusions about Grebel and his brethren (see Epi.G, below), but never quite resorted to this kind of indictment.

28. Rebaptism was made punishable by death in Zurich on March 7, 1526 (see 71M/448/15-19). On that very day Zwingli wrote to Vadian, praising the decision (71N/449).

29. Lat. *quocunque animo*, "some way or other in your mind," i.e., "partial assent."

30. This is an interesting reference to the doctrine of divine election and refers to another dialogue with Vadian (see lines 11-13, below): evidently another letter from Vadian which has been lost or perhaps a quotation from Vadian's *Schrift Wider die Täufer* which Vadian may have sent to Grebel. If the latter, it is the only indication that has survived of the content of this nonextant tract. Evidence that Grebel may have been quoting from the tract is his reference to the St. Gallen Council (line 17), to which Vadian had presented the tract on May 19. On the idea of the "divine election" of the Anabaptists, see 71K/fn.49. On Zwingli's discussion of his differences with the Anabaptists on the doctrine of election, see Part 3 of the *Elenchus* (Jackson, 1901, pp. 237ff.) and 71P/fn.1.

31. Grebel is asserting that striving against God's elect is a sure indication that the one doing the striving is not himself elected.

32. See previous sentence.

33. Martha Grebel, Vadian's wife.

70A. The Reactions to Anabaptism in St. Gallen, May and June, 1525

1. The walled city of St. Gallen had six gates: the Multerthor on the west, the Müllerthor on the south, the Spiserthor on the east, the Brühlthor on the northeast, the Blatzthor on the north, and the Scheibenthor on the northwest.

2. See Mt. 7:15.

3. See Mt. 5:34.

4. For this hearsay about Mantz, see 68L/353/32ff. and 71K/437/25ff. For Mantz's rather different version of the conversation with Zwingli in Hujuff's garden in the latter reference, see 441/31ff.

5. On the Church of St. Lawrence, see 35/fn.20.

6. Fast (Quellen 2, p. 609, fn. 75) states that such a mandate is found only in his document No. 435 (dated Feb. 17) and No. 457 (dated June 6), neither of which fits this reference to judicial appearance. He adds that either the mandate mentioned by Kessler is no longer extant, or (more likely) Kessler put the mandate of June 6 (70B, below) into an incorrect order.

7. On the location of the shooting lodge, see 69E/377/11 and 69E/fn.8.

8. For Uliman's court appearances on these charges, see Fast (Quellen 2) No. 444, dated April 25-26, and No. 465, dated June 26. It was in the latter hearing that his reference to the city officials as "heathen" was examined.

9. See Fast (Quellen 2) Nos. 446 and 449.

10. See 70B, below (Fast, Quellen 2, Nos. 456 and 457).

11. See 69C, above.

12. On Zili, see 35/fn.19, 69A/fn.15, and Cast of Characters No. 104.

13. Ger. *die borchirchen.* Fast (Quellen 2, p. 389, fn. 12) writes that "it was the back balcony, called the *Haldige Porkirche* [sloping Gallery]."

14. Kessler was in error. The interruption on this occasion came from Gabriel Giger and not from Uliman. Kessler confused this occurrence with a similar one in Teufen, at which Uliman was the spokesman (see 68K/fn.2, Fast, Quellen 2, No. 456, fn. 13 and No. 465, fn. 10, and Cast of Characters Nos. 27 and 89).

15. By "God's Word" was meant in this context the contents of a letter the Anabaptists received from Conrad Grebel (see fns. 16 and 17 below).

16. Grebel's letter to the burgomaster and council has been lost, but see 70B/fn.1.

17. It was apparently handed over forthwith, because it was read before the council on June 5 (see 70B/384/34).

18. The mobilization of not 100 but 200 men for special police duty against further Anabaptist demonstrations was carried out on June 8 (see Fast, Quellen 2, No. 460, pp. 391-92).

70B. Court Proceedings in St. Gallen, June 5 and 6, 1525

1. Referred to here is a lost letter that Grebel wrote to the St. Gallen burgomaster and council. As we read in 70A/384/6-8, the Anabaptists interrupted Zili's reading of Zwingli's *Taufbüchlein* with the statement that they wanted to read Grebel's letter, but they were not permitted to do so. Instead, they were made to submit the letter without further delay so that it could be read before the City Council.

2. Krom was burgomaster from 1509 to 1524, and altburgomaster from 1524 to 1527.

3. Rainsperg was a member of the Large Council from 1515, and became burgomaster in 1531.

4. There is no record of this ever being done.

5. Vadian's *Schrift Wider die Täufer* had apparently been written earlier in first draft at least (see 66/fn.4 and 67D/fn.8). It was complete in its present form as early as May 19 (see Fast, Quellen 2, No. 449, p. 383, fn. 4) and was apparently given to the Anabaptists for response prior to the June 5 meeting.

6. If Grebel was indeed the author of the response, this "writer" was only the copyist. It seems more likely that Grebel sent suggestions and this Anabaptist representative put them into final form for reading to the council. Fast (Quellen 2, p. 383, fn. 5) reports that the Anabaptist defense was written in the home of Jacob Spicherman.

7. "Outside" refers to areas in the hinterland of St. Gallen, i.e., "Goldach to the east, Teufen to the south, Oberdorf and Gosau to the southwest, and Cappel and Fredorf to the south" (see 71E/423/7-10).

8. See last sentence, below.

9. On Giger and his "sacrilege in the balcony of the church," see 68K/fn.2, 70A/383/31ff. (although Kessler mistook Uliman for Giger), and Cast of Characters No. 27. Concerning the outcome of Giger's sacrilege, see Fast, Quellen 2, No. 460, p. 392, fn. 6.

10. See 70A/fn.13.

11. Unknown.

12. Uli Mayer was guildmaster of the tailors' guild.

13. Fast (Quellen 2, No. 457, p. 389, fn. 1) surmises that the assembly was held in the Church of St. Lawrence followed by a session of the Large Council.

14. See fn. 6, above.

15. "Books" refers to Vadian's treatise and the Anabaptist response.

16. I.e., call a halt to the disputation.

17. See fn. 1, above.

18. For a discussion of the corresponding days of the week, see Fast, Quellen 2, p. 390, fn. 14.

1. Toggenburg was a district in the canton of St. Gallen in eastern Switzerland, purchased by the abbot of St. Gallen in 1468.

2. Zwingli came from Toggenburg, village of Wildhaus.

3. Ger. *den götzendienst*, referring to statutes and pictures used in private and public worship by Roman Catholics. Toggenburg had accepted the Reformation in July 1524, and Zwingli had written a special letter of congratulations to the Councillors of his home district at that time.

4. Zwingli has Anabaptism in mind.

5. Both, i.e., preaching and baptizing.

6. See 69C/fn.18, etc.

7. *Von dem touff, vom widertouff unnd vom kindertouff,* published May 27, 1525 (see 69C).

8. Compare with 69C/364/28-30.

9. Ger. *die widertöuffer yetz ertrencker nampte.* See Epi. C/fn.8.

10. Zwingli refers here to Conrad Grebel and Felix Mantz, who were citizens of Zurich.

11. The movement spread rapidly beyond Zurich.

12. Zwingli refers to six private and two public disputations to date. See 68B/Intro.

13. Zwingli often used the term "bishop" to refer to the head pastor of a local church.

14. Carthusian, a member of an austere contemplative religious order of hermit monks founded in AD 1084 by St. Bruno.

15. It is difficult to know on first reading whether the pronoun refers to the Carthusians or to the Anabaptists. If the former, Zwingli would seem to have a theory about the participation of the Carthusians in the destruction of their own monastery (see fn. 18, below, and Zwingli's own "Expert Opinion in the Ittinger Affair," ZW, III, pp. 511-38). If the latter, this would be the only known accusation that the proto-Anabaptists were involved in the vandalizing of the monastery at Ittingen on July 17, 1524. It would be an incredible claim in view of Zwingli's earlier sympathy with the men who were arrested and executed on Sept. 28, because their views were purely Zwinglian, and in view of the fact that one of the indictments against Jacob Grebel in November 1527 was that he gave secret testimony against one of those executed (see Epi.A/466/37-38).

16. Ittinger uprising, see 65/fn.24 and Epi. A/fn.83.

17. The Diet of the Swiss Republic meeting at Luzern in December 1524, had exacted a payment of 12,000 guilders for replacing the Ittinger tower. But there is nothing in the proceedings to link the decision to the rise of the Anabaptists. See *Eidg. Absch.* IV, la, pp. 534ff.

18. The French order of Carthusian monks purchased and took over the impoverished Augustinian monastery at Ittingen in 1461. Under Carthusian management, the monastery grew and became wealthy.

19. Ger. *das sy den Armen uff dem hals ligende von inen erhalten wärind.* To "lie on someone's neck" was a proverbial expression.

20. For Grebel's comments on this, see 63/289/5-12.

21. Ger. *in'n ermel geschoppet,* another proverbial expression.

22. Nickname for the Franciscan monks.

23. The editors of the text (ZW, IV, p. 387, fn. 22) think that this refers to Grebel and Mantz and their desire for professional chairs in the new theological school in Zurich, as Bullinger (I, p. 237) wrote (see 68F/fn.34 and 69/fn.40). Zwingli more likely had in mind a person like Simon Stumpf, who after being deprived of his parish at Höngg on Nov. 3, 1523, wrote a penitent letter to Zwingli saying, "I cannot dig ditches and have nothing to dig even if I were able." For the rest of the letter see ME, IV, p. 648.

24. See Zwingli's "Ratschlag betreffend Ausschliessung von Abendmahl für Ehebrecher, Wucherer, usw." (ZW, IV, pp. 25ff.) and his "Wer Ursache gebe zu Aufruhr, usw" (ZW, III, pp. 385.5ff.). Also see 53/fn.4.

25. See fn. 13, above.

26. A proverbial expression, "so manch Haupt, so mancher Sinn."

27. Another proverbial expression, "seinen Schalk verbergen können."

28. The editors of the text cite previous writings of Zwingli in which he made such a comment (ZW, IV, p. 393, fn. 16).

29. On the opening of a theological seminary in Zurich on June 5, two days after the publication of this treatise, see 69/fn.40. Jackson (1900, p. 293) describes the curriculum as follows: "The textbook was the Bible. Instruction began at eight o'clock in the morning. One teacher read the Hebrew text and translated it into Latin with a brief interpretation. Then Zwingli translated the same text from the Greek of the Septuagint into Latin. Leo Jud then commented in German upon what had been read, and explained in Latin. This theological seminary was attended not only by regular students but by the clergy of the city, and Leo Jud's lectures were attended by the people generally. Instruction from the Greek New Testament was given in the afternoon at three o'clock by Myconius.... He [Zwingli] called this institute 'The Prophecy.' "

30. Concerning the plans for the reformation of the chapter, dated September 1523, see "Vortrag und Gutachten Betreffend die Reformation des Stiftes," ZW, II, pp. 609-16. A digest is given in ZW, IV, p. 398, fn. 5.

31. Zwingli denies the multiplicity and plurality of ministries in the church, thus distorting the meaning of the Ephesian text because he is intent on preserving the centralized authority of the "office" of bishop-pastor (e.g., himself) in whom all these ministries allegedly accrue (see 47B/176/20-22). For an interpretation of the Anabaptist view of the shared ministry, see Paul Peachey, MQR, XXX, pp. 213-228.

32. Ger. *publicanen,* not in the sense of tax collector but of money-grabber.

33. The controversy between Grebel and Zwingli was not the issue of the financial support of pastors but the sources of that support, i.e., benefices which were based on compulsory tithes and interest and salaries paid by the state.

34. See 389/22-23, above.

35. The Ger. word-play, *geist ... gyt* is retained.

36. Ger. *sechtzehen stück.* A "Stück" consisted of a *Mütt,* one dry measure equal to one fourth of a Malter (rye measure), applied either to rye or to a pale of wine.

37. This is one of the few places Zwingli mentions his wife. Born the same year, 1484, she was the daughter of a wealthy landlord in Zurich, Oswald Reinhard. She was married in 1504 to Hans Meyer, who died in 1517, leaving three children: Margaret, b. 1505, Agatha, b. 1507, and Gerold, b. 1509. Her children to Zwingli were Regula, b. 1524, Huldreich, b. 1528, Wilhelm, b. 1529, and Anna, b. 1530.

38. On April 3, 1525, an agreement had been reached between Anna Reinhard, her children, their administrator, and Burgomaster Effinger, that she turn over her estate to the children who would in turn pay her an annuity of 30 guilders.

39. See fn. 35, above.

40. She was in fact 41.

41. Not her own, but indigent children.

42. Proverbial phrase, "Er hat das Nest zu früh verlassen."

43. Eris, the Greek goddess of discord.

44. Zwingli was undoubtedly thinking of Hubmaier and Carlstadt, perhaps also Müntzer.

45. On Momus, see 67C/fn.6.

46. See above 392/35ff.

47. I.e., the psalms and other songs.

48. Reference to the three people's priests in Zurich: Zwingli, Engelhart, and Jud.

49. I.e., Cardinals in the Roman Catholic hierarchy.

50. See above 392/16ff.

51. Zwingli interprets speaking in tongues not as glossolalia, but as linguistics, an accomplishment in languages.

52. See 67/302/22-23.

53. Ger. *kupleren*. For similar remarks elsewhere by Zwingli, see ZW, III, 45.5ff., III, 412.17ff., and I, 517.11ff.

54. Zwingli had previously made this statement. See ZW, II, 276.23ff.

55. See 67C/316/35-37.

56. This statement represents a clear difference in the doctrine of the ministry between Reformed Protestantism and Anabaptism.

57. Zwingli here bypasses Luther's doctrine of the priesthood of all believers.

58. See fn. 42, above.

59. Ger. *wo man iro schonet, als wir gethon habend*. For Zwingli's view of sparing or forbearance in relation to his radical followers, see 57A/fn.2. For his more recent comment concerning his forbearance for them, see 69C/fn.14.

70D. Procession of Zollikon Prophets to Zurich, after June 12, 1525

1. Blanke (p. 77) gives this date, based on Quellen 1, No. 74, p. 81: "From this source (council decision of June 12, 1525) we learn that the Council of Zurich expected this procession. Evidently the intention of the Zollikon prophets had been made known (by an informer?) to the council before it was carried out."

2. Lat. *salice aut reste*. Blanke (p. 62) was unable to trace the source for this preference for ropes and willow rods to belts. "Perhaps it is to be understood as a symbolic representation of the rod of divine chastisement. 'Then will I visit their transgression with a rod' (Psalm 89:32)."

3. Refers to Rev. 12:3ff. This reference reminds us of Myconius's comment that "whatever revelation of evils John makes, they piled upon Zwingli" (Jackson, 1912, p. 15).

4. Hans Hottinger's proclamation about the "false prophet" (see 70E/Intro., above) was aimed at the local Zollikon pastor, not Zwingli. But just a month before this, Grebel had written from his home in Zurich that "this is my asylum from captivity by Zwingli, who is himself going into captivity according to the Apocalypse.... While these gospel purveyors who had come into their reign after the beast, while these kings with one consent hand over their power to the beast, while they fight against the Lamb that will defeat them in his own time, may you meanwhile be strong in the peace and patience of the Lord" (69/357/33-34, 358/23-27).

5. I.e., to avoid arrest. The City Council minute for June 12 (Quellen 1, No. 74) tells how the appearance of the Zollikon demonstrators was awaited: the council appointed several men "to make a strike," indicating strategy they were to use when the Anabaptists came to Zurich crying woes.

70E. Grebel and Hottinger in Waldshut, Zollikon, June, 1525

1. On Jacob Hottinger, see 68/fn.3 and Cast of Characters No. 50.

2. They separated somewhere on the return trip, Grebel apparently heading in the direction of Grüningen.

70F. Grebel's Mission to the District of Grüningen, after June 29, 1525

1. Little is known about Jacob Schnider, except that he was a weaver from St. Gallen (Quellen 1, No. 89, p. 95) and a former priest, and that he came to Zollikon from St. Gallen on April 23 (see Quellen 1, No. 93) with Anthony Roggenacher and Bolt Eberli (see Cast of Characters Nos. 77 and 6). Fast (Quellen 2, No. 443, fns. 1 and 4) speculates that he was the unnamed priest who was martyred with Eberli in May (see 69E/376/28 and 377/36), but this seems unlikely inasmuch as he was arrested and fined in Zurich in August for his Anabaptist activities (Quellen 1, No. 93) and was mentioned in a letter written the following November (Quellen 1, No. 119).

2. Easter Sunday was April 16.

3. Unknown. This is the only entry for him in the Quellen 1 source volume.

4. June 24.

5. On Heine Merger and his son, see 68J/fn.12.

6. On Felix Lehman, see Cast of Characters No. 62.

7. June 28.

8. On Hans Hottinger, see 68I/fn.1 and Cast of Characters No. 49.

9. June 29.

10. It is difficult to determine whether the pronoun refers to Grebel or Schnider, probably the latter, although he obviously does not mean "home" to St. Gallen.

11. For some reason this testimony was not received into the record until March 12, 1526; but it pertains mostly to the events of July 2, 1525. Included here are only selected excerpts interspersed by other testimony regarding Anabaptism and the tithes.

12. This and lines 18 and 21, below, are the only entries for Hans Kasper in the Quellen 1 source volume. Otherwise unknown.

13. Also unknown, except for line 21, below.

14. On Max Bosshart, see Cast of Characters No. 7.

15. Ger. *her Ulrichen:* Ulrich Zingg, pastor at Dürnten 1522-42.

16. Hans Brennwald, pastor at Hinwil 1521-30. See 71C/fn.2.

17. Benedict Landenberger, pastor at Bäretswil 1526-29.

18. Uli Bluntschli was the brother of Anna Widerkerin (see 71M/fn.54)

19. Hans Golpacher, also known as Rudolf Golpacher, alias von Tobel, was a shoe-maker in Grüningen. See line 18, below.

20. Unknown.

21. Ger. *ein kappen gschroten.*

22. Unknown, probably a relative of Hans and Jörg (see fn. 23, below).

23. On Hans Hotz, carpenter in the Grüningen district, see Cast of Characters No. 53.

24. See fn. 22, above.

25. This was apparently a disputational question, using the child as a foil.

26. Zancker is unknown, except for this entry.

27. Also unknown.

28. See fn. 14, above.

29. This gives us the date for this entry, since it is known from Quellen 1, No. 85, p. 91, that Grebel and Bosshart preached at Hinwil "the Sunday before St. Ulrich's Day," which was July 2 (see 71C/420/8-10). Therefore, Zancker's testimony came after that date.

30. On the peasants' movement in the Hinwil district, see ME, II, pp. 604-5. Von Muralt writes that "the soil had been truly prepared for it ever since this territory had been incorporated into the canton [and] had become a center of opposition for those who favored economic autonomy and self-government by the peasants over against the centralization which the city of Zurich was promoting.... Many preachers complained against their manorial lord, the abbot of Rüti, and in line with the radical wing of the Reformation demanded the abolition of the tithe, grounding their demands in the gospel. The ferment was so strong that in April 1525 the peasants attacked and plundered the Rüti monastery.... The Zurich Council promised to examine their complaints, but the peasants were not satisfied. Consequently the government decided, on the advice of the magistrate Jörg Berger, not to yield any further to the demands of the peasants, although they had made concessions to the peasants of other districts."

31. Von Muralt writes that although "the Anabaptists are not responsible at all for the peasant troubles," statements like these attributed to Grebel "certainly kept alive the revolutionary mood against the authorities" (ME, II, p. 605; see also 71K/440/29-30).

32. Although this is the only entry for Ryhener in the Quellen 1 source collection, the document itself indicates (1) that he was a close friend of Anabaptist Marx Bosshart, (2) that he served as a messenger on various occasions, and (3) that one of these occasions was the delivery of the court summons to Bosshart and Grebel. Thus this hearing necessarily had to take place after July 5, and the date when the summons was delivered (see fn. 37, below, and 71/416/20-21).

33. Bosshart, see fn. 14, above.

34. Inasmuch as the proclamation was delivered on Thursday, July 6 (see fn. 32, above),

it is likely that it was issued the previous day, and that Ryhener immediately took it to Winterthur, sixteen miles northeast of Zurich. The proclamation itself has not been preserved.

35. See 71/416/19: "lies in his book on baptism."

36. Hans Wüest was the deputy bailiff and president of the village of Zollikon. His wife had become an Anabaptist the previous March (see Blanke, p. 54).

37. I.e., July 5.

38. It is more likely that Bailiff Cornell Schultheiss was meant than the Deputy Bailiff Wüest (see fn. 36, above).

71. Grebel and Bosshart to the Zurich Council, Winterthur or Zollikon, July 6, 1525

1. The place of origin of the letter is not given. It was likely either Winterthur, where the summons was delivered (see 70F/415/36), or Zollikon, where the reply of the council was requested to be sent (see line 14, below).

2. On Bosshart, see 70F/fn.14 and Cast of Characters No. 7.

3. The summons has not been preserved.

4. For Zwingli's *Taufbüchlein*, see 69C.

5. A document of safe conduct refers to the legal immunity against arrest given a person summoned to a court appearance.

6. July 8.

7. Rudy Thomann, Bosshart's aged father-in-law, became an Anabaptist with Bosshart on January 25, 1525 (70F/fn.14). The house at Gstadstrasse 23-25 is still preserved.

71A. Imprisonment of Four Anabaptists, Zurich, July 11, 1525

1. On Heinrich Walder, see Cast of Characters No. 94.

2. On Bosshart, see Cast of Characters No. 7.

3. The Felix Kienast home (today Rütistrasse 43) was one of the numerous meeting places for the Zollikon Anabaptists beginning the previous January (see 68G/fn.2 and Blanke, p. 29). He was in the first group arrested on January 30 (p. 43). In June he was one of a three-person Bible-reading mission to Wassberg and Nänikon (p. 67). We hear about him once more in June 1527, when four Zollikon Anabaptists go to Grüningen to encourage the two imprisoned Anabaptists, Falk and Reimann, prior to their execution (p. 69 and Epi.E).

4. Zwingli's *Taufbüchlein* (see 69C).

5. See No. 71, above.

6. On Fridli Schumacher, see 68G/fn.7 and Cast of Characters No. 84.

7. On Hans Ockenfuss, see 63/fn.95 and Cast of Characters No. 71.

8. July 15, 1525.

71B. The Visit of Finsterbach and Friends, Zurich, July 1525

1. The names of the three are given in Finsterbach's testimony below. The other two (Müller and Strasser) had been sentenced earlier: Strasser on August 2 (Quellen 1, No. 92, p. 96) and Müller on August 16 (Quellen 1, No. 97, p. 100). The date of Finsterbach's sentence was August 19 (No. 98, pp. 100-1). The court records on these three appeared on the same document, indicating that the date of their hearing might have occurred some days earlier than their sentencing. We know nothing about the three apart from the contents of these documents.

2. Easter was on April 16. This was the first of three visits of these men to Zollikon implied in Finsterbach's testimony, the first at Eastertime, the second following Bosshart's imprisonment on July 11, and the third in answer to the court's summons to appear.

3. See 71A, above, dated July 11.

4. The house is today Gstadstrasse 23-25 in Zollikon (see 71/fn.7), then the home of Bosshart's aged father-in-law, Rudy Thomann.

5. It is unclear what "before this" means. It could mean "before their first visit to Zollikon at Eastertime," which would indicate that Grebel visited Finsterbach on his way

back from St. Gallen prior to Easter, as Bender concluded (1950, p. 146). Or it could mean "before the second visit following Bosshart's imprisonment on July 11," as the editors of Quellen 1 (p. 100, fn. 4) supposed, in which case the Grebel visit occurred the first week in July (see 70F/415/35-37).

71C. The Bailiff's Report of Anabaptists in Grüningen, Grüningen, July 12, 1525
1. Ger. *dess heren halb von Humberächtikon.* The lord of Hombrechtikon to 1546 was Konrad Schörli. It is not clear from the context why he was being arrested, but it seems that the Zurich Council wanted him for questioning concerning Anabaptism or his public opposition to the payment of tithes (see fn. 15, below).
2. On July 9, 1525.
3. Ger. *nach fil handlung.*
4. Stäfa, in the district of Meilen.
5. July 2.
6. See 70F/fn.13.
7. Ger. *uf suntag nechst ferschinen.*
8. Such as calling for heretical, divine, and civil justice, none of which he receives (see 71D/421/16-18, 23-25, 422/10-16, 20-22) and that he challenged Zwingli to a written disputation (see 71D/421/17-21, 26-31, 422/16-19, 23-26).
9. The "enclosed note" is identical to 71D/422/20-26, written in Berger's handwriting and appended to the prior testimony taken in Grüningen and recorded by the Grüningen court secretary. See Quellen 1, No. 84, p. 90, fn. 7 and No. 86, p. 92, fn. 5.
10. The pronoun refers to Hansliss Uli of Ringwil (see 71D/422/20).
11. Ger. *zwen boten.*
12. "The twelve" refers to "den zwölf Richter" (the twelve judges of the district of Grüningen).
13. Ger. *unser eignosen von Bern,* i.e., the next session of the Diet of the Swiss Confederacy.
14. Ger. *nie kein garb ufgstelt.*
15. The two main issues in the Grüningen and Zurich courts at this time were Anabaptism and the system of forced tithes, which included not only the church tax but the so-called "small tithe"—the tax on the production and consumption of vegetables and fruits. With the support of their pastors, the peasants in the district of Grüningen were rebelling against the system in various ways. The exact relationship between these two issues has not been thoroughly studied. Von Muralt wrote, "In my judgment the Anabaptists are not responsible at all for the peasant troubles. On the other hand, their teachings ... found a ready hearing among the peasants" (ME, II, p. 605). The Zurich Council had conducted a public debate on tithes on July 22, three weeks prior to Berger's letter. Zwingli was generally open to the peasants' complaints but the council cited biblical grounds for keeping the tithes, ordered the peasants to pay them and be quiet, and warned the pastors against fomenting disturbances by erroneous Bible teaching. Cf. 52A, above.

71D. Investigation of Grebel's Activities, Zurich, July 12, 1525
1. Unknown, except not to be confused with Hans Müller of Oberwinterthur (71A/418/12).
2. Hans Brennwald, pastor at Hinwil 1521-30 (see 70F/fn.15).
3. Ger. *burger recht,* which refers to the local government of city states and districts, usually including some form of representation.
4. Here and below (421/24, 422/11,15,21) the German adjective is clearly *ketzerlich* (heretical); but the editors of the text ask whether *kaiserlich* (imperial) was intended. In either case, a "higher" level of justice than *burger recht* is meant, whether vested in the Diet of the Swiss Confederacy or in the Holy Roman Empire.
5. Ger. *göttlich recht.* It is not clear whether Grebel was referring to canonical-eccle-

siastical law or to the laws of God based in the Bible. According to the Roman Catholic Church, these are identical levels of justice.

6. Probably refers to the prison tower in the governor's castle in Grüningen, not to the prison tower in Zurich. See 422/17, below.

7. The reference is probably to the first public disputation of Jan. 17 (68B), although there were four Councillors present also at the Tuesday Disputations (66A and 67).

8. Grebel does not mean that Zwingli did not speak, but that he did not refute Grebel's arguments.

9. On Jacob Falk, a farmer from Gossau, see Cast of Characters No. 23 and Epi.E/ 514.

10. Ger. *aber keins mogen verfolgen noch glanzen,* "but was unable to follow or reach him."

11. Cf. 71M/444/37.

12. Unknown, perhaps a relative of Fridli Wolfensperg (422/6).

13. See 67C/fn.22.

14. Hans Brennwald, see fn. 12, above.

15. Unknown (see fn. 12, above).

16. Unknown.

17. Ger. *Und habe im dero keins mogen verfolgen noch verlangen.*

18. Unknown.

19. See fn. 6, above.

20. Up to this point, the record is in the handwriting of the Grüningen court reporter, the rest of the document in the handwriting of Bailiff Berger (see Quellen 1, p. 90, fn. 7).

21. Unknown.

71E. The Third Swiss Anabaptist Martyr: Hans Krüsi, Luzern, July 27, 1525

1. Ger. *als gegen morgen,* "as toward morning." Goldach is a village between St. Gallen and Lake Constance to the east, located in the district of the Abbey of St. Gallen.

2. Ger. *als gegen mittag,* "as toward noon." Teufen, a strong center of Anabaptist activity, lies between St. Gallen and Appenzell to the south.

3. Ger. *als gegen abend,* "as toward evening." The Gossau referred to is in the canton of St. Gallen, not Zurich, and is located about six miles west of St. Gallen. Oberdorf was located near Gossau. It belonged to the city of St. Gallen until 1590, afterward to the Abbey of St. Gallen.

4. Ger. *als gegen mittnacht,* "as toward midnight." The Cappel mentioned here was in St. Gallen, not the Cappel in the canton of Zurich. It was formerly the name of the parish of Wittenbach, three miles north of St. Gallen.

5. On Hans Krüsi, alias Hans Nagel and Hans Kern, see Cast of Characters No. 60.

6. Jacob Schurtanner was the pastor in Teufen and the chief promoter of the Reformation in the territory in Appenzell. In March 1524, Zwingli dedicated to him his published treatise on *The Shepherd* (see ZW, III, No. 30), a revision of the sermon he preached during the Second Disputation (see 57C/fn.43).

7. Fast (Quellen 2, p. 396, fn. 10) comments on another document dated June 26, which reported a confrontation in Teufen between Schurtanner and Wolfgang Uliman (see Cast of Characters No. 89), thus casting doubt on the accuracy of Kessler's assertion that Krüsi deposed Schurtanner. Moreover, in a letter dated in February 1526, Zwingli inquired of Vadian after Schurtanner, presuming that he was still in Appenzell. Fast hypothesizes that Kessler confused (1) the selection of Krüsi as pastor of an existing congregation in Tablat with the confrontation between Uliman and Schurtanner to the disadvantage of the latter and (2) the appearance of Uliman in Teufen with Giger's sacrilege in the balcony of the Church of St. Lawrence in St. Gallen (see 70A/fn.14).

8. Michael Degen was in charge of the police force that had jurisdiction in the political district governed by the abbot of St. Gallen.

9. Although technically the trial in Luzern was legitimized by the fact that this canton was one of the four protectorates of the Abbey of St. Gallen, it was irregular to transport a prisoner away from his place of citizenship and offense for trial elsewhere.

10. See fn. 5, above.

11. He was released from prison on June 16, 1525.

12. For the evidence in support of this charge, see Fast, Quellen 2, No. 466, pp. 397-98, and No. 210, p. 178.

13. See Fast, Quellen 2, No. 349, fn. 9.

14. Ger. *inn die püren uffgewysen und geheissen.*

15. Ger. *Beda der träger* [Drechsler], refers to Beda Miles, a woodworker turned Anabaptist (see 60/fn.2), who was released from prison with Krüsi on June 16.

16. At the time of their release, Miles and Krüsi had promised to give up their Anabaptist activities. Apparently Miles intended from the beginning not to comply and reproached Krüsi for making the promise of compliance in earnest.

17. It is not clear what work is meant, whether his role as preacher at Tablat or his occupation as a weaver. Or perhaps Miles was referring to his own work as a woodworker.

18. On the identity of these four persons, see Fast, Quellen 2, p. 262, fn. 11.

19. Ger. *gotzhus lütt,* "people of the house of God [abbey]."

20. Nicholas Guldin (see Fast, Quellen 2, No. 470, p. 400, fn. 1).

21. On Kürsiner (Roggenacher), see Cast of Characters No. 77.

22. On Giger, see Cast of Characters No. 27, although a son to this Giger may be meant here.

23. On Dominic Zili, see Cast of Characters No. 104.

24. Brändly (1, p. 68, fn. 8) assumes that the pronouns refer to the schoolmaster at St. Gallen, Zili; but Fast (Quellen 2, p. 262, fn. 16) is probably correct in inferring that Krüsi is meant. The Latin noun *provisor* (in the text, *provoser*) refers to a teacher's helper or assistant (*ibid.,* p. 263, fn. 17.)

25. These three are unknown to Fast or Brändly.

26. Fast (Quellen 2, p. 263, fn. 19) hypothesizes that one of two persons is meant here: Michael Wüst (see 71P/Intro.) or Mathias Nagel, the father of Hans Nagel (Krüsi).

27. Hans Nüsch is unknown. The Schnecken area was a jurisdiction of the district of Wil.

28. The name of Krüsi's wife is unknown. This is the only reference to her in the sources.

29. Hensli Studer was the son of Christian Studer, the burgomaster of St. Gallen. He was the representative of the Weavers' Guild in the Large Council since 1517, a member of the City Court or Tribunal 1524-25, and became burgomaster in 1542.

30. Jacob Spichermann was also a representative of the Weavers' Guild to the Large Council 1516-25. Fast (Quellen 2, p. 350, fn. 6) lists among other details that from 1525 to 1527 he had various associations with the Anabaptists; and Brändly (1, p. 68, fn. 10) states that in 1526, Spichermann was fined 200 guilders for Anabaptist sympathies.

31. See 71E/427/23, where Krüsi is described as a tanner. Fast (Quellen 2, p. 263, fn. 24) believes that the present reference is the more accurate.

32. Ger. *das halltum und die hellgen und götzen.*

33. Vadian wrote in his *Chronicle of the Abbey of St. Gallen* that Teufer and Gais removed the images from the church in 1525, but Krüsi may have been referring to the church at St. George.

34. This name was transcribed "Schorent" by Brändly, "Schwent" by Fast. Neither scholar could identify the person, although Brändly (1, p. 68, fn. 11) surmises that he was related to Uliman, also known as "Schorant" (see 69A/fn.11) and Fast [Quellen], p. 414, fn. 10) surmises that he was the same person cited in a court hearing in St. Gallen on March 11, 1526: Jung Swend Othmar, assuming that Swend is the surname of Othmar.

35. Ger. *gotzhusman.* See fn. 19, above.

36. I.e., the remains of saints worshiped as relics.

37. Melchior Degen (see fn. 8, above).

38. Krüsi may have had 1 Cor. 6:2ff. in mind.

39. See Acts 5:29.

40. See preface to this document regarding the dissension over tithes in the Abbey of St. Gallen.

41. Straubenzell lay directly west of St. Gallen in the abbey district, a suburban parish today.

42. Rotmonten was a parish in the abbey district directly northeast of St. Gallen, later belonging to Tablat and together annexed to St. Gallen.

43. Bernhardszell was also a parish in the abbey district west of St. Gallen near Gossau, belonging to Waldkirch today.

44. Fast (Quellen 2, p. 264, fn. 39) indicates that the number seems high and would have included every village in the whole abbey district if not the entire Toggenburg Valley. He refers to another court reference to "16 villages" (p. 375/fn.33).

45. One other court document dated March 31, 1524, in the Fast collection (No. 407, fn. 7) refers to Heini Locher, who was a linen worker in the service of the city of St. Gallen. In 1528 he became a representative of the Weavers' Guild to the Large Council; in 1548, guildmaster; and in 1556 a member of the Small Council.

46. Aberli (Albrecht) Schlumpf was a participant in the first Bible study group led by Kessler in the beginning of 1524. He served later as Stadtammann.

47. One of the two themes of the Grebel-Krüsi collection of Bible verses (see No. 71F, below).

48. See Mt. 10:28; Lk. 12:4; and Fast, Quellen 2, No. 445, p. 380, fn. 3.

49. Wolfgang Uliman, see 69A/fn.11 and Cast of Characters No. 89.

50. Sebastian Rugglisberger, a citizen of St. Gallen, was prior of the Williamite Monastery near Klingnau. He was a friend of Hubmaier, with whom he took a journey to St. Gallen and Zurich in the spring of 1523. At both places, the issue of infant baptism came up for discussion (see Fast, Quellen 2, No. 403, p. 330, fn. 4 and No. 466, p. 397, fn. 26). On his involvement in the Anabaptist movement, see Fast, Nos. 469, 497, 527, and 529.

51. Ger. anzöggt, modern Ger. angezeigt, "announced," "notified," "advised," "declared," "proclaimed." Johann Rütiner wrote in his diary in 1538 that Johann Ramseyer and Martin Baumgartner led Krüsi into Anabaptism (Fast, 1962, p. 583). These two men were among the first members of the movement in St. Gallen and probably took Krüsi to one of Grebel's meetings in the fortnight before Easter, April 9.

52. Same word as in fn. 51, above.

53. Fast, 1962, has demonstrated the probability that this manuscript was identical to that mentioned by Grebel himself in 62/283/19-20 and 69/358/13. See 62/fns. 7 and 8, and 69/fn.25.

54. "One Hundred" refers to the combined assembly of the Small and Large Councils of Luzern.

71F. The Grebel-Krüsi Collection of Bible Passages, Augsburg, 1525

1. A thorough study has not been made concerning the Bible edition used for this collection but a comment by Zwingli in the *Elenchus* (Epi.C/fn.167) indicates that Grebel made his own translation "even when those fellows struggle and stammer in the German tongue." Fast (1962, 456-75) reports showing the document to Dr. Joseph Benzing, an expert on sixteenth-century typography, who definitely identified the printer as Heinrich Steiner of Augsburg. The woodcuts were probably done by Jörg Breu. It is not known how he received the manuscript for printing, but Fast hypothesizes that after Krüsi's death, one or more of his followers with whom he had used the booklet saw to its printing. There was a close connection at that time between St. Gallen and Augsburg. Hans Denk, for example, attended an Anabaptist meeting in St. Gallen in the fall of 1525 and then traveled directly to Augsburg. It is even possible that he took it along for printing.

2. See 71E/fn.5.

3. Krüsi's occupations were identified in 71E/fn.5 as teacher and weaver. Fast *(ibid.)* hypothesizes that whoever saw to the printing of the booklet after Krüsi's death was mistaken in describing him as a *Ledergerber* (tanner).

4. Fast *(ibid.)* concluded erroneously that the words *dann du hast gnad funden vor mir* were not in the Genesis text, but a commentary inserted between verses 14a and 22. Actually they are the words of verse 8.

5. The following commentary was added: "That was a true trust in God concerning the sacrifice of Abel."

6. The following commentary was added: "And he believed the Lord."

7. Commentary added: "[So Lot went out] with his whole household. That you may comprehend according to the true faith."

8. Commentary added: "That is a truly heartfelt trustful hope and faith of the prophet Moses, through whom God the Father has done many wonders."

9. Commentary added: "Here we recognize the true faith that proceeds from the heart."

10. The Ger. word *vatterschafft* for *ritterschaft* contrasts with the Basel Bible edition of Adam Petri, 1523.

11. The following commentary was added concerning Thomas: "who previously was an unbeliever."

12. This verse was introduced with the comment, "Apply all your diligence and direct your faith and virtue in this way. . . ."

13. The following commentary was added: "And not through the world."

14. Commentary added: "Therein lies the faith."

15. Commentary added: "Thus she believed the angel. Now faith is only from heaven."

16. Commentary added: "[And nothing will be impossible to you] who believe." [But this kind never comes out except by prayer and fasting], "that is, we must pray for the Spirit of God."

17. Commentary added: "And the disciples of Jesus gave witness to him."

18. Commentary added: "[And Paul said, John baptized with the baptism of repentance] but you shall now be baptized in the name of Jesus Christ."

71G. Jud to Vadian, Zurich, August 8, 1525

1. The reference is to the decree of the St. Gallen Council dated June 5-6, 1525 (see 70B/385/19ff.).

2. "Our fault" refers to the leading preachers in the three main churches of Zurich in distinction to the Zurich magistrates.

3. The "two plagues" refer to "quarrel" and "hypocrisy" of the preceding phrase.

4. "Antichrist" refers to the pope and papal system.

5. The name "Sophist" originally applied to a class of teachers of rhetoric and conduct in ancient Greece about the middle of the fifth century after Christ. As masters of adroit and specious reasoning, the official doctrinal defenders of the Roman Catholic position—Johann Eck of Ingolstadt and Johann Faber of Constance—are the ones to whom Jud applies the name vis-à-vis the Protestant Reformers. See 49/fn.8 and 58A/fn.14.

6. The Greek word *epistomizein* is quoted from Tit. 1:11.

7. Compare with 68L/355/21 and Epi.D/508/4-5.

8. Mt. 13:25.

9. See Mt. 2:16.

10. See Mt. 7:15; 24:16, 24; Acts 13:6; Rev. 16:13; 19:20; 20:10.

11. 2 Pet. 2:1; 1 Jn. 4:1.

71H. The Arrest of Grebel and Blaurock, Grüningen, October 8, 1525

1. Apparently Berger had sent some kind of report to Zurich about his efforts to control the movement on Thursday, Oct. 5.

2. Oct. 8, the date of the present report.

3. On Brennwald, see 70F/fn.16 and 71D/fns. 2 and 14.

4. Ger. *der kilchher,* "church master."

5. Brennwald may have been in trouble with the authorities at an earlier date for supporting the agitation of the local peasants against the payment of taxes and perhaps even for conversing with the Anabaptists about the issue of baptism.

6. Ger. *der weibel,* "summoner" or "apparitor," identical to the *Untervogt* of fn. 11, below.

7. The two: Brennwald and the sergeant of Hinwil.

8. Jörg Blaurock, see Cast of Characters No. 5.

9. I.e., Brennwald, *der kilchher* (fn. 4, above).

10. I.e., Blaurock.

11. Ger. *unndervogt,* identical to the *weibel* in fn. 6, above.

12. I.e., Brennwald, the priest.

13. *Der kilchher* in this instance probably refers to Blaurock not to Brennwald.

14. I.e., the arrest of Blaurock.

15. Betzholz was in the parish and district of Hinwil.

16. Mantz had just been released from custody in Zurich on the previous day.

17. The editors of Quellen 1 (p. 110, fn. 6) write that it is not clear whether a place name or house name is meant. If the former, several place names come to mind, but all on the way from Betzholz to Edikon, while Berger's ride led from Betzholz to Ottikon and from there to Grüningen.

18. Ottikon was in the parish of Gossau, district of Hinwil.

19. The meaning of Berger's apology is not clear. It may be merely a general kind of self-depreciation.

711. Zwingli to Vadian, Zurich, October 11, 1525

1. Zwingli refers to the writing of Johann Bugenhagen of Pomerania entitled "An Epistle Against the New Opinions about the Sacrament of the Body and Blood of Our Lord Jesus Christ." For Zwingli's response, see his "Response to the Epistle of Johann Bugenhagen, dated October 23, 1525 (ZW, IV. No. 67, pp. 546-76).

2. According to Blanke (ZW, VI, pp. 21-22, fn. 1), Zwingli was still searching for a "party name . . . to give to his Anabaptist opponents." He had used the Ger. *widertouff* ("rebaptism"; see 69C/363) and its Lat. equivalent *rebaptisantium* (69D/fn.7). His later, preferred term will be the Greek word καταΒαπτισμός, Latinized to *catabaptismus* ("Catabaptism"; see Epi.C/fn.8), a term which Oecolampad got from the fourth-century Eastern Church Father, Gregory of Nazianzus. For Blanke's thorough discussion of these and other names used by Zwingli, see Epi.C/fn.8.

3. Hubmaier's booklet *Vom christlichen Tauf der Gläubigen,* published July 7 was directed against Zwingli's *Taufbüchlein* published the end of May (69C, above). Zwingli's reply under the title "Truthful, Well-Grounded Answer to Dr. Balthasar [Hubmaier's] Booklet on Baptism" was published on November 5 (see ZW, IV, No. 68, pp. 577-647).

4. Sertorious is Christoph Schappeler of St. Gallen, then preacher in Münster (see Cast of Characters No. 81).

5. The accusation that Schappeler had written the famous "Twelve Articles" of the peasants' revolt was made by Jacob Holzwart, a student in Wittenberg (ZW, VIII, p. 382, fn. 8). Fast (Quellen 2, p. 590, fn. 44) writes that Sebastian Lotzer authored the articles but under Schappeler's influence.

6. The reference is probably to Luther's venomous tract entitled "Against the Robbing and Murdering Hordes of Peasants" (LW, Vol. 46, pp. 45-56). See also 64/fn.7. Zwingli apparently did not approve of the *invectionis* of Luther against the peasants.

7. Zwingli refers to the tract entitled *Ein Schrift Philippi Melanchthon wider die Artickel der Bawerschaft,* 1525.

8. Oecolampad to Zwingli, Basel, October 2, 1525 (see ZW, VIII, No. 387.)

9. See 71N/fn.13.

10. Lat. *mota mente homine.*

11. Lat. *malis avibus bene ingeniatus,* "thoroughly constituted under birds of ill omen."

12. The allusion is to Jacob Grebel, Vadian's father-in-law and Conrad's father (see Cast of Characters No. 38). A number of interpretations of this reference to Jacob in the context of Conrad's arrest are possible. One is that Jacob was to some degree sympathetic toward his son's Anabaptist activities (see John Horsch, MQR, VII, 142-61). In support of this position is Zwingli's comment after Grebel's life imprisonment, "Your father-in-law senator implored mercy in vain" (71N/449/24-26). Another interpretation is that Jacob was a hopeless and faithless adherent of the old faith; and therefore Conrad was predestined to his own form of evil (Von Muralt, 1934, p. 80). In support of this position is Zwingli's reference of September 22, 1525, to "that false clerk [Joachim Amgrüt], the play-fellow of your father-in-law" (ZW, VIII, 371). Amgrüt was one of the few remaining members of the council who strictly adhered to the old Roman Catholic faith. A third interpretation is that Jacob was a moderate, who while supporting the Zwinglian Reformation was conciliatory toward both the old faith party and the radical dissenters (see Schelbert, p. 50, and the footnotes to Epi.A, below, on the execution of Jacob Grebel).

71J. The Third Public Disputation on Baptism, Zurich, November 6-8, 1525

1. This comment by Bullinger was part of his attempt to identify Grebel and the Anabaptists with the Peasants' Revolt. For Bender's refutation of this charge see 1950, pp. 111-16, 154-55.

2. For comments by Grebel and Mantz in this regard, see 67/301/33ff. and 67B/312/6-12.

3. Pastors at the Grossmünster, St. Peter's, and the Hospital Church, respectively.

4. On Joner, see 57F/fn.4 and Cast of Characters No. 57.

5. On Schmid, see 57C/fn.6c and Cast of Characters No. 83.

6. On Hofmeister, see 68J/fn.10 and Cast of Characters No. 46.

7. On Vadian, see Cast of Characters No. 93.

8. The Twelve Judges (magistrates) who conducted trials and settled disputes within their local district of Grüningen under the centralized authority of the Council of Zurich. Disputes with Zurich itself could be appealed to the Diet of the Swiss Confederacy.

9. The reference is to Zwingli's *Antwort über Doctor Balthasars Taufbüchlein,* published Nov. 5, 1525 (see ZW, IV, 577-647).

10. See document 4 in the present 71J series, below.

11. See 71K, below.

12. *Vom Christlichen Tauf der Gläubigen.*

13. See fn. 9, above.

14. Kessler is in error. The disputation started on Nov. 6, not 10.

15. Kessler was referring to Jörg Blaurock, although as stated in 68F/fn.21, he did not know that these names referred to the same person. For the derivation of these names, see ZW, VI, p. 153, fn. 3.

16. The actual occupation of Waldshut by the forces of the Austrian government occurred on Dec. 6, 1525. Hubmaier fled to Zurich on the 5th.

17. Unknown. Fast (Quellen 2, p. 612, fn. 91) wonders whether Kessler meant Lienhart Fessler, in which case, see Muralt and Schmid (Quellen 1, pp. 83, 161).

18. Junker Conrad Mayer was a delegate of the Tailors' Guild to the Large Council in St. Gallen 1520-21 and a member of the Small Council following that. He was burgomaster 1527-30. Concerning his interest in the Anabaptist movement, see Fast (Quellen 2, No. 481, fn. 5).

19. Mainrat Weniger, a tailor, was guildmaster of the Weavers' Guild from 1525, and later a Councillor. For his prior interest in Anabaptism, see Fast, Quellen 2, p. 396, fn. 21.

20. For similar eschatological references, see 67/302/18, 69/357/33•34, 70/378/17, etc.

21. Bullinger described this same scene. See Fast, Quellen 2, p. 613, fn. 94.

22. Although the disputation was held in the Grossmünster, Zwingli probably refers here to the three main parishes of Zurich.

23. Blanke (ZW, VI, p. 45, fn. 1) writes that "we are dealing here with the Disputation of Nov. 6-8, 1525."

24. For the First and Second Public Disputations on Baptism, see 68B and 68L, above.

25. The pastors of the three main parishes in Zurich—the Grossmünster, St. Peter's, and the Fraumünster.

26. As Bullinger reported (71J/434/1-3), the Disputation was moved from the Rathaus to the Grossmünster because of the crowds.

27. See fn. 9, above. The foreword to the booklet was dated Nov. 5, but according to this letter the actual date of publication was Nov. 14.

71K. The Trial of Grebel, Mantz, and Blaurock, Zurich, between November 9 and 18, 1525

1. On the problem of dating the trial, see Quellen 1, p. 120, fn. 1; p. 122, fn. 1; p. 124, fn. 1; p. 125, fn. 1; and p. 126, fn. 1.

2. On Simon Stumpf, see 57C/fn.12 and Cast of Characters No. 85.

3. I.e., Zwingli and Jud.

4. For another version of this charge by Zwingli, see 59A, above. Hofmeister repeats the charge in 438/39-40.

5. This is the only reference to the usury-tithes issue in the following testimony against the Anabaptists. For Blaurock's reply, under pressure of cross-examination, see 440/27-29.

6. Ger. *nüwen statt*. According to ZW, IV, p. 169, fn. 16, the Neustadt was not a city quarter but a street near the Grossmünster. This was probably the home of Felix Mantz (see Bender, 1950, p. 256, fn. 256).

7. For another version of this charge by Zwingli, see 67C/316/39.

8. Caspar Grossmann, alias Megander, preacher at the Hospital Church. See 68/fn. 1 and Cast of Characters No. 42.

9. I.e., the twelve judges or magistrates of the district of Höngg, where Stumpf was pastor at that time.

10. For another version of this charge by Zwingli, see 69C/365/34-36. For the reference to Grebel's reply, see fn. 17, below.

11. Muralt and Schmid date this contact prior to March 18, 1525, after which he was either in custody in Zurich or in flight (Quellen 1, p. 121, fn. 5).

12. The reference is to Hans Hujuff, one of the co-signers of Grebel's letter to Müntzer (see 63/fns. 50 and 72, 64/fn.31, and Cast of Characters No. 55).

13. For another version of this charge by Zwingli, see 69C/364/37-39. Hofmeister repeats the charge in 438/37. For Mantz's alternate version of this conversation with Zwingli in Hujuff's garden, see below, 441/31ff.

14. For Mantz's reply to this charge, see 442/6-8. For Grebel's reply to the same charge, see 439/28-31. A comparison of the two replies indicates that the issue was not "discussing it *with him*" (Mantz) but "discussing it *with one another*" (Grebel).

15. Muralt and Schmid (Quellen 1, p. 122, fn. 6) cannot identify either the man from Bern or the one called Martin, adding that the letter is not extant; but see fn. 79, below, concerning one named Martin Lingg, who was an Anabaptist spokesman at the Zofingen Disputation near Bern in 1532. For Grebel's reply to the alleged conversation, see 439/33-34.

16. Zwingli repeats the charge in lines 18-20, below. For an earlier version of the same charge, see 67C/316/35-37. Hofmeister repeats the charge in 438/33-34. For Grebel's reply, see 439/32-33, and for Mantz's reply to the same charge, see 442/9-10.

17. See fn. 10, above. For Grebel's reply, see 439/23-24, 34.

18. Heinrich Brennwald, provost of the chapter of the Church at Embrach (see 57E/fn.5 and Cast of Characters No. 8). Brennwald repeats this allegation in 439/2-5 and Blaurock denies it in 71M/441/8-10.

19. Apparently the prisoners were being held in the former Dominican (Preachers') Monastery since being transferred from the Grüningen Castle. See fn. 74, below.

20. From 438/41ff. we discover that Zwingli got this from Brennwald, who got it from George Sitz, who got it from Blaurock.

21. The reference is evidently to a comment that Grebel made on Monday.

22. On Sebastian Hofmeister, see 68J/fn.10, 71J/fn.5, and Cast of Characters No. 46.

23. On Anemund de Coct, French nobleman, see 69/fn.31 and Cast of Characters No. 15.

24. The identity of this prison escape is uncertain, but Muralt and Schmid (Quellen 1, p. 123, fn. 4) connect it with the first Anabaptist imprisonment at the beginning of February 1525.

25. For Grebel's reply to this charge, see 439/39-40.

26. For Grebel's reply, see 440/1-2.

27. See fn. 23, above.

28. See fn. 16, above. Mantz does not specifically deny the charge, but see fn. 29, below.

29. For Mantz's reply to this charge, see 442/9-10. The issue is not that the sword could not be used *per se,* but not by Christians; and that is why the doctrine of Christian nonresistance was meaningless "unless infant baptism [the main symbol of the state church] was abandoned."

30. See fn. 13, above.

31. See fn. 4, above.

32. On Heinrich Brennwald, see fn. 18, above.

33. Muralt and Schmid were unable to identify this name.

34. Trinkler (see Cast of Characters No. 86) and Stollen were members of the Small Council in Zurich.

35. See 437/38-41, above, to note how Zwingli used this hearsay evidence passed on from George Sitz to Brennwald, Trinkler, and Stollen, and from them to Zwingli. For Blaurock's reply to this charge, see 441/9-11, below.

36. Anthony Walder was a canon in the Grossmünster. He died at Cappel with Zwingli.

37. See fns. 10 and 17, above.

38. See fn. 14, above.

39. See fn. 15, above.

40. The particular Hofmeister testimony to which Grebel alludes was not recorded in 438/7ff., but see fns. 16 and 28, above.

41. See fn. 24, above.

42. See fn. 25, above.

43. See fn. 26, above.

44. The following remarks by Blaurock were apparently presented in the form of a letter "to the preachers in the churches" (see 71M/444/29-30). The reference to the "Tower" may indicate that it should be dated following Nov. 18, when the male Anabaptists were transferred from the Preachers' Monastery to the Tower (see 442/16, below).

45. Blaurock is quoting Jn. 10:7ff.

46. Blaurock's fourfold reference to *ein dieb und ein merder* ("a thief and murderer") comes from his German text of Jn. 10:1 and 8, referring to "false shepherds" (see 71M/444/ 29-30) who "climb in by another way." Zwingli used this same text against the papists in Jan. 1523 (see Meyer, p. 37): "4. Whoever seeks or points out another door errs, yes, he is a murderer of souls and a thief."

47. Blaurock is quoting Jn. 10:11ff.

48. Ger. *anfenger.* This and its translation as "beginner" could have two meanings: (1) disciple, learner, and (2) initiator, innovator.

49. Blaurock had inserted "in Christ," indicating that the idea of election was his main thought here. See 70/fn.30.

50. Ger. *disputieren.* Blaurock does not accept the custodial hearings, which Zwingli called "disputations" (68B/Intro.), as true debates.

51. Ger. *verornet.* a predestinarian reference for further study. See Hubmaier's tract on

"free will" in Williams, 1957, pp. 114-36.

52. On the relation between Anabaptism and the tithes issue, see 70F/fns. 30 and 31.

53. On Blaurock's work in Zollikon, see Blanke, 1961, pp. 30-32, 36.

54. On Margaret Hottinger, see Cast of Characters No. 51.

55. The question to which an answer was required was "whether or not she intends to persist in Anabaptism and the teachings of Grebel and Mantz" (see 442/20-21).

56. This is not quite accurate. Blanke (1961, p. 22) cites Brötli's baptism of Fridli Schumacher as "the first rebaptism administered to a citizen of Zollikon."

57. Ger. *anschlegenn,* "strikes," "attacks," "uprisings."

58. Ger. *verpüntnussenn,* "pacts," "alliances," "confederations."

59. Ger. *söndrungen,* "schisms," "separations," "divisions."

60. See fn. 46, above.

61. Another basic Zwinglian principle enunciated in Article 22 at the First Zurich Disputation: "... insofar, however, as they [our works] are ours, they are not right, not good" (Meyer, p. 41).

62. This refers to Brennwald's testimony (439/3-5).

63. See the council judgment of March 25 in Quellen 1, No. 65: "Concerning the aliens, namely, Peter Forster, schoolmaster from Luzern, Gabriel Giger from St. Gallen, Valentin Gredig from Savoy, Hans Bichtler from Walmenschwil, Jörg from Chur called Blaurock, and the brother in the white coat named [Michael Sattler], it is decided that they shall swear out of Milords' jurisdiction and territory immediately on their [good] will not to return." Apparently Blaurock was allowed to leave Zurich without actually swearing the oath. See also ZW, VI, 152-54. Incidentally, there is a gap in the manuscript following "brother in the white coat named," but the reference is clearly to Michael Sattler.

64. Ps. 24:1.

65. Master Wädischwiler was a member of the Zurich Council (see Quellen 1, No. 180, p. 199, line 29).

66. Ger. *gantz lougenbar und abred.* Just what Blaurock has "disavowed and agreed to" is not clear, but perhaps it represents a bit of conciliation on his part at the end of his November cross-examination.

67. This statement represents a clarification on Zwingli's arguments against rebaptism, that Scripture makes no warrant for two baptisms of the same person. Although on occasion they attempted to find a proof text for two baptisms (see 69C/370/17ff.), their more considered argument was that infant baptism was "no baptism" at all (see Epi.E/516/10).

68. The charge here is against unlawful secret meetings.

69. This is Mantz's version of the same conversation earlier reported by Zwingli in 71K/437/24ff.

70. Probably Hans Conrad Escher, a member of the Large Council, and also Conrad Grebel's brother-in-law (see Cast of Characters No. 21).

71. Rudolf Kambli, also a member of the Zurich Council, had earlier attended some Anabaptist meetings, although he had not allowed himself to be rebaptized (see Quellen 1, No. 56, p. 65.22, and No. 57, p. 66.13).

72. Refers to 437/30-32.

73. A clear statement of the nonresistant position, reminiscent of 63/290/10-11.

74. I.e., the prisoners are to be moved from their custodial confinement in the former Dominican (Preachers') Monastery to permanent imprisonment in the New Tower (also called "Witches' Tower," "Murder Tower," and "Heretics' Tower" in honor of the Anabaptists), located on the city wall between the two gates, Neumarkt and Niederdorf, near the cemetery of the Preachers' Monastery. See fn. 77, below.

75. On "mush" as a prison diet, see 32A/fn.5 and 54/fn.17.

76. On Margaret Hottinger, see fn. 54, above. Since this was the question to which she was asked to reply in 440/32-38, Muralt and Schmid (Quellen 1, p. 126, fn. 1) think that this minute may have preceded the one above in the sequence. The fact that her final judgment is still pending here would support that assumption. Nevertheless, she evidently refused the terms of her release (*ibid.,* No. 134) because she was transferred to the Wellenberg for

permanent imprisonment (see 71M/447/24).

77. The Wellenberg (Wave Tower) was located in the middle of the Limmat River within sight of the Rathaus, where the hearings were held. This Tower held only nine cells and was thus too small to house all of the Anabaptists (see 68H/fn.9), so the men were put into the New Tower (see fn. 74, above).

78. Ulrich Teck and Jacob Gross of Waldshut had been seized by Bailiff Berger on Sept. 20 (Quellen 1, No. 107, pp. 108-9) because of their Anabaptist activity. Among those baptized by Teck was Hans Küntzi of Klingnau (see 71Q/455/2).

79. On Marty Lingg, alias Martin Weniger, an articulate Anabaptist spokesman from Schaffhausen, see Cast of Characters No. 64.

80. On Michael Sattler, see Cast of Characters No. 80. He first appeared in Zurich the previous March (see Quellen No. 64, p. 73, and fn. 63, above) and apparently joined the Anabaptists at this time. His imprisonment with Grebel *et al.* implies participation in the November Disputation.

71L. Mandate of the Zurich Council to the Grüningen Magistrates, Zurich, November 30, 1525

1. The two previous "public disputations" of Jan. 17 and March 20-22 (see 68B and 68L, above).

2. Research is needed on the number and percentage of recantations by the early Anabaptists in the process of trial. In spite of such themes as "steadfastness and courage of the Anabaptists" and "the sources of their strength," the author of the article on Anabaptist "Martyrs" in ME, III, pp. 521-25 adds that "there were, however, a considerable number of recantations" (p. 524).

3. Ger. *rückfällig.* "Backslidden" in this context means a return to their Anabaptist commitment.

4. The Third Public Disputation of Nov. 6-8 (see 71J, above).

5. See 71J/fn.3.

6. Up to this point, the wording of the mandate is an abbreviated revision of the Nov. 15 letter of the Zurich Council to the Grüningen magistrates (Quellen 1, No. 129) taken from the *Actensammlung,* No. 873. What follows is the wording of the injunction as preserved in Bullinger's *Reformationsgeschichte,* I, p. 296.

7. Ger. *man und frowen, knaben und dochtern.* This is a rare reference in the documents to the role of dependent children in the movement; and its meaning in the present context is the obvious shift in public policy at this point to make the mandate applicable to all cases, present and future (see fn. 10, below).

8. For monetary equivalences, see Fast, Quellen 2, p. 722.

9. Ger. *büssen,* "to pray for," "to suffer for," "to do penance for."

10. Ger. *und nüt nachlassen,* "and not relax [slacken, soften, ease off, let go, yield, remit, abate, unbend, give way]." The mandate is characterized by a new measure of serious intent.

71M. The Tenth Disputation with the Anabaptists: Their Retrial and Sentencing, Zurich, March 5-7, 1526

1. The Third Public Disputation on Baptism, Nov. 6-8, 1525 (see 71J, below).

2. Lat. *noctue,* "the night owls."

3. For statistics on the spread of Anabaptism in the Zurich area, see Egli, 1878, pp. 98-99.

4. Lat. *pro virili,* "in proportion to their virility."

5. Lat. *post eam collationem,* "after that conference" or "the conference after that." Neither rendering is possible in this context. The former would imply that the Nov. 6-8 disputation was the tenth, but Myconius knew that it was the ninth (see Jackson, 1912, p. 15). The latter would be accurate chronologically but grammatically faulty because *collationem* is in the accusative case, not nominative. The rendering selected here is a legitimate translation of *post* when used to indicate rank order: "next after."

6. The tenth *collatio* was different from any of the other nine in that it was the *Täufer-*

prozess (the retrial) itself, unless perhaps the prosecution conducted by Huber, Trüb, and Usteri, was preceded by a private conversation between the Zurich pastors and the prisoners, in which case this should have been listed as a "private disputation" in the Intro. to 68B, below.

7. This is the point at which the execution of Anabaptists was first mandated in Zurich, with the consequence that ten months later, Felix Mantz was drowned in Zurich for the crime of rebaptism (see Epi.B).

8. Mantz's testimony was given in writing.

9. Mantz left no published writing, but his "Protestation und Schutzschrift" (67B) is included in the present collection.

10. See 71K/fns. 46 and 60.

11. See 71K/440/5ff and 71K/fn.44.

12. Bender (1950, p. 269, fn. 90) wrote that this comment was "very important for the dating of Grebel's booklet which Zwingli discusses in the *Elenchus*" (see Epi.C, below), i.e., Grebel wrote his *libellum confutatio* (Booklet of Counter Arguments) sometime between March and August 1526.

13. Five members of the Hottinger family (see Nuesch-Bruppacher, pp. 49ff. and 69E/fn.5) are included among the defendants. Uli Hottinger of Zollikon (to be distinguished from Uli Hottinger of Hirslanden) led some of the earlier meetings in his home (Blanke, 1961, p. 53). He was a brother of Heini (see Quellen 1, No. 170b, and 71-O/451/25), in whose home the Zollikon group finally decided to disband in August 1525 (Quellen 1, No. 105). But Uli dared again to testify against infant baptism (Quellen 1, No. 170b), for which he was imprisoned with Grebel *et al.,* but he subsequently recanted (No. 173) and was released. In June 1527 he was one of a five-man delegation sent to Grüningen to encourage the Anabaptist prisoners there (No. 219). Uli said that "he had given the imprisoned brothers his hands and had encouraged them and said that they should be steadfast and brave and not recant."

14. Ernst von Glätz, who Muralt and Schmid believe is the same person as *zur Eichs Knecht* (servant of zur Eichs), had been baptized on Feb. 22, 1526, by Karl Brennwald in the house (inn) of Anna Widerker (see fn. 53, below). Nothing more is known about him, but see Quellen 1, No. 170 and 71-O/451/1-3.

15. Ger. *acht tag,* "eight days."

16. Karl Brennwald was converted to Anabaptism on Jan. 28, 1526, by Anthony Roggenacher (see Cast of Characters Nos. 9 and 77).

17. On Widerkerin, see fn. 53, below.

18. The furrier's wife was Dorothea Roggenacher, wife of Anthony Roggenacher (see fn. 22, below, and Quellen 1, p. 179).

19. Probably Regula Gletzli (see Cast of Characters No. 98).

20. On Hubmaier, see Cast of Characters No. 54. Among the Anabaptist testimonies here recorded, Hubmaier expresses the most submissive attitude, having undergone severe interrogation under torture on the rack. Upon release, he returned to the leadership of the movement in Augsburg and Moravia.

21. See Quellen 1, No. 147, p. 148.

22. On Anthony Roggenacher [Kürsiner], see Cast of Characters No. 77.

23. On Hans Hottinger, see Cast of Characters No. 49.

24. On Rudolf Hottinger, see Cast of Characters No. 52.

25. On Hans Ockenfuss, see Cast of Characters No. 71.

26. Ger. *sin forfar.*

27. Brennwald, see fn. 16, above, and Cast of Characters No. 9.

28. Roggenacher, see fn. 22, above, and Cast of Characters No. 77.

29. Ernst von Glatz, see fn. 14, above.

30. Widerkerin, see fn. 53, below.

31. Agli Ockenfuss, perhaps the wife of Hans (fn. 25, above), may have been one of eight wives or daughters of Zollikon Anabaptists who were baptized in the house of Hans Murer on Feb. 26, 1525 (Quellen 1, No. 48). Hans was present.

32. On Ab-Iberg, see fn. 40, below.

33. Wilhelm Exell, see 71-O/fn.1.

34. A later recantation dated April 4 is here inserted into the text.

35. Apart from the fact that Elizabeth Hottinger came from Hirslanden, nothing is known about her, except that she recanted on April 25 and was released (Quellen 1, p. 182). Perhaps she was the wife of "Uli Hottinger of Hirslanden" (Quellen 1, pp. 105, 106, 161).

36. On Margaret Hottinger, see 71K/fn.54 and Cast of Characters No. 51.

37. Unknown, except see fns. 38 and 39.

38. In his letter to Müntzer, Grebel used the same play on the German words *gerutted* and *gepflantzet* (see 63/fn.32).

39. A later supplement dated Easter Monday, April 2, 1526, was added that "the brother of the above-mentioned Winbrat appeared before Milords, Councillors, and representatives, and begged that they be generous and gracious and release his sister to him, that he will provide for her and guarantee that Milords would have no further disturbance regarding her. Upon this petition, she was paroled to him by Milords and admonished that if she were ever to appear before them again because of Anabaptism, she would be drowned without mercy that very hour."

40. On Fridli Ab-Iberg, see Cast of Characters No. 2.

41. Probably Anthony Roggenacher (Cast of Characters No. 77).

42. Probably public inns outside of Zurich.

43. See fn. 25.

44. Wilhelm Exell, see fn. 33, above.

45. Unknown.

46. On the Lindenhoff, see 47A/fn.1.

47. Roggenacher, see fns. 16, 22, 28, and 41, above.

48. Probably Fridli Ab-Iberg, see fn. 40, above.

49. See fn. 27, above.

50. See fn. 42, above.

51. On Anna Mantz, see fn. 73, below, and Cast of Characters No. 66.

52. On Heinrich Aberli; see Cast of Characters No. 1.

53. On Anna Widerker, see Cast of Characters No. 98.

54. Guildmaster Uli Bluntschli, who with his wife also lived at the Green Shield.

55. Ernst von Glatz, see fn. 14, above.

56. Brennwald, see fn. 27, above.

57. Ger. *anschlegen nüdts.*

58. Heinrich Walder, see Cast of Characters No. 94.

59. Eighteen persons are here under sentencing, twelve men and six women. Probably with reference to the men only, Jörg Binder, former friend and classmate of Grebel's, wrote that "our Conrad has been judged most pitifully with 12 others to perpetual imprisonment" (Binder to Vadian, March 11, 1526; VB, IV, 9).

60. See fn. 13, above.

61. See fn. 14, above.

62. See fn. 22, above.

63. See fn. 23, above.

64. See fn. 24, above.

65. See fn. 25, above.

66. See fn. 27, above.

67. See fn. 40, above.

68. See fn. 45, above.

69. See fn. 31, above.

70. See fn. 35, above.

71. See fn. 36, above.

72. See fn. 37, above.

73. See fn. 51, above.

74. See fn. 53, above.

75. See Quellen 1, Nos. 170, pp. 174-77, and 170b, pp. 178-80.

76. On the New Tower, see 71K/fn.74.

77. Ger. *den frouwen und tochterenn,* "wives and daughters," but Regeli Gletzli, although probably a young woman, was not Widerkerin's daughter.

78. The women were probably returned to the Wellenberg (see 71K/fn.77).

79. The first mandate of execution for recidivist Anabaptists.

80. See 58/fn.11.

81. See fn. 34, above.

82. Zwingli also rationalized that it was not the state that caused the execution of the Anabaptists, but the latter themselves (see Epi.C/478/41-42).

83. Grossmünster, Fraumünster, and St. Peter's.

84. Hermann Miles (1464-1533) came from a respected Toggenburger family. Since 1484 he was provost of St. Mangen's Church in St. Gallen, later also treasurer of the abbey and dean of the territorial chapter. He was a fatherly friend of Vadian but since 1525 closed to the Reformation. His *Chronicle* is still in the form of a 1571 revision through the St. Galler, Martin Murer, and this only in a copy made in the 18th century.

85. Miles refers to the Lenten season of 1526, but actually Grebel had been imprisoned since October 8 and Hubmaier since December 20.

86. Murder Tower, see 71K/fn.74.

87. 210 denari equivalent to 1 guilder.

88. Actually, the mandate of March 7, 1526 (see above) specified death by drowning for the one performing the baptism rather than the one being baptized.

71N. Zwingli to Vadian, Zurich, after March 7, 1526

1. On the Council of Two Hundred, see 58/fn.11. The decree refers to 71M/466/27ff.

2. Lat. *catabaptistarum coryphaei.* This is the first of several usages of this label in Zwingli's letters and writings. In Epi.A/473/2 he uses it with particular reference to Grebel.

3. On the New Tower, see 71K/fn.74.

4. See 71M/447/32-33.

5. This second decree is 71M/448/5ff.

6. I.e., in the three Zurich parishes (see 448/20).

7. Jacob Grebel, father to Conrad (see Cast of Characters No. 38).

8. Lat. *tum dolet, tum displicet,* "first grieves, then angers."

9. Lat. *crepundia,* "rattle" (a child's plaything). Compare with *lusus* in 69D/375/15-16, "child's play."

10. I.e., by the decree of execution for incorrigible Anabaptists.

11. Acts 5:1ff.

12. Zwingli, the novice at punishing deceitful members in contrast to God (*trucidavit:* "who slaughtered them"). The omitted two paragraphs deal with current Swiss Confederate agenda in the struggle between the Reformed and Catholic cantons leading up to the Baden Disputation of May 21-June 18 (see ZW, VIII, pp. 542-43, fns. 3-5; Jackson, 1900, pp. 270-74).

13. Zwingli is referring here to comments Luther made in support of a treatise written by John Brenz on behalf of fourteen pastors of Swabia entitled *Syngramma Suevicum* (Swabian Symposium), published in October 1525 in rejection of the position of Oecolampad in his book on the Lord's Supper ("On the Original Meaning of the Words of Institution According to the Fathers of the Church"), published in late summer 1525. Oecolampad had dedicated his book to the Swabian pastors in the attempt to win their support to a figurative interpretation of the Lord's Supper, against the consubstantiationist view of Luther. Luther had reprinted the "Swabian Symposium" with his own letter of introduction to which Oecolampad replied in his *Antisyngramma.* Then in a letter of Jan. 4, 1526, which was printed and circulated, Luther replied to the Oecolampad rebuttal, labeling Zwingli's views of the Lord's Supper as the work of the devil. See LW, Vol. 49.

14. *Hyperaspistes Diatribae adversus Servum Arbitrium Martini Lutheri per Des. Erasmum Roterodamum* (A Defense of the Diatribe Against Martin Luther's "Bondage of the

Will" by Des[iderius] Erasmus of Rotterdam), published by Froben in Basel in two parts, June 1526 and September 1527.

15. *De servo arbitrio* (The Bondage of the Will), published in December 1525. For an English translation see LW, Vol. 33.

16. *De libero arbitrio diatribe sive collatio* (Diatribe or Discourse Concerning Free Will), published in September 1524. For an English translation see Rupp and Marlow, pp. 33-97.

71-O. *The Prison Escape of the Anabaptists, Zurich, March 21, 1526*

1. Wilhelm Exell came from Wallis (Fr. Valais), an archdiocese of the Roman Catholic Church (also called Sion or Sitten), located in southwest Switzerland, bordering on France and Italy. Little is known about Exell, except that on March 7 he testified in court that he had been baptized by Fridli Ab-Iberg "and he will stay with this baptism" (Quellen 1, No. 170b, p. 179.3). For this steadfastness, he was imprisoned with Grebel *et al.*

2. Felix Bischoff was one of the guards assigned to the New Tower.

3. Wednesday, March 21. See Quellen 1, p. 191, fn. 2.

4. Karl Brennwald, see 71M/fn.23 and Cast of Characters No. 9.

5. Ockenfuss, see 71M/fn.22 and Cast of Characters No. 71.

6. I.e., Ernst von Glätz, see 71M/fn.15.

7. Ger. *blutschinenn.* See Quellen 1, p. 191, fn. 3.

8. Kürsiner (Anthony Roggenacher), see Cast of Characters No. 77.

9. See fn. 2, above.

10. See fn. 6, above.

11. See fn. 5, above.

12. Ger. *roten indenn über das mer.*

13. Ockenfuss, the guard at the gate, was the brother of the prisoner, Hans Ockenfuss.

14. In distinction to his brother, the guard at the gate.

15. I.e., Anthony Roggenacher, see fn. 8, above.

16. Hottinger, see 71M/fn.13.

17. See fn. 15, above.

18. See fn. 4, above.

19. Ab-Iberg, see 71M/fn.24 and Cast of Characters No. 2.

71P. *Zwingli to Michael Wüst, Zurich, April 10, 1526*

1. Egli (ZW, VIII, No. 467, p. ·561, fn. 2) assumes that this refers to a lost letter to which Wüst's letter (ZW, VIII, No. 468) was the reply. At the beginning of his reply to Zwingli, Wüst referred to "your recent admonitions against the vacillating and dubious mind of the Anabaptists." Wüst's reply was written at about the time that Zwingli wrote the present (i.e., second) letter to Wüst, and their letters must have crossed en route, for they deal with different matters. One gathers from Wüst's reply that Zwingli's earlier letter dealt with their differences on the doctrine of election and predestination. Contrary to certain present-day interpretations of the idea of voluntarism among the Anabaptists, Wüst represented a view of predestination that was more rigorous than Zwingli's, reporting that certain Anabaptists were downplaying prayer as a human effort: "I hear some say that in the future times, they will not be praying, for the Spirit will perform this function according to Romans 8[:26]. And as God prays in them, they will live free of sin, for His Spirit is able to do all things, to the end that they will be led either to prayer or to sermon" (ZW, VIII, No. 468, p. 563.16ff.; see also Staehelin, II, pp. 698-99, and Jackson, 1901, pp. 237ff.).

2. Zwingli was otherwise occupied preparing memoranda for the Baden Disputation held May 21 to June 18 (see ZW, V, Nos. 80-81).

3. See 69C/fn.4.

4. Lat. *corium ac renum.* See Psalm 7:9.

5. Lat. *supra alios . . . debere.* This refers to the Zwinglian-Anabaptist debate then current regarding election and predestination (see fn. 1, above).

6. See Mt. 6:1, 23:5.

71Q. The Flight of Grebel, Glattfelden, April 11, 1526

1. Hans Küntzi was a wool weaver from Klingnau, baptized by Ulrich Teck (see fn. 2, below) and presently residing in Oberglatt with other Anabaptists, including his son, Kleinhans (or Junghans). Kleinhans appears to have been the more radical member of the two, for he was banished from the canton in April 1529 and executed at Liechtenstein sometime before Dec. 26, 1529 (see Quellen 1, pp. 304, 314). In spite of the appearance of submission in his following testimony, the father had given aid to both Brennwald and Grebel; and it is hard to believe "that he has never baptized nor been present when one baptized another."

2. Ulrich Teck of Waldshut had been arrested in Grüningen the previous September (Quellen 1, p. 109) and expelled from Zurich on Nov. 18, 1525, with Michael Sattler and Martin Lingg (see 71K/442/25-26). He was closely associated with fellow Anabaptist missioner from Waldshut, Jacob Gross, who baptized hundreds of persons in Grüningen and various towns in the canton of Bern and in Lahr, Strasbourg, and Augsburg. Both Bender (1950, p. 161) and Ruth (p. 138) erroneously have Teck instead of Küntzi giving testimony about Grebel's flight.

71R. The Death of Grebel, Maienfeld, August 1526

1. Ger. *evangelischen predicanten.*
2. See Fast, Quellen 2, p. 617, fn. 117.
3. 2 Cor. 3:6.
4. Jer. 31:33.
5. Grebel's letter to Müntzer of September 1524, containing 25 articles signed by five of his brethren (see No. 63, above), had been returned to Vadian in St. Gallen; and perhaps Kessler had them in mind in this reference.
6. Kessler had given thirteen pages of specific examples of Anabaptist fantasies, including such things as Bible-burning, Spirit-preempted prayer, rejection of greetings, speaking in tongues, messianic claims, and apocalyptic fraticide.
7. Refers not to villages but to the jurisdictions of Appenzell and the Provostship of St. Gallen, i.e., *Gotteshauses* (chapter church). See 69E/377/31-33.
8. For other secondary evidence, see Bender, 1950, p. 162.
9. See Epi.C, below.
10. Bergsten, p. 323, calls this a "gross exaggeration."

Epi.A. The Trial and Execution of Jacob Grebel, Zurich, October 30, 1526

1. This letter was primarily a reply to Capito's letter of Nov. 12 (see ZW, VIII, No. 550) concerning the trial of Jacob Grebel.

2. Capito got his information from Jodocus Brennwald, son of Heinrich Brennwald (see Cast of Characters No. 8), the former provost of Embrach. The father had written to the son, who was living in Strasbourg, about the imprisonment not only of Grebel but also of Felix Brennwald (see next fn.).

3. Felix Brennwald, brother of Heinrich and uncle of Jodocus. He had returned to Zurich in 1515 gravely wounded in the Battle of Marignano (see fns. 89 and 136). He became a member of the Large Council in 1516, the bailiff of Sargans, 1518-20. He was married to the daughter of Felix Schmid, the late burgomaster, who stood for caution about precipitous reform of the church and social customs. With an attitude similar to his father-in-law's, Felix Brennwald had opposed the abolition of the mass and was suspected of taking pensions. He was arrested at about the same time as Grebel but had escaped with the help of a friend, who had hidden him in a manure wagon. He was arrested again in Storchen, fined 100 pounds, and released. He was then summoned back to Zurich on promise of safe conduct, tried on Sept. 25, 1527, and fully reinstated into his offices on Oct. 16. He died in 1536.

4. Lucius Sergius Catilina (108-62 BC), Roman governor of Africa (67 BC), was organizer of an unsuccessful conspiracy to murder the leaders of the republic (66 BC) and to overthrow the republic and assume control (64 BC). He was exposed by Cicero and slain by the troops of Antonius.

5. May 14, 1526.

6. According to the minutes of the Diet (*Eidg. Abschiede* IV, la, p. 890), some deputies from the Roman Catholic cantons had replied to the deputies from Schaffhausen and Appenzell, who had tried to mediate, that "they might try with Zurich [to see] if it will tolerate the mass and decorate the churches again; then there would probably be yielding on the other points."

7. The knight, Caspar von Mülinen.

8. Identity unknown.

9. I.e., the trouble of mediating between Zurich and the Catholic cantons was "useless" if Zurich itself is divided.

10. Persons like Jacob Grebel and Felix Brennwald were prime suspects.

11. I.e., the king of France, etc.

12. See fn. 4, above.

13. Caius Sallustius Crispus (86-34 BC) was a noted Roman historian and politician best known for his interpretation of the conspiracy of Catiline.

14. Cicero Marcus Tullius (106-43 BC) was a distinguished Roman statesman and orator who in his undying efforts to serve the Roman Republic crushed the conspiracy of Catiline. His great speech to the Roman Senate in this connection was the "First Oration against Catiline."

15. Lat. *trito*, "grated," "threshed." The analogy is given five lines later. Hemp is grown for seed or fiber but requires a threshing process in either case. The traitors and bribe-takers will live off of foreign pensions until they, too, are threshed by the torture rack and made to confess their crimes.

16. These were probably letters that Conrad had written to Zwingli from Vienna (see 3/64/3ff.) and/or to Myconius from Paris (see 13/97/37ff., which was written to Vadian but might also have been written to Myconius in a letter that was now available to Zwingli as evidence against Conrad's father). See Schelbert, 55-56, and fn. 41, below.

17. "Thus Zwingli set out in great secrecy to gather incriminating material" (Schelbert, p. 55). See fn. 36, below.

18. Lat. *constituitur ergo dictatura ad praesens malum.* Between 1527 and his death on the battlefield in 1531, Zwingli virtually acted as the political dictator in Zurich, using the "secret council" as the institutional expression of his power. See fn. 30, below, Schelbert, fn. 137, and Alfred Farner, 1930, pp. 3, 123.

19. This judicial body of eleven men was specially appointed to conduct the prosecution of Grebel and nine other defendants. Their mandate was clearly more than to lead an inquiry but to destroy the religious and political enemies of Zwingli within Zurich who allegedly were undermining his Reformation and had gained reinforcement especially since the Baden Disputation of May 21-June 18, 1526 (see Staehelin, II, pp. 42ff.).

20. Lat. *catabaptistarum coryphaeus.*

21. See 47/fn.1.

22. See 71R/Intro. and fn. 8.

23. See fns. 116 and 157.

24. See fns. 40, 46, 71, and 157, below.

25. Lat. *Fugiunt Grebelio interfecto quidam alii,* "Grebel having been put to death, certain others fled." Felix Brennwald is the only known escapee (see fn. 3), and he fled prior to Grebel's execution, probably on Wednesday evening, Oct. 10 (see *Aktens.*, No. 1050, p. 507; 464/9-10).

26. See fn. 3, above.

27. See fns. 25, above, and 37, below.

28. His case was retried on Sept. 25, 1525, after which he was fully rehabilitated and restored to office. See fn. 3, above.

29. According to ZW, No. 557, fn. 3, this was Thomas Wellenberg (1470-1536), the "proprietor of Pfungen, [who] had recruited mercenaries in 1519 for Duke Ulrich of Württemberg. He was now accused of pension-taking, of having fomented an insurrection among

subjects of the Zürich commonwealth, and of having granted refuge to a certain Trebitz, who was a declared 'enemy of the imperial cities and a wayfarer.' On November 21, 1526, Wellenberg was fined 400 guilders, had to pay the cost of the prosecution, lost all his offices and rights, and was expelled from the commonwealth. He had to make a written promise, backed by a deposit of 2,000 guilders, that he would not prosecute those who had been involved in his trial" (Schelbert, p. 59).

30. See fn. 18, above.

31. Eleven names are given here, which raises the question whether this was the judicial body of "eleven," to which, according to Zwingli, was given "the jurisdiction for trial and sentencing" (462/36-38, above). Schelbert (pp. 56-57) makes a distinction between this group meeting on Oct. 11, which he thinks might be the "secret council," and the judicial body of eleven set up by the Large Council on Oct. 13. On Walder, Röist, and Binder, see Cast of Characters Nos. 94, 78, and 4.

32. On Saturday, Sept. 22, four council members had been appointed to investigate the charges Zwingli had made in his sermons (see 462/20, above). Zwingli told them what he knew, but they apparently did very little with the information. From 464/37-39, it is clear that the members of the original committee are here also present among the eleven.

33. See 462/20-21, above.

34. For the three extant mandates against pension-taking, see fn. 133, below.

35. Probably Felix Brennwald (see fns. 3 and 25, above).

36. Schelbert (p. 56) describes Zwingli's strategy here as a "tactical masterpiece." Because he had given pertinent information three weeks earlier without any action being taken, he would speak only briefly now. He had much more incriminating information to give, not as an accuser but as a witness, but not until he was "convinced that they will pursue the matter in earnest." This "display of hesitancy, disappointment, and moral indignation" had the intended effect; and the outcome of the trial was a personal achievement.

37. These four apparently represent a subcommittee of the group of eleven that met on Thursday (see 463/31-32 and 469/fn.30).

38. On the previous day, Zwingli had told the larger committee of eleven about a conversation with Ludwig Tschudi.

39. Ger. *das alt "Grübelin" had grüblet,* a play on Grebel's name. Ger. *grübeln,* "to dig," "to scratch," "to ruminate over," "to brood over," "to rack one's brains about." Ger. *Grübelei* is "minute searching or inquiry," "brooding."

40. The three-year French grant totaled 900 crowns, or 300 crowns a year (see 467/31-33, below). Thus, according to this testimony, Jacob still owed his son a little more than one third of the grant; but see fns. 46, 71, and 157, below.

41. It is impossible to identify this document with certainty. In his letter to Capito *et al.,* Zwingli referred to certain "letters" that had been found (see 462/30, above). Of Conrad's extant letters, the one that would have been most incriminating to his father would be Letter 13, above; but that was written to Vadian. It is possible that Conrad wrote to Myconius also, using wording similar to that found in Letter 13: "I still hope that he [father] who has sworn by the sacred stone of Jupiter has not accepted forbidden gifts" (97/40-41). "Everyone is aware of the matter . . . that time . . . will disclose all, though Father tries to hide it like the ill-omened Harpocrates" (98/10-13). "It seems to me that I was more prudent in accepting it [the grant] reluctantly than he [father] was in forwarding it promptly" (98/31-32).

42. On Heinrich Utinger, see 47E/fn.5 and Cast of Characters No. 92. As provost of the Grossmünster chapter, he was one of the most powerful figures in the Zurich religious establishment. It was through his influence that Zwingli received his call to Zurich in 1518, in spite of serious objections about the latter's sex life (see ZW, VII, No. 48, and Potter, 1978, pp. 10-12). He was godfather to Zwingli's first child and remained a loyal adviser and assistant in the work of the Reformation.

43. On Jörg Binder, see Cast of Characters No. 4.

44. Enderli (Andreas) Kramer was a local shopkeeper of some kind (see 466/3ff., below).

45. Conrad's wife, Barbara (see Cast of Characters No. 33 and fns. 40, 71, and 157, below).

46. 800 guilders are approximately equivalent to 400 crowns, but see fns. 40, 71, and 157.

47. The son-in-law refers either to Vadian (see 29/Intro., 29/fn.2, and 30/fn.8) or to Junker Hans Conrad Escher of Luchs (see Cast of Characters No. 21), the husband of Conrad's youngest sister, Dorothy. Schelbert (p. 57, line 8) assumes that it refers to Vadian, although he seems not to know that Escher, who was arrested with Jacob Grebel (see line 27, below), was also his son-in-law. This allegation that one of the sons-in-law also received 50 guilders is repeated in 466/33; but in 465/36, the witness testified that Grebel got all 50 crowns (100 guilders). Also in 468/20 and 471/17-18, the question boiled down to whether or not Jacob had sent his son to de Falconibus, and no mention is made anymore of having also sent his son-in-law.

48. On de Falconibus, see 36/fn.16, fn. 75, below, and Cast of Characters No. 22.

49. The figure of 50 guilders is confirmed in 466/33, but in 465/36 Binder claimed that it was 50 crowns (100 guilders). In 39/151/18-19, Conrad tells Vadian that he had received 100 francs from de Falconibus, but adds in the same context that his father knew nothing about it (13-14; see fns. 60 and 77, below).

50. Hedinger was Grebel's servant (see Cast of Characters No. 44).

51. Stoffel Bodmer, unknown; but see fns. 79 and 106, below.

52. Lat. *ad praetorium,* "to the quarters of the praetor or magistrate."

53. Hans Escher, see fn. 47, above, and Cast of Characters No. 21.

54. Hans Löw was accused of similar charges but especially of his supposed participation in the nighttime attack on the character of Zwingli at Conrad Baumann's house. He was subsequently released on 200 guilders bail (see Schelbert, p. 57).

55. On the Wellenberg, see 68H/fn.9 and 71K/fn.77.

56. The dating for the trial records here excerpted is not given by Egli, but it is obvious that the proceedings occurred sometime between the dates given here.

57. On Binder, see fns. 31 and 43, above, and Cast of Characters No. 4.

58. Conrad received 90-100 crowns on his way to Paris, October 1518, and another 200 crowns delivered by Alexander Stamp (see 479/34ff.).

59. See fn. 46, above. Schelbert (p. 42, fn. 64, para. 4) thinks that this was in truth the amount Jacob still owed to his son, but the judicial court computed it at 400 guilders (200 crowns; see 471/32-33). Zwingli thought it was 335 crowns (465/9-11) and Landös thought it was 1,000 crowns (466/22-23).

60. 50 crowns (100 guilders), but apparently his brother-in-law got half of this (see fns. 49 and 77). In 39/151/18-19, Conrad admitted that de Falconibus gave him 50 francs (guilders).

61. See fn. 49, above.

62. On Myconius, see Cast of Characters No. 70.

63. Egli (*Aktens.,* p. 494, last line) assumes that this refers to Enderli (Andreas) Kramer, referred to above (465/12) and below (466/3). It seems more likely, however, that Andreas Castelberger (see Cast of Characters No. 13) was meant here (see 41/fn.2 and 51/fn.23).

64. Man from Kronburg, William de Falconibus.

65. Ger. *Zinsen.* Myconius was probably confronting Conrad about the contradiction between his speaking out against the injustices of "zins und zehenden" (interest and tithes; see 52/fn.7, 53/fns. 3 and 5, 63/fn.54) and his own acceptance of money from the papal envoy, some of which probably came from this very source. It should be pointed out, however, that Conrad's acceptance of the papal grant (August 1521) antedated his development of concern for the plight of the peasants (June 1523ff.).

66. Kramer, see fn. 44, above, and 41/fn.2.

67. I.e., Euphrosine Grebel (Cast of Characters No. 36).

68. One guilder (seven-eighths of a pound). The meaning of this sentence is confusing because the sum of money mentioned represents more than half the total amount of the three-year grant.

69. On Utinger, see fn. 42, above, and 47E/fn.5.

70. Hans Landös, unknown, but see Quellen 1, p. 162.

71. This sum exceeds the total amount of the three-year grant, and again lacks credibility. For the contradictions, see fns. 40, 47, and 157.

72. Hans Hab, unknown.

73. Refers to Maximilian Sforza, through whom Jacob Grebel allegedly secured the grant for Conrad's education in Vienna from Emperor Maximilian, the duke's brother-in-law (see fns. 75 and 91, below).

74. See 465/2-3, above.

75. Refers to William de Falconibus, administrator to the papal legates in Switzerland (see Cast of Characters No. 22).

76. See fn. 114, below.

77. See fns. 49 and 60, above.

78. Hedinger, see fns. 50, above, and 105, below.

79. Stoffel Bodmer, see fns. 51, above, and 106, below.

80. Ger. *der Schaffner,* meaning Hans Wirz (Cast of Characters No. 99), who was present at the "nighttime disturbance" at Conrad Baumann's house, but apparently confronted his stepbrother, Jacob Grebel, about his acceptance of foreign monies (see 9A/ fn.2, 11/fns. 1 and 10, 13/fn.44, and 28/fn.8).

81. Conrad Baumann, see Cast of Characters No. 21. Baumann was under investigation along with Hans Escher and Hans Leu for sponsoring the nighttime disturbance in his house at which disparaging remarks and threats were made against Zwingli (see fns. 86 and 111, below). It was alleged "that he carried money from M[aster] Röuchlin's house; [and that] he often took money back and forth on his and others' orders" (*Aktens.,* No. 1050, p. 504). He was also accused of attending mass and sermons defending the old faith. He was found innocent and released on promise of nonretaliation against his accusers.

82. Hans Meyer, unknown.

83. The bailiff of Stammheim was Hans Wirth, and Zwingli blamed Grebel in part for his execution at the hands of anti-Zwingli Confederates. Concerning the Ittinger affair, see 65/fn.24, 66/fn.10, and fns. 87 and 166, below. Schelbert (pp. 51-52) gives the fuller story as follows: "As a result of the decree to remove the sacred images, the people of Stammheim, a village near Stein am Rhein, decided to imitate the example of Zürich, partly under the influence of two reform-minded priests, Hans and Adrian Wirth [see Pro.A/fns. 1, 17a, and 39]. Stammheim was then under two jurisdictions. The lower courts were under the supervision of Zürich while the higher courts, especially criminal cases involving the death penalty *(Malefizgericht),* were under the jurisdiction of the Confederate Diet. Thus the dispute arose whether the destruction of sacred images involved the higher or the lower courts. The Diet which was dominated by opponents of Zwingli's reform measures, considered the removal of sacred images a matter of the higher courts. The threat to capture the pastor of Stein am Rhein, one of the reform-minded priests, led Stammheim to conclude a defensive alliance with the town Stein am Rhein, which was under the exclusive jurisdiction and protection of Zürich. When on July 17, 1524, the pastor Johann Ulrich Oechsli was actually captured, the alarm bells rang out. Large crowds gathered to pursue the captors, but when this proved futile the masses moved in the early morning hours against the monastery of Ittingen which was first looted and then partly demolished. These events put Zürich on the defensive. The Diet was able to pressure Zürich into the capture and extradition of the leaders in the Ittingen affair despite strong opposition of Zwingli and his associates. In spite of remonstrances of the Zürich deputies, the captives were questioned about their religious beliefs, which were purely Zwinglian. Some were tortured and three of them were executed on September 28, 1524. Jacob Grebel was intimately involved in these affairs. In July he negotiated in the matter in Bern and Solothurn; from August 16 to 21 and during September he attended the Diet in Baden. His diplomatic experience and his conciliatory temperament seemed well fitted to calm the tense and conflict-laden atmosphere. But Grebel's efforts seem to have displeased Zwingli, who apparently made the Zürich deputy responsible for the negative outcome of the Ittingen affair. He may have been informed in this sense by other members of the Zürich dele-

751

gation."

84. These are probably the recorder's shorthand notes which he later used to write up the fuller testimony that follows.

85. For the wording of the remark allegedly made by Escher (see fn. 53, above) at Aarburg, a town between Zurich and Bern, see 472/15-16, below.

86. Refers to question No. 7 (466/36-37). For the wording of the remarks made by Escher in Baumann's house, see Cast of Characters No. 21.

87. Refers to question No. 8 (466/37-38). See fn. 83, above.

88. Conrad Engelhart, bailiff of Hyburg (see Cast of Characters No. 18). He was either a fellow delegate to these official meetings or just went along with his first cousin, Jacob Grebel.

89. Geneva was the place of the signing of the peace treaty with France on Nov. 29, 1516, following the ill-fated Battle of Marignano (1515). In the unpopular "Treaty of Perpetual Peace," all thirteen Swiss cantons had been forced to agree henceforth never again to go to war against France, to pay a million crowns in reparations, and to allow France to continue to recruit Swiss mercenaries. The French defeat of the papal troops was a blow to the ever-victorious Swiss soldiers. Zwingli was serving as chaplain of the Glarus contingent and was well aware that their defeat was due in large measure to the defection in the Swiss ranks, some of whose battle commanders had allegedly been in secret communication with King Francis I, through whose persuasion, sweetened with payoffs in money, they agreed not to oppose the French occupation of Milan. Without waiting for ratification from the Swiss Diet, other Swiss contingents regarded the campaign as ended and set out for home. Zwingli's contingent refused to leave the field until ordered to do so; and most of his men, pressed into battle by Cardinal Schinner, were killed. Zwingli vowed henceforth to oppose the whole demonic mercenary system.

90. This denial is a response to the testimony of his servant, Jörg Hedinger, that Grebel had received 100 crowns in advance of the 900-crown grant for his son. See 469/22, where Hedinger's testimony of Oct. 23 is inserted, and see fn. 129, below.

91. This apparently refers either to a fellow Councillor, Erhard Wyss (see 468/8 and 26), or to a certain Felix Wyss (see fn. 47, above), who was present at the nighttime disturbance at Baumann's house.

92. Freiburg (see 470/19, below) was the meeting place of the Swiss Diet that ratified the peace treaty with the French in 1517. It is located twenty miles southwest of Bern.

93. Stamp's cousin is probably the person Conrad Grebel referred to as Scampius (see 28/136/28,40, 109/10), a representative of the French monarch at various meetings with Swiss officials, beginning with the peace negotiations at Geneva (see fn. 119, below).

94. According to Schelbert (p. 58), "Heinrich Rubli was accused of anti-Zwinglian activities, but seems to have gone free at the time. Only much later, on January 1, 1529, was he expelled from the Large Council for separatist behavior and for having eaten fish on New Year's Day which had fallen on a Friday; both charges were taken as evidence for Rubli's old-faith sympathies."

95. This was the first installment of Conrad's 900-crown grant, which was a 90-crown down-payment (see 469/34-35). For the remaining installments, see fns. 120, 121, and 132, below.

96. This was a partial reply to question No. 4 (466/34-35), in which Grebel admitted a remaining debt to the dependents of his deceased son.

97. This is later contradicted by Grebel's admission in 468/29-30 that "he has invested his son's money in his business, but hopes that such use would not be a disadvantage to him."

98. Apparently the questioning took place in the bailiff's quarters in the Rathaus, where Grebel was held in confinement.

99. In view of the way the trial proceeded, including the application of torture and the admission of much contradictory hearsay evidence, this appeal was not out of order.

100. On Helbing's role, see 468/38-40, and fn. 121.

101. See fn. 75, above.

102. Refers to question No. 2 (466/30-31).

103. Probably Latin.

104. See fn. 75, above. Refers to question No. 2 (466/30-31).

105. Refers to question No. 5 (466/34), specified in 469/9ff.

106. Refers to question No. 6 (466/35).

107. The accusation was that Grebel called his son home in order to receive the French grant. On July 31, 1518, Conrad had indeed written to Zwingli that "Father ordered me to return from Vienna at once" (3/64/5-7), but because he was wounded and not because of the French stipend.

108. On Antonio Pucci, successor to Cardinal Schinner, see 23/fn.22 and Cast of Characters No. 72. This contact was made sometime prior to Oct. 17, 1520, when Jacob wrote to Vadian about the conversation with Pucci (see 23A/122/8ff.)/Although in that letter, it sounds as though a two-year grant was likely, he is here alleging that his request came too late to be approved, except for a retainer of 30 guilders to help with travel expenses and a promise of a position in Bologna or Pisa. This is confirmed in a letter Conrad wrote dated March 19, 1521 (30/139/13-16), in which Conrad also reports his final rejection of Pucci's offer. (This is not to be confused with his subsequent acceptance of a grant of 50 francs from Pucci's administrator, William de Falconibus.) Conrad, incidentally, made an earlier interesting reference to Pucci dated Nov. 11, 1520, which seems to indicate that Vadian had suggested that he send Pucci an original poem entitled "Choriambic Ode to Pucci" (24/124/25-26).

109. See fn. 94.

110. See fn. 3, above.

111. See fns. 81 and 86.

112. See fn. 75.

113. The pronoun could be in apposition either to Grebel or to de Falconibus, but the context favors the former interpretation.

114. Refers to question No. 3 (466/31-32).

115. Ger. *Papstzug.* the papal expedition probably refers to the meeting of the Swiss Diet in Freiburg (see fn. 92, above) at which the papal legate, Cardinal Schinner, urged the Swiss cantonal delegates to fulfill their promises and persist in the defense of the duchy of Milan from a new attack by Francis I.

116. Again (see fn. 95), this is an incomplete reply to question No. 4 (466/34-35), which sounds like an evasion.

117. This was one of Grebel's most incriminating confessions, following his earlier claim that "he took or received nothing for himself" (467/35-36). His rationalization here was that he invested the money in his business for the sake of his son's future estate, but note the way it was interpreted by the court in 471/29-30.

118. See fn. 94.

119. See fn. 97.

120. Four hundred guilders (200 crowns). Although in the next sentence called the "first payment," this was in reality the second installment of the "first year's payment of 300 crowns." See fn. 88b, above.

121. This is the second year's installment on the grant (see fns. 95 and 120, above). The identity of the man named Helbing is unknown, but see Muralt and Schmid, p. 122, regarding a Peter Helbing. Schelbert (p. 42, fn. 64) is in error that this was the final, third-year installment.

122. Ger. *alle Fronfasten,* "every ember-fast," days set apart for fasting and prayer in each of the four seasons of the year.

123. See 5/fn.40.

124. See 468/12ff.

125. See fn. 91 and 469/25-26, below.

126. Only the last of the following four questions pertains directly to the Jacob Grebel case.

127. See fn. 29, above.

128. See 89, above.

129. This particular allegation was denied by Grebel. See fn. 90, above. Schelbert (p. 42, fn. 64) writes that "one must keep in mind that Hedinger, Grebel's servant, testified under the stress of imprisonment and threat of torture, and that seven to nine years had elapsed since the event in question; an uncertain memory is thus easily understood."

130. Felix Schmid, burgomaster. See 47C/fn.4.

131. See fn. 95, above.

132. This is the third and final installment on Conrad's French grant (see fns. 95, 120, and 121). Ninety crowns (fns. 95 and 131) plus 200 crowns (fn. 120) plus 300 crowns (fn. 121) plus 300 crowns (present fn.) equals 900 crowns less 10. Probably the first collection totalled 100 crowns, which "when Jörg asked him, Conrad admitted getting about 90 crowns" (469/34-35).

133. As paragraphs 1, 9, and 11 reveal, the three mandates were dated 1513, 1518, and 1522, respectively. The middle one was the "milder" of the three, and the third was similar to the first. The third enacted Nov. 15, 1522, "provided that an offender would lose all offices and become ineligible for any participation in government; in a very serious case even higher penalties might be inflicted" (Schelbert, p. 60, fn. 194).

134. In the Battle of Novara, thirty miles west of Milan, 21,000 French cavalrymen were defeated by 7,000 Swiss foot soldiers fighting on behalf of the pope; but at such a great cost in casualties that Swiss patriots turned against the mercenary system, giving impetus to the enactment of the first of the three statutes prohibiting pension-taking.

135. Piedmont (It. Piemonte), a region in Northwest Italy bordering on France and Switzerland in the Alpine foothills.

136. More often known as the Battle of Marignano (see fn. 89).

137. Freiburg, see fn. 92, above.

138. Stamp, see fn. 93, above.

139. See 467/22-24, above.

140. Grebel denied this allegation (see 468/10-11).

141. See fn. 140, above.

142. Perhaps Zwingli himself (see 3/64/5-7), but more likely Jörg Berger (see 465/31-37).

143. See 469/29-30.

144. Hedinger specified 90 crowns (see 468/34-35 and fn. 131).

145. See 469/36-37, fn. 132.

146. See 468/38-40, fn. 121.

147. I.e., the stricter statute.

148. Puccius, see fn. 108, above.

149. De Falconibus, see fn. 75, above.

150. Grebel consistently denied this charge (468/14-15, 20-23, 469/6-7) and Conrad very explicitly told Vadian that his father knew nothing about the grant and would be very angry if he did (see fn. 49, above).

151. See 468/22-23, which Grebel had said more in jest than in seriousness.

152. The witness was Jörg Binder (see 465/35-36).

153. I.e., from the emperor, the king of France, and the pope.

154. This was, in effect, the verdict of guilty by the judicial court.

155. This is a new allegation in the trial proceedings, contradictory to Grebel's statement (467/34-35) that he still owed "a certain amount" to his son's dependents.

156. Grebel confessed only to the receipt of the 900 crowns for Conrad's education in Paris, only some of which he had invested in his business on behalf of his son's future inheritance (see 468/29-32).

157. Zwingli had put the figure at 335 crowns (465/1), Jörg Binder at 400 crowns (465/34), Landös at 1,000 crowns (466/22-23).

158. See fn. 38, above.

159. Unknown.

160. See fn. 38, above.

161. See 469/9ff.

162. See fns. 51, 79, 106, and 162.

163. See 465/22-23.

164. See 468/24-27.

165. See 466/39-40.

166. See fn. 83, above.

167. See 466/37-38 and 467/1-3.

168. The fishmart was located opposite the Rathaus in Zurich. In his *Chronicle*, Bernhard Wyss (p. 74) follows this sentence with the added comment, "He had a snow-white beard and snow-white hair, for he was about 60 years of age and well preserved."

169. This statement plus the fact that most of the other defendants were released and restored to their positions confirms Grebel's complaint that something less than justice was being given him in the proceedings.

170. In his *Chronicle* (p. 74), Wyss added "who had died this year before the execution."

171. The pronoun could refer either to Jacob or to Conrad. Schelbert (p. 33, fn. 7) concludes the former.

172. On Johann Wanner see Cast of Characters No. 95.

Epi.B. The Banishment of Blaurock and Execution of Mantz, Fourth Martyr of the Swiss Anabaptists, Zurich, January 5, 1527

1. Part Two of Zwingli's *Elenchus* is a critical commentary and point-by-point refutation of the Anabaptist Confession of Faith written by Michael Sattler (see Cast of Characters No. 80 and Yoder, 1973, pp. 27-54) and corporately adopted at Schleitheim on the northern Swiss border on Feb. 24, 1527. Its earliest circulated text contained the title "Brotherly Union of a Number of Children of God Concerning Seven Articles." The following excerpt comes from Zwingli's commentary on the Seventh Article dealing with the oath. For discussion of Zwingli's entire commentary, see Harder, 1980, pp. 51-66.

2. Article Seven (see above) had cited Mt. 5:34-37.

3. See Jn. 8:44.

4. See 68F/fn.21 and 71J/fn.15. For Blanke's discussion of the derivation of this name, see ZW, VI, p. 153, fn. 3.

5. At Blaurock's last trial in Zurich prior to Jan. 5, 1527, Zwingli gave testimony that an Anabaptist had told him he saw Jörg Blaurock as a "second Paul," and that "the spirit of Paul was in him" (Quellen 1, No. 198, p. 215).

6. Lat. *caederetur*, "hack at," "strike," "beat," "chop."

7. Lat. *virgis*, "stick" (used as a weapon), "bundle of twigs" (used to punish), "switch" (for flogging), "cudgel." The original official sentence read, *"mit ruten ... schlachen"* (Quellen 1, p. 227).

8. Lat. *portam infernam*. The original official sentence read, "The executioner is ordered to remove his clothes to the waist, bind his hands, and then beat him with rods down the street from the Fish Market to the Niederdorf Gate until the blood flows" (*ibid.*). In relation to this wording, Blanke (ZW, VI, p. 153, fn. 5) presents two possible interpretations of Zwingli's Latin term. One is that *infernam* ("infernal") is a printer's mistake for *inferam* ("lower," "southern"), and that Zwingli meant nothing more than a literal translation of *"Niederdorf"* (Lower or Southern Gate). The other is to take the text as printed as a mocking designation of Blaurock's destiny, i.e., the "gate of hell." One could still assume in this case that Zwingli intended a play on the name "Niederdorf Gate." In support of this interpretation is the fact that in Part One of the *Elenchus*, Zwingli also referred to Grebel (anonymously) as the "head in hell" (see Epi.C/487/28), "baptized among the shades on the Phlegethon" (488/9-10). A third possible translation would be "the gate of death," i.e., that he was beaten to the point of death, according to the letter of the sentence, "until the blood flows."

9. Lat. *servo senatus,* refers to the *Oberste Knecht* (Bullinger, I, p. 382), a senior officer of the council (ZW, VI, p. 154, fn. 2).

10. The last step in the execution of the sentence was the administration of the oath of truce before the gate or border where the banishment took effect that the offender would never criticize or avenge his sentence, and that he was herewith banished from the city, region, and jurisdiction of Zurich "upon punishment by drowning if he ever returned" (ZW, VI, p. 153, fn. 6; Quellen 1, pp. 227-28).

11. The preface to the official sentence of the council reported that Blaurock in an earlier release from prison had requested that he would not have to swear an oath, but that he would be allowed to give a simple promise (see 71K/fn.63).

12. This story that out of fear of extended imprisonment and corporal punishment, Blaurock finally consented to swear the oath that he insisted he could not swear was repeated by Bullinger, I, p. 382: "When the senior officer commanded that Jörg be led inside again and laid in the Wellenberg, pending further deliberation by the honorable Council [and] when he experienced this, he swore, set off down the street, and shook his blue coat and shoes over the city of Zurich" (*ibid.*).

13. On Bernhard Wyss, see 47B/fn.1 and Cast of Characters No. 102.

14. Hans Mantz presided over the Grossmünster Chapter from 1495 to 1518.

15. See 71K/fn.16.

16. See 63/290/7-9.

17. The Third Public Disputation on Baptism (see 71J).

Epi.C. Zwingli's Dialogue with Grebel's Ghost, Zurich, July 31, 1527

1. For the references to the *umbra* ("shade," "ghost") with whom he was contending, see fn. 116, below. The actual title of the tract was "Refutation of the Tricks of the Anabaptists." For commentaries on the three nouns in the title, see fns. 30-32, below.

2. Not only the Swiss but "all" evangelical pastors in central Europe are allegedly threatened by the spread of Anabaptism. This is the only one of Zwingli's writings addressed to all Protestant preachers.

3. Lat. *euangelii Christi ministeris* is Zwingli's term for the Reformed Protestant pastor, based on such New Testament texts as 1 Thess. 3:2, etc.

4. The saying goes back to the *Agamemnon* of Aeschylus 758 and 763.

5. Lat. *studiis,* which Jackson's translator renders "desires," perhaps because the noun is plural. A more literal rendering would be "enthusiasms" or "fervors."

6. I.e., *studiis,* "passions."

7. Zwingli argued more than once that the Anabaptists were primarily responsible for their own executions.

8. Lat. *catabaptistarum* ("of the Anabaptists") and its derivative, *catabaptismum* ("Anabaptism"), which Zwingli uses later in the book (see 68F/340/38, 39, 40), were derived from a Greek word first used in the fourth century AD by Gregory of Nazianzus, theologian of the Eastern Church, who coined many new terms in witty but overloaded rhetoric (see Oratio 40 in *sanctum baptisma Migne* SG 36, 421c, quoted by Blanke, ZW, VI, p. 22). Zwingli did not get the term from the Anabaptists themselves, as he implies in the next sentence, but from Oecolampad, whose letter of Oct. 13, 1525 (ZW, VIII, No. 391) made reference to Gregory's preference for this more contemptuous, cynical label ("immersers," "drowners"). Nevertheless, as Blanke documents (ZW, VI, pp. 21-22, fn. 1), modern scholars have not agreed on how the term "catabaptist" was to be interpreted: (1) Rudolf Staehelin (I, p. 527) maintains that *Katabaptisten* means *"Widertäufer"* ("Counterview Baptists"; *wider*=against) and is to be distinguished from *Anabaptisten,* meaning *"Wiedertäufer"* ("Re-baptizers"; *wieder*=again). (2) August Lang (1913, p. 45) translated the title of Zwingli's book, *Widergelung der Ränke der Taufzerstörer* ("Refutation of the Intrigues of the Baptism Abolitionists"), whereby he clearly conceives of the "cata" in *catabaptistae* as "contra" (i.e., *catabaptistae=contrabaptistae=Taufzerstörer,* meaning "Antibaptists" or "Baptism Abolitionists"). This interpretation is similar to that of Staehelin. (3) Walther Koehler (1918, p.

678), on the other hand, identifies *catabaptistae* in Zwingli's title with *"Wiedertäufer"* ("Re-baptizers" or "Anabaptists"). Which interpretation is correct? Immersers, Antibaptists, or Anabaptists? The answer can be found by examining page 114 in the text [ZW, VI, 114.28; Jackson, 1901, 183.29]. Here it says, "Since then you do not recognize rebaptism [rebap-tismum] or contrabaptism [contrabaptismum], though nevertheless against the standing custom of Christ's church and against the divine law, by your rebaptism [retinctionem] you crucify Christ again.... You do not dare, I say, to call your rebaptism [retinctionem] catabaptism [catabaptismum], but you call 'baptism' [baptismum] that which is rebaptism [rebaptismus]." According to the second part of the sentence, which begins with "you do not dare," one would expect the wording, "you call baptism that which is catabaptism." But instead of "catabaptism" there is the term "rebaptism." This substitution is clearly possible because both terms have equal meaning, which the passage, "to call your rebaptism catabap-tism" has already shown. Zwingli here uses three words for one thing: *retinctio, catabap-tismus, rebaptismus*. The words, therefore, are synonymous. But what does *rebaptismus* mean in this larger context? For one thing it surely means "rebaptism" or "Anabaptism" (see ZW, VI, 115.8: *ni retinctus sit*, "unless he has been rebaptized"). That this does not exhaust the content of the term is shown by the beginning of the first half of this sentence, "Since then you do not recognize rebaptism or contrabaptism, etc." Here "rebaptism" and "contrabap-tism" are closely related. In addition, this sentence beginning with "Since" is taken up again after a parenthesis and inscribed with the following words, "You do not dare, I say, to call your rebaptism [retinctionem] 'catabaptism.' " But if *retinctio* and *catabaptismus* are a repiti-tion of *rebaptismus* and *contrabaptismus*, it must follow that all these terms mean the same thing, i.e., "Catabaptism" means equally "Anabaptism" and "Antibaptism." Certainly Zwingli could readily have derived both meanings from the word, *"wider."* The sharply dif-ferentiated usage between *"wieder"* (Lat. *denuo*, "again") and *"wider"* or *"zuwieder"* (lat. *contra*, "against") was not yet known to him. *"Widertouf"* or *"Widertoufer"* mean to him si-multaneously "second baptism" and "one who practices counterview baptism," and therefore it must be his intention to find a word that expresses this double meaning in Latin. That word was *rebaptismus*. In the Latin, "re" implied both *wieder* ("again") and *gegen* ("against"), e.g., *reclamo, rebello, recanto*. Now the Greek word which he uses to express this same double meaning, which he got from Gregory of Nazianzus in the passage cited by Oecolampad, is καταβαπτισμός, Latinized as *catabaptismus*. But *cata* (equivalent to *contra*, is not *denuo* ("again"); and strictly speaking *catabaptismus* means only *contrabaptismus*, not *anabaptismus*. But this does not seem to have bothered Zwingli. It is enough for him that Oe-colampad pointed out to him that according to Gregory of Nazianzus, it was more correct to speak of Catabaptists than of Anabaptists. The literal meaning of his Greek term is *"Ersäufer"* ("drowners"), and it was in this contemptuous, cynical sense that Oecolampad wanted to apply this word to the Anabaptists. Blanke, whose foregoing commentary has been translated from the German nearly verbatim, concluded that while Zwingli used the term in a broad sense, its meaning to him was not quite as comprehensive as to Oecolampad, an expert on the church Fathers, who conceived of *catabaptismus* as *Ertränkung*, "drowning" or "sub-mersion," while Zwingli, according to Blanke, only thought of the term in its twofold sense of "rebaptism" and "contrabaptism." Blanke apparently overlooked Zwingli's passage, "just as if one were now to call the Anabaptists "drowners," because by that means they are trying to cause great disunity among the believers and ... great harm and suppression to the gospel" (70C/387/40-388/2).

9. It is not likely, and there is no evidence, that the Anabaptists used the Greek word *catabaptist* as a self designation. In fact, Zwingli contradicts this claim in a later sentence, "You do not dare to call your rebaptism 'catabaptism,' but you call 'baptism' that which is rebaptism" (ZW, VI, 115.3; Jackson, 1901, 183.34-184.1). Nevertheless, it is possible that they were already using the Greek name, ἀναβαπτισμός, "Anabaptist" (see 711/431/19 and 711/ fn.2) in the inclusive sense that Zwingli gave to the term (see previous fn.) but without the pejorative connotations.

10. Mt. 10:16.

11. I.e., since December 1523, when the Grebel-Stumpf alternative plan of an *ecclesia piorum,* a church of the devoted, free of state auspices, was first presented in Zurich (see 59A, above).

12. Zwingli was then probably thinking of such cities as Waldshut, St. Gallen, Schaffhausen, Basel, Bern, Chur, Constance, Strasbourg, etc.

13. The palace of Jove (Jupiter) in Rome was far removed not just from its corresponding location in Greece (Mt. Olympus, home of Zeus) but was especially remote from the hall of Pluto, Greek god of the lower world.

14. Zwingli's original wording was "not man but demons." The latter two words were stricken and the parenthetical question was inserted instead.

15. Lat. *immanium praestigiatorum.* Zwingli tried unsuccessfully to restrain his wording.

16. Mt. 13:3.

17. Mt. 13:25.

18. Mt. 7:15.

19. Eph. 4:14.

20. "Like the angels," which was Zwingli's original wording!

21. For the chronology of when the "heresy" of Anabaptism became a "sedition" against the state in Zwingli's thinking, see 69C/fn.8.

22. This sentence is not just another way to affirm the Protestant doctrine of grace, but a personal expression of Zwingli's own repentance of past immorality (see Hillerbrand, 1964, pp. 114-17 and Potter, 1978, 10-11), in contrast to his allegation that the Anabaptists not only whitewashed their own past immoralities but continue to live licentiously.

23. The particular referent for "shame" here is the case of the *Halbtäufer* Thomas Schuggers, who murdered his brother in St. Gallen in 1526. Zwingli does not say that the murder grew out of the spirit of Anabaptism but that the crime was not publicly recognized as such by the Anabaptists. Zwingli follows literary sources that describe the lioness and horse as having naturally shameful feelings (see Plinius, *Natural History,* VIII, 17 and 64). Evidence that Zwingli was following such an assumption is the fact that he corrected *leo* (lion) to *leena* (lioness). His accusation of the shamelessness of the Anabaptists is a two-edged sword. None of the beasts here named were guilty of burning, beheading, and drowning other members of their species for their faith.

24. Lat. *Illa enim Empusam.* Empusa, the ghost who attends Hekate in Aristophanes, *The Frogs,* appears in inconsistent forms, first as a mighty animal, then as a child, then as a donkey, then as a beautiful woman, finally as a dog.

25. Proteus, the sea god in Greek mythology capable of assuming different forms.

26. Any of a group of old world lizards having the unusual ability to change the color of the skin; hence, a fickle or changeable person.

27. Tarandus, according to Pliny's *Natural History,* VIII, 123, is an animal (reindeer, elk, etc.) living in Skythien, that is able to change its colors. Zwingli cited four examples of changeable figures with which to compare the Anabaptists.

28. The "Father of lights with whom there is no variation of shadow due to change" (Jas. 1:17).

29. Lat. *herbam veritati tribueris,* i.e., "you will have declared yourself conquered by handing over a blade of grass as a sign of subjection."

30. Lat. *elenchus,* "rebuttal," "disproving," "confutation," "controversion."

31. Lat. *strophas,* "cunning," "intrigues," "artifices." Zwingli first used this word with reference to the Anabaptists in his letter to Vadian of May 28, 1525 (see 69D/375/1, 69D/ fn.5). Later in the present tract he explains his use of this term as follows: "This work is called a 'Refutation of the Tricks, etc.' because this class of men so abounds and works in artificial means that I have never seen anything equally oily or changeable" (see below 480/39ff.).

32. See fn. 8, above.

33. Lat. *calumnias,* "calumnies," the malicious uttering of false charges, misrepresentations calculated to damage another's reputation. Zwingli refers specifically not to spoken abuses, but to a libelous writing (the *libellus,* "booklet") referred to in 481/2-3, below, written

758

by a single author and containing misrepresentations against Zwingli's defense of infant baptism. For documentation of Grebel's authorship, see Intro., above, and fns. 57, 97, 115, 116, 119, 143, 151, 179, and 187, below. The booklet "had for a long time been passing through the hands of their brotherhood, who everywhere boasted that they could so tear up Zwingli's positions that there would be nothing left" (481/4-7). Blanke is in error (29/fn.4) that Zwingli's comment, "you have never published them" refers to the *libellum confutatio;* it refers rather to the articles of the Schleitheim Confession of Faith (see Harder, 1980, p. 53). It is not entirely clear therefore that the *libellum* had been printed; the reference to "passing through the hands" may imply manuscript form. Nevertheless, after "looking and searching everywhere," Zwingli finally received a copy from his Basel colleague, Oecolampad. To be mentioned in this connection is that in his writing of 1530 *De Convitiis Eccii* (Schuler-Schulthess, 4, p. 40), Zwingli related that two years after the founding of the Anabaptist movement, he suppressed "in a friendly way" some Anabaptist *lucubrationes* (nighttime writings) against infant baptism. He was probably referring to Grebel's *libellum confutatio* and the Schleitheim articles which he refuted in Parts 1 and 2 of the *Elenchus.* The *libellum confutatio* as it circulated originally is no longer extant, but a substantial part of its content has been preserved in the excerpts that Zwingli translated word for word into Latin in Parts 1 and 3 of the *Elenchus.* Following is a summary of the content of the *libellum,* gleaned from those excerpts: In eleven numbered theses, it combatted *fundamentorum Zuinglii unum* ("one of Zwingli's bases," see below 480/27) for infant baptism, i.e., the family of Stephanas (1 Cor. 1:16) and other baptized families in the New Testament for which a quotation from Zwingli's first anti-Anabaptist tract of 1524 (67C/320/8ff.) forms the point of contact. With thesis 12, the *confutatio* proceeds to combat *Zuinglii alterum fundamentum* (Zwingli's second basis; see 494/27), i.e., the thesis of synecdoche which Zwingli had used to reply to Hubmaier's *Taufbüchlein* (see Zwingli's "Answer Concerning Balthasar's *Taufbüchlein,*" ZW, IV, No. 68, pp. 577-647). This brings us to the end of Part 1, at which point Zwingli interrupts his translation of the *libellum confutatio,* which he resumes in Part 3. The third part, however, yields only a few brief direct translations of the *confutatio* into Latin, which moreover are not placed into the explicit dialogical format of Part 1. In Part 3, Zwingli mainly gives the content of the *confutatio* in his own summary words.

34. Lat. *superstitionis ipsorum fundamenta subruam,* "I shall undermine the grounds of their fanaticism." By *fundamenta,* Zwingli refers to the Schleitheim articles, refuted in Part 2.

35. Lat. *Postremo de foedere iungam deque eo, quod firma manet electio dei,* "Next I will make a synthesis out of covenant and with that in view out of the election of God which remains fixed." These are the two main subjects for Part 3 of the *Elenchus.*

36. The Appendix, found in English translation in Jackson (1901, pp. 251-58) covers the four doctrines allegedly held by the Anabaptists—sleep of the soul, universal salvation, multiple ministry, and spiritualism. Zwingli also added a one-paragraph *Peroratio* (Conclusion).

37. Lat. *Omnia vero levi manu.* This phrase is susceptible to several interpretations: "But all with tongue in cheek" (which is hardly credible); "But all with gestures of the hand" (for maximum emphasis); "But all with sleight of hand" (for maximum disdain).

38. Zwingli twice emphasized the fidelity of his translation, here and in 493/3ff.: "I translate faithfully and literally, perverting nothing, even when these fellows struggle and stammer in the German tongue."

39. The excerpts from the *confutatio* in Part 1 of the *Elenchus* deal with two bases for Zwingli's biblical defense of infant baptism: (1) the "household baptism" (1 Cor. 1:16; Acts 16:33, etc.), which Grebel attempted to refute in his first eleven numbered theses (482/24 to 494/5-6), and (2) the "second foundation" (494/27-28), synecdochic figures of speech (Acts 2:46-47; 1 Cor. 10:1-4); which Grebel refuted in his twelfth thesis (494/20ff.).

40. See 1 Cor. 1:16; 16:15.

41. The following is almost a verbatim quotation from Zwingli's first anti-Anabaptist tract, "Who Gives Cause for Rebellion" (see 67C/320/7-13). Notice that Zwingli elects to excerpt only the quotation from his earlier writing, because it gives him the opportunity to

expand on it before he takes up Grebel's refutation.

42. Lat. *artibus*, "artificial means," "cunning." Notice that the word shifts from *strophas* (tricks) to *artes*, the latter defining the former.

43. Mt. 25:24.

44. Lat. *libellum confutationis nostrorum*, "booklet of refutation of our positions." The rendering "booklet of counter arguments" is preferred here because Zwingli uses another term, *elenchus*, to refer to his own "refutation" of Grebel's "confutation."

45. See fn. 33, above.

46. On Oecolampad, Reformer in Basel, see 57/fn.3.

47. On April 24, 1527, Oecolampad had written to Zwingli, *Mitto hic decreta catabaptistarum et quaedam in te scripta* ("I am sending to you herewith the doctrines of the Anabaptists and certain writings against you" (ZW, IX, No. 607, p. 101.15). He had gotten the documents from some rural preacher. The former was the Schleitheim Articles (see fn. 212, below, and Harder, 1980, pp. 51-66) and the latter the *libellum confutatio* (see Blanke, VI, p. 31, fn. 2).

48. Lat. *lusciosi . . . caeci,* "purblind . . . blind" or "intellectually blind . . . morally blind.

49. Lat. *sic adfectu ampliandae sectae.*

50. Zwingli repeated this accusation with reference to the Schleitheim Articles: "Although you have never published them, yet hardly any of your people exist who do not have a copy of these well-founded laws, as you call them. Why, pray, do you not publish what is so divine and so salutary?" (ZW, VI, p. 104; Jackson, 1901, p. 177). These were taunting comments in light of the fact that the Anabaptists were denied access to the printing presses, not to mention the confiscation of their documents, published or not.

51. See Jn. 3:20.

52. Lat. *sua ecclesiae judicio submitterent.* The first reproach Zwingli makes against the Anabaptists is not that they introduced rebaptism but that they bypassed the jurisdiction of the established church in doing so. In his *Taufbüchlein,* he had written, "Let every devout Christian judge whether they have acted in a Christian way or not when they have everywhere in actual fact, without the consent of the established church, brought forth one of their own (see above 69C/364/24-27 and 68L/355/34-39). Of course, the Anabaptists did not accept the authority of the state in church polity and therefore were unable *sua ecclesae judicio submittere* ("to submit to the jurisdiction of the church").

53. Lat. *sua* ("theirs") refers back to *opera* ("works") of the preceding sentence.

54. Lat. *haec,* which refers to the seven episodes in the founding and early history of the Anabaptist movement just chronicled by Zwingli, which we have excerpted earlier in our collection (59A, 66A, 68F, 68L, 70D, 71J, and 71M). Thus, the three dots preceding "Perhaps" signify the "details" of the seven episodes here omitted.

55. Fines, banishments, imprisonments, and by this time the execution of an Anabaptist leader, Felix Mantz (Epi.B, above).

56. Zwingli apparently got some of his unfavorable reports about the Anabaptists from disillusioned ex-members.

57. Zwingli may here be thinking of Grebel, whose leadership was characterized by high mobility and absentee authority (see 69A/360/17ff., 361/14ff., 361/30ff., 70A/384/3ff., etc.). Grebel was directly or indirectly involved in the recruitment of a number of early Anabaptist martyrs (see 69E, 71E, Epi.B, and Epi.E). For Zwingli, however, to lay the blame for their executions on the Anabaptist leadership is an example of what Peter Berger calls "moral alibi" and "bad faith" (1961, chs. 5, 10), by means of which one attempts to avoid responsibility for one's own actions.

58. Lat. *magistro.* Zwingli refers to the devil. In an omitted subsequent sentence, he refers to the leaders as *cacodaemonis apostolos,* "apostles of the devil." The term is stronger than the usual names for devil: *diabolus, daemon.* It has the profane connotation of a "defiling, defecating demon."

59. Compare with 71G/428/23-30.

60. 1 Jn. 2:19.

61. See fn. 40, above.

62. Although it is true that in his treatise of 1524 on rebels, he referred to the case of Stephanas as *ein Beispiel*, "an example" (67C/320/12-13) and not *pro fundamento*, "as a foundation," his reference in that context to "baptism as taking the place of circumcision" (319/39-40) was certainly his most basic argument or principle for infant baptism, of which the case of Stephanas was the first example. Perhaps Zwingli is thinking of his *Taufbüchlein* of March 1525, which he begins to review here, overlooking the source of Grebel's comment in the 1524 treatise on rebels.

63. The three examples cited from 1 Cor. 1:16; Acts 16:15, 33 (see 67C/320/8-12).

64. This comes from the part entitled "On Infant Baptism" in Zwingli's *Taufbüchlein*, not included in the present collection, in which Zwingli reiterated arguments he used in the First and Second Public Disputations with the Anabaptists (see 68B and 68L). For the original text, see ZW, IV, p. 301. 24ff. But see also 69C/366/1ff.

65. Mt. 7:3.

66. Quotation from Hubmaier's *Vom Christlichen Tauf der Gläubigen*, written in response to Zwingli's *Taufbüchlein*. See also Zwingli's *Antwort über Doctor Balthasars Taufbüchlein* (ZW, IV, No. 68, p. 604.11).

67. Grebel begins to number twelve theses, the first eleven of which deal with household baptisms (see fn. 39, above), and the twelfth of which deals with Zwingli's principle of synecdoche (see fn. 152, below).

68. Another paraphrase (see 480/27-34) from Zwingli's tract on rebels (67C/319/23-25).

69. See 483/33, below.

70. Zwingli used this same example in the last part of the *Taufbüchlein*, "Vom Kindertouff": "Where do we read that the Holy Mother of Jesus Christ was baptized? Yet if one were as obstinate as you, one would have to say, 'she was not baptized.' But would that not be blasphemy? Where does it state that the apostles were baptized? Excepting maybe two in John chapter 1? And even there, it is not a clear word but only an inference. Should one say therefore that they were not baptized, on the basis of their proof, 'It is not written, therefore it did not happen'? So must one separate the Holy Mother and the apostles from the issue of baptism" (ZW, IV, p. 308.28).

71. Antecedent to 482/26, above.

72. *Antistrephon*, "argumentation" which an opponent to whom it is directed can turn around and use against the one who is using it.

73. Lat. *imperite malignus ... maligne imperitus*.

74. The two instances recorded in Lk. 13:1-5.

75. Mk. 9:36; 10:16.

76. Grebel would more likely have written, "None of the testimonies that mention families includes children."

77. Mt. 1:1-17; Lk. 3:23-38.

78. Lk. 19:9.

79. Ex. 1:21.

80. Lat. *quasi vero asinus ullus ad lyram sic oscitaverit unquam*, i.e., "would have been so sleepy [or unaware] at the playing of a harp." *Asinus* refers to a simpleton or ludicrous person.

81. Refers to Zwingli's Reformation argument stated at the First Zurich Disputation of January 1523: "God does not desire our decree and doctrine when they do not originate with Him" (ZW, I, p. 549.12ff. and Jackson, 1901, p. 96.4ff.).

82. The vicar general of the bishop of Constance, Johannes Faber (see 51A/fn.14 and ZW, IV, 296.18ff.).

83. See Jn. 8:44. On the use of this hermeneutical principle in the earlier debates in Zurich, see 57A/fns. 33 and 36, 57C/fns. 31 and 57.

84. See Gal. 1:6-8; 2 Cor. 11:4.

85. Lat. *sub incude sudabant*, "they were sweating under the anvil," "they were in the

process of being forged."

86. Zwingli leaves the context of Grebel's writing for a moment and shifts to two later contexts, one continuous with his work and one quite unconnected. In this sentence, those Anabaptist leaders who have most recently appeared to deny the Old Testament are not immediately identified while some others who undermine the New Testament are named. But in the following sentence the former are also identified as certain Grüningen spokesmen (see fns. 93-96, below).

87. Lat. *Vangionas*. The term was used by Caesar, Plinius, and Tacitus, with reference to a people living on the Rhine in the vicinity of the present-day Worms. Zwingli calls the three men here named *Vangionas* because Kautz was a minister in Worms and the other two completed their translation of the prophets here in the spring of 1527.

88. Hans Denk of Augsburg (*ca.* 1500-27) was a leader of the South German Anabaptists of the spiritualist type, and therefore has not figured in the events of the movement in Switzerland to date. In the 415 documents of the Zurich origins in the Muralt-Schmid collection (Quellen 1), he was named in only one document: a letter from Zurich to Augsburg dated Aug. 10, 1527. He died of the plague in Basel in November of that year, three months after Zwingli referred to him in the *Elenchus*. His motto had been, "No one may truly know Christ unless one follows him in life" (see 48/fn.18). Zwingli's comment refers to the views of universal salvation held by Denk and the other named persons. Zwingli attempts to refute this doctrine in the Appendix to the *Elenchus,* but without quoting from the Anabaptist writings: "They have learned that ... the Hebrew word for 'forever' does not mean interminable duration. Here they do just as they do everywhere, when they have learned one thing, what they do not know or will not see they turn aside and reject. Let them therefore take Lk. 1:33: " 'He shall reign over the house of Jacob forever.' Is this 'forever' used for some ages? Another witness is Mt. 25:41, 'Depart from me, ye cursed, into eternal fire, prepared for the devil and his angels.' Tell me here, when will that fire have an end if 'eternal' is always a definite time?" (Jackson, 1901, p. 256). Denk interprets his universalist views in his treatise, *Wer die Wahrheit wahrlich lieb hat* (Gegenschrift 16, 17, and 28). He mentions it also in his *Vom Gesetz Gottes*. His thesis was that because God's nature is love and mercy, he cannot keep his anger forever. He used a number of passages from Isaiah and Jeremiah and the New Testament epistles to support this doctrine.

89. On Ludwig Hätzer, see Cast of Characters No. 43.

90. *Cutiis* is the Latin name for Jacob Kautz, Lutheran preacher at Worms for the two years 1526-27, who joined the Anabaptists during this time and was greatly influenced by Denk and Hätzer. Kautz's spiritualist/universalist ideas were expressed chiefly in seven theses which he attached to the door of the Preachers' Church in Worms after the manner of Luther (see Jackson, 1901, pp. 148-49). Three of the articles read as follows: "V. All that was lost in the first Adam is and will be found more richly restored in the second Adam, Christ; yea, in Christ shall all men be quickened and blessed forever. VI. Jesus Christ of Nazareth suffered on the cross and made satisfaction for us in no other way than that we should stand in his footsteps and walk in the way he has opened, and obey the command of the Father, even as the Son did. They who speak, think, or believe otherwise of Christ, each in his own way makes out of Christ an idol. VIII. Just as the literal bite of the forbidden fruit would have harmed neither [Adam] himself nor his descendants if he had not eaten of the same with his mind, so also the bodily suffering of Jesus Christ is not real satisfaction and reconciliation with the Father without internal obedience and the greatest desire to yield to the eternal will" (Jackson, 1901, pp. 148-49). It was in the light of such doctrines as these that Zwingli mockingly wrote, "I know not which Kautz."

91. The information that the three men named denied the satisfaction of Christ had come to Zwingli in two letters from Wolfgang Capito dated July 7 and 19, 1527: "They deny Christ very openly." He referred particularly to Hätzer and enclosed Kautz's seven articles, who he thought had gotten them from Denk and Hätzer (ZW, IX, 167.13 and 172.8). To be mentioned in this connection is that the preface to the Zurich translation of the prophets published in Zurich in 1529 by Froschauer makes the charge that Denk and Hätzer deny the Godhead of Christ in their translation of the prophets. This accusation has been found to

have no basis (see Blanke, ZW, VI, p. 57, fn. 1).

92. On the rise of the Anabaptist movement in Grüningen, see 71C/Intro.

93. Zwingli refers here to the Grüninger Eingabe, published below in English translation (Epi.E). It was written as the personal testimony of Jacob Falk and Heine Reimann, the fifth and sixth Anabaptist martyrs in Switzerland, the second and third to be drowned in Zurich. It was not directly addressed to their Zurich magistrates but to the Grüningen Diet as part of their petition to be released from custody and not turned over to the Zurich authorities for prosecution, a petition that was finally denied after two years of imprisonment in Grüningen. Zwingli's abstract from the *Eingabe* is not an accurate quotation but a prejudiced paraphrase of Epi.E/516/39ff., below. The sentence in question made an attack on the "false prophet Zwingli," who desperately attempts to derive baptism from the Old Testament. It is no wonder that Zwingli reacted with such hostility.

94. The shift from third- to second-person pronouns for the next fifteen sentences is an address to the two men who were martyred in Zurich on Sept. 5, 1528. As Zwingli prophesies in two of those sentences, "I will prove it then by the very power of him who silences the kind of spirit in which you abound so that it no longer dares to assert, 'Thou art the Son of God' ... for it is time to prove your spirit."

95. The Grüninger Eingabe, written by two unlettered farmers, has been described as a truly spiritual statement (see von Muralt, *Zwingliana,* V, 107, and Bender, 1950, p. 156).

96. The authors of the Grüninger Eingabe had asserted "that baptism belongs to those believers who devote themselves to the Son of God" (Epi.E/516/19-21). Zwingli's quotation tries to make a connection between this assertion and the prayer of the demon in the man of Gerasene to "Jesus, Son of the most High God" (Mk. 5:7).

97. Lat. *coryphaeis.* In November 1526, Zwingli referred to Grebel as the *catabaptistarum coryphaeus,* "the ringleader of the Anabaptists" (see Epi.A/463/2); but in the present context he probably means Denk, Hätzer and Kautz. The *coryphaeis* of the past are not mentioned by name in the *Elenchus.* Blanke points out that "it is noteworthy that Zwingli makes a distinction between the Anabaptist leaders *(coryphaie)* and the mass of the Anabaptists with reference to the confession of Christ. Only with the leaders does he doubt the sincerity of this expression of belief in Christ."

98. By "above," Zwingli refers to a paragraph in his dedicatory letter, which was omitted in our edition.

99. Not long after Zwingli wrote this, the Grüningen prisoners were turned over to the Zurich authorities for prosecution and execution on Sept. 5, 1528.

100. In a subsequent passage omitted in our edition, Zwingli identifies those Anabaptist leaders who teach a works righteousness. They are the *Vangionas* (fn. 87, above)—the three men of Worms previously named: "At Worms you deny Christ and lead the way back to trust in works, because the people there who have recently become interested in religion are little trained in the wiles of hypocrisy, and so are susceptible to your tricks" (ZW, VI, 61.14ff., Jackson, 1901, 151.26ff.). Later in Part 2, Zwingli seeks to discredit the first article of Schleitheim on the same grounds of works-righteousness (see Jackson, 1901, 178.32ff.); but it is doubtful that he was also thinking of the Schleitheim articles at the present point of writing.

101. After his brief digression to refute the Anabaptist writers of Grüningen and Worms, Zwingli returns to Grebel's *libellum confutatio.*

102. Jn. 17:20.

103. Heb. 5:14.

104. Lat. *cornicantur,* see Persius 5, 12.

105. Jn. 17:19.

106. See fn. 100, above.

107. Compare with 479/28-29, above, where Zwingli first wrote that the Anabaptists "appear angelic," but then changed the adjective to "divine."

108. Lat. *cacodaemonis nuncii.* See fn. 58, above, where the label was *dacodaemonis apostolos.*

109. Lat. *apud inferos, scit princep eorum.* The *princeps* "leader" of the Anabaptists refers to the author of the *libellum confutatio,* who has died and allegedly gone to the infernal

abode below, where he is "among the shades" *(inferni,* (see fns. 116 and 145, below).

110. The antecedent is 67C/320/7-8, above.

111. The phrase with which the students of Pythagoras praised their master's teachings. See Cicero, *De deorum natura,* 1, 5, 10.

112. Lat. *magister ille noster.* Blanke (ZW, VI, p. 65, fn. 3) cites Baur (II, p. 205, fn. 1), who said that Zwingli must have had a scholastic in mind when he used this term because the scholastic theologians loved to designate themselves as *magister;* but Blanke points back to an earlier reference in the *Elenchus* to *magistros omnium* ("masters of all"; see ZW, VI, p. 63.7), adding that "it is in this wider ironical sense that the term *magister* is used in this place to designate a man who wishes to be a schoolmaster to other men and also to the Holy Scriptures."

113. Lat. *furiose onager.*

114. Lat. *arbitror,* which can mean either "I think," "I suppose," reflecting a measure of uncertainty, or "I judge," "I decide," reflecting a more definite discernment. If the former was meant, it could indicate some uncertainty on Zwingli's part as to whether or not the author of the *confutatio* had died. Blanke (see fn. 115, below) rejects this interpretation and concludes that Zwingli, knowing the author to have died, was making a judgment as to his eternal destiny (see fns. 144 and 145 below).

115. Lat. *arbitror ... baptizari,* "I judge to be baptized." Zwingli is saying two things: (1) that the author of the *libellus confutatio* has died and (2) that in Zwingli's judgment he has gone to live in hell. As Blanke points out (ZW, VI, p. 65, fn. 6) the word *arbitror* ("I judge" or "I think") should not qualify the death of the author as if Zwingli had only thought on the basis of rumor that he had died, but should interpret the baptism on the Phlegethon as a judgment on Zwingli's part about the eternal state of the author's soul.

116. Lat. *umbras,* not just "shades" or "ghosts" but residents of hell (see fn. 109, above). This is Zwingli's most frequently used designation for the author of the *confutatio* (see 490/33, 494/33, and 496/9, below).

117. The Phlegethon is one of the rivers of the underworld. The name means "the burning one." The *umbrae* are the shadows of the dead along the Phlegethon.

118. Lat. *larvis,* meaning the spirits of those who have died. The author of the *libellum confutatio* is now one of the *larvae,* i.e., he has died and is no longer among the residents of earth.

119. Zwingli is not absolutely certain who wrote the *libellum confutatio,* but he has some strong surmises. As Blanke points out (ZW, VI, p. 66, fn. 1) this presents a double research assignment: (1) to discover whom Zwingli suspected as the author and (2) to determine whether that suspicion is correct. See fns. 143, 147, 179, and 187, below, for Blanke's conclusions. This and fn. 147 cite the two reasons why Zwingli was reluctant to name the author, even though he was fairly certain who he was: (1) he could not be sure and (2) since he had consigned him to hell it would not be nice to name him.

120. Zwingli means that it would do little good to load scriptural proofs upon "a frenzied wild ass" who would only throw them off in fury.

121. Lat. *Christianae familiae.* It is not clear whether here and in fn. 122 below, Zwingli means the biological family or the spiritual family, i.e., the church. In either case, he seems to know that the Anabaptists had a view on the status of unbaptized children within the believers' church, but not to know that Grebel had enunciated a doctrine that all children are covered by the atonement of Christ prior to the age of accountability and are thus fully included in both the biological and spiritual families (see 63/290/36ff.).

122. See fn. 121, above.

123. Lat. *tam pulchre funem ex arena didicistis texere.* Zwingli had used this same figure with Luther the previous February (see ZW, V, No. 104, p. 616, fn. 1).

124. Lat. *ubi leonina deficit, vulpinam adsuitis,* "where the lion's hide runs out, you sew on a fox's pelt," an ancient Greek and Latin proverb.

125. Gen. 21:9ff.

126. Gal. 4:30.

127. Blanke tried in vain to find Zwingli's source for this theory about pearls (see ZW, VI, p. 67, fn. 1).

128. Ex. 12:48.

129. Lat. *Isthmum perfodere.* Zwingli also used this figure with Luther (see fn. 123, above, and ZW, V, No. 104, p. 661, fn. 1).

130. Not foolishness but malice.

131. See fn. 88, above.

132. See fn. 89, above.

133. See fn. 90, above.

134. Lat. *mirabile avitium,* "remarkable species of birds." *Kauz* means "owl" and Hätzler *(Elster)* means "magpie."

135. Lat. *ab ipsis unguiculis,* has two meanings: *de tenero ungui,* "from earliest child" and *ad unguen,* "to a tee," "to a hair," "completely."

136. 1 Cor. 1:16.

137. Acts 16:15.

138. Acts 16:33.

139. Lat. *genus,* "class," "category," "race," "stock," "family," "house."

140. Ex. 12:48.

141. Lat. *sesquipedalia* (see Horace, *De arte poetica,* 97).

142. 1 Cor. 16:15-16. Grebel's argument was that "firstfruits" meant first converts and "appointed themselves to the ministry of the saints" implied adults, not children; and that therefore "household of Stephanas" also referred to adults.

143. Scholars differ as to how the fact that the *confutatio* was written in Swiss German was the "greatest proof" as to who the author was. August Baur *(Zeitschrift für Kirchenges-chichte,* 10, 1889, p. 337) assumed that the author was not Swiss by birth but was trying unsuccessfully to write in the Swiss dialect; therefore Hubmaier, not Grebel, was the author. In the following issue of the same journal (11, 1890, pp. 162-65), Johann Usteri refuted Baur's assumption and argued that the fact that Zwingli found nothing trans-Rhenish in the wording of Anabaptist point No. 8, above, proves that the author was a native Swiss, e.g., Conrad Grebel.

144. See 488/8-10.

145. Lat. *apud inferos* (see fns. 109 and 116, above). Blanke (ZW, VI, p. 69, fn. 5) comments as follows: "Baur *Zeitschrift für Kirchengeschichte,* 1889, p. 336) allows the word *in-dubie* [undoubtedly] of this sentence to express Zwingli's doubt whether his opponent has actually died. In opposition to this interpretation, both Usteri (ZK, 1890, p. 162) and R. Stae-helin (I, 1895, p. 528, fn. 1) have rightly objected that as above on p. 65.14 [see fn. 114, above] the uncertain *arbitror* ["I judge" or "I surmise";] refers to the baptism of the author of the *confutatio* on the Phlegethon, and not to his death. So here the *indubie* also refers to his being devoured by the fires of the underworld, and not to his death. In my opinion, Zwingli supposes that his dead opponent (whose death as ZW, VI, p. 80.6 [494/32-33] clearly shows is most certainly true) has come into hell and not into heaven. We have here a counterpiece to Luther's judgment of the dead Zwingli (see O Farner, *Das Zwinglibild Luthers,* 1931, p. 24).

146. Lat. *catabaptismo perlutus,* "Anabaptist bathing." Blanke (ZW, VI, p. 69, fn. 6) interprets this as a reference to baptism by immersion, the form used by Grebel in St. Gallen and elsewhere (see 69A/360/22-23 and fn. 13, and 69B/362/11 and fn. 3).

147. See fn. 119, above, for the other reason why Zwingli did not identify the author.

148. This is the second of four references to the author of the *confutatio* as *umbra* (see fns. 116, 181, and 195).

149. On Hatzer, see fn. 89, above, and Cast of Characters No. 43.

150. Zwingli refers here to the Tuesday Disputations, which he had described earlier in the *Elenchus* (see 66A/300/33-38) and which we have dated Dec. 6 and 13, 1524.

151. The author of the *confutatio* had implied that Zwingli "dishonestly" withheld reference to the passage in 1 Cor. 16:15-16 (see 490/18-19) with which the Anabaptists had

previously confronted him. Zwingli here combats this accusation by pointing out that he had refuted this objection when Hätzer raised it at the first Tuesday Disputation. It was therefore an "impudence" of the "shade" (line 8) to scold him now for ignoring this passage, when (as Zwingli implies) the "shade" was present when this discussion took place. Zwingli's evident intent here is to remind the author of the *confutatio* of something he had already heard. This inference narrows the search for the author's identity. He is someone who was present at the Tuesday Disputations, other than Ludwig Hätzer. Moreover, he is now a "shade," i.e., he has died since then. Unfortunately, only the names of those on Zwingli's side of the Tuesday meetings were identified by name (66A/fn.9); but we can be almost certain from documents 67 and 67B that Grebel and Mantz were both present. It is likely, moreover, that all the pre-Anabaptist leaders living in the Zurich bailiwick at the time took part—Andreas Castelberger, Johann Brötli, Hans Ockenfuss, Bartlime Pur, perhaps the elder Jacob Hottinger, and Wilhelm Reublin (although he may still have been in prison since August 1524). The following would *not* have been present: Simon Stumpf, who had been exiled in December 1523, Jörg Blaurock, who did not appear in Zurich until January 1525, Balthasar Hubmaier, who was back in Waldshut by then, leading the resistance movement there. Of those who might have been present, the only two who are known to have died subsequently are Mantz and Grebel; and Brötli, Aberli, Ockenfuss, Hottinger, and Reublin are known to have still been alive at the time Zwingli wrote the *Elenchus*. Therefore, either Mantz or Grebel was the *umbra* to whom Zwingli refers as the author of the *confutatio*. As stated in the Introduction, above, in June 1536 Heinrich Bullinger identified Grebel as the author.

152. Synecdoche is a figure of speech in which a part is put for the whole, or a whole for the part, e.g., "I baptized the household of Stephanas" (1 Cor. 1:16) is a whole put for the part, "I baptized the children of the household of Stephanas" (see ZW, IV, p. 239, fn. 5). Zwingli gives examples from two New Testament passages: (1) 1 Cor. 10:1-3: "all under the cloud," "all through the sea," "all baptized into Moses," "all ate the spiritual food," and (2) Acts 2:44-47: "all who believed." In his thesis 12, below, Grebel attempted to refute these synecdochic arguments. For Zwingli's own definition of synecdoche, see below 491/14ff. and 497/5ff.

153. 1 Cor. 16:15.

154. Zwingli's tangential comments are here omitted for lack of space.

155. See fn. 152, above.

156. See fns. 149 and 150, above.

157. I.e., "pretty large," if, as the Anabaptists argue, it contained only adults.

158. 1 Cor. 1:14-15.

159. Zwingli assumes that a group of such simplistic persons cannot be a church. In Part 2 of the *Elenchus* (see ZW, VI, p. 118.14), he argues that it is untenable that the Anabaptists could be a church, for they are a *cacoecclesia et conjuratio,* "a defiled church and a conspiracy."

160. 1 Cor. 1:15.

161. 1 Cor. 1:12.

162. See fn. 152, above.

163. The formula, *Bona verba, questo!* comes from Terence, *Andria,* 204, and means something like "Take it easy, please!"

164. Lat. *exclusivam.* Zwingli elsewhere (ZW, VI, p. 77.19) speaks of *propositionem exclusivam.* The first word means "a proposition" or "a basic assumption" used to introduce a syllogism in logic. The two words together refer to an exclusively valid proposition.

165. Lat. *Parturiunt montes.* The complete proverb from Horace, *Ars Poetica,* 139, adds *et nascetur ridiculus mus,* "and a ridiculous mouse will be born."

166. For a similar comment, see 480/21.

167. Zwingli is apparently criticizing Grebel's wording, not only for the addition of the word *gleichzeitig (simul),* "at the same time," which is not in the Latin Vulgate or in Luther's translation, but also for the use of the verb *lauschen (auscultare),* "to listen," instead of the verb *hören (audire),* "to hear," as in the Latin Vulgate and/or Luther's translation.

168. See Gal. 2:2ff.; Acts 15:1ff.

169. Acts 16:32.

170. Acts 16:33ff.

171. Grebel apparently reverted from the verb *lauschen (auscultare),* "to listen," to hören (audire), "to hear," in conformity with the Latin Vulgate and/or Luther's translation. See fn. 167, above.

172. Acts 16:34b.

173. See fn. 167, above. The infidelity in the translation in this case pertains to Grebel's translation of Acts 16:34b, which put the prepositional phrase after "rejoiced" rather than after "believed in God."

174. See fn. 152, above.

175. Deut. 6:4.

176. Grebel devoted eleven theses to the question of household baptisms, and now in his twelfth point shifts to the "second basis" for Zwingli's doctrine of infant baptism: synecdoche.

177. Acts 8:5ff.

178. Acts 8:12.

179. The "Wittenberg sophist" refers to Erhard Hegenwald, who wrote to Conrad Grebel on Jan. 1, 1525. This letter (see 67D) does not deal with infant baptism, but Hegenwald writes that he had written several conclusions concerning baptism to Myconius, which Grebel could read (see 67D/329/38-39). It is likely that the cited interpretation of Acts 8:12 in the *confutatio* was taken from this lost letter to Myconius. This would add another substantial proof for Grebel's authorship of the *confutatio.*

180. See fn. 152, above.

181. The third of four references to Grebel as the *umbra* (see fns. 116, 148, and 195).

182. See fn. 179, above.

183. See fn. 152, above. Zwingli means that it would have been more appropriate to use Greek rather than Latin lettering.

184. Grebel here quotes a passage from Zwingli's *Antwort über Doctor Balthasars Taufbüchlein:* "Therefore this passage in Acts 2[:46-47] is also synecdoche, where it states that the believers were all together breaking bread and praying, etc., and there is nothing stated there about the children. But it is certain that they were counted in the number of the parents or else we are forced to think that the parents had forsaken their children when they became Christians. Not even animals do this" (ZW, IV, p. 631.16-31). Zwingli subsequently drew the conclusion, "Since it cannot be denied that their children came through the Red Sea, it cannot be denied that their children were baptized" (ZW, IV, p. 632.9-11).

185. See 63/290/36ff.

186. Acts 2:44. Grebel here proposes a radical communitarian structure of the church in which children would be treated as the shared responsibility of the community of believers.

187. Grebel's reference to the way "believers had all things in common" touched a sensitive nerve in Zwingli's responses concerning this previously debated but unresolved issue in their disputations: "community of goods" (see 69C/365/34-36, 71K/437/22-23, 36-37, 439, 23-24, 34). Zwingli here claims that this doctrine led the Anabaptists into "wives in common" and other sexual license, citing two stories of alleged adultery which are here omitted (but see Jackson, 1901, pp. 168-71).

188. See fn. 186, above.

189. Blanke (ZW, VI, p. 81, fn. 2) writes that "the designation of children as 'pledges' *(pignora)* of wedded love is found in Ovid and other poets of the Augustinian period."

190. Gen. 37:27.

191. Compare with 479/15-17, above.

192. "They" does not refer to the Anabaptists but to the stories Zwingli is about to tell about them (see fn. 187, above), which are not here included.

193. 2 Tim. 4:14.

194. For an English translation of the omitted text, see Jackson, 1901, pp. 168-71.

195. This is the fourth reference to Grebel as an *umbra* (see fns. 116, 148, and 181, above).

196. Wesen, or Weesen, on Lake Walen, in the canton of St. Gallen. Blanke (ZW, VI, p. 93, fn. 4) writes that "Zwingli's mention of an act of adultery in Wesen, as well as his quotation of Grebel, can be supported by no other sources."

197. See Eph. 4:4.

198. Acts 2:42, 46.

199. See fn. 152, above.

200. Zwingli refers to Parts 2 and 3, which follow.

201. The subject of *argutantur* ("are arguing") is *catabaptistae* ("Anabaptists") (line 6, above), by which Zwingli means the author of the *confutatio,* i.e., Grebel. When Zwingli says that this Anabaptist talks also about "covenant," he implies that the *confutatio* also dealt with the covenant concept which Zwingli had used to support his idea of infant baptism. It is evident from this that Zwingli had not so far abstracted all of the content of the *confutatio,* which still contained other points, especially concerning his use of the Old Testament in support of infant baptism. We can therefore conclude that his defense not only of the covenant idea but also of his doctrine of the election in Part 3 was directed specifically against Grebel. The content of Grebel's *confutatio,* therefore, included refutations of four of Zwingli's arguments for infant baptism: (1) household baptisms like the families of Stephanas and the Philippian jailer, (2) covenant, (3) synedoche, and (4) election.

202. Lat. *testamentum,* which together with *foedere* are the two words Zwingli used for "covenant." See 498/12-13 where the two words are given synonymously.

203. I.e., in part 3 (see p. 498, below).

204. Evidently, after the author of the *confutatio* had combatted Zwingli's argument that Acts 2:44 is to be interpreted as synedoche, he went on to Zwingli's second example of synecdoche, 1 Cor. 10:1ff., but Zwingli now wants "to draw to a close" (line 6, above) without excerpting any more from Grebel on this subject. He simply writes them off as "so foolish and faulty that they are not to be taken seriously."

205. This is evidently another quotation from the *confutatio* at the end of Grebel's refutation of Zwingli's second example of synecdochic interpretation, i.e., 1 Cor. 10:1-3. Compare with 496/33-35. The accusation that Zwingli was the enemy of truth was earlier expressed by Grebel in his last letter to Vadian (see 70/379/10-11 and 380/3-4). The assertion that Zwingli shied away from following the cross of Christ occurred again in the *Chronicle of the Hutterian Brethren* (see 68F/fn.37).

206. See fn. 152, above.

207. Refers to ZW, VI, p. 78, line 4, omitted from our excerpt of the *Elenchus.*

208. This refers to a comment Zwingli had made earlier in the *Elenchus* that "they promised also that [if we set up a church of believers only] our forces would be far superior to the army of unbelievers" (59A/278/16-17).

209. 1 Cor. 10:2-3. See above 490/35ff. and 497/19ff.

210. Zwingli had not yet exhausted the contents of the *confutatio,* but he interrupts his translation at this point to tackle the Confession of Faith drawn up by the Anabaptists at Schleitheim the previous February (1527). He resumes his replies to Grebel's *confutatio* in the third part to the *Elenchus,* where, however, for the sake of brevity, he fails to fulfill his promise "to put their words first, faithfully translated from the German into Latin" (480/23-24).

211. Zwingli refers to the seven articles of the "Brotherly Union of a Number of Children of God," the Schleitheim Confession of Faith. See Yoder, 1973, pp. 25-54.

212. Berchtold Haller enclosed a copy of the articles in a letter to Zwingli dated April 25, 1527, reporting that the Anabaptists who had recently come to Bern from Basel had already won a following of twenty persons, that a house search of these persons had brought the handwritten document to light, and that an evaluation of them by Zwingli would be appreciated (ZW, IX, No. 609, p. 104). Zwingli apparently received another handwritten copy of the articles at about the same time from Oecolampad (ZW, IX, No. 607, p. 101). See fn. 47,

above. Thus, his comment that the articles were already being widely distributed in such a short period of time.

213. For the English translation of Part 2 of the *Elenchus,* see Jackson, 1901, pp. 177-219.

214. The third and final part of the *Elenchus* embraced pp. 219-58 in Jackson's English edition. In this section, Zwingli attempts to refute not only Grebel's ideas regarding the subjects of covenant and election (in reply to the *confutatio),* but also some additional Anabaptist arguments against infant baptism. Part 3 also contains an appendix in which Zwingli alleged Anabaptist doctrines of soul sleep, universal salvation, multiple ministry, and spiritualism.

215. Lat. *de foedere sive testamento* (see fn. 202, above).

216. For the complete translation of this section of Zwingli's comments, see Jackson, 1901, pp. 219-27. It includes a detailed exposition of the covenant concept in the Bible on the basis of which and together with Zwingli's other writings on the subject Gottlob Schrenk wrote, "Zwingli is the person who revitalized the biblical idea of the covenant for Reformed theology." Johann Martin, on the other hand, commented critically about Zwingli's attempt "to justify infant baptism by the concept of the covenant." For the citations of these two commentaries see Blanke, ZW, VI, p. 155, fn. 3.

217. In this section, Zwingli speaks to fourteen additional quotations from the *confutatio* (see fn. 210, above), which however, Zwingli did not set apart so distinctly in dialogical format as in Parts 1 and 2, but he still identified them with the use of quotation marks. Therefore, for the sake of consistency and clarity, we here put these Anabaptist comments, which were undoubtedly also taken from Grebel's *confutatio,* in a similar dialogical format as found in Part 1, above. This quotation is actually placed in the context not of the *confutatio,* but of a hypothetical Anabaptist objection; but because it follows the projection of 497/17-18, above, it is evident that the sentence is a continuation of the arguments in the *confutatio.*

218. See Rom. 9:13.

219. This sentence was not set within quotation marks, and thus it is less clear in this instance that Zwingli is quoting directly from the *confutatio* or whether he is merely implying Anabaptist argument; but see ZW, VI, p. 165, fn. 1.

220. Gal. 2:21.

221. See Gal. 4:4; Eph. 1:10.

222. Lk. 16:22.

223. See Lk. 2:25-35.

224. See Jn. 5:24.

225. Lat. *umbrae ablatae sunt,* perhaps "shadows were tolerated."

226. Heb. 8:5; 10:1.

227. Lat. *testamentum* (see fn. 202, above).

228. See Heb. 9:11-14.

229. The text reads, "The Anabaptists object here that Paul wrote. . . . " Although there are no encircling quotation marks in this instance, it is evident that this represents another excerpt in the series on "covenant" from the *confutatio* (see ZW, VI, p. 170, fn. 1).

230. See Rom. 4:3; Gal. 3:6.

231. Zwingli's principle of correlation between the New Testament baptism and the Old Testament circumcision was first enunciated in his tract of December 1524 (see 67C/319/40-320/2 and 69C/366/32-34).

232. Blanke (ZW, VI, p. 172, fn. 1) points out that Zwingli first became aware of the parallelism of the Old Testament Passover meal and the New Testament communion in April 1525.

233. Zwingli was compelled to deal with the subject of election because Grebel, in one passage of the *confutatio,* had used election as an argument against infant baptism (see 501/35-36, below). Zwingli replies by arguing that election can indeed be seen as a basis for infant baptism. This is the first time in all of Zwingli's anti-Anabaptist writings that he uses election as an argument for infant baptism (see Blanke, VI, p. 172, fn.2).

234. See 498/13, above.

235. Although Zwingli states here that he did not intend to present full treatment of the doctrine of election, it is nevertheless his fullest treatment of the subject to date. Concerning his earlier references on the subject, see Bauer, II, p. 235, fn. 1, and p. 686ff. (See also the important passage in ZW, IX, p. 207, line 9ff.).

236. For an English translation of the arguments here omitted, see Jackson, 1901, pp. 237-40.

237. For the English translation of the text here omitted, see Jackson, 1901, pp. 241-44.

238. See 498/13, above.

239. According to Blanke (ZW, VI, p. 170, fn. 3) this sentence is an established legal formula to the effect that "privileges or exceptions do not necessarily establish precedents."

240. See Acts 8:37; 1 Jn. 5:10.

241. See Acts 8:9-25.

242. See Gal. 2:4.

243. See Ps. 7:9; Jer. 11:20.

244. Mt. 8:11.

245. See Mk. 26:16.

246. Lat. *Lydius lapis,* a flinty slate used as a touchstone when testing gold.

247. See 1 Cor. 1:17.

248. For the English translation of the text here omitted, see Jackson, 1901, pp. 246-47.

249. See 286/2-5 above.

250. Zwingli's four arguments that follow here appear for the first time in the *Elenchus.*

251. See Acts 15:1-29; Gal. 2:1-10.

252. See Acts 15:28.

253. See Gal. 2:11; Acts 15:22-31.

254. See above 490/35-36.

255. 1 Cor. 10:2-3.

256. This may have been another of Grebel's arguments against Zwingli's synecdochic interpretation of 1 Cor. 10:1ff. (see 497/16, above).

257. 1 Cor. 11:28.

258. See Ex. 16:13-14; 17:1-7.

259. See 1 Cor. 10:2.

260. See Gal. 6:13.

Epi. D. Joint Decree for the Suppression of the Anabaptists, Zurich, September 9, 1527

1. Bern did not attend the ratification session in Zurich on Sept. 9 but had sent a memorandum on Sept. 6, indicating general agreement with the decree as written Aug. 12-14. On Sept. 14, however, Bern withdrew its consent to the printing, but by this time the decree had already been printed with its name attached.

2. Ger. *ain sect und sündrung.* These were Zwingli's often-used terms for the Anabaptists (see 69C/fn.4, 367/25. 59A/fn.3, etc.).

3. See 68L/355/21 and 71G/428/29-30.

4. A reference to the ten public and private disputations with the Anabaptists (see 71M/fn.6).

5. See fn. 2, above.

6. See 71M/444/16, etc.

7. See 71M/444/16, etc.

8. Ger. *lanndtschafft und gebieten.* See fns. 34 and 35, below.

9. See Epi.C/495/37ff. and Epi.C/fn.194.

10. This is a reference to the Schugger slaying (see Epi.C/fn.23).

11. See 70A/381/41 and 71K/439/39-40.

12. Zwingli had appended a paragraph to the *Elenchus* (see Jackson, 1901, p. 256) regarding this allegation, in which he probably had Hans Denk's writings in mind (see Intro. to Epi.G, below).

13. See 68L/353/22, etc.

14. See 70A/381/16, etc. The rejection of the sword for personal defense was part of Articles IV and VI of the Schleitheim Confession to which Zwingli replied in the *Elenchus* (see

Jackson, 1901, pp. 189ff.).

15. See 70C/389/20-36.
16. See 51B/fn.10, 63/fn.54, 70/fn.17, 70C/389/31-35, 70F/fns. 30 and 31.
17. See 71K/fns. 10 and 17.
18. See 68H/345/22-30. The "no Christian can be a magistrate" was part of Article VI of the Schleitheim Confession. For Zwingli's response, see Jackson, 1901, pp. 197ff.
19. "No Christian may swear an oath" was Article VII of the Schleitheim Confession. For Zwingli's response, see Jackson, 1901, pp. 208ff.
20. See 67B/315/5ff. and 69C/368/17ff.
21. Ger. *ainer oder aine,* meaning "he or she."
22. Ger. *der oder die* (see fn. 21, above).
23. Ger. *unser bürger, underthanen und hindersessen.*
24. See fn. 21, above.
25. Ger. *insässen,* "inhabitants" or "tenants" (see fn. 22, above).
26. See fns. 2 and 5, above.
27. Ger. *der oder dieselbigen.* See fn. 22, above.
28. This was the first mandate of the execution of Anabaptists in the canons of Bern and St. Gallen. The mandate was in force until July 31, 1531, when a new one was written, providing the death penalty for illegal return to the canton following a second banishment. Zurich had first mandated execution on March 7, 1526 (see 71M/448/15-17).
29. See fn. 25, above.
30. See fn. 21, above.
31. Ger. *der oder dieselbigen* (see fn. 27, above).
32. See fn. 28, above.
33. Ger. *eingefürt und verfürt.*
34. Ger. *stett, landtschafft und gebieten* (see fns. 8 and 35).
35. Ger. *stett, landtschafften und commun* (see fns. 8 and 34).
36. Ger. *unsern lieben aydtgnossen.* Politically this included the Catholic cantons from whom the Protestant cantons were otherwise alienated over the issue of the Reformation. Actually, however, the invitation to the joint consultation had gone out only to the Protestant cantons of Basel, Schaffhausen, Chur, and Appenzell, in addition to the three who ratified the decree; and it is probably only these four who are here designated as "dear confederates."
37. Ger. *unsern obern- und unndervögten.*

Epi.E. The Fifth and Sixth Swiss Anabaptist Martyrs: Jacob Falk and Heine Reimann, Zurich, September 5, 1528

1. Acts 5:29.
2. Lk. 3:23.
3. Mt. 3:13.
4. Mt. 3:14.
5. Mt. 3:15.
6. Lk. 4:9.
7. Mk. 4:9.
8. Mt. 28:19.
9. Mk. 16:16.
10. See fn. 7, above.
11. Mk. 10:14.
12. Mk. 13:22.
13. Mt. 3:15.
14. Lk. 7:30.
15. Acts 2:38.
16. Acts 2:41.
17. Acts 8:36-38.
18. Acts 19:1-2a.
19. Acts 19:2b.

20. Acts 19:3a.
21. Acts 19:3b.
22. Acts 19:4.
23. Acts 19:5-7.
24. Eph. 4:4.
25. Rom. 6:2-4.
26. Rom. 6:19.
27. Mt. 18:15-18.
28. Rom. 8:4.
29. Gal. 5:22.
30. Rom. 12:5.
31. Gen. 17:4, 8, 10-12.
32. Mk. 1:11.
33. Mt. 17:5.
34. Mt. 11:13.
35. Rom. 10:4.
36. Heb. 10:9.
37. Jn. 14:6.
38. Jn. 10:7-8.
39. See fn. 11, above.
40. Mt. 12:33.
41. Free reference to Gal. 5:19-21, where fifteen vices are listed.
42. 2 Jn. 9.
43. One of his earliest and apparently still one of Zwingli's main arguments against the Anabaptists was that they sanctioned two baptisms without biblical precedent (see 681/347/ 22-23, 347/31-32, 348/5, etc.). One of the Anabaptist replies had lacked credibility, namely, that an isolated case of rebaptism can be found in the account of the dual baptism of John and Paul in Acts 19:1-7. An alternate reply, found already in 681/348/6-7, and repeated here by Falk and Reimann, is that infant baptism, which is really no baptism at all, is at the very most the rebaptism against which Zwingli argued.
44. See 71M/448/18ff.
45. The wording of this sentence of execution is nearly identical to that pronounced in the case of Felix Mantz on Jan. 5, 1527 (Quellen 1, No. 204, p. 226, lines 20-25, compared with No. 273, p. 290, bottom six lines).

Epi.F. The Preachers' Disputation with the Anabaptists, Bern, March 11-17, 1538
1. Peter Kuntz was one of the four pastors in Bern, having previously served as pastor in Erlenbach in the Simmental and in Zweisimmen. An early adherent of the Reformation, he accompanied Haller to the Baden Disputation in May 1526 between the Swiss Reformers and spokesmen for the Roman Catholic Church. He was active in the Doctrinal Disputation of Bern in January 1528.
2. Two of the main issues of the debate were the concept of the church and the call to the ministry *(die Sendung)*. The statement by Kuntz is reminiscent of one of the earliest discussions between Zwingli and Grebel in connection with the "Turning Point in the Zwinglian Reformation" (see 59A, above).
3. On Hans Hotz, see Cast of Characters No. 53.
4. Ger. *die bücher.* The reference is probably to the books of the Bible, published in the German vernacular in Zurich beginning in 1524. The Froschauer Testaments were originally reprints of Luther's translation edited for Swiss readers.
5. See fn. 13, below.
6. See Rom. 6:4.
7. Mt. 3:2.
8. Mt. 4:17; Mk. 1:15.
9. Acts 2:37.

10. Acts 2:38.

11. Grebel, Mantz, and Blaurock (see fn. 13, below).

12. Ger. *den erstenn töuffer oder den Grebel.*

13. Ger. *Grebell hatt mich zum erstenn gelertt.* Compare this to Hotz's testimony to the Zurich court in August 1528, "Der Blawrock habe inn zum ersten gelert unnd daby gesterckt, dessglichenn der Felix Mantz" ("Blaurock first taught him and also strengthened him, likewise Felix Mantz"). In these two testimonies, Hotz is referring to separate periods. The one goes back to Grebel's mission to Grüningen between late June and early October 1525, and the other refers to his imprisonment with Blaurock and Mantz in Zurich between Dec. 3, 1526, and Jan. 5, 1527, although Hotz probably also heard Blaurock in Grüningen on the latter's return from Chur in October 1525.

14. According to the manuscript version No. C (see Intro., above), Hotz's response was interrupted by a repetition of Kuntz's question, "Who commissioned Grebel?" To which Kuntz replied with the counter-question, "who commissioned Zwingli?" In the present text A, Hotz argues from his experience of faith a point he had tried to prove from the Bible in the 1532 Disputation at Zofingen (see Quellen IV, p. 80ff.).

15. Erasmus Ritter, see 69/fn.30 and Cast of Characters No. 76.

16. See 2 Cor. 11:13-14.

17. Gal. 1:8.

18. This question by Hotz is missing in manuscript versions A, B, and D, but is found in C.

19. Ger. *verendert* (verändert).

Epi.G. Vadian's Critique of the Lives of Grebel and other Anabaptists, St. Gallen, August 19, 1540

1. Lat. *delicatissime morosa et morosimmima delicata,* a typical humanist expression.

2. Vadian may have had Thomas Müntzer in mind, since he became the custodian of Grebel's undelivered letters to Müntzer of Sept. 5 and 6, 1524 (see 63 and 64, above).

3. See 70 and 70B, above.

4. Hans Denk, see Epi.C/fn.88. Denk attended Anabaptist meetings in St. Gallen in June 1525, at the time such meetings were being outlawed. Apparently he gave free expression to his ideas on Universalism while here. Fast (Quellen 2, p. 403, fn. 5 and p. 480, fn. 3) gives evidence for the thesis that Vadian knew Denk personally.

5. Origen (AD 185-251) was one of the great early church fathers, whose theology was an amalgamation of Christianity and Platonism. In his *De Principiis,* his main theological treatise, he taught that the nature of God is love, and that the divine mercy cannot be satisfied with partial salvation or everlasting punishment. This doctrine became heretical about the sixth century.

6. Ludwig Hätzer (see Cast of Characters No. 43), first encountered as the able recorder of the Second Zurich Disputation and author of its crucial study document on the worship of images. See also 68E, where he is banished from Zurich following the First Public Disputation on Baptism in January 1525. Thereafter, however, he was a marginal figure in the movement.

7. On Balthasar Hubmaier, see Cast of Characters No. 54 and 68/fn.7, when Hubmaier first rejected infant baptism following contacts with Grebel. Vadian met Hubmaier at the Second Disputation in Zurich in 1523, although he may have met him in St. Gallen at the end of April 1523, when Hubmaier preached here on the subject of baptism (see Fast, Quellen 2, p. 330, fn. 4), on his way to Zurich where he conferred with Zwingli on the same subject.

8. Aulus Persius Flaccus, AD 34-62, Roman satirical poet. In the first of his six satires (lines 193-94) he wrote, "Could this be borne! this cuckoo-spit of Rome, which gathers round the lips in froth and foam!"

9. Vadian is undoubtedly thinking of the Grebel family and himself as having married into it.

10. Phaethon, a son of Helios, god of the sun, was permitted for a day to drive the chariot of the sun across the heavens until Zeus struck him down with a thunderbolt to keep the earth from being set on fire.

Literature Cited
in Notes, by Abbreviation

Akten[sammlung]   Emil Egli, *Aktensammlung zur Geschichte der Zürcher Reformation in den Jahren 1519-1533.* Zürich, J. Schabelitz, 1879.

Allen   Percy S. Allen et al., eds., *Opus Epistolarum des Erasmi Roterdami,* 11 vols. Oxford: Clarendon Press, 1906-1947.

Aschbach   Joseph Aschbach, *Geschichte der Wiener Universität im ersten Jahrhundert ihres Bestehens.* Vienna, 1865.

Bender   Harold S. Bender, *Conrad Grebel: The Founder of the Swiss Brethren Sometimes Called Anabaptists.* Scottdale: Herald Press, 1950.

Bauer   August Bauer, *Zwinglis Theologie, Ihr Werden und ihr System,* 2 vols. Halle, 1885-88.

Berger   Peter Berger, *The Precarious Vision.* New York: Doubleday, 1961.

Bergsten   Torsten Bergsten, *Balthasar Hubmaier: Anabaptist Theologian and Martyr,* ed. W. R. Estep, Jr., Valley Forge: Judson Press, 1978.

Blakeney   E. J. Blakeney, ed., *A Small Classical Dictionary.* London: Dent & Sons, 1910.

Blanke   Fritz Blanke, *Brothers in Christ: The History of the Oldest Anabaptist Congregation, Zollikon, near Zurich, Switzerland.* Scottdale: Herald Press, 1961.

Bluntschli   J. C. Bluntschli, *Staats- und Rechtsgeschichte der Stadt und Landschaft Zürich,* Vol. I. Zürich: Orell, Fussli, 1838.

Böcking   Eduard Böcking, ed., *Ulrich von Hutten Schriften.* Aalen: Otto Zeller, 1963.

Bonarand   Conradin Bonarand, *Vadians Weg vom Humanismus zur Reformation und seine Vorträge über die Apostelgeschichte,* 1523. Vadian-Studien 7, St. Gallen, 1962.

Brändly, 1   Willy Brändly, "Täuferprozesse in XVI. Jahrhundert," *Zwingliana,* VIII, 1947, 67ff.

Brändly, 2   Willy Brändly, "Wann war Vadian auf dem Pilatus?" *Zwingliana,* VIII, 1947, 425ff.

Bromiley   G. W. Bromiley, ed., *Zwingli and Bullinger: Selected Translations with Introductions and Notes.* The Library of Christian Classics, XXIV. Philadelphia: Westminster Press, 1953.

Bullinger	Heinrich Bullinger, *Reformationsgeschichte nach dem Autographon*, eds., J. J. Hottinger and H. H. Vögeli, 3 vols. Frauenfeld, 1838-40.
Burrage	Henry S. Burrage, *A History of the Anabaptists in Switzerland.* Philadelphia: American Baptist Publication Society, 1882.
Claassen	W. Claassen, "Schweizer Bauernpolitik im Zeitalter U. Zwinglis," *Sozialgeschichtliche Forschungen*, eds. H. Bauer and M. J. Hartmann. Berlin, 1899.
Clasen	Claus-Peter Clasen, *Anabaptism: A Social History, 1525-1618.* Ithaca: Cornell University Press, 1972.
Clemen	Otto Clemen, "Ein Strassburger Sammeldruck von 1523," *Zeitschrift für Kirchengeschichte*, XLIII:VI, 1924, 219-26.
Collins	*Rudolf Collins Schilderung seines Lebens*, ed. Salomon Voegelin, Zürich, 1859.
Correll	Ernst Correll, *Das Schweizerische Täufermennonitentum.* Tübingen, 1925.
Correll-Bender, 1	Ernst Correll and H. S. Bender, "Conrad Grebel's Petition of Protest and Defense to the Zurich Council in 1524." *Goshen College Record Review Supplement*, January 1926, 23-32.
Correll-Bender, 2	Ernst Correll and H. S. Bender, "Conrad Grebel and Marx Bosshart's Petition to the Great Council of Zurich for a Letter of Safe Conduct," *Goshen College Record Review Supplement*, January 1926, 31-32.
Correll-Bender-Yoder, 1	Ernst Correll, H. S. Bender, and Edward Yoder, "A Letter of Conrad Grebel to Zwingli, September 8, 1517," *Goshen College Record Review Supplement*, January 1926, 33-37.
Correll-Bender-Yoder, 2	Ernst Correll, H. S. Bender, and Edward Yoder, "A Letter of Conrad Grebel to Andreas Castelberger, May 1525." *Mennonite Quarterly Review*, I, July 1927, 41-53.
Corrodi-Sulzer	Corrodi-Sulzer, "Das Haus zum Kroenenthor in Zürich," *Zürcher Taschenbuch auf das Jahr 1525.*
DLL	James. H. Mantinband, *Dictionary of Latin Literature.* New York: Philosophical Library, 1956.
Egli, 1877	Emil Egli, *Die St. Galler Täufer. Geschildert im Rahmen der stadtischen Reformationsgeschichte.* Zurich, 1887.
Egli, 1878	Emil Egli, *Die Züricher Wiedertäufer zur reformationszeit.* Zürich, 1878.
Egli, 1879	Emil Eli, ed., *Aktensammlung* (see Akten, above).
Egli, 1910	Emil Egli, *Schweizerische Reformationsgeschichte*, I: 1519-25. Zurich, 1910.
Egli-Schock	Emil Egli and Rudolf Schock, eds., *Johannes Kesslers Sabbata mit kleineren Schriften und Briefen.* St. Gallen: Historischen Verein, 1902.
Erasmus Letters	*The Correspondence of Erasmus*, mult. vols., eds. R. A. B. Mynors and D. F. S. Thomson. Toronto: University Press, 1974ff.
Erasmus Works	*The Collected Works of Erasmus*, ed. Craid R. Thompson, mult. vols. Toronto: University Press, 1978ff.

Farner, 1930	Alfred Farner, *Die Lehre von Kirche und Staat bei Zwingli.* Tübingen, 1930.
Farner, 1918	Oskar Farner, *Huldrych Zwinglis Briefe, 1512-26.* Zürich, 1918.
Farner, 1943ff.	Oskar Farner, *Huldrych Zwingli, Seine Verkündigung und ihre ersten Früchte, 1520-25.* Zürich: Zwingli-Verlag, 1943-60.
Fast, 1962	Heinold Fast, "Hans Krüsis Büchlein über Glauben und Taufe," *Zwingliana* XI:7, 1962, 456-75.
Fast, 1973	Heinold Fast, *Quellen zur Geschichte der Täufer in der Schweiz,* Vol. 2. Zürich: Theologischer Verlag, 1973.
Fast, 1975	Heinold Fast, "Reformation durch Provokation: Predigtstörungen in den ersten Jahren der Reformation in der Schweiz," in Goertz (see below), pp. 70-110.
Ferm	Vergilius Ferm, ed., *An Encyclopedia of Religion.* New York: The Philosophical Library, 1945.
Feyler	Anna Feyler, *Die Beziehungen des Hauses Württemberg zur Schweizerischen Eidgenössenschaft in der ersten Hälfte des 16. Jahrhunderts.* Zürich: Muller and Werder, 1905.
Fritzsche	Otto F. Fritzsche, *Glarean, Sein Leben und seine Schriften.* Frauenfeld: J. Huber, 1890.
Geschichtbuch	A. J. F. Zieglschmid, ed., *Die älteste Chronik der Hutterischen Brüder.* Philadelphia, 1943.
Goertz	Hans-Jurgen Goertz, ed., *Umstrittenes Täufertum 1525-75, Neue Forschungen.* Göttengen: Vandenhoeck and Ruprecht, 1975.
Goeters	J. F. Gerhard Goeters, "Die Vorgeschichte des Täufertums in Zürich," *Studien zur Geschichte und Theologie der Reformation,* eds. Luise Abramowski and J. F. Gerhard Goeters. Neukirchen-Vluyn: Neukirchener Verlag, 1969, pp. 239-81.
Götzinger	Ernst Götzinger, *Joachim Vadian, der Reformator und Geschichts-schreiber von St. Gallen.* Halle, 1895.
Guyer	Paul Guyer, *Verfassungszustände der Stadt Zürich im 16., 17., und 18. Jahrhundert unter der Einwirkung der sozialen Umschichtung der Bevölkerung.* Zurich: Schulthess, 1943.
Harder	Leland Harder, "Zwingli's Reaction to the Schleitheim Confession of Faith of the Anabaptists," *Sixteenth Century Journal,* XI:4, 1980, pp. 51-66.
Haas	Martin Haas, ed., *Quellen zur Geschichte der Täufer in der Schweiz.* IV. Zurich: theologischer Verlag, 1974.
Heller	Clarence Nevin Heller, ed., *The Latin Works of Huldreich Zwingli,* Vol. 2 (see Jackson, 1912, below). Philadelphia: Heidelberg Press, 1929.
Hershberger	Guy F. Hershberger, ed., *The Recovery of the Anabaptist Vision.* Scottdale: Herald Press, 1957.
Herzog	Johann J. Herzog, *Das leben Johannes Oekolampads und die Reformation der Kirche zu Basel,* 2 vols., 1843.
Hillerbrand, 1964	Hans J. Hillerbrand, ed., *The Reformation: A Narrative History related by Contemporary Observers and Participants.* New York: Harper & Row, 1964.

Hillerbrand, 1967	Hans J. Hillerbrand, *A Fellowship of Discontent.* New York: Harper & Row, 1967.
Hillerbrand, 1970	Hans J. Hillerbrand, ed., *Erasmus and His Age: Selected Letters of Desiderius Erasmus.* New York: Harper & Row, 1970.
Holborn	Hajo Holborn, *Ulrich von Hutten and the German Reformation,* tr. Roland Bainton. New York: Harper Torchbooks, 1966.
Horsch 1932, 1	John Horsch, "The Rise and Early History of the Swiss Brethren Church, 1: The Rise of State Church Protestantism," *Mennonite Quarterly Review,* VI, 1932, 169-91.
Horsch, 1932, 2	John Horsch, "The Rise and Early History of the Swiss Brethren Church, 2: The Beginnings in Zurich," *Mennonite Quarterly Review,* VI, 1932, 227-49.
Horsch, 1933, 1	John Horsch, "The Struggle between Zwingli and the Swiss Brethren in Zurich," *Mennonite Quarterly Review,* VII, 1933, 142-61.
Horsch 1933, 2	John Horsch, "The Swiss Brethren in St. Gall and Appenzell," *Mennonite Quarterly Review,* VII, 1933, 205-26.
Horsch, 1934	John Horsch, "An Inquiry into the Truth of the Accusations of Fanaticism and Crime against the Early Swiss Brethren," *Mennonite Quarterly Review,* VIII, 1934, 18-31, 73-89.
Jackson, 1900	Samuel Macauley Jackson, *Huldreich Zwingli: The Reformer of German Switzerland.* New York: G. P. Putnam's Sons, 1900.
Jackson, 1901	Samuel Macauley Jackson, ed., *Selected Works of Huldreich Zwingli.* Philadelphia: University Press, 1901.
Jackson, 1912.	Samuel Macauley Jackson, ed., *The Latin Works and Correspondence of Huldreich Zwingli, together with Selections from his German Works,* Vol. 1, 1510-1522. New York: Putnam's Sons, 1912.
Jones	Hugh P. Jones, ed., *Dictionary of Foreign Phrases and Classical Quotations.* Edinburgh: John Grant, Ltd., 1958.
Kauffman-Harder	J. Howard Kauffman and Leland Harder, *Anabaptists Four Centuries Later.* Scottdale: Herald Press, 1975.
Keller-Escher	Caspar Keller-Escher, *Die Familie Grebel: Blätter aus ihrer Geschichte gesammelt zur Erinnerung an die am 27. Oktober 1386 erfolgte Einbürgerung.* Fraunfeld, 1886.
Kessler	Johannes Kessler, *Sabbata* (see Egli-Schock, above).
Kidd	B. J. Kidd, ed., *Documents Illustrative of the Continental Reformation.* Oxford: Clarendon Press, 1911.
Köhler, 1962	Walther Köhler et al., *Ulrich Zwingli, Eine Auswahl aus seinen Schriften.* Zurich: Zwingli Verlag, 1962.
Köhler 1937	Walter Köhler, "Der Verfasser des Libellum Confutationis," *Mennonitische Geschichsblätter,* 2. Jahrgang, 1937.
Krajewski	Ekkehard Krajewski, *Leben und Sterben des Züricher Täuferführers Felix Mantz.* Kassel: J. G. Oncken Verlag, 1957.

Lang	August Lang, *Zwingli und Calvin*. Bielefeld & Leipzig: Welhagen & Klasing, 1913.
LW	*Luther's Works,* Vols. 1-54, ed. Jaroslav Pelikan *et al.* St. Louis: Concordia Publishing House, 1958-67.
ME	*Mennonite Encyclopedia,* ed. H. S. Bender *et al.,* 4 vols. Scottdale: Mennonite Publishing House, 1955-59.
Meyer	Carl S. Meyer, *Luther's and Zwingli's Propositions for Debate.* Leiden: E. J. Brill, 1963.
Miles	Herman Miles, *Die Chronik des Herman Miles.* St. Gallen: MVG, 1902, 275-386.
Milt	Bernhart Milt, *Vadian als Arzt,* Vadian-Studien 6. St. Gallen: Verlag der Fehr'schen Buchhandlung, 1959.
MQR	*Mennonite Quarterly Review,* published quarterly 1927ff. by the Mennonite Historical Society, Goshen, Indiana.
Muralt, 1929	Leonhard von Muralt, "Jörg Berger," *Zwingliana,* V, 1929-30, 66-71, 103-26.
Muralt, 1934	Leonhard von Muralt, "Zum Problem Reformation und Täufertum," *Zwingliana,* VI, 2, 1934, 65-85.
Muralt, 1937	Leonhard von Muralt, "Konrad Grebel als Student in Paris," *Zürcher Taschenbuch auf das Jahr 1937,* 113-36.
M[uralt]-S[chmid]	Leonhard von Muralt and Walter Schmid, *Quellen zur Geschichte der Täufer in der Schweiz,* Vol. 1 Zurich: Hirzel Verlag, 1952.
Näf	Werner Näf, *Vadian und seine Stadt St. Gallen,* 2 vols. St. Gallen: Fehr'sche Buchlandlung, 1944, 1957.
Nüesch-Bruppacher	Alexander Nüesch and Heinrich Bruppacher, *Das alte Zollikon.* Zurich, 1899.
Otto	A. Otto, *Die Sprichwörter und sprichwörtlichen Redensarten der Römer.* Leipzig: B. G. Teubner, 1890.
Potter, 1976	G. R. Potter, *Zwingli.* London: Cambridge University Press, 1976.
Potter, 1978	G. R. Potter, *Huldrych Zwingli.* London: Edward Arnold Ltd., 1978.
Quellen 1	Same as M[uralt]-S[chmid], above.
Quellen 2	Same as Fast, 1973, above.
Quellen 4	Same as Haas, above.
Rauschenbusch	Walter Rauschenbusch, "The Zürich Anabaptists and Thomas Müntzer," *American Journal of Theology,* IX, 1905, 91-106.
Reichenbach	Alicide Reichenbach, *The Christian Education of Youth,* translation of and introduction to Zwingli's *Quo pacto ingeui adolescentes formandi sint* of August 1, 1523. Collegeville: Thompson Brothers, 1899.
Rupp	Gordon Rupp, *Patterns of Reformation.* Philadelphia: Fortress Press, 1969
Rupp-Marlow	Gordon Rupp and A. N. Marlow, eds., *Luther and Erasmus: Free Will and Salvation.* Philadelphia: Westminster Press, 1969.

Ruth John L. Ruth, *Conrad Grebel, Son of Zurich.* Scottdale: Herald Press, 1975.

Sachsse C. Sachsse, *D. Balthasar Hubmaier als Theologie.* Berlin, 1914.

Schelbert Leo Schelbert, "Jacob Grebel's Trial Revised," *Archiv für Reformationsgeschichte,* 60:1, 1969, 32-64.

Schiff Otto Schiff, "Thomas Müntzer als Prediger in Halle," *Archiv für Reformationsgeschichte,* XXII, 1926.

Schlabach Erwin Schlabach, *The Rule of Christ Among the Early Swiss Anabaptists.* PhD Dissertation, Chicago Theological Seminary, 1978.

Schlatter Theodor Schlatter, "Die Exkursion Vadians an den Pilatussee," *Die Alpen,* Vol. 11, 1955, 263-65.

Schmid Walter Schmid, "Der Autor der sogenannten Protestation und Schutzscrift," *Zwingliana,* IX, 1, 1950, 139-49.

Schuler-Schultess Melchior Schuler and Johannes Schulthess, eds., *Huldreich Zwinglis Werke.* Zurich, 1828-42.

Schulte Aloys Schulte, *Geschichte der grossen Ravensburger Handelsgesellschaft, 1380-1530.* Stuttgard, 1924.

Segesser Anton P. von Segesser, ed., *Amtliche Sammlung der ältern Eidgenössischen Abschiede,* I-IV, Luzern, 1865-82.

Sehling Emil Sehling, *Die evangelsichen Kirchenordnungen des 16. Jahrhunderts,* I. Leipzig, 1903.

Sider Ronald J. Sider, *Andreas Bodenstein von Karlstadt: The Development of His Thought, 1517-25.* Leidin: Brill, 1974.

Simon Karl Simon, "Die Züricher Täufer und der Hofgoldschmied Kardinal Albrechts," *Zwingliana,* VI:1, 1934, 50-54.

Smith William Smith, *Classical Dictionary of Biography, Mythology, and Geography.* London: John Murray, 1868.

Staehelin Rudolf Staehelin, *Huldreich Zwingli, sei Leben und Wirken,* 2 vols. Basel, 1895, 1897.

Staub Max Staub, *Die Beziehungen des Täufers Conrad Grebel zu seinem Schwager Vadian auf Grund ihres Briefwechsels.* Zürich, 1895.

Stayer James M. Stayer, *Anabaptists and the Sword.* Lawrence: Coronodo Press, 1972.

Strickler Johannes Strickler, ed., *Die Eidgenössischen Abschiede aus dem Zeitraume von 1521 bis 1528,* IV. Brugg: Fisch, Wild, und Co., 1813.

Studer Bernard Studer, *Geschichte der physischen Geographie der Schweiz bis 1815.* Bern, 1863.

VB Emil Arbenz and Hermann Wartmann, eds., *Die Vadianische Briefsammlung der Stadtbibliothek St. Gallen,* Vols. I-VII. St. Gallen: Historischer Verein, 1888-1913.

Vedder Henry C. Vedder, *Balthasar Hubmaier: The Leader of the Anabaptists.* New York: Putnam's Sons, 1905.

Walton Robert C. Walton, *Zwingli's Theocracy.* Toronto: University Press, 1967.

Weber P. X. Weber, *Der Pilatus und seine Geschichte.* Luzern, 1913.

Wenger,   J. C. Wenger, *Even Unto Death: The Heroic Witness of the*
1961   *Sixteenth Century Anabaptists.* Richmond: John Knox
                   Press, 1961.
Wenger,   J. C. Wenger, *Conrad Grebel's Programmatic Letters of 1524.*
1970   Scottdale: Herald Press, 1970.
Williams,   George H. Williams, ed., *Spiritual and Anabaptist Writers:*
1957   *Documents Illustrative of the Radical Reformation.* The Li-
                   brary of Christian Classics, Vol. XXV. Philadelphia:
                   Westminster Press, 1957.
Williams,   George H. Williams, *The Radical Reformation.* Philadelphia:
1962   Westminster Press, 1962.
Wyss   Bernhard Wyss, *Chronik des Bernhard Wyss 1519-30*, ed.,
                   Georg Finsler. Quellen zur Schweizerischen Reforma-
                   tionsgeschichte, I. Basel, 1901.
Yoder,   Edward Yoder, "Nine Letters of Conrad Grebel," *Mennonite*
1928   *Quarterly Review*, II, 1928, 229-59.
Yoder,   Edward Yoder, "Conrad Grebel as Humanist," *Mennonite*
1929   *Quarterly Review*, III, 1929, 132-46.
Yoder,   John H. Yoder, "The Turning Point in the Zwinglian
1958   Reformation," *Mennonite Quarterly Review*, XXII:2,
                   1958, 128-40.
Yoder,   John H. Yoder, "Balthasar Hubmaier and the Beginnings of
1959   Swiss Anabaptism," *Mennonite Quarterly Review*,
                   XXXIII:1, 1959, 5-17.
Yoder,   John H. Yoder, Täufertum und Reformation in der Schweiz, I:
1962   *Die Gespräche zwischen Täufern und Reformatoren, 1523-*
                   38. Karlsruhe, 1962.
Yoder,   John H. Yoder, *Täufertum und Reformation im Gespräch.*
1968   Basler Studien zur historischen und systematischen
                   Theologie, Bd. 13. Zurich, 1968.
Yoder,   John H. Yoder, "The Evolution of the Zwinglian Reforma-
1969   tion," *Mennonite Quarterly Review*, XLIII:1, 1969, 95-122.
Yoder,   John H. Yoder, *The Legacy of Michael Sattler.* Scottdale:
1973   Herald Press, 1973.
ZW   Emil Egli et al., *Huldreich Zwinglis sämtliche Werke*, I-XIV.
                   Corpus Reformatorum Vols. 88-101. Berlin and Leipzig,
                   1905-1959.
Zwingliana   *Zwingliana, Beiträge zur Geschichte Zwinglis, der Reformation*
                   und des Protestantismus in der Schweiz, mult. vols., 1897ff.

Index of Biblical References

NOTE: The first reference refers to Genesis chapter 1, verses 14-16, document 47D, note 6, pages 181 and 636. Sometimes only pages are given.

20:25-27 (387)
22:29 (67C/19; 319, 697)
23:5 (71P/6; 454, 746)
23:14 (56/4; 225, 654)
24 (412)
24:6 (65/25; 296, 687)
24:15 (66A/3; 300, 689)
24:15 (52/10; 208, 648)
24:16, 24 (71G/10; 429, 736)
24:42 (401)
25:1ff. 59A/20; 279, 674)
25:1-13 (239)
25:24 (Epi.C/43; 481, 760)
25:41 (Epi.C/88; 486, 762)
26 (287)
26:26 (67E/65; 329, 702)
26:26 (57C/66; 247, 663)
26:26-28 (57C/49; 245, 662)
26:26-29 (57A/47; 231, 657)
26:26-29 (270)
26:39-44 (57A/40; 230, 657)
27:2 (3A/5; 65, 585)
28 (65A/6; 298, 687)
28 (298)
28:18-20 (428)
28:19ff. (366)
28:19 (Epi.E/8; 514, 771)
28:19 (67B–13; 312, 695)
28:19; 67C/25; 319, 697)

Mark
1:9ff. (312)
1:11 (Epi.E/32; 517, 772)
1:15 (Epi.F/8; 521, 772)
2:28 (67E/63; 329, 702)
4:9 (Epi.E/7; 514, 771)
5:22-24,35b (427)
5:25-26a,27a,28,34a (427)
6:3 (69B/1; 362, 719)
9:33-37 (63/79; 290, 682)
9:36 (Epi.C/75;484/761)
9:40 (59A/14; 278, 674)
9-10 (290)
10:13-16 (63/79; 290, 682)
10:14 (Epi.E/11; 515, 771)
10:14 (65A/7; 298, 687)
10:15 (70/20; 379, 724)
10:16 (Epi.C/75; 484, 761)
10:16 (307)
10:18 (57A/37; 230, 657)
10:25 (52B/11; 215, 649)
13:7 (65/25; 296, 687)
13:7 (65/24; 296, 686)
13:9 (52B/4; 214, 649)
13:13 (19A/7; 113, 605)
13:14 (52/10; 208, 648)
13:22 (Epi.E/12; 515, 771)
14 (287)
14:22 (67E/65; 329, 702)
14:22 (57C/66; 247, 663)
14:22-24 (57C/49; 245, 662)

14:22-24 (244)
14:22-25 (270)
14:26 (63/33; 286, 678)
16:15b-16a (47D/9; 182, 636)
16:15-16 (428)
16:16 (309)
16:16 (65A/6; 298, 687)
16:16 (67B/14; 312, 695)
16:16 (68F/36; 342, 709)
16:16 (Epi.E/9; 514, 771)

Luke
1:26-29,31,35a,38a (427)
1:33 (Epi.C/88; 486, 762)
2:21, 3:21 (67B/24; 314, 695)
2:25-35 (Epi.C/223; 500, 769)
3:9 (312)
3:21-23a (428)
3:23 (Epi.E/2; 514, 771)
3:23-38 (Epi.C/77; 484, 761)
4:9 (Epi.E/6; 514, 771)
6:5 (67E/63; 329, 702)
6:13 (391)
6:35 (52B/14; 215, 649)
6:35 (52B–8; 214, 649)
7:29-30 (428)
7:30 (Epi.E/14; 515, 771)
9 (51A/17; 199, 646)
9:35 (67E/34; 327, 699)
10:2 (67/24; 302, 692)
10:5-7 (57A/46; 231, 657)
10:7 (396)
10:8 (47D/30; 185, 637)
12:4 (71E/48; 425, 735)
12:4 (52B/5; 214, 649)
12:49 (19A/12; 113, 605)
12:49 (19A/13; 113, 605)
12:49-50 (428)
13:1-5 (Epi.C/74; 484, 761)
14:5 (238)
14:26 (19A/14; 113, 605)
16:15 (67E/17; 325, 699)
16:22 (Epi.C/222; 499, 767)
17:5 (57A/42; 230, 657)
18 (290)
18:15 (65A/7; 298, 687)
18:15-17 (63/79; 290, 682)
18:17 (70/20; 379, 724)
18:25 (52B/11; 215, 649)
19:9 (Epi.C/78; 484, 761)
21:12 (52B/4; 214, 649)
21:19 (56:12; 226, 655)
22 (287)
22:17-19 (57C/49; 245, 662)
22:19 (67E/65; 329, 702)
22:19 (57C/66; 247, 663)
22:29ff. (244)

John
1:4 (312)
1:4 (67B/12; 312, 695)
1:26 (304)
1:27 (305)
1:29 (67B/11; 312, 695)
1:29 (305)
1:29 (67B/12; 312, 695)
1:30-31 (305)
1:47-50 (427)
3 (293)3:1ff. 67E/65; 329, 702)
3:5 (428)
3:16-18a (427)
3:20 (Epi.C/51; 481, 760)
3:22 (428)
3:34 (407)
5:24 (Epi.C/224; 500, 769)
5:39 (411)
5:39,46 (238)
6:25ff. (67E/65; 329, 702)
6:52-63 (63/37; 287, 679)
6:63 (67E/53; 328, 700)
6:67-69 (427)
8:31-32 (48/18, 190, 640)
8:32b,36 (47D/10, 182, 636)
8:44 (Epi.C/83; 484, 761)
8:44 (409)
8:56 (499)
9:1ff. (309)
9:35ff. (309)
9:36 (67C/39; 320, 698)
10:1 (47D/12; 182, 636)
10:1 (47D/13; 182, 636)
10:1,8 (54A/17; 223, 653)
10:1,8 (71K/46; 440, 740)
10:7-8 (Epi.E/38; 517, 772)
10:11-30 (401)
10:14 (68F/59; 342, 710)
10:34 (548)
11:25-26b (427)
12:47-49 (238)
13:17 (262)
13:15 (371)
13:35 (19A/9; 113, 605)
14 (413)
14:1ff. (57A–43, 230, 657)
14:6 (Epi.E/37; 517, 772)
14:21 (19A/9; 113, 605)
15 (412)
15:10 (548)
16 (51A/19; 200, 646)
16:2 (19A/8; 113, 605)
16:8 (67E/15; 325, 699)
16:23 (57A/41; 230, 657)
16:33 (19A/6; 113, 605)
17:19 (Epi.C/105; 487, 763)
17:20 (Epi.C./102; 487, 763)
17:20 (487)
18:14,28 (57A/10; 227, 656)
19:30 (57C/73; 248, 664)
19:34 (57C/69; 247, 663)

786

1:17 (Epi.C/247; 503, 770)
2:2 (67E/35; 327, 699)
2:15 (408)
3:1ff. (58B/27; 272, 671)
3:10-15 (57A/17; 228, 656)
3:13-15 (394)
4:10 (70/19; 379, 724)
5:5 (63/69; 290, 681)
5:7-8 (501)
6:2ff. (71E/38; 424, 735)
7 (320)
7:7 (373)
7:14 (307)
7:14 (308)
7:14 (67C/37; 320, 698)
7:15 (57A/50; 232, 658)
7:16 (308)
8 (327)
8:1ff. (308)
8:1 (57A/51; 232, 658)
8:2a (67E/36; 327, 699)
8:2b (67E/38; 237, 700)
9:5 (400)
9:24 (19A/16; 114, 605)
10:1 (505)
10:1ff. (Epi.C/204; 497, 768)
10:1ff. (Epi.C/256; 504, 770)
10:1-3 (497)
10:1-3 (Epi.C/152; 490, 776)
10:1-3 (Epi.C/205; 497, 768)
10:1-4 (Epi.C/39; 480, 759)
10:2 (427)
10:2 (Epi.C/259; 505, 770)
10:2,3 (504)
10:2-3 (Epi.C/209; 498, 768)
10:2-3 (Epi.C/255; 504, 770)
10:11 (287)
10:12 (19A/27; 115, 606)
10:16-22 (63/38; 287, 679)
10:18 (501)
11 (287)
11 (321)
11:5 (400)
11:12ff. (57A/49; 232, 658)
11:20-29 (63/38; 287, 679)
11:22 (397)
11:23 (57C/66; 247, 663)
11:23-26 (244)
11:23-29 (270)
11:24 (67E/65; 329, 702)
11:24b (57C/48; 244, 662)
11:25 (57A/47; 231, 657)
11:27-29 (51/20; 195, 644)
11:28 (67C/40; 321, 698)
11:28 (Epi.C/257; 504, 770)
11:29 (63/40; 288, 679)

11:34 (397)
11:34 (57A/48; 231, 658)
12 (318)
12:2 (67C/17; 318, 697)
12:6 (58/15; 256, 668)
12:10 (62/8; 283, 676)
12:28 (407)
12:29 (403)
12:29 (408)
13:7 (58B/31; 272, 671)
13:13 (427)
14 (289)
14 (290)
14:5 (402)
14:9,16 (63/23; 286, 678)
14:11,17,26 (57A/29; 229, 657)
14:13 (63/22; 286, 678)
14:20 (63/79; 290, 682)
14:26 (401)
14:26-33 (393)
14:26-33 (392)
14:29 (364)
14:30-33 (393)
14:31 (406)
14:31 (400)
14:33 (406)
14:35-36 (400)
14:36 (63/63; 289, 681)
15:22,45 (67E/74; 330, 703)
16:15 (Epi.C/40; 480, 759)
16:15 (Epi.C/153; 491, 766)
16:15-16 (Epi.C/142; 490, 765)
16:15-16 (Epi.C/151; 490, 765)

2 Corinthians
3 (289)
3:3 (63/59; 289, 681)
3:6 (71R/2; 455, 747)
3:17 (260)
4:13 (57A/12; 228, 656)
5:17 (57A/11; 227, 656)
5:17 (51/19; 195, 644)
11:4 (Epi.C/84; 485, 761)
11:13-14 (Epi.F/16; 522, 773)
11:14 (408-409)
11:24ff. (57A/39; 230, 657)
12:7 (57A/39; 230, 657).

Galatians
1:6ff. (67C/55; 245, 662)
1:6-8 (Epi.C/84; 485, 761)
1:8 (67B/26; 314, 696)
1:8 (485)
1:8 (Epi.F/17; 522, 773)
1:10 (19A/19; 114, 606)
2:1-10 (Epi.C/251; 504, 770)
2:2 (402)

2:2ff. (Epi.C/168; 493, 767)
2:4 (Epi.C/242; 502, 770)
2:11 (Epi.C/253; 504, 770)
2:16 (427)
2:21 (Epi.C/220; 499, 769)
3:2 (382)
3:7 (500)
3:13 (548)
3:15 (57C/55; 245, 662)
3:27 (51/19; 195, 644)
4:4 (Epi.C/221; 449, 769)
4:22-37 (498)
4:30 (Epi.C/126; 488, 764)
5 (316)
5:13 (67C/4; 316, 696)
5:19-21 (Epi.E/41; 518, 772)
5:22 (Epi.E/29; 516, 772)
6:1 (67E/22; 326, 699)
6:2 (67E/78; 330, 703)
6:9 (409)
6:13 (Epi.C/260; 505, 770)

Ephesians
1:3-8 (503)
1:10 (Epi.C/221; 499, 769)
1:17 (67E/22; 326, 699)
4:2 (67E/77; 330, 703)
4:3 (57A/24; 229, 657)
4:4 (Epi.C/197; 496, 768)
4:4 (Epi.E/24; 516, 772)
4:4a,5-6 (427)
4:11 (392)
4:11 (401)
4:11-14 (390)
4:11 (394)
4:11 (407)
4:11 (62/8; 283, 676)
4:14 (Epi.C/19; 479, 758)
4:17ff. (57A/29; 229, 657)
4:22-24 (531)
4:22-24 (67B/22; 314, 695)
4:24 (51/19; 195, 644)
5 (287)
5:19 (63/22; 280, 678)
5:19 (63/24; 287, 678)
6:5-9 (405)
6:11ff. (19A/10; 113, 605)

Philippians
1:1-2 (68J/2; 350, 711)
1:21 (427)
2:4 (52/13; 208, 649)
2:21 (52/13; 208, 649)
3:2 (387)
3:13 (67E/27; 326, 699)
3:13-14 (19A/17; 114, 605)
3:16 (364)
3:16 (397)
3:19 (389)

Colossians
1 (327)

1:9-10 (67E/40; 327, 700)
1:11 (67E/39; 327, 700)
1:22 (264)
2 (319)
2 (359)
2:11 (306)
2:11 (67C/30; 319, 697)
2:11 (501)
2:11 (505)
2:12 (427)
2:17 (57A/11; 227, 656)
2:18 (365)
2:18 (389)
3 (287)
3 (289)
3:10 (51/19; 195, 644)
3:11 (57A/28; 229, 657)
3:13 (67E/77; 330, 703)
3:16 (63/22; 286, 678)
3:16 (63/25; 287, 678)
3:16 (63/26; 287, 678)
3:16 (63/63; 289, 681)
3:16 (67E/76; 330, 703)
4:17 (409)

1 Thessalonians
1:9 (67C/17; 318, 697)
3:2 (Epi.C/3; 478, 756)
5:14 (67E/79; 330, 703)

2 Thessalonians
3:15 (67E/79; 330, 703)

1 Timothy
1:18-20 (427)
1:2b (63/2; 285, 276)
2:2 (402)
3:3 (49/13; 191, 641)
3:4 (395)
3:5 (395)
4 (403)
5:20 (47D/14; 182, 636)
6:2 (405)

2 Timothy
1:2b (63/2; 285, 676)
2 (317)

2:10 (65/14; 295, 685)
2:23 (67C/12; 317, 696)
2:24 (67E/79; 330, 703)
3:16 (48/11; 190, 640)
4:2 (394)
4:5 (394)
4:14 (Epi.C/193; 495, 767)

Titus
1:4b (63/2; 285, 676)
1:5 (405)
1:5-9 (395)
1:11 (71G/6; 428, 736)
1:12 (34/8; 145, 622)
1:14 (366)

Hebrews
2:12 (63/22; 286, 678)
5:14 (58B/27; 272, 671)
5:14 (Epi.C/103; 487, 763)
6 (382)
6:1-6 (427)
7:15ff. (244)
8 (289)
8:5 (Epi.C/226; 500, 769)
8:5 (500)
8:10 (63/61; 289, 681)
9:11ff. (244)
9:11-14 (Epi.C/228; 500, 769)
10:1 (57A/11; 227, 656)
10:1 (57A/13; 228, 656)
10:1 (500)
10:1 (Epi.C/226; 500, 769)
10:9 (Epi.E/36; 517, 772)
13:14 (47E/17; 187, 638)
13:17 (52B/25; 217, 650)

James
1:17 (Epi.C/28; 480, 758)
3:1 (408)
5:13 (63/22; 286, 678)

1 Peter
1:7 (427)
1:13-25 (67C/15; 317, 697)
2 (290)

2:1-12 (67C/15; 317, 697)
2:2 (63/79; 290, 682)
2:5,9 (408)
2:6-8 (427)
2:7 (47D/7; 181, 636)
2:13-18 (405)
3:3-29 (67C/15; 317, 697)
3:21 (67C/31; 320, 697)
3:21 (310)
3:21 (320)
4:1-19 (67C/15; 317, 697)

2 Peter
2:1 (71G/11; 429, 736)
3:10,12 (70/9; 379, 723)

1 John
1:8 (69C/10; 364, 720)
1:8 (353)
2 (413)
2:19 (364)
2:19 (Epi.C/60; 481, 760)
4 (328)
4:1 (410)
4:1 (67E/14; 325, 699)
4:1 (71G/11; 429, 736)
5 (318)
5:10 (Epi.C/240; 502, 770)
5:21 (67C/17; 318, 697)
10 (67C/11; 317, 696)

2 John
9 (Epi.E/42; 518, 772)

Revelation
5:9 (63/22; 286, 678)
9:1-11 (47D/30; 185, 637)
12:3ff. (70D/3; 410, 729)
13 (435)
13:10 (69/17; 357, 716)
16:13 (71G/10; 429, 736)
17:13,14,17 (69/32; 358, 717)
19:20 (71G/10; 429, 736)
20:10 (71G/10; 429, 736)
22:18-19 (57C/70; 247, 663)

General Index

Aarburg, 466, 472, 519, 752
Aargau, 572, 642
Aaron, 293
Aarwaggen, 519
Abbot of Cappel, 276, 352, 357, 665, 666, 672, 716
Abbey (Abbot) of St. Gallen, 423, 555, 556, 563, 640, 658, 727, 730, 733
Abbot of Rüti, 730
Abbot of Wettingen, 208, 565, 566
Aberli, Heinrich, 166, 168, 170-171, 175, 177, 203-206, 292, 294, 447, 527, 534, 546, 550-551, 558, 560-561, 569, 572, 633, 635-636, 647, 683-684, 744
Ab-Iberg, Caspar, 528
Ab-Iberg, Fridli, 446-447, 450, 452, 528, 743-744, 746
abominable fates, 72
abomination, 456, 648, 689
Abraham, 181, 306, 319-320, 366, 490, 499
Abraham's children, 320, 500
absolution, 214, 382, 532, 714-715
abuse of elders, 653
abyss of Fortune, 93
Achilles, 111, 143, 599, 605, 638
Adagia, 595-596, 599, 602, 633
Adam, 240, 330, 335
adoration of Mary, 172
Adrian VI, Pope, 564
adult baptism, 377, 434, 568, 681
adultery, 438, 440, 508
advocate, 188-189
aegis-bearer, 110, 605

Aegeria, 590
Aeneas, 134, 596, 616
Aeneid, 596, 614, 616
Africa, 109, 114, 317
Aeschylus, 599
Aesculapius, 141, 620
Aesop, 120, 609
Agammemnon, 599, 756
age of accountability, 381, 682, 764
age of the Lord, 410
Aglaia, 590
Agricola, Rudolph, 58, 580, 582, 588
Ahenarius, 554
ailment, Grebel's, 61, 67, 71, 77, 79, 86-87, 102-103, 135-136, 140, 142-143, 148, 154-155, 224, 284, 357, 586, 596, 602, 617, 620, 628, 654, 676, 683, 716
Ajax, 187, 638
Atlantsee, Lucas, 49, 150, 580, 619, 626, 628
Albert the Great, 54
Alcibiades, 145, 622
Alcmene, 616
Aldine Press, 56, 101, 578, 580, 602
Alexander the Great, 53, 163, 495, 578, 624
Alexander of Abnoteiches, 720
Aleander, 624
A'Liliis, 69, 605
Allen, P. S., 536, 589
Allstedt, 285, 559, 683
Alphonso, the Magnanimous, 578
Alsace, 553, 580, 610, 622, 638
Alstätten, 533
altburgomaster, 570
Altenbach, Hans, 532
alter ego, 90

Amalthea, 579, 605
deAbroise, Lord, 469
Ambrose, 663
ambrosia, 52, 577
Ambrosius, Captain, 194, 644
Amgrüt, Joachim, 337, 738
Ammann, John Jacob, 84-87, 147, 157, 186, 208, 282, 528, 535, 541, 567, 586, 592, 595, 624, 630, 638, 649, 670, 675, 718
Amphictyons, 576
Anabaptism, 112, 211, 359-360; 370, 374-375, 377, 418-419, 431, 442, 445-446, 456, 506-509, 511, 534, 536, 538, 547-548, 551, 555, 568, 577, 673, 694, 719, 722, 727, 732, 756-757
Anabaptist(s), 213, 235, 297, 334-335, 344, 353-354, 361-362, 367-368, 371-372, 377, 381-385, 387, 389, 393-394, 402, 415, 418, 423, 428, 430, 432-435, 437, 443, 448, 453-454, 456, 458, 472, 474, 476, 478-480, 497, 500-502, 505-511, 513, 528, 532-533, 541, 546, 554, 653, 661, 673, 679, 727, 757
Anabaptist beginnings in St. Gallen, 297-298
Anabaptist brethren, 355
Anabaptist church, 338
Anabaptist dissent, 337
Anabaptist doctrines, 534
Anabaptist movement, 204, 367, 674
Anabaptist position, 333
Anabaptist ringleaders, 449, 745, 748
Anabaptist washings, 490

789

795

Haupterneurer, 573
"head in hell," 487, 755
heathen, 214, 361, 383
Hebrew(s), 51, 115, 186,
    237, 264, 342, 392, 402-
    403, 331, 501, 529, 558,
    710, 728
Hedinger, Jörg, 70, 74, 465-
    466, 468-472, 544, 586-
    587, 589, 750-752, 754
Hedinger, Konrad, 618
Hedio, 602-603, 608
Hedylus, 642
Hege, Christian, 426
Hegenwald, Erhart, 22, 30,
    196, 322-331, 324, 478,
    558, 645, 675, 684, 698-
    702, 767
Heidelberg, 580
Heigerlin, 645
Heiligmaier, Wolfgang, 68,
    81, 587
Heine, 712
Heingarter, Hans, 446-447
Hekate, 758
Helbing, Peter, 467-468,
    471, 752-753
Helen, 584
Heliogabalus, 454
Helios, 774
Heller, 705
Helvetian, 59, 576
hemp seed, 462
hen's milk, 56
Hera, 583, 590, 616
Hercules, 114, 135, 157,
    188, 191, 255, 583, 597,
    606, 616, 629, 641, 667
heresy, 168, 190, 198, 505,
    524, 538, 708, 711, 721,
    758
heretic(s), 114, 198, 348-
    349, 363-364, 367-368,
    424, 681, 720-721
heretical (church, sects,
    violence), 191, 732, 505,
    682
heretical justice, 421-422,
    732
Heretics Tower, 741
heremeneutical principle,
    657, 663, 678-679, 720,
    761
Hermes, 60, 603
Hermoleos, 583
Herodotus, 580
Herrliberg Forest, 177, 512,
    538
Hershberger, Guy F., 18,
    673
Herzog, Hans, 514, 682
Hesse, 556

Hexenturm, 352
Hickey-Williams, John, 22-
    23, 50
Hilary, 114
Hillerbrand, Hans, 166,
    187, 235, 608, 661, 676,
    680, 704, 706-707, 758
Hilwil, 412-415, 418, 420-
    422, 429-430, 529, 537,
    722, 730, 732, 737
Hinwiler, John, 81, 582, 593
Hippocrates, 643
Hirslanden, 209, 343, 349,
    412, 556, 634, 648, 744,
    710, 722
History, Livy's, 137
Historia Naturalis, 580
Hochrütiner, Lorenz, 203-
    206, 232-233, 254-256,
    280, 297-298, 359-360,
    363, 520, 527, 544, 560,
    566, 568, 647, 653, 664-
    667, 675, 687
Hochrütiner, Jacob, 520,
    544
Hof, 430
Hoffman, Rudolf, 666
Hofmann, Conrad, 174,
    279, 564, 666
Hofmann, Melchior, 340
Hofmeister, Sebastian, 350-
    351, 433, 436, 438-439,
    520, 534-535, 544, 564,
    659-660, 664, 696, 712,
    717, 738-740
von Hohenlandenberg,
    Hugo, 178, 180, 197-198,
    545, 571, 620, 636, 642,
    645
Holbein, Hans, 559
Holborn, 607, 651, 686
holiness, 479
holocaust, 525
holokosmos, 29, 149, 154,
    161-162, 622, 625, 631-
    632
Holtzhalben, 70, 586
holy days, 86
holy fathers, 200
Holy Roman Empire
    (emperor), 558, 579-580,
    593, 601, 617, 683, 732
Holy Scriptures, 271, 336,
    377
Holy Spirit, 190, 198, 201,
    216, 249, 307, 365, 501,
    504
Holzwart, Jacob, 737
Hombrechtikon, 420
Homer, 72, 102, 110, 576,
    588, 596, 602-605, 607,
    609, 620-621, 624, 632,

639, 686
Homeric Thunderer, 110
Homer's Achilles, 143
Homer's *Iliad,* 630
Homer's *Odyssey,* 583, 599
Homer's poems, 581
Höngg, 170, 208, 233, 276,
    278, 436-437, 565-566,
    633, 662, 666, 672, 727,
    739
Höngg congregation, 634
Hör, Clemens, 621
Horace, 53, 358, 540, 578,
    598, 626, 630-631, 640-
    641, 718, 766
Horb, 562
Horgeberg, 451, 561
Horgen, 452, 666
Horner, Felix, 348
Horner, Heine, 348
Horsch, John, 707, 738
horse(s), 65-66, 107, 109,
    122, 125, 146, 148, 161,
    191, 468, 480, 603, 613,
    758
horseback, 65, 159
Hospital Church, 543, 703,
    738-739
Hottinger, 256, 344, 376,
    439, 560, 635, 664
Hottinger, Claus, 166, 168-
    171, 175, 177, 233, 527,
    545-546, 548, 561, 566-
    567, 633-634, 636, 666,
    696
Hottinger, Conrad, 349,
    548
Hottinger, Elizabeth (of
    Hirslanden), 446
Hottinger, Elizabeth, 447,
    744
Hottinger family, 743
Hottinger, Hans, 346-347,
    410, 413, 445, 447, 527,
    546, 548, 551, 556, 671,
    711, 723, 729-730, 743,
    772
Hottinger, Heini, 451, 513,
    723, 743, 746
Hottinger, Jacob, 169-170,
    332, 343-344, 458, 411-
    412, 513, 527-528, 530,
    545-546, 548, 561, 563,
    634, 691, 703, 710, 716,
    723, 729, 766
Hottinger, Jacob, Jr., 723
Hottinger, Margaret, 440,
    442, 446-447, 545-546,
    548, 741, 744
Hottinger, Rudolf, 445,
    447, 548, 707, 743
Hottinger, Rutsch, 723

799

557, 563-564, 570, 593, 608, 610, 747, 752, 754
Mariolotry, 193
Marius, Augustinus, 532
mark of the crescent, 99
market(place), 119, 360
Marnay s. Seine, 89
Marpeck, Pilgram, 15
Marpeck's Testamentserläuterung, 426
Marranos (Spain), 320, 697
Mars, 118, 124, 583, 608
Marti of Teuffen, 423
Martin (from Bern), 739
Martin, Johann, 769
martyrdom, 719, 723
Martyrs Mirror, 558
Mary, 376 (see Our Lady, Virgin Mother)
masculine, 181
mass, 189, 195, 199-200, 214, 226, 233-235, 238-240, 242-246, 248-249, 251-253, 255, 257-260, 263, 265-270, 272-273, 275-281, 287-288, 291, 331, 424, 461, 521, 532, 545-546, 550, 562, 574, 637, 646-647, 649, 656-658, 660-662, 664-665, 670-672, 679, 684, 690, 697, 701, 704, 747, 751
massacre in Thuringia, 559
mass-annuals, 669
Master Jacob, 141
Matsuda, Rosemarie, 24
matzoth, 663
Mauroticheus, Jodocus, 87
Maximilian I, Emperor, 56-57, 534, 538, 552, 558, 568-569, 579, 581, 589, 593, 703, 751
May family (Bern), 374, 722
Mayer, Conrad, 435, 738
Mayer, Uli, 385
Macedonia, 576
Mecklenburg, duke of, 140, 620
de Medici, Giovanni, 556
medicine, 52, 577
Meersburg, 545
Megander, Caspar, 346, 543, 547, 638, 689-691, 739
Meier, Jacob, 177
Meiers, Hans, 531
Meihuizen, H. W., 339-340, 706, 708
Meilen, 666, 732
Meis, Lady, 357, 537, 716
Meisen (inn), 171, 634

Mela, Pomponius, 59, 69, 580, 615
Melanchton, 187, 189-190, 431, 554, 615, 640, 651, 655, 680, 683, 737
Meluntichens, 87
Melpomene, 579
Melun, 89, 91, 102, 567, 596, 602
Memmingen, 189, 192, 563-564, 640
memorial, 270
medicant friars, 51, 577
mens (mentula), 616
mercenaries, 204, 206, 574, 579, 597, 618, 623
merchant at Basel, 111, 118
merchants of Ravensburg, 68
Mercury, 108, 120, 583, 603
Merger, 350-351, 551
Merger, Heine, 352, 412, 556, 712-713, 729
Merger, Jacob, 712
Merger, Uli, 348, 712
Messiah, 438
messianic claims, 747
Messmer, Jacob, 177
Metamorphoses, 358, 576, 580, 611, 717
metaphysics, 51, 577
Meyer, 645-646, 648, 663, 678, 697, 724-741
Meyers, The, 399
Meyer, Agatha, 728
Meyer, Gerold, 169, 728
Meyer, Hans, 466, 728, 751
Meyer, Lorenz, 232
Meyer, Margaret, 728
Meyer, Peter, 636
Meyer, Sebastian, 350, 562, 640, 712
Michael, 283-284, 675
Midas, 190, 639
Milan, 535, 564, 593, 596, 623-624, 752-754
Milan, Battle of, 470
Milan, castle of, 146
Miles, Beda, 280, 423, 555, 674, 734
Miles, Hermann, 674, 745
Milords, 139, 170, 176-177, 201, 209, 233, 242, 244, 248, 269, 274, 299, 301, 332, 349, 397, 411, 413-415, 419-422, 429-430, 440, 442, 444-447, 451-452, 455, 463-464, 662
Minerva, 120, 609
minister(s), 287, 345, 478
ministry, 190, 195, 225, 389, 480

missa, 200-201
Mnemosyne, 75, 590
mob, 511
Moera, 130, 615
Momus(es), 316, 400, 696, 728
Monachus, Johann, 163
monasteries, 176, 210
Monastery (Augustinian, Dominican, Franciscan), 112
monastic (garb, orders), 172, 174
monasticism, 174
money, 93-95, 97-99, 101, 138, 151, 160, 189, 194, 248, 265, 280, 379
monks, 157, 172, 176, 189, 191, 239-240, 340, 354-355, 454, 546, 608, 639, 661
monosyllable, 71
Mons Fractus, 585
Mons Pileatus, 585
Montbeliard, 534
Morat, 563
Moravia, 456, 546, 551, 562, 568, 743
More, Sir Thomas, 536
mores, 577
Morhart, Ulrich, 644
Morillon, 536
Moser, Adam, 143, 621
Moser, Conrad, 57, 102-103, 107, 579, 581-582, 602
Moses, 228, 230, 238, 293, 319, 329, 488, 491
motes, 97
mother, 93-94, 100, 109, 122, 141, 143-145, 165, 195, 221, 223-224, 296
mother-in-law, 140, 281
mother of God, 424
mouse, 161
Mt. Olympus, 758
Mt. Parnassus, 590
Mt. Pilatus, 28, 64, 115, 585-587, 560, 570, 600
Mühlhausen, 285, 559
Mulciber, 624
von Mültinen, Caspar, 748
Müller, E. F. K., 258
Müller, Hans, 418, 421, 731-732
Müllerthor, 725
Multerthor, 381, 725
multiple ministry, 478, 759, 769
de Mundo, 50
Munich, 425, 563
Münster Church, 543, 639, 737

813

The Editor

Leland Harder was born in 1926 in Hillsboro, Kansas, where his great grandfather taught in the Krimmer Mennonite Brethren village school following the immigration of this group from Russia in 1874, and where his grandfather and father, at different periods, taught at Tabor College, a school of the Mennonite Brethren Conference.

Leland graduated from Bethel College, Newton, Kansas, a school of the General Conference Mennonite Church, and taught social science in the nearby Mennonite community of Moundridge. He was awarded a research fellowship at Michigan State University, where he earned the M.A. degree in sociology and anthropology and where he also sensed a call into the Christian ministry.

Following seminary training in Chicago, where he met and married Bertha Fast, he served as pastor of the First Mennonite Church of Chicago for five years. He then entered a doctoral program in the sociology of religion at Northwestern University, after which he and Bertha joined the faculty of Mennonite Biblical Seminary in Elkhart, Indiana.

They are the parents of two sons: John, who presently teaches math in Peabody, Kansas, near his father's home town, and Thomas, who presently teaches classical guitar at Wichita State University. After twenty-five years of seminary teaching, Leland and Bertha have moved to North Newton, Kansas. Leland now serves as director of the Great Plains Seminary Education Program sponsored jointly by the Western District Conference and the South Central Mennonite Conference in cooperation with the Associated Mennonite Biblical Seminaries.